Image Technology

Springer
*Berlin
Heidelberg
New York
Barcelona
Budapest
Hong Kong
London
Milan
Paris
Santa Clara
Singapore
Tokyo*

Jorge L.C. Sanz (Ed.)

Image Technology
Advances in Image Processing, Multimedia and Machine Vision

With 344 Figures, Some in Color and 41 Tables

 Springer

Dr. Jorge L.C. Sanz
Coordinated Science Laboratory
University of Illinois at Urbana-Champaign
Urbana, IL 61801
USA

IBM Argentina
Ingeniero Enrique Butty 275
1300 Buenos Aires
Argentina

ISBN 3-540-58306-8 Springer-Verlag Berlin Heidelberg New York

Library of Congress Cataloging-in-Publication Data. Image technology: advances in image processing, multimedia and machine vision/Jorge L.C. Sanz, (ed). p. cm. Includes bibliographical references. ISBN 3-540-58306-8 (Hardcover: alk. paper) 1. Image processing. 2. Multimedia systems. 3. Computer vision. I. Sanz, J.L.C. (Jorge L.C.), 1955– . TA1637.I45 1995 006.4'2—dc20 95-42729

This work is subject to copyright. All rights are reserved, whether the whole or part of the material is concerned, specifically the rights of translation, reprinting, reuse of illustrations, recitation, broadcasting, reproduction on microfilm or in any other way, and storage in data banks. Duplication of this publication or parts thereof is permitted only under the provisions of the German Copyright Law of September 9, 1965, in its current version, and permission for use must always be obtained from Springer-Verlag. Violations are liable for prosecution under the German Copyright Law.

© Springer-Verlag Berlin Heidelberg 1996
Printed in Germany

The use of general descriptive names, registered names, trademarks, etc. in this publication does not imply, even in the absence of a specific statement, that such names are exempt from the relevant protective laws and regulations and therefore free for general use.

Typesetting: Best-set Typesetter Ltd., Hong Kong

SPIN: 10085832   33/3020/SPS-5 4 3 2 1 0–Printed on acid-free paper

*To my wife Diana,
to whom I owe all what
I have in my life*
                    June 1994

Introduction

Almost seven years have elapsed since I edited the book *Advances in Machine Vision*, published by Springer-Verlag in 1988. In spite of the tough economic times of the early 1990s, image processing and machine vision continue to be areas of active research and development. Commercial and industrial applications are widespread, and gaining more acceptance in different business environments. The advent of new algorithms and electronics clears the way to larger and more complex image applications.

In this book, several areas of continued interest and work are visited, covering some fundamentals as well as technology-oriented contributions. The book emphasizes concrete applications and promising technologies, although it also includes a few reviews of fundamental subjects that are relevant to both specialists and newcomers to this exciting field. The chapters by no means cover all areas in image processing and machine vision, but hopefully provide a solid start for a graduate student or the specialist who wants to gain some insight into the chosen subjects.

The book starts with an in-depth treatment of machine vision and mobile robots. The chapter "Vision for Mobile Robots" by Bartlett, Hampapur, Huber, Kortenkamp, Moezzi, and Weymouth presents an extensive review of work done in this area. The authors describe optical flow algorithms from a critical perspective and propose new approaches for mobile robots that take advantage of constraints unique to this domain. They go further into depth computation through egomotion complex logarithmic mapping. The results of the stereo techniques are improved by a new computational model in which spatial information is integrated over time without the direct computation of camera motion. This idea is tested on stereo image sequences coming from a mobile robot. The chapter ends with a discussion of collision avoidance using visual information, and coordination among multiple mobile robots, with concrete experiences obtained from the CARMEL project.

As in the case of mobile robots, deriving 3-dimensional information about a scene from its images is a challenging general problem. The chapter "3D Constraints on Monocular Image Sequences: Theory and Algorithms" by Sawhney and Anandan presents a critical appraisal of the techniques for problems involving geometric constraints between a scene and its monocular images when the scene is viewed from various positions and orientations of the camera.

The chapter "Integrating Selective Attention and Space-Variant Sensing in Machine Vision" by Colombo, Rucci, and Dario describes the simultaneous use of selective attention mechanisms and retina-like sensing in a system for machine perception.

The processing and understanding of color images has received a great deal of attention in recent years. The chapter "Modeling Color Images for Machine Vision" by Healey presents a review and an evaluation of color image models that have been used in machine vision. A detailed account of recent work on color texture is also shown.

Another subject that has attracted the interest of many image processing and computer vision researchers is the use of the Minimum Description Length (MDL) principle for different estimation problems in the field. MDL is explained in general terms in the chapter by Kanungo, Dom, Niblack, and Steele. Their chapter "A Fast Algorithm for MDL-Based Multi-Band Image Segmentation" also deals with the application of MDL to the segmentation of color images. They introduce novel methods to deal with the complexity of the optimization problems arising from the proposed functional.

With increasing interest in making transportation more efficient, a number of projects have been launched worldwide. One important aspect of public transportation is to provide large cities with efficient schedules for public buses. Counting people flow is an important way to determine the need for more buses, to measure congestion, and so on. The chapter "A Vision System for Estimating People Flow" by Del Bimbo and Nesi deals with new methods for counting people getting on and off a bus or other mass transportation vehicle.

The chapter "A Bayesian Network for Automatic Visual Crowding Estimation in Underground Stations" by Regazzoni, Tesei, and Vernazza also deals with the problem of counting people, this time in subway stations. The paper presents new techniques for estimating people congestion by means of multiple cameras and statistical approaches based on visual features. Applications to real data obtained from the underground system in Genoa, Italy, are given.

Another important aspect of transportation systems relies on the improvement of highway control, and in particular, on the ability to automate the job done at toll gates. The ideal system will be one that can bill a passing car through a toll directly to the owner without manual intervention and without traffic congestion. An important technology that may enable this process is the automatic reading of the license plate of a car passing through a toll gate. The chapter "Recognition of Motor Vehicle License Plates in Rear-View Images" by

Granieri, Stabile, and Comelli describes a system based on customized optical character recognition, suitably adapted to the varying scene situations arising from different illumination, weather conditions, and so on.

Using image processing and image understanding techniques to automate tasks of industrial inspection has been a research effort for many years. Its potential for improving quality and reducing costs of industrial production has been demonstrated by many working systems used in production environments.

The next four chapters cover different aspects of the many issues involved in inspection. They have been selected from papers submitted to the 11th International Conference on Pattern Recognition at the Hague, The Netherlands. The topics covered are quality control of hybrid circuits, evaluation of gravure paper quality, underwater inspection of pipelines, and dimensional inspection of machine parts. These different topics indicate the breadth of problems and applications for industrial inspection tasks.

The chapter "Automatic System of Quality Control by Vision of Hybrid Circuits" by Chehdi and Corazza describes a system for checking the production of hybrid circuits. The position of the circuit links and the quality of the solder joints are controlled by using a model of non-defective circuits. Experimental results show that about 97% of the flaws can be detected under the imposed time constraints.

The chapter "An Image Analysis Based Method to Evaluate Gravure Paper Quality" by Langinmaa describes a method to measure paper quality on the basis of measuring the quality of gravure printing. The problem is to measure defects quickly and objectively. Three different nonlinear processing methods are evaluated and it is shown that about 90% of defects can be detected. Also, the approach is reasonably insensitive to small parameter changes.

The chapter "A Vision System for an Autonomous Underwater Vehicle" by Hallset describes the vision component for a pipeline inspection system. Problems involved are light absorption, a non-uniform background on the sea bed, marine materials covering parts of the pipeline, and more than one pipeline in the field of view. The system employs a pipeline map to match pipeline segments with model segments. Experimental results show that the system can find and analyze moderately complex configurations and is robust against scaling and rotation errors.

The chapter "Visual Inspection of Machined Parts" by Modayur, Shapiro, and Haralick addresses the problem of defining and measuring geometric tolerances of machined parts. Presently, tolerances of industrial parts are usually evaluated by precision measurement devices. A promising future approach is to use optical precision measurement, based on image processing approaches. The paper gives a thorough definition of tolerances and works out propagation of uncertainties from low-level image processing up to tolerance decision. It is demonstrated experimentally that the error probabilities obtained by this approach are lower than those obtained without uncertainty propagation.

In summary, these chapters demonstrate that industrial inspection tasks can be handled successfully by image processing approaches. It is another question whether the approaches are already economically competitive. However, the cost of labor is steadily increasing and the cost of hardware is decreasing. In addition, automatic inspection is objective, not subject to fatigue, and readily applicable also in hazardous environments.

Important applications of texture measures include the inspection of finished surfaces, the assessment of wear of different materials in textile production, and quality of wood logs for commercial use, among many others. Finnish industries have a long record in the exploitation of machine vision technologies in order to better control production quality. The chapter "Texture Analysis in Industrial Applications" by Pietikaeinen and Ojala presents a thorough review of texture measures and their application to different inspection problems.

Two chapters reviewing and presenting new material relevant to the practitioner in machine vision are "Methods for Illumination-Invariant Image Processing" by Miller and Shridhar, and "A Comparison of Algorithms for Subpixel Peak Detection" by Fisher and Naidu. These chapters have techniques often used in different practical problems arising in 2-dimensional image processing. On a similar track is the chapter "Splines and Spline Fitting Revisited" by Vargas, E. Rodriguez, Flickner, and Sanz. Splines are frequently involved in fitting tasks and shape modeling in image processing, and the close relationship between them and multi-resolution periodic wavelets will attract renewed interest in spline fundamentals.

The chapters on visual inspection from ICPR in Holland are complemented by the chapter "Algorithms for a Fast Confocal Optical Inspection System" by Rao, Ramesh, Wu, Mandeville, and Kerstens, in which the authors present a system for surface topography measurement by means of confocal imaging. An image processing module is designed to detect surfaces in the incoming signal as well as to improve its resolution.

A long-standing and important 2-dimensional computer vision problem is the recognition of aircraft on the ground. The chapter "Qualitative Recognition of Aircraft in Perspective Aerial Images" by Das, Bhanu, Wu, and Braithwaite gives a summary of existing systems and presents a new system based on the use of a hierarchical object model data base using geometric entities.

Non-conventional imaging presents new challenges to the image processing and machine vision fields. Conversely, breakthroughs in robust algorithms for image processing and machine vision may unleash the power of new sensing methods for sub-micron metrology problems. The chapter "Scanning Probe Microscopy: Trends and Image Processing Issues" by Pingali and Jain demonstrates the importance of image processing techniques in scanning probe microscopy, and surveys different scanning probe microscopes such as scanning tunneling microscopy, magnetic force microscopy, atomic force microscopy, and scanning ion conductance microscopy, all from the perspective of image processing algorithms.

Images are at the heart of the new information management systems. The diversity of image data is paramount: from typed documents to color maps, and from detail-sensitive imagery to highly redundant video sequences. The representation and handling of this diversity, and its combination with other forms of data such as graphics and text, bring important new problems to information handling systems. The storage, modeling, and representation of image information is an active area of research.

The chapter "Advances in Image Information Modeling" by Grosky and Mehrotra discusses some of the key issues involved in image formation modeling, representation, and information represented in image management systems. Some future directions for research are discussed. Related material on this important topic can be found in the summary of the NSF Workshop on Visual Information Management Systems, published by R. Jain in SIGMOD Record, Vol. 22, Sept. 1993.

An important aspect of image representation is the volume of storage required in very large applications. Several commercial applications do not tolerate the loss associated with conventional compression algorithms. Such applications include archiving and retrieval systems for medical images, fingerprint storage systems, and many others. The massive number of images and high image resolution necessary in these applications call for judicious image compression techniques. Aiazzi, Alparone, and Baronti illustrate some of these issues in the chapter "Lossless Compression of Medical Images by Content-Driven Laplacian Pyramid Splitting".

A central image processing research and development subject of the 1990s is video compression. Applications of video storage and retrieval are commonly referred to as "multimedia". Two last two chapters of the book are devoted to the subject of video compression.

The chapter "Video Compression for Multimedia Applications" by A. Rodriguez, Fogg, and Delp describes algorithms and techniques commonly used in both software-only and hardware-assisted compression categories. A practical description of the technology is given to the point that newcomers to the field should be able to get a quick understanding of the discussed algorithms.

In the last chapter of the book, "Directionality and Scalability in Subband Image and Video Compression" by Taubman, Chang, and Zakhor, an in-depth view of new sub-band image compression techniques is presented. The authors also give an excellent summary of some of the conventional building blocks used in image and video compression algorithms and review key compression standards such as MPEG, JPEG, and H.261.

I would like to express my gratitude to several people who have made this book possible. I am indebted to Professor Niemann who provided the selected papers from authors attending the 11th International Conference on Pattern Recognition. Also, I would like to express my thanks to Professor Del Bimbo for his help in selecting the papers from some of the best on-going work in applied image processing and machine vision in Italy. My gratitude also goes to N. Venckus for her endless assistance in putting the book into a publishable form. Finally, I would like to thank Springer-Verlag's editors both for their kind invitation to prepare this book and for their help in finishing it.

Buenos Aires, January 1996   Jorge L. C. Sanz

Contents

Vision for Mobile Robots
S.L. Bartlett, A. Hampapur, M.J. Huber, D. Kortenkamp,
S. Moezzi, and T. Weymouth (With 41 Figures) 1

3D Constraints on Monocular Image Sequences:
Theory and Algorithms
H.S. Sawhney and P. Anandan (With 5 Figures) 83

Integrating Selective Attention and Space-Variant Sensing
in Machine Vision
C. Colombo, M. Rucci, and P. Dario (With 13 Figures) 109

Modeling Color Images for Machine Vision
G. Healey (With 14 Figures) 129

A Fast Algorithm
for MDL-Based Multi-Band Image Segmentation
T. Kanungo, B. Dom, W. Niblack, and D. Steele
(With 7 Figures) 147

A Vision System for Estimating People Flow
P. Nesi and A. Del Bimbo (With 16 Figures) 179

A Bayesian Network
for Automatic Visual Crowding Estimation
in Underground Stations
C.S. Regazzoni, A. Tesei, and G. Vernazza
(With 10 Figures) 203

Recognition of Motor Vehicle License Plates
in Rear-View Images
M.N. Granieri, F. Stabile, and P. Comelli (With 10 Figures) 231

Automatic System of Quality Control
by Vision of Hybird Circuits
K. Chehdi and M. Corazza (With 14 Figures) 253

An Image Analysis Based Method
to Evaluate Gravure Paper Quality
A. Langinmaa (With 14 Figures) 269

A Vision System for an Autonomous Underwater Vehicle
J.O. Hallset (With 16 Figures) 285

Visual Inspection of Machined Parts
B.R. Modayur, L.G. Shapiro, and R.M. Haralick
(With 17 Figures) 307

Texture Analysis in Industrial Applications
M. Pietikäinen and T. Ojala (With 7 Figures) 337

Methods for Illumination-Invariant Image Processing
J.W.V. Miller and M. Shridhar (With 9 Figures) 361

A Comparison of Algorithms for Subpixel Peak Detection
R.B. Fisher and D.K. Naidu (With 14 Figures) 385

Splines and Spline Fitting Revisited
D.C. Vargas, E.J. Rodríguez, M. Flickner, and J.L.C. Sanz
(With 3 Figures) 405

Algorithms for a Fast Confocal Optical Inspection System
A.R. Rao, N. Ramesh, F.Y. Wu, J.R. Mandeville, and P. Kerstens
(With 20 Figures) 439

Qualitative Recognition of Aircraft in Perspective Aerial Images
S. Das, B. Bhanu, X. Wu, and R.N. Braithwaite
(With 16 Figures) 475

Scanning Probe Microscopy:
Trends and Image Processing Issues
G.S. Pingali and R. Jain (With 21 Figures) 519

Advances in Image Information Modeling
W.I. Grosky and R. Mehrotra (With 1 Figure) 579

Lossless Compression of Medical Images
by Content-Driven Laplacian Pyramid Splitting
B. Aiazzi, L. Alparone, and S. Baronti (With 7 Figures) 595

Video Compression for Multimedia Applications
A.A. Rodriguez, C.E. Fogg, and E.J. Delp (With 32 Figures) 613

Directionality and Scalability in Subband Image
and Video Compression
D. Taubman, E. Chang, and A. Zakhor (With 37 Figures) 681

List of Contributors

Aiazzi, B.
Dipartimento di Ingegneria Elettronica, Università di Firenze,
Via di S. Marta 3, 50139 Firenze, Italy

Alparone, L.
Dipartimento di Ingegneria Elettronica, Università di Firenze,
Via di S. Marta 3, 50139 Firenze, Italy

Anandan, P.
David Sarnoff Research Center, Princeton, NJ 08544, USA

Baronti, S.
Dipartimento di Ingegneria Elettronica, Università di Firenze,
Via di S. Marta 3, 50139 Firenze, Italy

Bartlett, S.L.
Artificial Intelligence Laboratory, 1101 Beal Avenue,
Ann Arbor, MI 48109-2110, USA

Bhanu, B.
Visualization and Intelligent Systems Laboratory,
College of Engineering, University of California,
Riverside, CA 92521-0425, USA

Braithwaite, R.N.
Visualization and Intelligent Systems Laboratory,
College of Engineering, University of California,
Riverside, CA 92521-0425, USA

Chang, E.
Cory Hall, University of California, Berkeley, CA 94720, USA

Chehdi, K.
ENSSAT, LASTI/Groupe Image, B.P.447, 6 rue de Kerampont,
22300 Lannion, France

Colombo, C.
ARTS Lab, Scuola Superiore S. Anna, Via Carducci 40,
56127 Pisa, Italy

Comelli, P.
IBM SEMEA, Scientific Solution-Unit,
Viale Oceano Pacifico 171, 00144 Rome, Italy

Corazza, M.
ENSSAT, LASTI/Groupe Image, B.P.447, 6 rue de Kerampont,
22300 Lannion, France

Dario, P.
ARTS Lab, Scuola Superiore S. Anna, Via Carducci 40,
56127 Pisa, Italy

Das, S.
Visualization and Intelligent Systems Laboratory,
College of Engineering, University of California,
Riverside, CA 92521-0425, USA

Del Bimbo, A.
Department of Systems and Informatics,
University of Florence, Italy

Delp, E.J.
Purdue University

Dom, B.
Katholieke Universiteit Leuven,
Department of Electrical Engineering ESAT/M12,
Kardinaal Mercierlaan 94, 3001 Heverlee,
Belgium

Fisher, R.B.
Department of Artificial Intelligence, University of Edinburgh,
5 Forrest Hill, Edinburgh EH1 2QL, Scotland, UK

Flickner, M.
IBM Almaden Research Center K54-802, 650 Harry Road,
San Jose, CA 95120-6099, USA

Fogg, C.E.
Xenon Corporation

List of Contributors

Granieri, M.N.
IBM SEMEA, Scientific Solution-Unit,
Viale Oceano Pacifico 171, 00144 Rome, Italy

Grosky, W.I.
Computer Science Department, Wayne State University,
Detroit, MI 48202, USA

Hallset, J.O.
Oceaneering A/S, P.O. Box 638, 4001 Stavanger, Norway

Hampapur, A.
Artificial Intelligence Laboratory, 1101 Beal Avenue,
Ann Arbor, MI 48109-2110, USA

Haralick, R.M.
Intelligent Systems Laboratory,
Electrical Engineering Department, FT-10,
University of Washington, Seattle, WA 98195, USA

Healey, G.
Department of Electrical and Computer Engineering,
University of California, Irvine, CA 92717-2625, USA

Huber, M.J.
Artificial Intelligence Laboratory, 1101 Beal Avenue,
Ann Arbor, MI 48109-2110, USA

Jain, R.
University of California at San Diego,
Department of Electrical and Computer Engineering,
9500 Gilman Drive,
La Jolla, CA 92093-0407, USA

Kanungo, T.
Intelligent Systems Laboratory,
Department of Electrical Engineering, FT-10,
University of Washington, Seattle, WA 98195, USA

Kerstens, P.
IBM General Technology Division, Rt. 52, Hopewell Jct.,
New York, NY 12533, USA

Kortenkamp, D.
Artificial Intelligence Laboratory, 1101 Beal Avenue,
Ann Arbor, MI 48109-2110, USA

Langinmaa, A.
Technical Research Centre of Finland, Graphic Arts Laboratory,
P.O. Box 106, 02151 Espoo, Finland

Mandeville, J.R.
IBM Research Division, T.J. Watson Research Center,
Yorktown Heights, New York, NY 10598, USA

Mehrotra, R.
Center for Robotics and Manufacturing Systems,
University of Kentucky, Lexington, KY 40506, USA

Miller, J.W.V.
Department of Electrical and Computer Engineering,
School of Engineering, The University of Michigan-Dearborn,
4901 Evergreen Road, Dearborn, MI 48128-1491, USA

Modayur, B.R.
Intelligent Systems Laboratory,
Electrical Engineering Department, FT-10,
University of Washington, Seattle, WA 98195, USA

Moezzi, S.
Artificial Intelligence Laboratory, 1101 Beal Avenue,
Ann Arbor, MI 48109-2110, USA

Naidu, D.K.
Department of Artificial Intelligence, University of Edinburgh,
5 Forrest Hill, Edinburgh EH1 2QL, Scotland, UK

Nesi, P.
Department of Systems and Informatics,
University of Florence, Italy

Niblack, W.
IBM Almaden Research Centre K54-802, 650 Harry Road, San Jose,
CA 95120-6099, USA

Ojala, T.
Department of Electrical Engineering, University of Oulu,
90570 Oulu, Finland

Pietikäinen, M.
Department of Electrical Engineering, University of Oulu,
90570 Oulu, Finland

List of Contributors

Pingali, G.S.

Ramesh, N.
IBM Research Division, T.J. Watson Research Center,
Yorktown Heights, New York, NY 10598, USA

Rao, A.R.
IBM Research Division, T.J. Watson Research Center,
Yorktown Heights, New York, NY 10598, USA

Regazzoni, C.S.
Department of Biophysical and Electronic Engineering,
University of Genova, Via Opera Pia 11A,
16145 Genova, Italy

Rodriguez, A.A.
Scientific Atlanta Inc., 4357 Park Drive, MS: ATL-33H,
Norcross, GA 30093-2990, USA

Rodriguez, E.J.
IBM Argentina, Ing. Enrique Butty 275, 1300 Buenos Aires,
Argentina

Rucci, M.
ARTS Lab, Scuola Superiore S. Anna, Via Carducci 40,
56127 Pisa, Italy

Sanz, J.L.C.
Coordinated Science Laboratory, University of Illinois, Urbana, IL
61801, USA
IBM Argentina, Ing. Enrique Butty 275, 1300 Buenos Aires,
Argentina

Sawhney, H.S.
Machine Vision Group, IBM Almaden Research Center,
650 Harry Road, San Jose, CA 95120, USA

Shapiro, L.G.
Intelligent Systems Laboratory,
Electrical Engineering Department, FT-10,
University of Washington, Seattle, WA 98195, USA

Shridhar, M.
Department of Electrical and Computer Engineering,
School of Engineering, The University of Michigan-Dearborn,
4901 Evergreen Road, Dearborn, MI 48128-1491, USA

Stabile, F.
IBM SEMEA, Scientific Solution-Unit,
Viale Oceano Pacifico 171, 00144 Rome, Italy

Steele, D.
IBM Almaden Research Center K54-802, 650 Harry Road, San Jose,
CA 95120-6099, USA

Taubman, D.
Cory Hall, University of California, Berkeley, CA 94720, USA

Tesei, A.
Department of Biophysical and Electronic Engineering,
University of Genova, Via Opera Pia 11A,
16145 Genova, Italy

Vargas, D.C.
IBM Argentina, Ing. Enrique Butty 275, 1300 Buenos Aires,
Argentina

Vernazza, G.
Department of Biophysical and Electronic Engineering,
University of Genova, Via Opera Pia 11A,
16145 Genova, Italy

Weymouth, T.
Artificial Intelligence Laboratory, 1101 Beal Avenue,
Ann Arbor, MI 48109-2110, USA

Wu, F.Y.
IBM Research Division, T.J. Watson Research Center,
Yorktown Heights, New York, NY 10598, USA

Wu, X.
Visualization and Intelligent Systems Laboratory,
College of Engineering, University of California,
Riverside, CA 92521-0425, USA

Zakhor, A.
Cory Hall, University of California, Berkeley, CA 94720, USA

Vision for Mobile Robots

S.L. Bartlett, A. Hampapur, M.J. Huber, D. Kortenkamp, S. Moezzi, and T. Weymouth

1 Introduction

Mobile robots operate in a wide variety of environments, and the tasks they are being designed to perform vary from the simplest pick-and-place factory jobs to space station construction, maintenance, and repair. Vision systems for mobile robots are used to help locate goal objects or locations, plan paths to the goal, avoid obstacles along the chosen path, monitor the robot's progress along the path, locate landmarks, recognize objects, compute motion parameters, etc. The vision capability required for any robot depends heavily on its environment and its assigned tasks. A robot that works in a factory picking and placing objects whose geometry, location, and orientation are known and constant may not need any vision capabilities at all. On the other hand, a robot working autonomously in a dynamic 3D environment like space or under water, with possibly unknown objects moving with arbitrary accelerations and rotations, in the presence of humans would need complex visual perception capabilities.

Computer vision systems for mobile robots tend to be hierarchical. First, low level vision operators do feature detection, smoothing, morphological operations, etc., filtering out unnecessary details in the camera images. At the next level of perception, groups of pixels are given symbolic labels which are then used by the high level operators to make decisions about how the robot will move to perform its tasks. Computer vision researchers have invented a multitude of vision operators. Unfortunately, no subset of them is sufficient to solve all the vision problems. So, a key to good vision for mobile robots is choosing the right subset of operators based on the robot's working environment and the tasks it must perform. For example, if the environment is an empty corridor with a few open doorways and the task is to enter the third doorway, then a possible choice for a low level operator would be a vertical edge detector. Two vertical lines close together might be labeled a doorway. Then the distance to the third doorway would have to be computed and the correct commands issued to the actuators on the robot. If the environment or the task was more complicated (obstacles in the environment or an object to place in the doorway) the choice of operators at all levels of the vision system hierarchy might be different.

After a set of operators has been chosen, knowledge about the environment and the tasks almost always must be included, at least implicity. Even in our simple example, edge detectors always have thresholds that determine how faint an edge to consider. A doorway that was almost the same intensity at the wall would require a much lower threshold than one that was much darker or lighter than the wall. Knowledge about the size of the doorways compared to the space between the doorways is necessary for the doorway labeler. Knowledge about which is darker would make it even more robust. Finally, some knowledge about the accuracy of the drive mechanism and the relative sizes of the robot and the doorway would have to be used to decide how accurately the vision system much compute the distance to be traveled. If the robot's environment is more complex or its tasks are more difficult, explicit knowledge of object geometry and behavior, maps of the environment, etc., might be necessary.

A classic example of a working mobile robot is the Stanford Cart. It was designed to navigate through a cluttered indoor or outdoor environment and avoid obstacles. In an early version [Mor77, Gen77], the robot acquired stereo images of the environment, found and tracked distant features, computed the current location of the robot from the feature motion since the last image pair was taken, and finally computed steering and motor commands to move the robot 2 more feet. After moving, the robot stopped, took another image pair, did its computations, and then moved again. The system used vision operators such as an image size reducer to make images smaller so other operators would take less time to execute, an interest operator to find features to track and match, a correlator to find matching features for tracking and stereo matching, a camera solver that used camera geometry to compute robot motion and feature distances, a geometric distortion corrector for camera nonlinearities, a high pass filter, a point noise remover, a contrast normalizer, a vertical roll corrector, a picture comparator, and a ground surface finder. Very little explicit knowledge of the environment was included.

Ten years later research had taken on a new flavor. The work done at the University of Maryland [WJD+87] illustrates some of the differences. Instead of the generic, cluttered environment of the Stanford Cart, they chose automobile highways. The Cart did exactly the same processing on every image, but the Maryland system has two modes of visual processing: bootstrap mode, where appropriate image operators are applied to the entire image, and feedforward mode, in which the operators are applied to the areas of the image where the system expects to find features of interest. Unlike the Stanford Cart, a map of the local environment is created using the stereo data; the system "remembers" what it perceives. This map is used to plan robot motion and to locate areas of interest in the next image. The system also includes *a priori* knowledge of the area through which the vehicle will travel. In general, the trend in robot visions systems is to choose a constrained environment and build explicit knowledge of the environment into the vision system. The computer knows what to look for and where in the image to find it.

No single volume, much less a single chapter, can hope to describe all the vision operators and which combination should be used for each situation. Even describing just the current research would be an impossible task. In this chapter we present a sampler of work being done at various levels of the vision system hierarchy. We start with a discussion of optic flow in Sect. 2 and then present an approach to computing optic flow designed for mobile robot applications. In Sect. 3 we discuss techniques for determining the depths of objects in a scene with special emphasis on those appropriate for a moving camera. Section 4 presents an method for refining depth estimates over time. Section 5 shows how vision can be used for avoiding obstacles, determining the robot's position and orientation, and choosing appropriate actions. In Sect. 6 we discuss the use of vision for coordinating the activities of multiple robots working together.

2 Extraction of Pixel Motion

Extracting motion information in the image space is a common type of processing in dynamic vision systems. This process of image motion extraction generates an intermediate representation which contains information about the motion of pixels in the image plane. This image motion representation is normally referred to as *optic flow*. Given the reflectance properties of the objects in the scene, the characteristics and positions of the light sources, the camera parameters, and motion information for the camera and the objects, the motion field of the pixels in an image of the scene can be computed.

Ideally, this process would be reversible so the optic flow from the images could be used to compute the 3D structure and motion of the objects in the scene. Unfortunately, the problem is illposed. Attributes of objects in the scene often confound the structure and motion recovery process. For example, if a uniform sphere in the scene is rotating, the successive images of the sphere will all look the same – there will be no evidence of motion in the image space, even though the object is moving. In addition, limitations of the imaging process can cause further problems. One of these, called the aperture problem, is due to the fact that a camera has a limited field of view. Consider a vertical black line moving up and to the right against a white background. If only the central part of the line can be imaged by the camera, there will be no way to detect the vertical component of the motion – the line will seem to be simply moving right. Even if the whole line was within the camera's field of view, the aperture problem would confound the results. It is too computationally intensive to use information from the whole image to compute the optic flow at each pixel, so a relatively small neighborhood surrounding the pixel is used. If the feature is larger than this neighborhood, only the component of motion in the direction of the brightness gradient can be computed. Finally, researchers often have to make assumptions about the irradiance, the motion field, the image intensity function, etc. to make the mathematics tractable. These assumptions are often violated in the real world. In spite of all these problems, there is much interest in computing optic flow because it contains such an the abundance of information about the scene.

2.1 Review of Existing Techniques

There are numerous techniques for the estimation of optic flow from a sequences of images. All these techniques begin with a given sequence of images and perform various operations on the sequence. The result of these operations is a two dimensional vector field, where each vector in the field corresponds to the velocity of the point in image space. In this section we review some of the important techniques that are available for the computation of optic flow. We also review other techniques for motion analysis which do not use optic flow, with the intent of exploring an alternate view to the optic flow formulation.

Typically the process of optic flow extraction can be decomposed as follows:

- **Image Sequence Preprocessing.** In this stage the intensity image sequence is processed to generate an intermediate representation. All the following processes use this intermediate representation instead of the original intensity sequence. The most common transformation used in this stage is Gaussian filtering which is used to decrease the image noise. In many techniques this stage may not exist; in such cases we can treat it as an identity transformation which yields back the original image.
- **Initial Velocity Estimation.** The output of this stage is normally a noisy two dimensional vector field. Due to the local nature of the processing (the aperture problem) and noise in the image sequence, errors are introduced in to the initial velocity estimates. In addition, the reliability of the velocity information is not uniform through out the field.
- **Velocity Correction.** The main function in this stage is to use some non-local criteria to correct the errors in the velocity values due to the aperture problem. Many different criteria have been used to apply the correction, some of the most popular being the use of some form of spatio-temporal smoothness of velocity.
- **Velocity Propagation.** The output of this stage is a dense two dimensional vector field. The information that is available at some locations in the image is used to fill in the information at other image locations. This filling in operation is also done using some form of smoothness criteria. If the technique initially produces dense data, this stage may not exist, in which case we can treat it as an identity transformation.
- **Velocity Field Processing.** This is the final stage in the estimation of optic flow. Here some measurements are made on the vector field that has been estimated. One example is finding the location of the critical point of the vector field (Focus of Expansion/Contraction).

2.2 Review of Literature

We present a brief outline of some of the important techniques available for optic flow estimation. These techniques have been grouped under the following categories:

- **Derivative Based Methods.** These techniques use the derivatives of the image intensity function, along with additional criteria, for the extraction of image velocities from a sequence. These techniques assume a continuous differentiable image intensity function. The various differential formulations use one constraint derived from the image sequence and a second constraint which imposes some assumption on the velocities extracted. These techniques are in most cases formulated as an iterative minimization of some property of the velocity to be extracted.
- **Matching Based Approaches.** There are several techniques which use image intensity matching between frames to derive the initial motion vectors. These velocities are propagated to other regions by the use of some additional assumptions.
- **Spatio-Temporal Filtering.** These methods treat the image sequence as a spatio-temporal volume. they transform this volume from the spatio-temporal domain into a velocity space and use this representation to extract the velocity and smooth it.
- **Other Techniques.** Some researchers have developed unique approaches for computing optic flow and a few of these will also be presented.

We will also discuss other research which is relevant to the computation of optic flow.

- **Direct Methods for Motion Computations.** These approaches are significantly different from most of the optic flow estimation techniques, the critical difference being the goal. These techniques do not aim to generate optic flow as an intermediate representation in the extraction of information from image sequences. Their goal is to directly compute motion parameters using the spatio-temporal image intensity functions. This difference leads to a significantly different formulation of the problem. The study of these techniques is important to get an alternative view to the formalism of using optic flow as an intermediate representation.
- **Psychophysics.** The field of Psychophysics deals with the analysis of mechanisms that are used in the human perceptual systems. Specifically, researchers dealing with human perception of visual motion propose and analyze mechanisms for various aspects of human motion perception. A study of these theories can provide us with valuable insights into the problem of motion perception. The research in psychophysics related to visual motion and specifically optic flow is very extensive. We review only the work that is most relevant to our approach.

2.2.1 Derivative Based Techniques

One of the first techniques for computing optic flow from a sequence of images was developed by Horn and Schunck [HS81]. They use two constraints in the estimation of optic flow. The first constraint called the *brightness constraint* is available from the data. The second is called the *spatial smoothness of velocity*.

The brightness constraint is based on the assumption that the appearance of an object, and hence the brightness pattern of the object in the image, does not change due to the motion of the object. Since they assume a smooth reflectance function and a high sampling rate, they treat the image sequence as a continuous, differentiable, spatio-temporal function. For such an image intensity function, they formulate the brightness constraint as follows:

$$E_b = \frac{\partial E}{\partial x}u + \frac{\partial E}{\partial y}v + \frac{\partial E}{\partial t} = 0 \quad (1)$$

where $U = (u, v)$ is the image velocity of a pixel and $E(x, y, t)$ is the spatiotemporal image intensity function. This equation gives us a constraint on the normal velocity of a point, i.e., the velocity of a point along the direction of the spatial gradient at that point. In order to compute the two components of the image velocity, we require an additional constraint. Horn and Schunck formulated and used the spatial smoothness of velocity as a constraint. This constraint forces the image velocity to be a smooth function across the image. They formulated this constraint as the minimization of the Laplacian of the image velocity as follows:

$$\nabla^2 u = \frac{\partial^2 u}{\partial x^2} + \frac{\partial^2 u}{\partial y^2} \qquad \nabla^2 v = \frac{\partial^2 v}{\partial x^2} + \frac{\partial^2 v}{\partial y^2} \quad (2)$$

$$E_c = \nabla^2 v + \nabla^2 v \quad (3)$$

E_b and E_c are the errors in the brightness and smoothness constraints respectively. The complete problem of extracting velocities was formulated as an iterative minimization problem using the calculus of variations. The quantity for minimization was

$$\iint (w^2 E_c^2 + E_b^2) \quad (4)$$

where w was the smoothness factor for the velocity. In their approach, image regions with small gradients would be filled in with the average velocity of the neighboring regions. They presented results for a number of synthetic image sequences.

Nagel and Enkleman [Nag83, Nag87, NE86] have performed a rigorous theoretical analysis and a number of experiments using real world sequences on the effects of additional constraints used in the estimation of optic flow. Based on this analysis they propose a new constraint called the *oriented smoothness constraint*. Their technique is based on the following ideas:

- In an image sequence, the structure of the intensity function has a direct effect on the amount of velocity information it conveys locally. For example, a gray level corner provides complete constraints on the velocity at that point, meaning that both components of the velocity can be determined without any additional assumptions.

- Since the velocity information content at any point in the image depends on the underlying image intensity structure, the intensity function must influence the smoothness constraint at each point, i.e., the smoothness constraint should have no effect on the velocity at corners and points of high curvature, but should have a significant influence at points in the image where the intensity function is relatively smooth.

They formulate the problem of velocity extraction as the minimization of the brightness constraint term and the oriented smoothness term. They provide results on a sequence with a moving car.

Schunck [Sch86a, Sch86b, Sch89, Sch84a, Sch84b, Sch85] has analyzed the brightness constraint equation and the effects of noise and sampling on this constraint. He proposed different constraints for handling the following different types of motion phenomenon:

- Simple image flows involving only translation of image brightness patterns, with no discontinuities.
- Discontinuous image flows for situations involving multiple motions and discontinuities in the optic flow field due to occlusions of moving objects in the scene.
- Structural image flows for scenes in which the object motion results in arbitrary motion of the brightness pattern.

He uses a *constraint line clustering* approach which treats the brightness constraint as a line in velocity space. The velocity at a point in the image has to lie along this line. To determine the actual velocity at a point in the image, it is necessary to select a point on this velocity line which satisfies all the constraints available at a point. The key ideas in this research are as follows:

- The image velocity of a point is given by the intersection of the constraint lines from a local neighborhood around that point, when lines used come from points in the image which have the same velocity.
- The intersection of the constraint lines is computed based on robust statistics. This allows the algorithm to tolerate outliers in the points of intersection. The tolerance to outliers allows the algorithm to estimate the correct velocity even when the neighborhood under consideration contains two different velocity distributions.
- The velocity field generated by constraint line clustering is smooth in regions of continuous velocity. Regions of continuous velocity are detected by locating the edges in the velocity field generated by the constraint line clustering.

Verri et al. [CV92, VGT89a, VGT89b, VGT90, VP87a, VP87b, VP89] have viewed optic flow from the perspective of dynamical systems. This view permits them to look at optic flow as a vector field. They have presented techniques for computing the qualitative stable properties of these fields.

Verri and Poggio [VP89] have studied the relationship between the motion field and the optic flow field. The motion field is the projection of the actual 3D displacement vectors onto the image plane. The optic flow field is the set of displacement vectors computed from the image intensity variations. The imaging process acts as a transformation between the motion flow field and the optic flow field. They have analyzed this relationship for various imaging assumptions like Lambertian reflectance and specular reflectance and for various motions like translations and rotations. Based on this analysis they make the following claims:

- In general the optic flow field is different from the motion flow field. They are equivalent only in some specific cases which are not valid for most real scenes. From this result they conclude that using a dense optic flow estimate is ill suited for extracting structure from motion.
- The qualitative properties of optic flow fields and motion flow fields are the same in general. By qualitative properties they mean the critical points (singular points) of the velocity field and the type of the flow field.

Verri, Girosi and Torre [VGT89a, VGT89b] have developed a theory relating the singular points of motion fields to the motion parameters. They formulate the problem of computing visual motion as an analysis of the phase portrait of a dynamical system and relate the changes in the local structure of the singular points over time to the motion parameters. They present derivations for recovering pure translation and pure rotation from the behavior of singular points. They also present results for restricted cases of both translation and rotation. The emphasis of their entire research is on using the qualitative properties of the flow fields to analyze the motion.

Verri et al. [VGT90, CV92] present a differential technique for the extraction of the optic flow. The singular points of this flow are then used to compute the motion parameters. The key ideas used in this work are as follows:

- The optic flow field from a sequence of images can be modeled by the local deformations of the image intensity function.
- The variations of the intensity function (the function and its partial derivatives) are constrained by the type of local deformation that the intensity function is undergoing. these constraints are used to solve the aperture problem.

They also smooth the flow that is recovered and perform segmentation of the scene based on the optic flow field. They have presented results with several real image sequences.

Tretiak and Pastor [TP84] have proposed an approach to computing optic flow based on the second derivatives of the image intensity function. The basic steps in this approach are:

- Compute the flow by solving two second order differential equations generated by differentiating the brightness constraint equation.
- Average the estimates over a local neighborhood to get the final flow field.

They perform smoothing of the sequence before computing the partial derivatives. No results on image sequences are presented in the paper.

Hildreth [Hil83] proposes a technique for computing optic flow using information along contours. This technique is a variant of the Horn and Schunck [HS81] approach of using velocity smoothness as the additional constraint for estimating optic flow. She extracts zero-crossing contours in the image and minimizes a velocity functional along this contour. The justification for using contours is that the information in the image is contained at locations which contain significant gradient activity. The author suggests different types of functionals for minimization, e.g., the direction of the velocity vectors along the contours, the magnitude of the vector along the contour, or the complete velocity along the contour. The problem is formulated as a constrained optimization problem and solved using the conjugate gradient algorithm. No experimental results are provided.

2.2.2 Matching Based Techniques

Anandan et al. [Ana89, Gla87, GRA83] use a matching approach to the computation of optic flow. The fundamental idea on which these techniques are based is that an image contains information at various scales. They extract information at coarser scales of resolution and use it to guide the extraction process at finer scales. The technique they present is a hierarchical scheme for the extraction of image plane velocities. To determine the displacement vectors between two frames of a sequence, they perform the following steps:

- Create a hierarchical scale pyramid of the two images to be matched.
- Begin the matching process at the highest level in the pyramid and use the displacement vectors estimated at the higher level to constrain the matching process at the lower levels.

The matching process also generates a confidence of the match. They use a smoothness constraint similar to that of Horn and Schunck [HS81] to propagate information from areas of high confidence to areas of low confidence in the image. They also provide results with several image sequences.

Lucas and Kanade [LK81, Luc84] propose an iterative matching technique for the estimation of optic flow. They formulate the matching as a differential equation, and use a weighted average of the velocities as the second constraint for the extraction process. The second derivative of the intensity function is the weight for the averaging. They provide results for a sequence of real images.

Lawton [Law80, Law83, Law84] proposes a technique for processing translatory sensor motion which is based on feature matching. Its goal is to determine the axis of translation. First the zero-crossings of the Laplacian of the Gaussian are computed and interesting points which lie on these zero-crossings are identified. Then a search process is used which minimizes the match error to find a direction. This direction lies on a unit sphere. The search process generates an error surface in terms of the matching coefficient. This surface represents the error in the match for different directions of translation on the unit sphere. The direction with the minimum error is declared as the direction of transltion.

2.2.3 Spatio-Temporal Techniques

Waxman, Wu and Bergholm [WWB88] propose a technique called *convected activation profiles* for computing the image velocities from a sequence. The key ideas in their research are as follows:

- Associate activation profiles with several significant image intensity structures like edge and feature points.
- Convect or move these activation profiles as the feature moves in the sequence.
- Use spatio-temporal filtering on these convected activation profiles to extract the actual velocities.

They have implemented their technique on a parallel machine, to obtain real-time operation. They provide results for a synthetic sequence.

Fleet and Jepson [FJ90] propose a technique for the computation of *component image velocities* from a sequence of images. They convert the spatiotemporal data into velocity space by using filtering and then use the phase of the filter outputs to compute the component velocities in the image sequence. They claim that the phase information is more robust than the magnitude information in the filter outputs. They provide results on synthetic and real image sequences.

Heeger [Hee88] proposes a spatio-temporal filtering approach for the extraction of image velocities. They convert the spatio-temporal data available in the image sequence into motion-energy data through the use of 3D Gabor filters and then minimize the difference between the predicted energy and the actual output of the filter. The technique is applied across various scales. They present results on real texture images and synthetic images of scenes.

2.2.4 Other Techniques

Haralick and Lee [HL86] present a facet approach to computing optic flow. Their view of optic flow in terms of the facet model can be summarized as follows:

- The brightness constraint equation can be interpreted as the intersection of the isocontour plane with the successive frames. This plane can be determined by fitting a local facet model to the image intensity function.
- The additional constraint they use is that the point that lies along this line must have the same brightness as the point at which the flow is being computed.

They present results in the case of a synthetic sequence with translation.

Yachida [Yac83] proposes a method of combining feature based methods and gradient based methods. The velocity at feature points is estimated by solving the feature correspondence problem using matching techniques. These velocities are used in the Horn and Schunck [HS81] type of iterative formulation to propagate the velocities. The magnitude of the gradient is used as a weight in the propagation process. The process of propagation is terminated when the errors in the velocity stops decreasing. The error is measured in terms of the departure of the velocity of a point from the average velocities of the neighborhood. The velocities of the previous frames are used to predict the velocities in the next frame. The previous frame is first transformed by its velocity map before the velocities are used in the prediction. The assumption in the prediction is that the motion between frames is smooth.

Singh [Sin91, SA92] uses tools from estimation theory in the extraction of optic flow. Two estimates of the velocity are computed at each point: one corresponding to the brightness constraint and the other corresponding to the spatial neighborhood constraint. The initial velocity extraction is based on image matching. These brightness and neighborhood estimates are then combined in a minimization formulation to obtain the exact velocity at a point. The match coefficients over the search neighborhood are treated as responses and covarience matrices (confidence values) are associated with them. The covariances from the two estimates can be used to detect neighborhoods which have multiple motions. This prevents the blurring at motion boundaries. The use of covariance matrices allows these estimates to be used in further processing with techniques like Kalman filtering.

2.2.5 Other Research

To put the computation of optic flow in proper perspective, we will review two other areas of research: direct computation of motion parameters and psychophysics. We review the former because optic flow is not an end in itself, but just a preliminary step in the computation of more immediately useful quantities like object motion paramenters. So it is necessary to consider direct methods for computing these quantities. We review psychophysics because these theories about human motion perception can provide us with valuable insights into the problem of machine motion perception.

Direct Methods for Motion Computations

These techniques do not aim to generate optic flow as an intermediate representation in the extraction of information from image sequences. Their goal is to directly compute motion parameters of the sequence using the spatiotemporal image intensity functions. This leads to a significantly different formulation of the problem. The study of these techniques is important to get an alternative view to the formalism of using optic flow as an intermediate representation.

Neghadharipour et al. [NH87a, NL91] formulate motion parameter recovery in terms of the image intensity function and its derivatives. They propose a formulation for directly recovering the motion parameters of a plane, i.e., its translation and rotation, from a sequence of images. The main steps involved in this procedure are as follows:

- Use the brightness constraint equation and the constraints provided by a plane undergoing rigid body transformation to set up a system of nonlinear equations in terms of the translation and rotation.
- Solve these equations to recover the motion parameters.

They have derived closed form solutions for the case of planar rigid body motion. They presents results on a simulated image.

Horn and Weldon [HW87, HW88] propose a method for the direct recovery of motion parameters for the cases of pure rotation, pure translation, and arbitrary motion with known rotation. They do not make any assumptions about the structure of the scene. The key ideas on which this research is based are as follows:

- A minimization of the error between the predicted time derivative of the brightness function and the actual time derivative of the brightness function.
- The imaged surface has to be in front of the viewer.

They present algorithms for recovery of motion parameters in several cases like known depth, pure rotation and pure translation. They have also studied the distribution of the velocities generated by the brightness constraint equation. Their techniques are sensitive to the range of depth values, the field of view and the amount of smoothing applied on the image.

Neghadharipour and Horn [NH87b] use an hypothesize and test technique for recovering the Focus of Expanison (singular point of the flow field) from a sequence of images generated by either pure translation or translation with known rotation. Since the location of the FOE can be used to compute the depth at any point, they hypothesize a location for the FOE and test the sign of the depths computed using that location. Since all objects in the field of view must have positive depths, locations that generate negative depth values are eliminated. They present results on sequences with the FOE both inside and outside the image.

Psychophysics

The field of Psychophysics deals with the analysis of mechanism that are used in the human perceptual system. Researchers propose and analyze mechanisms for various aspects of human motion perception. A study of these theories can provide us with valuable insights into the problem of motion perception. The research in psychophysics related to visual motion and specifically optic flow is very extensive.

In this subsection we review only the work that is most relevant to the new approach we propose for computing optic flow for mobile robots.

Koenderink and van Doorn [KvD75, KvD76] have derived the local invariant properties of the flow field due to visual motion. They decompose the flow field into its local invariants (properties that are independent of coordinate system), namely the curl, divergence and deformation of the field. They show that any flow field can be canonically represented in terms of these local properties. They also show that these differential invariants capture the orientation of the surface elements in 3D space. They suggest that these properties are important in several tasks like aircraft landing and automobile steering. They have used these differential invariants to classify the visual flow fields into several types. They provide the exact solution for the case of an observer moving in an environment which contains a plane at a known depth.

2.2.6 Discussions of Existing Techniques

In this section we briefly comment on the various techniques we reviewed in the previous section. Many of the techniques we have reviewed do not present results with image sequences obtained from the real world. This makes the process of commenting on their performance difficult. The synthetic images on which these techniques have been evaluated do not capture some of the essential features of real images.

Derivative based techniques [HS81, Nag83, Sch86a, TP84, Hil83] use the intensity derivative of the image sequence as the initial measurement from the sequence. The derivative operation on images is known to yield poor results as the intensity surfaces in images are discontinuous and have a significant amount of nose. Most of the techniques which use derivatives overcome this problem by using Gaussian filtering to smooth the intensity function, before computing its derivative. But the use of smoothing immediately raises the question of the scale of the filter to be used. The above problems cause intensity derivative based techniques to be very sensitive to noise. Some of the techniques we have reviewed use the second derivatives of the intensity function as a basis in their computations. In these cases the problem of noisy derivative estimates is more pronounced. In addition to the problem of noisy derivative estimates, these techniques also face the problem of temporal aliasing. Since they assume that the spatio-temporal volume is continuous and differentiable, the temporal sampling rate of the sequence needs to be very high. In many practical applications like robot navigation such a high temporal sampling rate may not be possible.

The traditional approach to dealing with the aperture problem has been to compute the image plane motion where it is available and to use this information to fill in the gaps, thus creating a dense image motion estimate. This interpolation of information has been based on various cirteria like smoothness, oriented smoothness or some other property of the veloicty [HS81, NE86, TP84, Hil83]. The use of such criteria causes problems at many image locations where there are gray level or motion discontinuities. Since the image sequences inherently lack dense motion information, we need to be able to extract the required information based on sparse estimates of the image velocity.

The clustering techniques used in some of the approaches [Sch89, Gla81] tend to provide better results as they use information from a significant area around a point to estimate the correct velocity at a point. The use of robust methods to compute the intersection make the technique significantly immune to noise in the estimation process. But the computation of robust statistics is an expensive process and makes the algorithm very costly.

Some of the techniques rely on invariant properties [KvD75, KvD76] of the flow fields for the process of estimation. Such techniques tend to be fairly stable. Techniques which use qualitative stable properties of images [VGT89a, VGT89b, VGT90, VP87a, VP87b, VP89] in the process of extracting and analyzing image velocities are in general better than techniques which rely on accurate quantitative measurements from the image data, since image data is more often than not extremely noisy.

Matching based techniques [Ana89, Gla87, GRA83, LK81, Luc84, Law80, Law83, Law84] provide reliable information at some image locations. But these techniques have the drawback that they rely on extensive interpolation to fill in the entire velocity field.

The spatio-temporal techniques face many of the problems of the derivative based techniques, as they essentially make the same assumptions about the spatio-temporal data as the derivative techniques.

Barron, Fleet, Beauchemin and Burkitt [BFBB92a, BFBB92b] have presented results on an experimental evaluation of several of the popular optic flow techniques. They have performed experiments with several synthetic and real sequences in which the ground truth of the camera motion is known. In the case of the synthetic images the ground truth of the exact pixel motions is available. Using this information they have compared the technique in terms of the accuracy of the velocity estimates generated. Below we list their main conclusions:

- The degree of smoothing applied to the image sequence is very critical to the performance of the techniques which rely on differentiation.
- Use of confidence measures to filter out bad velocity estimates is of considerable importance.
- Local techniques of velocity correction were better than the global techniques like smoothness constraints.

The image sequences used in these experiments are fairly realistic, but are not close to the images that will be acquired from a camera mounted on a robot, navigating through an environment.

The approaches we have reviewed are applicable to any general sequence of images. If the sequence of images is obtained by a robot navigating through an environment, several additional constraints can be used to formulate the problem with a different emphasis. The next section presents one such technique which is under development.

2.3 Motion Analysis for Mobile Robots

Most of the techniques discussed so far start with a sequence of images, extract the flow between the images, and use some additional assumption like smoothness to solve the aperture problem. In the context of robot navigation, constraints about the motion of the camera and the objects in the environment can be used to solve the aperture problem instead of using assumptions about the structure of the world. The use of camera motion constraints makes the resulting algorithms specific to robot navigation applications in a stationary world. In the approach proposed below, simple matching based techniques are used to extract the initial flow. Given a particular kind of robot motion and stationary objects, the appropriate kind of 2D linear vector field model is used as a model of the extracted flow. The model parameters are estimated from the initial flow and regenerative iteration is used to refine the initial flow. Thus this algorithm results in a mathematical model of the flow rather than the 2D flow itself, as is the case in most other optic flow alogrithms.

In this approach, the process of extracting vectors and estimating the vector field model are performed in an iterative manner, making the local flow vector extraction process more reliable. The use of predictions based on the previous model of the image motion reduces the number of errors generated by the velocity extraction process. Unlike most techniques for solving the aperture problem, the approach proposed here does not impose an arbitrary smoothness constraint on the vectors. The type of motion between frames, which is a global parameter, is used as the additional constraint to solve the aperture problem.

The equations that govern the motion of points in the image plane are derived in this section. The procedure for estimating the parameters of these equations are also presented. The standard camera geometry is assumed, where the optic center is at the origin of the coordinate system. The image plane is at a unit distance from the origin along the positive Z axis. All objects in the world lie in front of the image plane, i.e., for any point in the world $Z > 1$. Figure 1 illustrates the camera geometry and various motion parameters of the camera. Let $\vec{V} = [V_x, V_y, V_z]$ be the translational velocity of the camera with reference to the coordinate axes. Let $\vec{R} = [R_x, R_y, R_z]$ be the rotational velocity of the camera about the coordinate axes. Let $\vec{P} = [X, Y, Z]$ be the position of a point in space. Let $\vec{p} = \left[\frac{X}{Z}, \frac{Y}{Z}, 1\right]$ be the projection of $\vec{P}$ onto the image plane. Let $\vec{v} = [u, v]$ be the velocity of the point $\vec{p}$ in the image plane due to the motion of the point $\vec{P}$ in the world. Then the image motion of the point $\vec{p}$ is given by the following equations

$$u = x\frac{V_z}{Z} - \frac{V_x}{Z} + xyR_x - (1+x^2)R_y + yR_z \tag{5}$$

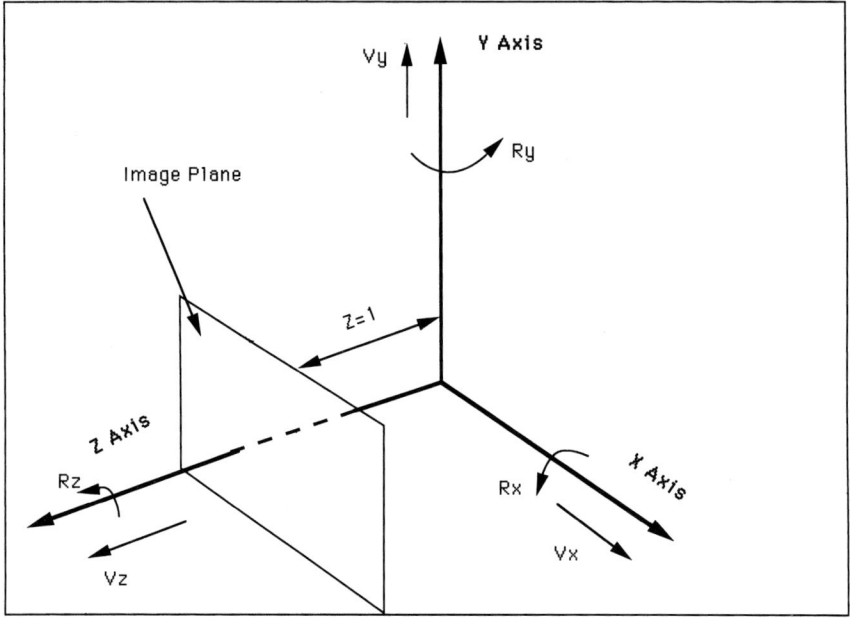

Fig. 1. Camera geometry

$$v = y\frac{V_z}{Z} - \frac{V_y}{Z} - xyR_y + (1+y^2)R_x - xR_z \qquad (6)$$

where $\vec{v}$ gives the velocity of any point on the image plane due to the motion of the camera. The above equations can be decomposed into two components, one corresponding to pure translation and the other to pure rotation. The translation component depends on the scene structure and the rotation equations are independent of the scene structure. In the following subsections the design of estimators for estimating the parameters of translation and rotation fields are presented.

2.3.1 Pure Translation

Given that the camera motion is pure translation $\vec{R} = [0, 0, 0]$. The image flow equations (5, 6) now reduce to the following:

$$u = x\frac{V_z}{Z} - \frac{V_x}{Z} \qquad v = y\frac{V_z}{Z} - \frac{V_y}{Z} \qquad (7)$$

The critical point of the vector field is the point where both the components of the flow vanish. This point can be located by setting $\vec{v} = \vec{0}$ and solving the equations for the location of the critical point (x_c, y_c). For equation (7) the critical point is

$$(x_c, y_c) = \left(\frac{V_x}{V_z}, \frac{V_y}{V_z}\right) \tag{8}$$

In the case of pure translation the critical point is called *Focus of Expansion* or *Focus of Contraction* for approaching or receding motion respectively. From equation (7)

$$tan(\theta) = \frac{u}{v} = \frac{xV_z - V_x}{yV_z - V_y} \tag{9}$$

This equation demonstrates that the orientation of the flow vectors at each point is independent of the scene depth at that point. Translation parameters can therefore be estimated using only the orientation of the flow vector at each point.

Least squares estimation is used to estimate the parameters of the flow field from the sparse image motion. A complete discussion of the design of the estimator can be found in [SJ92]. The orientation of a first order motion field is given by

$$t = tan(\theta) = \frac{a_1 x + b_1 y + c_1}{a_2 x + b_2 y + c_2} \tag{10}$$

which can be rewritten as

$$(a_1 - a_2 t) x + (b_1 - b_2 t) y + (c_1 - c_2 t) = 0 \tag{11}$$

The parameters of the flow field should satisfy the above equation. The estimator used minimizes the following weighted expression:

$$\sum_{i=1}^{N} w_i^2 (a_1 x_i - a_2 t_i x_i + b_1 y_i - b_2 t_i y_i + c_1 - c_2 t_i)^2 \tag{12}$$

where w_i is the reliability of the orientation of each point (x_i, y_i) and N is the number of points at which the image motion is measured. The reliability is computed as follows:

$$w_i = cos(\theta_i) \times \sqrt{\left(\frac{\partial E}{\partial x}\right)^2 + \left(\frac{\partial E}{\partial y}\right)^2} \tag{13}$$

where $E(x, y)$ is the image intensity function. The constraint on the minimization is

$$\sqrt{a_1^2 + b_1^2 + a_2^2 + b_2^2} = 1 \tag{14}$$

It is important to note that the estimator uses only the orientation of the sparse flow at each point. This makes the procedure independent of the scene depth at each point, giving a global model of the direction of pixel motion.

2.3.2 Pure Rotation

This section presents the design of an estimator for extracting the rotation parameters of a camera undergoing pure rotary motion. Given that the camera motion is pure rotation, $\vec{V} = [0, 0, 0]$. The image flow equations (5, 6) now reduce to the following:

$$u = xyR_x - (1 + x^2)R_y + yR_z \tag{15}$$

$$v = -xyR_y + (1 + y^2)R_x - xR_z \tag{16}$$

The above equations are linear in their parameters (R_x, R_y, R_z) and second order in terms of the spatial variables (x, y). A formulation similar to the translation estimator is used. The orientation of the vectors is used as the data to estimate the parameters.

A weighted linear least squares estimator is used to estimate the rotation parameters. The orientation of the vector at each point is used to estimate the rotation parameters. The following cost function is minimized in the estimation process:

$$\sum_{i=1}^{N} w_i^2 ((t_i x_i y_i - y_i^2 - 1)R_x - (t_i + t_i x_i^2 + x_i y_i)R_y + ((t_i y_i)R_z))^2 \tag{17}$$

where

$$t = tan(\theta) = \frac{-xyR_y + (1 + y^2)R_x - xR_z}{xyR_x - (1 + x^2)R_y + yR_z} \tag{18}$$

and the weight for the estimation is given by

$$w_i = cos(\theta_i) \times \sqrt{\left(\frac{\partial E}{\partial x}\right)^2 + \left(\frac{\partial E}{\partial y}\right)^2} \tag{19}$$

The estimation is subject to the constraint $\sqrt{R_x^2 + R_y^2 + R_z^2} = 1$.

2.3.3 Iterative Refinement

This subsection discusses the main steps in this approach for estimating a model for the image plane motion. The motivation for an iterative refinement process is to correct the errors generated by the initial matching process. A local matching process is bound to be error prone due to the aperture problem [Ana89]. By using the initial model to constrain the matching process, a global motion constraint is imposed on the local matching process, thus generating better matches.

The first step in the algorithm is to extract from the image sequence a set of velocity vectors at locations in the image where the information is reliable. This set

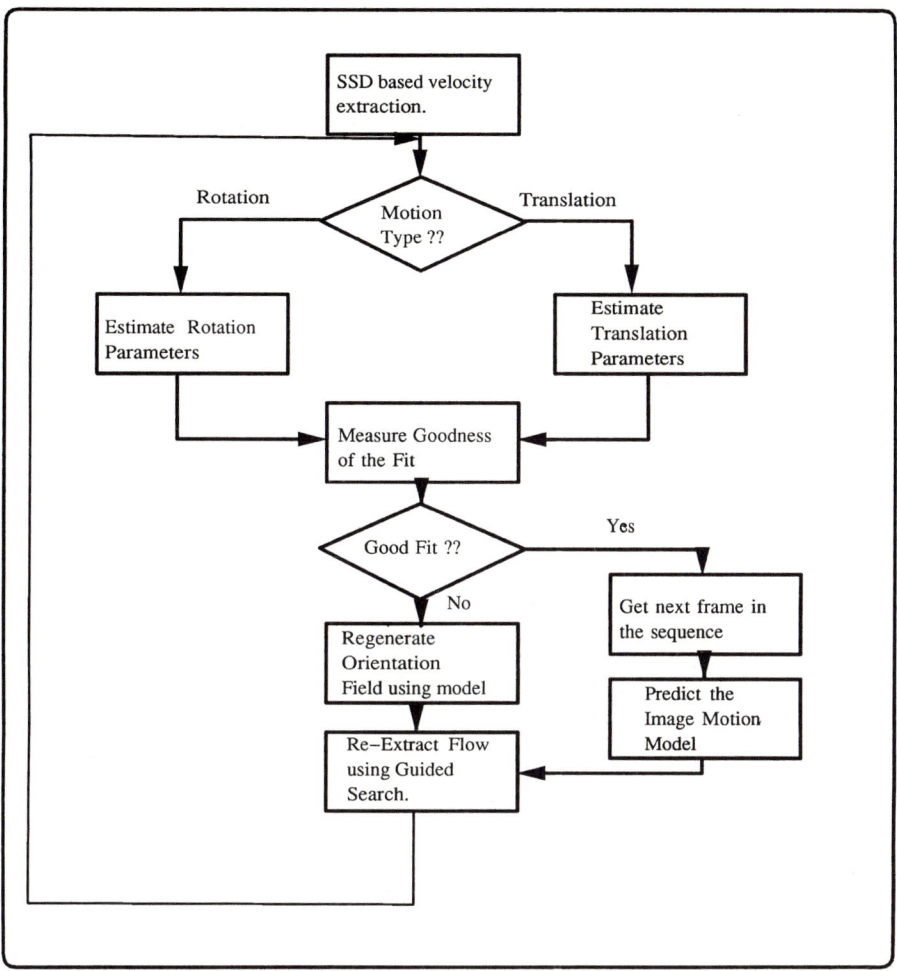

Fig. 2. Flow chart of the algorithm

of vectors is referred as the *sparse flow*. The orientation of this sparse flow field is used to estimate the *global* model of the flow field, i.e., the parameters of equations (7, 15, 16). The model used depends on the type of motion that the camera undergoes. This global model is then used to regenerate the vector field at various image locations. The local process for extracting the image plane motion is constrained based on this regenerated vector. This re-extracted sparse flow cycles again through the iteration process. A flow chart of the algorithm is given in Fig. 2. The first step is to extract sparse image velocities using the first two frames of the sequence. Depending on the type of motion, this sparse velocity field is modeled either as a translation field or rotation field. The goodness of the fit is evaluated and iterative refinement is performed if a better fit is required. The goodness of fit can be measured in terms of the condition number of the recovered parameters and the residue of the minimization process. Once a model for the image motion between two frames has been obtained, this is used to predict and estimate the model for the next frame in the sequence. Each of the steps are presented in the following subsections.

2.3.4 Sparse Flow Extraction

The extraction of the initial velocity vectors is based on a *sum of squared differences* (SSD) [Ana89] of intensity patches between successive images in the sequence. Since motion information is not uniformly distributed through out the image [Nag83], velocity vectors are extracted only at points of high gradient. This factor of non-uniform distribution of motion information has been taken into account in the design of the estimator in terms of the weighting factor which is proportional to the magnitude of the intensity gradient as in equations (13, 19). The points for data extraction are chosen using an empirically determined threshold on the magnitude of the intensity gradient. The correct match is determined based on a search for a minimum in the SSD value in a neighborhood as shown in Fig. 3. The use of the SSD of the intensity to match intensity patches allows for the violation of the brightness constraint [HS81]. These violations occur when the brightness of a patch changes due to reasons other than the motion. The velocity extraction process is followed by the estimation of the model as outlined in Sect. 2.3.

2.3.5 Guided Search

If the parameters for a flow field are known, it can be regenerated using equations (9) and (18). The orientation of the regenerated vectors is used to guide the search

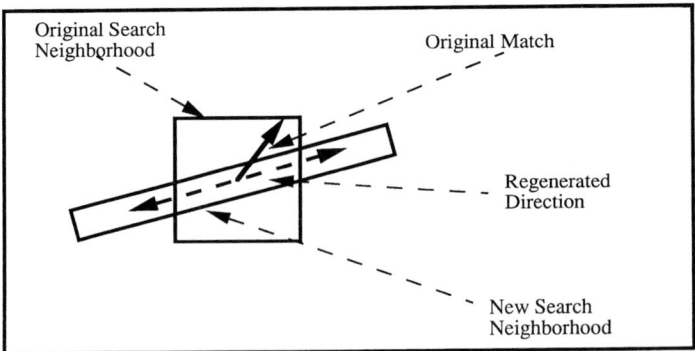

Fig. 3. Search neighborhoods for guided search

for better matches in the two images. Figure 3 illustrates the rationale behind using the regenerated flow. The idea of guided or directed search can be summarized as follows. The results obtained from the SSD based matching algorithm depend on the size of the search neighborhood used and the size of the intensity patch used for matching. Given a particular template (intensity patch) size to use in the matching process, the possibility of mismatch increases with the size of the search area. This is especially true of image locations, like uniform regions, where the aperture problem is severe. If the search area is constrained to a very small neighborhood, the possibility of excluding the correct match increases. Guided search represents a trade-off in the size and shape of the search area based on the global image motion characteristics in the image.

The model obtained from the initial fitting is used to predict the orientation of the displacement vector at each point in the image. The search neighborhood at each point is then constrained along the direction of this predicted orientation as shown in Fig. 3.

2.3.6 Experimental Results

Experiments were conducted using both real images and simulations. The iterative estimation procedure has been applied to a sequence of images in which the camera has a pure translatory motion. One frame of the sequence is shown in Fig. 4. The sequence was obtained from the *IEEE 1991 Motion Workshop* database. Figures 5, 6, 7, and 8 show the progress of the iterative refinement process. Figure

Fig. 4. Coke can image sequence

Fig. 5. Extracted sparse flow

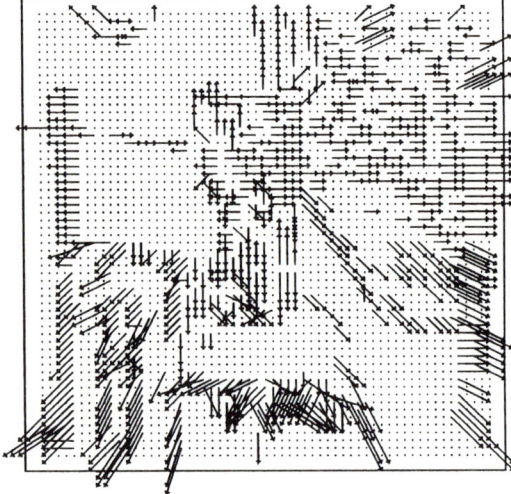

Fig. 6. Refined sparse flow: iteration 1

5 shows the initial flow extracted using SSD matching. Figures 6 and 7 show the improvement over the first two iterations. Figure 8, shows the reconstructed flow using the recovered parameters. The iterative algorithm has also been applied to predict and extract the motion model for subsequent images in the coke image sequence. Experiments with image sequences in which the location of the critical point changes are in progress.

The rotation estimator presented has been tested using simulated flow vectors. Figure 9 shows the simulated flow generated using $(R_x, R_y, R_z = 0.1, 0.2, 0.3)$. This flow was used as data to the rotation estimator. The recovered flow is shown in Fig. 10. The estimation procedure performs well on simulated data. The estimator is

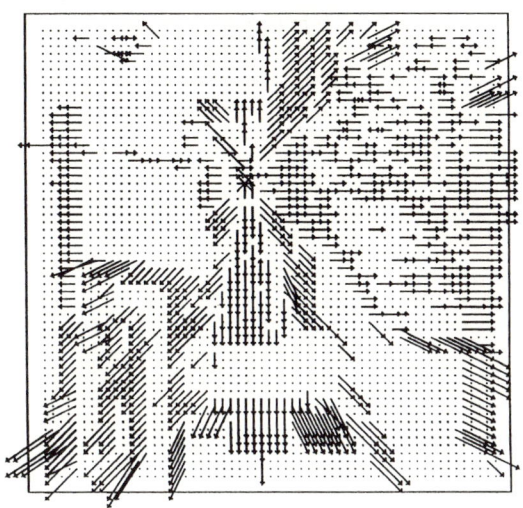

Fig. 7. Refined sparse flow: iteration 2

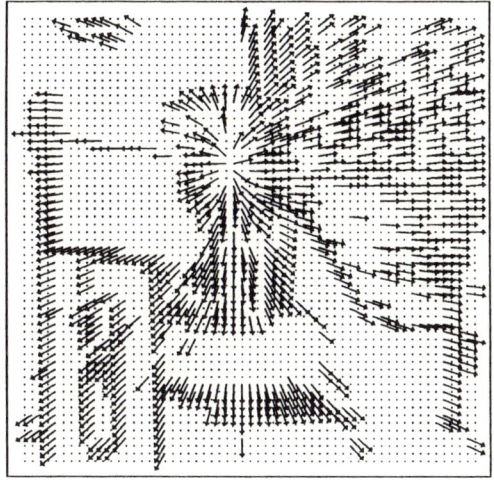

Fig. 8. Reconstructed flow

currently being evaluated on real image sequences with pure rotation, and known ground truth.

2.4 Conclusions and Future Work

We have presented a review and critique of optic flow computation algorithms and proposed an approach for mobile robots that takes advantage of constraints unique to that domain. This approach presented an iterative technique for estimat-

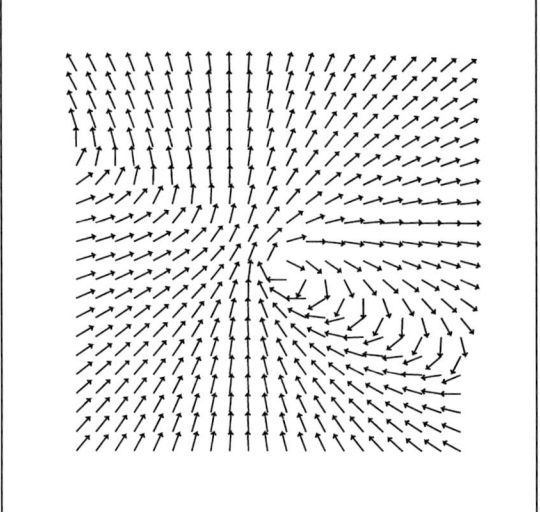

Fig. 9. Simulated flow

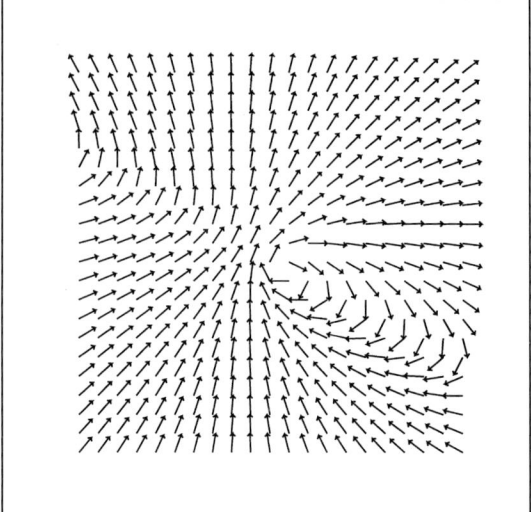

Fig. 10. Recovered flow

ing a global model for the image plane motion from a sequence of intensity images. The technique uses pixel motion which is extracted from the image sequence. The technique does not need dense image plane motion to estimate the image velocity orientation field. The use of information from all parts of the image in estimating the image velocity orientation field model makes the estimation process reliable and insensitive to noise in the local computations. The unique feature of the proposed approach is the use of the global model to modify local processing. Since the global model is based on information from all regions in the image, the information it captures is the stable behavior of the pixel motion. The use of global information to constrain local processing, ensures that the velocities generated by the local processes are globally consistent. Choosing the estimation procedure based on the type of robot motion allows the technique to handle both translation and rotation. The results obtained on both real images and in simulation are very encouraging. Future research will address problems involving both translation and rotation.

3 Stereo and the Ego-Motion Complex Logarithmic Mapping

Determining the depths of objects in the scene is often a necessary part of a robot vision system. The problem inherent in finding depths from a single image is to correctly reconstruct the 3D scene from the 2D images. The difficulty arises from the fact that an infinity of 3D scenes can produce a given 2D image. Figure 11 illustrates the problem in two dimensions. The image of point P, P_I, could also have been formed by any identical point along the line of sight. There is not enough information in one image alone to determine the 3D locations of the points in the scene uniquely. One way of getting the needed information is to use two images, as shown in Fig. 12. With two images, depth can be computed by using triangulation or by reversing the perspective projection. To find the depth of a point in the scene, it is necessary to find the pixels that correspond to that point in both images. This can be viewed as a matching problem, which usually results in sparse depth data, or as an optic flow problem which gives dense data.

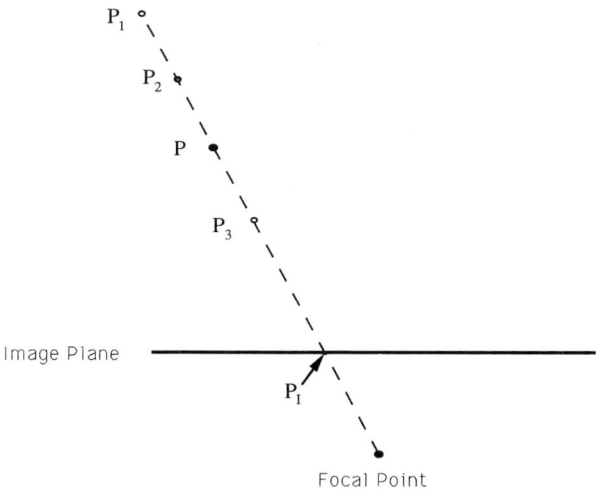

Fig. 11. This simple 2D example illustrates the problem with finding depths of objects from a single view. The image of point P, P_I, could also have been formed by any identical point along the line of sight

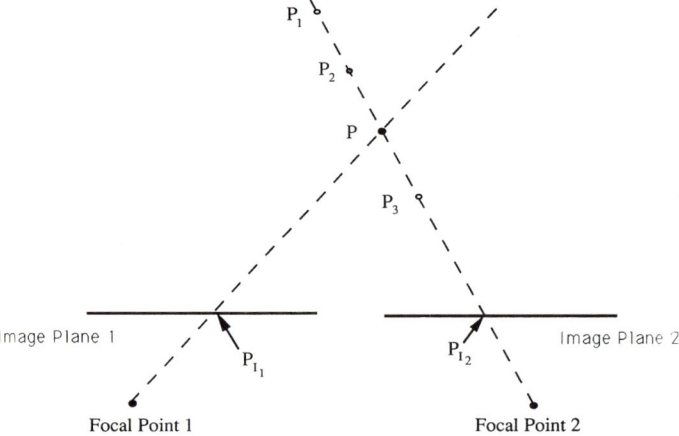

Fig. 12. If two images are used, the point can be identified uniquely

Constraints on the camera geometry are used to simplify the computations. The most commonly used constraints are: the two cameras must point in the same direction and they are displaced along only the x-axis. This arrangement mimics the placement of our eyes in our head and is known as binocular stereo. The advantage of this camera configuration is that the matches or the flow vectors will be along the image scan lines. This makes finding matches or computing optic flow easier. Binocular stereo is a popular passive depth determination technique, but, because two new images are needed to determine depth, the approach requires a lot of hardware (two camera, etc.) or a lot of time (to move one camera to a second location). This makes it less appealing for mobile robot navigation where the extra weight or extra time can be a problem.

We can relax the constraints on the camera geometry and define a type of stereo that capitalizes on camera motion. Instead of allowing only displacement along the x-axis, let us allow arbitrary translation of the camera as long as there is some motion along the z-axis. This is called motion stereo and requires only a single camera and only one new image after the first pair is obtained. The drawback to this approach is that the stereo matches are no longer constrained to be long an image scan line, as they are in binocular stereo. Thus matching is much more time consuming. The complex logarithmic mapping (CLM) is useful for motion stereo because it can be used to orient the flow vectors along image rows so matching is as easy as in binocular stereo. At the same time, using the mapping makes the actual depth computation less complex. If the camera images are transformed into CLM space, computing depth in motion stereo becomes as simple as in binocular stereo.

First we will define the mapping mathematically, explain how it can be used to transform images, and outline its usefulness. Then we will show how it can be used for finding depths.

Vision for Mobile Robots

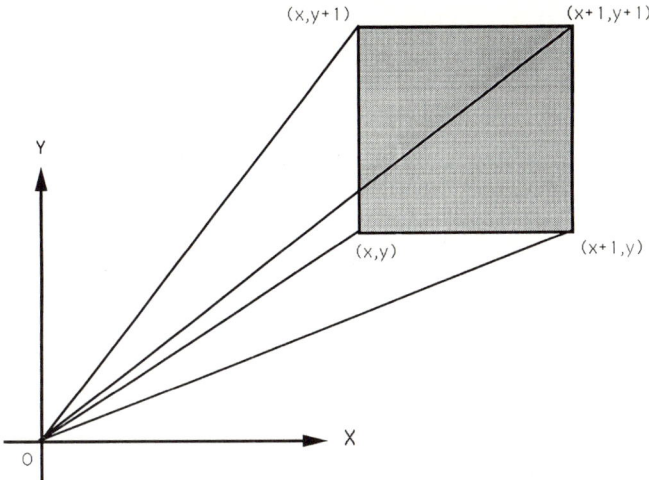

Fig. 13. Since a single image pixel has a measurable size, it maps to a range of values in CLM space

3.1 The Mapping

The complex log mapping may be written as

$$w = \log z \tag{20}$$

where w and z are complex variables:

$$z = x + iy = r(\cos\theta + i\sin\theta) = re^{i\theta} \tag{21}$$

and

$$w = u(z) + iv(z) \tag{22}$$

In this way, a function or image in z-space with coordinates x and y is mapped to w-space with coordinates u and v. The mapping is obtained from the simplified equations:

$$u(r, \theta) = \log r = \log\sqrt{x^2 + y^2} \tag{23}$$

$$v(r, \theta) = \theta = \tan^{-1}\frac{y}{x} \tag{24}$$

To map an image, in a simplistic way, take each pixel's image coordinates, (x, y), and use them to compute the coordinates (u, v) in the new mapped image. Then take the intensity value at (x, y) in the original image and assign it to pixel (u, v) in the mapping. In the continuous case, each point in the image space corresponds to exactly one point in the CLM space. However, in computer vision systems, an image can only be stored as a finite number of pixels. In addition, only a finite number of intensities are representable. This quantization of the image leads to ambiguity in the mapping. An illustration of this is shown in Fig. 13. Close to the

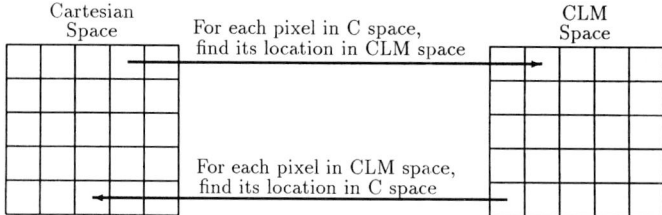

Fig. 14. The mapping from a Cartesian image to a CLM image can be performed 2 different ways

origin of the mapping, these ranges can be quite wide causing such an image pixel to map to a range of pixels in CLM space. At the periphery of the image, these ranges are practically negligible, so several pixels in the image may map to a single pixel in the transformed space. To overcome this problem each pixel in the CLM image can be assigned the pixel value in the corresponding location in the Cartesian (C) space represented by the camera image. Figure 14 shows the underlying difference between the two approaches. In the discretized domain of digital images, the mapping is not 1-to-1 as it is in the continuous domain, so each approach will produce different results. Figure 15 shows these differences. The images are square (128×128) and the mapping origin is the center of the original image, with the x axis horizontal and the y axis vertical. The mapped image is the same size as the original image, with the u axis ($\log r$) horizontal and the v axis (Θ) vertical. The origin of the mapped image is the lower left corner. Theta is measured counter-clockwise from the positive x axis in the original image. If we want to use standard computer vision algorithms on the mapped images, it is obvious that the mapping in the bottom row is more suitable.

There are many attractive features of this mapping [CW79, BGT81, ST80], even though it looks strange. From the mathematical viewpoint, it is the only analytic function which maps a circular region, such as an image on the retina, into a rectangular region. This is a desirable feature for the study and modeling of the human visual system. The mappings of two regular patterns are shown in Fig. 16 to result in similarly regular patterns. Figure 16a shows that concentric circles in an image or in the z-plane become vertical lines in the mapped w-plane. This is because the constant radius, r, at all angles, θ, of the circle gives a constant u coordinate for all v coordinates in the mapped space. Similarly in Fig. 16b, an image of radial lines, which have constant angle but variable radii, result in a map of horizontal lines.

Through the mappings in Fig. 16, we can demonstrate some interesting properties of CLM. First, it is rotation invariant. In Fig. 16a, we saw that for a circle, all possible angular orientations of a point at the given radius will map to the same vertical line. Thus, if an object is rotated between successive images, this will result in only a vertical displacement of the mapped image. This same result can be seen in Fig. 16b. As a radial line rotates about the origin, the horizontal line in CLM moves only vertically.

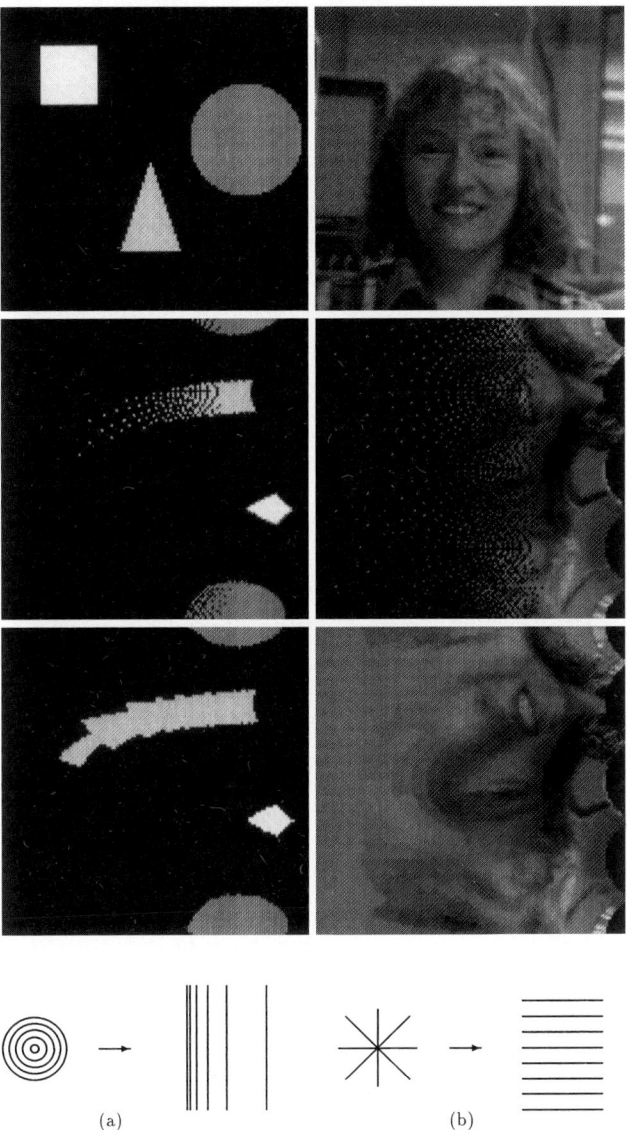

Fig. 15. The top row shows 2 sample images, one synthetic and one real. The second row shows the two images mapped using the C space to CLM space algorithm. The bottom row shows the same images mapped using the CLM space to C space algorithm

Fig. 16. The CLM results in the transformation of certain regular patterns in the z-plane into other regular patterns in the w-place. **a** Shows that concentric circles are mapped into vertical lines; **b** Shows that radial lines are mapped into horizontal lines

Another property is size invariance. This also can be seen in Fig. 16. The mappings of the concentric circles of Fig. 16a remain vertical lines and only move horizontally as the circles change in size. As a point moves out from the origin along a radial line in Fig. 16b, its mapping stays on the same horizontal line moving only from left to right.

A third important property is projection invariance. When an observer translates in space, the images of stationary objects change on the retina, but the object perceived on the striate cortex does not change. This is due to the fact that in CLM space, translation of the observer only causes the object image to be displaced in the horizontal direction; the size and shape of the object image remain unchanged.

Given these invariences, CLM can be useful for depth perception. Suppose an observer is looking at the center of a circle and moving toward it along his direction of gaze. As he moves, the circle seems to get bigger. If the observer took some pictures of the circle as he moved, they would look much like Fig. 16a. As time passes, the vertical line that represents the circle would move in CLM space. How far the circle moves is a function of its depth. Another thing to note is that the size of the circle in CLM space remains the same, even though the size in the image changes, which is very useful for matching.

Unfortunately, these useful properties occur only under certain conditions. Cavanaugh [Cav78, Cav81] showed that the rotation and scale invariances are obtained only if the object is in the center of the image and the rotation and scale changes are with respect to the origin. The projection invariance is obtained only if the direction of the observer's gaze and motion are the same. However, these constraints are easily satisfied in many computer vision tasks, e.g., a vehicle traveling along a straight road, a space craft docking, or a robot arm approaching the part to be inspected or grasped. Thus a single operation on the images obtained by a camera mounted on such a moving vehicle or robot can simplify both object recognition and depth determination.

3.2 Depth Determination

It has been shown [JBO87] that the depth of a static object can be obtained using CLM if images of the object are obtained by a translating camera. The images are mapped into the CLM space using the focus of expansion (FOE) as the origin for computing image coordinates. When the FOE is used as the origin, the mapping becomes the ego-motion complex logarithmic mapping (ECLM), since it is based on the motion of the camera itself. Estimates of ego-motion parameters are usually available for moving vehicles and robots, so ECLM can be used in these cases. For those applications where the FOE is unknown, there are several techniques available for computing it [Jai83, Law82, DMRS88, NH89].

If ECLM is used, the depth, Z, of a feature on a static object can be obtained based on the following relation [JBO87]:

$$\frac{du}{dZ} = -\frac{1}{Z} \tag{25}$$

where du is the displacement of the feature along the u axis in the ECLM space and dZ is the distance in depth that the camera moves between frames. Note that

$$\frac{dv}{dZ} = 0 \qquad (26)$$

where dv is the displacement along the v axis. This simplification results from the projection invariance of the mapping. Thus the matching features can be found by searching in a line parallel to the axis in ECLM space, rather than searching in a line at an arbitrary angle in the image.

Depth determination using ECLM is similar to binocular stereo in the sense that both methods rely on matching between images – the mapped images for ECLM and the scene images themselves for binocular stereo. ECLM has several advantages, however. First, the search is always along an axis of the image, making it faster and easier to do on the computer. For binocular stereo this is only possible if the two images are obtained from camera positions that are only horizontally or only vertically displaced from each other. Second, the search range for a point in the second image is smaller for ECLM [Alv87]. And finally, the problem of features with no matches is reduced because all the stationary objects in the closer image are also in the farther image.

Using ECLM for real-time depth determination applications requires that the images be mapped into the complex log space in real time. Hardware exists for transforming images at frame rates [Wei88, Wei89]. CCD sensors which simulate the mapping have been built [TS90].

For a given camera, using binocular stereo, the only way to increase the accuracy and/or range of the computed depths is to use a larger baseline. This parameter is difficult to change, especially dynamically. Fortunately, using ECLM, there are several ways to get more accurate depth estimates or a broader range of detected depths. One method is to use a larger map size. An image can be transformed into a map of any size. Map size affects the range of detectable depths, the largest detectable depth, and the time it takes to process the map. Table 1 shows relative recoverable depth data for a 128 × 128 image transformed to maps of different sizes. Note that the units of the depths in the table are the same as the units used to measure the distance the camera moved. Note that the larger the map, the larger the detectable depth and the finer the depth resolution. If the mapping is done with software, this simply means that a single mapping parameter has to be changed to get improved results. This would be easy to do on the fly, if necessary.

Another way to increase the available depth information is to process the current image with several previous ones. Conceptually, this provides depths computed with larger values of dZ, equivalent to having a longer baseline. For example, assume a camera is moving at a constant speed of 1 cm per second and an image is obtained every second. If 128 × 128 images are obtained and mapped to 128 × 128, then values in row 2 of Table 1 can be used to obtain depths. Using the current image and the previous one, depths between 0.22 cm and 28.41 cm can be recovered. Using the current image and the one before the previous one, depths between 0.44 cm and 56.82 cm can be recovered. Using even earlier images further expands the range and resolution of detectable depths. If there is enough memory in the

Table 1. This table shows the relative recoverable depths for a 128 × 128 image transformed into various sized mappings. The relative depth represented by a displacement of different numbers of pixels in the ECLM images is given. These values must be multiplied by dZ to give the absolute depth and the units

Map size	Feature displacement in pixels							
	1	2	3	4	5	6	7	max
64	14.20	7.10	4.73	3.55	2.84	2.37	2.03	0.23
128	28.41	14.20	9.47	7.10	5.68	4.73	4.06	0.22
256	56.82	28.41	18.94	14.20	11.36	9.47	8.12	0.22
480	106.54	53.27	35.51	26.63	21.31	17.76	15.22	0.22
512	113.64	56.82	37.88	28.41	22.73	18.94	16.23	0.22
640	142.05	71.02	47.35	35.51	28.41	23.67	20.29	0.22
1024	227.28	113.64	75.76	56.82	45.46	37.88	32.47	0.22

system, this can be done easily by saving previous images and processing them with the current one.

Another option for improving the depth information is to use a blind spot at the origin of the mapping. In the derivation for computing detectable depths given above, the u axis of the ECLM image ranged from 0 to u_{max}, distributed over R_m pixels. Using a blind spot, the u axis represents values ranging from some value $u_{min} > 0$ to u_{max}. Now the smallest Δu that can be measured is $\frac{u_{max} - u_{min}}{R_m}$ and, therefore the greatest distance that is recoverable is $-dZ \cdot \frac{R_m}{u_{max} - u_{min}}$. Using a blind spot, the changes in u that can be detected are

$$\Delta u = n \cdot \frac{u_{max} - u_{min}}{R_m} \quad \text{for } n = 1, 2, 3, \ldots \tag{27}$$

which means that the depths that can be computed are

$$Z = -\frac{dZ}{n} \cdot \frac{R_m}{u_{max} - u_{min}} \quad \text{for } n = 1, 2, 3, \ldots \tag{28}$$

Since $u_{max} - u_{min} < u_{max}$, larger depths can be detected.

Depending on the size of the blind spot, the range $[u_{min}, u_{max}]$ will change and hence the resolution will also change. Table 2 shows the effects of various sized blind spots on the recoverable depths using a 128 × 128 mapping as the exemplar. Again, the units used to measure the distance the camera moved determine the units of the depths in the table.

For practical applications, minimizing computer computation and memory requirements is an important issue. The constraints of a given application and tables like the ones in this section can be used to choose the camera motion parameters and mapping parameters to measure the required range of depths to the required accuracy.

Table 2. This table shows the relative recoverable depths for various blind spot sizes. The table is computed for a 128 × 128 image transformed to a 128 × 128 mapping. These values must be multiplied by dZ to give the absolute depth and the units

Spot size	Pixel displacement						
	1	2	3	4	5	6	max
0–1	28.4	14.2	9.5	7.1	5.7	4.7	0.22
2.0	33.6	16.8	11.2	8.4	6.7	5.6	0.26
3.0	37.6	18.8	12.5	9.4	7.5	6.3	0.30
4.0	41.0	20.5	13.7	10.3	8.2	6.8	0.32
5.0	44.2	22.1	14.7	11.0	8.8	7.4	0.35
6.0	47.2	23.6	15.7	11.8	9.4	7.9	0.37
7.0	50.0	25.0	16.7	12.5	10.0	8.3	0.39
8.0	52.8	26.4	17.6	13.2	10.6	8.8	0.42
9.0	55.5	27.7	18.5	13.9	11.1	9.2	0.44
10.0	58.1	29.1	19.4	14.5	11.6	9.7	0.46
11.0	60.7	30.4	20.2	15.2	12.1	10.1	0.48
12.0	63.3	31.7	21.1	15.8	12.7	10.6	0.50
13.0	66.0	33.0	22.0	16.5	13.2	11.0	0.52
14.0	68.6	34.3	22.9	17.1	13.7	11.4	0.54

3.3 Results

A lab scene with simple objects was used to test the approach. A camera was mounted on a PUMA robot arm. This set-up allowed us to move the camera in a known direction by a known amount. The objects used were wooden blocks with dimensions less than 6 inches. The scene was constructed so most of the background and foreground was black. Due to the limited depth of field of the camera, the objects had to be placed relatively near each other. The camera moved 6 inches along its optical axis toward the blocks, putting the focus of expansion in the center of the image. A set of five 512 × 512 images were obtained and then shrunk to 128 × 128 to decrease computation time and storage space. The FOE was assumed to be in the center of the image. A point matching algorithm was used to compute depths in this experiment, but any feature matching or optic flow algorithm could be used.

The first four frames of the sequence are shown in Fig. 17. In this experiment, we found corners in the image and then mapped the corners to ECLM space. Corners of the objects found using Moravec's interest operator [Mor81b] are shown in Fig. 18. Figure 19 shows the corners of Fig. 18 mapped into the ECLM space.

The correspondence between features was established in the ECLM space. Since the number of points is small, the matching was done in the continuous, real ECLM space rather than the ECLM image space shown in Fig. 19. This helped eliminate some of the quantization error. For each pair of images, the coordinates in the ECLM space were calculated for all the interesting points and saved in a list.

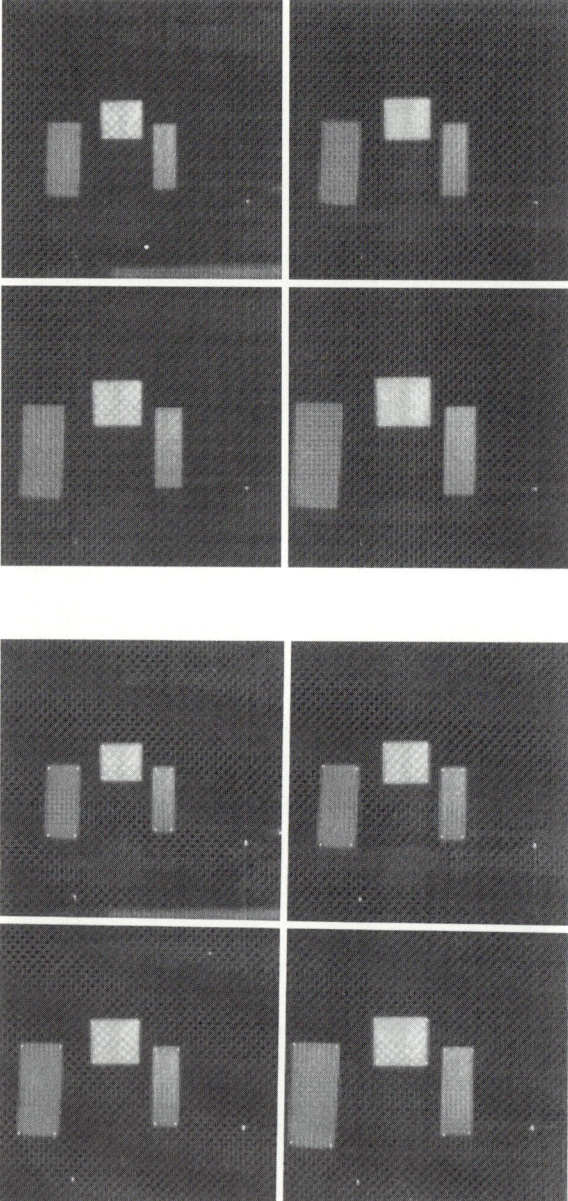

Fig. 17. These are the first 4 of the sequence of images of blocks taken in the laboratory with a camera mounted on a Puma robot arm. The camera moves along its optical axis

Fig. 18. These are the corners found in the images in Fig. 17

Theoretically, two matching points should have the same Θ value (v coordinate). Due to digitization error, blurring in the images from shrinking, and errors in feature detection, matching points do not have the same Θ value. A threshold for the maximum possible dv between corresponding features (the difference between the Θ values) was used. In addition, some heuristics were used to establish the

Vision for Mobile Robots

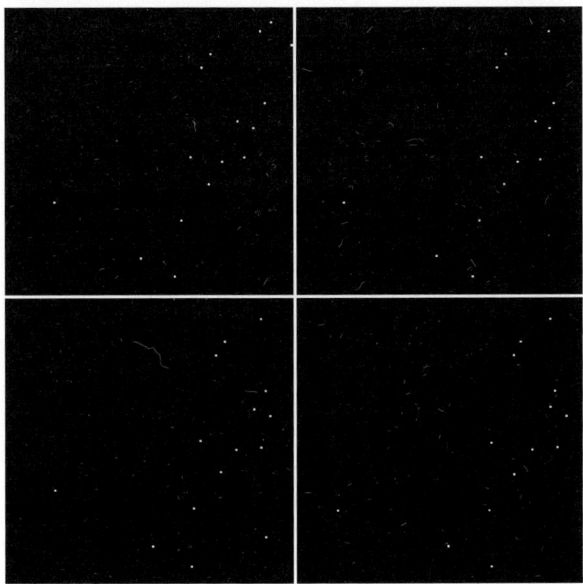

Fig. 19. These are ECLM mappings of the corners found in the images in Fig. 17

correspondence of points within the selected threshold. These are described in the following paragraph.

The algorithm was run on every pair of images using three different thresholds for dv: 0.01, 0.02 and 0.05. Since ground truth data is available for the images, matches can be objectively evaluated. A match is considered correct if the points belong to the same object. By using two simple rules, most match errors in these images were detected by the system. The rules are: a camera cannot see behind itself ($z > 0$); and, if you pass an object, it won't be in the second image ($z > dz$). This eliminates all matches with a distance less than the amount the camera moved.

The effect on the average depth determination with a tighter bound on allowable depths for individual pairs was also studied. An arbitrary value larger than the distance the camera moved was chosen as the lower bound. An arbitrary value of 100 was chosen as the upper bound. This is a valid assumption for indoor scenes, since the distance to the far wall can be measured and a camera can't see through walls. The depth of an object was obtained by averaging the depth obtained for its corners. The results are shown in Table 3.

For each object the distances were computed using the two simple rules and an upper bound of 130 inches and a lower bound of 20 inches to eliminate false matches. Using the upper and lower bound usually made no difference in the depth determination. However, this heuristic corrected a few errors that the simple rules did not catch. Increasing the threshold for dv increases the number of matches found. Often this means that a depth can be computed for an object. Whether or not the additional points improve the depth estimate depends on various factors discussed in the next chapter.

Table 3. This table shows the relative recoverable depths for various image/mapping sizes. For each image transformed into an ECLM image of the same size, the relative depth represented by a displacement of different numbers of pixels in the ECLM images is given. These values must be multiplied by dZ to give the absolute depth

Image pairs	dv = 0.01			dv = 0.02			dv = 0.05		
	obj 1	obj 2	obj 3	obj 1	obj 2	obj 3	obj 1	obj 2	obj 3
1–2	54	79	47	58	79	47	58	79	62
	−16%	−4%	−36%	−10%	−4%	−36%	−10%	−4%	−16%
1–3	61	82	79	63	79	76	63	79	72
	−4%	0%	6%	−2%	−4%	1%	−2%	−4%	−3%
1–4	69	–	81	70	98	75	65	98	74
	6%	–	8%	9%	19%	0%	0%	19%	−1%
1–5	–	–	–	78	94	77	78	94	77
	–	–	–	21%	13%	3%	21%	13%	3%
2–3	62	123	60	62	123	60	62	106	66
	−4%	49%	−19%	−3%	49%	−19%	−3%	28%	−11%
2–4	71	100	66	71	100	66	64	100	66
	10%	21%	−11%	10%	21%	−11%	0%	21%	−11%
2–5	77	–	–	77	101	74	77	101	74
	18%	–	–	18%	22%	0%	18%	22%	0%
3–4	76	–	62	74	–	60	74	122	61
	17%	–	−17%	15%	–	−19%	15%	47%	−17%
3–5	78	93	74	78	93	73	78	97	73
	20%	12%	0%	20%	12%	−1%	20%	17%	−1%
4–5	75	92	86	75	92	80	75	92	85
	16%	10%	13%	16%	10%	5%	16%	10%	12%

3.4 Summary

This has been a brief discussion of the ego-motion complex logarithmic mapping. We have shown that it can be used to make matching and depth computation easier for motion stereo. A fuller discussion and error analysis of the approach can be found in [Bar93].

4 Dynamic Stereo

Information about objects in the scene is very important for robot navigation. However, the information obtained from using any of the stereo methods described in Sect. 3 is not very reliable due to digitization error, noise in the images, occlusion of one object by another, etc. One way to overcome these problems is to compute new depth estimates as the robot moves in the environment and combine them over time. The redundancy in the data can be exploited to correct the errors.

This section is primarily concerned with developing a computational framework for recovering reliable and timely depth information from a stream of stereo images that are obtained over time by a robot vision system in a stationary environment. The wealth of information available in dynamic stereo affords us many options for processing methodologies to overcome some of its inherent problems. Recovering reliable depth information from image sequences, by integrating depth information computed from each stereo pair, has been investigated by several researchers. The problem with most previous approaches is the need for knowing or computing the exact camera motion (or displacement) between frames [Jen84, LD89, Gam90]. The importance of knowing such information cannot be underestimated. In applications that involve stationary sliders or robot arms, this camera displacement information can be obtained accurately. But for mobile robots that wander around a scene, it is a completely different story. In such applications, camera motion information that can be obtained from odometry is inaccurate and uncertain due to wheel slippage, finite shaft encoder resolution, etc. Furthermore, in outdoor experiments the camera platform is generally unstable due to small obstacles on the navigation course or changes in the ground slope. The projective geometry is such that the small camera rotations induced by these imperfections can cause drastic, unexpected changes on the image plane. Such rotations are the single most profound obstacle that many current approaches face.

We present a new computational model for fusion of time-varying spatial information. The novel aspect of the model is that it provides a framework for integrating spatial information over time without the direct use of camera motion. At the heart of the model is the transformation of viewer-centered information into what we call a *Referent-centered* representation. The central idea behind Referent-centered dynamic vision analysis is the representation of spatial information of all scene points with respect to a few prominent scene features which are tracked over time. Much of the power of this approach is derived from the fact that relative spatial information does not change when the point of observation moves and, therefore, the need for computing exact camera displacement during robot motion is eliminated. Our particular objective here is computing reliable depth information or, more precisely, *disparity maps*. A disparity map is a map that is registered to the left or right image and specifies the binocular disparity of the corresponding pixel in the image, from which depths can be computed using camera system parameters.

4.1 A Dynamic Binocular Vision System for General Camera Motion

The dynamic binocular vision system (DBV-1) described here computes reliable depth information by integrating data over time. The process is based on the Referent-centered dynamic vision model and therefore is carried out without the use of camera displacement information. The main objective of the process is to discard inconsistent disparity data using a corresponding confidence map that is

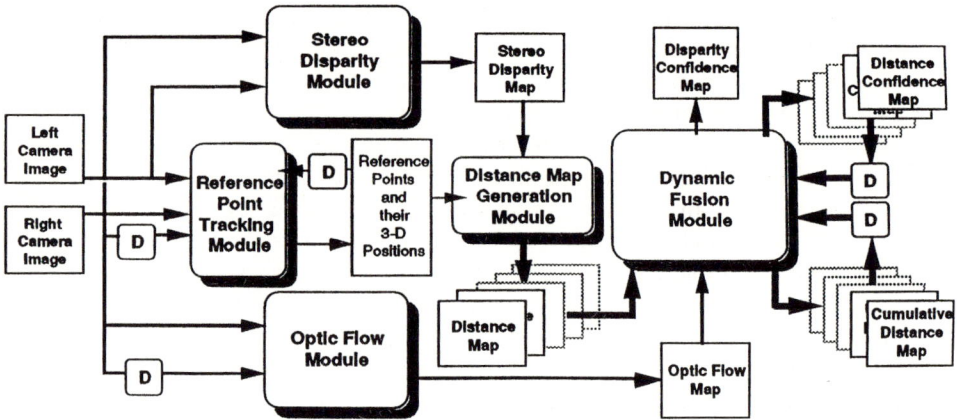

Fig. 20. Block diagram of the Dynamic DBV-1 system for computing reliable depth information from stereo images of a camera undergoing general motion

updated over time. The only assumptions are that the scene is stationary and the camera displacements between frames are relatively small.

The general procedure DBV-1 uses to compute reliable depth information over time is shown in Fig. 20. Each stereo image pair is first analyzed and a disparity map is computed. A parallel process finds and tracks a set of Reference Depth Points. A third process uses the right image sequence and computes an optic flow map for each consecutive temporal pair. The stereo disparity map is transformed into a set of invariant maps, in this case distance maps, using the current positions of the reference points. Newly computed distance maps are evaluated and updated by the dynamic fusion process using the optic flow maps. The fusion process generates a confidence map for the current disparity map, allowing the selection of disparity values that are the most reliable. A complete explanation of each of these processes follows.

4.1.1 Reference Point Tracking

The Reference Point Tracking process selects and tracks a set of Reference Depth Points in the stereo image sequence. The 3D positions of these reference points, in the camera-coordinate system, are also computed at each time step.

The selection process proceeds as follows. Using the Moravec operator [Mor81b] we find a set of interesting points in the right camera image. For every interesting point, area-based correlation matching is used to find the corresponding image of the point in the left camera image. Three criteria are used to select a set of reference points from these interesting points. First, they must have a strong match in the left image. The value of the correlation is used to determine the strength of the match. The second criteria is that the match must be unique. This is determined based on the number peaks in the correlation. The third criteria used in selecting a reference point is that it must not be "too far" from the camera. Since the Reference Depth Points are used to compute the distances of all other objects in the scene, the positional uncertainty of these points must be small. In general, the further an object is from the camera, the higher its positional uncertainty. Therefore, Reference Depth Points are generally selected from among points that are estimated to be within a certain range of the cameras.

Area-based correlation matching is used to track the Reference Depth Points in the right camera image sequence. At each time step, once the position of every reference point is found in the current right camera image, the tracking process uses the epipolar constraint to find a stereo match in the left camera image for each reference point. The 3D position of each reference point, in the camera-coordinate system, is then computed using the disparity of the match, the image location of the point, and the camera parameters.

A number of problems can occur. A reference point may not be tracked correctly in the right image sequence. The match found in the left image at any time step may be wrong. A reference point may disappear from either or both images, either temporarily or permanently. As will be shown later, given enough points, the dynamic stereo vision procedure can recover from all of the above errors.

4.1.2 Stereo Disparity Computation

A modified version of the coarse-to-fine disparity computation algorithm introduced by Anandan [Ana87b, Ana87a] is used for the Stereo Disparity Computation. This algorithm uses a Laplacian pyramid transform for decomposing each intensity image into a set of spatial-frequency tuned channels. The disparity information obtained by matching low-frequency images are used to guide the disparity computation at higher-frequency levels of the pyramid. The algorithm uses correlation-based matching by minimization of the sum-of-squared differences measure (SSD).

In this implementation of the algorithm, matching starts with the Laplacian of the Gaussian image pairs at the coarsest level of the pyramid. The stereo camera system uses a pair of cameras mounted such that their optical axes are parallel; therefore, we can use the epipolar constraint. Thus the search area is only in the horizontal direction. The matches found at this level are constrained to be unique, that is, no two pixels in one image have the same match in the other. These disparities are then filtered using a median filter for discarding outliers. The disparity map found at this level is then used to guide the same process at the next finer level. The finest level of the pyramid is the intensity images themselves.

4.1.3 Optic Flow Computation

The optic flow process analyzes two temporally consecutive images obtained by the same camera and computes the displacement vector for each pixel. This is done using a coarse-to-fine algorithm similar to that for the stereo disparity computation described above. The main difference is the search area is not constrained along the epipolar line. We assume small rotation and translation in order to minimize the search area. In our case for each pixel, P, at time t the search area in the image of $t + 1$ is a window of 30×30 pixels centered on P at the lowest level of the pyramid.

The input is the stream of intensity images obtained by the right camera. The output is two maps (optic flow maps) which contain the two components of the displacement vector, horizontal and vertical. Since the disparity maps computed by the stereo disparity process are also registered to the right image, the optic flow maps can be viewed as describing the pixel-by-pixel correspondence between two consecutive disparity maps as well.

4.1.4 Invariant Map Generation

Each Reference Depth Point found using the process described above, is used to transfer the disparity map into an invariant map. For general camera motion, the distance measure is used as the invariant and therefore the process generates a distance map. The distance values in each of these maps are computed using the Cartesian distance formula:

$$D = \sqrt{(x_r - x)^2 + (y_r - y)^2 + (z_r - z)^2}$$

where x_r, y_r, and z_r are the 3D coordinates of the Reference Depth Point and x, y, z are the 3D coordinates of the pixel, both in the camera coordinate system. These coordinates are computed using the pin-hole camera model in the following manner. The relation between disparity and depth is

$$z = \frac{bf}{d}$$

where z is the depth, b is the separation between cameras, f is the focal length of the cameras, and d is the disparity. Once z is found, the x and y coordinates are computed in the following manner.

$$x = \frac{z}{f} \times x'$$

$$y = \frac{z}{f} \times y'$$

where x' and y' are the image coordinate of the pixel.

4.1.5 Dynamic Fusion

The central role of the Dynamic Fusion module is the integration of the corresponding invariant maps, in this case distance maps, over time. The main objective of the fusion process is to determine the reliability of the new disparity data. The reliability of the disparity data is determined based on the consistency of the distance values over time, and is represented in the form of a confidence map that is directly registered to the current disparity map.

Since the camera motion is unknown, there is no way of knowing *a priori* how a point's stereo disparity should vary over time. However, no matter what the camera motion, its distance from any "correct" Reference Depth Point (RDP) must be the same throughout the sequence. In order to gain a general understanding of the fusion process, consider the following experiment. Two points, A and B, were selected in the right image of a stereo image sequence pair taken at $t1$ and their disparity values were extracted from the associated stereo disparity map. As more images are processed, we can determine the position and the disparity of both points throughout the entire sequence from the optic flow maps and new disparity maps. Figure 21 shows the disparity values of both of these points over 20 frames. Since we make no assumption about the direction, speed or acceleration of the mobile robot while the image sequence was obtained, there is no way of knowing if the disparity values obtained for A and B are correct.

In the Dynamic Fusion module, the reliability of these disparity values are determined using their associated invariants, in this case, the relative distances of these points from a set of Reference Depth Points. These distance are available in the invariant maps that are computed directly from the disparity maps. Figures 22

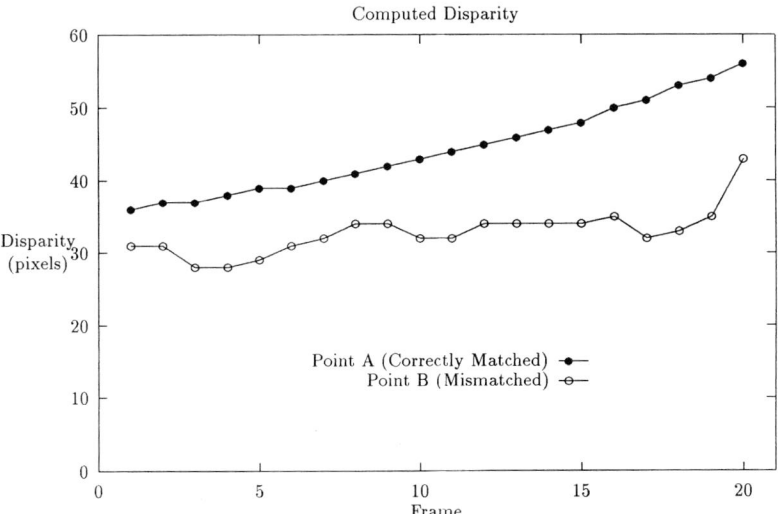

Fig. 21. Disparity values for two pixels tracked over time

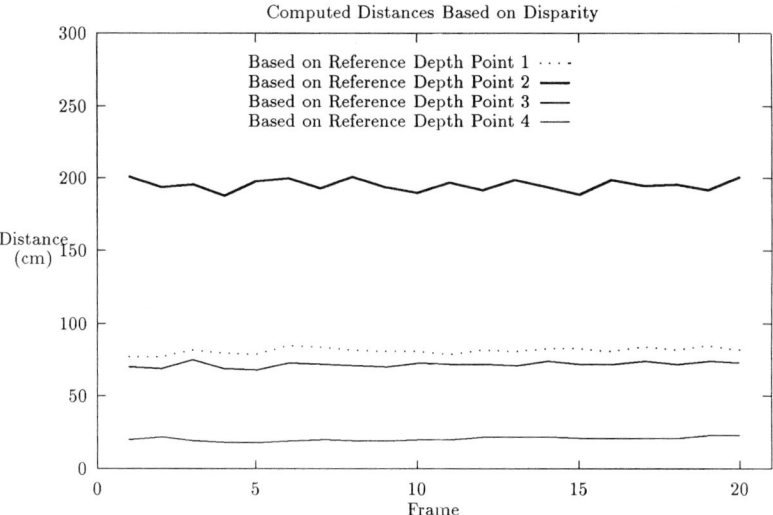

Fig. 22. Distances of point A to four of the Reference Depth Points. They are essentially constant over time

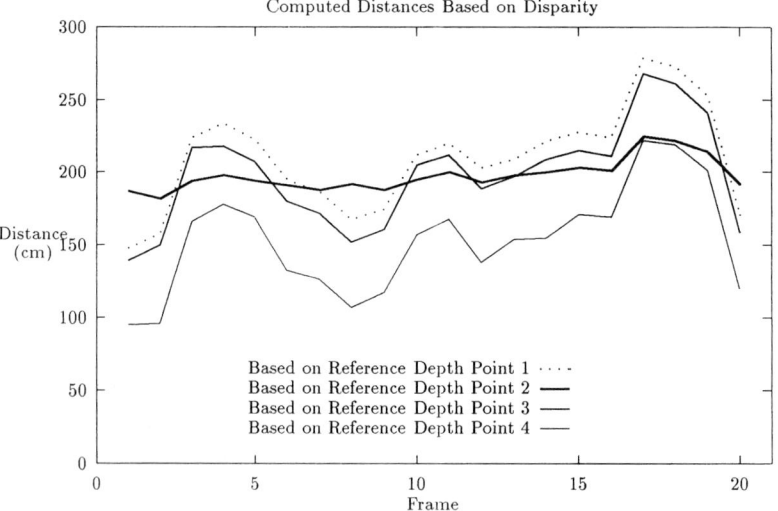

Fig. 23. Distances of point B to four of the Reference Depth Points. They are definitely not constant over time

and 23 show the relative distances of A and B respectively, using four different Reference Depth Points. By studying these figures, it is immediately apparent that the stereo disparity values computed for point A are reliable since the distance values to all four points remain constant throughout the entire 20 frames. The information obtained for point B however, must be in error since the distance values computed are definitely not constant over time.

Note that in the beginning we said "correct" Reference Depth Point. This is because inconsistencies in the distance values computed for a point may be due to error in the Reference Depth Points. If, however, at least four RDPs are correct, we can be confident of the reliability of the computed disparity value of the pixel in question. This is true because 4 points define a unique point in three dimensional space. Therefore, the fusion process starts with integrating distance maps over time and uses this information to assign a confidence to the corresponding disparity values obtained by the stereo matching process.

The Dynamic Fusion module consists of identical processes running in parallel, one process for each Reference Depth Point. Each of these identical processes takes an incoming distance map and integrates this map with the distance map predicted at the previous step. Two maps are undated at each time step, a cumulative distance map and a corresponding confidence map. The cumulative distance maps represent the integrated distance values over time, and the confidence maps represent the confidence in the validity of these values. Each confidence map reports the reliability of the original disparity values based on one of the Reference Depth Point. The overall confidence in the disparity information is derived by combining all the internal confidence maps. For a given pixel in the disparity map, at least four of the parallel processes must support its validity with high confidence. The predicted distance maps are generated using the two-dimensional displacement vector computed at each point by the Optic Flow module. The displacement vectors relate every pixel in the current intensity image, as well as the current distance map, with a pixel in the previous image, or the cumulative distance map. Therefore, at each time step t, the prediction process takes the cumulative distance map of $t-1$ and transforms it according to the optic flow vectors. Consider a given pixel in the current distance map, P, with image coordinate (x, y). Let D and D' be the distances values at (x, y) in the current and the predicted distance maps respectively. Assuming a perfect measurement system, D and D' must be equal. The integration process uses the degree to which D and D' differ in order to determine the reliability of the distance value D. A new cumulative distance map and its corresponding confidence map are then updated based on this decision.

Integration of the current and the predicted distance values, D and D', is done using weighted averaging. The predicted value (D') is weighted according to the number of past measurements it represents. Let n be the number of past measurements combined to compute D', then the integrated distance value (D'_{cum}) is computed as follows:

$$D'_{cum} = \frac{D + n \times D'}{n+1}$$

$$n = n + 1$$

The confidence measure for D'_{cum} is always set to the new value of n. Before D and D' can be combined, we have to make sure that these values represent the same physical entity. For computational ease, this is accomplished by taking the difference between D and D'. If the difference is less than a set threshold then they are integrated. When this difference exceeds the threshold, if the confidence value for D' is high, D is ignored and D'_{cum} is set to D', but the confidence value is reduced by one. If the confidence for D' is low, then D'_{cum} is set to D and the confidence is set to one.

For a given Reference Depth Point, the discrepancies between the current and the predicted distance values can come from a number of sources. Either the new or the previous disparity value assigned to an image feature may be erroneous. The optic flow process may be incorrect, i.e., the two dimensional displacement vector is wrong. Finally, the reference point itself may be incorrect. The fusion module does not determine the source of the discrepancy; it only recognizes that some discrepancy exists. Thus the system only recognizes the dynamic persistence of correct data, and when doing so increases the confidence measure associated with the data.

Fig. 24. These are frames from Image Set #1

a

b

Fig. 25. These are frames from Image Set #2

4.2 Experimental Results

DBV-1 was applied to two binocular image sequences. The scene for Image Set #1 was a set of Styrofoam panels that had black, spray-paint designs attached. This image sequence is accompanied by a synthetic sequence generated based on the ground truth data. The two frames used in this experiment are shown in Fig. 24. Samples from Image Set #2 are shown in Fig. 25.

For Image Set #1, eight Reference Depth Points were manually selected and then tracked using the algorithm described in the previous section. The tracked positions of these points are shown in Fig. 26. The figure shows that there is jitter

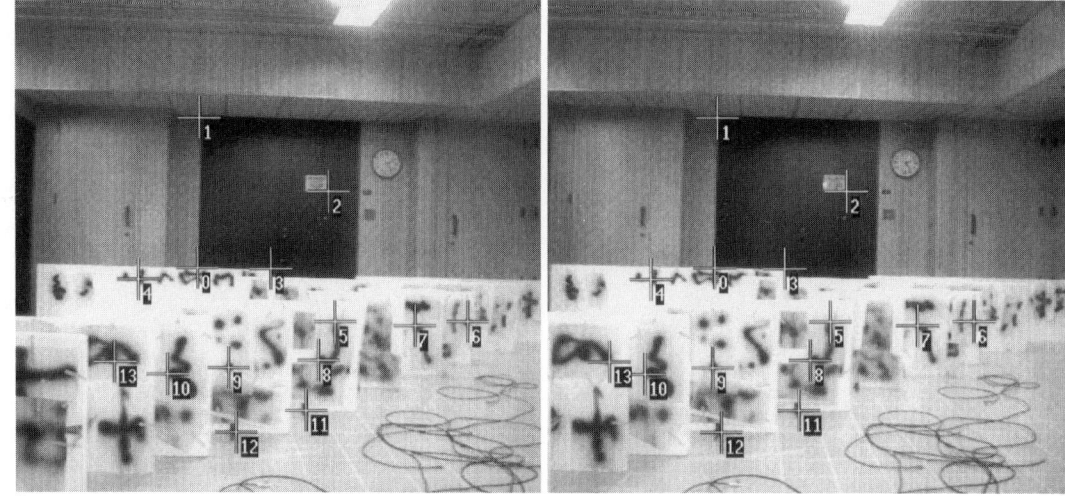

Fig. 26. The stereo image pair obtained at *t*1 in Image Set #1 and the positions of tracked Reference Depth Points

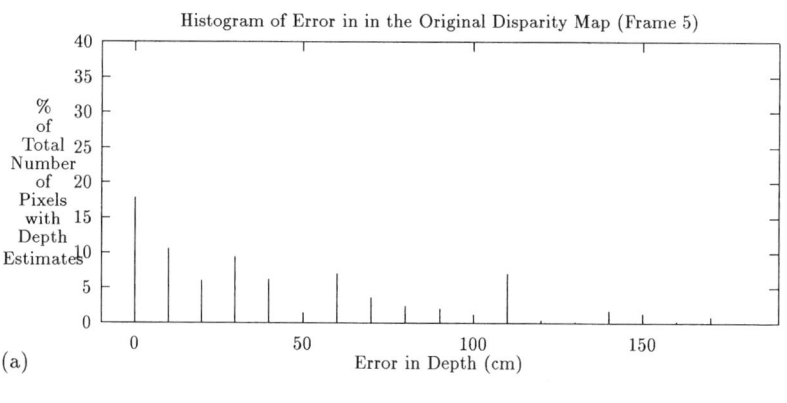

(a)

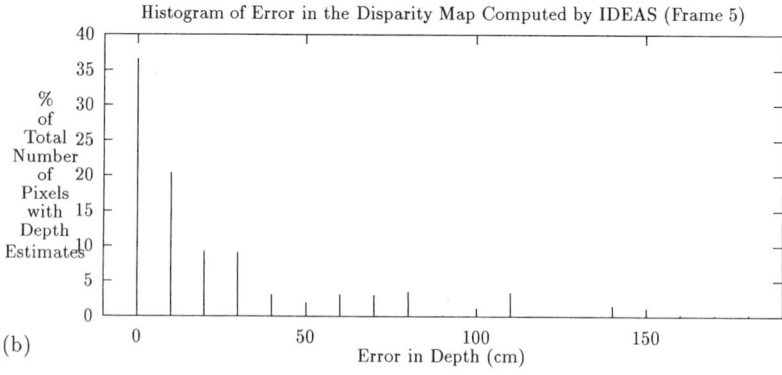

(b)

Fig. 27. These graphs show the percent of pixels in the disparity map that have a given error in disparity. **a** The original disparity map computed from a single stereo pair obtained at *t*5 for Image Set #1; **b** The disparity map computed by the DBV-1 system of IDEAS. Note that a much larger percent of the IDEAS disparity map values have small errors, and a smaller percent have large errors

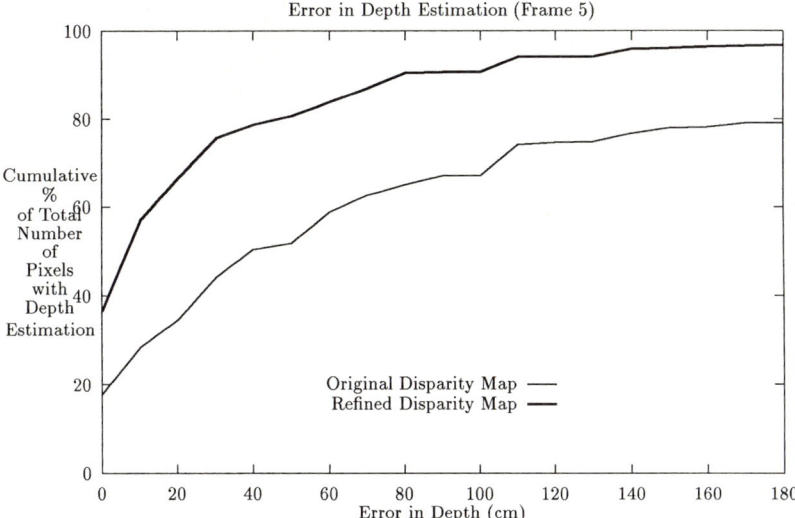

Fig. 28. This graph shows the cumulative error in depth at frame 5 of the first image sequence with and without refinement. Note that almost 80% of the pixels in the refined disparity map have errors less than 40 cm, while less than 45% of the original values have such small errors

in the camera motion and errors in both tracking and stereo matching. For example, close examination of the left and right tracks shows that point 5 is mismatched between stereo pairs at almost every time step. Although point 7 seems to be accurately tracked and matched, it is an artifact created by the accidental line up of one of the panels and the door at the rear of the room, which changes as the camera moves.

To evaluate the effectiveness of our approach, we studied how information obtained at time t_2 helped select reliable depth information at time t_5, using the eight Reference Depth Points mentioned above. First, raw disparity maps were obtained for frames t_2 and t_5 using a stereo algorithm. For each Reference Depth Point, a distance map was computed from each disparity map. Using the optic flow maps and the distance maps from t_2, a predicted distance map for t_5 was generated for each Reference Depth Point. The predicted distance maps for t_5 and the distance maps computed from the disparity map obtained at time t_5 were then integrated using the fusion process described in the previous section. The confidence maps produced by the fusion process were then used to eliminate pixels in the disparity map of t_5 which had low confidence. A median filter operation was also performed to propagate good values to areas with no data. The resulting improvement is quantified in Figs. 27 and 28. Results on the entire image sequence are available in [Moe92].

We also applied the complete procedure to the more complex images in Image Set #2. Figure 29 shows the positions of the selected Reference Depth Points and the tracked positions superimposed on the first frame of the sequence. A close

Fig. 29. The positions of selected RDPs in the left image of Image Set #2 and their tracked positions through the entire sequence

scrutiny of the tracked points shows that some points are incorrectly matched or tracked. Figures 30 through 32 show the right image, the raw disparity map and the refined disparity map for frame 10. As can be seen most erroneous values which appear in the original raw disparity map have been eliminated in the refined map produced by the DBV-1 system. Results on the entire image sequence are available in [Moe92].

4.3 Conclusions

This section described a new general framework for recovering spatial information from time-varying images obtained by a moving observer. The most important

Fig. 30. Right image for Image Set #2, frame 10

Fig. 31. The original raw disparity map for Image Set #2, frame 10. This map was generated using a single stereo pair

Fig. 32. The disparity map generated by the DBV-1 system for Image Set #2, frame 10. This map was generated by integrating depth information obtained at frames 0 through 10

aspect of this model is that it allows integration of spatial information over time without the explicit computation of camera motion. The system was tested on real stereo image sequences obtained by a mobile robot, and numerical and visual proofs are presented showing that the computational model is both practical and robust. We were able to show that relative depth is a powerful tool for integrating spatial information in dynamic vision.

5 Navigating Using Visual Information

For a robot to be mobile it must navigate. Navigating requires a variety of information – the robot must know where free space is so that it can avoid obstacles, the robot must know where it is and how it is oriented, and the robot must know what action to take to lead it towards its goal location. There are many ways of acquiring this information, for example, many robots use sonar sensors to determine free space [ME85, BK91a]. However, in keeping with the theme of this book, this section will examine the use of vision to aid mobile robot navigation. Three different uses of vision for navigation will be examined in detail. The first use of vision is to avoid obstacles. The second is to determine the robot's position and orientation in the world, both in conjunction with a 3-D CAD model of the environment and through the use of landmarks. The final use of vision that will be examined is using visual information to select an appropriate action that will lead the robot towards a goal location. In each of these cases, specific examples of working robot systems will be given and analyzed.

5.1 Obstacle Avoidance Using Vision

Sections 2, 3, and 4 of this chapter presented various ways to determine information about objects in the robot's environment. This information can be used to help the robot avoid hitting obstacles. For example, depth information can be projected onto the ground plane to create a two-dimensional representation of the robot's environment. Then any one of several path planners can be used to guide the robot through the obstacles [LPW79, Bro82, KZB85]. Many early robots used just this approach [Nil69, Mor81a]. Some of these two-dimensional representations can be extended to three-dimensions by dividing the environment into *voxels* (cubes representing some fixed volume of space) and labeling each voxel as empty, filled or unknown, depending on the depth information returned by vision.

A different approach to using vision for obstacle avoidance is not to represent obstacles explicitly, but to use each image frame to determine the location of the free space in the environment and then direct the robot toward it. This can be called the *reactive* or *behavioral* approach and is motivated by the subsumption architecture [Bro86]. An example of a robot that uses this approach is Polly [Hor93b, Hor93a]. Polly uses a 64×48 pixel gray-scale image to navigate corridors. It aligns along the axis of the corridor using the vanishing point of the parallel lines formed by the edges of the corridor. It detects the distances to obstacles by assuming that the floor of the corridor is homogeneous and then finding the height of non-floor pixels by scanning up each column of the image until an edge is detected, signifying a break in the homogeneity of the floor. The height of non-floor pixels can be directly translated into distances using the ground-plan constraint (i.e., if all things rest on the floor then the further away something is the higher it will appear in the image). Using these environmental constraints and simple algorithms, Polly can process 15 frames per second, allowing it to travel at 1 m/sec. Because they don't have the overhead of building and maintaining a world model, reactive systems can run quickly and robustly.

5.2 Determining Position and Orientation

Just doing obstacle avoidance is rarely enough for a mobile robot. In order to perform tasks in the environment the robot needs to know where it is in the environment, i.e., the robot must determine its position and orientation with respect to the environment. This section will look at three different approaches to this problem. The first approach is to use visual features in conjunction with a detailed CAD-like world model that is given to the robot. The second approach is to triangulate the robot's position and orientation from known landmarks. The final approach is to determine when the robot is at predetermined places in the environment (this is called *place recognition*). For each approach, a working robot system will be examined in detail.

5.2.1 Model-Based Approaches

A popular and successful way of determining position and orientation is to match visual features to a 3-D, CAD-like world model that has been given to the robot. There are several different, working instantiation of this approach including Harvey [FH90], Mobi [KB88, KTB89], FINALE [KK92] and COSIM [RWA+92]. The basic approach of each system is the same: 1) The robot has a detailed, 3-D model of its environment; 2) A robot action is preformed and the model is used to predict the location of visual features that the robot should see after performing the action; 3) The locations of these visual features are compared with corresponding features in an actual image taken by the robot and the robot position is then updated. The major difference between systems is in the visual features that they use. Harvey uses vertices, Mobi uses vertical edges that fall within a small band across the center of the image, FINALE uses horizontal and vertical edges and COSIM uses horizontal edges. Because many of these systems are similar and in the interest of brevity, only one will be examined in detail – COSIM.

The COSIM system consists of a mobile robot with a single black and white camera and a 3D model of the robot's environment. COSIM determines its position and orientation by comparing a simulated image generated from the 3D model with an actual camera image. This process consists of five components:

1. Camera calibration routines that use the model and images to determine effective focal length, and the x and y pixel dimensions.
2. A fast and crude orientation corrector that uses vanishing point analysis.
3. An algorithm to match 2D image points to 3D model features.
4. A reverse projection algorithm to produce two sets of 3D match points from a 3D model and 2D image points.
5. An algorithm for determining a registration vector that gives the rotation and translation necessary to align the two sets of 3D points. This registration vector can be used to determine the camera's position and orientation relative to some fixed coordinate frame that is inherent to the 3D model.

These five components work together as follows: First, camera calibration is performed to obtain the camera's intrinsic values, which are crucial in all of the other calculations. Calibration will have to be repeated anytime the camera is

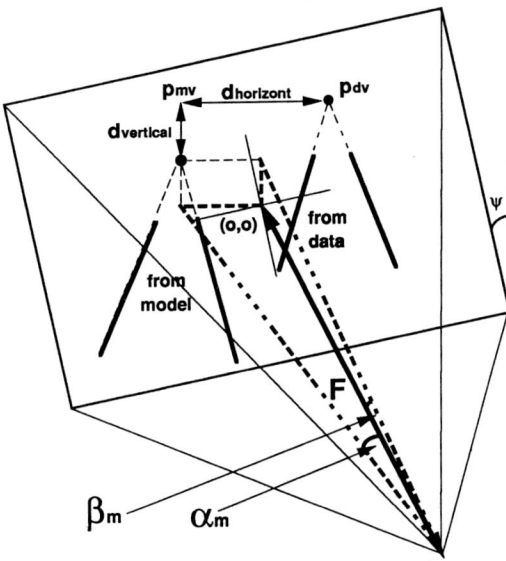

Fig. 33. Variables used by COSIM to calculate the vanishing point

replaced or when the optical system is adjusted. Next the robot starts moving through the modeled environment and takes images. Each image is analyzed to determine the deviation between the position of the vanishing point in the image from its expected position based on the model and dead reckoning information. This step assumes that there exists a pair or more of dominant parallel lines in the environment (the baseboard lines between the walls and the floor are used in the actual implementation).

Given a set of parallel lines in the 3D model, their location in the image plane can be projected using the expected camera position supplied by the dead reckoning sensors of the robot. Let (x_{m_v}, y_{m_v}) represent the 2D intersection point of these lines in the image plane in pixel units. Then let (x_{d_v}, y_{d_v}) represent that intersection point of the two parallel lines in the actual image (see Fig. 33).

Let $dx = x_{d_v} - x_{m_v}$ and $dy = y_{d_v} - y_{m_v}$. Since the image may be tilted (say by φ) dx and dy are converted to horizontal and vertical deviations, $d_{horizontal} = dx \cos \varphi - dy \sin \varphi$ and $d_{vertical} = dx \sin \varphi + dy \cos \varphi$.

The expected horizontal angle to the vanishing point is:

$$\alpha_m = \arctan\left(\frac{-(x_{m_v} \cos \varphi - y_{m_v} \sin \varphi)}{F}\right)$$

where F is the focal length of the camera. The actual horizontal angle to the vanishing point is:

$$\alpha_d = \arctan\left(\frac{-(x_{m_v} \cos \varphi - y_{m_v} \sin \varphi) + d_{horizontal}}{F}\right)$$

The expected pan angle is corrected as follows:

$$\theta = \theta_e - (\alpha_d - \alpha_m)$$

where θ_e is the expected pan angle.

A similar operation is performed for the tilt angle. The expected vertical angle to the vanishing point is:

$$\beta_m = \arctan\left(\frac{(x_{m_v}\cos\varphi - y_{m_v}\sin\varphi)}{F}\right)$$

The actual vertical angle to the vanishing point is:

$$\beta_d = \arctan\left(\frac{(x_{m_v}\cos\varphi - y_{m_v}\sin\varphi) + d_{vertical}}{F}\right)$$

The expected tilt angle is corrected as follows:

$$\phi = \phi_e - (\beta_d - \beta_m)$$

where ϕ_e is the expected pan angle.

This technique corrects gross orientation errors very quickly, which allows for expectation matching of features to be performed robustly. COSIM matches image features to model features using a technique based on searching small regions in the image space for particular oriented features (lines) and their intersections. Then a global consistency check is performed in 2D space that eliminates gross matching errors. This produces a set of image points *imagepoints* and a matching set of *modelpoints*. These points are then reverse projected to 3D space. Finally, using a technique based on [BM92] the two sets of matched 3D points are used to find a correction vector $\vec{q}$. The correction vector is made up of two vectors, a unit rotational quaternion and a translation vector. The correction vector can be used to align the robot with the model, both in position and orientation, the goal of this approach.

5.2.2 Using Landmarks

Sometimes a system cannot tolerate the overhead of the 3D model required in the above technique. In these cases triangulating to fixed landmarks in the environment can provide position and orientation information. Landmark-based systems rely on a small set of distinctive landmarks that can be seen over a large portion of the environment. Triangulation requires distinct, point-like landmarks that can be recognized from any direction and from long distances. These landmarks can be natural (see [LL90] for a system that uses natural landmarks for triangulation) or artificial. Much research has been done using triangulation, including [Sug88, Kro89]. The triangulation approach will be demonstrated in this subsection by examining a robot system, CARMEL [KHC+93], which uses artificial landmarks whose locations have been acquired previous by the robot. First, the landmark recognition system will be described and then the landmark triangulation algorithm will be given.

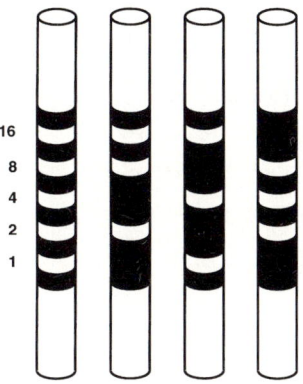

Fig. 34. Example object tags showing the basic pattern and objects with bit pattern of 0, 5, 10, and 17

CARMEL's vision system consists of an object tag design and an algorithm for detecting and distinguishing those tags. The object tag design used for CARMEL consists of a black and white stripe pattern placed upon PVC tubing with a four inch diameter, allowing the tags to be slipped over the object poles. An example object tag is shown in Fig. 34. The basic stripe pattern is six evenly spaced horizontal black bands of 50 mm width, with the top of the top band and the bottom of the bottom band spaced 1000 mm apart. The white gaps between the black bands correspond to the bit positions in a five-bit word. A white space between two bands corresponds to an "off" bit, while filling the space with black corresponds to an "on" bit. The five bits between the six bands can then represent 32 unique objects.

The actual algorithm for extracting objects from an image requires no preprocessing of the image. The algorithm makes a single pass over the image, going down each column of the image looking for a white-to-black transition that would mark the start of a potential object. A finite state machine keeps track of the number and spacing of the bands. After finding enough bands to comprise a tag the algorithm stores the tag id and pixel length. Once a column is complete, the eligible objects are heuristically merged with objects found in previous columns. The distance between the top of the top band and the bottom of the bottom band, in terms of the number of pixels in the image, is then used to estimate the actual distance from the camera to the object. The algorithm has an effective range of about 12 meters. See [HBM+93] or [KHC+93] for a detailed description and analysis of the vision algorithm.

The landmark recognition algorithm returns a heading and a distance to any landmark. The triangulation algorithm requires only the relative heading between any three known landmarks to determine the robot's location and orientation. Referring to Fig. 35, landmark 1, landmark 2, and the robot form one circle (circle A). Even though the robot's location is not known, there are only two possible circles because the angle between landmarks as viewed by the robot is known. Landmark 2, landmark 3, and the robot also form another unique circle (B). From the information available (landmark locations and the angles α and β) the equa-

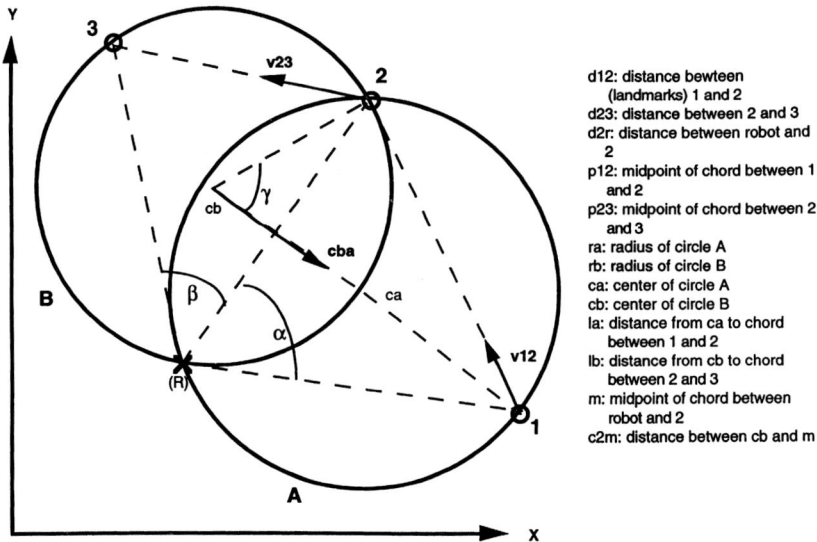

Fig. 35. CARMEL's three object triangulation using the circles method

tions of the circles can be determined. The two circles intersect at landmark 2 and the robot's location. Landmark 2's location is already known and the robot's location is the other intersection point. Below is the algorithm for circle intersection. Refer to Fig. 35 for the definitions of the variables used to explain the algorithm. A landmark's orientation is denoted by (Lxi, Lyi) where i represents the number of the landmark. A landmark's orientation from the robot is denoted by Loi.

1. Properly order landmarks, see below.
2. $\alpha = Lo2 - Lo1$. if α is too small or equals 90° or 270°, return with error because division by 0 will occur.
3. $\beta = Lo3 - Lo2$, if β is too small or equals 90° or 270°, return with error because division by 0 will occur.
4. $ra = \dfrac{d12}{2\sin(\alpha)}$; 5. $rb = \dfrac{d23}{2\sin(\beta)}$; 6. $la = \dfrac{d12}{2\tan(\alpha)}$; 7. $lb = \dfrac{d12}{2\tan(\beta)}$
8. Let $v12x$ and $v12y$ be the unit vector from landmark 1 to landmark 2.
9. Let $v23x$ and $v23y$ be the unit vector from landmark 2 to landmark 3.
10. $cax = p12x - la(v12y)$
11. $cay = p12y + la(v12x)$
12. $cbx = p23x - lb(v23y)$
13. $cby = p23y + lb(v23x)$
14. Return an error if the centers of the two circles are too close (we used 10 unit).
15. If γ is very large, then return error.
16. Let $cbax$ and $cbay$ be the unit vector from the center of circle B to the center of circle A.

Vision for Mobile Robots

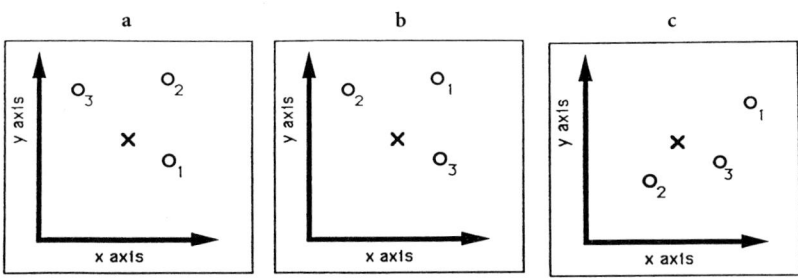

Fig. 36. a Properly ordered landmarks; b and c improperly ordered landmarks

17. $d2r = 2rb\sin(\gamma)$
18. $c2m = rb\cos(\gamma)$
19. Robot x position = $Rx = 2mx - Lx2 + 0.5$
20. Robot y position = $Ry = 2my - Ly2 + 0.5$
21. $\phi = \arctan\left(\dfrac{Ly1 - Ry}{Lx1 - Rx}\right)$, the heading of landmark 1 from the true robot position.
22. If $\phi > 0.0$ then robot orientation error $= -(Lo1 - \phi)$ else robot orientation error $360° + \phi - Lo1$
23. Return with solution

For this algorithm to work properly, both α and β must be less than 180°. When this condition holds we say that the landmarks are "ordered" properly. Properly ordered landmarks assure that the desired solution (out of the two solution possible) is found. Properly ordered landmarks have the following two features:

1. They are labeled consecutively (1, 2, 3) in a counterclockwise fashion,
2. The angle between landmarks 1 and 2 (β) and the angle between landmarks 1 and 3 (α) must be less than 180°.

This triangulation algorithm is analyzed and compared with other triangulation algorithms in [CK93].

One drawback to landmark triangulation is the need to be able to recognize distinctive landmarks. Often landmarks are specially designed objects that have been placed in the environment by users (such as the barcoded objects used by CARMEL). However, some work is being done on automatically acquired landmarks from visual scenes. Some examples of this work are [TL93, ZT90, LL90].

5.2.3 Place Recognition

While landmark triangulation systems can provide very accurate position and orientation information, they require distinctive landmarks that are visible from anywhere in the environment. In many environments, for example indoors, he robot field of vision is too narrow to allow for triangulation from distant landmarks. In these cases, the robot may have to be restricted to determining that it is at certain specific places, instead of being able to determine its position and orientation at any place in the environment. This is called *place recognition*. Much work has been done is place recognition using sonar sensors [DBC+90, MA90, Mat92, KB91]. Relatively little work has been done using visual place recognition. This subsection will examine place recognition by looking at an implemented, hybrid robot system, RPLAN [Kor93], which is designed to operate in structured, office building environments.

RPLAN uses sonar sensors to find interesting places and vision sensing to distinguish those places. The vision component of place recognition relies on the sonar system to position the robot in approximately the same place each time. The vision system uses vertical edges as cues for recognition. Each vertical edge in an image has two features: it's direction (i.e., is it an edge from dark to light or light to dark) and it's distance, obtained using simple stereo matching. Additionally, each edge is stored in an abstracted representation that preserves its location in the scene. During training runs in an environment a number of scenes are accumulated and associated with particular places. During trial runs, these scenes are matched with the actual image taken by the robot. The matching process is as follows: For each cell in which there is a cue in the current abstracted scene, if there is a cue in the corresponding cell in the stored abstracted scene that has the same direction and approximately the same distance (the threshold for a distance match is set at 200 mm in these experiments) then there is a match for that cell. The total number of matching cells is divided by the total number of full cells in the current abstracted scene to get a match percentage.

Table 4 shows experimental results using an actual robot. The robot took sixteen different images in its environment. Each image was taken at five different

Table 4. Results from scene matching

	A1	A2	B1	B2	B3	C1	C2	D1	D2	E1	E2	E3	F1	F2	G1	G2
A1	1.0	0.14	0	0	0	0	0	0	0	0	0	0	0	0	0.11	0.14
A2	0	0.78	0.16	0.16	0.2	0.44	0.4	0	0.2	0	0	0	0.25	0.18	0.11	0
B1	0	0	1.0	0	0.8	0.33	0.4	0.11	0	0.66	0	0	0	0	0	0
B2	0	0	0	1.0	0	0	0	0	0.4	0.16	0	0	0	0.18	0	0
B3	1.0	0	0.25	0	0.6	0.22	0.20	0.22	0	0.33	0	0	0.25	0.27	0.22	0.28
C1	0	0.42	0	0	0	0	0	0	0	0	0	0	0.62	0	0.11	0.14
C2	0	0.28	0.33	0	0.6	0.77	1.0	0.55	0.2	0.16	0	0	0	0.36	0.11	0
D1	0	0.28	0	0.16	0.2	0.22	0.5	0.88	0.4	0.33	0	0	0	0.09	0.11	0
D2	0	0.14	0	0.83	0	0.44	0.20	0.22	0.6	0.16	0	0	0	0.72	0	0
E1	1.0	0	0.16	0	0.4	0	0.2	0	0	0.3	0	0	0.12	0	0	0.14
E2	0	0	0	0	0	0	0	0	0	0	0	0	0	0	0	0
E3	0	0	0	0	0	0.2	0	0	0	0.16	0	0.6	0	0.27	0	0
F1	0	0.7	0	0	0	0.11	0	0	0	0	0	0	0.62	0	0	0.28
F2	0	0	0	0	0	0	0.11	0.2	0	0	0	0	0	0	0	0
G1	0	0	0	0	0	0	0	0	0	0	0	0	0	0	0.11	0.28
G2	0	0.7	0	0	0	0	0	0.1	0	0	0	0	0.12	0	0	0.14

Vision for Mobile Robots

times and edges that appeared in less than half of those images were eliminated from the scene. The robot then took a sixth set of images and tried to match them against the images that it had stored. The percentage of cues that matched between the stored image and the current image is shown in each cell of the table. As the table shows, in nine of the images the highest match percentage is with the correct stored scene. In the actual RPLAN system, the visual information would be combined with sonar information to increase the accuracy of the system.

5.2.4 Conclusions

The choice of whether to use 3-D models, landmark triangulation or place recognition to perform localization depends greatly on the task and the environment. Constructing an accurate CAD-model is time consuming and expensive to store and access. Therefore, 3-D model localization is limited to small, unchanging environments where the robot will be living for a long time. Landmark triangulation requires much less storage and can be used in larger environments. However, it requires omni-directional landmarks that can be easily distinguished and it requires clear sightlines to these landmarks. This is difficult in the real world, especially indoors, but in environments where artificial landmarks can be placed it offers the best performance. Place recognition is restricted to environments in which the robot doesn't need to know its location at any point in the environment, but only at specific places. Of course, there is nothing to prevent a hybrid system that uses a model for well-known areas, landmark triangulation within certain artificially constructed places and place recognition in highly structured, office-type environments. Finally, there is a fourth method of localization, not discussed here, which is using an external camera to locate a robot in a work space [FB93].

5.3 Action Selection

Once the robot's location and orientation have been determined, it needs to select an action that will take it towards its destination. If the robot is using a world coordinate system, like CARMEL does, then once the robot knows its current (x, y) location and its orientation, it can simply move to another (x, y) position using its internal dead reckoning, possibly updating its location and orientation along the way using landmarks. Place recognition systems, such as RPLAN, often have a network of places that they search to determine a path to a goal place. Neither of these approaches use vision except to determine the initial starting location and orientation. There are, however, some interesting vision-based approaches to action selection. The first is a qualitative navigation system called Qualnav [LL90] and the others fall under the title of "homing" robots. Each will be examined separately.

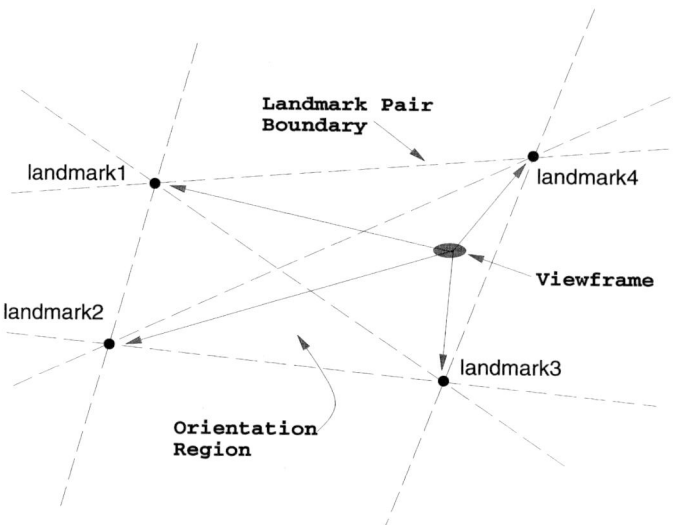

Fig. 37. Qualnav's representation of space

5.3.1 Qualnav

Qualnav uses relative angles and estimated ranges to natural landmarks to define regions of space called *viewframes*. Transformations between different viewframes containing common landmarks gives rise to headings that will move the robot from one viewframe to the next. Landmarks also lead to a topological division of the ground space into regions. Two landmarks create a virtual boundary, called a Landmark Pair Boundary (LPB). Several LPBs create *orientation regions* (Fig. 37 shows Qualnav's spatial representation). To move from one orientation region to the next, Qualnav simply has to cross the LPB separating them, which it does by sighting the two landmarks and plotting a vector that passes between them. Qualnav continues to track each landmark until they have both passed behind it and then it knows that it has crossed the LPB and is in a new orientation region. Once it is within the same orientation region as its goal, it can move from one viewframe to the next until it reaches its goal location.

5.3.2 Homing

The basic idea of homing is that the robot stores sensory data about the environment and associates movements with sensory events. As sensory events trigger movements the robot navigates the environment. There are two significant systems that use this approach. In the first system, Nelson [Nel89] uses abstracted scenes of the environment, each of which is stored with a movement vector that will take the robot from the location of that scene to the goal location. In this system, the robot (actually a robot arm, holding a camera and moving through a miniature town called "Tinytown") compares each new scene against all stored scenes and choses the best match. The second system [HTP+92, HTP+90] uses a location signature instead of an abstracted scene. A 360 degree panorama is converted into a one dimensional vector that is the location signature. Differences between the signature of the robot's current location and the goal location are used to compute movements that will take the robot closer to the goal location.

5.4 Conclusion

Vision-based navigation is an important area in mobile robotics. While other sensing modalities, such as sonar sensors, can provide rough estimates of obstacles surrounding a robot, vision sensing has the advantage of greater angular resolution and range. However, the current state-of-the-art in vision-based navigation requires many assumptions about the robot and the environment. For example, most vision-based navigation systems require extensive camera calibration. Also, most systems have significant a-priori knowledge about the environment. Some of this knowledge is explicit, such as the case of needing a CAD-like world model. Some of this knowledge is implicit, such as assuming that there will be vertical edges or that the floor will not change its pattern. There is still, of course, a great deal of work to be done in vision-based navigation. For example, landmark recognition is currently very limited and usually restricted to artificial objects. There is also work to be done in integrating vision sensing with other sensors while performing navigation tasks. As mobile robots become more common and operate in more environments, the need for effective vision-based navigation will grow.

6 Distributed AI and Mobile Robots

All of the vision techniques discussed to this point have been from the perspective of a single mobile robot. In the near future, however, there will be a great number of autonomous mobile robots going about their business. While vision-based behavior such as obstacle detection will permit these robots to interact safely (hopefully), some extra effort will be required before there robots can work or compete *together*. Although there will be a number of sensing modalities that a mobile robot can draw upon, optical sensing will probably be the primary sensor-based information source. Since coordination of the robots is the goal, the resulting behavior of the robots has been the primary research focus so far, not the sensing. The significant issues in coordination of mobile robots are that 1) the robots have to first detect the presence of other robots in their vicinity, 2) the robots have to have some way of coordinating so that conflicts – not simply collisions, but conflicts over resources in general – are avoided. If possible, the same mechanism should provide for detection of situations where the robots could actually help (or harm) each other, and not simply detect interactions.

6.1 Related Work

Research concerning the coordination of multiple mobile robots comes primarily from three research veins: robotics (obviously), distributed AI (DAI), and plan recognition. We will discuss each of these, in turn.

Until very recently, little research within the robotics field has addressed the coordination of multiple mobile robots. Some of the exceptions include [Ark92, BMMM90, CCL+90, Gro88, PY90], none of which, however, uses vision as a coordination resources. The only known research that involves using computer vision for coordinating multiple robots is that currently being done by Huber and Durfee in [HD92, HD93], which will be discussed in a little more detail later. In this research, multiple mobile robots utilize computer vision to make observations of the behavior of other robots in the vicinity and then coordinate with the other robots from information (hypothesis about the other robot's goals) based upon inferences from the observations[1].

Coordination of multiple agents (a generalization of robots), however, has received a great deal of research in such fields as DAI. DAI researchers have been keenly devoted to general coordination issues such as: explicit, implicit, or no communication [RG84]; conflict detection and resolution [DL87]; communication protocol used by the agents [DM90]; the type, quantity, and representation of information exchanged [Smi80]; the type, quantity and representation of information maintained by agents about other agents (modeling information) [RG91]; and the organization of the agents, if any, and the impact upon coordination [Fox81].

Many of the coordination techniques developed from the DAI field however, have required intentional, explicit communication between the involved agents (see [DL91, LC81, DS81, Smi80, CP79, CML88]) to exchange the information required to coordinate. Coordination without explicit communication has received

---

[1] And, while sensor systems for making observations of other robots could be based upon a number of modalities, including sonar and infrared, the best overall modality for mobile robots is computer vision. Vision provides the capability for both long and short range observation of other agents, while at the same time providing a large amount of sensory data from which to extract the behaviors (actions) of the other robots.

Vision for Mobile Robots

much less attention [GGR84, GDW91], and does not explicitly involve the use of information gained through sensors such as vision systems. Perhaps one reason why sensor-based coordination has not been actively investigated is the additional difficulties of dealing with sensor uncertainty and with having to perform computationally expensive processing to extract the information necessary for intelligent coordination with other robots (or agents).

The expensive processing that is required might take one or more forms. It might consist of specially designed algorithms for detecting signals between robots during explicit communication. "Body" language, special signs or flags, etc., might be used to do this, depending upon the domain and the amount of information that is being passed. To date, there is no work that we knew of that involves using robots explicitly communicating via vision.

Heavy processing may also be involved in performing inferencing of another robot's goals and plans based upon the visually detectable behavior of the other robot. The latter may involve "keyhole" observation, where the observed robot does not know that it is being watched; or, it may involve "passive" communication, where the observed robot is not actively sending information to the watching robot, but may be accentuating certain aspects of its behavior to make it clear what it is doing. In both explicit and non-explicit communication, vision processing to detect and identify critical objects and relationships between objects in the scene is required. With explicit communication, the details of the communicating robot's goals can be passed explicitly. With non-explicit communication, however, inferencing is also required, as information only indirectly related to the observed robot's goals and plans can be determined by the vision processing.

Without the inferencing step, even if the inferencing is to simply determine where the other robot is going to be in the next second so that collisions can be avoided, there can be no intelligent coordination between the robots. Inferring plans and/or goals based upon observations of the other robots going about their business goes by the name of plan recognition, and has been the focus of a great deal of research (see [AFH89, KA86, GL90, CG90, CG91] for just a small sample), although in a number of domains substantially different from mobile robotics such as story understanding, discourse analysis, and intelligent interfaces.

6.2 Sensor Requirements

So just what is required of a robot's sensing system to be able to perform sensor-based coordination? Obviously, a robot must be able to detect objects in the world that are in close proximity to it. With this minimal information it is then possible for a robot to avoid collisions with other robots nearby. While this may be all that is necessary to "coordinate" robots in some domains, in general it will be necessary to have much more intelligent coordination. More intelligent coordination requires more information, of which some, or perhaps most, can more from the visual sensing system.

6.2.1 Vision–Determinable Information

Information currently gleanable from computer vision systems that might be useful for coordinating robots includes range, change of position, direction of motion, orientation, and velocity. This list is not meant to be complete, but to simply introduce some of the useful information extractable by vision system. As indicated earlier in the chapter, there has been a great deal of research to extract this kind of information.

Mobile robots may also be capable of signaling to each other visually, so that special purpose software can be developed for identifying these signals, although no research has yet used explicit visual communication.

Visual information not directly related to the robot(s) can also be useful, such as the relationship of the robot to landmarks, other robots (including the observing robot), and objects in its vicinity [KL88]. These relationships may obtained from second-level computations on the information already extracted from the image. And finally, if an observed robot is physically complex (e.g., an android), the motion and physical relationship of various body parts to each other can also be informative.

6.2.2 Levels of Sensory Information

Another way of looking at coordinating mobile robots with visual information is to categorize the visual processes discussed above according to the level of reactivity associated with the coordination that is based upon the information gained from the processing. At the lowest, most reactive level, computer vision processing can be tied directly to very reactive behaviors such as obstacle avoidance, where the vision system's output is a model of obstructions immediately surrounding the robot (which would include other robots) [TG90]. At a higher level, quantitative information such as another robot's location can be used during longer term planning. At even more deliberative levels, the computer vision system would need to supply more abstract, symbolic information about objects in a scene, such as identifying labels. Further processing can reveal meta-level information about the visual information for higher level deliberation by the mobile robot, such as the relationships between objects.

In terms of the interaction of multiple robots, low-level reactivity alone will never be a useful coordination mechanism for mobile robots of any sophistication. So called "emergent" behavior from groups of very simple robots using only reactive processing can only lead to short term and very short-sighted "coordination." As symbolic processing is the hallmark of intelligence, efficient and effective coordination of robots will become possible when the robots involved in interactions reason with (and possibly exchange) more abstract information. This information must be related to the goals and/or plans of the other robots, of

Vision for Mobile Robots

course, as it is the analysis of this type of information that permits planning for coordination.

6.3 How Can this Information Be Used?

So how can robots coordinate with each other, even once they have obtained information from their vision systems? As discussed above, many coordination techniques have been proposed, most of which involve intentional, explicit communication between the involved agents (e.g., signaling).

6.3.1 Explicit Visual Communication

If explicit communication is feasible, two robots will be able to "talk" to each other through some form of signaling, perhaps body motions or special signs that are displayed. The only limitation to the degree of coordination possible is the amount (or perhaps quality) of information that can be communicated; currently the bandwidth associated with visual communication is very limited compared to methods based upon radio, for instance. If the information obtained from vision consists of velocity, direction, and range, the amount of information is in the order of a few bytes of data. In contrast, communication using radios can easily result in the exchange of kilobytes of data in a short period of time and with far fewer computational resource requirements. In order to effectively coordinate, the robots involved must have some idea of the goals and future intentions of at least some of the other robots. With explicit communication, the goals and intentions can be communicated directly, and in general may require a large amount of data. With vision's bandwidth, this information cannot usually be explicitly communicated[2].

6.3.2 Plan Recognition

Explicit communication is not always possible, however. Especially in the near future, mobile robots will not have a common language with which to communicate with each other (primarily due to the lack of standardization between research and/or commercial sources of these robots). There are also many situations where explicit communication is not possible, such as between military vehicles on a

---

[2] In certain situations where there are only a small set of possible goals, it might be feasible to devise a simple code that can then be signaled to communicate which goal is currently being pursued.

battlefield, where signaling might give away the vehicle's position to an "enemy" robot.

An alternative to using explicit communication to transfer information about goals between robots is to have the robots *infer* the same information, a process called *plan recognition*. Each of the mobile robots that are interacting are executing plans in order to accomplish certain goals; to satisfy of some of these goals the robot must perform physical actions in the world which may manifest themselves as visible behavior. With this information *and* some model of the observed robot's goals and what the observed robot will do in various situations while attempting to fulfill those goals, the observing robot should be able to hypothesize *why* the robot it is observing is performing those actions. This knowledge is extremely useful, as information about what the robot will do in the future facilitates planning for coordination.

Simple plan recognition can be performed using information directly from the vision system (e.g., range, change of position, etc., as mentioned above) and performing only simple inferencing. Range information would be useful when determining the responsiveness required to coordinate; generally, if agents are very close to each other they need to be able to react to each other more quickly. Observing a robot's change of position is useful, since it could indicate that the robot is moving to a nearby strategic location; the observing robot might then choose to rendezvous at the same place. Similarly, information about the direction of motion and/or orientation might indicate the direction to an enemy vehicle without needing to explicitly communicate this fact. A robot's velocity can be revealing, possibly indicating that a rendezvous is required very quickly.

The most important thing to note is that both methods (explicit and non-explicit communication) produce information that is used for the same purpose: determining what the observed robot is going to be doing in the future. Once the observing robot has determined the goals of the watched robot, it may then attempt to coordinate with the other robot by looking for harmful conflicts or helpful interactions. If explicit communication is used, the goals of the communicating robot are explicitly represented in the communicated information and conflict between the involved agents' goals can be checked immediately. Inferred goal information can be used in exactly the same manner, although the information is likely to be (more) uncertain due to uncertainty in the vision processing and the inferencing process.

6.4 An Implemented System

As mentioned earlier, plan recognition research has primarily been conducted in domains such as story understanding. The only known research that involves using computer vision for multiple robots is that currently being done by Huber and Durfee in [HD92, HD93]. In this work, multiple robots use vision as their only

Vision for Mobile Robots

source of "coordinating" information, use plan recognition to infer the goals of the observed robots, and plan to coordinate their activities. The goals of the robots in the experiments are locations within a bounded area that are of "interest" to the robots. The vision system on the robots detect other robots in their vicinity and determine the observed robots' current positions. Using the observations, the observing robot can then infer the target location the observed robot is attempting to reach and plan its own actions accordingly. For example, if the observing robot's goal is to rendezvous with the another robot, it hypothesis of the observed robot's destination gives it a head start toward the rendezvous point. Currently, only two robots are involved in the research, where one of the robots is performing keyhole observations, and the observed robot is attempting to attain a particular goal location without regard to the observing robot. Uncertainties are imposed upon the system from two separate sources: dead reckoning errors that accumulate whenever the robots move, and estimation errors by the computer vision system that is used to sense the other robot's actions. A detailed description of the research is given below.

6.4.1 Spatial Representation

Our work to date has dealt with agents moving and navigating through a flat world. Representing the goals of the observed robot requires some form of spatial representation of the environment in which the robots operate, with particular distinction given to special goal locations (those deemed interesting for some reason). For operation in very small areas, or where the granularity of representation can be quite large, enumeration of possible locations (e.g., at some quantization level such as centimeter intervals) might be useful. Larger areas, or the need for a finer granularity of representation, require some form of abstraction, as the system can become bogged down by the sheer number of possibilities. We have developed a spatial representation that employs a multiple resolution hierarchical scheme to make plan recognition feasible in our domain by reducing the computational demands upon the plan recognition system.

The representation scheme that we have developed is similar to quad trees in that the "map" of the world in which the robots operate is subdivided into quadrants. In this scheme, quadrants are further broken down to higher resolution levels in order to differentiate the region occupied by the observed robot from any of the regions in which there are possible destination locations. This heuristic is necessary so that the observing agent can determine if the watched robot is actually "at" a destination, or merely close to one. Quadrants are not broken into higher resolution levels if some prespecified maximum resolution level has been reached (a function of how accurate sensors are, what makes sense for the given environment, etc.). Two examples of representations are shown in Fig. 38a. In the top representation in Fig. 38a, the highest resolution level used was very detailed close to the robot (the hollow square) in order to distinguish its location from the

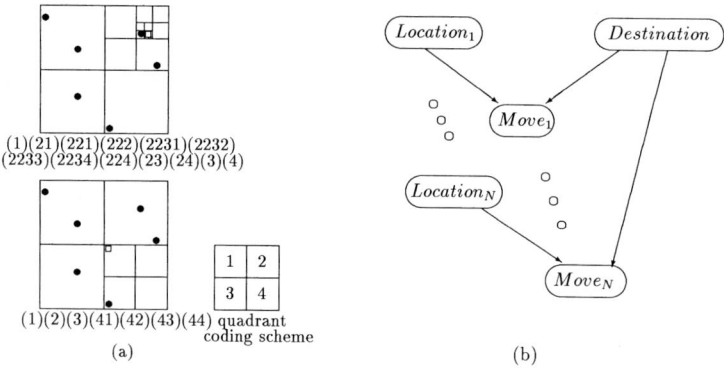

Fig. 38. a Examples of representations. The filled circles are possible destination locations, the hollow square is the observed robot; **b** Belief network architecture

possible destination closest to it (the filled-in circle immediately to its left)[3]. In the bottom example, the representation did not have to go to such a high level of detail since the robot was quite far from any of the possible destinations.

6.4.2 Plan Recognition Architecture

Our plan recognition system is based upon belief networks, a graph-oriented probabilistic representation of causal and dependency relationships between concepts (see [Cha91] for a gentle introduction). Belief networks allow us to model actions (observable activities of an agent), plans, and goals, and the relationships between them.

The belief network that we have started with is shown in Fig. 38b. This network is a model of a simple agent plan: an agent that has a goal of moving to a particular location in the world will examine its current location and plan a sequence of movements that will take it to its goal destination. In causal terms, the belief network states that the current location of the observed robot and the destination that it wishes to attain determines the motion that the robot will take to get to its destination. Our model of motion is that the robot will try to move directly towards its goal, thereby moving in a straight line from its current location toward the destination.

Each node in the belief network shown in Fig. 38b contains the various values that are possible for that particular concept. The *Location* node has as possible states all of the possible location regions (of the current spatial representation such

---

[3] Had the representation not been so detailed, the observing robot would have had to reason that the other robot was *at* a destination, an observation significantly different from being "close" to a destination.

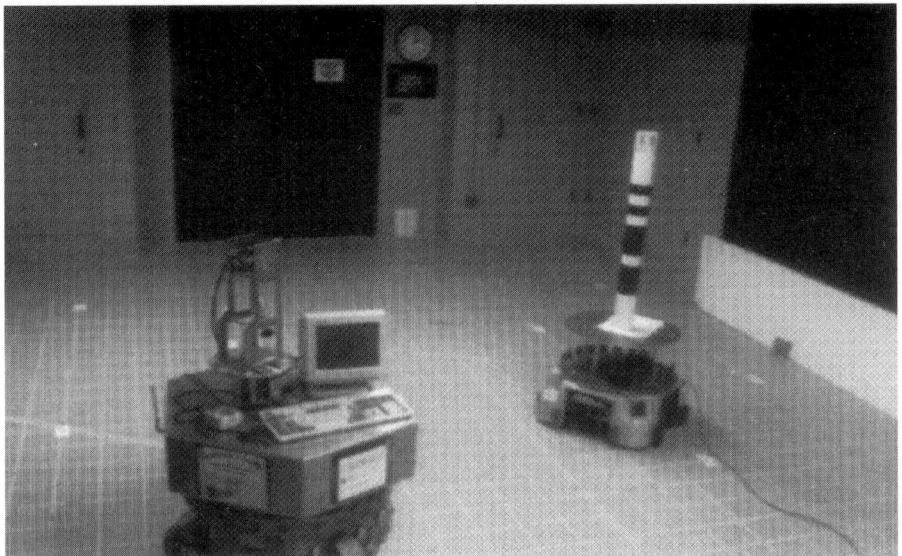

Fig. 39. The plan recognition testbed

as that seen in Fig. 38a) that the observed agent might have while it is trying to attain its goal destination. The *Destination* node contains all of these possible regions that contain one or more destination locations (i.e., a subset of the *Location* node). The *Motion* node is evidence for the agent having moved NORTH, SOUTH, EAST, WEST, or staying in the same location, and is calculated based upon the current and previous observed locations.

The belief network is used to perform plan recognition through the propagation of beliefs from evidence, in the form of observations of the other robot's activities, to the possible goals. By observing the robot's location and by calculating the motion exhibited by the other robot since the last observation, we can then propagate this evidence through the belief network to update the beliefs of where it is going.

6.4.3 Observational Uncertainty

In Fig. 41 we illustrate the uncertainties that arise in our system. Robot 1, the observing robot, starts at position $(X1_{R1}, Y1_{R1})$, while the observed robot, Robot 2, starts at $(X1_{R2}, Y1_{R2})$. In the figure, we show the position uncertainty computed by Robot 1 for itself and the other robot at their initial positions and after both robots have moved to their second positions. In the figure, Robot 1 starts with no uncertainty in its position, perhaps having just been homed to this position. Robot 1's estimate of where Robot 2 starts is not quite so certain[4]. This uncertainty is a function of the distance between the two agents; the farther apart the two robots, the greater the possible error in the localization. Furthermore, after each robot moves to its respective second position, dead reckoning errors also become a factor. The dead reckoning error accumulated by Robot 1 is shown by the increased uncertainty bounds surrounding Robot 1's second position. Visual localization of Robot 2 again introduces error. The two errors are additive, so that Robot 1's uncertainty in the position of Robot 2 is potentially even greater from its new position. This positional uncertainty will continue to increase unless Robot 1 manages to more accurately determine its own position or the agents move sufficiently close together to offset the larger dead reckoning error[5].

The impact of the observational uncertainty on the performance of the system is dramatic. Experiments in which no method for dealing with the uncertainty was used show that the system can be entirely baffled, even broken, by the positional error that arises from the dead reckoning and the computer vision system's uncertainty [HD92]. The system, being committed to assuming observations are correct and exact, occasionally miscalculates the location, and therefore the motion. This results in an observed motion of NORTH instead of SOUTH (for instance), contradicting previous, correct observations, and violating the motion model of the belief network.

To deal with the uncertainties associated with this domain, we needed to relax the assumption that observations were accurate and correct and, instead, allow a probabilistic mix of possible observation values. By simple modeling of the dead reckoning and computer vision errors as error bounds, we can then calculate the possible motion and location values. The two errors are additive, and are proportional (with different constants) to the distance traveled by the observing robot (in the case of dead reckoning) and the visual distance between the two robots (in the case of the computer vision system). Roughly, dead reckoning errors accumulate at approximately 1 meter for every 30 meters of travel, and the computer vision system is in error approximately 20 millimeters for every meter of visual distance for CARMEL, our robot (see Sect. 6.4.4).

The effect of this upon modeling where the observed agent is at any time can be seen in Fig. 40a. Instead of making an observation that the current location of the observed agent is at a single region in the hierarchical representations, we now have to allow for the possibility that it can be in any region that the uncertainty bounds overlap, weighted by the amount of overlap.

The motion between two locations with uncertainty is depicted in Fig. 40b. The calculations of the observed agent's motion to incorporate the uncertainty is

---

[4] The computer vision system that is used to make observations returns an estimate of the location of other agents in the current field of view, and this estimate is known to be incorrect due to quantization error, noise, poor lighting, etc.

[5] Note that the dead reckoning error accumulated by Robot 2 does not affect Robot 1's uncertainty in Robot 2's position. If Robot 2 was also doing plan recognition, its own dead reckoning would contribute to its uncertainty about Robot 1's location.

Vision for Mobile Robots

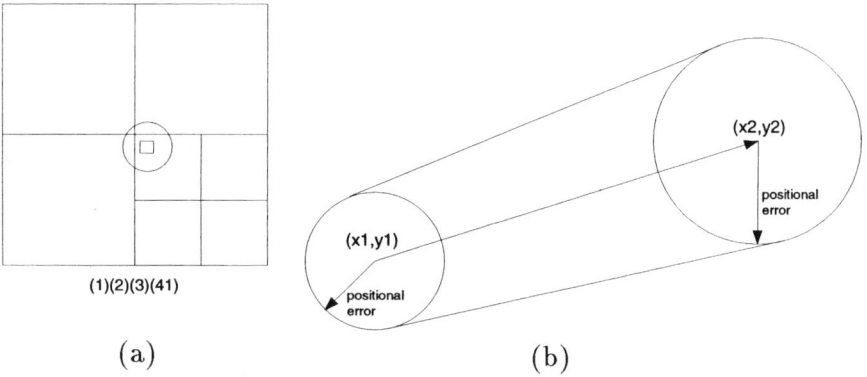

Fig. 40. a Uncertainty in the location of the observed agent caused by the accumulation of dead reckoning and computer vision errors means that the agent could be in any of the regions indicated; **b** Motion between two uncertain locations

a function of the amount of overlap of the error bounds and the magnitude of the motion in the cardinal directions. For example, given the motion of the other agent as that depicted in Fig. 40b, the agent could have moved NORTH or SOUTH, and EAST, but not WEST. We have implemented a simple approximation of the motion uncertainty for our experiments, weighting each direction by the distance of travel along that direction, relative to the level of uncertainty. Long motion relative to the uncertainty bounds, then, helps in reducing the ambiguity of the motion. As the accumulation of dead reckoning errors grows, however, the ambiguity of the motion increases, and the observations becomes more uncertain.

6.4.4 CARMEL: The Implemented System

We have implemented our system on CARMEL, a Cybermation K2A mobile robot used previously in research on obstacle avoidance [BK91b] and autonomous robotics [CHK+93]. CARMEL serves as the observer, performing plan recognition based on observations of other agents in its environment with which it may interact. CARMEL performs these observations using a computer vision system that detects and calculates the position of objects marked with a special bar code [HBK+92]. The "agents" that CARMEL has observed include another robot (a TRC Labmate) and various people. CARMEL and the TRC in the middle of run are shown in Fig. 39. As mentioned earlier, CARMEL's purpose is to determine where the other agent is moving and then rendezvous at that location.

In our implementation, the observing robot periodically looks for the other robot, detects its new location, and calculates the motion that brought the robot to that new position. This data is given to the belief network as evidence and is propagated through it, resulting in new posterior probabilities for each of the

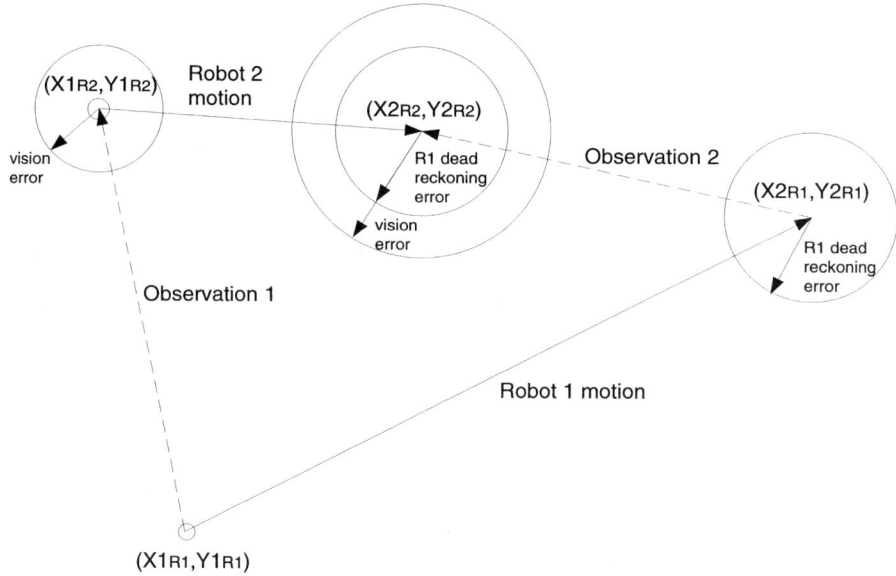

Fig. 41. Uncertainty bounds as the observing and observed robots move

destination regions in the *Destination* node of the network. Probabilities for individual destinations (as more than one destination location may be contained in a single region) are then determined, either by associating the probability associated with a region to a lone destination within that region or by equally dividing the probability of a region among all of the destinations within it. The destination that has the highest probability is taken to be the most likely goal of the observed agent. CARMEL then calculates a path of that location in order to rendezvous with the agent.

CARMEL only travels a short distance toward the destination, however. By periodically stopping along the way, CARMEL can make new observations and continually update its beliefs about the observed agent's intentions. Early, incorrect guesses about the goal location can then be corrected by further observations. The plan recognition system even works in situations where the agent "feints" toward a particular destination for a while and then heads for another goal. The system, having settled on a particular destination, becomes temporarily confused by the change of direction until enough supporting evidence for the new goal is accumulated.

6.5 Application Areas

Robotic agents would find computer vision-based coordination skills effective and useful in a large number of domains and environments. Some possible application areas include:

Vision for Mobile Robots

- Intelligent Vehicle Highway Systems (IVHS) – autonomous vehicles will be able to use their vision systems to perform simple plan recognition to determine whether other vehicles are trying to make an exit from a highway, changing lanes, passing, etc. They will also be able to use vision to detect traffic backups, accidents, and pedestrians.
- Military – a large number of military applications exist that would benefit from the ability of autonomous mobile robots to coordinate using only vision. Some of these include forward reconnaissance and battlefield situations, where radio contact is limited due to radio silence or because of intentional jamming by enemy forces. Using plan recognition on enemy forces is also a highly interesting application.
- As backup – In any environment and domain, it might be very useful to augment other information exchange and acquisition mechanisms with a vision-based system that uses some of the techniques described earlier. The vision-based system would become active whenever it became infeasible to utilize more efficient and effective communication means such as radio. This would allow the robot to continue operating, although perhaps with degraded performance.

6.6 Limitations

There are several disadvantages associated with using visual information for coordinating multiple mobile robots. One is the relatively high level of computation required to do state of the art vision processing. Much of the information useful for coordinating the robots (motion, object recognition, signal recognition, etc.) requires computer vision algorithms that are very computationally expensive. In many cases it might be too expensive to use vision for this purpose. Explicit communication with specialized signs or tags may not fall prey to this limitation, as the signs can be engineered to be easy to detect and identify.

Uncertainty in results of the vision system, in terms of ambiguity of object and relationship and characteristic information extracted from a scene, also introduces uncertainty into the planning process that does not, in general, occur when using explicit communication over modalities that do not introduce ambiguity, such as radio.

Also, the robots need to be within sensor range of each other, at least some of the time, for vision-based coordination to be of use. If this condition is not met, however, it is because other agents are so far away that they cannot be seen or that the environment is very cluttered with obstructing objects. In the first case, there may be no need to have the robots spend time trying to coordinate their actions as they might be distant enough to not be "interacting" in any way. In the second case, the agents will not become aware of each other until they are *very* close to each other, such that they will have to rely on reactions more than on a deliberative approach to avoid harmful interactions.

6.7 Future Directions

There are a number of research areas that deserve immediate attention. While a certain amount of research has been done that touches upon coordinating robots with vision, hardly any has been done specifically for that purpose. Vision algorithms and techniques need to be created and implemented that are specific to the extraction of information from images that is directly useful for coordinating robots. Some of this information, such as the motion of a robot's arm for instance, might be domain specific and require specialized software and/or hardware. People are wonderfully adept at detecting subtle but very revealing details about other people's behavior; mobile robots need to have the same capability.

Research also needs to be directed toward coordination issues that are raised by using vision to gather the coordination information. Image resolution, processing speeds, recognition and detection uncertainty, and other vision related issues will have an impact upon coordination, and these relationships need to be studied.

6.8 Conclusion

The current state of the art in multi-agent computer vision is still in its infancy. Very little research has been done toward using computer vision explicitly for the purpose of coordinating multiple robotic agents. Some researchers have used computer vision for obstacle avoidance, which can be considered a very low level of coordination. The results of this "reactive" co-ordination is not particularly a multi-agent solution, it simply works because the robots are trying to stay away from anything that might hit them, and do not reason explicitly about the obstacles as being static or dynamic, and certainly not having "agenthood". Even less work has been directed toward using vision in more intelligent coordination. A great deal of research will be required before mobile robots will be able to work effectively together based upon information gathered from their vision systems.

References

[AFH89] J. Azarewicz, G. Fala, and C. Heithecker. Template-based multi-agent plan recognition for tactical situation assessment. In *Proceedings of the Sixth Conference on Artificial Intelligence Applications*, pp. 247–254, 1989.

[Alv87] N. Alvertos. Stereo camera modeling and image correspondence for three-dimensional machine vision. Technical report TR-ECE-87-18, University of Tennessee, August 1987.

[Ana87a] Padmanabhan Anandan. Measuring visual motion from image sequences. COINS Technical Report 87-21, University of Massachusetts as Amherst, Computer and Information Science, Amherst, Mass, March 1987.

[Ana87b]   Padmanabhan Anandan. A unified perspective on computational techniques fot the measurement of visual motion. In *DARPA Image Understanding Workship*, pp. 719–732, February 1987.

[Ana89]   P. Anandan. A computational framework and an algorithm for the measurement of visual motion. *International Journal of Computer Vision*, Vol 2: 283–310, 1989.

[Ark92]   Ronald C. Arkin. Cooperation without communication: Multiagent schema-based robot navigation. *Journal of Robotic Systems*, 3(9):351–364, 1992.

[Bar93]   Sandra L. Bartlett. *USING THE EGO-MOTION COMPLEX LOGARITHMIC MAPPING FOR DYNAMIC VISION*. PhD thesis, The University of Michigan, Ann Arbor, MI, 1993.

[BFBB92a]   J.L. Barron, D.J. Fleet, S.S. Beauchemin, and T.A. Burkitt. Performance of optical flow techniques. Technical Report 299, Department of Computer Science, The University of Western Ontario, London, Ontario, 1992.

[BFBB92b]   J.L. Barron, D.J. Fleet, S.S. Beauchemin, and T.A. Burkitt. Performance of optical flow techniques. In *Proceedings of the IEEE Computer Society Conference on Computer Vision and Pattern Recognition*, pp. 236–242, 1992.

[BGT82]   C. Braccini, G. Gamberdella, and V. Tagliasco. A model of the early stages of human visual system. *Biological Cybernetics*, 44:47–88, 1982.

[BK91]   Johann Borenstein and Yoram Koren. Histogramic in-motion mapping for moblie robot obstacle avoidance. *IEEE Journal of Robotics and Automation*, 7(4), 1991.

[BM92]   Paul J. Besl and Neil D. Mckay. A method for registration of 3-D shapes. *IEEE Trans. on Pattern Analysis and Machine Intelligence*, 14(2):239–256, February 1992.

[BMMM90]   R. Brooks, P. Maes, M. Mataric, and G. More. Lunar base construction robots. In Tsuchiura, editor, *IEEE Int. Workshop on Intelligent Robots and Systems (IROS '90)*, pp. 389–392, Japan, 1990.

[Bro82]   Rodney A. Brooks. Solving the find-path problem by good representation of free space. In *Proceedings of the National Conference on Artificial Intelligence (AAAI)*, 1982.

[Bro86]   Rodney A. Brooks. A Robust Layered Control System for a Mobile Robot. *IEEE Journal of Robotics and Automation*, 2(1), 1986.

[Cav78]   P. Cavanaugh. Size and position invariance in the visual system. *Perception*, 7(2):167–177, 1978.

[Cav81]   P. Cavanaugh. Size invariance: reply to Schwartz. *Perception*, 10(4):469–474, 1981.

[CCL+90]   P. Caloud, W. Chio, J. Latombe, C. LePape, and M. Yim. Indoor automation with many mobile robots. In Tsuchiura, editor, *IEEE Int. Workshop on Intelligent Robots and Systems (IROS '90)*, pp. 67–72, Japan, 1990.

[CG90]   Eugene Charniak and Robert Goodman. *Plan Recognition in Stories and in Life*, Uncertainty in Artificial Intelligence (5). Elsevier Science Publishers, 1990.

[CG91]   Eugene Charniak and Robert Goldman. A probabilistic model of plan recognition. In *Proceedings Ninth National Conference on Artificial Intelligence*, pp. 160–165, Anaheim, CA, July 1991. American Association for Artificial Intelligence.

[Cha91]   Eugene Charniak. Bayesian networks without tears. *AI Magazine*, 12(4):50–63, Winter 1991.

[CHK+93]   Clare Congdon, Marcus Huber, David Kortenkamp, Kurt Konolige, Karen Myers, Alessandro Saffiotti, and Enrique Ruspini. CARMEL vs. flakey: A comparison of two winners. *AI Magazine*, 14(1):49–57, Spring 1993.

[CK93]   Charles Cohen and Frank Koss. A comprehensive study of three-object triangulation. In William J. Wolfe and Wendell H. Chun, editors, *Mobile Robots VII*. SPIE, Bellingham, Washington, 1993.

[CML88]   Susan E. Conry, Robert A. Meyer, and Victor R. Lesser. Multistage negotiation in distributed planning. In Alan H. Bond and Les Gasser, editors, *Readings in Distributed Artificial Intelligence*, pp. 367–384, Morgan Kaufman, 1988.

[CP79]   Philip R. Cohen and C. Raymond Perrault. Elements of a plan-based theory of speech acts. *Cognitive Science*, 3(3):177–212, 1979.

[CV92]   Marco Campani and Alessandro Verri. Motion analysis from first-order properties of optical flow. *Computer Vision, Graphics and Image Processing: Image Understanding*, Vol 56(No 1):90–107, July 1992.

[CW79]   G. Chaikin and C. Weiman. Log spiral grids in computer pattern recognition. *Computer Graphics and Pattern Recognition*, 4:197–226, 1979.

[DBC+90]   Thomas Dean, Kenneth Basye, Robert Chekaluk, Seungseok Hyun, Moises Lejter, and Margaret Randazza. Coping with uncertainty in a control system for navigation and exploration. In *Proceedings of the National Conference on Artificial Intelligence (AAAI)*, 1990.

[DL87]   Edmund H. Durfee and Victor R. Lesser. Using partial global plans to co-ordinate distributed problem solvers. In *Proceedings of the Tenth International Joint Conference on Artificial Intelligence*, pp. 875–883, Milan, Italy, August 1987. (Also published in *Readings in Distributed Artificial Intelligence*, Alan H. Bond and Les Gasser, editors, pp. 285–293, Morgan Kaufmann, 1988.).

[DL91]   Edmund H. Durfee and Victor R. Lesser. Partial global planning: A coordination framework for distributed hypothesis formation. *IEEE Transactions on Systems, Man, and Cybernetics*, 21(5):1167–1183, September 1991. (Special Issue on Distributed Sensor Networks).

[DM90]   Edmund H. Durfee and Thomas A. Montgomery. A hierarchical protocol for coordinating multiagent behaviors. In *Proceedings of the National Conference on Artificial Intelligence*, pp. 86–93, July 1990.

[DMRS88]   R. Dutta, R. Manmatha, Edward M. Riseman, and M.A. Snyder. Issues is extracting motion parameters and depth from approximate translational motion. In *Proc. DARPA Image Understanding Workshop*, pp. 945–960, April 1988.

[DS81]   Randall Davis and Reid G. Smith. Negotiation as a metaphor for distributed problem solving. AI Memo 624, Artificial Intelligence Laboratory, Massachusetts Institute of Technology, Cambridge, Massachusetts 02139, May 1981. (Also published in *Readings in Distributed Artificial Intelligence*, Alan H. Bond and Les Gasser, editors, pp. 333–356, Morgan Kaufmann, 1988.)

[FB93]   Sara Fleury and Thierry Baron. Absolute external mobile robot localization using a single image. In William J. Wolfe and Wendell H. Chun, editors, *Mobile Robots VII*. SPIE, Bellingham, Washington, 1993.

[FH90]   Claude Fennema and Allan R. Hanson. Experiments in autonomous navigation. In *Proceedings Image Understanding Workshop*, 1990.

[FJ90]   David J. Fleet and Allan D. Jepson. Computation of component image velocity from local phase information. *International Journal of Computer Vision*, 5(1):77–104, August 1990.

[Fox81]   Mark S. Fox. An organizational view of distributed systems. *IEEE Transactions on Systems, Man, and Cybernetics*, 11(1):70–80, January 1981. (Also published in *Readings in Distributed Artificial Intelligence*, Alan H. Bond and Les Gasser, editors, pp. 140–150, Morgan Kaufmann, 1988.)

[Gam90]   Jean-Pierre Gambotto. Determining stereo correspondence and egomotion from s sequence of stereo images. In *10th International Conference on Pattern Recognition*, pp. 259–262, Atlantic City, New Jersey, June 1990.

[GDW91] Piotr J. Gmytrasiewicz, Edmund H. Durfee, and David K. Wehe. A decision-theoretic approach to coordinating multiagent interactions. In *Proceedings of the Twelfth International Joint Conference on Artificial Intelligence*, August 1991.

[Gen77] Donald B. Gennery. A stereo vision system for an autonomous vehicle. In *5th International Joint Conference on Artificial Intelligence*, volume 2, page 584, Cambridge, Massachusetts, August 1977.

[GGR84] M.R. Genesereth, M.L. Ginsberg, and J.S. Rosenschein. Cooperation without communications. Technical Report 81-36, Stanford Heuristic Programming Project, Computer Science Department, Stanford University, Stanford, California 94305, 1984. (Also published in *Readings in Distributed Artificial Intelligence*, Alan H. Bond and Les Gasser, editors, pp. 220–226, Morgan Kaufmann, 1988.)

[GL90] Bradley A. Goodman and Diane J. Litman. Plan recognition for intelligent interfaces. In *Proceedings of the Sixth Conference on Artificial Intelligence Applications*, pp. 297–303, 1990.

[Gla81] Frank Glazer. Computing optic flow. In *International Joint Conference on Artificial Intelligence*, 1981.

[Gla87] Frank Glazer. Hierarchical motion detection. Technical Report COINS Technical Report 87-02, Department of Computer and Information Sciences, University of Massachusetts, 1987.

[GRA83] Frank Glazer, G. Reynolds, and P. Anandan. Scene matching through hierarchical correlation. In *Proceedings of the IEEE Computer Society Conference on Computer Vision and Pattern Recognition*, pp. 432–441, 1983.

[Gro88] D. Grossman. Traffic control of multiple robot vehicles. *IEEE Journal of Robotics and Automation*, 4(5):491–497, 1988.

[HBK+92] Marcus Huber, Clint Bidlack, David Kortenkamp, Kevin Mangis, Doug Baker, Annie Wu, and Terry Weymouth. Computer vision for CARMEL. In *Mobile Robots VII*, Boston, MA, November 1992. SPIE.

[HBM+93] Marcus J. Huber, Clint Bidlack, Kevin Mangis, David Kortenkamp, L. Douglas Baker, Annie Wu, and Terry Weymouth. Computer vision for CARMEL. In William J. Wolfe and Wendell H. Chun, editors, *Mobile Robots VII*. SPIE, Bellingham, Washington, 1993.

[HD92] Marcus J. Huber and Edmund H. Durfee. Plan recognition for real-world autonomous agents: Work in progress. In *Working Notes: Applications of Artificial Intelligence to Real-World Autonomous Robots*, pp. 68–75, Boston, MA, October 1992. American Association for Artificial Intelligence.

[HD93] Marcus J. Huber and Edmund H. Durfee. Observational uncertainty in plan recognition among interacting robots. In *Working Notes: Workshop on Dynamically Interacting Robots*, Chambery, France, August 1993. International Joint Conference on Artificial Intelligence.

[Hee88] David J. Heeger. Optical flow using spatiotemporal filters. *International Journal of Computer Vision*, 1:279–302, 1988.

[Hil83] E.C. Hildreth. Computing the velocity field along contours. In *ACM Siggraph/Sigart, Interdisciplinary Workshop, Motion: Representation and Perception*, pp. 26–32, 1983.

[HL86] R.M. Haralick and J.S. Lee. The facet approach to optic flow. In *IEEE Workshop on Computer Vision*, 1986.

[Hor93a] Ian Horswill. Polly: A vision-based artificial agent. In *National Conference On Artificial Intelligence (AAAI-93)*, 1993.

[Hor93b] Ian Horswill. A simple, cheap, and robust visual navigation system. In Jean-Arcady Meyer, Herbert L. Roitblat, and Stewart W. Wilson, editors, *From Animals to Animats 2: Proceedings of the Second International Conference on Simulation of Adaptive Behavior*. MIT Press, Cambridge, MA, 1993.

[HS81]   Berthold K.P. Horn and Brian G. Schunck. Determining optical flow. *Artificial Intelligence*, 17:185–203, 1981.
[HTP+90] Jia-Wei Hong, Xiaonan Tan, Brian Pinette, Richard Weiss, and Edward M. Riseman. Image-based navigation using 360 degree views. In *Proceedings of the Image Understanding Workshop*, 1990.
[HTP+92] Jia-Wei Hong, Xiaonan Tan, Brian Pinette, Richard Weiss, and Edward M. Riseman. Image-based homing. *IEEE Control Systems*, 12(1):38–45, 1992.
[HW87]   Berthold K.P. Horn and E.J. Weldon. Computational efficient methods for recovering translational motion. In *International Conference on Computer Vision*, pp. 2–11, 1987.
[HW88]   Berthold K.P. Horn and E.J. Weldon. Direct methods for recovering motion. *International Journal of Computer Vision*, 2:51–76, 1988.
[Jai83] R. Jain. Direct computation of the focus of expansion. *IEEE Transactions on Pattern Analysis and Machine Intelligence*, 5(1):58–64, January 1983.
[JBO87] R. Jain, S.L. Bartlett, and Nancy O'Brien. Motion stereo using ego-motion complex logarithmic mapping. *IEEE Transactions on Pattern Analysis and Machine Intelligence*, 9(3):356–369, May 1987.
[Jen84] Michael R.M. Jenkins. The stereopsis of time-varying images. Technical report RBCV-TR-84-3, Department of Computer Science, University of Toronto, Toronto, Ont., Canada, September 1984.
[KA86]   H.A. Kautz and J.F. Allen. Generalized plan recognition. In *Proceedings of the Fifth National Conference on Artificial Intelligence*, pp. 32–37, Philadelphia, PA, August 1986.
[KB88]   David J. Kriegman and Thomas O. Binford. Generic models for robot navigation. In *IEEE International Conference on Robotics and Automation*, 1988.
[KB91]   Benjamin J. Kuipers and Yung-Tai Byun. A robot exploration and mapping strategy based on a semantic hierarchy of spatial representations. *Robotics and Autonomous Systems*, 8, 1991.
[KHC+93] David Kortenkamp, Marcus Huber, Charles Cohen, Ulrich Raschke, Clint Bidlack, Clare Bates Congdon, Frank Koss, and Terry Weymouth. Integrated mobile robot design: Winning the AAAI-92 robot competition. *IEEE Expert*, August 1993.
[KK92]   A. Kosaka and Avi C. Kak. Fast vision-guided mobile robot navigation using model-based reasoning and prediction of uncertainties. *Computer Vision, Graphics, and Image Processing*, 56(2), 1992.
[KL88]   Benjamin J. Kuipers and Tod S. Levitt. Navigation and mapping in large-scale space. *AI Magazine*, 9(2), 1988.
[Kor93] David Kortenkamp. *Cognitive maps for mobile robots: A representation for mapping and navigation.* PhD thesis, The University of Michigan, 1993.
[Kro89] E. Krotkov. Mobile robot localization using a single image. In *Proceedings IEEE Conference on Robotics and Automation*, 1989.
[KTB89] David J. Kriegman, Ernst Triendl, and Thomas O. Binford. Stereo vision and navigation in buildings for mobile robots. *IEEE Transactions on Robotics and Automation*, 5(6), 1989.
[KvD75] J.J. Koenderink and A.J. van Doorn. Invariant properties of the motion parallax field due to the movement of rigid bodies relative to an observer. *Optica Acta*, 22:773–791, 1975.
[KvD76] J.J. Koenderink and A.J. van Doorn. Local structure of movement parallax of the plane. *J. Opt. Soc. Amer.*, 66:717–723, 1976.
[KZB85] Darwin T. Kuan, James C. Zamiska, and Rodney A. Brooks. Natural decomposition of free space for path planning. In *Proceedings of the IEEE International Conference on Robotics and Automation*, 1985.

[Law80] D.T. Lawton. Constraint-based inference from image motion. In *The First Anual National Conference on Artificial Intelligence*, pp. 31, 34, 1980.

[Law82] Daryl T. Lawton. Motion analysis via local translational processing. In *Proc. Workshop on Computer Vision: Representation and Control*, pp. 59–72, Rindge, NH, August 1982.

[Law83] D.T. Lawton. Processing restricted sensor motion. in *Image Understanding Workshop*, pp. 266, 281, 1983.

[Law84] Daryl T. Lawton. Processing dynamic image sequences from a moving sensor. Technical Report COINS Technical Report 84-05, Department of Computer and Information Sciences, University of Massachusetts, 1984.

[LC81] Victor R. Lesser and Daniel D. Corkill. Functionally accurate, cooperative distributed systems. *IEEE Transactions on Systems, Man, and Cybernetics*, SMC-11(1):81–96, January 1981.

[LD89] Lingxiao Li and James H. Duncan. Recovering 3-d translation motion and establishing stereo correspondence from binocular flows. In *IEEE Workshop on Visual Motion*, pp. 329–336, Irvine, CA, March 1989.

[LK81] B.D. Lucas and T. Kanade. An iterative image registration technique with an application to stereo vision. In *Seventh International Joint Conference on Artificial Intelligence*, pp. 674, 679, 1981.

[LL90] Tod S. Levitt and Daryl T. Lawton. Qualitative navigation for mobile robots. *Artificial Intelligence*, 44(3), 1990.

[LPW79] Tomas Lozano-Perez and Michael A. Wesley. An algorithm for planning collision-free paths among polyhedral obstacles. *Communications of the ACM*, 22(10), 1979.

[Luc84] Bruce D. Lucas. Generalized image matching by the method of differences. Technical Report CMU-CS-85-160, Department of Computer Science, Carnegie-Mellon University, 1984.

[MA90] Peter K. Malkin and Sanjaya Addanki. LOGnets: A hybrid graph spatial representation for robot navigation. In *Proceedings of the National Conference on Artificial Intelligence (AAAI)*, 1990.

[Mat92] Maja K. Mataric. Integration of representation into goal-driven behavior-based robots. *IEEE Transactions on Robotics and Automation*, 8(3), 1992.

[ME85] Hans P. Moravec and Alberta Elfes. High resolution maps from wide angle sonar. In *Proceedings IEEE Conference on Robotics and Automation*, 1985.

[Moe92] Saied Moezzi. *Dynamic Stereo Vision*. PhD thesis, The University of Michigan, Ann Arbor, 1992.

[Mor77] Hans P. Moravec. Towards automatic visual obstacle avoidance. In *5th International Joint Conference on Artificial Intelligence*, volume 2, pp 584, Cambridge, Massachusetts, August 1977.

[Mor81a] Hans P. Moravec. *Robot Rover Visual Navigation*. UMI Research Press, Ann Arbor, MI, 1981.

[Mor81b] H.P. Moravec. *Robot Rover Visual Navigation*. UMI Research Press, Ann Arbor, 1981.

[Nag83] Hans-Hellmut Nagel. Constraints for the estimation of displacement vector fields from image sequences. In *International Joint Conference on Artificial Intelligence*, 1983.

[Nag87] Hans-Hellmut Nagel. On the estimation of optical flow: Relations between different approaches and some new results. *Artificial Intelligence*, 33:299–324, 1987.

[NE86] Hans-Hellmut Nagel and Wilfried Enkelmann. An investigation of smoothness constraints for the estimation of displacement vector fields from image sequences. *IEEE Transactions on Pattern Analysis and Machine Intelligence*, (5):565–593, Sep 1986.

[Nel89] Randal C. Nelson. Visual homing using an associative memory. In *Proceedings of the Image Understanding Workshop*, 1989.

[NH87a] Shahriar Negahdaripour and Berthold K.P. Horn. Direct passive navigation. *IEEE Transactions on Pattern Analysis and Machine Intelligence*, 9(1):168–176, January 1987.

[NH87b] S. Neghadharipour and B.K.P. Horn. Using depth-is-positive constraint to recover translational motion. Technical Report AI Memo No 939, The MIT AI Lab, Cambridge, MA, 1987.

[NH89] Shahriar Negahdaripour and Berthold K.P. Horn. A direct method for locating the focus of expansion. *Computer Vision, Graphics and Image Processing*, 46(3):303–326, June 1989.

[Nil69] Nils J. Nilsson. A mobile automation: An application of AI techniques. In *Proceedings of the International Joint Conference on Artificial Intelligence*, 1969.

[NL91] S. Neghadaripour and S. Lee. Motion recovery from image sequences using first-order optical flow information. In *Proceedings of the IEEE Workshop on Visual Motion*, pp. 132–139, October 1991.

[PY90] S. Premvuti and S. Yuta. Consideration on the Cooperation of multiple autonomous mobile robots. In Tsuchiura, editor, *IEEE Int. Workshop on Intelligent Robots and Systems (IROS '90)*, pp. 59–63, Japan, 1990.

[RG84] Jeffrey S. Rosenschein and Michael R. Genesereth. Communication and cooperation. Technical Report HPP-84-5, Stanford Heuristic Programming Project, Stanford University, October 1984.

[RG91] A.S. Rao and M.P. Georgeff. Modeling rational agents within a BDI-architecture. In J. Allen, R. Fikes, and E. Sandewall, editors, *Proceedings of the Second International Conference on Principles of Knowledge Representation and Reasoning*. Morgan Kaufman Publishers, San Mateo, CA, 1991.

[RWA$^+$92] Yuval Roth, Annie S. Wu, Remzi H. Arpaci, Terry Weymouth, and Ramesh Jain. Model-driven pose correction. In *Proceedings IEEE International Conference on Robotics and Automation*, 1992.

[SA92] A. Singh and P. Allen. Image-flow computation: An estimation-theoretic framework, and a unified perspective. *Computer Vision, Graphics and Image Processing: Image Understanding*, 56(2):152–177, 1992.

[Sch84a] Brian G. Schunck. The motion constraint equation for optical flow. In *IEEE International Conference on Pattern Recognition*, pp. 20–22, 1984.

[Sch84b] Brian G. Schunck. Motion Segmentation and estimation by constraint line clustering. In *IEEE Workshop on Computer Vision*, pp. 58–62, 1984.

[Sch85] Brian G. Schunck. Image flow: Fundamentals and future research. In *Proceedings of the IEEE Computer Society Conference on Computer Vision and Pattern Recognition*, June 1985.

[Sch86a] Brian G. Schunck. The image flow constraint equation. *Computer Vision, Graphics and Image Processing*, Vol 35: 20–46, 1986.

[Sch86b] Brian G. Schunck. Image flow continuity equations for motion and density. *Proceedings of the Workshop on Motion*, 1986.

[Sch89] Brian G. Schunck. Image flow segmentation and estimation by constraint line clustering *IEEE Trans. Pattern Analysis and Machine Intelligence*, 11(10), October 1989.

[Sin91] A. Singh. Image-flow computation: An estimation-theoretic framework, unification and integration. *Machine Vision and Applications*, 4:55, 1991.

[SJ92] Chiao-Fe Shu and Ramesh Jain. Vector field analysis of oriented patterns. Technical Report CSE-TR-120-92, Department of Electrical Engineering and Computer Science, The University of Michigan, Ann, Arbor, 1992.

[Smi80] Reid G. Smith. The contract net protocol: High-level communication and control in a distributed problem solver. *IEEE Transactions on Computers*, C-29(12):1104–1113, December 1980.

[ST80]   G. Sandini and V. Tagliasco. An anthropomorphic cretin-like structure for scene analysis. *Computer Graphics and Image Processing*, 14(4):365–372, December 1980.

[Sug88] K. Sugihara. Some location problems for robot navigation using a single camera. *Computer Vision, Graphics, and Image Processing*, 42(3), 1988.

[TG90]   Charles Thorpe and Jay Gowdy. Annotated maps for autonomous land vehicles. In *Proceedings Image Understanding Workshop*, 1990.

[TL93]   Saburo Tsuji and Shigang Li. Memorizing and representing route scenes. In Jean-Arcady Meyer, Herbert L. Roitblat, and Stewart W. Wilson, editors, *From Animals to Animats 2: Proceedings of the Second International Conference on Simulation of Adaptive Behavior*. MIT Press, Cambridge, MA, 1993.

[TP84]   O. Tretiak and L. Pastor. Velocity estimation from image sequences with second order differential operators. In *IEEE International Conference on Pattern Recognition*, pp. 20–22, 1984.

[TS90]   Massimo Tistarelli and Giulio Sandini. Robot navigation using an anthromorphic visual sensor. In *IEEE Transactions on Robotics and Automation*, pp. 374–381, Cincinnati, Ohio, May 1990.

[VGT89a] A. Verri, F. Girosi, and V. Torre. Mathematical properties of 2d motion field: From singular points to motion parameters. In *Proceedings of the IEEE Workshop on Visual Motion*, pp. 190–200, March 1989.

[VGT89b] A. Verri, F. Girosi, and V. Torre. Mathematical properties of the two-dimensional motion field: From singular points to motion parameters. *Journal of the Optical Society of America*, 6(5), 1989.

[VGT90] A. Verri, F. Girosi, and V. Torre. Differential techniques for optical flow. *Journal of the Optical Society of America*, 7(5), 1990.

[VP87a] Alessandro Verri and Tomaso Poggio. Against quantitative optical flow. In *International Conference on Computer Vision*, pp. 171–180, 1987.

[VP87b] Alessandro Verri and Tomaso Poggio. Qualitative information in the optical flow. *Proceedings of the DARPA Image Understanding Workshop*, pp. 825–834, 1987.

[VP89]   Alessandro Verri and Tomaso Poggio. Motion field and optical flow: Qualitative properties. *IEEE Transactions on Pattern Analysis and Machine Intelligence*, Vol 11(No 5):490–498, May 1989.

[Wei88] R. Weiss. Researchers eye retinal remapping. *Science News*, 134(8):119, August 1988.

[Wei89] Carl F.R. Weiman. Private correspondance, September 1989.

[WJD+87] Allen M. Waxman, Jacqueline J. LaMoigne, Larry S. Davis, Babu Srinivasan, Todd R. Kushner, Eli Liang, and Tharakesh Siddalingaiah. A visual navigation system for autonomous land vehicles. *IEEE Journal of Robotics and Automation*, RA-3(2):124–141, April 1987.

[WWB88] Allen M. Waxman, Jian Wu, and Fredrik Bergholm. Convected activation profiles and the measurement of visual motion. In *Proceedings of the IEEE Computer Society Conference on Computer Vision and Pattern Recognition*, 1988.

[Yac83] Masahiko Yachida. Determining velocity maps by spatiotemporal neighborhoods from image sequences. *Computer Vision, Graphics and Image Processing*, 21:262–279, 1983.

[ZT90]   Jiang Yu Zheng and Saburo Tsuji. Panoramic representations of scenes for route understanding. In *Proceedings of the Tenth International Conference on Pattern Recognition*, 1990.

3D Constraints on Monocular Image Sequences: Theory and Algorithms

H.S. Sawhney and P. Anandan

Abstract. Deriving three-dimensional information about a scene from its images is a challenging problem in computer vision. Multiple views of a scene/object from a moving camera can be used for this task. This paper presents a critical appraisal of the theory and algorithms for problems involving 3D geometric constraints between a scene and its multiple views. The essential constraints between the 3D shape, the view transformations and the 2D image projections are presented for various widely applicable models of projection. The recent trend in representing 3D shape in a fixed object-centered coordinate system figures prominently in this paper. It is shown how this approach nicely separates the contribution of 3D shape and motion as manifested in the image motion. This is contrasted with the traditional approach of computing 3D motion as a precursor to the computation of 3D structure. Methods that incorporate these constraints using discrete features (like points) and spatio-temporal intensity gradients are presented.

1 Introduction

Images of a scene captured from time-varying viewpoints are an important source of three-dimensional (3D) information about the scene. In addition to varying viewpoints due to a moving sensor, objects in the world move independently. Analyzing the motion of such objects through their images can provide information about their 3D motion and structure. Creating 3D representations of the structure and motion of objects and the world relative to the camera can facilitate building autonomous robotic systems for navigation in complex environments, grasping and dexterous manipulation for flexible assembly tasks, and building 3D world models through visual exploration.

Three-dimensional reconstruction is only one of the possible goals for analyzing images from varying viewpoints. Multiple views of an object can be used to acquire a model of the object in an intrinsic coordinate system. The shape of the object in this coordinate system can be used to match and predict its appearance from novel views. Thus an intrinsic object representation maybe derived from a set of images which in turn is used for matching.

A third set of applications that can benefit from 3D motion and structure analysis involves video/image management and analysis for video annotation, content-based indexing, and coding and compression. Some of the image analysis tasks involved in these applications are scene change detection, grouping of video frames into clips based on an event, segregation of the stable scene from independently moving objects, and novel view generation. Again, these tasks do not involve an explicit 3D reconstruction of the scene but have to take into account constraints on the changing appearance of scenes and objects due to varying viewpoints.

This paper presents a critical appraisal of the theory and algorithms for problems involving geometric constraints between a scene and its images when the scene is viewed from varying positions and orientations of the imaging device. We will limit this presentation to the analysis of monocular image sequences. Many of the approaches to be discussed are useful for stereo or multi-ocular sequences too. However, a large body of work that exploits constraints for specific multiple camera configuration (like stereo) will not be discussed here.

We are not attempting a survey of the body of literature related to the problems discussed above. The endeavour here is to highlight the essential geometric constraints between the 3D geometry and the changing 2D projections, and present salient algorithms that have attempted to exploit these constraints. Even in this task, we in no way claim to be exhaustive in presenting the literature.

The approaches discussed in this paper highlight the following technical aspects of the multiple view analysis problem:

1. Constraints on the 2D images from projections of 3D scenes/objects in relative motion with respect to a camera.
2. Models of projection – perspective and weak/paraperspective.
3. Two-frame and multi-frame analysis.
4. Feature correspondence based and direct spatio-temporal intensity change based analysis.

2 Overview

The trend in 3D reconstruction from image motion (or multiple views) has rapidly moved in the past few years from camera-centered depth and motion recovery to scene-centered shape and pose recovery. We first present the latter, more recent trend for three widely used models of projection from 3D to the 2D image plane: weak perspective (**WP**), paraperspective (**PP**) and (full) perspective (**FP**).

The 3D reconstruction problem turns out to be linear for the **WP/PP** models. An elegant approach for the simultaneous estimation of shape and motion is presented first. The essential structure of the 3D constraints for the problem are laid bare by this approach – it is shown that the overconstraining set of image measurements can be factorized into a motion part and a structure part. The shape of the viewed object, represented in an object-centered coordinate system, and the view transformations for each view are simultaneously computed from the images.

Alternatively, when a reference plane is available in the scene, then the 3D estimation problem becomes linear for both the **WP** and **PP** cases. This is the subject of Sect. 5. The underlying idea here is to use the motion parallax for the scene with respect to the reference plane resulting in a factorization of the parallax motion into a component dependent on the non-planar structure and another dependent on motion (rotation for **WP** and translation for **PP**).

In order to contrast the linear approaches with the general case (when an identified plane is not assumed), Sect. 6 presents the non-linear problem of extracting motion and structure under perspective projection. The key constraint – the coplanarity or the essential matrix constraint – relating the projections of 3D points in the scene in two images is first derived. This constraint captures the complete epipolar geometry of the two-view imaging situation. Two possible ways of computing the relative camera transformations from a number of corresponding imaged points are presented. When the camera calibration is known, an ideal pin-hole camera model can be used to derive the 3D Euclidean transformation and the corresponding Euclidean structure of the scene. When the camera calibration is unknown or assumed arbitrary, then the camera transformations and the corresponding scene structure can be recovered up to an arbitrary projective transformation in P^3.

Two-frame reconstruction of the 3D coordinates of the scene will in general be unreliable in the presence of imperfect feature extraction and correspondence. Multiple views of the same scene lead to more robust and accurate reconstruction. This is the subject of Sects. 6.2 and 6.3.

Feature correspondence and tracking are important ingredients for algorithms involving 3D reconstruction. Section 7 summarizes the salient issues in feature selection and correspondence. For correspondence two approaches are contrasted – one that uses purely image plane motion heuristics for tracking features and another that uses constraints from 3D motion/structure.

Finally, Sect. 8 is devoted to direct methods for 3D estimation. These methods need not use discrete features, the spatio-temporal gradients of intensities are used directly to compute parameters that capture the 3D motion and structure of the scene.

3 Projection Models

Consider a scene represented in a fixed scene-centered coordinate system, (X_w, Y_w, Z_w). Let (X, Y, Z) represent a camera-centered coordinate system that changes with relative motion between the camera and the scene. A point $\mathbf{P}_w$ in the w-coordinates is represented as $\mathbf{P}$ in the camera coordinates as

$$\mathbf{P} = \mathbf{R}\mathbf{P}_w + \mathbf{T}, \qquad (1)$$

where $\mathbf{R}$ is the rotation matrix and $\mathbf{T}$ the translation vector that represent the coordinate transformation between the two coordinate systems. If $\mathbf{i}^T$, $\mathbf{j}^T$ and $\mathbf{k}^T$ are the three rows of $\mathbf{R}$, then the above equation can be written componentwise, for instance for the x component,

$$P_x = \mathbf{i}^T \mathbf{P}_w + T_x. \qquad (2)$$

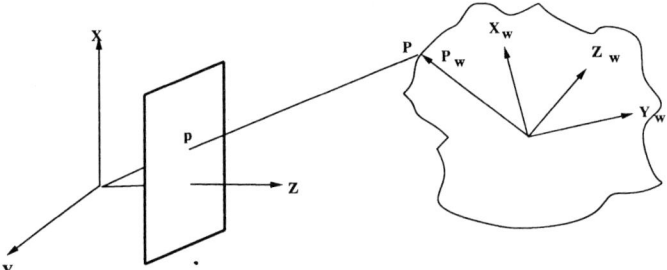

Fig. 1. The perspective projection

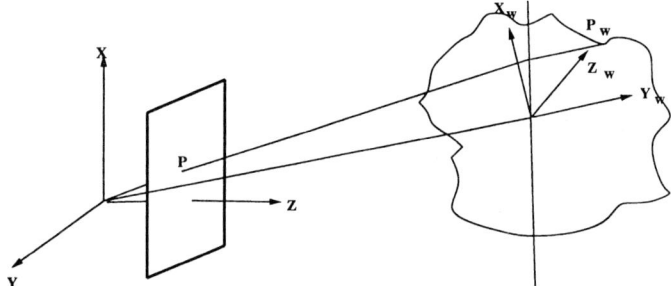

Fig. 2. The paraperspective projection

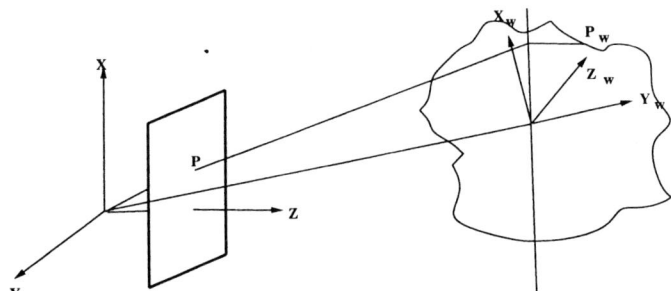

Fig. 3. The weak perspective projection

In (full) perspective projection (**FP**), depicted in Fig. 1, a pin-hole model of the camera is used. Assuming that the focal length of the camera is unity, the 2D image projection p of **P** can be written componentwise as

$$p_x = \frac{P_x}{P_z} = \frac{\mathbf{i}^T \mathbf{P_w} + T_x}{\mathbf{k}^T \mathbf{P_w} + T_z}, \quad p_y = \frac{P_y}{P_z} = \frac{\mathbf{j}^T \mathbf{P_w} + T_y}{\mathbf{k}^T \mathbf{P_w} + T_z}. \tag{3}$$

That is, the x and y 2D components are the ratios, respectively, of the x and y components of **P** with its z component.

Clearly, under **FP**, each point projects with its own scale factor, its z component. It will be seen that this creates the non-linearities in the inverse process of inferring 3D information from the 2D projections. Alternatively, approximations to **FP** can be used. Paraperspective (**PP**) is a particular first order approximation to **FP**. If the extent of the scene/object is small compared to its average distance from the camera, that is $|\mathbf{P}_w|^2/P_{0_z}^2 \approx 0$ ($\mathbf{P}_0$ is the centroid of the object in the camera coordinates), and the object is significantly off-centered, that is, $|\mathbf{P}_w|^2/P_{0_z}^2 \ll |\mathbf{P}_w||T_x|/P_{0_x}^2, |\mathbf{P}_w|^2/P_{0_x}^2 \ll |\mathbf{P}_w||T_y|/P_{0_z}^2$ then, the 2D projections can be approximated by [36]

$$\mathbf{p} = \frac{1}{T_z}\left(\begin{bmatrix} \mathbf{i}^T - \frac{T_x}{T_z}\mathbf{k}^T \\ \mathbf{j}^T - \frac{T_y}{T_z}\mathbf{k}^T \end{bmatrix}\mathbf{P}_w + \begin{bmatrix} T_x \\ T_y \end{bmatrix}\right). \tag{4}$$

Note that **PP** allows for a global scale factor for all points corresponding to the z component of the centroid, and also allows for changes in the view angle for the object. Geometrically, **PP** is shown in Fig. 2. Each point is first projected, along the view direction of the centroid, on a frontal plane passing through the centroid. All the projections from this frontal plane are projected to the image plane resulting in a common scale factor.

If only the zeroth order term in the Taylor series expansion of the perspective equations around the z component of the object centroid is significant, then the resulting projection is called the weak perspective projection, **WP**. Geometrically (Fig. 3), each point is first projected along the optical axis (z direction of the camera) on to a frontal plane passing through the centroid. All projections from this plane are then projected on to the image plane. The projection equations are

$$\mathbf{p} = \frac{1}{T_z}\left(\begin{bmatrix} \mathbf{i}^T \\ \mathbf{j}^T \end{bmatrix}\mathbf{P}_w + \begin{bmatrix} T_x \\ T_y \end{bmatrix}\right). \tag{5}$$

4 Shape and Motion Under Weak/Paraperspective

Tomasi and Kanade [52] developed an elegant approach to simultaneously compute the shape of a scene/object and camera transformation (pose/motion) from multiple frames imaged under orthographic projection. The formulation presented here is essentially based on their work but includes the case of weak perspective (scaled orthographic). This formulation has been generalized to paraperspective too [36].

Let $\mathbf{P}_k$ denote the *k*th 3D point on an object in a fixed object-centered coordinate system, C_W, and let $\mathbf{p}_{fk}$ be its weak perspective projection in the *f*th frame, C_F, whose rigid body transformation with respect to the object coordinate system is given by the rotation $\mathbf{R}_f$ and translation $\mathbf{T}_f$.

$$\mathbf{p}_{fk} = s_f \begin{bmatrix} \mathbf{i}_f^T \\ \mathbf{j}_f^T \end{bmatrix} \mathbf{P}_k + s_f \mathbf{T}_f, \tag{6}$$

where s_f is the scale factor for frame f, and $\mathbf{i}_f$, $\mathbf{j}_f$ are the first and second row vectors of $\mathbf{R}_f$ (see equation (5)).

Without loss of generality, the origin of C_W can be chosen to be the centroid of the object. $\mathbf{p}_{fk}$ then can be written without the translational part when referred to the centroid of the object's image.

Give F frames and N points, the $2F \times N$ image measurements can be written as a matrix $\mathbf{W}$,

$$\mathbf{W} = \begin{bmatrix} \vdots \\ s_f \mathbf{i}_f^T \\ s_f \mathbf{j}_f^T \\ \vdots \end{bmatrix} [\cdots \mathbf{P}_k \cdots], \tag{7}$$

or $\mathbf{W} = \mathbf{MS}$, that is the measurement matrix $\mathbf{W}$ can be factorized into a $2F \times 3$ motion matrix $\mathbf{M}$ and a $3 \times N$ shape matrix $\mathbf{S}$. This representation lays bare the essential structure of the problem in that the $\mathbf{W}$ defined for any number of frames F and points N has rank no bigger than three. Thus, the best shape and motion estimates can be extracted from $\mathbf{W}$ through its best rank three approximation.

The best rank three approximation to $\mathbf{W}$, in the least squares sense, is given by the Singular Value Decomposition (SVD) $\mathbf{W} = \mathbf{U\Sigma V}^T$, where $\mathbf{U}$ $(2F \times 3)$, Σ (3×3) and $\mathbf{V}^T$ $(3 \times N)$ correspond to the most significant three singular values.

From the SVD factorization, the affine shape (that is, the object-centered 3D coordinates up to an arbitrary 3D affine transformation) as well as the rigid 3D shape can be obtained. $\mathbf{V}^T$ or $\mathbf{AV}^T$ for any arbitrary 3×3 non-singular $\mathbf{A}$ gives the affine shape. In particular, $\mathbf{A}$ can be chosen so that any three of the 3D points form the standard basis [57].

In order to compute the rigid (metric) shape, $\mathbf{A}$ can be fixed by constraining the rows of $\mathbf{M}$ to correspond to scalings of rows of rotation (orthonormal) matrices. In particular, if $\hat{\mathbf{M}} = \mathbf{MA}$ is to be the motion matrix, then

$$\mathbf{m}_i^T \mathbf{AA}^T \mathbf{m}_i = \mathbf{m}_{i+1}^T \mathbf{AA}^T \mathbf{m}_{i+1} \tag{8}$$

$$\mathbf{m}_i^T \mathbf{AA}^T \mathbf{m}_{i+1} = 0 \tag{9}$$

for $i = 0, 2, \ldots F$. $\mathbf{A}$ can be computed from this over-constrained system of equations. Any particular camera frame, C_F, can be chosen to be aligned with C_W. This fixes the 3D shape matrix completely.

Weak perspective approximation allows for a global scale factor in the projection. This is primarily responsible for the nice linear decomposition of the measurements into a motion and a shape component. Poelman and Kanade [36] extended the factorization method to paraperspective projection. Unfortunately, the nice linear structure of the problem is lost under perspective projection. However, a similar structure is revealed when the reconstruction problem is posed using the notion of parallax with respect to a plane. We present this idea first for weak perspective and then go on to the perspective case.

5 Shape from Planar Motion Parallax

Instead of defining the 3D shape with respect to an arbitrary coordinate system, a reference surface, for instance a plane, in the scene can be used to define the shape. Any arbitrary 3D point can then be defined with the in-plane and the non-planar coordinates. It will be shown here that this method of specifying shape leads to a linear method for shape and motion computation not only for the weak perspective case but also for the perspective case.

The essential principle behind planar motion parallax is that if the image motion of a plane in the environment can be subtracted from the actual motion of points in a scene, then the residual image motion can be factorized into a component that depends only on the non-planar shape and another that depends only on the motion/view transformation (translation in the case of perspective and rotation for weak perspective). This is called the *planar motion parallax*. It is a specific instance of the well-known notion of motion parallax. In general, it can be shown [28, 38] that if two distinct points in 3D project to the same point in an image (that is are along the same view ray), then the difference in their image displacements due to a change in the viewpoint (that is the vector joining the two in another view) depends only on the 3D translation (perspective) or rotation (weak perspective) between the views and the relative depth of the 3D points. In general, there may not be coincident points in images. However, if the image motion of a set of points lying on a plane can be computed, then virtual points coincident with real points in a reference view can be created. That is, the points of intersection of an arbitrary 3D point's view ray with the plane can be chosen as the point whose projection coincides with the original 3D point (Fig. 4). The motion of the virtual point can be predicted using the computed motion of the plane. Thus, knowing the projection of an arbitrary 3D point in the second view, its difference with the predicted planar motion of the virtual point leads to the desired motion parallax vector.

In fact, the surface with respect to which the parallax vector is defined could be any arbitrary surface as shown in Fig. 4. However, the motion corresponding to a planar surface can be parameterized with a small number of parameters (6 for **PP**/**WP** and 8 for **PP**). Therefore, the parallax can be relatively easy to compute. Figure 4 clearly shows that the parallax vector $\vec{qp}$ defined as the difference between a real point **P** and a corresponding *pseudo-point*, **Q**, on the surface S (for instance, a plane), lies along the *epipolar direction*. Epipolar directions for various points intersect at the *epipole*, which is the projection of the displacement (**OM**) between the two camera centers on to the image plane. Thus, the parallax vectors are all

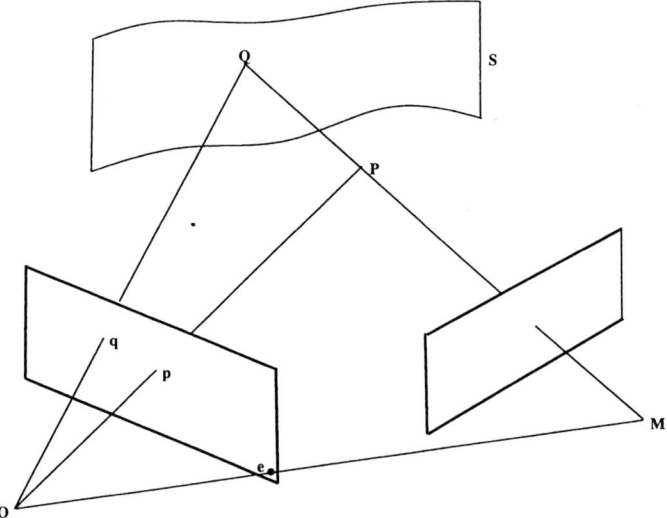

Fig. 4. Motion parallax with respect to a surface S

directed towards the epipole and their magnitude is related to the 3D location of the corresponding point. We now present the algebraic derivation.

5.1 The Weak/Paraperspective Case

The theory of planar parallax structure has been derived in various forms in [24], [26], [45], and [56]. The formulation presented here is different in that it makes the planar (affine) and the non-planar components of the image motion explicit in terms of the view transformation and the 3D shape.

Given the scene to camera coordinate transformation of equation (1), the image projection, **p**, of P under **WP** is

$$\mathbf{p} = s(\mathbf{R}_{23}\mathbf{P}_w + \mathbf{T}_{xy}), \tag{10}$$

where $s = 1/T_z$ is the weak perspective scale factor, $\mathbf{R}_{23}$ is the top left 2×3 submatrix of **R**, and **Txy** is the vector $[T_x \ T_y]^T$. Clearly, the centroid of the image projections of a set of points is the same as the projection of the object centroid. Therefore, if **p** now refers to the difference vector between an imaged point and the centroid, the above equation can be simplified to:

$$\mathbf{p} = s(\mathbf{R}_{23}\mathbf{P}_w) \tag{11}$$

We can choose the scene coordinate frame to be aligned with an arbitrary image frame, called the reference frame. In this frame, the projection equation simplifies to:

$$\mathbf{p} = s\mathbf{P}_{w_{xy}} \tag{12}$$

Projections in any other arbitrary view, whose coordinates are denoted as $\mathbf{p}'$, can be written as:

$$\mathbf{p}' = \frac{s'}{s}\mathbf{R}_{22}\mathbf{p} + s'[r_{13}\ r_{23}]^T P_{w_z} \qquad (13)$$

where $\mathbf{R}_{22}$ is the top-left 2×2 sub-matrix and and r_{ij} the ijth element of $\mathbf{R}$.

If all the scene points lie on a plane $\mathbf{g}^T\mathbf{P}_{w_{xy}} + P_{w_z} = 0$, then the relation between projections in the reference view and an arbitrary view can be written as:

$$\mathbf{p}' = \frac{s'}{s}\left(\mathbf{R}_{22} - \begin{bmatrix} r_{13} \\ r_{23} \end{bmatrix}\mathbf{g}^T\right)\mathbf{p} \qquad (14)$$

This is the well known result that projections of a plane under weak perspective transformation are related through an affine transformation.

Let $\mathbf{g}^T\mathbf{P}_{w_{xy}} + P_{w_z} = 0$ be a reference plane defined in the scene coordinate system. Consider an arbitrary point (not lying on the reference plane, in general) in the reference view. The view ray for this point intersects the reference plane at some point. So, the reference image projection for both these points (the original point and its planar intersection) is the same as shown in Fig. 4. P_{w_z} for the arbitrary point can be written as a sum of the z-component of the corresponding planar point, say $P_{w_z}^{pl}$, and the out-of-plane z-component, $P_{w_z}^{np}$. Since, the planar component satisfies equation (14), the projection relation for the arbitrary point in two views is:

$$\mathbf{p}' = \frac{s'}{s}\left(\mathbf{R}_{22} - \begin{bmatrix} r_{13} \\ r_{23} \end{bmatrix}\mathbf{g}^T\right)\mathbf{p} + s'[r_{13}\ r_{23}]^T P_{w_z}^{np} \qquad (15)$$

We write this more compactly as

$$\mathbf{p}' = \mathbf{A}\mathbf{p} + Z_{np}\mathbf{b} \qquad (16)$$

where the new symbols have the obvious correspondence with those in equation (15). The first part of the transformation is due to the affine planar component and the second is due to the non-planar component. Thus, the image motion of points has been decomposed into a planar component with respect to a reference plane in a reference view, and an out-of-plane component. Furthermore, the non-planar motion is decomposed into a component that depends on the relative structure of the scene in the reference view, and another component that depends on the view transformation. Also note that for any arbitrary view, the vector $\mathbf{b}$ is fixed for all the points. So, the non-planar vectors for each point in the view are parallel. Their magnitude is directly proportional to the out-of-plane depth component. If an additional reference point is chosen, then the relative magnitude of the non-planar displacement of any other point with respect to this reference point gives a view-invariant representation of the structure of the scene.

In the formulation above, the orthonormality of the rotation matrix was not utilized anywhere. In the view transformation (equation (1)), $\mathbf{R}$ could be an arbitrary 3×3 matrix representing a 3D general linear transformation. Therefore, the view-invariant representation of structure derived above is invariant to general affine view transformations. Also, since the projection transformations in equations (5) and (4) for **WP** and **PP** are similar in that they have a linear and a translational part, the above decomposition of image motion into planar and non-planar components is valid for **PP** too.

Any three points present both in the reference view and an arbitrary view can be used to define a 2D affine transformation corresponding to the reference plane passing through those three points. The correspondence of a fourth point specifies the invariant structure completely. Three coordinates are being specified from two views to compute an invariant structure representation of the object. The in-plane 2D affine coordinates can be computed in the reference view itself and the third coordinate is computed using the additional view. Alternately, if the image plane coordinate system in an arbitrary view is warped to account for the planar 2D affine transformation of the reference plane, then the residual motion is due only to the non-planar structure. This represents the one parameter of scene structure with respect to an intrinsic coordinate system of the reference plane.

5.2 The Perspective Case

In the following formulation, a reference view and any other arbitrary view are chosen to present the motion parallax equations. The 3D coordinate transformation between the primed coordinates, **P'**, in view 2 and the reference coordinates, **P**, in view 1 is written as:

$$\mathbf{P} = \mathbf{R}\mathbf{P'} + \mathbf{T} \tag{17}$$

Let $\mathbf{N'}^T\mathbf{P'} = d$ represent a plane in the second coordinate system. Substituting this in the above equation, one can write the view transformation for the plane as [15]:

$$\mathbf{P}^w = \mathbf{R}[\mathbf{I} + \mathbf{R}^T\mathbf{T}\mathbf{N'}^T/d]\mathbf{P'} \tag{18}$$

Note that this represents the general 8-parameter projective relationship for plane-to-plane projection. Using the identity $[\mathbf{I} + \mathbf{R}^T\mathbf{T}\mathbf{N'}^T/d]_{-1} = [\mathbf{I} - \beta\mathbf{R}^T\mathbf{T}\mathbf{N'}^T/d]$ (see [14]), where $\beta = (1/(1 + \mathbf{N'}^T\mathbf{R}^T\mathbf{T}/d))$, the above relationship can be written as the follow projective transformation:

$$\rho\mathbf{p'} = [\mathbf{I} - \beta\mathbf{R}^T\mathbf{T}\mathbf{N'}^T/d]\mathbf{R}^T\mathbf{P}^w \tag{19}$$

p' is the image plane vector $(p'_x, p'_y, 1)$ in the reference view, and ρ is an unknown scale factor. Equation (17) can be written in terms of **p'** and an unknown scale factor k as:

$$\mathbf{P} = \mathbf{R}k\mathbf{p'} + \mathbf{T} \tag{20}$$

Substituting for **p'** from equation (19), after some algebraic manipulations, we get:

$$\mathbf{P}^w = \frac{\rho}{k}[\mathbf{I} + \mathbf{T}\mathbf{N}^T/d](\mathbf{P} - \mathbf{T}) \tag{21}$$

where $\mathbf{N} = \mathbf{R}\mathbf{N}'$ is the plane normal in the reference view. Given a view ray $\mathbf{p}'$ in an arbitrary view, with the knowledge of the plane projective transformation of equation (19), the projection of the virtual planar point (intersection of $\mathbf{p}'$ with the plane) in the reference view can be computed using equation (19). In other words, points in any arbitrary view can be transformed (or warped) so that they project to the corresponding virtual planar points in the reference view. For points that do lie on the plane, the warping transformation leads to their real projection in the reference view. For the non-planar points, the planar motion parallax vector (the difference between the virtual planar projection and the actual projection) is given by:

$$p - p^w = \left(1 \Big/ \left(1 + P_z \Big/ d_N \frac{T_z}{d}\right)\right)(p - t) \qquad (22)$$

where the lower case bold letters represent the respective image vectors with their z-components unity, $d_N = P_N - T_N - d$ is the perpendicular distance of $\mathbf{P}$ from the plane, P_N and T_N being the dot products of $\mathbf{P}$ and $\mathbf{T}$ with the plane normal $\mathbf{N}$, respectively.

When T_z is zero, the parallax equation becomes:

$$\mathbf{p} - \mathbf{p}^w = (-d_N/P_z)[T_x\ T_y\ 0]^T \qquad (23)$$

For an alternative derivation of the above results see [25].

We have shown that the parallax vector defined with respect to an arbitrary plane is directed towards the epipole in the reference image. Thus, the parallax vector field is due only to the translational component of the 3D view transformation, as is expected of any motion parallax field. The effect of rotations on the image motion has been eliminated by choosing a warping transformation corresponding to a plane in the environment. In the warped coordinate system, the motion disparity of the plane is zero. In other words, the points on the plane have been fixated through a coordinate transformation. The residual image motion is due only to the non-planar component of the environment and translational motion.

5.3 View-Invariant Representation

The magnitude of the parallax vector is a function of the non-planar distance, d_N of $\mathbf{P}$, and the z-components of $\mathbf{P}$ and $\mathbf{T}$. Let $\eta = 1 \Big/ \left(1 + P_z/d_N \frac{T_z}{d}\right)$ be the magnitude and let $\tau = 1/\eta - 1$. If a point P_0 not lying on the fixated plane is chosen as a reference then for any other point P_i:

$$\tau_i / \tau 0 = \frac{P_{iz}}{d_{iN}} \Big/ \frac{P_{0z}}{d_{0N}} \qquad (24)$$

That is, the ratio of the magnitudes of the non-planar parallax motion components are dependent only on the relative structure of the environmental points not lying on the reference plane. This ratio represents a view-independent "coordinate" of the structure of the environment that does not lie no the reference plane. Given any arbitrary viewpoint, if the new view can be warped using the transformation corresponding to the reference plane, then the relative magnitude of the residual parallax vectors is always that given in equation (24). Thus, fixation with respect to the reference plane not only compensates for the effects of rotations, but also provides an environment centered reference surface with respect to which the complete shape of the environment can be specified. The in-plane coordinates of a point can be computed in the reference view itself given at least four points lying on the reference plane. This can be done in a number of ways [25]. Essentially the four reference points define a plane projective basis for the projective plane P^2, and any other point lying in the plane has two view-invariant coordinates in this basis [33]. Therefore, the two in-plane and one non-planar relative coordinate for an arbitrary environmental point specifies the shape in an intrinsic environment-centered coordinate system.

The derived representation contains the necessary representations both for motion and structure reconstruction and matching. If the absolute metric motion and structure information is required, then the translation can be computed from the parallax field leading subsequently to the rotation [25] and the absolute coordinates in any particular view reference frame. If the goal is recognition and matching, then absolute metric structure need not be computed. From two views, given four planar and two out-of-plane points, the intrinsic structure representation can be computed. For any arbitrary view, if the six points can be matched, then a synthetic image for the new viewpoint can be created using the intrinsic structure. This can then be compared with the given view. Similarly for new view generation, if the mapping of the six points is available, then a new view can be created without knowing the absolute structure and the motion between the views.

The derivation of 3D information from planar motion parallax requires that a reference plane be available for defining the residual motion. In the absence of such information, one has to resort to a general method for computing structure and motion under perspective projection. Any of the general methods for this problem are inherently non-linear. Some salient methods are presented now to contrast them with the simplicity of the linear weak perspective and planar parallax methods.

6 Structure and Motion Under Perspective Projection

There are two classes of methods for computing general structure and motion under perspective projection. One set of methods compute first the motion transformation on a two-frame basis, and then use this to compute the 3D structure.

3D Constraints on Monocular Image Sequences: Theory and Algorithms

The 3D structure can be refined over many frames by representing it in a stable coordinate system. In the second set of methods, both the structure (represented in a fixed coordinate system) and the motion transformations are solved for simultaneously from image measurements over many frames. Both sets of methods use iterative non-linear minimization techniques. Representative algorithms for the two classes, and the essential mathematical nature of the problem are presented here.

6.1 Two-Frame Motion Estimation

The problem of estimating the rigid motion of a camera from two-views of an arbitrary scene is called the *two-frame* motion estimation problem or the *relative orientation* problem. One way to derive the 3D structure of a scene is to first estimate the the relative rigid rotation and translation between two different views of the scene, and then compute the 3D coordinates of scene features in a camera-centered coordinate system. Two-view motion estimation is important in its own right for applications in camera localization and motion compensation.

6.1.1 The Essential Matrix Constraint

The geometry of the two-view motion problem is illustrated in Fig. 5. A static scene is observed from two distinct camera positions that are related through a rotation, R, and a translation t. For the purposes of the development in this paper, it will be assumed that point features in the scene are observed in the two views and that correspondences between the two view rays for the same 3D point are available.

Given the rigid displacement between the two views, a 3D point in the two distinct coordinate systems can be written as:

$$P_2 = RP_1 + t \qquad (25)$$

The two image space points in homogeneous coordinates can be written as:

$$p_1 = P_1 \qquad p_2 = RP_1 + t \qquad (26)$$

From the figure, it is evident that the view-ray in the second view is constrained to lie in the plane defined by the corresponding ray in the first view and the translation vector. This is called the *co-planarity* constraint in the Euclidean interpretation. In projective terms, the first view ray and the camera displacement define an epipolar line in the second image that is the image of all the points along the first view ray. This is called the *epipolar constraint*. The two equivalent constraints can be written as:

$$p_2 \cdot (t \times Rp_1) = 0 \qquad (27)$$

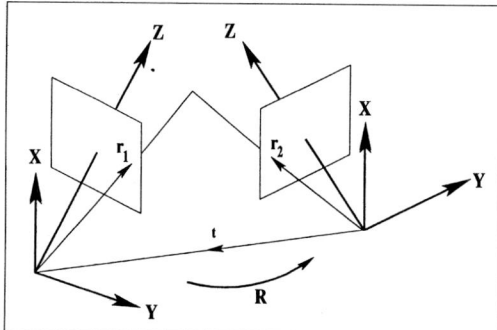

Fig. 5. The coplanarity constraint

The above equation can also be written as:

$$\mathbf{p}_2^T T_X R \mathbf{p}_1 = 0 \qquad (28)$$

where T_X is the matrix operator for the cross-product operation with the vector $\mathbf{t}$. The 3×3 product matrix $T_X R$ is called the *Essential Matrix* or the E-matrix derived originally by Longuet-Higgins [27]. Under the rigidity constraint, this matrix encodes the complete information about the viewing geometry.

6.1.2 Computing the View Transformation

Note that in the derivation of the E-matrix constraint above, a *pin-hole* or *perspective* camera model was assumed. That is, the view rays in the images are assumed to be measured with a calibrated camera so that they are known with respect to an absolute calibrated coordinate system centered at the cameras. This allows estimation of absolute metric information from the two views. When arbitrary unknown calibration parameters are allowed for the two cameras, the E-matrix can be generalized in a projective formulation. We will discuss that in a later section. Presently, we discuss methods of computing the rigid displacement parameters from the epipolar constraint.

The E-matrix has nine parameters defined up to an arbitrary scale factor because equation (28) is homogeneous in the parameters. There are three additional constraints on the E-matrix. There exist two orthogonal triad of vectors $[\mathbf{v}_1, \mathbf{v}_2, \mathbf{v}_3]$ and $[\mathbf{t}\ \mathbf{u}_2\ \mathbf{u}_3]$ such that $R[\mathbf{v}_1\ \mathbf{v}_2\ \mathbf{v}_3] = [\mathbf{t}\ \mathbf{u}_2\ \mathbf{u}_3]$. Therefore, by inspection, E can be written as:

$$E = [\mathbf{t} -\mathbf{u}_2\ \mathbf{u}_3] diag(0, 1, 1)[\mathbf{v}_1\ \mathbf{v}_2\ \mathbf{v}_3]^T \qquad (29)$$

Thus, the E-matrix has one zero singular value and two other equal singular values [23, 31].

Equation (28) is linear and homogeneous in the nine unknowns of the E-matrix. Many researchers have attempted to solve for the E-matrix (up to a scale factor) from at least eight point correspondences of non-degenerate configurations in the two views without imposing the above constraints on the decomposability of the E-matrix. The E-matrix is first solved assuming independence amongst its nine components. Subsequently, the closest matrix decomposable into a product $T_x R$ is computed to derive the corresponding translation **t** and the rotation **R**. However, even with small magnitudes of noise in the point correspondences, the unconstrained E-matrix can be very different from the original decomposable matrix. Thus, the rotation and translation derived from the unconstrained E-matrix are themselves quite erroneous [18, 53].

The correct way to solve for the two-view transformation is to impose the decomposability constraint on the E-matrix in the solution process. One possible way to do this is to impose the constraint that **t** is a unit vector and **R** is an orgthonormal (rotation) matrix in the equation (27). Here we briefly present one such elegant treatment due to Horn [19] (also see [20]).

Given the coplanarity (or the E-matrix) constraint, the following sum of squares error measure can be minimized to compute the best two-view transformation:

$$E = \sum_i w_i (\mathbf{t} \cdot (\mathbf{R} \mathbf{p}_{i_1} \times \mathbf{p}_{i_2}))^2 \tag{30}$$

where i refers to the *ith* point and w_i is a weight factor that is the inverse of the variance of the *ith* term in the error measure given independent, zero-mean Gaussian noise in each of the point correspondences. Horn uses an iterative Gauss-Newton optimization method to compute the R and t. Given an initial estimate **t**, **R**, the best increment in the unknowns can be obtained by solving for the extremum of the following linearized error measure:

$$E_{linear} = \sum_i w_i (a_i + \mathbf{b}_i^T \delta \mathbf{t} + \mathbf{c}_i^T \delta \omega)^2 + \lambda (\mathbf{t}^T \delta \mathbf{t}) \tag{31}$$

where $\delta \mathbf{t}$ and $\delta \omega$ are the unknown increments in the translation and rotation, $a_i = w_i \mathbf{t} \cdot (\mathbf{R} \mathbf{p}_{i_1} \times \mathbf{p}_{i_2})$, $\mathbf{b}_i = w_i \mathbf{R} \mathbf{p}_{i_1} \times \mathbf{p}_{i_2}$, $\mathbf{c}_i = w_i \mathbf{R} \mathbf{p}_{i_1} \times (\mathbf{p}_{i_2} \times \mathbf{t})$, and λ is a Lagrange multiplier that is used to impose the unit translation vector constraint. The following 7×7 system of equations is solved to compute the increments:

$$\begin{bmatrix} A & B & \mathbf{t} \\ B^T & C & 0 \\ \mathbf{t}^T & 0^T & 0 \end{bmatrix} \begin{bmatrix} \delta \mathbf{t} \\ \delta \omega \\ \lambda \end{bmatrix} = - \begin{bmatrix} \mathbf{b} \\ \mathbf{c} \\ 0 \end{bmatrix} \tag{32}$$

where $A = \Sigma_i w_i \mathbf{b}_i \mathbf{b}_i^T$, $B = \Sigma_i w_i \mathbf{b}_i \mathbf{c}_i^T$, $C = \Sigma_i w_i \mathbf{c}_i \mathbf{c}_i^T$, $\mathbf{b} = \Sigma_i w_i a_i \mathbf{b}_i$, $\mathbf{c} = \Sigma_i w_i a_i \mathbf{c}_i$.

In each iteration, the computed increments are added to the existing **t** and **R** estimates. **t** is normalized to the closest unit vector and the new **R** is normalized to the closest unit quaternion. The converged values are the final computed estimates.

The non-linear least squares estimate requires an initial guess for the unknown rotation and translation. In many situations the approximate intended motion of the moving camera is known. This can serve as the initial guess to the iterative algorithm. Alternately, as Horn suggests, the 3D unit hemisphere in 4D space representing unit quaternions could be randomly or systematically sampled to provide initial guesses for rotation [19]. Given a rotation, the corresponding optimal translation can be solved for in closed-form from the quadratic error measure in equation (30). Either of these methods of specifying the initial guess leads to rapid convergence to a local minimum in most situations. The best local minimum (amongst various starting points) is usually close to the true solution.

There are situations, however, when even with tens of point correspondences, none of the local minimum is close to the desired solution. In some cases, the local minimum closest to the correct solution has a higher error residual than the one with the wrong solution [39]. These situations reflect some of the inherent ambiguities in two-frame motion estimation. These have been discussed extensively in the literature. We will mention the highlights here.

When the field of view is small and the motion has significant rotations around axes parallel to the image plane (rotations in depth), then small perturbations in the point correspondences can lead to large perturbations in the computed motion parameters. In this situation, it is hard to decompose the observed image motion into its constituent rotational and translational components. Adiv [2] demonstrated this ambiguity for motion displacements arising out of small rotations. Recently Daniilidis and Nagel [9] showed this analytically for planar surfaces by deriving the covariance matrix of the computed motion parameters. Sawhney and Hanson [39] give an experimental demonstration of this ambiguity.

A second source of convergence to the wrong minimum arises out of the use of the coplanarity constraint as an error measure. Again, when the field of view is small, translation along the optical axis (along the direction of depth) almost always leads to a local minimum solution which is often the global minimum too [39]. This has been observed and analyzed by Spetsakis and Aloimonos [47] and Daniilidis and Nagel [8]. This local minimum solution can be avoided by normalizing the coplanarity error measure so that it represents the error between the expected projection of the second view ray and the observed projection *in the image plane* and not the 3D distance measure that it represents in the unnormalized form (equation (30)). This normalization, however, leads to a more complex error function whose convergence behavior is worse than for the unnormalized function [43].

6.2 3D Structure/Depth Reconstruction

When the relative orientation, **R** and **T**, between two camera positions is known, then the 3D vector for each of the points observed with correspondence between the two views can be reconstructed. For instance, in the reference frame of the first camera,

$$\mathbf{P}_1 = \frac{\|\mathbf{T}\|(\hat{\mathbf{T}} \times \mathbf{R}\mathbf{p}_1) \cdot (\mathbf{p}_2 \times \mathbf{R}\mathbf{p}_1)}{(\mathbf{p}_2 \times \mathbf{R}\mathbf{p}_1) \cdot (\mathbf{p}_2 \times \mathbf{R}\mathbf{p}_1)} \mathbf{p}_1 \tag{33}$$

Note that the magnitude of **T** has been made explicit in the equation because only the unit vector $\hat{\mathbf{T}}$ can be determined from the monocular motion relative orientation constraint. Since only the depth component of the view ray is unknown, the above equation represents depth or 3D structure estimation.

Computing the 3D coordinates of a point from only two measurements is prone to large errors in the computed coordinates even when the computed motion parameters might be quite accurate [11]. With the computed motion parameters themselves being erroneous due both to random errors in the measurements, and due to the inherent ambiguities in their estimation, the resulting two-frame depth estimates are, in general, very unreliable. This problem has been addressed by using multiple frames and integrating the 3D structure estimates thus obtained.

An alternative to the batch method is the sequential (recursive) method that processes multiple frames frame-by-frame. For every new frame of measurements, the new structure estimates with the associated covariance are combined with the estimates from the previous frames using Kalman filtering. The key idea in this technique is to incorporate the errors in computing relative orientation (motion) parameters into the covariances of the structure parameters which can then be combined with new measurements. Oliensis and Thomas [35] were the first to point out that traditionally, the effect of the motion parameters on the 3D structure has ignored the cross-correlations between the estimates of various points. That is, the $3N \times 3N$ covariance matrix of the N 3D points has been approximated by N 3×3 matrices, each of which is the covariance matrix of a point computed using equation (33). Given that the same motion parameters are used to compute the N 3D coordinates, the covariance of the motion parameters will lead to cross-correlations in the covariances of the coordinates.

If $\mathbf{P} = [\mathbf{P}_1\mathbf{T} \dots \mathbf{P}_N\mathbf{T}]^T$ is the vector of all the 3D coordinates, then [35]:

$$d\mathbf{P} = \frac{\partial \mathbf{P}}{\partial (\mathbf{R},\mathbf{T})} \frac{\partial (\mathbf{R},\mathbf{T})}{\partial \mathbf{p}} d\mathbf{p} + \frac{\partial \mathbf{P}}{\partial \mathbf{p}} d\mathbf{p} \tag{34}$$

The $3N \times 3N$ covariance matrix of **P** can be calculated using the above equation and equation (33). Oliensis and Thomas [35, 50] provide ample experimental and analytical evaluation of their approach and contrast it with the ones that omit the cross-correlation terms in the covariance matrix.

Oliensis and Thomas represent the 3D structure in a moving coordinate system that is the coordinate system of the most recent frame. Thus, their method suffers from two potential problems:

1. there are additional errors introduced due to the linearization of the equation for the propagation of the 3D coordinates to the new view, and
2. they are unable to take advantage of the possibly larger baseline of motion between the reference frame and an arbitrary frame because they compute motion parameters always between successive frames.

In a recent paper, Azarbayejani et al. [5] address these issues by representing the structure in a fixed coordinate system.

6.3 Simultaneous Structure and Motion Reconstruction

The essential idea behind estimating 3D structure from many views of the same scene is that scene structure remains static (fixed) while changing viewpoints provide many measurements of the fixed scene parameters. We will present approaches that do not assume a particular model of motion relating the position and orientation the camera from successive viewpoints. It is assumed that each viewpoint of the camera is independent.

There are two major approaches. In one, the scene structure is represented as the 3D coordinates of points in a fixed coordinate system, for instance the first camera frame. The corresponding points observed in an image from an arbitrary view can be expressed as a rigid transformation (25) followed by a perspective projection. Thus, M (excluding the reference image) images of N points provide $6M + N$ unknowns and $2NM + 1$ (one to fix the arbitrary scale) equations. These are solved in a batch method involving all the frames and the points using non-linear least squares techniques [46, 48]. When camera calibration (the linear camera parameters) are unknown, it has been reported that the non-linear optimization problem is better behaved [32, 48]. In this case, the unknown camera calibration, the projection and the coordinate transformation can be combined into a single 3×4 unknown projective transformation:

$$\rho \mathbf{p} = \mathbf{KP} \tag{35}$$

where ρ is an unknown scale factor for each imaged point in each frame. Again, knowing the imaged $\mathbf{p}$'s for M frames and N points, the M view transformations K, and the projective coordinates of the N points can be computed using non-linear optimization. Note that the reconstructed coordinates are defined up to an unknown 4×4 projective transformation in P^3. This can be left unspecified if metric structure is not required. Alternatively, five or more known 3D points can be used to fix this transformation.

7 Establishing Correspondence/Tracking

In all the algorithms for shape and motion estimation presented above, it was implicitly assumed that the image projections of any point over many frames have been identified. This is called the *correspondence* problem. There are two major issues underlying the correspondence problem: i) detection of features like points and lines that remain stable over changes in viewpoint over time, and ii) finding correspondence of each feature over time as it moves on the image plane (i.e., maintaining identity of a feature).

7.1 Feature Selection

Point and line features that are distinctive enough have been the features of choice in most structure from motion algorithms. Alternative approaches that avoid the use of discrete features will be discussed later. Various operators that measure the "cornerness" of the intensity surface have been used. For instance, Tomasi [51] uses the curvatures of the sum-of-squared-differences (SSD) surface [3] defined as a function of image displacements. High values of the principal curvatures implies a distinctive point-like feature. Szeliski and Kang [49] use a measure of monotonicity in local regions to define blobs whose centroids are the features that are tracked. Sawhney et al. [42] use corners defined as intersection of line segments to obtain trackable point features. Line features are more stable than point features as they derive their support from an extended one-dimensional region in the intensity surface. Sawhney and Hanson [40] and Williams and Hanson [59] have used lines extracted through a hierarchical grouping process developed by Boldt et al. [6].

7.2 Correspondence/Tracking

For the purposes of deriving 3D information from motion, only features that remain stable over time are useful. Stability of features can be measured by their *trackability*, that is those features that can be tracked reliably are stable [40, 51]. Reliable tracking can be defined as consistency with respect to a constraint. Ullman [54] and Williams and Hanson [59] solve the correspondence problem on a two-frame basis by setting up minimal graph matching problems between local neighborhoods defined over point/lines in two consecutive frames. Most long-range (multi-frame) feature tracking methods look for consistency within a constraint of smooth motion *in the image plane*. For instance, locally constant velocity and acceleration are commonly used constraints [7, 10]. Sethi and Jain [44] and Rangarajan and Shah [37] use a trajectory smoothness match measure to find smooth trajectories defined over sets of points from multiple frames.

A fundamental problem with most of the above correspondence/tracking methods is that no explicit 3D constraints are used to constrain potential matches between frames. Almost all the methods have used smoothness and similarity of image motion as a heuristic to constrain the search for correspondences. For stereo date, 3D constraints from the 3D structure and motion of the scene have been utilized to constrain the correspondences [60]. For monocular motion, Sawhney and Hanson [40] formulated the correspondence problem to allow for similarity (or affine) transformations between aggregate sets of features. Every small set of features is hypothesized as an *affine describable* set. Consistency over time with the modeled transformation is used to track the aggregate features (and hence the points and lines constituting them). Another novel aspect of this approach is that aggregate features (defined as collections of lines/points) are matched *as a whole* across frames rather than the traditional independent feature matching. The measurement and motion modeling uncertainties in the tracking problem are explicitly modeled for the aggregate feature. These are used to define a match measure for correspondence. (This similarity/affine constraint based tracking was subsequently used to segment and reconstruct objects that are well-approximated as fronto-parallel planes [41].)

8 Direct Methods

The algorithms and theory for 3D reconstruction presented earlier leads to robust results only if reliable feature correspondences are available. Moreover, discrete feature-based reconstruction leads to only sparse 3D structure. Direct methods for 3D reconstruction avoid the necessity of isolating discrete features, working directly with spatio-temporal gradients of image intensities. Negahdaripour and Horn [34] were one of the first to propose a direct method for computing 3D information for a moving plane. Their approach has been generalized by Horn and Weldon [22], Heel [17], Hanna [13] and Bergen et al. [12] amongst others for general 3D reconstruction. Our presentation here is primarily based on the work of Bergen et al. [12].

Underlying the direct approach to 3D reconstruction is the basic assumption that an image intensity patch at one time instant moves to another location at the next instant *purely due to the relative motion between the camera and the corresponding patch in the scene*. This can be expressed as:

$$I_1(\mathbf{p}) = I_2(\mathbf{p}') \tag{36}$$

where I_1 and I_2 are the two image intensity functions, and $\mathbf{p}$ and $\mathbf{p}'$ are the two corresponding 2D points. This is called the brightness constancy assumption. Traditionally, brightness constancy has been used to compute an *explicit* representation of the *optical flow field* as a precursor to 3D reconstruction and interpretation [1, 4, 6, 21]. Obviously, optical flow represents the motion of the image intensities under the brightness constancy assumption. This is different from the 3D *motion field* (that is, the field of 3D displacement vectors of points in the scene) or even from a 2D projection of the 3D motion field. (For an analysis of the conditions under which the two are similar and different, see [55].) Note that equation (36) represents a one-dimensional constraint on the flow at a point, the *normal flow*, that along the gradient at the point.

The brightness constraint is represented directly in terms of the parameters that define the projection of the 3D motion field. Under the assumption that the motion between two frames is small, a first order approximation to equation (36) is written as:

$$\nabla I_1(\mathbf{p})^T \delta \mathbf{u}(\mathbf{p}) = I_2(\mathbf{p} - \mathbf{u}_0(\mathbf{p})) - I_1(\mathbf{p}) \quad (37)$$

where $\mathbf{u}_0(\mathbf{p})$ is a known estimate of the displacement, and $\delta \mathbf{u}(\mathbf{p})$ is the unknown increment that is to be solved for. This equation represents a one-dimensional constraint on the image flow at any point. It constrains the *normal flow*, the flow along the direction of the image gradient, but leaves the flow perpendicular to the gradient unconstrained. Local and/or global models of 3D motion and structure can be used to constrain the flow completely.

Bergen et al. [12] use various models of $\delta \mathbf{u}(\mathbf{p})$ parametrized in terms of global 2D motion models or 3D motion models and 3D structure parameters. For instance, for a 2D 6-parameter affine model of motion (see also [58], in a given region for each point, the following is true:

$$\nabla I_1(\mathbf{p})^T \mathbf{X} \delta \mathbf{a} = I_2(\mathbf{p} - \mathbf{u}_0(\mathbf{p})) - I_1(\mathbf{p}) \quad (38)$$

where $\mathbf{X} = \begin{bmatrix} 1 & x & y & 0 & 0 & 0 \\ 0 & 0 & 0 & 1 & x & y \end{bmatrix}$ with x, y being the image coordinates of $\mathbf{p}$, and $\delta \mathbf{a}$ is the 6-dimensional vector of incremental affine parameters. In order to satisfy the small motion approximation, the iterative solution of the parameters is implemented hierarchically. Gaussian/Laplacian pyramids of appropriate number of levels are created for the two images. Estimates of the unknown parameters derived at a coarse level are used as initial estimates at the next finer level to create a warped image $I_2(\mathbf{p} - \mathbf{u}_0(\mathbf{p}))$. At any level, iterations of equation (38) are used to compute the refined parameters. General models of 3D motion and their corresponding image transformations (discussed in the development of theory in the earlier part of this paper) can also be used in the direct methods [12]. Note that the affine deformation case is important in its own right because, as was shown earlier, a plane to plane projection under weak/paraperspective is an affine transformation, and the same for full perspective can often be approximated as one[1].

The obvious advantage with the direct methods is that discrete feature extraction and correspondence is avoided. However, the brightness constancy assumption and the assumption of small motion in the linearization step limit the applicability of these methods to small interframe deformations. Also a theoretical and experimental analysis of the quantitative performance of the direct methods for structure and motion estimation has not been done. The inherent ambiguities and noise sensitivity [11, 9] associated with the feature-based algorithms should apply to the direct methods too because both use the same image displacement models. The performance of both the direct and feature-based methods using planar parallax is still open to investigation.

---

[1] Especially when the field of view, and rotations, and translation in depth are small.

An alternative to the linearization of the intensity function in spatial coordinates in equation (37) has recently been proposed by Manmatha for the cases of affine [29] and similarity transformations [30]. Instead of matching linearized intensity functions defined over an unknown coordinate deformation, it is proposed to match intensities convolved with deformations of a *known* windowing function. For instance, if two images are related through an affine deformation of the 2D coordinate system, $I_1(\mathbf{p}) = I_2(\mathbf{Ap})$, then the unknown deformation can be computed by matching with affine deformed Gaussians:

$$G(\mathbf{p}; \Sigma) * I_1(\mathbf{p}) = G(\mathbf{p}'; \mathbf{A}\Sigma\mathbf{A}^T) * I_2(\mathbf{p}') \tag{39}$$

where $\mathbf{p}' = \mathbf{Ap}$. Note that this equation expresses an exact relation for the unknown $\mathbf{A}$ without approximating the intensity functions through linearization. Thus, in principle large deformations can be handled in contrast with the methods that use equation (37). Instead, linearizations of a known analytical function, the Gaussian, about some sample values of $\mathbf{A}$ can be used to solve for the unknown $\mathbf{A}$. This has been solved for the case of arbitrarily large similarity deformations in [30]. Extension of this idea to more general deformations (for instance those for a general 3D to 2D projection) is open for research.

Direct methods when combined with 3D constraints from shape and motion can be generalized to incorporate not just the normal flow constraints but also flow constraints for features like points and edges. Specifically, the structure of the covariance matrix of image gradients in a local region can be used to incorporate various generalized image features in the estimation process.

9 Conclusions

A lot of progress has been made in the last few years in developing an understanding of how geometric information about three-dimensional world can be derived from multiple two-dimensional images. In this paper, an attempt has been made to present the essential 3D constraints on 2D projections, along with salient algorithms that exploit these constraints to robustly derive the 3D information.

In recent years, there has been a convergence of ideas on the derivation of shape and motion information. Approaches that represent 3D shape in a fixed scene-centered coordinate system have shown a lot more promise compared to the traditional depth and motion estimation methods. With this viewpoint, derivation of 3D shape from multiple views and recognition of 3D objects under varying viewpoints are seen as complementary questions [45, 56]. If 3D shape can be derived from a few views, even up to some unknown geometric transformations, it can be used to predict novel views that can then be used for matching and recognition. The methods based on motion parallax make this relationship especially explicit.

The correspondence problem also can now be viewed as a matching problem with the shape derived from a few views providing sufficient 3D constraints for an object's appearance from novel views. Thus, 3D constraints can enrich or replace purely heuristic approaches to tracking and correspondence.

References

[1] G. Adiv. Determining 3D motion and structure from optical flows generated by several moving objects. *IEEE Transactions on Pattern Analysis and Machine Intelligence*, 7(4):384–401, 1985.
[2] G. Adiv. Inherent ambiguities in recovering 3D information from a noisy flow field. *IEEE Transactions on Pattern Analysis and Machine Intelligence*, 11(5):477–489, 1989.
[3] P. Anandan, *Measuring Visual Motion from Image Sequences* PhD thesis, University of Massachusetts at Amherst, MA, 1987. COINS TR 87-21.
[4] P. Anandan. A computational framework and an algorithm for the measurement of visual motion. *International Journal of Computer Vision*, 2(3):283–310, 1989.
[5] A. Azarbayejani, B. Horowitz, and A. Pentland. Recursive estimation of structure and motion using relative orientation constraints. In *Proc. Computer Vision and Pattern Recognition Conference*, pp. 294–299, 1993.
[6] M. Boldt, R. Weiss, and E. Riseman. Token-based extraction of straight lines. *IEEE Transactions on Systems Man and Cybernetics*, 19(6):1581–1594, 1989.
[7] J.L. Crowley, P. Stelmaszyk, and C. Discours. Measuring image flow by tracking edge-lines. In *Proc. 2nd Intl. Conf. on Computer Vision*, pp. 658–664, 1988.
[8] K. Daniilidis and H.H. Nagel. Analytical results on error sensitivity of motion estimation from two views. In *Proc. 1st European Conference on Computer Vision*, pp. 199–208, 1990.
[9] K. Daniilidis and H.H. Nagel. The coupling of rotation and translation in motion estimation of planar surfaces. In *Proc. Computer Vision and Pattern Recognition Conference*, pp. 188–193, 1993.
[10] R. Deriche and O. Faugeras. Tracking line segments. In *Proc. 1st European Conference on Computer Vision*, pp. 259–268, 1990.
[11] R. Dutta and M.A. Snyder. Robustness of correspondence-based structure from motion. In *Proc. 3rd Intl. Conf. on Computer Vision*, pp. 106–110, 1990.
[12] J.R. Bergen et al. Hierarchial model-based motion estimation. In *Proc. 2nd European Conference on Computer Vision*, pp. 237–252, 1992.
[13] K.J. Hanna. Direct multi-resolution estimation of ego-motion and structure from motion. In *Proc. IEEE Wkshp. on Visual Motion*, pp. 156–162, 1991.
[14] R. Hartley and R. Gupta. Computing matched epipolar projections. In *Proc. Computer Vision and Pattern Recongnition Conference*, pp. 549–555, 1993.
[15] J.C. Hay. Optical motions and space perception: An extension of Gibson's analysis. *Psychological Review*, 73:550–565, 1966.
[16] D.J. Heeger and A.D. Jepson. Subspace methods for recovering rigid motion I: Algorithm and implementation. Technical Report RBCV-TR-90-35, University of Toronto, 1990.
[17] J. Heel. Temporally integrated surface reconstruction. In *Proc. 3rd Intl. Conf. on Computer Vision*, pp. 292–295, 1990.
[18] B.K.P. Horn. Recovering baseline and orientation from essential matrix. Internal Report, 1990.
[19] B.K.P. Horn. Relative orientation. *International Journal of Computer Vision*, 4(1):59–78, 1990.
[20] B.K.P. Horn. Relative orientation revisited. *Journal of the Optical Society of America A*, 8(10):1630–1638, 1991.

[21] B.K.P. Horn and B.G. Schunck. Determining optical flow. *Artificial Intelligence*, 17(1-3):185-203, 1981.
[22] B.K.P. Horn and E.J. Weldon. Direct methods for recovering motion. *International Journal of Computer Vision*, 2(1):51-76, 1988.
[23] T.S. Huang and O.D. Faugeras. Some properties of the E matrix in two-view motion estimation. *IEEE Transactions on Pattern Analysis and Machine Intelligence*, 11(12):1310-1312, 1989.
[24] J.J. Kowenderink and Andrea J. van Doorn. Affine structure from motion. *Journal of the Optical Society of America A*, 81:377-385, 1991.
[25] Chia-Hoang Lee. Structure and motion from two perspective views via planar patch. In *Proc. 2nd Intl. Conf. on Computer Vision*, pp. 158-164, 1988.
[26] Chia-Hoang Lee and T. Huang. Finding point correspondences and determining motion of a rigid object from two weak perspective views. *Computer Vision Graphics and Image Processing*, 52:309-327, 1990.
[27] H.C. Longuet-Higgins. A computer algorithm for reconstructing a scene from two projections. *Nature*, 293:133-135, 1981.
[28] H.C. Longuet-Higgins and K. Prazdny. The interpretation of a moving retinal image. In *Proc. Royal Society of London B*, pp. 385-397, 1980.
[29] R. Manmatha. Thesis Proposal, Univ. of Massachusetts, 1992.
[30] R. Manmatha and J. Oliensis. Extracting affine defformations from image patches – i. finding scale and rotation. In *Proc. Computer Vision and Pattern Recognition Conference*, pp. 754-755, 1933.
[31] S. Maybank, *Theory of Reconstruction from Image Motion*. Springer-Verlag, 1993.
[32] R. Mohr, F. Veillon, and L. Quan. Relative 3D reconstruction using multiple uncalibrated images. In *Proc. Computer Vision and Pattern Recongnition Conference*, pp. 543-548, 1993.
[33] J.L. Mundy and A. Zisserman, *Geometric Invariance in Computer Vision*. The MIT Press, MA, 1992.
[34] S. Negahdaripour and B.K.P. Horn. Direct passive navigation. *IEEE Transactions on Pattern Analysis and Machine Intelligence*, 9(1):168-176, 1987.
[35] J. Oliensis and J.I. Thomas. Incorporating motion error in multi-frame structure from motion. In *Proc. IEEE Wkshp. on Visual Motion*, pp. 8-13. 1991.
[36] C.J. Poelman and T. Kanade. A paraperspective factorization method for shape and motion recovery. Technical Report CMU-CS-92-208, Carnegie Mellon University, 1992.
[37] K. Rangarajan and M. Shah. Establishing motion correspondence. In *Proc. Computer Vision and Pattern Recognition Conference*, pp. 103-108, 1991.
[38] J.H. Rieger and D.T. Lawton. Processing differential image motion. *Journal of the Optical Society of America A*, 2(2):354-360, 1985.
[39] H.S. Sawhney and A.R. Hanson. Comparative results of some motion algorithms on real image sequences. In *Proc. DARPA Image Understanding Workshop*, 1990.
[40] H.S. Sawhney and A.R. Hanson. Identification and 3D description of "shallow" environmental structure in a sequence of images. In *Proc. Computer Vision and Pattern Recognition Conference*, pp. 179-186, 1991.
[41] H.S. Sawhney and A.R. Hanson. Trackability as a cue for potential obstacle identification and 3D description. *International Journal of Computer Vision*, 1993.
[42] H.S. Sawhney J. Oliensis, and A.R. Hanson. Image description and 3D reconstruction from image trajectories of rotational motion. *IEEE Transactions on Pattern Analysis and Machine Intelligence*, 15(9), 1993.
[43] Harpreet S. Sawhney. *Spatial and Temporal Grouping in the Interpretation of Image Motion*. PhD thesis, University of Massachusetts at Amherst, MA, 1992. COINS TR 92-05.

[44] S.K. Sethi and R. Jain. Finding trajectories of feature points in a monocular image sequence. *IEEE Transactions on Pattern Analysis and Machine Intelligence*, 9(1):56–73, 1987.
[45] Amnon Shashua. Correspondence and affine shape from two orthographic views: Motion and recognition. Technical Report AI Meno No. 1327, Massachusetts Institute of Technology, 1991.
[46] M. Spetsakis and Y. Aloimonos. A multi-frame approach to visual motion perception. *International Journal of Computer Vision*, 6(3):245–255, 1991.
[47] M.E. Spetsakis and J. Aloimonos. Optimal computing of structure from motion using point correspondences in two frames. In *Proc. 2nd Intl. Conf. on Computer Vision*, pp. 449–453, 1988.
[48] R. Szeliski and S.B. Kang. Recovering 3D shape and motion from image streams using non-linear least squares. In *Proc. Computer Vision and Pattern Recognition Conference*, pp. 752–753, 1993.
[49] R. Szeliski and S.B. Kang. Recovering 3D shape and motion from image streams using non-linear least squares. Technical Report CRL93/3, DEC Cambridge Research Lab., 1993.
[50] J.I. Thomas, A. Hanson, and J. Oliensis. Understanding noise: The critical role of motion error in scene reconstruction. In *Proc. 4th Intl. Conf. On Computer Vision*, pp. 325–329, 1993.
[51] C. Tomasi. *Shape and Motion from Image Streams: A Factorization Method*. PhD thesis, Carnegie Mellon University, 1991. CMU-CS-91-172.
[52] C. Tomasi and T. Kanade. Shape and motion from image streams under orthography: A factorization method. *International Journal of Computer Vision*, 9(2):137–154, 1992.
[53] R.Y. Tsai and T.S. Huang. Uniqueness and estimation of 3D motion parameters and surface structures of rigid objects. In Whitman Richards and Shimon Ullman, editors, *Image Understanding 1984*, pp. 135–171. Ablex Corporation, NJ, 1984.
[54] S. Ullman. *The Interpretation of Visual Motion*. The MIT Press, Cambridge, MA, 1979.
[55] A. Verri and T. Poggio. Motion field and optical flow: Qualitative properties. *IEEE Transactions on Pattern Analysis and Machine Intelligence*, 11(5):490–498, 1989.
[56] D. Weinshall. Model based invariants for 3D vision. *International Journal of Computer Vision*, 10(1):27–42, 1993.
[57] D. Weinshall and C. Tomasi. Linear and incremental acquisition of invariant shape models from image sequences. In *Proc. 4th Intl. Conf. On Computer Vision*, pp. 675–682, 1993.
[58] P. Werkhoven and J.J. Koenderink. Extraction of motion parallax structure in the visual system I. *Biological Cybernetics*, 59, 1990.
[59] L.R. Williams and A.R. Hanson. Translating optical flow into token matches and depth from looming. In *ICCV*, pp. 441–448, 1988.
[60] Z. Zhang and O. Faugeras. *3D Dynamic Scene Analysis: A Stereo Approach*. Springer, Berlin, Heidelberg, 1992.

Integrating Selective Attention and Space-Variant Sensing in Machine Vision

C. Colombo, M. Rucci, and P. Dario

Abstract. Studies on visual perception have demonstrated that selective attention mechanisms and space-variant sensing are powerful tools for focusing available computing resources to the process of relevant data. In this paper an overall architecture for an active, anthropomorphic robot vision system which integrates retina-like sensing and attention mechanisms is proposed. Gaze direction is shifted both on the basis of sensory and semantic characteristics of the visual input, which are extracted separately by means of a parallel and serial analysis. An implementation of the system by means of optical flow and neural network techniques is described, and the results of its application are discussed.

1 Introduction

During the last few decades, machine vision applications have often been hampered by the need of processing huge amounts of data. This led to the common belief that the major bottleneck in solving problems in vision was the computing power and image acquisition facilities [17]. Yet, only a small fraction of the raw image data may be relevant to the task at hand. That is, vision systems usually do not need to understand the scenes with which they deal, but they only need to extract the information required to accomplish specific tasks [7]. The idea of a system that purposively selects among visual data the relevant information and ignores irrelevant details is common to several recently proposed machine vision paradigms (e.g., [2, 4]), and it is crucial when a real time performance is required.

Specific mechanisms for data reduction and selection are also present at different levels of the human visual system, and play a major role to dramatically simplify visual computations. At the earliest stage of vision, the particular layout of the receptors of the retina – which are organized into a *space-variant* sampling structure including a high-resolution, small central *fovea*, and a *periphery* whose resolution linearly decreases with eccentricity – yields a good compromise between spatial acuity and field of view [34]. The mechanisms of *selective attention*, which allow for selectively processing simultaneous sources of visual information, act at later stages of human vision. By means of attention, computational resources are allocated to the processing of data included into a limited extent *spotlight*; the spotlight can be shifted through the visual field and can vary in size [19, 28]. Due to the space-variant structure of the retina, visual exploration in humans occurs by actively shifting the fixation point, so as to exploit the high-resolution capabilities of the fovea [38]. Gaze control is mainly provided by attentional mechanisms, even if it has been shown that the spotlight can be voluntarily shifted independently of eye fixations [14]. As already hypothesized in 1890 by William James, attention can be drawn both by the *sensory* and *semantic* characteristics of a visual stimulus [18].

Due to the fact that the processing power of current computers is still by far lower than that of the brain, implementing similar mechanisms in machine vision is extremely important towards the development of effective, real time systems.

Recently, the space-variant structure of the human retina has received the interest of the research community, and a number of applications based on its simulations have been described [37, 16]. Furthermore, a hardware sensor mimicking the geometry of the human eye has been designed and developed, and it has been applied to bidimensional pattern recognition and motion estimation [32, 33, 35]. A few architectures have also been proposed, which attempt to replicate selective attention in machine vision systems, by the use of multi-resolution image data structures, or *pyramids* [29, 6, 10]. Data selection with such hierarchical structures is the result of a coarse-to-fine search through certain paths of the pyramids [7, 11, 27]. Also the concept of *saliency map* – a topographical map which combines individual sensory outputs into a global measure of attentional conspicuity, as first defined in 1987 by Koch and Ullman [21] – has been found useful for the implementation of attentive systems in robotics [9].

So far, research on attention in machines has been based on traditional high-resolution cameras, thus not exploiting the further data reduction advantages achievable by space-variant sensing. Furthermore, apart from some speculative considerations, the work has been focused either on the sensory (*bottom-up*) or the semantic (*top-down*) characteristics of the input data, while their combined use into a single architecture has been neglected.

In this paper, the integration of selective attention mechanisms and space-variant sensing towards the development of a real-time anthropomorphic vision system is proposed. The focus here is on merging both semantic and sensory cues in order to achieve active gaze control with a robotic head. The architecture includes a simplified saliency map, which is activated simultaneously by bottom-up and top-down cues, as resulting from a parallel and a serial analysis of the visual input, respectively.

The system is designed so as to attend to different visual tasks, and to change the way it interacts with the environment depending on them. The system implementation is based on a hybrid architecture, including neural and conventional image analysis techniques, such as optical flow and edge extraction. Thanks to its intrinsic modularity, the architecture is suitable to be expanded so as to include different tasks and to be adapted to other requirements. In the present implementation, particular interest has been devoted to motion cues at the sensory level and to object recognition at the semantic level, so that the head is able to foveate on and explore moving objects, which can be eventually recognized as far as they are already known to the system. As the system's goal is to control the motion of the sensors according to a predefined task, the architecture proposed in this paper can be included in the *active vision* paradigm [1, 3].

The paper is organized as follows: in Sect. 2 the system architecture is presented and theoretical issues are discussed, then in Sect. 3 implementation details are provided and the results of a simulation of system behavior are described. Finally, in Sect. 4 conclusions are drawn.

2 The System Architecture

A general scheme of system architecture is shown in Fig. 1. This includes a robotic head including retina-like sensors, two modules for visual analysis and an attention controller. A basic assumption of this scheme is that shifts of attention are always accompanied by corresponding movements of the sensors, i.e. that *the attentional spotlight is kept centered on the fovea*. Due to this constraint, controlling attention also implies gaze control.

The system is organized as a loop. The raw image data coming from the whole visual field of the space-variant sensors are analyzed by a *parallel processing module*, and a set of salient locations of the image space (*sensory cues*) which are candidates for drawing attention are produced. At the same time, the visual region covered by the attentional spotlight is analyzed by a *serial processing module*, which produces *semantic cues* as the result of knowledge-based expectations. The role of the attention controller is to combine current proprioceptive data and

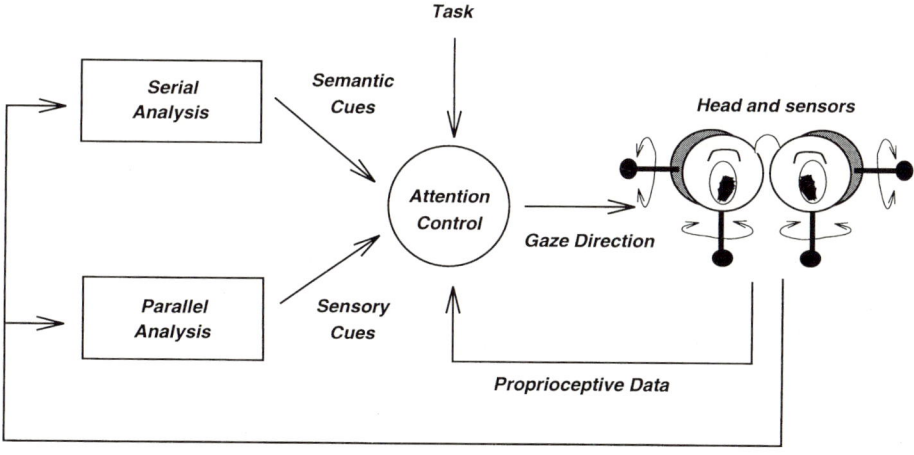

Fig. 1. The system architecture. Sensory and semantic cues are the result of a parallel and serial analysis of raw image data. The new direction of gaze is selected by the attention controller on the basis of the task at hand

salient cues so as to activate, also on the basis of the current task, a simplified version of the saliency map. Gaze direction is selected as the map location with maximum activation.

It is worth nothing that, as far as attention control is concerned, no formal distinction is made between sensory and semantic cues. These typically alternate in drawing attention. In face, after the detection and localization of a sensory relevant region of the visual field, movements of the eyes play an important role for its analysis and classification.

A number of theories of visual recognition have been proposed, based on the sequence of gaze directions [26, 25, 38]. According to these theories, the system performs recognition by serially looking at different parts and features of the examined object. The identification of a feature which characterizes a known object can stimulate the system to look in different directions searching for other features of that object, so as to better assess object identity. To this aim, the system incorporates a fragmentary representation of the objects to recognize.

The way the system responds to visual input changes according to the task at hand. That is, on the basis of the task, a priority can be assigned to different visual features.

In the following paragraphs, a detailed description of the elements of the architecture is given, in the case of a monocular implementation.

2.1 Head and Retina-Like Sensing

The sampling structure for retina-like sensing is shown in Fig. 2. The periphery around the central fovea is partitioned into M annuli $\times N$ angular sectors. The ratio of the outer and inner radii of each annulus is equal to a constant $a > 1$. By suitably scanning the sensing elements, the retinal periphery space (x, y) can be mapped onto a *cortical plane* (ξ, γ) by means of a *log-polar* (or *retino-cortical*) transformation [33]. Figure 3 gives an example of a space-variant image representation in both the retinal and the cortical planes. The log-polar transformation can be analytically expressed as:

$$\begin{cases} \xi = \log_a(\sqrt{x^2 + y^2}) - p \\ \gamma = q \ \arctan(y/x) \end{cases} \quad (1)$$

where p and q are constants determined by the size and layout of the sensing elements.

Figure 4 illustrates the geometry of a monocular head-eye system. In the case of a space-variant sensor characterized by equation (1), the field of view is 2δ, where

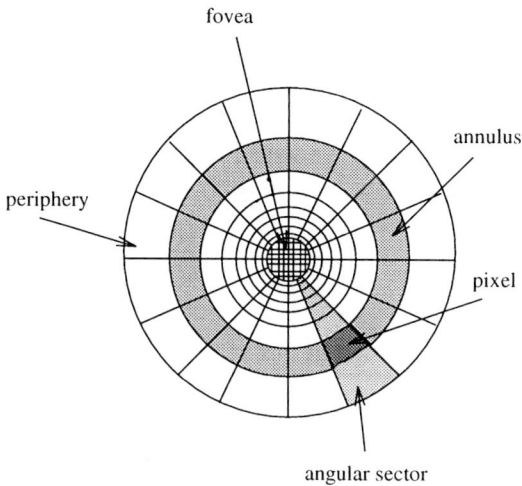

Fig. 2. The sampling structure of retina-like sensing

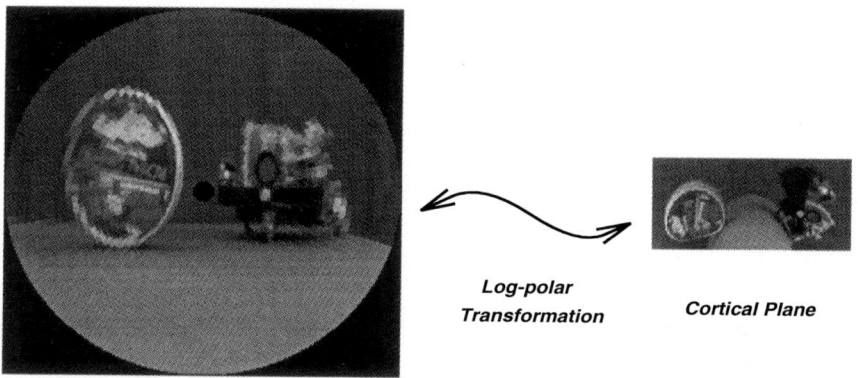

Fig. 3. Example of retina-like sensing. The objects imaged in the retinal plane (a cookie-box and a mini-robot) undergo a strong deformation after the log-polar transformation that maps them into the cortical plane. Notice also that image degradation is increasingly higher moving outwards from the fovea

$$\delta = \arctan(a^{M+p}/f), \qquad (2)$$

and f denotes the focal length of perspective projection. The exponential term allows one to achieve either a wider field of view than with traditional cameras, if image resolution is kept fixed, or a reduction of the overall image data for a given field of view.

Figure 5 shows an hardware implementation of the retina-like sensor, which has been included in a binocular vision system recently developed at the ARTS Lab [12].

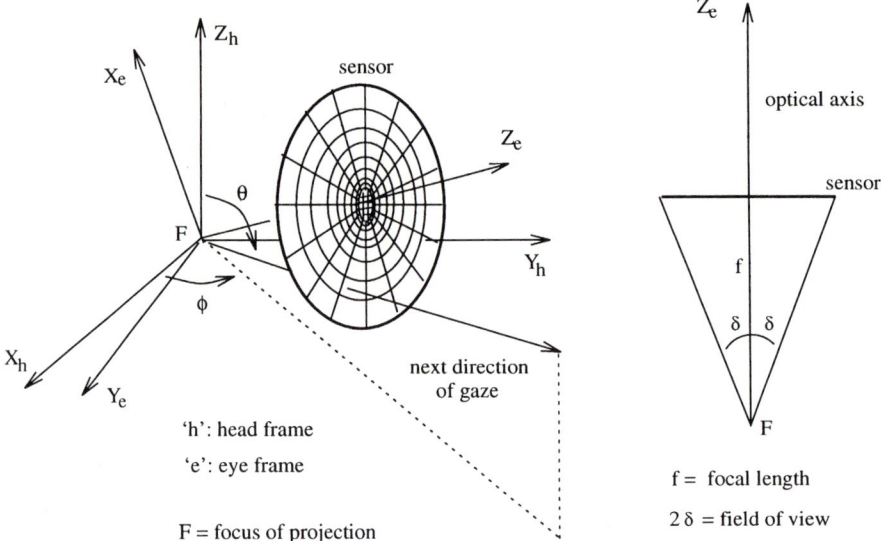

Fig. 4. The geometry of a monocular head-eye system. The two d.o.f. of the sensor are the *pan* (ϕ) and *tilt* (θ) angles. The head (fixed) and the eye (mobile) frame origins are assumed here to be coincident

Fig. 5. *Left*: the CCD retina-like sensor built at IMEC, Leuven, Belgium. Several partners were involved in the design and development of the sensor: DIST – University of Genoa, Italy; University of Pennsylvania; ARTS Lab Pisa, Italy. *Right*: the robotic head developed at the ARTS Lab. The system is composed of a mechanical unit which includes two retina-like sensors, each actuated with two DOFs through DC servomotors, and a transputer-based control architecture

2.2 Parallel Analysis

Figure 6 presents the schematic organization of the parallel analysis module. The module includes as many pyramids as the number of different sensory features that are candidates for drawing system attention – e.g., image brightness, color, motion features, edge density, texture, etc.

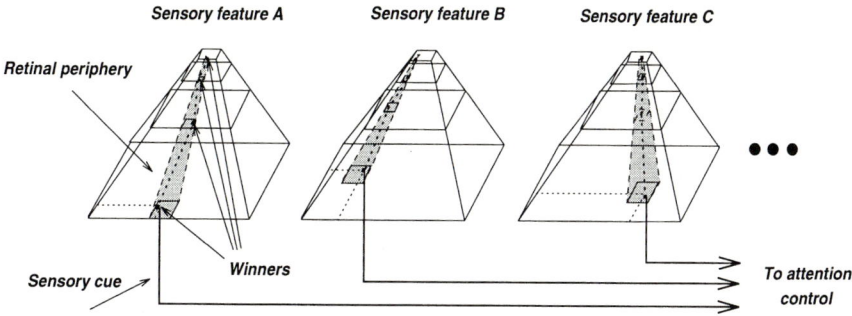

Fig. 6. Sensory pyramids and the Winner-Take-All mechanism at the parallel stage of analysis

A sensory cue is produced for each pyramid as the result of a coarse-to-fine search through all of its levels. All pyramids are scanned in parallel, and at a generic level L a *Winner-Take-All* mechanism acts so that only one "winner" is propagated to level $L - 1$, while "loosers" are inhibited [11, 36]. In such a way computations are greatly reduced, as only a small part of the visual data is processed at high resolution, while the rest is explored only at low resolution. The image coordinates of the 0th level winner of a pyramid are delivered to the attention control module as the sensory cue for that pyramid.

A characteristic of the pyramids used in this system is that they are built *on cortical images rather than on retinal images.* Such hierarchical structures will be referred to as "cortical pyramids." Note that, since cortical images encode only information from the periphery of the retina, data from the fovea are not considered at the parallel stage, but their analysis is left to the serial analysis module. Pixels in the retinal plane have nonuniform layout and dimensions – they are in fact distributed according to a polar-exponential geometry. Nonetheless, the corresponding pixels in the cortical plane are distibuted according to the same Cartesian geometry as the pixels of traditional raster cameras, thus allowing one to build up the cortical pyramids according to a classical algorithm [6, 29]. That is, the generic level $L + 1$, $L \geq 0$ of the pyramid is constructed by first smoothing and then subsampling by a factor of two in both the ξ and γ directions the cortical image at level L. As a result, as shown in Fig. 7, the new level of the hierarchy can be interpreted in the retinal plane as a novel retina with characteristic parameters $M_{L+1} = M_L/2$, $N_{L+1} = N_L/2$, $a_{L+1} = a_L^2$, $p_{L+1} = p_L/2$, $q_{L+1} = q_L/2$. Figure 8 shows a three-level cortical pyramid, and the corresponding retinal pyramid.

Note that, although constructing cortical pyramids has of course a smoothing effect, which contributes to reduce the noise in the raw image data, sensory cues are usually very noisy, and thus inadequate for a quantitative (absolute) analysis of

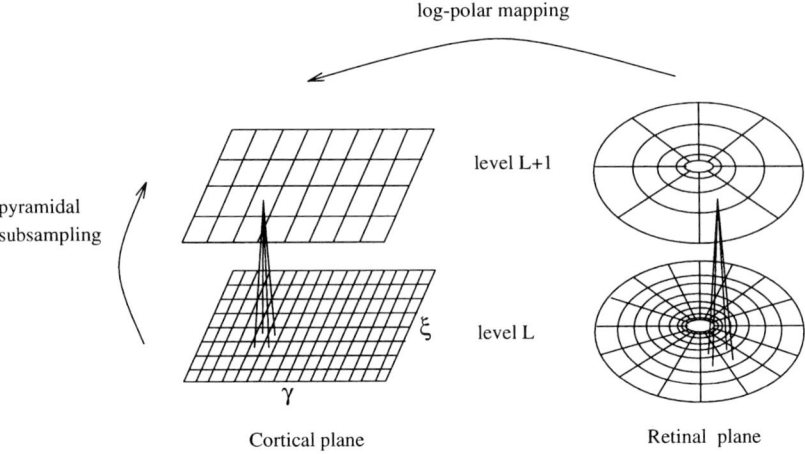

Fig. 7. *Left*: building binary cortical pyramids. *Right*: backtransforming a cortical pyramid yields a retinal pyramid: notice the presence of a hollow inner region corrensponding to the fovea

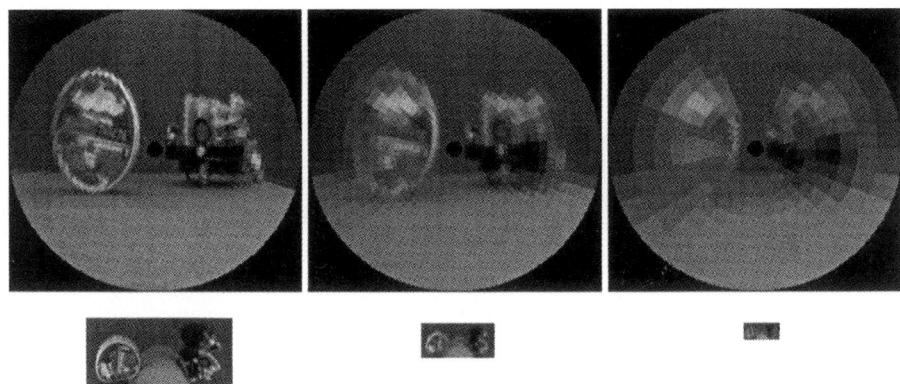

Fig. 8. An example of cortical pyramid. *Top*: retinal plane. *Bottom*: cortical plane

the visual scene[1]. The system is though robust enough to exploit the information present in the *relative* feature magnitude, and to draw attention to specific objects that have to be recognized.

Note also that, as far as a b/w sensor is considered, sensory pyramids related to features of increasing complexity can all be built starting from an image brightness pyramid. This leads to a further simplification, in that pyramid level L for a

---

[1] A related problem is the generation of spurious cues produced by image noise, which could produce gaze shifts to irrelevant visual directions. To avoid that, a simple thresholding mechanism is used at the lowest level of each sensory pyramid, in order to discriminate the signal from noise.

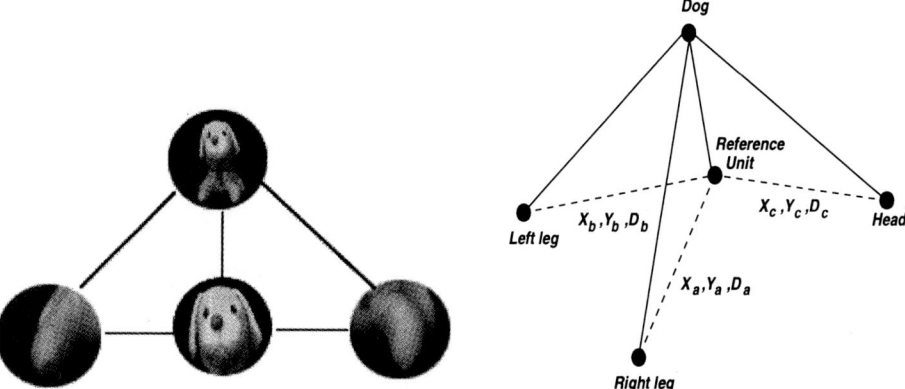

Fig. 9. *Left*: the fragmentary representation used for object recognition is composed of a set of icons having different levels of resolution, and linked by spatial relationships. *Right*: the representation is implemented with a neural network which includes a set of feature units (dashed circles) and an object unit (solid circle)

given sensory feature is actually constructed only when – and if – required by the top-down search mechanism. In the Appendix, the case of motion analysis is discussed, and the recursive construction of sensory pyramids for the *optical flow* and related features – such as its first-order *differential invariants* and the *immediacy of collision* – starting directly from cortical data is described. Such motion features provide powerful cues for the attentive control of a robot head. They can be effectively used to implement several different system tasks – such as searching for specific kinds of motions (e.g., pure translations or rotations), shifting gaze on the image feature with largest immediacy of collision, or pointing out the object in the scene with largest speed. In Sect. 3, some experiments are described in which the parallel analysis is based on the optical flow magnitude and the immediacy of collision.

2.3 Serial Analysis

As emphasized at the beginning of this section, semantic cues correspond to visual field locations where characteristics of the hypothesized object are expected to be found. The system includes a fragmentary representation of each object to recognize. As shown in the left part of Fig. 9, an *object representation* is basically a graph composed of fixed-dimension images (*icons*) reproducing different parts (or *features*[2]) and views of the object at varying level of resolution. The icons are linked

---

[2] The term "feature" indicates in this paragraph a characteristic part of an object and should not be confused with the sensory feature of the previous paragraph.

by means of spatial relationships, which specify how they are located with respect to other icons, and the relative dimensions of their features.

An object representation has been implemented in the system by means of a neural network which includes a set of *feature units* linked to a single *object unit* with excitatory connections (see the right part of Fig. 9). Each feature unit is sensitive to a specific part of the object, that is to all the icons reproducing that feature, and it acts as a cumulator, by storing and cumulating the activation provided by a matching network. As shown in the figure, the spatial relationships among the features are given with respect to the feature unit sensitive to the icons centered on the object centroid and enclosing the whole object (*reference unit*). For each object representation, the parameters (x_i, y_i) and D_i indicate the position of feature i with respect to object centroid and the dimension that the attentional spotlight should have for its examination, respectively. All the parameters are given in the retinal space, and they are normalized with respect to the object size. In this way, if the reference unit is activated when the width of the attentional spotlight is equal to D_s, so that gaze is shifted, with respect to feature i by an amount proportional to $(x_i D_s, y_i D_s)$ in the image plane and the spotlight size is correspondingly set to $D_i D_s$.

Starting from each feature, the parameters for the examination of each other part of the object are determined by following the graph and passing through the reference unit. As will be explained later on, when required the spatial relationships are estimated by a neural network so as to adapt to the actual orientation of the examined object. The use of a scale-independent object representation allows object recognition capabilities even with different focal lengths and object distances.

All object units inhibit each other in a Winner-Take-All fashion, so that only one of them has a positive value of activation at a given time, while all the others are inhibited (output equal to zero). This is equivalent to the formulation of an hypothesis on the identity of the observed object. In this terms, recognition is intended as the eventual determination of a winning object unit.

The structure of the serial analysis module is illustrated in Fig. 10 – a preliminary of its application to a simple case of object recognition using conventional sensors is described in detail in [30]. Image data are organized into a multi-resolution edge pyramid, which represents image edges at different levels of resolution. The pyramid is built on both data coming from the fovea and the periphery of the sensor. The edges are extracted at the lowest pyramid level by a gradient operator and data are then propagated at successive stages by means of Gaussian smoothing. As shown in the figure, the pyramid is scanned by an attentional spotlight centered on the fovea which, by moving through a "fovea-centered cylinder," samples a fixed amount of information at different levels of resolution. As a result, a trade-off is built between the resolution level and the spatial extension of the considered area, and an increment of the width of the area implies a corresponding decrement of the level of resolution at which data are examined. The spotlight performs an expansion of the gray-level dynamic and produces a fixed dimension *attentional icon*. By means of the expansion, parts of the examined area

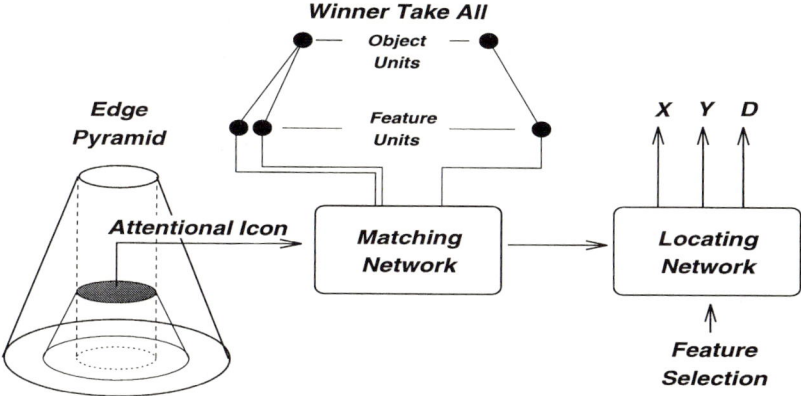

Fig. 10. The architecture for visual recognition (serial processing module)

with stronger edges and/or higher edge concentration are emphasized with respect the others. When it is not involved in a recognition sequence, the spotlight scans the cylinder from the bottom to the top of the pyramid. This is equivalent to performing a radial expansion of the considered region, starting from the fovea and moving towards the periphery. The resulting attentional icon is compared at each time with all the icons included in the object representation. If a "semantic match" is found, the pyramid scanning process stops and the spotlight dimension is stored into a short-term memory (not shown in the figure). The size of the attentional spotlight is later used for calculating the spatial parameters of subsequent fixations.

The attentional icon is matched in parallel with all the icons of the memory, so as to activate hypotheses on object identity. Hypotheses are ordered according to their plausibility and their are sequentially verified. Each verification involves the serial analysis of all the parts and features of the hypothesized object so as to test if other matches are achieved.

The matching process is carried out by a *matching net*[3], which is implemented with the counterpropagation paradigm [13]. The matching network has as many output units as are the features to identify, and each output is linked with the corresponding feature unit in the object representations. As proposed by Kohonen [23], the topological self-organizing map at the second layer of the net is trained by means of an unsupervised learning process which requires the recursive presentation of patterns of the training set to the net. During the training, the weight vectors of the maximally responding unit and those of its immediate neighborhood are modified towards the input pattern, whereas the size of the neighborhood and the parameters regulating weight changes decrease. The train-

---

[3] A "Weak perspective" projection model [24] is assumed here, thus avoiding significant deformations of the peripheral parts of the foveated objects; such deformations could seriously complicate the iconic representation.

ing set includes all the icons reproducing the features selected for representing the objects, extracted in a large number of images. By means of learning, the map selects actually which icons to use for the representations on the basis of their statistical relevance, and stores generalized versions of them in the first layer of weights. In this way, the map self-organizes so as produce several disconnected areas where units are sensitive to similar icons.

The spatial parameters are estimated by a *locating net* which is trained with the back-propagation algorithm [31]. The network, illustrated in Fig. 11, includes four full-connected layers of weights and it is split in two parts in the first layer, where different input information are processed separately. The first set of inputs has as many inputs as the feature units' number. The number of input of the second set is equal to the sum of the dimensions of the self-organizing map. Three sets of outputs code, with a sparse coding, the coordinates of the spatial location of the feature and the spotlight dimension required for its examination, respectively. The locating net is trained so as to produce the spatial parameters of a feature when the feature is selected with the first set of inputs, while the position of the winning unit on the self-organizing map which activated the reference unit (stored in the short-term memory) is specified with the second set. If a feature not corresponding to the reference unit is examined, the location of the centroid and the object size – i.e., the parameters needed for activating the reference unit in the subsequent fixation – are found by coding the current winning position and the desired feature. In this way it is always possible to reach a global analysis starting from a detail, and to search then again for other details.

The basic strategy followed by the system for recognition is to examine sequentially all the features of an hypothesized object. When a feature to be analyzed is chosen, its spatial location and the spotlight size required for its

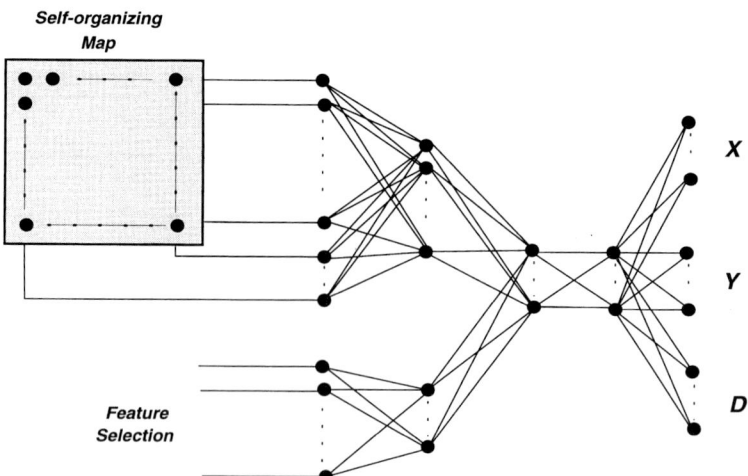

Fig. 11. The locating network is a five-layer full-connected net, which has been trained with the backpropagation algorithm to provide the spatial parameters of the representation

examination are found by converting the numerical values provided by the locating net by means of the parameters stored in the short term memory. Recognition is achieved if the global input to the object unit is larger than a predetermined threshold. If an hypothesis fails to be confirmed by successive attentional fixations, all the feature units in the representation of the rejected object are reset. In this way, the second most probable hypothesis wins the competition and its features are then analyzed. The cycle is repeated until recognition is achieved or all the formulated hypotheses are sequentially examined.

2.4 Attention Control

The sensory cues generated by parallel analysis and the semantic cues produced by the serial analysis activate spatial locations in the saliency map. The saliency map can be seen as a not retinotopic plane including all visual directions. Each gaze direction is represented in the map by the point identified by the spherical coordinates θ (co-latitude) and ϕ (longitude) relative to a head frame centered on the focus of perspective projection – see Fig. 4.

Salient cues are expressed by the processing stages in retinotopic coordinates, and they are transformed later into visual directions on the basis of the focal length – sensor plane-eye coordinate transformation – and of "proprioceptive" data – the relative rotation between the eye and the head coordinate systems – obtained from the position sensors of the actuation subsystem. Specifically, if g_s is a vector that represents the next direction of gaze as expressed in the sensor coordinate frame, its expression g_h in the head reference frame, which has to be provided to the motor subsystem, can be simply evaluated as

$$g_h = {}^e_h T \, {}^s_e T \, g_s, \qquad (3)$$

where the matrices ${}^e_h T$ and ${}^s_e T$ encode the homogeneous transformations between the eye/head and between the sensor/eye frames, respectively – refer again to Fig. 4.

It should be noted that the set of directions of gaze explored by the sensor at a given time is a subset of the map, whose size depends on the field of view. At everytime, the activations provided to the saliency map (salient cues) are gated by the considered task. That is, the task selects the level of priority for a generical cue c by assigning it a weight $w_c \in [0, 1]$. By properly arranging the weight values, it is possible to select a sensory feature with respect to others and/or to inhibit irrelevant cues. In this way, the task currently accomplished by the system changes the way it responds to visual stimuli and, eventually, the way it interacts with the external world.

3 Simulation Results

In this section, experimental results obtained with a simulation of the system behavior are described and discussed. The simulation has been carried out on a

SUN SPARCstation, with a program written in C. Space-variant images have been obtained by resampling high-resolution 256 × 256 images acquired with a b/w raster camera.

Three toy-objects, which are shown in the sequence of Fig. 12, were included into the system memory for recognition: a dog, a train, and a cat. The icons were circles of 156 pixels – approximately the size of the fovea – and they were classified by a topological self-organized map composed of 400 units (20 units along each axis). Each object representation included 5 feature units. The locating network was composed of 55 (40 + 15) input units, 15 units in both the hidden layers and 15 (5 + 5 + 5) units in the output layer. A number of images for each object were used to train the nets of the system: windows located on the representative features were extracted from the images and their positions and dimensions were stored. The topological feature map was trained by means of the icons corresponding to the selected windows and the locating net with their spatial relationships. To achieve a further computational gain, only the considered part – i.e., the attentional icon – of the edge pyramid was produced.

The retina was composed of $M = 64$ annuli and $N = 128$ angular sectors, the radii-ratio was $a = 1.04621$, and p was set to 43.32067. The field of view was approximately 45 deg. Three pyramid levels were built in the cortical plane, using a Gaussian-shaped smoothing filter with a mask size of 3 pixels. At the top pyramid level, which was the only one to be completely processed, a data reduction of approximately two orders of magnitude was achieved with respect to raster images. Two motion features were used as sensory features for the system: the magnitude of the optical flow, and the upper bound on the immediacy of collision,

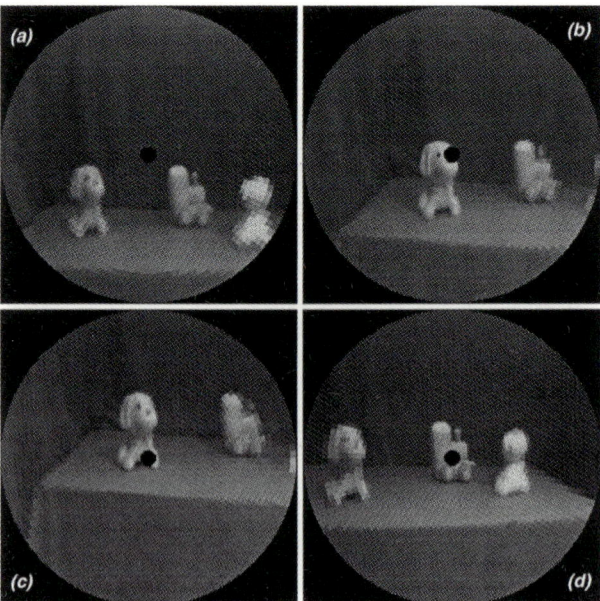

Fig. 12. Some frames taken by the system at work. Black dots indicate the foveal region, that surrounds the fixation point

obtained from the cortical flow and its derivatives using equations (5) and (9), respectively – see Appendix. The cortical flow was computed on a three-frame basis, by means of a motion-boundary preserving algorithm based on a multiwindow least squares technique [5]. The cortical flow was regularized by a vector median filter, having a filter mask size of 3 pixels.

In the following, an experiment illustrating the system behavior is described. The three objects represented into the system were located in the scene, and different motions were assigned to each of them. In a first phase, the dog approaches the camera, the cat goes away, and the train is still. After a while, the dog stops and the train departs moving parallel to the camera. Task weights are assigned so that recognition has the highest priority ($w_r = 1.0$), followed by immediacy detection ($w_i = 0.6$) and speed detection ($w_s = 0.2$).

At the beginning, as shown in Fig. 12a, none of the objects is foveated, so that no semantic cues are produced by the serial analysis stage. The results of the parallel analysis are shown in Fig. 13a,b. As it can be noticed, the magnitude of the optic flow field is greater for the cat than for the dog. Nonetheless, system attention is drawn by the approaching dog, due to its larger value of immediacy of collision. The train is not considered at all in this phase, because it is not in motion.

After the first foveation on the dog (Fig. 12b), a semantic match occurs, so that a recognition sequence is activated. Figure 12c shows the last of the four foveations required for the recognition process.

While the system is involved in the recognition "scanpath," the train starts moving, but the corresponding sensory cue (Fig. 13c,d) does not gain the system

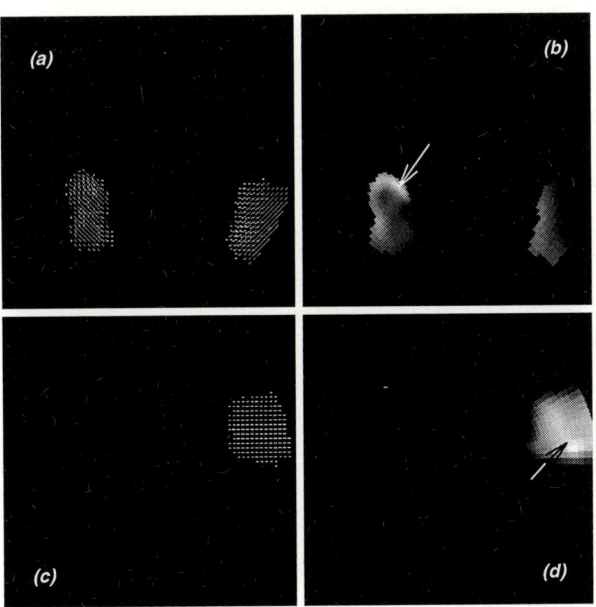

Fig. 13. Optical flow and sensory features. Brighter areas correspond to higher feature values. Features are as they would look if the whole 0th level of the pyramid was processed. Actually, only the cues indicated by the arrows were computed

attention. However, after that object identity is assessed, no more semantic cues are available and optical flow magnitude becomes the most prominent cue. As a result, gaze direction is shifted to the train (Fig. 12d).

Other experiments have shown that recognition performance is good, in that objects are correctly identified in more than 90 percent of the cases, all the errors being due to the failing of the first semantic match during the pyramid scanning.

4 Conclusions

Studies on visual perception have demonstrated that evolution has developed powerful tools – such as selective attention mechanisms and space-variant sensing – for focusing the available computing resources to the process of relevant data. Implementing similar mechanisms in machine vision is extremely important towards the development of effective systems. In fact, in spite of the great improvements of the recent years, the processing power of current computers is still by far lower than that of the brain.

The system described in this paper is an example of how biological theories and concepts can be effectively exploited in machine vision applications. The simultaneous use of selective attention mechanisms and retina-like sensing allows a dramatical computational gain, which encourages complex real-time applications. Besides, the integration of sensory and semantic characteristics of the visual data and the dependency on the task at hand are indicated as fundamental issues for the development of an "intelligent" behavior.

Basically, two directions of future research can be outlined. On the one side, other visual features and even other sensory modalities, such as touch and hearing, could be included in the system processing stages so as to produce new cues for the saliency map. On the other, the learning capabilities of the system could be improved. By means of on-line learning, achievable among other techniques also by different neural network paradigms, the system could be able to autonomously select relevant features and to create new object representations.

Acknowledgements. The work described in this paper has been supported by MURST and by the Special Project on Robotics of the National Research Council of Italy. We thank Dr. D.M. De Micheli for providing us the implementation details of the ARTS head.

References

[1] J. Aloimonos, I. Weiss, and A. Bandyopadhyay. *Active vision.* International Journal of Computer Vision 1(4), pp. 333–356, 1988.
[2] Y. Aloimonos. *Purposive and qualitative active vision.* In: "Artificial Intelligence and Computer Vision", Y.A. Feldman and A. Bruckstein eds., Elsevier, 1991.
[3] R. Bajcsy. *Active perception.* Proc. of the IEEE 76(8), pp. 996–1005, 1988.
[4] D.H. Ballard. *Animate vision.* Artificial Intelligence 48, pp. 57–86, 1991.

[5] F. Bartolini, V. Cappellini, C. Colombo, and A. Mecocci. *Multiwindow least squares approach to the estimation of optical flow with discontinuities.* Optical Engineering, 32(6), pp. 1250–1256, 1993.
[6] P.J. Burt and E.H. Adelson. *The Laplacian pyramid as a compact image code.* IEEE Transactions on Communications 31(4), pp. 532–540, 1983.
[7] P.J. Burt. *Smart sensing within a pyramid vision machine.* Proc, of the IEEE 76(8), pp. 1006–1015, 1988.
[8] R. Cipolla and A. Blake. *Surface orientation and time to contact from image divergence and deformation.* Proc. 2nd European Conference on Computer Vision, pp. 187–202, S. Margherita Ligure (Italy) 1992.
[9] J.J. Clark and N.J. Ferrier. *Attentive visual servoing.* In: "Active vision", A. Blake and A. Yuille eds., MIT Press, 1992.
[10] J.L. Crowley. *A representation for visual information.* Tech. Rep. CMU-RI-TR-82-7, Carnegie-Mellon University, 1987.
[11] S.M. Culhane and J.K. Tsotsos. *An attentional prototype for early vision.* Proc. 2nd European conference on Computer Vision, pp. 551–560, S. Margherita Ligure (Italy) 1992.
[12] D.M. De Micheli, M. Bergamasco, and P. Dario. *An anthropomorphic active vision system based on a retina-like sensor.* Proc. 3rd International Symposium on Measurement and Control in Robotics, Torino (Italy) September 1993.
[13] R. Hect-Nielsen. *Applications of the counter-propagation networks.* Neural Networks 2(1), 1988.
[14] H. von Helmholtz. "Psychological optics". J.P.C. Sothall ed., Dover, New York, 1866/1925.
[15] B.K.P. Horn and B.G. Schunck. *Determining optical flow.* Artificial Intelligence 17, pp. 185–203, 1981.
[16] R. Jain, S.L. Bartlett, and N. O'Brien. *Motion stereo using ego-motion complex logarithmic mapping.* IEEE Transactions on Pattern Analysis and Machine Intelligence 9(3), pp. 356–369, 1987.
[17] R.C. Jain and T.O. Binford. *Ignorance, myopia, and naiveté in computer vision systems.* Computer Vision, Graphics and Image Processing: Image Understanding 53(1), pp. 112–117, 1991.
[18] W. James. "The principles of psychology", Harvard University Press, Cambridge, 1890/1983.
[19] W.A. Johnston and V.J. Dark. *Selective attention.* Annual Review of Psychology 37, pp. 43–75, 1986.
[20] K. Kanatani. "Group-theoretical methods in image understanding", Springer, 1990.
[21] C. Koch and S. Ullman. *Shifts in selective visual attention: toward the underlying neural circuitry.* In: "Matters of intelligence". L.M. Vaina ed., D. Reidel Pub. Comp., 1987.
[22] J.J. Koenderink and A.J. van Doorn. *Invariant properties of the motion parallax field due to the movement of rigid bodies relative to an observer.* Optica Acta 22(9), pp. 773–791, 1975.
[23] T. Kohonen. *Self-organized formation of topologically correct feature maps.* Biological Cybernetics 43, pp. 59–69, 1982.
[24] J.L. Mundy and A. Zisserman. *Projective geometry for machine vision.* In: "Geometric invariance in computer vision", J.L. Mundy and A. Zisserman eds., MIT Press, 1992.
[25] K. Nakayama. *The iconic bottleneck and the tenuous link between early visual processing and perception.* In: "Vision: coding and efficiency", C. Blakemore ed., University Press, 1991.
[26] D. Noton and L. Stark. *Eye movements and visual perception.* Scientific American, 224(6), pp. 34–43, 1971.
[27] B. Olshausen. *A neural model of visual attention and invariant pattern recognition.* Tech. Rep. CalTech, CNS Memo 18, September 1992.

[28] M. Posner. *Orienting of attention*. Quarterly Journal of Experimental Psychology 32, pp. 3–25, 1980.
[29] A. Rosenfeld et al. "Multiresolution image processing and analysis", A. Rosenfeld ed., Springer, 1984.
[30] M. Rucci and P. Dario. *Selective attention mechanisms in a vision system based on neural networks*. Proc. International Conference on Intelligent Robots and Systems, Yokohama (Japan) July 1993.
[31] D.E. Rumelhart, G.E. Hinton, and R.J. Williams. *Learning internal representations by error propagation*. In: "Parallel Distributed Processing", MIT Press, 1986.
[32] G. Sandini and V. Tagliasco. *An anthropomorphic retina-like structure for scene analysis*. Computer Graphic and Image Processing 14(3), pp. 365–372, 1980.
[33] G. Sandini and P. Dario. *Active vision based on space-variant sensing*. Proc. 5th International Symposium of Roboticsw Research, pp. 408–417, Tokio 1989.
[34] E.L. Schwartz. *Spatial mapping in the primate sensory projection: analytic structure and relevance to perception*. Biological Cybernetics 25, pp. 181–194, 1977.
[35] M. Tistarelli and G. Sandini. *Estimation of depth from motion using an anthropomorphic visual sensor*. Image and Vision Computing 8(4), pp. 271–278, 1990.
[36] J.K. Tsotsos. *Analyzing vision at the complexity level*. The Behavioral and Brain Sciences 13, pp. 423–469, 1990.
[37] C.F.R. Weiman. *Tracking algorithms using log-polar mapped image coordinates*. Proc. SPIE Intelligent Robots and Computer Vision VIII: Algorithms and Techniques, pp. 843–853, Philadelphia (Pennsylvania) 1989.
[38] A.L. Yarbus. "Eye movements and vision", Plenum Press, 1967.

A Space-Variant Motion Analysis

In this Appendix, the case of motion analysis, and specifically the construction of cortical pyramids for the optical flow and related features, is described.

Although defined as an approximation of the velocity field $(\dot{x}, \dot{y})$ – the projection onto the retinal plane of the tridimensional speed of the objects in the scene relative to the sensor –, the optical flow of points of the retinal periphery can be computed directly from cortical image data using the log-polar transformation (1). Let us define the "cortical flow" as the optical flow-like field $(\dot{\xi}, \dot{\gamma})$ arising due to brightness changes in the cortical plane. This field satisfies the equation [15]:

$$\frac{\partial E}{\partial \xi}\dot{\xi} + \frac{\partial E}{\partial \gamma}\dot{\gamma} + \frac{\partial E}{\partial t} = 0, \qquad (4)$$

where $E(\xi, \gamma, t)$ is the cortical image brightness. Then, assuming that $(\dot{\xi}, \dot{\gamma})$ is the cortical flow at a generic pyramid level L (the subscript $_L$ from the retinal parameters is omitted for the sake of simplicity), the corresponding optical flow is evaluated as

$$\begin{cases} \dot{x} = a^{\xi+p}\left[(\ln a\, \dot{\xi})\cos(\gamma/q) - \left(\frac{1}{q}\dot{\gamma}\right)\sin(\gamma/q)\right] \\ \dot{y} = a^{\xi+p}\left[(\ln a\, \dot{\xi})\sin(\gamma/q) + \left(\frac{1}{q}\dot{\gamma}\right)\cos(\gamma/q)\right]. \end{cases} \qquad (5)$$

In the same way – that is, by exploiting the retino-cortical transformation –, other interesting motion parameters can be computed from the cortical flow pyramid. The *differential invariants* of the optical flow, which are nothing but proper combinations of the first spatial derivatives of the flow [20]:

$$\begin{cases} \text{divergence} = \dfrac{\partial \dot{x}}{\partial x} + \dfrac{\partial \dot{y}}{\partial y} \\ \text{curl} = -\dfrac{\partial \dot{x}}{\partial y} + \dfrac{\partial \dot{y}}{\partial x} \\ \text{shear} = \left[\left(\dfrac{\partial \dot{x}}{\partial x} - \dfrac{\partial \dot{y}}{\partial y} \right)^2 + \left(\dfrac{\partial \dot{x}}{\partial y} + \dfrac{\partial \dot{y}}{\partial x} \right)^2 \right]^{1/2} \end{cases}, \quad (6)$$

are related to some simple geometrical and kinematic characteristics of the imaged scene [22]. Using again equation (1), it can be easily shown that the optical flow invariants can be computed from the cortical flow and its spatial derivatives as:

$$\begin{cases} \text{divergence} = 2 \ln a \, \dot{\xi} + \dfrac{\partial \dot{\xi}}{\partial \xi} + \dfrac{\partial \dot{\gamma}}{\partial \gamma} \\ \text{curl} = \dfrac{2}{q} \dot{\gamma} - q \ln a \dfrac{\partial \dot{\xi}}{\partial \gamma} + \dfrac{1}{q \ln a} \dfrac{\partial \dot{\gamma}}{\partial \xi} \\ \text{shear} = \left[\left(\dfrac{\partial \dot{\xi}}{\partial \xi} - \dfrac{\partial \dot{\gamma}}{\partial \gamma} \right)^2 + \left(q \ln a \dfrac{\partial \dot{\xi}}{\partial \gamma} + \dfrac{1}{q \ln a} \dfrac{\partial \dot{\gamma}}{\partial \xi} \right)^2 \right]^{1/2} \end{cases}. \quad (7)$$

Besides, simple linear combinations of the optical flow invariants can be directly related to the *immediacy of collision* (the reciprocal of the *time to collision*, or the time it takes before the object and sensor collide) and the *cyclotorsion* – the rotational component of the sensor speed along the optical axis. If the field of view is sufficiently small, these two quantities can be bounded by [8]:

$$\text{immediacy} \approx \dfrac{\text{divergence} \pm \text{shear}}{2} \quad (8)$$

$$\text{cyclotorsion} \approx \dfrac{\text{curl} \pm \text{shear}}{2}. \quad (9)$$

Modeling Color Images for Machine Vision

G. Healey

Abstract. This chapter reviews and evaluates color image models that have been used in machine vision. Color image formation is described using models for image sensors, surfaces, and reflection processes. These models have been used to predict properties of color pixel distributions that will result for various classes of scenes. Several algorithms are described that use these distribution models for applications such as image segmentation, illuminant color estimation, and illumination invariant recognition. For textured images that are common in outdoor applications, benefits can be derived from using spatial interaction models for color images. A detailed summary is presented of recent work that introduces color texture models and applies these models to image segmentation and geometry invariant surface identification.

1 Introduction

The modeling of color images in Machine Vision has a relatively short history. Although color images contain considerably more information than intensity images, researchers have only recently devoted significant attention to understanding the structure of this information. Much of the progress in modeling color images has resulted from the study of physical models for image formation that describe color pixel measurements in terms of properties of light sources, surfaces, and image sensors. These physical models have led to improved color image models which have been exploited by Machine Vision algorithms.

Color provides useful information for several different visual processes. The capability of segmentation algorithms, for example, has been significantly advanced by using color image models. The purpose of these algorithms is to partition an image into physically meaningful regions. Several phenomena that are common in images of three dimensional scenes have been modeled and accounted for by segmentation algorithms. These phenomena include highlights, shading, interreflection, and texture. In each case, the utilization of color information has been an important element in the analysis.

Color image models are also useful during object recognition. Since the measured color of a surface depends on contextual factors such as illuminant color, the recovery of invariant surface descriptors is an important step in object recognition. Several researchers have used color reflection models to derive algorithms for locating highlights to estimate illuminant color. From these estimates, illumination invariant color surface descriptions can be computed. Another body of work uses physically motivated linear model approximations for spectral reflectance functions and illumination spectral power distributions to compute illumination invariant color properties of surfaces. Algorithms have also been developed that exploit color texture models for geometry invariant surface recognition.

Much of the research that uses color reflection models in Machine Vision can be found in an edited collection of papers published in 1992 [14]. In this chapter, I emphasize the role of color image modeling in this research. Section 2 summarizes the underlying physics and Sect. 3 traces the corresponding evolution of color image models and their applications. Although the color pixel distribution models presented in Sect. 3 have many uses, these models do not capture the spatial structure that is present in textured color images. In Sect. 4, I describe recently developed color texture models and their application to image segmentation and surface recognition.

2 Color Image Formation

2.1 Image Sensing

A digital color image is represented by three discrete functions $R(i, j)$, $G(i, j)$, and $B(i, j)$ which describe the amount of light in red, green, and blue color bands striking each location on a sensor plane. For an ideal camera, the functions $R(i,j)$, $G(i, j)$, and $B(i, j)$ can be modeled using

$$R(i, j) = \int_\lambda \int_y \int_x E(x, y, \lambda) f_R(\lambda) dx dy d\lambda \tag{1}$$

$$G(i, j) = \int_\lambda \int_y \int_x E(x, y, \lambda) f_G(\lambda) dx dy d\lambda \tag{2}$$

$$B(i, j) = \int_\lambda \int_y \int_x E(x, y, \lambda) f_B(\lambda) dx dy d\lambda \tag{3}$$

where λ denotes wavelength, $E(x, y, \lambda)$ is the incoming spectral irradiance, $f_R(\lambda)$, $f_G(\lambda)$, and $f_B(\lambda)$, are the sensitivities of the red, green, and blue sensing elements, and the integrals are evaluated over the area on the sensor plane corresponding to image coordinate (i, j). The functions $f_R(\lambda)$, $f_G(\lambda)$, and $f_B(\lambda)$, are typically the combination of the quantum efficiency of the imaging device, the spectral transmission of a color filter, and the spectral transmission of the optics. More detailed camera models that account for effects such as chromatic aberration, noise, and response nonlinearity are useful in various contexts [13] [29]. The discrete functions $R(i, j)$, $G(i, j)$, and $B(i, j)$ are often referred to as the red, green, and blue color planes.

2.2 Color Reflection Models

For a surface patch in the field of view of the camera, the sensor spectral irradiance $E(x, y, \lambda)$ is proportional to the scene spectral radiance L which describes the light that the surface reflects in the direction of the sensor [17]. Scene spectral radiance can be computed using a color reflection model which quantifies the spectral and geometric attributes of the light reflected from a surface as a function of properties of the incident light. For many years, Machine Vision researchers showed little interest in considering reflection models during algorithm development. The recent study of reflection models, however, has provided important insight into the structure of pixel distributions in color images.

Since the mid-1980s, machine vision researchers have studied the spectral and geometric properties of light reflected and scattered from objects. The interaction of light with material has been classified into two distinct processes. Interface reflection describes the light that is reflected at the surface of an object. Body scattering refers to light that is not reflected at the surface but which penetrates into the body of the material and eventually exits back through the surface. In general, both interface reflection and body scattering transform the spectral and geometric properties and the incident light.

In [38], Shafer introduced the dichromatic reflection model that describes reflection and scattering from inhomogeneous dielectric materials. The model characterizes the radiance L of the light leaving an object as the superposition of a radiance L_i due to interface reflection and a radiance L_b due to body scattering. In general, L is a function of the illumination and viewing angles and wavelength. The dichromatic model, however, assumes that both L_i and L_b factor into two terms such that one term depends only on the photometric geometry Θ and the other term depends only on wavelength λ. Note that the vector Θ represents the illumination direction and viewing direction. The dichromatic model may be written

$$L(\lambda, \Theta) = L_i(\lambda, \Theta) + L_b(\lambda, \Theta) \tag{4}$$

$$= m_i(\Theta)c_i(\lambda) + m_b(\Theta)c_b(\lambda) \tag{5}$$

The spectral terms $c_i(\lambda)$ and $c_b(\lambda)$ incorporate the spectral composition of the illumination and spectral properties of the material reflectance so that

$$c_i(\lambda) = P(\lambda)r_i(\lambda) \tag{6}$$

$$c_b(\lambda) = P(\lambda)r_b(\lambda) \tag{7}$$

where $r_i(\lambda)$ and $r_b(\lambda)$ are proportional to the material's interface and body reflectance functions and $P(\lambda)$ is the spectral power distribution of the illumination.

In 1989, Healey [10] summarized reflection models in the optics literature including the Torrance-Sparrow model [44] for interface reflection and the Reichman model [34] [35] for body scattering. Using these models, he confirmed the accuracy of the dichromatic reflection model for inhomogeneous dielectrics and showed that the reflected radiance from metal surfaces can also be accurately characterized by a model that factors according to

$$L(\lambda, \Theta) = m(\Theta)c(\lambda) \tag{8}$$

for nearly all values of the photometric geometry vector Θ.

The dichromatic reflection model for inhomogeneous dielectrics is often augmented by the assumption that $r_i(\lambda)$ is constant for visible wavelengths. This assumption implies that the reflected spectral radiance from the interface $L_i(\lambda, \Theta)$ is proportional to the spectral power distribution of the illumination $P(\lambda)$ for any Θ. We observe this as highlights on dielectric surfaces appearing to have the same color as the light source. Tominaga and Wandell [42] have shown experimentally that this assumption is accurate for certain kinds of plastics and fruits. H.C. Lee et al. [23] conducted further experiments that confirmed the accuracy of the model for a set of plastics, leaves, painted surfaces, and fruits. They also showed, however, that the constant $r_i(\lambda)$ assumption fails for other inhomogeneous dielectrics including some papers and ceramics.

2.3 Linear Models

Another assumption that is often applied in modeling color images is that the body reflectance $r_b(\lambda)$ can be represented as a linear combination of a small number of basis functions. Thus, the body reflectance $r_b(\lambda)$ is approximated by a representation of the form

$$r_b(\lambda) = \sum_{1 \leq i \leq n} a_i b_i(\lambda) \tag{9}$$

where the $b_i(\lambda)$ are fixed basis functions defining an n-dimensional linear model. Similar linear models are often also used to approximate the spectral power distribution of the illumination $P(\lambda)$. The linear model assumption is an important part of several algorithms for color constancy [7] [16] [25] which endeavor to recover surface descriptors from color images that do not change as the color of the illumination changes. Cohen [3] and Maloney [24] have studied large reflectance data sets to analyze the accuracy of linear approximations. D'Zmura and Lennie [6] use an extended version of (9) that includes interface reflection after making the assumption that $r_i(\lambda)$ is constant.

3 Modeling Color Image Distributions

Each component of a color pixel vector (R, G, B) measured at an image location is typically quantized to eight bits. The set of all possible color vectors defines a three dimensional space called color space or RGB space. The set of color pixel vectors measured over an image region occupies some subset of color space and defines a color distribution. This distribution is sometimes referred to as a color histogram.

3.1 Statistical Models

Early work in processing color images treated measured color pixel vectors as features with statistical properties. These features were often used as input to clustering algorithms for segmenting images into regions with approximately uniform color. Several clustering procedures have been used to segment color images [4] [9] [37] in situations where characteristic colors are *a priori* unknown. These procedures find clusters of pixels in color space and then assign color pixels to one of these clusters. In these techniques, color space distributions are typically modeled using standard probability densities such as multivariate Gaussian. The use of color in these systems often improved segmentation accuracy by providing additional features. The RGB measurements, however, were treated as generic features and physical constraints on color distributions were not utilized.

Region splitting is another technique used for color image segmentation. During region splitting an image is recursively split into smaller and smaller regions until each region is uniform according to some criterion. Ohlander [30] developed a region splitting algorithm that splits regions after finding peaks in histograms of nine features computed from RGB measurements. Ohta [31] worked to reduce the number of features required by Ohlander's algorithm. He analyzed a set of color images using the Karhunen-Loeve transform to derive a small set of effective color features. Ohta determined that the most effective linear combinations of RGB values are given by $I_1 = (R+G+B)/3$, $I_2 = R-B$, and $I_3 = (2G-R-B)/2$ can this equation $I_3 = (2G - R - B)/2$. As with clustering techniques, these algorithms implicitly assume that the color space distribution corresponding to a surface has a single mode and is reasonably localized in color space. The color features used are not derived from physical considerations. Thus, for example, feature I_1 is dependent on surface orientation and can cause a curved surface of uniform color to be split during segmentation. Such undesired splitting is dramatically illustrated in an image of a color cylinder shown in [31].

Color distributions have also been used for recognition. Color signatures are often used for the classification of regions in aerial images [26]. For recognizing objects with complex color distributions, Swain and Ballard [40] developed a technique called color indexing that represents objects in a database using color histograms. Efficient object recognition is performed by matching observed histograms to stored histograms using a procedure called histogram intersection. These methods are useful in many situations, but can fail when scene parameters such as the illumination spectral content are allowed to vary.

3.2 Physical Models

Shafer [38] made the first prediction for color image distributions using a model for reflection. From the dichromatic reflection model, he showed that color pixels in the image of an inhomogeneous dielectric material will lie on a parallelogram in color space defined by directions corresponding to the colors of interface and body reflection. This parallelogram can be determined from color image data and the location of a particular color pixel can be used to determine the contributions of interface and body reflection for that pixel. This allows the computation of intrinsic images that separate the interface reflection (highlight) component and body reflection component at each pixel.

Using the dichromatic reflection model, Klinker et al. [18] and Gershon et al. [8] showed that color pixel distributions for inhomogeneous dielectrics tend to lie in a subset of the dichromatic parallelogram. This subset is described geometrically as a skewed T [18] or dogleg [8] that is spanned by the directions corresponding to interface and body reflection. Using the assumption that $r_i(\lambda)$ is constant for visible wavelengths, Klinker [18] further pointed out that the direction of the highlight cluster in the skewed T can be used to determine the illumination color. In subsequent work, Healey [10] showed that color pixel distributions for metal surfaces tend to lie along linear segments in color space.

Novak and Shafer [28] provided a more comprehensive study of the structure of color histograms for inhomogeneous dielectric materials by identifying structures within the skewed T that relate to scene properties. Using the Torrance-Sparrow model [44] for reflection from rough surfaces, they showed that certain structures within a color histogram can be used to estimate surface roughness. They also showed that certain dimensions of the color histogram can be used to determine scene geometry. By using a more detailed color histogram model, the analysis in [28] can be used to compute improved estimates for illumination color.

3.3 Using Physical Models for Segmentation

The importance of using image models for segmentation has long been recognized [36]. Many segmentation algorithms are based on models for image distributions. These algorithms will often fail on images for which the models do not accurately describe the actual distributions. Thus, there has been interest in using image models during segmentation that take into account various physical effects such as shading, highlights, nonuniform illumination, and surface texture. Segmentation algorithms that use such physics-based models have been applied successfully to color images of complex scenes.

Klinker et al. [19] used knowledge about the color distributions predicted by the dichromatic reflection model to implement a segmentation algorithm that correctly processes highlights and shading effects while using a physical camera model to correct for sensor deficiencies. The algorithm uses physical constraints to interpret color clusters based on eigenvalue magnitudes computed for image regions. Hypotheses are generated from these interpretations and used to guide a region growing process. The algorithm has been used to generate accurate segmentation results for complex arrangements of plastic objects.

Healey [12] used the dichromatic reflection model and the reflection model for metals of (8) to derive a segmentation algorithm that accounts for changes in surface orientation and highlights in color images of metal and dielectric materials. The algorithm is based on the principle [10] that normalized color is a relatively invariant surface property over different surface orientations and source locations. The technique exploits both region properties and local edge properties during processing. This allows the computation of reliable region statistics and the accurate localization of region boundaries. The approach was demonstrated on images of metals, plastics, and painted surfaces.

Bajcsy, Lee, and Leonardis [1] developed a segmentation algorithm using the dichromatic reflection model that is designed to segment accurately highlight and interreflection regions. The algorithm assumes the availability of a white reference card which allows the image to be adjusted to its appearance under white light. The researchers have analyzed color space distributions in the hue, saturation, and intensity (HSI) space corresponding to shading, highlights, shadows, and interreflection. The segmentation algorithm makes use of this analysis and has been applied successfully to a range of images.

3.4 Using Physical Models for Recognition

Several researchers have used the assumption that $r_i(\lambda)$ is constant for visible wavelengths to develop algorithms for estimating the color of the illuminant and the body reflectance $r_b(\lambda)$. The function $r_b(\lambda)$ is useful for recognizing materials since it is independent of both the ambient illumination $P(\lambda)$ and the photometric geometry Θ. H.C. Lee [22] showed that in an image of two or more surfaces under the same illuminant, the linear clusters in chromaticity space corresponding to each surface will intersect at the chromaticity of the light source. Tominaga and Wandell [42] developed a method for estimating $P(\lambda)$ by finding the intersection of planes in color space. They extended this method [43] to develop an algorithm for estimating $r_b(\lambda)$. This work used sampled spectral radiance data obtained using a spectroradiometer. Healey [11] demonstrated a method for approximating $r_b(\lambda)$ from the color image of a single surface with a highlight.

Finite dimensional linear models for spectral reflectance and illumination spectral power distribution have been used to develop algorithms for recovering illumination invariant descriptions of surfaces and objects. Maloney and Wandell [25] assumed linear models for $r_b(\lambda)$ and $P(\lambda)$ to show that if the number of degrees of freedom in the spectral reflectance model (n in (9)) is less than the number of color bands, then $P(\lambda)$ and $r_b(\lambda)$ can be estimated at each image location. Forsyth [7] extended this algorithm to recover a higher dimensional approximation to $P(\lambda)$ using the same number of color bands. Another algorithm developed in [7] recovers illumination invariant surface descriptions by assuming constraints on $P(\lambda)$ while allowing arbitrary surface reflectance functions. Ho, Funt, and Drew [16] used linear models for $r_b(\lambda)$ and $P(\lambda)$ to recover three parameter models for both functions using the sampled reflected radiance $L(\lambda)$. Novak and Shafer [27] assumed linear models and the availability of a color chart with known reflectance properties to derive an algorithm for estimating $P(\lambda)$. By assuming a three parameter linear model for $r_b(\lambda)$, Healey and Slater [15] developed a method for computing invariants of color image distributions that are independent of $P(\lambda)$.

4 Modeling Color Textures

The models presented in Sect. 3 characterize distributions of color pixel values in images. Several of these models relate properties of these distributions to physical aspects of image formation. Many different color images, however, have the same color pixel distributions. Therefore, it is often useful to represent information about a color image that is not captured by these distributions. In particular, the spatial structure or texture present in a color image provides important additional information in many contexts. In this section, I present recently developed color texture models and describe their use for segmentation and recognition in images of complex scenes.

4.1 Color Texture Segmentation

The segmentation of textured color images has received some attention by treating a color image as three separate intensity images and applying standard techniques [5] [45]. A more accurate representation for color texture, however, should also model spatial interaction between the planes of a color image. Panjwani and Healey [33] developed a general model for color textures using Markov random fields [2] that characterizes the spatial interaction within and between the red, green, and blue planes of a color image. This model makes use of a generalized neighbor set that represents the red, green, and blue measurements at a pixel as a linear combination of neighbors in all three color bands plus noise. A total of nine possible neighbor sets are used to define the model with, for example, the set N_{rg} denoting the neighbors in the green band used in the representation of a red pixel component.

A color pixel vector in a region S is represented by $C(i, j) = [R(i, j)\ G(i, j)\ B(i, j)]$ with μ_R, μ_G, and μ_B denoting mean color intensities. Using a Gaussian Markov random field (GMRF) for the color texture, the conditional probability density of $C(i, j)$ is given by

$$P(C(i,j)/S) = \frac{1}{\left(8\pi^3 |\Sigma|\right)^{\frac{1}{2}}} \exp\left\{-\frac{1}{2}[e_r(i,j)\ e_g(i,j)\ e_b(i,j)]\Sigma^{-1}[e_r(i,j)\ e_g(i,j)\ e_b(i,j)]^t\right\} \quad (10)$$

where $[e_r(i,j)\ e_g(i,j)\ e_b(i,j)]$ is a zero mean gaussian noise vector and

$$\Sigma = \begin{bmatrix} v_{rr} & v_{rg} & v_{rb} \\ v_{gr} & v_{gg} & v_{gb} \\ v_{br} & v_{bg} & v_{bb} \end{bmatrix} \quad (11)$$

is the noise correlation matrix with the expected value of $e_p e_q$ denoted by v_{pq}. The RGB measurements are represented as a linear combination of neighbors in all three color planes and noise according to

$$\begin{aligned} e_r(i,j) = (R(i,j) - \mu_R) &- \sum_{(m,n) \in N_{rr}} \alpha_{RR}(m,n)(R(i+m, j+n) - \mu_R) \\ &- \sum_{(m,n) \in N_{rg}} \alpha_{RG}(m,n)(G(i+m, j+n) - \mu_G) \\ &- \sum_{(m,n) \in N_{rb}} \alpha_{RB}(m,n)(B(i+m, j+n) - \mu_B) \end{aligned} \quad (12)$$

$$\begin{aligned} e_g(i,j) = (G(i,j) - \mu_G) &- \sum_{(m,n) \in N_{gr}} \beta_{GR}(m,n)(R(i+m, j+n) - \mu_R) \\ &- \sum_{(i,j) \in N_{gg}} \beta_{GG}(m,n)(G(i+m, j+n) - \mu_G) \\ &- \sum_{(i,j) \in N_{gb}} \beta_{GB}(m,n)(B(i+m, j+n) - \mu_B) \end{aligned} \quad (13)$$

$$\begin{aligned} e_b(i,j) = (B(i,j) - \mu_B) &- \sum_{(i,j) \in N_{br}} \gamma_{BR}(m,n)(R(i+m, j+n) - \mu_R) \\ &- \sum_{(i,j) \in N_{bg}} \gamma_{BG}(m,n)(G(i+m, j+n) - \mu_G) \\ &- \sum_{(i,j) \in N_{bb}} \gamma_{BB}(m,n)(B(i+m, j+n) - \mu_B) \end{aligned} \quad (14)$$

where the α's, β's, and γ's are the parameters of the color GMRF and $N_{rr}, N_{rg}, \ldots, N_{bb}$ define the different neighborhood sets. There are many possible approaches to estimating the α, β, and γ parameters of a GMRF from an image region S. An approach that has been useful for image segmentation is based on maximizing the pseudolikelihood function [32].

The color texture model of (10)–(14) has been incorporated into a color texture segmentation algorithm [33]. The algorithm uses an agglomerative clustering process that endeavors to maximize the pseudolikelihood of the image. After partitioning an image into a set of initial regions, adjacent regions are merged so that each merger causes the smallest possible decrease in the image pseudolikelihood. A similar merging criterion has been used by Silverman and Cooper [39]. At each step in agglomerative clustering, a candidate best merge is selected over all possible merges of adjacent regions. Rules for deciding when to stop agglomerative clustering have been developed [32].

Before applying agglomerative clustering, an image must be partitioned into initial regions of uniform texture. These initial regions must be sufficiently large to estimate the color GMRF parameters. Several steps are used to prepare for agglomerative clustering. First, the image is partitioned into square blocks of the minimum size required to estimate reliable GMRF parameters. Each block is tested for uniformity by comparing the color mean vectors and covariance matrices for its four component subblocks. Nonuniform blocks are recursively split into subblocks until each remaining block is uniform or a minimum size is reached. This region splitting process results in blocks of uniform texture. A conservative merging process is used following region splitting . During this phase, adjacent regions that are similar in color mean and covariance as well as color texture are merged. This process reduces the number of regions that must be processed during agglomerative clustering. Conservative merging provides significant computational advantage since it is applied locally whereas agglomerative clustering selects the best merge over the entire image.

Figure 1-6 illustrate the performance of the segmentation algorithm on a color image of a lake, beach, grass, and dense foliage. Boundaries are drawn in the images to show the segmented regions at different stages in the processing. Figure 1 is the original image and Fig. 2 is the result following region splitting. The regions after conservative merging are shown in Fig. 3. Figure 4 is the intermediate result after 137 merges during agglomerative clustering and Fig. 5 is the intermediate result after 157 merges. Figure 6 is the final segmentation and demonstrates the capability of the algorithm for segmenting textured color imagery. This algorithm has been applied successfully to a range of images of natural scenes [32].

Fig. 1. Image of a beach, water, and foliage. See Color Plate I (inserted after p. 178) for illustration in color

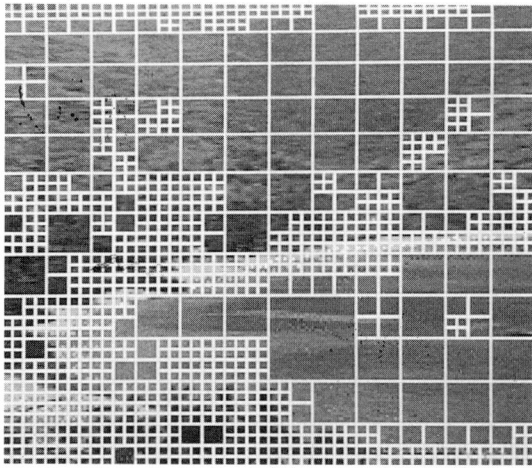

Fig. 2. Result after the region splitting phase. See Color Plate I (inserted after p. 178) for illustration in color

Fig. 3. Result after the conservative merging phase. See Color Plate II (inserted after p. 178) for illustration in color

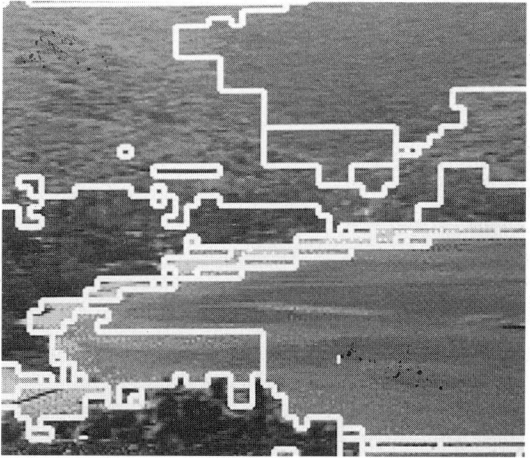

Fig. 4. Result after merge 137 during agglomerative clustering. See Color Plate II (inserted after p. 178) for illustration in color

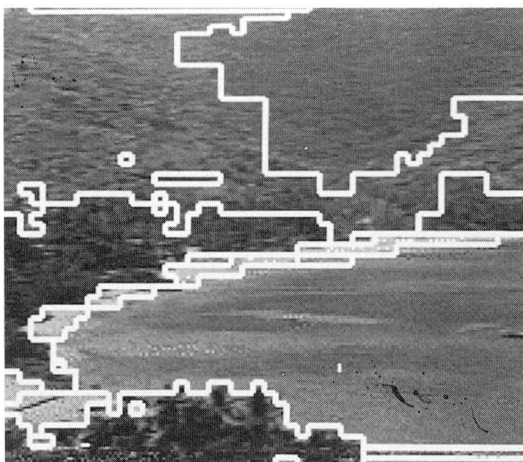

Fig. 5. Result after merge 157 during agglomerative clustering. See Color Plate III (inserted after p. 178) for illustration in color

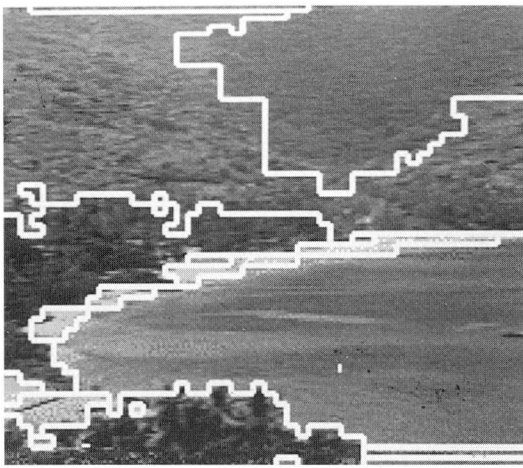

Fig. 6. Final segmentation. See Color Plate III (inserted after p. 178) for illustration in color

4.2 Color Texture Identification

Another important problem is the recognition of textured surfaces in three dimensional scenes. Kondepudy and Healey [20] have developed a correlation model for color textures. This model describes the appearance of a textured color surface in terms of its position and orientation in the scene. A set of geometric invariants has been developed for identifying a surface from estimated color correlation functions. These invariants are useful during 3-D object recognition or image database searching. Following surface identification, a search process is used to determine surface location and orientation.

Color textures are assumed to be wide sense stationary processes. The color correlation model is defined by six functions

$$F_{RR}(n, m) = E\{(R(i, j) - \mu_R)(R(i + n, j + m) - \mu_R)\} \quad (15)$$

$$F_{RG}(n, m) = E\{(R(i, j) - \mu_R)(G(i + n, j + m) - \mu_G)\} \quad (16)$$

$$F_{RB}(n, m) = E\{(R(i, j) - \mu_R)(B(i + n, j + m) - \mu_B)\} \quad (17)$$

$$F_{GG}(n, m) = E\{(G(i, j) - \mu_G)(G(i + n, j + m) - \mu_G)\} \quad (18)$$

$$F_{GB}(n, m) = E\{(G(i, j) - \mu_G)(B(i + n, j + m) - \mu_B)\} \quad (19)$$

$$F_{BB}(n, m) = E\{(B(i, j) - \mu_B)(B(i + n, j + m) - \mu_B)\} \quad (20)$$

where E denotes expected value.

Consider a planar surface in the scene whose six image correlation functions are denoted by $F_{ij}(\bar{n})$ where $\bar{n} = (n, m)$. If the surface is given a new location and orientation, this will lead to a transformed set of correlations functions $F'_{ij}(\bar{n})$. The correlation function transformation can be written

$$F'_{ij}(\bar{n}) = F_{ij}(M\bar{n}) \quad (21)$$

where M is a 2×2 matrix with elements dependent on the geometric transformation of the surface. Recognizing a surface from its estimated color correlation functions $F'_{ij}(\bar{n})$ requires determining if a matrix M exists that transforms a known set of correlation functions $F_{ij}(\bar{n})$ into $F'_{ij}(\bar{n})$. Since the single matrix M represents the transformation for each of the six correlation functions in (21), recognition using color texture has much improved certainty over recognition in intensity images using only a single autocorrelation function. A minimization process can be used with (21) to determine the parameters of the geometric transformation corresponding to identified surfaces.

Certain quantities that are invariant to surface position and orientation can be computed from the first and second moments of a color distribution. These invariants can be used to eliminate efficiently many potential matches. One set of invariant quantities is the ratio of the color means μ_R, μ_G, μ_B. In addition, ratios of the six elements of the covariance matrix defining the color distribution are also invariant. These elements are the zero lag points on the color correlation functions given by $F_{RR}(0, 0)$, $F_{RG}(0, 0)$, $F_{RB}(0, 0)$, $F_{GG}(0, 0)$, $F_{GB}(0, 0)$, and $F_{BB}(0, 0)$.

Geometric invariants have also been derived that depend on the structure of the color correlation functions. From (21), three dimensional transformations of a surface in the scene result in an affine transformation of the axes for the color correlation functions. Using this relationship, moment invariants can be computed that characterize the color correlation functions independent of the transformation matrix M. Efficient algebraic methods for computing moment invariants have been derived by Taubin and Cooper [41].

Kondepudy and Healey [21] have applied moment invariants to the task of color texture identification. A small vector of moment invariants is computed for each color correlation function and the set of these vectors is used as an invariant for recognition. The moment invariants are typically eigenvalues of matrices of moments of the correlation functions. These invariants have been used for reliable surface identification in the presence of geometric transformations in the three dimensional scene.

The invariants have been used for recognition in a database of images. Figures 7 and 9 are rotated images of a sweater and Figs. 8 and 10 are two of the corresponding correlation functions. Figures 11 and 13 are two views of the Grand Canyon and Figs. 12 and 14 are two of the corresponding correlation functions. These images are examples of color textures that have been interpreted successfully using moment invariants for recognition and conjugate gradient search to recover geometric transformations. Additional examples are given in [21].

Fig. 7. Sweater. See Color Plate IV (inserted after p. 178) for illustration in color

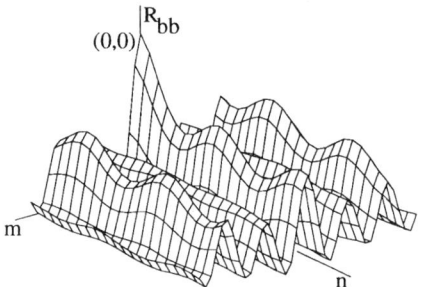

Fig. 8. Correlation function of Fig. 7

Fig. 9. Rotated sweater. See Color Plate IV (inserted after p. 178) for illustration in color

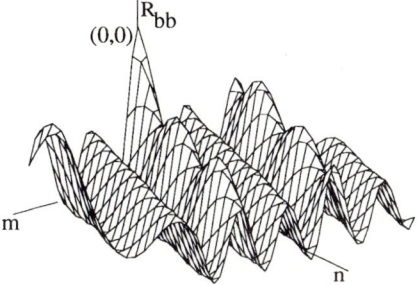

Fig. 10. Correlation function of Fig. 9

Fig. 11. Grand Canyon. See Color Plate V (inserted after p. 178) for illustration in color

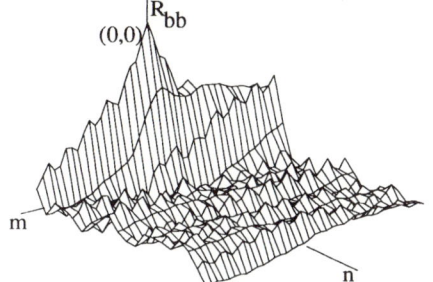

Fig. 12. Correlation function of Fig. 11

Fig. 13. Different view of Grand Canyon. See Color Plate V (inserted after p. 178) for illustration in color

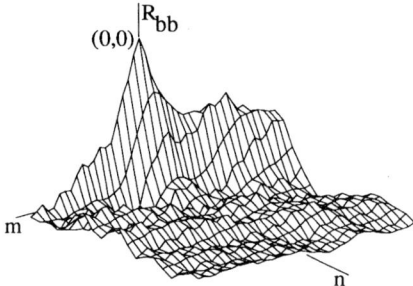

Fig. 14. Correlation function of Fig. 13

5 Summary

Recent activity in Physics-based vision has led to the realization that color images contain significant information about a scene that is not present in intensity images. Researchers in this area have developed increasingly accurate models for color pixel distributions that account for surface properties such as material and roughness as well as phenomena such as highlights and interreflection. Illumination and sensor models have also contributed to improved color image models. In addition, spatial interaction models that describe textured color images have been developed that can be applied to images of outdoor scenes.

Image segmentation is an important early step in the description of images and in the recognition of objects. As shown in Sect. 3, improvements in physics-based color pixel distribution models have been accompanied by corresponding advances in the capability of segmentation algorithms. Recently developed color texture models described in Sect. 4 have led to color segmentation algorithms that extend the class of images that can be segmented accurately. An important challenge for future research will be to develop segmentation algorithms that use integrated physics-based texture models.

Improved color image models have also led to progress in scene description algorithms. Color highlight analysis using the reflection models in Sect. 2 has led to algorithms for estimating illuminant chromaticity and computing illumination invariant color surface descriptions. Linear models for spectral reflectance and illumination spectral power distribution have been the foundation of several approaches to color constancy described in Sect. 3. A color correlation texture model described in Sect. 4 has been used to compute geometry invariant descriptions of textured color surfaces.

Acknowledgement. I thank Raghava Kondepudy and Dileep Panjwani for their contributions to the section on color texture modeling. This work has been supported in part by the Office of Naval Research under grant N00014-93-1-0540.

References

[1] R. Bajcsy, S.W. Lee, and A. Leonardis. Color image segmentation with detection of highlights and local illumination induced by inter-reflections. In *Proceedings of the International Conference on Pattern Recognition*, pp. 785–790, Atlantic City, 1990.

[2] R. Chellappa and A.K. Jain, editors. *Markov Random Fields, theory and applications.* Academic Press, San Diego, 1993.

[3] J. Cohen. Dependency of the spectral reflectance curves of the munsell color chips. *Psychonomic Sci.*, 1:369, 1964.

[4] G.B. Coleman and H.C. Andrews. Image segmentation by clustering. *Proceedings of the IEEE*, 67(5):773–785, May 1979.

[5] M. Daily. Color image segmentation using markov random fields. *IEEE Conference on Computer Vision and Pattern Recognition*, pp. 304–312, 1989.

[6] M. D'Zmura and P. Lennie. Mechanisms of color constancy. *J. Opt. Soc. Am. A*, 3(10):1662–1672, 1986.

[7] D. Forsyth. A novel algorithm for color constancy. *International Journal of Computer Vision*, 5(1):5–36, 1990.

[8] R. Gershon, A. Jepson, and J. Tsotsos. Highlight identification using chromatic information. In *Proceedings of the First International Conference on Computer Vision*, pp. 161–170, London, June 1987.

[9] R. Haralick and G. Kelly. Pattern recognition with measurement space and spatial clustering for multiple images. *Proceedings IEEE*, 57:654–665, April 1969.

[10] G. Healey. Using color for geometry insensitive segmentation. *J. Opt. Soc. Am. A*, 6:920–937, June 1989.

[11] G. Healey. Estimating spectral reflectance using highlights. *Image and Vision Computing*, 9(5):333–337, October 1991.

[12] G. Healey. Segmenting images using normalized color. *IEEE Transactions on Systems, Man, and Cybernetics*, 22(1):64–73, Jan/Feb 1992.

[13] G. Healey and R. Kondepudy. Radiometric CCD camera calibration and noise estimation. *IEEE Transactions on Pattern Analysis and Machine Intelligence*, 1994. Vol. 16, No. 3, March, 267–276.

[14] G. Healey, S. Shafer, and L. Wolff, editors. *Physics-Based Vision: Principles and Practice, COLOR.* Jones and Bartlett, Boston, 1992.

[15] G. Healey and D. Slater. Global color constancy: recognition of objects by use of illumination – invariant properties of color distributions. *J. Opt. Soc. Am. A*, 11(11):3003–3010, November 1994.

[16] J. Ho, B.V. Funt, and M.S. Drew. Separating a color signal into illumination and surface reflectance components: Theory and applications. *IEEE Transactions on Pattern Analysis and Machine Intelligence*, 12(10):966–997, October 1990.

[17] B.K.P. Horn and R. Sjoberg. Calculating the reflectance map. *Applied Optics*, 18:1770–1779, 1979.

[18] G.J. Klinker, S.A. Shafer, and T. Kanade. The measurement of highlights in color images. *International Journal of Computer Vision*, 2:7–32, 1988.

[19] G.J. Klinker, S.A. Shafer, and T. Kanade. A physical approach to color image understanding. *International Journal of Computer Vision*, 4:7–38, 1990.

[20] R. Kondepudy and G. Healey. Modeling and identifying 3-D color textures. In *Proceedings of IEEE Conference on Computer Vision and Pattern Recognition*, pp. 577–582, New York City, 1993.

[21] R. Kondepudy and G. Healey. Use of invariants for recognition of three-dimensional color textures. *J. Opt. Soc. Am. A*, 11(11):3037–3049, November 1994.

[22] H.C. Lee. Method for computing the scene-illuminant chromaticity from specular highlights. *J. Opt. Soc. Am. A*, 3(10):1694–1699, October 1986.

[23] H.C. Lee, E. Breneman, and C. Schulte. Modeling light reflection for color computer vision. *IEEE Trans. on Pattern Analysis and Machine Intelligence*, 12(4):402–409, April 1990.
[24] L. Maloney. Evaluation of linear models of surface spectral reflectance with small numbers of parameters. *J. Opt. Soc. Am. A*, 3(10):1673–1683, October 1986.
[25] L. Maloney and B. Wandell. Color constancy: A method for recovering surface spectral reflectance. *J. Opt. Soc. Am. A*, 3:1673–1683, October 1986.
[26] M. Nagao, T. Matsuyama, and Y. Ikeda. Region extraction and shape analysis in aerial photographs. *Computer Graphics and Image Processing*, 10:195–223, 1979.
[27] C. Novak and S. Shafer. Supervised color constancy for machine vision. In *SPIE Proceedings Vol. 1453 on Human Vision, Visual Processing, and Digital Display II*, pp. 353–368, 1991.
[28] C. Novak and S. Shafer. Method for estimating scene parameters from color histograms. *J. Opt. Soc. Am. A*, 11(11):3020–3036, November 1994.
[29] C. Novak, S. Shafer, and R. Willson. Obtaining accurate color images for machine vision research. In *SPIE Proceedings Vol. 1250 on Perceiving, Measuring, and Using Color*, pp. 54–68, Santa Clara, 1990.
[30] R. Ohlander, K. Price, and D.R. Reddy. Picture segmentation using a recursive region splitting method. *Computer Graphics and Image Processing*, 8:313–333, 1978.
[31] Y. Ohta, T. Kanade, and T. Sakai. Color information for region segmentation. *Computer Graphics and Image Processing*, 13:222–241, 1980.
[32] D. Panjwani and G. Healey. Segmentation of Textured Color Images. Technical report, University of California, Irvine, 1993.
[33] D. Panjwani and G. Healey. Results using random field models for the segmentation of color images of natural scenes. In *Proceedings of Fifth International Conference on Computer Vision*, 714–719, Cambridge, 1995.
[34] J. Reichman. Determination of absorption and scattering coefficients for nonhomogeneous media. 1: Theory. *Applied Optics*, 12(8):1811–1815, August 1973.
[35] J. Reichman. Determination of absorption and scattering coefficients for nonhomogeneous media. 2: Experiment. *Applied Optics*, 12(8):1816–1823, August 1973.
[36] A. Rosenfeld and L. Davis. Image segmentation and image models. *Proceedings of the IEEE*, 67(5):253–261, May 1979.
[37] A. Sarabi and J. Aggarwal. Segmentation of chromatic images. *Pattern Recognition*, 13(6):417–427, 1981.
[38] S. Shafer. Using color to separate reflection components. *COLOR Research and Application*, 10(4):210–218, Winter 1985.
[39] J. Silverman and D. Cooper. Bayesian clustering for unsupervised estimation of surface and texture models. *IEEE Trans. on Pattern Analysis and Machine Intelligence*, 10(4):482–495, July 1988.
[40] M. Swain and D. Ballard. Color indexing. *Int. J. Comp. Vision*, 7:11–32, 1991.
[41] G. Taubin and D. Cooper. Object recognition based on moment (or algebraic) invariants. In J. Mundy and A. Zisserman, editors, *Geometric Invariance in Computer Vision*, pp. 375–397. MIT Press, Cambridge, Mass, 1992.
[42] S. Tominaga and B. Wandell. Standard surface-reflectance model and illuminant estimation. *J. Opt. Soc. Am. A*, 6(4):576–584, April 1989.
[43] S. Tominaga and B. Wandell. Component estimation of surface spectral reflectance. *J. Opt. Soc. Am. A*, 7(2):312–317, 1990.
[44] K. Torrance and E. Sparrow. Theory for off-specular reflection from roughened surfaces. *J. Opt. Soc. Am.*, 57:1105–1114, 1967.
[45] W. Wright. A markov random field approach to data fusion and color segmentation. *Image and Vision Computing*, 7:144–150, 1989.

A Fast Algorithm for MDL-Based Multi-Band Image Segmentation

T. Kanungo, B. Dom, W. Niblack, and D. Steele

Abstract. We consider the problem of image segmentation and describe an algorithm that is based on the Minimum Description Length (MDL) principle, is fast, is applicable to multi-band images, and guarantees closed regions. We construct an objective function that, when minimized, yields a partitioning of the image into regions where the pixel values in each band of each region are described by a polynomial surface plus noise. The polynomial orders and their coefficients are determined by the algorithm. The minimization is difficult because (1) it involves a search over a very large space and (2) there is extensive computation required at each stage of the search. To address the first of these problems we use a region-merging minimization algorithm. To address the second we use an incremental polynomial regression that uses computations from the previous stage to compute results in the current stage, resulting in a significant speed up over the non-incremental technique. The segmentation result obtained is suboptimal in general but of high quality. Results on real images are shown.

1 Introduction

1.1 The General Image Segmentation Problem

This paper[1] describes a solution to the problem of unsupervised multiband image segmentation. This is an extension of a previous algorithm[SDNS92]. More precisely, the problem we address is the following. We are given an image in which the ith pixel has associated with it two vectors: $\mathbf{y}_i \in \Re^d$ and $\mathbf{x}_i \in \mathbf{Z}^q$. The components of $\mathbf{x}_i$ are the pixel coordinates in a discrete, q-dimensional space. The components of $\mathbf{y}_i$ represent the measured intensity levels (greylevels) in d different "bands". These may be spectral bands (e.g., "red", "green" and "blue"), different imaging modalities (e.g., an optical image and a range image), "features" (using pattern recognition parlance) computed from the greylevels of the pixels in some neighborhood of pixel i[2], and so on. We assume that the image represents a real scene consisting of objects, regions, surfaces, etc. Our task is to divide this image into a number of non-overlapping regions whose union is the entire image. The

---

[1] This is an expanded version of a conference paper to be presented in June 1994[KDNS94].
[2] Some examples are the local mean, median, maximum, gradient magnitude/direction, Laplacian. More complicated measures are, of course, also possible.

goal is for these regions to correspond to actual regions, objects, surfaces, etc., in the real scene. We want the regions produced by the algorithm to be homogeneous in some sense. There may be a precise measure of homogeneity corresponding to a particular application or we may want the grouping into regions to be similar to one that would be produced by a human given the same task. We consider this to be an important problem that is still open in the sense that a truly general solution has not been found. Our approach here will be to propose a precisely defined problem whose solution is, in many cases of interest, consistent with this more general but somewhat imprecise definition. In doing so, we will make certain assumptions about the images being segmented. In practice these frequently may not hold of course, but, taking a pragmatic view, we will judge the algorithm by how well it does in segmenting images of real scenes.

The solution to the segmentation problem that we present uses the Minimum Description Length Principle (MDL), a natural and powerful tool for regularizing underconstrained optimization problems, to obtain a complexity-based objective function. The originality of our approach is in its combination of generality (multi-band, high-order polynomial surfaces), speed, and this fixed (no adjustable thresholds) MDL-based objective function.

1.2 Related Work

Before beginning a detailed description of our approach, we will briefly survey related work. We will review here only closely related work. For a more complete survey of image segmentation techniques see [HS85, HS92]. The MDL criterion was first used for the problem of image segmentation by Leclerc[Lec89a] where a graylevel image was partitioned into regions, with a two-dimensional polynomial model defined on each region. A continuation minimization procedure[BZ87] led to an algorithm for finding the regions and polynomials, yielding very promising results. This work is the most closely related to ours. There are, however, important differences between his approach and ours: (1) we use a region-merging-based optimization procedure whereas Leclerc uses a continuation scheme. Although the continuation approach is less likely to result in a suboptimal (local minimum) solution than ours, it is much slower and if not allowed to run to convergence, may leave boundary fragments that aren't closed. Our approach never does this; (2) ours treats multiple band images; (3) we explicitly count the cost of the encoding parameters in our MDL formulation; (4) ours is implemented by a fast, incremental computation; (5) Leclerc's algorithm, through its application of the continuation approach has a "relaxation" flavor where pixels determine their new (next iteration) parameter values based on the values of those parameters and the greyvalues of neighboring pixels (and their own) for the current iteration. Our approach is region based, however, always maintaining and merging regions based on their statistics and boundaries. In more recent work[Lec90]

Leclerc applied the same approach to region grouping. Our approach lends itself naturally to that problem as well; see [SDNS92].

Other authors have also used MDL for image segmentation. Keeler[Kee90] describes a method in which he segments an image by encoding the topology of the segments (for which he has an efficient encoding), their specific boundaries, and the pixel values in each segment as a noise-corrupted constant grey level. The segmentation is the one for which the encoding length of the topology, boundaries, means, and deviations from means is minimum. Fua and Hanson[FH88] use MDL for a model-based image segmentation. They use geometric constraints on object boundaries (e.g., they are straight lines), allow certain outlying pixels to be excluded to account for shadows, etc., and model only the "objects" in a scene, not the background. Pentland, Darrel and Sclaroff have applied MDL in image and motion segmentation[Pen89, DSP90, DP91]. They use part-based models combined with an optimization algorithm that uses a modified Hopfield-Tank network and a continuation scheme.

MDL has been used to achieve segmentation by simple feature-space clustering. See for example the work of Wallace and Kanade[WK90]. Zhang and Modestino[ZM90] use the AIC (Akaike's information criterion [Aka74]), an information-theoretic criterion that is an alternative to MDL, for image segmentation, also by simple feature-space clustering.

Keren et al. [KMWP90] apply MDL to the problem of 1D waveform segmentation and experiment with extensions of the technique to images by operating on 1D projections of those images.

Besl and Jain [BJ88] also addressed image segmentation using polynomial surface fitting, but the criterion function uses a user-specified threshold for acceptable noise variance and does not account for the model complexity as the MDL principle does. Another approach that uses a similar image model (polynomial surfaces plus Gaussian noise) is applied to 2D images in [LCJ91] and 3D surfaces in [LJ91]. This work is also not based on MDL however, and uses a different optimization algorithm.

1.3 The Problem We Solve

Similar to many of these approaches, to solve this problem we will use the common general approach of formulating an *objective function*, whose global minimum (we assume) corresponds to the best segmentation of the image, then devising an *optimization procedure* that attempts to find this minimum. In formulating this objective function we will assume that the images to be analyzed come from a certain stochastic process, characterized by a family of stochastic models (probability distributions, $p(\mathbf{y}_i)$). The model we assume for this process consists of an ideal partitioning (the segmentation we seek) of the image into regions, $\{\omega_j\}$ (denote this segmentation by $\Omega = \{\omega_j\}$) and a separate probability density $p(Y_j|\beta_j)$ for each region, where Y_j represents the collection of y_i's within region j and β_j is a vector of parameters characterizing the distribution. For example, β_j may consist of the mean vector and covariance matrix of a Gaussian distribution or the parameters of a Markov random field. We will use $\beta \triangleq \{\beta_j\}$ to denote the collection of all the parameters for all the regions in Ω. More specifically, in the work described here we will assume that the pixel values of the regions of the image can be described by polynomial (in spatial coordinates) greyscale surfaces (one per band) to which "white" (spatially uncorrelated) "noise" has been added. We further assume that this noise is Gaussian distributed with (in general) a non-diagonal covariance matrix, i.e., there can be correlation among the bands[3]. For this model we may write:

$$p(Y_j | \beta_j) = \prod_{i \in \omega_j} p(y_i | \beta_j), \tag{1.1}$$

where

$$p(y_i | \beta_j) = \frac{1}{(2\pi)^{d/2} |\Sigma_j|^{1/2}} \exp\left\{-\frac{1}{2} [y_i - \mu_j(\mathbf{x}_i)]^t \Sigma_j^{-1} [y_i - \mu_j(\mathbf{x}_i)]\right\} \tag{1.2}$$

$\mu_j(\mathbf{x})$, the spatially dependent mean of this distribution, is a d-dimensional vector-valued function, whose components are the values of the underlying polynomial surfaces mentioned above; and Σ_j is the covariance matrix for the region ω_j. Note that for this model β consists of the polynomial coefficients of the greyscale surfaces and the components of the covariance matrices. Notice also that in this description, the region boundaries are composed of the "cracks" between the pixels. In many images, for example those where the optical resolution of the imaging system (lenses, etc.), expressed in units of length, is large than the pixel size, this may seem like an unjustified assumption. Our use of polynomial models allows the existence of "edge" regions in such cases, however.

We have just specified a parametric model for the image. This model has a large number of degrees of freedom that can be adjusted to "fit" (in the sense of statistical estimation) the model to the image. The adjustable parameters consist of the segmentation, Ω, and the collection of parameters, β, for the probability densities associated with all the regions comprising Ω. Thus, viewing this abstractly, a by-product of the process of this model-fitting exercise is a segmentation of the image. That "by-product" is, of course, the end result we seek. The common way to perform such fitting is to specify a goodness-of-fit measure (the most common being mean-square error) which is then minimized by adjusting the various parameters. The values of the so-obtained parameters constitute the best-fit model. This procedure, when expressed in precise statistical terms, is known *as maximum likelihood* (ML) estimation. Specifically ML estimation maximizes the probability,

---

[3] This inter-band correlation will be especially strong in cases where, for example the "noise" actually corresponds to material texture in the scene.

$p(Y|M)$[4], where Y symbolizes the entire collection of **y** values for the image and M is a vector variable whose value completely specifies the model.

A problem with performing ML estimation in a case such as this is that there is no bound on the complexity of the model, M, and the more complex it is made, the better the fit obtained until the ridiculous limit of every pixel being a separate region is reached. We say that such problems are "ill-posed" or "under-constrained". To correct such problems some way of "regularizing" them must be found. The approach we have chosen to address this problem is to apply the Minimum Description Length Principle (MDL)[Ris78, Ris89]. In this approach the objective function to be minimized is the description length of the data in a suitable "language." We choose MDL for two reasons: (1)It has a strong fundamental grounding, being based on information-theoretic arguments that can be viewed as a formalization of the physicist's *Ockham's razor*: the simplest model explaining the observations is the best[5]; and (2) It results in an objective function with no arbitrary thresholds. To formalize this, the model is used to *encode* (in the sense of data compression) the data in such a way that it can be decoded by a decoder that "knows" only about the model class (the image size, the number of bands and the fact that polynomial Gaussian models will be used)[6]. The model that gives the shortest description length in bits is then chosen as optimum.

There are different ways to reduce this general methodology to an algorithm that can be applied to a given problem (see [Ris89]). The one we use is conceptually straightforward and typically the easiest computationally. It is based on a two-part encoding, where one part consists of an encoding of the model and the other consists of an encoding of the data using the model. Thus the codelength we seek to minimize is:

$$L(Y, M) = L(M) + L(Y|M), \qquad (1.3)$$

where $L(...)$ denotes codelength. This codelength *is* our objective function. In the following section we will derive detailed expressions for the terms in this equation. If the set of possible models were discrete (countable) and we had a prior probability, $P(M)$, on those models we could let[7] $L(M) = -\log P(M)$ and let $L(Y|M) = -\log P(Y|M)$[8]. In this case minimizing equation (1.3) is equivalent to performing Bayesian *maximum a posteriori* (MAP) estimation. If the set of possible models is not countable (the more usual case, which is also the case in this work), however,

---

[4] Actually, doing ML estimation, the goodness-of-fit measure *is* the value of $p(Y|M)$. In certain cases (e.g., Gaussian models) this is equivalent to minimizing the mean-square error.
[5] Attributed to William of Ockham (1285–1349).
[6] No actual compression or encoding of the image data is performed, but we must outline the process by which it would be encoded in order to derive the expression for the codelength that we require for our objective function.
[7] This $L(M) = -\log P(M)$ connection between codelength's and probabilities comes from one of Shannon's theorems. See [CT91, Abr63] for a discussion.
[8] This connection with conditional probabilities is why we use the conditional notation, $L(Y|M)$.

the situation is more complicated. An expanded discussion of MDL is presented in Appendix A.

2 The Objective Function

As discussed in the introduction, our objective funtion will be divided into two parts: the codelength of the model, $L(M)$, and the codelength of the data given the model (i.e., encoded using the model), $L(Y|M)$. In our approach the specification of the model divides naturally into two components, $M = \{\Omega, \beta\}$: the segmentation, Ω, and the distribution parameters, β. Thus our total code length (equation (1.3)) may be written as:

$$L(Y, \Omega, \beta) = L(\Omega) + L(\beta|\Omega) + L(Y|\Omega, \beta) \qquad (2.1)$$

We begin by deriving an expression for $L(\Omega)$.

2.1 Encoding Region Boundaries: The Codelength for the Segmentation, $L(\Omega)$

We can encode the boundaries by encoding a graph whose nodes represent the boundaries' intersections (either with each other, or with the image frame), and whose edges represent the boundary branches lying between those intersections[9]. To make the boundaries reconstructable from such a graph, we choose one node from each connected component of this graph to be a reference node. To describe a given connected component we start by specifying the location of the reference node, followed by the number of branches from that node, followed by length of the first boundary branch (corresponding to a graph edge), followed by a chain code representing its path along the rectangular grid between the pixels (this chain-code description was also used in [Lec89a]). Thus the description of the entire graph (image partition) has the form:

1. number of connected components
2. description of first connected component
3. description of second connected component
4. and so on ...

where the description of each connected component has the form:

1. the location of the reference node, x_0
2. the number of branches from the reference node, v_0

---

[9] The boundary of a region that forms an "island" within a larger region does not have any natural node. We can circumvent this problem by assigning one of its points, say the upper rightmost, to be a node, with a loop edge attached to it.

3. length of the first boundary branch, l_{01}
4. chain code description of first boundary branch, λ_{01}
5. Length of the second boundary branch, l_{01}
6. chain code description of second boundary branch, λ_{02}
7. length of the third boundary branch[10] (if applicable), l_{03}
8. chain code description of third boundary branch, λ_{03}
9. the number of branches from the node at the end of branch (01), v_{01}
10. length of the first boundary branch from node (01), l_{011}
11. chain code description of first boundary branch, λ_{011}
12. and so on ...

Following this for the entire graph would result in duplication because every branch has two ends and can therefore be seen as originating from the nodes at either of these ends. The simple solution to this, however, is to simply not encode a branch that has already been encoded via another path (from the node at its opposite end), in a sense, pretending, at that point, that it doesn't exist.

Each element of the chain-code description of a branch represents the direction of the next step in the chain. Since the number of possible direction is 3, i.e., the number of adjacent grid points (excluding the last visited grid point)[11], the number of bits required for the chain code is $l_i \log 3$. To encode the length of the boundary segment we use Rissanen's "universal prior" for integers[Ris83], which gives the following code length:

$$L^0(l_i) = \log^*(l_i) + \log(2.865064) \tag{2.2}$$

where $\log^*(x) = \log x + \log \log x + \log \log \log x \ldots$ up to all positive terms. Thus, associated with arc i, whose length is l_i, is an encoding $L^0(l_i) + l_i \log 3$.

When the regions are large, the bulk of the resulting codelength will be the length of description of the branches, so that we can approximate the description length of the boundaries (neglecting the description length of the graph) by $\sum_{\text{all branches}} [l_i \log 3 + L^0(l_i)]$, yielding:

$$L(\Omega) \approx \sum_i (l_i \log 3 + L^0(l_i))$$

Other boundary-encoding schemes are possible, but this one has two main advantages: its regularizing action and its tractability. It is clear that this scheme results in a relatively simple expression for the segmentation codelength and, as will be shown, it is also tractable. The regularizing question is somewhat deeper. Somehow we want our objective function to favor segmentations that are more likely to occur in nature[12]. The scheme we have chosen favors segmentations with

---

[10] It is possible (but not necessary) to choose a reference node with four branches, but we will assume three.
[11] For the branch starting point, the number of possible directions may be less or more than 3, but we ignore this fact.
[12] In some cases, of course, one might replace "nature" with a particular application of interest. In this case, however, we seek an objective function and associated algorithm with general applicability.

shorter total boundary length for a given image size. This means it favors a small number of regions with smooth boundaries. This also seems to be a reasonable measure of complexity, though it does differentiate between some cases where the complexity difference is not clear such as charging a heavier penalty for a large square than for a small one. A more in-depth discussion of this boundary encoding scheme is presented in Appendix B.

2.2 Encoding the Parameters:
The Codelength for the Real-Valued Distribution Parameters, $L(\beta|\Omega)$

For the coding cost of the real-valued parameters, β, we use the expression derived by Rissanen in his optimal-precision analysis[Ris83]. For encoding K independent real-valued parameters characterizing a distribution used to describe/encode n data points the codelength he derives is: $(K/2)\log n$. Rissanen derives this expression for the encoding cost of real-valued parameters by optimizing the precision to which they are encoded. Encoding them to infinite precision would require an infinite number of bits and there is a trade-off point at which the gain (i.e., decrease) in the codelength of the data due to increasing the precision of the parameters is exactly offset by increased codelength for the parameters. This codelength corresponds to that optimal precision, but is an asymptotic form for large n. During the writing of this paper we have become aware of recent results in this area[Noh93, Ris93]. These results derive better expressions valid for small n. In future work we will utilize these new results.

Applying this result in our case we will have one such term for each region, which results in a total parameter codelength of:

$$L(\beta|\Omega) = \frac{1}{2}\sum_i K_{\beta_j} \log n_j, \tag{2.3}$$

where K_{β_j} is the number of free parameters in β_j and n_j is the number of pixels in region j. For our model we have:

$$K_{\beta_j} = \frac{d(d+1)}{2} + dm_j, \tag{2.4}$$

where m_j is the number of polynomial coefficients per band in region j. The first term on the right hand side of equation (2.4) is the number of free parameters in the covariance matrix, Σ_j. The second term is the number of polynomial coefficients in the spatially varying mean vector, $\mu_j(\mathbf{x})$, which is equal to the number of terms in Θ. For maximum polynomial degree k_j and a two-dimensional ($q = 2$) image $m_j = (k_j + 1)(k_j + 2)/2$. See Appendix E for the proof and extension to the general case when the image is q-dimensional. Substituting into equation (2.4) yields, for a two dimensional image:

$$K_{\beta_j} = \frac{d}{2}[(d+1) + (k_j+1)(k_j+2)]. \tag{2.5}$$

It should be mentioned that we have neglected the cost of encoding the polynomial orders $\{k_j\}$. This would add a small, constant number of bits for each region[13].

2.3 Encoding the Residuals:
The Codelength for the Greyvalues Within the Regions, $L(Y|\Omega, \beta)$

In this section we will describe the encoding of the residuals (the data given the model) and derive an expression for $L(Y|M) = L(Y|\Omega, \beta)$. Since our model includes polynomial surfaces fit to the greyvalues in each region, we might think of this step as that of encoding the residuals between the polynomial surface and the actual data. For this reason we will refer to this as the process of "encoding the residuals".

Now let $Y = [y_1 y_2 \ldots y_n]^t$ (the total collection of pixel values for the entire image), let Y_j denote those belonging to the jth region and let n_j the number of pixels in region j. Bear in mind that both n_j and Y_j are functions of the image partitioning, Ω. To facilitate the notation, however, we will omit the Ω dependence, allowing it to be implicit. Let $p(y|\beta_j)$ be the conditional distribution of a sample y belonging to the jth region which is characterized by the parameter vector β_j and let the parameter set $\beta \triangleq \{\beta_1, \ldots, \beta_J\}$, where J is the total number of regions in Ω. Then, the conditional distribution $p(Y|\Omega, \beta)$ is obtained by forming a product of the individual conditional distributions for all the regions in Ω.

$$p(Y|\Omega, \beta) = \prod_j p(Y_j|\beta_j) \tag{2.6}$$

From Shannon's theorems (see [Abr63]) we know that, when such a distribution is known, the shortest codelength for Y is given by

$$L(Y|M) = -\log p(Y|\Omega, \beta) = \sum_j -\log p(Y_j/\beta_j), \tag{2.7}$$

where the logarithms are base-two.

We now derive an expression for this codelength using the specific assumptions of our model. We use the assumed Gaussian distributions (equations (1.1) and (1.2)), but in order to use these equations, we need an expression for $\mu_j(x)$, which is a vector-valued function whose components are polynomial greyvalue surfaces of the form:

$$\mu_{jl}(x) = \sum_{k=1}^m \theta_{jlk} \phi_k(x) \tag{2.8}$$

---

[13] If we allow any order, we could us L^0, but, in practice, it won't add more than three bits per region.

where μ_{jl} is the lth component of the vector μ_j and θ_{jlk} is the scalar coefficient for the jth region, the lth band and the kth polynomial basis function. The basis functions $\{\phi_k(\mathbf{x})\}$ are products of various powers of the components of $\mathbf{x}$. (i.e., the two image spatial coordinates). In matrix form this may be written as: $\mu_j = \Phi_j \Theta_j$ where μ_j is an $n_j \times d$ matrix of the fitted polynomial surface values (μ values); one for each of the d bands for each of the n_j points in region ω_j. Also, Φ_j is an $n_j \times m$ matrix of basis function values; one for each of the m basis functions for each of the n_j points. The $n_j \times m$ matrix of regression coefficients is represented by Θ_j. Then, using these definitions, we may rewrite equation (1.1) obtaining:

$$p(Y_j | \beta_j) = (2\pi)^{-dn_j/2} \left|\Sigma_j\right|^{-n_j/2} \exp\left[-\frac{n_j}{2} \operatorname{trace}\left\{\Sigma_j^{-1} S_j\right\}\right] \qquad (2.9)$$

where $|\ldots|$ denotes the determinant and S_j is the *sample* covariance matrix defined by: $S_j \triangleq \frac{1}{n_j}(Y_j - \Phi_j \Theta_j)(Y_j - \Phi_j \Theta_j)^t$. A proof of this result has been provided in Appendix B. See also [And84].

Using the results presented thus far we can write our objective function as follows.

$$L(Y, \Omega, \beta) = \sum_i (l_i \log 3 + \overset{0}{L}(l_i)) + \sum \frac{K_{\beta_j}}{2} \log n_j$$
$$+ \sum_j \frac{n_j}{2}\left[d \log(2\pi) + \log|\Sigma_j| + \operatorname{trace}\left\{\Sigma_j^{-1} S_j\right\}\right], \qquad (2.10)$$

where Σ_i is a sum over all boundary segments and Σ_j is a sum over all regions (not to be confused with the covariance matrix Σ_j). The three summations correspond to $L(\Omega)$, $L(\beta|\Omega)$ and $L(Y|\Omega, \beta)$ from left to right in that order.

Since Y is fixed, we can think of this as an objective function that must be minimized over Ω and β. Fortunately, part of this minimization can be performed analytically. In fact, for a given Ω all the real-valued components (everything except the polynomial orders) of β have analytical expressions. For example, for Gaussian distributions the ML estimate (which is also minimum-codelength) for Σ_j is $\hat{\Sigma}_j = S_j$. Using this result gives trace $\{\hat{\Sigma}_j^{-1} S_j\} = d$. The remaining components of β are the polynomial coefficients, $\{\Theta_j\}$, which don't appear explicitly in equation (2.10), but are required to compute S_j. Expressions for these are derived in the following section.

Further simplifying equation (2.10) yields the following objective function that can be minimized over all Ω. We use the notation, $\mathscr{L}(\Omega)$ (i.e., no functional dependence on Y and β) to emphasize the point that during the minimization process, the data, Y, are fixed and the parameters, β, have analytical expressions in terms of Y that would appear in an expanded expression for S_j. These are derived in the following section.

$$\mathscr{L}(\Omega) = \frac{n}{2} d(1 + \log 2\pi) + \sum_i [l_i \log 3 + \overset{0}{L}(l_i)] + \frac{1}{2} \sum_j [n_j \log |S_j| + K_{\beta_j} \log n_j] \qquad (2.11)$$

Evaluating this expression (equation (2.11)) requires computing the sample covariance matrices, $\{S_j\}$. This can be done as follows (omitting the region subscript j for simplicity of notation).

$$\begin{aligned} n \cdot S &= [Y - \Phi\hat{\Theta}]^t[Y - \Phi\hat{\Theta}] \\ &= Y^tY - Y^t\Phi\hat{\Theta} - \hat{\Theta}^t\Phi^tY + \hat{\Theta}^t\Phi^t\Phi\hat{\Theta} \end{aligned} \quad (2.12)$$

But we know that $\Phi^t\Phi\hat{\Theta} = \Phi^tY$. Thus,

$$\begin{aligned} n \cdot S &= Y^tY - Y\Phi\hat{\Theta} - \hat{\Theta}^t\Phi^tY + \hat{\Theta}^t\Phi^tY \\ &= Y^tY - Y^t\Phi\hat{\Theta} \\ &= Y^tY - \hat{\Theta}^t[\Phi^tY], \end{aligned} \quad (2.13)$$

since S is symmetric.

To evaluate this expression for S we need an expression for $\hat{\Theta}$. This is derived in the next section, but as will be discussed in that section, it won't be directly computed for each new region formed during region merging. Rather, incremental formulas will be derived. Using these, $\hat{\Theta}$ and S for a new combined region will be computed in terms of the results for the two merged regions.

An important feature of this objective function is that it contains no adjustable thresholds or arbitrary parameters of any kind. It is simply derived from "first principles" and applied directly to images. The only choices at our discretion in deriving it were the class of distributions (Gaussian), the functional form (polynomial) of the surfaces and the boundary encoding scheme.

3 The Regression Problem

In the previous section we obtained an expression for our objective function, ($\mathcal{L}(\Omega)$; equation (2.11)), which we would like to minimize over all Ω. The sample covariance matrices, $\{S_j\}$ appear in this equation and their calculation involves the problem of fitting multi-variate polynomial functions (surfaces) to discrete multi-variate data (i.e., Y). In fact they (the S_j) partially characterize the statistics of the deviations of the data from these surfaces. Before describing the algorithm for finding the best segmentation in the following section, in this section we derive the expression to be used in calculating S_j.

Here we treat the general problem of fitting multi-variate polynomial functions (surfaces) to discrete multi-variate data of the form $f: \mathbf{Z}^q \to \mathbf{Z}^d$, where $\mathbf{Z}$ is the set of integers. In the case of one band, 2-D grayscale images, $q = 2$ and $d = 1$.

3.1 Uni-Variate Regression

First consider the case where $f: \mathbf{Z}^q \to \mathbf{Z}$, i.e., the number of bands $d = 1$. Assume that we are given n ordered data points $(\mathbf{x}_i, y_i)$, $1 \leq i \leq n$ where $\mathbf{x}_i \in \mathbf{Z}^q$ is the spatial coordinate of the ith pixel and $y_i \in \mathbf{Z}$ is its greyvalue. Let $\phi_j(\mathbf{x})$, $1 \leq j \leq m$ be a set of m basis functions such that y_i can be modeled as

$$y_i = \sum_{j=1}^{m} \theta_j \phi_j(\mathbf{x}_i) + \psi_i \qquad (3.1)$$

where ψ_i is zero-mean Gaussian noise with variance σ^2, and θ_j are scalar coefficients. The basis functions $\phi_j(\mathbf{x})$ in our case are products of various powers of components of $\mathbf{x}$. e.g., if $\mathbf{x}_1 = (x_{11} \ldots x_{1q})^t \in \mathbf{Z}^q$, then some examples of $\phi(\mathbf{x}_1)$ are 1, x_{11}, $(x_{11})^3$, $(x_{11})^2(x_{1q})^3$, etc. Using this model we can write an an expression for all the data as follows:

$$\begin{bmatrix} y_1 \\ y_2 \\ \vdots \\ y_n \end{bmatrix} = \begin{bmatrix} \phi_1(\mathbf{x}_1) & \phi_2(\mathbf{x}_1) & \cdots & \phi_m(\mathbf{x}_1) \\ \phi_1(\mathbf{x}_2) & \phi_2(\mathbf{x}_2) & \cdots & \phi_m(\mathbf{x}_2) \\ \vdots & \vdots & \vdots & \vdots \\ \phi_1(\mathbf{x}_n) & \phi_2(\mathbf{x}_n) & \cdots & \phi_m(\mathbf{x}_n) \end{bmatrix} \cdot \begin{bmatrix} \theta_1 \\ \theta_2 \\ \vdots \\ \theta_m \end{bmatrix} + \begin{bmatrix} \psi_1 \\ \psi_2 \\ \vdots \\ \psi_n \end{bmatrix} \qquad (3.2)$$

We represented the above equation in matrix form as

$$Y = \Phi \cdot \theta + \psi \qquad (3.3)$$

where Y and ψ are $n \times 1$ vectors, θ is an $m \times 1$ vector and Φ is an $n \times m$ matrix. Here ψ is assumed to be zero-mean Gaussian-distributed as $N(0, \sigma^2 I)$, where I is the $n \times n$ identity matrix (i.e., we assume the samples to be uncorrelated).

The regression problem, then, is to find the $\hat{\theta}$ that minimizes

$$\varepsilon^2 = \|Y - \Phi\theta\|^2. \qquad (3.4)$$

The solution to this minimization problem is

$$\hat{\theta} = [\Phi^t\Phi]^{-1}\Phi^t Y. \qquad (3.5)$$

Although the above equation is correct, it is sensitive numerically, because computing the inverse of $[\Phi^t\Phi]$ can be unstable [Gv83, PTaBPF92]. It is better to solve the system:

$$\Phi^t y = \Phi^t \Phi \theta. \qquad (3.6)$$

The solution $\hat{\theta}$ for the system of equations $\Phi^t Y = \Phi^t \Phi \theta$ is the same as the $\hat{\theta}$ that minimizes $\|Y - \Phi\theta\|^2$. (See Appendix A for a proof). Asymptotically, both the techniques are of the same order of complexity but for smaller systems of equations, a considerable amount of computation time can be saved.

3.2 Multi-Variate Regression

Now consider the case when: $f: \mathbf{Z}^q \to \mathbf{Z}^d$, i.e., the number of bands d, is greater than one. In this case we can represent the regression problem as:

$$[y_1 y_2 \ldots y_n]^t = \Phi \cdot [\theta_1 \theta_2 \ldots \theta_d] + [\psi_1 \psi_2 \ldots \psi_d], \qquad (3.7)$$

where they y_i are $d \times 1$ vectors representing the gray values in the d bands at the ith pixel, θ_i are $m \times 1$ vector of regression coefficients for the ith band, and ψ_i are $n \times 1$ vector of Gaussian noise values in the ith band are distributed as $N(0, \sigma^2 I)$, (I is an $n \times n$ identity matrix[14]) and Φ is a $n \times m$ matrix. We can write the above equation in a more compact form as

$$Y = \Phi \cdot \Theta + \Psi \qquad (3.8)$$

where Y and Ψ are $n \times d$ matrices, Θ is a $m \times d$ matrix and Φ is a $n \times m$ matrix.

The multi-variate regression problem, then, is to find the $\hat{\Theta}$ that minimizes the sum of squared residuals

$$\varepsilon^2 = \text{trace}\{(Y - \Phi \cdot \Theta)^t (Y - \Phi \cdot \Theta)\}. \qquad (3.9)$$

The above operator in this case is essentially the sum of squares of all entires of the error matrix $\varepsilon = (Y - \Phi \cdot \Theta)$. The solution to the minimization problem is

$$\hat{\Theta} = [\Phi^t \Phi]^{-1} \Phi^t Y, \qquad (3.10)$$

and the same solution is also obtained by solving the system of equations

$$\Phi^t Y = \Phi^t \Phi \Theta. \qquad (3.11)$$

Substituting the expression for $\hat{\Theta}$ (equation (3.10)) into our expression for S (equation (2.13)) yields:

$$nS = Y^t Y - \{[\Phi^t \Phi]^{-1} \Phi^t Y\}^t [\Phi^t Y].$$

For numerical reasons this expression will not be evaluated directly, but rather $\hat{\Theta}$ will be calculated and then substituted into equation (2.13).

3.3 The Incremental Regression Problem

Because we seek only the image segmentation Ω, we would not need to compute the regression coefficients, Θ (they do not appear explicitly in equation (4.1)) if it were not for the fact that they are required to compute the covariance matrix estimates $\{\hat{\Sigma}_j\}$. For this reason, anything that can be done to improve the efficiency of their calculation and that of the $\{\hat{\Sigma}_j\}$ will be valuable. In this section we derive *incremental* formulas for computing these polynomial regression coefficients and the covariance matrix of a new merged region from those of the two individual

---

[14] Some confusion is possible here. We are saying that the noise samples in the same band are uncorrelated with each other (i.e., no pixel-to-pixel correlation). This is the "white-noise" assumption. One the other hand the various bands may be correlated with each other when measured for the same pixel. We have assumed that the distribution that characterizes that relationship is $N(\mu(x), \Sigma)$, where Σ is $d \times d$.

regions merged without having to perform an explicit regression on the data of the merged region.

Consider the following two independent multi-variate regressions:

$$Y_1 = \Phi_1 \cdot \Theta_1 + \Psi_1 \tag{3.12}$$

$$Y_2 = \Phi_2 \cdot \Theta_2 + \Psi_2, \tag{3.13}$$

where Y_i is a $n_i \times d$ data vector, Φ_i is a $n_i \times m$ regression matrix, Ψ_i is a $n_i \times d$ noise matrix, and Θ is a $m \times d$ regression coefficient matrix.

Assume that the optimal $\hat{\Theta}_1$ and $\hat{\Theta}_2$ have already been computed. Now consider the following "concatenated" problem:

$$\begin{bmatrix} Y_1 \\ Y_2 \end{bmatrix} = \begin{bmatrix} \Phi_1 \\ \Phi_2 \end{bmatrix} \cdot \Theta + \Psi. \tag{3.14}$$

Let $Y = [Y_1^t \; Y_2^t]^t$ and let $\Phi = [\Phi_1^t \; \Phi_2^t]^t$. Then the above equation can be written as

$$Y = \Phi\Theta + \Psi. \tag{3.15}$$

The problem: find a computationally efficient method for computing $\hat{\Theta}$ and $(n_1 + n_2)S = [Y - \Phi\hat{\Theta}]^t[Y - \Phi\hat{\Theta}]$ for the concatenated system.

3.3.1 Incremental Computation of $\hat{\Theta}$

As discussed earlier, matrix inverse computations can be unstable and it is better to compute $\hat{\Theta}$ by solving the linear system of equations

$$\Phi^t Y = \Phi^t \Phi \Theta. \tag{3.16}$$

Expanding Φ and Y we get

$$\Phi^t Y = [\Phi_1^t \; \Phi_2^t] \cdot \begin{bmatrix} Y_1 \\ Y_2 \end{bmatrix} = [\Phi_1^t Y_1 + \Phi_2^t Y_2] \tag{3.17}$$

and,

$$\Phi^t \Phi = [\Phi_1^t \; \Phi_2^t] \cdot \begin{bmatrix} \Phi_1 \\ \Phi_2 \end{bmatrix} = [\Phi_1^t \Phi_1 + \Phi_2^t \Phi_2]. \tag{3.18}$$

Notice that the matrix products $\Phi_i^t Y_i$ and $\Phi_i^t \Phi_i$ are available since they must have been computed for the individual systems. Moreover, although the matrices Φ and Y are of varying dimensions, the matrix products $\Phi^t Y$ and $\Phi^t \Phi$ are of always of constant small (relative to the number of pixels in most regions) dimensions, independent of the dimensions of Φ and Y, which change with the number of pixels in a region. That is, the matrix product $\Phi^t Y$ is $m \times d$ and $\Phi^t \Phi$ is $m \times m$. The elements of these matrices are given by:

$$(\Phi^t Y)_{ij} = \sum_{l=1}^{n} \phi_i(\mathbf{x}_l) y_{jl} \qquad (3.19)$$

$$(\Phi^t \Phi)_{ij} = \sum_{l=1}^{n} \phi_i(\mathbf{x}_l) \phi_j(\mathbf{x}_l), \qquad (3.20)$$

where y_{jl} is the value of the jth band for the lth pixel.

3.3.2 Incremental Computation of S

In this section we give expressions for incrementally computing the covariance matrices, $\{S_j\}$. From equation (2.13) we have:

$$nS = Y^t Y - \hat{\Theta}^t [\Phi^t Y]. \qquad (3.21)$$

In the incremental computation we utilize the fact that $Y^t Y = Y_1^t Y_1 + Y_2^t Y_2$, and $\Phi^t Y = [\Phi_1^t Y_1 + \Phi_2^t Y_2]$, which reduces the number of computations in the incremental computation of the covariance matrix. Furthermore, all the matrices involved in the computation of S ($\hat{\Sigma}$) and Θ have fixed dimensions and therefore the bookkeeping involved with dynamically changing region sizes is reduced.

4 Segmentation Algorithm

The problem our algorithm must solve is one of finding the minimum of equation (2.11) over all Ω. Obtaining the absolute (global) minimum is infeasible because the search space is so large. For this reason we use a hierarchical algorithm similar to that used in [SDNS92, BG89] to find a good, though perhaps local, minimum. It starts with an initial segmentation of the image. This may be just the image itself, with each pixel considered to be a separate region, or it may consist of larger regions produced by some heuristic device. Starting with this initial segmentation, the algorithm successively merges pairs of neighboring regions provided that the mergers decrease the total code-length. At each step the pair of regions producing the greatest codelength decrease are merged.

The MDL codelength decrease, δ_{tv}, due to a merger between two neighboring regions, ω_t and ω_v, can be deduced from equation (2.11):

$$\begin{aligned}\delta_{tv} =& [l_{tv} \log 3 + \log l_{tv}] \\ &+ \frac{1}{2}[n_t \log |S_t| + n_v \log |S_v| - (n_t + n_v) \log |S_{tv}|] \\ &+ \frac{1}{2}[K_{\beta_t} \log n_t + K_{\beta_v} \log n_v - K_{\beta_{tv}} \log(n_t + n_v)]\end{aligned} \qquad (4.1)$$

where S_{tv} denotes the sample covariance matrix of the combined region $\omega_t \cup \omega_v$. As mentioned above, at each step in the algorithm we search for the two regions ω_t, ω_v

that yield the greatest code length decrease δ_{tv} when merged. The first term expresses the savings due to the fact that a boundary branch drops when the merger occurs. The second term is the increase in the codelength of the actual data values themselves. This results from going to a single distribution from a separate distribution for each region. The third term is the savings associated with the fact that we have fewer model parameters to described after the merger. K_{β_t}, K_{β_v} and $K_{\beta_{tv}}$ represent the number of parameters in the models representing the regions t, v, and tv respectively.

The total number of merger steps needed to reach the final classification equals the number of initial regions r_0 minus the final number of regions R (usually $R \ll r_0$). The regions are ordered with a *heap-based priority queue* [Sed90] to select the best merger and at each step a time proportional to $\log r_0$ is required to maintain the queue, thus making the run time proportional to $r_0 \log r_0$. The memory size required by the algorithm equals the total number of regions (both the initial and the newly created, summing up, in the worst case, to $2r_0$) multiplied by the memory size required by the data set of a single region, which is roughly proportional to the average number of neighbors of a single region. This last number is usually much smaller than r_0, and therefore the memory requirements of this hierarchical algorithm are also proportional to r_0, being modest when compared to conventional hierarchical clustering procedures that try to merge every possible pair regardless of spatial location, and therefore requiring a memory size proportional to $\frac{1}{2} r_0 (r_0 - 1)$. Moreover, some of the items of the data sets of inactive regions may be erased to save memory space.

The algorithm is run by first fixing the maximum degree of regression polynomials to 0. That is, region greyvalues are represented by piece-wise constant functions. After the algorithm converges to a segmentation (because it is more expensive to encode the image if any further merging is done), merging is attempted with first order polynomials representing the merged regions. This is continued until the merging converges. The process of incrementing the regression polynomial order and merging until convergence is continued until no merging is accomplished for a particular degree of the polynomial. Note that this process can be stopped at any degree of fit and will still result in closed region boundaries.

5 Experimental Results

To test the algorithm, we implemented it in C on an IBM RISC-System/6000 model 970 and ran it on both synthetic and real images. The synthetic images that were used fit the model assumptions of piece-wise constant, linear and quadratic regions with Gaussian noise. Here we show results on two real images. The segmentation results for various maximum polynomial order fits are shown. The computation time for images of size 128 × 128 was on the order of 180 seconds.

Our first real image test case (Fig. 1) was a real 128 × 128 two-band (red and blue) image of a small fragment of an electronic circuit. Figures 2, 3, and 4 are the

A Fast Algorithm for MDL-Based Multi-Band Image Segmentation

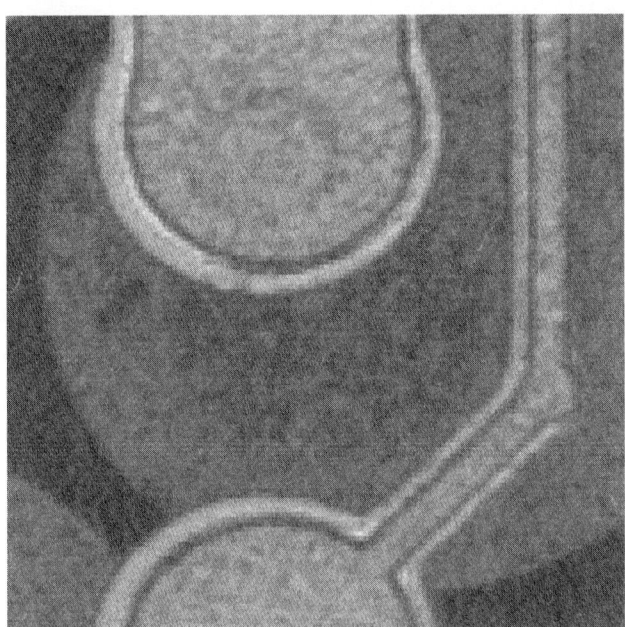

Fig. 1. The grayscale image of the red band of a real, two-band (red and blue), image of a small fragment of an electronic circuit

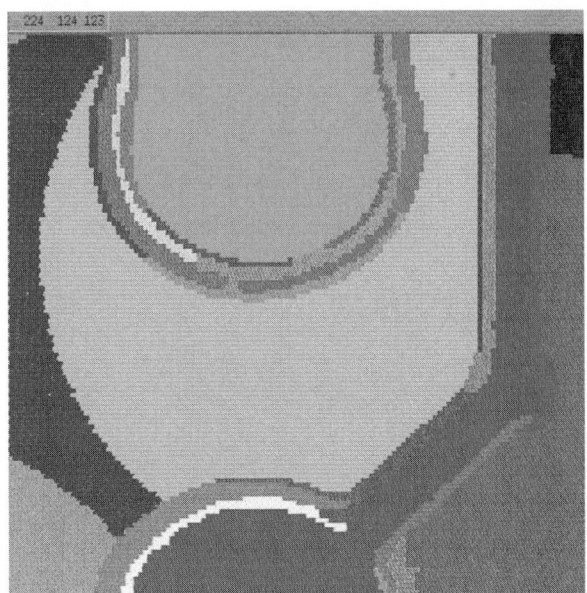

Fig. 2. Segmentation result for the electronic circuit image. In this run, the maximum degree of polynomial was zero. That is, a piece-wise constant model was used for each region. See Color Plate VI (inserted after p. 178) for illustration in color

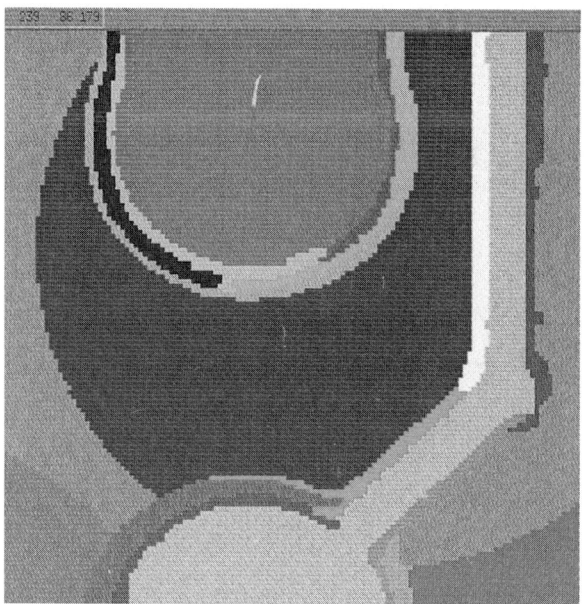

Fig. 3. Segmentation result for the electronic circuit image. In this run, the maximum degree of polynomial was one. That is, a piece-wise linear model was used for each region. Notice that some of the regions in the piece-wise constant result have been merged in this result. See Color Plate VI (inserted after p. 178) for illustration in color

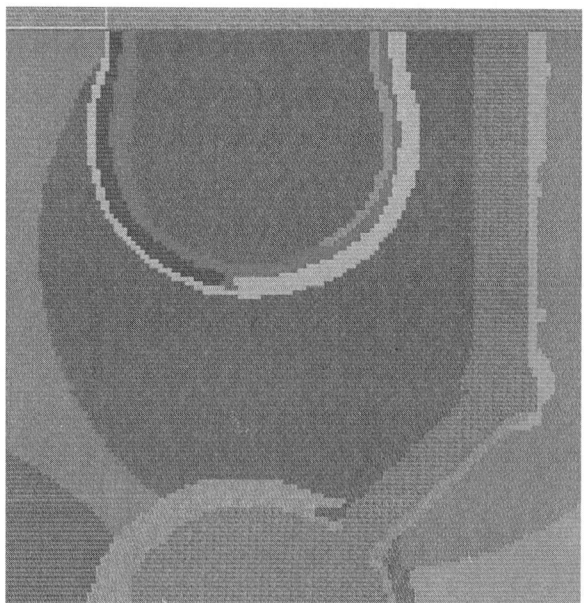

Fig. 4. Segmentation result for the electronic circuit image. In this run, the maximum degree of polynomial was two. That is, a piece-wise quadratic model was used for each region. Some of the regions in the piece-wise linear result have been merged in this result. See Color Plate VII (inserted after p. 178) for illustration in color

Fig. 5. A real, 128 × 128, grayscale image of a house

segmentation result when the maximum degree of polynomial allowed is zero, one, and two, respectively. As can be seen in the figure, the result for zero-order polynomials (i.e., piece-wise constant) is quite good, but contains many small regions in the boundary areas. This is due partially to the inadequacy of the piecewise-constant model in these areas. Many of these fragments get merged when the maximum degree of the polynomial allowed is increased to linear, and then quadratic.

Our second real image test case was the real 128 × 128 pixel image of a house in Fig. 5. This is a single-band grayscale image. The results are quite good for the piece-wise constant case in Fig. 6, but there are certain region boundaries that appear inappropriate. This is a kind of contouring effect that is, again, an artifact of the piecewise-constant assumption/model. This problem is partially solved when the maximum degree is allowed to go to piecewise linear as shown in Fig. 7.

Note that when maximum allowed degree of fit is two (quadratic surfaces), some of the regions still can have piece-wise constant and linear surfaces since the MDL criterion might find it cheaper to encode those regions that way. This model selection is, of course, done automatically using the MDL criterion – there are no heuristic thresholds.

It is interesting to note that a very high percentage of time is spent in merging neighbor lists (37%). An efficient implementation of merge procedure could speed up the software further. Other sections of the algorithm that take considerable amounts of time are: computing logarithms (10%), and computation of the codelength change, δ_{tv} (15%).

Fig. 6. Segmentation result for the house image. In this run, the maximum degree of polynomial was zero. That is, a piece-wise constant model was used for each region. See Color Plate VII (inserted after p. 178) for illustration in color

Fig. 7. Segmentation result for the house image. In this run, the maximum degree of polynomial was one. That is, a piece-wise linear model was used for each region. Notice that some of the regions in piece-wise constant result been merged in this result. See Color Plate VIII (inserted after p. 178) for illustration in color

6 Discussion and Conclusions

We have developed an MDL-based objective function for multi-band image segmentation and an efficient segmentation algorithm that performs a sub-optimal minimization of this criterion. The algorithm is incremental and makes use of computations performed in previous stages. The algorithm was tested on both synthetic and real images. The speed and performance of the algorithm on the test images were quite good and no manually adjusted thresholds were required. It should be mentioned that this algorithm can be used to treat texture-based segmentation by using the appropriate texture operators to compute the input bands for this algorithm. An alternate approach to texture will be mentioned below. Natural extensions of this algorithm/work include:

- alternate coding schemes for segment boundaries. For example polygonal coding will be more efficient for images that have polygonal shapes (e.g., aerial images of buildings), and Fourier descriptors for images which have shapes with smooth contours (e.g., images of organs).
- a way of incorporating prior information (e.g., vertical lines may be more probable than horizontal, or, the probability of 90 degree angle between lines might be higher than other angles), into the MDL objective function.
- other (than polynomial Gaussian) stochastic models. For example, Markov random field models could be used for encoding textures. This would then simultaneously segment images into textured and piece-wise smooth regions.
- extend the boundary coding scheme to allow coding of three-dimensional surfaces. This would help in segmenting three-dimensional objects in multidimensional (volume) data, e.g., CT images of the heart or other organs.
- a more rigorous analysis of small-sample-size effects on the covariance matrix estimate (and therefore the objective function) when the region sizes are small in the initial states of clustering.
- using recent results that obtain better (*sharper*) MDL formulas for small data sets that have appeared in the literature [Noh93, Ris93]. Applying these for the encoding cost of the parameters, β, may produce better results. This is especially true of the results in [Noh93], which apply specifically to the problem of polynomial regression.
- explore the possibility of using our algorithm for lossless image compression.

Acknowledgement. The authors would like to thank Jacob Shienvald, Nimrod Meggidio, Jorma Rissanen, Myron Flickner and Harpreet Sawhney for illuminating discussions.

References

[Abr63]   N. Abramson. *Information Theory and Coding*. McGraw-Hill, 1963.
[Aka74]   H. Akaike. A new look at statistical model identification. *IEEE Trans.*, AC-19:716–723, 1974.

[And84]   T.W. Anderson. *An Introduction to Multivariate Statistical Analysis*. Wiley, New York, second edition, 1984.
[Ber85]   James O. Berger. *Statistical Decision Theory and Bayesian Analysis*. Springer-Verlag, New York, second edition, 1985.
[BG89]   J.M. Beaulieu and M. Goldberg. Hierarchy in picture segmentation: A stepwise optimization approach. *IEEE PAMI*, 11(2):150–163, February 1989.
[BJ88]   P.J. Besl and R.C. Jain. Segmentation through variable-order surface fitting. *IEEE Trans PAMI*, 10(2):167–192, March 1988.
[BZ87]   A. Blake and A. Zisserman. *Visual Reconstruction*. MIT Press, Cambridge, MA, 1987.
[CT91]   Thomas M. Cover and Joy A. Thomas. *Elements of Information Theory*. Wiley, New York, 1991.
[DP91]   Trevor Darrell and Alex Pentland. Recovery of minimal descriptions using parallel robust estimation. Technical Report 163, 1991.
[DS90]   Byron Dom and David Steele. 2^n – tree classifiers and realtime image segmentation. In *MVA '90: IAPR Workshop on Machine Vision Applications*, Tokyo, Japan, 1990. IAPR (for expanded version see IBM Research Report 7558 (70424) 7/2/90).
[DSP90]   Trevor Darrel, Stan Sclaroff, and Alex Pentland. Segmentation by minimal description. In *ICCV 90*, Osaka, Japan, pp. 112–116, 1990.
[FH88]   P. Fua and A.J. Hanson. Extracting generic shapes using model driven optimization. In *Proceedings of the Image Understanding Workshop*, pp. 994–1004, Boston, 1988.
[GR80]   I.S. Gradshteyn and I.M. Ryzhik. *Table of Integrals, Series, and Products*. Academic Press, New York, corrected and enlarged edition, 1980.
[Gv83]   G.H. Golub and C.F. van Loan. *Matrix Computations*. The Johns Hopkins University Press, Baltimore, MD, 1983.
[HS85]   R.M. Haralick and L. Shapiro. Image segmentation techniques. *Computer Vision, Graphics, and Image Processing*, 29:100–132, 1985.
[HS92]   R.M. Haralick and L.G. Shapiro. *Computer and Robot Vision*, volume 1. Addison-Wesley, 1992.
[Jay83]   Edwin T. Jaynes. Prior probabilities. In R.D. Rosenkrantz, editor, *E.T. Jaynes: Papers on Probability, Statistics and Statistical Physics*, chapter 7. D. Reidel, Boston, 1983 (original paper published in 1968).
[KDNS94] T. Kanungo, B. Dom, W. Niblack, and D. Steele. A fast algorithm for MDL-based multi-band image segmentation. In *International Conference on Computer Vision and Pattern Recognition*. IEEE Computer Society, 1994 (to appear).
[Kee90]   K. Keeler. Minimal length encoding of planar subdivision topologies with application to image segmentation. In *AAAI 1990 Spring Symposium of the Theory and Application of Minimal Length Encoding*, 1990.
[KMWP90] Daniel Keren, Ruth Marcus, Michael Werman, and Shmuel Peleg. Segmentation by minimum length encoding. In *ICPR 90*, pp. 681–683, 1990.
[LCJ91]   S. Liou, A.H. Chin, and R. Jain. A parallel technique for signal-level perceptual organization. *IEEE Trans PAMI*, 13(4):317–325, 1991.
[Lec89a] Y.G. Leclerc. Constructing simple stable descriptions for image partitioning. *International Journal of Computer Vision*, 3:73–102, 1989.
[Lec89b] Y.G. Leclerc. *The Local Structure of Image Intensity Discontinuities*. PhD thesis, McGill University, Montréal, Québec, Canada, May 1989.
[Lec90]   Y.G. Leclerc. Region grouping using the minimum-description-length principle. In *DARPA Image Understanding Workshop*, 1990.
[Liu77]   C.L. Liu. *Elements of Discrete Mathematics*. McGraw Hill, New York, 1977.
[LJ91]   S. Liou and R. Jain. An approach to three-dimensional image segmentation. *CVGIP: Image Understanding*, 53(3):237–252, 1991.

[Noh93] Ragnar Nohre. *Topics in Descriptive Complexity*. PhD thesis, Technical University of Linkoping, 1993. See Chap. 2 Coding Small Data Sets.
[Pen89] Alex Pentland. Part segmentation for objects recognition. *Neural Computation*, 1:82–91, 1989.
[PTaBPF92] W.H. Press, S.A. Teukolsky, W.T. Vetterling, and B.P. Flannery. *Numerical Recipes in C (2 ed.)*. Cambridge University Press, 1992.
[Ris78] J. Rissanen. Modelling by shortest data description. *Automatica*, 14:465–471, 1978.
[Ris83] J. Rissanen. A universal prior for integers and estimation by minimum description length. *The Annals of Statistics*, 2(11):211–222, 1983.
[Ris89] J. Rissanen. *Stochastic Complexity in Statistical Inquiry*, volume 15. World Scientific Series in Computer Science, 1989.
[Ris93] Jorma Rissanen. Fisher information and stochastic complexity. Research Report RJ 9547, IBM Research Division, 1993.
[SDNS92] J. Sheinvald, B. Dom, W. Niblack, and D. Steele. Unsupervised image segmentation using the minimum description length principle. In *Proceedings of ICPR 92*, August 1992. For an expanded version see: *IBM Research Report RJ 8474 (76695)*, (11/1/91).
[Sed90] R. Sedgewick. *Algorithms in C*. Addison Wesley, 1990.
[Sha48] C.E. Shannon. A mathematical theory of communication. *Bell Syst Tech J.*, (3):379–423, 1948.
[Str80] G. Strang. *Linear Algebra and its Applications*. Academic Press, New York, NY, 1980.
[WK90] R.S. Wallace and T. Kanade. Finding natural clusters having minimum description length. In *AAAI 1990 Spring Symposium on the Theory and Application of Minimum Length Methods*, Stanford University, Stanford, CA, 1990.
[ZM90] J. Zhang and J.W. Modestino. A model fitting approach to cluster validation with application to stochastic model-based image segmentation. *IEEE PAMI*, 12(10):1009–1017, October 1990.

A MDL Principle for Estimation

Here we present a brief tutorial discussion of the Minimum Description Length principle (MDL) [Ris78] for estimation or model selection. It has been described in depth in [Ris89] and an interesting historical account of its development is presented in [Lec89b]. The MDL principle addresses the following general problem: Given a set of observations $Y = \{y_1, \ldots, y_n\}$ (e.g., a set of pixel measurement vectors corresponding to a greyscale or multiband image) and a set of competing candidate models $\{M \in \mathcal{M}\}$, select the best model, where, in principle, "best" refers to the purpose for which the model is to be used; for example (in our case) for unsupervised image segmentation. The MDL approach defines at *best* the model that yields the shortest codelength for the given observations, when used in an ideal coding-theoretic scheme. It is based on information-theoretic arguments, and can (as mentioned in the body of this paper) be viewed as a formalization of *Ockham's razor*: the simplest model explaining a set of observations is the best[15].

---

[15] Attributed to William of Ockham (1285-1349). The exact quote usually given is: "entities are not to be multiplied beyond necessity". This is also referred to as the *law of economy* or the *law of parsimony*.

Much of the work on this topic by Rissanen [Ris89] and others might be described as addressing the issue of how one formalizes this minimum description length principle mathematically. This formalization is achieved by building on the work of Shannon [Sha48] and others (information theory [Abr63, CT91]), associating codelengths with probabilities. The MDL criterion we use, which is based on a two-part coding scheme, represents one such formalization. We derive this criterion as follows. One envisions a scheme that uses a class of parametric probability models, $\{p(Y|M)\}$ ("indexed" by M) to encode the data, Y. The data is encoded by first encoding the model and then encoding the data using ("conditioned on") the model. Thus the total codelength is given by: $L(M) + L(Y|M)$. The codelength we use for the data (2nd term) is given by[16]: $L(Y|M) = -\log p(Y|M)$[17]. There is a certain redundancy hidden in this coding formulation, however. This can be seen as follows. The model M is selected to minimize this codelength. However, only a subset of the possible Y values could have resulted in the selection of a particular M, whereas this codelength implies a code that would allow any Y to be encoded using M, even one that couldn't possibly have led to its selection.

To correct this redundancy we can, in principle, given M, construct a normalized density over only these allowable Y values by simply dividing $p(Y|M)$ by $\Sigma_{Y \in R(M)} p(Y|M)$, where $R(M)$ is the set of allowable Y values. Then a code whose lengths are given approximately by logarithms of this normalized density can be constructed. Because of the problem in computing this sum, however, we ignore it and (as has been the usual practice) thus use a somewhat less efficient encoding scheme, which (one would assume) will result in slightly worse estimates. Recent results in this area[Noh93, Ris93] would appear to improve on this criterion by addressing this redundancy and other issues. In future work we will utilize these new results. Here we will only describe and use the older results.

The issue of how to encode the model is not quite as straightforward, as that of encoding the data using the model. If M is a discrete set (either finite or countably infinite)[18] and we have an associated prior[19] $p(M)$, we may simply use it

---

[16] A minor point is being swept under the rug here. Throughout our development we will treat Y as real-valued and $p(Y|M)$ as a continuous probability *density*. The coding paradigm applies only to discrete "symbols" however. Implicit in our development is that the scalar values composing Y have been truncated to the appropriate precision and can, therefore, be represented by integers. It would therefore be more correct to write $L(Y|M) = -\log[p(Y|M) \cdot \delta Y]$, where (because y values are integers) $\delta Y = 1$.

[17] The notation used here might seem a little confusing when first encountered. The variable M may be thought of as a specification of the model and since we follow the Bayesian notion of considering this to be a random variable, we use the *conditional* notation, $(\ldots | \ldots)$. In this context, $p(Y|M)$, denotes the value of the probability density one obtains for Y using the model specified by M.

[18] The decision trees of [DS90] for example.

[19] This term is used in the paradigm of Bayesian estimation [Ber85] where the model M (or its specification) is considered to be a random variable with its own probability distribution, $P(M)$, usually referred to as the *prior* because it presumably embodies prior knowledge about the likelihood of various values of M. Occasionally, there is a known process

to accomplish this encoding (i.e., $L(M) = -\log p(M)$). If we have no such prior, then one must be constructed. Techniques have been developed for constructing priors using limited prior knowledge. For example see [Ber85] and [Jay83]. In cases where there is essentially no prior knowledge, Rissanen's *Universal Prior for Integers* may be used[20]. It should be pointed out that in this discrete-model case constructing a prior and constructing an encoding scheme are equivalent; the length of the latter being essentially the logarithm of the former.

In the more common case the model specification, M, is divided into a *structure parameter* (usually integer-valued), κ (which indexes the discrete part of the model), and a vector of real-valued parameters[21] $\beta^{(\kappa)}$, where the dimensionality of $\beta^{(\kappa)}$ is $K^{(\kappa)}$. As a simple example consider the problem of polynomial (in one variable) curve fitting. In this case κ is the polynomial order, $K^{(\kappa)} = \kappa + 1$, and $\beta^{(\kappa)}$ is the set of $\kappa + 1$ coefficients. In our image-segmentation application κ specifies the partitioning (segmentation) of the image into regions and the orders of the 2D polynomial surfaces for all the regions, while the components of $\beta^{(\kappa)}$ are the polynomial coefficients and the variances and covariances (components of the covariance matrix).

When the model structure is fixed, the two most common criteria for estimating β are *maximum likelihood* (ML) (choosing β to maximize $p(Y|\beta)$) and the Bayesian *maximum a posteriori* (MAP) estimation (choosing β to maximize the *posterior* density: $p(\beta|Y) = p(Y, \beta)/p(Y)$). From the coding perspective assumed by MDL, however, these estimates beg the question of what precision is to be used in encoding β. Since β is real-valued, infinite precision is required (in general) to represent it with complete accuracy. This problem is, in a sense, an opportunity for the MDL principle to exert its influence. Rissanen has developed a technique for determining the optimal precision for encoding real-valued parameters[Ris83]. This technique is based on a universal scheme for encoding discretized real-valued vectors. The codelengths associated with this scheme cannot be considered negative logarithms of a prior (in the Bayesian sense), because the codes and associated codelengths depend on the data, Y. For the case of ML estimation (i.e., no prior

---

[19] (*Contd.*) characterizable by a known distribution, $P(M)$. In the more usual situation, $P(M)$, is not known precisely. In such cases it is chosen to be consistent with whatever is known (both qualitatively and quantitatively) and, within those constraints, in the most computationally convenient form.

[20] This provides a prior (or, equivalently, a coding scheme) for the positive integers. If the models of the discrete set $\mathcal{M}$ have no natural ordering, then their association with the positive integers is arbitrary and this creates a minor problem because Rissanen't prior slightly favors small integers. If the set $\mathcal{M}$ is countably infinite (the usual case for using Rissanen's prior), then it almost certainly has a natural ordering and (if this isn't already the case) its indexing should be transformed such that the complexity of the models increases with the index.

[21] In this tutorial section we use the supersript (κ) to remind the reader that the dimensionality of β depends on the model structure κ. In the main body of the paper, we drop this superscript and the symbol, κ, for ease of notation.

$p(\beta)$ is available), when this is taken to a suitable asymptotic ($n \to \infty$)[22] form, it may be written as[23]:

$$L(\hat{\beta}^{(\kappa)} | \kappa, Y) = \frac{1}{2} K^{(\kappa)} \log n \qquad (A.1)$$

where $\hat{\beta}^{(\kappa)}$ is the maximum likelihood estimator of $\beta^{(\kappa)}$ (i.e., the minimizing value for $-\log p(Y|\beta^{(\kappa)})$) and $K^{(\kappa)}$ is the number of "free" components in $\beta^{(\kappa)}$. Note that the only remaining dependence on the data in equation (A.1) is on the number of data points n.

For the case of MAP estimation we have:

$$L(\hat{\beta}^{(\kappa)} | \kappa) = -\log p(\hat{\beta}^{(\kappa)}) + \frac{1}{2} K^{(\kappa)} \log n \qquad (A.2)$$

In this case $\hat{\beta}^{(\kappa)}$ is the MAP estimate, which will, in general, be different from the ML estimate. The $\frac{1}{2} K^{(\kappa)} \log n$ term is usually called the "penalty term", since it penalizes models with many parameters. Some workers use the term "MDL criterion" to refer to the ML form of the minimum description length, using this asymptotic form for the description length of β. This may be written as:

$$MDL(\kappa) = -\log p(Y | \hat{\beta}^{(\kappa)}) + \frac{1}{2} K^{(\kappa)} \log n + L(\kappa) \qquad (A.3)$$

where $L(\kappa)$ is the encoding length for κ based on whatever encoding scheme is used for the particular problem. In some cases (e.g., polynomial curve fitting) $L(\kappa)$ is dropped because it is either the same for all κ or insignificant. In our image-segmentation application we ignore the polynomial orders and κ reduces to Ω, the segmentation of the image.

B A Discussion of the Encoding Scheme for Region Boundaries

One might be concerned about an apparent inefficiency in chain-code-based boundary (image-partition) encoding scheme we use. There is a subtle point here. This encoding scheme allows the description of impossible partitionings (segmentations) (e.g., boundary segments that intersect themselves, go outside the image, etc.) and is thus inefficient from the viewpoint of coding. If this coding scheme were used directly as part of a practical scheme for image compression, this inefficiency would be real. In doing model selection (estimation), however, we

---

[22] The recent results mentioned above [Noh93, Ris93] also eliminate the parameter-precision issue and offer an expression valid for small n.

[23] There is a subtle flaw in this notation, but it is fine for our purposes. Using this term, the total code length is given by: $L(Y|\hat{\beta}^{(\kappa)}) + L(\hat{\beta}^{(\kappa)}|\kappa, Y)$. This seems to imply that the value of $\hat{\beta}^{(\kappa)}$ is used to encode the data and that $\hat{\beta}^{(\kappa)}$ is then encoded with $L(\hat{\beta}^{(\kappa)}|\kappa, Y)$ bits. In reality, of course, the optimal-precision approximation to $\hat{\beta}^{(\kappa)}$ is used to encode the data, Y. For an in-depth discussion see Rissanen's original paper [Ris83] or the discussion on pp. 54–58 of his book [Ris89].

A Fast Algorithm for MDL-Based Multi-Band Image Segmentation

need not be concerned with this kind of inefficiency for the following reason. Let $L(\Omega)$ represent the length function for our encoding scheme. L is defined for all valid segmentations. Using the Kraft inequality [Abr63], we can construct a probability function $P(\Omega)$ as follows:

$$p(\Omega) = 2^{-L(\Omega)} / \sum_{\Omega} 2^{-L(\Omega)}, \tag{B.1}$$

where the sum is over all possible segmentations. Using p, we may now, in principle, construct a new coding scheme with code lengths given approximately by: $-\log p(\Omega)$, which means that they will differ only by an additive constant (the logarithm of denominator in the RHS of equation (B.1)) from $L(\Omega)$. Because this constant is the same for all models it will have no effect on which model (i.e., which segmentation) we select and no harm comes, therefore, from omitting it and using our original $L(\Omega)$.

This reasoning may be misleading, however. Suppose we were to construct codes for Ω that linearly increase with boundary length, but are longer than the ones we've described here. That is, the lengths of these new codes are equal to a constant ($\alpha > 1$), times the ones described here. In that case the derivative of our code length with respect to the boundary length of Ω is $\alpha \log_2 3$. Thus, the larger we make α the greater the degree to which our objective function will favor segmentations with a shorter total boundary length. If we think of this $p(\Omega)$ as a *prior* probability in the Bayesian sense, increasing α is equivalent to concentrating more of the probability in the region of shorter boundary lengths. The probability associated with the zero-boundary-length segmentation, Ω_0 (i.e., a single region that is the entire image) is given by:

$$p(\Omega_0) = \left[\sum_{\Omega} 2^{-L(\Omega)} \right]^{-1}, \tag{B.2}$$

An alternate coding scheme that is possible in principle is to specify the total boundary length corresponding to Ω, $l(\Omega)$, and then to specify which of the possible partitionings with that total boundary length is used. This can be done by ordering all the partitionings for a given l in any arbitrary way (the encoder and decoder just need to use the same ordering) and then specifying the partitioning by its index (position in the list). The number of bits required to specify this index is the logarithm of the number of possible partitionings with the specified total boundary length.

This has no inefficiency of the type described above (i.e., allowing the description of impossible boundaries), but is less tractable because it cannot be written as a sum of terms, each corresponding to a single boundary segment, and therefore doesn't lend itself as well to our region-merging optimization scheme because the codelength change associated with merging two regions (and thus eliminating their common boundary segment) depends on the boundary length of the entire segmentation and not just that of shared segment as is the case for our chain-code-based scheme. This scheme also has the problem that is has a maximum with respect to codelength that doesn't correspond to the maximum boundary length. In fact, the codelength for a complete "checker board" (where every pixel is a separate region) is the same as that for Ω_0 because in each case the number of possible partitionings with the corresponding total boundary length is one. This maximum is a problem for us, because we have chosen total boundary length as our measure of complexity.

C A Proof for Equivalence of Two Solutions

In this appendix we show that regression solutions obtained by matrix inverse and by solving a linear system of equations are one and the same.

First we need the following lemma (from Strand [Str80]).

Lemma C.1. *Let Φ be a $N \times M$ full rank matrix with $N > M$. That is, $rank(\Phi) = M$. Then $rank(\Phi^t\Phi) = M$, and thus $\Phi^t\Phi$ is invertible and has the null space $\{0\}$.*

Proof. We prove the lemma by (i) showing that the null space of Φ and the null space of $\Phi^t\Phi$ are of same dimensions, and (ii) using the fact that the number of colums of Φ and $\Phi^t\Phi$ are the same.

Let $\mathbf{x}$ be in the null space of Φ. Therefore $\Phi\mathbf{x} = 0$. Multiplying by Φ^t we have $\Phi^t\Phi\mathbf{x} = 0$. That is, if $\mathbf{x}$ is in the null space of Φ, then it is in the null space of $\Phi^t\Phi$. Now the converse. Let $\Phi^t\Phi\mathbf{x} = 0$. Then, if we take the inner product with $\mathbf{x}$ we have $\mathbf{x}^t\Phi^t\Phi\mathbf{x} = 0$. That is, $\|\Phi\mathbf{x}\|^2 = 0$, or, $\Phi\mathbf{x} = 0$. Thus Φ and $\Phi^t\Phi$ have the same null space.

But $M = rank(\Phi) = M - dim(\text{null space of } \Phi) = M - dim(\text{null space of } \Phi^t\Phi) = rank(\Phi^t\Phi)$. Thus, the rank of $\Phi^t\Phi$ is M and hence it is invertible and has the null space $\{0\}$.

Proposition C.1. *Let Φ be a $N \times M$ full rank matrix with $N > M$; that is $rank(\Phi) = M$. Then if $\hat{\theta}$ minimizes*

$$\|\mathbf{y} - \Phi\theta\|^2,$$

then $\hat{\theta}$ also minimizes

$$\|\Phi^t\mathbf{y} - \Phi^t\Phi\theta\|^2.$$

Proof. $\hat{\theta}$ minimizes the fitting error if and only if the error vector is orthogonal to the space spanned by the basis vectors. Thus, $\hat{\theta}$ minimizes $\|\Phi^t\mathbf{y} - \Phi^t\Phi\theta\|^2$ if and only if $(\Phi^t\Phi)^t(\Phi^t\mathbf{y} - \Phi^t\Phi\hat{\theta}) = 0$. But since Φ is full rank, the null space of $\Phi^t\Phi$ is $\{0\}$ (from Lemma C.1). This implies that $\hat{\theta}$ minimizes $\|\Phi^t\mathbf{y} - \Phi^t\Phi\theta\|^2$ if and only if $\Phi^t\mathbf{y} - \Phi^t\Phi\hat{\theta} = 0$. Factoring out Φ^t we have $\Phi^t(\mathbf{y} - \Phi\hat{\theta}) = 0$. But this is true if and only if $\hat{\theta}$ minimizes $\|\mathbf{y} - \Phi\theta\|^2$. Thus we have proved our claim.

D Computation of $-\log p(Y_j|\hat{\beta}_j)$

In this appendix we will prove some of the results used in the section on residual encoding. First, we will need the following proposition which represents the exponent of a multivariate Gaussian maximum likelihood formulation in terms of sample covariance matrices.

Proposition D.1. Let $y_1, y_2, \ldots, y_n$ and $\mu_1, \mu_2, \ldots, \mu_n$ (in our application/notation $\mu_i \equiv \mu(x_i)$) be n d-dimensional vectors and let Σ be a positive definite matrix. Then,

$$\sum_{i=1}^{n}(y_i - \mu_i)^t \Sigma^{-1}(y_i - \mu_i) = n \cdot \text{trace}\left\{\Sigma^{-1} S\right\}$$

where

$$S = \sum_{i=1}^{n}(y_i - \mu_i)(y_i - \mu_i)^t.$$

Proof. Let y_{ij} be the jth component of the vector y_i. Similarly, let μ_{ij} represent the jth component of the vector μ_i. Now we will try to simplify the left had side and the right hand side of the proposition and show that they are the same.

$$\text{L.H.S.} = \sum_{i=1}^{n}(y_i - \mu_i)^t \Sigma^{-1}(y_i - \mu_i)$$

$$= \sum_{i=1}^{n}\sum_{j=1}^{d}\sum_{k=1}^{d}(y_{ij} - \mu_{ij})\sigma_{jk}^{-1}(y_{ik} - \mu_{ik}). \quad (D.1)$$

Now, s_{ij}, the $(i, j)^{th}$ component of the matrix S can be computed as

$$s_{jk} = \frac{1}{n}\sum_{i=1}^{n}(y_{ij} - \mu_{ij})(y_{ik} - \mu_{ik}).$$

We will use the above equation to simplify the right hand side of the proposition.

$$\text{R.H.S.} = n \cdot \text{trace}\left\{\Sigma^{-1} S\right\}$$

$$= n\sum_{j=1}^{d}\sum_{k=1}^{d}\sigma_{jk}^{-1} s_{jk}$$

$$= n\sum_{j=1}^{d}\sum_{k=1}^{d}\sigma_{jk}^{-1} \sum_{i=1}^{n}(y_{ij} - \mu_{ij})(y_{ik} - \mu_{ik})$$

$$= \sum_{i=1}^{n}\sum_{j=1}^{d}\sum_{k=1}^{d}(y_{ij} - \mu_{ij})\sigma_{jk}^{-1}(y_{ik} - \mu_{ik})$$

$$= \text{L.H.S.}$$

Thus proved.

Proposition D.2. *Let* $Y = [y_1, y_2, \ldots, y_n]^t$ *where* $y_i \in R^d$, *and let* y_i *be samples from the Gaussian distribution*[24] $N(\Phi\Theta, \Sigma)$, *where* Φ *is a constant matrix. Then*

$$-\log p(Y | \Phi\hat{\Theta}, \hat{\Sigma}) = \frac{1}{2} dn(1 + \log 2\pi) + \frac{1}{2} n |\hat{\Sigma}|.$$

Proof. Since y is Gaussian distributed, we have

$$-\log p(Y | \Phi\Theta, \Sigma) = \frac{n}{2}\left(d \log 2\pi + |\Sigma|\right) + \frac{1}{2} \sum_{i=1}^{n} (y_i - \Phi\Theta)^t \Sigma^{-1} (y_i - \Phi\Theta).$$

From proposition D.1 we have

$$-\log p(Y | \Phi\Theta, \Sigma) = \frac{n}{2}\left(d \log 2\pi + \log |\Sigma|\right) + \frac{n}{2} \cdot \text{trace}\left\{\Sigma^{-1} S\right\},$$

where $S = \frac{1}{n} \sum_{i=1}^{n} (y_i - \Phi\Theta)(y_i - \Phi\Theta)^t$. But, $\hat{\Theta}$ and $\hat{\Sigma}$ minimize $-\log p(Y|\Phi\Theta, \Sigma)$. Substituting for $\Phi\hat{\Theta}$ for $\Phi\Theta$ in the computation of S and $\hat{\Sigma}$ for Σ, we have,

$$-\log p(Y | \Phi\hat{\Theta}, \hat{\Sigma}) = \frac{n}{2}(d \log 2\pi + \log |\hat{\Sigma}|) + \frac{n}{2} \cdot \text{trace}\{\hat{\Sigma}^{-1}\hat{\Sigma}\}$$

$$= \frac{n}{2}(d \log 2\pi + \log |\hat{\Sigma}|) + \frac{n}{2} \cdot d$$

$$= \frac{1}{2} dn(1 + \log 2\pi) + \frac{1}{2} n \log |\hat{\Sigma}|$$

Thus proved.

E Number of Terms in a Kth-Degree Polynomial in q Variables

In this appendix we compute an expression for the number of terms in a kth-degree polynomial in q variables. This is necessary in order to compute the surface regression, and the encoding cost of the model. The q in our context is the dimensionality of the pixel coordinates, and not the number of bands d of the image. For example, for CT volume data $q = 3$. As usual, k represents the degree of the polynomial that is fit to the data in each band.

We will use the method of generating functions for the computation (see [Liu77]). Notice that the number of terms with degree j in a kth-degree polynomial ($j \leq k$) in q variables $x_1, \ldots, x_q$, is given by the coefficient of z^j in the expansion[25]

---

[24] The appearance of $\Phi\Theta$ as the mean in the Gaussian distribution, $N(\Phi\Theta, \Sigma)$ might warrant some explanation. This corresponds to our position-dependent non-stationary mean, $\mu(x)$. The $(i, j)^{th}$ element of $\Phi\Theta$ is the μ value for the $(i, j)^{th}$ element of Y.
[25] The generating function in this case is $A(z)$.

$$A(z) = (1 + z + \cdots + z^k)^q.$$

This is because the coefficient of z^j is the number of ways we can make up z^j as a product of q factors taken from the set $\{1, z, \ldots, z^k\}$. Now, putting $A(z)$ in a form where it is possible to isolate the z^j term, we use the partial summation formula to obtain:

$$(1 + z + \cdots + z^k)^q = \left(\frac{1 - z^{k+1}}{1 - z}\right)^q$$

$$= (1 - z)^{-q} \cdot (1 - z^{k+1})^q$$

$$= \left[\sum_{l=0}^{\infty} \binom{q + l - 1}{l}(-1)^l z^l\right] \cdot \left[\sum_{i=0}^{q} \binom{q}{i}(-1)^i (z^{k+1})^i\right].$$

By inspection it can be seen that the number of terms of degree j, $0 \leq j \leq k$ is given by

$$\binom{q + j - 1}{j}.$$

Thus the total number of terms, m, is just the summation of the above quantity from $j = 0$ to $j = k$. That is,

$$m = \sum_{j=0}^{k} \binom{q + j - 1}{j}.$$

Using the closed-form expression for the above summation (see [GR80]), we obtain a general expression of the number of terms m in a kth-degree polynomial in q variables.

$$m = \binom{k + q}{k}. \tag{E.1}$$

In particular, when the image is two dimensional, that is, $q = 2$ and the pixel coordinates can be expressed by the row and column, we have,

$$m = \frac{(k + 1)(k + 2)}{2}. \tag{E.2}$$

Color Plate I

Fig. 1. Image of a beach, water, and foliage

Fig. 2. Result after the region splitting phase

Color Plate II

Fig. 3. Result after the conservative merging phase

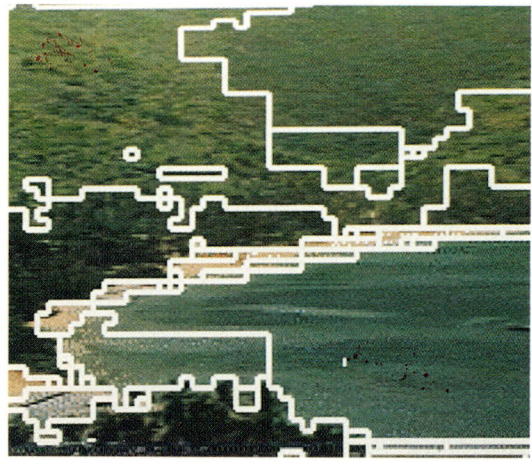

Fig. 4. Result after merge 137 during agglomerative clustering

Color Plate III

Fig. 5. Result after merge 157 during agglomerative clustering

Fig. 6. Final segmentation

Color Plate IV

Fig. 7. Sweater

Fig. 9. Rotated sweater

Color Plate V

Fig. 11. Grand Canyon

Fig. 13. Different view of Grand Canyon

Color Plate VI

Fig. 2. Segmentation result for the electronic circuit image. In this run, the maximum degree of polynomial was zero. That is, a piece-wise constant model was used for each region

Fig. 3. Segmentation result for the electronic circuit image. In this run, the maximum degree of polynomial was one. That is, a piece-wise linear model was used for each region. Notice that some of the regions in the piece-wise constant result have been merged in this result

Color Plate VII

Fig. 4. Segmentation result for the electronic circuit image. In this run, the maximum degree of polynomial was two. That is, a piece-wise quadratic model was used for each region. Some of the regions in the piece-wise linear result have been merged in this result

Fig. 6. Segmentation result for the house image. In this run, the maximum degree of polynomial was zero. That is, a piece-wise constant model was used for each region

Color Plate VIII

Fig. 7. Segmentation result for the house image. In this run, the maximum degree of polynomial was one. That is, a piece-wise linear model was used for each region. Notice that some of the regions in piece-wise constant result been merged in this result

A Vision System for Estimating People Flow

P. Nesi and A. Del Bimbo

Abstract. Counting the number of people crossing a public area can be very useful for properly scheduling the frequency of a service. Mechanical and photosensitive systems, such as rotating tripod gates, short iron doors, weight-sensitive boards, and photoelectric cells, have often been used for such estimates. Since these methods are not efficient in critical conditions, vision-based approaches have been provided. Many of them identify moving objects through a segmentation process. Once the objects are identified, they are tracked in the sequence of images and counted. These approaches have some drawbacks when they are used in critical conditions such as for counting the people getting on and off a public bus. In this paper, a new technique for counting passing people which is based on motion estimation and spatio-temporal interpretation of the estimated motion is proposed, with its implementation on prototype DSP-based architecture.

1 Introduction

Estimating the number of people getting on and off a given place is of interest in many contexts, among these: public services as buses and metros, to properly scheduling the frequence of service; museums, to limit the number of people in certain areas; shops and supermarkets, to control the consumers' interest with respect to certain products, etc.

Technical solutions have often used mechanical systems, such as rotating tripod gates, and short iron doors. These methods are not recommended when the flow of people is high, as usually occurs at the exit of public places or when people try to catch a bus, because such methods could create a slowing down in the flow, and this in turn could cause accidents. Alternative solutions are based on photo-electric cells or weight-sensitive boards placed on the ground, but these solutions are not robust enough when the people flow is not constant in direction and intensity – e.g., when people arrive under the sensor, stay without motion for some time instants, and then move in the same or opposite direction afterward.

A different approach for counting moving people for solving the above-mentioned problems is the use of a microprocessor-based system connected to a camera. Several experiences have been reported in literature, in which vision systems for counting moving objects are used. Many of these identify moving objects through a segmentation process. Once the objects are identified, they are tracked in the sequence of images, and counted according to their behavior.

The segmentation process may be based on either (i) traditional algorithms for image segmentation, or (ii) the estimation of an approximated projection on the image plane of 3D object motion (usually called "image flow" or "optical flow") [1], [2]).

The main drawback to the first approach is its high computational complexity due to the fact that edges must be extracted [3]. Since, the edges which belong to non-moving objects are also detected, it is even more difficult to select the moving objects. Several different techniques using the second approach have been proposed: cumulative differences among frames have been used in [4], and [5] to extract the moving objects' shape; the clustering of image brightness features having the same optical flow field has been proposed in [6], [7]. Bayesian and entropy formulations for moving object segmentation starting from the image sequences [8], or from the motion fields [2], have also been reported in literature.

Most of these motion-based segmentation approaches are not completely satisfactory. Typically, when different objects having the same velocity are very close or connected to each other, they are recognized as a single object. In addition, these are strongly sensitive to noise.

As to tracking segmented objects, one problem is related to the fact that shapes representing bodies of moving people cannot be regarded as rigid objects, and therefore object tracking cannot be simply based on shape matching.

As an alternative approach, spatio-temporal reasoning has often been applied to analyse pedestrian and vehicle flows. Several researchers have studied the spatio-temporal surfaces of selected objects under motion [9], [10], [11]; works based on the Epipolar Plane Image (EPI) [12], [13], [14], [15], [16]; have been also presented.

Limitations on the use of the above techniques partially depend on the constraining assumptions that are to be made. Most of the techniques require that the moving objects be completely visible (i.e., their size is much smaller than the view area of the acquisition system), and that the moving objects never stop (in order to maintain the conditions for motion-based tracking). In an uncontrolled outdoor environment both these two assumptions are usually false. A further limitation, regarding most of the above-mentioned approaches is that they are computationally too complex to be implemented in a low-cost automatic counting system.

In this paper, we present the principles and experimental proofs of a system for counting moving people in order to estimate input/output flow on city buses. It is a substantial improvement on the prototypical version described in [17]. The system proposed is based on optical flow field estimation [1], [2], and follows a new method for spatio-temporal analysis of optical flow fields, so that the previously presented problems concerning shape visibility, and behavior of people flow are avoided. The system was developed in a joint project involving industries in the Florence area and was partially sponsored by CESVIT (Agency for Technology Development of Industry in the Florence Area). A prototype of a DSP-based embedded system was developed.

The paper is organized as follows. In Sect. 2, the system's working conditions and general architecture are discussed. In Sect. 3, the fundamentals of optical flow estimation with some techniques for motion estimation are briefly reviewed. In the same section the algorithm for motion estimation employed in our system is described, and some experimental results are given. In Sect. 4, the features of spatio-temporal domain are explained, and the algorithm for counting moving people who pass under the image acquisition system is proposed. In Sect. 5, a brief description of system implementation is given. Conclusions are drawn in Sect. 6.

2 System Architecture and Working Environment

In this section, the environmental conditions necessary to proper functioning of the system will be discussed. Moreover, a brief overview of the system architecture will be given.

2.1 System Requirements

A vision system for counting people getting on/off a bus must satisfy the following requirements:

1. Low-cost. This guarantees wide applicability. This requirement is mainly satisfied by limiting the computational complexity of the algorithm used for counting people in real-time;
2. Robustness with respect to critical conditions in the acquisition system, such as noise in the image acquisition system, and out-of-focus moving regions;
3. Robustness with respect to the optical flow estimation problems discussed in Sect. 3;
4. Robustness with respect to changes in environmental conditions (i.e., illumination, weather, etc.). The system must work both under sunlight and the artificial light generated inside the bus after sunset;
5. Robustness with respect to the people size, because the moving people are not completely included in the image acquisition view area and cannot be considered as rigid objects;
6. Robustness with respect to people's behavior.

2.2 System Operation

In our approach requirements expressed in Sect. 2.1 are coped through motion estimation with an optical flow technique and spatio-temporal domain analysis. In Fig. 1, the general schema of the counting process is reported.

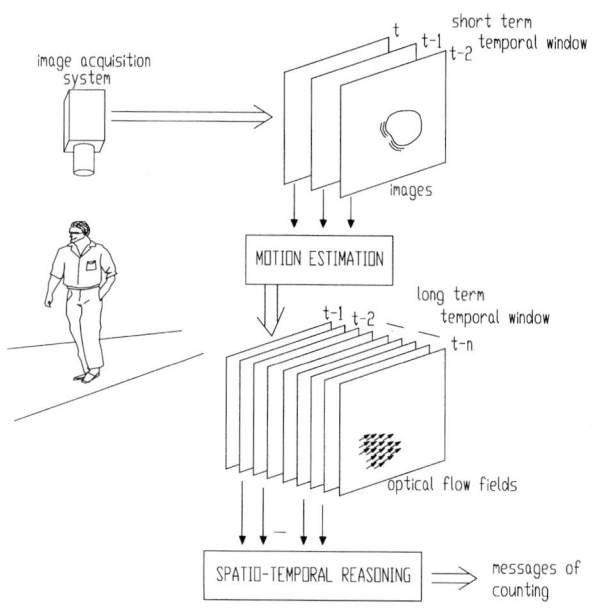

Fig. 1. The overall process

Optical flow is obtained by analysing the image sequence on a short-term temporal window. It provides support for the identification of image features velocity. The collection of optical flow fields on a long-term temporal window is considered to be the spatio-temporal description of object behavior. Spatio-temporal domain analysis supports the counting of people getting on/off the bus through tracking of image features traces. Since this information is too noisy to be automatically interpreted for counting moving objects, the spatio-temporal domain is smoothed by means of a regularization-based approach for rejecting noise [18]. Tracking of simple features on a discrete version of the smoothed spatio-temporal is performed in order to understand if the moving objects observed are getting on/off the bus or are standing still under the image acquisition view area.

The optical flow estimation technique is expounded in Sect. 3. Spatio-temporal domain analysis is reported in Sect. 4.

2.3 Working Environment

The working environment is shown in Fig. 2. In order to count people getting on and off a bus, two image acquisition systems (CCD-based cameras) are placed on the bus's ceiling, just over the stairs, one for each entrance lane divided by an iron barrier.

It is reasonably assumed that only one person at a time can go through each entrance lane, but several people can be present at the same time in the view area more or less close to each other (this is what usually occurs in crowding condi-

Fig. 2. A two lane bus door and the view areas

tions). These people can be doing different things (such as getting on or getting off the bus from the same door), either *without stopping in the view area* or *stopping in the view area (and perhaps swinging), and moving again to get on or off the bus*. Since image acquisition systems are very close to the heads of moving people, the image acquisition view area cannot include the full shape of the moving objects.

The sequence in Fig. 3 shows a person which is getting onto a bus. The stair steps and the metallic barrier dividing the door into two lanes can be noted. The shapes of the passing people are not completely focused and are only partially included in the image frames; their form also changes in the sequence of frames.

3 Optical Flow Estimation

3.1 Fundamentals of Optical Flow

Optical flow techniques provide a solution for the motion estimation problem starting from the observation of brightness changes in the image plane [1], [19], [20], [21], [22], [23], [24], [2], [25].

The optical flow is the field of the image brightness feature velocities, and therefore, differs from the perspective projection of 3D motion on the image plane (i.e., the velocity field) [26], [22], [25]. However, the estimation of an approximate velocity field, such as optical flow, can be very useful for many applications not requiring precision as in our case.

Most of the techniques described in literature for estimating optical flow fields use the so-called Optical Flow Constraint (OFC) equation, which derives from the observation that the changes in image brightness $E(x(t), y(t), t)$ of each point

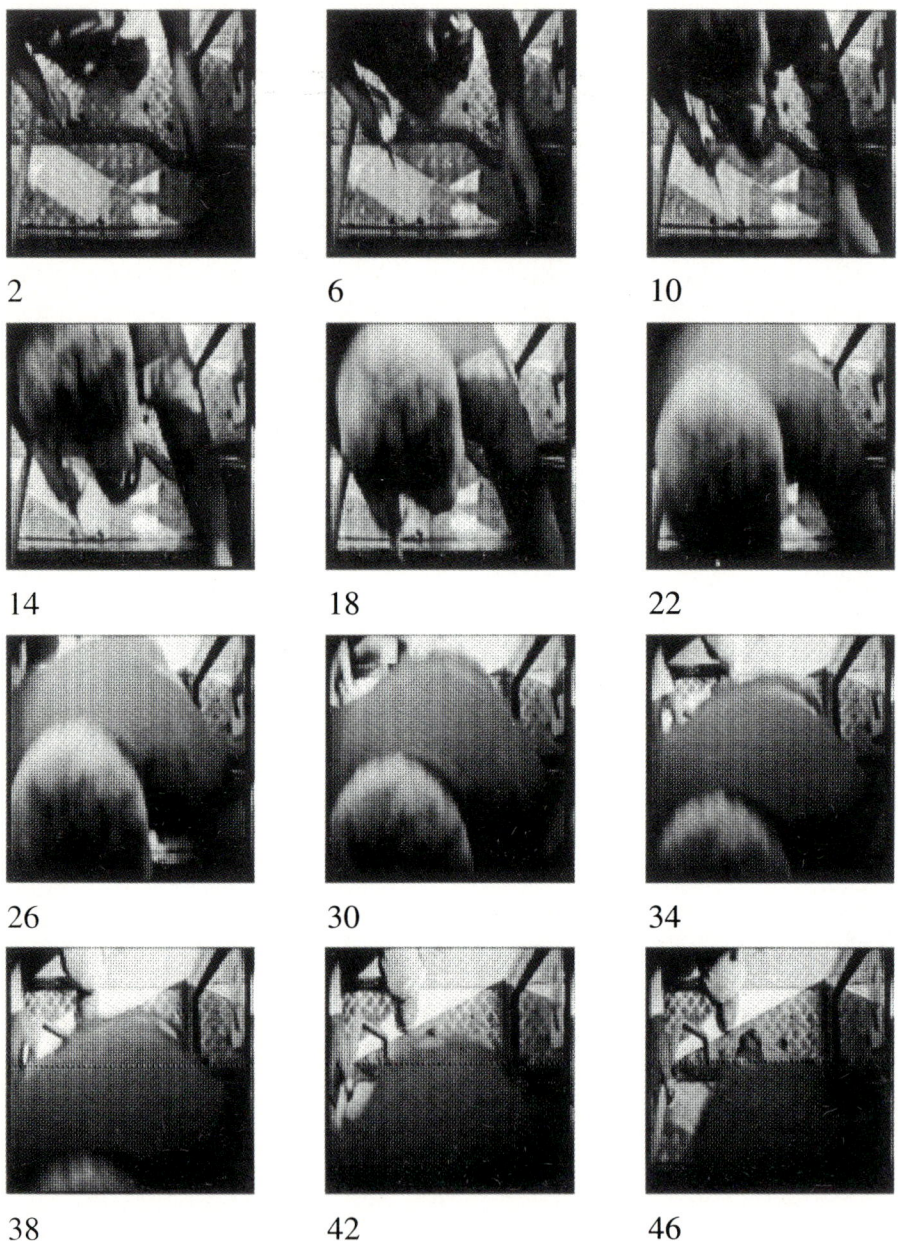

Fig. 3. Typical sequence of images where people are getting on a bus (frames: 2, 6, 10, 14, 18, 22, 26, 30, 34, 38, 42, 46) (image resolution: 128 × 128 pixels)

in the image are supposed to be stationary with respect to the time variable (i.e., $dE/dt = 0$):

$$E_x u + E_y v + E_t = 0, \qquad (1)$$

in which the abbreviation for partial derivatives of image brightness had been introduced, and u, v correspond to dx/dt, dy/dt, and represent the components of the local velocity vector $\mathbf{V}$ along the x and y directions on the image plane, respectively.

In the literature, two main approaches for optical flow estimation are identified: the *regularization-* and the *multiconstraint-based* approaches.

The *regularization-based* approaches consider optical flow estimation as an ill-posed problem. Solutions are obtained by minimizing a functional where a smoothness constraint is appropriately weighted to regularize the solution. The functional is minimized by using calculus of variations, and leads to define iterative solutions [1], [19], [27], [28].

The *multiconstraint-based* approaches for estimating optical flow fields are based on the fact that it is usually possible to define more than one constraint equation [29], [30]. They can be used to define an over-determined system of equations with u and v as unknowns evaluated at the same point in the image [20], [21], [23], [24], or considering that all the constraint equations which can be defined in the neighborhood around the estimation point represent the same optical flow field [31], [32], [2], [33]. The latter approach is commonly referred to as a "multipoint" approach. The overdetermined system of equations can be solved by using the least-square technique or by other means [18], [2], [34].

In general, optical flow estimations present two main problems.

The first is the presence of discontinuities in the optical flow field: these are due to image brightness discontinuities which are originated by the presence noise, too crisp patterns on the moving object surfaces, occlusions between moving objects, and object velocities which are too fast for the measuring system. Generally speaking, the presence of discontinuities can be overcome (or at least attenuated) by filtering the image with a 2D or 3D Gaussian smoothing operator at the expense of computational effort [35].

The second problem is the so-called "problem of aperture," found in the human vision, too. It derives from the impossibility to recover the direction of motion univocally if the object is observed through an aperture which is smaller than the object size. In this context, the references of the object under observation (such as textures – e.g., patterns) are not enough to make perception of the transversal component of the object motion, and only the component of apparent velocity which is parallel to ∇E can be detected [36], [37].

3.2 Estimation Technique

In our counting system we use a multipoint-based technique for optical flow estimation. Robustness with respect to noise and behavior coherent with the human vision in the presence of aperture conditions have been discussed by the authors in [38], [37], and [33].

The *multipoint* approach for optical flow estimation used in the system is based on the fact that, considering that the optical flow changes follow a law which is approximatively linear, a smoothed solution for optical flow estimation can be obtained from a linear approximation of the OFC equation in the neighborhood of the point under consideration [31], [32], [2] (this assumption is valid only if the optical flow field under observation is smooth). Consequently, a set of similar constraints in the neighborhood of a pixel yields an over-determined system of equations.

A multipoint solution based on the OFC equation (1) is obtained in the discrete domain at the finite differences. Thus, for the estimation of velocity components for the pixel under consideration, an over-determined system of $N \times N$ constraint equations in 2 unknowns, is defined,

$$E_{t(i,j,t)} + E_{x(i,j,t)}u + E_{y(i,j,t)}v = 0,$$

for all (i, j) in an $N \times N$ neighborhood of the estimation point; where N is the dimension of the image segment side of the neighboring pixels, and $N \geq 2$.

In this technique, a large value of N will lead to smooth optical flow estimations, and loss in resolution in the estimation of velocity vectors.

The over-determined system of equations is solved by using a least-squares technique. In particular, after the estimation of image brightness derivatives in each pixel an over-determined system of $N \times N$ OFC equations in 2 unknowns is defined:

$$A\mathbf{V} + K = 0,$$

where $\mathbf{V}$ is the optical flow vector with components u, v; $A \in R_{N^2 \times 2}$ matrix of coefficients, with $a_{r,1} = E_{xr}$ and $a_{r,2} = E_{yr}$; and $K \in R_{N^2}$ vector with known terms $k_r = E_{tr}$ for $r = 1, \ldots, N^2$.

The solution of the over-determined system of equations by means of the least-squares technique can be obtained by using the pseudo-inverse technique, which transforms the above system of equations into a determined system of equations:

$$\hat{A}\mathbf{V} + \hat{K} = 0, \tag{2}$$

where $\hat{A} = A^T A$, and $\hat{K} = A^T K$ (i.e., A^T is the transpose of A). This system of equations can be solved by using traditional techniques such as LU decomposition, Gauss Jordan, etc. In our case the system (2) is composed of 2 equations in 2 unknowns, and the direct solution is used.

Among the N^2 OFC equations, those which have the E_t under a chosen threshold are ignored and considered as insignificant constraints. Moreover, the constraint equations which have too large values for E_x and E_y are also neglected, hypothesising that there is a high probability that such large values are originated by noise.

3.2.1 Computational Complexity

The explicit complexity of the solution proposed for estimating an optical flow field on an $M \times M$ image on a sequential machine is:

$$C() = 3M^2 + 8N^2 \left[\frac{M-d}{G}\right]^2 + 8\left[\frac{M-d}{G}\right]^2, \qquad (3)$$

where $d = 2\left(1 + \frac{N-1}{2}\right)$ is due to the image boundaries, and the first term is due to the estimation of the partial derivatives of image brightness, which are obtained by using central differences.

The second additive term of (3) is due to the least-squares technique for calculating $\hat{a}_{i,j}$ and $\hat{k}_i$ (for $i = 1, 2$, and $j = 1, 2$), where G is the distance between two spatially consecutive estimation points, and $[x]$ is the greatest integer number lower than x; and the third term is determined by the method for solving the final system of equations (2). By improving the G value, less smooth optical flow fields are obtained.

As can be seen from (3), the asymptotical complexity of the solution proposed is:

$$O\left(\frac{M^2 N^2}{G^2}\right).$$

The computational cost in terms of floating point operations is reported in the following table. This cost is useful in order to evaluate the computational power required for performing optical flow estimation with the proposed solution. In Table 1 the number of floating point operations (expressed in millions, MFLOP), with $G = 1$, and $N = 5$ as a function of the image dimension M, is reported. In this case, $(M - 6)^2$ velocity vectors are estimated at each time interval. It has been used $G = 1$, $N = 5$ since these values represent a good compromise between the estimation quality, noise robustness and the computational cost. For this reason, these values have been used in our experiments.

Table 2 shows the number of MFLOP per second (MFLOPS) needed to estimate optical flow fields in real-time – i.e., at video-rate frequency, 25 optical flow estimations per second – as a function of the dimension of the image, M.

Figures in Table 2, show that it is possible to implement both the algorithm proposed by using low-cost processors with a floating point unit such as Analog Device ADSP 21020, Motorola 96000, Intel i860, etc., provided that the image size

Table 1. Millions of floating point operations (MFLOP), with $G = 1$, $N = 5$, for different image dimensions

M	512	256	128	64	32	16	8
OFC-based	70	17.5	4.3	1.1	0.27	0.068	0.017

Table 2. Millions of floating poihnt operations for second (MFLOPS), with $G=1$, $N=5$, for different image size

M	512	256	128	64	32	16	8
OFC-based	1750	437	107	27.5	6.7	1.7	0.42

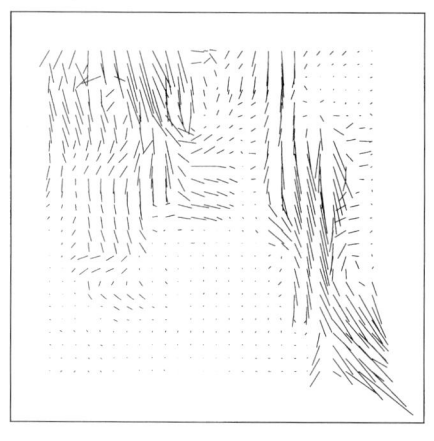 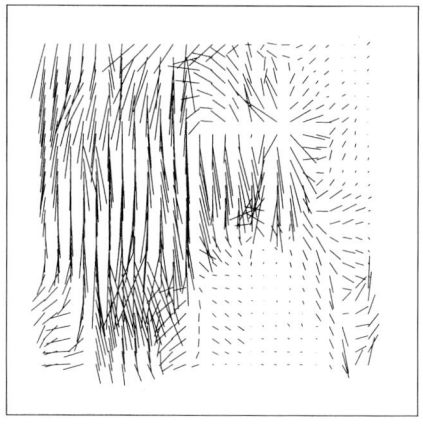

6 18

Fig. 4. Optical flow fields estimated from the sequence of images presented in Fig. 2 by using the proposed solution with $G=1$ and $N=5$ (frames: 6 and 18 with resolution of 32×32)

is not too large. The number of MFLOPS should be divided by at least G^2 if the estimation of velocity vectors is required only every G pixels, in both x and y direction.

3.2.2 Results of Optical Flow Estimation

In order to test the robustness of the optical flow estimation technique used, several experiments were performed. Particular attention was given to testing algorithm responses with respect to changes in illumination and weather, deformations due to non-rigidity of moving objects, and critical effects due to the out-of-focus and the incomplete vision of the moving objects' shape in the view area.

Figure 4 illustrates optical flow fields estimated by using the method proposed on the sequence reported in Fig. 3.

As can be seen, the shape of the moving person is not immediately detectable from the optical flow fields. This is mainly due to the fact that the body of the person is *non-completely focused and included* in the view area of the image acquisition system. In addition, the moving object is *non-rigid* and its parts are moving at *different velocities* in intensity and direction. In such conditions, the same moving object has regions of its shape characterized by contrasting velocities which change from one image to the successive. Therefore, segmentation process based on the optical flow fields leads to estimate moving object shapes in one image which are strongly different with respect to those obtained in the successive one, and is not suitable to be used as a basis to track the moving objects.

In addition, optical flow estimation cannot solve the problems related to all moving objects' behaviors, as required by a system that performs people counting. These problems can be solved only by long-term analysis which interprets optical flow fields in time. People's flow should be interpreted as flow of elementary moving particles (each of which has its own optical flow vector) and not as sequence of single passages of large objects. Then, the number of passing people should be estimated by knowing the geometry of the acquisition system (i.e., distance from moving objects, etc., as in our case) and the dimensions (in terms of projected shape) of moving people. The sum of the flow of particles divided by the median flow due to a person should give the number of people passed through the door. This subject is addressed in detail in the next Section.

4 Interpreting Optical Flow Fields in Time

Let $\mathbf{V}_{(i,j,t)}$ with components $u_{(i,j,t)}$, and $v_{(i,j,t)}$ be the velocity in an image point with coordinates i, j, at the time t. In the working environment taken into consideration, the flow of the people is constrained by metallic barriers along the direction of the y-axis of the image plane (see Sect. 2), and therefore, the motion of interest is only described by the component $v_{(i,j,t)}$ of optical flow.

The problem of counting moving objects which only move along a direction parallel to the y-axis has been solved by estimating the flow of the image brightness features in time through a transversal section S on the image plane, usually called slit [16], [39] (this could be performed by using a simple linear CCD placed along section S). By collecting these sections in time, an EPI is obtained [14], [15], [16]. Unfortunately, this type of spatio-temporal image is not suitable for solving the above-mentioned problems. In fact, in such images it is not possible to distinguish between *two consecutive and fast moving objects which cross the view area without stopping* from a *single object which enters in the view area, stops its motion and then restarts*, which both are common situations when entering a bus. It is evident that this approach should lead to incorrect results in counting people.

To solve this problem, a different form of spatio-temporal reasoning is proposed, which makes it is possible to measure feature flow and analyze the spatio-temporal behavior of moving objects.

4.1 Spatio-Temporal Feature Flow Domain

The feature flow at time t through a section S, which is parallel to the x-axis, can be estimated by:

$$F_{(S,t)} = \int_S \mathbf{V}(t) \cdot \hat{\mathbf{y}}\, dx \tag{4}$$

where $\hat{y}$ is the unit vector of the y-axis. In the discrete field, a measure of features' flow can be obtained by dividing the optical flow field into s horizontal segments (rows along the y-axis, $s = [(M-d)/G]$, see Fig. 5), and by collecting one value for each segment:

$$f_{(j,t)} = \sum_{i=1}^{h} v_{(i,j,t)}, \quad \text{for} \quad j=1,\ldots,s,$$

where h is the number of optical flow vectors present in each row of the full optical flow field ($h = [(M-d)/G] = 26$ in the optical flow fields presented in Fig. 4). This approximation is obtained when the dimension of each segment along the section S is taken to be unitary, while smoother feature flows can be computed by considering multiple rows for each estimation of $f_{(j,t)}$.

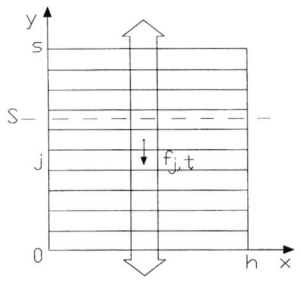

Fig. 5. Optical flow field segments in the image plane at time t

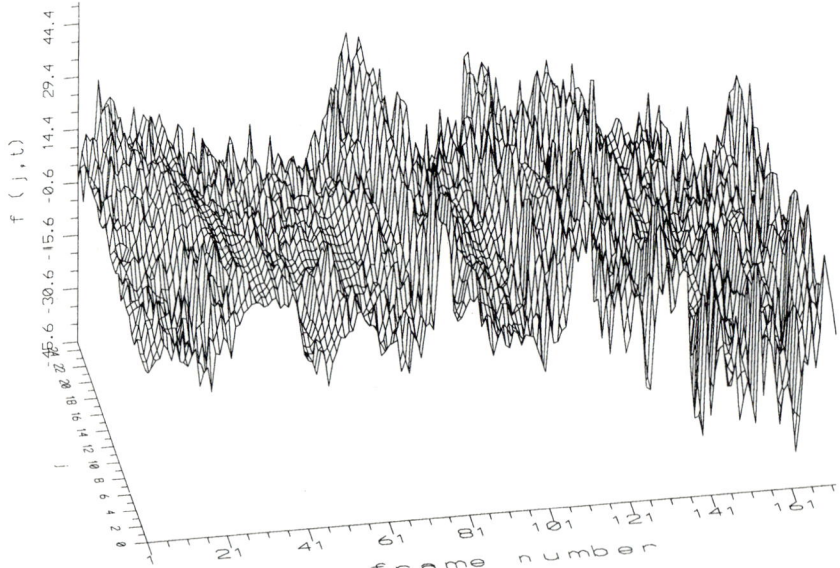

Fig. 6. The spatio-temporal behavior of $f_{(j,t)}$

In Fig. 6, the spatio-temporal behavior of $f_{(j,t)}$ for the test sequence of Fig. 3 is reported. Positive hills correspond to people who are getting onto a bus (e.g., around frame 20), while negative hills correspond to people who are getting off a bus (e.g., aroung frame 150). In Fig. 6, they can be recognized 4 people who get into a bus (around the 20th, 71st, 110th, and the 120th frame, the last two people are very close connected to each other (see Fig. 7)), and 3 people who are quickly getting off (around the 141th, 150st, and the 160th frame).

Simply counting peaks in a transversal slice $f_{(j,t)}$ (e.g., Fig. 8 shows a transversal slice of the surface of Fig. 6) of $f_{(j,t)}$ that are higher than a predefined threshold leads to incorrect results when people stop in the view area, because each restart produces a new peak. To avoid this problem, and understand what people are really doing when they cross the view area, it is necessary to analyse a large spatio-

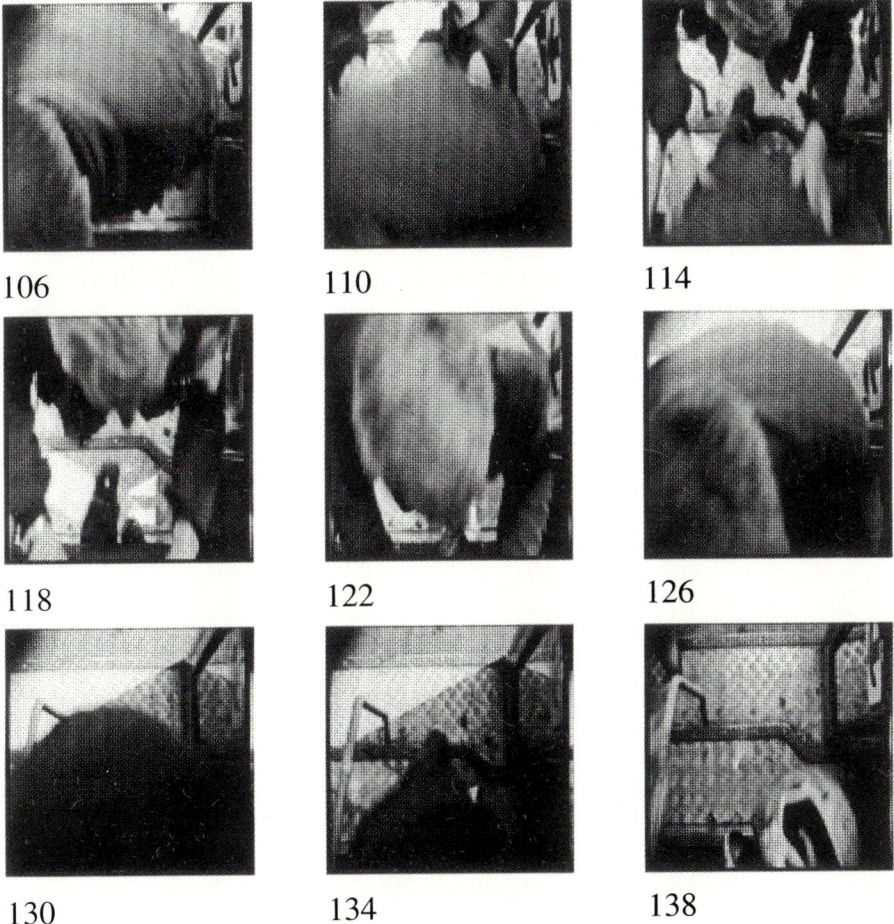

Fig. 7. Sequence in which two close people are getting on a bus (frames: 106, 110, 114, 118, 122, 126, 130, 134, 138) (image resolution: 128 × 128)

temporal window of a feature flow surface. A threshold for identifying the most prominent feature flow regions can also be defined on this surface. Figure 9 illustrates the map representing $\mathcal{F}_{(j,t)}$ obtained from surface $f_{(j,t)}$ of Fig. 6 according to:

$$\mathcal{F}_{(j,t)} = \begin{cases} +1 & \text{if } f_{(j,t)} > D_{in} \quad \text{"entering"} \\ -1 & \text{if } f_{(j,t)} < D_{out} \quad \text{"exiting"} \\ 0 & \text{otherwise} \quad \text{"motionless"}; \end{cases}$$

two different thresholds D_{in} and D_{out} were imposed for the feature flow values generated by inputs and outputs, respectively. This map was obtained by coloring the entering flow of gray, the absence of flow black, and the exiting flow white. The moving objects are identified by transversal segments (referred to as *traces* in the rest of the paper) connecting the upper and lower map limits.

Nevertheless, even when the thresholds are imposed carefully, the maps obtained are affected by too much noise to allow automatic interpretation (see Fig. 9). Hence, a smoothing action must be performed on feature flow $f_{(j,t)}$ before its transformation into the map, $\mathcal{F}_{(j,t)}$. Then, the smoothed map obtained can be interpreted in order to count the passing people.

Please note, that imposing a threshold on the feature flow $f_{(j,t)}$ is very different from imposing a threshold on the optical flow field itself. In the latter case, threshold imposition leads to neglecting objects which are moving slower than a given value (this condition in not acceptable for the application proposed, because people usually get on a bus very slowly). On the contrary, threshold imposition on the feature flow $f_{(j,t)}$, leads to neglecting objects which generate a feature flow lower than a given value. This limitation is not restrictive because people's dimensions

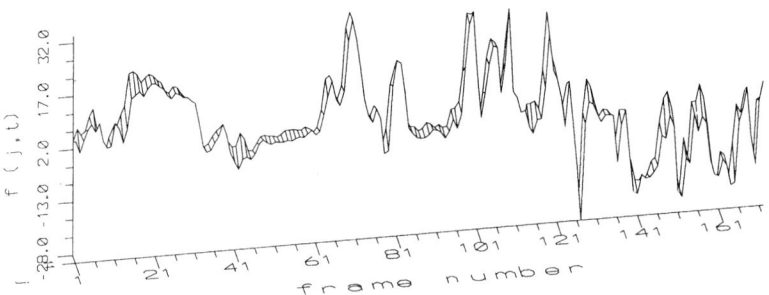

Fig. 8. Temporal behavior of $f_{(j,t)}$, for $j = 12$, of Fig. 6

Fig. 9. Map $\mathcal{F}_{(j,t)}$ of feature flow obtained with $D_{in} = 10$ and $D_{out} = -10$ from $f_{(j,t)}$, of Fig. 6

do not change significantly, therefore only the presence of very small objects (even if they are moving very quickly) is neglected.

We observed in our experiments that a suitable value for such thresholds is about 1/3 of h; with these values, people moving very slowly are detected even when they are very small. Lower values make noise too prominent, while high threshold values must not be set because they lead to losing people's movements, such as when a passing person swings under the view area. Since people usually get off a bus faster than they get onto it, it is appropriate to impose different values on threshold D_{in} and D_{out} in order to detect the entering and the exiting conditions.

In Fig. 10 an ideal noise-free map $\mathcal{F}_{(j,t)}$ is illustrated. It has been obtained by using a synthetic image sequence in which a rigid object crosses the view area. It contains several traces corresponding to typical, object behaviors. The first trace refers to an object entering in the view area and standing still before going out of it later. The second trace refers to a moving object which stops during the crossing and then moves again in the same direction. The last trace is very fragmentary, and corresponds to a crossing object which makes various stops and direction changes (swinging) under the view area.

In order to count people reliably we must be able to manage common ambiguous situations such as those in which there are two closely connected objects crossing the view area (such as around the 115th frame in Fig. 7). To this end, it could be useful to have a measure of the moving object velocity and dimension to find out when the trace under observation is due to a slow single object or to two objects moving at normal velocity.

Object velocity can also be determined from a feature flow map. Figure 11 illustrates a map in which an object, having constant dimensions, crosses the view area when getting off the bus, at different velocities. The slope of a trace corresponds to the object's velocity. The first trace represents an object which crosses the view area at a velocity equal to 1 pixel/frame, in the second trace the object goes at 2 pixel/frame, and, in the third it goes at 3 pixel/frame. Thus, considering the acquisition system geometry is possible to recover the true moving object velocity from a feature flow map.

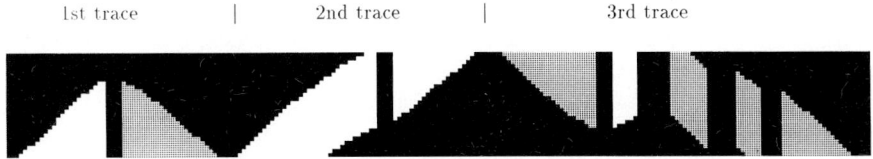

Fig. 10. Typical behaviors in the spatio-temporal feature flow domain

Fig. 11. Traces of moving objects in the spatio-temporal feature flow domain

If the moving objects have a constant area size, l (i.e., if we assume that do not change their dimension with time), integrating $F_{(S,t)}$ on a generic section S the area dimension of the moving object going through the section S on the image plane is obtained. In the discrete domain the integration is $m_{(j,T)} = \Sigma_{t=t_0}^{T} f_{(j,t)}$ and thus $m_{(j,T)}/l$ could be interpreted as the number of objects getting on, minus the number of objects getting off during the time interval $T - t_0$.

This technique cannot be used in our working environment, because the objects to be counted do not have a constant dimension. Moreover, due to the approximations adopted to estimate the first-order partial derivative of the image brightness, with gradient-based techniques produce reliable estimations of optical flow only when object displacements between two consecutive frames are not wider than 1 pixel. Therefore, to have a reliable detection of a moving object crossing the view area, the corresponding trace in the feature flow domain must be "tracked" in time.

In the following section the techniques used for smoothing the feature flow domain and tracking traces with continuous labeling are expounded in detail.

4.2 Smoothing the Feature Flow Domain

The presence of noise on a map can be reduced by using a traditional low-pass filter (e.g., average, median, etc.) directly on the $F_{(S,t)}$, or by using stochastic relaxation with clips [40], [2], [7] on $\mathcal{F}_{(S,t)}$. The first method does not permit an adequate control of smoothing in different ways along the y- and t-axes of map, without a strong reduction of the signal level; the latter method could solve these problems but is computationally heavy.

We propose a deterministic relaxation as a solution for these problems, that is a regularization-based approach: the problem is posed as the minimization of the functional:

$$\int\int (F-W)^2 + \alpha^2 (W_y)^2 + \beta^2 (W_t)^2 \, dy \, dt, \tag{5}$$

where $F = F_{(S,t)}$ is the feature flow; $W = W_{(S,t)}$ is the smoothed feature flow function; $(W_y)^2$, $(W_t)^2$ are the smoothness constraints on $W_{(S,t)}$; α, β are the weighting factors which are used to handle the smoothing at different intensities along y- and t-axes.

The functional (5) is minimized by using the calculus of variations [41]; this leads to the partial derivative equation:

$$F - W + \alpha^2 W_{yy} + \beta^2 W_{tt} = 0,$$

which can be solved by using natural boundary conditions. By discretizing the above equation, by means of the finite difference method we obtain:

$$W_{(j,t)y} = W_{(j+1/2,t)} - W_{(j-1/2,t)},$$
$$W_{(j,t)yy} = W_{(j+1,t)} - 2W_{(j,t)} + W_{(j-1,t)}.$$

A Vision System for Estimating People Flow

Hence, the iterative solution is obtained:

$$W_{(j,t)}^{n+1} = \frac{f_{(j,t)}^n + \alpha^2 (W_{(j+1,t)}^n + W_{(j-1,t)}^n) + \beta^2 (W_{(j,t+1)}^n + W_{(j,t-1)}^n)}{2\alpha^2 + 2\beta^2 + 1}, \qquad (6)$$

in which the same finite difference technique is also used along the t axis. In the estimation, the discrete version of $F_{(s,t)}$, that is $f_{(j,t)}$, is considered, and $f_{(j,t)}^n = W_{(j,t)}^n$. This smoothing equation is used for regularizing the function $f_{(j,t)}$. The regularization process is performed on a running window of a map having a $\Delta T \times s$ dimension during its production in time as depicted in Fig. 12. Since the regularization process is performed on the running window, the number of iterations performed on a given neighborhood is equal to $I\Delta T$, where I is the number of iterations preformed at each time instant in the window ΔT in time, by using (6).

Figure 13 shows the surface $W_{(j,t)}$, obtained by smoothing function $f_{(j,t)}$, of Fig. 6. After smoothing, thresholding is performed on the $W_{(j,t)}$ domain to obtain a discrete map $\mathscr{W}_{(j,t)}$ preserving the main moving objects' traces (see Fig. 14):

$$\mathscr{W}_{(j,t)} = \begin{cases} +1 & \text{if } W_{(j,t)} > D_{in} \\ -1 & \text{if } W_{(j,t)} < D_{out} \\ 0 & \text{otherwise} \end{cases}$$

As can be noted comparing the map of Fig. 14 with that of Fig. 9, the weighting factors α and β are used to obtain a propagation effect with good regularization along the j-axis and a slight regularization along the t-axis. In this way, each trace crossing the view area is evidenced. By our experiments we have been observed that a good effect of smoothing rejecting noise without to loss too much in resolution is to adopt $I = 2$, $\Delta T = 4$, $\beta = 0.2$ and $\alpha = 2$.

In the regularized map of Fig. 14 we can count four objects getting on the bus, at different velocities, and three objects getting off the bus at a higher velocity (as usually happen when people leave the bus).

After having obtained $\mathscr{W}_{(j,t)}$ the detection and tracking of traces on the map make it possible to count the moving people. Trace tracking is based on continuous labeling as shown in the next subsection.

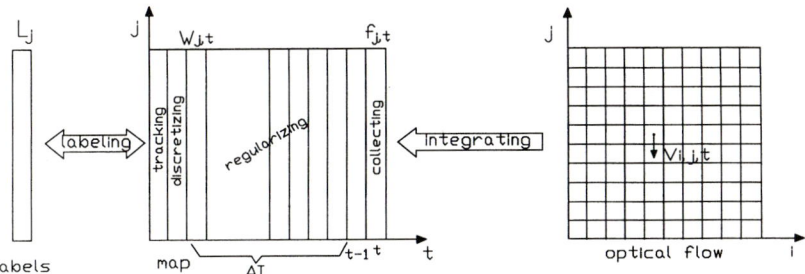

Fig. 12. The collecting, smoothing and interpretation processes in time

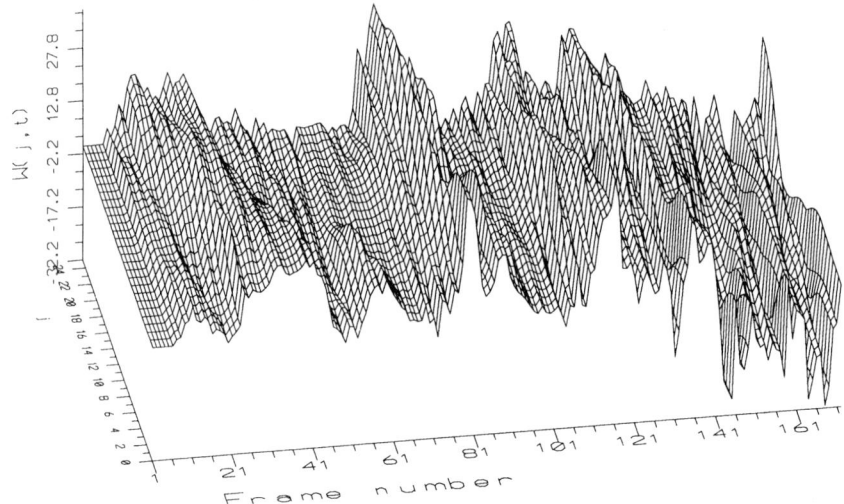

Fig. 13. Regularized spatio-temporal behavior $W_{(j,t)}$, of feature flow $f_{(j,t)}$, obtained with $\alpha = 2$, $\beta = 0.2$, $I = 2$, and $\Delta T = 4$

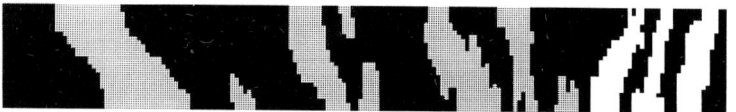

Fig. 14. Map $\mathcal{W}_{(j,t)}$ of feature flow obtained with $D_{in} = 10$ and $D_{out} = -10$ from $W_{(j,t)}$, of Fig. 13

4.3 Tracking with Continuous Labeling

The tracking of traces in the map is performed by means of the technique of continuous labeling. Figure 15a–c illustrates the typical result of the continuous labelling technique applied to a fragmented map with $s = 9$.

Each label is activated when a new arrival from the lower or upper limits appears in the map. The labeling process (see Fig. 15b) consists in comparing an old labelled *slice* of the map, $L_{(j)}$, with the feature flow map, $\mathcal{W}_{(j,t)}$, at time $t - \Delta T - 3$ at each time instant (see Fig. 12). With this mechanism a trace is followed also when the object stay motionless (see label 1 in the history of the labelled *slices* Fig. 15c), because positions are stored in the slice of labels, $L_{(j)}$. The same label, that has been used to track a crossing object, can be used again later.

Simple rules based on label movements in $L_{(j)}$, are applied for counting the passing people, In other words the passage of a person results in the labelled space as a simple segment which connects the lower with the upper limits of the map, even if the trace was very fragmented.

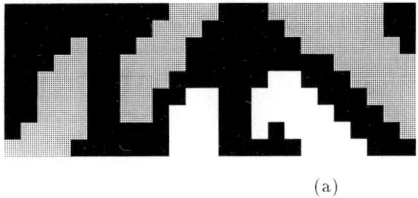

(a)

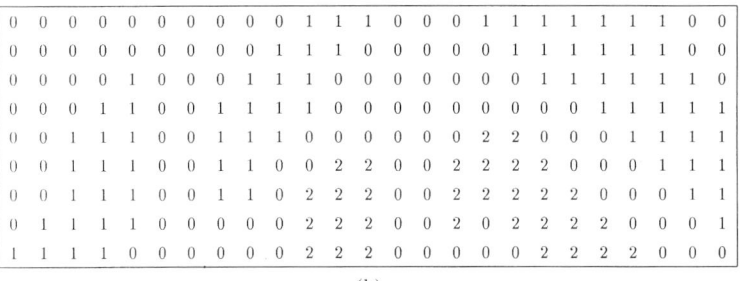

(b)

(c)

Fig. 15. Typical history of the continuous labelling process: **a** several instants of a fragmented map $\mathcal{W}_{(j,t-\Delta T-3)}$; **b** labels associated with the map; **c** history values for the slice of labels, $L_{(j)}$, corresponding to the time instants of **b**

4.4 Computational Complexity

The computational cost of interpreting the optical flow fields at each time instant (considering $s = h = [(M - d)/G]$), is given by the summation of distinct sequential costs related to:

- estimating of the feature flow map, $f_{(j,t)}$, for $j = 1, \ldots, s$: $O([(M - d)/G]^2)$;
- spatio-temporal smoothing of $f_{(j,t)}$, to obtain $W_{(j,t)}$, for $j = 1, \ldots, s$; this process consists in I iterations on a temporal window of ΔT instants: $O(I\Delta T[(M - d)/G])$;
- thresholding of $W_{(j,t)}$, in order to obtain $\mathcal{W}_{(j,t)}$, for $j = 1, \ldots, s$: $O([(M - d)/G])$;
- continuous labelling, which consists in comparing the position of the labels in $L_{(j)}$ with $\mathcal{W}_{(j,t-\Delta T-3)}$, for $j = 1, \ldots, s$: $O([M - d)/G])$.

Table 3. Millions of floating point operations per second (MFLOPS), with $G = 1$, $N = 5$, $I = 2$, $\Delta T = 4$, for different image sizes

M	512	256	128	64	32	16	8
OFC-based	7.13	1.92	0.549	0.168	0.054	0.017	0.003

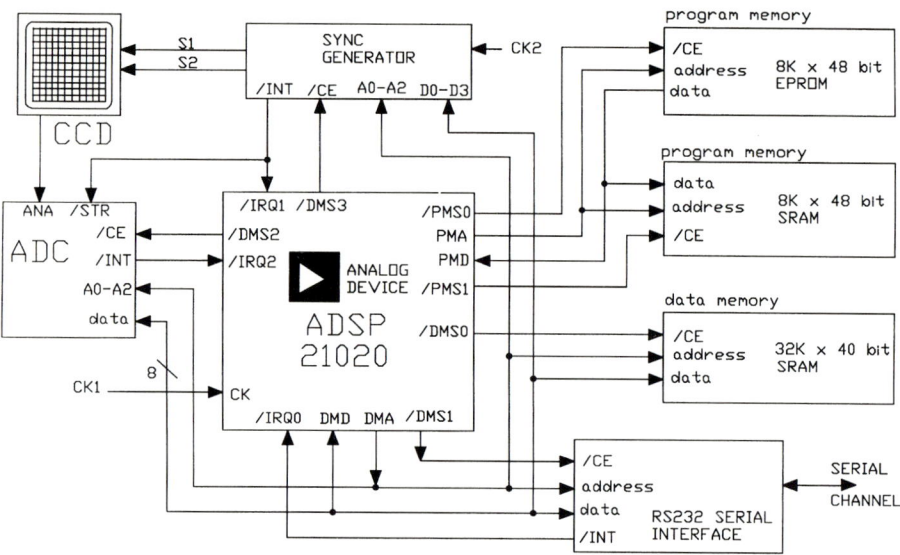

Fig. 16. Physical system architecture. Only the main signals are reported

According to this, the asymptotical complexity of optical flow interpretation for counting moving objects is an

$$O\left(\frac{M^2}{G^2}\right),$$

where $M/G > I\Delta T$ because in our experiments: $I = 2$ and $\Delta T = 4$ while $G = 1$, $N = 5$, and $M = 32$.

It can be noted that, the computational complexity of interpretation is negligible compared to the complexity of optical flow estimation, which is an $O(M^2 N^2 / G^2)$. This can be seen comparing Table 2 with Table 3, in which the number of MFLOP per second (MFLOPS) needed for interpreting the optical flow at a videorate frequency as a function of the dimension of the image are shown.

5 Notes on Hardware Implementation

A general schema of the hardware architecture of our system is shown in Fig. 16. The system is based on a floating point DSP, the Analog Device ADSP 21020, which sustains 66 MFLOPS. In our application, it processes images of 64 × 64 pixels (i.e., $M = 64$) with 8 bits per pixel. The image acquisition system (a CCD with a low cost lens) is directly integrated in the architecture.

Synchronisms used for the CCD are not consistent with neither the standard PAL nor NTSC, but are custom-defined. The generation of synchronisms is delegated to a specialized hardware (instead of using the DSP itself), in order to save CPU time and support a regular rate of 20 frames per second. The analog to digital converter (ADC) receives the signla/STR to start the analog to digital conversion directly by the synchronism generator, and only when conversion is terminated it sends an interrupt to the DSP, which reads the pixel value.

An RS232 serial interface communicates the number of people which passed through the supervised door to the system which controls the vehicle. A reset of the counting can be forced through this port. In a regular city bus, 6 of these sensors are mounted, one for each door lane. A microprocessor-based system for each bus collects the information from these and other sensors, and sends these data to the monitoring center of the town by means of a radio transmitter.

6 Conclusions

In this paper, a system for solving the problem of counting people getting on/off a public bus has been presented; the system is based on optical flow estimation with associated spatio-temporal analysis. The system proposed can count passing people with high confidence even when they are not completely focused, and visible within the view area. Moreover, it is very robust with respect to noise due to image acquisition and people's behavior.

The low computational effort assocaited with the used technique allowed its implementation on a DSP based hardware architecture which is currently under testing.

Acknowledgments. Authors acknowledge ANALOG DEVICE Inc. for the support provided in the hardware implementation of the system.

References

[1] B.K.P. Horn and B.G. Schunck, "Determining optical flow," *Artificial Intelligence*, vol. 17, pp. 185–203, 1981.
[2] P. Nesi, A. Del Bimbo, and J.L.C. Sanz, "Multiconstraints-based optical flow estimation and segmentation," in *International Workshop on Computer Architecture for Machine Perception*, (Paris), pp. 419–426, DGA/ETCA, CNRS/IEF and MEN/DRED, December 1991.
[3] W.K. Pratt, *Digital Image Processing*. New York, USA: John Wiley & Sons, 1978.
[4] R. Jain, W.N. Martin, and J.K. Aggarwal, "Segmentation through the detection of changes due to motion," *Computer Vision, Graphics, and Image Processing*, vol. 11, pp. 13–34, 1979.

[5] R. Jain, "Difference and accumulative difference pictures in dynamic scene analysis," *Image and Vision Computing*, vol. 2, pp. 99–108, May 1984.

[6] A. Shio and J. Sklansky, "Segmentation of people in motion," in *Proc. of the IEEE Workshop on Visual Motion*, (Nassau Inn, Princeton, NJ, USA), pp. 325–332, IEEE Computer Society, 7–9 October 1991.

[7] D.W. Murray and B.F. Buxton, "Scene segmentation from visual motion using global optimization," *IEEE Transactions on Pattern Analysis and Machine Intelligence*, vol. 9, pp. 220–228, March 1987.

[8] P. Lalande and P. Bouthemy, "A statical approach to the detection and tracking of moving objects in an image sequence," in *proc. of V European Signal Processing Conference, EUSIPCO'90 Barcelona, Spain*, pp. 947–950, 18–21 Sept. 1990.

[9] H.H. Baker and T.D. Garvey, "Motion tracking on spatiotemporal surface," in *Proc. of the IEEE Workshop on Visual Motion*, (Nassau Inn, Princeton, NJ, USA), pp. 340–345, IEEE Computer Society, 7–9 October 1991.

[10] M. Allmen and C.R. Dyer, "Computing spatiotemporal surface flow," tech. rep., Computer Science Technical Report 935 University of Wisconsin, Madison, USA, May 1990.

[11] S.-L. Peng and G. Medioni, "Interpretation of image sequence by spatio-temporal analysis," in *Proc. of the IEEE Workshop on Visual Motion*, pp. 344–351, Irvine, California, USA: IEEE Computer Society, 20–22 March 1989.

[12] H. Baker and R. Bolles, "Generalising epipolar-plane image analysis on the spatiotemporal surface," *International Journal of Computer Vision*, vol. 3, pp. 33–49, 1989.

[13] S.-L. Peng, "Temporal slice analysis of image sequences," in *Proc. IEEE Computer Vision and Pattern Recognition Conference, CVPR'91*, pp. 283–288, 1991.

[14] T.E. Boult and L.G. Brown, "Factorization-based segmentation of motion," in *Proc. of the IEEE Workshop on Visual Motion*, (Nassau Inn, Princeton, NJ, USA), pp. 179–186, IEEE Computer Society, 7–9 October 1991.

[15] H. Tamamoto, Y. Narita, A. Yanase, F. Saito, and K. Komatsu, "A measuring system for traffic flow of passers-by by processing itv image in real time," in *Proc. of MVA'92 IAPR Workshop on Machine Vision Applications, Tokyo*, pp. 343–347, 7–9 Dec. 1992.

[16] T. Nakanishi and K. Ishii, "Automatic vehicle image extraction based on spatio-temporal image analysis," in *Proc. of 11th IAPR IEEE International Conference on Pattern Recognition, ICPR'92*, pp. 500–504, 30 Aug.–3 Sept. 1992.

[17] A. Del Bimbo, P. Nesi, and J.L.C. Sanz, "Estimation and interpretation of optical flow fields for counting moving objects," in *Proc. of MVA'92 IAPR Workshop on Machine Vision Applications Tokyo*, (NEC Super Tower, Minato-ku, Tokyo, Japan), 7–9 Dec. 1992.

[18] B.G. Schunck, "Image flow segmentation and estimation by constraints line and clustering," *IEEE Transactions on Pattern Analysis and Machine Intelligence*, vol. 11, pp. 1010–1027, Oct. 1989.

[19] H.-H. Nagel, "Displacement vectors derived from second-order intensity variations in image sequences," *Computer Vision, Graphics, and Image Processing*, vol. 21, pp. 85–117, 1983.

[20] R.M. Haralick and J.S. Lee, "The facet approach to optical flow," in *Proc. of Image Understanding Workshop (Science Applications Arlington), Va* (L. S. Baumann, ed.), 1983.

[21] O. Tretiak and L. Pastor, "Velocity estimation from image sequences with second order differential operators," in *Proc. Of 7th IEEE International Conference on Pattern Recognition*, pp. 16–19, 1984.

[22] H.-H. Nagel, "On a constraint equation for the estimation of displacement rates in image sequences," *IEEE Transactions on Pattern Analysis and Machine Intelligence*, vol. 11, pp. 13–30, January 1989.

[23] A. Verri, F. Girosi, and V. Torre, "Mathematical properties of the two-dimensional motion field: from singular points to motion parameters," *J. Opt. Soc. Am. A*, vol. 6, pp. 698–712, May 1989.

[24] A. Verri, F. Girosi, and V. Torre, "Differential techniques for optical flow," *J. Opt. Soc. Am. A*, vol. 7, pp. 912–922, May 1990.
[25] A. Del Bimbo, P. Nesi, and J.L.C. Sanz, "Analysis of optical flow constraints," *IEEE Transactions on Image Processing*, Jan 1995.
[26] A. Verri and T. Poggio, "Motion field and optical flow: Qualitative properties," *IEEE Transactions on Pattern Analysis and Machine Intelligence*, vol. 11, pp. 490–498, May 1989.
[27] E.C. Hildreth, "Computations underlying the measurement of visual motion," *Artificial Intelligence*, vol. 23, pp. 309–354, 1984.
[28] P. Nesi, "Variational approach for optical flow estimation managing discontinuities," *Image and Vision Computing*, vol. 11, no. 7, pp. 419–439, 1993.
[29] H.-H. Nagel, "On the estimation of optical flow: Relations between different approaches and some new results," *Artificial Intelligence*, vol. 33, pp. 299–324, 1987.
[30] A. Mitiche, Y.F. Wang, and J.K. Aggarwal, "Experiments in computing optical flow with the gradient-based multiconstraint method," *Pattern Recognition*, vol. 20, no. 2, pp. 173–179, 1987.
[31] C. Cafforio and F. Rocca, "Tracking moving objects in television images," *Signal Processing*, vol. 1, pp. 133–140, 1979.
[32] M. Campani and A. Verri, "Computing optical flow from an overconstrained system of linear algebraic equations," in *Proc. of 3rd IEEE International Conference on Computer Vision ICCV'90, Osaka, Japan*, pp. 22–26, 4–7 Dec. 1990.
[33] A. Del Bimbo, P. Nesi, and J.L.C. Sanz, "Optical flow computation using extended constraints," tech. rep., Dipartimento di Sistemi e Informatica, Facolta' di Ingegneria, Universita' di Firenze, DSI-RT 19/92, Florence, Italy, 1992.
[34] D. Ben-Tzvi, A. DelBimbo, and P. Nesi, "Optical flow from constraint lines parametrization," *Pattern Recognition*, vol. 26, pp. 1549–1561, Nov. 1993.
[35] A. Del Bimbo and P. Nesi, "Real-time optical flow estimation," in *Proc. of 1993 IEEE Systems, Man and Cybernetics Conference, Le Touquet, France*, 17–20 October 1993.
[36] A. Singh, *Optic Flow Computation: A Unified Perspective*. Los Alamitos, California, USA: IEEE Computer Society Press, 1991.
[37] A. Del Bimbo, P. Nesi, and J.L.C. Sanz, "Optical flow estimation by using classical and extended constraints," in *Proc. of 4th International Workshop on Time-Varying Image Processing and Moving Object Recognition*, 10–11 June 1993.
[38] A. Del Bimbo, P. Nesi, and J.L.C. Sanz, "Innovative multipoint solutions for optical flow estimation with different constraints," in *Proc. of International Conference on Image Analysis and Processing, IAPR, Bari, Italy*, 20–23 September 1993.
[39] K. Mase, A. Sato, Y. Suenaga, and K. Ishii, "A fast object flow estimation method based on spacetime image analysis," in *Proc. of MVA'92 IAPR Workshop on Machine Vision Applications, Tokyo*, pp. 199–202, 7–9 Dec. 1992.
[40] S. Geman and D. Geman, "Stochastic relaxation, gibbs distributions, and bayesian restoration of images," *IEEE Transactions on Pattern Analysis and Machine Intelligence*, vol. 6, pp. 721–741, Nov. 1984.
[41] R. Courant and D. Hilbert, *Methods of Mathematical Physic*, vol. 1. New York, London: Interscience Publisher, Inc., 1955.

A Bayesian Network for Automatic Visual Crowding Estimation in Underground Stations

C.S. Regazzoni, A. Tesei, and G. Vernazza

Abstract. A system for crowding evaluation in complex environments is presented. The system acquires and processes data from a set of cameras monitoring an underground scene. The processing structure is modelled as a hierarchical Bayesian network of interacting nodes; each node aims at obtaining the probabilistic value of the number of people, detected within either local areas or the whole station, starting from suitable features extracted from images. Piece-wise linear models allow mapping from the feature value space to the number of people to be performed. The modelling algorithm, based on the Bellman Principle, is discussed. Results obtained after an extended test phase in a station of Genova's underground are reported.

1 Introduction

Visual surveillance systems using image processing capabilities aim at providing attention focusing messages to human operators responsible for observing and controlling different environments. A challenging problem that current technology is facing within several fields such as transport applications, public events, large demonstrations, etc., is monitoring crowd behaviour.

In the transportation field, one of the main problem is quantitative evaluation of people number within the environment to be controlled. This information can be useful for two aspects: a) detection of overcrowded situations; b) statistical temporal evaluation of people number for traffic planning purposes. The first problem has tighter time and performance requirements, as it is related to potentially dangerous situations that must be signalled to the operator within few seconds. On the other hand, the technique chosen to solve the second problem can provide responses within a greater time delay, but it is required to be characterized by a higher precision.

The two aspects can be considered as problems of increasing complexity.

Evaluation of overcrowded situations requires the study of processing techniques providing a qualitative output. This output can be considered as a binary answer to a query about the crowd status. Attempts to solve this problem by using Neural Networks (NNs) (Fahlman 1988) have been done for the London metro and by using Regularization Networks (Poggio and Girosi 1990) in the ESPRIT project P-5345, DIMUS (Ferrettino and Bozzoli 1992).

Quantitative estimation of the people number requires a finer processing of visual information, i.e., the capability of a more precise mapping from the image space to a quantized solution space, which is represented by a numerical evaluation of the status of the observed system in terms of an integer number.

In both cases information acquired by a single sensor is not sufficient to acquire a complete knowledge about the status of the system. For example, in the case we deal with in this paper (i.e., a subway station), it is very difficult, mainly due to occlusions, that a single camera is sufficient to monitor the whole environment. In general, it is possible that some areas does not fall in the field of view of any sensor. Further problems are represented by the difficulty of current image processing techniques to provide a good response under different environmental conditions: change in illuminations and scene structure must be considered as a part of the problem to be solved. At the same time, one should realize that perspective transformation makes it possible that different 3D-scenes with the same number of people can be perceived in a very different way by the camera. These aspects make it difficult the problem of selecting features to be extracted from an image to perform the mapping; in order to provide a robust mapping, such features should behave in an invariant way under different transformations.

The problem of crowding monitoring has been considered in literature from the point of view of image processing since few years. Previous works mainly concerned with attempts to simulate people behaviour by using knowledge-based (Hartley, Ravenscroft, and Williams 1992) or statistical models. Other attempts have been done to use non-visual sensors as a basic information source for crowding evaluation: strain gages and displacement transducers have been proposed (Ebrahimpour et al. 1991) to determine and predict loads generated by a crowd in buildings; tactile sensors (Allen 1986; Bar-Shalom 1990) have been proposed to monitor people number on transportation vehicles. All this methods rely on sensors which basically provide less information than the visual ones at equal cost: this is their strength (from a computational point of view) but also their weakness. In fact, as a consequence of their lower information power, they are characterized by a minor degree of adaptability to provide information in different environmental situations. Moreover, if a similar information capability is considered, their installation costs become higher than those ones of visual cameras. In this sense, a further advantage of visual surveillance is that monitor systems are already present in control rooms of all subway stations: consequently, image processing capabilities can be added by avoiding installation costs.

From the point of view of image processing, to our knowledge few attempts have been reported in literature for considering the specific problem. A method for passenger stream evaluation has been proposed to roughly estimate the degree of crowding (Sasama and Ukay 1989) in a railway application. The method is based on evaluation of inter-frame differences and on the hypothesis of human motion in the observed environment: thanks to the application of a simple change detection mechanism, the number of changing pixels is detected and related to people number.

Research has been performed in the direction of studying and characterizing the behaviour of individuals (Aranda et al. 1993; Yuhua et al. 1992; Altwood et al. 1989; Levine 1992; Yee-Hong et al. 1992). However, such techniques are of few interest in the present application, as they assume a good isolation of single human body from the background and the absence of significant occlusions in the scene: these hypotheses cannot be definitely assumed when looking at crowded scenes.

Other related research is ongoing in the direction of traffic monitoring: in the ESPRIT project P2152 VIEWS (Corral 1991) monitoring of traffic knots implies the capability of evaluating the presence of individual vehicles as well as of queues. The latter one can be considered as a problem of "car overcrowding" detection, and is solved by image processing techniques involving the use of spatial knowledge. However, knowledge about the constraints on the traffic flow and the restriction of the search to rigid objects allows more hypotheses to be taken in such a case.

1.1 Description of the Approach

In this paper, the problem of crowding monitoring is considered by following a distributed multisensor data-fusion approach. The goal of the proposed system is to integrate multiple observations acquired in a synchronized way by either a single or multiple visual cameras in order to provide a quantitative estimate of the number of people both inside areas monitored by a single sensor and within the overall station. To this end, an architecture composed by two groups of modules is used (Ottonello et al. 1992; Bozzano et al. 1993; Peri et al. 1993), as shown in Fig. 1.

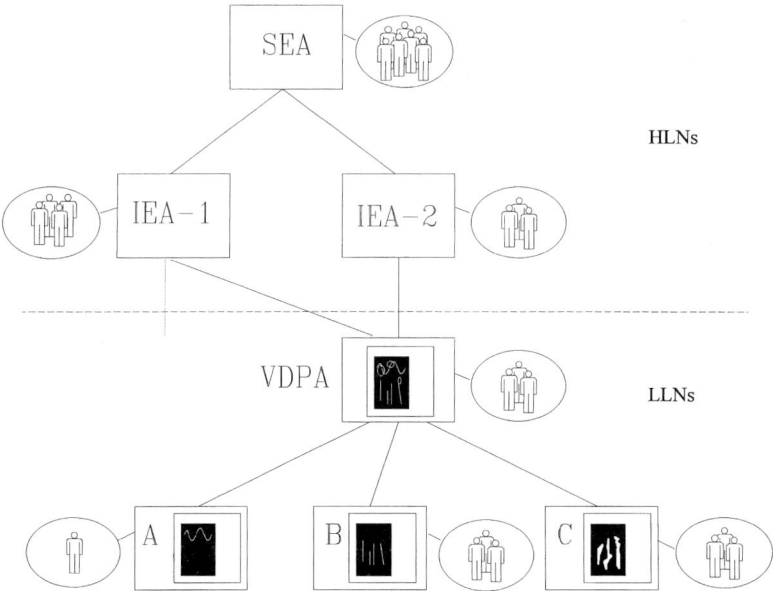

Fig. 1. Fragment of the hierarchical inference architecture

The first subnetwork, constituted by Low-Level Nodes (LLNs), is devoted to provide a quantitative estimate of the number of people within the field of view of a single camera. In this sense, each LLN can be considered as an intelligent sensor whose observations are virtual fused data, i.e., observations of different kinds obtained from the same physical sensor.

The second group of linked nodes, here indicated as High Level Nodes (HLNs), has the role of referring estimates (coming from multiple cameras) to the subway-station reference map by using both a-priori knowledge about the spatial displacement of the field of view of each sensor and fusion techniques. Moreover, the highest level module of the HLN has to provide to the surveillance system an estimate about the global number of people within the overall station.

Both networks are described as Bayesian Belief Networks (BBN) (Pearl 1987; Pearl 1988; Peot and Shachter 1991). This means that each module of the network is associated with a random variable estimated according to the distributed probabilistic inference algorithm presented in (Ottonello et al. 1992). This algorithm can be considered as a special case of the more general algorithm presented in (Pearl 1988). The random variables used inside the BBN assume the meaning of people number.

One can say that each subnetwork composed of LLNs is organized according to a *functional* fusion criterion, i.e., devoted to provide a robust single sensor observation. On the contrary, the subnetwork of HLNs is organized according to a *spatial* criterion. Each node is related to the people number present inside *a specific observed area* of the subway.

Two aspects must be observed. First, the approach is per-se highly modular in respect to the insertion of new visual sensors to monitor a new area: this implies the insertion of a new LLN subnetwork and the insertion of new nodes among the HLNs according to the spatial displacement of the related field of view.

The second point is that the basic estimates which the whole network functioning depends on are those ones provided by the LLNs: if such estimates are sufficiently precise and fast, i.e., characterized by a low uncertainty and obtained by means of computationally efficient algorithms, the whole performances of the net are good.

This motivation, together with the consideration that for many small environments a single sensor is sufficient to provide an estimate, carried us to follow a scaled-up strategy in the implementation of the network. This strategy, which is the same followed during our participation to the ESPRIT project P5345, DIMUS, whose first phase terminated in February 1992, implied focusing research first on the development of LLNs and on the proof of feasibility of a subnetwork of HLNs with few sensors. Results from this phase of the research justified the need of a second phase of the project, which is now ongoing to install in a permanent way a multi-sensor surveillance system within the underground station of Genova-Di Negro, whose simplified 2D map is drawn in Fig. 2.

This paper reports results concerning with the first phase of the DIMUS project, by focusing attention on feature extraction, feature vs. people number mapping, and functional fusion among different estimates inside a LLN. For the

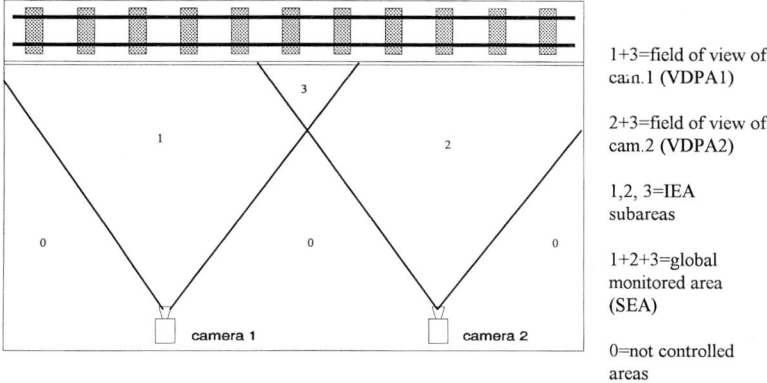

Fig. 2. Example of spatial subdivision of a scene in subareas (horizontal plane): simplified 2D map of the monitored scene at the Di Negro station of Genova's underground

sake of generality, some of the experiments carried out for demonstrating the feasibility of HLNs are also shown.

The paper is organized into seven sections. In Sect. 2 an overview of the inference mechanisms and the topology of the system architecture is given. In Sect. 3 the modelling phase to correlate feature values and the number of people is presented. In Sect. 4 the solutions for image-processing and feature-extraction algorithms are discussed. Section 5 is devoted to detail the inference mechanism. In Sect. 6 experimental results of people estimates are reported and conclusions are drawn in Sect. 7.

2 The Knowledge-Based System

The evaluation approach presented in the paper is based on the implementation of a distributed hierarchical architecture modelled as a Bayesian Belief Network (BBN) (Pearl 1988) of message-passing nodes.

2.1 Information Processing and Propagation in the Bayesian Network

Each architecture node is seen as a probabilistic processor working on a stochastic variable X, which represents the locally estimated number of people, i.e., the local status variable of the system. Local estimation is based on information derived from the interactions of the node with its neighbours and from internal data processing. The system architecture also provides a global status variable that defines the number of people detected in the whole monitored environment and that coincides with the local variable at the root of the hierarchical tree (the highest level node, or Station Environment Analyzer).

The representation of the status X of each node is completely defined by two probabilistic parameters: the expectation π and the likelihood λ, which are received, updated, and propagated during the recognition process. According to BBN theory, based on Pearl's formalization (Pearl 1988) for discrete random variables, whenever a node is activated by new evidence derived from data or by expectations from the operator, its belief value is updated according to the formula

$$BEL(X) = \alpha \pi(X) \lambda(X)$$

where α is a normalizing constant, $\pi(X) = \mathrm{Prob}(X|e_x^+)$ and $\lambda(X) = \mathrm{Prob}(e_x^-|X)$.

In the present application, the random variable X, i.e., the number of people, is assumed to be continuous. However, from BBN theory, one can deduce that the belief-updating process for continuous variables derives from that for discrete variables only under some conditions and, in the case of this particular application, is well-founded, as proved in (Ottonello et al. 1992; Peri et al. 1993).

2.2 Network Node Typologies

Network nodes are labelled according to two main criteria: Low Level Nodes (LLNs) aim at providing the people estimates of each physical sensor separately; High Level Nodes (HLNs) deal with spatial areas and subareas of the whole monitored zone (see Fig. 1).

Low Level Nodes

They are organized into two abstraction layers of the tree, according to a *functional* taxonomy related to:

1) extraction of features and mapping of feature values into rough estimates of the number of people;
2) fusion of these first estimates into a single, more precise evaluation of people present in the field of action of a single sensor.

In particular, the lower layer is composed of a set of nodes (Descriptive Primitive Analyzers – DPAs), each performing two sequential main tasks:

1) extraction of the value of a certain feature type (one for each DPA associated with the same camera) from the analyzed image (e.g., straight edges, points of edge, etc.);
2) mapping of each obtained value into the corresponding Gaussian probability density function (pdf), related to the detected number of people, by using a local piecewise linear model.

Details about the feature types used for the estimation process and about the feature extraction algorithms are presented in Sect. 4. The mapping process is detailed in Sect. 5.

The higher layer is composed of nodes (Virtual Descriptive Primitive Analyzers – VDPAs) devoted to fusing estimates derived from the lower level into a single, data-dependent pdf. The fusion inference phase is described in Sect. 5.

A subnetwork of the LLN type exists for each physical sensor monitoring the environment and its nodes extract and process information coming from the same image. So, at the top of each subnetwork, an estimate of the number of people present in the area controlled by each sensor is available together with an uncertainty degree.

High Level Nodes

HLNs are organized into two layers, by following a *spatial* taxonomy.

At the lower layer, each node (called Isle Environment Analyzer – IEA) is associated with a different subarea of the observed environment; each subarea is given by the intersection among the fields of action of different cameras. In particular, the whole area subdivision is carried out by considering a horizontal section of the 3-D environment geometrical representation, based on a-priori spatial knowledge about the monitored scene. The method, used to mapping the 3-D knowledge about the geometrical description of the area and the sensors spatial parameters (3-D fields of action) into a 2-D representation on the horizontal plan, is shown in details in (Ferrettino and Bozzoli 1992).

For example, the simplified 2-D map drawn in Fig. 2 shows an area monitored by two cameras, whose fields of actions are overlapped. In this case, three isles are present, one of them (that one with label 3) controlled by both the sensors. Isle 1 is monitored only by camera 1, isle 2 by camera 2. Anyway, some uncontrolled subareas (shadow zones, with label 0) usually remain, about which the system can not provide any crowding evaluation.

Each IEA performs the following sequential actions:

1) it receives the set of likelihood λ pdfs relative to the whole field of action of each VDPA concurrent in monitoring the same isle area;
2) it uses spatial knowledge (the ratio between the size of its monitored sub-area and any field of action of the VDPA children) and a uniform distribution hypothesis, in order to make each propagated λ pdf evaluate the number of people only inside the local isle;
3) it fuses the resulting pdfs in order to obtain a single more correct estimate about the isle.

The main purpose of the nodes at this level is the splitting of previous results (the contribution of each sensor) according to the spatial knowledge about the controlled area.

The higher layer consists of a single node, the Station Environment Analyzer (SEA), associated with the whole environment. This root node is associated with a variable representing the people number in the station as the sum of the people number present in the different station areas. It receives as input a set of pdfs from its sons (all IEAs), from which it can estimate the total number of people present in the whole area, using again spatial knowledge (see Fig. 2). Thanks to fusion among the received set of partial estimates, it provides a global evaluation of the crowding.

Details about inference process inside LLNs and HLNs are provided in Sect. 5.

3 Virtual-Sensor Modelling at the DPA Level

Virtual sensor modelling is an off-line phase with respect to the inference process for crowding estimation. It aims to allow a DPA to associate the value of the feature extracted from each occupancy rectangle in an image with the number of people inside the field of view related to the rectangle itself.

3.1 The Non-Linear Modelling Algorithm

The model (feature value extracted from the rectangle vs. number of people inside the rectangle) is computed for each feature type employed in the system architecture.

The algorithm goal is to provide the mapping between the feature space and the number of people to be estimated; the goal is reached by analyzing a set of association pairs (measurement points, number of people) derived from a training set. The first choice for the model shape was a linear function (Ottonello et al. 1992; Peri et al. 1993), whose main advantages are:

a) simple model building (based on an LSM interpolation algorithm);
b) constant, low memory occupancy (the number of parameters to describe each model completely is constant: the angular coefficient and the ordinate in the origin are the only two quantities to be stored);
c) fast and simple mapping in the on-line inference phase.

On the other hand, extensive experiments at the application site showed that this model shape does not fit real data well, especially when the number of people increases (reciprocal people occlusions from the camera point of view imply the occurrence of a feature saturation phenomenon, as Fig. 3 shows). So, a piece-wise linear model has been selected, obtaining better results. Its main characteristics are:

a) algorithm simplicity (the algorithm is based on the Bellman Principle (Bellman 1967; Bellman and Dreyfus 1969) to solve a deterministic linear dynamic system with a quadratic cost);

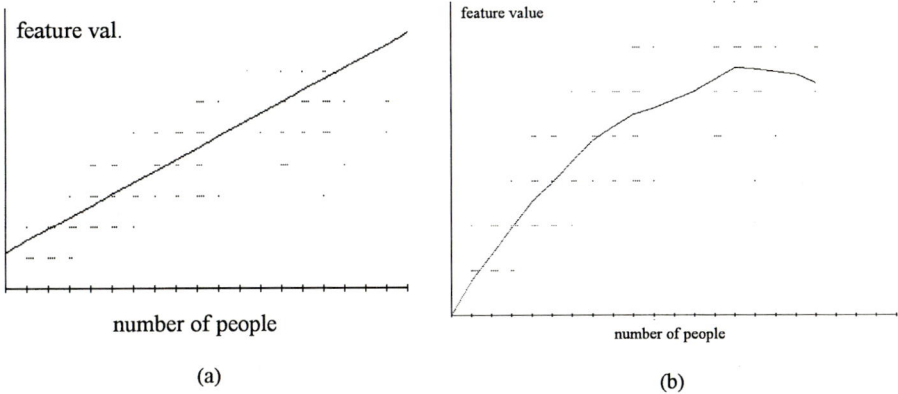

Fig. 3. Measure pairs (people vs. feature values) respectively fitted by a linear **a** and piecewise linear **b** model

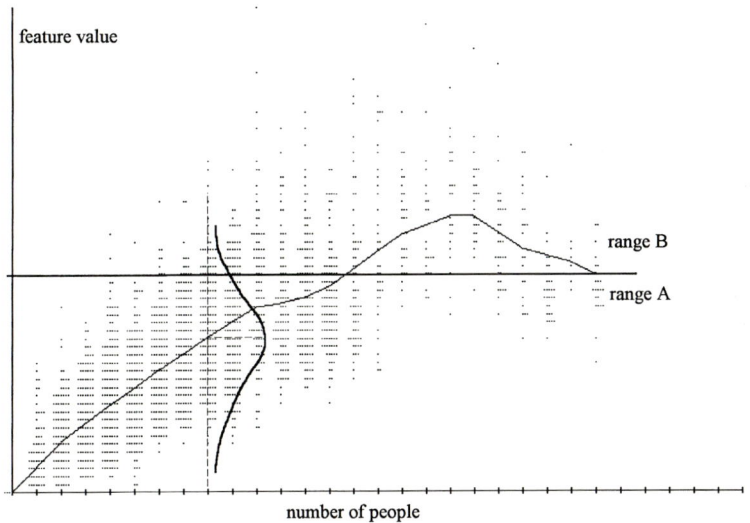

Fig. 4. Gaussian pdf of a feature value, according to the nonlinear model

b) low memory occupancy vs. increasing information (since storing few segment-junction points implies quite a limited occupancy, even when the maximum value of the extracted feature or of the counted people increases);
c) similar mapping capabilities;
d) better fitting with real data, with a consequent smaller spread of the measures from the model shape itself; hence less uncertainty and roughness can be obtained in the estimation results (see Figs. 3, 4 and 5).

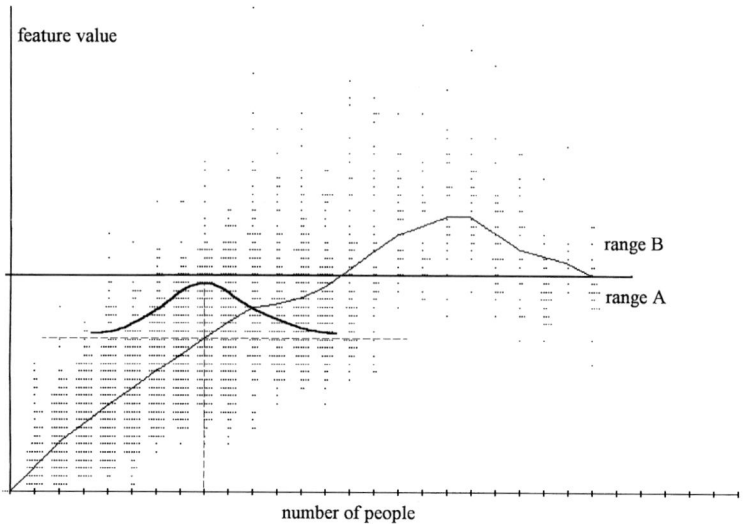

Fig. 5. Gaussian pdf of the estimated number of people mapped on the nonlinear model

Description of the Algorithm

Model building is considered as the problem of searching for the optimal trajectory between point P_B and point P_E (both of them fixed) in a piece-wise linear way, in order to minimize the following quadratic cost

$$J = \sum_{x=0}^{N-1} h_x(y_x, y_{x+1}) + h_N(y_N),$$

with

$$h_x(y_x, y_{x+1}) = \frac{1}{K_x} \sum_{m=1}^{K_x} (y_x - y_x^m)^2 + (y_x - y_{x+1})^2,$$

$$h_N(y_N) = (y_N - \mu_N)^2,$$

where x represents the current step and the number of people, N is its maximum value, K_x is the number of training measures for the current step, y_x^m is the current feature value for that x, and μ_N is the mean feature value for the last step.

The cost function is defined in such a way that it penalizes the distance of the optimal current tracking point from the measure values at that step and from the optimal tracking point at the next step. This cost is built to allow model continuity and favour the presence of at most one mode. Algorithm details are presented in Appendix A.

The resulting optimal model has no constraint about monotonicity. A further modelling phase makes the shape of the model to be monotone or, at least, unimodal. In this way a feature value can be mapped into a maximum of two possible values of number of people: this kind of post-processing on the resulting shape has the advantage of making the next estimation-inference phase easier by reducing estimate choices, while allowing a multi-hypothesis inference process and preserving a best-fitting with the measure points distribution (see Fig. 3). To this end, a simple interpolation algorithm, able to smooth peaks and fill holes, is used.

A final modelling step consists in computing the uncertainty degree associated with each model feature value corresponding to a certain number of people. Since measures are spread around the model for each number of people, the variables x and y on the plane are considered stochastic, so a certain probability density function (pdf) is associated with such variables. For a fixed number of people, the feature value pdf is assumed to be Gaussian, but asymmetric (upper and lower standard deviations may be different); its mean value is the corresponding model value, its upper deviation is computed from the spread of the measures higher than the model, its lower deviation from the spread of the lower measures.

Figure 4 shows the pdf associated with a feature value fallen into range A, in the case of a unimodal model.

3.2 Operating Modelling Conditions

The modelling process is an off-line phase carried out by means of a training set of about 750 images (per physical sensor), acquired in different crowding situations (this amounts to an average of 1000 occupancy rectangles and points on the modelling plane – one for each feature type). The training images have been selected in such a way that they form a set that is as complete and as varied as possible in terms of the number of people, and their positions and distribution in the scene monitored by each sensor. To this aim, the collected images show small, medium, and large numbers of people, divided into groups, isolated, or forming a crowd, dressed in different ways and colours, located at various points of a scene (closer to or more distant from the point of view of each camera), showing different kinds of behaviour.

Feature types suitable for crowding estimation have been selected, taking into special account robustness and invariance of results to changes in the above parameters and in the natural or artificial light present in the scene (as stressed in Sect. 3). However, the modelling phase has to be repeated every time geometrical acquisition conditions change in a significant way in terms of intrinsic and extrinsic sensor parameters. Figure 3 shows a comparison of the linear model with the non-linear shape for one of the employed sensors, after the second modelling phase, with respect to the measure points distribution and spread on the plane (number of people, feature value). In this example the obtained model is a unimodal function. It is the local model used by the corresponding network node in the people-estimation inference phase.

4 Low- and Middle-Level Image Processing

Crowding estimates are based on data acquired by a number of visual b/w cameras oriented towards a zone to be monitored. Images have been acquired in the Genova's underground station in which the system is going to be installed. The video signals coming from cameras are multiplexed and acquired by means of an Image Technology 150 board, processed and finally transmitted to a host workstation (a SUN SPARC Station 2) through a VME bus (Ferrettino and Bozzoli 1992). Image processing algorithm are applied both directly on IT 150 board and on the host computer.

The object "crowd" is modelled as a collection of groups of one or more people. Each group is characterized by its occupancy rectangle on the image plane: the extraction of the occupied areas allows the recognition process to be applied only to the corresponding part of the image (windowing) with the consequent saving of computational resources. In order to obtain as accurate as possible evaluations of the number of people in the station, each sub-crowding area is characterized by several hints, which are matched with the data obtained by using proper Low- and Middle-Level algorithms. Change detection and focus of attention are the basis for feature extraction.

4.1 Change Detection

Change detection algorithms produce a *foreground* image which outlines those image subareas presenting remarkable differences in respect of background image (Capocaccia et al. 1990). Two possible algorithms of change detection have been considered: change detection at pixel level and at edge level. The former operates by simply computing for every pixel the absolute value of the difference between actual and background images and selecting foreground pixels by an hysteresis criterion that takes neighbouring pixels assignments into account. This algorithm even though theoretically valid is unsatisfying for the images in use because is very hard to find a pair of thresholds which allow to reasonably eliminate shades of people on the background and, at the same time, to detect objects in a poor contrast with the background of the scene. Therefore change detection at edge level has been chosen: actual and background images are considered after the edge extraction phase. A Sobel based edge detector (Davies 1990) is used. Those pixels having high gradient amplitude values (i.e., greater than a fixed threshold) are considered as edge points. Other edge detection algorithms (in particular Marr and Canny (Canny 1986) algorithms) have been tested, but the Sobel one has been chosen because required time efforts are very low (unlike Canny's), and it computes an estimate of the image gradient, which is very useful for further processing.

A Bayesian Network for Automatic Visual Crowding Estimation

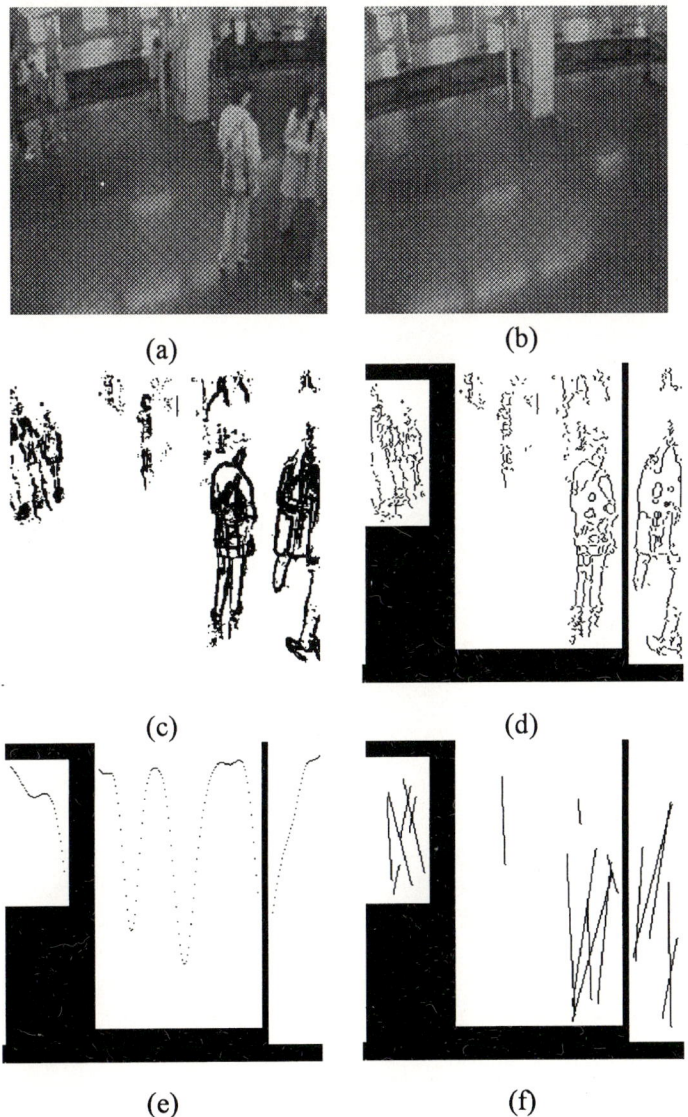

Fig. 6. Example of Low- and Middle-Level processing on real-life images: current image **a**, background **b**, filtered edges **c**, extracted occupancy rectangles **d**, 1D-profiles **e**, vertical linear edges **f**

4.2 Focus of Attention

The goal of focus of attention algorithms is to divide foreground image into logically self-standing subareas. The used algorithm first searches for the minimum boundary rectangle that contains all foreground edges (i.e., all the changes

Table 1. List of most of the tested kinds of features, the performances of their extraction algorithms and the consequent choice

feature type	fast?	accurate?	selected?
num. of edge points	yes	yes	yes (DPA C)
num. of vertical edges	no	yes	yes (DPA B)
rectangle area	yes	no	no
num. max in 1D-profile	yes	yes	yes (DPA A)
rectangle y-dim/x-dim	yes	no	no
num. of circle edges	no	no	no
num. of edges	yes	no	no

vs. background). Subsequently, edge thinning and filtering phases follow, in order to eliminate noisy, very short and isolated edges, and finally iterated minimum boundary rectangle splitting (threshold controlled) is applied to detect a minimum boundary rectangle for each change subarea. During this last phase, very small rectangles are eliminated.

4.3 Feature Extraction

Many feature-extraction algorithms (to be applied to each rectangle of the foreground image) have been tested in terms of time response and estimation accuracy (see Table 1). The latter parameter is mainly evaluated by analysing the fitting of feature data with the corresponding piecewise model, obtained as seen in Sect. 4. From the analysis of performance responses, three feature types (and suitable extraction algorithms) have been selected, getting the best trade-off between the mentioned performance parameters:

1) number of maxima in the 1-D upper profile of the change area (associated with head profile),
2) number of pixels belonging to edges,
3) number of vertical linear edges.

Figure 7 shows a block diagram representing the logical sequence of steps of the used Low-Level algorithms; in Fig. 8 a similar diagram shows the Middle-Level image processing.

Table 2 shows the CPU-time consume of each step of the Low- and Middle-Level image processing, with reference to a SUN SPARC Station 2. Image-processing phase takes most of the time spent for the whole estimation process and their computational loads depend on the complexity of the scene analysed (i.e., number of the present people). In the worst case, this phase requires about 15 seconds of CPU time per sensor. The inference phase is faster; its computational load is independent of the number of people actually present in the image, and it takes

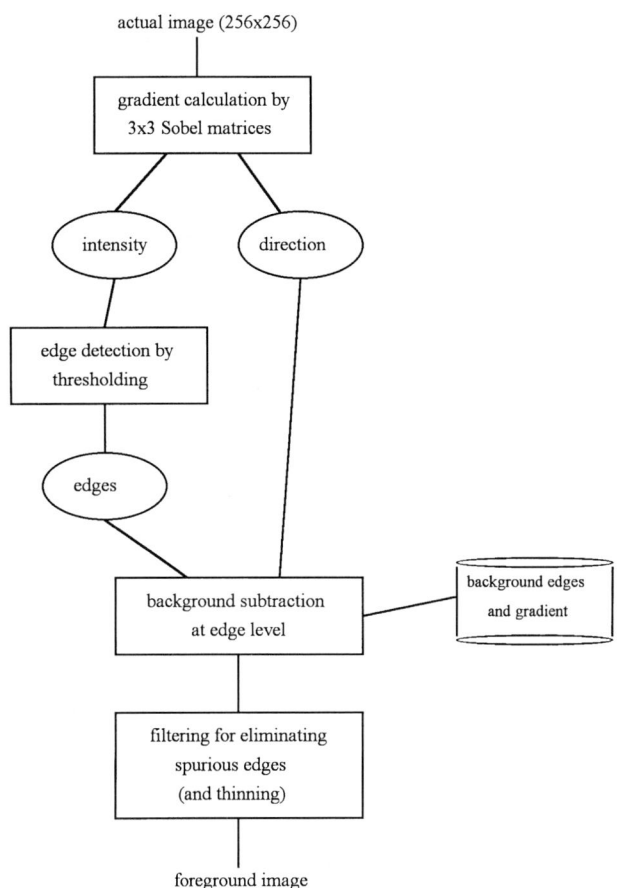

Fig. 7. Block diagram for Low-Level Processing

less than 2 seconds of CPU time. In conclusion, the whole estimation process takes less than 18 seconds for each sensor in the worst case of a large people number. These performances are considered acceptable by end-users because the behaviour of the people-number changes in the field of view of a sensor is estimated to have comparable dynamics. This estimate is based on knowledge that typical frequency of trains in the considered subway (0.2–1 train per minute), and of the total amount of passengers during a working day. Analysing the changes of the monitored scene in time (from a video sequence of frames acquired with a sampling period of 2.5 seconds), an auto-correlation function $R(\tau)$ has been drawn (see Fig. 9). It reveals that at average a strong change in a scene is detectable only after about 18 seconds: this means that giving a crowding estimate every 17–18 seconds is acceptable.

Both figures and tables concern the change detection phase and the only selected and used features.

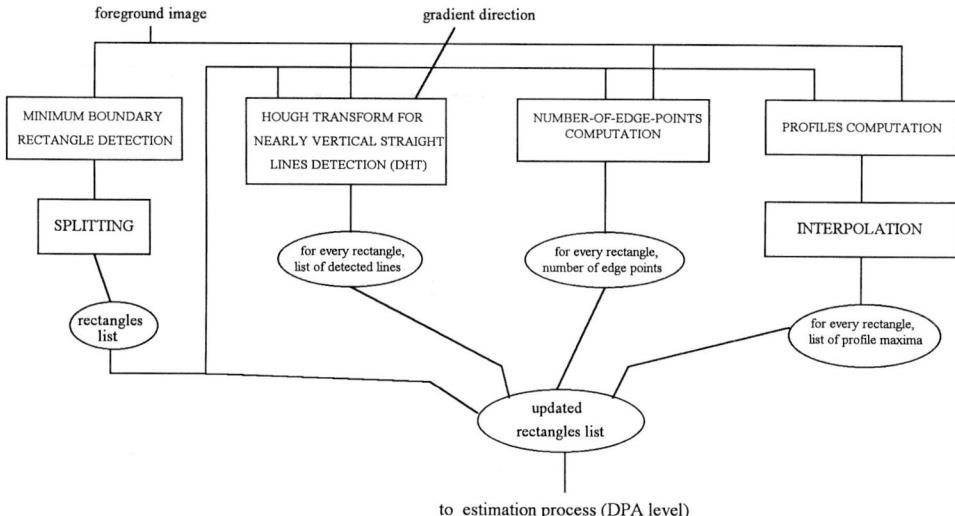

Fig. 8. Block diagram for Middle-Level Processing

Table 2. CPU time for KBS Low- and Middle-Level Modules

MODULES	ONE PERSON per image	FEW PEOPLE per image	MANY PEOPLE per image
gradient calculation	1.33 s	1.3 s	1.24 s
edges filtering	1.18 s	1.15 s	1.20 s
edges thinning	1.09 s	0.79 s	1.15 s
vertical lines detection	0.96 s	2.35 s	6.30 s
background subtraction at edge level	0.12 s	0.17 s	0.28 s
minimum boundary rectangle detection	0.03 s	0.00 s	0.00 s
edge detection	0.03 s	0.03 s	0.03 s
1D profile and maxima detection	0.01 s	0.03 s	0.02 s
rectangles splitting	0.00 s	0.02 s	0.03 s
main	3.4 s	5.1 s	11.1 s
total	5.58 s	8.0 s	15.09 s

4.4 Specific Selected Algorithms

The number of edges is a very convenient feature because it detects very well the presence of people in the whole scene and its extraction is immediate, since edge detection is the basis of the chosen algorithm of focus of attention.

Vertical line extraction has been chosen in spite of time consume because straight lines are really important for detecting the bodies (i.e., legs and arms) of

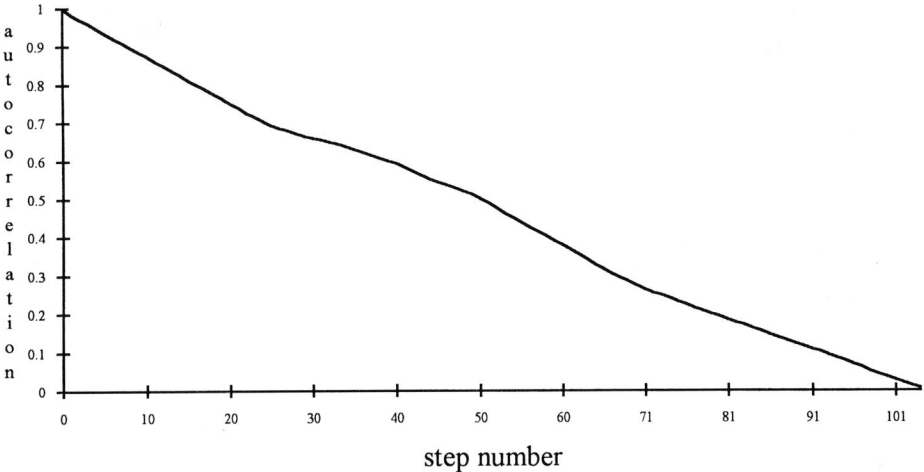

Fig. 9. Example of auto-correlation function about the speed of change of the number of people in a scene

nearly "unoccluded" people present in the environment. Lines detection is operated by using a Hough Transform based algorithm (Foresti et al. 1993; Pao et al. 1992). The algorithm transforms numerical information contained in a scene discontinuities image into a relational graph, whose nodes are represented by segments, and whose arcs are represented by relational properties holding between nodes. It operates on edge image and on gradient phase image.

Monodimensional profile analysis has been implemented in order to define a method for detecting and locating the heads of persons either isolated or very far from the sensor. In general, the presence of a lot of heads against the background implies the presence of people also in the foreground of the scene. The algorithm operates on every minimum boundary rectangle which is obtained by previously described focus of attention procedures. First, a monodimensional profile formed by as many points as the rectangle width is calculated considering for every column the distance between the rectangle top side and the first edge point. An interpolation phase follows in order to "regularise" the profile. To detect heads, a robust algorithm for calculating maxima has been implemented: for every maximum, it consider the local pattern in its neighbourhood in order to discriminate between "lonely" maximum (isolated person) and "composite" maximum (close people).

5 Estimation Inference Process

As mentioned before, most critical parameters in inference process are response time and estimate accuracy: to reach a satisfactory compromise between them, the chosen approach of information propagation through the network uses a *one-shot* Top-Down/Bottom-Up flow: after a first Top-Down initialisation phase, once likelihood has risen up from the lowest to the highest nodes, the inference mechanism stops, without any further expectation updating and propagation.

5.1 Top Down Propagation of Expectations

When the human operator of the surveillance system provides a certain a-priori probability knowledge about the expected number of people to estimate, this kind of information is considered as the expectation about the status variable of the root of the architecture tree.

It is propagated downwards, through the network, according to the spatial links existing among nodes. Indeed, the spatial link between a node i and its son j is represented by the ratio k_{ij} between their respectively monitored areas; under the hypothesis of uniform distribution of people in the whole controlled zone, the same ratio characterises also the relationship between the numbers of people X_i and X_j, respectevely present inside the areas of the father i and the son j, $X_j = X_i/k_{ij}$.

The propagation formula linking two expectation pdfs is $\pi(X_j) = k_{ij}\pi(X_i)$.

Whenever a father i and a child j monitor the same area, their linking k_{ij} is 1.

In the paper, to avoiding any possible influence of external suggestion in testing actual estimation capabilities of LLNs, no a-priori knowledge is provided; this means that the expectation π of any node X is uniformly distributed and $BEL(X) = \alpha\lambda(X)$.

5.2 Inference Procedure Local to DPA Nodes

After the initialisation phase, when new data from Low and Middle Level algorithms applied to the current image are available, crowding estimation at the DPA level starts.

The local inference phase employs the non-linear model in the following way: first of all, the Low- and Middle-Level algorithms give the value of the local feature. It is employed as input y on the model plane xy, and may be associated to a maximum of two x values. As told previously and shown in Figs. 4 and 5, the number of possible estimates depends on the shape (monotonic or unimodal) of the model and, only in the latter case, on the range including the current y (cases A and B). In any case, each estimated number of people x may fall

1) inside one of the linear segments, or
2) at a junction point between two adjacent segments of the model.

In the first case, in order to compute the pdf for x as a function of that for y, fundamental theorem of stochastic variables (Papoulis 1984) is used, in accordance with the method presented in detail in (Ottonello et al. 1992). An example of this mapping is shown in Fig. 5 with respect to Fig. 4.

In the second case, two pdfs for the variable x may be computed: the left and right sides of the junction point belong to two different linear segments, to each of which the previous mapping method can be applied. The pdf with the least standard deviation (the average between the left deviation and the right one) is chosen for the junction point estimate.

In any case, if a Gaussian function regarding the pdf for y is asymmetric, also the derived Gaussian function representing the pdf for x is asymmetric.

Finally, the result of each DPA node is the pdf of the locally estimated number of people, in terms of either one or two asymmetric Gaussian functions, expressed by their three characteristic parameters (mean value and left and right standard deviations).

This result is the local Belief about the status variable "number of people" in the controlled subarea the node is related to; it is propagated as a Bayesian likelihood towards the parent node VDPA, referring to the same physical sensor (hence to the same monitored area, i.e., the sensor field of action), and located at a higher level of the network.

5.3 Data-Fusion Algorithm at the VDPA Level

Any partial estimate coming from the K DPAs referring to the same camera is collected by the common parent VDPA i, characterized by functional taxonomy. Locally, each VDPA fuses all propagated λ_{ij} pdfs, to obtain a unique estimate of crowding for the monitored field of action. The process is carried out in two phases.

1) From any DPA j a pdf per rectangle is propagated upwards. Since each DPA is concurrent with the other ones in estimating the crowding in the same area, the stochastic variable X_{ir}, local to the extracted rectangle r inside the node VDPA i, is seen as the weighted sum of the children contributes X_{jr}:

$$X_{ir} = \sum_{j=1}^{K} b_{ij} X_{ij,r}$$

The parameters b_{ij} have to be computed during the training phase on the basis of the feasibility of each feature extractor model with respect to the others. In this application, no virtual sensor model is considered more robust and efficient than the others, so $b_{ij} = 1/K$.

Hence, the fusion algorithm consists in computing

$$\lambda(X_{ir}) = \alpha \prod_{j=1}^{K} \lambda(X_{ij,r}),$$

with a normalization constant α.

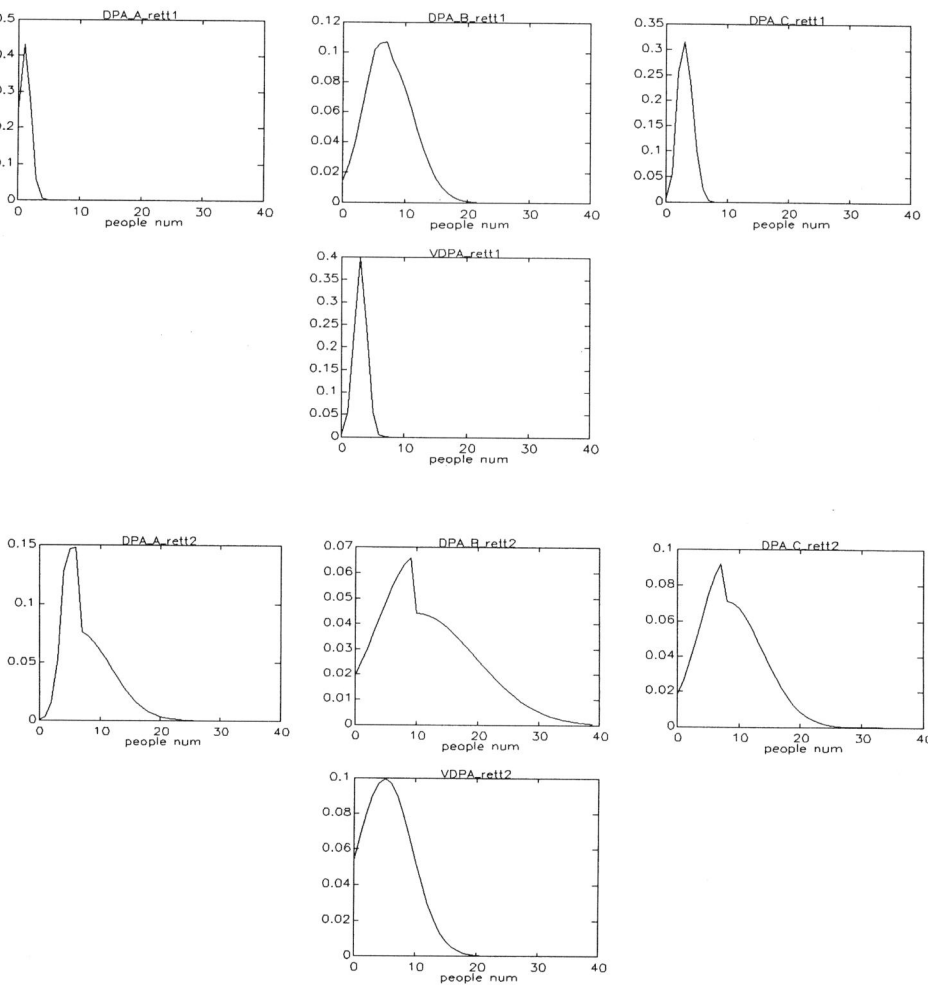

Fig. 10. The fusion and propagation mechanism through a LLN network for image in Fig. 6 a. The estimates at the VDPA level (both on the three rectangles and in total) are correct: 11 people in the whole field of view

It should be noted that estimates in close mutual agreement confirm one another, thus making the result more certain, whereas a propagated estimate too different from the others zeros them, thus producing a complete uncertainty about the evaluation result. Intermediate cases may give rise to a multi-hypothesis result (a pdf approximately composed of a certain number of Gaussian functions), from which only the two most probable Gaussian shapes are selected in order to maintain the same conditions as at the DPA level.

2) The people number X_i to be estimated in the local field of action is computed from the sum of the people numbers evaluated inside each of the R rectangles of the image:

A Bayesian Network for Automatic Visual Crowding Estimation

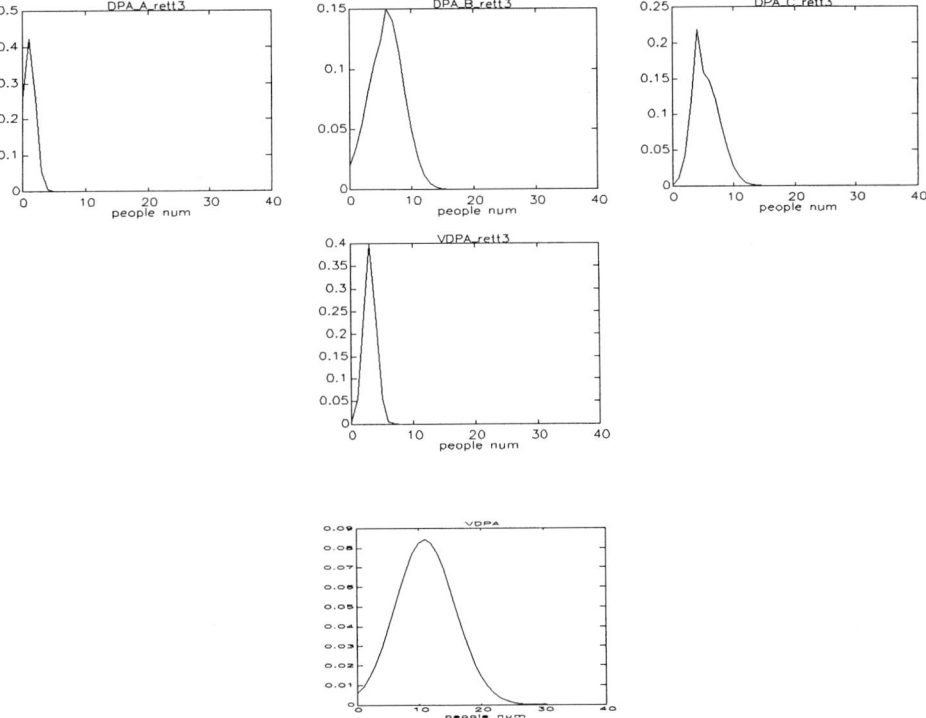

Fig. 10. (*Contd.*)

$$X_i = \sum_{r=1}^{R} X_{ir}.$$

So, the corresponding pdfs about each rectangle $\lambda(X_{ir})$ are fused by convolution to obtaining $\lambda(X_i)$:

$$\lambda(X_i) = (\,..\,((\lambda(X_{i1})*\lambda(X_{i2}))*\lambda(X_{i3}))\,..\,*\lambda(X_{iR})).$$

From this fusion step up to the final result at SEA level, each propagated and updated pdf is referred to the whole area locally monitored by the node (rectangles are not considered any longer). Figure 10 shows an example of fusion of three DPA estimates at the VDPA level. This result refers to the image in Fig. 6.

5.4 Extension to Multisensor Fusion

When a global scene is monitored by more than one camera, the system network is extended to higher levels (dealing with spatial knowledge) in order to have crowding evaluations for the whole area and separately for different subareas under control.

Isles formed by the overlapping of the fields of action of K concurrent VDPAs are characterised by a people number X_i given by the weighted sum:

$$X_i = \sum_{j=1}^{K} b_{ij} k_{ij} X_{ij}$$

(the formula is similar to that deriving from the fusion process per rectangle at the VDPA level, but here X_i depends on each variable X_j according to the spatial links k_{ij}). In terms of pdfs, the formula becomes:

$$\lambda(X_i) = \alpha \sum_{j=1}^{K} X_{ij} / k_{ij},$$

with a normalising parameter α.

Finally, at the SEA level, each isle contribution X_m is complementary with respect to all the other in the global area estimation X, i.e., $X = \sum_{m=1}^{M} X_m$.

This sum of stochastic variables implies a convolution in terms of pdfs:

$$\lambda(X) = (\,..\,((\lambda(X)_1)*\lambda(X_2))*\lambda(X_3))..*\lambda(X_M)).$$

6 Experimental Results

In this section the results of an extensive phase of on-line tests on performances of the proposed system are presented.

Experimental tests about time performances of the system have been shown in Sect. 4, where they have been compared with an estimation of the dynamics in changes of the number of people (see Fig. 10 and Table 3); therefore, here attention is focused only on the final estimates results with respect to the number of people really present in the monitored scene.

Tests concern estimates on the field of view of each physical sensor separately and are carried out by means of a set of about 700 images per camera, showing a wide range both of people configurations (in terms of location, grouping and number of people) and of environmental conditions (acquisitions in presence of different lighting situations), according to the same criteria followed in the training phase.

Tests show that an accurate evaluation can be achieved by using the proposed modelling, image processing and inference mechanism. Crowding-estimation performances are evaluated in terms of deviation from the ideal correct behaviour, as the number of people varies.

The system performance are in terms of (number of people really present inside an occupancy rectangle vs. estimated number of people per rectangle). From a quantitative statistical point of view, the results have been summarised in the Table 3, where the mean error e_i (in terms of the number of people per rectangle) is computed according to the following expression, as the real number of people varies with the index i:

A Bayesian Network for Automatic Visual Crowding Estimation

Table 3. Mean error in crowding estimation local to DPA_A, DPA_B, DPA_C, VDPA per rectangle

real peo.	error	real peo.	error	real peo.	error	real peo.	error
0	1.000000	0	1.000000	0	0.500000	0	0.000000
1	0.299595	1	0.910931	1	0.510121	1	0.973684
2	1.326705	2	1.602273	2	0.795455	2	1.215909
3	1.442688	3	2.059289	3	0.964427	3	0.952569
4	3.699187	4	2.747967	4	1.626016	4	1.682927
5	3.040541	5	3.500000	5	2.121622	5	2.081081
6	4.000000	6	3.700000	6	2.200000	6	2.625000
7	5.333333	7	4.814815	7	3.111111	7	3.074074
8	4.352941	8	4.500000	8	3.147059	8	3.617647
9	4.525000	9	4.475000	9	3.325000	9	3.875000
10	5.303571	10	4.660714	10	4.089286	10	4.267857
11	5.931034	11	2.965517	11	2.896552	11	3.275862
12	4.875000	12	3.750000	12	3.375000	12	3.312500
13	6.166667	13	3.000000	13	3.888889	13	3.888889
14	8.800000	14	2.700000	14	4.000000	14	4.000000
15	5.428571	15	3.142857	15	2.285714	15	1.785714
16	8.200000	16	3.200000	16	1.000000	16	1.400000
17	13.000000	17	1.000000	17	0.000000	17	0.000000
18	5.333333	18	4.000000	18	2.000000	18	1.000000
19	9.666667	19	5.833333	19	4.333333	19	3.500000
20	6.750000	20	5.750000	20	3.625000	20	3.375000
21	6.750000	21	6.500000	21	4.500000	21	4.625000
22	8.666667	22	7.777778	22	5.777778	22	6.666667
23	7.625000	23	1.875000	23	2.750000	23	6.000000
24	8.000000	24	6.000000	24	2.000000	24	3.500000
25	9.833333	25	5.833333	25	3.166667	25	3.666667
26	7.500000	26	4.000000	26	0.100000	26	4.500000
27	5.666667	27	6.333333	27	3.666667	27	3.666667
28	2.000000	28	4.000000	28	10.000000	28	5.000000
29	5.666667	29	3.000000	29	5.666667	29	4.000000
30	0.000000	30	3.000000	30	4.000000	30	4.000000

$$e_i = \frac{1}{M} \sum_{m=1}^{M_i} \left| \hat{x}_i^m - i \right|.$$

where M_i is the number of test rectangles containing i people and $\hat{x}_i^m$ is the system estimate of the number of people present in the test rectangle m (really containing i people). The tables (a), (b), (c) are referred to estimates at the DPA layer, (d) presents the fused result at the VDPA level.

On the basis of the test results, it has to be noted that, in most cases:

a) the deviation from ideal behaviour increases as the number of people present in the scene increases (this is a consequence of the feature saturation phenomenon, due to people reciprocal occlusions);

b) the estimation certainty increases from the DPA layer to the VDPA one, where fusion mechanism is applied.

7 Conclusions and Future Works

The paper presents a system able to provide accurate quantitative estimates of the number of people present in a scene monitored by a set of cameras. The problem of providing precise estimation of crowding present in an underground station (as well as in a railway station, an airport, and so on) is critical for surveillance and useful for activity-planning aims, but is difficult to solve because of the complexity and variability of the scenes. The task is performed by following a distributed multisensor data-fusion approach. A probabilistic Bayesian network implements the crowding-estimation system.

Among the most interested aspects presented in the paper, the inference mechanism at the lowest layer of the architecture is based on the mapping between the value of a feature extracted from an image and the number of people to be estimated, in accordance with a piecewise model; moreover, different local data-fusion methods are applied inside the nodes at different levels of the network, according to the BBN theory.

About future work, test phase is going to be extended to that part of the system network dealing with spatial knowledge (HLNs) in order to validate the implemented spatial-scaling approach in terms of medium error of estimates. To improve the system performances in terms of both time response and estimate robustness and accuracy, several approaches are going to be tested.

First, new features are being tested according to the previous criteria and thanks to modularity of the system the nodes analysing them will be able to be substituted to the present ones or added to the system network in a very simple way. Moreover, it is worth noting that the present estimation approach has no memory in terms of time; actually, estimation based on previously obtained estimates could be useful:

a) to predict crowding values when new data to process are not available between two successive estimates, both derived from data processing;
b) to improve accuracy of the estimation performed when also data are available.

Proof of feasibility of such a time extension of the system is already given by the behaviour of the auto-correlation function shown in Fig. 9 (a too abrupt change in a scene does not allow to base an estimate on the result of the previous one); but, at the present, integrating into the system this estimation approach (so closely connected to time-response performances) needs a significant speeding-up of Low- and Middle-Level algorithms of feature extraction.

The employment of information deriving from the history of estimates may be achieved by the application of Kalman filtering and prediction phases (Kalman 1960; Bittanti 1991).

Some of these improvements are going to be tested on a system prototype installed at the underground station of Genova Di-Negro, in the context of the second phase of DIMUS (ESPRIT Project P-7809).

Acknowledgements. This paper has been partially funded by the European Community under contract no.ESPRIT-P5345 (DIMUS). Authors wish to thank all partners of the DIMUS project and, in particular, Ansaldo Ricerche, and IRST for their valuable co-operation in data acquisition. They are also grateful to Roberto Bozzano, Paolo Delucca and Paolo Moretti for their assistance in the implementation and tests of the Low- and Middle-Level algorithms.

Appendix A

The first step of modelling phase, regarding the search of the optimal piecewise trajectory linking two points according to certain constraints, is solved by means of the Bellman Principle (Dynamic Programming) applied to the linear dynamic system:

$$\begin{cases} y_{x+1} = u_x & x = 0,.., N-1 \\ y_0 = 0 \end{cases}$$

where

x is the number of people in each occupancy rectangle extracted from each training image (in the optimal trajectory problem it represents the current discrete step),

y is the integer part of the feature value extracted in the occupancy rectangle itself (status variable of the dynamic system),

N is the maximum number of people counted in the training set of rectangles (so the number of problem steps is equal to N + 1),

u_x = control variable, that represents the decision to get in order to go from a point of the step x to a point of the step (x + 1), for any $x \in [0, N-1]$.

The first point to be connected is (0, 0), according to the hypothesis that the absence of people implies the absence of features.

Another constant interested in the problem is:

μ_x = mean value computed on feature values measured for the people number x.

The end point of the trajectory is (N, μ_N).

The optimal sequence of u_x has to be chosen in order to minimise the quadratic cost function

$$J = \sum_{x=0}^{N-1} h_x(y_x, y_{x+1}) + h_N(y_N).$$

In this case

$$h_x(y_x, y_{x+1}) = \frac{1}{K_x} \sum_{m=1}^{K_x} (y_x - y_x^m)^2 + (y_x - y_{x+1})^2,$$

$h_N(y_N) = (y_N - \mu_N)^2$.

According to Bellman Principle, a partial optimal cost-to-go is defined as follows:

$$J_x^o(y_x) = \min_{y_{x+1},\ldots,y_{N-1}} [h_x(y_x, y_{x+1}) + J_{x+1}^o(y_{x+1})]$$

$$J_N^o(y_N) = h_N(y_N)$$

(it is the cost referred to an optimal sub-trajectory from stage y_x to the end stage).

The problem is solved in two phases.

A) in the Backward Phase, at any stage from $N-1$ to 0, the minimum problem

$$\begin{cases} J_x^o(y_x) = \min_{y_{x+1}} [h_x(y_x, y_{x+1}) + J_{x+1}^o(y_{x+1})] & x = N-1, \ldots, 0 \\ J_{N-1}^o(y_{N-1}) = h_{N-1}(y_{N-1}, y_N) \end{cases}$$

gives as result the optimal sub-trajectory from stage x to stage x+1, depending on the still variable current start point y_x:

$$y_{x+1}^o = y_{x+1}^o(y_x).$$

In this application:

$$\begin{cases} y_N^o = \dfrac{1}{2}(y_{N-1}^o + \mu_N) \\ y_{x+1}^o = \left(y_x^o + \mu_{x+1} + \sum_{k=x+2}^{N} \dfrac{a_k}{a_{x+1}} \mu_k \right) \dfrac{1}{1 + 1 + \sum_{k=x+2}^{N} \dfrac{a_k}{a_{x+1}}} & x = N-2, \ldots, 0 \end{cases}$$

with

$$\begin{cases} a_N = 1 \\ a_{N-1} = 2a_N \\ a_x = 2a_{x+1} + \sum_{k=x+2}^{N} a_k & x = N-2, \ldots, 0 \end{cases}$$

B) Using the sequence of optimal sub-trajectory obtained in A), the global optimal trajectory can be built in the Forward Phase from the start point (fixed by the dynamic system boundary condition $y_0 = 0$) to the end point:

$$y_1^o = y_1^o(y_0), \Rightarrow y_2^o = y_2^o(y_1^o), \Rightarrow \ldots \Rightarrow y_N^o = y_N^o(y_{N-1}^o).$$

References

Allen PK (1986) Integrating vision and touch for object recognition tasks. International Journal Robot. Res. 7(6): 15–33.

Antognetti P, De Gloria A, Delucca P, Tesei A, Vernazza G (1992) DIBE activities after Intermediate Demo. DIMUS Project Internal Report (ESPRIT Project P-5345).

Aranda J, Amat J, Frigola M (1993) A multitracking system for trajectory analysis of people in a restricted area. In: Proc. of 4th International Workshop on Time-varying image processing and moving object recognition (in press).

Attwood CI, Sullivan GD, Baker KD (1989) Model-based recognition of human posture using single synthetic images. In: Fifth Alvey Vision Conference AVC89. Proc. of the 5th AVC. Univ. Sheffield, Sheffield, 25–30.

Bar-Shalom Y (1990) Multi-target multi-sensor tracking. Artec House.

Bellman R (1967) Introduction to the mathematical theory of control processes-Vol.1. Academic Press, New York.

Bellman R, Dreyfus SE (1969) Applied dynamic programming. Princeton University Press, New Jersey.

Bittanti S (1991) Teoria della Predizione e del Filtraggio. Pitagora Editrice Bologna, Bologna.

Bozzano R, Regazzoni CS, Tesei A (1993) A Bayesian network for crowding estimation in underground stations. In: Proc. of 7th International Conference on Image Analysis and Processing (in press).

Canny J (1986) A Computational Approach to Edge Detection. IEEE Transactions on Pattern Analysis and Machine Intelligence 8:679–698.

Capocaccia G, Damasio A, Regazzoni CS and Vernazza G (1990) Dynamic evaluation of multiple sensors for obstacle detection and identification. In: Time-Varying Image Processing and Moving Object Recognition, vol. 2, Proceedings of the 3rd International Workshop, Elsevier.

Chen Z, Lee HJ (1992) Knowledge-guided visual perception of 3D human gait from a single image sequence. IEEE Transactions on Systems, Man and Cybernetics 22(2):336–42.

Corrall D (1991) VIEW: Computer vision for surveillance applications. In: IEE Colloquium on Active and Passive Techniques for 3D Vision (Digest 045). IEE, London, 8/1–3.

Davies ER (1990) Machine Vision. Academic Press.

Ebrahimpour A, Sack RL, van Kleek PD (1991) Computing crowd loads using a nonlinear equation of motion. Computers and Structures 41(6):1313–19.

Fahlman SE (1988) Faster-learning variations on back propagation: An empirical study. In: Proc. of the 1988 Connectionist Models Summer School. Morgan-Kaufmann, San Mateo.

Ferrettino M, Bozzoli A (1992) A surveillance system project. In: ESPRIT Day ECCV.

Foresti GL, Murino V, Regazzoni CS and Vernazza G (1993) Distributed Spatial Reasoning for Multisensory Image Interpretation. Signal Processing 32 (1–2):217–255.

Hartley JR, Ravenscroft A, Williams RJ (1992) CACTUS: Command and control training using knowledge-based simulations. Interactive Learning International 8(2):127–136.

Kalman RE (1960) A New Approach to Linear Filtering and Prediction Problems. Trans. ASME, Series D, J. Basic Eng.: 35–45.

Ottonello C, Peri M, Regazzoni CS, Tesei A (1992) Integration o f multisensor data for crowding evaluation. In: Proc. of IEEE International Conference on System, Man and Cybernetics, pp. 791–796.

Pao DCW, Li HF and Jayakumar (1992) Shapes recognition using straight line Hough Transform: Theory and generalization. IEEE Transactions on Pattern Analysis and Machine Intelligence 14(11):1076–1089.

Papoulis A (1984) Probability, random variables, and stochastic processes. McGraw-Hill International Editions.

Pearl J (1987) Distributed revision of composite beliefs. Artificial Intelligence 33:173–215.

Pearl J (1988) Probabilistic Reasoning in Intelligent Systems: Networks of Plausible Inference. Morgan-Kaufmann, San Mateo, CA.

Peot MA, Shachter RD (1991) Fusion and propagation with multiple observations in belief networks. Artificial Intelligence 48:299–318.

Peri M, Regazzoni CS, Tesei A, Vernazza G (1993) Crowding estimation in underground stations: a Bayesian probabilistic approach. In: ESPRIT Workshop on data fusion. Springer Verlag (in press).

Poggio T, Girosi F (1990) Networks for approximation and learning. Proceedings of the IEEE 78(9).

Sasama H, Ukai M (1989) Application of image processing for railways. QR of RTRI 30(2):74–81.

Yee-Hong Y, Levine MD (1992) The background primal sketch: an approach for tracking moving objects. Machine Vision and Applications 5(1):17–34.

Yuhua L, Perales LFJ, Villanueva PJJ (1992) An automatic rotoscopy system for human motion based on a biomechanic graphical model. Computers & Graphics 16(4):355–62.

Recognition of Motor Vehicle License Plates in Rear-View Images

M. Notturmo Granieri, F. Stabile, and P. Comelli

Abstract. In this paper a system for the recognition of car license plates is presented. The aim of the system is to read automatically the Italian license number of a car passing through a toll-gate. A TV camera and a frame grabber card are used to acquire a rear-view image of the vehicle. First, a segmentation phase locates the license plate within the image. Then a procedure based on feature projection estimates some image parameters needed to normalize, by a bilinear resampling, the license plate characters. Finally, the character recognition extracts the desired information. Feature points and template matching operators are used to get a robust solution under multiple acquisition condition. The system is able to reject an image if some conditions are not met, as, for instance, the passage of a foreign car through the tollgate. A test has been done on more than three thousand real images acquired under different weather and illumination conditions. Within a test set the system has discarded all the unrecognizable images, i.e., not provided with the required characteristics. The recognition rate has been close to 91%. The final percentage may increase if a more accurate drawing of the templates is performed.

1 Introduction

Automatic recognition of car license plates is a necessary capability for the realization of unattended toll-gates. A vision system for the car identification can also help a human operator and improve the overall quality of a service. Highways, parking areas, bridges or tunnels are places where such a system can be applied. Any situation requiring the automatic control of the presence and identification of a motor vehicle provided with a license number may represent a potential application. If a payment operation is also expected then the use of a credit card or of an automatic cashier could be a solution but a number of different situations has to be considered. If some default conditions are not verified, as, for instance, the machine is out of order or the customer has not proper money, a rear-view picture of the car can be taken using a TV camera. The picture can be subsequently analyzed by a human operator or by a vision system to send an invoice to the car owner.

An interesting application of machine vision to traffic control can be found in (Iñigo 1989) where an algorithm for vehicle detection as well as an algorithm for vehicle tracking is presented. By this technique is possible the monitoring of vehicle traffic, although no car identification is expected.

In this paper a vision system for the Italian license number recognition is presented. The paper mainly addresses the image processing and the pattern recognition techniques used to read the license number within an acquired image. Even if the system has been designed for the specific case of the Italian licence plate, it can be adapted to different models (i.e., foreign licence plates). This system has been designed to be applied on a real service, called *TELEPASS*®[1], offered by the main company that manages the Italian highways. *TELEPASS*® is a new and efficient way to pay the imposed toll on the Italian highways by means a radio link between the motor vehicle and the toll-station. Only the vehicles equipped with a suitable radio transmitter may use the *TELEPASS*® toll-gates. When the vehicle passes through the gate transmits its identification number through a coded signal to the toll-station and an automatic payment is performed. The main goal of this service is to pay without stopping at the gate, thus avoiding queues. This implies the absence of a physical barrier to stop the cars. A *TELEPASS*® toll-gate is unattended, and so there are no human operators to solve "on line" possible problem. Several situations may lead to an unproper payment and therefore to a financial damage for the highway company. A TV camera is used to frame the cars, while they are exiting the toll-gate and all the unsuccessful transits are recorded. A vision system can be successfully applied to process these images in order to show the human operator each one of them, the recognized characters and more information retrieved from a license numbers database. This approach leads to a faster and more accurate data analysis and therefore improves the overall quality of the service.

To design a real vision system and to realize a well functioning prototype a great amount of test real images is required. A severe test set must be considered in order to choose or design the right algorithms by which the field problem may be solved. More than three thousand images have been available for this study. The images were chosen to obtain an unbiased set: in fact all the installed toll-stations and various weather and illumination conditions were considered. Even if a toll-gate is equipped with an illumination system night frames are less recognizable depending on their very low contrast.

The paper is organized as follows. Section 2 describes the main modules and their goals; in Sect. 3 the Italian licence plate model is given and the problem of its location within the image is briefly described; Sect. 4 deals with the image processing and the normalization process needed to precondition the data for the recognition; in Sect. 5 the character recognition problem is treated; experimental results and conclusions appear in the last two sections.

2 System Overview

The presented system, called unofficially RITA, *RIconoscitore di Targhe Automobilistiche* (licence plate recognizer), has been designed to recognize auto-

---

[1]*TELEPASS*® is a registered mark of Autostrade S.p.A.

matically the characters written on the license plate placed on the rearside of motor vehicles. The goal is to read only the Italian license plates and reject all the others.

The image acquisition is performed by a CCD TV camera mounted on the framework of a toll-gate. In such a way it is possible to frame a rear-view of a passing vehicle, whose presence is reported by an ending-race sensor. Image acquisition is made while the vehicle is passing through the toll-gate, i.e., the vehicle being in motion. In these conditions, even if a limit on the vehicle speed exists, to obtain good results it is necessary to store only half a frame (the odd rows or the even ones) because of the acquisition time delay between two adjacent image rows. A quasi-static image is so obtained. The analog image is then converted into a digital signal to be processed later by a computer. A frame grabber is used to obtain the proper data. The working area for the TV camera is about $180 \times 180\,cm^2$. The acquired image size is 256×512 using 256 gray levels (8 bit/pixel).

The variety of acquisition conditions makes the recognition task not easy to solve. In fact, the examined images are different under illumination, perspective and geometrical conditions; the TV camera can be mounted in different position, depending on the examined toll-gate; the scene can be acquired at any time, thus generating images with different contrast solutions. An illumination system is available for night frames. The framed vehicle could be not always at the same distance from the TV camera, depending on the vehicle speed. As a consequence the license plate may appear greater or smaller than expected depending on several acquisition parameters.

Weather conditions can influence images quality too as in the case of a rainy or foggy day. It is possible to summarize the main defects in the images as *out of focus, geometrical distorsion and noise presence*. The resulting licence plate characters are very small (about 15 pixels high and 10 pixels large) and noisy.

RITA is a software application composed by three modules corresponding to the three main computational phases: the licence-plate area location module, the preprocessing module and the recognition one (see Fig. 1).

The estimation of the image portion containing the license plate is not very accurate, because the utilized algorithm does not segment the single characters but the whole license plate area. Nevertheless the results are very encouraging and the error rate for locating the license plate area is close to zero.

The preprocessing phase removes the noise, enhances the image, detects, centers and normalizes the licence-plate image. Within the cut area it is possible to find all the information necessary for the recognition. It is important to have the characters of constant size because of the chosen recognition technique. Therefore the output of this module is still an image representing the isolated and normalized license plate.

In the recognition phase, through a template matching technique a match for the characters of the license plate is found or a reject message is generated. The template matching has given satisfactory results under normal work conditions.

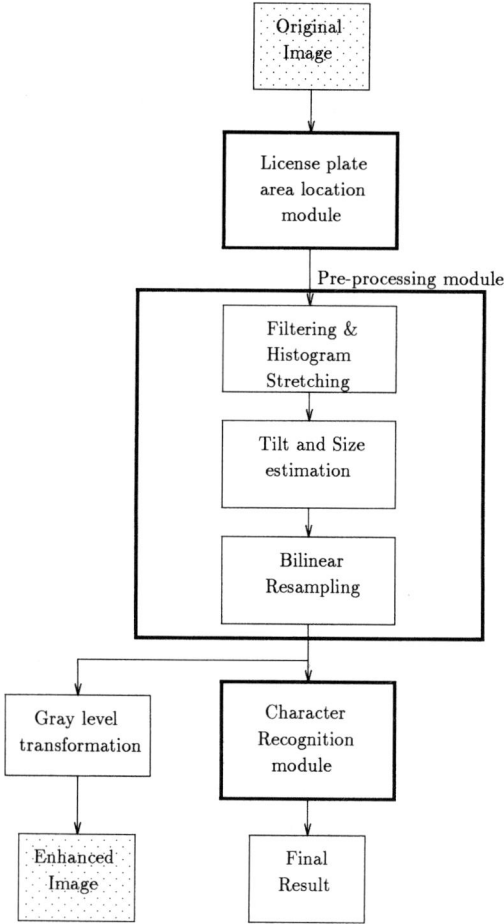

Fig. 1. RITA architecture: the system is composed by three modules, correponding to the three main computational phases: the license plate area location module, the pre-processing module, and the recognition module. An enhanced image is generated to be presented to a human operator

3 The Italian License Plates

In this section a brief description of the Italian license plates is given and the technique to locate it within the input image is also presented.

An Italian car license number consists of two main fields: the first, on the left, contains the province initials; the second, on the right, a six character string. The initials refer to one of the 95 main Italian province and the six characters represent an identifier for each registered vehicle in that province. Because of the large number of registered cars in the largest provinces, digits and letters appear in the string. For all the provinces, except one case, the initials are represented by two characters; only for the province of Rome, all the characters in the name are used.

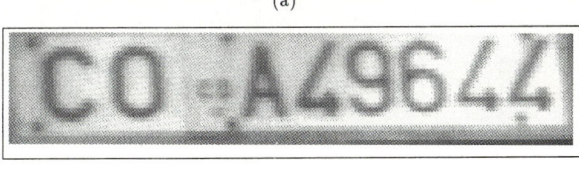

Fig. 2. a An example of input image acquired under normal illumination conditions; **b** The licence plate area automatically located

(a)

(b)

The license plate, placed on the rear-side of a vehicle, consists of two separate metal plates: one for the initials and one for the string. These metal plates are usually mounted as shown in Fig. 2, placed side by side to form a single row: in this case the license plate assumes a rectangular form.

Sometimes (less than 1% of the car population) the metal plates are mounted stacking the province field on top of the six characters, giving the license plate a square form. The characters used either for the initials or for the numbers are black on a reflecting white background. However, the province initials are thicker than the string characters.

Foreign cars can be presented to the system too. The algorithm, locating the area containing the license plate, does not distinguish among the various license plates, i.e., of different countries. Foreign license plates have different structure: different character font, different character displacement, different colours. All these factors make our system able to reject, in the recognition phase, license plates out of interest. License plate location is based on the observation of some peculiar characteristics presented by the image function. The algorithm picks, within the picture, the area presenting the maximum local contrast. A gradient analysis on the whole image leads to estimate the most probable rectangle containing the license plate, which is then isolated. The main information obtained is the knowledge of the center coordinates of the window containing the license plate. It is indispensable to gain this information for the following phase of normalization. The window center coordinates represent a preliminary exstimation of the license plate center ones.

4 Image Normalization

The preprocessing phase consists of conventional techniques like image filtering, enhancement and resampling as well as specific processes tied to the character size or the license plate baseline orientation. First of all a filtering operation is applied; this is followed by a process of histogram stretching, to produce an enhanced image; the last operation resamples the image to obtain standard dimension characters. The whole set of steps is applied only to the license plate area in order to evaluate the parameters related to the character size and to the license plate orientation to achieve a high recognition rate. These parameters will be discussed later in Sect. 4.2. The chosen algorithms are justified by the particular character recognition technique: template matching using cross-correlation measures between the gray level image and the gray level templates (Rosenfeld and Kak 1982). Fixed size and unrotated characters are required to be correctly recognized.

4.1 Filtering and Enhancement

The original images, acquired by black and white commercial TV camera, are gray level images. The idea of tresholding in some way has been discarded after having observed that the large amount of the examined subimages presented a great variety of illumination conditions. In some cases, in particular with images uniformly illuminated and not too noisy, it is possible to find automatically a good threshold to isolate the various characters from the background. Such good images present a bimodal gray level histogram. A threshold can be selected finding the two local maxima of the histogram, provided that they are some minimum distance apart. A significant valley between these two peaks could be an useful threshold to segment the scene (Rosenfeld and Kak 1982; Duda and Hart 1973). But, as already noted, such images are only a small percentage.

Other binarization techniques were considered, based on iterative methods founded on homomorphic filtering (Perez and Gonzalez 1987; Parker 1991) or on adaptive thresholding as in chromosome images (Castelman and Wall 1973) or on edge enhancement as in cardioangiograms thresholding (Chow and Kaneko 1972). Each one of these interesting techniques provided satisfactory results for a good amount of images; nonetheless the final choice has been to avoid any thresholding.

The first operation is represented by a classical gaussian filtering along the rows of the original image, with the convolution kernel

$$\frac{1}{4.1}[0.25 \ 0.5 \ 0.8 \ 1 \ 0.8 \ 0.5 \ 0.25]. \tag{1}$$

The contrast of the sub-image roughly containing the license plate is, at this point, the same of the original image. To visualize better and recognize the characters an enhancement operation is needed.

Enhancement operations modify the gray scale of the given picture. Among them a *gray level transformation* has been chosen; by changing the image gray scale the contrast is increased and the details of the picture are more easily visible (Rosenfeld and Kak 1982).

Let's indicate a mapping from the given gray scale i into a transformed gray scale i' with

$$i' = t(i) \tag{2}$$

where the allowable co-range of gray level values is equal to $[A, B]$.

If $f(x, y)$ is an image with values limited in $[a, b] \subset [A, B]$, a linear gray scale transformation that stretches and shifts the gray scale to occupy the full range $[A, B]$ may be represented as

$$i' = \frac{B-A}{b-a}(i-a) + A = \frac{B-A}{b-a}i + \frac{Ab-Ba}{b-a}. \tag{3}$$

In the same way a piecewise linear transformation may be indicated as

$$i' = \begin{cases} \frac{B-A}{b-a}i + \frac{Ab-Ba}{b-a}, & a \le i \le b \\ A, & i < a \\ B, & i > b \end{cases} \tag{4}$$

when most of the gray levels of the given image lie in $[a, b]$. RITA's transformation function is based on (4) with $A = 0$ and $B = 255$. Let's assume that the image is $n \times m$ pixels. It is possible to compute the histogram function $h(i)$ and to calculate two particular gray level values. The first, a, corresponds to the smallest integer that satisfies the following condition:

$$\sum_{i=0}^{a} h(i) \ge \frac{nm}{10} \tag{5}$$

the second, b, is the greatest integer that satisfies the following condition:

$$\sum_{i=0}^{b} h(i) \le \frac{9}{10} nm. \tag{6}$$

Let a' and b' be

$$a' = 0.1 \times 255 \tag{7}$$

$$b' = 0.9 \times 255 \tag{8}$$

and let's define the transformation as follows

$$i' = \begin{cases} f_1(i), & A \le i < a \\ g(i), & a \le i \le b \\ f_2(i), & b < i \le B. \end{cases} \tag{9}$$

with

$$g(i) = \frac{B-A}{b-a}i + \frac{Ab-Ba}{b-a} \tag{10}$$

$$f_1(i) = \begin{cases} g(i) & \text{if } a \leq a' \\ \dfrac{a'}{a}i & \text{if } a > a' \end{cases} \tag{11}$$

$$f_2(i) = \begin{cases} g(i) & \text{if } b \geq b' \\ \dfrac{b'-B}{b-B}i + \dfrac{b-b'}{b-B}B & \text{if } b < b'. \end{cases} \tag{12}$$

The enhanced image is thus available for further processing. The resulting piecewise linear transformation function appears as in Fig. 3, for each case.

An example of the image enhancement is presented in Figs. 4 and 5.

4.2 Character Size and License Plate Tilt Estimation

The following step concerns the character size estimation as well as the evaluation of the license plate tilt. In fact, due to the presence of perspective distorsions in the acquired image an inclination of the license plate with respect to the usual image

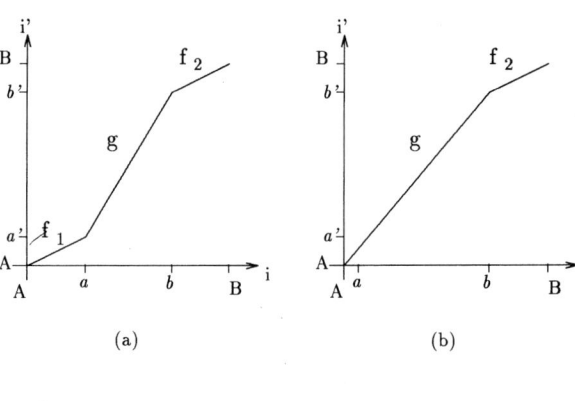

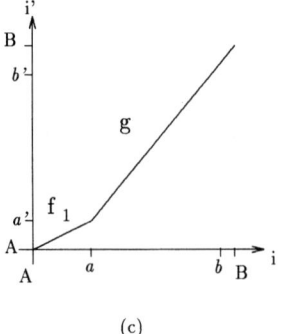

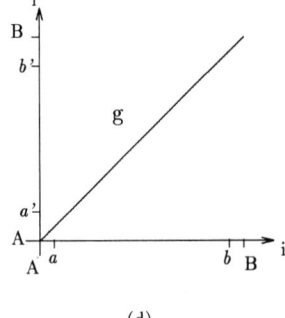

Fig. 3. The four possible gray level transformations to increase the contrast in the license plate area: **a** $a > a'$ and $b < b'$; **b** $a \leq a'$ and $b < b'$; **c** $a > a'$ and $b \geq b'$; **d** $a \leq a'$ and $b \geq b'$

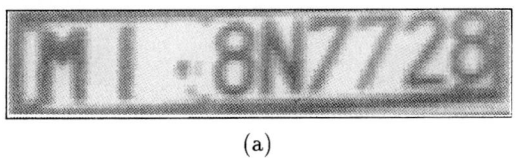

(a)

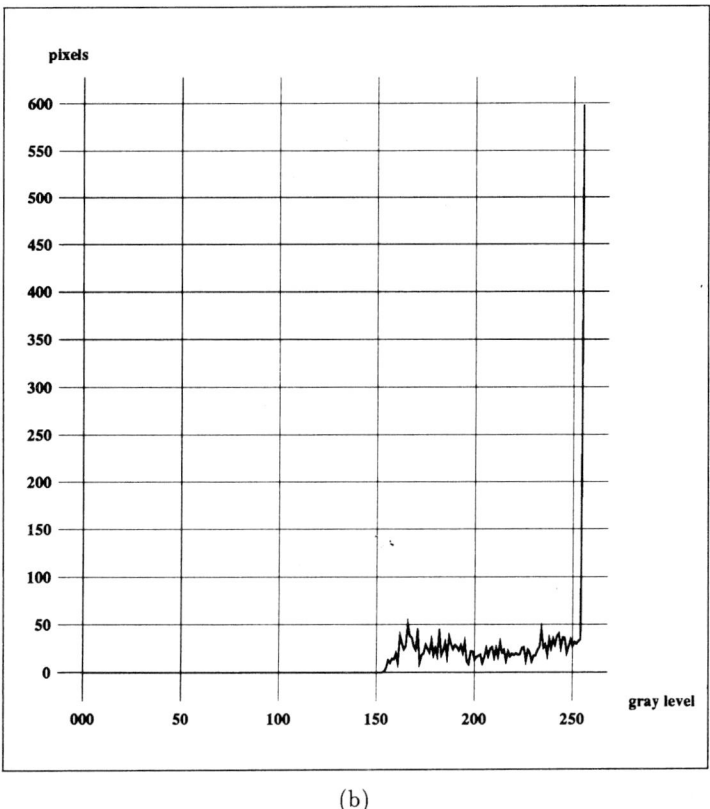

(b)

Fig. 4. In **a** is reported a license plate before the enhancement process, and in **b** its histogram

reference system may be evident. The segmentation process has to evaluate a preliminary approximation of the license plate position within the image. Let's examine the way the system estimates the character height in the enhanced image. Some particular features have to be found to characterize the size of numbers and letters in the license plate. A possibility is to consider the edge points by which it is possible to evaluate the horizontal and vertical dimension of each single character. An attempt was made using the usual techniques for edge detection but the results were not satisfactory. Therefore, as features, two classes of image points were considered.

Given the input image $f(x, y)$, we label *local minima* and *local maxima points* any couple (x, y) for which the following conditions are respectively satisfied:

(a)

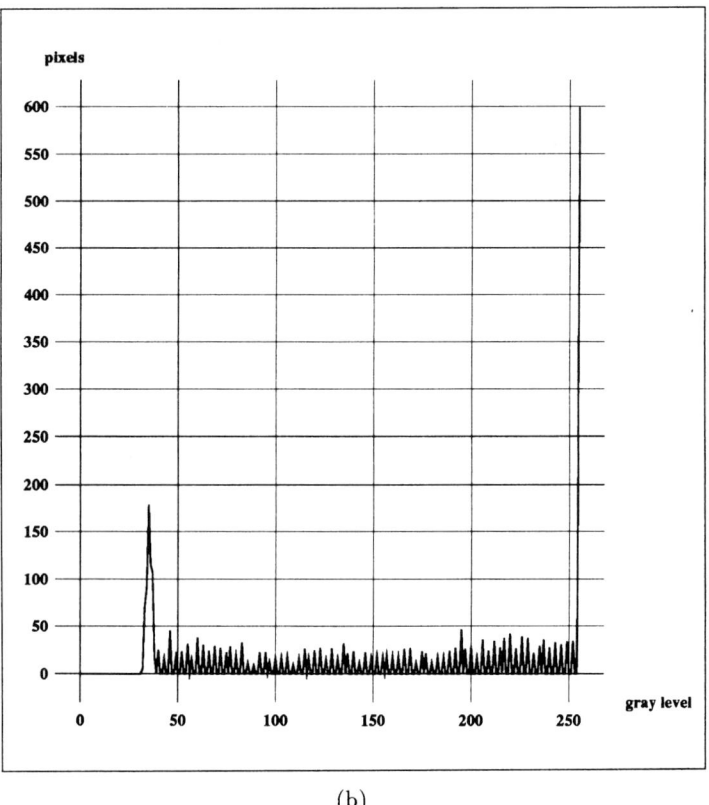

(b)

Fig. 5. In **a** the license plate of Fig. 4 after the enhancement process; it has been applied the gray level transformation of Fig. 3c. In **b** the new histogram of the license plate

$$\left.\begin{array}{l}f(x-2,y)>f(x-1,y)>f(x,y)\\f(x+2,y)>f(x+1,y)>f(x,y)\end{array}\right\} local\ minima$$

$$\left.\begin{array}{l}f(x-2,y)<f(x-1,y)<f(x,y)\\f(x+2,y)<f(x+1,y)<f(x,y)\end{array}\right\} local\ maxima$$

It has to be noted that these features are extracted only along the rows of the function $f(x, y)$.

As experimentally observed these feature points are mostly located into the characters body and between two adjacent ones. An analysis of their distribution lets to determine, through a set of orthogonal projections, an approximation of the character height.

To retrieve it let's fix a Cartesian system whose origin coincides with the center of the segmented area and whose axes x and y are oriented as in Fig. 6b.

Let's now consider a second Cartesian system whose origin coincides with the previous and whose axes x' and y' are rotated of a certain angle, say α. Once the features are extracted into the segmented area a set of points is obtained grouping all the *local minima* and *local maxima* (Fig. 6b). Each point $P(x, y)$ in the set can be projected onto the y' axis to represent a new point $P'(0, y')$ where

$$y' = -x\cos(\alpha) + y\sin(\alpha). \tag{13}$$

All these projected points are collected to form a histogram distribution, along the y' axis, whose bar width is chosen 0.1 pixel. This histogram depends on the chosen angle α: in fact the histogram range is expected to be minimum when α is close to the real license plate tilt. A possible measure of the histogram range may be obtained by its spread, defined as the difference between two values, say a and b which are evaluated using formulas similar to (5) and (6). For any variation $d\alpha$ of the angle α inside an interval $[-\alpha_1, +\alpha_1]$ the histogram spread is evaluated. The particular angle $\bar{\alpha}$, for which the spread measure is minimum, is chosen to be the license plate tilt. The character height is proportional to the minimum spread.

The presented method, experimentally tested, has given good results even if it returns only an approximation of the character height.

4.3 Normalization by Resampling

A normalized image of the license plate is obtained applying both a geometrical transformation and a bilinear interpolation for the resampling.

A geometrical transformation of the picture f may be represented as

$$x' = h_1(x, y) \tag{14}$$
$$y' = h_2(x, y) \tag{15}$$

The new image takes into account a possible rotation given by the estimated tilt angle. As to the presence of a possible inclination of the license plate in the acquired image, the first step consists on a geometrical transformation which compensates this rotation. Size estimation requires us to apply a second geometrical transformation, substantially a magnification or a demagnification.

In the first case

$$x' = x\cos(\bar{\alpha}) - y\sin(\bar{\alpha}) \tag{16}$$
$$y' = x\sin(\bar{\alpha}) + y\cos(\bar{\alpha}) \tag{17}$$

where $\bar{\alpha}$ is the license plate estimated tilt.

In the second case the transformation is

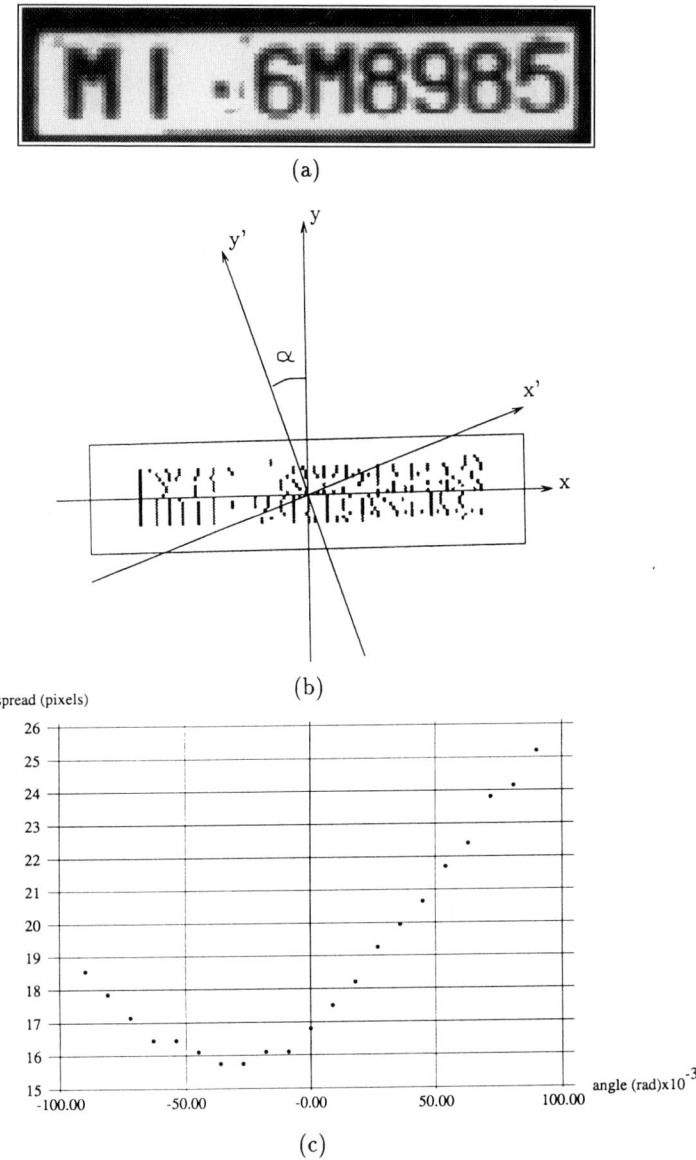

Fig. 6. The segmented area containing the whole license plate **a** and two Cartesian coordinate systems superimposed over the extracted features referring to the above license plate **b**. Each feature point is projected onto the y' axis; the extreme projected points define the histogram range; **c** The histogram spread values vs. angle α: the minimum spread is obtained for a particular angle value $\bar{\alpha}$

$$x' = kx \tag{18}$$

$$y' = ky \tag{19}$$

where k is evaluated as the ratio between the desidered character size and the original one. To associate a gray level to any new point, the bilinear interpolation method is applied. Applying the gray level transformation described in Sect. 4.1 the desidered image is obtained.

The dimension of the resampled image is 20×200 and the resampled characters fit the vertical dimension, having the same aspect ratio of the original ones. The horizontal size is really larger than required because a fine character height estimation is made but their position is still unknown.

5 Character Recognition

The objects to be recognized are characters, both numbers and letters, written in the license plate. They are single font and black coloured on a white background. Any attempt made for thresholding vanished as to the very low visual quality. So the idea of isolating a single character through any possible expensive segmentation technique has been discarded. It has to be noted, observing the images, that often a black frame is placed around the license plate (see Fig. 7a) in a way that it results adjacent to the characters body. It becomes really difficult, even for a human being, to distinguish the various characters, or better, to isolate them. Even if a good enhancement operation is realized on the original image, the frame illumination conditions may vary so that the final characters in the enhanced image may present different thickness. A dark image usually contains adjacent characters (see Fig. 7b). This is a typical situation for night frames or underexposed images. The same problem may be encountered for images much noisy as those in Fig. 7c. Exactly the contrary is the case of bright images deriving from sunny or overexposed frames. The result will be the presence of characters whose silhouettes will coincide with their skeletons (see Fig. 7d). In both cases any attempt to isolate the single characters has led to unsatisfactory results.

5.1 Pattern Matching and Templates

A suitable technique for the recognition of single font, not rotated and fixed size characters is the pattern matching, (Kittler 1988; Pavel 1988). Although this one is preferably utilized with binary images (Gader et al. 1991; Tubbs 1989), properly realized templates allowed to obtain very good results also for gray level images.

The normalization phase has generated standard size characters. Gray level instead of binary prototypes for numbers and letters were realized, to make them more similar to the original gray level images. An operator for detecting a given

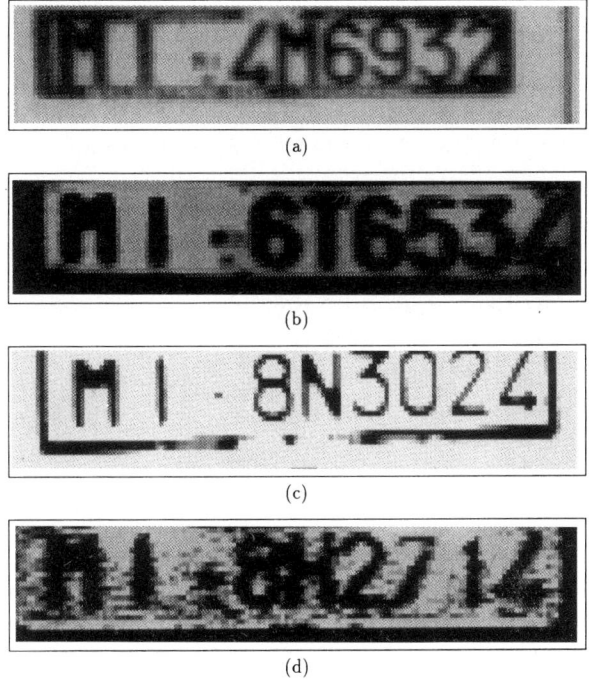

Fig. 7. Examples of license plates correctly recognized by RITA: **a** a clear image with a black frame around the license plate; **b** a dark image with adjacent characters; **c** a bright image with skeletonized characters; **d** a noisy image with destroyed characters

pattern in the picture was chosen: the cross-correlation (Rosenfeld and Kak 1982). This operator can be used to measure the degree of match between two images: in the present case it is applied between a sub-area of the normalized image and each prototype, one at a time.

Let g be a generic template and $\bar{g}$ its average gray level and let f be a sub-image of the same size of the template and $\bar{f}$ its average gray level: the normalized cross-correlation operator in the discrete case is defined as:

$$C_{fg} = \frac{\sum\sum(f-\bar{f})(g-\bar{g})}{\sqrt{\sum\sum(f-\bar{f})^2(g-\bar{g})^2}}. \tag{20}$$

The recognition process is based on the calculation of all the possible normalized cross-correlation values. This is done shifting the template g into all the possible positions relative to f.

Due to the difference between the character thickness of the province initials, on the left, and of the right string, different size prototypes were realized. Instead of recognizing the two letters separately, RITA tries to recognize the pair once for all. This implies the realization of as many templates as all the possible provinces. So 95 composite-prototypes, instead of 26 single-prototypes, has been realized as shown in Fig. 8a.

For 94 provinces two-letters templates has been realized and only in one case, for the province of Rome, a complete-name template has been prepared.

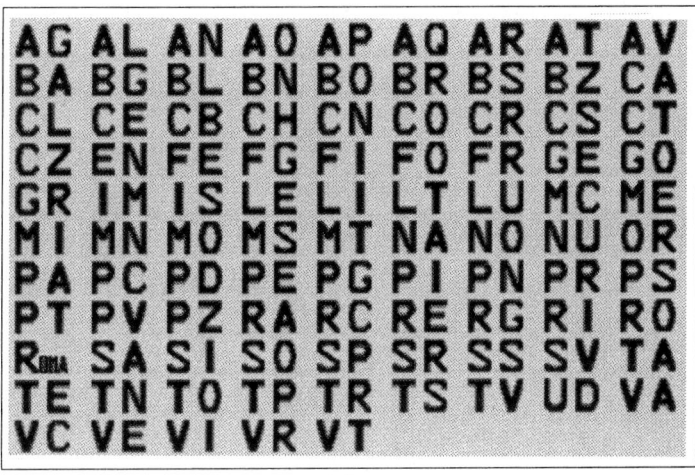

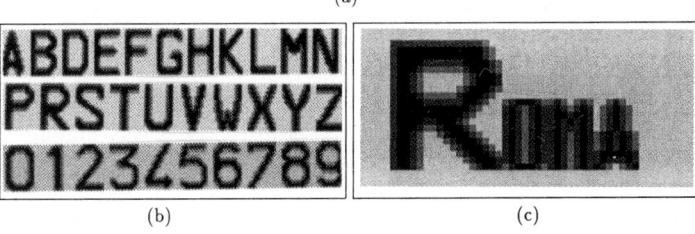

Fig. 8. Templates used for pattern matching: **a** 95 pair-prototypes for the province initials; **b** 31 single prototypes for the right string: 10 digits and 21 letters; **c** The template for Rome in more details. Note the four gray levels used also for the other templates

The recognition of the six characters, either numbers or letters, is done searching one at a time. The number of the needed templates is 31:10 for the numbers and 21 for the possible letters, i.e., only those used in the Italian license plates. They are shown in Fig. 8b.

The realization of the templates has been done using four gray levels; as known, image data consists of an array of pixels with intensity data. Usually the image is represented as 8 bits of data per pixel, thus having 256 levels of intensity: the level 0 corresponds to black, the level 255 to white; all the intermediate levels correspond to different gray levels. For the realized templates the level 0 has been chosen to draw the skeleton of the character, while the level 200 has been chosen for the background. Two intermediate levels, 62 and 152, have been used to create the character edge. In such a way it has been possible to create a sort of shading off of the character templates. This may be seen in Fig. 8c, for the province of Rome, where a specific template with four characters has been realized. In fact, as already noted, for this province, the complete name, instead of an abbreviation, appears in license plates. The size of the templates is 20×50 pixels for the province initials and 20×17 pixels for the single characters. The choice of the value for each pixel in the array representing a template has been done exploring the original images of the license plates in a training set through a graphic tool. Each character has been drawn manually, having the original one as reference displayed on a graphic terminal. An alternative way would require to extract the characters from a great amount of original images and to use the mean among them as a template. This kind of procedure requires the possibility to extract exactly the needed character in the resampled image.

5.2 Recognition Algorithm

The first step of the recognition algorithm examines the province initials in the license plate. Due to the elevate computational cost required by the cross-correlation measure, the search for the template that matches in the best way a sub-image containing exactly the two characters, must be done in a portion of the normalized image.

The normalization phase has given a resampled image of 20 × 230 pixels after having estimated the character height in the input image. The resampled image contains entirely the license plate, but the normalization process has made the license plate exactly with characters 20 pixels high, while their position is unknown. In fact if the estimated center of the license plate area is assumed to be the center of the license plate only the coordinate y may considered certain; this is not true for the coordinate x, which may be affected by uncertainty. When a window is placed over the image to contain the license plate, a larger horizontal dimension must be considered to take into account a possible horizontal shift of the license plate. So the final resampled image, 230 pixels large, will contain also other portions of the original image. Looking at the picture as a matrix of 20 rows and 230 columns, it has been decided that the search for the province initials must be done into the first 64 columns. An area of 115 pixels is explored to find the best match between one of the 95 templates and a sub-image of the same size. Each one of the 95 prototypes is shifted over the image with step of 1 pixel. A correlation matrix 95 × 64 is prepared: the columns correspond to the image ones and the rows contains the 95 templates. Each matrix element reports the cross-correlation value (ccv) beetwen the template in that row with the sub-image starting at that column. The maximum among the matrix elements is searched and, if this value is greater than a fixed threshold, the province is recognized otherwise the image is rejected. In Fig. 9 the greatest ccv along each matrix column is reported for each position over the tested image. The summit of the resulting polyline is evident with a ccv greater than 0.8 and close to column 40.

Once the province has been recognized, the system proceeds to calculate the ccv for each of the 31 character templates in any relative position within the rightmost. In fact, starting from a new position, which includes the column at which the province has been recognized, the width of the province template, and the blank space between the province field and the first character of the right

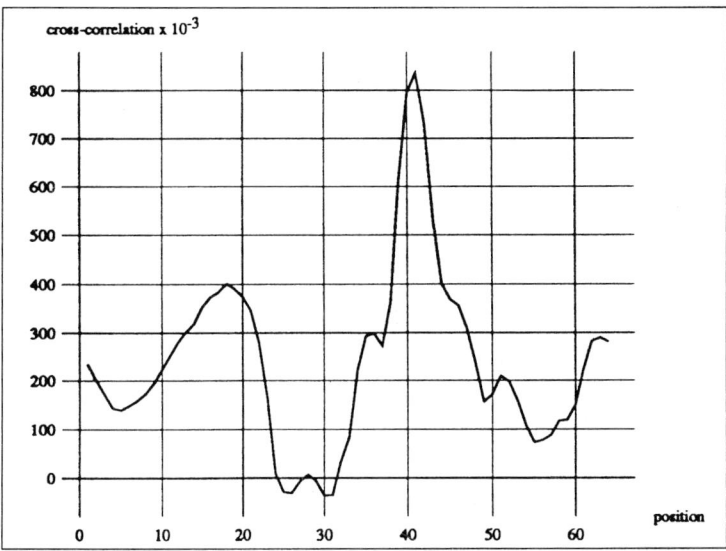

Fig. 9. An example of trend of the greatest cross-correlation values, each one obtained along the matrix columns. Only the province templates are considered in this part of the license plate. The summit of the polyline represent the recognized province initials at that position. The correspondent template has given the best match with a ccv greater than 0.8 in a position close to column 40

string, and going on as far as column 213, each one of the 31 single-templates is shifted over the image with step of 1 pixel. At each step the ccv between each template and the correspondent sub-image is saved in a new matrix with 31×163 elements. Each matrix row contains the ccv of the template arranged in that row in any position over the image. Each matrix column contains the list of ccvs of all the templates in that position over the image. The six character positions within the license plate image is unknown.

First, for each matrix column the template with the greatest ccv is searched to obtain a list of potential solution candidates; each of them has given the best match with the sub-image from a certain position onwards. Searching the six greatest values in the above list of templates, is not a good idea. In fact there is no certainty that the six positions, corresponding to six found templates, coincide exactly with the character positions in the license plate.

A study of the normalized license plate image has emphasized that the suitable conditions for the exact character recognition require a character distance that may vary from 15 to 19 pixels, when the estimated character dimension is 20×17. If the character size in the resampled image is very close to the template one, the conditions for a correct recognition are satisfied. This constraint is put on the choice of the six characters: their relative distance, cannot be smaller than 15 pixels or greater than 19. A set of potential 6-ples of characters may be constructed: each 6-ple is composed by six characters with the greatest local ccv and whose intercharacter distance is constant in an admitted range. Finally the estimated solution will be the one showing the greatest mean cross-correlation value.

In Fig. 10 the greatest ccv along each matrix is reported for each position over the same image previously used. Now the six local greatest ccvs are evident and the correspondent templates represent the solution for the recognition of the right string.

5.3 Image Rejection

RITA's output is the answer about the contents of the license plate, if recognized, or a rejection message. We wished to have the highest recognition rate with the lowest rate of errors. The last situation may be obtained even if the rejection rate may get worse. Even if the complete recognition has been performed it may happen that the solution has to be discarded. It may be a "doubt" in the answer justified by the low mean ccv for the right string or by the low ccv for the province initial: the use of sperimental thresholds for the ccv of the province initials and of the string character let to discard the final solution. In this case it is preferable to loose a right answer instead of giving a wrong one.

A good system has to be able to reject the images which are unrecognizable. Therefore the first requirement is the capability to discard those images that do not

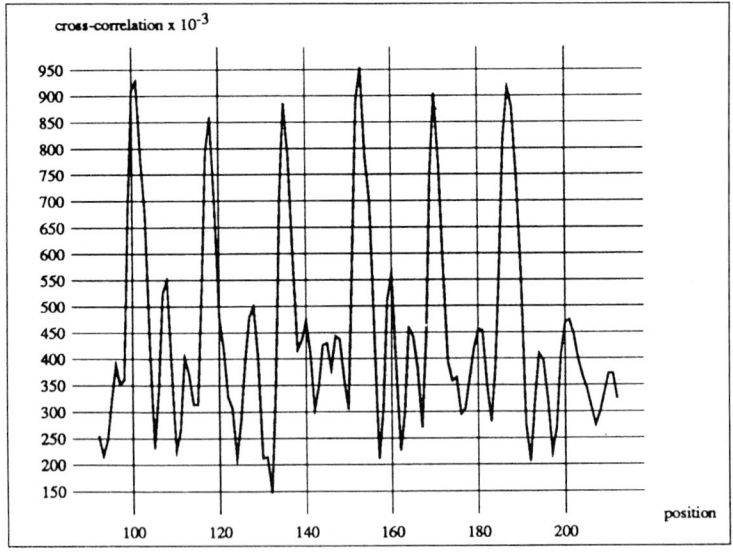

Fig. 10. The trend of the greatest cross-correlation values, each one obtained along the matrix columns. Only the character templates are considered in this part of the license plate. The six local greatest ccvs represent the recognized string of characters in the right area of the license plate

contain the license plate at all. In the case of foreign license plates, even if similar to the Italian ones, the system must discard the images.

There are also a variety of particular vehicle license plates, such as those of public services, i.e., police cars or ambulances, that are our of interest and must be rejected. The last situation refers to the Italian licence plates of old realization. They differ from the new ones because the characters are white on a black background and the font is different too. The system rejects images containing these license plates. The reject capability of RITA is based not only on the template matching peculiar characteristics, but also on some heuristic knowledge. For example, in the license plate string may appear only one letter: so the rest of the string must be composed by numbers. In the case of solutions with more than one letter in the string, the image is automatically discarded and a reject message is given. In such a case, the reject capability is increased with the aim to maintain low the error rate.

6 Experimental Results

The rear-view images used for this project are representatives of the most probable work conditions. Among the tested images there are some unrecognizable ones. They represent a good test for the system reject. More exactly RITA was tested on 3,092 images out of which 2,779 had the characteristics to be automatically recognized. The remaining 313 were unrecognizable because: there was not any license plate in the image; it was a foreign vehicle; it was a public service vehicle, etc. RITA successfully rejected the entire set of unrecognizable images.

In the set of recognizable images the system rejected 439 pictures (15.80%). For the remaining 2,340 good images it gave a correct answer for 2,131 images and a wrong one for 209 images; i.e., in the 91.07% of the cases RITA has successfully recognized both the province initials and the six characters, while in the 8.93% of the cases RITA has proposed a wrong recognition for at least one character.

It is possible to divide either the reject cases or the mistake ones into two classes. In the first class there are rejects and mistakes caused respectively by a doubt or a mistake about the province initials; there were 156 rejects and 77 mistakes. In the second class there are cases caused by a doubt or a mistake about at least one of the six solution characters: in this case there were 283 rejects and 132 mistakes.

In Tables 1 and 2 the results about the single characters recognition are reported. The results refer only to the string characters, both numbers and letters. The system is implemented on an IBM RS/6000 running AIX (a version of UNIX). Programs modules are written in C. More than 90% of CPU time is spent to compute the cross-correlation measures between the various templates and the relative sub-images. In fact the time spent to run the complete system is about 2.3 seconds per image on a RS/6000 mod. 560: it takes about 2.1 seconds to compute all the cross-correlation measures.

Table 1. Recognition statistics of the right-string numbers. For all the 2340 images for which RITA gave a recognition answer the occurrence, the recognition, and the mistake rate are presented. Note the low mistake percentage obtained having automatically rejected 439 pictures of the recognizable set

Number	Occurences	Successes	Mistakes
0	1297	1281	16
1	1166	1157	9
2	1131	1121	10
3	1182	1164	18
4	1208	1202	6
5	1129	1105	24
6	1220	1181	39
7	1298	1287	11
8	1191	1175	16
9	1395	1387	8
Total	12217	12060 (98.7%)	157 (1.3%)

Table 2. Recognition statistics of the right-string letters. For all examined images, for which RITA gave a recognition answer, the occurrence, the recognition, and the mistake rate are presented

Letter	Occurrences	Successes	Mistakes
A	354	352	2
B	428	410	18
D	148	144	4
E	25	25	–
F	30	29	1
G	36	35	1
H	41	41	–
K	35	35	–
L	23	23	–
M	41	41	–
N	76	76	–
P	54	54	–
R	83	81	2
S	110	110	–
T	102	102	–
U	74	73	1
V	89	89	–
W	38	38	–
X	1	1	–
Y	13	9	4
Z	22	18	4
Total	1823	1786 (97.97%)	37 (2.03%)

7 Conclusions and Further Applications

The algorithms were defined on a training set of images different from those later used for testing it. So, if the definition phase involved about 320 images, the following test phase required an amount of images an order of magnitude greater. The images included in the second phase are representative of the real work conditions.

It has to be pointed out that RITA's task is not easy since the image acquisition process is done in the open air and in possible conditions of reduced visibility. On the contrary the Italian license plates characteristics are optimum in terms of characters readability.

The presented results are satisfactory and make the system able to work efficently as a real application. The error rate is low and even if the human intervention is required, only one character of the proposed solution has to be corrected.

Future efforts are directed to improve RITA's performances above all in terms of the recognition rate. With this goal it is possible to investigate other character recognition techniques which work on not binarized images. It is possible to use other linear operators to measure the degree of match in the template matching.

As possible applications one may think to apply the system for the traffic control into reserved areas (i.e., parking areas) either public or private. As pointed out, RITA has been conceived for the recognition of Italian license plates. It is not difficult to adapt, by the same technique, the base algorithm to different but similar models. Due to the low resolution of the CCD camera used for the images acquisition the recognition of foreign license plates may be more difficult. Because of the small size of characters in many foreign plates, HDTV cameras may be necessary.

Acknowledgements. The authors would like to thank Silvano Di Zenzo, Mauro Maier and all the Robotic Vision Laboratory staff for their continuos assistance in making this work possible. They also would like to thank the contacted people at the Autostrade S.p.A. for the provided information and for many helpful discussions.

References

Castleman K., Wall R. (1973), Automatic systems for chromosome identification, Nobel Symposium 23 - Chromosome Identification. New York, Academy.
Chow C.K., Kaneko T. (1972), Automatic boundary detection of the left ventricle from cineangiograms, Comput. Biomed. Res., vol. 5, pp. 388–410.
Duda R.O., Hart P.E. (1973), Pattern classification and scene analysis, New York, Wiley.
Gader P., Forester B., Ganzberger M., Gillies A., Mitchell B., Whalen M., Yocum T. (1991), Recognition of handwritten digits using template and model matching, Pattern recognition, Vol. 24, No. 5, pp. 421–431.
Haralick R.M. (1983), Pictorial data analysis, Berlin, Springer Verlag.
Iñigo R.M. (1989), Application of machine vision to traffic monitoring and control, IEEE Transactions On Vehicular Technology, Vol. 38, No. 3, pp. 112–122.
Kittler J. (1988), Pattern recognition, Berlin, Springer.

Parker J.R. (1991), Gray level thresholding in badly illuminated images, IEEE Transactions on Pattern Analysis and Machine Intelligence, Vol. 13, No. 8, pp. 813–819.
Pavel M. (1988), Fundamentals of pattern recognition, New York, Dekker.
Perez A., Gonzalez R.C. (1987), An iterative thresholding algorithm for image processing, IEEE Transactions on Pattern Analisys and Machine Intelligence, Vol. 9, No. 6, pp. 742–751.
Rosenfeld A., Kak C.A. (1982), Digital picture processing – Second edition. Vols. 1 e 2, London, Academic Press.
Tubbs J.D., (1989), A note on binary template matching, Pattern Recognition, Vol. 22, pp. 359–365.

Automatic System of Quality Control by Vision of Hybrid Circuits

K. Chehdi and M. Corazza

Abstract. In this paper we present a control system by vision of hybrid circuit production. It concerns controlling the position of the circuit links and the quality of the solder joints. The control procedure consists of extracting the parameters characterising each type of circuit and comparing each circuit in relation to that of the prior known model. This system is integrated into the production line taking into account the constrained real time. These circuits are intended for industrial purposes, for professional equipment and the general public where the controls imposed are severe. This system therefore allows automatic control of electronic circuits performed manually up until this day.

1 Introduction

In a production line, several people are often immobilized in order to carry out quality controls during and at the end of the chain. This is why the automatic inspection of the electronic circuits constitutes one of the principle sectors of the artificial vision application. The inspection of a production line of hybrid circuits is often carried out either by the naked eye, in order to verify the position of the components, or by a microscope in order to control the quality of the solder joints. A control with the aid of a microscope is a tedious task. Furthermore, the quality control is subject on the one hand to the subjectivity of the operator, and on the other hand to the fact that the ability of the operator performing the work diminishes in relationship to work load. At the moment there are a lot of automatic control systems to perform such tasks for example the method of detecting defects in printed circuit boards developed by Darawish et al. (1988) and the method of automatic inspection of integrated circuits, the detection of cracks in the ferrite, developed by Chapron (1985). On the other hand several control methods were developed for other fields of application. From amongst these methods, we can quote the method which detects faults in the wood by means of a camera developed by Maloigne-Fernandez et al. (1988), and the automatic inspection method in textile material developed by Lelièvre (1979).

In order to respond to these needs we have studied and carried out an automatic control system, by image analysis, for controlling the quality of hybrid circuits (parallelism of the circuit links and the quality of the solder joints). We have developed a general binarisation method (Chehdi et al. 1992) that we have applied to the control of the solder joints. The significance of the study of such a

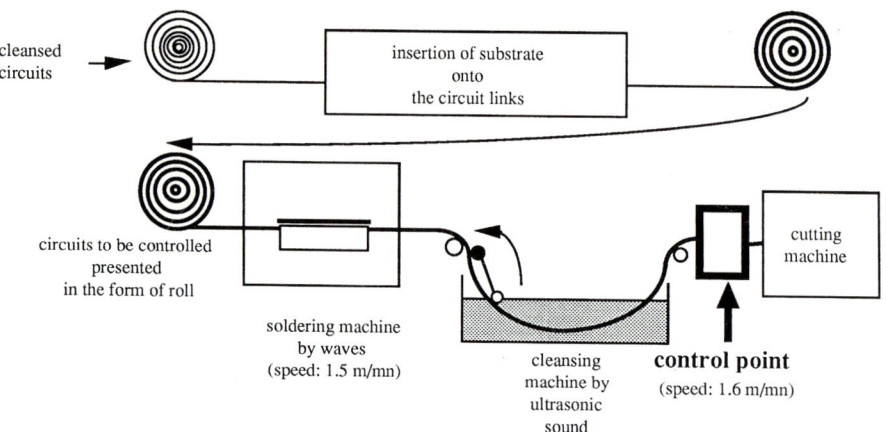

Fig. 1. Diagram of the production line

system is twofold: it allows an increase in the turnover of production by avoiding the final control and finally it allows difficult and repetitive tasks to be avoided because the control represents 20% of the total manufacturing time of one batch of hybrid circuits.

2 Criteria of Control and Constrained Real Time

The producion line for the circuits is, in general, composed of several operations, with each operation being carried out by a specific machine with a limited production time span. The integration of a control system in such a line is therefore a delicate task, due to two constraints generally imposed: the first is linked to the calculation time and the second to the quality control carried out.

At the time of conception of an inspection system by image analysis, one of the major worries is to speed up the processing time and thus to reduce the volume of information used, so as not to disturb the production line. However, this reduction must not in any way undermine the quality of the extracted information at the time of the image analysis. Before starting on the constrained real time, we show the circuits to be controlled and the criteria of control used.

The band of circuits to be controlled is at the beginning of the line in the form of a roll. This band is unrolled and then guided into the wave of the solder joints. The diagram of the production line for the circuits and the position of the control point in this line is shown in Fig. 1.

Before the control point, the circuits are spread out and joined together by circuit links (Fig. 2).

At the end of the production line the circuits to be controlled come in two forms (Fig. 3).

Fig. 2. Example of circuits spread out and linked up before control

 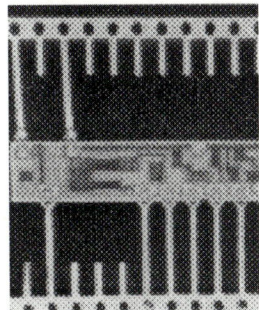

Single in line (SIL) circuit   Double in line (DIL) circuit

Fig. 3. Circuits to be controlled

The inspection of the circuits is based on two criteria:

- the parallelism of the circuit links
- the quality of the solder joints

Figures 4 and 5 represent those criteria used for the detection of faults.

The objective is to control the circuits at the end of the production line without slowing it down. The time that one has for the inspection is in that case included between 1.5 and 2 seconds per circuit. In this study we limit ourselves to the control of simple sided circuit boards.

In order to detect the flaws in the different circuits, it appeared very important to determine the objective criteria. We have therefore developed two analysis techniques in order to bring the anomalies that a circuit can show to the fore. One concerns the detection of badly positioned links and the second localises the poor solder joints of these links.

3 Material Composition

In the whole system of vision one is faced with the problems of acquisition, where the choices of captor and of lighting are primordial.

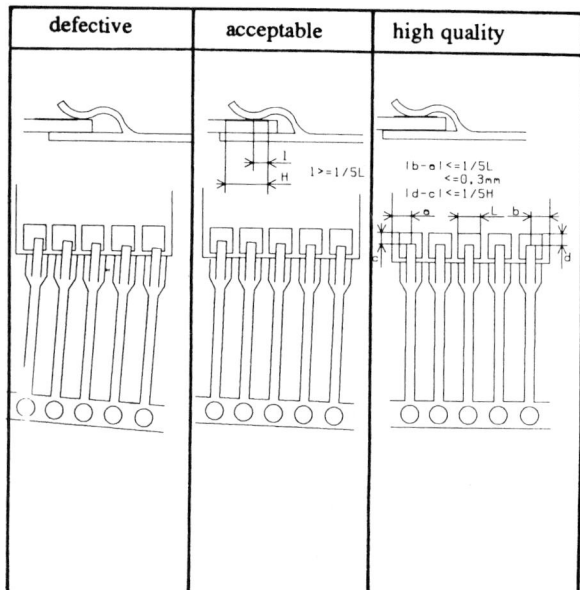

Fig. 4. Control criteria of the links

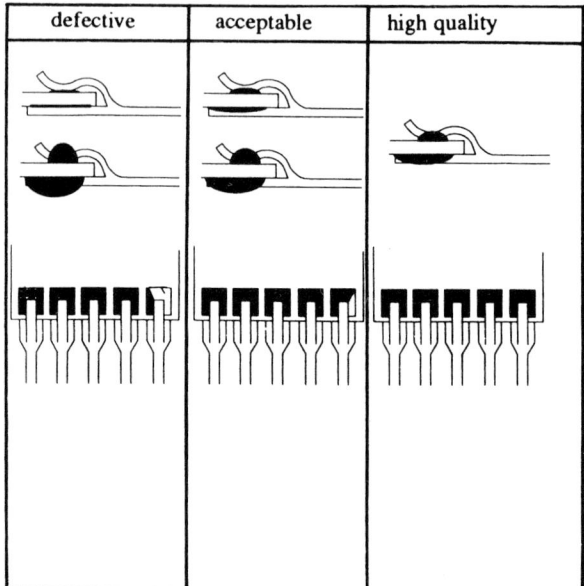

Fig. 5. Control criteria of the solder joints of the links

Acquisition of the Images

In the framework of this study we have chosen a CCD IMC562 (I2S) camera (256 × 256), more adaptable for industrial high rate inspection systems and which can be activated by an exterior signal and only provides a single synchronised image

Automatic System of Quality Control by Vision of Hybrid Circuits

Fig. 6. Outside view of the control system

frame with a display time of 1 ms. This therefore allows us to obtain images without blurring. The camera is equiped with a 11×110 m zoom. This allows sufficient magnification to obtain a good resolution on the small components and an important adjustment range for the different variations of these.

Concerning the lighting of the scene, we have chosen DULUX lamps. They offer the advantage of having a uniform spectral distribution of light from 400 to 1000 nm and give a sufficient brightness of diffused light. This allows us to bring the light variations of the solder joints of the links to the fore.

The lighting system releases itself by a signal coming from an infra red detector.

In order to avoid ambient light and surrounding luminous disruptions, the lighting system is integrated into a tunnel adapted to the control system.

The camera is coupled with an IBM PC AT 386 host computer through the medium of a MATROX MVP/AT image processing card. Finally the system is equiped with a mechanic system of circuit guidance. Figure 6 shows an outside view of the control system.

Synchronization of Operations

In order to synchronize the different operations, hardware and software interruption procedures were brought into focus. The synchronization takes into account

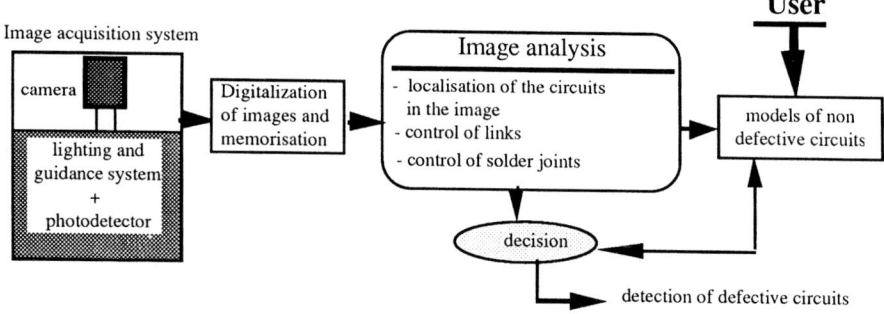

Fig. 7. Diagram of the control point

the speed of the movement of the pieces to be inspected and the duration of the controls for each type of circuit.

The information exchanges of the acquisition system are directed towards the PC by hardware interruptions and in the other direction by writing on the Input/Output ports of the PC.

The detector chosen is an infra red transmitter receiver. When a circuit arrives at the control setting it cuts the beam of the photodetector and activates the control.

The study of the control system includes several stages as shown in the Fig. 7.

4 Procedure of Measuring Interlinking Distances

After acquisition and numerisation of images, the different stages for localising links and measuring the distances which separate them are represented in the Fig. 8.

The position of the circuit is defined by 6 or 8 points according to the type of circuit (SIL or DIL); the determination of the coordinate axes is fulfilled starting from the binary images. The points that allow the circuit to be localised are given in Fig. 9.

These points are determined by reading the lines and the significant coordinates of the binary image. Once this procedure is accomplished, the circuit to be controlled is localised in a precise manner.

In order to measure the distance separating the links, firstly we localise the zone containing the links (Fig. 9). This zone is delimited in the case of the DIL circuit on the one hand, by the lower side of the substrate and the metallic strip of the bottom, and on the other hand by the higher side of the substrate and the upper metallic strip. In the case of the SIL circuit this zone is delimited by the lower side of the substrate and the lower bottom metallic strip. Next, in this zone we place one or two parallel lines at the sides of the substrate (according to the type of circuit)

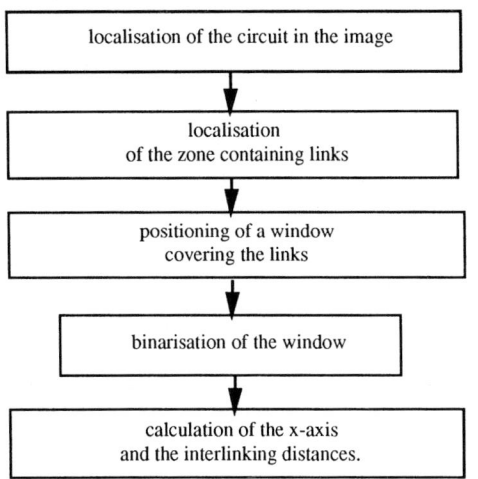

Fig. 8. Stages of verification of the links' parallelism

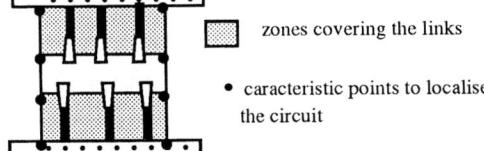

Fig. 9. Localisation of the links

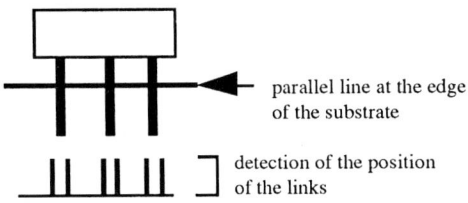

Fig. 10. Analysis of the position of the links

(Fig. 10). The aim of this operation is to considerably limit the analysis zone and thus the calculation time; while retaining useful information to verify the parallelism of the links.

Given that the background of the image in the zone containing the links is homogeneous whatever the type of circuit, we apply a fixed threshold to binarise the line or lines.

In order to determine the position of the links, we calculate the x-axis of the median axis of the links on the binary image, by determining the positions of their edges (black/white and white/black transition), then we calculate the position of the median axis of the links by the average of the position of two successive transitions (Fig. 10).

The relative positions of the links are determined with precision by measuring the interlinking distances.

5 Solder Joint Control

The solder joints of the links can be controlled by identification of the different textures (Chehdi and Liao 1991) of the solder, of the connection area and of the link. We therefore determine, by this medium, the covering of the connection area by the solder. We can also define good or poor solder according to the number of pixels contained in each homogeneous region.

In the framework of this application, recognition by texture analysis requires a calculation time beyond constrained real time set by the production line. We have opted for the binarisation technique for differentiating the connection area from the link. In this case there are two solutions:

a) Localisation of the band of the image containing all the solder, calculation of the histogram, then binarisation of this band so as to compare the number of black pixels to the number of white pixels. In this case it is necessary to know the average number of black (or white) pixels contained in this band for a circuit that does not show soldering flaws. This solution allows us to detect the flaws of the circuit in general, on the other hand it does not allow identification of the faulty solder joint or joints of the band.

b) The second solution is based on prior knowledge of the position and the limits of the solder joints (lower edge of the substrate, x-axis of the links, size of the connection area). The procedure used in this case is presented in the Fig. 11.

We chose the second solution as it has the advantage of being more precise than the preceding one. This solution, like the first, requires the average number of pixels to be known (white/black pixels) after the binarisation step of the zone containing the connection area.

In order to obtain a precise binarisation, we have developed an automatic thresholding method which we will go through.

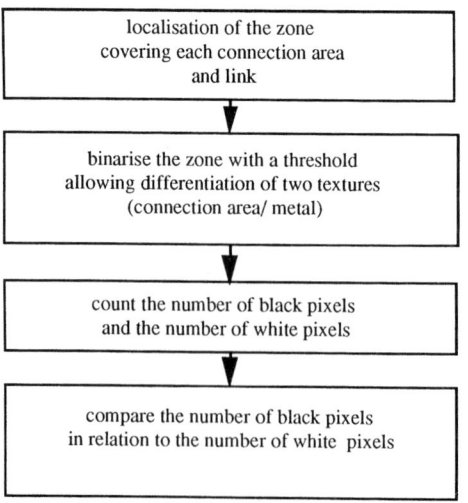

Fig. 11. Stages of quality control of the solder joints

5.1 Binarisation Problems

The main difficulty to be found in applying the threshold method to images lies in the non homogeneity of the captor's response, the problems of shading effects and the type of image to be processed. The threshold method is a classical technique frequently used in image processing. Several local or global thresholding methods have been used to date; the majority of which have been used for specific applications. Global thresholding methods (Sahoo et al. 1988) may be used if the grey level of the background is uniform as well as that of the object. However, in practice this situation rarely occurs. For local thresholding several methods exist. They use either segmentation techniques in region (Wu et al. 1982; Kittler and Illingworth 1985; Chow and Kaneko 1971; Haralick and Shapiro 1986; Pun 1980; Johannsen and Bille 1983) or edge detectors (Milgram and Herman 1979; White and Rohrer 1986) or relaxation techniques (Fetecke et al. 1981; Rosenfeld and Smith 1981); or a multifrequency analysis or learning criteria of a local threshold (Chehikian 1986). Some techniques are time consuming and occupy memory space, or are sensitive to high frequency noise. Other techniques are reliable for a class of images representative of weak reflectance objects set against a background of a higher reflectance. However, their performance is affected by the presence of the shading effects.

A rigorous threshold method should be applicable to several types of images, economical from a computing and memory space point of view, non sensitive to the shading effects, precise enough to be able to retain the details of the region, and should be able to take into account the heterogenous aspect of each image. The method developed is based on the automatic detection of the different local thresholds of the image, taking into consideration the local properties of each histogram (unimodal, bimodal or multimodal). Validation criteria are used in obtaining each optimal threshold.

5.2 Developed Method of Binarisation

Let F be an image or a zone of image of size NxN to be processed, subdivided into several W_j windows, the size of which is equal to nxn. Let L be a set of positive integers representing the k grey levels of W_j; $L = \{0, 1, \ldots, k-1\}$. The set L is composed of two sub sets O and G, corresponding respectively to the objects and to the background.

The method that we have developed requires two stages:

- modification of the local histograms
- location of local thresholds

Stage 1. Modification of the Local Histograms

The aim of the transformation operation of the original histogram of a window is to characterise each W_j window by an ideal H_i histogram unimodal, bimodal or

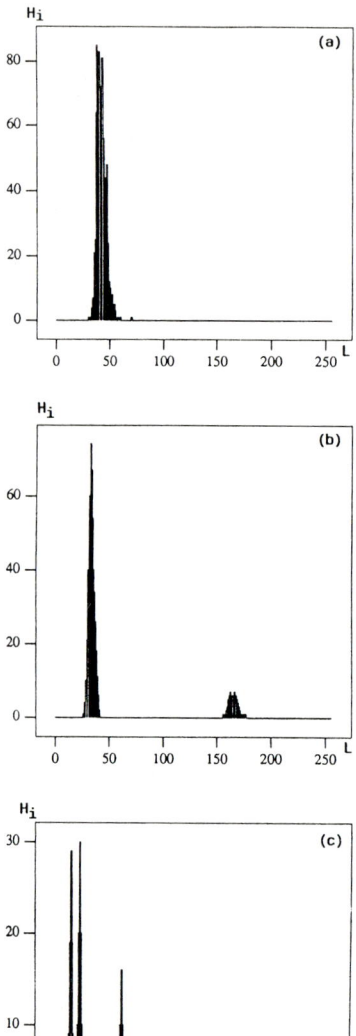

Fig. 12. Ideal local histograms: (a) unimodal histogram; (b) bimodal histogram; (c) multimodal histogram

multimodal (Fig. 12) where the modes are distinctly separated. The histogram in Fig. 12a represents either an object or a background. Figure 12b represents an object and a background and Fig. 12c reflects the non homogeneity of the objects and of the background.

This procedure is necessary for the determination of the thresholds. In fact, most classical local histograms being bimodal or multimodal, the boundaries of

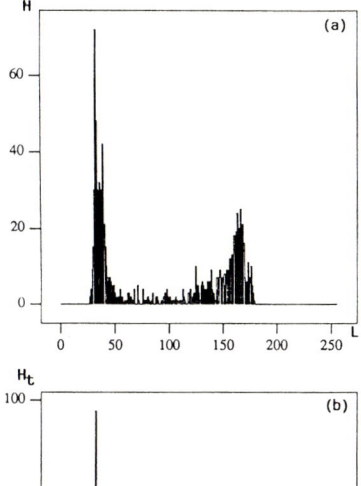

Fig. 13. Transformation of histogram: (a) original local histogram; (b) transformed histogram

each mode are not well defined and the calculation of the thresholds becomes delicate (example as in Fig. 13a).

Transformation of Histograms

In order to highlight the most important classes of each histogram, two criteria noted C_1 and C_2, based on the fluctuation measurement of the grey levels, are used for each pixel of the window Wj.

Let $l = f(x, y)$ be the grey level at (x, y). Let p_l be the appearance frequency of the grey level l calculated in the window Wj ($l \in L$). The two criteria C_1 and C_2 defined at (x, y) are:

$C_{1l}(x, y) = |f(x, y) - f(x - 1, y)| \leq 1$

$C_{2l}(x, y) = |f(x, y) - f(x, y - 1)| \leq 1$; with $f(.,.) \in Wj$

These two criteria are calculated for each pixel of the grey level l belonging to Wj. $C_{1l}(x, y)$ and $C_{2l}(x, y)$ each give an indication of the homogeneity of a point (x, y) in relation to the nearest neighbouring points. According to these criteria, p_l is modified in the following manner:

$$p_l = \begin{cases} p_l + 1; & \text{if } C_{1l} \text{ or } C_{2l} \text{ is true} \\ p_l + 2; & \text{if } C_{1l} \text{ and } C_{2l} \text{ are true} \\ p_l; & \text{otherwise} \end{cases}$$

The transformation is repeated for all grey levels of Wj. Figure 13 illustrates this transformation: two distinct modes of the grey level are created, compared with the classical histogram (Fig. 13a). The Histogram of Fig. 13b corresponds to the ideal histogram sought H_i.

Smoothing of Transformed Histograms

Before detecting the main extrema the modified H_t histogram is smoothed. This operation is necessary in order to eliminate the non significant grey level. This processing consists in replacing each appearance frequency p_l of the grey level l of H_t ($l \in L$) by the average value of neighbouring p_l.

Stage 2. Location of Local Thresholds

In order to locate the extrema enabling the optimal thresholds, the grey levels of the smoothed histogram are eliminated whose appearance frequencies are inferior or equal to the average of p_l.

If the histogram obtained is unimodal, a zero is affected to the value of the threshold. If the histogram is bimodal or multimodal two techniques can be used in order to determine the local thresholds:

First Solution. If the histogram is bimodal the theshold is equal to:

$$sj = (l_1 + l_2)/2$$

where l_1 and l_2, correspond respectively to the grey levels of the p_{l_1} and p_{l_2} maxima.

In the case where the histogram is multimodal, the M maxima are localised and regrouped by using the d_i criteria thus minimising the difference of levels corresponding to the p_{li} ($i \in [1,M]$).

Procedure. Compute: $d_i = l_{i+1} - l_i$; $i = 1,2, \ldots, M$; for minimum d_i, perform:

$$li = (l_{i+1} + l_i)/2 \text{ and cancel } l_{i+1}$$

reorder the indexes following the increasing values of l_i decrement M by one unit if $M > 2$, recommence the procedure otherwise perform

$$sj = (l_1 + l_2)/2$$

Second solution. To determine the different local thresholds, a homogenous criterion can be used. This criterion enables the local window to be separated into two more or less homogenous classes. The homogeneity criterion corresponds to the following function:

$$U(l) = 1 - \frac{var_1^2 + var_2^2}{var_T^2}$$

var_i and var_T correspond respectively to the variance of the class i and to the total variance of the local window. This assumes that in the local area of the image there are only two homogeneous regions and each region is characterised by its statistical parameters.

The Fig. 14 represents the bimodal and multimodal histograms and the corresponding functions of homogeneity $U(l)$. The maximum of each function is indicated by an asterix (*).

Note that in the case where the histogram is bimodal or multimodal, the grey level where the homogeneity function $U(l)$ is maximal, allows a more satisfactory separation of the histogram into two homogenous classes (optimal threshold).

This solution gives noticeably better results than the first, but the calculation time is relatively long. We have therefore opted for the first solution to detect the local thresholds in the case where the histogram is bimodal or multimodal.

The threshold values obtained following the three cases (histogram unimodal, bimodal, multimodal), create a *nxn* size matrix. The null values of the thresholds of this matrix are recomputed by interpolation, as they characterise the homogenous zones of an object or a background.

The resulting matrix is characterised by its average (m) and standard deviation (σ). In order to validate or reject the different thresholds of the matrix the criterion used is:

If the threshold $sj \in [m - \sigma, m + \sigma]$, it is retained
otherwise: sj is rejected ($sj = 0$)

Finally, in order to homogenise the matrix values, each null threshold value is replaced by the average value of the eight neighbouring thresholds non equal to zero. Thus each window shall be thresholded.

This method enables the optimal binarisation threshold to be determined for each production series of the circuits.

6 Modelisation of the Circuits

For the modelisation stage, we have used circuits satisfying the different criteria of control. A file containing the characteristics of each model is saved on disk under a directory chosen by the user.

Each series of circuits is thus characterised by:

- the type of circuit
- the size of the circuit
- the number of links
- the dimensions of the interlinking spaces

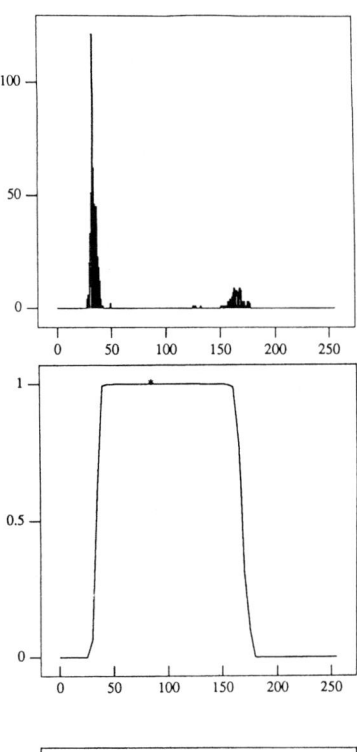
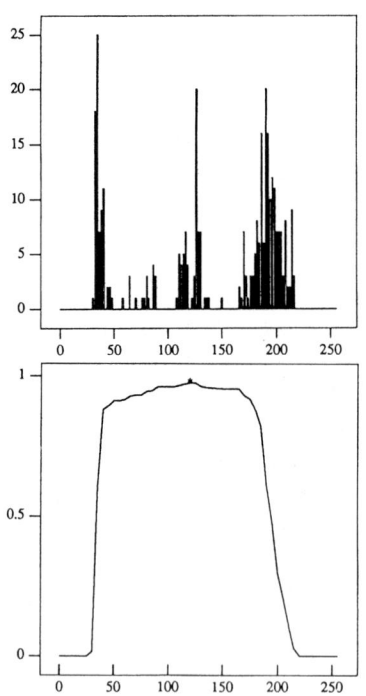

Fig. 14. Histograms and corresponding functions of homogeneity

- size of connection area
- number of rows of links
- number of black pixels / number of white pixels, after binarisation of the window covering the solder joint.

The information saved in this way allows us to modelise each type of circuit.

We have also included a set of procedures allowing the consultation of characteristics saved in order to check, know, indeed modify the information that we hold on the listed circuits or to add new models corresponding to the new series.

7 Detection of Faulty Circuits and Marking

The principle of the control that we have adapted is the comparison of significant characteristics (distance between the median axis of different links, number of black or white pixels of each solder joint) of the circuit being tested with those of the model circuits.

In order to detect faulty solder joints, the severity of the control depends on the number of black and white pixels fixed beforehand. When a faulty circuit is detected, it is automatically numbered by a marker.

After a faulty circuit is detected, the system sends a signal to the point of marking so that the user can easily repair the circuits.

To ensure the exchanges of information between the host micro-computer and the point of marking, a card has been realized which allows the generation of interruption signals coming from the photodetector.

8 Conclusion

The proposed control system allows us to automatically check the position of the links and their solder joints. It takes into account the different types of circuits corresponding to the manufactured series; moreover, it is adaptable to other types of circuits. The configuration, the use of the control system can be assured by someone not specialised in the field of image analysis.

This system outstandingly controls one side of the circuits passing at the same cadence as the production line. The execution of the programs is carried out in an arborescent way following the options of the clear and precise menus. Moreover, the adjustable parameters determining the severity of the controls are chosen by the operator who knows the characteristics of the circuits to be controlled. We tested the system on a significant sample of circuits showing a variety of flaws most often come across, and the rate of recognition is 97%. The tests are satisfactory as much for the level of the rapid execution as for the level of the results obtained.

References

Chapron (1985) Contribution à l'inspection automatique par traitement d'images. Application au montage de circuits integrés et à la détection de fissures sur des ferrites, Thèse de docteur-ingenieur. Rapport LAAS n° 85/57.

K. Chehdi and Q.M. Liao (1991) A new approach to the improvement of texture modelisation, in International Symposium on Electronics and Information Sciences, Kobe, Japan, pp. 24.1–24.10.

K. Chehdi and D. Coquin (1991) Bianarisation of various images by detecting local thresholds with a validation test, in IEEE pacific Rim Conference on Communications Computer and Signal Processing, Victoria, Canada, pp. 611–614.

A. Chehikian (1989) Binarisation d'images: deux solutions à ce problèmes, Revue de Traitement du Signal, vol. 6, n° 1. pp. 59–67.

C.K. Chow and T. Kaneko (1971) Boundary detection of radiographic images by a threshold method, in Proceedings of the IFIP Congress, pp. 130–134.

A.M. Darwish and A.K. Jain (1988) A rule-based approach for visual pattern inspection, IEEE Transactions on Pattern Analysis and Machine Intelligence; vol. 10, n°1, pp. 56–68.

G. Fetecke, G.O. Eklundh and A. Rosenfeld (1981) Relaxation: evaluation and application, IEEE Transactions on Pattern Analysis and Machine Intelligence, vol. 3, pp. 460–469.

R.M. Haralick and L.G. Shapiro (1986) Survey, image segmentation techniques, Computer Vision, Graphics, and Image Processing, vol. 29, pp. 100–132.

G. Johannsen and J. Bille (1983) A threshold selection method using information measures, in Proc. V.I. International Conference on Pattern Recognition, Munich.

J. Kittler and J. Illingworth (1985) On threshold selection using clustering criterion, IEEE Transactions on Systems, Man, Cybenetics, vol. 15, pp. 652–655.

Le Lièvre (1979) Processus d'acquisition et de traitement d'images en temps réel. Application à l'inspection automatique en matériau textile, Thèse de doctorat d'ingénieur, Université des sciences et techniques de Lille.

R. Maloigne-Fernandez, Croche (1988) Classification des défauts observés dans le bois par caméra, Traitement du Signal vol. 5, n° 1, pp. 41–48.

D.L. Milgram and D.J. Herman (1979) Clustering edge values for threshold selection, Computer Graphics, Vision, and Image Processing, vol. 10, pp. 272–280.

T. Pun (1980) A new method for gray-level picture thresholding using the entropy of histogram, Signal Processing, vol. 2, pp. 223–237.

A. Rosenfeld and R.C. Smith (1981) Thresholding using relaxation, IEEE Transactions on Pattern Analysis and Machine Intelligence, vol. 3, pp. 598–606.

P.K. Sahoo, S. Soltani and A.K.C. Wong (1988) A survey of thresholding techniques, Computer Vision, Graphics, and Image Processing, vol. 41, pp. 233–260.

J.M. White and G.D. Rohrer (1986) Image thresholding for optical character recognition and other applications requiring character image extraction, IBM J. Res. Development, 27, pp. 400–411.

A.Y. Wu, T.-H. Hong and A. Rosenfeld (1982) threshold selection using quadtrees, IEEE Transactions on Pattern Analysis and Machine Intelligence, vol. 4, pp. 90–94.

An Image Analysis Based Method to Evaluate Gravure Paper Quality

A. Langinmaa

Abstract. A method has been developed to find the so-called missing dots in a heliotest strip. Heliotest is a test print method which is used to determine the quality of gravure print paper. The developed method is based on image processing and supervised learning, requiring a 386-based MS/DOS computer, a commercial image processing board and software, a commercial co-ordinate table, a CCD camera, and lighting equipment.

1 Introduction

1.1 Gravure Printing

Printing, i.e., the transfer of ink on the paper includes three steps. These are the contact between paper and the printing ink, the penetration of the ink into the paper and the splitting of the print layer. The transfer of ink to paper takes place in the nip between two cylinder or plates. The quality of the print can be regarded as the degree to which the appearance and other properties of a print approach those of the desired result [1]. The unevenness of print quality is mostly related to the evenness of paper. Furthermore, the printing process also introduces unevenness to the print.

In the printing process the transfer of ink to paper takes place in the nip between two cylinders or plates. Gravure (intaglio) printing is a process of printing from engraved surfaces in which the areas to be printed are etched or engraved on a plate or a copper cylinder. The image and text to be printed are sunken below the surface. The depth of the depressions is proportional to the amount of ink which is to be transferred. A heavy ink is smeared over the print surface and the excess is wiped off by a doctor blade, thus leaving the engraved areas filled with ink. As the paper passes through the press, it removes the ink from the depressions.

If the contact between the paper and the printing surface is not close enough, i.e., the paper is too rough, the ink does not transfer to the paper properly and the print will be lacking in colour, strength and detail. Smoothness is therefore one of the most important paper properties in gravure printing [2].

The etchings of Rembrandt and all other engravings are early examples of the intaglio process. Originally the gravure process was confined entirely to illustrations while letterpress was confined to type. Today gravure printing is most often used for long runs on high quality paper.

1.2 Gravure Print Quality Evaluation

The most severe quality problems of gravure paper include blistering of the contact surface, missing dots, mottling, granularity and wiremarking. There exists so far no reliable, objective method of directly measuring defects quickly for quality control purpose. Conventional paper smoothness test instruments which measure the time for a common known volume of air to leak across a surface or instruments which actually measure air flow have been found to correlate poorly with gravure print smoothness.

Today the gravure printability of paper can be predicted most reliably from developed tests on laboratory gravure presses. The oldest method to evaluate the overall quality of proof prints is to use visual evaluation. Several methods to rank the results of visual inspection exist. They include the absolute evaluation on the basis of depreciation points, putting the samples in order, paired comparison and classifying the samples into classes, like superior, very good, . . . , bad, useless. Except the depreciation point method all the methods yield only a ranked order of the proof prints. It is not possible to know, whether the quality difference between classes two and three is greater or smaller than between classes three and four. Nevertheless, the paired comparison method has been developed to establish ordinal relation, i.e., pair-comparison indices, between two different prints. This modified evaluation of the paired comparison allows to represent the quality distances of a great amount of proof prints isomorpholously on a scale [3].

The print quality can be evaluated by measuring the contrast and optical density of the print. Another method is to determine the information capacity of the print [4], i.e., the capability of processes and prints to reproduce different levels of tone and colour.

Granularity and mottling introduce respectively high-frequency medium- and low-contrast variations to the print density. Their amount is most often characterised visually. Another image analysis based method is to filter the image using 2-dimensional bandpass filters [5]. Recently a method to evaluate the mottling using texture analysis has been introduced [6].

Missing dots are white spots in the print which are caused by roughness in the paper surface. Missing dots are often called gravure speckle or cell skipping. The missing dots occurring in a solid print are most often measured as the total area of missing dots per unit area [7, 8, 9].

1.3 Heliotest Method

Heliotest is a standard method to test the smoothness of gravure printing paper [10]. Dots are printed on a strip of paper with a special heliotest ink so that the dot frequency remains the same but the size of the dots decreases towards the end of the strip. Looking at the strip, the intensity of the colour is found to be greater at the beginning of the strip than at the end of the strip. The quality of the paper is determined by searching for the first 20 missing dots. When the 20th missing dot is found the distance from the beginning of the strip is measured. The better the quality of the paper the bigger the measure in centimetres. Until now the search for missing dots has been made manually, i.e., laboratory operator has examined the strips with a magnifying glass or a video camera to produce a magnification. This is, however, a very laborious and error prone procedure. Besides the inspection strains the eyes and a large number of strips cannot be tested consecutively.

For the above reasons the application of image analysis to find the missing dots automatically is a natural approach. There are, however, problems. The available contrast of the heliotest strip is not very good. Ink diffusion makes the strips spotty. Part of the dot is often missing or the dot intensity is very weak, i.e., the contact between the paper surface and the ink has been only partial. In these cases it is difficult for the viewer to decide whether to accept or reject the dot. To make the quality control repeatable and the results comparable, these problems should be solved in a consistent and repeatable way, which is difficult when a human being makes the decision.

There are some restriction which had to be noticed when the algorithm was designed [11]. The quality control station is aimed to daily-base use, thus the algorithm must provide reliable results. The algorithm must for example not be too sensitive to image variations due to uneven and varying illumination. Thus the algorithm must be on the other hand sufficiently sophisticated to find the missing dots and sufficiently robust to withstand errors in the heliotest preparation and image acquisition process.

Attempts have been made before to apply the image analysis to the heliotest problem. The difficulty with these methods is that they require expensive equipment and they take a lot of processing time.

2 The Proposed Method

2.1 Equipment

The images were acquired using a CCD camera with 512×512 pixels. A heliotest strip is 11 cm long and 0.8 cm wide. As the acquired image is far less than 11 cm high, one strip has to be processed little by little.

The quality control is carried out by setting the strips on the surface of a commercial co-ordinate table. An image of the first part of the first strip is acquired and processed to find the number of the missing dots. The acquired image is digitised and stored by a commercial image processing board and software. A 386-based MS/DOS computer is used for the processing. Between the image acquisitions the camera is moved by the co-ordinate table. When the 20th missing dot is found the process is terminated for that strip and the next strip is processed.

Fig. 1. Part of a heliotest strip, beginning of the strip

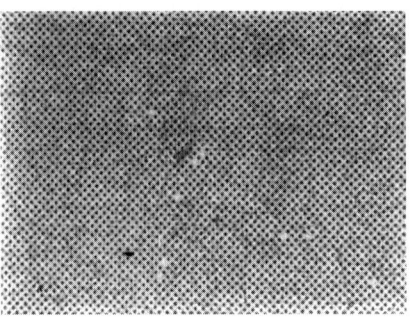

Fig. 2. Part of a heliotest strip, 7 cm from the beginning of the strip

2.2 Algorithm

As discussed in Sect. 1, the contrast of the images is bad, showing defects. The dots which are not thoroughly dark appear at the beginning of the strip as can be seen in Fig. 1 (the beginning of the strip). Towards the end of the strip the dots become smaller and the contrast gets worse as seen in Fig. 2 (about 7 cm from the beginning). Spots appear throughout the strip.

The images are first filtered using a combination of median and grey level morphological eroding filter.

Let g(x) denote a structuring element. The grey scale erosion of image f( ) by structuring element g( ) is defined by [12]

$$[f \ominus g](x) = \min_{z \in D, z-x \in G} \{f(z) - g(z-x)\} \quad (1)$$

where g(x) is a structuring function and G is a subset of R^n indicating the domain of G. The hybrid filter is defined as

$$y = \text{med}(z_1, z_2, z_3, z_4) \quad (2)$$

$$z_1 = [f \ominus g_h](x)$$

$$z_2 = [f \ominus g_v](x)$$

$$z_3 = [f \ominus g_{d_1}](x)$$

$$z_4 = [f \ominus g_{d_2}](x)$$

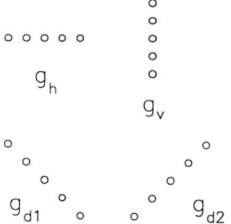

Fig. 3. Structuring elements of (2)

Table 1. Konvolution kernal used in the matched filtering

-2	-1	0	0	0	0	0	0	0	0	-1	-2
-1	0	0	0	0	0	0	0	0	0	0	-1
0	0	0	0	0	0	0	0	0	0	0	0
0	0	0	0	0	0	0	0	0	0	0	0
0	0	0	0	0	0	0	0	0	0	0	0
0	0	0	0	0	2	2	0	0	0	0	0
0	0	0	0	0	2	2	0	0	0	0	0
0	0	0	0	0	0	0	0	0	0	0	0
0	0	0	0	0	0	0	0	0	0	0	0
0	0	0	0	0	0	0	0	0	0	0	0
-1	0	0	0	0	0	0	0	0	0	0	-1
-2	-1	0	0	0	0	0	0	0	0	-1	-2

where the subsections g_h, g_v, g_{d1} and g_{d2} span the horizontal, vertical and diagonal structural elements which pass through the pixel as shown in Fig. 3 and med( ) denotes the median.

Besides the filtering at the pre-processing stage the image is filtered using a matched filter designed to find the white areas which are surrounded by dark dots, i.e., the missing dots. Template matching can be implemented using convolutional filtering [13]

$$g(x, y) = \sum_{m=0}^{M-1} \sum_{n=0}^{N-1} h(x-m, y-n) f(m, n) \qquad (3)$$

where f( ) is the original image, h( ) denotes the convolution kernel and g( ) the convoluted image. The convolution kernel is shown in Table 1.

The decision whether to accept a response as a missing dot is made on the basis of the size of the reponse. Supervised learning [14, 15] has been used to teach a proper threshold value for the size of the response.

2.3 Experimental Analysis of the Proposed Pre-Processing Filter with Artificial Data

The filter of (2) is a very nonlinear one. The filter was analysed by generating an image consisting of Gaussian noise. This image was filtered using the introduced

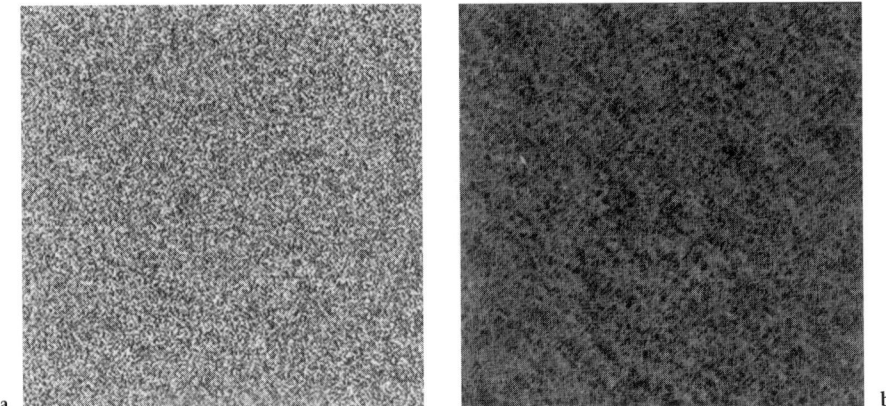

Fig. 4. a An image consisting of Gaussian noise; **b** Filtered Gaussian noise image

Fig. 5. a Magnitude spectrum of the Gaussian noise image; **b** Magnitude spectrum of the filtered Gaussian noise image

filter. In Figs. 4a and 4b we see the original image and filtered image respectively. Figures 5a and 5b show the magnitude spectra of the original noise image and the filtered image respectively. Figure 6 shows the histograms of these images. Figure 5 shows that the spectral contents of the noise image are smoothed. Figure 6 shows that the grey level contents of the image are shifted towards lower values.

Figure 7 shows an image representing Gaussian distribution. Figures 8a and 8b show the magnitude spectrums of the Gaussian image and its filtered counterpart respectively. Figure 9 shows the histograms of the original and filtered image.

From Figs. 8 and 9 it can be seen that the histogram of the image is not affected and that the higher order frequencies are removed.

An Image Analysis Based Method to Evaluate Gravure Paper Quality

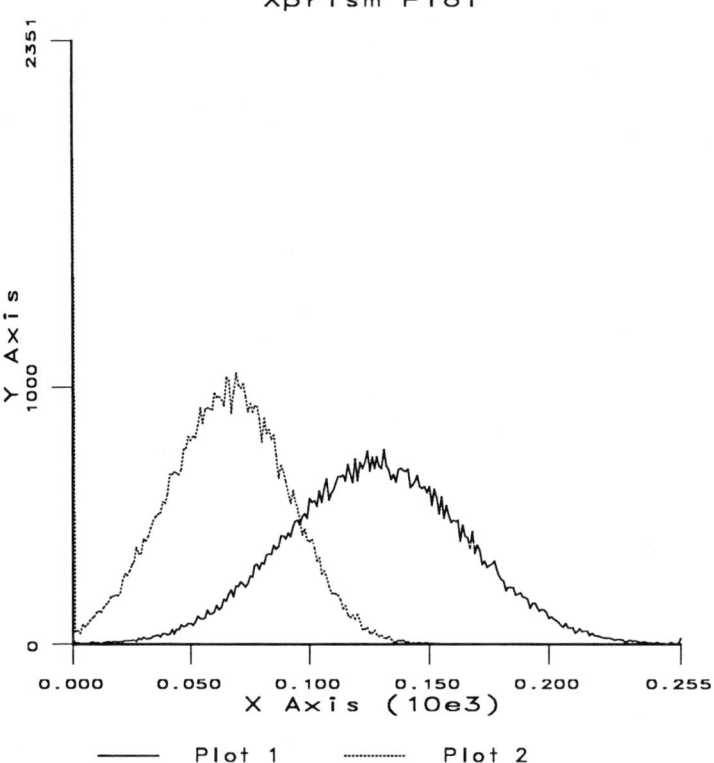

Fig. 6. Histograms of the images 4a (solid line) and 4b (dotted line)

Fig. 7. A Gaussian distribution image

Fig. 8. a Magnitude spectrum of the Gaussian distribution image; **b** Magnitude spectrum of the filtered Gaussian distribution image

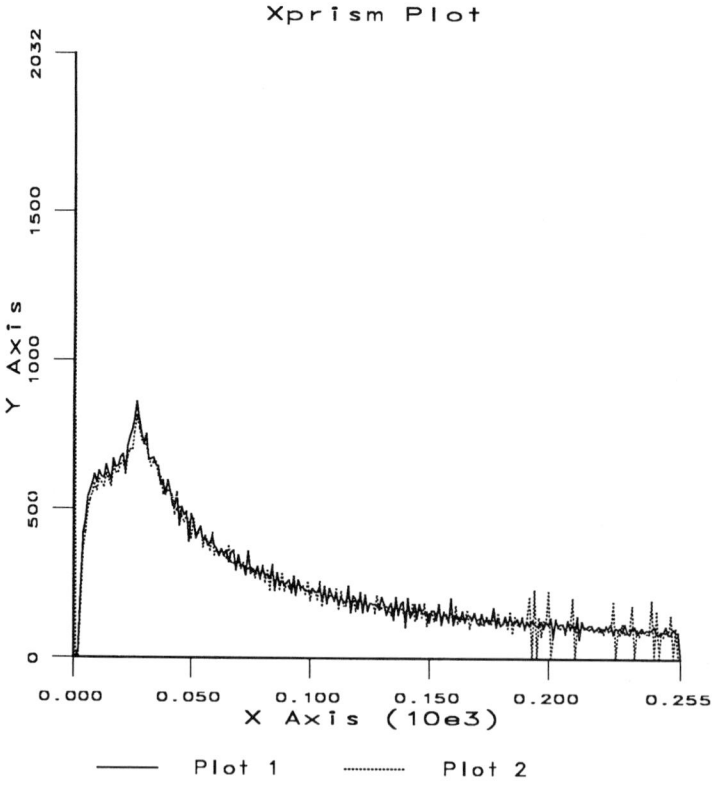

Fig. 9. Histograms of the Gaussian distribution image (solid line) and the filtered Gaussian distribution image (dotted line)

Fig. 10. The heliotest image of Fig. 1 filtered with the hybrid filter

Fig. 11. a Original image filtered with 3 × 3 median filter; **b** Original image filtered with 3 × 3 eroding filter

2.4 Analysis of the Proposed Pre-Processing Filter with Real Data

In Fig. 10 we see the Fig. 1 filtered with the hybrid filter of equation (2). Figures 11a and 11b show the original image filtered with 3 × 3 median and purely erosion filter operating with a 3 × 3 structuring element. Figures 12a and 12b show the magnitude spectrums of the original and filtered images respectively.

The hybrid filter strengthens the large dark areas, i.e., dots but it does not expand small dark defects and the borders of the dots as the pure erosion filter does. Compared to the pure erosion filter the hybrid filter alleviates its robustness and the strong characteristics of the pure erosion filter which has the disadvantage of stressing and expanding dark areas.

3 Evaluation of the Method

3.1 The Classification Algorithm

The classification procedure consisted of three steps:

1. Pre-processing: The image was pre-processed to enhance the feature extraction performance. Besides the hybrid filter of equation (2) the performance of

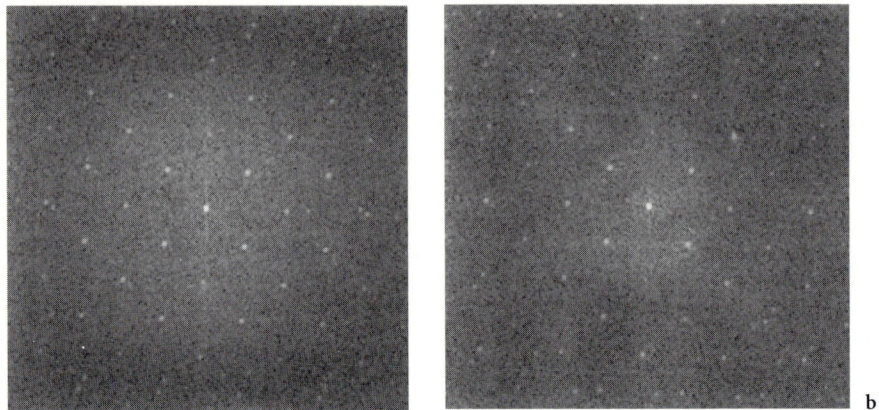

Fig. 12. a Magnitude spectrum of the heliotest image of Fig. 1; **b** Magnitude spectrum of the filtered heliotest image (Fig. 10)

Table 2. Tested pre-processing methods

Method	Description of the method
1	no pre-processing
2	grey level erosion filter
3	3 × 3 median filtering
4	5 × 5 median/erosion filering

two other filters was tested. The tested methods are shown in Table 2. In addition to these filters also four other nonlinear filtering methods have been tested [16].

2. Feature extraction: The feature extraction was done by applying a matched filter designed to find the white areas which are surrounded by dark dots, i.e., the missing dots. Several templates were tested but the exact design of the template seemed to have little significance provided that it was of right type.

3. Decision: The decision whether to accept a response of the matched filter as a missing dot or not is made on the basis of the size of the response. For each part of the strip an own threshold value was determined by supervised learning. The determination of the threshold values was done for the learning data.

The method 1 is the reference method and is the no-filtering method, i.e., only the mask is applied and pre-processing is omitted. Method 2 represents pure morphological filtering. The idea of using min filter was to get rid of the holes inside the dots. It was further thought that the min filter would increase the contrast between the dots and the background area. Filter 3 is a pure median filter, filter 4 is the hybrid filter consisting of a median and erosion filter part.

3.2 Evaluation Criteria

The results were evaluated by computing for each strip the percentile recognition rate. After that the average deviation from perfect recognition was computed for both the learning and for the test set.

In this case small errors (recognition deviation smaller than 10%) are acceptable but greater error undesirable. The errors were divided into classes and for each method an error histogram was computed for both the learning and for the test set. A cost was given for each error and the misclassification costs for each method were computed using the formula

$$cf = \sum_{i=1}^{nb \text{ of strips}} n_i c_i \qquad (4)$$

where n_i is the number of strips in error class i and c_i the cost associated with that particular error class.

In practice an tolerable error is the centimetre measure is about 0.5 cm. Errors greater than 1 cm are highly undesirable. According to this fact the errors were partitioned into classes and a cost was given to each class. From Table 2 it can be noted that the cost for the small errors is negligible but greater errors are strongly stressed.

3.3 Test Material

The methods were tested using 24 strips as learning data and 24 strips as test data. The strips were processed to the image in which the 20 missing point was found.

The learning data consisted of four different grades of super calendered gravure paper. The learning set consisted also of four grades of super calendered paper although the differences between the various grades were smaller than in the case of learning data.

3.4 Results

In Fig. 13 we see the response of the unprocessed image of 1 to the matched filter. It can be seen that several responses exist. When the original image was filtered with the hybrid filter of equation (2) the response image changes as can be seen from Fig. 14. It can be seen that several amount of nonlinear noise has been disposed and the number of false responses is radically reduced.

The results for the learning set are shown in Table 2 and the results for the test set in Table 3.

Fig. 13. Response of the heliotest image (Fig. 1) to the matched filter

Fig. 14. Response of the filtered heliotest image (Fig. 10) to the matched filter

Table 3. The error classes and their respective costs

Error class	1	2	3	4	5	6	7	8
Error %	0%	0–5%	5–10%	10–15%	15–20%	20–30%	30–40%	>40%
Cost	0	0.1	0.3	0.9	1.5	4	8	12

Table 4. Performance test results for the learning data

Method	1	2	3	4
Mean error, %	7.5	6.7	5.9	3.9
Cost	9.5	11.2	7.5	3.7

By comparing Tables 2 and 3 it can be seen that the pre-processing methods have the same effect for both the learning and test data results. The mean errors and costs are greater for the test data but their order of superiority is about the same.

We see that the without any pre-processing (method 1) it is possible to get quite promising results. As a matter of fact the cost row reveals that the erosion filtering procedure introduced severe misrecognitions. The reason for its fail is probable that it is too strong and introduces new potential error locations to the image.

Table 5. Performance test results for the test data

Method	1	2	3	4
Mean error, %	11.4	13.9	8.6	7.8
Cost	32.9	41.6	23.8	18.4

Table 6. Sensitivity analysis results for the learning data

Method	1	2	3	4
Mean error I	7.5	6.7	5.9	3.9
Mean error II	12.2	9.5	7.8	5.8
Cost I	9.5	11.2	7.5	3.7
Cost II	40.3	34.0	13.7	7.3

Table 7. Sensitivity analysis results for the test data

Method	1	2	3	4
Mean error I	11.4	13.9	8.6	7.8
Mean error II	20.9	22.1	12.3	11.2
Cost I	32.9	41.6	23.8	18.4
Cost II	86.0	96.0	34.7	31.8

3.5 Sensitivity Analysis

The sensitivity of the method regarding the threshold selection was tested by increasing and decreasing each threshold by 10 percents and computing the recognition percents and costs for this case.

In the following tables I refers to the optimised thresholds, II to the increased thresholds.

The results for the learning data are shown in Table 4 and results for the test data in Table 5.

When the mean error I and II rows as well as the corresponding cost rows of Table 4 and Table 5 are compared it can be seen that the promising performance of the no-filtering method deteriorates radically and the performance of the pure erosion filter is further reduced. On the other hand the results show that the data pre-processed with the hybrid filter as well as with the median filter resist little changes in the threshold selection essentially better than the other methods.

4 Discussion

The proposed method is universal, i.e., it can be applied to all grades of gravure paper under heliotest. The supervised learning procedure which was used to find suitable threshold values was applied to a learning set consisting of samples of very different grades. Thus the scheme was very ambitious because the resulting classification procedure is able to treat the whole spectrum of gravure papers. It is, however possible to determine for each gravure paper grade an own set of threshold values. This procedure is surely able to decrease the recognition errors. Because each paper mill has a certain assortment of gravure paper grades in production this is certainly the way to be recommended for the practical threshold selection.

The results for the learning data show that most cases are handled correctly without any pre-processing. This is a typical observation when image analysis problems are concerned. Often a simple solution optimised for a particular data set is able to handle 90% of cases correctly, the rest 10% form the most difficult cases. This sort of simple solutions tend also to be sensitive to parameter, image data and/or image formation changes. These general experiences were found to be true also in this case. When the matched filter without pre-processing was applied to the test set the results were deteriorated relatively more than with the other methods (excluding the pure eroding filter). The sensitivity analysis also revealed that the good results obtained without any pre-processing are due more to result of parameter optimisation for a particular set than to the general usability of the method.

In the work three different non-linear filtering methods were compared regarding their ability to improve feature extraction. The results show that the robust non-linear filter, i.e., eroding filter and median filters do not help the feature recognition. The results show that the performance of the 5×5 hybrid filter is superior to the other pre-processing methods concerning both feature extraction improvement and sensitivity. The good performance of the 5×5 hybrid filter is due to its ability to stress the dots and remove small-sized dark defects at the same time.

There exist no systematic study of the reliability of the conventional evaluation of the heliotest strip and the automatic and human evaluations can thus not be compared. The automatic evaluation has, however, the advantage over its human counterpart that it acts in a consistent and predictable way. The recognition rates obtained with the automatic method are acceptable for most cases. The greatest errors occur when the strip contains a cluster of missing points. The proposed method is unable to solve this sort of a case correctly and none of the pre-processing filter remedies the situation. Theses type of errors are fortunately uncommon and they are easy to recognise visually because of the large light blotch on the strip.

References

[1] G.A. Smook. Handbook of pulp & paper terminology. Angus Wilde Publications, Vancouver, Bellingham, 1990.
[2] A. Glassman. Printing fundamentals. Tappi Press, 1985.
[3] C. Chareza, T. Greve, and L. Göttsching. Einstufung von Probedrucken nach visueller Beurteilung mittels Paarvergleichs-Index. Das Papier, 39. Jahrgang, Heft 7, 1985 (in German), pp. 293-302.
[4] P.T. Oittinen and H.J. Saarelma. Application of information theory to characterize print quality. Tappi Journal, August 1991, pp. 197-203.
[5] I.M. Kajanto and K. Niemi. Measurement of print unevenness with an image analyzer. Paperi ja puu 73 (1991):770-772.
[6] A. Visa and A. Langinmaa. A Texture-based Method to Evaluate Solid Print Quality in "Advances in printing science and technology", pp. 168-173.
[7] P.A. Gartaganis, H.U. Heintze, and R.W. Gordon. From printrograph to videoscanner. Tappi Journal, Vol. 59, No. 12, December 1976, pp. 113-117.
[8] H.U. Heintze and R.W. Gordon. Reliability of videoscanner measurement of gravure speckle on coated paper. Tappi Journal, Vol. 63, No. 9, September 1980, pp. 125-128.
[9] H. Praast and L. Göttsching. Analyse und Ursachen von Missing Dots im Tiefdruck. To be published in "Das Papier".
[10] Paperin ja kartongin syväpainatussileyden määritys, heliotest menetelmä. Keskuslaboratorion käyttämät analyysimenetelmät, No: 224:88. KCL 1988 (in Finnish).
[11] B.G. Batchelor, D.A. Hill, and D.C. Hodgson (editors), Automated Visual Inspection. IFS (Publications) Ltd, 1985.
[12] I. Pitas and A.N. Venetsanapoulis. Nonlinear Digital Filters, Principles and Applications. Kluwer Academic Publishers, Massachusetts, 1990.
[13] R.J. Schalkoff. Digital image proccessing and computer vision. John Wiley & Sons, Inc. 1989.
[14] T.Y. Young and T.W. Calvert, Classification, Estimation and Pattern Recognition. American Elsevier Publishing Company, New York, 1974.
[15] C.W. Therrien. Desicion, Estimation and Classification. John Wiley & Sons, New York, 1989.
[16] A. Langinmaa. Automatic visual inspection of heliotest strips. Licentiate's thesis, Helsinki University of Technology, Finland, 1992.

A Vision System
for an Autonomous Underwater Vehicle

J.O. Hallset

Abstract. A vision system for our PISCIS project is described. This is a proposed project for the use of an untethered autonomous underwater vehicle (AUV) for pipeline inspection. The vision system is termed PVS (the PISCIS vision system). It will assist the AUV in finding and following pipelines. A salient feature of the PVS is that it is designed to find all pipelines within the field of view and, thus, the AUV can follow any of them. Robust image interpretation is important as humans can not interact with the PVS and correct errors. Furthermore, the image quality is reduced by backscatter, light absorption, a non-uniform background (the sea-bed), and marine material on the pipelines. The PVS is fixed to a vehicle and must rely on a heading sensor and an altitude sonar to match image features with pipeline models. The models are retrieved from a map based on the vehicle's position.

1 Introduction

The PISCIS vehicle is shown inspecting a pipeline in Fig. 1. The camera's field of view (FOV) is indicated with the dark square, the light source's coverage with the shaded circle, and an altitude sonar with a vertical "ray" at the back of the vehicle. A video will be recorded, possibly using the same camera as the PVS, while the AUV is moving along the pipeline. A human operator will later do the actual pipeline inspection by replaying the video.

After being launched somewhere near the pipeline, the AUV has to transit to the start of it. The AUV will then search for the pipeline and follow it by means of the PVS. During the mission the AUV must circumvent subsea installations, and then continue tracking a pipeline on another side of an installation. Finally, upon mission completion, the AUV must land at a predetermined base. In the transit, circumvention, and landing phase the vehicle is assisted by a map-based navigation system rather than the PVS. The PISCIS project is described in more detail by Hallset and Rødseth (1991), and Hallset (1992). The background for the project can be found in Rødseth (1990), and Rødseth and Hallset (1991a; 1991b).

The task of the PVS will be to use a camera to continuously find the position and heading of all nearby pipelines relative to the AUV. The positions and headings are used in a control loop to move the vehicle to a chosen pipeline. They are also used to keep the vehicle over this chosen pipeline during the inspection.

To make a simple and low-cost system it is profitable to use the same CCD-camera for both video recording and relative positioning. The three alternative systems for recognition and relative positioning are magnetic trackers, sonars, and

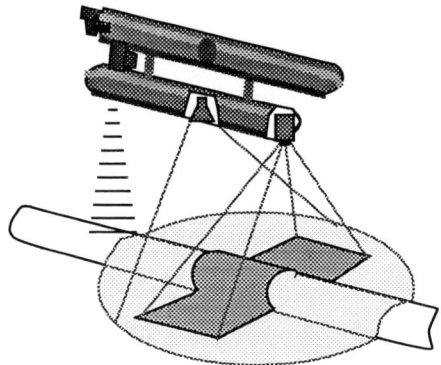

Fig. 1. Pipeline inspection

structured light sensors. They are all either bulky, expensive, or use too much energy compared to a CCD-camera in a pressure housing.

Little has been published on complete systems that use cameras for underwater object-tracking. However, the PVS has been inspired by two land-based systems for road-following: Turk et al. (1988) present the VITS vision system for their ALV vehicle. The system has a colour camera and a laser range scanner; Dickmanns et al. (1990) presents the similar VaMoRs system, equipped with tele- and wide-angle cameras. Both projects have been extensively tested under realistic outdoor conditions and can, therefore, contribute invaluable experience.

The next Sect. 2 presents the environment the PVS faces. Section 3 presents the PVS itself, and the following Sects. 4 to 6 presents the details of the PVS' segmentation-, matching-, and interpretation-stage. Section 7 gives some experimental results, and finally Sect. 8 presents a summary and discussion.

2 The PVS' Environment

The PVS is to operate in an underwater environment, which is highly unstructured and can not be controlled. Six basic problems arise from operating in this environment:

(1) The outline of pipelines are broken by marine growth, mud, or sand cover. The background, i.e., the sea-bed is non-uniform and may introduce false image-features that makes image analysis difficult.
(2) Ambient light decreases rapidly as a function of water depth and the vehicle has to bring its own light source as illustrated in Fig. 1. The light intensity from this source will decrease with the distance to the sea-bed, as the light energy then will be spread over a larger area. Even worse is it that the visual range is reduced by light absorption resulting in faint light and, thus, low contrast at ranges of a few metres.

(3) The light intensity will vary slowly over the covered area. It will be relative constant, for a given distance, in the centre of the scene and will then drop abruptly at the edges. The problem is made worse as the surface-reflectance is not the same for all the objects or the background. The two problems are difficult to handle and will probably have to be accepted. However, they are made less by the fact that marine material will smooth the objects and the background.
(4) By using an active light-source the quality of images is degraded by backscatter from the water. The image will have small bright spots in them caused by reflections (backscatter) from organic material floating in the water between the scene of interest and the camera. This effect is predominant in shallow waters.
(5) The system is fixed to a moving vehicle. The vehicle will find and follow pipelines at known locations. This suggest that models of pipelines should be retrieved from a pipeline-map and made available to the PVS based on the vehicle's position.
(6) Scenes with many, possibly overlapping, objects are difficult to interpret. The problem gets worse if there are similar objects, or objects that look the same from a given viewpoint. Underwater pipelines are not expected to overlap, but they can have the same diameter, and, thus, look the same. Their known relative position and heading must be used to differentiate between them.

The PVS that is presented in the following and described fully in Hallset (1992), will handle these difficulties by adapting known image analysis techniques to the underwater environment. It is argued in Sect. 4 that edge based image segmentation is well suited. Edge points should be assembled into short lines, which again are used for recognition of a pipeline's outline. The assumption is that enough short lines will be generated to enable recognition of the pipeline's heading and position, even though the outline is broken.

3 The PISCIS Vision System

The PVS takes its inputs from a camera, an altitude sonar, a heading sensor, a position sensor, and a pipeline map, and presents its results to the PISCIS mission control system (PMC) as shown in Fig. 2. The PVS is a classical pipeline vision-system. Its four main modules are found in the figure: A segmentation pipeline with a *Filter*, an *Edge* and a *MHough* function; A *Predict* module for finding pipeline segments within the FOV; A *Match* module that matches image lines with pipeline segments; An *Interpret* module for validating matches. An overview of the PVS is given in the following (refer to Fig. 2) before further details are given in Sects. 4 to 6.

The PVS' light source can reach pipelines on the seabed if the altitude is less than 5 metres. The Predict module must in addition find that there are possible pipelines within the FOV. Assume that these two preconditions are OK. Then the

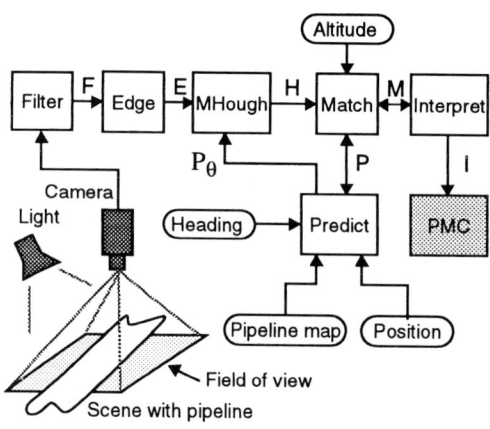

Fig. 2. The PISCIS vision system

vehicle state-variables *position*, *altitude*, and *heading* will be read simultaneously with an image-frame from the camera. Thereafter, lines are extracted from the image by the segmentation module functions: The digitised image is smoothed by the *Filter* function. The smoothed image F will be turned into an edge point image E by the Edge function. The MHough function requires input from the Predict module in addition to E.

The Edge and MHough functions are based on known algorithms that are adapted to the underwater environment: (1) The edge-detection algorithm is based on the Sobel operator (Gonzalez and Wints 1987, page 337); (2) The MHough algorithm is based on a modification of the Hough transform (Gonzalez and Wints 1987, page 130). The first algorithm enables the PVS to find image edgepoints as the contrast in the scene varies with the AUV's distance to the scene. The second algorithm finds the position and orientation of short line-segments from these edges. The lines are found even though there are spurious edge-points caused by backscatter from the water and a natural features in the environment.

The Predict module will find a list P of pipeline segments from the pipeline map, based on the vehicle's position. The segments in P are rotated to vehicle coordinates by the Predict module based on the vehicle's heading. A list P_θ of the vehicle-relative headings of the segments in P are input to the MHough function. It will search for image lines in the directions given by P_θ and produce a list of lines H, which will be scaled to vehicle-relative coordinates by the Match module, based on the vehicle's altitude.

All the pipeline-segments, that are found to be within the camera's FOV, will be retrieved from the pipeline-map. There may be retrieved segments that are outside the FOV due to the vehicle's position uncertainty. The segments will, therefore, be matched one by one with image lines. The matching process could have failed, because of too many false segments, if all were simultaneously matched. Another consequence of the uncertain pipeline-segment position is that the matching in the PVS must be based solely on the pipeline-heading and -diameter, which are assumed to be known.

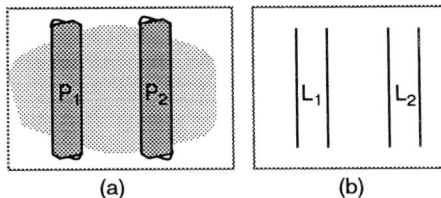

Fig. 3. a A scene with two parallel pipeline segments with the same diameter; b The resulting line image

The Match module will match one and one segment from P with the scaled images lines and store the result in a list M as (P_i, L_i)-pairs of image-line clusters and pipeline-segment parameters. There may exist false lines which do not belong to any pipeline segment. The PVS simply ignores spurious lines which can not be matched to a pipeline segment. The matching algorithm is a variant of Agglomerative clustering (Duda and Hart 1973, pp. 230–235).

The chosen matching method will in general result in false or ambiguous matches caused by segments that have the same diameter and heading as shown in Fig. 3a. The figure shows an image from a simple scene with two parallel pipelines P_1 and P_2. They will look exactly the same in an edge image. This is indicated in Fig. 3b by the two sets of line clusters L_1 and L_2. The matching stage will end up with four matches: (P_1, L_1), (P_1, L_2), (P_2, L_1), (P_2, L_2).

The Interpret module resolves the ambiguity after matching by assuming that the relative positions of pipelines are accurate. It will search for the set of (P_i, L_i)-pairs which in combination gives the "best" geometric fit of pipeline segments and line clusters. Pairs which increase an error function to much are rejected. By observing the relative position in Fig. 3 it is obvious that the correct matches are (P_1, L_1) and (P_2, L_2). The two other matches are discarded. The accepted pairs are the final interpretation of an image. The Interpret module will deliver the valid matches in the list I to the PMC.

4 Segmentation

The segmentation stage is the basis for image analysis and must be reliable. It faces four problems: (1) The outline of pipelines will be distorted or broken by marine growth, and mud or sand cover; (2) Furthermore, it is expected that their interior will be covered with patches of marine material; (3) The pipeline's colour is expected to be blurred by marine material; (4) The colour balance is shifted with the distance to the object. A natural balance can only be obtained within a distance of 2–3 metres (MacKay 1991), as the absorption of the red wavelength is higher than that of the blue/green wavelength.

From the above discussion I will conclude that the boundary of pipelines should be used for recognition. The boundary will of course be distorted, but it is expected that big objects like pipelines always will have a distinguishable contour and that they can be recognised by their contrast against the sea-bed: The marine life and marine material on the pipeline will differ from that on the sea-bed. Thus, the best viewpoint for recognition is from above such that the sea-bed can be seen on both sides of the pipeline. Boundary detection has the additional advantage that fast high-level analysis is possible as the number of edge points usually is at least two orders of magnitude less than the original number of image pixels.

Boundary detection starts by finding edge points in an image that can be grouped or rather linked into boundaries. There are in general two problems that must be handled: (1) The contrast in an image can change which makes it difficult to find a threshold that can be used to discriminate between edge- and non-edge-pixels. If it is too high, edges that are searched for are lost. If the threshold is set too low, unwanted edges are introduced by noise in the image. The threshold should ideally be found directly from the image data; (2) The other problem is that the boundary-linking algorithm may be lead astray by spurious edges or be stopped at missing edge points.

The proposed segmentation pipeline, which solves these two problems for the PVS, can be seen in Fig. 2 and is described in the following Sects. 4.1 to 4.3. It consists of a pre-processing stage including an average filter, an edge-detection stage that can set a threshold automatically, and a modified Hough line-detector that is robust.

4.1 Pre-Processing

An auto-iris lens will try to keep the light-intensity in an scene constant as the AUV's distance to the sea-bed changes. Note that the contrast still will change even though the average intensity will be fine. A problem with these lenses, as with all lenses, is to retain a sharp and detailed image at high aperture. This should not be a problem, as the PVS is to detect large pipeline-objects where details are of less interest.

A second problem with auto-iris lenses is that they may use too small aperture, when there are spots of high light-intensity in a scene. This will result in an image with low contrast, as the automatic iris-control is based on measuring the average intensity in the scene. If this proves to be a problem, a lens with a controllable iris can be chosen and a more sophisticated iris control can be implemented. However, underwater images are dominated by a sandy sea-bed and surfaces with marine material, and it is unlikely that there will be highly reflecting surfaces causing such spots.

A averaging filter will reduce the effect of backscatter and, in addition, the slight gain differences in the individual cells of a CCD-camera, Backscatter spots, which are smaller than the mask size (3 by 3 pixels) of the averaging filter, will be smoothed. However, the effect of heavy backscatter or large bright spots on objects are difficult to handle. The engineering solution is to make the best of it and reduce the effect of the backscatter by separating the light source and the camera (Jaffe 1990).

4.2 Edge Detection

There are numerous ways of computing the gradient for edge detection (Pratt 1991, pp. 491–556). It seems that most detectors perform well on images with a high signal-to-noise ratio, and poorly on images with a low one. Alas, there are practically no objective measures available to specify the performance of a detector (Jain and Binford, 1991, p. 116).

The Sobel operator is popular because of its computational simplicity. Kitchen and Malin (1989) have compared it with other similar operators and found that it has the most uniform magnitude response as a function of edge direction. This is important when searching for boundaries that can have any direction in an image.

The problem of finding an edge-threshold remains, and a new method for doing this is proposed here. It is based on a suggestion by Lacroix (1988). She proposes to calculate the edge-magnitude for all image pixels and to keep the x percent of them that have the highest magnitude. The problem is that too many or too few edge-points may be accepted. More serious is it that edges will be found in images where there are none.

In the method, that is proposed here, it will be assumed that x percent of the edge points, those with the least magnitude, are noise. The assumption is that it is easier to guess the maximum content of edges than how many there really are.

Underwater images are expected to have relative few man-made objects that can generate edges, and a reasonably safe value for x is 60–70%. It is further assumed that the magnitude of the noise edges has a Gaussian distribution with a mean m and a standard deviation σ. Denote the Sobel-magnitude of a pixel with e_i, the number of pixels in an image with n, and the edge threshold by t. Edge pixels will be those that have:

$$e_i > t = m + 3\sigma \tag{1}$$

where m and σ are given by:

$$m = \frac{1}{n}\sum_i e_i$$
$$\sigma^2 = \frac{1}{n}\sum_i (e_i - m)^2 \tag{2}$$

When the noise has a Gaussian distribution only 0.5% of the noise edges will be misjudged as "real" edges. The threshold will be found based on maybe 70 percent of the background. There will be found few edges in these 70 percent. If there are no objects in the image, and the background is modestly uniform, there will be found equally few edges in the remaining 30 percent of the image. However, a few outliers must always be expected in images of natural scenes.

A problem is that boundaries, after thresholding, will appear to be more than one pixel thick. Several algorithms have been proposed that place the boundary point where the magnitude has a peak value in the gradient-direction. Fleck (1992) compares the performance of some of the algorithms and finds that the output from them are surprisingly similar. The PVS uses the Sobel operator for finding the edge-magnitude and -gradient. They are the input to the boundary-point detection scheme in the PVS (Canny 1987; Fleck 1992). This straight-forward scheme (Hallset 1992) will produce an edge-point image with one pixel thick boundaries.

The proposed thresholding method is fast and surprisingly robust, but it will, as all other methods, encounter problems with images that have extremely low contrast. This can happen if an image is saturated with light or if it gets too little light. This must be handled by the PMC by not allowing the vehicle to get too near or too far from the pipelines on the sea-bed.

4.3 Line Detection

A pipeline segment will occur in an edge images as two parallel lines, which are separated with the diameter of the segment (see Fig. 3). Furthermore, it is assumed that the segments can extend beyond the edges of the image such that closed contours can not be found.

Apparent lines in the edge-point image will have gaps as marine material will distort the outline of the segments and the image will contain unwanted edge points, which must be rejected. They are caused by backscatter and natural features in the environment. The Hough transform offers, according to Illingworth and Kittler (1988), an almost unique ability to handle images containing noise, missing, and extraneous data.

The use of the Hough transform has three problems: (1) Lines will be indicated by clusters of almost the same (θ, d) values, rather than a single strong value. A method for detecting these clusters and finding the most probable line from one has to be found. The interaction between the cluster size, the number of clusters, and the threshold is not obvious; (2) Although line angles and the perpendicular distances from the image centre are readily found, there is no indication of line length and position; (3) The basic transform searches for all possible lines in the edge image which is time-consuming and unnecessarily when the directions of expected lines are known. This problem is of course easy to solve by restricting θ to be within the range of expected line-angles.

The algorithm, which is proposed in the following, will solve the three above problems. The modified transform will be referred to as MHough.

The basic Hough transform keeps track of what lines a certain edge pixel can be part of. The MHough transform will do it the other way around by keeping track of what pixels that can be included in a line with a given length, midpoint, and angle.

MHough may be seen as a search algorithm that uses line templates. It will reduce the processing time by restricting the line-template angles to the directions of expected pipelines. MHough will start by assuming that every edge pixel that is not already part of a line can be a line centre. It will then place a template line with a fixed length and a fixed angle θ over that edge pixel at (x_c, y_c) as shown in Fig. 4. MHough will count the number of edge points under the template. If the number

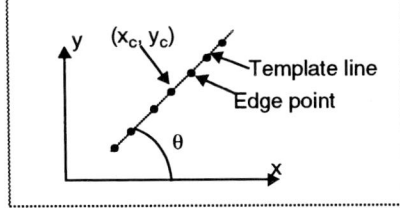

Fig. 4. A line template laid "over" points in an edge image

```
1. Let c' = n and K_i = {x_i}, i = 1,...,n.
2. If c' ≤ c, stop.
3. Find the nearest clusters K_i and K_j.
4. Merge K_i and K_j.
5. Delete K_j, and decrement c' by one.
6. Goto 2.
```

Fig. 5. The basic Agglomerative Clustering Algorithm

exceeds a given percentage of the template length these pixels will be accepted as a line. The accepted line will now have a known position, length, and angle. The accepted edge pixels will be marked such that they will not be counted for inclusion in another line.

This way of setting a threshold may not seem to be any different from picking a "good" threshold in the basic Hough transform, *but it is*. A line is now based on a given percentage of edge pixels within a *known* length. Long "dotted" lines will not be accepted together with short "solid" ones. The result of the MHough transform will be a list of fixed-length lines with midpoint- and heading-parameters of (x_i, y_i) and θ_i.

5 Matching

This module matches image lines with pipeline-segments from the pipeline map. Matching is done in vehicle coordinates and image lines must be scaled, based on the vehicle, altitude, to their real-world size before comparison. Two alternatives for matching have been considered. The first is a classical tree-search method proposed by Grimson and Lozano-Perez (1987). It will have problems with keeping the image-processing time down. This is caused be the combinatorial explosion when there are many segments and image-lines.

The PVS uses an alternative method for matching. It is a variant of the Agglomerative Clustering Algorithm (ACA) described by Duda and Hart (1973, pp. 230–235). Figure 5 shows the main steps of the basic ACA.

In the above algorithm it is assumed that there are n samples which are to be merged into exactly c clusters. The algorithm starts by letting all samples x_i be a cluster kernel K_i. It then finds the two nearest clusters K_i and K_j, according to some

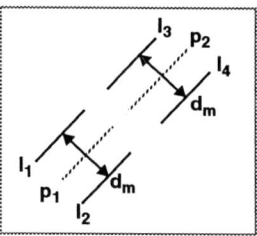

Fig. 6. Pairing of image lines into pipeline segment kernels

criterion, and merges these two into the cluster K_i. K_j is deleted and the cluster counter c' is decremented by one. The merging of clusters is continued until the desired number of clusters c is reached.

The ACA must be modified if the number of clusters is unknown as it is here. This can be done by choosing a suitable "nearest" criterion. It must be cast such that the merging is stopped when the remaining clusters are too far separated. The criterion must be based on one or more of the pipeline-segment parameters: The position, the length, the heading, and the diameter. The exact position of a segment is not known and the segment will, in addition, usually extend over the whole image such that the length can not be used. However, it is assumed that the vehicle-relative heading θ_m and the diameter d_m are known. Thus, these two parameters can be used for clustering.

The PVS does the clustering in two steps by first pairing two and two image-lines, which both must have the heading θ_m and be separated by d_m. This is illustrated in Fig. 6 where first l_1 and l_2 is made into the pair p_1, and l_3 and l_4 to p_2. The pairs will now be the centre lines of short candidate pipeline-segments, which can be merged with other candidates into a longer segment centre-line. Figure 6 shows that p_1 and p_2 are aligned and, thus, they can be combined into a longer line. The result of the matching will be one or more such long lines for each pipeline segment. Note that the pipeline segments are matched one and one with the image lines. Thus, when there are two segments that have the same θ_m and d_m they will be matched with the same image lines. The Interpret module (Sect. 6) will resolve the conflicting matches based on the segments' relative position.

The pairing of lines and the clustering of these pairs into longer centre-lines are guided by a series of tests. These tests are similar to the ones presented by Grimson and Lozano-Perez (1987, p. 451). Three tests are used to find the line pair:

(1) The first is on the angle deviation between θ_m and an image line's heading θ_i. Two image lines must be found to form a pair. The deviation must be less than a threshold t_θ:

$$|\theta_i - \theta_m| < t_\theta \qquad (3)$$

(2) The second test is on scale. The distance between two image lines should be about the same as d_m. A threshold t_{dd} will be set for the maximum allowed deviation. It will be scaled by d_m as the error in the diameter found from the image, is

expected to be proportional to the error in the altitude measurement. Denote the signed perpendicular distance from the origin of the vehicle's coordinate system to the two lines by r_i and r_j, where r_i is found by:

$$r_i = y_i \cos \theta_i - x_i \sin \theta_i \tag{4}$$

The following condition must then be met if the two lines are to be paired into a centre-line candidate:

$$\left| |r_i - r_j| - d_m \right| < t_{dd} \cdot d_m \tag{5}$$

(3) The third test is on the distance between the two image lines that are to be paired. The midpoints of the two lines must not be too far separated and a scalable threshold t_{md} will be set for the maximum allowed distance. The assumption is that close lines are more probably generated by the same pipeline segment than lines that are wide apart. The least possible distance will be the pipeline's diameter, thus, it is reasonable to let t_{md} be scaled by d_m. Denote the midpoints of the two lines by respectively (x_i, y_i) and (x_j, y_j). To be paired the two must meet the following condition:

$$\sqrt{(x_i - x_j)^2 - (y_i - y_j)^2} < t_{md} \cdot d_m \tag{6}$$

The parameters (x_p, y_p, θ_p) of a pair that met the conditions in (3), (5), and (6) are given by:

$$\begin{aligned} x_p &= (x_i + x_j) / 2 \\ y_p &= (y_i + y_j) / 2 \\ \theta_p &= (\theta_i + \theta_j) / 2 \end{aligned} \tag{7}$$

Every possible pair of lines will be found guided by the three tests given above. An image line will be allowed to be part of only one pair, and lines that can not be paired, will be ignored.

The clustering will be started with one of the found pairs as a cluster kernel. The kernel will be merged with other pairs into a longer line that will be a possible pipeline segment centre-line. The clustering will be guided by two tests that checks the lengthwise-distance d_{lw}, and the crosswise-distance d_{xw}, between a cluster's midpoint and a pair's midpoint. The cluster and the pair can be merged if d_{lw} is less than a threshold and d_{xw} is less than another. Both the lengthwise threshold t_{lwd} and the crosswise threshold t_{xwd} are scaled by d_m just as t_{dd} and t_{md} are.

Figure 7 shows the parameter of a cluster and a pair. Denote the parameters of the cluster by $(x_c, y_c, \theta_c, n_c)$ where n_c is the number of pairs in the cluter. Denote the parameters of one of the pairs already in the cluster by (x_q, y_q, θ_q), and the parameters of a pair that is a candidate for merging by (x_p, y_p, θ_p). Assume that (4) is used to find r_c for the cluster and r_p for the pair. The cluster and the pair can then be merged if the two following conditions are met:

$$d_{xw} = |r_c - r_p| < t_{xwd} \cdot d_m \tag{8}$$

and

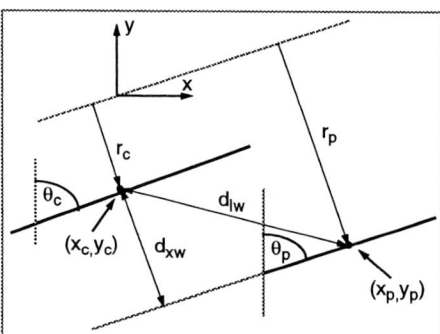

Fig. 7. The parameters of a cluster and a pair

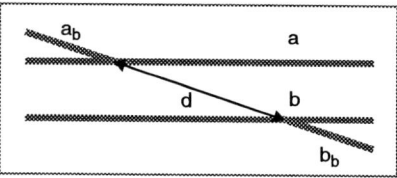

Fig. 8. A pipeline configuration where two short pipeline segments can be merged into a long false one

$$d_{lw} = \sqrt{(x_q - x_p)^2 - (y_q - y_p)^2} < t_{twd} \cdot d_m \qquad (9)$$

The lengthwise distance is approximated as the diagonal distance in (9) as $t_{xwd} \ll t_{lwd}$. Pairs will be merged with the cluster until no more pairs can be included in it. A new pair will then be picked as a cluster kernel and new cluster will made in the same way. This will continue until there are no more pairs that can be clustered. The parameters of the cluster are updated every time a new pair is included in it and the pair will be marked as a part of that cluster such that it can not be included in another one. The cluster parameters, which are the result of the matching stage, are updated by:

$$\begin{aligned} x_c &= (x_c \cdot n_c + x_p) / (n_c + 1) \\ y_c &= (y_c \cdot n_c + y_p) / (n_c + 1) \\ \theta_c &= (\theta_c \cdot n_c + \theta_p) / (n_c + 1) \\ n_c &= n_c + 1 \end{aligned} \qquad (10)$$

The importance of the test against d_{lw} is illustrated in Fig. 8, which contains four pipeline segments. Assume that they all have the same diameter. Segment a_b is a branch of segment a, and b_b is a branch of segment b. Furthermore, segment b_b is parallel with and an extension of a_b, but their endpoints are separated by the distance d. The two segments would always have been merged without the test of d against $t_{lwd} \cdot d_m$.

Note that step 3 in the ACA (Fig. 5) have been simplified. The criterions for merging as given in (8) and (9) are of the "near enough" type rather than "nearest." This can be done as it is expected that pipelines will not overlap and, thus, clusters will be well separated. As a consequence of this the clustering process will be faster.

A Vision System for an Autonomous Underwater Vehicle

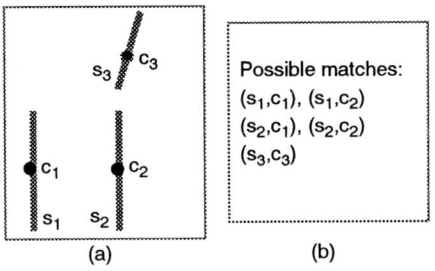

Fig. 9. A possible set of matches between image clusters c and pipeline segments s

The alternative would have been to find the "distance" between every possible pair of clusters before the pair with the least "distance" could have been merged.

6 Interpretation

The name of this module is probably somewhat presumptuous as it indicates that the module has some, perhaps primitive, intelligence. What the module really will do is to search for the combination of matches with the best fit between image line-clusters and pipeline segments. The set of matches that has the least error will be accepted as a valid interpretation and the rest of them will be discarded. The Interpret module will check that all segments of the interpretation are inside the FOV before it finds the fit error.

6.1 Interpretation Based on "Coupled Constraints"

Grimson and Lozano-Perez (1987, pp. 487–492) describes the fundament for a method, referred to as "coupled constraints". They want to find an assignment of image *patches* with model *faces*. They propose to find an initial interpretation by finding a range of probable assignments between two *faces* and two *patches*. This range will be further constrained when a third *face* and *patch* are assigned. By including more *patches* and *faces* the range of possible assignments will be quickly reduced. If the range becomes empty the interpretation can be discarded. The method, which will be proposed here, will use the idea of coupled constraints as the basis for a blind search for the best range of assignments. The search problem is illustrated in Fig. 9.

Figure 9a shows three pipeline segments $s_1 - s_3$ that are found to be within the FOV by the Predict module. Assume that $s_1 - s_3$ have the same diameter, that s_1 and s_2 have the same heading, and that the Match algorithm finds three image line-clusters $c_1 - c_3$ corresponding to $s_1 - s_3$. A cluster is shown in Fig. 9a as a point that indicates its midpoint. The Match module will find a list M of five matches which can be seen in Fig. 9b. A match m_i from M will consist of a pair (c_j, s_i) where c_j

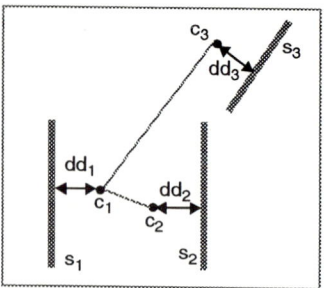

Fig. 10. Position independent matching

contains the parameters of an image cluster and s_i the parameters of the corresponding pipeline segment. The five matches are: s_3 are represented by and matched with c_3; c_1 is matched with both s_1 and s_2. This happens are the Match module clusters image lines with segments solely based on their heading and diameter; c_2 will be matched with s_1 and s_2 for the same reason. The Interpret module must solve two problems in order to find a valid interpretation from the five matches:

(1) There is an offset between the origin of the image line-clusters and the pipeline segments which is caused by the position uncertainty of the vehicle. Thus, the relative positions of segments must be compared with the relative positions of their corresponding line-clusters. As an example consider the two matches (s_1, c_2) and (s_2, c_1) in Fig. 9: the signed distance between s_1 and s_2 is the negative of the signed distance between c_2 and c_1. Thus, the combination of the two is inconsistent and the two matches must be discarded as a valid interpretation.

Assume now that the valid interpretation is the three matches in Fig. 10: (c_1, s_1), (c_2, s_2), and (c_3, s_3). This solution will be found by checking that the signed distance between s_1 and s_2 are about the same as the signed distance between c_1 and c_2. The (c_3, s_3)-match must also be consistent with (c_1, s_1). The difference in signed distances are given as the dd_i-values in Fig. 10. Note that their sizes are strongly exaggerated.

This method, where the matches must be consistent with each other if they are to be accepted as a valid interpretation, has the flavour of Grimson and Lozano-Perez's "coupled constraints". The method can be more formally stated when it is assumed that the signed distance is found with a function D. We would like to find the segment s_r for which the accumulated distance-difference DD_r has its minimum. It is given by the following equation:

$$DD_r = \sum dd_i \tag{11}$$

where the distance difference dd_i is defined as:

$$dd_i = \|D(s_r, s_i) - D(c_r, c_i)\| \tag{12}$$

Wild points will be removed by defining a threshold t_{dd} and requiring that:

$$dd_i = MIN(dd_i, t_{dd}) \tag{13}$$

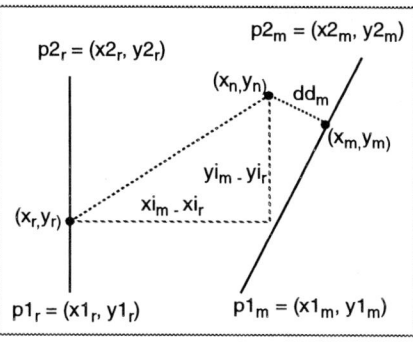

Fig. 11. The parameters used for checking if a reference segment r and a segment m can be parts of the same interpretation

(2) The second problem concerns how to find dd_i. An image line-cluster is described by its (x, y)-midpoint (see (10)) while a pipeline segment is described by a line. Their headings are assumed to be the same as the cluster is found based on the segment's heading. We would like to find the point, on each segment in a possible interpretation, that results in the minimum DD_r. This will be done by appointing one and one segment in M as a reference segment r, and computing DD_r at all possible positions along r. If DD_r is less than the current DD_{min} it will be noted as the new DD_{min} together with the current position along r. The noted position will, after all the segments in M have been traversed, give the valid interpretation: Namely the segments in M that has $dd_i < t_{dd}$, for that position.

The error distance dd_i can be detailed by referring to Fig. 11. The centre-lines of two segments r and m can be seen, where r is the reference segment and m is another segment of a match in M. The two corresponding image clusters have the midpoint coordinates (xi_r, yi_r) and (xi_m, yi_m). The endpoints of the segments are respectively $(p1_r, p2_r)$ and $(p1_m, p2_m)$. The point on r, for which the dd_i's are to be computed, is shown as (x_r, y_r). The two segments can be part of a valid interpretation if the distance dd_m meets the following condition:

$$dd_m = \sqrt{(x_n - x_m)^2 + (y_n - y_m)^2} < t_{dd} \qquad (14)$$

where

$$\begin{aligned} x_n &= x_r + (xi_m - xi_r) \\ y_n &= y_r + (yi_m - yi_r) \end{aligned} \qquad (15)$$

and (x_m, y_m) is the point on m, which is nearest to (x_n, y_n) when the finite length of m is accounted for (Hallset 1992).

6.2 Limitations of the Interpretation Strategy

A problem arises when only one pipeline segment really is within the FOV, and two are found by the Prediction module. This will happen if pipeline A has been

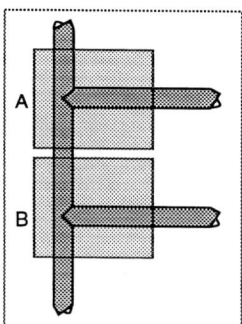

Fig. 12. An ambiguous pipeline configuration where images taken at position A and B, with a FOV as indicated by the shaded squares, can not be distinguished

tracked for same time, and the position uncertainty has increased. Then pipeline B may also be inside the FOV according to the navigation system. However, from historical data and physical restrictions it is clear that a sudden jump from A to B can not occur, and that a match with pipeline B must be rejected.

A second problem is illustrated with Fig. 12 where a pipeline with two branches can be seen. Imagine that both the branches are found to be within the FOV, but that the real FOV is limited as shown by the light-shaded squares at positions A and B in the figure. It will then be impossible to distinguish between an image taken at position A and B.

The solution to the two problems, described above, is to introduce prediction (Dickmanns et al. 1990). For the PISCIS vehicle this will mean that PMC must predict, based on the vehicle dynamics and the pipelines' positions in the previous image, where they are expected to occur in the next one. The PVS must use the predicted positions of the pipeline segments to restrict the search for the valid interpretation. A problem is of course how to find the pipelines' positions the first time: The PMC must then make the vehicle search for the pipelines at positions where ambiguous configurations can not occur. The implementation of the prediction scheme will be the next natural step when experience have been gained with the robustness of this PVS-version.

7 Results

It will be shown here that the PVS can find the centre lines of pipelines based on "sensor" input and the three scenes in Figs. 15 and 16. The PVS must in addition do this under rotation- and scaling-errors, and skewed light. This will not be covered here due to space limitations, but can be found in Hallset (1992).

The centre-lines are found by telling the PVS that it is at 4 metres altitude, and giving it a proper heading and scaling factor, for each image and position. The altitude and heading are assumed to be exact, while the position is assumed to be known within an error circle. The three images, that are used, have 8 bit grey-level resolution and a size of 256 by 182 pixels.

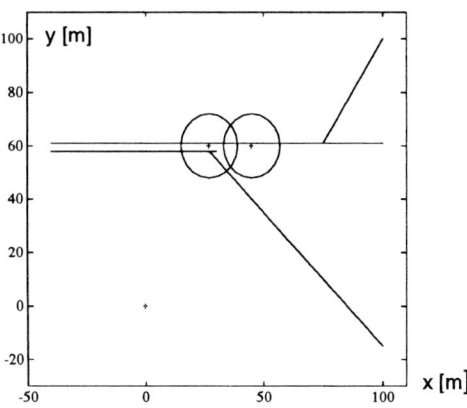

Fig. 13. A simple world model of pipelines, with the AUV at the two circled positions

Images are by their nature diverse and, thus, a complete test of the PVS can not be done. The test must be restricted to the processing of "representative" images. It has been a problem that real underwater-scenes are unavailable. The test will, however, show that the PVS can handle effects that are expected to be present under water. They have, like real underwater-images, highly varying contrast, "pipelines" with a broken outline, and a non-uniform background. Three images will be used: (1) The first image, which will be referred to as Scene1, is shown in Fig. 15a. It is a black plastic tube that is laid out on a background of sand. The midpoint of the tube is partly covered with sand; (2) Scene2 in Fig. 15b is a slightly more complex configuration of three plastic-tubes; (3) Scene3 in Fig. 16 is of a grey plastic tube deployed in the Ocean Basin Laboratory (OBL) at MARINTEK here in Trondheim. OBL is basically a freshwater tank which is 50 by 80 metres wide and 10 metres deep. Note that the centre-lines that the PVS have found is drawn into Figs. 15 and 16.

The pipeline map in Fig. 13, which is used in the test of the PVS, makes up a rather small world. The map shows two branched pipelines laid out on a flat seabed. All the pipeline segments in the map has a diameter of 1 metre. The map is purely artificial and pre-programmed as a fixed list of pipeline-segments into the PVS. The segments that are found within the left-most circle will be matched with Scene2, and the segments within the right-most circle will be matched with Scene1 and Scene3.

Some problems are ignored in the test. Plastic tubes are used for building the lab scenes instead of concrete and steel pipes which are expected to appear under water. This was done since plastic tubes were at hand, concrete- and steel-tubes were not. The lab scenes will, therefore, appear with better contrast between the pipes and the background than in real underwater-scenes. Light distribution is not the same for the lab scenes and for underwater scenes. However, it is shown in Hallset (1992) that the PVS can handle an uneven light distribution.

The parameters of the PVS have been set to fixed values and are the same for all the three scenes. The choice of these parameters are discussed thoroughly in

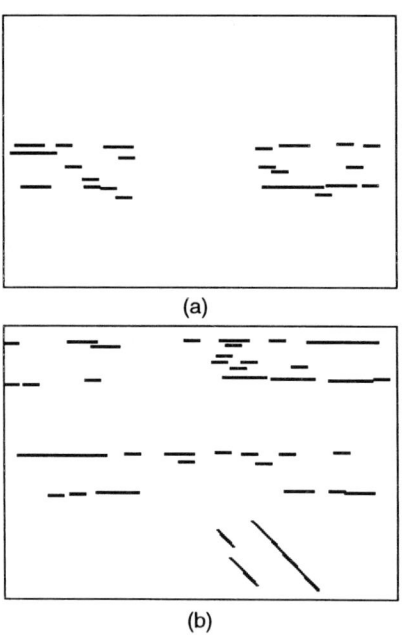

Fig. 14. Line images after using the MHough algorithm on the edge-point images of **a** Scene1, and **b** Scene2

Hallset (1992). This section shows that the chosen values gives a reasonable robust PVS although I would have preferred a lower number of parameters in order to make PVS more robust. However, it seems that a high number of parameters are the curse of most vision-systems (Snyder 1991, p. 118).

7.1 The PVS Used on "Dry" Images

Figure 14 shows that the MHough function have found lines at 0° relative to image's horizontal axis for Scene1, and at both 0° and 45° for Scene2.

There are two observations that can be made based on the two line images in Fig. 14: (1) The number of false lines are reduced to a minimum by restricting the search for lines to the expected directions of pipes. This again reduces the computational burden and complexity of the following matching stage; (2) The line images are not an exact representation the pipe-boundaries. They have many of the expected properties of underwater line-images: (a) Many of the lines in the interior of the pipes are clearly false caused by spurious edge-points; (b) The boundaries of the pipes have holes and are even completely missing at places where the pipes are covered with sand; (c) The boundaries are somewhat misplaced. Thus, if the PVS can find pipe centre-lines from these line images it is probable that it can find pipes from real underwater-scenes.

Figure 15 shows the centre-lines for Scene1 and Scene2, that are found based on the line images in Fig. 14. The white centre-lines are drawn directly by the PVS. The found matches for Scene1 and Scene2 are quite satisfactory as there are no

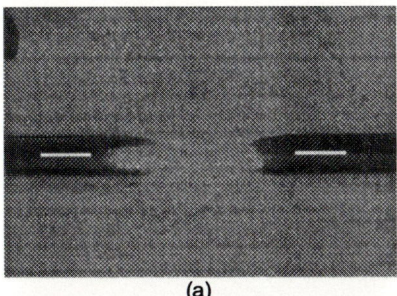

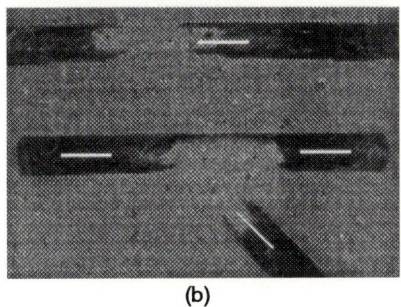

Fig. 15. Found pipeline centre lines for a Scene1, and b Scene2

apparently false centre-lines. The problem that the same segments are assigned to several centre-lines and vice versa appears to have been solved by the Interpret module. In Hallset (1992) it is shown that it indeed finds a set of matches based on the known relative position of the segments. The remaining matches are discarded.

Figure 15a shows that the PVS has found two centre-lines for the single pipeline segment in the scene. It is no surprise that two matches are found as the pipe in Scene1 is broken in two by a sand cover. The two parts that can be seen will naturally have the same diameter and heading and, thus, will both be plausible matches. However, if the two lines had been closer they might have been merged into one. This merging is guided by t_{lwd}. As the two centre-lines are consistent there will be no problems, for the PMC, to use them for pipeline-following.

Figure 15b shows that the PVS has found one centre-line for the upper segment, two for the middle, and one for the lower. The sand cover for the upper pipe is slightly shorter than the one for the lower and, thus, the result is that the upper two parts gets merged as they are close enough guided by t_{lwd}, while the middle ones remains separated. As with Scene1 this will not cause problems for the PMC, since the found centre-lines are consistent.

7.2 An Underwater Image

Figure 16 shows Scene3 that is taken with a camera that was vertically mounted on a moving underwater vehicle. Scene3 has low contrast which can be seen by noting that the image appear to be dim. Still the PVS manages to find a suitable threshold

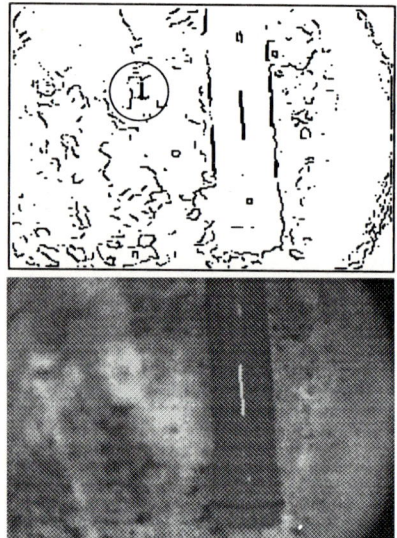

Fig. 16. An underwater scene from the Ocean Basin Laboratories. It contains a grey plastic tube deployed on the steel-plated bottom of the basin. The upper image is the original one with the centre-line that the PVS finds. The lower black- and-white image shows the edge-points that the Edge algorithm finds, the lines that the MHough algorithm finds, and the centre-line. The edgepoints are one pixel thick while the lines are two

for edge-point detection and to find lines that can be combined into a valid interpretation of the scene. This image is a good illustration of the powerful concept of letting the MHough function use the expected heading of the pipes together with a fixed line-length to ignore unwanted edge-points: There is only one apparent false line in the edge/line-image even though there are many unwanted edge-points. This line is circled in Fig. 16. However, it is expected that there will be more than one false line in most images.

8 Conclusion

The application of a vision system (the PVS) in a proposed pipeline inspection AUV has been presented. The PVS is intended as a low-cost sensor for pipeline tracking: The pipeline's position and heading relative to the vehicle is found by the PVS and used to guide the vehicle along the pipe. The PVS is presented, and the essential scheme for the inclusion of orientation-, altitude-, and position-sensors is given. It is pointed out that robust image interpretation is important in the unstructured underwater environment. Here automatic edge-thresholding and a modified Hough transform is proposed for robust segmentation. The following robust interpretation is ensured with a matching stage that accounts for the vehicle position uncertainty by doing position independent matching. This may lead to ambiguous matches. The final interpretation stage validates the matches by discarding improbable combination of matches.

It is shown here that the PVS can interpret moderately complex pipeline-configurations even when the vehicle's position is not known exactly. The PVS is in addition shown, in Hallset (1992), to be robust against scaling- and rotation-errors, and a skewed light-source. However, it is pointed out in Hallset (1992) that there are things that can and should be improved: The error handling could be better and the number of parameters in the PVS should have been reduced. These improvements are not crucial in a prototype vehicle, where reliability is of less priority, but they are essential in a future production version of the PISCIS.

The plan is to build a prototype vehicle and implement the PVS. We foresee few theoretical, but many practical problems concerning reliability, error handling, light conditions, and energy consumption. These problems are best detected and, thereafter, overcome by building the prototype vehicle with the PVS and testing it. The experience gained will point out where the real problems are in making reliable vision-systems for AUVs.

Acknowledgements. This work is done by members of the staff of the Foundation for Scientific Research at The Norwegian Institute of Technology (SINTEF). The project has in part been funded by the The Royal Norwegian Council for Scientific and Industrial Research (NTNF).

References

Canny, J. (1986). A computational Approach to Edge Detection. *IEEE Transactions on Pattern analysis and Machine Intelligence*, vol. 8, no. 6, November, 1986, pp. 679–698.

Dickmanns, E. D., Mysliwetz, B., and Christians, T. (1990). An integrated spatio-temporal approach to automatic visual guidance of autonomous vehicles. *IEEE Transactions on Systems, Man, and Cybernetics*, vol. 20, no. 6, November / December 1990, pp. 1273–1284.

Duda, R.O. and Hart, P.E. (1973). *Pattern classification and scene analysis.* John Wiley and Sons, New York, 1973.

Fleck M.M. (1992). Some defects in finite-difference edge finders. *IEEE Transactions on Pattern analysis and Machine Intelligence*, vol. 14, no. 3, March 1992, pp. 337–345.

Gonzalez, R. C. and Wintz, P. (1987). *Digital image processing.* Addison Wesley.

Grimson, W. E. L. and Lozano-Perez, T. (1987). Recognition and Localization of Overlapping Parts From Sparse Data. In Kanade, T. (Ed.), *Three-Dimensional Machine Vision*. Kluwer Academic Press, pp. 451–510.

Hallset, J.O. (1992). *A vision system for an autonomous underwater vehicle.* Dr. ing. thesis, the Norwegian Institute of Technology, Trondheim Norway, ITK report 1992:109-W.

Hallset, J.O. and Rødseth, Ø.J. (1991). PISCIS – An autonomous underwater vehicle for pipeline inspection. *Proceedings of the 7h international symposium on unmanned untethered submersible technology*, Durham, New Hampshire, 23–25 September, 1991, pp. 51–59.

Illingworth, J. and Kittler, J. (1988). A survey of the Hough transform. *Computer vision, graphics, and image processing*, No. 44, 1988, pp. 87–116.

Jaffe, J.J. (1990). Computer modelling and the design of optimal underwater imaging systems. *IEEE Journal of Oceanic Engineering*, vol. 15, no. 2, April 1990, pp. 101–111.

Jain, R.C. and Binford, T.O. (1991). Ignorance, myopia, and naivete in computer vision systems. *Computer Vision, Graphics and Image Processing: Image understanding*, vol. 53, No. 1, January 1991, pp. 112–117.

Kitchen, L.J. and Malin, J.A. (1988). The effect of spatial discretization on the magnitude and direction response of simple differential edge operators on a step edge. *Computer Vision, Graphics and Image Processing* xx, pp. 243–258.

Lacroix, V. (1988). A three-module Strategy for Edge Detection. *IEEE Transactions on Pattern Analysis and Machine Intelligence*, pp. 803–810, vol. 10, no. 6, November 1988.

Pratt, W.K. (1991). *Digital image processing*. John Wiley and Sons Inc., New York.

Rødseth, Ø.J. (1990). Research on autonomous underwater vehicles in Norway. *Seminar on autonomous underwater vehicles*, The association for structural improvement of the shipbuilding industry, Tokyo, November 1990.

Rødseth, Ø.J. and Hallset, J.O. (1991a). ROV90 – A prototype autonomous inspection vehicle. *Proceedings of the first international offshore and polar engineering conference*, Edinburgh, 11–15 August, 1991, pp. 42–47.

Rødseth, Ø.J. and Hallset, J.O. (1991b). ROV90 – A pragmatic approach to autonomous underwater design. *Proceedings of Oceans 91*, Honolulu, Hawaii, 1–3 October 1991, pp. 1075–1081.

Snyder, M.A. (1991). A commentary on the Paper by Jain and Binford. *Computer Vision, Graphics and Image Processing: Image understanding*, vol. 53, No. 1, January 1991, pp. 118–119.

Turk, M.A., Morgenthaler, D.G., Gremban, K.D., and Marra, M. (1988). VITS- A Vision System for Autonomous Land Vehicle Navigation. *IEEE transactions on pattern analysis and machine Intelligence*, vol. 10, No. 3, May 1988, pp. 342–361.

Visual Inspection of Machined Parts

B.R. Modayur, L.G. Shapiro, and R.M. Haralick

Abstract. The problem of automating industrial inspection tasks is an interesting and challenging one. Since modern design techniques produce geometric models of the parts being designed, it is natural to extend these models to the task of inspecting the parts that are manufactured. Although many special purpose inspection systems have been developed, general purpose systems utilizing CAD models of the parts are still in the research stage. While it is easy to define *ad hoc* algorithms for inspection, it is much more difficult to justify the algorithms with solid theory. In this paper we describe a CAD-model-based machine vision system for dimensional inspection of machined parts, with emphasis on the theory behind the system. The original contributions of our work are: 1) the use of precise definitions of geometric tolerances suitable for use in image processing, 2) the development of measurement algorithms corresponding directly to these definitions, 3) the derivation of the uncertainties in the measurement tasks, and 4) the use of this uncertainty information in the decision-making process. Our experimental results have verified the uncertainty derivations statistically, proved that the error probabilities obtained by propagating uncertainties are lower than those obtainable without uncertainty propagation, and demonstrated that the inspection system responds in a predictable manner when applied to deformed objects.

1 Introduction

The problem of automating industrial inspection tasks is an interesting and challenging one. Modern design techniques are performed via computer and produce a geometric model of the part being designed. Three-dimensional graphics techniques can be applied to this model to generate various views of the object for the designer to look at. It is clearly desirable to develop machine vision techniques to inspect the finished, or partially finished, part.

CAD-based vision is the automatic production of vision procedures for a specific task, given CAD models of the objects involved in the task and knowledge of the environment in which the task is to be performed. This approach is much more cost-effective than the older approach of designing specialized techniques for each new part and has been advocated by a number of people (e.g., [LS89], [Ike87], [BHT85]) for use in machine vision systems. Most of the CAD-based vision systems have been for part recognition and pose estimation, not for inspection, but a few inspection systems ([H.D88], [WFD91]) have been built.

There are two major problems involved in automating the inspection process. The first problem is technique. The techniques to be used in the inspection system must satisfy a set of standards. But the standards for conventional inspection tasks were not designed for machine vision and are, in most cases, unsuitable. For example, consider the task of determining if a planar surface is flat enough. There are several methods used in industry to do this. One method is to dye (with ink) the irregular surface and measure the area of the dyed portion imprinted on a known planar surface. A second method is to use a mechanical stylus. This stylus is similar to a pen in a plotter. The stylus is run all over the irregular surface and the highest and lowest points are measured. This gives an idea of the irregularity of the surface. These procedures are not immediately adaptable to a machine vision system, because the criteria for success are not standardized. The second problem is interpretation of results. The error of the final measurement depends on the error at each step of the processing. Most machine vision work has not seriously considered the propagation of error.

Many special purpose inspection systems have been developed; some are even in use on the factory floor. General purpose systems are still in the research stage. While it is easy to define *ad hoc* algorithms for inspection, it is much more difficult to justify the algorithms with solid theory. This section motivates our approach to the problem and discusses related work. Section 2 starts with a discussion on conventional and geometric tolerancing schemes, defines the simulated datum features used in this work, and explains the construction of these datum features. Section 2 also defines the different tolerance types and describes the algorithms that carry out the inspection tasks. Section 3 explains the need to propagate uncertainty information in measurement tasks and carries the reader through one task, namely measurement of straightness of edges. Section 3 also describes how this uncertainty information is used in the decision making process to rule a feature as acceptable or not. Section 4 describes the design of our experimental interactive inspection system. Section 5 explains the relevant image processing operators and sequences used in extracting the required features from an image. Section 6 discusses the experiments and results.

1.1 Statement of the Problem

Consider an ideal unit cube. For computer-aided design, this solid can be unambiguously represented by either constructive solid geometry or a boundary representation with a corresponding set of parameters. Now consider a set of cubes which are "close" to the ideal cube but with varying edge lengths, vertex positions, edge orientations, and surface areas. It would be possible to represent all these solids in terms of the original (ideal) cube, but with all the parameters varying over a range of values.

This closeness of the non-ideal solids to the ideal solid could be defined in terms of a variational class [Req83]. All the solids belonging to a variational class are functionally interchangeable. A non-ideal solid is considered acceptable if its features are contained in the "tolerance zones" of the ideal model. The purpose of

Visual Inspection of Machined Parts

tolerance specifications is to enable us to decide whether a manufactured part is acceptable. This will be the case if all its features are within the corresponding tolerance zones, the size, shape and orientation of which are dictated by the tolerance assertions.

In our present work, we consider only edge and vertex features. Assume there is 1) a solid model M with vertex set V^M and edge set E^M and 2) a part P to be inspected with vertex set V^P and edge set E^P. This part P has a one-one feature correspondence with the model M. It will pass the inspection test if all its features in sets V^P and E^P satisfy the tolerance specification(s) imposed on the corresponding features of the ideal model M. The pose and orientation of the part P is known with some uncertainty. We have one or more images of the part. The problem is to determine whether the part P passes the inpection test.

1.2 Motivation for Our Work

An inspection task can be broken down into three stages: the object recognition/pose determination stage, the inspection stage, and the decision-making stage. In the object recognition stage, a correspondence between the features of the object model and the features extracted from the image is determined. The output of the recognition stage is the identity of the object being inspected and a transformation matrix, which defines the position and orientation of the object. In the inspection stage image processing, feature extraction, and measurement routines are employed to access and text those features required by the inspection task. The decision-making stage determines whether the manufactured part being inspected is satisfactory, ("in spec") or not ("out of spec"). Since a real part is never perfect and a real image is never noise free, the position and orientation obtained from the recognition stage have uncertainty associated with them. Noise in the image creates uncertainty in the estimated attributes of the entities obtained as a result of image processing. For example, the positions of edge pixels obtained as the output of an edge detector are uncertain.

It is our belief that it is absolutely necessary to propagate this uncertainty in lower-level entities upward to the inspection stage in order to improve the accuracy in the decision-making stage. Thus all the measurements that are made at the inspection stage have uncertainties associated with them. The final decision is not whether a part is "good" or "bad," but rather how certain we are that the part is "good" or "bad."

Our beliefs about the need for propagation of uncertainty are an important factor in this work. A second key factor that has motivated the work is the need to have precise definitions for the various types of tolerances and the need to have measurement algorithms that perform a measurement task *exactly* the way it is laid out in the tolerance definitions. The one common inadequacy of a number of related works has been the fact that the measurement algorithms do not follow the guidelines set up in the formal definition of tolerances. There is thus inconsistency between the definition of tolerances and the way measurements are carried out to verify these tolerances. In this work, we try to bridge the gap and make the measurements correspond exactly to the definition of tolerances.

1.3 Related Literature

Though there is an abundance of literature in the area of automatic visual inspection for specific domains (e.g., solder joints, printed circuit boards, light bulb filaments, etc.), literature on inspection systems (specifically CAD-based) for general machine parts is hard to come by. Requicha [Req83] was the first to lay down a formal theory of tolerancing. The formalization was done with a view to an efficient incorporation of tolerancing facilities in geometric solid modelers, which otherwise can handle only ideal objects. We draw on the ideas in this seminal work and the guidelines prescribed in the ANSI standards [ANS73] to set up formal definitions of the various tolerances. Park et al. [PM90] discussed issues in developing an automated inspection system with emphasis on achieving an integrated CAD-Vision model, not on the tolerance theory or the measurement tasks. The system employs a rule-based approach to automatic generation of inspection procedures.

West et al. discussed an automated CAD-based inspection system with emphasis (as in [PM90]) on bridging the gap between CAD and vision models. Using their vision model data structures, they were able to generate exact inspection procedures, given an inspection task. The work described several inspection tasks and briefly assessed the issue of accuracy obtainable from a visual inspection system. Etesami et al. [EU85] described a technique for automatic inspection of machine part contours. They used a curve fitting scheme employing Fourier series and normalized Fourier coefficients to obtain dimensional error between the measured and theoretical parts. Although a number of coordinate measurement machine (CMM) vendors claim to have solved the inspection problem, they work by fitting surfaces and curves to image data and inspecting the parameters of the fit. This, however, is not what the industrial standards prescribe.

2 Tolerancing Schemes

Conventional tolerancing schemes resort to excessive use of implicit datum, leaving the designer resolve inherent ambiguities. We reproduce an illustration from [Req83] in Fig. 1. Two different interpretations are given for the dimensional constraint 6.0 ± 0.2. In the first interpretation a plane tangent to the left face of the actual object is treated as the reference datum. The right face is then expected to lie within the tolerance zone defined by two planes parallel to the reference datum. In

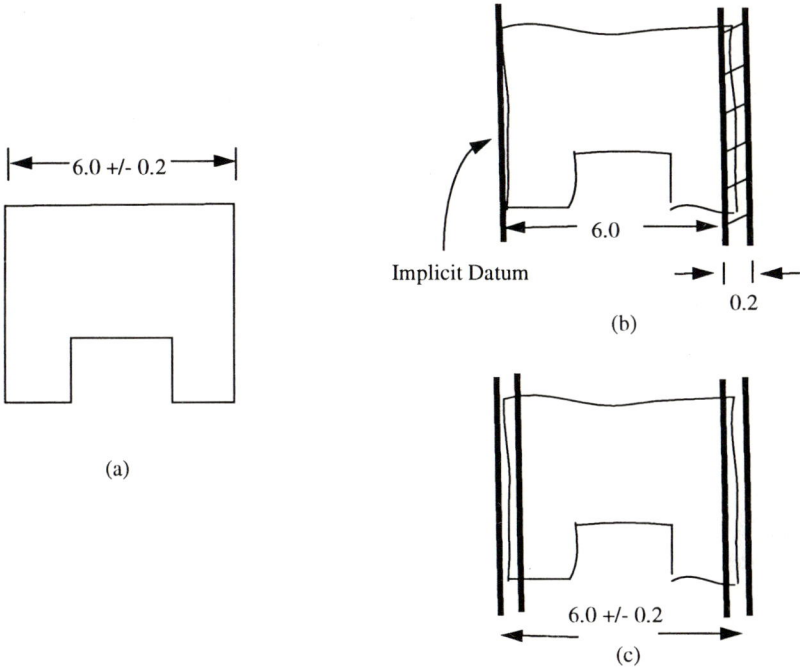

Fig. 1. a shows the original engineering drawing; **b** shows one of the many interpretations with an implicit datum; **c** shows another interpretation without any datum

the second interpretation, no references are assumed. The two imperfect planes are expected to lie within the two zones as illustrated. Yet another interpretation is to treat the right plane as the reference and check to see if the left plane is within two planes parallel to the reference plane. It is clear that the lack of explicit datums leads to varying interpretations of what the designer really intended.

Geometric tolerancing, which is widely used in industry, is well-defined in the ANSI standards. In this scheme, as opposed to conventional tolerancing, use is made of explicit datum features. We make a simple extension to the guidelines laid out in the ANSI standards and the formal theory proposed by Requicha to enable the imposition of tolerances on two-dimensional object features that are observable in an image. We decide if an object feature is acceptable or not depending on whether the feature lies within zones created by offsetting the feature's ideal shape.

It is not always possible to define dimensions exactly on an imperfect object feature. Features of a real object are never perfect. For example, how do we define the distance between two edges that are not straight? How do we define the angle between two imperfect edges? How do we define the coordinates of a vertex with respect to a coordinate system formed by two imperfect edges? The solution to these problems employed by the geometric tolerancing paradigm is the use of "simulated datum features."

A *simulated datum feature* is a perfectly formed geometric entity that is associated with an imperfectly shaped, manufactured object feature. It is called "simulated" because it does not exist in reality. Measurements made using imperfect object features are not well-defined. The standards suggest the use of simulated datum features in order to make the measurements well-defined. Thus, our inspection system must associate with imperfect, real features, corresponding perfectly-formed features so that measurements can be made. Simulated datum features are used in most cases to construct partial or complete coordinate systems. These coordinates systems are then used as the basis for doing subsequent measurements on other object features. Thus, simulated datum features (henceforth referred to as just datum features) serve as the starting point for establishing a dimensional relationship between features of the manufactured part.

We consider five geometric features in our inspection tasks. They are: straight lines, circles with the material side external to the circle, circles with the material side internal to the circle, rectangles with the material side external to the rectangle, and rectangles with the material side internal to the rectangle. These correspond to the two-dimensional counterparts of a planar feature, a cylindrical slot, a cylindrical part, a rectangular slot, and a rectangular part, respectively. In order to implement our measurement tasks, datum features have to be associated with these five geometric features.

In the reminder of this section we will (i) define the datum features associated with each of the five geometric features and explain the construction of these datum features, (ii) use these datum feature definitions to define the associated tolerances, and finally (iii) use these definitions of datum features and tolerances to define the measurement algorithms that carry out the inspection tasks.

2.1 Datum Features – Definition and Construction

A datum feature is selected on the basis of its geometric relationship to the toleranced feature and the requirements of the design. The following guidelines will be used to relate a perfectly-formed feature to an object feature.

1. There must be a meaningful geometric and physical relationship between the simulated datum feature and the object feature. ANSI standards state that the simulated datum to a plane should be an ideal plane that makes contact with the high points of the object plane. Though datum #2 in Fig. 2 is geometrically meaningful, it does not make sense physically to construct a planar datum feature that makes contact with the object internally.
2. Proper part interface and assembly must be ensured. This is a requirement that has to do with the functionality of the part. The purpose of imposing tolerances on a part is to guarantee that the manufactured part would perform its designated function even though the features of the part may be imperfect. Consider the illustration of Fig. 3. Since the slot has to interface with a protrusion, it makes sense to have the internal circle as the datum feature.

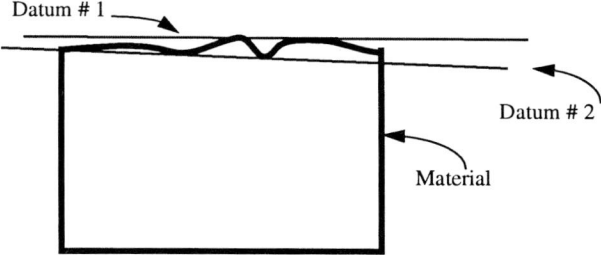

Fig. 2. A simulated datum should be physically meaningful. Datum #2 does not make sense physically, since it makes contact with the object surface internally

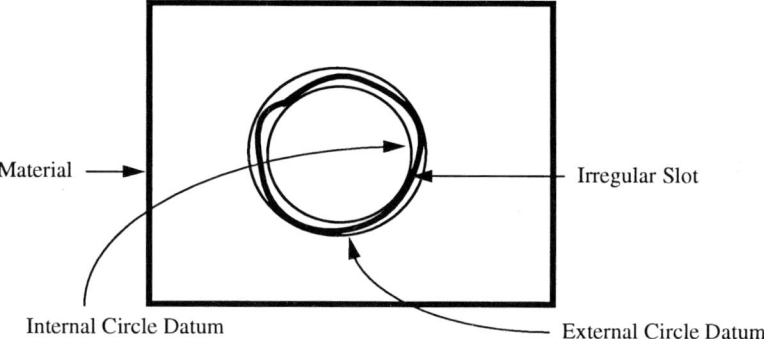

Fig. 3. A simulated datum should ensure proper part interface. Since the slot has to interface with a protrusion, it makes sense to have the internal circle as the datum

2.1.1 Definitions

Planar Object Features. Planar object features in 3D are just planar surfaces of the part. A popular industrial practice used to associate a planar datum to an irregular surface is to let a known planar object rest on the irregular surface. We are going to inspect edges which are 2D projections of planar surfaces. The simulated datum feature for an edge is a straight line positioned so as to minimize the integral sum of distances between points on the edge to straight line.

Cylindrical Parts. The 2D profile of a cylindrical part is a circle with the material side internal to the circle. The associated simulated datum is the smallest circumscribing circle.

Cylindrical Slots. The 2D counterpart of a cylindrical slot is a circle with the material side external to the circle. In ANSI terminology, a cylindrical slot is an internal feature. The associated simulated datum is the largest inscribing circle.

Rectangular Slots. This is an internal features. According to the ANSI guidelines, the datum to be associated with rectangular slots should be two parallel planes at

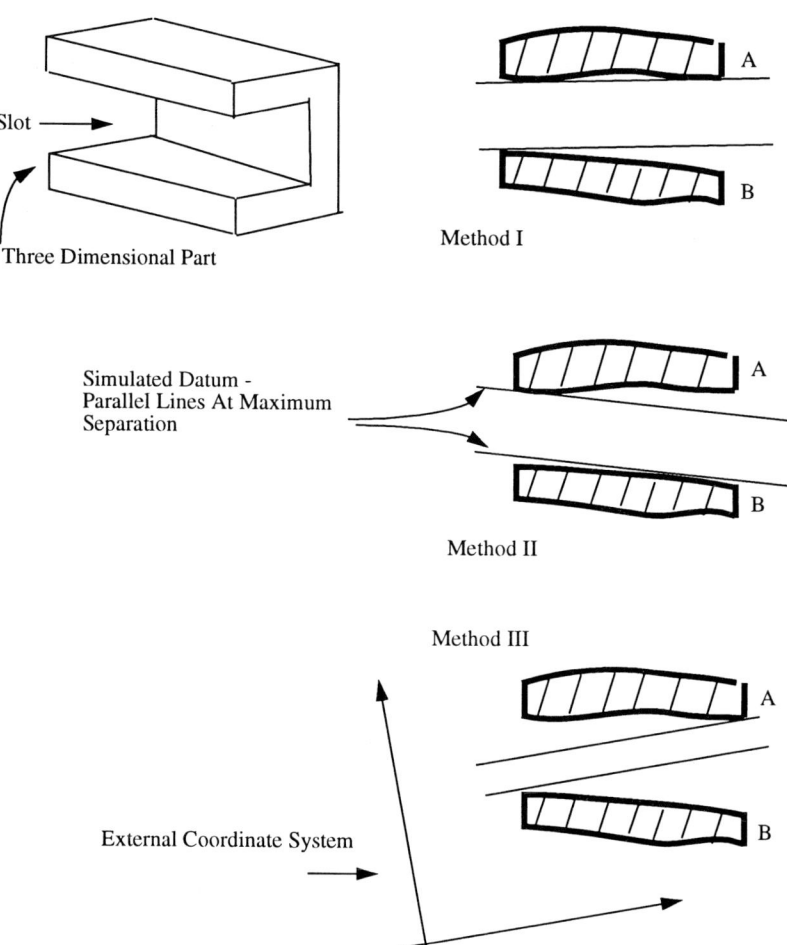

Fig. 4. Order dependencies in datum construction

maximum separation that make contact with the internal part surface. In two dimensions, there are two straight lines instead of two planes. There are three different ways to choose this datum:

  I. Fix a straight line datum to part surface A. Extend out a parallel line until it makes contact with part surface B.
  II. Start with part surface B by fixing a straight line datum to it. This can now be extended until contact is made with the opposite surface A.
  III. Start with a line of known orientation with respect to an external coordinate system. Extend two parallel lines in opposite directions until contact is made with both A and B.

Figure 4 illustrates these methods.

The datum features built using one of these three methods need not necessarily be identical to the ones built using the other methods. Thus when an object feature meets tolerance specifications, the inspection system has to notify the user as to what datum features were used in each of those measurements. We will see later that for positional tolerance measurements, method 3 is most suitable. For size and form tolerance measurements, method 1 or method 2 would suffice.

2.1.2 Construction of Datum Features

It is not enough to merely define datum features. In addition, we must specify how these features are to be constructed, and their constructions must be suitable for implementation in the digital image domain. This section deals with the actual construction of the different datum features we discussed before.

Straight Line Datum. According to ANSI standard Y14.5M, where a nominally flat surface (in two dimension, a straight line) is specified as a datum feature, the corresponding datum is simulated by a plane (a straight line in 2D) contacting the high points of the surface. This gives us a simulated datum that is physically and geometrically meaningful and the datum is "close" to the irregular surface in some sense. Refining this idea further, we can require that the integral sum of distances from the simulated plane to the irregular surface be a minimum. This makes the datum plane "the closest" to the actual manufactured surface. Thus, in two-dimensions, we have the following problem.

Problem. *Given N points in 2 space, construct a supporting line L^1 to these N points such that the sum of perpendicular distances from the N points to this line L is a minimum. The following theorem gives the solution to this problem. Our proof is given in the Appendix.*

Theorem. *Given N points in 2 space, the supporting line that minimizes the sum of perpendicular distances to these N points passes through an edge of the convex hull of the N points.*

Thus, given N points in 2 space belonging to an edge, the simulated datum straight line is contructed the following way. Construct the convex hull CH_N. The supporting line that minimizes the sum of perpendicular distances is an edge E_i of the hull. So, we can compute the sum of perpendicular distances for all the edges of CH_N. Choose the edge yielding the lowest sum of distances. This is the required straight line datum. Figure 5 illustrates the construction of the straight line datum feature.

---

[1] We require L to be a supporting line because we want the datum to "completely enclose" the irregular edge.

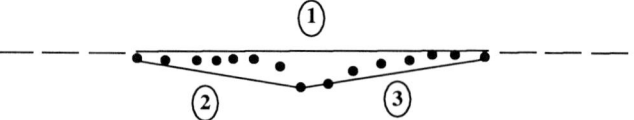

Fig. 5. Line segments (1), (2) and (3) form the edges of the convex hull of the set of edge points. Edge (1) minimizes the sum of the perpendicular distances to the edge points and hence is selected as the required datum line

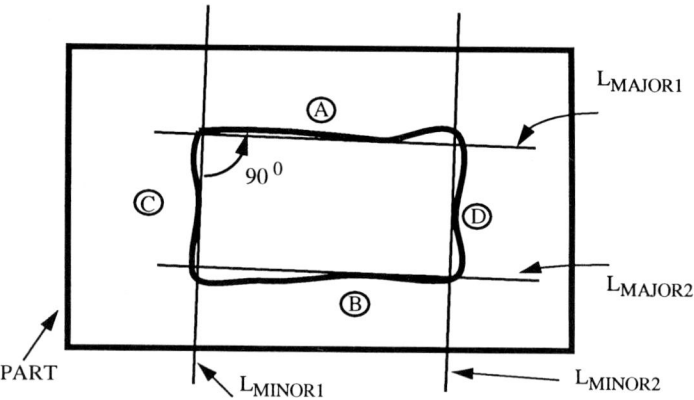

Fig. 6. Datum construction for a rectangular slot. Datum construction is started with L_{MAJOR1}. L_{MAJOR2} is constrained to be parallel to L_{MAJOR1}. L_{MINOR1} and L_{MINOR2} are constrained to be perpendicular to L_{MAJOR1}

Circular Part. The required simulated datum is the smallest circumscribing circle to the set of edge points constituting the circle.

Circular Slot. The sinmulated datum is the largest inscribing circle for the set of edge points constituting the slot outline.

Constructing the smallest circumscribing circle and the largest inscribing circle for a set of 2D data points is a well-defined computational geometry problem. The reader is referred to [PS85] for a description of these algorithms.

Rectangular Datum. We start with one of the major sides (side A in Fig. 6). A simulated straight line datum L_{MAJOR1} is fixed to this edge using the procedure outlined earlier. This straight line datum is translated away from the material side (towards major side B) until contact is made with major side B. This translated datum that is parallel to L_{MAJOR1} can be denoted by L_{MAJOR2}. L_{MAJOR1} and L_{MAJOR2} constitute two parallel lines at maximum separation that make contact with edges A and B. We repeat the procedure with the minor sides now. We start with minor side C and construct datum L_{MINOR1}. But we constrain L_{MINOR1} to be perpendicular to the primary datum L_{MAJOR1}. Then we construct datum L_{MINOR2} parallel to L_{MINOR1}. L_{MINOR1} and L_{MINOR2} constitute two parallel lines at maximum separation and per-

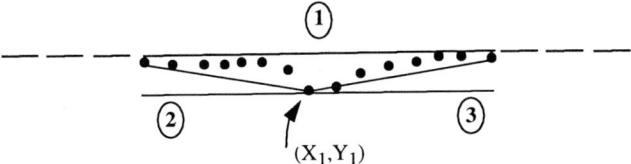

Fig. 7. Line segments (1), (2), and (3) form the convex hull of the set of edge points. Edge (1), since it minimizes the sum of the perpendicular distances to the edge points, is the required datum line. Point (X_1, Y_1) is the farthest from the datum line in terms of perpendicular distance. The perpendicular distance of (X_1, Y_1) from datum line (1) should conform to the straightness tolerance

pendicular to L_{MAJOR1} that make contact with edges C and D. The four straight line datum features L_{MAJOR1}, L_{MAJOR2}, L_{MINOR1} and L_{MINOR2} together constitute the simulated datum for the rectangular slot.

2.2 Tolerance Definitions and Measurements

In this section, we will define a few of the tolerance types and give a brief account of the algorithms to make those tolerance measurements on an object feature.

Straightness of an Edge

Definition. *An edge with straightness tolerance, T_s conforms to the specification if it can be enclosed completely by two parallel lines at a separation less than T_s.*

Measurement. We check for the straightness in the following way. The required simulated datum feature (in this case, a straight line) is first constructed. This datum line is then translated until all the edge points are on or between the simulated datum and this translated version. If the distance between these two parallel lines is less than T_s, the edge conforms to the straightness specification. This is illustrated in Fig. 7.

Angularity of Edges

Definition. *Let the ideal angle between two edges be θ_{id} and let the angular tolerance be specified by T_a. The two edges satisfy the angular tolerance, if the angle between the two associated simulated datum features is θ_{obs}, satisfying*

$$\theta_{id} - T_a/2 \leq \theta_{obs} \leq \theta_{id} + T_a/2.$$

Measurement. We construct the simulated datum features associated with the two edges as outlined before. Then we measure the angle between the two resultant straight lines. The measured angle has to lie within the interval

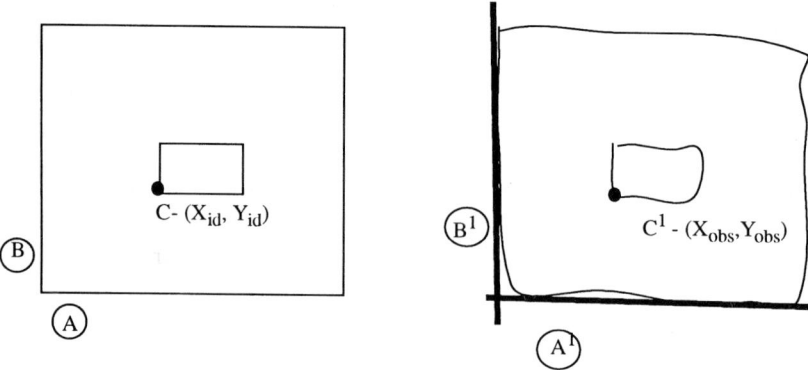

Fig. 8. (a) shows the model. Edges A and B form the coordinate system. The coordinates of the corner point C are (X_{id}, Y_{id}); (b) shows the manufactured part. Edges A_1 and B_1, corresponding to model edges A and B, form the coordinate system. The coordinates of corner point C_1, with respect to this coordinate system, are (X_{obs}, Y_{obs})

$$[\theta_{id} - T_a/2, \theta_{id} + T_a/2]$$

for the edges to conform to the angularity tolerance.

Corner Point Position

Definition. *Let the ideal corner point coordinate with respect to a coordinate system formed by two mutually perpendicular edges A and B be* (x_{id}, y_{id}). *Let the positional tolerance be specified by* T_{px} *along the primary axis (assume it is defined as edge A in this case) and by* T_{py} *along the secondary axis (edge B in this case). Now, the corner point (in a real part) satisfies the position tolerance if its coordinate with respect to a coordinate system formed by edges A and B on the image is* (x_{obs}, y_{obs}) *such that* $x_{obs} \in (x_{id} - T_{px}/2, x_{id} + T_{px}/2)$ *and* $y_{obs} \in (y_{id} - T_{py}/2, y_{id} + T_{py}/2)$.

Measurement. Simulated datum features are constructed for the edges A_1 and B_1 of the real part corresponding to edges A and B in the ideal model. There is one basic constraint. The primary datum feature (we assume that to be A_1) is constructed as before, but the secondary datum feature (edge B_1) is constrained to be perpendicular to the primary datum. Hence, instead of looking for the support line that minimizes the sum of distances, we look for the support line that is parallel to the primary datum line. Now, the coordinate of the corner point in the image is evaluated with respect to the coordinate system we just established. Let this be (x_{obs}, y_{obs}). The corner point satisfies the position tolerance if it satisfies $x_{obs} \in (x_{id} - T_{px}/2, x_{id} + T_{px}/2)$ and $y_{obs} \in (y_{id} - T_{py}/2, y_{id} + T_{py}/2)$. This is illustrated in Fig. 8.

Circularity

We associate three distinct types of tolerances with circularity: size, form and position tolerance. We start by defining the tolerances and then give brief algorithms to make the actual measurements.

Size Tolerance. Let the ideal radius of the circle be r_{ideal} and let the imposed size tolerance be T_s. An imperfect circle satisfies this tolerance if the circle can be completely enclosed by two concentric circles of radii r_{in} (for inner circle) and r_{ext} (for the external circle), such that

$$r_{ideal} - T_s/2 \leq r_{in} \text{ and } r_{ext} \leq r_{ideal} + T_s/2$$

The positions of the two concentric circles with respect to any coordinate system are immaterial.

Form Tolerance. Let the form tolerance be specified by T_f. An imperfect circle satisfies the form tolerance if the circle can be completely enclosed by two concentric circles of radii r_{in} (for the inner circle) and r_{ext} (for the external circle), such that

$$(r_{ext} - r_{in}) \leq T_f$$

Here, the actual value of r_{in} or r_{ext} is immaterial. What is of consequence is the difference in their values. As with size tolerance, the position of the concentric circles is immaterial.

Position Tolerance. Let the center of the ideal circle be positioned at coordinates (a, b) with respect to a coordinate system formed by two ideal object edges A and B. Assume that the object coordinate system on the imperfect part has been built using edges A_1 and B_1 which correspond to A and B on the ideal object. If two concentric circles with the center at (a, b) relative to this object coordinate system can be found, such that the ideal circle of radius r_{ideal} with center at (a, b) is completely enclosed by these two concentric circles, then the circle satisfies position tolerance with respect to this particular coordinate system. The actual procedures to measure these tolerances are as follows.

Size Tolerance Measurement. We start by constructing the simulated datum associated with this circular feature. If the feature is a circular part, we construct the datum as the smallest circumscribing circle. For a circular slot, we fix the datum as the largest inscribing circle. Let the radius of the simulated circular datum be r_{dat} and its center be at $C_r = (X_r, Y_r)$.

For a circular slot, we expand the datum of radius r_{dat} to get a concentric circle of radius r_{circum} that is the smallest circumscribing circle with center at C_r. Now, we have two concentric circles of radii r_{dat} and r_{circum} that enclose the irregular circular feature completely. With ideal radius r_{ideal} and an imposed size tolerance T_s, the size tolerance is satisfied if the conditions $r_{ideal} - T_s/2 \leq r_{rat}$ and $r_{circum} \leq r_{ideal} + T_s/2$ are satisfied.

For a circular solid part, we shrink the datum circle to get a concentric circle that is the largest inscribing circle with center at C_r. Let the radius of this inner circle be r_{ins}. Now, we have two concentric circles of radii r_{ins} and r_{dat} that completely enclose the irregular circular feature. The size tolerance for this feature is satisfied if the conditions $r_{ideal} - T_s/2 \leq r_{ins}$ and $r_{dat} \leq r_{ideal} + T_s/2$ are satisfied.

Form Tolerance Measurement. Let the form tolerance imposed on the circular feature be T_F. We use the same method as before in constructing the two concentric circles whose annulus completely contains the circular feature. For a circular slot to satisfy the form tolerance requirement, the condition $r_{circum} - r_{dat} \leq T_F$ should be met. For a circular part, the condition $r_{dat} - r_{ins} \leq T_F$ should be met.

Position Tolerance Measurement. Positional tolerance relies on a reference coordinate system. We assume that an object reference coordinate system using some object features has already been established. Let the positional tolerance imposed on this circular feature be denoted by T_p. We begin by constructing the smallest circumscribing circle and the largest inscribing circle to the imperfect circle, but with one constraint – the center position of these circles with respect to the object coordinate system *should be exactly the same as that of the nominal feature (circle) with respect to the ideal, model coordinate system.* The text is now the same as that for size tolerance. We check to see whether the radii of the two concentric circles is within the interval $(r_{ideal} - T_p/2, r_{ideal} + T_p/2)$.

3 Uncertainty Propagation in Measurements

A real image is seldom absolutely noise free. Noise in the image leads to uncertainties in the attributes of the entities output by image processing algorithms. Typically, an edge pixel output from an edge detector would be contaminated by noise in the image. This in addition to the inaccuracies in the detector algorithm makes the position of the edge pixel uncertain. The observed edge pixel position can thus be thought of as the true edge pixel perturbed by a random process. Thus, instead of a single 2D position for the edge pixel, we have a zone of uncertainty.

The starting point of our measurement process is the construction of simulated datum lines (supporting lines) to edges. This was proved to be an edge of the convex hull of the edge points. Thus, the required datum line passes through two end points of an edge of the hull. Because of noise in the image, the position of these two end points is uncertain. This uncertainty in the end point position makes the parameters of the line passing through them uncertain. Going one step further, the uncertainty in the parameters of this datum line causes uncertainty in the coordinate system that is created based on this line as a reference. The coordinates of a corner point with respect to this uncertain coordinate system are also uncertain. Thus, uncertainty in the lower-level edge pixels leads up to uncertainty in the tolerance measurement tasks. The purpose of this section is to expound on the

Visual Inspection of Machined Parts

propagation of this uncertainty to our measurement tasks. We will take the reader through one task, namely measurement of straightness of an edge. The derivations for variances of other measurements are similar in principle.

3.1 Noise Model

Let the true edge pixel position be denoted by (x_i, y_i). Let the observed edge pixel position be denoted by $(\hat{x}_i, \hat{y}_i)$. Our model for the noisy, observed edge pixel is,

$$\hat{x}_i = x_i + \varepsilon_i$$
$$\hat{y}_i = y_i + \xi_i$$

where, ε_i and ξ_i are samples from independent distributions that are even functions [Yi90], with mean zero and variances σ_{ε_i} and σ_{ξ_i}, respectively.

3.2 Datum Line Uncertainty

The simulated datum line for straight edges is the nearest-supporting line that passes through an edge L_1 of the convex hull of the edge pixels. Let us denote the end points of this hull edge by (x_1, y_1) and (x_2, y_2). We can write the line equation as $L_1: \alpha x + \beta y + \gamma = 0$, where

$$\alpha = \frac{(y_2 - y_1)}{d}$$

$$\beta = \frac{-(x_2 - x_1)}{d}$$

$$\gamma = \frac{(x_2 y_1 - y_2 x_1)}{d}$$

$$d = \sqrt{(x_2 - x_1)^2 + (y_2 - y_1)^2}$$

Since, we only have noisy observations $(\hat{x}_1, \hat{y}_1)$ and $(\hat{x}_2, \hat{y}_2)$, the observed line parameters are

$$\hat{\alpha} = \frac{(\hat{y}_2 - \hat{y}_1)}{\hat{d}}$$

$$\hat{\beta} = \frac{-(\hat{x}_2 - \hat{x}_1)}{\hat{d}}$$

$$\hat{\gamma} = \frac{(\hat{x}_2 \hat{y}_1 - \hat{y}_2 \hat{x}_1)}{d}$$

$$\hat{d} = \sqrt{(\hat{x}_2 - \hat{x}_1)^2 + (\hat{y}_2 - \hat{y}_1)^2}$$

Let us estimate the behaviour of one of the line parameters α as a result of noise on the edge pixels. We can see that α is a function of the coordinates of the two edge pixels that the line passes through, (x_1, y_1) and (x_2, y_2). We will represent α by a Taylor series expansion around the true edge points (x_1, y_1) and (x_2, y_2). We will truncate the Taylor series as an approximation and include only the linear terms. As a result

$$\hat{\alpha} = \frac{(\hat{y}_2 - \hat{y}_1)}{\hat{d}} \quad (1)$$

$$\hat{\alpha} = \alpha + (\hat{x}_1 - x_1)\frac{\partial \alpha}{\partial x_1} + (\hat{y}_1 - y_1)\frac{\partial \alpha}{\partial y_1} + (\hat{x}_2 - x_2)\frac{\partial \alpha}{\partial x_2} + (\hat{y}_2 - y_2)\frac{\partial \alpha}{\partial y_2} \quad (2)$$

Evaluating the partials, and plugging them into (2), we get the following approximation for $\hat{\alpha}$ in terms of the edge pixel coordinates.

$$\hat{\alpha} = \alpha + \frac{(y_2 - y_1)^2}{d^3}[(\hat{y}_1 - y_1) - (\hat{y}_2 - y_2)] + \frac{(x_2 - x_1)(y_2 - y_1)}{d^3}$$

$$[(\hat{x}_1 - x_1) - (\hat{x}_2 - x_2)] + \frac{1}{d}[(\hat{y}_2 - y_2) - (\hat{y}_1 - y_1)]$$

Squaring the above equation and taking expectations on both sides results in

$$E[(\hat{\alpha} - \alpha)^2] =$$

$$V[\hat{\alpha}] = [V[\hat{y}_1] + V[\hat{y}_2]]\left(\frac{(y_2 - y_1)^4}{d^6} - \frac{(y_2 - y_1)^2}{d^4} + \frac{1}{d^2}\right) + [V[\hat{x}_1] + V[\hat{x}_2]]$$

$$\left(\frac{(x_2 - x_1)^2(y_2 - y_1)^2}{d^6}\right)2[Cov[\hat{x}_1, \hat{y}_1] + Cov[\hat{x}_2, \hat{y}_2]]$$

$$\left(\frac{(y_2 - y_1)^3(x_2 - x_1)}{d^6} - \frac{(x_2 - x_1)(y_2 - y_1)}{d^4}\right)$$

This is assuming that the coordinates (x_1, y_1) are independent of (x_2, y_2), which would make the expectations of the cross terms void. That is,

$$E[(\hat{x}_i - x_i)(\hat{y}_j - y_j)] = 0$$

when $i \neq j$.

In a similar way, we can estimate the variances of the parameters $\hat{\beta}$ and $\hat{\gamma}$ in terms of the coordinates (x_1, y_1) and (x_2, y_2). Now, we have the variances of the parameters of the datum line L_1. To measure the straightness of this edge, we have to find another line parallel to this datum line and such that all the edge pixels are on or between the two lines. To accomplish this, we determine the edge point whose perpendicular distance to L_1 is the highest among all the edge points. Call this edge point (x_3, y_3). Denote the line passing through this point, parallel to the datum line L_1 by L_2. The equation for L_2 is

L_2: $\hat{\alpha}x + \hat{\beta}y - (\hat{\alpha}x_3 + \hat{\beta}y_3) = 0.$

The distance between the two parallel lines which should conform to the straightness tolerance is

$$\hat{d} = \hat{\alpha}x_3 + \hat{\beta}y_3 + \hat{\gamma}. \tag{3}$$

Since α and β are themselves functions of θ which is the angle that the line makes with the X-axis, we rewrite d as a function of θ and γ.

$$\hat{d} = x_3 \sin\hat{\theta} - y_3 \cos\hat{\theta} + \hat{\gamma}$$

Proceeding with the truncated Taylor series expansion as before,

$$\hat{d} = d + (\hat{\theta} - \theta)[x_3 \cos\theta + y_3 \sin\theta] + (\hat{\gamma} - \gamma)$$

Squaring and taking expectations on both sides,

$$V[\hat{d}] = V[\hat{\theta}][x_3 \cos\theta + y_3 \sin\theta]^2 + V[\hat{\gamma}] + 2[x_3 \cos\theta + y_3 \sin\theta]Cov[\hat{\theta},\hat{\gamma}] \tag{4}$$

Equation (4) expresses the uncertainty of the straightness measurement. Given the observed coordinates of the two edge pixels that support the datum line ($(\hat{x}_1, \hat{y}_1)$ and $(\hat{x}_2, \hat{y}_2)$) and the third edge pixel $(\hat{x}_3, \hat{y}_3)$ that is farthest away from this datum line, and the variances of the observed edge pixel positions ($V[\hat{x}_1]$, $V[\hat{y}_1]$, $V[\hat{x}_2]$ and $V[\hat{y}_2]$) all the quantities on the right-hand side of equation (4) can be computed and hence $V[\hat{d}]$ can be determined. Thus, the uncertainties in the edge pixel positions have been propagated all the way up to the measurement task. A similar approach is employed to determine the variances of all the other measurement tasks.

3.3 Decision Making

Once the inspection system has the measured straightness $\hat{d}$ and the associated variance $V[\hat{d}]$, a decision has to be made as to the acceptability of the edge with respect to straightness. The following assumptions are made.

1. The edge pixels are perturbed by Gaussian noise and the measured straightness is a normal random variable with variance $V[\hat{d}]$ and standard deviation $\sigma_{\hat{d}}$.
2. A straightness threshold T_{str} is specified. In the simple case without error propagation, if the estimated straightness is below T_{str} the edge is accepted.

The measured straightness is a normal random variable, thus it can be modeled as a normal curve with mean $\hat{d}$ and standard deviation $\sigma_{\hat{d}}$. If the normal curve is truncated at a significance level of $s\%$ corresponding to r standard deviations for a real number r, then the edge should be accepted if

$$\hat{d} + \gamma\sigma_{\hat{d}} \leq T_{str}.$$

Two kinds of errors can occur in the decision making process. An edge can be accepted when the true straightness is actually higher than T_{str}. We call this error misdetection. The second type of error called false alarm occurs when an edge is rejected but the true straightness was below T_{str}. For example, with a confidence level of 80% corresponding to $1.3\sigma_{\hat{d}}$, the edge is accepted if $\hat{d} + 1.3\sigma \leq T_{str}$, or $T_{str} - \hat{d} \geq 1.3\sigma$. When $T_{str} - \hat{d} = 1.3\sigma$, the probability that the true straightness is greater than T_{str} equals the area under the normal curve to the right of T_{str}. Since we chose a significance level of 80% in this illustration, this probability would be 0.1. As $T_{str} - \hat{d}$ becomes greater than 1.3σ, the area of the normal curve to the right of T_{str} decreases. Thus, 0.1 is an upper bound on the misdetection probability.

If $T_{str} - \hat{d} < 1.3\sigma$, the edge is rejected. For a rejected edge, we are interested in the probability that the true straightness was really less than T_{str} (False Alarm). When $T_{str} - \hat{d} = 1.3\sigma - \varepsilon$, for an infinitesimal ε, the edge is rejected. Now, the false alarm probability would be the area under the normal curve to the left of T_{str}. This would equal 0.9. As $T_{str} - \hat{d}$ becomes smaller, this area to the left of T_{str} would also become smaller. Thus, at the 80% significance level, 0.9 is an upper bound on the false alarm probability, and 0.1 is an upper bound on the misdetection probability.

4 System Design

We have built a system called ICIS (Interactive CAD-based Inspection System) to test our concepts and to illustrate how we think automated inspection should be carried out. ICIS consists of two parts: an interactive front end and a set of computer programs to handle the actual inspection tasks. The interactive front end allows the user of the system to select the inspection tasks required for the part to be inspected. The user first selects the part from a database of CAD models. A wire-frame view of the object is then displayed on the screen. The user employs a virtual sphere device [CMS88] to interactively rotate the object so that he/she can view the various features to be inspected. A combination of menus and mouse clicks on the wire-frame image is used to select the actual tasks to be performed. Figure 9 gives an example of a typical screen displayed to the user by ICIS.

The interactive system works with a 3D vision model of the object, derived from the original CAD model. The vision model is a hierarchical, relational model of the part in terms of its surfaces, its edges, and their interrelationships. This vision model has been used in our automatic pose estimation work [CSH91]. For use in the inspection system, we have augmented the model to include inspection specifications and tolerances. For example, each edge has an associated straightness tolerance. The system derives this information from its interaction with the user.

The second part of the system is the set of inspection procedures. We are initially focusing on measurement tasks. The measurement procedures call on image processing procedures to extract the required information from the

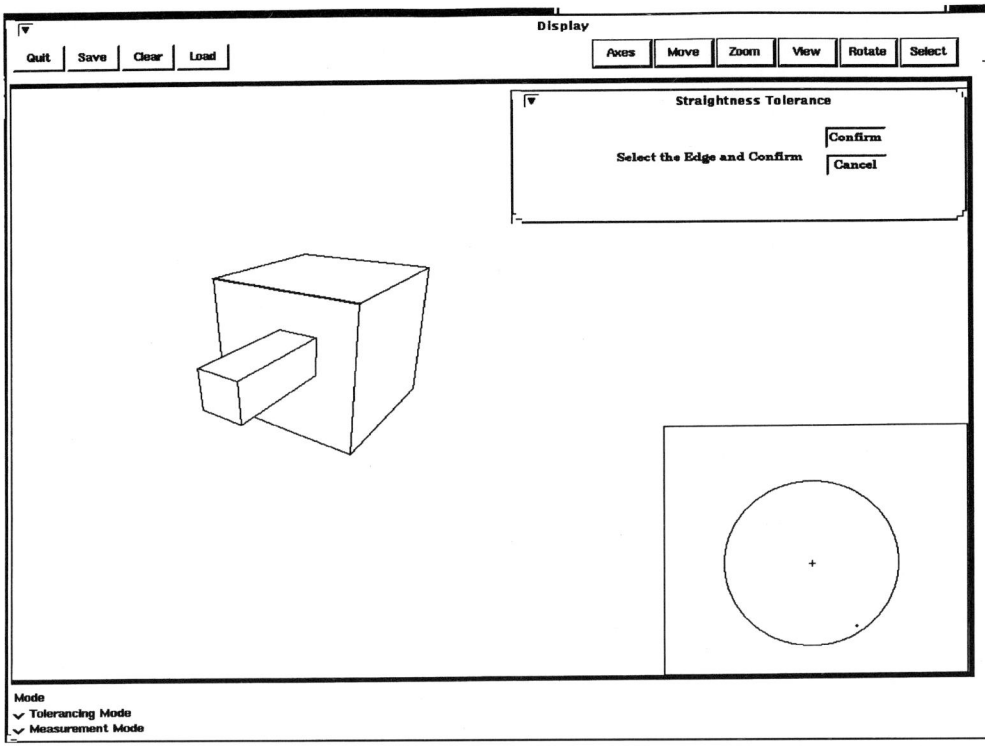

Fig. 9. A typical screen displayed by ICIS. An edge has been selected from the hidden-line-removed object. Straightness tolerance has been selected. On the bottom right is the "virtual sphere" with the current viewpoint highlighted

image(s) of the object and then make the decisions as to the acceptability of the part.

5 Image Processing for Inspection Tasks

The transformation matrix from the object recognition stage yields information, with a degree of uncertainty, about approximately where to expect features of the object to appear on the image. The image processing operators, instead of operating on the entire image, operate only in specific regions where we expect features (such as edges) to lie. We call these specific regions "search windows." Given the uncertain transformation matrix and an estimate of the noise in the image, an accurate estimate of the size and position of these search windows can be obtained. We have developed an adaptive Kalman-filter-based algorithm [Mod91] to fuse these two uncertainties to get an estimate of the size and position of the search windows. All the measurement tasks in this work require just two basic low-level entities. They are, (1) edge pixels and (2) corner pixels. The sequence of image processing operations employed is geared toward extracting these two primitive features from selected regions in the image that are defined by the search windows.

The first step in our image processing sequence is edge detection. We employ the Haralick edge operator [Har84], which uses the zero crossings of the second directional derivative to classify edge pixels. The edge detector output is contaminated with stray noise specks, spurious edge pixels and small segments that cannot be grouped with other segments on the basis of adjacency or orientation. Thus, a necessary step after edge detection is symbolic grouping of edge pixels to form a higher-level entity. As a preliminary step we perform a connected shrink operation. The output of the shrink operator is a symbolic image of arc segments that are one pixel wide. After very small segments are removed, the remaining segments are grouped according to adjacency and orientation. The adjacency condition can be relaxed to group edge segments that are broken because of noise. The set of edge segments output by the grouping process is directly used by the measurement procedures. Corner pixels are obtained as a by-product of the grouping process described above. Points of high curvature on the arc segments are classified as corners.

6 Experiments and Results

Our experiments consisted of three phases. In the first phase, the accuracy of the variance formulas derived for the various measurement tasks were checked. In particular, we were interested in the conditions under which the first order Taylor series approximation would fail. We employed a statistical testing procedure for this purpose, taking straightness measurement as an example task. In the second phase, the performance of the measurement algorithms was determined with and without error propagation. The straightness and angularity measurement tasks were utilized as representative tasks. The goal of the third phase was to test the inspection system with machined objects having varying degrees of deformation. To do this for the straightness measurement task would require a method of progressively deforming the straightness of an edge. Since this type of deformation is not well-defined, we chose the angle-measurement task, for which it was possible to introduce systematic deformations to the machined object. By repeated machining of the object, we progressively varied the angle of one edge with respect to another.

Phase 1

In order to test whether $\sigma^2_{\hat{d}}$, the variance of the straightness measure $\hat{d}$ is equal to $V[\hat{d}]$, the analytic formula derived for the variance of the straightness measure, the null and alternate hypotheses were formulated to be

$$H_0: \sigma_{\hat{d}}^2 = V[\hat{d}]$$
$$H_a: \sigma_{\hat{d}}^2 \neq V[\hat{d}],$$

and the test statistic to be

$$Test = \frac{\sigma_{\hat{d}}^2 - V[\hat{d}]}{\sigma_{\sigma_{\hat{d}}^2}^2}.$$

Since the distribution of $\sigma^2_{\hat{d}}$ is not known, we approximate the mean and variance of $\sigma^2_{\hat{d}}$ by the experimental mean straightness variance and the mean variance of the straightness variance, respectively. The statistical test was carried out with the significance level $\alpha = 0.05$ (corresponding to a value of ± 1.96 for a normalized Gaussian random variable). Thus the null hypothesis would be accepted if the test statistic were between ± 1.96.

Straightness is measured as the perpendicular distance between the datum line (a line passing through two edge pixels) and the edge pixel that is farthest away from this line. Figure 10 shows the result of the statistical test for a line oriented at 45°, with perpendicular distance to the farthest edge point being 35 pixels. The distance between the two points through which the datum line passes was varied from 10 to 25 pixels. The standard deviation σ of the Gaussian noise on the two edge points supporting the datum line was varied from 0.0 to 3.0. The statistical test value fell below the significance level when the distance between the two points fell below 12. Thus, for the linearization approximations made in the variance derivations to hold, the two points that support the datum line must be separated by at least four standard deviations.

Phase 2

The second stage of our experiments focused on determining the performance of the measurement algorithms with and without error propagation. We tested the straightness measurement and the angularity measurement algorithms. We will illustrate the experimental methodology, however, using the straightness measurement algorithm. Our experimental object is shown in Fig. 11. The object was modeled using PADL-2 and machined on a CAMM-3 modeling machine (with some apparent gross errors in a couple of edges). We selected two edges in this image: a "good" edge (in terms of straightness) and a "bad" edge. We determined the datum lines passing through P_1 and P_2 for the good edge and P_3 and P_4 for the bad edge. We measure the farthest point for the good edge and the bad edge.

The following evaluation process, influenced by [KJHP90] was then used.

1. The points P_1, P_2, P_3, and P_4 are perturbed with independent samples from a normal distribution with variance σ^2. The straightness is measured for both edges.

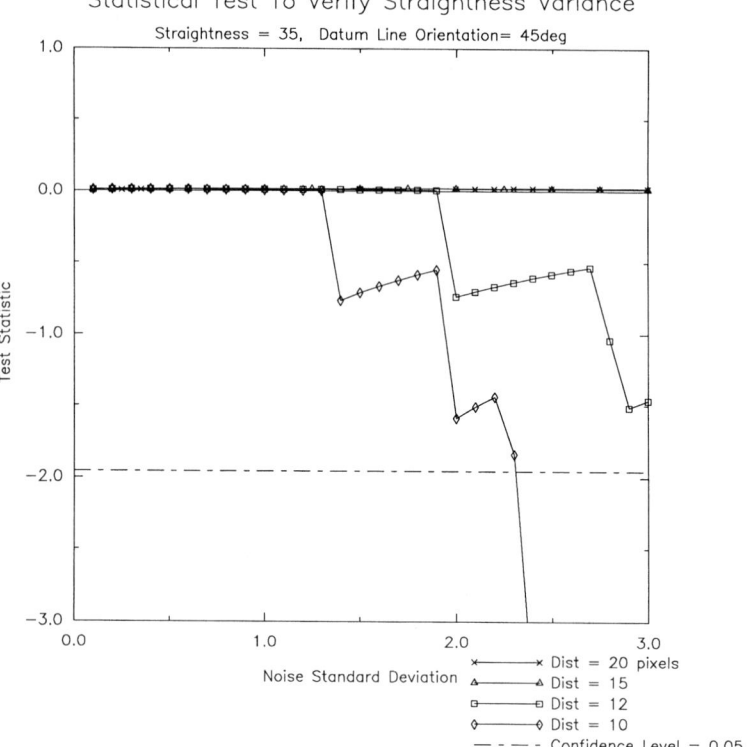

Fig. 10. Results of the statistical test to verify straightness variance. The value of the test statistic is plotted as a function of noise standard deviation. The datum line used was oriented at 45°. The straightness of the synthetic edge used in this test was 35 pixels. The distance between the two edge points that support the datum line was varied from 20 pixels down to 10 pixels. The test fails when the absolute value of the test statistic becomes higher than 1.96 (significance level $\alpha = 0.05$). The test comes close to a breakdown when the distance is 12 pixels (4 times σ) and breaks down when the distance is 10 pixels

Fig. 11. The machined object

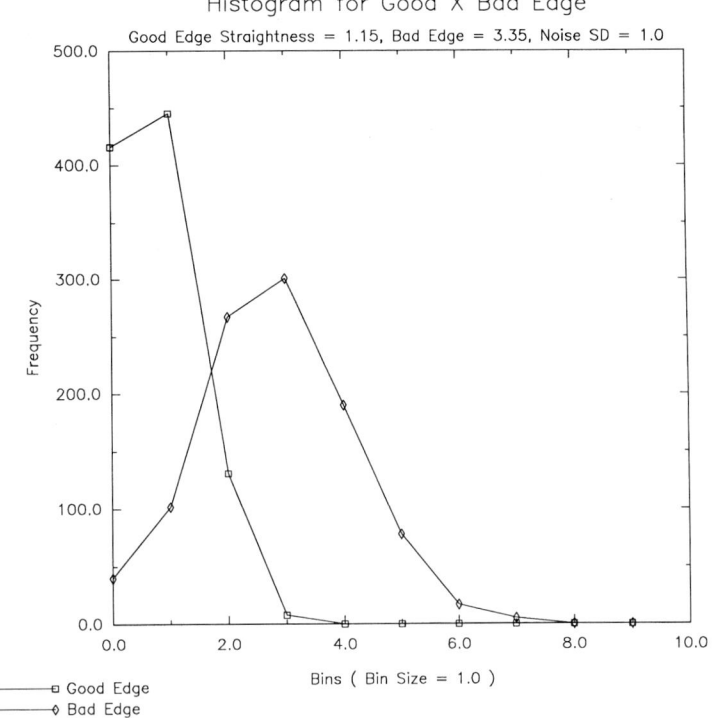

Fig. 12. Histogram for the good versus bad edge. Given any straightness threshold, the area of the "good" curve to the right of this threshold indicates false alarm. The area of the "bad" curve to the left of this threshold indicates misdetection

2. Step 1 is repeated 1000 times to obtain 1000 samples of straightness measures with noise variance σ^2.
3. A histogram is computed with this set of straightness measures for the good and bad edges as shown in Fig. 12.
4. Let T_{str} be a straightness threshold. If the straightness measure is above this threshold, the edge is bad, and if the measure is below the threshold, the edge is good. For a particular threshold value T, the area under the good curve to the right of T indicates false alarms, and the area under the bad curve to the left of T indicates misdetections. The threshold T is varied over a range and the false alarm and misdetection probabilities are determined.
5. The noise level is changed and steps 1 to 4 are repeated.
6. The entire procedure is repeated with error propagation taken into account. The only difference in deciding whether an edge is classified as good or bad is that instead of checking whether the measured straightness M_{str} is below the threshold, we check to see if $M_{str} \pm k\sigma$, for constant k, is below the threshold.

The false alarm and misdetection probabilities we obtained for various noise levels have been plotted in Figs. 13 and 14. Our results show that the decision

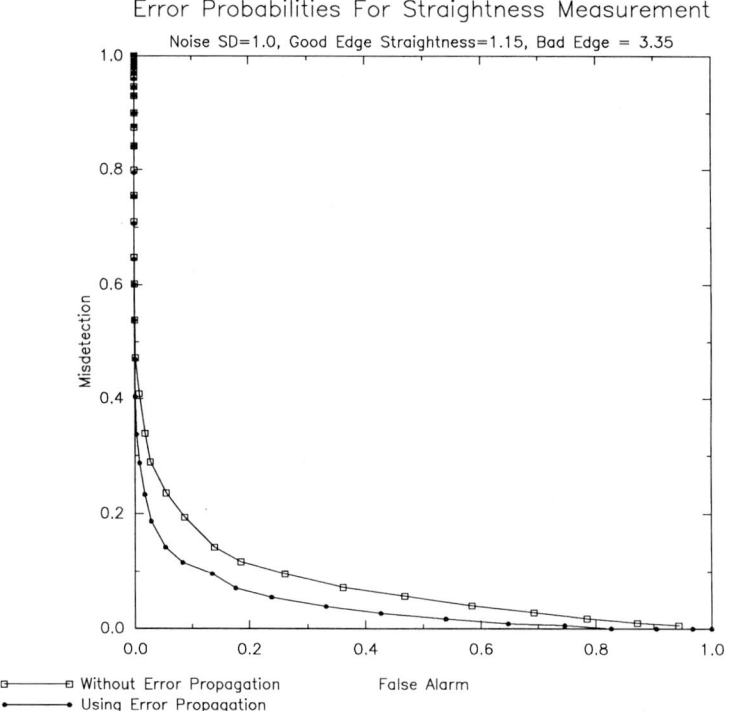

Fig. 13. Straightness measurement – error probabilities with noise $\sigma = 1.0$

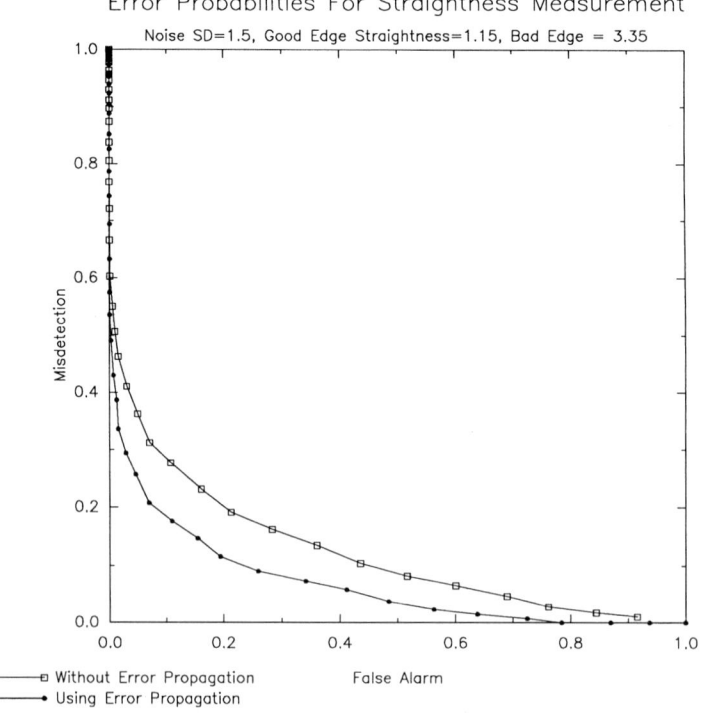

Fig. 14. Straightness measurement – error probabilities with noise $\sigma = 1.5$

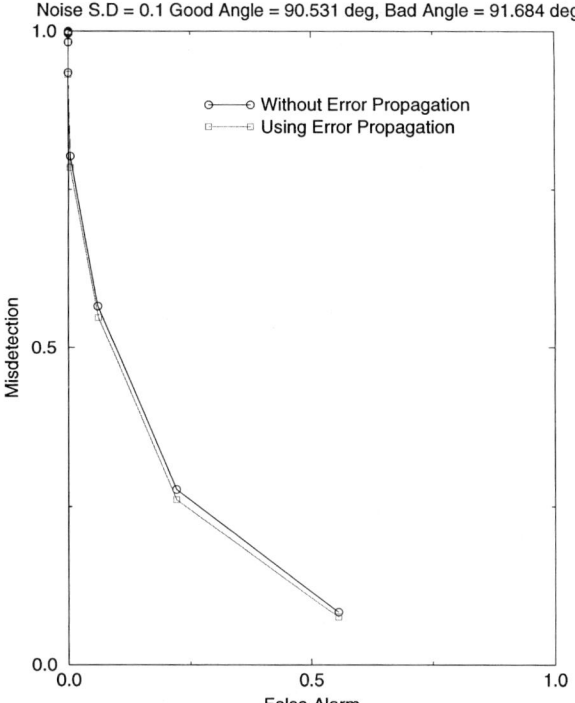

Fig. 15. Angularity measurement – error probabilities with noise $\sigma = 0.1$

making procedure that takes error propagation into account yields lower error probabilities than the one that does not propagate errors. The same process was repeated for the angularity measurement algorithm. Here, two pairs of mutually perpendicular edges were selected from the machined object – the "good" angle being 90.531° and the "bad" angle being 91.684°. With such a small difference between the good and the bad entities, the performance of the algorithm with and without error propagation becomes comparable. But the error probabilities are still smaller when uncertainty propagation is utilized. The results for angularity measurement are plotted in Figs. 15 and 16.

Phase 3

In the third stage of experiments, the inspection system was tested with machined objects at varying degrees of deformation. Consider the visual inspection system to be a black box whose input is in the form of images of machined objects. Given a particular measurement task to perform (e.g., measurement of angularity of a pair of edges), the system outputs a numerical measure along with the associated variance. The numerical measure and the associated variance are

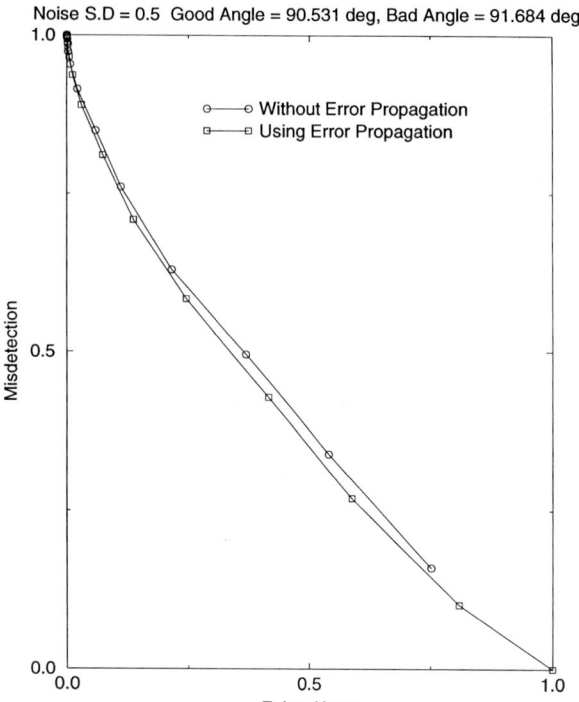

Fig. 16. Angularity measurement – error probabilities with noise $\sigma = 0.5$

used in conjunction with the tolerance specifications in deciding the goodness of the feature(s). In our experiments, we were not directly interested in the actual value of the numerical measure, because 1) we do not possess accurate tactile measurement devices that could perform the same procedures manually for comparison, and 2) the actual values of the tolerance specifications are decided by the manufacturer and are arbitrary. In the light of these factors, what we were interested in observing was the behavior of the numerical measure output by the inspection system as the machined object underwent deformation.

The object shown in Fig. 11 was machined on our CAMM-3 modeling machine to the best possible accuracy of the machine. A pair of mutually perpendicular edges were selected. One of the edges was systematically deformed by additional machining such that the angle between the two edges increased (Fig. 17). With this monotonic increase in the angle, the output measure of the system was observed. Each deformation produced an increase in angle of approximately two degrees and there were ten such deformations. The output of the system as shown in Table 1 clearly indicates that the angularity measure output by the inspection system is also monotonic.

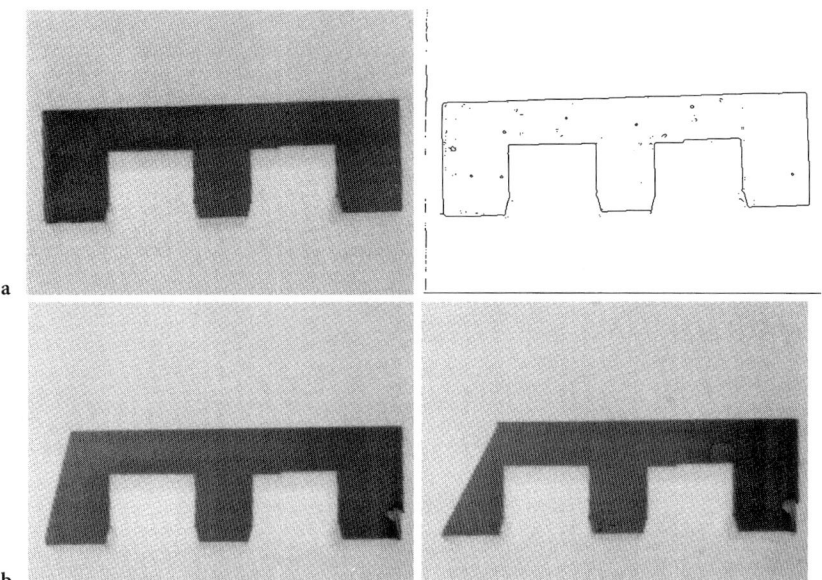

Fig. 17. a The original object and the corresponding edge image after connected shrinking; **b** The same object after the fifth angular deformation; **c** The object after the tenth deformation

Table 1. Progressive angular deformation of the test object produces monotonic change in the angular measure output by the inspection system

Deformation #	Angular measure output by system
1	1.553
2	1.530
3	1.474
4	1.429
5	1.392
6	1.310
7	1.275
8	1.218
9	1.148
10	1.077

7 Conclusions

In this paper, we described a CAD-based machine vision system for dimensional inspection of machined parts. The system performs inspection by strictly adhering to well-defined tolerance definitions. Hence all the measurements made by the system have a strong underlying theoretical basis. We extended our three-dimensional vision models originally developed for pose determination to include the tolerance information. We propagated uncertainties from lower-level edge pixels all the way up to the measurement tasks. We then incorporated these uncertainties in our decision making to rule a feature acceptable or not. Our experimental results verified the uncertainty derivations statistically, proved that the error probabilities obtained by propagating uncertainties are lower than those obtainable without uncertainty propagation, and demonstrated that the system responds in a predictable manner to progressively deformed objects.

This work sets up a theoretical and operational framework for a CAD-based inspection system. Additional measurement tasks can be included by setting up precise tolerance definitions adhering to the guidelines described. Uncertainty propagation for these additional tasks can be done by following the methodology outlined for the straightness of edge task.

References

[ANS73]   *American National Standards Institute (ANSI). 1973. Dimensioning and Tolerancing. ANSI Standard Y 14.5.* American Soc. of Mech. Engg., 1973.

[BHT85]   B. Bhanu, T. Henderson, and S. Thomas. 3-d model building using cagd techniques. In *IEEE Conference on Computer Vision and Pattern Recognition*, pages 234–239, Jun 1985.

[CMS88]   M. Chen, S.J. Mountford, and A. Sellen. A study in interactive 3-d rotation using 2-d control devices. *Computer Graphics*, 22:121–128, Aug 1988.

[CSH91]   O. Camps, L.G. Shapiro, and R.M. Haralick. Premio: An overview. In *IEEE Workshop on Directions in Automated CAD Based Vision*, pages 11–21, 1991.

[EU85]   F. Etesami and J. Uicker. Automatic dimensional inspection of machine part cross-sections using fourier analysis. *Computer Vision, Graphics and Image Processing*, 29:216–247, 1985.

[Har84]   R.M. Haralick. Digital step edges from zero crossings of second directional derivatives. *IEEE Trans. on Pattern Analysis and Machine Intelligence*, Jan 1984.

[H.D88]   H.D. Park. Cavis- cad based automated visual inspection system. *PhD Thesis, Purdue University*, Dec 1988.

[Ike87]   K. Ikeuchi. Generating an interpretation tree from a cad model for 3d-object recognition in bin-picking tasks. *International Journal of Computer Vision*, 1(2):145–165, 1987.

[KJHP90] T. Kanungo, M.Y. Jaisimha, R.M. Haralick, and R. Palmer. An experimental methodology for performance characterization of a line detection algorithm. *SPIE Optics, Illumination and Image sensing for Machine Vision*, 1385, 1990.

[LS89]   H. Lu and L.G. Shapiro. Model-based vision using relational summaries. In *SPIE Conference on Applications of Artificial Intelligence*, 1989.

[Mod91]   B. R. Modayur. Visual inspection of machined parts. *MSEE Thesis, Dept of EE, Univ. of Wash.*, Seattle, 1991.

[PM90]   H.D. Park and O.R. Mitchell. Cad-based planning and execution of inspection. *IEEE Conference on Computer Vision and Pattern Recognition*, 1385, 1990.

[PS85]   F.P. Preparata and M.I. Shamos. *Computational Geometry: An Introduction.* Springer-Verlag N.Y. Inc, 1985.

[Req83] A.A.G. Requicha. Toward a theory of geometric tolerancing. *International Journal of Robotics Research*, 2(4):45–60, 1983.
[WFD91] G.A.W. West, T. Fernando, and P.M. Dew. Cad based inspection: Using a vision cell demonstrator. In *IEEE Workshop on Directions in Automated CAD Based Vision*, pages 155–164, 1991.
[Yi90] S. Yi. Illumination control expert for machine vision: A goal driven approach. PhD Thesis, Dept. of EE, Univ. of Wash., Seattle, 1990.

Appendix

Proof that the Required Support Line is an Edge of the Convex Hull

Problem. *Given N points in 2 space, construct a line L that is a supporting line[2] for these N points such that the sum of perpendicular distances from the N points to this line L is a minimum.*

Theorem. *Given N points in 2 space, the supporting line that minimizes the sum of perpendicular distances to these N points passes through an edge of the convex hull of the N points.*

Proof. The supporting line L that minimizes the sum of perpendicular distances has to pass through at least one vertex of the convex hull CH_N. Let this vertex be V. Let U and W be the two adjacent vertices. Let P be any point on or inside the convex hull CH_N.

Now, the perpendicular distance from P to the line L would be

$$d = |PV| \sin Z$$

where $|PV|$ is the Euclidean distance from V to P, Z is the angle between VP and VC, and C is the closest point on L from P.

Let θ_1 be the value of Z when L is flush with UV and let θ_2 be the value of Z when L coincides with VW[3]. Since $|PV|$ remains a constant as L rotates around the pivotal point V from VW to UV, the distance d is a function of $\sin Z$. The sin function is concave-down in the region 0 to 180 degrees. This means that the perpendicular distance from any one of the N points to L is a concave-down function. Thus the sum of perpendicular distances is also a concave-down function and the sum of distances function attains a minimum either when L = UV or when L = VW.

---

[2] We require L to be a supporting line because we want the datum to "completely enclose" the irregular edge.
[3] The range of Z is from 0 to 180 degrees since U, V and W are adjacent vertices of a convex hull.

Texture Analysis in Industrial Applications

M. Pietikäinen and T. Ojala

Abstract. Problems of texture analysis in industry are considered. First, a literature survey of proposed industrial applications is presented and, then, some popular texture measures which have been successfully used in various applications and new promising approaches proposed recently are described. Finally, a comparative study of the texture measures is carried out by using a classification principle based on comparing sample distribution of feature values to predefined model distributions with known true class labels.

1 Introduction

Texture is an important characteristic for the analysis of many types of images. A textured area in an image can be characterized by non-uniform or varying spatial distribution of intensity. The intensity variation reflects some variation in the scene being imaged. Important applications include industrial and biomedical surface inspection, for example for defects and disease, ground classification and segmentation of satellite or aerial imagery, and segmentation of textured regions in document analysis.

A wide variety of measures for discriminating textures have been proposed. For recent surveys of texture analysis, see Van Gool et al. (1985), Rao (1990), Tomita and Tsuji (1990), Haralick and Shapiro (1992), Reed and Du Buf (1993), and Tuceryan and Jain (1993). The methods can be divided into three main categories: statistical, structural, and a combination of both. Among the most widely used texture measures are those derived from co-occurrence matrices of second-order gray level statistics, or from first-order statistics of local property values (difference histograms), "texture energy" measures obtained by local linear transforms, edge-based measures, and features based on multi-channel Gabor filtering, random field models, fractal models or mathematical morphology. Comparative studies to evaluate the performance of some texture measures have been carried out by, among others, Weszka et al. (1976), Conners and Harlow (1980), Pietikäinen (1982), Du Buf et al. (1990), and Ohanian and Dubes (1992).

There are many potential areas of application for texture analysis in industry. A major problem with the application of texture analysis to real problems is that textures in the real world are often not uniform, due to changes in orientation, scale or other visual appearance. In addition, the degree of computational complexity of many of the proposed texture measures is very high. The popular texture measures derived from co-occurrence matrices of second-order gray level statistics, for example, are too complex for many on-line visual inspection applications. Further discussion on approaches and problems dealing with texture analysis in industrial applications is presented by Song et al. (1992) and Chetverikov (1987).

This paper is concerned with problems of texture analysis in industry. In Sect. 2 a literature survey of proposed industrial applications is given. Section 3 describes some popular texture measures which have been successfully used in various applications and new promising approaches proposed recently. In Sect. 4, experiments with different types of texture measures are carried out to evaluate their performance in texture classification. A classification principle based on comparing sample distribution of feature values to predefined model distributions with true class labels is employed. Two different data sets are used in experiments: images used in a recent comparative study by Ohanian and Dubes (1992), and images taken from Brodatz's (1966) album. Section 5 contains a discussion, and Sect. 6 concludes the paper.

2 Survey of Industrial Applications

Classification of wood defects is one of the most challenging areas of application for texture analysis, due to high variability of image data within and between species. Conners et al. (1983) applied texture analysis methods for the identification and location of surface defects on lumber boards. The digital image of a board was divided into non-overlapping rectangular sub-images and each of these was classified separately. Different tonal properties and texture measures were computed for each region and fed into a statistical pattern recognition procedure. Their study indicated that measures of tonal and pattern related qualities of wood are needed to obtain good performance. The tonal measures employed were derived from the gray scale histogram of the sub-image under consideration. The pattern related (texture) measures were derived from co-occurrence matrices of second-order gray level statistics. A two-stage sequential classification scheme was proposed which first separated clear wood samples from the defective ones by using computationally simple tonal measures. The second stage classified the defects using both the tonal measures and the texture measures. Similar tonal measures were also used by Sobey and Semple (1989) to detect the presence of visual features (defects) in radiata pinewood boards. Ojala et al. (1992) studied the performance of edge-based texture measures in the classification of plywood defects. The edge-based approach performed about equally well as the co-occurrence method. The importance of the tonal measures also became clear in this study.

Segmentation of defects in textile fabric has been studied among others by Ade et al. (1984), Dewaele et al. (1988) and Neubauer (1992). Ade et al. used different types of local transforms (including Laws' masks) to measure textural properties. Statistics on the outputs of the transforms in macro-windows of a certain size were used to arrive at a set of feature planes. The values of these feature planes at each pixel location were combined into a Mahalanobis distance which is a measure for the intensity of the defect at this location. Dewaele et al. used a similar approach to that of Ade et al. The most important novelty of their approach was that the filters used for local transforms did not have a prespecified form. The texture was first investigated in order to extract its overall repetitiveness. Recently, Neubauer has applied multiple FIR-filters similar to Laws' concept and computed histograms of features for non-overlapping sub-images. Histograms were then classified by a Perceptron Net trained by backpropagation.

Texture analysis in semiconductor wafer manufacturing has been considered by Brecher (1992) and Rao (1990) for example. Brecher presented two techniques for detecting defects on patterned wafers. The methods are based on comparisons of local to global first order statistics of edge orientation and contrast. The techniques chosen were motivated by the principles of human pre-attentive visual detection. Rao studied a certain category of defects consisting of abnormally rough surfaces. The fractal dimension of the surface was used as a measure of its roughness.

Texture properties of cast metals to discriminate a rough surface from a normal iron surface were studied by Okawa (1984). The standard deviation of the gray levels, two features derived from the differences of two adjacent pixels, and two features derived from the horizontal and vertical profiles were used. Dinstein et al. (1984) studied the problem of discriminating textured and homogeneous regions required in the inspection of magnetic disc heads. A simple gray-level difference operator was used for texture detection. Fast implementations of the method were discussed to enable real-time operation. Borghesi et al. (1984) used the co-occurrence matrix method to detect faulty (broken, loose, missing, etc.) cords in the regular pattern of a pneumatic tyre. An architecture for real-time implementation of the proposed solution was also presented.

Jain et al. (1990) used texture features based on Gabor filtering to classify the quality of painted metallic surfaces with an application in the automotive industry. Non-defective paint has a smooth texture, but defective paint may have "mottle" or "blotchy" appearance (Tuceryan and Jain 1993). Jain and Bhattacharjee (1992) successfully used Gabor filter features for segmenting textured areas in document images.

Kegelmeyer and Hansen (1992) showed that acceptable and unacceptable chemical vapor deposition (CVD) diamond films can be distinguished automatically by using texture analysis. They used a texture feature which measures the homogeneity of the edge orientations in a local window for this task and proposed an architecture for real-time operation. The use of texture analysis for carpet wear assessment was studied by Siew et al. (1988), with potential applications in carpet grading and quality control in carpet manufacturing. Four sets of carpet samples exposed to different degrees of wear were analyzed by using texture measures derived from the second-order gray level statistics, and from first-order statistics of gray level differences, respectively.

The development of new approaches for wheat hardness assessment may have an impact on the grain industry in marketing, milling and breeding. Zayas et al. (1991) studied the use of texture features for wheat hardness evaluation. Parameters which characterize texture were determined and used to classify images of crushed wheat kernels into six wheat classes. Texture measures derived from co-occurrence matrices were used in this study. Kjell (1992) used texture energy operators to measure the proportion of constituents in mixtures of two types of small particles, barley and rice. Two approaches were tested: multi-linear regression, and linear classification into discrete composition classes. A simple classification procedure using features computed by 3×3 Laws' operators gave a sufficiently good performance.

The size of a structure is an intuitively observable and quantitative feature useful for many applications, e.g., in materials science and biology. Mathematical morphology has been the most widely used approach. Serra (1982) described in his book examples which use binary morphology. A generalization of global binary size distribution determination to local gray value size distribution determination was presented by Behrens and Dengler (1990) with applications in medical image analysis. Gerhardt et al. (1989) applied texture analysis for identifying and classifying sandpaper samples on the basis of the amount of sizing coat. Placing too much sizing coat will cause the product to be too smooth, and placing too little will cause the product to be too gritty. Methods based on mathematical morphology and neighboring gray level dependence matrices were used.

3 Texture Measures

3.1 Spatial Gray Level Dependence Method

The spatial gray level dependence method (SGLDM) is the most widely used method for texture analysis. It has performed favorably in the comparative studies of Weszka et al. (1976), Conners and Harlow (1980), Du Buf et al. (1990), and Ohanian and Dubes (1992). The method has been successfully used in various applications, for example by Conners et al. (1983), Borghesi et al. (1984), Siew et al. (1988) and Zayas et al. (1991).

The SGLDM estimates the joint gray level distribution for two gray levels located at a specified distance and angle (second-order statistics). The second-order statistics are usually tabulated as a co-occurrence matrix $P(i,j;d,a)$ for each fixed distance and angular spatial relationship. Each matrix $P(i,j;d,a)$ is computed by counting the number of times each pair of gray levels occurs at given intersample spacing d and in the given direction a (a = 0, 45, 90, or 135 degrees). Usually the matrices are symmetrical, i.e., $P(i,j;d,a) = p(j,i;d,a)$. As an example, if the digital image is

0 1 2
3 2 1
0 3 1

and d = 1 and a = 0 (i.e., horizontal direction), the co-occurrence matrix is

0 1 0 1
1 0 2 1
0 2 0 1
1 1 1 0

Haralick et al. (1973) derived a set of 14 moments from these matrices; and some of them have been very successful in many application areas. Among the most widely used are energy, entropy, correlation, local homogeneity, and inertia. The first paper to report a direct use of co-occurrence matrices in classification was by Vickers and Modestino (1983).

3.2 Gray Level Difference Method

A class of simple image properties that can be used for texture analysis are first-order statistics of local property values, i.e., the means, variances, etc. In particular, a class of local properties based on absolute differences between pairs of gray levels or of average gray levels has been sometimes used; for example, in the comparative studies of Weszka et al. (1976) and Conners and Harlow (1980) and in the application study of Siew et al. (1988).

For any given displacement d = (dx, dy), where dx and dy are integers, let $f'(x, y) = |f(x, y) - f(x + dx, y + dy)|$. Let P' be the probability density function of f'. If the image has m gray levels, this has the form of an m-dimensional vector whose ith component is the probability that f' (x, y) will have value i. P' can be easily computed by counting the number of times each value of f' (x, y) occurs. For a small d the difference histograms will peak near zero, while for a larger d they are more spread out.

Usually different kinds of measures are derived from difference histograms, such as contrast, angular second moment, entropy, mean, and inverse difference moment. Weszka et al. found that the gray level differrence method (GLDM) performed about as well as the spatial gray level dependence method (SGLDM). Conners and Harlow concluded that the SGLDM is more powerful than the GLDM. They also suggested that the common set of five features employed with the SGLDM by Weszka et al. cannot measure all the important information from the co-occurrence matrices. In fact, it is clear that theoretically the SGLDM approach should be more powerful than the GLDM method, because the information contained in the difference histograms is also available in the co-occurrence matrices. From a practical point of view, however, the ease with which the most important texture information can be extracted from the texture representation used is of great importance.

Whole distributions of gray level differences (instead of absolute differences) in four different directions were used by Unser (1986). He considered the use of sum and difference histograms, jointly and on their own, as an alternative to the usual co-occurrence matrices. Experiments with twelve different Brodatz's textures showed that the sum and difference histograms jointly performed about as well as the co-occurrence matrices. Difference histograms appeared to be much more powerful than sum histograms and performed, even on their own, about as well as co-occurrence matrices.

3.3 Laws' Texture Measures

The "texture energy measures" developed by (Laws 1979; Laws 1980) or related measures developed by others have also performed well in some comparative studies (Laws 1980; Pietikäinen 1982; Du Buf et al. 1990). Recently, Ng et al. (1992) found that a local linear transform approach (used by Laws, for example) is more powerful for texture segmentation than an approach based on Gabor filtering. Laws' or related measures have been successfully used, for example, in the application studies of Ade et al. (1984), Dewaele et al. (1988), Neubauer (1992) and Kjell (1992).

Laws' properties, which he called "texture energy measures," are derived from three simple vectors of length 3, L3 = (1,2,1), E3 = (−1,0,1), and S3 = (−1,2,−1), which represent the one-dimensional operations of center-weighted local averaging, symmetric first differencing (edge detection), and second differencing (spot detection) (Laws 1980; Pietikäinen et al. 1983). If we now multiply the column vectors of length 3 by row vectors of the same length, we obtain Laws' 3×3 masks. The eight zero-sum 3×3 masks (i.e., all but L3L3) are shown in Fig. 1.

To use these masks to describe the texture in a (sub)image, we convolve them with the image and use statistics of the results as textural properties. Laws concluded that the most useful statistics are the sums of the squared or absolute values of the image after these masks are convolved with it. The sum of the squares

```
-1   0   1        -1  -2  -1        1   0  -1        1  -2   1
-2   0   2         0   0   0        0   0   0        0   0   0
-1   0   1         1   2   1       -1   0   1       -1   2  -1

     L3E3               E3L3             E3E3             E3S3

-1  -2  -1         1   0  -1        1  -2   1       -1   2  -1
 2   4   2        -2   0   2       -2   4  -2       -2   4  -2
-1  -2  -1         1   0  -1        1  -2   1       -1   2  -1

     S3L3               S3E3             S3S3             L3S3
```

Fig. 1. Eight 3×3 Laws' masks

justifies the terminology "texture energy measures," but the sum of the absolute values is preferable because it is computationally cheaper. The whole distribution of mask responses for describing textural properties was used by Harwood et al. (1985), Harwood et al. (1993) and Ojala et al. (1993).

3.4 Center-Symmetric Covariance Measures

Laws' and other related studies of texture analysis suggest that many natural and artificial textures are measurably "loaded" with distributions of various specific local patterns of texture having these abstract symmetrical forms. Moreover, to measure the local "loading" of gray level symmetric (positive) or antisymmetric (negative) texture, we have only to compute local auto-covariances or auto-correlations of center-symmetric pixel values of suitably sized neighborhoods.

In a recent study of Harwood et al. (1993), a set of related measures was introduced, including two local center-symmetric auto-correlation measures, with linear (SAC) and rank-order versions (SRAC), together with a related covariance measure (SCOV). All of these are rotation-invariant robust measures and, apart from SCOV, they are locally gray-scale invariant. These measures are abstract measures of texture pattern and gray-scale, providing very discriminating information about the amount of local texture. A mathematical description of these measures computed for center-symmetric pairs of pixels in a 3×3 neighborhood (see Fig. 2) is presented in equations (1) to (4). μ denotes the local mean and σ^2 the local variance in the equations.

SCOV is a measure of the pattern correlation as well as the local pattern contrast. Since it is not "normalized" in respect to local gray-scale variation, it provides more texture information than the normalized auto-correlation measures SAC and SRAC. SAC is an auto-correlation measure, a "normalized," gray-scale invariant version of the texture covariance measure SCOV. SAC is invariant under linear gray-scale shifts such as correction by mean and standard deviation. It should also be noted that the values of SAC are bound between -1 and 1.

$$\text{SCOV} = \frac{1}{4} \sum_{i}^{4} (x_i - \mu)(x_i' - \mu) \tag{1}$$

$$\text{SAC} = \frac{\text{SCOV}}{\sigma^2} \tag{2}$$

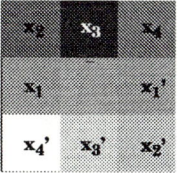

Fig. 2. 3×3 neighborhood with 4 center-symmetric pairs of pixels

Texture statistics based directly on the gray values of an image are sensitive to noise and monotonic shifts in the gray scale. With SRAC, the local rank order of the gray values is used instead of the gray values themselves. Hence, SRAC is invariant under any monotonic transformation including correction by mean and standard deviation and histogram equalization. The amount of auto-correlation in the ranked neighborhood is given by Spearman's rank correlation (Udny Yule and Kendall 1968). It is defined for the nxn neighborhood with 4 center-symmetric pairs of pixels as (3) where m is n^2 and each t_i is the number of ties at rank r_i in the ranked neighborhood. The values of SRAC are bound between -1 and 1.

$$\text{SRAC} = 1 - \frac{12\left\{\sum_{i}^{4}(r_i - r_i')^2 + T_x\right\}}{m^3 - m} \quad (3)$$

$$T_x = \frac{1}{12}\sum_{i}^{l}(t_i^3 - t_i) \quad (4)$$

The distributions of the feature values described above are used for classification (Harwood et al. 1993; Ojala et al. 1993).

3.5 Texture Units and Texture Spectrum

Recently, Wang and He (1990) introduced a new model of texture analysis based on the so-called texture unit, where a texture image can be characterized by its texture spectrum. A texture unit (TU) is represented by eight elements, each of which has one of three possible values (0,1,2) obtained from a neighborhood of 3 × 3 pixels. In total, there are $3^8 = 6561$ possible texture units describing spatial three-level patterns in a 3 × 3 neighborhood. The occurrence of distribution of texture units computed over a region is called the texture spectrum. Wang and He demonstrated that the different texture images have different spectra, which means that the texture aspect of an image can be characterized by its spectrum.

Figures 3a,b show an example of transforming a neighborhood to a texture unit. The value of a given pixel (Fig. 3a) is compared to the value of the center pixel in that neighborhood. Then, the original value will be transformed to 0,1 or 2, depending on if it is smaller, equal or greater than the value of the center pixel, respectively (Fig. 3b).

There is no unique way to label and order the 6561 texture units. We have used a principle which is illustrated Fig. 3c. The value of a pixel in the transformed image (Fig. 3b) is multiplied by the weight given to the corresponding pixel (Fig. 3c), and the result is shown in Fig. 3d. Then, a number for this texture unit is computed by summing the values of the eight pixels. In our example, a value of 4915 is obtained.

The texture unit number gives a description of the relative gray level relationships between the center pixel and its eight neighbors. By computing a histogram

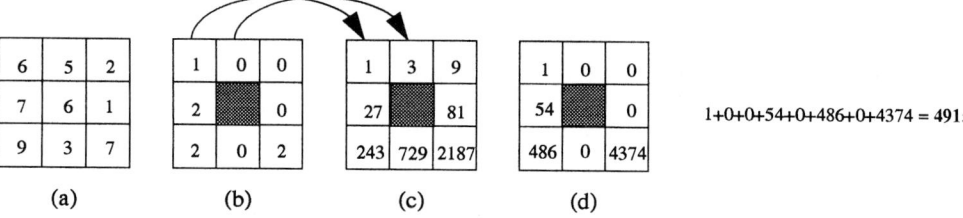

Fig. 3. Local neighborhood is transformed to a texture unit (TU)

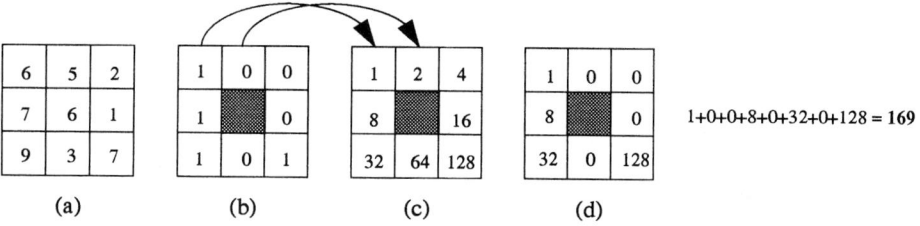

Fig. 4. Two-level version (LBP) the of texture unit

of all the texture unit numbers over a (sub)image, a texture spectrum is obtained. Wang and He demonstrated that the texture spectrum is very useful in discriminating different types of textures. In texture classification experiments they used a simple method of comparing two distributions based on computing the absolute differences between the sample and prototype distributions. Later they also defined a set of features derived from the distributions (He and Wang 1990). Some of these are rotation invariant.

3.6 Local Binary Patterns

Recently, Ojala et al. (1993) found that a simple two-level version of the method of Wang and He performs about as well as the original three-level approach. The method provides a robust way for describing pure local binary patterns (LBP) in a texture.

In the two-level version, there are only $2^8 = 256$ possible texture units instead of 6561. In binary case, the original 3×3 neighborhood (Fig. 4a) is thresholded by the value of the center pixel. The values of the pixels in the thresholded neighborhood (Fig. 4b) are multiplied by the weights given to the corresponding pixels (Fig. 4c). The result for this example is shown in Fig. 4d. Finally, the values of the eight pixels are summed to obtain the number (169) of this texture unit.

Figure 5b shows the LBP histogram computed over the image of Fig. 5a. The histogram has only 256 bins, which simplifies and speeds up the analysis compared

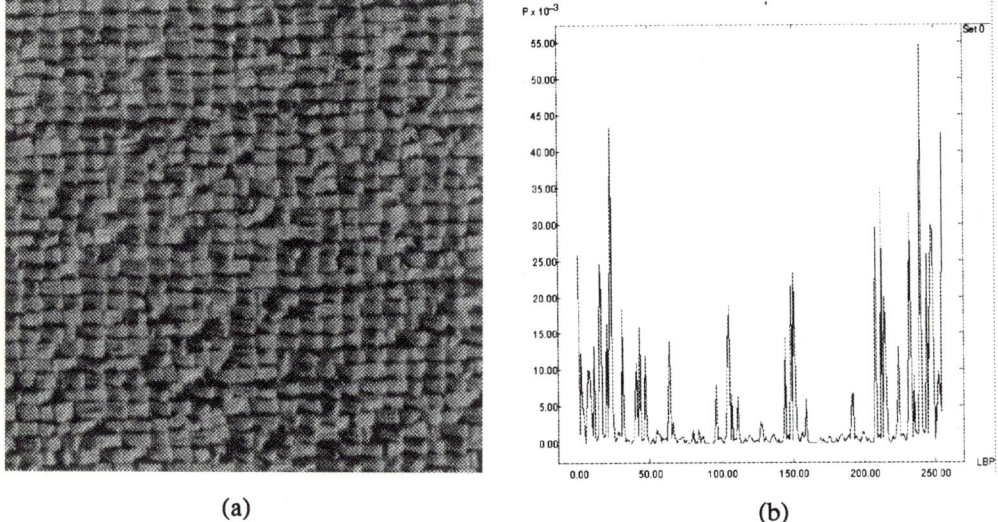

Fig. 5. a Texture image D84 from Brodatz's album, and **b** LBP histogram computed over the image

to the three-level approach. The LBP method is gray scale invariant and can be easily combined with a simple contrast measure in a two-dimensional classification scheme, as was shown by Ojala et al. (1993). Contrast information is obtained by computing for each neighborhood the difference of the average gray level of those pixels which have the value 1, and those which have the value 0, respectively (see Fig. 4b).

4 Performance Evaluation of Texture Measures

4.1 Classification Principle

Most of the approaches to texture analysis quantify the texture measures by single values (means, variances etc.). These values are used as elements of feature vectors in performing classification. In this way, much important information contained in the distributions of feature values might be lost.

There are some results which indicate that the whole distributions of feature values provide very discriminating information about the textures. Vickers and Modestino (1983), for example, used the co-occurrence matrix directly, and Unser (1986) the sum and difference histograms, jointly and on their own, in a maximum likelihood classifier. Harwood et al. (1985), Harwood et al. (1993) and Ojala et al. (1993) employed nearest neighbor classification based on Kullback (or related G test) discrimination of sample and model distributions using various texture measures.

In the experiments presented in this paper, the distributions of feature values were used for classification. A log-likelihood-ratio test, the G test, was used to compare the sample and model distributions (Sokal and Rohlf 1969; Kendall and Stuart 1979; Harwood et al. 1985). The G test is closely related to Kullback's minimum cross-entropy principle (Kullback 1968). The value of the computed G statistic indicates the probability that the two sample distributions come from the same population: the higher the value, the lower the probability that the two samples are from the same population. For a goodness-of-fit test the G statistic is (5):

$$G = 2 \sum_{i=1}^{n} s_i \log \frac{s_i}{m_i} \qquad (5)$$

where s and m are the sample and model distributions, n is the number of bins and s_i, m_i are the respective sample and model probabilities at bin i. In our experiments, a single model distribution for every class was not used. Every sample was in its turn classified using the other samples as models, hence the leave-one-out approach was applied. The sample was assigned the label of the model that minimized two-way test-of-independence (6);

$$G = 2 \left\{ \left[\sum_{s,m} \sum_{i=1}^{n} f_i \log f_i \right] - \left[\sum_{s,m} \left(\sum_{i=1}^{n} f_i \right) \log \left(\sum_{i=1}^{n} f_i \right) \right] - \left[\sum_{i=1}^{n} \left(\sum_{s,m} f_i \right) \log \left(\sum_{s,m} f_i \right) \right] \right.$$
$$\left. + \left[\left(\sum_{s,m} \sum_{i=1}^{n} f_i \right) \log \left(\sum_{s,m} \sum_{i=1}^{n} f_i \right) \right] \right\} \qquad (6)$$

where s, m are the two texture samples (test sample and model), n is the number of bins and f_i is the frequency at bin i.

The model distribution for each sample was obtained by scanning the texture image with the local texture operator. The distributions of local statistics were divided into histograms having a fixed number of bins; hence, the G tests for all pairings of a sample and a model had the same number of degrees-of-freedom. The number of bins used in quantization of the feature space plays a crucial role. Histograms with a too modest number of bins fail to provide enough discriminative information about the distributions. However, since the distributions have a finite amount of entries, it may not make sense to go to the other extreme. If histograms have too many bins, and the average number of entries per bin is very small, histograms become sparse and unstable. In most of our experiments, histograms with 32 bins were used. This corresponded to an average number of 32 entries per bin for samples 32 × 32 in size and 8 entries per bin for samples 16 × 16 in size, respectively.

The feature space was quantized by adding together feature distributions for every single model image in a total distribution which was divided into 32 bins having an equal number of entries. Hence, the cut values of the bins of the histograms corresponded to 3.125 (100/32) percentile of the combined data. Deriving the cut values from the total distribution, and allocating every bin the same amount of the combined data guarantees that the highest resolution of the quantization is used where the number of entries is largest and vice versa. It should be noted that the quantization of feature space is only required for texture operators with a continuous-valued output. Output of discrete operators like TU and LBP, where two successive values can have totally different meaning, does not require any further processing; operator outputs are just accumulated into a histogram. The empty bins were set to the value 1 in all of our experiments.

4.2 Features Used

The aim of the comparative study was to evaluate the performance both of some texture measures which have been successfully used in various applications and of some new approaches proposed recently. Most of the methods considered are computationally very simple, which is important in many industrial applications. A description of the texture measures was presented in Sect. 3. In this paper, we only present experimental results using one-dimensional distributions of single features in classification. We also considered joint occurrences of pairs of features, including the co-occurrence matrix method, using a two-dimensional version of the classifier described in equation (6). The results of this investigation are presented in a separate paper (Ojala et al. 1993).

The feature set contained four measures based on the gray level difference method: DIFFX and DIFFY are histograms of absolute gray level differences between neighboring pixels computed in horizontal and vertical directions, respectively, while DIFF2 accumulates absolute differences in horizontal and vertical directions and DIFF4 in all four principal directions, respectively, in a single histogram, providing rotation invariant texture measures.

Four Laws' operators were considered. L3E3 and E3L3 perform edge detection in vertical and horizontal directions, respectively, and L3S3 and S3L3 are line detectors in these two orthogonal directions. Other measures included in this study were the center-symmetric covariance measures, SCOV, SAC and SRAC, as well as the local binary patterns (LBP).

4.3 Experiments with Image Set I

Recently, Ohanian and Dubes (1992) studied the performance of four types of features: Markov Random Field parameters, Gabor multi-channel features, fractal-based features, and co-occurrence features. They used four classes of images in experiments: fractal images, Gaussian Markov Random Field (GMRF) images, leather images, and painted images. Each image class contained four types of images: the synthetic fractal and GRMF images were generated by using different parameter values and the natural images represented different types of leather or painted surface, respectively. The images are shown in Fig. 6. With these images four 4-class problems and a 16-class problem were established. Whitney's forward selection method was used for feature selection and a kNN (k = 9) decision rule for classification. The co-occurrence features generally outperformed other features followed by fractal features. The Gabor features, which have been widely used in the computer vision community, performed poorly. This result was later confirmed by Ng et al. (1992). Ohanian and Dubes (1992) concluded that the empirically derived non-linear transformation used by, for example, Jain and Farrokhnia (1991) instead of the energy from the raw Gabor filtered images seems to be crucial for the performance of these features. Anyway, the results of earlier studies of Weszka et al. (1976), Conners and Harlow (1980) and Pietikäinen (1982), for example, also support our belief that spatial frequency approaches perform poorer than many other methods (see also Haralick and Shapiro (1992)).

With co-occurrence features, the best results obtained by Ohanian and Dubes using single features and a best combination of multiple features were the following. For fractal images they achieved an error rate of 28.9% with one feature, and with the six best features, the result was 18.9%. The GMRF images were easiest to discriminate. The best feature gave an error rate of 5.1% and the best combination of two features 0.0%. The discrimination of leather images was a difficult problem. Ohanian and Dubes obtained an error rate of 45.5% with one feature, and with the six best features, the result was 11.3%. The error rates for the painted surfaces were 20.3% with one feature, and 3.5% with ten features, respectively. In the 16-class problem, they achieved 47.7% with one feature, and 9.3% with ten features. It should be noted that one should be careful when comparing our results to those of Ohanian and Dubes, because the methods of image preprocessing, and the methods of classification were different in the two studies.

In our study, the same set of images was used. The images were corrected by mean and standard deviation in order to reduce discrimination by overall gray-level variation which is unrelated to local image texture. Figure 6 shows the corrected images. The correction was applied to the whole images instead of correcting every sample window separately. The mean gray value of each corrected image was set to 256 and the standard deviation to 40. Like Ohanian and Dubes, we treated each of the four classes of images as a separate 4-class problem. 200 non-overlapping samples of size 32×32 were extracted from each image (texture type), resulting in a classification problem of 800 samples. Additionally, the 16-class problem including all 3200 non-overlapping samples extracted from all 16 images was considered. Every sample was in its turn classified using the other 799 samples as models (3199 models in the 16-class problem) by applying the leave-one-out approach. A 9-NN classifier resembling the principle of Ohanian and Dubes was used.

The error rates for the four 4-class problems and the 16-class problem using distributions of single features are summarized in Table 1.

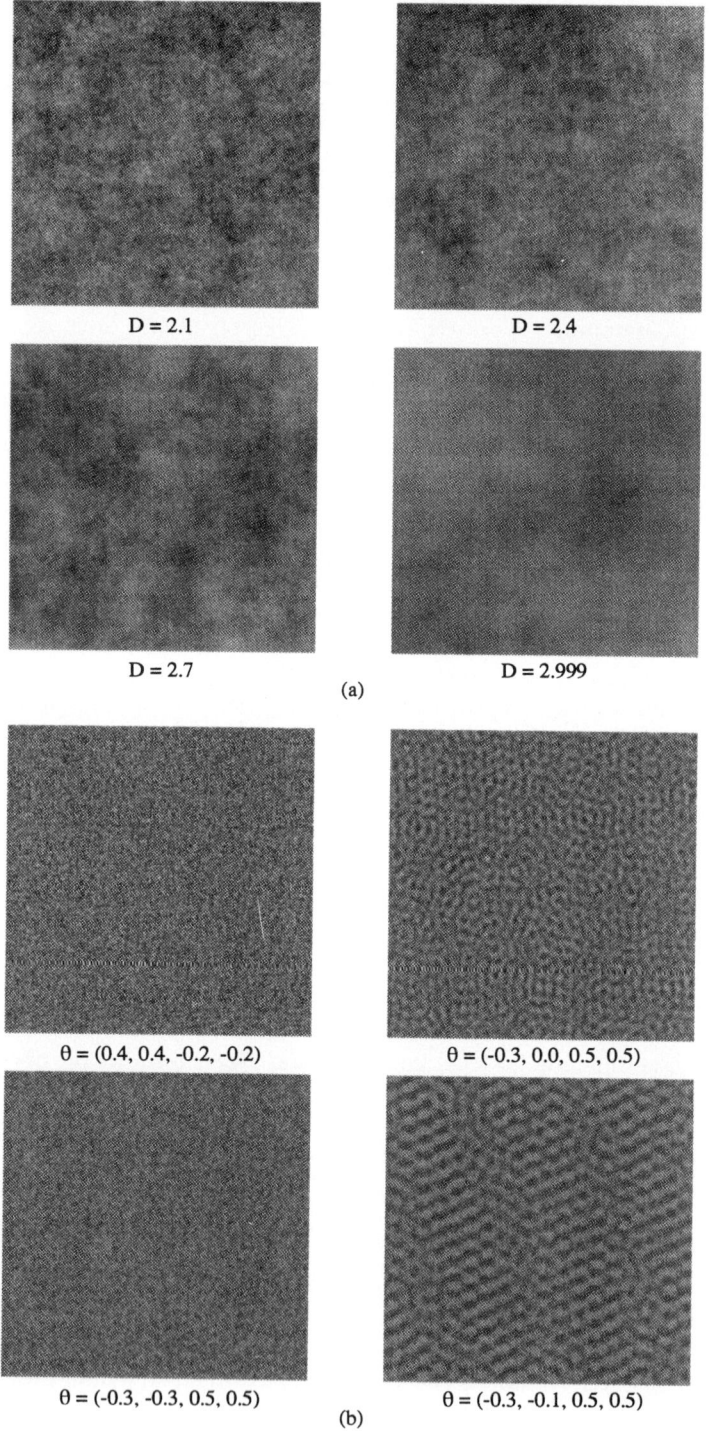

Fig. 6. a Fractal images with fractal dimension D; b Gaussian Markov Random Field images; c Leather images; d Painted surface images

Texture Analysis in Industrial Applications

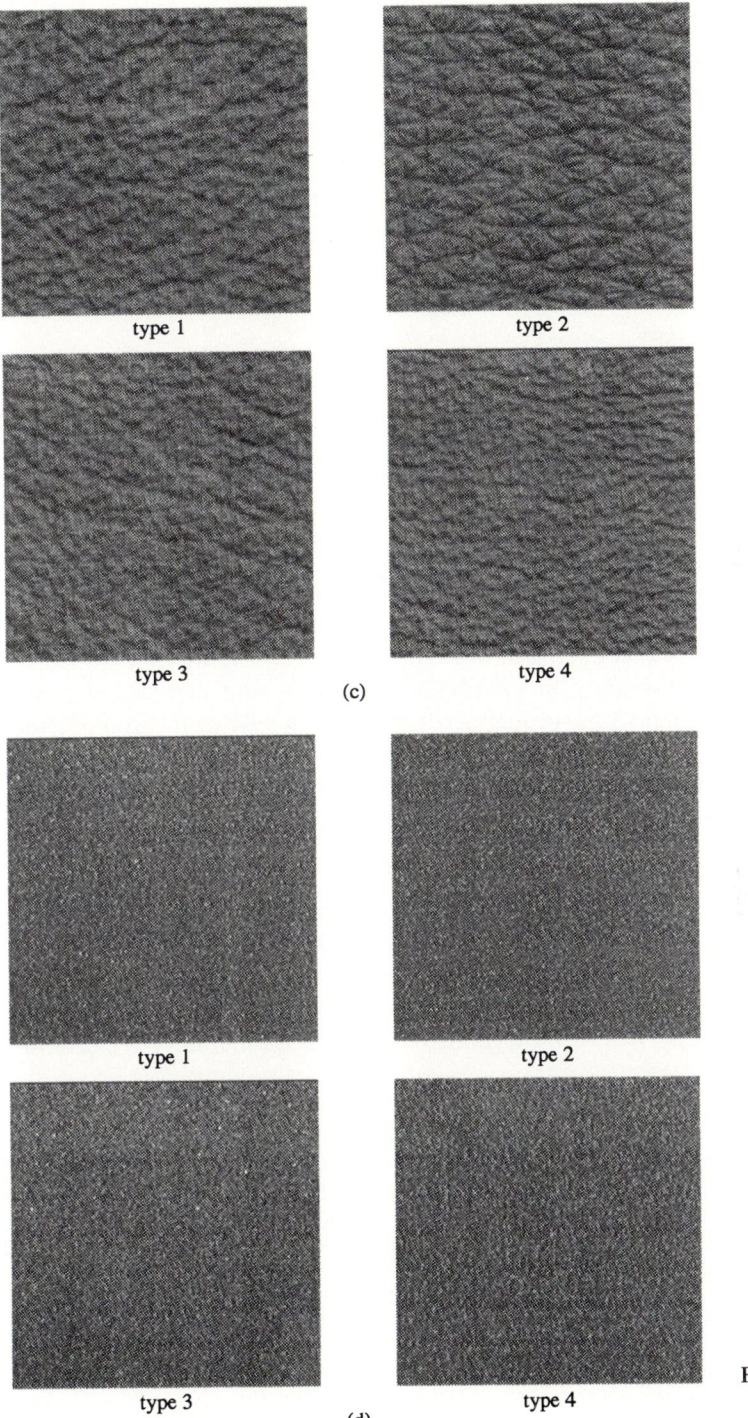

Fig. 6c,d

Table 1. Error rates for Image Set I

Feature	Fractal	GMRF	Leather	Painted	16-class
LBP	37.75	0.00	24.12	10.75	18.16
DIFFX	0.00	10.62	2.25	6.25	5.75
DIFFY	0.00	10.50	0.00	2.88	3.72
DIFF2	0.00	7.88	0.12	1.75	2.81
DIFF4	0.00	14.50	0.00	0.88	3.69
L3E3	1.00	6.88	23.12	40.62	33.06
E3L3	2.00	26.50	27.25	49.25	36.09
L3S3	0.00	7.38	39.25	50.12	31.53
S3L3	0.00	13.25	36.38	22.00	27.22
SCOV	0.00	3.38	28.38	31.37	16.56
SAC	43.25	10.88	46.12	34.00	46.28
SRAC	12.75	2.12	34.75	12.00	18.25

It can be seen that fractal images were quite easy to discriminate: all samples were correctly classified with DIFFX, DIFFY, DIFF2, DIFF4, L3S3, S3L3, and SCOV. LBP, SAC and SRAC did not perform well. This indicates that gray scale contrast is important for discriminating these images. It is surprising that Ohanian and Dubes achieved quite poor performance for these images. Their method of using histogram equalization for each 32×32 sample separately and reducing the number of gray levels to eight has obviously lost important contrast information from the fractal images. The results also indicate the discriminative power of our classification principle using distributions of feature values.

LBP, SRAC and SCOV performed best for GMRF images, achieving error rates of 0.00%, 2.12% and 3.38%, respectively. The worst results for the difference histogram features were obtained with these images, with error rates ranging from 7.88 (DIFF2) to 14.50 (DIFF4). The classification of leather images is somewhat more difficult. The excellent results obtained with DIFFY (0.00%), DIFF4 (0.00%) and DIFF2(0.12%) are surprisingly good. The results for the other features are much poorer.

The painted surfaces were also difficult for some features to discriminate. DIFF4, DIFF2 and DIFFY, again, achieved very low error rates of 0.88%, 1.75% and 2.88%, respectively. DIFFX, LBP and SRAC also performed quite well, but the results for the other features are much poorer.

The difference histogram features performed best in the 16-class problem, too, achieving error rates ranging from 2.81% to 5.75%. SCOV, LBP and SRAC also performed quite well with error rates of less than 20%. The poor performance of Laws' features, ranging from 27.22% to 36.09%, is mainly caused by the difficulty of discriminating leather and painted images with these measures. SCOV and SRAC performed better than Laws' measures, but, as expected, they also had problems with leather and painted images.

Table 2. The effect of quantization accuracy with Image Set I

# bins	DIFFX	DIFFY
2	53.00	44.88
4	26.53	21.78
8	17.22	11.16
16	8.06	5.62
32	5.75	3.72
64	3.94	2.97
128	3.16	2.75
256	3.25	2.53

The effect of the quantization accuracy on the results was also evaluated. In this study the DIFFX and DIFFY features with histograms ranging from 2 to 256 bins were used in the 16-class problem. The results are shown in Table 2. It can be seen that the accuracy of classification improves with the number of bins used. At least 32–64 histogram bins are required for a very good performance. A reason for selecting 32 bins for our experiments was that we also carried out experiments with a two-dimensional classifier using joint occurrences of pairs of features and, in this case, the 64×64 histograms, requiring much more computations, did not perform any better than the 32×32 histograms due to sparseness of the larger histograms.

4.4 Supplementary Study with Image Set II

Supplementary experiments with the set of Brodatz's textures used by Harwood et al. (1993) were also carried out. Nine classes of textures, grass, paper, waves, raffia, sand, wood, calf, herringbone and wool, were taken from Brodatz's album (1966). The texture images were corrected by mean and standard deviation as described in Sect. 4.3. Figure 7 shows the corrected images. The classification principle was the same as that used by Harwood et al. (1993). The sample was assigned the label of the model that optimized Kullback's minimum cross-entropy principle. This approach is similar to the goodness-of-fit G test (5). The model distribution for each class was obtained by scanning the corrected 256×256 texture image with the local texture operator. The test samples were obtained by randomly subsampling the original texture images. 1000 subsamples of 32×32 and 16×16 pixels in size were extracted from every texture class, resulting in a classification of 9000 random samples in total. When classifying a particular sample, the sample distribution was subtracted from the model distribution of the true class of this sample, so that an unbiased error estimate was obtained.

Table 3 shows the classification error rates for 32×32 and 16×16 samples from nine 256×256 images representing nine texture classes.

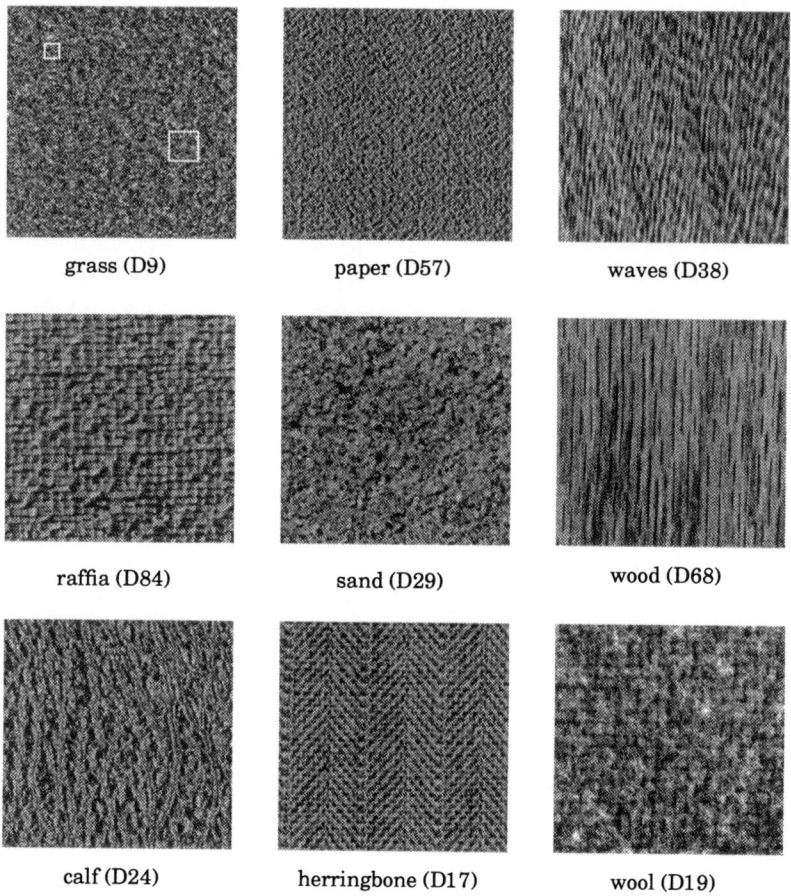

Fig. 7. Nine texture images from Brodatz's album. White rectangles in grass demonstrate the 16 × 16 and 32 × 32 sample sizes

Best performance was obtained for LBP feature with error rates of 2.30% for 32 × 32 samples and 12.52% for 16 × 16 samples, respectively. The difference histogram features also performed very well. The covariance measures performed better than Laws' measures, but the error rates for the 16 × 16 samples are quite poor for these two related approaches. This indicates that for good results the covariance and Laws' measures require larger sample sizes than the other approaches considered here. Harwood et al. (1993) obtained an error rate as small as 0.69% with the SRAC measure for 64 × 64 samples of the same textures.

Table 4 shows the effects of the quantization accuracy on the classification results using DIFFX and DIFFY feature distributions with 2–256 bins for the 16 × 16 samples of Brodatz's textures. We can observe that the accuracy of classification improves with the number of bins also for these textures. In fact, the results with 64 bins for DIFFY (9.94%) and 64 bins for DIFFX (11.53%) are better than were obtained with any feature in Table 3.

Table 3. Error rates for Image Set II

Feature	32 × 32	16 × 16
LBP	2.30	12.52
DIFFX	3.04	14.31
DIFFY	3.30	12.84
DIFF2	8.43	13.50
DIFF4	8.73	14.32
L3E3	19.82	42.46
E3L3	17.62	39.58
L3S3	14.28	33.78
S3L3	7.58	23.68
SCOV	8.07	29.62
SAC	11.83	36.92
SRAC	8.46	32.77

Table 4. The effect of quantization accuracy with Image Set II

# bins	DIFFX	DIFFY
2	58.46	43.44
4	47.01	32.91
8	36.58	26.37
16	27.00	19.53
32	14.31	12.84
64	11.53	9.94
128	10.67	8.91
256	10.22	8.72

5 Discussion

Most of the earlier approaches to texture classification quantify the texture measures by single values. These values are used as elements of feature vectors in performing classification. The very good results that we obtained by using distributions of simple texture measures suggest that distributions of feature values should be used instead of single values.

The gray level difference method (GLDM) achieved the best overall performance discriminating most of the textures very well. It is very easy to compute, and it performed well even with small 16 × 16 samples, which make this approach very attractive for many applications, including texture classification and segmentation. Our results support the conclusion of some earlier studies that the difference histograms contain most of the useful texture information available in the cooccurrence matrices. A disadvantage of GLDM is that it is not invariant with respect to gray scale variance, which means that the textures to be analyzed should be gray scale corrected. Due to its simplicity, however, the GLDM approach should be a method of choice for many practical applications.

The texture measures based on local binary patterns (LBP) are also computationally very simple. These measures performed very well, especially with the Brodatz textures. LBP is gray scale invariant and can be easily combined with a simple contrast measure, which makes it even more powerful. The use of LBP should be considered in problems in which the local spatial structure of texture is of importance. The method is rotation variant which is undesirable in certain applications. It should be noted, however, that is possible to derive rotation invariant features from the feature distributions (He and Wang 1990).

Center-symmetric covariance features performed very well for some of the textures being more powerful than Laws' measures. Both of these approaches require larger sample sizes than the GLDM and LBP methods. A reason of this is that most of the discriminative information for these kinds of measures is contained in the match maxima, as shown by Pietikäinen et al. (1983). To get statistically reliable information on the distributions of local exterema, quite large image windows may be needed. Covariance measures are computationally more complex than Laws' measures, but they are all rotation invariant while Laws' measures are not. In addition, the SRAC measure, which performed quite well, is invariant under any monotonic transformation, including correction by mean and standard deviation and histogram equalization.

There are many applications, for example in industrial inspection and remote sensing, in which the gray-scale invariance of a texture measure is of great importance due to uneven illumination or great within-class variability. Recent results which we have obtained with applying texture classification to a difficult metal sheet inspection problem have demonstrated that the gray-scale invariant LBP and SRAC measures can be more powerful in such applications than the other approaches considered in this paper.

The quite poor performance of Laws' approach indicates that the discriminative power of these measures is mostly contained in the variances of the feature distributions which have been used in most of the earlier studies. The whole distribution does not seem to provide much additional information. We would also suggest that Laws' or related approaches requiring quite large sample sizes are not as powerful in texture segmentation as, for example, the gray scale difference method. Our preliminary experiments with texture segmentation have supported this conclusion.

6 Conclusion

Texture analysis has many areas of potential application in industry. A survey of several proposed applications was presented. A major problem with the application of texture analysis to real problems is that textures in the real world are often not uniform, which tends to decrease the performance of most approaches. A comparative study to evaluate the performance of some commonly used and some recently proposed texture measures in texture classification was carried out. The results for different types of textures showed that a very good texture discrimination can be obtained by using simple texture measures and a classification principle based on a comparison of sample and prototype distributions of feature values.

Acknowledgements. The financial support of the Technology Development Center and the Academy of Finland is gratefully acknowledged. The authors also wish to thank David Harwood from the University of Maryland for his contributions in the early stages of this study, and Prof. Richard C. Dubes and John Lees from the Michigan State University for providing a set of test images used in this study.

References

Ade, F., N. Lins, and M. Unser (1984). Comparison of various filter sets for defect detection in textiles. Proc. 7th International Conference on Pattern Recognition, Montreal, Canada, pp. 428–431.
Behrens, S. and J. Dengler (1990). Analysing the structure of medical images with morphological size distributions. Proc. 10th International Conference on Pattern Recognition, Vol. I, Atlantic City, NJ, pp. 886–890.
Borghesi, M., V. Cantoni, and M. Diani (1984). An industrial application of texture analysis. Proc. 7th International Conference on Pattern Recognition, Montreal, Canada, pp. 420–423.
Brecher, V. (1992). New techniques for patterned wafer inspection based on a model of human preattentive vision. SPIE Vol. 1708 Applications of Artificial Intelligence X: Machine Vision and Robotics, pp. 452–459.
Brodatz, P. (1966). Textures: A Photographic Album for Artists and Designers. Dover Publications, New York.
Chetverikov, D. (1987). Texture imperfections. Pattern Recognition Letters, Vol. 6, pp. 45–50.
Conners, R.W. and C.A. Harlow (1980). A theoretical comparison of texture algorithms. IEEE Transactions on Pattern Analysis and Machine Intelligence, Vol. 2, No. 3, pp. 204–222.
Conners, R.W., C.W. McMillin, K. Lin, and R.E. Vasquez-Espinosa (1983). Identifying and locating surface defects in wood: part of an automatic lumber processing system. IEEE Transactions on Pattern Analysis and Machine Intelligence, Vol. 5, pp. 573–583.
Dewaele, P., L.Van Gool, P. Wambacq, and A. Oosterlinck (1988). Texture inspection with self-adaptive convolution filters. Proc. 9th International Conference on Pattern Recognition, Rome, Italy, pp. 56–60.
Dinstein, I., A. Fong, L. Ni, and K. Wong (1984). Fast discrimination between homogeneous and textured regions. Proc. 7th International Conference on Pattern Recognition, Montreal, Canada, pp. 361–363.
Du Buf, J.M.H., M. Kardan, and M. Spann (1990). Texture feature performance for image segmentation. Pattern Recognition, Vol. 23, No. 3/4, pp. 291–309.
Gerhardt, L.A., R.P. Kraft, P.D. Hill, and S. Neti (1989). Automated inspection of sandpaper products and processes using image processing. SPIE Vol. 1197 Automated Inspection and High-Speed Vision Architectures III, pp. 191–201.
Haralick, R.M., K. Shanmugam and I. Dinstein (1973). Textural features for image classification. IEEE Transactions on Systems, Man, and Cybernetics, Vol. SMC-3, pp. 610–621.

Haralick, R.M. and L.G. Shapiro (1992). Computer and Robot Vision, Vol. 1, Addison-Wesley.
Harwood, D., T. Ojala, M. Pietikäinen, S. Kelman, and L.S. Davis (1993). Texture classification by center-symmetric auto-correlation, using Kullback discrimination of distributions. University of Maryland, Center for Automation Research, Technical Report CAR-TR-678, 1993.
Harwood, D., M. Subbarao, and L.S. Davis (1985). Texture classification by local rank correlation. Computer Vision, Graphics, and Image Processing, Vol. 32, pp. 404–411.
He, D.C. and L. Wang (1990). Texture features based on texture spectrum. Pattern Recognition, Vol. 24, pp. 391–399.
Jain, A.K. and S.K. Bhattacharjee (1992). Text segmentation using Gabor filters for automatic document processing. Machine Vision and Applications, Vol. 5, pp. 169–184.
Jain, A.K. and F. Farrokhnia (1991). Unsupervised texture segmentation using Gabor filters. Pattern Recognition, Vol. 24, pp. 1167–1186.
Jain, A.K., F. Farrokhnia, and D.H. Altman (1990). Texture analysis of automotive finishes. Proc. of SME Machine Vision Applications Conference, Detroit, MI, pp. 1–16.
Kegelmeyer, W.P. and F. Hansen (1992). Automated visual quality evaluation of CVD film. SPIE Vol. 1708 Applications of Artificial Intelligence X: Machine Vision and Robotics, pp. 88–98.
Kendall, M. and A. Stuart (1979). The Advanced Theory of Statistics, Vol. 2. Macmillan Publishing Co., New York.
Kjell, B. (1992). Determining composition of grain mixtures using texture energy operators. SPIE Vol. 1825 Intelligent Robots and Computer Vision XI, pp. 395–400.
Kullback, S. (1968). Information Theory and Statistics, Dover Publications, New York.
Laws, K.I. (1979). Texture energy measures. Proc. Image Understanding Workshop, pp. 47–51.
Laws, K.I. (1980). Textured Image Segmentation. USCIPI Rep. 940, Image Processing Institute, University of Southern California.
Neubauer, C. (1992). Segmentation of defects in textile fabric. Proc. 11th International Conference on Pattern Recognition, Vol. I, The Hague, The Netherlands, pp. 688–691.
Ng., I, T. Tan and J. Kittler (1992). On local linear transform and Gabor filter representation of texture. Proc. 11th International Conference on Pattern Recognition, Vol. III, The Hague, The Netherlands, pp. 627–631.
Ohanian, P.P. and R.C. Dubes (1992). Performance evaluation for four classes of textural features. Pattern Recognition, Vol. 25, pp. 819–833.
Ojala, T., M. Pietikäinen, and D. Harwood (1993). A comparative study of texture measures with classification based on feature distributions. To appear in Pattern Recognition.
Ojala, T., M. Pietikäinen, and O. Silven (1992). Edge-based texture measures for surface inspection. Proc. 11th International Conference on Pattern Recognition, Vol. II, The Hague, The Netherlands, pp. 594–598.
Okawa, Y. (1984). Automatic inspection of the surface defects of cast metals. Computer Vision, Graphics, and Image Processing, Vol. 25, pp. 89–112.
Pietikäinen, M. (1982). Image Texture Analysis and Segmentation. Acta Universitatis Ouluensis, Series C, No. 21 (Dissertation).
Pietikäinen, M., A. Rosenfeld, and L.S. Davis (1983). Experiments with texture classification using averages of local pattern matches. IEEE Transactions on Systems, Man, and Cybernetics, Vol. SMC-13, pp. 421–426.
Rao, A.R. (1990). A Taxonomy for Texture Description and Identification, Springer-Verlag, New York.
Reed, T.R. and J.M.H. Du Buf (1993). A review of recent texture segmentation and feature extraction techniques. CVGIP Image Understanding, Vol. 57, No. 3, pp. 359–372.
Serra, J. (1982). Image Analysis and Mathematical Morphology, Academic Press.

Siew, L., R. Hodgson, and E. Wood (1988). Texture measures for carpet wear assessment. IEEE Transactions on Pattern Analysis and Machine Intelligence, Vol. 10, pp. 92–105.

Sobey, P. and E. Semple (1989). Detection and sizing visual features in wood using tonal measures and a classification algorithm. Pattern Recognition, Vol. 22, pp. 367–380.

Sokal, R.R. and F.J. Rohlf (1969). Biometry. W.H. Freeman and Co.

Song, K.Y., M. Petrou, and J. Kittler (1992). Texture defect detection: a review. SPIE Vol. 1708 Applications of Artificial Intelligence X: Machine Vision and Robotics, pp. 99–106.

Tomita, F. and S. Tsuji (1990). Computer Analysis of Visual Textures. Kluwer Academic Publishers.

Tuceryan, M. and A.K. Jain (1993). Texture analysis. In: Handbook of Pattern Recognition and Computer Vision (Eds. C.H. Chen, L.F. Pau, P.S.P. Wang), World Scientific Publishing Co.

Udny Yule, G. and M.G. Kendall (1968). An Introduction to the Theory of Statistics, Hafner Publishing, New York.

Unser, M. (1986). Sum and difference histograms for texture classification. IEEE Transactions on Pattern Analysis and Machine Intelligence, Vol. 8, No. 1, pp. 118–125.

Van Gool, L., P. Dewaele, and A. Oosterlinck (1985). Survey: texture analysis anno 1983. Computer Vision, Graphics, and Image Processing, Vol. 29, pp. 336–357.

Vickers, A.L. and J.W. Modestino (1982). A maximum likelihood approach to texture classification. IEEE Transactions on Pattern Analysis and Machine Intelligence, Vol. 4, No. 1, pp. 61–68.

Wang, L. and D.C. He (1990). Texture classification using texture spectrum. Pattern Recognition, Vol. 23, pp. 905–910.

Weszka, J., C. Dyer, and A. Rosenfeld (1976). A comparative study of texture measures for terrain classification. IEEE Transactions on Systems, Man, and Cybernetics, Vol. SMC-6, pp. 269–285.

Zayas, I.Y., C.R. Martin, J.L. Steele, and R.E. Dempster (1991). Image texture analysis of crushed wheat kernels. SPIE Vol. 1615 Machine Vision Architectures. Integration, and Applications, pp. 203–215.

Methods for Illumination-Invariant Image Processing

J.W.V. Miller and M. Shridhar

Abstract. Illumination-invariant image processing is an extension of the classical technique of homomorphic filtering using a logarithmic point transformation. In this paper, traditional approaches to illumination-invariant processing are briefly reviewed and then extended using newer image processing techniques. Relevant hardware considerations are also discussed including the number of bits per pixel required for digitization, minimizing the dynamic range of the data for image processing, and camera requirements. Three applications using illumination-invariant processing techniques are also provided.

1 Introduction

Scene illumination is one of the most important factors that determine success or failure for many imaging and machine vision applications. With appropriate lighting, irrelevant information can be eliminated, contrast of significant image features enhanced, and the sensor signal-to-noise ratio improved. Stringent requirements, however, may be placed on the lighting with regard to the need for very uniform and temporally constant levels of illumination unless suitable low-level processing is performed. Frequent lighting adjustments, tightly regulated power supplies or special feedback circuitry for controlling light level may be needed in these cases which can increase system cost and complexity significantly.

Even with ideal illumination, deficiencies in the optics and imaging hardware can introduce apparent variations in scene illumination that reduce the robustness and reliability of vision systems. Optical losses increase significantly from the center of the field to the edge due to the $\cos^4$ law and vignetting [12]. Imagers often exhibit sensitivity variations (shading) as a function of spatial position. While higher-quality system components reduce these problems, the added cost can be excessive.

Real-time gray-scale image processing hardware which is generally available in newer vision systems can alleviate the effects of these imperfections economically. Traditionally, linear high-pass filtering prior to thresholding has often been used to reduce the effects of these variations since they are most significant at low spatial frequencies. Because image features of interest such as edges predominate at high spatial frequencies, the effects of illumination variations can be reduced prior to further processing [8, 21].

Morphological processing also has been used to correct for illumination variations [4, 22]. In some applications, a closing operation will generate an image that is a good estimate of background illumination by suppressing dark features at higher spatial frequencies. Calculating the difference between the background image and the original image generates a high-pass-filtered image.

High-pass filtering alone, however, does not completely eliminate these effects because most images are approximately a function of the product of the illumination and reflectance properties of a given scene [23]. An image feature in a dim area of an image will have poorer contrast than the same feature in a bright area as a result of this modulation-like property. A number of techniques have been used to remove the gray-level distortion introduced by this effect including shading correction and homomorphic filtering.

The term "illumination invariance" will be used to describe these techniques since they attempt to generate an image in which gray-scale errors associated with illumination, optics and the imager have been eliminated. Errors associated with illumination and optics are presumed to be purely multiplicative while the imager may require both an additive and a multiplicative correction factor [5]. Compensation for the multiplicative effects from all three sources can be provided simultaneously after imager offset errors have been removed.

Shading correction can directly compensate for these error sources if an "empty" scene is available, that is, a scene that is only a function of the illumination, optics and imager. For purposes of this paper, such a scene is designated as the background. Scene elements of interest, such as objects or image features, comprise the foreground. Hence, if an image of the background can be acquired directly and stored, it can be divided into the foreground image data to compensate for existing nonuniformities [5, 12]. If imager offset errors are significant, a completely dark scene can be captured and subtracted from the imager data prior to multiplicative correction. Shading correction has been used in a variety of applications including thin-film disk inspection and the evaluation of lumber [3, 20].

Homomorphic filtering represents another approach to illumination-invariant processing [17, 23]. Here, gray-scale values of a given image are nonlinearly transformed, the resulting image is linearly filtered, and the inverse of the original nonlinear transformation is performed on the filtered image. Homomorphic filtering using a logarithmic transformation to linearize the multiplicative effect of illumination is a classical and well established image and signal processing technique [17]. Typical applications include enhancement of photographs containing scenes with wide illumination variations and edge detection [19, 21]. Homomorphic Wiener filtering has also been used for restoration [8].

In this paper, classical techniques for illumination-invariant processing are reviewed and a number of enhancements are proposed. Homomorphic filtering, for example, has very advantageous properties. However, obtaining linear filters that remove or pass specific scene elements in a given image can be very difficult to implement. Nonlinear filtering operations such as morphological closings can often be generated with the desired characteristics. By logarithmically transforming a given image prior to morphological filtering, illumination-invariance may also be achieved.

Implementation issues are also examined here. A detailed discussion regarding the minimization of quantization errors with applications that require large dynamic range is presented. The use of an analog logarithmic amplifier prior to digitization is shown to provide significant benefits. Additional techniques to minimize A/D resolution requirements are discussed here also.

A discussion of various aspects of illumination-invariant processing has been divided into four sections in this paper. In the next section, a basic approach to illumination-invariant processing based on background estimation with very general assumptions is developed along with a brief discussion of classical illumination-invariant processing approaches. A presentation of new techniques is given in Sect. 3 and hardware considerations for minimizing quantization errors are given in Sect. 4. In the last section of the paper, three applications using illumination-invariant processing techniques are discussed.

2 Classical Illumination-Invariant Processing Techniques

The basic concept for illumination invariance follows from the image formation model in which light reflected from an object is approximately the product of the incident light and surface properties [12, 17]. If the background illumination is known, it can be used to normalize the light reflected from the object and minimize errors caused by illumination variations.

The same approach also can be applied to back-illuminated translucent objects or with an image created by passing X rays through an object. In either case, the observed radiation is the product of the physical properties of the objects and the incident radiation. In this paper, a simple one-dimensional model will be presented that is suitable for both reflectance and transmittance. If desired, this model can be generalized to two dimensions easily.

2.1 A Simple Image Formation Model

Consider the expression for the incident light I[n] at the nth pixel of a sensor,

$$I[n] = I_0[n]s[n] \qquad (1)$$

where $I_0[n]$ is the illumination for an empty scene and $s[n]$ is the value of the transmission or reflectance for the object in the scene at that point. The value of $s[n]$ can range from zero when no light is reflected or transmitted to one for total light reflectance or transmittance. Note that $s[n]$ is rarely smaller than one percent for the reflectance case [23].

This simple model does not take into consideration the complex manner in which objects with both specular and diffuse components reflect light. Also, geometric considerations such as the angle of incident light upon the observed surface and angle of the camera to the observed surface affect the detected light pattern markedly [12]. However, for purely transmissive cases and reasonably flat surfaces illuminated so that specular reflections are not imaged, this model is appropriate.

If the assumption is made that the sensor linearly converts the illumination it receives into a voltage $v[n]$, then

$$v[n] = b[n]s[n] \qquad (2)$$

where $b[n]$ is proportional to $I_0[n]$.

The maximum illumination signal possible at the nth pixel, $b[n]$, is a function of both the light source and the optics. Typically, this function is slowly varying such that

$$b[n] \approx b[n+k], 0 < k < d \qquad (3)$$

in which d represents the number of sensor pixels over which illumination variations are relatively small. If the background illumination has significant high-frequency components, then d is correspondingly small.

To illustrate this concept further, consider one scan line of data from a simulated sensor plotted in Fig. 1. Here, small dark objects cause sharp drops in light level against the slowly varying background illumination. These objects have a transmission or reflectance value of 0.5 so that $s[n]$ is unity everywhere except in the presence of these objects. The background illumination level falls to zero at the edges of the scan. While this rarely happens in actual applications, similar but less severe illumination patterns are observed in typical applications due to optical and illumination properties [11, 12]. Note that no linear threshold exists that can differentiate between the background and all of the dark objects simultaneously.

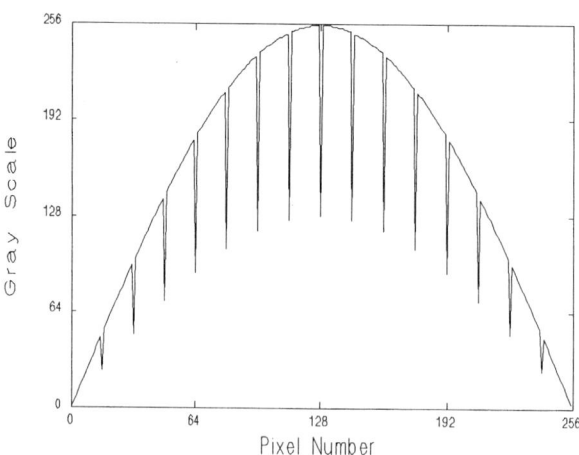

Fig. 1. Simulated scene containing small objects with $s[n] = 0.5$ against a slowly varying background

2.2 High-Pass Filtering

As mentioned in the introduction, high-pass filtering is often used to reduce the effects of such nonuniformities. The high-pass filter will remove DC and low-frequency components while retaining the high-frequency features of interest. In essence, the high-pass filter "subtracts" the low-frequency background from the image. Consider a high-pass filter which is implemented as the difference between a given signal and its filtered output obtained with a low-pass filter. Under the assumption that the low-pass filter will recover $b[n]$ (as shown in the upper trace of Fig. 2) from the expression $b[n]s[n]$ exactly for all n, the high-pass filter $y_{hp}[n]$ is defined as

$$y_{hp}[n] = b[n]s[n] - b[n] = b[n](s[n] - 1). \tag{4}$$

Since $s[n]$ is unity everywhere except in the presence of the dark objects, $y_{hp}[n]$ is nonzero only for pixels covered by these objects. The output of the filter will be zero except in the presence of the dark objects where its output will be positive. Negative output values implies that the foreground image is brighter than the background illumination which is impossible for backlit objects. Specular reflections with front illumination can be brighter than the background estimate if it was obtained with a diffuse reflector. Note that the assumption for the existence of a filter $f(\cdot)$ such that

$$b[n] = f(b[n]s[n]) \tag{5}$$

may prove to be very difficult to obtain in practice. If $f(\cdot)$ is to be a linear filter, serious implementation problems arise unless the power spectrums of the background and foreground are widely separated. Certain types of nonlinear filters, however, are likely to be much more suitable for estimating $b[n]$ accurately which are presented in Sect. 3.2.

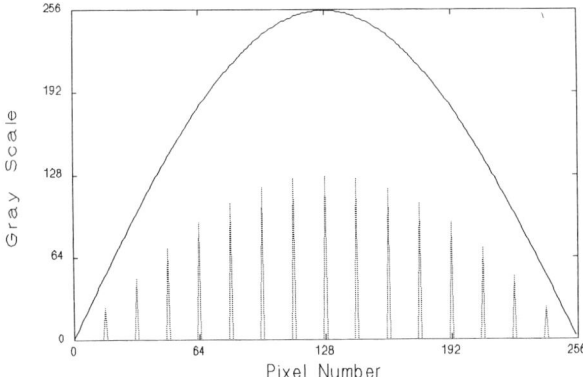

Fig. 2. By applying an ideal low-pass filter to the data of Fig. 1, the background illumination can be obtained as shown in the top trace. Subtracting the unfiltered data from it generates the lower trace

Using the filter given in (4) to process the data of Fig. 1 provides the results shown in the lower trace of Fig. 2. Although low threshold values exist that will detect the features of interest, the amplitudes of the dark objects vary significantly in proportion to the background light level. Low threshold values, however, will be very susceptible to noise and irrelevant features when $b[n]$ is large [11].

2.3 Illumination-Invariant Processing

Consider modifying (4) so that the low-pass filtered signal is divided into the original signal.

$$y_{ii}[n] = \frac{b[n]s[n]}{b[n]} = s[n] \qquad (6)$$

Here, $y_{ii}[n]$ is unaffected by illumination variations and thus is illumination-invariant. This technique is often referred to as shading correction and may include correcting for sensor offset errors prior to the division operation [5, 20]. From this simple model, it would appear that any value of illumination is satisfactory. However, because of sensor characteristics, random noise, and quantization effects, the acceptable range of light variations will always be limited. Typically, illumination variations of up to 16 to 1 can be tolerated for many vision applications with eight-bit uniform quantization since at least four bits are still available in the darkest portion of the scene to represent $s[n]$ digitally. Further quantization considerations are discussed in Sect. 4.1.

2.4 Processing Using a Logarithmic Gray-Scale Transformation

Illumination-invariant processing can also be obtained by logarithmically transforming the gray-scale data from the sensor prior to high-pass filtering. The basic approach here is to replace the division operation in (6) by the subtraction of two logarithmically transformed values. While the results are theoretically identical for the two methods, the logarithmic implementation has significant advantages with low-noise cameras which are considered in Sect. 4.2.

A linearly-digitized image is represented by a matrix of numbers which correspond to the light intensity of an image. Calculating the logarithm of each pixel results in a new image that is proportional to the density of a photograph of the same scene [23]. As will be seen, there are significant advantages to working with a density representation for achieving illumination-invariant processing.

To begin, consider a modification of (4)

$$y_{loghp}[n] = \log(b[n][s[n]]) - \log(b[n]) = \log(s[n]) \qquad (7)$$

If desired, exponentiation can be performed so that results identical to equation (5) are obtained. However, since the output of the filter is often only used for thresholding purposes, this additional operation is not required for many vision applications.

Applying (7) to the simulation data plotted in Fig. 1 gives the results plotted in Fig. 3. Here, the top trace is the logarithmically-transformed data from Fig. 1 and the bottom trace is the result of background subtraction after logarithmic transformation. Note that all amplitudes are equal regardless of the illumination level.

If the low-pass filter used to estimate $\log(b[n])$ is linear with impulse response $h_1[n]$, the resulting high-pass filtering operation will be homomorphic after its output is exponentiated. This can be demonstrated by convolving $h_1[n]$ with the density image to obtain the low-pass-filtered output signal $y_1[n]$,

$$y_1[n] = h_1[n]*\log(b[n]s[n]) \tag{8}$$

$$= h_1[n]*\log(b[n]) + h_1[n]*\log(s[n]) = \log(b[n]). \tag{9}$$

A new impulse response can be defined as

$$h_2[n] = \delta[n] - h_1[n] \tag{10}$$

Convolving $h_2[n]$ with $\log(b[n]s[n])$ generates the high-pass filtered output $y_2[n]$,

$$y_2[n] = h_2[n]*\log(b[n]s[n]) \tag{11}$$

$$= \log(b[n]s[n]) - h_1[n]*\log(b[n]s[n]) = \log(s[n]) \tag{12}$$

which is the same result as given in (8). As previously stated, $y_2[n]$ can be exponentiated to obtain a homomorphic filter.

2.5 Illumination-Invariant Filtering Using an FIR Filter

Values for $s[n]$ can be recovered very well from a scene if a good estimate of the background illumination $b[n]$ is available. The ability to generate this estimate is very application dependent and is essential if $s[n]$ is to be recovered accurately. For

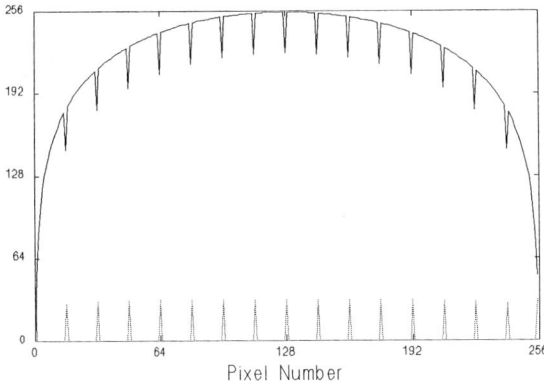

Fig. 3. The top trace has been generated by performing a logarithmic transformation of the data in Fig. 1. Low-pass filtering this trace and subtracting the top trace from it creates the bottom trace

other applications, however, it is only necessary that the filter remove the DC component in a local region of the image. The gradient operator is one example of a commonly used FIR filter in which $s[n]$ cannot be recovered although useful information is extracted by it.

Consider a high-pass FIR filter that removes the DC component over the extent of the filter and assume that it is small relative to the variation of the background illumination. If a density image is filtered by it, the resulting image will be illumination invariant. To show this, consider the basic FIR convolution operation

$$y[n] = \sum_{k=-K/2}^{K/2} C_k \log(x[n-k]) \tag{13}$$

in which C_k is the kth filter coefficient, $x[n]$ is the data to be filtered, and K is the kernel size. Since the output of the filter must be zero when the input signal is constant over the extent of the filter, let the constant a represent $x[n]$ over the extent of the filter.

$$y[n] = \sum_{k=-K/2}^{K/2} C_k \log(\alpha) = \log(\alpha) \sum_{k=-K/2}^{K/2} C_k = 0 \tag{14}$$

From this, it can be inferred that

$$\sum_{k=-K/2}^{K/2} C_k = 0. \tag{15}$$

This condition can now be used to illustrate that the output of the filter is independent of the background illumination. Since $v[n] = s[n]b[n]$,

$$y[n] = \sum_{k=-K/2}^{K/2} C_k \log(s[n-k]b[n-k]) \tag{16}$$

$$= \sum_{k=-K/2}^{K/2} C_k \log(s[n-k]) + \sum_{k=-K/2}^{K/2} C_k \log(b[n-k]) \tag{17}$$

Using the requirement for a DC removing filter from (14) and letting a = $b[n]$ over the extent of the filter (recall that $b[n] \cong b[n + k]$ for k small),

$$y[n] = \sum_{k=-K/2}^{K/2} C_k \log(s[n-k]) \tag{18}$$

Clearly, $y[n]$ is independent of the background illumination. Note that in general $y[n] \neq \log(s[n])$.

2.6 Shading Correction

Shading correction is another technique that can be used if background illumination levels can be obtained directly. The inspection of transparent or translucent objects which are backlit is a typical class of applications that can be addressed with this approach. Often, an object will not be in the field of view continuously so that an image of the empty scene is available. In some applications, this will provide a direct measurement of the effective scene illumination. If the illumination is temporally invariant, (6) can be used to obtain illumination invariance.

Alternatively, background subtraction can be performed between the background density image and a density image containing both background and foreground information as in (7). This approach is appropriate for both linear and matrix cameras. Implementation is usually easier with linear-camera systems since data from only one scan of the empty scene is required. For matrix cameras, a frame buffer can be used to store the background scene.

Note that no special assumptions about the spatial properties of the background relative to features of interest are required since spatial filtering is not used either to estimate the background illumination as in (5) or to remove its effects as in (12). If (7) is used for shading correction, a time-domain filtering operation is being performed by the subtraction of two sample images acquired at different times.

However, sampling the background only once, and subtracting that image from more recent images results in a time-varying filter. As time progresses, the frequency response of the filter changes because the effective sampling interval increases. In general, there is no loss of effectiveness provided that the background illumination level does not change significantly. It can be shown that adjusting for illumination changes is relatively straightforward if spatial and temporal illumination functions vary independently. A suitable approach for exploiting this is presented in the next section.

3 New Approaches for Illumination-Invariant Processing

While traditional approaches to illumination invariance are quite effective in many applications, significant enhancements can still be realized. In this section, extensions and improvements for realizing a more effective illumination invariance are described. To begin, a method for increasing the robustness of the direct background measurement approach is presented, based on the assumption that spatial and temporal illumination variations are independent. The basic objective here is to correct for short-term lighting variations without having to capture a new background image. The basic assumption is made that illumination variations occur proportionally and simultaneously over the entire scene.

3.1 Compensating for Short-Term Temporal Illumination Variations

While both long- and short-term illumination variations can occur, long-term variations due to darkening and similar aging effects can be ameliorated with relatively infrequent (daily or weekly) periodic sampling. However, short-term illumination variations associated with power line fluctuations require a different solution. These variations can occur over periods on the order of 10 ms. which makes background resampling impractical in most applications. Incandescent sources exhibit a pronounced 120 Hz ripple when powered by 60 Hz. sinusoidal power sources. This ripple is caused by lamp filament cooling during zero crossings. With DC voltage sources, even modest voltage changes cause significant light output variations due to the great sensitivity of black-body radiators to temperature changes [15].

A variety of techniques can be used to deal with short-term deviations. Regulated DC sources can provide power for the illumination sources although this solution can be quite expensive if power requirements are substantial. In some applications, cameras can be scanned synchronously with the power line although AC power regulation may still be required. Television-type cameras are often synchronized with the 60 Hz power source using phase-locked loop circuitry to minimize light-source ripple. This approach, however, is unsuitable for high-speed matrix and line-scan camera applications.

More robust compensation can be provided using an extension of concepts previously discussed here. To begin, consider modifying (1) so that the effective illumination reaching the sensor is a function of both time and spatial position,

$$I[j, n] = I_o[j, n]s[j, n] \qquad (19)$$

where $I[j, n]$ is the effective radiation for the jth time sample impinging on the nth camera pixel. Since illumination sources are usually driven from a common power source, the light output of each illumination source will vary temporally in exactly the same manner.

For this reason, $I_o[j, n]$ can be decomposed into the product

$$I_o[j,n] = I_t[j]I_s[n] \qquad (20)$$

where $I_t[j]$ is the relative illumination level for the *jth* sample and $I_s[n]$ is the value of the illumination for the *nth* pixel at a specific time sample, such as $j = 0$. Under the same assumptions as (2), the voltage output of the sensor becomes

$$v[j,n] = I_t[j]b[n]s[j, n] \qquad (21)$$

The density representation for (21) is

$$d[j, n] = \log(I_t[j]b[n]s[j, n]) = \log(I_t[j]) + \log(b[n]s[j, n]) \qquad (22)$$

Assume that some reference region R exists in the image that is temporally invariant except for variations due to $I_t[j]$. This region can be a fixed painted white strip that is always present in the field of view of the camera. The light reflected into the camera from this region will vary directly as a function of the illumination. Let $a[j]$ be the average value of the N density-image pixels in this region for the *jth* sample,

$$a[j] = \frac{1}{N}\sum_{n \in R}(\log[I_t[j]] + \log(b[n]s[j, n])) \tag{23}$$

$$= \frac{1}{N}\left(\sum_{n \in R}\log(I_t[j]) + \sum_{n \in R}\log(b[n]s[j, n])\right) \tag{24}$$

Note that $\log I_t[j]$ is constant for all pixels in region R since it only varies as a function of the sample number. Similarly, a constant k_R can be defined as

$$k_R = \frac{1}{N}\sum_{n \in R}\log(b[n]s[j, n]) \tag{25}$$

since region R is temporally invariant by definition except for $I_t[j]$. The average of region R becomes

$$a[j] = \log(I_t[j]) + k_R \tag{26}$$

This value can be used to generate a normalized version of the jth image, $d_n[j, n]$

$$d_n[j,n] = \log I_t[j] + \log(b[n]s[j, n]) - a[j] \tag{27}$$

$$= \log I_t[j] + \log(b[n]s[j, n]) - \log(I_t[j]) - k_R \tag{28}$$

$$= \log(b[n]s[j, n]) - k_R \tag{29}$$

Notice that the amount of processing required is relatively small. The region R need only be large enough to minimize errors due to camera signal noise. The image normalization operation simply requires that a constant value be added to each pixel which could be done easily with a lookup table.

There are a number of ways in which this approach can be applied. Consider a simple case in which spatial uniformity of the illumination source is relatively good and image features have sufficiently high contrast. Assume simple thresholding is sufficient for segmentation or identifying features of interest with a temporally constant light source. Given some initial image, the average grayscale value of the reference region can be found and used to normalize the image as given in (29). A threshold value can be found using a suitable technique and used on all succeeding images after they are normalized. Alternatively, the threshold T_0 could be found for the initial image and a new threshold value T_j calculated for the jth succeeding image as

$$T_j = T_0 - a[0] + a[j]. \tag{30}$$

Depending on the hardware available, this operation may be faster than normalizing each image and using a constant threshold.

Illumination-invariant template matching can be performed using this approach also. Assuming that the 0*th* image is the reference image, the difference image $d[j, n]$ is calculated as

$$d[j, n] = d_n[j, n] - d_n[0, n] \tag{31}$$

$$= \log(b[n]s[j, n]) - k_R - (\log(b[n]s[0, n] - k_R) \tag{32}$$

$$= s[j, n] - s[0, n] \tag{33}$$

Background subtraction results if the 0*th* image is empty, that is $s[0, n] = 1$ for all n. Substituting this into (33) gives

$$d[j, n] = s[j, n] \tag{34}$$

which is only a function of the foreground image.

3.2 Morphological Illumination-Invariant Processing

When the background cannot be measured directly, some means of background estimation by spatial filtering is very desirable. One effective technique for accomplishing this in many applications is gray-scale morphology. Given an image in which features of interest have limited spatial extent relative to a bright background, gray-scale morphology can provide an excellent estimate of the background.

Traditionally, the estimate of the background image obtained by morphological filtering is linearly subtracted from the original image prior to thresholding or some other segmentation operation. As discussed in Sect. 2, the result will not be illumination invariant since the modulating effects of the background illumination will still be present. However, using the background estimate with either (6) or (7) will provide illumination-invariant processing.

The basic approach advocated here is to use the closing operation on a density image. The closing operation consists of the sequential application of dilation and erosion using the same structuring element [4, 22]. The dilation operation fills in darker regions of an image as the brighter regions enlarge. If a given structuring element spans a dark region such as the narrow dips in Fig. 1, the dark region will disappear.

The inverse operation is then applied to remove biases caused by the dilation operation. Since the small dark objects have disappeared, this operation cannot restore them but instead will provide an estimate of the background illumination in the region of these objects based on adjacent pixels.

One word of caution should be stated with respect to the ability of a given morphological operation to extract the background successfully. Unlike homomorphic filtering, in which a linear filter is used, gray-scale morphological operations are highly nonlinear since they are based on min- and max-type functions. In addition, their output is generally biased so they do not preserve DC. Thus, no corresponding relationships exist comparable to the expressions in (13)-(18) for morphological filters unless the background can be estimated with relatively little distortion.

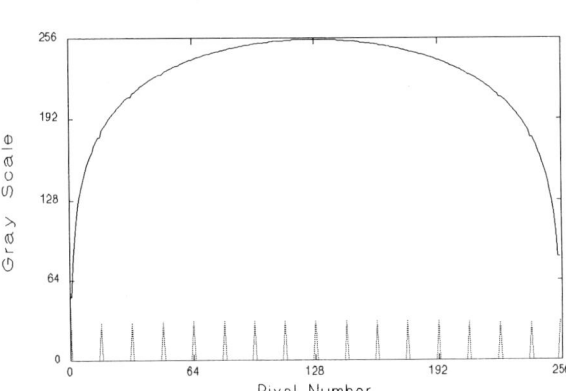

Fig. 4. The application of a gray-scale closing operation to the logarithmically-transformed data of Fig. 1 is shown in the top trace. The difference between the closed data and the logarithmically transformed data is given in the bottom trace

3.3 Illumination-Invariant Adaptive Thresholding

Like morphological filters, adaptive thresholding can also be modified for illumination invariance. As in the previous approach, working with a density representation allows a straightforward means of decoupling the illumination and reflectance components in an image under a variety of conditions. Here again, the objective with illumination-invariant adaptive thresholding is to ensure that if a given feature in a bright area exceeds the threshold, then an equivalent feature in a dim area will also exceed it. With adaptive thresholding, the threshold at any given point in the image is based on some local average which is usually obtained by low-pass filtering the original image [2].

Using a density representation as the starting point for adaptive threshold processing, consider a low-pass filter that can provide a good estimate of the background $b[n]$. The threshold function $t[n]$ can be given as

$$t[n] = y_{loglp}[n] + T = \log(b[n]) + T. \tag{35}$$

Here, T is a sensitivity parameter. If T is large, a given gray-scale value will have to deviate substantially from the local average before the threshold is exceeded. The threshold decision function is true if

$$t[n] - \log(b[n]s[n]) < 0 \tag{36}$$

$$\log(b[n]) + T - \log(s[n]) - \log(b[n]) < 0 \tag{37}$$

$$T - \log(s[n]) < 0. \tag{38}$$

Whether or not the decision function is true depends only on T and $s[n]$ and is independent of the background illumination.

This operation produces the same bilevel image that is obtained using a constant threshold T on an image generated by (7). However, an image obtained by applying (7) can provide more useful information for setup and adjustment. The high-pass filtered image can be viewed directly and the effect of threshold modification visualized immediately with standard image display hardware.

4 Hardware for Illumination-Invariant Processing

As can be seen from the previous discussion, there are a variety of ways to achieve illumination invariance. Some are significantly easier to implement in hardware than others or may have other advantages. Consider, for example, a hardware implementation of (7) in which the analog signal from the sensor is digitized by an analog-to-digital (A-D) converter and then filtered using a low-pass filter. Logarithmic conversion can be performed easily digitization by means of a lookup table (LUT) using a memory chip.

4.1 Logarithmic Transformation Techniques

A potential disadvantage, however, exists with this approach. The digital logarithmic transform results in a large number of unrealizable values for low input-signal levels while multiple values at high input-signal levels are assigned to the same transformed value. Hence, the quantization is very coarse for low-amplitude signals and too fine at higher amplitudes with a corresponding decrease in dynamic range.

To illustrate this problem more fully, consider Fig. 5. The two ramp functions shown represent background illumination (higher ramp) and the foreground scene (lower ramp) with $s[n] = 0.05$. The other two traces represent density difference images. The nearly uniform horizontal trace is the result of performing an analog logarithmic transformation prior to digitizing the signal to obtain $y_a[n]$

$$y_a[n] = \text{round}(k_s \log(b[n])) - \text{round}(k_s \log(s[n]b[n])) \tag{39}$$

The rounding function rounds its argument to the nearest integer to simulate the quantization error that results with A/D conversion. The scaling factor K_s is calculated as

$$k_s = \frac{255}{\log(b_{max})} \tag{40}$$

where b_{max} is the maximum value of the background signal.

The trace that oscillates in an approximately triangular fashion about the horizontal trace represents the results of digitization prior to logarithmic conversion. The output $y_d[n]$ is calculated as

Methods for Illumination-Invariant Image Processing

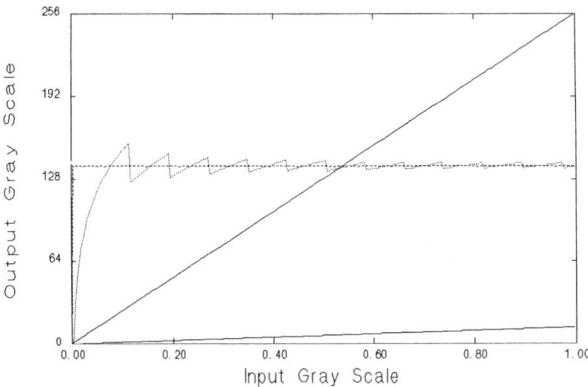

Fig. 5. Effects of quantization error when logarithmic transformation is performed before (nearly horizontal line) after (approximately triangular waveform). The lower and higher ramps represent background and foreground data

$$y_d[n] = k_s\log(\text{round}(b[n])) - k_s\log(\text{round}(s[n]b[n])) \tag{41}$$

Since $s[n]$ is constant for all n, the output signal should be constant. Clearly, (39) comes much closer to achieving this goal. Ignoring the meaningless result when the illumination is zero, a maximum error of two counts from the correct (rounded) value is observed. As indicated by the oscillating trace, however, digitization followed by logarithmic conversion causes substantially greater quantization errors, especially for low light-level conditions.

There are at least two ways to implement (39) in hardware. Use of an analog logarithmic amplifier prior to digitization represents one approach. Here, the logarithmically-transformed signal is uniformly digitized over the range of acceptable voltages to the A/D converter. Sufficient resolution can be obtained for some applications with this approach using only 6 bit conversion [14].

The second approach is to use a nonlinear quantizer whose output values correspond to a logarithmic representation of the input. Theory covering nonlinear and optimal quantizers is well represented in the literature [10, 18]. However, a review of various manufacturers' data sheets indicates that nearly all A/D converters are implemented with uniform quantization including flash converters that are commonly used in real-time imaging applications.

Given the limitations with existing hardware, the best option is to use an analog logarithmic amplifier with a uniform quantizer. Analog adjustments can be performed to control the resolution per decade of the input signal and the range of input signals that can be digitized. The degree of amplification of the signal after logarithmic conversion determines the voltage range that will be digitized. Offsetting the transformed signal by a certain amount establishes the actual voltage endpoints that correspond to the minimum and maximum outputs of the quantizer.

This can be illustrated by considering the output voltage V_{out} of a logarithmic amplifier,

$$V_{out} = A\log(V_{in}) + V_{offset} \tag{42}$$

where A is the amplification, V_{in} is the input voltage and V_{offset} is a constant offset voltage. As the gain is increased, the resolution of the input signal is increased while the range of input voltages that can be converted is reduced. Generally, the offset voltage is adjusted so that the maximum camera signal will correspond to the maximum output value of the A/D converter.

Logarithmic conversion can be performed with standard op-amp circuits using a diode or transistor in the feedback circuit along with temperature compensation circuitry [16]. Alternatively, a monolithic logarithmic amplifier may also be used [9]. The dynamic range required for vision applications is usually not large since most video cameras have dynamic ranges less than 80 db [6]. Therefore, except for band-width, performance requirements of logarithmic amplifier are fairly modest.

4.2 Camera Considerations

There are several factors that must be considered when designing a system with a logarithmic amplifier. Perhaps the most basic and obvious factor is the importance of minimizing DC offset errors. If very wide dynamic range is important in a given application, even relatively small DC offset errors can substantially reduce the accuracy of the results.

Video cameras often have substantial offset errors which can be measured by blocking all light from the sensor. The digitized results can be used to eliminate the offset errors by subtracting them on a pixel-by-pixel basis from the camera data [5, 12]. However, these techniques require the image to be digitized before correction is performed which is incompatible with analog logarithmic transformation. One approach that overcomes this limitation is to store the correction signal digitally but convert it back to analog format prior to subtraction and quantization.

Quantization errors can be minimized by increasing analog gain substantially when the offset errors are being acquired and rescaled for analog subtraction. By acquiring multiple images and averaging, the resulting dithering effect will also increase the effective resolution of the offset error image. Note that offset errors can be very temperature dependent with CCD cameras, especially if long integration times are used since correspondingly greater errors due to dark signal effects occur [6].

Background subtraction can be implemented in the same manner to increase the effective resolution of the system for detecting features with very low contrast [14]. The background image can be stored digitally in memory and converted back to analog format for subtraction and amplification prior to digitization. This provides even smaller quantization errors than digital subtraction after an analog logarithmic conversion. The background signal can be stored with substantially more resolution and converted back to analog form very cost effectively. The cost of a high-resolution D/A converter is relatively small compared to a flash converter with the same number of bits.

Note that this type of processing can only be justified with low-noise cameras. Typical television cameras have signal-to-noise ratios on the order of 43 to 50 db which do not require more than eight-bit representation [7]. With these cameras, lower amplitude signals are lost in the noise. The SNR for low-noise cameras, however, is on the order of 60 to 80 db which justifies the additional analog processing [6].

One other caveat is worth noting here. Many cameras provide gamma correction to compensate for the nonlinear (power-law) brightness response of typical CRT displays with increasing grid-drive voltage [1]. The brightness B is given as

$$B = KE^\gamma \tag{43}$$

where K is a constant, E is the grid-drive voltage and γ is the value of the gamma parameter. Cameras with gamma correction provide the inverse operation

$$E = E^{1/\gamma} \tag{44}$$

Values for γ range from 2.0 to 2.4 for typical CRT displays so cameras often use $1/2.2 = 0.45$ as the correction factor.

Generally, gamma correction should be disabled if it is available on a given camera since a density representation can be obtained from a linear camera response as previously discussed. Also, the precision and stability of gamma correction is not necessarily very high. For typical video applications such as surveillance operations, where a person will observe the resulting image, the exact camera response is relatively unimportant [1]. Gamma correction is generally achieved with simple analog circuitry using PN junction properties to generate the desired function and consequentially is error prone.

In certain noncritical vision applications, however, it may be appropriate to use the gamma-corrected camera signal in place of a logarithmic transformation. Its general shape is similar to the logarithmic transformation as illustrated in Fig. 6. Performing background subtraction with the original data of Fig. 1 after gamma

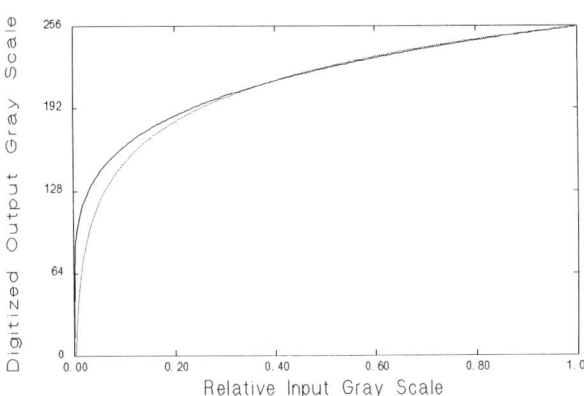

Fig. 6. Scaled gamma correction with an exponent of .45 (top curve) and logarithmic transformation function (bottom curve) are very similar except for low gray levels

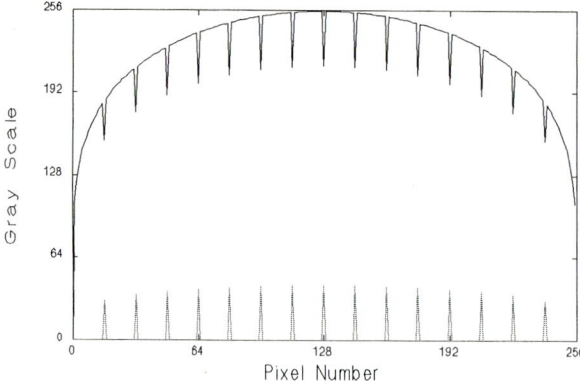

Fig. 7. If a camera provides gamma correction, the results are similar to those obtained with a logarithmic transformation shown in Fig. 3

correction provides the results in Fig. 7. While there is some variation as a function of background illumination, the results are significantly better than the linear differencing results illustrated in Fig. 2.

It is also possible to remove the gamma correction digitally [5]. Although traditionally the objective has been to obtain a linear response to light intensity, a logarithmic response can be obtained in the same manner. The similarity of the curves plotted in Fig. 6 indicate that relatively minor changes in signal levels are required. Quantization errors with this approach are almost as small as with a direct logarithmic transformation because of the similarity of the two curves. However, the problems noted earlier with regard to accuracy and stability may limit the usefulness with many cameras. Individual camera calibration may be performed if stability is not a problem [5].

5 Choice of Illumination-Invariant Techniques

A variety of approaches for achieving illumination invariance have been presented in this paper. In the following section, considerations and tradeoffs for making appropriate choices are discussed for three applications. The first two applications deal with glass inspection.

5.1 Plate Glass Inspection

Glass is used in a variety of applications from windows to packaging and quality is often very important. The quality requirements for plate glass in automotive and architectural applications are high because of safety considerations which justify automatic flaw-detection techniques. Defects such as scratches, embedded particles, and bubbles need to be detected so that defective glass can be rejected. Glass bottles used for carbonated beverages represents another area where safety is a primary concern. Bottles with defects may explode when handled by the consumer with severe liability consequences.

The generally uniform nature of glass makes it a relatively easy material to inspect since only significant gray-scale changes from the normal background need to be evaluated for defect detection. If defects have sufficient contrast and lighting is reasonably uniform, simple thresholding will provide adequate results and no illumination compensation is required. If the illumination source exhibits temporal variations, the use of a reference region in conjunction with (29) is appropriate.

Many defects do not have high contrast relative to spatial illumination variations so more sophisticated processing is required. Under these conditions, providing illumination compensation becomes highly advantageous. As stated earlier, the primary objective is to estimate the background illumination by some means or measure it directly.

Direct measurement of the background is very compatible with plate glass because of the highly uniform nature of the material with no defects. Since transmission through a normal glass panel is spatially invariant, the background illumination may be measured directly with a defect-free piece of glass in place.

One problem with this approach is that the presence of dust and similar contaminants will introduce inaccuracies in the background measurement. A number of different good panels may be used and combined to create an improved estimate of the background illumination. Note that averaging the measurements together on a pixel-by-pixel basis may not provide the best results. Selecting the maximum gray-scale value at each pixel location will eliminate the attenuating effects of any contaminants present.

Alternatively, some kind of low-pass filtering may be used to minimize the effects of contaminants, especially if they are likely to be small. Since processing the background image will only need to be performed infrequently, more sophisticated off-line algorithms may be implemented for better background estimation. Note that an estimate based on multiple sampling may be spatially low-pass filtered if desired. Low-pass filtering of the estimate should not be performed however, if the sensor exhibits significant pixel-to-pixel sensitivity variations. Once a good estimate of the background has been obtained, it may be used in conjunction with (30) and (34) to compensate for short-term illumination variations that may occur.

5.2 Amber Bottle Inspection

While many glass-inspection applications should be compatible with the direct background measurement approach, certain circumstances may require a different technique. Consider the amber bottle illustrated in Fig. 8. Large variations in light transmission are very evident due to normal sidewall glass-thickness differ-

Fig. 8. Significant variations in light transmission through amber bottle occur due to nonuniform glass thickness

ences that occur during manufacturing. Bottle inspection is typically performed by rotating the bottle in front of a linear camera to provide complete circumferential inspection [13]. As with plate glass, embedded defects are a serious concern and can be detected because they cause light levels to deviate from the normal background significantly. However, directly measuring the background is of no value here because glass thickness varies substantially in a random manner. Therefore, some type of real-time filtering is required to distinguish between normal background variations and defects.

Since the background variations occur at much lower spatial frequencies than defects do, linear high-pass filtering is very useful and effective. While a variety of filters may be useful here, consider the simple illumination-invariant filtering operation based on pixel differencing of a density image:

$$y_{diff}[n] = \log(b[n]s[n]) - \log(b[n-1]s[n-1]) \tag{45}$$

$$= \log(b[n]s[n]/(b[n-1]s[n-1])) \tag{46}$$

Since $b[n] \approx b[n-1]$ if the background if the background is slowly varying,

$$y_{diff}[n] \approx \log(s[n]/s[n-1]) \tag{47}$$

which is illumination invariant since the filter output is not a function of $b[n]$. Because the filtering operation is linear, exponentiation of the results will provide homomorphic filtering. This filter is also DC removing as defined in Sect. 2. It may also be noted that $s[n]$ is not recovered with this filter.

Glass inspection and the general class of uniform field objects represent one type of application that can benefit significantly from illumination-invariant processing. Another application that requires similar processing is automatic furnace batch charge monitoring. Here, it is desired to measure the presence of batch material is measured with a vision system.

5.3 Batch Charge Monitoring

The major difficulty with automatic batch charge monitoring is the very large and temporally varying illumination gradients that are created by the flaming gas jets that are used to heat the furnace. Processing is needed to transform the original image so that a single threshold can detect unmelted batch material on the surface of the molten glass as illustrated in Fig. 9A. Recently injected unmelted batch material is visible at the far end of the furnace where it is not obscured by the large flame. This material gradually melts and mixes with the molten glass as it moves towards the bubblers. The bubblers are the very dark circular areas which mix the remaining unmelted batch material with the melted glass. No unmelted batch material should be present past the bubblers.

The objective here is to identify the areas of the furnace which are covered by batch material and determine whether or not it is covering the bubblers. Using an octagonal structuring element a closing operation was performed on the original

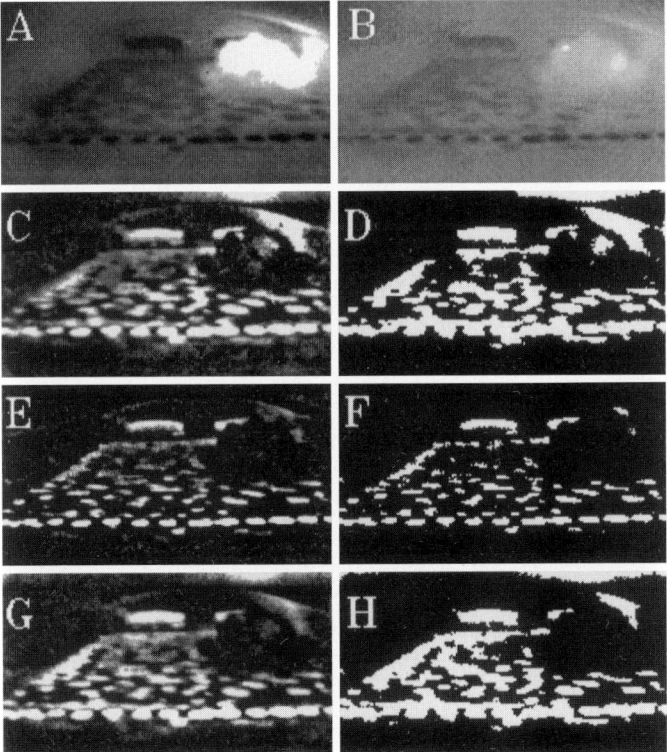

Fig. 9. Scene from a glass furnace is shown in **A** The same scene after logarithmic conversion is given in **B**. Results obtained by closing **A** and subtracting are given in **C**. Thresholding **C** provides the results shown in **D**. Linearly filtering **B** results in images given in **E** and **F**. Results obtained by closing **B** and subtracting are given in **G** and **H**

image to estimate the background. The difference between the background estimate and the original image is shown in Fig. 9C. While it is clear that the low-frequency illumination variations have been removed, significant contrast variations remain since there is considerable variation in the brightness of the batch material as a function of illumination.

Using a logarithmic transformation, a density representation of Fig. 9A was obtained as shown in Fig. 9B. The density image was filtered by applying a 3×3 averaging filter 18 times. The difference between this image and the density image is given in Fig. 9E. A thresholded version of this image is given in Fig. 9F. While the effects of the illumination variations have been eliminated, the results are actually inferior to the traditional morphological filter because the background estimate is much poorer.

Morphological filtering of the density image provides the best results as shown in Fig. 9G and in its thresholded version given in Fig. 9H. The same morphological filtering operation used to generate Fig. 9C was performed here. A comparison of the three thresholded images given in Figs. 9D, 9F and 9H shows that morphological filtering of the density image provides the best estimate for the presence of batch material.

6 Conclusion

Illumination-Invariant processing can be achieved in a variety of ways. The basic approach described here assumed that some method was available for measuring the background illumination. In some applications, background can be measured directly while in others low-pass filtering provides a good estimate. If direct but infrequent background measurements are performed, degradations associated with global short-term temporal variations can be removed by making adjustments based on invariant regions of a scene.

The use of a logarithmic transformation to convert images from an intensity representation to a density representation is very important for illumination-invariant processing. The multiplicative effects of illumination becomes additive for density images so that the effects of nonuniform illumination can be removed by subtraction.

There are a variety of ways to obtain a density representation of an image. The most straightforward approach is to digitize the image and use a look-up table to perform the logarithmic transformation. Using an analog logarithmic amplifier prior to digitization results in a uniform distribution of quantization errors in density images and provides a much larger dynamic range for a given number of bits. In noncritical applications, digitization after gamma correction may provide suitably accurate results.

Acknowledgement. The authors would like to acknowledge the support of National Science Foundation that awarded a research grant to the principal author (NSF - MIP 901 2298). The authors also acknowledge the support of the University of Michigan-Dearborn that awarded a seed grant to the authors for initiating this research.

References

1. K.B. Benson: Television Engineering Handbook, McGraw-Hill Book Company, 1986
2. P. Cielo: Optical Techniques for Industrial Inspection, Academic Press, Inc., 1988, pp. 234–5
3. R.W. Conners, C.W. McMillin, K. Lin, R.E. Vasquez-Espinosa: Identifying and locating surface defects in wood: Part of an automated lumber processing system. IEEE Transactions on Pattern Analysis and Machine Intelligence, PAMI5(6), 573–583 (1983)
4. D.G. Daut, D. Zhao: Mathematical morphology and its application in machine vision. Visual Communications and Image processing IV, SPIE Vol. 1199, pp. 181–191 (1989)
5. I. Dinstein, F. Merkle, T.D. Lam, K.Y. Wong: Imaging system response linearization and shading correction. Optical Engineering, pp. 788–93 (1984)
6. Fairchild Weston CCD Imaging Databook, Milpitas, CA (1989)
7. Fordham Radio Catalog, Vol. 16 No. 5, Hauppauge, NY (1990)
8. R.W. Fries, J.W. Modestino: Image enhancement by stochastic homomorphic filtering. Transactions on Acoustics, Speech, and Signal Processing, ASSP-27(6):625–37 (1979)
9. B. Gilbert, B. Clarke: Monolithic DC-to-120 MHz log-amp is stable and accurate. Analog Dialogue 23(3) (1989)
10. E.L. Hall: Computer Image Processing and Recognition, Academic Press (1979)
11. T.R. Hsing: Techniques of adaptive threshold setting for document scanning applications. Optical Engineering, 23(3):288–93 (1984)
12. B. Kleinemeier: Real-time restoration of image sensor photoresponse nonuniformity. Optical Engineering, 24(1):160–70 (1985)
13. J.W.V. Miller: Real-time system for the automatic inspection of uniform field objects. Proceedings of the Third Annual Applied Machine Vision Conference, Schaumburg, Illinois (1984)
14. J.W.V. Miller, P.S. Miller: Image Analysis System Employing Filter Look-Up Tables. U.S. Patent No. 4,941,191 (1990)
15. J.B. Murdoch: Illumination Engineering-From Edison's Lamp to the Laser. Macmillan Publishing Co. (1985)
16. National Semiconductor Corporation Linear Databook, Santa Clara, CA (1982)
17. A.V. Oppenheim, R.W. Schafer, T.G. Stockham: Nonlinear filtering of multiplied and convolved signals. Proceedings of the IEEE, 56(8):1264–91 (1968)
18. W.K. Pratt: Digital Image Processing, John Wiley & Sons, New York (1978)
19. R. Ray, J. Wilder: Visual and tactile sensing system for robotic acquisition of jumbled parts. Optical Engineering, 23(5):523–30 (1984)
20. J.L.C. Sanz, D. Petkovic: Machine vision algorithms for automated inspection of thin-film disk heads. IEEE Transactions on Pattern Analysis and Machine Intelligence, 10(6):830–48 (1988)
21. W.F. Schreiber: Image processing for quality improvement. Proceedings of the IEEE, Vol. 66, No. 12, pp. 1640–1651 (1978)
22. S. Sternberg: Biomedical image processing. Computer, 16(1):22–34 (1983)
23. T.G. Stockham: Image processing in the context of a visual model. Proceedings of the IEEE, 60(7):828–42 (1972)

A Comparison of Algorithms for Subpixel Peak Detection

R.B. Fisher and D.K. Naidu

Abstract. This paper compares the suitability and efficacy of five algorithms for determining the peak position of a line or light stripe to subpixel accuracy. The algorithms are compared in terms of accuracy, robustness and computational speed. In addition to empirical testing, a theoretical comparison is also presented to provide a framework for analysis of the empirical results.

1 Introduction

It is often necessary to make measurements that are outwith the precision of a visual measurement system which relies on locational accuracy to the nearest pixel. For example, in an imaging system which relies on accuracies to the nearest pixel while translating from 2-D camera coordinates to 3-D world coordinates, the accuracy of the estimated 3-D coordinates of a point in space will be limited by the image resolution. If a large spatial volume is projected onto the imaging surface, each single pixel on the imaging surface will record information from a range of positions. In our range sensor (working volume 20 cm on a side), each pixel images about 1 mm^2 of the scene. This limited resolution is not good enough for precision robotic image analysis. Therefore, algorithms that estimate feature positions to subpixel accuracy by interpolating the sensor response function (e.g., [4, 3, 5]) are useful. This paper compares five algorithms for determining the peak image position of a image line or stripe to subpixel accuracy.

To determine the stripe to subpixel accuracy, the image of the stripe width must be observed over more than one pixel. Here, we assume that the spread of intensity values across the width of the stripe is not simply random, but conforms to some kind of distribution and this pixel spread is exploited in the design of the subpixel interpolation algorithms. Some spread is almost always the case because, although it is possible optically to focus the stripe to less than a single pixel width, the operative response of individual sensor elements often leads to a measurement that is several pixels wide. If we did obtain an image of the stripe which was only a pixel wide, it would be impossible to determine where the peak of the stripe was located within the pixel because we would have data from only one pixel with which to interpolate. An example of a typical intensity response versus position is shown in Fig. 1.

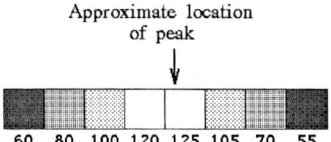

Fig. 1. Typical intensity values from contiguous pixels

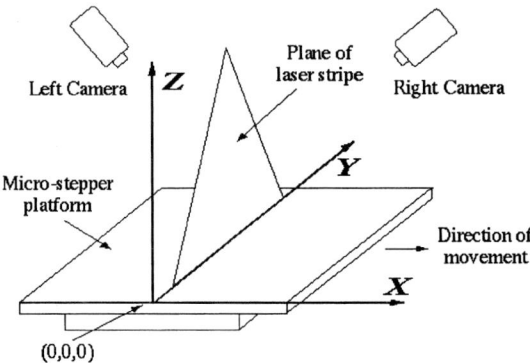

Fig. 2. Schematic of micro-stepper set-up

2 An Example Subpixel Stripe-Based Range Sensor

An example of where subpixel stripe detection methods are useful is in our laser stripe based triangulation sensor, which is used to acquire range images of objects (see Fig. 2). The target object is placed on a platform mounted on a linear microstepper which is activated under software control. The platform moves in small increments under a stationary laser stripe, and at each forward step of the platform a pair of digitized images of the laser stripe on the object is acquired using two cameras located on either side of the object. These images are then processed in software to derive a slice of range values of the object. Each successive step produces a fresh slice and these slices are accumulated to provide a complete range image of the object.

The digitized image from each camera is processed to determine the position of the stripe to subpixel precision. Because of the camera and stripe placement, the stripe is viewed in the image as a nearly vertical curve, the shape of which is determined by the shape of the object on which the stripe impinges. Since the curve is vertical, the scanning of the raster image is performed from left to right so as to process pixel values across the width of the perceived stripe. The y-coordinate of the pixel is determined by the vertical distance of the scan line from the top of the image. The x-coordinate is determined by the location of the pixel along a particular scan line. Therefore, when we refer to the subpixel position of the peak of the stripe, we are discussing the x-coordinate of the pixel.

Once the peak of the stripe has been detected, the image coordinates of the peak are used to determine the 3D, real-world coordinates of the point by using the known projective transform between the camera model and the real world in conjunction with the known 3D equation of the stripe plane. Greater accuracy in determining the peak position in 2D will automatically result in a more accurate determination of the location of the stripe in 3D coordinates, which in turn will produce more accurate estimates of object dimensions and location.

3 Description of Algorithms

All subpixel algorithms that we could locate in the literature plus a new one (Gaussian) are analyzed below.

In the analyses below, x is the pixel position of the observed peak sensor reading with value $f(x)$. $f(x-1)$ and $f(x+1)$ are the values of the adjacent pixels, etc. The true peak is at $x + \delta$ and we will estimate δ by $\hat{\delta}$. The calculations use intensity values that have had the background image intensity value subtracted.

3.1 Gaussian Approximation

This algorithm uses the three highest, contiguous intensity values around the observed peak of the stripe and assumes that the observed peak shape fits a Gaussian profile. This assumption is approximately true as the light incident on the scene is known to be nearly Gaussian distributed. The real distribution, of course, will not be Gaussian, because each pixel integrates light over its field of view, the physical sensor pads of the solid-state cameras we use have a gap between them, the sensor pads have internal structure that affects their sensitivity, and not all sensor pads are equally sensitive. None the less, while we do not know the exact form of the distribution, we assume that the composition of all these effects can be modeled by a Gaussian distribution. The subpixel offset ($\hat{\delta}$) of the peak is given by:

$$\hat{\delta} = \frac{1}{2} \frac{\ln(f(x-1)) - \ln(f(x+1))}{\ln(f(x-1)) - 2\ln(f(x)) + \ln(f(x+1))}$$

As the $f()$ are usually integers in the range 0–255, the log calculation can be performed by table lookup. We have not found any previous references to this form of peak detector in the literature.

3.2 Center of Mass

The center-of-mass algorithm also assumes that the spread of intensity values across the stripe conforms to a Gaussian distribution. Thus, the location of the peak can be computed by a simple weighted-average method. The subpixel location of the peak is given by:

$$\hat{\delta} = \frac{f(x+1) - f(x-1)}{f(x-1) + f(x) + f(x+1)}$$

The above equation describes the method using only three points. However, we have compared the same algorithm using 3, 5 and 7 points (denoted CoM3, CoM5 and CoM7) to compute the center of mass. The extension of the algorithm for the latter two cases is:

$$\hat{\delta} = \frac{2f(x+2) + f(x+1) - f(x-1) - 2f(x-2)}{f(x-2) + f(x-1) + f(x) + f(x+1) + f(x+2)}$$

for the CoM5 algorithm and for the CoM7 algorithm:

$$\hat{\delta} = \frac{3f(x+3) + 2f(x+2) + f(x+1) - f(x-1) - 2f(x-2) - 3f(x-3)}{f(x-3) + f(x-2) + f(x-1) + f(x) + f(x+1) + f(x+2) + f(x+3)}$$

Algorithms to use all points along the raster scan also exist (e.g., as used in [6]).

3.3 Linear Interpolation

This method assumes that a simple, linear relationship defines the spread of intensity values before and after the peak. Thus, if the three highest intensity values are identified as before, then:

If $f(x + 1) > f(x - 1)$

$$\hat{\delta} = \frac{1}{2} \frac{f(x+1) - f(x-1)}{f(x) - f(x-1)}$$

else

$$\hat{\delta} = \frac{1}{2} \frac{f(x+1) - f(x-1)}{f(x) - f(x+1)}$$

3.4 Parabolic Estimator

A continuous version of the peak finder is derivable from the Taylor series expansion of the signal intensity near the peak. If the peak is at $f(x + \delta)$ and we observe the signal at $f(x)$, then we have:

$$f'(x + \delta) = 0 = f'(x) + \delta f''(x) + O(\delta^2)$$

Hence, neglecting the higher order terms,

$$\delta \doteq -\frac{f'(x)}{f''(x)}$$

We can estimate the derivatives discretely, resulting in:

$$\hat{\delta} = \frac{1}{2} \frac{f(x-1) - f(x+1)}{(f(x+1) - 2f(x) + f(x-1))}$$

This estimator is also that found by fitting a parabolic (i.e., second-order) function to the points $f(x-1)$, $f(x)$ and $f(x+1)$. In the experiments below, we call this the **parabolic** estimator.

3.5 Blais and Rioux Detectors

Blais and Rioux [2] introduced fourth and eighth order linear filters:

$$g_4(x) = f(x-2) + f(x-1) - f(x+1) - f(x+2)$$
$$g_8(x) = f(x-4) + f(x-3) + f(x-2) + f(x-1)$$
$$\qquad - f(x+1) - f(x+2) - f(x+3) - f(x+4)$$

to which we also add a second order filter:

$$g_2(x) = f(x-1) - f(x+1)$$

These operators act like a form of numerical derivative operator. The peak position is estimated as above by:

$$\hat{\delta} = \frac{g(x)}{g(x) - g(x+1)}$$

The results of Blais and Rioux showed that the 4th order operator had better performance than the 8th order operator over the stripe widths that we are interested in here, so we only analyze it (called **BR4** below) and the simplified 2nd order operator (called **BR2** below). The 8th order operator has better performance for stripe widths with Gaussian width parameter larger than 2 pixels. Note that this operator is only applied in the given form for $f(x+1) > f(x-1)$. If $f(x+1) < f(x-1)$, then:

$$\delta = \frac{g(x-1)}{g(x-1) - g(x)} - 1$$

4 Maximum Error of Estimators

Assuming that the observed stripe has Gaussian form and the true peak position is near to an observed pixel, we determine the relationship between the estimated and true peak positions (i.e., offsets from that pixel), for each of the peak detectors. Assume that the continuous stripe is modeled by:

$$f(n) = e^{-\frac{(n-\delta)^2}{2\sigma^2}}$$

where $-\frac{1}{2} \leq \delta \leq \frac{1}{2}$ is the true peak position and f is sampled at $n = -2, -1, 0, 1, 2, \ldots$ We ignore the problems of pixels integrating their inputs over their spatial extent, as well as any shaping functions the camera and digitizer may apply.

We might ask what is the maximum deviation $|\delta - \hat{\delta}|$ over the range $-\frac{1}{2} \leq \delta \leq \frac{1}{2}$ for each estimator. We generated sampled stripes for values of δ over this interval and calculated the estimated $\hat{\delta}$. For three values of σ the maximum errors are:

σ	Gaussian	CoM3	CoM5	CoM7	Linear	Parabolic	BR2	BR4
0.5	0.0	0.026	0.023	0.023	0.087	0.169	0.009	0.015
1.0	0.0	0.223	0.042	0.003	0.043	0.047	0.034	0.018
1.5	0.0	0.350	0.178	0.060	0.067	0.021	0.019	0.014

Figure 3 (left) shows the error versus δ for the CoM7 estimator for $\sigma = 1.0$.

By weighting the estimator ($\hat{\delta}' = \alpha_{\text{estimator}} \hat{\delta}$) we can, for a given σ, reduce the maximum error by spreading the error across the full range. Figure 3 (right) shows the error for the resulting CoM7 estimator when $\alpha = 1.006$. This shows that the maximum error has been reduced by almost a factor of 10. By choosing an appropriate value of α for each algorithm and the expected value of σ, we can minimize the maximum error. Here, we choose the α that minimizes the error for stripe width $\sigma = 1.0$ pixel, and examine the maximum error for the same three real stripe widths:

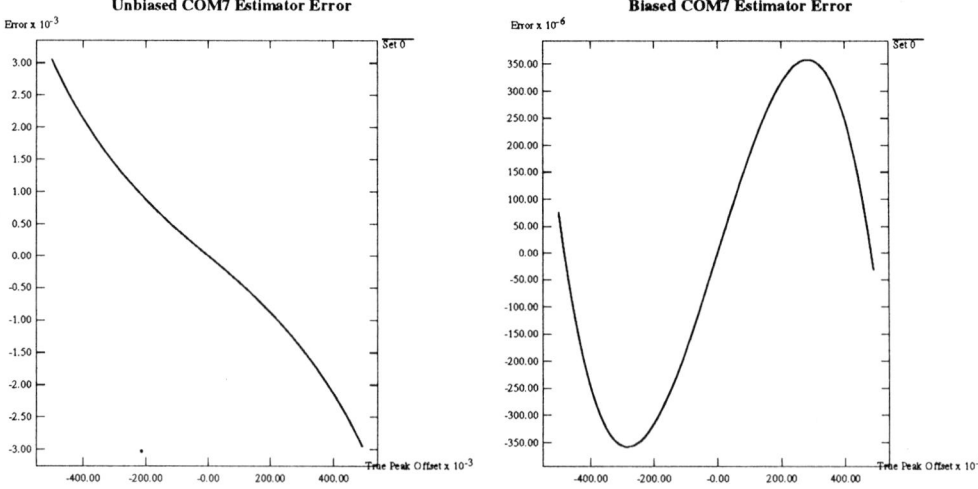

Fig. 3. Error versus δ for unbiased (*left*) and biased (*right*) COM7 estimator

σ	Gaussian	CoM3	CoM5	CoM7	Linear	Parabolic	BR2	BR4
0.5	0.0	0.380	0.041	0.021	0.103	0.156	0.026	0.023
1.0	0.0	0.005	0.002	0.000	0.030	0.029	0.024	0.013
1.5	0.0	0.239	0.150	0.057	0.049	0.034	0.022	0.011
α	1.0	1.85	1.093	1.006	0.93	1.08	0.95	0.975

This shows that, in at least the case of $\sigma = 1.0$, we can tune the estimator to have a very low error; however, setting the α values for one σ may produce reduced performance at other σs.

5 Bias of Estimators

Using the Gaussian stripe model in Sect. 4, we can determine an analytical model of the estimated peak offset $\hat{\delta}$ for a small, real offset, δ. Our analysis assumes first-order approximations:

$$e^x \doteq 1 + x$$
$$\log(1+x) \doteq x$$

So:

$$f(n) \doteq \left(1 + \frac{n\delta}{\sigma^2}\right) e^{-\frac{n^2}{2\sigma^2}}$$

We can now determine the form of $\hat{\delta}$ for each peak estimator. For the **Gaussian** estimator:

$$\hat{\delta} = \frac{1}{2} \frac{\log(f(-1)) - \log(f(1))}{\log(f(-1)) + \log(f(1)) - 2\log(f(0))}$$

$$\doteq \frac{1}{2} \frac{\log(e^{-\frac{1}{2\sigma^2}}(1 - \frac{\delta}{\sigma^2})) - \log(e^{-\frac{1}{2\sigma^2}}(1 + \frac{\delta}{\sigma^2}))}{\log(e^{-\frac{1}{2\sigma^2}}(1 - \frac{\delta}{\sigma^2})) + \log(e^{-\frac{1}{2\sigma^2}}(1 + \frac{\delta}{\sigma^2})) - 2\log(1)}$$

$$= \frac{1}{2} \frac{\log(1 - \frac{\delta}{\sigma^2}) - \log(1 + \frac{\delta}{\sigma^2})}{2\log(e^{-\frac{1}{2\sigma^2}}) + \log(1 - \frac{\delta}{\sigma^2}) + \log(1 + \frac{\delta}{\sigma^2})}$$

$$\doteq \frac{1}{2} \frac{-\frac{\delta}{\sigma^2} - \frac{\delta}{\sigma^2}}{2(-\frac{1}{2\sigma^2}) - \frac{\delta}{\sigma^2} + \frac{\delta}{\sigma^2}}$$

$$= \frac{1}{2} \frac{-2\frac{\delta}{\sigma^2}}{-\frac{1}{\sigma^2}}$$

$$= \delta$$

Hence, the **Gaussian** estimator has the ideal form for small δ. For the **Linear** estimator:

$$\hat{\delta} = \frac{f(1) - f(-1)}{2(f(0) - f(-1))}$$

$$\doteq \frac{e^{-\frac{1}{2\sigma^2}}(1 + \frac{\delta}{\sigma^2}) - e^{-\frac{1}{2\sigma^2}}(1 - \frac{\delta}{\sigma^2})}{2(1 - e^{-\frac{1}{2\sigma^2}}(1 - \frac{\delta}{\sigma^2}))}$$

$$\doteq \frac{e^{-\frac{1}{2\sigma^2}}(2\frac{\delta}{\sigma^2})}{2(1 - e^{-\frac{1}{2\sigma^2}})}$$

$$= \frac{\delta}{\sigma^2} \frac{e^{-\frac{1}{2\sigma^2}}}{(1 - e^{-\frac{1}{2\sigma^2}})}$$

We skip the derivations for the other cases and summarize their results:

Estimator	Local Estimate	Estimator	Local Estimate
Gaussian	δ	CoM3	$\dfrac{2\delta}{\sigma^2} \dfrac{e^{-\frac{1}{2\sigma^2}}}{(1 + 2e^{-\frac{4}{2\sigma^2}})}$
Linear	$\dfrac{\delta}{\sigma^2} \dfrac{e^{-\frac{1}{2\sigma^2}}}{(1 - e^{-\frac{1}{2\sigma^2}})}$	CoM5	$\dfrac{2\delta}{\sigma^2} \dfrac{e^{-\frac{1}{2\sigma^2}} + 4e^{-\frac{4}{2\sigma^2}}}{(1 + 2e^{-\frac{4}{2\sigma^2}} + 2e^{-\frac{4}{2\sigma^2}})}$
Parabolic	$\dfrac{\delta}{2\sigma^2} \dfrac{e^{-\frac{1}{2\sigma^2}}}{(1 - e^{-\frac{1}{2\sigma^2}})}$	CoM7	$\dfrac{2\delta}{\sigma^2} \dfrac{e^{-\frac{1}{2\sigma^2}} + 4e^{-\frac{4}{2\sigma^2}} + 9e^{-\frac{9}{2\sigma^2}}}{(1 + 2e^{-\frac{1}{2\sigma^2}} + 2e^{-\frac{4}{2\sigma^2}} + 2e^{-\frac{9}{2\sigma^2}})}$
BR2	$\dfrac{2\delta}{\sigma^2} \dfrac{e^{-\frac{1}{2\sigma^2}}}{(1 - e^{-\frac{4}{2\sigma^2}})}$	BR4	$\dfrac{2\delta}{\sigma^2} \dfrac{e^{-\frac{1}{2\sigma^2}} + 2e^{-\frac{4}{2\sigma^2}}}{(1 + e^{-\frac{1}{2\sigma^2}} - e^{-\frac{4}{2\sigma^2}} - e^{-\frac{9}{2\sigma^2}})}$

From these results, we see that the **Parabolic** operator gives one half the estimate of the **Linear** operator. When $\sigma = 1.0$ (as is approximately our case), the estimators are now:

Estimator	Gauss	CoM3	CoM5	CoM7	Linear	Parabolic	BR2	BR4
Local Estimate	1.00δ	0.55δ	0.92δ	0.99δ	1.54δ	0.77δ	1.40δ	1.20δ

A Comparison of Algorithms for Subpixel Peak Detection

However, in light of the results from Sect. 4, we use the α estimator bias to change the overall bias according to the algorithm. When $\sigma = 1.0$ (as approximately in our case), the resulting $\hat{\delta}$ is:

Estimator	Gauss	CoM3	CoM5	CoM7	Linear	Parabolic	BR2	BR4
$\hat{\delta}$	1.00δ	1.01δ	1.00δ	1.00δ	1.40δ	0.83δ	1.33δ	1.17δ

Hence, all but the **Linear** and **BR2** estimators are reasonably unbiased. Overall, this noise-free theoretical and empirical analysis suggests that the **Linear**, and **BR2** estimators are not particularly good. However, given typical sensor substructure, pixel spatial integration and cross-talk, non-gaussian stripe formation and non-linear sensor transfer functions, errors of less than 5% seem unlikely in any case. Hence, the **Gauss**, **CoM5**, **CoM7**, **Parabolic** and **BR4** estimators still seem like good candidates.

6 Errors in the Presence of Noise

In line with the experiments of Blais and Rioux [2], we investigated how error in the stripe data affected the estimated stripe position. These experiments were conducted by generating stripe data with a known, but randomly chosen stripe offset about an exact pixel position, and then corrupting the observed stripe intensity with noise. The main controlled variable was the stripe width. Uniform noise was added (following the model of Blais and Rioux). Point measurements were generated by:

$$f(n, \delta, \sigma, \beta) = e^{-\frac{(n-\delta)^2}{2\sigma^2}} + \beta\varepsilon$$

where:

$\delta \in U[-0.5, +0.5]$ is the stripe position.
$n \in \{-3, -2, -1, 0, 1, 2, 3\}$ are the measured pixel positions.
$\varepsilon \in U[0, 1]$ is the noise variable.
σ is the stripe width parameter (range 0.8 to 1.8).
β was the magnitude of the noise, and was considered for $\beta = 0.0, 0.1, 0.25$, which bounded our observed noise level (i.e., $\beta < 0.1$).

We measured both RMS error ($\sqrt{\frac{1}{N}\Sigma(\delta_i - \hat{\delta}_i)^2}$) and maximum deviation ($max\,|\delta_i - \hat{\delta}_i|$) as a function of σ for $N = 10,000$ samples. Figures 4, 5 and 6 show the RMS error for $\beta = 0.0, 0.1, 0.25$ respectively. Figures 7, 8 and 9 show the same for the maximum error. Immediately, we see that the **CoM3** and **CoM5** estimators are problematic. What is surprising is the error of the **CoM7** estimator in the presence of noise at low stripe widths. However, this is understandable as, when the stripe

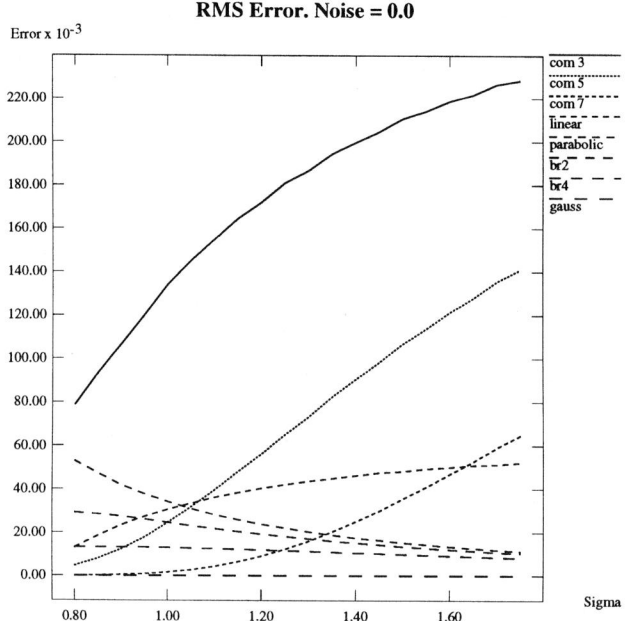

Fig. 4. RMS error versus σ for the estimators, noise = 0.0 (algorithms are listed large to small at maximum σ)

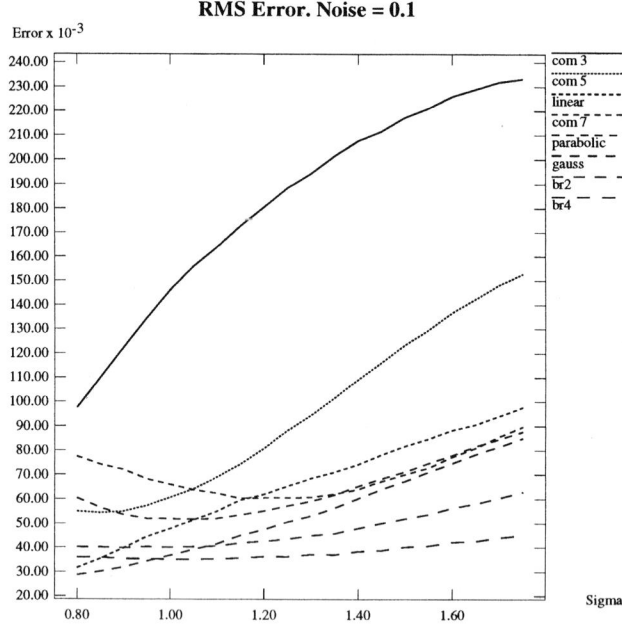

Fig. 5. RMS error versus σ for the estimators, noise = 0.1 (algorithms are listed large to small at maximum σ)

A Comparison of Algorithms for Subpixel Peak Detection

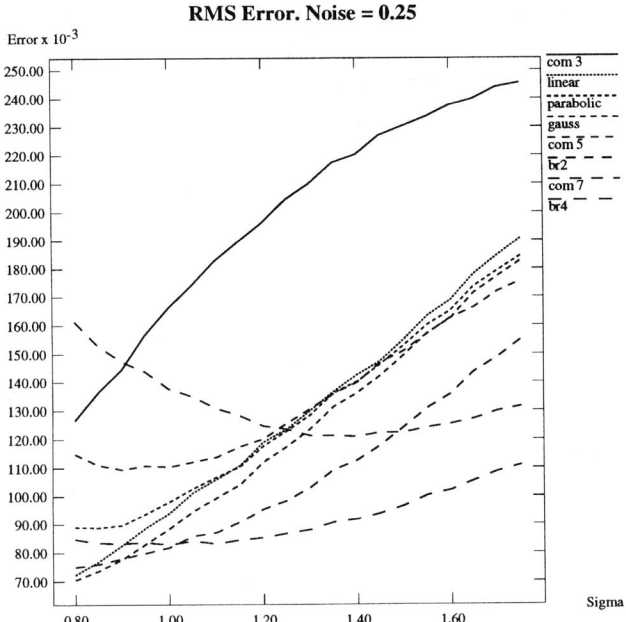

Fig. 6. RMS error versus σ for the estimators, noise = 0.25 (algorithms are listed large to small at maximum σ)

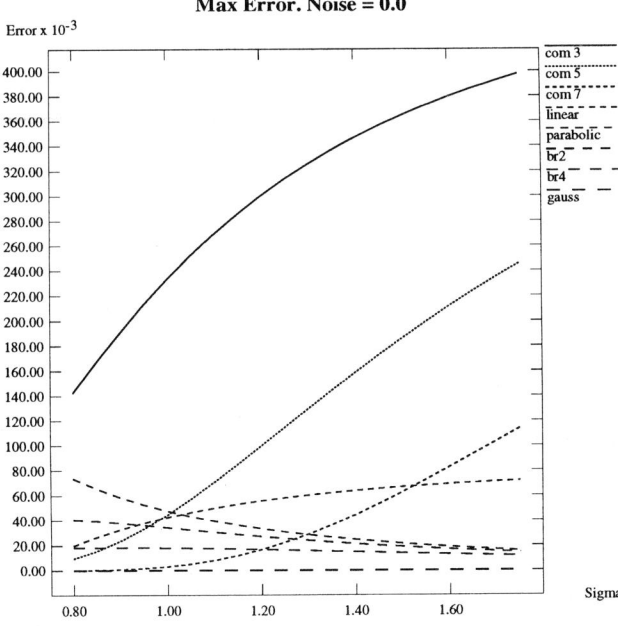

Fig. 7. Max error versus σ for the estimators, noise = 0.0 (algorithms are listed large to small at maximum σ)

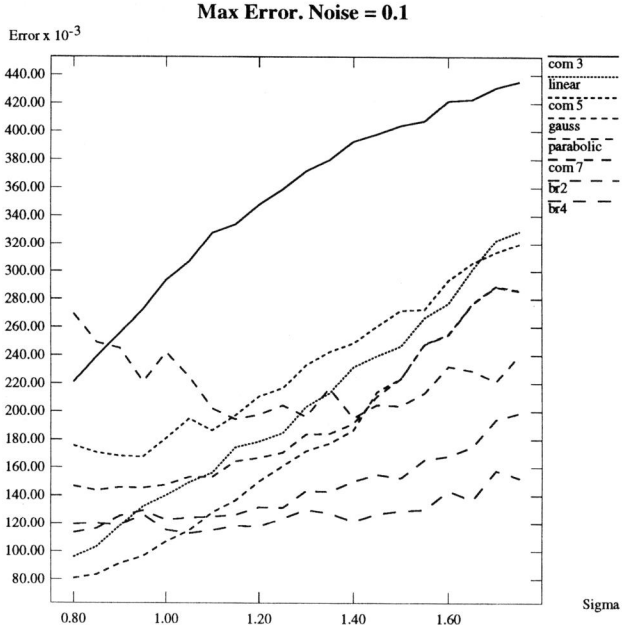

Fig. 8. Max error versus σ for the estimators, noise = 0.1 (algorithms are listed large to small at maximum σ)

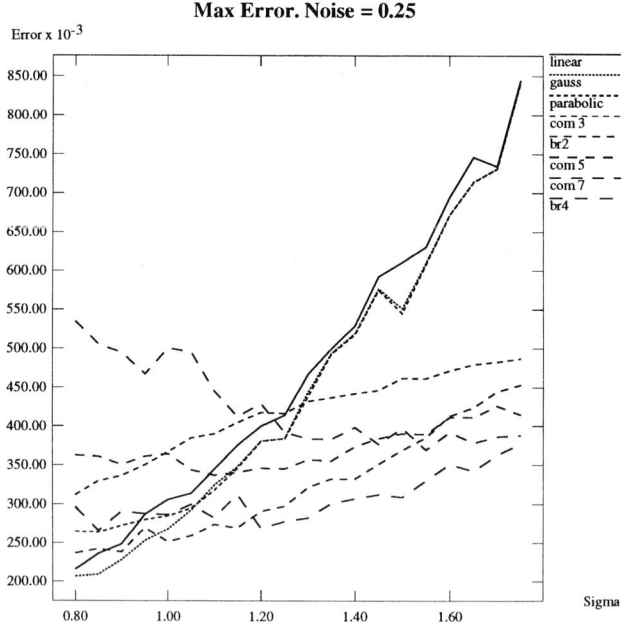

Fig. 9. Max error versus σ for the estimators, noise = 0.25 (algorithms are listed large to small at maximum σ)

width is low, the stripe intensities fall quickly at non-central pixels, causing the noise to more quickly dominate the signal and have a greater effect.

To compare the algorithms, we also summed the RMS error for $\sigma = 0.8 - 1.8$ (by 0.05) for the three values of β.

β	Gaussian	CoM3	CoM5	CoM7	Linear	Parabolic	BR2	BR4
0.00	0.00	3.71	1.36	0.31	0.87	0.49	0.39	0.24
0.10	1.07	3.90	1.86	1.32	1.36	1.23	0.93	0.77
0.25	2.49	4.25	2.67	2.63	2.62	2.61	2.12	1.86

From this, we can see good performance over a range of σ and β for the **BR2** and **BR4** estimators. This is also clear in Figs. 5 and 6, however, the **Gaussian** estimator has obvious benefits as the noise level or stripe width decreases. It is also interesting that the figures show to what extent the choice of estimator is linked to the specific stripe width and noise level. For our stripe system, we have observed:

Target color	Mean stripe peak intensity	Stripe σ	Background range
white	201	1.69	13–15
grey	165	1.31	11–12
black	60	1.22	10–12

Hence, for our striper, the noise seems to be about 2–3 quanta, or about 1–5% of the peak intensity. We think that the increase in σ as the intensity increases is explained by the gamma compression of the camera flattening the stripe peak.

7 Algorithm Behavior on Sensor Saturation

No algorithm should produce wildly unreasonable estimates of the peak position when the sensor is saturated. When saturation occurs, the measured intensity values at the peak and nearby pixels are usually at some limiting value (e.g., 255). Moreover, because of the effects of saturation on the physical sensor, adjacent pixels whose true signal is below saturation may also be affected or become saturated. Hence, use of these adjacent pixels may also not be possible.

The **Gaussian**, **Linear** and **Parabolic** algorithms given in Sect. 3 have a definite problem in this situation, resulting in a division by zero. We propose that these algorithms can be modified to use the midpoint of the saturated region:

```
if overflow-occurred
{
    peak_position = last_overflowed_pixel - overflow_length/2 + 0.5
}
else use_normal_algorithm
```

The other algorithms do not actually perform too badly, provided the region of saturation is only 1–3 pixels. We tested the behavior of the algorithms by an experiment where the pixel values were generated using the formula given in Sect. 4. Then, whenever the intensity value was greater than 0.5, it was set to 0.5 (i.e., the saturation limit). This limit allowed a maximum of three consecutive saturated pixels. The algorithms were applied at all subpixel offsets from -0.5 to 0.5, and the deviation of the estimated subpixel offset away from the true offset were recorded. Figure 10 shows the deviations for the **Gauss** and the **BR4** algorithms.

The maximum deviations for the algorithms are:

Algorithm	Gaussian	CoM3	CoM5	CoM7	Linear	Parabolic	BR2	BR4
Max Deviation	0.320	0.255	0.059	0.049	0.320	0.320	0.175	0.071

Some improvement might be possible by a function of the non-saturated pixels surrounding the saturated region, but the utility of these algorithms depends on how the sensor responds when saturated.

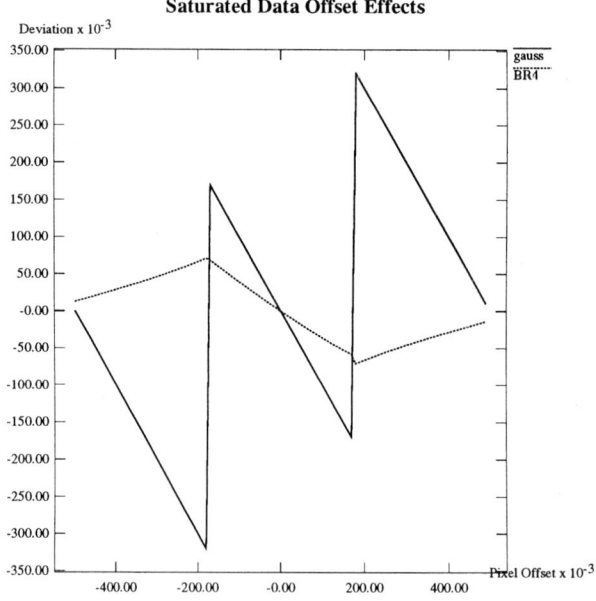

Fig. 10. Deviations of pixel offsets using saturated data

8 Empirical Testing

We tested all algorithms in the laser stripe range sensor described in Sect. 2. The experiments used three different test objects. These were a cube, a trapezoid with its top surface at an angle of 10° to the horizontal, and an equilateral prism (see Fig. 11). In all cases, the object was oriented so that all range values along the stripe were equal. The test objects were aligned so that their surface normals lay in the $X - Z$ plane. The coordinate system, the relative positioning of the cameras and the direction of motion of the micro-stepper are clarified in Fig. 2.

The experiments obtained a series of range images comprising 100 range stripes each. A single data point was chosen from each stripe, such that all the data points chosen lay along a line parallel to the x-axis. Secondly, the stripes were taken with a very small micro-stepper movement (0.2 mm for the prism and 0.3 mm for trapezoid and the cube), thereby leading to high data density. Also, the depth quantization was kept small (0.03 mm), so that the estimation errors would be of larger magnitude than the quantization errors.

For each surface, each algorithm was used to detect the stripe peak, and then the depth calculated from each camera was noted and their average computed. Having collected the data, a linear least-squares fit ($z = \hat{a} + \hat{b}x$) was computed for each set of data points. The slope of this fitted line was computed, and the minimum and maximum values of the errors were recorded. The variance of the errors was also computed. The comparative statistics are shown below.

Surface	Algorithm	$\hat{a}$	$\hat{b}$	Error(mm)		
				Min.	Max.	Variance
Flat Surface	Gaussian	49.7680	0.000112	−0.12762	0.09815	0.00249
	CoM – 3 pt	49.6466	0.000006	−0.06152	0.08812	0.00122
	CoM – 5 pt	49.7025	0.000130	−0.10121	0.09972	0.00156
	CoM – 7 pt	49.6239	0.000036	−0.09555	0.09658	0.00156
	Linear	49.7878	0.000090	−0.07676	0.08499	0.00120
	Parabolic	49.7397	0.000297	−0.14026	0.14496	0.00271
	BR – 2nd	49.6804	−0.000171	−0.21498	0.11769	0.00323
	BR – 4th	49.6808	−0.000411	−0.13912	0.16080	0.00343

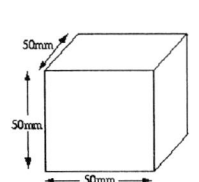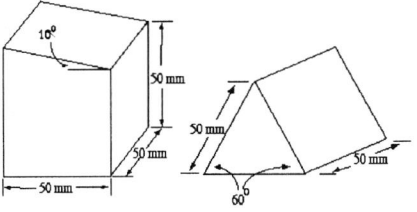

Fig. 11. Detail of experimental objects

Surface	Algorithm	$\hat{a}$	$\hat{b}$	Error(mm)		
				Min.	Max.	Variance
10° slope, left to right	Gaussian	57.2598	−0.05306	−0.24558	0.38329	0.02463
	CoM – 3 pt	57.7386	−0.05443	−0.45631	0.56070	0.05423
	CoM – 5 pt	57.6771	−0.05466	−0.37467	0.31389	0.03110
	CoM – 7 pt	57.6287	−0.05478	−0.29864	0.34434	0.02416
	Linear	57.6665	−0.05391	−0.30376	0.31999	0.01737
	Parabolic	57.7211	−0.05436	−0.23738	0.37868	0.01899
	BR – 2nd	57.8916	−0.05389	−0.27106	0.28737	0.01836
	BR – 4th	57.8261	−0.05382	−0.28686	0.33492	0.02110
10° slope, right to left	Gaussian	51.3929	0.05424	−0.31441	0.51424	0.03381
	CoM – 3 pt	51.8246	0.05257	−0.43193	0.47276	0.04573
	CoM – 5 pt	51.7356	0.05321	−0.34414	0.41777	0.03457
	CoM – 7 pt	51.6648	0.05277	−0.32581	0.42064	0.03128
	Linear	51.7305	0.05263	−0.35943	0.40299	0.03645
	Parabolic	51.7699	0.05281	−0.35278	0.41456	0.03496
	BR – 2nd	50.9346	0.05460	−0.33865	0.48187	0.03299
	BR – 4th	50.9251	0.05439	−0.30189	0.47461	0.03184

Surface	Algorithm	$\hat{a}$	$\hat{b}$	Error(mm)		
				Min.	Max.	Variance
60° slope, left to right	Gaussian	70.2352	−0.34806	0.43505	0.45969	0.04737
	CoM – 3 pt	70.3217	−0.34726	−0.42918	0.51835	0.05024
	CoM – 5 pt	70.3418	−0.34816	−0.37187	0.55610	0.04146
	CoM – 7 pt	70.1715	−0.34771	−0.39819	0.51866	0.04106
	Linear	70.2851	−0.34810	−0.43443	0.42978	0.04897
	Parabolic	70.3154	−0.34841	−0.39460	0.50010	0.04764
	BR – 2nd	70.1493	−0.34781	−0.46431	0.51234	0.05624
	BR – 4th	70.1202	−0.34813	−0.47256	0.47195	0.04401
60° slope, right to left	Gaussian	23.5725	0.34834	−0.34344	0.44277	0.03918
	CoM – 3 pt	23.5071	0.34925	−0.33353	0.41938	0.03397
	CoM – 5 pt	23.5518	0.34852	−0.31148	0.35788	0.03213
	CoM – 7 pt	23.3997	0.34865	−0.40910	0.48459	0.03624
	Linear	23.5029	0.34894	−0.38680	0.47643	0.03994
	Parabolic	23.5249	0.34873	−0.39773	0.44770	0.03675
	BR – 2nd	23.5494	0.34841	−0.31710	0.46174	0.03628
	BR – 4th	23.5244	0.34870	−0.34116	0.52795	0.02985

Flat Surface Residual Comparison

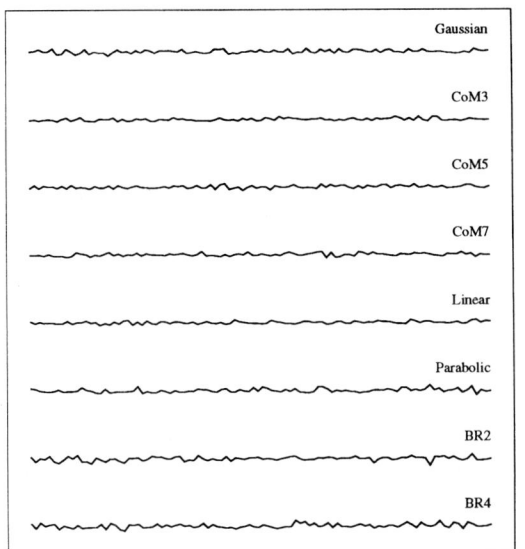

Fig. 12. Comparative depth residuals across a flat surface. The data is separated for clarity

The measured values for $\hat{a}$ are not particularly relevant. The values of $\hat{b}$ are of interest, because they specify the slope of the surface as measured by the algorithms used. The true value of $\hat{b}$ is 0 in the case of the cube, ±0.0538 in the case of the trapezoid, and ±0.3464 for the prism. These values were derived by careful physical measurements of the objects, but are still subject to the usual measurement errors. However, they provide us with a basis for comparing the accuracies of the different peak-picking methods.

The tabulated results are better illustrated by the comparative graphs shown in Figs. 12–14. The graphs are the plots of the variation of the residuals from the line of best fit applied to the measured data. The plots have each been offset by a different amount so that they are appear together on one graph. The scale on the Y-axis is the same for all the data sets. The maximum absolute variation of the plots from the line of best fit is about 0.5 mm.

Figure 12 shows the variation across the surface of the cube. The **CoM3** and **BR2** algorithms appear to show the least amount of perturbation, followed closely by the plots derived from the **Linear** and **BR4** methods.

The results with the trapezoid (see Fig. 13) clearly show systematic errors in the imaging system, particularly with all the **CoM** algorithms. These are caused by the aliasing of the image of the peak creeping from one pixel to the next, crossing the inter-pixel gap. We estimate this gap is itself almost as wide as a pixel. The non-uniform response across a pixel response is also a source of the observed periodic effect (see e.g., [1]).

The performance of all the algorithms deteriorates dramatically in the case of the prism (see Fig. 14). The variations are more pronounced and more frequent than in the previous two examples. This is because the acute angle of the object,

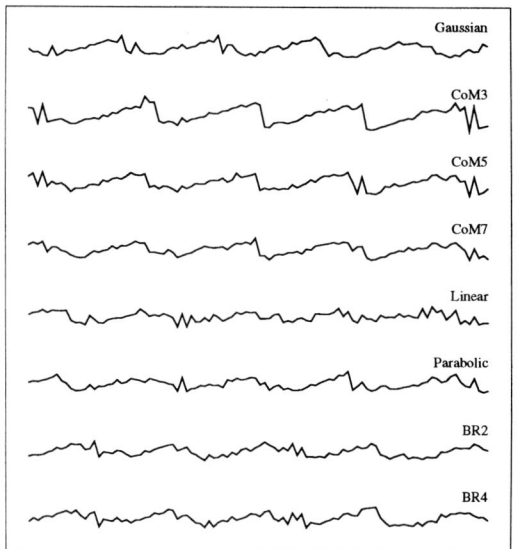

Fig. 13. Comparative depth residuals across a 10°, left-to-right slope. The data is separated for clarity

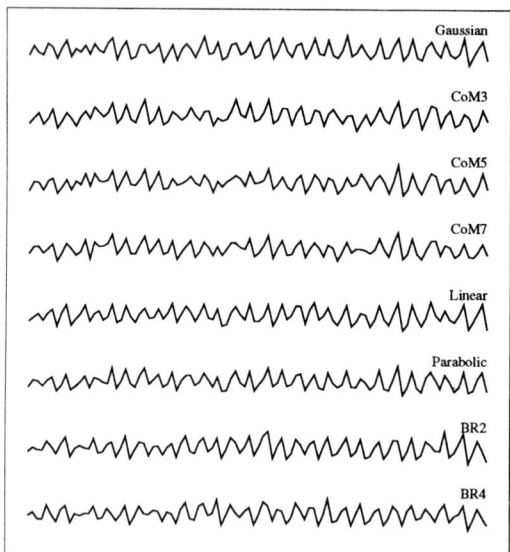

Fig. 14. Comparative depth residuals across a 60°, left-to-right slope. The data is separated for clarity

which is very close to the angle of the camera axis to the horizontal, causes the stripe to move across the imaging sensors pixels more quickly.

The aliasing gives a periodic structure to the estimators. Some portion of this periodic, and systematic error could probably be reduced by modeling the effect as a function of local surface slope and uncorrected estimated subpixel position. In the case of our sensor, the errors observed here are symptomatic of the sensor structure and dominate most of the theoretical results discussed above. We have investigated using subpixel algorithms that fit an observed stripe profile to an empirically derived real stripe profile; however, the stripe profiles that we observed varied from pixel to pixel with little systematic character, and we concluded that modeling each pixel's response individually was unprofitable for our application.

9 Conclusions

The empirical results show that the **CoM3** algorithm has poor performance. The other methods display performance within the same range probably because of factors such as sensor structure, inter-pixel gaps, cross-talk, and integration of the sensor response over the width of the pixel. The **Linear** and **BR2** methods have been shown to possess high bias (Sect. 5). When we consider the errors produced, the sum of the RMS errors are highest for the **CoM3** and **CoM5** algorithms. They are joined by the **Parabolic** algorithm when we consider the maximum errors. This leaves us with only the **Gaussian**, **CoM7** and **BR4** algorithms as suitable candidates.

In the case of algorithms like the **CoM7** and **BR4**, which rely on a large number of points around the peak, we observe that specular reflections and transparency may cause problems since the outlying pixels have a substantial effect on the computation of the location of the peak. Also, in the case where the object has holes in it, causing internal reflections and mutual illumination, the weighted average method of the **CoM** algorithms will deliver a skewed estimate of the peak position. That is, when random noise levels are low, estimators using a small number of ponts will have advantages in avoiding effects arising from the structure of the sensed object.

We can see good performance over a range of σ and β for the **BR4** estimator. This is also clear in Fig. 5; however, the **Gaussian** estimator has obvious benefits as the noise level or stripe width decreases. It is also interesting that the figures show to what extent the choice of estimator is linked to the specific stripe width and noise level. For our striper, the noise seems to be about 2–3 quanta, or about 1–5% of the peak intensity. Note that in all cases we assumed that the intensity levels were below the saturation level of the sensor.

When comparing the speeds of the algorithms, the **Gaussian** is the slowest by about a factor of 2 over the **Linear** algorithm, which is the fastest in our implementation. However, the peak detection sub-process takes up only a small percentage of the total range image acquisition and peak detection time, so the speed of the algorithms is not a factor in their comparison.

In addition to these results, we have not seen published before a bias analysis (cf. Sect. 5) and a bias factor on the estimator (cf. Sect. 4). Finally, the aliasing effect observed in Sect. 8 does not seem to have been reported before in conjunction with subpixel range sensors.

These results apply to sampled and digitized signals, whereas some algorithms, namely the center-of-mass algorithm, can be applied directly to the video signal [3, 6]. Real-time digitized stripe detection and subpixel location can be achieved by scanning for the peak as the digitized signal is acquired. Both approaches have been implemented (elsewhere) in hardware and thus remove computational expense as a consideration, because the subpixel calculations are fast enough to be completed in the time before the next pixel is acquired, and one has to wait for the complete video scan anyway, when using standard video equipment.

Acknowledgements. The authors gratefully acknowledge the assistance of the University of Edinburgh and the European Institute of Technology (Grant EIT-061) for funding the research described in this paper.

References

1. B. G. Batchelor, D. A. Hill and D. C. Hodgson, "Automated Visual Inspection", IFS (Publications) Ltd, UK, North Holland, 1985.
2. F. Blais & M. Rioux, "Real-Time Numerical Peak Detector", Signal Processing 11, pp 145–155, 1986.
3. D. Braggins, "Achieving subpixel precision", Sensor Review, Volume 10, No. 4, pp 174–177, 1990.
4. P. J. MacVicar-Whelan & T. O. Binford, "Intensity Discontinuity Location to Subpixel Precision", Proceedings of the 7th International Joint Conference on Artificial Intelligence, pp 752–754, 1981.
5. D. K. Naidu, R. B. Fisher, "A Comparitive Analysis of Algorithms for Determining the Peak Position of a Stripe to Sub-Pixel Accuracy", Proc. 1991 British Machine Vision Association Conf., pp 217–225, Glasgow, 1991.
6. S. J. White, "Method and Apparatus for Locating Center of Reference Pulse in a Measurement System", U.S. Patent No. 4,628,469, December 1986.

Splines and Spline Fitting Revisited

D.C. Vargas, E.J. Rodríguez, M. Flickner, and J.L.C. Sanz

Abstract. This paper presents a detailed summary of the properties and basic facts about spline spaces and their B-spline bases. Examination is made of the many different joint-continuity conditions. Geometric continuity constraints are of special interest, as they appear to satisfy visual needs of the human observers. Least-squares approximation of analytic curves and discrete point sets is also discussed. Special attention is devoted to the problem of selecting the bast fit to a closed curve, considering all the possible shifted parametric descriptions of the curve.

1 Introduction

The word *spline* is an Anglian term that names the bending laths, thin strips of wood or metal, that were used to design the complex shapes of ships and aircrafts [3, 28]. Spline curves are piecewise curves, each piece belonging to a certain family of (generally polynomial or rational polynomial) functions. Since almost all published work on spline curves refers to polynomial spline or rational polynomial spline curves, the term spline is generally used in this restricted sense. Spline curves have been studied, as early as in the 19th century, in the form of probability densities.

Spline interpolation is the natural generalization of polynomial interpolation. It overcomes deficiencies – such as the oscillatory character (Runge phenomenon) of high degree polynomials used when the number of data points increases [9], – and ameliorates the computational complexity of the interpolating procedure [11]. Spline interpolation allows the specification of discontinuities on the derivatives of the function. Splines are also employed as collocation patterns in ODE solving and in quadrature rules of numerical integration. An early application of spline functions (1928; see [11]) was the approximation of the Fourier coefficients of a function g from the DFT of samples of g using a spline interpolant. Spline functions also arise as the solution of variational regularization techniques for ill-posed problems [8, 35].

From another point of view, splines are generalization of the Bézier curves [14] that have made a powerful impact in computer-aided geometric modeling (CAGM) systems [5]. Spline use has spread in CAGM, since they allow stable and efficient rendering procedures [10] while maintaining the continuity of the curve under control. Splines can also provide interactive design capabilities since they can be represented as linear combinations of B-splines, a proper generalization of the Bernstein polynomials [2].

The available literature on splines is rapidly expanding, and there exist a wealth of good surveys and textbooks on the subject. Good introductions to spline theory are in [11] and [14]. Practical details of the use of splines for curve synthesis is exposed in tutorial form in [3], along with a discussion of geometric continuous β-splines, and the computational aspects of rendering splines.

Spline approximation has been used in the image processing field in a variety of tasks. Image magnification can be done by fitting a spline through the pixels in each row and resampling the resulting curve up to the desired resolution. The process can be repeated for each column [20]. Also, splines can be used in image restoration. In this case, the picture is corrupted due to the point spread function of the imaging device, sampling and quantization errors. Spline modeling seeks to restore the underlying noiseless image. The fast and accurate evaluation of splines in B-spline form has favored their use to synthesize smooth digital filters [15]. Regularizing splines have been used in early vision [4] for optical flow computation, shape from shading, stereo matching, edge detection, and other topics.

A key step in a scene analysis system is the extraction of features that facilitate the identification and description of objects. Raw digital data may be used, or a functional model can be defined to comprise relevant information about the picture. Usual approaches are a Fourier description of the boundary data, or shape representation as a parametric function, selected from a certain class, for example piecewise polynomials splines [27, 38, 43]. Using polynomial splines, good compression rates have been achieved, since coding the control points resulting from a least-squares fitting is much less expensive than coding the original boundary points [26]. Control point-based feature extraction is generally straightforward [39]. Spline models have been used to compute moments and projections of binary shapes [27], curvatures [44] and gradients [43]. Typical applications include matching and segmentation of shapes, optical character recognition (OCR), font design and boundary compression.

The outline of this work is as follows. Section 2 introduces some terminology and basic facts on splines, discussing spline bases appropriate to both open and closed curve modeling. The next section analyzes different continuity conditions between pieces of a spline, in particular, the relationship between *parametric* and *geometric* continuity is studied. Section 4 reviews regularization techniques, which, given the problem of finding the best fit to a given set of samples within a usually broad class of functions (like $L^2(R)$), add constraints, for instance, continuity of the derivatives, in order to ensure smoothness of the solution. Section 5 is devoted to discussing fitting with splines; how different inner products, *continuous* or *discrete*, over the function space, give rise to different fitting methods. A comparison between continuous and discrete inner product methods is presented. When considering approximations to a closed curve, the selection of the starting point of its parameterization is of concern, since different starting points result in different fits. In Sect. 6, the selection of the best fitting to a closed curve for all the possible shifted parameterizations of the curve is studied. This question seems not to have been addressed before, although in the context of shape analysis [52] a related topic is considered: a shift invariant descriptor set for image samples, based on multidimensional orthogonal polynomials.

The last section draws some conclusions and suggests related topics of future research.

2 Splines: Definition and Basic Facts

The concept of *spline* [3, 11] involves a piecewise defined parametric curve over a given interval $[a, b]$

$$P(u) = \begin{cases} P_0(u) & \text{if } t_0 \leq u < t_1 \\ \vdots \\ P_{k-1}(u) & \text{if } t_{k-1} \leq u < t_k \end{cases} \tag{2.1}$$

where each piece $P_i(u) = (x_i(u), y_i(u))$ belongs to a certain class of curves P, (e.g., n-degree polynomials, rational curves, etc.) and $t = [a = t_0 \leq \ldots < t_k = b]$ is a non decreasing sequence of parameter values called *knots*. When dealing with closed curves, periodic parametric functions with period $b - a$, will be considered. Specified continuity conditions (C^0, C^1, tangent continuity, etc.) are required on every joint.

In this work, P will be the space of n-degree polynomials. In this case, if no continuity conditions are enforced at the knots t_i, it is easy to see that the set of the $P(u)$ defined over t by (2.1) is a vector space P_t with dimension kn. On the other hand, the requirement of different constraints on the continuity of the consecutive derivatives, leads to the definition of several subspaces of P_t. The most common situation is when each piece is joined to its neighbors with C^{n-1} continuity[1]. This space will be denoted as P_t^{n-1}. In the next subsection, an adequate basis for P_t^{n-1} will be constructed using B-splines.

2.1 B-Spline Basis

For the sake of simplicity, the open curve case will be dealt with first. Given a fixed knot-sequence $t = [a = t_0 < \ldots < t_k = b]$ of length $k + 1$, the set of n-degree B-spline functions can be obtained recursively [17]:

$$N_i^0(u) = \begin{cases} 1, & t_i \leq u \leq t_{i+1} \\ 0, & \text{otherwise} \end{cases} \tag{2.2a}$$

$$N_i^r(u) = \frac{(u - t_i) N_i^{r-1}(u)}{t_{i+r} - t_i} + \frac{(t_{i+r+1} - u) N_{i+1}^{r-1}(u)}{t_{i+r+1} - t_{i+1}}, \quad r = 1, \ldots, n. \tag{2.2b}$$

---

[1] with the convention that C^{-1} means no continuity at all.

for $i = 0, \ldots, k - n - 1$. These piecewise polynomial functions have C^{n-1} continuity at the knots. Any C^{n-1} polynomial spline over $[t_n, t_{k-n}]$ may then be written using the B-spline representation

$$P(u) = \sum_{i=0}^{k-n-1} c_i N_i^n(u), \quad u \in [t_n, t_{k-n}]. \tag{2.3}$$

Note that this linear combination is valid only when $u \in [t_n, t_{k-n}]$. It can be proven [3, 11] that the set of B-splines $\{N_i^n\}_{i=0}^{k-n+1}$ form a basis of the $(k-n)$-dimensional space of piecewise polynomials with C^{n-1} continuity at the knots, over that interval. Moreover, $\{N_{j-s}^n\}_{s=0}^n$ is a basis of the n-degree polynomials restricted to the interval $[t_j, t_{j+1}]$.

The weights c_i are 2D vectors when curves in R^2 are being considered, and may be understood as points that locally control the shape of the curve being modeled, since each $P_i(u)$ is a linear combination of only $n + 1$ of these weights. They will be referred to as *control points* and are usually not interpolated by P. The extension to curves in higher dimensions is straightforward, and will not be considered.

Since the problem is to have the spline defined over the whole interval $[a, b]$, an ingenious solution is to add n extra knots t'_j at the beginning and n at the end of the knot sequence

$$\mathbf{t}' = [t'_0 = \ldots = t'_n = a, \ldots, b = t'_{k+n} = \cdots = t'_{k+2n}].$$

The knots in-between remain equal to the original knots: $t'_{n+j} = t_j, j = 0, \ldots, k$. The new length of the knot sequence is $k' = k + 2n + 1$. The number of pieces in the spline is now k, and the dimension of the space over $[a, b]$ is $k + n$. The first and the last control points are interpolated: $P(a) = c_0$ and $P(b) = c_{k+n-1}$ [14].

Lower degree continuity at the joints can be obtained when consecutive knots are made coincident. In this case, the recurrence (2.2) is used to define the basis and the curve is represented as in (2.3). If $t_l = \ldots = t_{l+\mu}$, the knot t_l is said to have *multiplicity* μ and, in this case, the curve $P(u)$ will be $n - \mu - 1$-continuous at t_l [3].

When dealing with closed curves, the set of polynomial splines over $[a, b]$ is a vector space of dimension k. The recursive definition (2.2) can be used to construct a basis for this space. First of all, the knot sequence $\mathbf{t}'$ is infinitely extended to $[t_j]_{j \in Z}$ with $t_{i+ks} = t_i + sT$, where $T = b - a$ is the period. Now, an infinite number of B-splines $\{N_i^n\}_{i \in Z}$ are derived from (2.2), each N_i^n having finite support $[t_i, t_{i+n+1}]$. These functions verify $N_{i+ks}^n(u) = N_i^n(u - sT)$, $0 \leq i < k$. Thus, defining $\tilde{N}_i^n$ as

$$\tilde{N}_i^n(u) = \sum_{j \in Z} N_{i+jk}^n(u), \quad 0 \leq i < k,$$

a periodic function, with period T, is obtained. This function coincides with N_{i+jk}^n in $[t_{i+jk}, \ldots, t_{i+jk+n+1}]$, and

- $\tilde{N}_i^n$ is a spline, with C^{n-1} continuity at the knots and C^∞ continuity between them.
- The set $\{\tilde{N}_i^n\}_{i=0}^{k-1}$ is linearly independent.
- The set $\{\tilde{N}_{j-s}^n\}_{s=0}^n$ generates all the n-degree polynomials in $[t_j, t_{j+1}]$

Splines and Spline Fitting Revisited

hence, $\{\tilde{N}_i^n\}_{i=0}^{k-1}$ is the sought basis. Once again, the spline P may be written as a B-spline superposition

$$P(u) = \sum_{i=0}^{k-1} c_i \tilde{N}_i^n(u), \quad \forall u. \tag{2.4}$$

2.2 Further Properties

Selected properties of B-splines and B-spline representations are listed below [3, 14].

1. The open basis function N_i^n is non-zero and non-negative only in a limited region of the real line. The closed basis function $\tilde{N}_i^n$ is non-zero and non-negative in a limited region of the real line in each period. These regions are the intervals (t_i, t_{i+n+1}), in the open case and $(t_{i+sT}, t_{i+sT+n+1})$, $s \in Z$, in the closed case. This fact is known as *local control property*: each control point affects only a limited section of the curve.

2. $\sum_{s=0}^{n} N_{j-s}^n(u) = 1$ or $\sum_{s=0}^{n} \tilde{N}_{j-s}^n(u) = 1$, $t_j \le u < t_{j+1}$

   and, from Property 1 above,

   $\sum_{s=0}^{k-n+1} N_s^n(u) = 1$, $t_n \le u < t_{k-n}$ or $\sum_{s=0}^{k-1} \tilde{N}_s^n(u) = 1$, $\forall u$.

   This motivates the fact that the functions defined by (2.2) sometimes are referred to as *normalized* B-splines.

3. From 1 and 2, the B-spline representations (2.3) and (2.4) are convex combinations of the basis functions. Consequently, $P(u)$ lies in the convex hull of the $n+1$ control points $c_{j-n}, \ldots, c_n$. This means that the position of the control points location gives a rough idea of the shape of the curve being modeled.

4. Control points are invariant to affine maps and other spatial transformations
   - $c_i' = c_i A \Rightarrow P'(u) = P(u)A$, where $A = \text{diag}[A_x, A_y]$ is a given scale matrix.
   - $c_i' = c_i + \bar{r}, \Rightarrow P'(u) = P(u) + \bar{r}$, where $\bar{r} = [r_x, r_y]$ is a translation vector.
   - $c_i' = c_i R \Rightarrow P'(u) = P(u)R$ where R is a rotation matrix of angle θ:

   $$R = \begin{bmatrix} \cos\theta & -\sin\theta \\ \sin\theta & \cos\theta \end{bmatrix}$$

   - If the control points are reflected about a given straight line, the curve is reflected about the same axis.

5. Values of splines of arbitrary degree can be found by repeated linear interpolation. If P, given by (2.3) or (2.4), is to be evaluated in x such that $t_p \le x < t_{p+1}$, it can be proven [10] that $P(u) = c_p^{[0]}$, where $c_p^{[0]}$ is obtained from the recursion (with $p - r \le i \le p$)

$$c_i^{[n]} = c_i$$
$$c_i^{[r-1]} = (1-\omega_i^r)c_{i-1}^{[r]} + \omega_i^r c_i^{[r]}$$
$$\omega_i^r = \frac{u-t_i}{t_{i+n}-t_i}.$$

This procedure is referred to as *de-Boor evaluation*. Of course, explicit expressions for the various polynomials can also be employed.

2.3 Uniform Splines

The curves $P(u)$ generated by (2.3) and (2.4) are called *uniform splines* when the basis functions are defined on a uniformly spaced knot sequence $t_u = [t_0 + i\Delta t]_{i=0}^k$. From the recursive definition (2.2), it is easy to see that the uniform B-splines defined on t_u are shifted versions of each other, i.e.,

$$N_{i+1}^n(u) = N_i^n(u - \Delta T) \quad \text{and} \quad \tilde{N}_{i+1}^n(u) = \tilde{N}_i^n(u - \Delta T). \tag{2.5}$$

It means that the uniform B-spline representation can be written in terms of the *0th* basis function

$$P(u) = \sum_{i=0}^{k-1-n} c_i N(u - i\Delta t), \tag{2.6}$$

where N is N_0^n or $\tilde{N}_0^n$ in the aperiodic or periodic case, respectively.

Alternatively, the *0th* closed uniform basis function can be obtained as the convolution of lower degree B-splines [45]. Let M^r stand for the *0th* r-degree closed B-spline, defined over the k knots $t_r = [a = -\frac{1+r}{2}, \ldots, b = k - \frac{1+r}{2}]$. Each knot is one unit apart from its neighbors. Starting with the periodic continuation of the 'window'

$$M^0(u) = \begin{cases} 1 & \text{if } -1/2 \leq u < 1/2, \\ 0 & \text{otherwise,} \end{cases} \tag{2.7}$$

it has been shown that [41]

$$\tilde{M}^r(u) = (\tilde{M}^{r-1} * \tilde{M}^0)(u) = \int_a^b \tilde{M}^{r-1}(\tau)\tilde{M}^0(u-\tau)d\tau \tag{2.8}$$

generates the desired function for all u, where $*$ is the circular convolution product over one period. This statement provides a handy way of evaluating the inner product

$$\langle f, g \rangle = \int_a^b f(\tau)g(\tau)d\tau,$$

of two uniform n-degree closed B-splines defined over t_r. This property is summarized in the next equation [42]

$$\left\langle \tilde{N}_i^n, \tilde{N}_j^n \right\rangle = \int_a^b \tilde{N}_i^n(\tau)\tilde{N}_j^n(\tau)d\tau = \tilde{N}_0^{2n-1}(j-i) = \tilde{N}_0^{2n-1}(i-j). \tag{2.9}$$

The following fact will be needed later:

Proposition 1. *The integral over a whole period of any uniform closed spline is equal to 1.*

Proof. By induction:

$$\int_a^b M^0(u)du = \int_{-1/2}^{1/2} du = 1$$

Assuming that $\int_a^b \tilde{M}^{r-1}(u)du = 1$, it follows from (2.8):

$$\int_a^b \tilde{M}^r(u)du = \int_a^b \int_a^b \tilde{M}^{r-1}(\tau)\tilde{M}^0(u-\tau)d\tau du$$
$$= \int_a^b \left(\int_a^b \tilde{M}^0(u-\tau)du \right) \tilde{M}^{r-1}(\tau)d\tau$$
$$= \int_a^b \tilde{M}^{r-1}(\tau)d\tau = 1.$$

3 Geometric Continuity Conditions

The continuity constraints on the parametric spline are not always suitable from the point of view of visual continuity of a continuous curve in R^2. Hence, different conditions are sought, involving the existence of a tangent space in every point (the so-called G^1 continuity) or the continuity of the curvature vector (G^2 continuity). Formally,

Definition 1. *A curve f is G^1 continuous at a given u iff its tangent vector*

$$T(u) = \lim_{h \to 0} \frac{f'(u+h)}{\|f'(u+h)\|} \tag{3.1}$$

is defined.

A curve is said to be G^1 continuous if it is G^1 at each point of its domain. The spline, being a piecewise smooth function, satisfies (3.1) everywhere, except possibly at the knots.

Stress will now be put on the relationship between C^1 and G^1 continuity:

- A C^1 curve is G^1 at a given point if the parametric derivative does not vanish at that point.
- On the other hand, if the derivative is zero, the tangent vector space may or may not exist:
  1. Consider the following curve [3]:

$$P(u) = \begin{cases} (2u-u^2,\ 2u-u^2) & \text{if } 0 \leq u < 1 \\ (2-2u+u^2,\ 2u-u^2) & \text{if } 1 \leq u < 2 \end{cases}$$

At $u = 1$,

$$\lim_{u \to 1^-} P'(u) = \lim_{u \to 1^+} P'(u) = 0.$$

Thus, P is C^1. Nevertheless

$$\lim_{u \to 1^-} T(u) = \frac{1}{\sqrt{2}}(1,\ 1)$$

$$\lim_{u \to 1^+} T(u) = \frac{1}{\sqrt{2}}(1,\ -1)$$

and therefore, P is not G^1 at 1.

2. Let P be the composite 3rd degree Bézier curve whose two pieces are[2]

$$P_1(t) = \sum_{i=0}^{3} C_i B_i^3(t), \quad 0 \leq t \leq 1$$

$$P_2(t) = \sum_{i=0}^{3} D_i B_i^3(t), \quad 0 \leq t \leq 1$$

where its control points satisfy the following constraints

$$C_2 = C_3 = D_0 = D_1 \qquad (3.2\text{a})$$

$$C_1 \neq C_2 \qquad (3.2\text{b})$$

$$D_1 \neq D_2 \qquad (3.2\text{c})$$

$$D_2 - D_1 - \alpha(C_2 - C_1), \quad \alpha > 0 \qquad (3.2\text{d})$$

It is easy to see that $P_1'(1) = 3(C_3 - C_2)$ and $P_2'(0) = 3(D_1 - D_0)$. Thus,

$$P_1'(1) = P_2'(0) = 0$$

and P is C^1. It is also true that

$$\lim_{u \to 1^-} T_1(u) = \frac{C_2 - C_1}{\|C_2 - C_1\|}; \qquad \lim_{u \to 0^+} T_2(u) = \frac{D_2 - D_1}{\|D_2 - D_1\|}.$$

Because of (3.2) it follows that P is G^1 as well. Note that enough degrees of freedom are available in this example, so as to join two *different* polynomial segments and still satisfy (3.2).

---

[2] Recall that B_i^n are the *Bernstein polynomials* $B_i^n(t) = \binom{n}{i} t^i (1-t)^{n-i}$.

Splines and Spline Fitting Revisited

- Generally a G^1 parameterization of a curve is not C^1. However, there always exists a suitable C^1 reparameterization, namely arc-length parameterization (**ALP**).

  Given a G^1 spline, its **ALP** usually does not belong to the same family, since it will still be a piecewise defined curve, but its pieces will not be in the same function space S as before. For example, a piecewise n-degree polynomial, whose **ALP** is generally not piecewise polynomial.

Nevertheless, if the spline is open, there exists a linear reparameterization that is C^1 and in general, each piece belongs to the same function space, because of linearity.

Suppose the following curve is given

$$P(u) = \begin{cases} P_0(u) & \text{if } t_0 \leq u < t_1 \\ \vdots & \\ P_{k-1}(u) & \text{if } t_{k-1} \leq u < t_k \end{cases}$$

where in each knot $t_i (1 \leq i \leq k-1)$ the following equations are satisfied:

$$P_{i-1}(t_i) = P_i(t_i) \tag{3.3a}$$
$$P'_{i-1}(t_i) = \alpha_i P'_i(t_i), \quad \alpha_i > 0 \tag{3.3b}$$

The constraints (3.3) force each piece to be joined to its neighbors with C^0 as well as G^1 continuity (if $P'_i(t_i) \neq 0$ for all $1 \leq i \leq k$)[3]. A new knot sequence $v_0, \ldots, v_{k+1}$ and a spline $\tilde{P}$ over this sequence will be defined, which not only will be C^1 but will also describe the same geometrical entity as P:

$$v_0 = t_0$$
$$v_1 = v_0 + (t_1 - t_0)$$
$$v_2 = v_1 + \frac{t_2 - t_1}{\alpha_1}$$
$$\vdots$$
$$v_i = v_{i-1} + \frac{t_i - t_{i-1}}{\alpha_1 \cdots \alpha_{i-1}}$$

where $i \leq k$.

It should be noted that this knot sequence starts at the same point as the old one, but the relative distance between consecutive knots is stretched.

If

$$\Delta_i = t_i - t_{i-1}; \; \Delta'_i = v_i - v_{i-1}$$

then

$$\Delta'_i = \frac{\Delta_i}{\alpha_1 \cdots \alpha_{i-1}}$$

---

[3] If however, $P'_i(t_i) = 0$ for some i in $0 \leq i \leq k$, neither the tangent space, nor a linear reparameterization may exist.

The spline is given by

$$\tilde{P}(v) = \begin{cases} \tilde{P}_0(v) & \text{if } v_0 \leq v < v_1 \\ \vdots \\ \tilde{P}_{k-1}(v) & \text{if } v_{k-1} \leq v < v_k \end{cases}$$

where

$$\tilde{P}_0(v) = P_0(v)$$
$$\tilde{P}_1(v) = P_1(\alpha_1(v - v_1) + t_1)$$
$$\tilde{P}_2(v) = P_2(\alpha_1\alpha_2(v - v_2) + t_2)$$
$$\vdots$$
$$\tilde{P}_i(v) = P_i(\alpha_1\alpha_2 \ldots \alpha_i(v - v_i) + t_i), \quad i \leq k - 1.$$

Each new piece $\tilde{P}_i$ is the composition of the corresponding piece P_i in the previous spline, with a linear function

$$g_i(v) = \alpha_1\alpha_2 \ldots \alpha_i(v - v_i) + t_i$$

that maps the interval $[v_i, v_{i+1}]$ into $[t_i, t_{i+1}]$ and thus the image of $\tilde{P}$ is the same as the image of P. At knot v_i $(1 \leq i \leq k - 1)$

$$\tilde{P}_{i-1}(v_i) = P_{i-1}(\alpha_1 \ldots \alpha_{i-1}(v_i - v_{i-1}) + t_{i-1})$$
$$= P_{i-1}((t_i - t_{i-1}) + t_{i-1})$$
$$= P_{i-1}(t_i)$$

$$\tilde{P}_i(v_i) = P_i(\alpha_1 \ldots \alpha_i(v_i - v_i) + t_i) = P_i(t_i).$$

Because of the continuity of P (see 3.3),

$$\tilde{P}_{i-1}(v_i) = \tilde{P}_i(v_i)$$

thus ensuring C^0 continuity. Moreover,

$$\tilde{P}'_{i-1}(v_i) = \alpha_1 \ldots \alpha_{i-1} P'_{i-1}(t_i)$$

and

$$\tilde{P}'_i(v_i) = \alpha_1 \ldots \alpha_i P'_i(t_i).$$

Because of (3.3), it can be concluded that

$$\tilde{P}'_{i-1}(v_i) = \tilde{P}'_i(v_i).$$

Thus, a linear reparametrization has been found that is C^1 continuous. For closed curves, the situation is different: a special condition has to be satisfied for a linear reparameterization to exist. Along with constraint (3.3), an additional constraint relating the first and last knots must be satisfied:

$$P_k(t_{k+1}) = P_0(t_0) \tag{3.4a}$$
$$P'_k(t_{k+1}) = \alpha_0 P'_0(t_0), \quad \alpha_0 > 0 \tag{3.4b}$$

When trying to reparameterize the spline, strictly increasing C^1 functions, f_i, are sought, that map each interval $[t_i, t_{i+1}]$ into some new interval $[v_i, v_{i+1}]$. Over each new interval, the new spline is defined to be:

$$\tilde{P}_i(v) = P_i(f_i^{-1}(v)).$$

If $\tilde{P}$ is required to be C^1 continuous then at each knot v_i, $1 \le i \le k-1$,

$$\tilde{P}'_{i-1}(v_i) = \tilde{P}'_i(v_i)$$

applying the chain rule, this is equivalent to

$$\frac{1}{f'_{i-1}(f_{i-1}^{-1}(v_i))} P'_{i-1}(f_{i-1}^{-1}(v_i)) = \frac{1}{f'_i(f_i^{-1}(v_i))} P'_i(f_i^{-1}(v_i))$$

Since $f_{i-1}^{-1}(v_i) = f_i^{-1}(v_i) = t_i$ and $P'_{i-1}(t_i) = \alpha_i P'_i(t_i)$,

$$\frac{f'_{i-1}(t_i)}{f'_i(t_i)} = \alpha_i.$$

The same reasoning makes (3.4) valid. So every set of functions leading to a C^1 parameterization must satisfy the following set of equations:

$$\frac{f'_0(t_1)}{f'_1(t_1)} = \alpha_1; \quad \frac{f'_1(t_2)}{f'_2(t_2)} = \alpha_2; \quad \ldots; \quad \frac{f'_{k-2}(t_{k-1})}{f'_{k-1}(t_{k-1})} = \alpha_{k-1}; \quad \frac{f'_{k-1}(t_k)}{f'_0(t_0)} = \alpha_0$$

Multiplying each side,

$$\frac{f'_{k-1}(t_k)}{f'_0(t_0)} \cdot \frac{f'_0(t_1)}{f'_1(t_1)} \cdot \ldots \cdot \frac{f'_{k-2}(t_{k-1})}{f'_{k-1}(t_{k-1})} = \alpha_0 \alpha_1 \ldots \alpha_{k-1}. \tag{3.5}$$

If each f_i is required to be linear, then f'_i is constant, thus (3.5) reduces to

$$\alpha_0 \alpha_1 \ldots \alpha_{k-1} = 1. \tag{3.6}$$

In summary, given a G^1 spline, there exists a linear reparameterization that yields C^1 continuity if and only if (3.6) holds. This does not exclude the existence of a non-linear function on the parameter providing the desired C^1 continuity, but this non-linearity is of little practical interest.

Definition 2. *A curve f is G^2 continuous at a given u iff its tangent vector and its curvature vector*

$$K(u) = \frac{f''(u) \times f'(u) \times f''(u)}{\|f'(u+h)\|^4} \tag{3.7}$$

are defined and continuous in u, where $\times$ is the vector cross product.

All that has been said about G^1 continuity may be extended to the G^2 case, and adequate examples can be shown. In [18], definitions of higher degree continuities have been proposed.

4 Regularization Techniques and Splines

Two related disciplines, computer graphics and computer vision, deal with images as their object of study. Computer graphics is concerned with the construction of a desired image from an adequate description. On the other hand, many tasks in computer vision are described as inverse problems, where the goal is to recover the description of the original physical process, given a discrete set of noisy samples. Often, inverse problems are ill-posed, in the sense that either a unique solution is not attainable, or the solution is extremely sensitive to small data perturbations. One approach to overcome such difficulties is to *regularize* the problem by requiring additional constraints for the intended solution, such as smoothness of derivatives [4, 33].

Spline models frequently arise as regularized solutions of ill-posed problems [4]. The method may be illustrated using regularization of the data fitting problem. Given a set of noisy samples, $\{y_i = f(t_i) + \varepsilon_i; i = 0, \ldots, n-1\}$, the best L_2 approximation for f in an appropriate function space S is the minimizer of the *sample mean square error*

$$\sum_{i=0}^{n-1} w_i (y_i - g(t_i))^2; \quad g \in S. \tag{4.1}$$

Here, the weights w_i may be related to the distribution of the residuals ε_i, as in $w_i = \sigma_i^{-2}$, or be set to one. Depending on the space S, the solution may not be unique or may be noise-sensitive, and fail to accurately estimate the true function f.

Usually, S is the space of functions with $m-1$ absolutely continuous derivatives and square-integrable mth derivative. In this case, a stable unique solution $\hat{g}$ results from minimizing

$$\int (g^{(m)})^2 dt$$

among all functions g such that

$$\sum_{i=0}^{n-1} w_i (y_i - g(t_i))^2 \leq K,$$

where K is a constant which controls the degree of smoothing [35].

An equivalent formulation [11] describes $\hat{g}$ as the minimizer of

$$\sum_{i=0}^{n-1} w_i (y_i - g(t_i))^2 + \lambda \int (g^{(m)})^2 dt, \tag{4.2}$$

where $\int (g^{(m)})^2 dt$ is a *stabilizer* that penalizes functions with non-smooth mth-derivatives.

The solution to both problems, for fixed K or λ is a *natural* mth-order polynomial spline with simple knots at the abscissae t_i; $i = 1, n-2$, and boundary conditions

$\hat{g}^{(j)}(t_i) = 0;\quad i = 0, n-1;\quad j = 0, \ldots, m-1.$

This curve is usually referred to as *smoothing spline*. Algorithmic details of its construction can be found in [35, 36].

A more general technique for data fitting [31] introduces the objective function

$$\sum_{i=0}^{n-1} w_i (y_i - g(t_i))^2 + \lambda \|Pf\|^2$$

where P is a differential operator, and $\|\cdot\|$ is a norm on S.

4.1 Choosing the Best Smoothing Parameter

As it was mentioned before, (4.2) has an unique solution for a fixed value of the smoothing parameter λ. When λ varies from 0 to $+\infty$, different solutions $\hat{g}_\lambda$ arise. If $\lambda = 0$, a subjacent noiseless signal is assumed, and the solution is the natural spline interpolant to the data. On the other hand, when $\lambda \to +\infty$, the least squares $m-1$-degree polynomial approximation is obtained [11]. Due to this diversity, it is relevant to search for the optimal value of λ.

A measure of the quality of the estimation $\hat{g}_\lambda$ is given by the *true mean square error*.

$$TMS(\lambda) = \sum_{i=0}^{n-1} (\hat{g}_\lambda(t_i) - f(t_i))^2.$$

The optimum value λ^* is defined as the minimizer of this expression. A different choice of λ will result in fitting the noise (*under-smoothing*), or in the loss of relevant curve information (*over-smoothing*).

When the deviation of the noise is known, it has been suggested [35] that the sample mean square error $S(\lambda^*)$ – given by (4.1) – should lie inside the confidence interval

$$1 - \sqrt{\left(\frac{2}{n}\right)} \sigma^2 \leq S(\lambda^*) \leq 1 + \sqrt{\left(\frac{2}{n}\right)} \sigma^2$$

but this criterium has been criticized because of over-smoothing [50]. Instead, choosing λ^* such that

$$S(\lambda^*) = k\sigma^2$$

with $k = 1.5, \ldots, 1.8$, is a criteria supported by a large set of Monte Carlo experiments [50].

In most practical cases, σ is not known. Cross-validation has been proposed [50] for estimating the best λ using the samples themselves, as the minimizer of

$$CVMSE(\lambda) = \sum_{k=0}^{n-1}(y_k - \hat{g}_\lambda^{|k|}(t_k))^2,$$

where $\hat{g}_\lambda^{|k|}$ is the smoothing spline for all but the *k*th-sample. A generalization of the *CVMSE* criterion (*GCVMSE*) is introduced in [8], and efficient methods for its computational implementation are presented in [12, 19, 44]. Several methods of choosing λ are compared in [48] for a simplified penalty term, and the *GCVMSE* criterion is criticized because of undersmoothing.

4.2 Smoothing Surfaces and Regularized Edge Detection

The approach exposed above has been extended to 3D data. *Thin plate* splines [49] are non-polynomial C^1 piecewise functions that minimize

$$\sum_{i=0}^{n-1}(z_i - f(x_i, y_i))^2 + \lambda \iint (f_{xx}^2 + 2f_{xy}^2 + f_{yy}^2) dx dy.$$

Rubber sheet or membrane C^0 splines were also defined when the stabilizer reduces to

$$\iint (f_x^2 + f_y^2) dx dy.$$

Unfortunately, these functionals impose global smoothing restrictions, and this may be a drawback if discontinuity detection is desired.

To attack this problem, edge finding can be merged into the optimization procedure, or a preprocessing step can be added. In [47], controlled-continuity constraints are introduced. These are weighting functions that regulate which derivatives are to be considered in the stabilizer functional, at a given point (x, y). As a special case, *thin plate surfaces under tension* arise when

$$\iint \rho(x, y)\{[1 - \tau(x, y)](f_x^2 + f_y^2) + \tau(x, y)(f_{xx}^2 + 2f_{xy}^2 + f_{yy}^2)\} dx dy$$

is adopted as the stabilizer. Here, $\rho(x, y)$ and $1 - \tau(x, y)$ measure surface cohesion and surface tension, respectively. They can be specified by a discontinuity estimation coprocess, or adding a third term to the objective functional. A discrete regularization scheme is adopted in [22] to detect discontinuity constraints at the (one-dimensional) data points. These restrictions are then embedded in the residual term of (4.2).

In [32] a convolutional spline filter is devised to solve

$$\sum_{t=0}^{n-1}(z_i - f(x_i, y_i))^2 + \lambda \iint \nabla^2 \overline{\nabla}(f)^2 dx dy$$

for regular data. This kernel is similar to a Gaussian filter and, in consequence, the zero crossings of the Laplacian of the filtered image allow the identification of edges as insufficient smoothing locations. Edges may then serve as boundaries for a second regularization step.

4.3 Further Details and Discussion

Regularizing splines have been used as a description method in early vision tasks such as surface reconstruction, optical flow computation and edge detection [31, 33]. Feature extraction has benefited from smoothing splines models in the computation of curvature [44] and derivatives [34], among others. Also, splines have been used for spectral density estimation [51], and meteorological modeling [49]. Moreover, there are additional developments of smoothing solutions for closed intervals [46] and *complete smoothing* – fitting with fixed derivatives at the boundary. A statistical point of view on regularization methods for ill-posed problems can be found in [25]. Regularization methods are related to Bayesian estimation [21] and the minimum description length (MDL) principle, although thus far no published record comparing this last method to regularization is known. Although smoothing techniques have proven its relevance when hard problems are being considered, its use in shape analysis suffers from a major drawback. As pointed out in [11], the smoothing spline needs more degrees of freedom than there are data points, to be able to cope with the stabilizer term. This is a disadvantage when compressing and reconstructing curves. Also, the selection of both the stabilizer and the λ parameter are somewhat dictated by mathematical convenience, rather than by independent physical knowledge of the process under study. Least-squares spline fitting is developed as an adequate alternative when a concise approximating description is needed.

5 Least Squares Approximation

5.1 Continuous Least Squares Approximation

Given a function f, its least-squares approximation with respect to a norm $\|\cdot\|$ in a linear space S of functions is obtained by minimizing the norm of the *residual*

$$\min_{g \in S} \| f - g \|. \tag{5.1}$$

The case of interest is the L_2 norm induced by the integral inner product

$$\langle s, t \rangle = \int_a^b s(u) t(u) du. \tag{5.2}$$

If $\{\phi_i\}_{i=0}^{N-1}$ is a basis of S, and $f: [a, b] \to R^2$ is a parametric curve, then the following matrix equation is the *least-squares* problem

$$HC = P \tag{5.3}$$

where P is a vector with coordinates $P_i = \langle f, \phi_i \rangle$, C is a vector with coordinates c_i, and H is the $N \times N$ *Gram* matrix with coefficients $H_{ij} = \langle \phi_i, \phi_j \rangle$. Since H is associated to the bilinear form $\langle x, y \rangle$, $x, y \in S$, it is a positive definite symmetric matrix. The least-squares solution is given by $\hat{f} = \sum_{i=0}^{N-1} c_i \phi_i$ [11].

When S is the space of n-degree polynomial splines over the knot sequence $[t_0, \ldots, t_k]^4$, one system for each coordinate is solved. When the B-spline basis is used, H has a band structure, because of the local support of the basis functions $N_{i,r}$. Moreover, if the knot sequence is uniform, i.e., $t_{i+1} = t_i + \Delta t$, (2.5) holds and it follows that $H_{(i+1)(j+1)} = H_{ij} = H_{i-j}$. Hence, H is a Toeplitz matrix.

For closed curves the matrix is "almost" banded, since at the top right and bottom left corners there are non-zero elements. When the knot sequence is uniform, H is also a circulant matrix.

The system in (5.3) is a non-singular system of linear equations, and it can be solved by any of the well-known methods. However, as it can be seen in [37], the system is ill-conditioned for large values of n, so special care must be taken when working with high-order splines.

5.2 Discrete Least Squares Approximation

The situation here is similar but, instead of a continuous curve, a set $\{Y_j\}_{j=1}^m$ of data points is now given. It will be assumed that these are the values of an (unknown) function f at a increasing sequence of arbitrary points $\{u_j\}_{j=1}^m$ belonging to the interval $[a, b]$

$$Y_j = f(u_j), \quad j = 1, \ldots, m. \tag{5.4}$$

A different inner product must be considered

$$\langle s, t \rangle = \sum_{j=1}^m s(u_j) t(u_j) w_j. \tag{5.5}$$

The w_j are *weights* chosen so as to allow this sum to approximate the integral inner product (quadrature formula), if desired. Often, they are all set equal to one.

The normal equations (5.3) are the same, but with the new inner product definition

$$H_{ij} = \sum_{r=1}^m \phi_i(u_r) \phi_j(u_r) w_r \tag{5.6}$$

$$P_i = \sum_{r=1}^m \phi_i(u_r) Y_r w_r. \tag{5.7}$$

---

[4] with $a = t_n$, $b = t_{k-n}$ in the open case and $a = t_0$, $b = t_k$ in the closed case.

Again, when S is the space of n-degree polynomial splines over the knot sequence $[t_0, \ldots, t_k]$, H has a band structure, because of the local support of the basis functions $N_{i,r}$. A system for each dimension is solved.

The elements of matrix H are computed using the recurrence relation (2.2) for the values u_r of the parameter.

It is worth noting that if the data point parameters u_j are not chosen so that there is at least one in each interval $[t_i, t_{i+n+1}]$ one or more columns of H will be equal to zero, resulting in non-uniqueness of the solution. On the other hand, if the condition stated above holds, then a unique solution exists [11].

Unlike the continuous case, the Toeplitz structure of H for uniform knot sequences, is not ensured. But, in the closed curve case, distributing uniformly the data point parameters along the domain, and enforcing the following conditions

$$t_{i+1} = t_i + \Delta t \tag{5.8a}$$

$$u_{j+1} = u_j + \Delta u \tag{5.8b}$$

$$\frac{\Delta t}{\Delta u} = p \in 1, 2, 3, \ldots. \tag{5.8c}$$

H is not only Toeplitz but also circulant. This distribution of the data points is not unrealistic. For instance, when the data points are the result of digitizing a continuous contour, it is quite reasonable to suppose that they are uniform samples of a function f that describes the curve with constant speed.

Other parameterizations are possible. For instance, *chord-length parameterization* profits from the geometry of the problem [7], setting

$$\Delta u_i = \gamma \, d(Y_i, Y_{i+1}), \quad 1 \leq i \leq m$$

with

$$\gamma = \frac{u_m - u_1}{\sum_1^m d(Y_i, Y_{i+1})}$$

and $d(A, B)$ being the Euclidean distance between A and B. Also, heuristic criteria guided by curve segmentation schemes based on critical points detection have been proposed [26].

5.3 Continuous vs. Discrete Approximation

When fitting with splines a number of decisions have to be made: class of splines to be used: polynomial, rational, etc., degree of the pieces and number and location of the knots. Each of these decisions requires serious thought and there is no exact answer to them yet, although a plethora of criteria have been suggested [3, 6, 13, 14, 16, 23, 24, 29, 30, 40, 41].

Even after resolving these questions, one is still confronted with choosing between two different fitting techniques, discrete and continous. It is obvious that when an analytic expression of the function to be approximated is available, continuous fitting should be used. But what does one do when discrete samples of the function are all that is available? This is the most common situation in digital image processing and other applications.

The simplest solution is to use discrete fitting. But it suffers from some drawbacks, the most serious being where to locate the abscissae of the samples. Finding a smart way to convert the samples into an analytic function would allow to use continuous fitting, and thus overcome the above mentioned problem. The most straightforward way is to join each pair of contiguous samples by a line. It should be noted however that this does not eliminate the problem of locating the preimages of the samples, since now the speed with which each line segment is traversed determines the "moment of time" at which the samples are visited.

Experiments were carried out fitting uniform cubic B-splines over the knot sequence $[0, 1, \ldots, k]$ to samples extracted from the contour of a Chinese character, using both techniques, discrete and continuous.

In the discrete case, uniform sampling was used. Similarly, in the continuous case samples were uniformly interpolated, at a distance $1/p$, with

$$p = \frac{\#\,of\,samples}{\#\,of\,pieces\,of\,the\,spline}.$$

In order to be able to compare the errors obtained in both cases, a normalized measure: the ratio between the fitting error and the norm of the approximated function, was used.

$$err_{disc} = \frac{\sum_{i=1}^{kp}(Y_i - f(u_i))^2}{\sum_{i=1}^{kp} Y_i^2}$$

$$err_{cont} = \frac{\int_0^k (y(t) - f(t))^2\,dt}{\int_0^k y(t)^2\,dt}.$$

The results of fitting using 40 pieces to 200 samples of the contour of a Chinese character may be observed in Fig. 1. Differences are undistinguishable to the eye and the normalized errors are very similar:

$err_{disc} = 0.000597\ldots$ $err_{cont} = 0.000514\ldots$

The algorithmic complexity of both methods is the same. For the discrete case, C can be computed as a sum over all samples of the product between the ith basis function and the approximated function:

$$c_i = \sum_{j=ip}^{(i+n+1)p-1} \phi_i(u_j) Y_j.$$

For the continuous case, since the function is piecewise linear with breakpoints $u_j = a + \frac{j}{p}, j = 0, \ldots, kp - 1$, c_i can be computed as

Splines and Spline Fitting Revisited

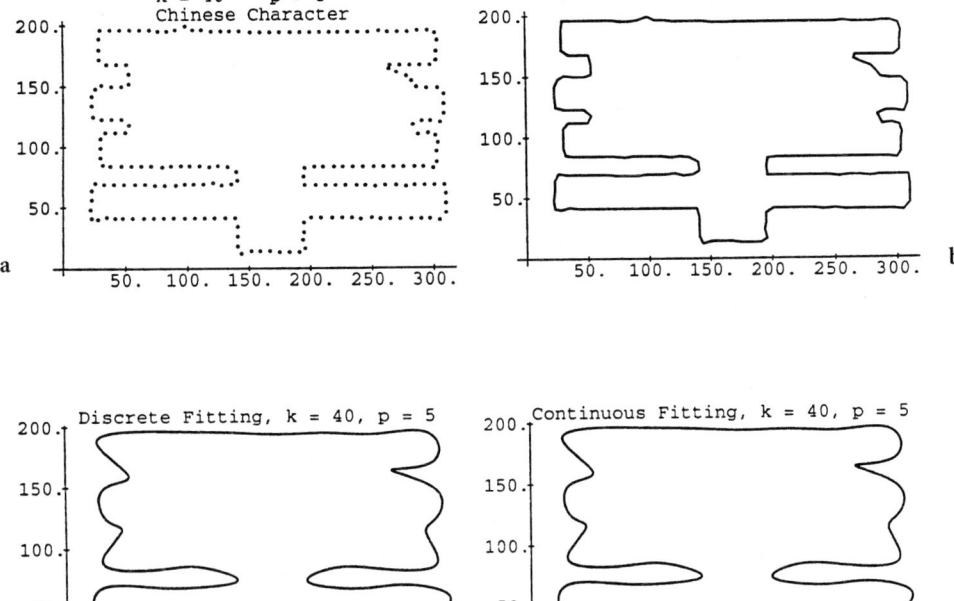

Fig. 1. Continuous vs. discrete approximation: **a** original samples; **b** linear interpolation of the samples; **c** discrete approximation to samples in **a**; **d** continuous approximation to function in **b**

$$c_i = \sum_{j=ip}^{(i+n+1)p-1} \int_{u_j}^{u_{j+1}} \phi_i(t)(a_j t + b_j)dt.$$

Knowing ϕ_i, this integral can be computed beforehand, leaving as parameters a_j and b_j, the coefficients of the line joining the samples Y_j and Y_{j+1}.

So, which method should be chosen? Having a sounder mathematical basis, the continuous technique should be preferred. Besides, in the discrete method, the norm induced by the inner product employed is not in general a true norm, but a *seminorm*, since there may be non-zero functions f in the spline space with $\|f\| = 0$. This apparent disadvantage is nevertheless easily overcome by choosing appropiately the data point parameters u_j: if there is at least one in each interval $[t_i, t_{i+n+1}]$ the seminorm will be a true norm, and there will be a unique solution to the least squares problem [11].

On the other hand, when p, the ratio between the number of samples and the number of spline pieces is small (no greater than 2), discrete fitting should be preferred. This is because when $p = 1$, all samples are exactly interpolated by the discrete technique [11], while in the continuous case the approximated function does not belong to the space of approximating splines, causing nonzero error.

5.4 Invariant Properties of Least Squares Uniform Spline Fitting

Least-squares B-spline approximation is invariant to affine maps (i.e., translations, scalings and rotations) of the function f to be fitted. In each case, a new system

$$HC' = P' \tag{5.9}$$

is required, where the meaning of each term is the same that in (5.3)[5]. These facts should not be confused with Property 4 in Sect. 2.2, where no input data is considered.

Translational Invariance. *Let Ψ be a constant function $\Psi(u) = \psi$, $\forall u$, and $\bar{\psi}$ a constant k-element vector. Then, to obtain the least-squares approximation of a translation $f' = f + \Psi$, the right hand side of (5.9) is given by:*

$$P'_i = \langle N^r_i(u), f' \rangle = \langle N^r_i(u), f \rangle + \langle N^r_i(u), \Psi \rangle = P_i + \psi \tag{5.10}$$

Then, from the original system,

$$HC' = P' = P + \bar{\psi} = HC + \bar{\psi} \rightarrow H(C' - C) = \bar{\psi}$$

But $\bar{\psi}$ is an eigenvector of H:

$$(H\bar{\psi})_i = \psi \sum_{j=0}^{k-1} H_{ij} = \psi \sum_{j=0}^{k-1} \langle N_i, N_j \rangle = \psi \left\langle N_i, \sum_{j=0}^{k-1} N_j \right\rangle = \langle N_i, \bar{\psi} \rangle = \psi$$

Hence, $C' - C = \bar{\psi} \rightarrow C' = C + \psi$.

Scaling Invariance. *If the input function is a scaled version of f, the rhs of (5.9) turns to be:*

$$P'_i = \langle N_i, af \rangle = a \langle N_i, f \rangle = aP_i$$

Then,

$$HC' = \mathrm{diag}(a, \ldots, a)P = \mathrm{diag}(a, \ldots, a)HC \rightarrow$$
$$C' = H^{-1}\mathrm{diag}(a, \ldots, a)HC = \mathrm{diag}(a, \ldots, a)C$$

Rotational Invariance. *In this case a parametric curve $f = [f^1, f^2]$ has been rotated by a matrix $R = R(\theta) = [[\cos\theta\ \sin\theta], [-\sin\theta, \cos\theta]]$ yielding a new curve f'. The dimension of both C' and P' in (5.9) is $k \times 2$. The rhs is given by:*

$$P'_{io} = \langle N_i, f^1\cos\theta - f^2\sin\theta \rangle$$
$$= \langle N_i, f^1 \rangle\cos\theta - \langle N_i, f^2 \rangle\sin\theta$$
$$= P_{io}\cos\theta - P_{il}\sin\theta$$

$$P'_{il} = \langle N_i, f^1\sin\theta - f^2\cos\theta \rangle$$
$$= P_{io}\sin\theta - P_{il}\cos\theta$$

Hence,

---

[5] In the first two cases, each coordinate can be dealt with separately.

$$P'_i = P_i R$$

and

$$HC' = P' = PR = HCR \rightarrow C' = CR$$

Applying Property 4 of Sect. 2.2 in each of the previous caes, it follows that the B-spline least-squares fitting of a function is invariant to its arbitrary affine mapping.

A similar analysis can be made for uniform least-squares fitting using a discrete inner product, relying on the fact that

$$\sum_j N_i(t_j) = 1$$

with j in a period of period of N_i.

6 Choosing the Best Starting Point

Given an arbitrary parametric closed curve β on the plane, there exist many shifted versions of β describing the same locus. Let f be the least-squares approximation of β on the spline function space S over the knot sequence $[a = t_0, \ldots, t_k = b]$. The aim of this section is to study the solutions of the fitting problem for the shifted versions of β, and to choose the one with the least residual.

6.1 Continuous Case

Definition 3. *The shift of a periodic curve $\beta(t)$ with period $b - a$ is*

$$\beta_\varepsilon(t) = \beta(t - \varepsilon). \tag{6.1}$$

Proposition 2. *If f is the least squares approximation in S to β and f_ε is a spline defined over the same knot sequence[6], then the least-squares approximation in S to $\beta_\varepsilon(t)$ will be f_ε.*

Proof. Suppose there exists $g \in S$ such that

$$\|g - \beta_\varepsilon\| < \|f_\varepsilon - \beta_\varepsilon\|.$$

Notice that

$$g_{-\varepsilon}(t) = g(t + \varepsilon)$$

is a spline over the knot sequence $[t_0 - \varepsilon, \ldots, t_k - \varepsilon]$ but, by hypothesis, this knot sequence is the same as $[t_0, \ldots, t_{k+1}]$; thus $g_{-\varepsilon} \in S$.

---

[6] f_ε is always a spline, but over the knot sequence $[t_0 + \varepsilon, \ldots, t_k + \varepsilon]$.

It will now be shown that $||g - \beta_\varepsilon||^2 = ||g_{-\varepsilon} - \beta||^2$ and that $||f_\varepsilon - \beta_\varepsilon||^2 = ||f - \beta||^2$, contradicting the fact that f is the least squares approximation to β in S.

$$||f_\varepsilon - \beta_\varepsilon||^2 = \int_a^b (f_\varepsilon(t) - \beta_\varepsilon(t))^2 \, dt = \int_a^b (f(t-\varepsilon) - \beta(t-\varepsilon))^2 \, dt.$$

Making the replacement $u = t - \varepsilon$ and remembering that $(f - \beta)$ is periodical,

$$||f_\varepsilon - \beta_\varepsilon||^2 = \int_{a-\varepsilon}^{b-\varepsilon} (f(u) - \beta(u))^2 \, du = \int_a^b (f(u) - \beta(u))^2 \, du = ||f - \beta||^2.$$

Analogously,

$$||g - \beta_\varepsilon||^2 = \int_a^b (g(t) - \beta_\varepsilon(t))^2 \, dt = \int_a^b (g_{-\varepsilon}(t-\varepsilon) - \beta(t-\varepsilon))^2 \, dt$$
$$= \int_{a-\varepsilon}^{b-\varepsilon} (g_{-\varepsilon}(u) - \beta(u))^2 \, du = \int_a^b (g_{-\varepsilon}(u) - \beta(u))^2 \, du$$
$$= ||g_{-\varepsilon} - \beta||^2.$$

If different shifted versions of β are chosen the same geometrical entity is still being described, nevertheless the aproximation error may vary. Therefore, the goal is to find:

$$\min_{0 \leq \varepsilon \leq b-a} ||f_\varepsilon - \beta_\varepsilon||^2. \tag{6.2}$$

Expanding out this norm:

$$||f_\varepsilon - \beta_\varepsilon||^2 = ||\beta_\varepsilon||^2 + ||f_\varepsilon||^2 - 2\langle \beta_\varepsilon, f_\varepsilon \rangle. \tag{6.3}$$

The right hand terms are:

- The norm of β_ε is

$$||\beta_\varepsilon||^2 = \int_a^b (\beta_\varepsilon(t))^2 \, dt = \int_a^b (\beta(t-\varepsilon))^2 \, dt$$
$$= \int_{a-\varepsilon}^{b-\varepsilon} (\beta(u))^2 \, du = \int_a^b (\beta(u))^2 \, du = ||\beta||^2$$

- f_ε is the least squares approximation to β_ε, therefore f_ε is given by

$$f_\varepsilon = \sum_{i=0}^{N-1} c_{\varepsilon_i} \Phi_i$$

where c_ε is the vector of points obtained by solving the linear system(s) of equations:

$$Hc_\varepsilon = P_\varepsilon$$

with $H_{ij} = \langle \Phi_i, \Phi_j \rangle$ and $P_{\varepsilon_i} = \langle \Phi_i, \beta_\varepsilon \rangle$

Therefore,

$$\|f_\varepsilon\|^2 = \left\langle \sum_i c_{\varepsilon_i} \Phi_i, \sum_j c_{\varepsilon_j} \Phi_j \right\rangle = \sum_i c_{\varepsilon_i} \sum_j c_{\varepsilon_j} \langle \Phi_i, \Phi_j \rangle$$
$$= \sum_i c_{\varepsilon_i} \sum_j c_{\varepsilon_j} H_{ij} = \sum_i c_{\varepsilon_i} (Hc_\varepsilon)_i \quad (6.4)$$
$$= \sum_i c_{\varepsilon_i} P_{\varepsilon_i} = c_\varepsilon^t P_\varepsilon$$

- The inner product between β_ε and f_ε is

$$\langle \beta_\varepsilon, f_\varepsilon \rangle = \left\langle \beta_\varepsilon, \sum_i c_{\varepsilon_i} \Phi_i \right\rangle = \sum_i c_{\varepsilon_i} \langle \beta_\varepsilon, \Phi_i \rangle$$
$$= \sum_i c_{\varepsilon_i} P_{\varepsilon_i} = c_\varepsilon^t P_\varepsilon. \quad (6.5)$$

From (6.4) and (6.5) it can be concluded that

$$\|f_\varepsilon\|^2 = \langle \beta_\varepsilon, f_\varepsilon \rangle,$$

and therefore,

$$\|f_\varepsilon - \beta_\varepsilon\|^2 = \|\beta\|^2 - \|f_\varepsilon\|^2. \quad (6.6)$$

The original problem (6.2) now reduces to finding

$$\max_{0 \le \varepsilon < b-a} \|f_\varepsilon\|^2 = \max_{0 \le \varepsilon < b-a} c_\varepsilon^t P_\varepsilon. \quad (6.7)$$

6.1.1 A Special Case: Uniform Knot Sequences

When the knot sequence $[t_0, \ldots, t_k]$ is *uniform*, that is, when

$$t_{i+1} = t_i + \Delta, \quad \text{with } \Delta = \frac{b-a}{k}$$

the search space for the best starting point may be significantly reduced.

When the shift ε is an integer multiple of the knot spacing Δ

$$\varepsilon = q\Delta$$

then the knot sequence $[t_0 - \varepsilon, \ldots, t_k - \varepsilon]$ is a periodic shift of $[t_0, \ldots, t_k]$. Therefore the conditions of proposition 2 are satisfied, and the best approximation for β_ε is f_ε. The error in this approximation is $\|f_\varepsilon - \beta_\varepsilon\|^2$ which is the same as the original error $\|f - \beta\|^2$.

Consider now an arbitrary shift ε, with $0 \le \varepsilon < b-a$; there exist integer q and rational r, $0 \le r < \Delta$, such that

$$\varepsilon = q\Delta + r.$$

By the above reasoning, shifting the curve β_r by $q\Delta$ yields the same error as when β_r is not shifted.

Now, shifting β_r by $q\Delta$ is equivalent to shifting the original curve β by $r + q\Delta = \varepsilon$. Therefore, the minimum error will be achieved somewhere between 0 and Δ.

Hence, for **uniform** knot sequences with knot-spacing Δ the problem (6.7) reduces to finding

$$\max_{0 \leq \varepsilon < \Delta} \|f_\varepsilon\|^2 = \max_{0 \leq \varepsilon < \Delta} c_\varepsilon^t P_\varepsilon = \max_{0 \leq \varepsilon < \Delta} P_\varepsilon^t H^{-1} P_\varepsilon. \qquad (6.8)$$

6.1.2 Numerical Experiments

A uniform cubic splice over the knot sequence $[0, 1, \ldots, 12]$ was fitted to a periodic parameterization with period $T = 12$ of a 12 unit square, given by:

$$\beta(t) = \begin{cases} (4t, 0) & 0 \leq t < 3 \\ (12, 4t - 12) & 3 \leq t < 6 \\ (36 - 4t, 12) & 6 \leq t < 9 \\ (0, 48 - 4t) & 9 \leq t < 12. \end{cases}$$

Approximations were computed to different shifted versions of the square.

As the knot sequence was uniform, only values of ε in $[0, 1]$ were considered (see Sect. 6.1.1). As can be seen in Fig. 2b, the fittings are noticeably different, depending on the starting point of the parameterization. Figure 2c shows a graph of the fitting error as a function of the shift. In this case, the minimum error is obtained for $\varepsilon = 0$, i.e., the original curve; this by no means indicates that the original curve always gives the best fitting, it is rather a coincidence probably arising from the fact that the irregularities (corners) of the approximated curve are located at parameter values which are also knots (0, 3, 6 and 9).

The minimum error fitting looks more appealing to the eye also, being less oscillating than the other example ($\varepsilon = \frac{1}{3}$). It also better models the corners of the square.

The experiments suggest there is no a-priori way of knowing which starting point yields the best fit. Thus, it is better to try fittings for different values of ε and choose the one yielding the minimum error. A smarter technique than blind search could be applied, like a gradient descent method on ε, since the error function is smooth.

6.2 Discrete Case

Unlike the continuous case, a *known* function β which can be shifted so as to obtain the best approximation is unavailable. A vector of **samples** given by

Splines and Spline Fitting Revisited

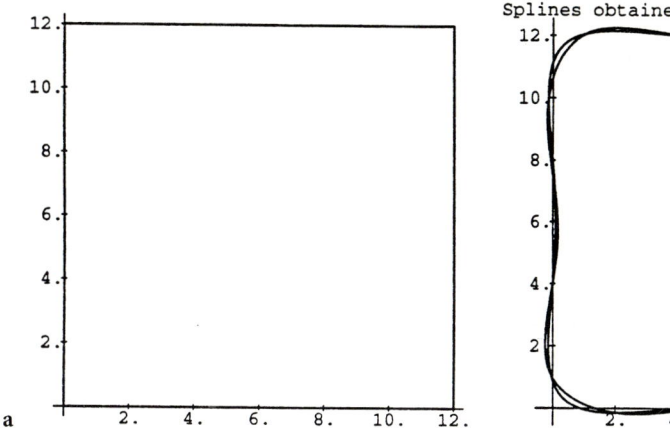
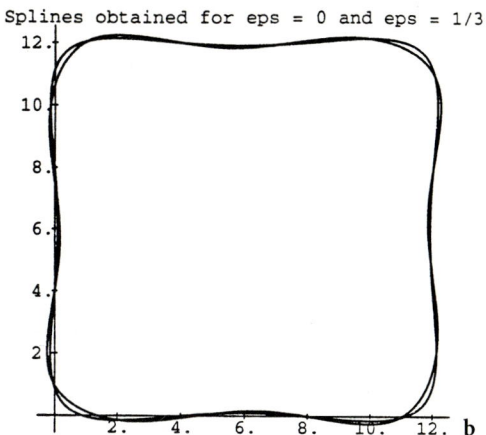
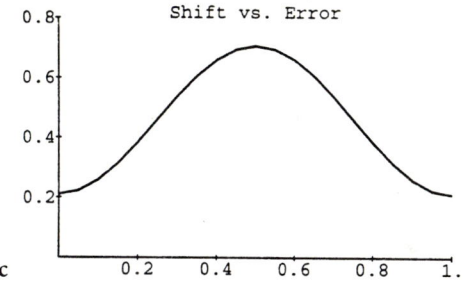

Fig. 2. Dependency of the fitting on the starting point: **a** original curve; **b** fittings for $\varepsilon = 0$ and $\varepsilon = \frac{1}{3}$; **c** approximation error as a function of the shift

$$\mathbf{y} = (y_1, \ldots, y_m)$$

are supposed to be the values of an (*unknown*) periodical function β at a nondecreasing sequence of points $\{u_i\}_{i=1}^m$ in the interval $[a, b]$.

Since the function being approximatied is unknown, there is no reason that the least-squares approximation obtained for **y** will be any better than the approximation of the same samples for a shifted version of the vector **y**:

$$\mathbf{y}_l = (y_{l+1}, \ldots, y_m, y_1, \ldots, y_l).$$

The elements of $\mathbf{y}_l$ are given by:

$$y_{li} = y_{(i+l-1)(\bmod m)+1} = \begin{cases} y_{i+l}, & 1 \leq i \leq m - l \\ y_{i+l-m}, & \text{otherwise.} \end{cases} \tag{6.9}$$

Again, $\mathbf{y}_l$ are considered to be samples of an unknown periodical function β_{yl},

$$y_{li} = \beta_{yl}(u_i).$$

If f_{y_l} is the best approximation is S for the vector $\mathbf{y}_l$, the aim is to find

$$\min_{0\le l<m}|| f_{y_l} - \beta_{y_l} ||^2 = \min_{0\le l<m}\sum_{i=1}^{m}(f_{y_l}(u_i)- y_{l_i})^2 w_i. \qquad (6.10)$$

The search is restricted to $0, \ldots, m-1$, since shifting m times the vector **y** yields **y** again.

As in the continuous case,

$$||f_{y_l} - \beta_{y_l}||^2 = ||\beta_{y_l}||^2 + ||f_{y_l}||^2 - 2\langle\beta_{y_l}, f_{y_l}\rangle. \qquad (6.11)$$

Looking at the right hand terms, the following results, analogous to the continuous case, will hold if the inner product weights w_i are all equal to a constant w.

- The norm of the (unknown) function β_{y_l} is equal to the norm of β:

$$\begin{aligned}
|| \beta_{y_l} ||^2 &= \sum_{i=1}^{m}(\beta_{y_l}(u_i))^2 w_i = w\sum_{i=1}^{m}(y_{(i+l-1)(\mathrm{mod}\,m)+1})^2 \\
&= w\sum_{i=1}^{m-l}(y_{i+l})^2 + w\sum_{i=m-l+1}^{m}(y_{i+l-m})^2 \\
&= w\sum_{j=l+1}^{m}(y_j)^2 + w\sum_{j=1}^{l}(y_j)^2 \\
&= \sum_{j=1}^{m}(y_j)^2 w_j = || \beta ||^2
\end{aligned}$$

- f_{y_l} is the least squares approximation to β_{y_l} in S, therefore f_{y_l} is given by

$$f_{yl} = \sum_{i=0}^{k}c_{li}\Phi_i$$

where c_l is the vector of points obtained by solving the linear system(s) of equations:

$$Hc_l = P_l$$

with

$$H_{ij} = \langle\Phi_i, \Phi_j\rangle = w\sum_{r=1}^{m}\Phi_i(u_r)\Phi_j(u_r)$$

and

$$P_{li} = \langle\Phi_i, \beta_{y_l}\rangle$$

Therefore,

$$\begin{aligned}
|| f_{y_l} ||^2 &= \left\langle\sum_i c_{l_i}\Phi_i, \sum_j c_{l_j}\Phi_j\right\rangle = \sum_i c_{l_i}\sum_j c_{l_j}\langle\Phi_i, \Phi_j\rangle \\
&= \sum_i c_{l_i}\sum_j c_{l_j}H_{ij} = \sum_i c_{l_i}(Hc_l)_i \\
&= \sum_i c_{l_i}P_{l_i} = c_l^t P_l.
\end{aligned} \qquad (6.12)$$

Splines and Spline Fitting Revisited

- Again,

$$\langle \beta_{y_i}, f_{y_i} \rangle = \left\langle \beta_{y_i}, \sum_i c_{l_i} \Phi_i \right\rangle$$
$$= \sum_i c_{l_i} \langle \beta_{l_i}, \Phi_i \rangle = \sum_i c_{l_i} P_{l_i} = c_l^t P_l \quad (6.13)$$

Therefore,

$$\|f_{y_i} - \beta_{y_i}\|^2 = \|\beta\|^2 - \|f_{y_i}\|^2 \quad (6.14)$$

The original problem (6.10) now reduces to finding

$$\max_{0 \le l < m} \|f_{y_i}\|^2 = \max_{0 \le l < m} c_l^t P_l = \max_{0 \le l < m} P_l^t H^{-1} P_l. \quad (6.15)$$

6.2.1 A Special Case: Uniform Knot Sequences and Uniform Sampling

This section examines what happens when the knot sequence is uniform. The samples y are assumed to be taken uniformly, (that is, when the points u_j at which the unknown curve β is sampled are uniformly spaced) and, between knots, the same number of sample points found.

More specifically, the case:

$$t_{i+1} = t_i + \Delta t, \quad \Delta t = \frac{b-a}{k}$$
$$u_{i+1} = u_i + \Delta u, \quad \Delta u = \frac{b-a}{m} \quad (6.16)$$
$$\frac{\Delta t}{\Delta u} = p \in 1, 2, 3, \ldots$$

will be studied, where k is the number of pieces of the curve (i.e., number of knots minus one). As it was stated in Sect. 5, the assumption that the sequence $\{u_j\}_{j=1}^m$ is uniform is adequate in many practical cases.

It will be shown, using (6.16), that the minimum error will occur in the integer interval [0, p-1], proving there is no need to search over the whole integer interval [0, m-1] (see (6.15)). Since $m = pk$, it turns out that the search space is reduced $k - 1$ times.

Proposition 3. *If f is the spline in S that best approximates the samples $y = (y_1, \ldots, y_m)$, then f_{y_p}, the spline over the same space S which best approximates*

$$y_p = (y_{p+1}, \ldots, y_m, y_1, \ldots, y_p)$$

is given by

$$f_{y_p}(t) = f(t + \Delta t); \text{ where } \Delta t = p \Delta u, p \in \{1, 2, 3, \ldots\}. \tag{6.17}$$

Proof. 1. f_{y_p} is a spline over the knot sequence

$$[t_0 - \Delta t, \ldots, t_{k-1} - \Delta t, t_k - \Delta t] = [t_{k-1} - (b-a), t_0, \ldots, t_{k-2}, t_{k-1}].$$

Since f_{y_p} is periodic, this turns out to be the same knot sequence as

$$[t_0, t_1, \ldots, t_{k-1}, t_k].$$

2. The error of the approximation is:

$$\sum_{i=1}^{m}(f_{y_p}(u_i) - y_{P_i})^2 = \sum_{i=1}^{m-p}(f(u_i + \Delta t) - y_{i+p})^2$$
$$+ \sum_{i=m-p+1}^{m}(f(u_i + \Delta t) - y_{i+p-m})^2.$$

Now, if $1 \leq i \leq m - p$,

$$f(u_i + \Delta t) = f(u_i + p\Delta u) = f(u_{i+p})$$

and, if $m - p < i \leq m$,

$$\begin{aligned} f(u_i - \Delta t) &= f(u_i + p\Delta u) \\ &= f(u_i + p\Delta u - (b-a)) \\ &= f(u_i + p\Delta u - m\Delta u) \\ &= f(u_i + (p-m)\Delta u) \\ &= f(u_{i+p-m}). \end{aligned}$$

Thus,

$$\sum_{i=1}^{m}(f_{y_p}(u_i) - y_{P_i})^2 = \sum_{i=1}^{m-p}(f(u_{i+p}) - y_{i+p})^2$$
$$+ \sum_{i=m-p+1}^{m}(f(u_{i+p-m}) - y_{i+p-m})^2$$
$$= \sum_{j=p+1}^{m}(f(u_j) - y_j)^2$$
$$+ \sum_{l=1}^{p}(f(u_l) - y_l)^2$$
$$= \sum_{j=1}^{m}(f(u_j) - y_j)^2.$$

Thus, the error obtained approximating y_p with f_p is *equal* to the optimal error obtained approximating **y** with splines in S.

3. Suppose there exists $g \in S$ such that

$$\sum_{i=1}^{m}(g(u_i)-\mathbf{y}_{\mathrm{p}_i})^2 < \sum_{i=1}^{m}(f_{y_p}(u_i)-\mathbf{y}_{\mathrm{p}_i})^2.$$

Define h by $h(t) = g(t - \Delta t)$. It is easy to see that h is a spline over the *same* knot sequence as g and $h \in S$.

If $1 \le i \le m - p$,

$$g(u_i) - \mathbf{y}_{\mathrm{p}_i} = h(u_i + \Delta t) - \mathbf{y}_{i+p} = h(u_i + p\Delta u) - \mathbf{y}_{i+p} = h(u_{i+p}) - \mathbf{y}_{i+p}$$

and, if $m - p < i \le m$

$$\begin{aligned}g(u_i) &= h(u_i + \Delta t) = h(u_i + p\Delta u) = h(u_i + p\Delta u - m\Delta u) \\ &= h(u_i + (p-m)\Delta u) = h(u_{i+p-m}).\end{aligned}$$

Thus,

$$\begin{aligned}\sum_{i=1}^{m}(g_{y_p}(u_i)-\mathbf{y}_{\mathrm{p}_i})^2 &= \sum_{i=1}^{m-p}(h(u_{i+p})-\mathbf{y}_{i+p})^2 \\ &\quad + \sum_{i=m-p+1}^{m-p}(h(u_{i+p-m})-\mathbf{y}_{i+p-m})^2 \\ &= \sum_{j=p+1}^{m}(h(u_j)-\mathbf{y}_j)^2 \\ &\quad + \sum_{l=1}^{p}(h(u_l)-\mathbf{y}_l)^2 \\ &= \sum_{j=1}^{m}(h(u_j)-\mathbf{y}_j)^2.\end{aligned}$$

If g existed, there would be another spline in S which approximated y better that f does. This is impossible, since f is the best approximation by definition. Thus, f_{y_p} is the least-squares approximation to the samples y_p.

Consider now an arbitrary shift $l = sp + r$, with $0 \le r \le p$; by the above reasoning, shifting the vector y_r by sp yields the same error as when y_r is not shifted. Therefore, as in the continuous case, the search space is reduced.

To summarize, for **uniform** knot sequences with knot-spacing Δt and uniform sample points separated by Δu, with $\frac{\Delta t}{\Delta u} = p \in \{1, 2, 3, \ldots\}$, finding the best fitting over all starting points reduces to finding

$$\max_{0 \le l < p} \| f_l \|^2 = \max_{0 \le l < p} c_l^t P_l. \tag{6.18}$$

6.2.2 Numerical Experiments: Discrete Fitting on Real Images

To see how the approximation varies as a function of the starting point on a real object, the following experiment was performed. Samples were extracted from the contour of a Chinese character and an approximation was made, using uniform cubic **B**-splines over the knot sequence $[0, 1, \ldots, k]$.

Figure 3 shows the results of fitting a spline with $k = 50$ pieces to 1500 samples, yielding a total of $p = 30$ samples per piece. In Fig. 3a the original samples are displayed, whereas in Fig. 3b the fittings which produced the minimum and maximum errors are shown. The differences between both approximations are very noticeable.

Figure 3b plots the fitting error as a function of the shift of the original sample vector. Note that the shape of this function is similar to the corresponding shift vs. error plot in the continuous fitting (Fig. 3c). The ratio between the minimum and maximum squared errors is approximately

$$\frac{err_{min}}{err_{max}} = 0.826 \ldots$$

This confirms the variability of an approximation to the same geometrical entity, depending on the starting point of the description of this object.

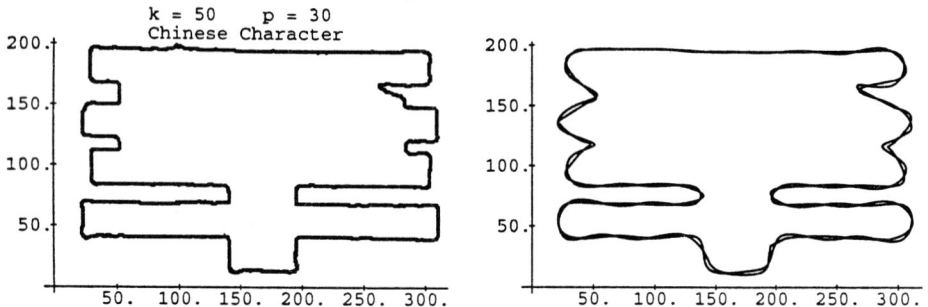

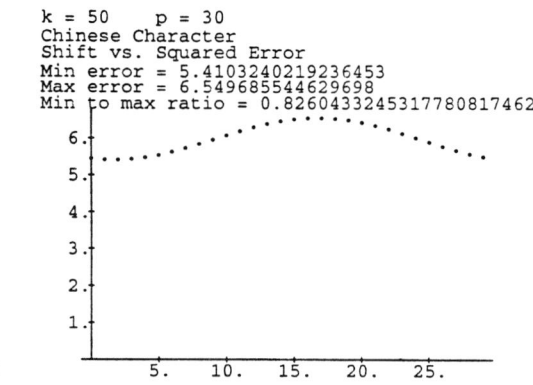

Fig. 3. Dependency of the fitting on the starting point: **a** original samples; **b** minimum (shift = 2) and maximum (shift = 17) error fittings; **c** approximation error as a function of the shift

7 Conclusions

This work was motivated by the increasing applications of spline fitting in shape analysis tasks. Although the literature on this subject is quite extensive, it seemed a good idea to collect the most relevant matters on fitting as well on splines in general.

A question never addressed in the surveyed literature was whether fitting a closed curve varies because of starting point for a given parameterization. It turns out to be that it *does* depend on the starting point, as can be seen in Sect. 6. There, it was shown that it is not enough to fit the original samples or continuous curve; instead, to obtain the best fit, it is necessary to consider all the possible shifts of the data. It was seen that there exist some simplifications for particular cases, like uniform knot spacing. Nevertheless, a good heuristics still has to be devised in order to help find the best approximation. A gradient descent method might be a promising technique for the continuous case.

References

[1] R. Barnhill and R. Riesenfeld, editors. *Computer Aided Geometric Design*. Academic Press, 1974.
[2] P. Barry and R. Goldman. What is the natural generalization of a Bézier curve? In T. Lyche and L. Shumaker, editors, *Curves and Surfaces for Computer Aided Geometric Design*, pages 71–85, San Diego, CA, 1989. Academic Press, Inc.
[3] R. Bartels, J. Beatty, and B. Barsky. *An Introduction to Splines for use in Computer Graphics and Geometric Modeling*. Morgan Kaufmann Publishers, Inc, Los Altos, CA, 1987.
[4] M. Bertero, T.A. Poggio, and V. Torre. Ill posed problems in early vision. *Proceedings of the IEEE*, 76(8):869–889, 1988. Special Issue on Computer Vision.
[5] P. Bézier. Mathematical and practical possibilities of UNISURF. In Barnhill and Riesenfeld [1], pages 127–152.
[6] W. Boehm. On cubics: A survey. *CGIP*, 19:201–226, 1982.
[7] W. Böhm, G. Farin, and J. Kahmann. A survey of curve and surface methods in CAGD. *CAGD*, 1:1–60, 1984.
[8] P. Craven and G. Wahba. Smoothing noisy data with spline functions. *Numer. Math.*, 31:377–403, 1979.
[9] G. Dahlquist and Å. Björk. *Numerical Methods*. Prentice Hall, Englewoods Cliffs, NJ, 1974.
[10] C. de Boor. On calculating with B-splines. *J. of Approx. Theory.*, 6:50–62, 1972.
[11] C. de Boor. *A Practical Guide to Splines*, volume 27 of *Applied Mathematical Sciences*. Springer Verlag, New York, NY, 1978.
[12] F. R. de Hoog and M. F. Hutchinson. An efficient method for calculating smoothing splines using orthogonal transformations. *Numer. Math.*, 50:311–319, 1987.
[13] M. Epstein. On the influence of parameterization in parametric interpolation. *SIAM Journal Numer. Anal.*, 13(2):261–268, 1976.
[14] G. Farin. *Curves and Surfaces for Computer Aided Geometric Design*. Academic Press, Inc, San Diego, CA, 1988.
[15] L. A. Ferrari, P. V. Sankar, and J. Sklansky. Efficient two-dimensional filters using B-spline functions. *CVGIP*, 35:152–169, 1986.

[16] F. N. Fritsch and R. Carlson. Monotone piecewise cubic interpolation. *SIAM Journal Numer. Anal.*, 17(2):238–246, 1980.
[17] W. Gordon and R. Riesenfeld. B-splines curves and surfaces. In Barnhill and Riesenfeld [1], pages 95–126.
[18] M. Hohmeyer and B. Barsky. Rational continuity: Parametric, geometric and Frenet frame continuity of rational curves. *ACM Trans. on Graphics*, 8(4):335–359, 1989.
[19] M. F. Hutchinson and F.R. de Hoog. Smoothing noisy data with spline functions. *Numer. Math.*, 47:99–106, 1985.
[20] A. K. Jain. *Fundamentals of Digital Image Processing*. Prentice Hall, Inc, Englewood Cliff, 1989.
[21] G. S. Kimeldorf and G. Wahba. A correspondence between bayesian estimation on stochastic processes and smoothing by splines. *The Annals of Mathematical Statistics*, 41:495–502, 1970.
[22] D. Lee and T. Pavlidis. One dimensional regularization with discontinuities. In *Proc. 1st Intern. Conf. Computer Vision, London*, 1987.
[23] F. Lu and E. E. Milios. Optimal local spline approximation of planar shape. In *Proceedings of the ICASSP*, 1991.
[24] G. Nürnberger. Chebyshev approximation by splines with free knots and computation. In C. K. Chui, L. L. Shumaker, and J. D. Ward, editors, *Approximation Theory V. Proceedings, College Station, Texas 1986*, pages 511–514. Academic Press, 1986.
[25] F. O'Sullivan. A statistical perspective on ill-posed inverse problems. *Statistical Science*, 1(4):502–527, 1986. With comments.
[26] D. Paglieroni. *Control Point Algorithms for Contour Processing and Shape Analysis*. PhD thesis, University of California at Davis, 1986.
[27] D. Paglieroni and A. K. Jain. Control point transforms for shape representation and measurement. *CVGIP*, 42:87–111, 1988.
[28] T. Pavlidis. *Algorithms for Graphics and Image Processing*. Computer Science Press Inc., Rockville, MA, 1982.
[29] T. Pavlidis. Curve fitting as a pattern recognition problem. In *Proc. 6th Int. Conf. Pattern Recognition*, pages 853–859. IEEE Computer Society Press, 1982.
[30] M. Plass and M. Stone. Curve fitting with piecewise parametric cubics. *Computer Graphics – SIGGRAPH '83 Conf. Proc.*, 17(3):229–239, 1983.
[31] T. Poggio and F. Girosi. Regularization algorithms for learning that are equivalent to multilayer networks. *Science*, 247:978–982, 1990.
[32] T. Poggio, H. Voorhees, and A. Yuille. A regularized solution to edge detection. *Journal of Complexity*, 4:106–123, 1988.
[33] T. A. Paggio, V. Torre, and Ch. Koch. Computational vision and regularization theory. *Nature*, 317(26):314–319, 1985.
[34] D. L. Ragozin. Error bounds for derivatives estimates based on spline smoothing of exact or noisy data. *J. of Approx. Theory*, 37:335–355, 1983.
[35] C. H. Reinsch. Smoothing by spline functions. *Numer. Math.*, 10:177–183, 1966.
[36] C. H. Reinsch. Smoothing by spline functions. II. *Numer. Math.*, 16:451–454, 1971.
[37] E. J. Rodríguez, J.L.C. Sanz, D.C. Vargas, and M. Flickner. Fast least squares orthogonal spline fitting and its applications to shape analysis. TR 14-91, CRAAG – IBM Argentina, 1991.
[38] P. Saint-Marc and G. Medioni. B-spline contour representation and symmetry detection. IRIS 262, Institute for Robotics and Intelligent Systems. University of Southern California, 1990.
[39] E. Salari and S. Balaji. Recognition of partially ocluded objects using B-spline representation. *Pattern Recognition*, 24(7):653–660, 1991.
[40] K. Šalkauskas. C^1 splines for interpolation of rapidly varying data. *Rocky Mountain Journal of Math.*, 14(1):239–250, 1974.
[41] I. J. Schoenberg. Cardinal interpolation and spline functions. *J. of Approx. Theory*, 2:167–206, 1969.

[42] I. J. Schoenberg. Notes on spline functions V. Orthogonal or Legendre splines. *J. of Approx. Theory*, 13:84–104, 1975.
[43] I. Sekita, K. Toraichi, R. Mori, K. Yamamoto, and H. Yamada. Feature extraction of handwritten Japanese characters by splines functions for relaxation matching. *Pattern Recognition*, 21:9–17, 1988.
[44] B. Shahraray and D. J. Anderson. Optimal estimation of contour properties by cross-validated regularization. *IEEE Transactions on PAMI*, 11(6):600–610, 1989.
[45] L. Shumaker. *Spline Functions: Basic Facts*. John Wiley & Sons, New York, NY, 1981.
[46] H. Späth and J. Meier. Flexible smoothing with periodic cubic splines and fitting with closed curves. *Computing*, 40:293–300, 1988.
[47] D. Terzopoulos. Regularization of inverse visual problems involving discontinuities. *IEEE PAMI*, 8:413–424, 1986.
[48] A. M. Thompson, J. C. Brown, J. W. Kay, and D.M. Titterington. A study of methods of choosing the smoothing parameter in image restoration by regularization. *IEEE Transactions on PAMI*, 13(4):326–339, 1991.
[49] G. Wahba. Spline bases, regularization, and generalized cross validation for solving approximation problems with large quantities of noisy data. In E.W. Cheney, editor, *Approximation Theory III, Proceedings, Austin, Texas*. Academic Press, 1980.
[50] G. Wahba and S. Wold. A completely automatic french curve: Fitting spline functions by cross validation. *Communications in Statistics*, 4:1–17, 1975.
[51] G. Wahba and S. Wold. Periodic splines for spectral density estimation: the use of cross validation for determining the degree of smoothing. *Communications in Statistics*, 4:125–141, 1975.
[52] J. Xu and Y. H. Yang. Generalized multidimensional orthogonal polynomials with applications to shape analysis. *IEEE PAMI*, 12(9):906–913, 1990.

Algorithms for a Fast Confocal Optical Inspection System

A.R. Rao, N. Ramesh, F.Y. Wu, J.R. Mandeville, and P. Kerstens

Abstract. The measurement of surface topography is an important inspection task as it provides useful information for process and quality control. A candidate technique for such an application is confocal imaging. The advantages of confocal imaging are that it is a non-contact measurement, can be operated at high speed (greater than 10 megapixels/sec) and submicron resolution, and provides height information in multi-layered semi-transparent materials.

In this paper we present a system designed for fast acquisition and processing of confocal images. The system consists of an optical front end that uses tilted confocal scanning, and an image processing module. The function of the image processing module is to improve signal resolution, perform smoothing and detect surfaces in the incoming signal. The input signal is first deconvolved in order to improve the depth resolution, and then processed to identify significant peaks. These peaks represent the positions of different surfaces in the object being inspected. These peak locations are smoothed using a cluster based smoothing scheme to combat noise. For semi-transparent materials, our system is capable of detecting up to two surfaces at a given location.

1 Introduction

Surface topography measurement is critical in many manufacturing processes, especially in semiconductor manufacturing and packaging. These measurements are used for quality and process control. Surface measurements carried out by inspection techniques must keep pace with increasing circuit density and complexity, increasing number of mask levels and shrinking pattern dimensions of semiconductor devices. These techniques have to be cost effective, fast and reliable.

Electrical testing and vision based inspection are the two most widely used techniques to monitor the quality of semiconductor devices. While electrical methods are used to test for proper connectivity between components, visual inspection techniques are used to identify locations in the circuit that may cause failures and to check dimensional tolerances. For instance, one can visually verify the presence of extraneous material which can cause potential shorts. Another advantage of visual inspection is that it can be done while the circuitry is still incomplete. Electrical and visual methods of inspection complement one another, and together they can ensure the reliability of the device. This paper focuses on visual inspection methods that use confocal microscopes to acquire 3-D data from the device being imaged.

Confocal microscopy compares favorably against many other 3-D sensing techniques, when evaluated on the basis of speed, resolution, cost effectiveness and ease of operation. Other techniques for gathering 3-D information include laser triangulation [1], SEM (Scanning Electron Microscope) stereo [2], scanning probe microscopy [3] and stylus profilometry. Confocal microscopy [4], with its ability to offer higher resolutions than that of conventional light microscopes, has recently become a viable option.

In addition, the use of confocal microscopes is preferred in a manufacturing environment. Their non-contact and non-destructive modes of operation and their ability to generate a high resolution image of a thin slice of a thick object [4] makes them suitable for acquiring 3-D data of multi-layered devices. 3-D measurements are made by optically scanning a point source and a point detector across the object at different focal places. By doing so, regions that are out of focus contribute very little light to the sensor while those regions "in focus" contribute maximum light. High speed operation (greater than 10 megapixels/sec), submicron resolution, and the uniformity of focus for a particular optical section are other advantages of confocal microscopy.

The quality of the images acquired from the confocal microscope can be enhanced by digital image processing. Images of optical slices at different planes of the object may be blurred due to the presence of other translucent or even opaque interfering surfaces. Additional scattering of light may occur because of the light scattering properties of the materials in the object. Image processing techniques can be used to filter out extraneous signals. These techniques have been successfully applied in a number of domains.

Currently most confocal imaging systems are used in biomedical imaging [5]. In this paper we discuss the special challenges of using confocal imaging in a manufacturing environment.

In the next section of the paper we discuss two current domains of applications. Current surface topography measurements are discussed in Sect. 3. The overview of our system for semiconductor inspection is then followed by detailed descriptions. The theory of operation is the subject of Sect. 5. The processing algorithms are discussed in the three following sections: pre-processing in Sect. 6, deconvolution in Sect. 7, and post-deconvolution methods in Sect. 8. Section 9 deals with methods to resolve the results obtained from two channels of processing. This is followed by a discussion of the experimental results and our conclusions.

2 Background

Though the confocal microscope was invented in 1957 by Marvin Minsky [6], it was only after the mid 1970s that it came into wider usage. The reasons for this lag were that computers had very little memory and lasers had not yet been developed [6]. Improvements in the operation of the microscope were made by Petran [7], who developed a tandem scanning arrangement by using a modified version of the Nipkow disk [8], and Davidovits and Egger [9], who used a laser light source. Sheppard and Choudhury [10] provided a detailed analysis of the theory of operation. In the 1980s Alan Boyde [11] pioneered the use of confocal microscopy in biological applications to capture the 3-D structure of biological tissue. Confocal microscopy is now being used in a wide range of applications, some of which are reviewed in the following sections.

2.1 Biological Applications of Confocal Microscopy

Confocal microscopes are primarily used in biology for their ability to provide 3-D data about a specimen. They are less susceptible to stray light than conventional microscopes. Their high axial and lateral resolution, and uniformity of focus are other important features. Biological samples imaged under a microscope are by nature largely transparent. This property makes them amenable to confocal imaging. Since the microscope provides only sets of 2-D images, processing is required to combine the acquired 3-D data for volume visualization. Volume visualization through reconstruction is the most common application of confocal microscopy in the biological domain. A general system to do this is described by Richardson [12]. Kaufman et al. [13] have used optical sections of nerve cells that are rich in stainable actin, for 3-D visualization. Masters discusses visualization of the ocular tissue in [14].

Depending upon the specimen imaged, and the nature of the data required, different techniques are used either in the microscopy or on the specimen. For example, the microscope can be used in the white light imaging mode [15], in the polarization imaging mode [16], in the dark field mode, in the fluorescent [17], reflection and transmission modes [18] [19], and many other modes that can serve to emphasize or de-emphasize certain characteristics of the imaged specimen. Other factors that change the characteristics of the image obtained include lighting, fixation and mounting of the specimen, staining dyes, numerical aperture of the lens, type of detectors, and so on. Confocal fluourescent microscopy compares favorably compared to conventional fluourescent microscopy because of its ability to reduce the glare caused by out of focus light.

The fact that a confocal microscope is a non-destructive 3-D instrument has led to advances in stereology [21], for example to make measurements on microstructure. Other applications include the recording of temporal changes in the specimen under observation [22] [23] and particle counting [24].

2.2 Semiconductor Applications of Confocal Microscopy

In semiconductor metrology, confocal microscopy is primarily used for two purposes: inspection and measurement. Inspection is done for the purposes of defect detection and process control. The 3-D data available from the confocal microscope facilitate the detection of height related defects. Linewidth and overlay measurements are critical in the lithographic process. The shrinking dimensions of circuit features have resulted in the migration of some inspection and measurement tools from optical to SEM based methods. However, confocal microscopes still compete with low resolution SEMs [25] since they offer high lateral and axial resolutions which can be increased by controlling the wavelength of the light, through the use of pupil plane filters, and different sized detectors [26].

Current products in semiconductor manufacturing, from chips to the final packaging, are formed of multilayered structures, as shown in Fig. 1. These layers consist of both opaque (e.g., metal) and transparent materials (e.g., polyimide) that are sandwiched together. The 3-D measurement of these structures is an important part of process control and quality assurance. Furthermore, due to the multilayered nature of structures, it is not possible to get a single well focussed 2-D intensity image using a conventional microscope. The confocal microscope can generate a 2-D image that is well focussed at every point.

In biological applications, the data in all of the image slices may be significant because frequently the object contains continuous distributions of matter that fluoresce, scatter, or absorb the incident light [5]. However, in the inspection of manufactured electronic parts, there are typically only one or two interfaces at or near the top surface that need to be inspected at each step in the manufacturing process. The raw confocal image slices contain much more data than is needed for inspection, and cannot be efficiently processed by the algorithms that actually perform the inspection. Consequently, a preprocessing step which extracts the heights of the surfaces from the input data should be used to feed the inspection algorithms that check heights, linewidths, pattern accuracy, etc., against design data.

The trend in the semiconductor and packaging industry is towards smaller linewidths and denser circuitry. The increasing complexity of products demands

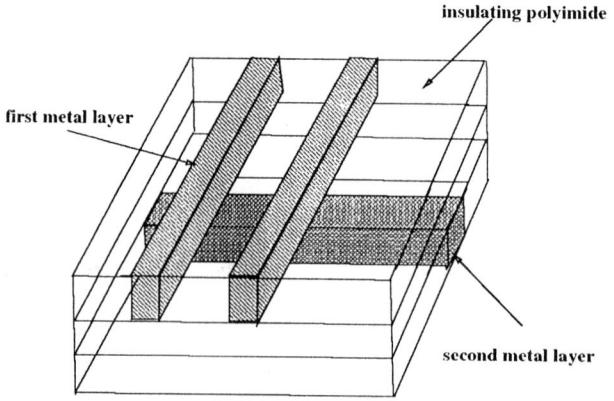

Fig. 1. A schematic of the part of be inspected

higher throughput, resolution and accuracy in the inspection systems, both for image acquisition and analysis. This fact, combined with the earlier observation that the confocal images have to be used by inspection algorithms imply stringent speed requirements. For instance, if the confocal microscope is operated at 10 megapixels/sec to produce sixteen 2-D slices, then we require a processing speed of 160 megapixels/sec. The requirement of high speed limits the choice of algorithms that can be used, and this will be discussed later.

3 Brief Survey of Surface Topography Measurement Methods

The measurement of surface topography can be broadly categorized into microscopic and macroscopic measurements. For example, the range sensors [27] are in general used for large objects, while scanning microscopes are used to acquire information about microscopic objects. In this section we shall very briefly mention some recent methods for the measurement of surface topography. A detailed survey of such techniques falls beyond the scope of this paper.

The use of acoustic microscopy in imaging of microstructures is discussed in [28] and has a height resolution in the range of 20 Å and lateral resolution in the range of 800 Å. In an atomic force microscope, usually a SiN (Silicon Nitride) tip [29] is attached to a cantilever beam that is moved on the surface and the deflections of the cantilever beam are measured by interferometric methods to characterize the surface [30].

Montgomery et al. [31] describe a phase stepping microscope that is most suitable for use with electronic and optoelectronic devices. A CCD sensor captures the data, and image processing techniques are used in the analysis of the fringes produced by interference. The vertical resolution is 1 nm and the horizontal resolution is 0.6 μm.

A survey of the applications of laser scanning tomography is given in [32], especially for semiconductors while Tome [33] discusses some applications of infrared interferometry. The use of an electron microscope for surface topography measurements is described in [34]. Corredera et al. [35] describe an interference system used to measure the "flatness" of the end of an optical fiber, with height resolution of 0.3 μm. Using ultrasound techniques, Blessing et al. [36] claim to be able to resolve "discrete asperities" of less than 1 μm. This system uses scattering and reflection techniques in a range of ultrasonic frequencies. Pidduck and Nayar [37] claim that a laser scanning optical microscope (SOM) in the differential phase contrast (DPC) mode can resolve heights in the order of a few nanometers. They examine surface textures on polished silicon wafers for microroughness measurements.

A theoretical analysis of a differential phase optical microscope is provided by Bozhevol'nyi et al. [38] where the various parameters of the optical system are taken into consideration. They also suggest ways to improve the resolution of the

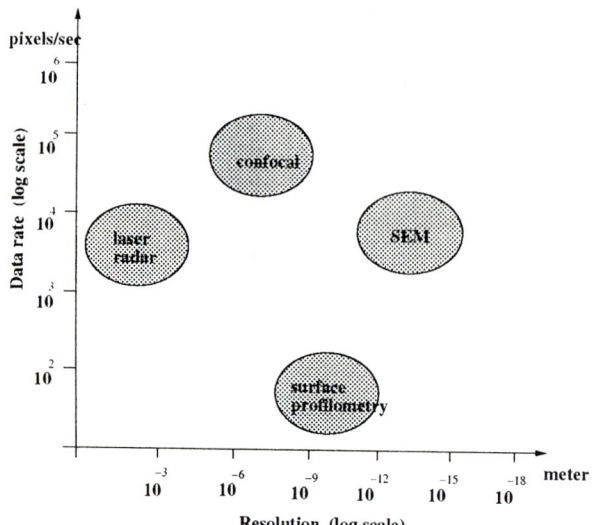

Fig. 2. Chart showing approximate resolutions (lateral and height) against the data capture rate of different technologies

instrument and achieved depth resolutions of 2 Å and lateral resolutions of 2.5 μm in an experimental study. The use of Moire profilometry for the imaging of large objects (esp. stamping dies) have been discussed in [39]. A three color laser diode interferometer is described in [40] while Wust and Capson [41] use the relative phase differences between the red, green and blue components of a color image obtained by projecting sinusoidal color fringes onto the object for height measurements. Offside [42] has developed a phase sensitive scanning optical microscope which is sensitive to height changes of less than 3 Å. Here a narrow focussed beam and a collimated beam are directed on the surface, and on reflection, interfere with a third beam that has been frequency shifted. The resulting parallel Michelson's interferometers produce the relative phase shifts that provide information about the surface structure.

An optical profiler with a height resolution of 1 nm and lateral resolution of 0.5 μm is described by Montgomery et al. [43]. It is based on interference microscopy with a high intensity LED as the light source and a CCD camera detector.

Methods to increase the lateral resolution of stylus profilometers are described by Song and Vorburger [44]. According to their study a very fine stylus with a small tip size is the most important factor in controlling the lateral resolution. However, typical scanning times for a stylus profilometer are in the order of several seconds for one scan line (1 to 50 seconds for scan lengths of 50 μm to 50 mm for the DEKTAK 3030 AUTO I, manufactured by Veeco Instruments Inc., Santa Barbara).

Besl [45] provides a good survey of range imaging sensors and compares different sensing techniques and commercially available sensors.

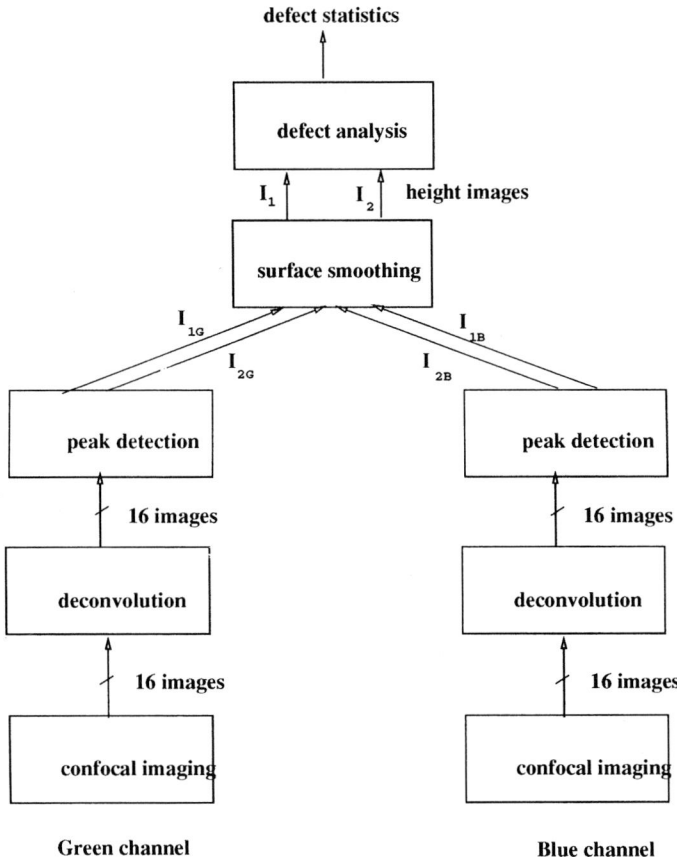

Fig. 3. The block diagram of the system with the various processing stages shown. The objective of the process is to obtain two height images that can be used for further evaluation

4 System Overview

The block diagram of the system is shown in Fig. 3.

The first part of our system is a confocal imaging subsystem that acquires optical slices of a device at different heights, and the second part is the image processing subsystem that processes the images acquired to give two height images. A semiconductor device goes through various manufacturing stages resulting in multiple layers of metallic circuits sandwiched between polyimide. Inspection of the device needs to be done each time a new physical film is added, resulting in multiple inspections before the device is completely fabricated. These inspections serve to detect and defects or exceeded tolerances inside or on top of the new film. Our inspection system yields two images that contain the information about any defects present in this film. We need to examine two surfaces to be able to identify any defects that occur within the transparent parts of the film. For example, if the top layer of polyimide has a raised area, then the next film may be affected.

Briefly, the two height images stated above are obtained as follows. A semiconductor device is imaged using a confocal system yielding a number of optical slices. Using the response function along the optical axis, the 1-D signal corresponding to the different slices along the z axis is deconvolved using a linear filter. The peaks of the deconvolved signal are detected to determine the location and nature of the surfaces. Ideally, each peak detected corresponds to either the top surface or an interface between films. However, even after deconvolution, noise can given rise to spurious peaks. So the top two peaks based on a quality measure are identified as the top two surfaces. There are two possibilities: only the top surface is present, in which case there is only one peak, or both the top and second surfaces are present, in which case we detect two peaks.

The device is imaged through green and blue light for two reasons. First, reflectance characteristics for a particular type of surface may be different for these two wavelengths. This is exploited to obtain images of different contrast. For instance, polyimide is relatively more transparent in green light than blue light. Secondly, noise and the use of an approximate response function can result in the detection of spurious peaks. Hence the results of processing the green and blue channels are used together to combat noise by smoothing. This results in two height images, I_1 and I_2. This stage is further followed by a defect analysis stage which indicates the presence of any defects, and if any tolerances have been exceeded, gives a "measure" of the error.

5 Principles of Operation

The basic principle exploited by the confocal microscope is that of defocus. When a conventionally imaged object is displaced from best focus, the image contrast decreases, but the spatially averaged intensity remains the same. However in a confocal imaging system, the image of a defocused surface appears *darker* than if it were in focus. Thus the confocal optics can be said to have axial resolution in addition to lateral resolution. As a consequence of this property, it is possible to extract topographic information from a set of confocal images taken over a range of focal planes. Figure 4 illustrates the principle. A further benefit is that a set of confocal images can be combined in any of several ways to generate an *extended focus image*, an image which appears to be sharply focused over a range much greater than the nominal depth of focus. Due to the rejection of light from defocused surfaces, confocal images also exhibit lower levels of stray light.

In a reflective confocal system, a point light source is imaged onto the object. Light reflected from the object and collected by the lens is re-imaged via a beamsplitter onto a point detector. When the object is in the focal plane of the lens, there is a maximum amount of light received by the point detector. When the object is defocused, the reflected light is spread out at the detector, and relatively

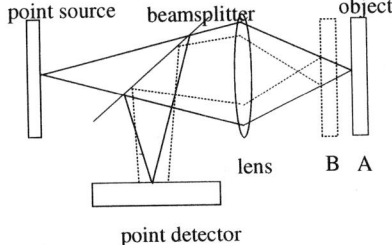

Fig. 4. Imaging of the object using a confocal microscope. At position A the object is in focus, while at B it is defocused

little is received by the point detector. For an ideal lens and a mirror-like object, the dependence of detected signal on defocus can be expressed as

$$I(z) = I_0 sinc^2(\pi NA^2/\lambda z) \tag{1}$$

where $I(z)$ is the light intensity along the axial direction, NA is the numerical aperture, λ is the wavelength, and $sinc(x)$ stands for $sin(x)/x$. The peak signal occurs when the object is in the focal plane, z = 0.

In order to form a confocal image, the signal is recorded as the object is scanned relative to the image of the point source in a plane parallel to the focal plane. Multiple confocal image slices are obtained by repeating the process at various levels of object defocus. Thus by focusing at different heights (along the z – axis) on the object, it is possible to obtain 3-D information about the object.

Confocal image processing must solve the inverse problem of determining the surface height(s) from a series of confocal images with varying defocus. The result is a map of the 3-D topography of the object.

5.1 The Confocal Optical System

The system described here is intended to adapt the 3-D imaging properties of confocal optics to automatic inspection. As described above, a confocal system images only one point at a time. Acquiring a complete two-dimensional image requires that either the illuminated spot or the object be scanned in two dimensions. Acquisition speed can be increased by illuminating and imaging multiple isolated spots simultaneously. This technique is used in the tandem scanning microscope [7], which employs a spiral pattern of holes etched into a "Nipkow" disk. The object is stationary while the disk rotates, scanning each pinhole image across the field of view. The observer's eye or camera integrates the image and yields a "real-time" image. Roughly speaking, the microscope generates a 2-D image of surfaces that are in or near the focal plane. Acquisition of 3-D image data requires repeated imaging at several parallel planes in object space. A point on the object surface will produce a signal of different strength in each of the images, in accordance with equation(1). The imaging system used in this work is intended for automatic optical inspection of electronic packaging, in which the areas to be

Fig. 5. The mask pattern

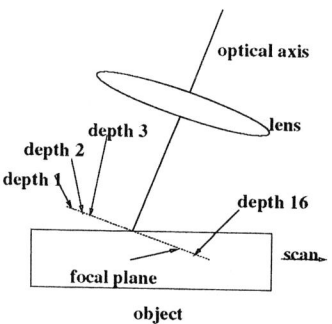

Fig. 6. Illustrating the principle of tilted scanning

inspected are much larger than the field of view of any real optical system capable of the necessary resolution. Consequently in this system, the object is moved across the field of view in a continuous motion as confocal image data are acquired, in a manner analogous to the use of a line-scan camera.

The confocal optical system is built around a modified microscope body. The viewing head has two camera ports which produce two planes conjugate to the object plane by means of a cube beamsplitter. A stationary mask containing numerous pinholes is positioned in each of the two planes. One of the masks is trans-illuminated and imaged onto the object, while the other filters the reflected light on its way to an area array CCD camera. The masks have the pattern shown in Fig. 5.

The pattern is analogous to a linear array camera pattern. The object must be scanned as the pixel data are read out; the sensor is read out once each time the object moves by one pixel distance. The part must be scanned some distance before a complete "frame" of data has been acquired. Unlike a line-scan camera the data from each read-out do not constitute one line in the image; the data must be stored at the proper locations in image memory.

The basic pattern of Fig. 5 is replicated several times on both pinhole masks to enable acquisition of multiple images at different focal planes simultaneously. In order to position the pinhole masks patterns at different focal planes, we tilt the object and its scanning stage so that the nominal object surface is not normal to the optical axis, as shown in Fig. 6. Each camera frame is analogous to one read-out of

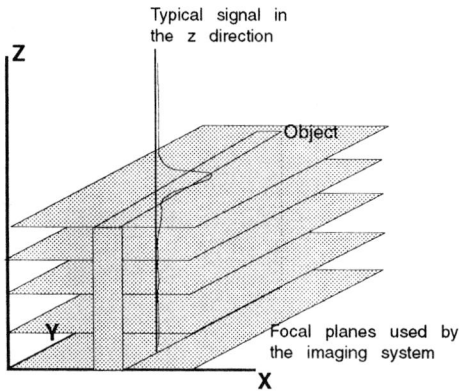

Fig. 7. The coordinate system used. Numerous confocal image slices are stacked along the z-direction. The object being imaged is a thick metal line. The top surface of the object causes a peak in the intensity signal measured along the z axis

multiple linear array cameras. Each time the scanning part moves by one pixel, the camera is read out and those pixels in the vicinity of a pinhole image are summed and the result stored in image buffers. Thus a single scan allows the acquisition of several confocal images at different focal plane heights.

Actually each *row* of each pattern focuses at a different plane; this is the reason for the "banding" that can be seen in the images shown in Fig. 15. This artifact is removed by the image processing algorithms that produce height and reflectance (extended focus) images.

For our application, we use the microscope to acquire a set of 16 confocal images, each at a different focal plane near the top surface of the object. Thus each pixel is associated with 16 values from which surface height(s) are to be calculated. The range of the 16 equally-spaced focal planes is selected to match the inspection requirements.

Figure 7 illustrates the coordinate system that we will use. Imaging from the top, we obtain sixteen slices ($x - y$ plane) of the object along the z direction. The z direction is parallel to the optical axis. Since the image obtained is a function of the reflectivity of the surface, for each pixel, the signal along the z axis will indicate the type of surface present along that axis.

5.2 Controllable Microscope Parameters

Equation (1) directly dictates the nature of the intensity signal observed along the optical axis for a confocal arrangement. Three important parameters can be controlled to alter this signal: the intensity I_0 and wavelength λ, of the light source, and the numerical aperture (NA) of the lens. We shall in turn discuss how each of these parameters affect the behavior of the system.

A high-brightness source is required for confocal imaging because the instantaneously illuminated area is very small. Laser light sources are the preferred ones, as in the case of confocal laser scanning microscopes (CSLM). Since laser sources are coherent, simultaneous imaging of multiple points is susceptible to interference effects when lasers are used. High intensity mercury arc lamps are feasible alternatives. They also emit multiple wavelengths which can easily be selected with filters. The present application makes use of the green-yellow (577 nm) and blue (436 nm) lines.

The depth resolution of the microscope is a function of the NA. Higher NA values give rise to steeper response functions resulting in higher resolutions, as implied by equation(1). The NA of a lens can be increased by replacing the air medium between the object and the lens by oil. Though such a technique is frequently used in biological microscopy, it is infeasible for the examination of electronic parts. There is a tradeoff between the depth resolution of the system and the number of optical slices required to scan an object. The greater the resolution, the larger is the number of optical slices required to avoid missing entire surfaces. Since our main objective is fast processing speed, we would like to acquire a minimum number of optical slices. This means that we must sacrifice resolving power to obtain a small number of optical slices. Sixteen slices represents a suitable compromise for our system.

5.3 Special Requirements for Manufacturing Environments

The main thrust of our research is to develop accurate and reliable algorithms for height processing, which are able to run in real time. Several issues need to be considered which lead to the development of a desired solution.

1. Processing speed is one of the most important requirements in an inspection system. This requirement is even more crucial when the algorithms to be used are for the front end of the system. This is because the front end merely provides good signals, and the additional overhead of other inspection algorithms has to be incurred. Thus, this requirement implies that time consuming iterative algorithms (which may have superior performance in terms of quality) cannot by used.
2. The object can have multiple layers, some of which may be transparent. This case creates special degradations of the signal. In our application, at most two surfaces are to be detected, corresponding to the presence of a transparent film over opaque surface.
3. The microscope(s) can possess varying response functions. The image obtained is a convolution of the real data with the microscope's response function. The theoretical model for the response function in reflective confocal imaging is a $sinc^2$ function. However, with real lenses the response is usually quite different, and often asymmetrical. Hence, analytical methods based on the $sinc^2$ function are not applicable. Further-more, even nominally identical lenses may have different depth responses. Thus, the solution should be adaptable to different depth response functions.

4. The signal is usually noisy, and has to be filtered to get good results. At the same time, one must be careful not to smooth out small defects. The objective here is not to fit smooth surfaces to the data, but rather reproduce a given surface faithfully so that defects can be found.
5. The algorithms should be easily translatable into hardware implementations, in order to maximize processing speed.

6 Preprocessing the Image

As mentioned in Sect. 5.1 the optics introduces "banding" in the image. The nature of "banding" is important because it affects the result of preprocessing. For simplicity, consider a flat object of uniform reflectance. The signal at each pixel location is sampled at sixteen points (in our case) resulting in sixteen intensity images. Each column of a confocal is sampled at a slightly different phase from the previous column. The shift, δz, resets after every eight columns as shown in Fig. 8.

Let the continuous intensity signal, $f(z)$, be sampled at C points, each δz apart. The discrete form of $f(z)$ is then given by

$$f(u) = f(z_0 + u\delta z) \qquad (2)$$

where $u = 0, 1, \ldots, C - 1$. However, z_0 is different at each column and is given by

$$z_0 = mod\left(\frac{c\delta z}{p}, \delta z\right) \qquad (3)$$

where c is the column number and p is the width (number of columns) of the banding.

If preprocessing involves smoothing, the following approaches can be used:

6.1 Smoothing After Resampling

The signal along the optical axis (height axis) is reconstructed and resampled in the correct phase. This will remove the "banding" and a spatial smoothing operation can then be done. We studied two methods of signal reconstruction; *sinc* interpolation and a linear three point interpolation technique. The *sinc* interpolation is the more accurate and removes banding completely, but is computationally involved. The linear three point method is an approximation and is suitable in most cases. After the signal has been reconstructed, it is sampled at the same phase for all image points.

6.2 Smoothing Before Resampling

Let C be the number of optical slices obtained from the confocal microscope, and the images be denoted by $I_1, I_2, \ldots, I_i, \ldots, I_C$.

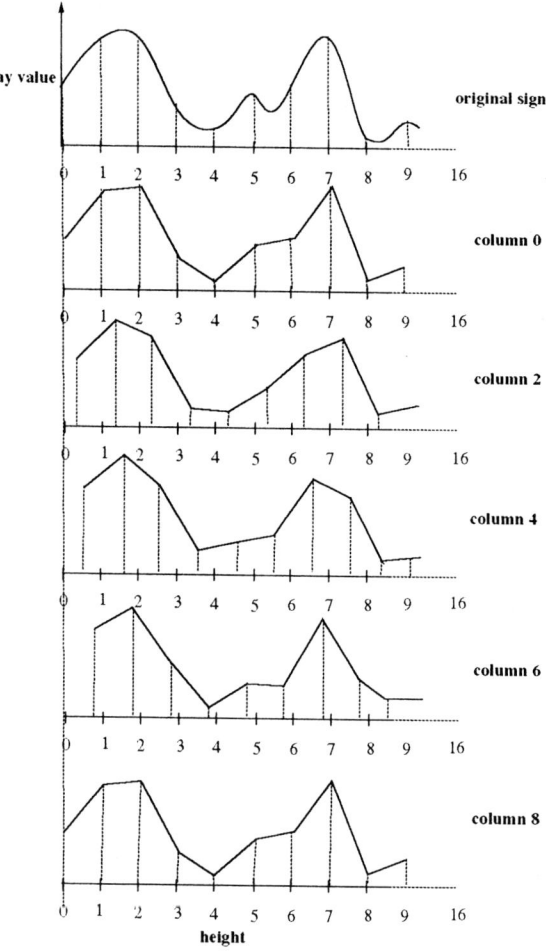

Fig. 8. The banding that occurs due to a phase shift in the sampling in each column. Ideally the same type of surfaces will give rise to the same signal over different columns. However, the signal is sampled with a phase shift in the adjacent columns, but this phase is reset after every eight columns. Each plot indicates the sampled points along one column

If the height signal had been sampled without a phase shift at fixed intervals of δz, then, each image I_k can be smoothed independently. When smoothing is done over a local neighborhood region R, the pixel under consideration is given by

$$p_k = \frac{\sum_R p_i^{I_k}}{N} \qquad (4)$$

where the $p_i^{I_k}$ are the pixels in the neighborhood of region R in the image I_k and N is the number of pixels in the region.

However, since there is an initial phase shift in the phase of the sampling, we make the following modification. If the R falls completely within the columns where the sampling phase has not been reset, then

Algorithms for a Fast Confocal Optical Inspection System

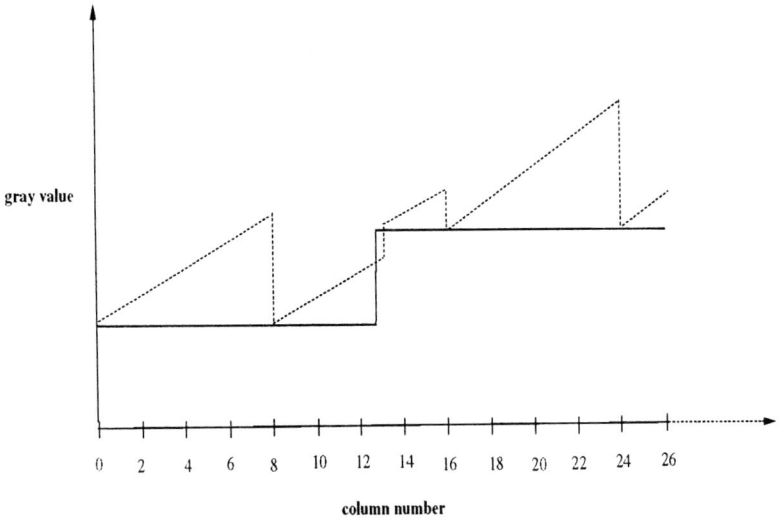

Fig. 9. This figure shows two surfaces at different heights, extending from column 0 to column 26. The unbroken lines indicate the line along which the signal should have been sampled. The broken lines indicate the height at which the signal has actually been sampled. Notice how the sampling resets after every 8 columns

$$p_k = \frac{\sum_R p_i^{I_k}}{N} \tag{5}$$

as above. However, if R includes a column where the phase shift has been reset, then R is divided into two regions R_1 and R_2, within each of which the phase has not be reset. In this case, the averaging is given by

$$p_k = \frac{\sum_{R_1} p_i^{I_k}}{N_1} + \frac{\sum_{R_2} p_i^{I_{k\pm1}}}{N_2} \tag{6}$$

where N_1 and N_2 are the number of pixels in the regions R_1 and R_2 respectively, and I_k is the kth image, and $I_{k\pm1}$ could be the "next" or "previous" image.

7 Deconvolution

An object imaged as described above will give rise to signal peaks at regions where a surface is within the range of the confocal slices as shown in Fig. 7. Sometimes, two close peaks may overlap to give rise to one single peak. Hence, a way of resolving such signals is required. The technique called deconvolution (also

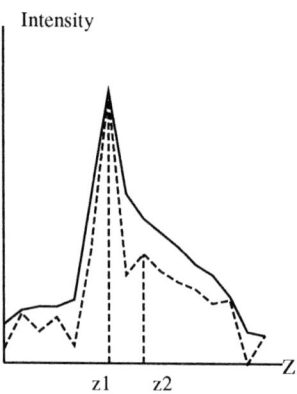

Fig. 10. This figure shows the signal resulting from two surfaces at heights z_1 and z_2. The curve in solid lines represents the original signal. Note that the surfaces at z_1 and z_2 are close enough for their responses to overlap. This causes the original signal to contain only one peak. The result after applying deconvolution (Wiener filtering) is shown in dashed lines. Note that we have now resolved the two peaks at z_1 and z_2

known as image restoration) [46, 47, 48] which can help separate close peaks, is a possible solution. Figure 10 illustrates the operation of deconvolution.

A simple degradation model is given by

$$g(z) = n(z) + \int f(z-\tau)h(\tau)d\tau \qquad (7)$$

where $f(z)$ is the original signal, $h(z)$ is the point spread function of the optical system (which introduces a blurring operation), $g(z)$ is the output signal, and $n(z)$ represents the additive noise term. Here a one-dimensional model is used. The above equation can be interpreted as a corruption of the original signal in two ways: first, it is convolved with a point spread function, and then noise is added.

The deconvolution or restoration problem is to recover $f(z)$ in equation(7), given $g(z)$ and $h(z)$. Due to the unknown nature of the noise, $n(z)$, equation(7) cannot be solved directly. The most that can be done is to produce an estimate $\hat{f}(z)$ of the solution.

Deconvolution or restoration techniques can be classified into two broad categories: linear techniques and non-linear techniques. Linear methods are concerned with applying a linear filter to the corrupted signal $g(z)$ in order to recover the original signal $f(z)$. Non-linear techniques allow the imposition of additional constraints on the restoration, such as positivity of the restored signal. In contrast to linear methods, non-linear methods are invariably iterative.

In the formation of confocal images, the values of the height samples are affected by the characteristics of the surfaces not only at one particular (x, y) coordinate, but also at nearby points. Of course the extent of the influence of neighboring regions on the value of a sample depends on how far from focus the sample is taken. Ideally, a full three-dimensional deconvolution should be performed to account for this crosstalk. Even so, such a three-dimensional deconvolution is valid only if the object is incoherent, as in the case of confocal fluorescence imaging. It is not strictly valid in the present application, where the surfaces are coherent reflectors. In spite of these limitations, we have found that acceptable performance can be achieved with a one-dimensional deconvolution, as described below.

7.1 Linear Deconvolution Techniques

Linear deconvolution techniques are concerned with the design of a linear filter $r(z)$, such that the convolution of $r(z)$ with $g(z)$ gives a "best" estimate for $f(z)$. Different goodness criteria can be used to define what a "best" estimate means.

7.1.1 Wiener Filtering

A common criterion used is the least squares criterion. The output of the restoring filter, $r(z)$ is

$$\hat{f}(z) = \int r(z-\tau)g(\tau)d\tau \tag{8}$$

The least squares criterion requires that

$$\int |\hat{f}(z) - f(z)|^2 \, dz = \int |\hat{F}(\omega) - F(\omega)|^2 \, d\omega \tag{9}$$

be minimized, where $F(\omega)$ is the Fourier transform of $f(z)$, and similarly for $\hat{F}(\omega)$.
Let $S(\omega) = H(\omega)F(\omega)$, and $R(\omega) = \Phi(\omega)/H(\omega)$. It can be shown that [49] [pg. 434] if $\Phi(\omega)$ is a real function, then

$$\Phi(\omega) = \frac{|S(\omega)|^2}{|S(\omega)|^2 + |N(\omega)|^2} \tag{10}$$

To determine the optimal filter, $R(\omega)$, the noise spectrum $N(\omega)$ is estimated as described in [49] [pg. 436]. Wiener filtering is in practice the most widely applicable deconvolutional method [46] [pg. 92].

Other linear techniques such as regularization can also be used, as described in [17]. The deconvolution filter derived from regularization is very similar to the Wiener filter.

7.2 Non-Linear Deconvolution

Non-linear deconvolution techniques have superior signal restoration properties [50]. One reason for this is that non-linear methods make use of additional constraints such as the positivity of the signal. Linear methods are not capable of guaranteeing this constraint.

Jansson [51, 52] developed an enhancement to Van Cittert's [53] scheme for deconvolution that ensures positivity of the restored signal. The technique is an iterative relaxation scheme, and is used in the deconvolution of spectra [48].

7.2.1 Subtractive Deconvolution

In this iterative technique, a fraction of the ideal response is repeatedly subtracted from the given signal. The advantage of this technique is that it involves only simple subtraction operations, and does not need any convolution operations [46] [pg. 80].

A 1-D observed signal with a noise component, can be modelled as follows

$$g(z) = \sum f(z)h(z) + \eta(z) \tag{11}$$

where $f(z)$ is the original signal, $h(z)$ the impulse response and $\eta(z)$ the noise component. While $f(z)$ can be considered as a ordered set of impulses, $f(z)h(z)$ can be considered to be thought of as a "spread impulse" [46]. Subtractive deconvolution derives its name from being able to "subtract out," gradually, the noise component of the observed signal.

Subtractive deconvolution is most useful when the observed signal has been reduced in contrast, but is still resolvable. Since it is an iterative operation it is also computationally intensive.

We implemented these non-linear techniques and found that they gave superior performance, both in terms of the ability to resolve proximate peaks and the ability to contain the amount of ringing in the deconvolved signal. However, improvement in performance comes at the cost of processing speed. Non-linear techniques are invariably iterative and thus unsuited for real-time applications like the one being addressed.

7.3 3-D Deconvolution

Since we obtain a 3-D data set of measurements, it seems logical to use 3-D deconvolution techniques. However, there are some problems associated with it.

The physics of optical image formation in our case is non linear. In reflectance confocal microscopy, the surface of the object in the neighborhood of each pixel has an effect on the image intensity due to the partial coherence of the source and the preservation of relative phase upon reflection from the surface. Since 3-D deconvolution is a linear operation, it cannot "reverse" the effects introduced in the image formation.

In most biological applications however, image formation is a linear process in the fluorescent mode. This is because, the phases of the light emitted from the adjacent molecules are random, and are not affected by the neighboring molecules when imaged. Therefore 3-D deconvolution is justifiable in biological applications that use fluorescent imaging.

8 Peak Detection

Reflection at the surfaces of the device gives rise to peaks along the z direction of the intensity signal, $g(z)$. The location of these surfaces can be identified by detecting the peaks of the signal $g(z)$.

8.1 With No Prior Deconvolution

Deconvolution may not be necessary in cases where a single peak or two well separated peaks have to be detected.

8.1.1 Inverting the Normalized Intensity

LaComb et al. [54] have developed a method based on the calibrated depth response curve. The normalized intensity of a signal is compared against the calibrated curve, which yields a height measurement. A problem with this approach is that the z value computed has a sign ambiguity. This arises from the symmetry of the depth response (which is approximately a $sinc^2$ function).

8.1.2 Matched Filtering

The ideal response (corresponding to a mirror-like surface) is correlated with a given signal, and the location of the maximum is found. For well-separated peaks in the presence of white noise, this method yields the optimum peak location accuracy.

A potential drawback of this technique is that it reduces the resolution as the signal is smoothed. Since correlation tends to broaden peaks and we search for local maxima, two proximate peaks may merge.

8.2 With Prior Deconvolution

Peak detection is an important component of the system, because while on one hand it should have a good tolerance to noise, it should also be able to extract the 'true' peaks. Further requirements on the algorithm are that its sensitivity should be controllable and it should be computationally inexpensive.

There are a number of different peak detection techniques available [55, 56] but we will restrict ourselves to discussing just two of them.

8.2.1 Peak Detection Through Cumulative Averaging

This technique [57] of locating peaks is based on the principle of finding the zero-crossings and then using the local extrema values of a peak detection signal to extract significant peaks. The peak detection signal is obtained by convolving a peak detection kernel with the original signal.

$$s_N = p_N \otimes f \qquad (12)$$

where s_N is the peak detection signal, p_N the peak detection kernel, f is the original signal and the parameter N denotes the width of the kernel, which Sezan calls the "peak detection parameter." p_N is obtained by convolving a smoothing filter with a differencing filter, and approximates first order differentiation. Peaks are determined from the sign and zero-crossings of the signal s_N. p_N is the convolution of a "difference" signal and a "smoothing" signal. p_N is defined in such a way that its convolution with f turns out to be equivalent to $c - \bar{c}_N$, where c is the cumulative distribution function (cdf) and $\bar{c}_N$ is the cdf averaged over a window of length N. The nice feature about this algorithm is the single controllable parameter N that controls the "coarseness" of the peaks considered. A larger value of N will tend to smooth out small variations whereas smaller values of N will pick out the smaller peaks.

However, we are always interested in extracting the two prominent peaks, and there is no way to directly control this in Sezan's method. After identifying the peaks, we still would have to define criteria to extract the two most prominent peaks.

8.2.2 Peak Detection Based on Strength of Zero Crossings

In our application, we have to detect up to two surfaces at a given (x, y) point. Furthermore, weak peaks due to noise have to be eliminated. One way of meeting both requirements is to define a peak strength measure for each peak in the signal. A peak is synonymous with a negatively sloped zero crossing (along the positive direction of the z axis), and is identified through a change in the sign of the first derivative. In addition to peaks, we identify valleys in the signal, which are positively sloped zero crossings. Each peak is flanked by a valley on either side, as shown in Fig. 11.

Note that a significant peak is characterized both by its sharpness (magnitude of the second derivative) and by the area under the peak (product of height and

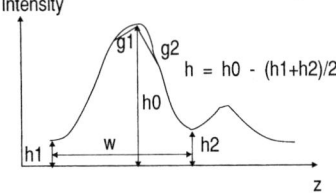

Fig. 11. Peaks and valleys are identified through changes in the sign of the gradient. The height of a peak is defined to be the average height above the two neighboring valleys (minima)

width). The area under the peak is a measure of the local energy of the signal. A simple way of combining both these desirable qualities of a peak is to take their product, yielding

$$P(h, w, g_1, g_2) = hw(g_1 - g_2) \qquad (13)$$

where P is the peak strength measure, h and w are the height and width of the peak as in Fig. 11, and g_1 and g_2 are the gradients on either side of the peak.

Weak peaks in the signal are eliminated through a threshold (the setting of this threshold is discussed later in Sect. 11.5) and the two surviving peaks that have the largest peak strength measure are interpreted as the two surfaces we seek. The elimination of weak peaks is similar in spirit to the elimination of weak edges in edge detection through hysteretic thresholding [58] or the authentication of zero crossings [59].

9 Smoothing of Height Images

After deconvolution and peak detection, we extract at most two peaks, say at z_1 and z_2 at a location (x, y) from each channel. Let j denote the channel, where j is either G or B for green or blue. These two peaks are stored in an upper height image, I_{1j}, and a lower height image, I_{2j}, ($I_{1j}(x, y) = z_1$ and $I_{2j}(x, y) = z_2$). We assume that the top surface of the object is positioned in the range of the system. Therefore, if only one peak is detected, it is the top surface, and we encode the lack of a peak with the z-value of 0. If the signal in channel j at location (x, y) contains only one peak at z_1, then $I_{1j}(x, y) = z_1$ and $I_{2j}(x, y) = 0$. If the signal at (x, y) contains no peaks, then $I_{1j}(x, y) = I_{2j}(x, y) = 0$.

Thus each channel (green and blue) produces two height images, giving a total of four: I_{1G} and I_{2G} corresponding to the green channel, and I_{1B} and I_{2B} corresponding to the blue channel. The heights measured at a location (x, y) can be different in the green and blue channels due to noise and systematic offsets, and have to be combined to produce a consistent height. One may expect a pairwise averaging of I_{1G} and I_{1B} to provide an averaged upper surface image, I_1, and averaging I_{2G} and I_{2B} to provide an averaged lower surface I_2.

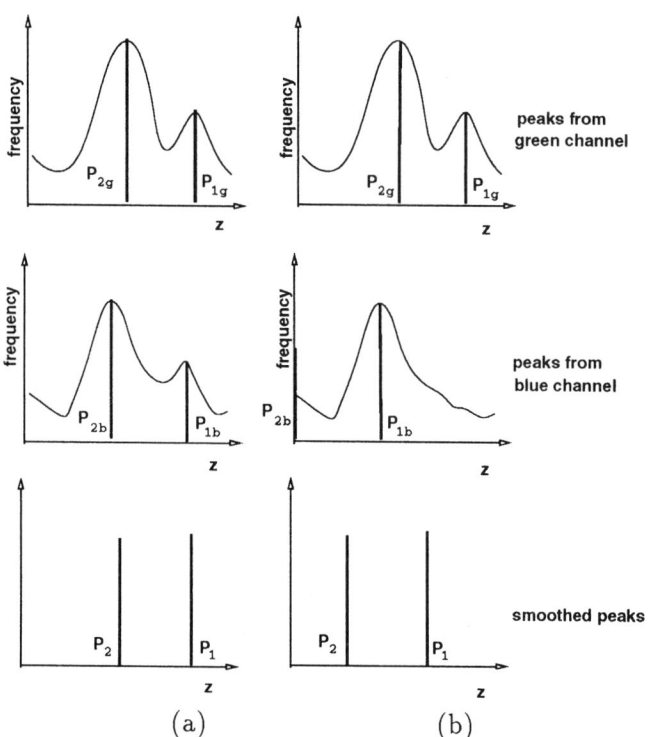

Fig. 12. Pairwise averaging of the peaks from the green and blue channel. **a** The peaks have been detected correctly; **b** One peak from the blue channel has been missed, resulting in wrong final peaks if pairwise averaging is used

However, this pairwise averaging does not work because there are two sources of measurement errors. There are minor variations due to noise, and major variations due to the fact that a surface may be detected in one channel but missed in the other. Pairwise averaging fails if there are such missing surfaces. Figure 12 illustrates this problem.

Since pairwise averaging does not work, we need a technique to smooth the four images *simultaneously*. Different methods can be applied here, and one such technique is described as follows. The essential idea is similar to conventional pattern recognition techniques [60] wherein we "cluster" a neighborhood region of the pixel and pick out the center of the cluster as the resulting height.

9.1 A Clustering Approach to Smoothing

Since the object contains at most two discernible surfaces at a given (x, y) location, we expect these surfaces to be manifested by two clusters in the z measurements made in the vicinity of (x, y).

Conventional clustering algorithms are iterative [60], and hence must be modified before use. We have devised a simpler scheme based on the following observation. The relation between the features of the object and the inter-slice sampling distance is typically chosen such that there is a reasonable separation (two or more samples) between the two surfaces. This implies that the two clusters that may be present are well separated[1]. This fact is made use of in the clustering algorithm.

The essential idea used in the clustering algorithm is the following. For each location (x, y), we form a neighborhood of size $N \times N$ (N is typically 3 or 5). A histogram of heights z from the four images within this neighborhood is created. The histogram is scanned to identify well separated clusters. The two clusters with the maximum number of data points are selected and the cluster centroids (in z) are taken to be the smoothed height values.

9.2 A 1-D Clustering Algorithm

We first review a general 1-D clustering algorithm [60] and then present an adaptation suitable for real-time processing.

The results of peak detection in two channels provide us with four images, I_{1_G}, I_{2_G}, I_{1_B} and I_{2_B} corresponding to the green and blue channels respectively. A histogram A, of heights z, consisting of 256 bins is created from these four images. We define two thresholds T_a and T_b. T_a arises from noise considerations, and its function is to suppress small contributions from noise. Thus, we ensure that the number of elements in every bin should be greater than T_a. T_b is the minimum inter-cluster distance, and depends on the resolution of the imaging system.

We also define $d[C_i, C_j]$, the inter-cluster distance between clusters C_i and C_j to be the distance between the centroids of C_i and C_j.

To partition our gray-value space into different clusters C_i, $i = 1, n$ we first do the following:

$A[i] = 0$, if $A[i] \leq T_a$

A merging technique can be used to group individual elements $A[i]$ into clusters. Initially, each non-zero element $A[i]$ is designated as the cluster center for the cluster. Thus, if we have p non-zero elements we have p clusters C_i, $i = 1, p$.

The algorithm then proceeds as follows:

1. $A[i] = 0$, if $A[i] < T_a$
2. For all elements of A
   if $A[i] \geq T_a$, designate it as a new cluster and initialize its centroids.
3. While the inter-cluster distance $d[C_i, C_j] \leq T_b$ merge C_i and C_j and update the centroids.

---

[1] If the two clusters corresponding to the two surfaces are close enough to merge, then the resolution limit of the system has been exceeded. This is detectable because of the interference phenomena described in Sect. 10.

4. Output the centroids of the two largest clusters. This gives the smoothed surface heights.

9.3 Efficient Implementation

All the above steps can be implemented in one scan of the array **A** with a single iteration. After accumulating the values of neighborhood pixels into the array **A** we set $A[i] = 0$ if $A[i] \leq T_a$. Instead of performing iterative merging, we look for islands of non-zero values, where the separation between islands consists of a string of zero values whose length exceeds $T_{b'}$. $T_{b'}$ is an approximation of T_b and is a slightly different definition of the inter-cluster distance. It is defined to be the distance between the end of one cluster and the beginning of the next. The use of $T_{b'}$ instead of T_b simplifies the computation.

In our system, $T_a = 1$ and $T_{b'} = 4$. The performance of the system is not critically dependent on these parameters. T_a could also have been set to 2. However, large values of T_a would destroy the information present in the signal.

10 Resolution of the Imaging System

We approach the issue of resolution from the viewpoint of being able to detect a defect in the object. There are two criteria here: the resolution along the optical axis, and lateral resolution.

10.1 Resolution Along the z Axis

As seen in Sect. 8, surfaces are identified as peaks in the set of slices. This raises the issue of what happens when two surfaces are close together, Linear deconvolution (Sect. 7) can separate proximate surfaces only if they are farther than two sample slices apart. Of course, bandwidth extrapolation schemes [61, 62] can be used to improve the resolution, but these methods are iterative and hence unsuitable for high speed applications. Thus, the resolution of our system is limited to the distance between two sample slices. However, defects below this resolution can be detected by alternate means, as follows.

If two surfaces are indeed very close together, then interference can be observed in the 2-D intensity image. For instance, if we have a polyimide layer on top of metal, then interference fringes can be observed if the polyimide layer is less than 5 microns thick. This phenomenon was studied using an optical simulator package [63]. Figure 13 shows a 2-D intensity image that exhibits interference fringes due to a thin polyimide film on top of metal. Thus, a height related defect

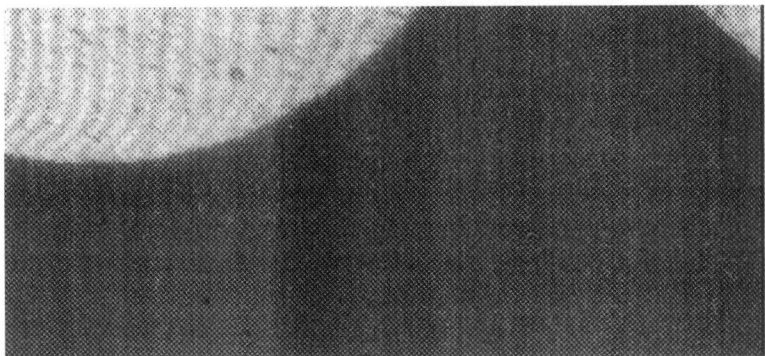

Fig. 13. This figure shows interference fringes due to a thin polyimide film of varying thickness. The polyimide film covers the entire image. The circular region to the upper left is a metal surface. The interference between the metal and polyimide gives rise to the fringes

(film thickness too small) manifests itself as a 2-D intensity defect, composed of interference fringes. These interference fringes could be detected by the back-end inspection algorithms to indicate the presence of the related height defect.

10.2 Lateral (x − y) Resolution

By lateral resolution we mean the smallest lateral extent of a height defect that the system can detect. The major factor determining the lateral resolution is the size of the window used in surface smoothing. There is a tradeoff between two factors: combating noise and preserving the ability to detect small defects. A larger window gives better immunity to noise, but smooths out small defects.

The lateral resolution (in pixels) is $\lceil N/2 \rceil$ where N is the size of the smoothing window. For instance, if the surface smoothing uses a 3×3 neighborhood, defects of sizes greater than 5 pixels can be detected.

11 Experimental Results

All the experiments were conducted on an IBM RS/6000 workstation running ALX 3.1.5. We used both synthetic and real images to test our image processing and surface detection algorithms.

11.1 Relative Reflectance Values

The following table gives the measured relative reflectances of the different surfaces. This information was used to generate synthetic images.

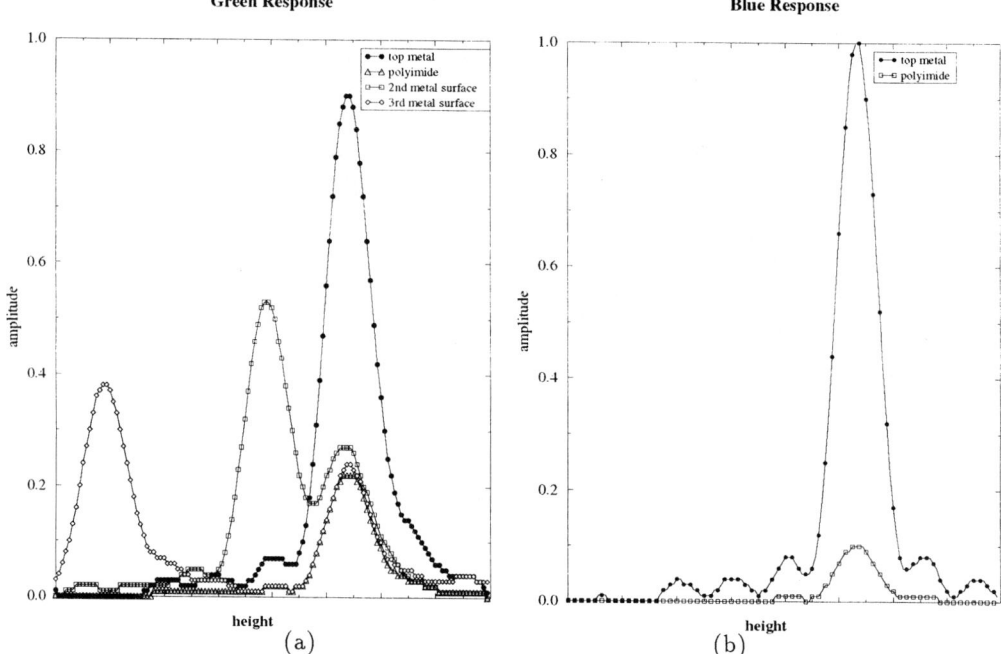

Fig.14. a The responses of the different surfaces as imaged through green light; **b** The responses of the different surfaces as imaged through blue light. Only the top metal and polyimide responses are shown because the responses of the other surfaces closely resembles that of the polyimide

	Blue	Green
top metal	230	179
top polyimide	44	30
second metal surface	35	102
third metal surface	6	68

11.2 Synthetic Image Generation

The synthetic images were generated from the optical characteristics of the current imaging system. The response characteristics of different surfaces (top metal, polyimide, and metal under polyimide) with respect to green and blue light were measured and are shown in Fig. 14. These responses, along with the their known locations (in height) were used to generate synthetic images. The refractive index of polyimide (1.74) was also taken into account.

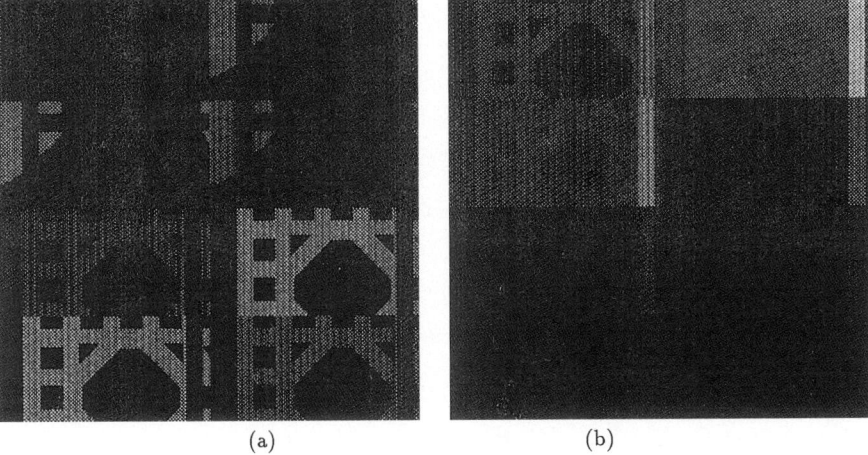

Fig. 15. A set of confocal images. Each confocal image is of size 256×128 pixels. The images in figure **a** and (**b**) are of size 512×512, and each contains eight confocal images. The first eight images are shown in (**a**) and the next eight images are shown in **b**. The sequencing is left to right and top to bottom. The banding in these images is an artifact caused by the image capturing mechanism, as described in Sect. 5.1. This banding is periodic along the x axis, and can be removed by a linearly varying offset

The set of 16 confocal slices was then created by mapping these different surface types via a mask layout pattern. Figure 15 shows the images created for the green band. The images for the blue band are similar, but attenuated.

11.3 Addition of Noise

Gaussian noise with zero mean and different standard deviations were added to the images generated to test the behavior of our algorithms at different noise levels, and at the same time determine the noise level at which the system meets all the design requirements. Also, the signal to noise ratio in the actual blue image was 0.6 times that of the green image. So as a close approximation, we worked with synthetic blue images of twice the standard deviation of the green images.

We plotted the different error types discussed in Sect. 11.5 as a function of noise and the peak measure threshold (described in Sect. 8.2). This determines the operating characteristic of the system, and can then be used to set the thresholds at the desired level. Figure 16 shows such an operating characteristic.

11.4 Introducing Artificial Defects

Artificial defects were also introduced in two ways. In the first technique, we shifted the response curves corresponding to each surface type away from their

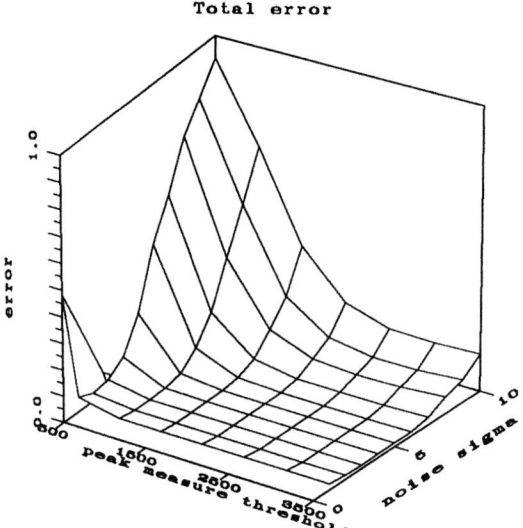

Fig. 16. Error measurements to determine the global operating region

ideal location. This was done in a small region and corresponds to assigning wrong heights to the different surfaces. The second type of artificial defect was introduced by moving the polyimide response curves closer to the second and third layer of metal. This translates to a dish-down where the polyimide has been laid improperly on the metal surface.

In principle, the peak measure threshold could be estimated from the images based on a technique developed by Voorhees and Poggio [64] to estimate the thresholds for the Canny edge detector. However, we prefer to use a pre-determined threshold here in the interests of saving computation time.

The performance required from the system is a total error of less than 5% up to a noise level of $\sigma = 5$. This requirement translated to a peak measure threshold of 2500, as this gives rise to the minimum total error in Fig. 16. The choice of this threshold is not critical, and any value between 2000 and 3000 could be used to provide acceptable performance.

11.5 Evaluation Criteria

The performance of the system is a function of the noise level present as well as the particular values selected for thresholds that may be needed. In order to evaluate the system performance, it is necessary to define a ground truth, and check the output of the system with respect to this. Since we did not have a real part whose dimensions were accurately known, we generated synthetic data, and added varying degrees of noise to it.

Algorithms for a Fast Confocal Optical Inspection System

Three major types of errors were categorized for each surface:

1. Extra surfaces detected
2. No surface detected where one should have been
3. Surface was detected but the height was outside the allowable tolerance value

Tolerance bands were specified for the different error types, based on final product specifications. For example, in the top metal, no pixel should exceed the height tolerance which was 0.5 microns, no extra surface should be detected and not more than 0.1% of the surface should be missing.

In other words, for the top metal, we had the following categories:

1. $h_1 \in [H_1 - \Delta_t, H_1 + \Delta_t]$, $h_2 = 0$ – criteria met
2. $h_1 = h_2 = 0$ – missing surface
3. $h_1 \in [H_1 - \Delta_t, H_1 + \Delta_t]$, $h_2 \neq 0$ – extra surface
4. $h_1 \notin [H_1 - \Delta_t, H_1 + \Delta_t]$, $h_2 = 0$ – exceed height tolerance
5. $h_1 \notin [H_1 - \Delta_t, H_1 + \Delta_t]$, $h_2 \neq 0$ – exceed height tolerance and extra surface

where h_1 and h_2 are the observed heights, H_1 is the actual height that should have been located, and Δ_t is the allowable tolerance.

11.6 Results of Processing the Synthetic Image

The following sequence of algorithms was applied: (a) deconvolution through Wiener filtering (Sect. 7.1.1), (b) peak detection (Sect. 8.2), (c) smoothing using cluster based smoothing over a 3 × 3 window (Sect. 9.1).

In order to employ deconvolution techniques such as Wiener filtering, we need to measure the point spread function of the system, $h(z)$. We used a one-dimensional model for the sake of simplicity, and in order to improve the processing speed of the system. The point spread function was measured by averaging several signals resulting from the reflection off of a mirror-like surface.

Figure 17 shows the result of processing the synthetic images of Fig. 15. The result is displayed as two grayscale encoded height images – an upper surface image and a lower surface image. Artificial defects had been introduced in the generated images by shifting the top polyimide layer down by a small amount in two rectangular regions. The system is able to correctly identify these defective regions on the top surface. This is illustrated in Figs. 17c and 18.

11.7 Results of Processing a Real Image

Figure 19 shows a set of 16 confocal images of metal lines. This image shows a two layered metal pattern on top of an insulating layer. Beneath the insulating layer is another metal plane.

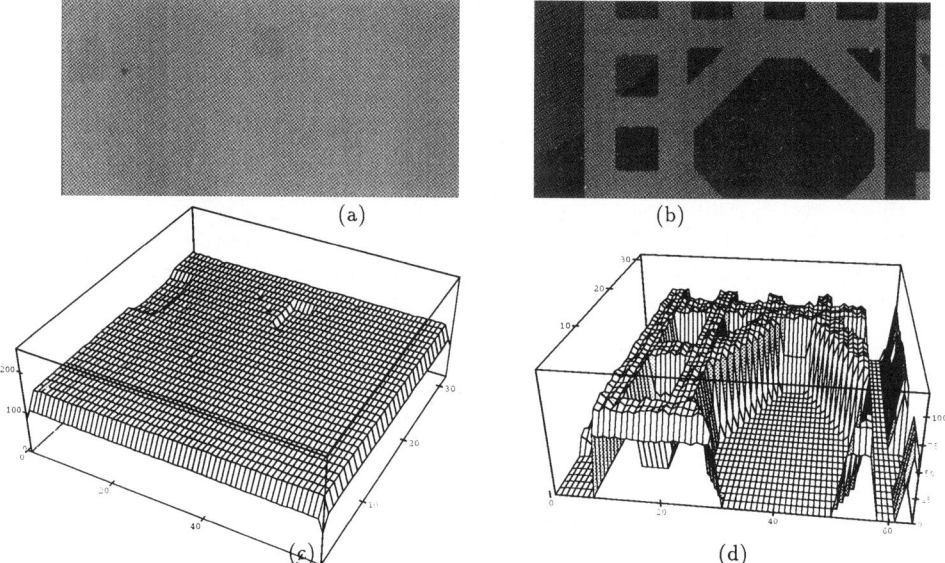

Fig. 17. The result of applying Wiener filtering followed by peak detection and smoothing. Height is encoded via intensity. **a** The upper height image; **b** The lower height image; **c** and **d** A wireframe plot of the surfaces in Fig. 17. The size of the images was reduced to 64 × 32 for ease of plotting

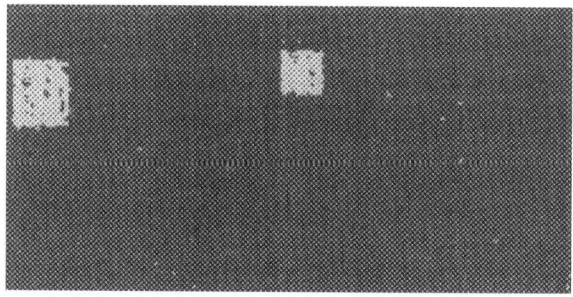

Fig. 18. Emphasizing the gray values between 128 and 132 (both included) of the upper image. The "depression" on the top layer is more clearly visible

Figure 20 shows the result of processing the set of 16 confocal images. These results prove that the system is capable of measuring heights of top surfaces and also of measuring the heights of surfaces under a semi-transparent layer.

Note that the lower height image is somewhat noisy – there are "holes" consisting of black pixels. If the signal is too low at a point (due to attenuation), we do not compute the surface height, but instead encode the pixel a having zero height. The metal film whose surface is being detected here is "grainy," possessing many small regions of low reflectivity. Similarly, the upper height image has flecks

Algorithms for a Fast Confocal Optical Inspection System 469

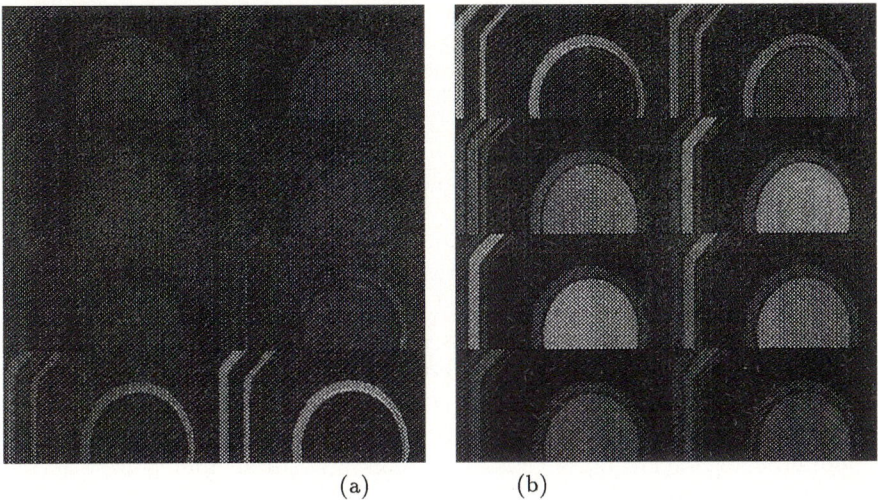

Fig. 19. A set of confocal images. Each confocal image is of size 256 × 120 pixels. The images in **a** and **b** are of size 512 × 480, and each contains eight confocal images. The first eight images are shown in **a** and the next eight images are shown in **b**. The sequencing is left to right and top to bottom

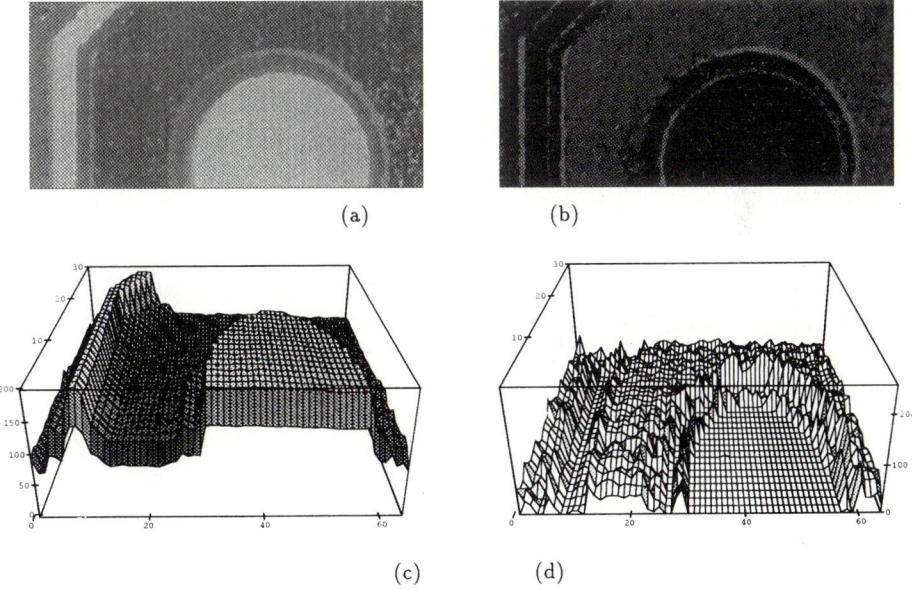

Fig. 20. The result of applying Wiener filtering followed by peak detection and smoothing. Height is encoded via intensity. **a** The upper height image; **b** The lower height image. The heights are displayed using a wireframe model in **c** and **d**. The size of the images was reduced to 64 × 30 for ease of plotting

of white. This occurs because of spurious peaks detected due to the presence of noise.

11.8 The PSF – Its Determination and Use

The PSF of the image can be obtained by three means – by direct measurement, by computation, or theoretical methods. By far, the most used way to find the PSF is by direct measurements [65]. This will take care of peculiar characteristics of the sensing equipment, noise and variations over different regions. The PSF may vary over the image because of the distortion effects of the imaging system. In order to correct for this, the distortion itself can be corrected to a certain extent, thereby indirectly making the PSF spatially invariant. Alternatively, it is possible to take in account the changing PSF in later stages of processing. This method is also referred to as *sectioning*, whereby the image is partitioned into different regions within each of which the PSF is invariant [46].

Not much work has been done in the computational methods to obtain the PSF. The relative motion of various parts of an object in a blurred image is used in the estimation of a spatially variant PSF by Trussell and Fogel [66]. Tan et al. [67] give another technique to estimate the PSF from motion blur. Methods of deconvolution that use PSF's that are not measured from the image, but are computed in some indirect way, are called blind-deconvolution.

Analytical expressions for the PSF can be derived if the aberrations of the system are known. However, aberrations are not usually easy to obtain.

11.9 Discussion

We have investigated the implementation of our algorithm on special purpose hardware. The deconvolution can be viewed as a 16×16 matrix multiply operation. This can be implemented by using commercially available chips such as the TRW TMC2250 which operates at 40 MHz. The peak detection operation can be implemented using comparators and lookup tables. The software simulations were mainly for the purposes of testing the algorithm. The hardware design suggested that operating the system at 32 MHz is feasible. The software simulations was done on a IBM RISC 6000 workstation where each pixel is encoded with 8 bits.

12 Conclusion

We demonstrated the feasibility of using confocal imaging to provide three dimensional information in industrial inspection tasks. The advantages of confocal imaging lie in its speed, non-contact operation and its ability to image semi-transparent objects.

We developed an algorithm which involves deconvolution with a linear filter (the Wiener filter) to improve signal resolution in the z direction. Though non-linear filters provide better signal restoration capabilities, they are not feasible for real time applications. The restored signal is then processed to detect peaks which in turn represent the heights of different points on the object. Finally, we use a cluster based smoothing technique to smooth the surface heights.

References

[1] G. West and T. Clarke, "A survey and examination of subpixel measurement techniques," in *Proc. SPIE*, vol. 1395, pp. 456–63, Sept 1990.
[2] A. Kayaalp, A. R. Rao, and R. Jain, "Scanning electron microscope based stereo analysis," *Machine Vision and Applications*, vol. 3, Fall 1990.
[3] H. Wickramasinghe, "Scanning probe microscopy: current status and future trends," *J. Vac. Sci. Technol. A, Vac. Surf. Films*, vol. 8, no. 1, pp. 363–8, 1990.
[4] T. Wilson, "Confocal scanning microscopes," in *Proc. SPIE, Optics in complex systems*, vol. 1319, pp. 460–1, 1990.
[5] S. Paddcok, P. DeVries, J. Holy, and G. Schatten, "On laser scanning confocal microscopy and three dimensional reconstruction," in *Proc. SPIE, Bioimaging and two dimensional spectroscopy*, vol. 1205, pp. 20–28, 1990.
[6] M. Minsky, "Memoir on inventing the confocal scanning microscope", *Scanning*, vol. 10, no. 4, pp. 128–138, 1988.
[7] M. Petran, M. Hadravsky, M. Egger, and R. Galambos, "Tandem scanning reflected light microscope," *J. Opt. Soc. Am.*, vol. 58, pp. 661–4, 1968.
[8] P. Nipkow, "German patent number 30, 105," 1884.
[9] P. Davidovits and M. Egger, "Scanning laser microscope for biological investigations," *Applied Optics*, vol. 10, pp. 1615–1619, 1971.
[10] C. Sheppard and A. Choudhury, "Image formation in the scanning microscope," *Optica*, vol. 24, pp. 1051, 1978.
[11] A. Boyde, "The tandem scanning reflected microscope," vol. 3, pp. 131–139, Proc. Royal Microscopy Society, 1985. Part2.-Pre micro '84 applications at UCL.
[12] M. Richardson, "Confocal microscopy and 3-d visualization," *Am. Lab.*, vol. 22, pp. 19–20, 22, 24, Nov 1990.
[13] A. Kaufman, R. Yagel, R. Bakalash, and I. Spector, "Volume visualization in cell biology," in *Proc. of the First IEEE Conference on Visualization*, pp. 160–168, 471–472, IEEE, IEEE Comp. Soc. Press, Oct 1990. San Francisco, CA.
[14] B. Masters, "Two and three dimensional visualization of the living cornea and ocular lens," *Machine Vision and Applications*, vol. 4, no. 4, pp. 227–232, 1991.
[15] T. Wilson and C. Sheppard, *Theory and Practice of Scanning Optical Microscopy*. Orlando, FL: Academic Press, 1984.
[16] Y. Howikawa, M. Yamamoto, and S. Dosaka, "Laser scanning microscope: differential phase images," *J. Microscopy*, vol. 148, pp. 1–10, 1987.
[17] M. Bertero et al. "Three dimensional image restoration and super-resolution in fluorescence confocal microscopy," *J. Microscopy*, vol. 157, pp. 3–20, 1989.
[18] A. Dixon, S. Damaskinos, and M. Atkinson, "A scanning confocal microscope for transmission and reflection imaging," *Nature*, vol. 351, pp. 551–3, June 1991.
[19] A. Dixon, S. Damaskinos, and M. Atkinson, "Transmission and double reflection scanning stage confocal microscope," *Scanning*, vol. 13, pp. 229–306, Jul/Aug 1991.

[20] A. Truneh and P. Machy, "Detection of very low receptor numbers on cells by flow cytometry using a sensitive staining method," *Cryometry*, vol. 8, pp. 562–567, 1987.
[21] V. Howard, *Confocal Microscopy*, ch. The confocal microscope as an instrument for measuring microstructural geometry, pp. 285–303. Academic Press, 1 ed. 1990.
[22] K. New, W. Petroll, A. Boyde, L. Martin, P. Corcuff, J. Leveque, M. Lemp, H. Cavanagh, and J. Jester, "In vivo imaging of human teeth and skin using real time confocal microscopy," *Scanning*, vol. 13, no. 5, pp. 369–72, 1991.
[23] W. Petroll, H. Cavanagh, M. Lemp, P. Andrews, and J. Jester, "Digital image acquisition in in vivo confocal microscopy," *J. Microscopy*, vol. 165, no. 1, pp. 61–69, 1992.
[24] L. Karlsson and M. C. Orive, "The new stereological tools in metallography: estimation of pore size and number in aluminium," *J. Microscopy*, vol. 165, pp. 391–415, March 1992.
[25] R. W. Wijnaendts-Van-Resandt, *Confocal Microscopy*, ch. Semiconductor metrology, pp. 339–360. Academic Press, 1 ed., 1990.
[26] S. Hewlett and T. Wilson, "Resolution enhancement in three-dimensional confocal microscopy," *Machine Vision and Applications*, vol. 4 pp. 233–242, 1991.
[27] P. J. Besl and R. Jain, "Three-dimensional object recognition," *ACM Computing Surveys*, vol. 17, pp. 75–145, March 1985.
[28] S. Akamine, B. Hadimioglu, B. K. Yakub, H. Yamada, and C. Quate, "Acoustic microscopy beyond the diffraction limit: an application of microfabrication," in *TRANSDUCERS '91. Int. Conf. on Solid State Sensors and Actuators*, (New York, NY), pp. 857–859, IEEE, 1991.
[29] K. Lee, D. Abraham, F. Secord, and L. Landstein, "Submicron si trench profiling with an electron beam fabricated atomic microscope tip," *J. Vacuum Science Technology B. Microelectron. Process. Phenom*, vol. 9, no. 6, pp. 3562–3568, 1991.
[30] M. Tortonese, H. Yamada, R. Barrett, and C. Quate, "Atomic force microscopy using a piezoresistive cantilever," in *TRANSDUCERS '91. Int. Conf. on Solid State Sensors and Actuators*, (New York, NY), pp. 448–51, IEEE, IEEE, 1991.
[31] P. Montgomery, J. Fillard, M. Castagne, and D. Montaner, "Phase stepping microscopy (psm): a qualification tool for electronic and optoelectronic devices," *Semiconductor Sci. Technology*, vol. 7, no. 1A, pp. PA237–42, 1992.
[32] J. Fillard, P. Gall, J. Bonnafe, M. Castagne, and T. Ogawa, "Laser scanning microscopy: a survey of recent investigations in semiconductor materials," *Semiconductor Sci. Technology*, vol. 7, pp. PA 283–87, Jan 1992.
[33] J. Tome, "Infrared interferometry cuts a swath," *Lasers Optronics*, vol. 10, pp. 21 3, Nov 1992.
[34] J. Thong and B. Breton, "A topography measurement intrument based on the scanning electron microscope," *Rev. Sci. Instrum.*, vol. 63, pp. 131–138, Jan 1992.
[35] P. Corredera, A. Pons, J. Campos, and A. Corrons, "Interferometric system for the inspection and measurement of the quality of optical fibre ends," in *Proc. SPIE – Int. Soc. Opt. Engg., Fibre Optic Metrology and Standards*, (The Hague, Neatherlands), SPIE, Mar 1991.
[36] G. Blessing, D. Eitzen, H. Ryan, and J. Slotwinski, "Surface micrometrology using ultrasound," in *IEEE 1990 Ultrasonics Symposium Proceedings*, (Honolulu, HI), pp. 1047–52, IEEE, Dec 1990.
[37] A. Pidduck and V. Nayar "Optical imaging of microroughness on polished silicon wafers," *Appl Physics A, Solid Surf.*, vol. A53, pp. 557–62, Dec 1991.
[38] S. Bozhevol'nyi, E. Zolotov, and P. Rad'ko, "Study of the differential phase optical microscope," *Sov. Phys. Tech. Phys.*, vol. 36, pp. 187–91, Feb 1991.
[39] J. Blatt, J. Hooker, and R. Belfatto, "3d inspection of large objects by moire profilometry," *in Southcon/90 Conference Record 1990*, (Orlando, FL), pp. 96–100, Electr. Conventions Manage, Mar 1990.
[40] P. D. Groot, "Three color laser diode interferometer," *Appl. Optics*, vol. 30, pp. 3612–16, Sep 1991.

[41] C. Wust and D. Capson, "Surface profile measurement using color fringe projection," *Machine Vision and Applications*, vol. 4, no. 3, pp. 193–203, 1991.
[42] M. Offside, "A phase sensitive optical heterodyne interferometer for surface height measurement," *Trans. Inst. Meas. Control*, vol. 13, no. 3, pp. 115–24, 1991.
[43] P. Montgomery, J. Fillard, N. Tchandjou, and S. Ardisasmita, "Three dimensional nanoprofiling of semiconductor surfaces," in *Proc. SPIE – Optical Testing and Metrology III: Recent advances in Industrial Optical Inspection*, (San Diego, CA), pp. 515–524, SPIE, July 1990.
[44] J. Song and T. Vorburger, "Stylus profiling at high resolution and low force," *Applied Optics*, vol. 30, pp. 42–50, Jan 1991.
[45] P. Besl, *Advances in Machine Vision: Applications and Architectures*, ch. Active optical range imaging sensors. Springer-Verlag, 1 ed., 1989.
[46] R. Bates and M. McDonnell, *Image Restoration and Reconstruction*. Clarendon Press, Oxford, 1986.
[47] H. Andrews and B. Hunt, *Digital Image Restoration*. Prentice Hall, Englewood Cliffs, NJ., 1977.
[48] W. Blass and G. Halsey, *Deconvolution of Absorption Spectra*. Academic Press, New York, 1981.
[49] W. H. Press, B. P. Flannery, S. A. Teukolsky, and W. T. Vetterling, *Numerical Recipes in C: The Art of Scientific Computing*. Cambridge University Press, 1988.
[50] B. Frieden, "Image enhancement and restoration," in *Picture Processing and Digital Filtering* (T. Huang, ed.), Springer-Verlag, New York, 1979.
[51] P. Jansson, R. Hunt, and E. Plyler, "Resolution enhancement of spectra," *J. Opt. Soc. Am. A*, vol. 60, no. 2, pp. 596–599, 1970.
[52] P. Jansson, "Method for determining the response function of a high-resolution infrared spectrometer," *J. Opt. Soc. Am. A*, vol. 60, no. 2, pp. 184–191, 1970.
[53] P. V. Cittert, *Z. Physik*, vol. 69, pp. 298, 1931.
[54] L. Lacomb, T. Corle, and N. Levine, "Three dimensional image visualization using the real time confocal scanning optical microscope," in *Proc. SPIE*, vol. 1261, pp. 91–101, Sept 1990.
[55] J. Eklundh and A. Rosenfeld, "Peak detection using difference operators," *IEEE Trans. Pattern Analysis and Machine Intelligence*, vol. PAMI-1, pp. 317–325, July 1979.
[56] A. Rosenfeld and P. D. L. Torre, "Histogram concavity analysis as an aid in threshold selection," *IEEE Trans. Systems, Man, and Cybernetics*, vol. 13, no. 3, pp. 231–235, 1983.
[57] M. I. Sezan, "A peak detection algorithm and its application to histogram-based image data reduction," *Computer Vision, Graphics and Image Processing*, vol. 49, pp. 36–51, 1990.
[58] J. F. Canny, "A computational approach to edge detection," *IEEE Trans. Pattern Analysis and Machine Intelligence*, vol. 8, pp. 679–698, November 1986.
[59] A. Rodriguez and J. Mandeville, "Image registration for automated inspection of 2d electronic circuit patterns," in *High-Speed Inspection Architectures, Barcoding and Character Recognition, Proc. SPIE 1384* (M. J. W. Chen, ed.), pp. 2–14, 1990.
[60] R. O. Duda and P. Hart, *Pattern classification and scene analysis*. John Wiley and Sons, 1973.
[61] R. Gerchberg, "Super-resolution through error energy reduction," *Optica Acta*, vol. 21, no. 9, pp. 709–720, 1974.
[62] A. Papoulis, "A new algorithm in spectral analysis and band-limited extrapolation," *CAS*, vol. CAS-22, pp. 735–742, Sep 1975.
[63] C.-M. Yuan and A. J. Strojwas, "User manual of an optical image profile modeling software," tech. rep., Carnegie Mellon University, 1990.
[64] H. Voorhees and T. Poggio, "Detecting textons and texture boundaries in natural images," in *First International Conference on Computer Vision*, pp. 250–258, 1987.

[65] P. Shaw and D. Rawlins, "The point spread function of a confocal microscope: its measurement and use in deconvolution of 3-d data," *J. Microscopy*, vol. 163, no. 2, pp. 151–165, 1991.

[66] H. Trussell and S. Fogel, "Identification and restoration of spatially variant motion blurs in sequential images," *IEEE Trans. Image Processing*, vol. 1, pp. 123–126, Jan 1992.

[67] K. Tan, H. Lim, and B. Tan, 'Restoration of real world motion blurred images," *Computer Vision, Graphics and Image Processing*, vol. 53, pp. 291–299, May 1991.

Qualitative Recognition of Aircraft in Perspective Aerial Images

S. Das, B. Bhanu, X. Wu, and R.N. Braithwaite

Abstract. Recognition of aircraft in complex, perspective aerial imagery is difficult because of occlusion, shadow, cloud cover, haze, seasonal variations, clutter and various forms of image degradation. This chapter describes a system for aircraft recognition that addresses some of these issues. The recognition system uses a hierarchical object model database that includes models represented using advance concepts to geometric entities. It involves three key processes: (a) The *qualitative object recognition* process is responsible for model-based *symbolic* feature extraction and *generic* object recognition; (b) The *refocused matching and evaluation* process accesses deeper levels of the database hierarchy with input from (a) to refine the extracted features and to perform more *specific* classification; and (c) the *primitive feature extraction* process regulates the extracted features based on their saliency and interacts with (a) and (b). Experimental results showing the qualitative recognition of aircraft in perspective, aerial images are presented.

1 Introduction

Photointerpretation (PI) has been an important application domain of image understanding (IU) techniques for about two decades. There have been several U.S. Government programs initiated in the past, e.g., SCORPIUS [8], RADIUS [16, 36], in this area. The importance of automating the PI process is underscored by the fact that a very small percentage of the available imagery in the intelligence community is currently being analyzed due to manpower limitations [1]. An important goal of PI is image exploitation or extraction of intelligence from image data, particularly aerial imagery, to aid reconnaissance tasks, such as airfield, port, and troop movement monitoring. The problem of PI is one of identifying instances of "known" object models in images acquired from a platform, such as by a satellite or a reconnaissance aircraft. The "known" objects are a collection of geometric (e.g., CAD-based) models available to the object recognition system. Model-based object recognition is a challenging task and requires *efficient* indexing of the stored object models for realistic-time performance.

In real-world PI scenarios, there are additional factors that complicate the overall model-based object recognition process. These include occlusion, shadow, cloud cover, haze, seasonal variations, clutter, and various other forms of image degradation. All of these problems put heavy requirements on any IU system to be robust. For example, the goal of the SCORPIUS program was to be demonstrate the object-oriented image exploitation capability over a wide range of imaging conditions with performance equivalent to a "novice" image analyst [8]. An IU system for photointerpretation is typically required to identify buildings, aircraft, ships, ground vehicles, bridges, and storage facilities. Of these, the first two object classes – buildings and aircraft – have received the maximum attention in the literature. Recognition of buildings has proved to be relatively easier than that of aircraft because of the structural simplicity of the former. Although there have been several aircraft recognition systems proposed in the past, very few of these have actually addressed the concerns of real-world, such as those mentioned earlier in this paragraph, or are demonstrated to be effective in practical scenarios.

In this chapter, we describe an IU system for aircraft recognition under development that addresses some of the issues related to geometric model-based object recognition and also the variabilities of real-world scenarios, such as shadow, clutter, and low contrast. We distinguish between two types of image features: *primitive* or low-level, features that are completely data-driven, e.g., edge segments, lines, regions; *symbolic* or intermediate-level, features that are data/goal driven, e.g., convex groups of lines, surfaces, ribbons. Symbolic features are usually derived from mappings of primitive features under geometrical and physical constraints. In addition to features, we shall also refer to *concepts* that are used to represent the system's knowledge about the domain of aircraft recognition and about the world. There are two types of concepts: *basic*, concepts that are independent of the domain, such as unary properties (e.g., small, large), binary properties (e.g., smaller, larger), spatial relationships (e.g., connected-to, left-of, front); *advance*, concepts that are domain dependent and are defined in terms of symbolic features, basic concepts, and other advance concepts, such as an aircraft wing which can be represented by a convex group of lines and which is known to be connected to the aircraft fuselage.

Our system uses a hierarchical representation, consisting of *qualitative-to-quantitative* descriptions, of object models (aircraft in this case). Such descriptions vary from advance concepts (e.g., aircraft wing) to primitive geometric entities (e.g., points, lines) and allow increasingly focused search of the precise models in the database to match the image features. The organization of our model database is in the form of a hierarchy of generic-to-specific information about generic objects (e.g., aircraft), object classes (e.g., jumbo aircraft), specific objects (e.g., Boeing 747), and aspects of an object. It is the *specificity* of the information available at any given level of the hierarchy that controls the focus of the search. Since the space for indices may be bounded [12], such distribution of information among the various levels enables one to derive a set of efficient indices for entities at each level. Besides, this representation allows partial recognition, such as determination of an object class, even when a precise object model is not available. Current model-based recognition systems do not have this capability, i.e., they do not exhibit graceful degradation when encountering a new model.

Additionally, our approach emphasizes the importance of using *symbolic features* which are known to be aspect invariant in majority of the real-world perspective imagery except for extreme viewpoint situations. To account for image variabilities, our system exploits *heterogeneous models* such as that of camera/

platform, sun, shadow to derive these symbolic features in a robust manner. Finally, we have brought in a novel aspect to the recognition problem by *regulating* the extracted *primitive features* based on their saliency. We demonstrate that this step helps to distinguish the relevant features from the image clutter, thereby reducing the complexity of the search problem.

The *main contributions* of this research are the extraction of perceptually salient primitive features and their use in a regulated fashion, the use of heterogeneous geometric and physical models associated with image formation for feature extraction and subsequent recognition, and the integration of high-level recognition processes with low-level feature extraction ones. Real-world data, highlighting the difficulties of aircraft recognition in practical situations, is used to demonstrate the effectiveness of our proposed approach. In the following sections, we will discuss the details of our approach to aircraft recognition. Section 2 describes the background and motivation behind the work reported in this paper. Section 3 describes the key features of our qualitative-to-quantitative approach to object recognition. Section 4 presents the details of an algorithm that integrates feature refinement and object classification. Section 5 gives the details of implementation and the experimental results for qualitative recognition of aircraft. Section 6 presents concluding remarks.

2 Background and Motivation

2.1 Background

There is a variety of object recognition and classification techniques that can possibly be applied to the domain of aircraft recognition. However, the algorithms reviewed in this section are those that have been applied to the specific problem of aircraft identification in both 2-D and 3-D.

The different approaches to aircraft recognition that have been proposed so far can be broadly classified into the following categories:

- *Moment Invariant Techniques* – These techniques use moment invariant features [26] of the aircraft silhouette and silhouette border to perform the classification task. The advantage of these techniques is that these invariants are unaffected by rotational, translational, and scaling differences between an object model and its observed image. The disadvantage is the sensitivity of the invariants to mass distribution inside the silhouette, occlusion, clutter, noise, and other image abnormalities.
- *Syntactic/Semantic Grammar Techniques* – These approaches use linguistic pattern recognition techniques to analyze shapes and classify aircraft using piecewise linear border approximations. Using a set of terminal symbols to represent image primitives (lines or arcs) and relationships (parallel, collinear, right angles) between these primitives, a grammar is derived to specify allowable

combinations of these primitives to construct complete aircraft borders. Other information, e.g., mean, variance, etc., about a particular object is represented by the semantics introduced into the grammar. Thus, recognition of individual aircraft reduces to the task of parsing a set of words (image primitives) to create legal sentences (aircraft borders). The advantages of syntactic/semantic grammar over moment invariants are that the former allows specification of local structure rather than global shape and the variations in object shapes can be explicitly incorporated into the models, thereby reducing the sensitivity to noise. However, these approaches are also inadequate in handling occlusion and clutter.

- *Fourier Descriptor Techniques* – In these approaches, the shape of the aircraft's closed contour in the image plane is represented using a Fourier descriptor (FD) which is subsequently used to recognize future instances of the aircraft. The principle of FD [51] is that the boundary of a closed planar figure can be expressed as a function of some variable and repeating this process multiple times will produce a periodic function that can be expressed in a Fourier series. This series is the Fourier descriptor of the planar figure. Various normalization procedures are used to derive feature sets that are invariant with respect to starting point, rotation, translation, and scale. The advantage of FD's is that partial shape matching in presence of occlusion can also lead to complete classification. However, there may be instances when the normalization for deriving invariant features is not uniquely determined. Other factors affecting FD-based approaches are number of sampling points used on the contour, uniformity of sample spacing, number of FD's used, quantization error, and the amount of perturbation of the contour.
- *Model and Knowledge-Based Techniques* – These techniques seek to represent an aircraft using advance concepts in a hierarchical part-subpart fashion, where the lowest-level representation is usually in terms of image primitives. The recognition process begins by locating these image primitives and then by combining them in a forward- or backward-chaining fashion using the system's model and knowledge base. The advantage of these techniques is that they rely on spatially local features which can be extracted from the sensory data with relative ease. Such features can lead to relatively robust model matching in presence of noise, occlusion, and missing data, when compared to the global shape representations, by incorporating appropriate object, sensory, and contextual information. The main drawbacks of these techniques are the "knowledge acquisition bottleneck" and the real-time implementation.
- *Other Techniques* – These are the techniques that do not exactly belong to any one of the categories described above.

Summaries of the specific algorithms that are representative of these groups appear in Table 1.

The "knowledge-free," global techniques are inadequate in the real-world recognition context, since these almost always treat the object of interest in isolation from the rest of the image, i.e., they assume a perfect segmentation of the

Table 1. Summary of various aircraft recognition techniques

Techniques	References	Descriptions
Moment Invariant	Gupta and Srinath [22]	2D; vector of a sequence of moment invariant functions computed from contour
	Gupta and Srinath [23]	2D; moment function based on distances between each contour pixel and object centroid
	Dudani et al. [15]	3D; invariant features computed from silhouette and its border for different views of each aircraft; Bayes and distance-weighted k-NN classification
	Reeves et al. [40]	3D; normalized moment invariants that are less sensitive to noise than conventional invariants; performance comparable to FD's with/without noise
Syntactic/Semantic Grammar	Tang and Huang [47]	2D; large, useful structures obtained by removing redundant terminal symbols; localization without classification
	Davis and Henderson [14]	2D; hierarchical approach using only grammatically correct fragment at all levels with constrainst propagation; classification into general categories
Fouries Descriptor	Lin and Chellappa [30]	2D; estimation of FD for the complete contour from partial data
	Wallace and Wintz [50]	3D; normalized FD's for global shape descriptions
	Wallace et al. [49]	3D; FD's for local shape descriptions
	Gorin [19]	3D; combines individual classification results from multiple frames to refine accuracy over time
	Gorman et al. [20]	3D; partical recognition of occluded or overlapping objects using FD's of local features
	Chen and Ho [10]	3D; elliptic FD's that are less sensitive to contour perturbation than regular FD's; reduced set of near neighbors in NN classification for speed
Model and Knowledge-Based	Ming and Bhanu [34]	2D; Explanation-Based Learning for model acquisition and refinement;

Table 1. (*Contd.*)

Techniques	References	Descriptions
	Brooks [9]	Conceptual Clustering for classification 3D; specific and generic objects, partially specified scene and camera models; iteration of prediction, description, and interpretation from coarse object subpart and class interpretations to fine distinctions among subclasses and precise 3D quantification
	Moldovan and Wu [35]	3D; hierarchical classification using object skeleton, boundary, surface, volume, and ancillary data; top-down reasoning from higher abstraction level of object details to lower level of greater object-related information
	COBIUS [7]	3D; hierarchical representation of objects and constrains; dynamic selection of region or edge segmentation for initial interpretation, followed by model-based resegmentation to extract expected objects
Other	Ma et al. [33]	2D; normalized shape descriptors faster than FD's and requiring less storage
	Gibbon [18]	2D; weighted chord functions to represent angle chords of an object
	Ben-Arie and Meiri [2]	3D; matching of n-ary relational graphs
	Thompson and Mundy [48]	3D; vertex-pairs as invariant features
	Chien and Aggarwal [11]	3D; quadtree and octree-based object representation; identification using occluding contours
	Reeves and Taylor [41]	3D; recognition based on contour, silhouette, and range imagery

object, which is generally not achieved. Among the past research in aircraft recognition, the ACRONYM system by Brooks [9] is closest to the system described in this paper. In ACRONYM, symbols called quantifiers act as place holders for variable quantities in the representation of generic objects. These quantifiers are provided restrictive set of constraints to model more specific subclasses. The constraints are usually ranges of numbers that determine the degree of specificity of the subclass models. Variations of size, structure, and spatial relations within object classes allow determination of observational invariants of objects that are useful for recognition. Additionally, rules aid in reasoning about geometric relationships between coordinate systems linked by multiple partially specified coordinate transforms. The combination of these two mechanisms provide ACRONYM the means for predicting the appearance of objects in the images. The interpretation process involves the merging of hypothesized local matches (of objects to image features) that provide a consistent global interpretation about the hypothesized object. Using the initial set of derived image primitives, the system searches small image regions for particular features for finer classification and pose estimation of objects.

In spite of its representational elegancy, the ACRONYM system falls short of addressing the real-world concerns posed by the PI problem. In particular, it has no mechanism for automatically acquiring and refining object models, and shadows, clutter and other image degradations are not adequately handled within its framework. In other words, this system is not applicable to real-world, complex images without significant enhancements and modifications.

The deficiencies of the current aircraft recognition techniques emphasize the need for a more practically oriented approach, the motivation for which is now presented in the following subsection.

2.2 Motivation

Central to the model-based approach to recognition lies the implicit assumption that each instance of an object is an accurate projection of the object of known dimensions and shape onto the image plane. Consequently, the focus of the model-based work has been to recover that *single* object from the model database subject to the condition that its descriptions agree best with the projected data for that unknown viewpoint.

The one-step recognition of single-model instances is bound for high complexity and inefficiency because of the lack of reliable low-level image analysis operations and tools. For example, in spite of the large number of image segmentation techniques presently available [25], no general methods have been found that perform adequately across a diverse set of imagery. It is well known that some form of segmentation of the raw image primitives into meaningful groups is essential for any model-based approach [21], whose complexity is exponential in the number of features and linear in the number of models used in recognition. In real-world, complex images, such as those encountered in the PI context, a good segmentation cannot be guaranteed in general. This difficulty is compounded by the fact that a specific aircraft type (e.g., a C-130) can have very different appearances depending on the imaging conditions. To reduce the search time during model matching and also to minimize the false alarm rate, an efficient *indexing* scheme needs to be devised. Such an indexing scheme still remains an important but elusive goal of model-based object recognition. Since one has little control on the imaging conditions and hence on the types of features that may be obtained in unstructured environments, a more pragmatic approach to reduce the burden on the indexing scheme would be to adopt a multi-step recognition approach that proceeds from identifying generic object classes to specific object instances. A nodal hierarchy of model database in which the terminal nodes are specific object models of *geometric entities* and successive higher levels are *symbolic conceptualization* of the lower-level nodes is well suited for this purpose. The conceptualization at any given node is responsible for aggregating the more *generic* (global/coarse/qualitative) object features spanning the lower nodes while leaving the more *specific* (local/fine/quantitative) features to the latter. Interestingly, the hierarchically structured model database and the nature of the associated recognition process are so much akin to the human behavior unlike the traditional model-based approaches. Categorization or the process of treating nonidentical stimuli as equivalent in the case of humans is performed in a highly deterministic way and very often occurs at a *basic level* [42]. Basic categories are those that carry most distinguishing features, such as aircraft, bridge, house, tree, and typically are the ones that are first discriminated in an environment and therefore are more efficiently indexed [42].

Recognition of objects in *real-world* scenarios is a difficult problem even if the best indexing scheme is available. The difficulty is caused by image variations due to noise, shadow, occlusion, weather condition, etc. Most geometric model-based object recognition approaches rely on spatially local image features, such as edges, for making coarse-level decisions that interact to arrive at a globally consistent interpretation of the observed scene. The aforementioned image variabilities cause missing, spurious, or ambiguous features that contribute to inefficient search of the decision space. Quite often a significant amount of contextual or other scene-specific information is required to alleviate this problem.

One of the key factors for poor recognition performance is the presence of *shadows*. Shadows may cause occasional loss in photometric information. However, shadows provide valuable 3D information, such as surface orientations [45], distance between surfaces in an image [17, 27, 32]. They have been successfully utilized in recognizing buildings in aerial photographs [28, 29], but have found little attention in aircraft recognition scenarios. One of the ways shadows can be helpful is in the identification of image features that are caused by raised structures, such as buildings, poles, or aircraft, and also in the determination of their 3D orientations, such as a vertically oriented structure (e.g., a pole) as opposed to a horizontally oriented structure (e.g., an aircraft). Occlusion is another factor which a robust IU system needs to address. In the scenario of aircraft recognition in aerial images, occlusion is primarily due to self-occlusion or close parking of aircraft.

There are significant merits in intelligent *feature selection* for any IU task. Feature selection is of prime importance in executing complex tasks like object recognition in unstructured environments. For the aircraft scenario, this implies an ability to distinguish between image features that are caused by the aircraft structure and those that constitute the clutter. An early selection of the relevant image features could significantly reduce the burden on the subsequent interpretation stage, which would otherwise need to distinguish among several alternatives hypothesized by the different groups of local features. One way to determine the relevant features is to identify the perceptually *salient* image contours (linked edge segments). As psychological evidences indicate, very often such contours are associated with objects that could be of interest or that attract our visual attention immediately. Detection of such salient contours in aerial images, which could very well be aircraft contours, should considerably simplify the segmentation and recognition tasks.

Further improvement in aircraft image understanding is possible by *integrating* the *feature selection* and *image interpretation* processes, so that the interpretation process is driven by the most salient contours first, followed by the less salient ones. Previous attempts at aircraft recognition have focused on a single type of image features, either edges (lines, closed boundaries, etc.) or regions (blobs, silhouettes, etc.). Some IU systems have incorporated both, but dynamically selected only one at any stage of processing, e.g., COBIUS [7]. However, since the extraction processes for these two types of features seek to maximize different criterion functions and are therefore affected by the image variabilities in different ways, the overall recognition process is benefited by combining these features in meaningful ways.

3 A Framework for Model-Based Object Recognition

The general problem of model-based object recognition encompasses the following issues: representation of object models, prediction of observables (mapping of models to images), selection of image features, matching of selected features to the predictions (mapping of images to models), and resolving inconsistencies during the matching process in order to deduce a globally consistent 3D interpretation of the image. We now describe our framework for geometric, model-based object recognition which addresses these issues. Subsequently, the framework forms the basis of our aircraft recognition system. The framework, which is schematically shown in Fig. 1, has four key features: (a) a qualitative-to-quantitative hierarchical object model database that provides the object models for the domain of recognition, and three recognition sub-processes that utilize these models – (b) saliency-based regulation of low-level features that extracts these features from the input images and makes them available to the subsequent steps of recognition in an incremental fashion, (c) model-based symbolic feature extraction and evaluation step that uses the regulated low-level features and the object models together with heterogeneous models of image segmentation, shadow casting, and image acquisition to derive symbolic features for generic object recognition, and (d) refocused matching and evaluation step to perform finer object classification using the hierarchical model database. These four features are now described in detail.

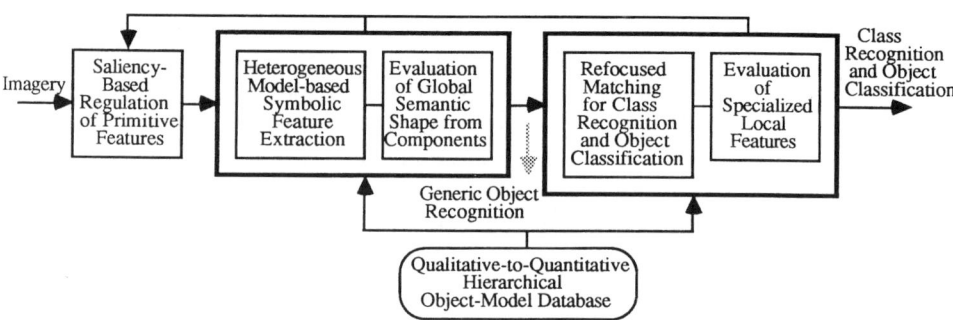

Fig. 1. A framework for model-based object recognition

3.1 Qualitative-to-Quantitative Hierarchical Object Model Database

Each level of the representation hierarchy indicates certain degree of conceptualization for the object entities. The conceptualization of objects at any given level has "class"-specific features sufficient enough to resolve classes at that level. The choice of generic object representation can be in the form of *structural models* [3, 6, 9] or it can be based on the *functional* aspect of the objects [46]. In our approach, we have adopted the former since it is the most natural way to express the part-whole relationships in an object model and also the conceptualization is based on the structural components of the model. However, it is almost intuitive that the best object recognition system for a given task should combine both of these representations.

The *top-level* of the hierarchy corresponds to the *basic categories* [42], e.g., chair, aircraft. According to Rosch et al. [42], the members of each basic category share most common attributes which may be used to form a definite image of that category in human memory. In contrast, the categories that are one level more abstract or the superordinate categories (e.g., furniture, vehicle) exhibit little commonality among its members, while those below the basic level or the subordinate categories (e.g., lounge chair, jumbo jet) demonstrate significant overlap of attributes with other similar categories (for example, jumbo jet shares most of its attributes with other kinds of jets). Thus, the basic categories in the object recognition context are those which can be described in the most conceptual form using *image-based structural* information. The description of a basic category includes its shape attributes and structural subparts in a symbolic (qualitative) form. The progressively deeper levels embody more specific knowledge that becomes completely quantitative once the terminal nodes (location of geometric models) have been reached. A partial hierarchy illustrating this particular database structure for the aircraft category is shown in Fig. 2.

There are two important considerations in designing such a hierarchical database from the point of view object recognition:

- the choice of features to represent a particular object class. In our framework, it is driven by the discriminating power of the features in distinguishing among objects at the same level of the hierarchy. Besides, these features of an object model are ranked according to their relative importance in recognizing that particular object and this order is followed during evidence accumulation to support that object hypothesis.
- the matching process. In our framework, the process can search a lower level for distinguishing features should a categorization be not possible at a particular level because of the lack of suitable features derived from the image (a realistic situation!). Thus, the flow of control during matching is bi-directional, between a generalized class and its more specialized subclasses.

The ACRONYM [9] system which also adopts a hierarchical representational scheme of generic and specific objects addresses these two issues in somewhat different ways. In ACRONYM, the representation scheme is based on the specialization (of an object class) primitive. In other words, all the features that are characteristics of a specialization are also present in the corresponding generic description, except that these feature values are replaced by symbols (quantifiers) in the generic model. In ACRONYM, the reasoning about object classes and their specializations is carried out at the same time, i.e., matches to some parts of an object class is automatically carried down to a match to the corresponding part of a specialization of that object class for the purpose of mensuration. In other words, the control flow is always from the generalized to the specialized classes and failure to recognize the generalized class causes failure of the subclass recognition.

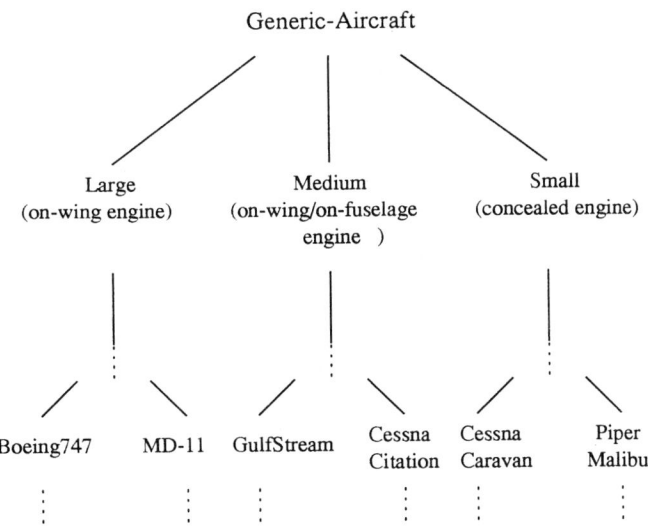

Fig. 2. A partial hierarchy of generic-to-specific aircraft

To specify a subclass of a selected object class, new structural features that are essential for subclass discrimination may be introduced in a qualitative manner or known features (belonging to the parent class) may be instantiated as in ACRONYM. For example, the engine is not an essential structural feature to detect a generic aircraft and is therefore not a part of the generic aircraft model, but it is required for subclass discrimination as shown in Fig. 2. Another important issue related to this hierarchical design is the degree of conceptualization that may be required at each level which in turn determines the number of levels. However, that is not the focus of this paper, instead the emphasis here is on given such a hierarchical database of advance concepts to geometric entities how one may utilize it to perform qualitative-to-quantitative recognition of objects.

3.2 Saliency-Based Regulation of Low-Level Features

Application of current model-based object recognition techniques to real-world, complex scenarios generally produces unsatisfactory results because of the large amount of image *clutter* that may be present in these cases. The clutter information misleads the recognition system to believe that it is associated with the target objects when actually it is not. A preprocessing step which is so important for any IU task has been ignored, by and large, in model-based object recognition approaches. At the same time, considerable effort has been directed towards segmentation and grouping of primitive features. The preprocessing step is necessary to improve object contrast and to reduce noise and clutter in the image. While noise and contrast may be improved by applying standard filtering techniques, clutter rejections is difficult using local image measures unless these measures have strong saliency, e.g., color.

One way to distinguish an object from its background clutter is by its *perceptual saliency*. Humans can visually attend to salient structures almost immediately without scanning an entire image. The different saliency measures can be length, curvature, or contrast of primitive features. Sha'ashua and Ullman [44] present an iterative method of extracting a collection of data that are globally salient using local measurements of curvature and curvature variation.

We adopt a *non-iterative* approach that utilizes simple local measures of saliency based on the *strengths* of detected edge pixels, and *lengths* and *local curvatures* of edge segments. As a first step, edge pixels at multiple thresholds are extracted. This is motivated by the fact that no single threshold is suitable for all the different images that may be encountered in practice, let alone for the different parts of a single image. Edge pixels are grouped based on the local curvature values and the continuity of edge segments. In addition, the flow of low-level features that are used to derive the symbolic features is regulated based on the edge-strength measure. Regulation may also be based on the "specialized" nature of the features as required by the refocused matching process.

3.3 Model-Based Symbolic Feature Extraction and Evaluation

This module is responsible for *generic object recognition* or categorization at the *basic level*. Because of the conceptual nature of the model descriptions at this level, it is crucial that symbolic features be extracted from the primitives and be used in the matching process. Symbolic features may be derived using perceptually grouped primitives. The attractive feature of perceptual grouping is that the groups are more useful for higher-level image interpretation processes, such as object recognition, than the individual primitive features of the group and the grouping process is domain independent. Although, the perceptually grouped primitives improve the efficiency of recognition search techniques, they do not have the discriminating power of symbolic features that are domain dependent. The main drawback of the perceptual groups is that these are based on local measures, such as proximity, collinearity, parallelism [31], while the desired symbolic features need to exhibit more global properties that are typical of a basic category. The extraction of symbolic features is goal-driven in our approach, based on the domain knowledge about generic objects.

Both symbolic features and advance concepts are represented in our system by *production rules*. Once the conditions of a rule have been satisfied, the rule action asserts the presence of the symbolic feature or the advance concept. There are two types of production rules:

- a qualitative rule, which measures the qualitative properties of symbolic features and advance concepts, and
- a quantitative rule, which computes values for the corresponding symbolic features or advance concepts.

For example, in the case of a base category, the conditions of the rule are essentially the part decompositions and the structural relationships among the parts, while the action is the name of the category. Each part is defined by a similar production rule. Such whole-to-part decomposition is essential for generic object recognition [3] and is central to the *Recognition By Components* (RBC) theory [6].

The *extraction* of symbolic features beyond perceptual grouping requires special consideration. This is because there exists no "meta-rule" of perceptual organization that will allow combination of its domain-independent rules. Consequently, the recognition search process is initiated at the top level of the database hierarchy and is allowed to loop through the production rules of the node being visited in a goal-decomposition fashion till it encounters a rule whose conditions involve perceptual groups. At this instant, the symbolic feature extraction process is started. In most practical situations, the need for recognition will be driven by *what matters in the environment*. Therefore, the perceiving agent will be able to reduce the number of base categories that need to be visited to initiate the symbolic feature extraction process by using some background/contextual knowledge.

The *evaluation process* involves the verification of the *global semantic shape* components to correspond to the qualitative object or the base category, i.e., the verification step is one of testing all the conditions of the highest level production rule associated with a base category. It is essentially a *reasoning process* based on *evidence accumulation* to infer the presence of the selected base category in the image. Such decision making process is typical of humans and constitutes the very last stage in the feature analysis model of human pattern recognition [43]. The key feature of this evaluation step in our framework is the use of *heterogeneous* models to accrue evidence for the semantic components of a base category. These models include:

- edge/grey scale-based model for image segmentation,
- models for shadow casting process, and
- models for image acquisition.

Also used are the *dominant axes* that characterize the shape of the generic object class. We assert that the use of such heterogeneous models is essential for any real-world aircraft recognition task and is exclusive to our recognition system.

Finally, our system provides a *feedback* path from the generic recognition module to a feature regulation module (see Fig. 1). The feedback control is used to acquire additional low-level features in the event of recognition failure or low recognition confidence. Integrating feature acquisition and recognition is essential for robust object recognition. However, this aspect has *not* been addressed by previous model-based recognition techniques. The output of the symbolic feature extraction and evaluation process is a known generic object class and labeled symbolic features that will be useful for finer classification.

3.4 Refocused Matching and Evaluation

This module is responsible for *further classification* of an object whose category has been determined by the generic recognition process. The key difference of this step and the multiresolution approaches to recognition is that the former views the object model database at increasing resolution instead of the image. The additional effort involved in our approach is the creation of the hierarchical database, while in the latter the resolution is varied by image resampling. It may be noted that in the absence of any higher-level control knowledge, the resampling process may exclude important object features while accommodating clutter. In our approach, the data reduction is achieved by deriving symbolic features that are more "focused" or localized with respect to a particular level.

During the course of *refocused recognition*, instances of new symbolic features of the object model may be identified in the image or old symbolic features extracted in previous cycles may be subjected to mensuration. Evaluation of the recognition results may require refinement of the features at the symbolic feature extraction level or new model features may prompt access to "special" local features (e.g., a curve at a certain image location) at the feature regulator level.

Usually, the derived symbolic features guide the search for these special features. The final result of refocused matching is object recognition/classification.

4 A Qualitative Recognition Algorithm

The emphasis of this paper is on qualitative recognition of aircraft using the framework described in the previous section. In our representational scheme, the volumetric shape of a generic aircraft is described using the linear RSHGC (Right Straight Homogeneous Generalized Cylinder, see Fig. 3) representation [4] and the structural components of a generic aircraft are wings, fuselage, tails, rudder, and nose (see Table 2). The corresponding (expected) image descriptions are indicated in Table 3. These predictions about image features follow the fact that linear RSHGC descriptors project to lines in a plane (see Appendix A.1). The symbolic definitions (simplified) of a generic aircraft and its three subclasses based on the hierarchy of Fig. 2 are illustrated in Fig. 4. Here, the action part is the assertion that the symbolic description is one of a generic aircraft or one of its subclasses. Similar production rules are used to define each of the subparts. One common feature of the shape descriptions of all the subparts is the convexity and another one is the single axis of symmetry. Examples of subpart-specific information include trapezoid-like shapes, one that monotonically decrease away from the fuselage, for the wings and tails, and the quantity of these subparts (see Table 3). At the subclass level, the distinctions are based on the engine location – on-wing (large), on-fuselage (large/medium), in-body (small) – which is still a qualitative information but is more specific. All of these symbolic definitions are stored in the hierarchical object model database described in Sect. 3.1.

Give an input 2-D image and ancillary data about the imaging parameters and scene conditions, the algorithm for qualitative recognition of aircraft consists of

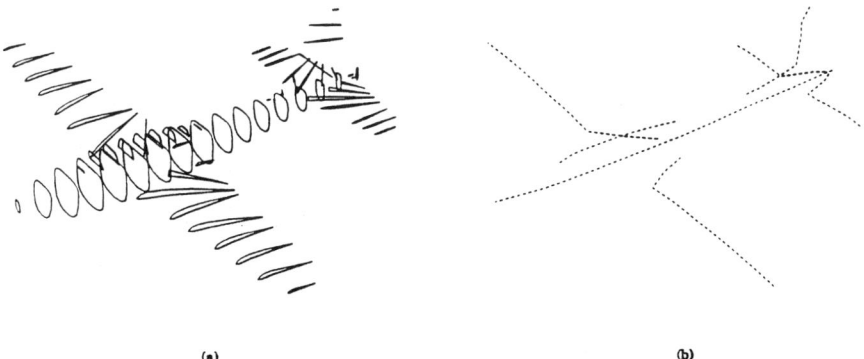

(a)   (b)

Fig. 3. Generalized Cylinders representation of the subparts of a generic aircraft: **a** cross-sections of GCs, and **b** axes of GCs in **a**

Table 2. The description of the form of a generic aircraft model

Model Part	Qualitative Definition	Inter-relationship
Nose	• one point of high curvature (nose tip) • one axis of symmetry through this high curvature point • monotonically increasing cross-section along this axis and at right angles to it starting at one end	connected to the fuselage
Fuselage	• elongated shape • one axis of symmetry • monotonically increasing right cross-section along this axis	connected to the nose, wings, tails, rudder
Wing	• one axis of symmetry • monotonically increasing right cross-section along this axis • two in number placed equidistant from the nose tip on either side of the fuselage axis	connected to the fuselage-the axis of symmetry of each wing makes the same angle with the fuselage axis
Tail	• one axis of symmetry • monotonically increasing right cross-section along this axis • two in number placed equidistant from the nose tip on either side of the fuselage axis	connected to the fuselage-the axis of symmetry of each tail makes the same angle with the fuselage axis
Rudder	• one axis of symmetry • monotonically increasing right cross-section along this axis	connected to the fuselage-the axis of symmetry is in a plane perpendicular to that of the fuselage axis

Table 3. Image descriptions of the different parts of the generic aircraft model

Model part	Model shape	Image contour shape	Connecting (to other parts) segment shape
Nose	Straight	Wedge	Straight
Fuselage	Straight	Linear	Straight
Wing	Straight	Trapezoid	Straight
Tail	Straight	Trapezoid	Straight
Rudder	Straight	Trapezoid	Straight

the steps illustrated in Fig. 5. Some of these steps, i.e., the critical ones, such as saliency-based features regulation, symbolic feature extraction and generic object recognition, and refocused matching based on specialized feature acquisition, have been discussed in Sect. 3 while describing our framework for model-based

```
(define-rule GENERIC-AIRCRAFT              (define-rule LARGE-AIRCRAFT
  "The description of a generic aircraft"    "The description of a large aircraft class"
  (shape-description = Linear RSHGC)         (symbolic-feature = ENGINE)
  (symbolic-feature = WING) (satisfy = TRUE) (location (ENGINE, WING)))
  (symbolic-feature = FUSELAGE) (satisfy = TRUE)
  (symbolic-feature = TAIL) (satisfy = ø)                    (b)
  (symbolic-feature = RUDDER) (satisfy = ø)
  (symbolic-feature = NOSE) (satisfy = ø)  (define-rule MID-AIRCRAFT
  (connected-to (WING, FUSELAGE))            "The description of a mid aircraft class"
  (connected-to (TAIL, FUSELAGE))            (symbolic-feature = ENGINE)
  (connected-to (RUDDER, FUSELAGE))          (location (ENGINE, WING)) v
  (connected-to (NOSE, FUSELAGE))            (location (ENGINE, FUSELAGE)))
  (closer-to (WING, NOSE, TAIL))
  (closer-to (WING, NOSE, RUDDER))                           (c)
  (closer-to (TAIL, RUDDER, WING))
  (closer-to (RUDDER, TAIL, WING)))        (define-rule SMALL-AIRCRAFT
                                             "The description of a small aircraft class"
                                             (symbolic-feature = ENGINE)
                                             (location (ENGINE, ø)))
              (a)
                                                             (d)
```

Fig. 4. Simplified examples of advance concepts: **a** a generic aircraft, and the three aircraft classes; **b** large; **c** medium; **d** small

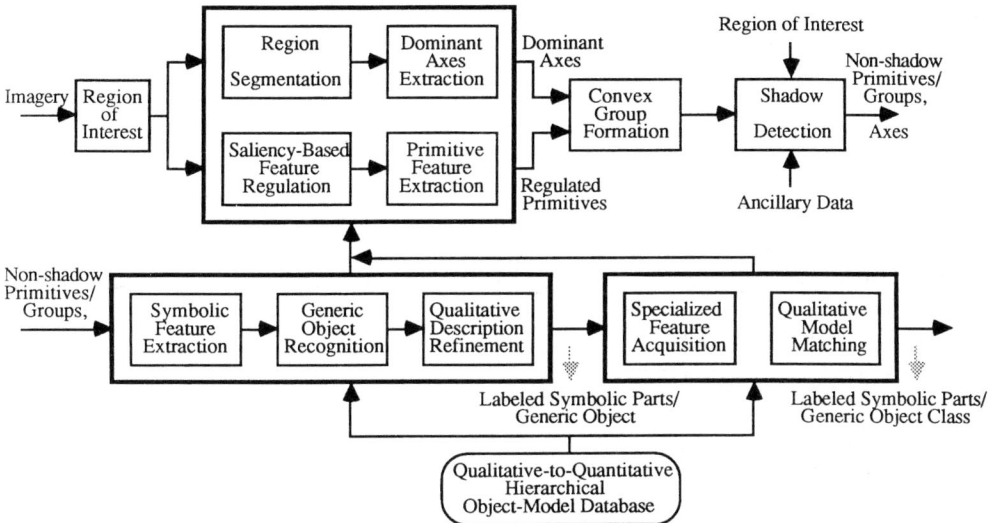

Fig. 5. A flow diagram of the *qualitative* object recognition algorithm

object recognition. These steps, along with others shown in Fig. 5, will now be detailed as part of the qualitative recognition algorithm.

4.1 Region of Interest Identification

In any 3D scene interpretation scenario, the objects of interest typically occupy a limited portion of the visual field. On the other hand, the input imagery in PI are usually of very high resolution, which puts significant burden on preprocessing, segmentation, and feature extractions steps. By performing intelligent search to direct the focus of attention at certain parts of the image, the regions of interest (ROIs) containing the target objects (aircraft in our case) can be identified. A traditional approach is to sample the image and submit the low resolution image to the recognition process, but such subsampling may loose important information regarding the object of interest. Alternately, we adopt a context-driven approach to isolate the basic categories or generic classes from the database that are likely to be present in the image. Our approach begins with a low resolution version of the original image and identifies different image parts that have a large concentration of perceptual groups of primitive feature types that are characteristic of the targeted generic classes. Next, each of these subimages are examined at increasingly higher resolution using similar argument until the original resolution is attained. Further details of this step appears in [38].

Once the ROIs have been identified, each of them is subjected to the recognition process in succession. The following discussions apply to every ROI.

4.2 Saliency-Based Feature Regulation

An ROI is first treated with a Gaussian filter for noise removal. Edge pixels in images are detected using six 5×5 masks sensitive to edge orientations in steps of 30° [39]. At each image location, the edge response is set to the magnitude (and the corresponding direction) of the 5×5 edge mask that gives the largest response. Edges are thinned to one-pixel width by retaining only those edge pixels that satisfy the following conditions: (a) the edge magnitude is larger than the magnitude of its two neighbors in a direction normal to the edge direction, and (b) the edge directions of the two neighboring pixels are within 30° of that of the central pixel. The thinned edge pixels are next used to extract perceptually salient contours and other primitive features. Intuitively speaking, the strongest edge pixels will typically lie on the object boundaries. However, what separates an object from the background in monochromatic images are the perceptually salient edge contours or linked edge segments. Our approach to identifying perceptually salient contours is based on finding *long, smooth* edge segments that are made up of *high-magnitude* edge pixels.

The above goal can be formulated as a problem of finding an edge segment of length N starting at a terminal pixel, corresponding to $s = 0$ (s being the segment parameter), subject to the following optimization:

$$\max_{C \in C_o^N} \left[\int_C [\omega_1 \Delta(s) + \omega_2 \lambda(s)] \, ds - \omega_3 \int_C (d\theta/ds)^2 \, ds \right]. \tag{1}$$

Here, C_o^N denotes the set of all contours, C, of length N beginning at $s = 0$. The variable $\Delta(s)$ is the magnitude of an edge pixel along the contour and denotes the *strength* component of the criterion function; $\lambda(s) = 1$, if $\Delta(s)$ is greater than a chosen threshold and $\lambda(s) = 0$, otherwise, and it represents the *length* component; the variable $d\theta/ds$ denotes the local curvature at the selected pixel, where $\theta(s)$ is the slope along the contour, and it is a measure of local roughness. The constants ω_1, ω_2, and ω_3 are the weights of the strength, length, and smoothness components of the criterion function, respectively, where $0 < \omega_1, \omega_2, \omega_3 < 1$. We note that (1) is a non-linear optimization in terms of the variable C, and an exhaustive search would span a space whose size is p^N, p being the number of pixels that needs to be considered at each point along the contour C. We therefore reduce the complexity of the above optimization problem by adopting a multi-step approach. To do this, we decompose (1) into several optimization steps:

$$\max_{C \in C_0^N} \left[\int_C [\omega_1 \Delta(s) + \omega_2 \lambda(s)] ds - \omega_3 \int_C (d\theta/ds)^2 ds \right]$$
$$= \max_{S \in C_0^{N_1}} \left[\int_S [\omega_1 \Delta(s) + \omega_2 \lambda(s)] ds - \omega_3 \int_S (d\theta/ds)^2 ds \right]$$
$$+ \max_{S \in C_{N_1}^{N_2}} \left[\int_S [\omega_1 \Delta(s) + \omega_2 \lambda(s)] ds - \omega_3 \int_S (d\theta/ds)^2 ds \right]$$
$$+ \ldots + \max_{S \in C_{N_n'}^{N_n}} \left[\int_S [\omega_1 \Delta(s) + \omega_2 \lambda(s)] ds - \omega_3 \int_S (d\theta/ds)^2 ds \right], \quad (2)$$

where $N_n' = \sum_{i=1}^{n-1} N_i$ and $N = \sum_{i=1}^{n} N_i$. Now, the multi-step optimization problem is concerned with finding segments, S, that are of lengths $N_1, \ldots, N_n$, each of which is smaller than the original contour, C, of length N. Further reduction in complexity is achieved if the number of pixels, p, that need to be considered at each point along the segment is lowered. Both of these conditions, viz., shorter edge segments and fewer neighboring pixels, are satisfied by thresholding a thinned edge image using multiple thresholds. The application of multiple edge-magnitude thresholds results in a set of edge images containing segments of edge contours in the original thinned edge image.

To create long chains of edge segments, we initiate edge segment-following at a terminal pixel (one which has a single neighboring edge pixel) in the edge image obtained with the highest threshold value. The edge-segment following process is accomplished by selecting a neighbor of a given edge pixel of the segment that maximizes the optimizing criterion of (1). To account for noise, our approach allows a gap length of two pixels to be covered by the edge segment-following process. Since a very long contour would rarely appear in a single edge image, the edge segment-following process continues across edge images obtained with progressively lower thresholds after it has been terminated within a single edge image. The process stops when the current edge image is the last of the edge image set, only to be reinitiated at another terminal pixel (belonging to a different contour) in the first image. This new starting pixel is selected through a raster scan and the subsequent repetition of the edge segment-following process yields a different contour. After all the terminal pixels in the first image have been scanned and a set of linked edge segments is obtained (to be referred to as the top-level configuration), the entire process is repeated beginning at the second edge image and so on. Each set of linked edge segments (length of each segment $\geq T_0$) constitutes perceptually salient contours which are handed over to the primitive feature extraction process in a regulated manner, starting with the top-level configuration (see Figs. 1 and 5).

4.3 Primitive Feature Extraction

In order to extract primitive features for generic object recognition, the feature extraction process is based on the expected image descriptions of the generic classes. According to Table 3, such descriptions for a generic aircraft consist of linear segments. In our system, we have implemented a line extraction algorithm, based upon the detection of significant instances of collinearity (scale-independent) among edge points, similar to the one proposed by Lowe [31]. The input to this line extraction algorithm is a set of regulated edge segments. In addition to lines, our algorithm also detects corners by obtaining gradient and curvature measurements at pixels in the grey scale image [37].

4.4 Region Segmentation and Dominant Axes Extraction

Given the input ROI image, the region segmentation process uses grey scale intensities together with edge information (magnitude and orientation) to extract image regions. It is based on the joint relaxation of a two-class (object/background) region-based approach and a two-class (edge/no edge) edge-based approach [5]. The joint relaxation provides edge and grey value interactions in the initial label (probability) assignment to each pixel. Only the edge orientation, and not the magnitude, is updated in each iteration. At the end of each iteration, the coincidence of edge and border values is determined. Requirement for a high degree of coincidence is necessary to obtain precise and accurate segmentation boundaries.

Extraction of dominant axes that characterize the shape of a generic object in the image, requires access to the model of the shape. In our algorithm, the potential dominant axes of the generic aircraft shape are generated by connecting the extremities of a labeled region within a segmented image. To determine the extreme points, the smallest convex polygon (in terms of area) that completely surrounds the object region is found. The smallest convex polygon is one whose vertices lie close to the local extrema of curvature points along the boundary of the labeled region. The extremities of the segmented region should correspond to these local extrema of curvature points that are near the vertices of the smallest polygon. Now, more than one "extreme" point may be identified within a small neighborhood along the region boundary in the vicinity of a polygon vertex, e.g., when there are multiple local extrema points in a certain segment of the boundary. In that case, nearby "extreme" points are grouped into clusters and the cluster centers are chosen to represent the region extremities. A potential dominant axis is a line that connects two such extreme points that are not the centers of adjacent clusters. Since a perfect segmentation is difficult to achieve in practice, the segmented region may not have the exact shape of a generic object or it may be fragmented. Thus, it is additionally ensured that a potential dominant axis is not located outside the segmented region. Lines whose significant portions are not contained within the segmented region are ignored.

4.5 Potential Shadow Identification

Shadows are unavoidable characteristics of outdoor scenes. Some have exploited shadow information in a scene-specific manner [28], while others have suggested general methods of shadow interpretation [24]. The shadow of an object has two parts: the object's dark side (or self-shadow) and its projected (or cast) shadow. The shadow boundary is defined by a brightness discontinuity between directly illuminated regions and regions receiving either no light or only indirectly scattered light. It is important to note that the information about the shadow casting object is contained only in the shadow boundaries. A shadow boundary has three basic types of segments (see Appendix A.2): *shadow*, *shadow-making*, and *occluding*. The first type belongs to the cast shadow, whereas the rest are associated with the shadow-casting object. The following are some useful properties of shadow edges (2-D projections of shadow boundaries) [32]:

- *Contrast* across a shadow edge is equal to the ratio of direct to indirect light. This ratio along the length of the shadow will change only smoothly and independently from the surface on which it falls. For a distant light source, the ratio is nearly constant.
- Each point on a shadow edge *corresponds* to some point on the shadow-making edge in the direction toward or away from the illumination vanishing point (projection of the point source).
- Shadow breaks (tangent discontinuities or corners) are *caused* by breaks in shadow-making edges unless the source of illumination is coincidently coplanar with the two tangents of the break or shadows cast by different objects intersect.

Assuming that any arbitrarily shaped shadow boundary can be locally represented by straight lines, we have developed an algorithm to detect potential shadow lines. It is based on the test of bimodality of the local histogram which is a consequence of the first property of a shadow edge mentioned above. A rectangular window is first set up on each side of a selected line. The dimensions of the window are $l \times w$, where l is the length of the line and the width w is chosen to be large enough for the histogram computation to be effective. Within each window, the region segmentation algorithm described above is applied and the largest region is retained. Next, a grey-level histogram is obtained for the region and the significant modes are identified.

Identification of modes involves locating the peaks and valleys in the 1-D histogram first, followed by clustering of the grey-levels between two consecutive valleys. Small clusters are removed from consideration. Given that the grey levels in the k-th cluster are between p_k and q_k, the mode of the cluster is obtained as

$$m_k = \frac{\sum_{i=p_k}^{q_k} i N(i)}{\sum_{i=p_k}^{q_k} N(i)}, \qquad (3)$$

where $N(i)$ denotes the frequency of the i-th grey level. For two adjacent clusters, whose modes are m_k and m_{k+1} and whose total number of pixels are N_k and N_{k+1}, respectively, the following averaged mode is computed:

$$\hat{m} = \frac{m_k N_k + m_{k+1} N_{k+1}}{N_T}, \qquad (4)$$

where $N_T = N_k + N_{k+1}$. The two clusters are merged if

$$(m_k - \hat{m})^2 N_k / N_T < T_1 \quad \text{and} \quad (m_{k+1} - \hat{m})^2 N_{k+1} / N_T < T_1.$$

The new mode for the merged clusters is obtained by applying (3). The process is continued until there is no change in the number of clusters. Finally, the mode corresponding to the largest cluster is retained as the significant mode. Since the histogram is based on the pixels of a single region, there is usually a single significant mode. The two most significant modes from either side of the line are then subjected to the bimodality test. If the separation between the modes is less than a threshold, T_2, or the smaller of the two is more than another threshold, T_3, the line is ignored. Otherwise, it is marked as a potential shadow edge.

4.6 Non-Shadow Feature Extraction

The shadow edges detected in the previous stage (Sect. 4.5) may include projections of shadow, shadow-making, and occluding boundaries. The focus of this step is to separate the shadow boundaries from the rest. In order to do this, we make use of the remaining properties of shadow edges stated in the preceding subsection. Additionally, we utilize the ancillary data about the camera-platform position/orientation and the illumination point source, I_s, (the sun in our case) position together with the imaging parameters to compute the image plane position of the illumination projection point, i_s. The shadow edges are identified by pairing them up with shadow-making edges while observing that the illumination rays diverge from i_s (I_s in front of the camera), converge to i_s (I_s behind the camera), or are parallel (I_s in the lens plane of the camera). However, the location of i_s itself is not a strong constraint to resolve correspondences between shadow and shadow-making boundaries except for specific aspects. e.g., direct overhead-view. The lines therefore need to be grouped in some meaningful way such that two groups would correspond to each other only when their members do.

One way to group the lines is to form their convex sets. A convex group of shadow-making lines would normally cast a convex group of shadow lines. Initially, groups of lines are formed based on the perceptual cues of proximity and collinearity [31]. Each group is then subjected to a convexity test for which we utilize the segmentation results for the entire ROI from Sect. 4.4. The motivation here is that if the elements of the group belong to a region boundary, then the segmentation results would help to determine the interior of the region and hence to verify the "convexity" of the group.

We recall that the convexity property requires that the line joining any two points on the boundary of a convex figure must be completely contained within that figure. A convexity test is performed for every pair of lines in a selected group. We, however, relax the "containment" condition since the region borders do not precisely coincide with the edge borders. For any two lines l_i and l_j in a selected group, we determine the two lines, ll_{14}^{ij} and ll_{23}^{ij}, botained by joining the end points (e_1, e_2) of l_i and (e_3, e_4) of l_j. If R denotes the corresponding segmented region, then ll_{14}^{ij} and ll_{23}^{ij} will be said to be completely contained in R if

$$\frac{N_{ll_{14}^{ij} \cap R}}{N_{ll_{14}^{ij}}} \geq T_4 \quad \text{and} \quad \frac{N_{ll_{23}^{ij} \cap R}}{N_{ll_{23}^{ij}}} \geq T_4.$$

Here, N_s denotes the number of pixels in the set s.

If there is a line in a group which fails the above convexity test when paired with any other line from the same group, then that line is removed and put in a new group by itself. After all the initial groups have been considered, this process creates the *first* set of convex groups and isolated lines removed during the convexity test. The *second* pass considers whether an isolated line can be put in a convex group based on proximity, collinearity, and convexity.

Once the convex groups of lines have been identified, for each marked shadow line in a group, a corresponding shadow-making line from another group is sought by searching in a direction towards (or away from) i_s. The matching score is determined by the degree of overlap of the two matching lines in the predicted direction. Let r be a shadow line from a convex group, G_A, and let t be another line (may or may not be marked as a shadow) belonging to a different convex group, G_B. Also, let $\hat{n}_{r_i}$ denote the unit vector connecting the ith pixel of r and i_s and let $\hat{n}_{t_j}$ denote that connecting the jth pixel of t and i_s. Then the total matching score of the pair (r, t) is

$$\phi_{rt} = \frac{\sum_{i=1}^{N_r}\sum_{i=1}^{N_t} \hat{n}_{r_i} \cdot \hat{n}_{t_j}}{N_r + N_t}, \tag{5}$$

where N_r and N_t denote the lengths (in pixels) of the lines r and t, respectively. In order to minimize the match of one pixel element of one pixel element of r with multiple elements of t, it is ensured that the angle $\theta_{ij} = \arccos(\hat{n}_{r_i} \cdot \hat{n}_{t_j}) < T_5$.

All the candidate matches of a selected shadow line are arranged according to the matching scores and marked with the corresponding group identifier. For example, the line t corresponding to the selected shadow line r is assigned the label (ϕ_{rt}, G_B). This entire matching process is repeated for all other shadow lines in that particular group (G_A in the above example). The most promising matching group is determined from the group identifiers of the candidate matches. Each line in the selected group is assigned a unique match from the candidate group based on the *matching scores* and enforcing *similarity* of *spatial ordering* of the selected lines and their matches. If most of the lines in the selected group have been assigned unique matches, then the group as a whole is marked as a shadow group and the matching group is marked as a shadow-making (i.e., non-shadow) group.

4.7 Symbolic Feature Extraction

Since symbolic features are characteristic of generic classes and are more global than the perceptually grouped features, their extraction tends to be domain-dependent or more specifically goal-driven. According to Table 3, the symbolic features for a generic aircraft class included trapezoid-like shapes for wings, tails, and rudder, and wedge-like shape for the nose part. In Sect. 3, we outlined the steps of our symbolic feature extraction step while describing the framework of our object recognition approach. Here, we additionally note that the perceptual groups that would be used in symbolic feature extraction must come from the non-shadow features. Our algorithm has already identified the convex groups of non-shadow features in the preceding step and convexity is a common characteristic of most geometric-modeled objects. These convex groups are now used to derive the specific types of symbolic features.

To identify the trapezoid-like shapes, groups of three (partially closed contour) and four (fully closed contour) lines are considered. The partially closed contours are typical of any aircraft wing, tail, and rudder sections, while the fully closed contours are a rarity. Any group of *three* lines must satisfy the following conditions:

- two lines are non-parallel (using parallelism measure of [31]),
- the third line is in between the two non-parallels,
- the intersections of the third line with the non-parallels occur near independently detected corners, and
- the third line is smaller in length than one of the non-parallels (at least).

On the other hand, a group of *four* lines must satisfy the following conditions:

- two lines are non-parallel, two are parallel,
- the parallels form the opposite sides of the trapezoid and so also the non-parallels,
- all pairwise line-intersections occur near detected corners, and
- the parallel lines are smaller than the non-parallels.

To overcome the problem due to oversegmentation, i.e., fragmentation of long lines into smaller parts, groups of lines that are found to satisfy any one of the above sets of conditions are merged based on collinearity measures. Non-overlapping line pairs that are far apart are prevented to have a high collinearity value by enforcing the condition that the average separation between the lines of a pair is proportional to the smaller line length. Since, the proximity measure defined in [31] is based on the Euclidean distance between the end points of a line pair and can therefore be similar for both parallel as well as non-parallel lines, we introduce an additional perceptual measure for determining the proximal non-parallel lines only. Given the point of intersection, p, of two lines l_1 and l_2, if $p1$ and $p2$ denote the endpoints of these lines closest to p, respectively, then the end point proximity measure, $prox_{NP}$, for non-parallel lines is

$$prox_{NP} = \frac{1}{(d_{p1p} + d_{p2p})/2.0},$$

where d_{ab} denotes the Euclidean distance between a and b. Finally, if the total length of the lines in a group is smaller than a certain fraction of the perimeter of the trapezoid-like shape obtained by connecting these lines, then the group is discarded. This step is motivated by the fact that no such group of lines can be due to an accidental alignment of the constituent lines satisfying the above conditions of a trapezoid-like shape. Finally, associated with each perceptual measure of parallelism, proximity, and collinearity is a range of threshold values. Initially, the threshold values are set to the maxima of the corresponding ranges. However, these values can be relaxed based on the flow of evidence when multiple mutually supporting hypotheses interact [13].

4.8 Generic Aircraft Recognition

Once the symbolic features have been derived, these need to be matched to the generic aircraft model through an evidence accumulation process. Since the features are derived in a class specific manner, the recognition amounts to satisfying the highest-level production rule associated with the generic aircraft description. This amounts to verifying the mutual connectedness of the symbolic features representing the different parts of a generic aircraft in a manner specified by this highest-level production rule.

Instead of associating evidence with primitive features and casting these evidences in a conflict resolution situation to support or refute hypotheses individually [32] or within a "blackboard" paradigm, our effort has been directed towards gradual accumulation of evidence through

- clutter rejection,
- non-shadow feature identification,
- symbolic feature extraction, and
- interaction of hypotheses.

This reduces the number of alternative hypotheses that need to be considered at this stage. We avoid using any probabilistic measure of confidence in a hypothesis since probablistic measures are highly context-dependent and vary widely from image to image. However, the ordering of the test conditions in the highest-level production rule are based on the likelihood of an individual test to support the evidence of a generic aircraft. One such test condition involves the most dominant structural parts of the generic model. As evidences of these structures, we make use of the dominant axes of the aircraft's shape that are extracted in the step described in Sect. 4.4.

Recognition confidence is said to be low if some of the important test conditions, called the *critical evidences*, of the production rule fail, such as non-identification of dominant features. The generic aircraft recognition process then needs to interact with the low-level feature regulator so that less salient symbolic features may now be available along with the existing ones. In other situations, not all the evidences associated with a hypothesis can be found, particularly when there are viewpoint-imposed constraints, such as missing structural parts due to self-occlusion. The generic recognition process then accesses deeper levels of the hierarchical database to look for alternate evidences, such as more "specialized" features, which can be verified from the data.

4.9 Qualitative Description Refinement

Since the generic aircraft recognition step is concerned with generating and testing hypotheses based on evidence and not on the "completeness" of symbolic information, further refinement of the detected aircraft shape is required to improve upon the extracted symbolic information. This usually involves completing the generic aircraft description by accounting for the missing elements of the symbolic features. This is followed by obtaining a skeleton of the model instance which is composed of the axes of symmetry of the individual components. The skeleton can be directly used for mensuration purposes when performing quantitative matching. The final output are the identified symbolic parts of the generic aircraft.

4.10 Refocused Matching

The labeled symbolic parts which capture the global shape description of a generic aircraft are now used to direct the image-based search for more localized features that are available at lower levels of the database hierarchy. Availability of these features allows more precise classification of the recognized generic aircraft. The refocused matching process may utilize the symbolic/primitive features that have not been utilized in the generic aircraft recognition step or may request new or less-salient primitive features. Currently, our algorithm handles only qualitative model features.

5 Experimental Results

The aircraft recognition system described in this paper is implemented in C programming language on Sun Sparcstation running UNIX 4.2BSD. There are ten *main* subcomponents (program modules) to the system implementing the various steps of the algorithm described in Sect. 4. Of these, the modules implementing the region segmentation and dominant axes extraction are written as KBVision[1] tasks that run under X windows. Currently, the remaining eight modules run as regular UNIX programs. However, these are also being converted into KBVision tasks so as to provide a homogeneous IU environment. A control program written in shell-level language monitors the interactions among the various modules and oversees the entire system. In our implementation, the hierarchical model database has three levels: the top-level consists of generic objects, the intermediate level comprises subclasses of a generic object, and the bottom level has the specific object models. The results reported in this paper are, however, based on the first two levels. The top level has one generic object – aircraft – and three classes at the intermediate-level – large, medium, and small. The non-image information is provided to the system in the form of an external file that contains the ancillary data: the camera-platform position/orientation, weather condition (sunny/cloudy/hazy), sun angle (if sunny), and camera parameters. The following values are used for the different thresholds mentioned in Sect. 4: $T_0 = 10$ pixels, $T_1 = 100$, $T_2 = 160$, $T_3 = 30$, $T_4 = 0.9$, and $T_5 = 30°$.

The experimental results of qualitative aircraft recognition are presented using aerial photographs ($4K \times 4K$) of an air-base. The examples are ordered according to increasing level of complexity.

Example 1. Figure 6a shows the first of the set of images which has several aircraft – four C-130's and one F-18. Using the multiresolution focusing approach, several

---

[1] KBVision is a registered trademark of Amerinex Artificial Intelligence, Inc.

Fig. 6. An aerial view of an airfield: **a** original image ($4K \times 4K$); **b** preliminary regions of interest (black regions); **c** new regions of interest (ROIs) found in the close-ups of the preliminary regions

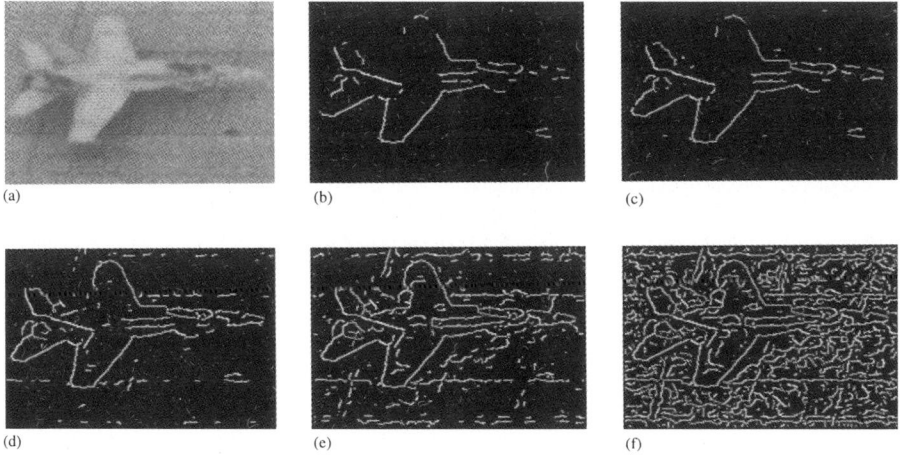

Fig. 7. Results of low-level processing of the bottom ROI in Fig. 6c: **a** original ROI image (162×240). Extraction of thinned edges using different thresholds for edge magnitude; **b** $t = 225$; **c** $t = 200$; **d** $t = 150$; **e** $t = 100$; **f** $t = 50$

regions of interest are identified and analyzed by the object recognition system in succession. Here, we present the results of analyzing one ROI (162×240) from Fig. 6 that contains the F-18 aircraft. The ROI and the output of the multi-threshold edge detection step are shown in Fig. 7. In our implementation, we have selected five threshold (t) values which are fixed for *all* images. As we observe, a significant part of one wing is missing from the edge image corresponding to the highest threshold value and too much of image clutter is present in the image corresponding to the lowest threshold value. This motivates the need for extracting globally salient structures. The result of this step is presented in Fig. 8a which shows the top-level (globally most salient) structure, the aircraft in this case. Figure 8b shows the next set of salient structures in addition to what has already been detected, most of which are due to the mosaic of the tarmac. The following step is to extract the primitive features from this global structure. The results of line fitting to the salient structures are shown in Figs. 8c,d.

The significance of salient feature selection is summarized in Table 4. Very often the feature extraction process can lead to undersegmentation (e.g., 18 lines for $t = 225$) or oversegmentation (e.g., 213 lines for $t = 50$). On the other hand, the set of lines belonging to the most salient structures constitutes only 17% of the total lines obtained from the edge image of Fig. 7f. At the same time, this set accounts for nearly 84% of the "useful" (that may be associated with the aircraft) lines of the latter set. This is a significant gain in terms of computational efficiency for any subsequent model-matching step. Segmented regions and the dominant axes of regions are shown in Figs. 8e,f.

According to the ancillary data, the weather condition for the image of Fig. 6a is cloudy, therefore shadow-line removal step is skipped. Since, the convex groups of lines are also required for the symbolic features like wings, these are determined next using perceptual cues of proximity, collinearity, cotermination (based on the incidence of line pairs on detected corners) and the region segmentation results. Figure 9a shows the six convex sets of lines identified in this manner. The symbolic descriptions of some of the subparts, such as wings, tails, and rudder, require extraction of trapezoid-like structures from the convex groups. Extracted trapezoid-like features are shown in Fig. 9b. In contrast to wings or tails, subparts, such

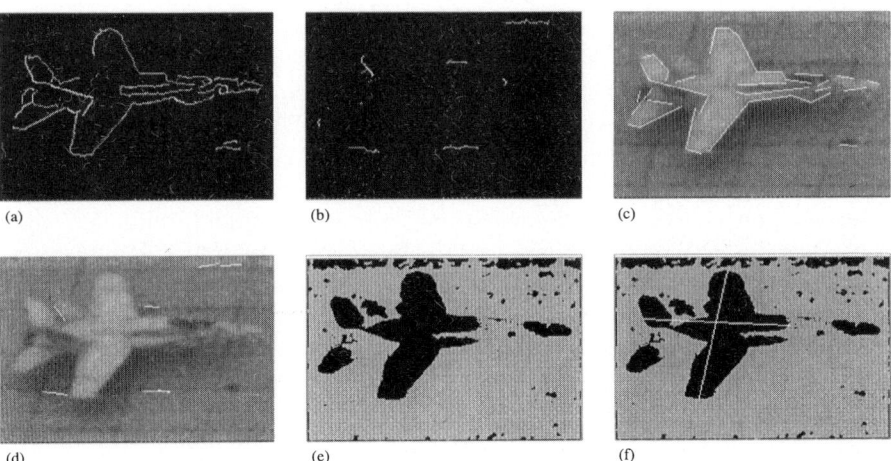

Fig. 8. Results of feature extraction: **a** detection of most salient structure; **b** detection of next incremental salient structure; **c** fitting straight lines to the structure of **a**; **d** fitting straight lines to the structure of **b**; **e** region segmentation results; **f** extracted dominant axes for the largest foreground region

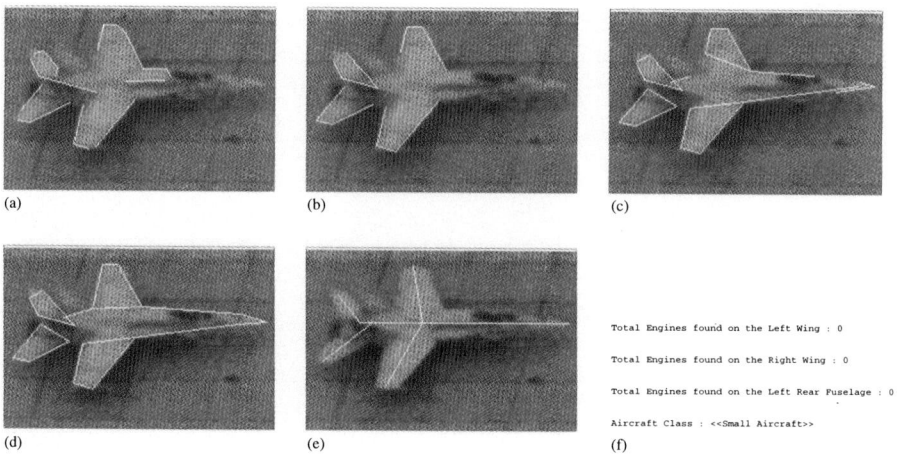

Fig. 9. Results of qualitative object recognition: **a** six convex groups of lines identified in Fig. 7a; **b** trapezoid-like shapes identified using these groups; **c** structural parts found during generic object recognition; **d** refined structural parts that are also labeled; **e** finding the skeleton of the shape; **f** class recognition

as fuselage, require less specialized features like perceptual groups of collinear, parallel lines.

During the generic object recognition step, the order of evidence accumulation is for the wings first, followed by that for the fuselage, with the nose last. The dominant axes are used to support or refute a selected symbolic feature as a wing of the aircraft or the fuselage. Once all the conditions of connectivity and relative localization of the different subparts have been satisfied, can their ensemble be recognized as a generic aircraft. The identified subparts are shown in Fig. 9c. Inability to identify both wings or the fuselage is considered to be a recognition failure for the generic aircraft class. In this case, since both wings are detected and so also the fuselage, the recognition of a generic aircraft is successful.

The computational advantage gained because of the use of symbolic features is evident from the results of Tables 4 and 5. The overall effect of salient structure determination (17% of the original set of lines retained) and symbolic feature grouping (50% of the salient lines used) is the retention of only 8.5% of the lines obtained from Fig. 7f for aircraft recognition. The connectivity information of the parts is exploited to obtain more complete descriptions of the subparts, followed by the extraction of the shape skeleton. These results are shown in Figs. 9d,e. Observe that the left tail of the aircraft has not yet been found, since it is not necessary for the recognition of a generic aircraft. Also, the nose-shape is not a characteristic of an F-18. The labeled symbolic features are only coarse descriptions of the object. Note that no *precise* model has been utilized in this recognition process.

The labeled symbolic parts are utilized by the refocused matching process which tries to perform an improved classification of the generic aircraft based on the engine location. The symbolic description of an engine is an elongated blob-like region, where the elongation axis is nearly perpendicular to the leading-edge (edge closer to the nose) of the wing when engines are located on wings, and the axis is nearly parallel to fuselage when engines are located on fuselage. The refocused matching stage interacts with the primitive feature extraction process to obtain segmented regions within a window along the leading-edges of the two wings and also the rear-part of the fuselage, separately. However, no elongated blob-like region is detected that may indicate presence of engines. Therefore, the generic aircraft is identified as belonging to a *small* class (Fig. 9f).

Example 2. A second aerial image is shown in Fig. 10a of which Fig. 10b constitutes an ROI containing a Hercules aircraft. The region segmentation results of Fig. 10c follow the observation that the gray-levels of the aircraft and its cast shadow are nearly similar in Fig 10b. The extracted dominant axes are also shown in Fig. 10c. In this case, three dominant axes have been determined one of which is actually due to the shadow cast by the wings. We will refer to this axis as the shadow axis in subsequent discussions.

Figure 11a shows the top-level structure obtained using the ROI of Fig. 10b. The line-fits to this structure and the next incremental salient structure are displayed in Figs. 11b,c. Once again, the computational advantage gained by using the salient structure detection step is indicated in Table 6. Here, the salient structures constitute only 26% of the lines obtained from the edge image corresponding to

Table 4. Significance of saliency-based feature regulation for the ROI of Fig. 7a. The lines referred to in this table are those that are at least 10 pixels long

No. of lines detected using edge magnitude threshold of					No. of lines from most salient	Ratio l_1/L_5 (l_1)	Fraction of aircraft contour (ground truth)
$t = 225$ (L_1)	$t = 200$ (L_2)	$t = 150$ (L_3)	$t = 100$ (L_4)	$t = 50$ (L_5)			
18	28	40	91	213	36	0.17	0.84

Table 5. Significance of symbolic feature extraction for the ROI of Fig. 7a. The lines referred to in this table are those that are at least 10 pixels long

No. of lines from most salient structures (l_1)	No. of distinct lines forming convex groups (l_2)	No. of distinct lines forming trapezoids (l_3)	No. of additional lines needed for recognition (l_4)	Ratio l_2/l_1	Ratio $(l_3 + l_4)/l_1$
36	18	13	5	0.5	0.5

Fig. 10. A second aerial image: **a** original image ($4K \times 4K$); **b** a ROI image (300×450) of the aircraft marked with a × in **a**; **c** extracted dominant axes

lowest edge threshold. Table 6 also illustrates the difficulty posed by the current scenario as nearly equal number of lines belong to the actual aircraft contour (38% of the salient structure lines) and the shadows (35% of the salient structure lines).

Convex groups are formed using the lines of Fig. 11b. The potential shadow lines identified among the lines of Fig. 11b are shown in Fig. 11d. In order to resolve the shadow lines more accurately, it is first determined whether one of the axes is due to a cast shadow. This procedure is similar to matching a potential shadow line with a non-shadow line which is outlined in Sect. 4.6. In this case, the rightmost of the two nearly parallel axes of Fig. 10c is determined to be due to shadow since it matched up with the leftmost of the two when the illumination projection point information is used. Assuming that the shadow is cast on a plane, the shadow axis demarcates an area in the image away from the illumination projection point (to the right of the shadow axis) and all the potential shadow lines that lie within this area are marked as true shadow lines. For the potential shadow lines that are outside this area, the usual correspondence-based matching discussed in Sect. 4.6 is carried out. The final shadow lines are displayed in Fig. 11e. The groups of non-shadow lines are next used to obtain the trapezoid-like symbolic features of Fig. 11f.

One of the symbolic features of Fig. 11f that aligned with one of the dominant axes, axis-1 (the wing axis), is hypothesized as the wing, wing-1 (say). This is shown in Fig. 12a. (Notice that the shadow axis is removed from consideration during the generic recognition process.) Now, this generic recognition process is confronted with a situation in which only one wing hypothesis could be formed. As a result, the system accesses the lower-level of the database hierarchy for "specialized" features, like engines, that are characteristic of some aircraft, viz., large-class aircraft. Further evidence of wing-1 is sought by searching for elongated blob-like regions (qualitative description of an engine) in the vicinity of wing-1. The search succeeds in this case, thereby improving the combined support of wing-1 hypothesis. Next, the system attempts to seek evidence of the other wing, wing-2 (say), by interpreting the current situation as one of missing data.

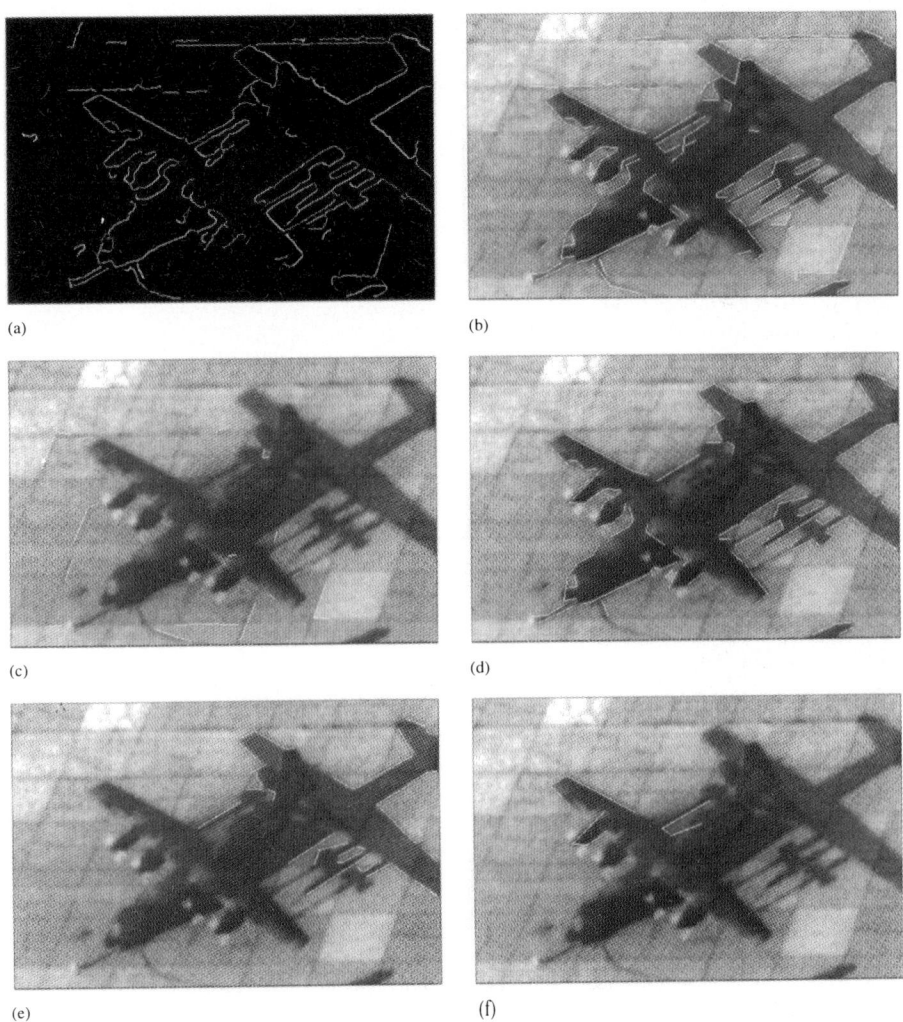

Fig. 11. Results of feature extraction: **a** detection of the most salient structure; **b** fitting straight lines to the structure of **a**; **c** straight line-fits to the next incremental salient structure; **d** potential shadow lines; **e** resolved shadow lines; **f** trapezoid-like shapes identified using non-shadow groups

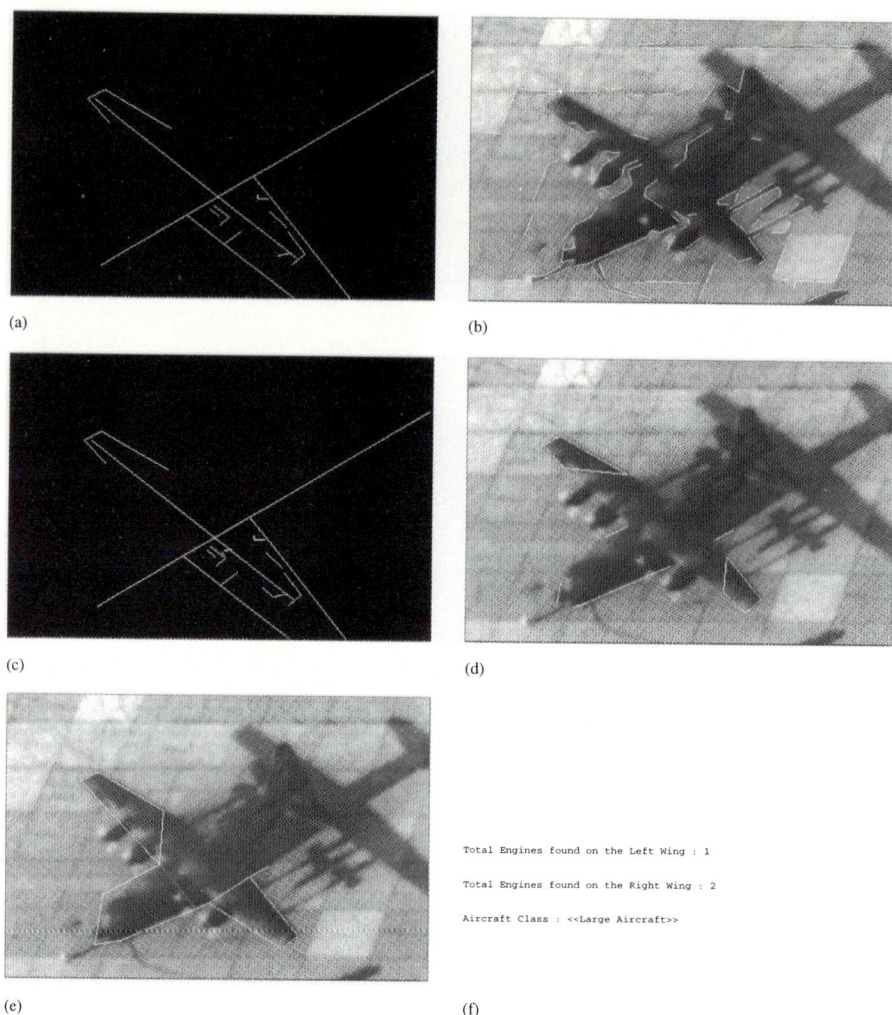

Fig. 12. Results of qualitative object recognition: **a** a hypothesized wing, a search region for the second wing and the non-shadow lines to support it; **b** the current non-shadow lines together with the lines of Fig. 11c obtained from the regulator; **c** emergence of additional non-shadow lines within the search region of **a**; **d** recognition success after lines within the search region have been grouped by relaxing the perceptual constraints thereby allowing the other wing to emerge; **e** refined structural parts; **f** class recognition

A search region is next set up, for this purpose, on the other side of the intersecting dominant axis, axis-2 (the fuselage axis), and along axis-1. The search region delineated in Fig. 12a is determined from the image location of wing-1 and the condition of symmetry of the wings about the fuselage axis. Next, a search for the lines that may support the evidence of the other wing is carried out within this region. However, the non-shadow lines contained within this region (Fig. 12a) fail to identify any symbolic feature that may support a wing hypothesis. The removed shadow lines are next considered, which also are inadequate in this case. Integration of subsequent symbolic feature extraction and recognition is therefore initiated by allowing the generic recognition process to interact with the feature regulator. The new primitive features together with the current non-shadow lines that are not utilized by the symbolic features of Fig. 11f are shown in Fig. 12b. The additional non-shadow lines together with the previous ones that are identified within the search region (Fig. 12c) are further subjected to the grouping process for symbolic feature extraction. The initial (maximum) values of the various perceptual constraints fail to produce any meaningful perceptual grouping as the line primitives are few in number and are separated apart. However, since the hypotheses wing-1 and wing-2 are mutually reinforcing, i.e., evidence for one makes the evidence for the other more likely, the constraints are relaxed in steps. Particularly, the lowering of the thresholds of the proximity of a line-pair intersection to a detected corner and the ratio of the total line length to the perimeter of a trapezoid-like shape (see Sect. 4.7) cause grouping of lines to occur. As a result, a trapezoid-like symbolic feature emerges (the left wing tip) that drives the subsequent steps of recognition.

The identified structural parts are the two wing tips, the front part (and a small portion of the rear) of the fuselage, and the nose. These are indicated in Fig. 12d and the refined parts are shown in Fig. 12e. The processes of shadow identification and symbolic feature extraction have reduced the number of useful lines for aircraft recognition to only 6% of the total number of lines (Table 6) that otherwise would have to be considered. Finally, the refocused matching process determines the class of this aircraft as *large* as indicated in Fig. 12f.

Table 6. Significance of shadow detection and symbolic feature extraction for the ROI of Fig. 10b. The lines referred to in this table are those that are at least 10 pixels long. The edge image obtained using a magnitude threshold of t = 50 is denoted by E_{50}

No. of lines from the most salient structures (l_1)	Fraction of l_1 from E_{50} in set l_1	Fraction of l_1 belonging to aircraft (ground truth)	Fraction of l_1 belonging to shadows (ground truth)	No. of shadow lines found (l_2)
150	0.26	0.38	0.35	36

No. of additional lines from the next salient structures (l_3)	No. of distinct lines forming trapezoids (l_4)	No. of additional lines needed for generic recognition (l_5)	Ratio $(l_4 + l_5)/(l_1 + l_3)$
24	6	5	0.06

6 Conclusions

In this chapter, we have presented an approach to qualitative recognition of aircraft in complex, perspective aerial imagery. Our approach is motivated by the difficulties posed by real-world scenarios, such as occlusion, shadow, cloud cover, haze, seasonal variations, clutter and various forms of image degradation. We have introduced a framework for geometric model-based object recognition that addresses some of these variabilities of the real-world and also the fundamental issues related to model-based recognition. In particular, our approach is capable of handling shadows, clutter, and low image contrast and it uses qualitative features of object (aircraft) models for recognition. The *main contributions* of this research are the extraction of perceptually salient primitive features and their use in a regulated fashion, use of heterogeneous geometric and physical models associated with image formation for feature extraction and subsequent recognition, and integration of high-level recognition processes with low-level feature extraction ones. Real-world data, highlighting the difficulties of aircraft recognition in practical situations, is used to demonstrate the effectiveness of our proposed approach. Implementing the final stage, that of quantitative recognition, is a future research issue.

A Generalized Cylinders for Model Representation

In this section, we discuss the properties of Straight Homogeneous Generalized Cylinders (SHGCs) that are used to model the volumetric shape of generic aircraft and also the shadow geometry. Subsequently, we present analysis of the occluding contours of these shape descriptors, the results of which are used directly in our algorithm.

A.1 Contour Analysis for SHGCs

In this subsection, we shall describe the properties of the occluding contours, i.e., the contours tangent to the line of sight, of SHGCs using some of the results of Shafter [45]. The occluding contour is a curve on the surface of an object that projects to the silhouette of the object in the image.

Recall that an SHGC is a subclass of Generalized Cylinder (GC), a shape descriptor of a large class of curved objects. It has a line segment in space for its axis and an uniformly-scaled cross-section along this axis. Figure 13a shows an SHGC which maps two parameters onto a set of points in the 3-D world: s, the parameter which measures distance along the axis of the shape; and t, the para-

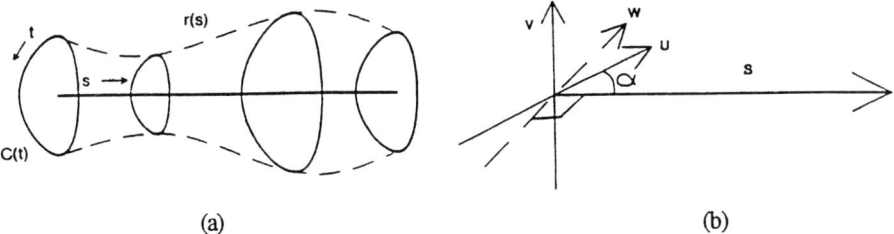

Fig. 13. Straight Homogeneous Generalized Cylinder: **a** representation, and **b** coordinate axes

meter which indirectly measures distance along the cross-section. Both s and t have as the domain the unit interval [0, 1]. Let $C(t)$ denote the cross-section function that describes the shape of the cross-section (constant for SHGC) and let $r(s)$ denote the radius function which describes the size of the cross-section along the axis. The function r is restricted to be continuous and differentiable everywhere and the function C is continuous and differentiable almost everywhere. The coordinate system for an SHGC is shown in Fig. 13b. The $u - v$ plane is the plane of the cross-section at a fixed angle α to the axis which passes through the origin. On the $u - v$ cross-section plane, for each value of s, the cross-section is the set of points $r(s)C(t)$ for $0 \leq t \leq 1$, where $C(t) = (u_c, v_c)(t)$. An orthogonal coordinate system $w - v - s$, whose axes are independent of the components of any particular shape, is also included in Fig. 13b. Thus, a point $(u, v, s)_{uvs}$ in the $u-v-s$ coordinate system is expressed as $(u\sin\alpha, v, s + u\cos\alpha)_{wvs}$ in the $w - v - s$ system. In the following, all coordinates will be expressed in the $w - v - s$ coordinate system, hence the subscript will be omitted.

Let $P(s, t)$ be a point on the surface of an SHGC as shown in Fig. 14a. Thus, for any values of s and t

$$P(s,t) = (u_c(t)r(s)\sin\alpha,\ v_c(t)r(s),\ s + u_c(t)r(s)\cos\alpha). \tag{6}$$

The outward surface normal, $N(s, t)$, at $P(s, t)$ is given by [45]

$$N(s,t) = \frac{\partial P}{\partial s} \times \frac{\partial P}{\partial t} = r(s)\left(W(t)\cos\alpha\frac{dr}{ds} + \frac{dv_c}{dt},\ -\sin\alpha\frac{du_c}{dt} - W(t)\sin\alpha\frac{dr}{ds}\right), \tag{7}$$

where $\partial P/\partial s$ is the tangent vector to the surface at the point $P(s, t)$ in the direction of increasing s and $\partial P/\partial s$ is the tangent vector in the direction of increasing t, as shown in Fig. 14b. Here, $W(t)$ is the Wronskian determinant of u_c and v_c, i.e.,

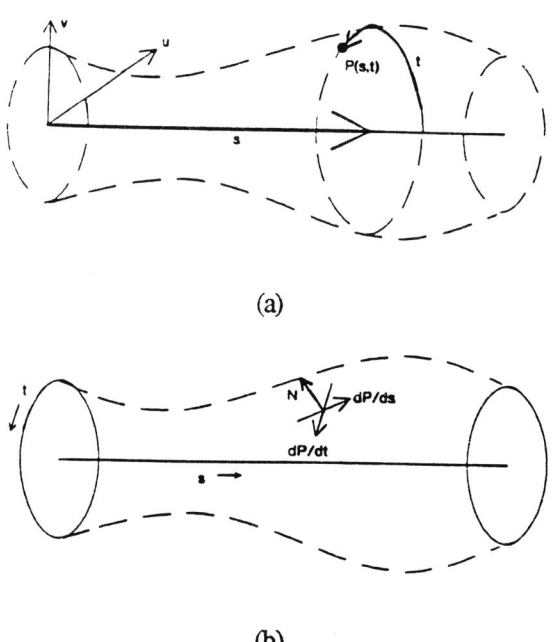

Fig. 14. Straight Homogeneous Generalized Cylinder: a coordinates of a point on the surface, and b surface normal at a point

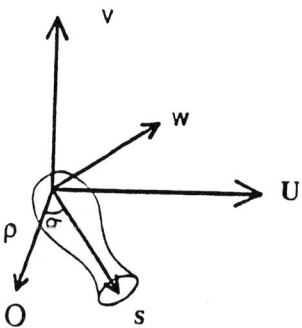

Fig. 15. Perspective projection of an SHGC onto an image plane where O is the viewpoint. $\rho = (\rho_w, \rho_v, \rho_s)$ is the view vector in the $w - v - s$ coordinate system

$$W(t) = \begin{vmatrix} u_c & v_c \\ \dfrac{du_c}{dt} & \dfrac{dv_c}{dt} \end{vmatrix}.$$

Figure 15 shows the perspective projection of an SHGC onto an image plane, in which the contour of the silhouette is the projection of the occluding contour. Since along the occluding contour the surface is tangent (i.e., the surface normal is perpendicular) to the viewing direction, the following relation is satisfied.

$$\mathbf{N} \cdot \rho = 0. \tag{8}$$

Now, in the case of a Right SHGC (RSHGC), $\alpha = \pi/2$, and for a Linear Homogeneous Generalized Cylinder (LHGC), $r = m(s - s_0)$, where s_0 is the apex and m is the gradient of the linear envelope. Thus, for a linear RSHGC, the occluding contour satisfies

$$\rho_w \frac{dv_C}{dt} - \rho_v \frac{du_C}{dt} - m\rho_s W(t) = 0. \tag{9}$$

Given an object whose shape is represented by a linear RSHGC, the viewing vector ρ (i.e., ρ_w, ρ_v, ρ_s), and the parameter m are fixed. Hence, (9) is a function of t only.

Lemma 1. *The occluding contour of a Linear RSHGC always lies in a plane.*

Proof. Let (9) hold true for some value of $t = t_0$ and let $\mathbf{P}(s, t_0)$ be any arbitrary point on the occluding contour such that

$$\mathbf{P}(s, t_0) = (w_P, v_P, s_P) = (u_C(t_0)r(s), v_C(t_0)r(s), s).$$

The corresponding normal is

$$\mathbf{N}(s, t_0) = r(s)\left(\frac{dv_C}{dt}, -\frac{du_C}{dt} - mW(t_0)\right).$$

We observe that

$$r(s)\left[(\rho_w - w_P)\frac{dv_C}{dt} - (\rho_v - v_P)\frac{du_C}{dt} - mW(t_0)(\rho_s - s_P)\right]$$

$$= r(s)\left[-w_P\frac{dv_C}{dt} + v_P\frac{du_C}{dt} - ms_P W(t_0)\right]$$

$$= r(s)\left[-u_C(t_0)r(s)\frac{dv_C}{dt} + v_C(t_0)r(s)\frac{du_C}{dt} + msW(t_0)\right]$$

$$= r(s)\left[-r(s)W(t_0) + msW(t_0)\right] = 0 \tag{10}$$

for $s_0 = 0$. But (10) is the equation of a plane through the occluding contour and containing the viewpoint.

Lemma 2. *The 2D image of the occluding contour of a Linear RSHGC is a line.*

Proof. The projection of a plane when viewed end-on is a line. The tangent plane passing through the viewpoint and containing the occluding contour of a Linear RSHGC therefore projects to a line which is the silhouette corresponding to the occluding contour.

Lemma 3. *The 2D image of a solid corner subtended at the apex of a Linear RSHGC or formed by two intersecting Linear RSHGCs is a corner.*

Proof. A solid corner at the apex of a Linear RSHGC or at the intersection of two Linear RSHGC is due to the dihedral angle between two intersecting tangent planes of the occluding contours. Now, each of the tangent planes projects as a line in the 2D image according to the above claim, and two lines corresponding to the two intersecting tangent planes subtend a corner between them in the image.

A.2 Shadow Models

In this subsection, we discuss the properties of shadow formation geometry which is modeled using SHGC shape descriptors. The shadow of an object has two parts: the object's dark side (or self-shadow) and its projected (or cast) shadow. The shadow boundary is defined by a brightness discontinuity between directly illuminated regions and regions receiving either no light or only indirectly scattered light. The apparent boundary is completely determined by the surface topography and the positions of the light source and the viewer.

A shadow boundary has three basic types of segments [24]: shadow-making, shadow, and occluding. These segments for an object illuminated by a point source are illustrated in Fig. 16. Each segment represents a certain profile of the object. The shadow-making boundary is essentially the occluding contour for the point source. For an object whose shape is represented by a Linear RSHGC, the shadow-making boundary is planar. The "shadow volume" (the volume of space shaded by an object) is an LSHGC with the point source as the apex. This may be seen from Fig. 16. The end of this LSHGC closer to the source is made up of the plane containing the shadow-making boundary.

Lemma 4. *The shadow boundary on a plane for a Linear RSHGC is linear.*

Proof. We note that the shadow boundary is the intersection of the tangent plane containing the shadow-making boundary and the plane on which the shadow is cast.

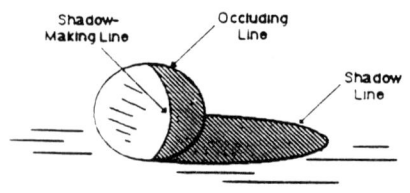

Fig. 16. Basic shadow boundary segments

Acknowledgment. This work was supported in part by a grant from Honeywell/ORD at the University of California at Riveride. Authors are thankful to Joe Mundy and Bany Roberts for providing us the imagely used in this work.

References

[1] *IEEE Spectrum*, 23(7) edition, July 1986.
[2] J. Ben-Arie and A. Z. Meiri. 3D object recognition by optimal matching search of multinary graphs. *Comp. Vis., Graphics, and Image Proc.*, 37:345–361, 1987.
[3] R. Bergevin and M. D. Levine. Generic object recognition: Building and matching coarse descriptions from line drawings. *IEEE Trans. Patt. Anal. and Mach. Intell.*, 15(1):19–36, 1993.
[4] B. Bhanu and C.-C. Ho. Building hierarchical vision model of objects with multiple representations. In *Proc. SPIE on Applications of Artificial Intell. X: Machine Vision and Robotics, vol. 1708*, pages 663–674, Orlando, FL, April 1992.
[5] B. Bhanu and R. D. Holben. Model-based segmentation of FLIR images. *IEEE Trans. Aerospace Elec. Sys.*, 26(1):2–11, 1990.
[6] I. Biederman. Human image understanding: Recent research and a theory. *Comp. Vis. Grap. Image Proc.*, 32(1):29–73, 1985.
[7] C. Bjorklund, M. Noga, E. Barrett, and D. Kuan. Lockheed imaging technology research for missiles and space. In *Proc. DARPA Image Understanding Workshop*, pages 332–352, Palo Alto, CA, May 1989.
[8] J. F. Bogdanowicz and A. Newman. Overview of the SCORPIUS program. In *Proc. DARPA Image Understanding Workshop*, pages 298–308, Palo Alto, CA, May 1989.
[9] R. A. Brooks. Symbolic reasoning among 3-dimensional models and 2-dimensional images. *Artificial Intell.*, 17:285–349, 1981.
[10] Z. Chen and S.-Y. Ho. Computer vision for robust 3d aircraft recognition with fast library search. *Pattern Recognition*, 24(5):375–390, 1991.
[11] C. H. Chien and J. K. Aggarwal. Model construction and shape recognition from occluding contours. *IEEE Trans. Patt. Anal. and Mach. Intell.*, PAMI-11(4):372–389, 1989.
[12] D. T. Clemens and D. W. Jacobs. Space and time bounds on indexing 3-D models from 2-D images. *IEEE Trans. Patt. Anal. and Mach. Intell.*, 13(10):1007–1017, 1991.
[13] S. Das and B. Bhanu. Reasoning with incremental data for qualitative object recognition. Technical Report, Visualization and Intelligent Systems Laboratory, University of California, Riverside, 1993.
[14] L. S. Davis and T. C. Henderson. Hierarchical constraint processes for shape analysis. *IEEE Trans. Patt. Anal. and Mach. Intell.*, PAMI-3(3):265–277, 1981.
[15] S. A. Dudani, K. J. Breeding, and R. B. McGhee. Aircraft identification by moment invariants. *IEEE Trans. on Computers*, C-26(1):39–46, 1977.
[16] J. Edwards, S. Gee, A. Newman, R. Onishi, A. Parks, M. Sleeth, and F. Vilnrotter. RADIUS: Research and development for image understanding systems phase 1. In *Proc. DARPA Image Understanding Workshop*, pages 177–184, San Diego, CA, Jan. 1992.
[17] M. A. Fischler, S. T. Barnard, R. C. Bolles, M. Lowry, L. Quam, S.G., and A. Witkin. Modeling and using physical constraints in scene analysis. In L. S. Baumann, editor, *Proc. ARPA Image Understanding Workshop*, pages 286–298, September 1982.
[18] G. Gibbon. Weighted chord functions, *Pattern Recognition*, 21(4):367–379, 1988.
[19] A. Gorin. Aspect-based aircraft classification from dynamic imagery. In *Proc. IEEE Conf. Patt. Recog. and Image Proc.*, pages 141–143, 1982.

[20] J. W. Gorman, O. R. Mitchell, and F. P. Kuhl. Partial shapre recognition using dynamic programming. *IEEE Trans. Patt. Anal. and Mach. Intell.*, 10(2):257–266, 1988.

[21] W. E. L. Grimson. *Object Recognition by Computer: The Role of Geometric Contraints.* Cambridge, Mass.: The MIT Press, 1990.

[22] L. Gupta and M. D. Srinath. Contour sequence moments for the classification of closed planar shapes. *Pattern Recognition*, 20(3):267–272, 1987.

[23] L. Gupta and M. D. Srinath. Invariant planar shape recognition using dynamic alignment. *Pattern Recognition*, 21(3):235–239, 1988.

[24] L. N. Hambrick, M. H. Loew, and R. L. Carroll Jr. The entry-exit method of shadow boundary segmentation. *IEEE Trans. Patt. Anal. Mach. Intell.*, PAMI-9(5):597–607, 1987.

[25] R. M. Haralick and L.G. Shapiro. Image segmentation techniques. *Comp. Vis. Graph. Image Proc.*, 29:100–132, 1985.

[26] M.-K. Hu. Visual pattern recognition by moment invariants. *IRE Trans. Inform. Theory*, IT-8:179–187, 1962.

[27] A. Huertas. An edge based system for detecting buildings in aerial images. In R. Nevatia, editor, *Image Understanding Research.* USC, 1982. Tech. Report ISG 101.

[28] A. Huertas and R. Nevatia. Detection of buildings in aerial images using shape and shadows. In *Proc. 8th IJCAI*, pages 1099–1103, Karlsruhe, West Germany, August 1983.

[29] R. B. Irvin and D. M. McKeown. Methods for exploiting the relationship between buildings and their shadows in aerial imagery. *IEEE Trans. Sys., Man, and Cyber.*, 19(6):1564–1575, 1989.

[30] C. C. Lin and R. Chellappa. Classification of partial 2-D shapes using Fourier descriptors. *IEEE Trans. Patt. Anal. Mach. Intell.*, PAMI-9(5):686–690, 1987.

[31] D. G. Lowe. *Perceptual Organization and Visual Recognition.* Boston, MA: Kluwer, 1985.

[32] D. G. Lowe and T. O. Binford. The interpretation of geometric structure from image boundaries. In L. S. Baumann, editor, *Proc. ARPA Image Understanding Workshop*, pages 39–46, April 1981.

[33] J. Ma, C. Wu, and X. Lu. A fast shape descriptor. *Comp. Vis., Graph., and Image Proc.*, 34:282–291, 1986.

[34] J. C. Ming and B. Bhanu. A multistrategy machine learning approach for target model recognition, acquisition, and refinement. In *Proc. DARPA Image Understanding Workshop*, pages 742–756, Pittsburgh, PA, Sept. 1990.

[35] D. I. Moldovan and C. Wu. A hierarchical knowledge based system for airplane classification. *IEEE Trans. on Software Engineering*, 14(12):1829–1834, 1988.

[36] J. L. Mundy, R. Welty, L. Quam, T. Strat, W. Bremner, M. Horwedel, D. Hackett, and A. Hoogs. The RADIUS common development environment. In *Proc. DARPA Image Understanding Workshop*, pages 215–226, San Diego, CA, Jan. 1992.

[37] H.-H. Nagel. Displacement vectors derived from second-order intensity variations in image sequences. *Computer Vision, Graphics, and Image Processing*, 9:203–214, 1983.

[38] H. Nasr, B. Bhanu, and S. Lee. Refocused recognition of aerial photographs at multiple resolution. In *Proc. SPIE*, vol. 1098, pp. 198–206, Orlando, FL, March 1989.

[39] R. Nevatia and K. R. Babu. Linear feature extraction and description. *Computer Graphics and Image Processing*, 13:257–269, 1980.

[40] A. P. Reeves, R. J. Prokop, S. E. Andrews, and F. P. Kuhl. Three-dimensional shape analysis using moments and Fourier descriptors. *IEEE Trans. Patt. Anal. and Mach. Intell.*, PAMI-10(6):937–943, 1988.

[41] A. P. Reeves and R. W. Taylor. Identification of three-dimensional object using range information. *IEEE Trans. Patt. Anal. and Mach. Intell.*, 11(4):403–410, 1989.

[42] E. Rosch, C. B. Mervis, W. D. Gray, D. M. Johnson, and P. Boyes-Braem. Basic objects in natural categories. *Cognit. Psychol.*, 8(3):382–439, 1976.

[43] O. G. Selfridge. Pandemonium: A paradigm for learning. In D. Blake and A. Uttley, editors, *Proc. Symp. Mechanization of Thought Processes*, pages 511–529. London: HMSO, 1959.
[44] A. Sha'ashua and S. Ullman. Structural saliency: The detection of globally salient structures using a locally connected network. In *Proc. IEEE Second Intl. Conf. Comp. Vision*, pages 321–327, Tarpon Springs, FL, Dec. 1988.
[45] S. A. Shafer. *Shadows and Silhouettes in Computer Vision*. Hingham, MA: Kluwer, 1985.
[46] L. Stark and K. Bowyer. Achieving generalized recognition through reasoning about association of function to structure. *IEEE Tran. Patt. Anal. and Mach. Intell.*, 13(10):1097–1104, 1991.
[47] G. Y. Tang and T. S. Huang. Using the creation machine to locate airplanes on aerial photos. *Pattern Recognition*, 12:431–442, 1980.
[48] D. W. Thompson and J. L. Mundy. Three-dimensional model matching from an unconstrained viewpoint. In *IEEE Int. Conf. Robotics Autom.*, pages 208–220, Raleigh, NC 1987.
[49] T. P. Wallace, O. P. Mitchell, and K. Fukunaga. Three-dimensional shape analysis using local shape descriptors. *IEEE Trans. Patt. Anal. and Mach. Intell.*, PAMI-3:310–323, 1981.
[50] T. P. Wallace and P. A. Wintz. An efficient three-dimensional aircraft recognition algorithm using normalized Fourier descriptors. *Comp. Graphics, Image Proc.*, 13:99–126, 1980.
[51] C. T. Zahn and R. Z. Roskies. Fourier descriptors for plane closed curves. *IEEE Trans. Comput.*, C-21:269–281, 1972.

Scanning Probe Microscopy: Trends and Image Processing Issues

G.S. Pingali and R. Jain

Abstract. Scanning probe microscopy (SPM) includes techniques such as scanning tunneling microscopy (STM), atomic force microscopy (AFM), magnetic force microscopy (MFM) and scanning ion conductance microscopy (SICM). Scanning probe microscopes have started a new era in microscopy by providing depth maps at an unprecedented resolution. These versatile devices work in vacuum, air, liquids, and aqueous solutions. Their resolution can be varied from the atomic range to the micrometer range. Scanning probe microscopy is being recognized as a powerful imaging technique in a variety of application areas. Not only can SPM image surface topography, but also other surface characteristics such as magnetic domains, electrical charge, local density of electron states, and surface temperature. Promising results using SPM have been obtained in imaging semiconductors, metals, organic materials, superconductors, and biological samples. SPM is already being used in some industrial applications and there is immense potential for applying it to surface characterization, metrology, and inspection in numerous applications. Image processing techniques are a vital complement to sensor technology in scanning probe microscopes. Image analysis and understanding techniques are essential if the potential of SPM for metrology and industrial inspection is to be realized. In this chapter, we present an overview of the state of the art in SPM with emphasis on image processing techniques for SPM. We outline the principle of operation of different scanning probe microscopes. Issues related to sensor technology are discussed. Commercially available scanning probe microscopes are listed and their features summarized. We review in detail the image processing work that has been done to date in relation to SPM and raise relevant issues. Existing and potential applications of SPM are discussed. Finally, we point out directions for future research in image processing related to SPM.

1 Introduction

Scanning probe microscopy marks a new era in the history of microscopy. Since the invention of the optical microscope by Antony van Leeuwenhoek in the seventeenth century, microscopes have improved in resolution and sophistication and aided mankind in its study of the minute. Optical microscopes have improved to the point where their resolution is hampered only by a fundamental limitation, which is half the wavelength of the light used. Since the average wavelength of visible light is about 2000 times the diameter of a typical atom, the optical microscope cannot image structures at the atomic level. The electron microscope broke this barrier by the use of high energy electrons which have low wavelengths. However, the use of high energy electrons means that the electrons used in imaging often penetrate the sample being imaged, making it hard to study the surface of the sample. Scanning probe microscopy started with the invention of the scanning tunneling microscope (STM) by Gerd Binning and Heinrich Rohrer [25] who won the Nobel Prize in Physics in 1986 for their invention. Since then, several variants of the scanning tunneling microscope have been developed which can be grouped under the title "Scanning Probe Microscopy" (SPM) or "Scanning 'X' Microscopy" (SXM). This form of microscopy achieves the feat of imaging surface structure of samples with a resolution of one Å, about half the diameter of an atom.

Some of the variants of scanning tunneling microscopy that fall under the category of scanning probe microscopy [189, 190] are:

- Atomic Force Microscopy (AFM)
- Laser Force Microscopy (LFM)
- Magnetic Force Microscopy (MFM)
- Electrostatic Force Microscopy (EFM)
- Scanning Thermal Microscopy
- Scanning Ion Conductance Microscopy (SICM)

Atomic force microscopy, laser force microscopy, magnetic force microscopy, electrostatic force microscopy and related force microscopies are sometimes collectively referred to as Scanning Force Microscopy (SFM) [161]. Scanning probe microscopes are becoming popular not only due to their ability to produce ultra-high resolution images, but also because they provide a three dimensional image of a surface profile (even at lower resolutions), and because they can produce images under a variety of conditions.

In this chapter we present an overview of the state of the art in scanning probe microscopy. Section 2 outlines the principle of operation of scanning probe microscopes. Section 3 points out the attractive features of these instruments. Section 4 discusses the sensor technology issues related to scanning probe microscopes. Tip technology, cantilever technology, and the technology of positioning devices are discussed in this section. Section 5 lists the commercially available scanning probe microscopes and compares their specifications. Section 6 discusses the existing and potential application areas for SPM's. Section 7 discusses image processing and visualization techniques for SPM's. This is the biggest section in the chapter. In this section we review the image processing work that has been done to date in relation to scanning probe microscopy and raise relevant issues. Section 7.1.1 discusses the enhancement of SPM images using spatial domain and frequency domain filtering techniques. Section 7.1.2 reviews the work in the area of visualization of SPM images. Section 7.2 reviews the work in restoration of scanning probe microscope images. This includes restoration using linear filters for high resolution images as well as geometric restoration that accounts for nonlinear distortion of images due to probe geometry. Section 7.3 discusses the issuue of correcting SPM images for the tilt of the sample with respect to the x-y plane of the scan-coordinate system. The issue of taking advantage of the sample inclination to improve surface recovery is also discussed. Section 7.4 reviews the work done in recovering the shape of the probe used in scanning from an image obtained using the probe. Section 7.5 considers the work done in making measurements from

SPM images. Section 7.6 discusses the work in tools that can simulate and animate the SPM imaging process. Section 8 points out directions for future research and Sect. 9 summarizes the discussion in this chapter.

2 Principle of Operation of SPMs

All scanning probe microscopes use a small and narrow stylus (probe) which is brought close to the material surface to be scanned. This probe is rastered across the surface of interest by means of a suitable mechanism. A physical effect that occurs due to the close proximity of the probe and the surface is monitored by a feedback system. The feedback system keeps the strength of the effect constant as the probe is rastered across the surface. For topographic imaging, the physical effect chosen is highly sensitive to the distance between the probe and the sample. In this case the feedback system is used to maintain a constant distance between the probe and the surface. The probe, in effect, "rides over" the surface at a constant distance. The height of the probe is used to image the topography of the surface.

2.1 The Scanning Tunneling Microscope (STM)

Figure 1 shows a schematic diagram of a scanning tunneling microscope (STM). The main components of the scanning tunneling microscope are:

i) A probe used for scanning.
ii) A scanning system for rastering the probe across the sample surface.
iii) A sensing mechanism for measuring the height of the probe over the sample surface.
iv) A feedback controller that maintains the probe at a constant height above the scanned surface.
v) A display system for visualization of the measured topography of the surface.

The scan generator applies voltages to the X and Y piezo crystals attached to the probe causing the probe to move across the sample in a raster fashion. The sensing mechanism used in the case of the STM is based on the tunneling current between the probe tip and the sample. The tunneling current falls exponentially with the distance between the probe tip and the sample, and can be used to measure the height of the probe over the sample. The feedback controller compares the tunneling current between the tip and the sample with a reference current value. The output of the feedback controller controls the z piezo crystal and, hence, monitors the height of the probe so as to maintain a constant tunneling current. This output voltage, which indicates the height of the probe as it scans the sample, is input to the display system along with the scan generator signals to

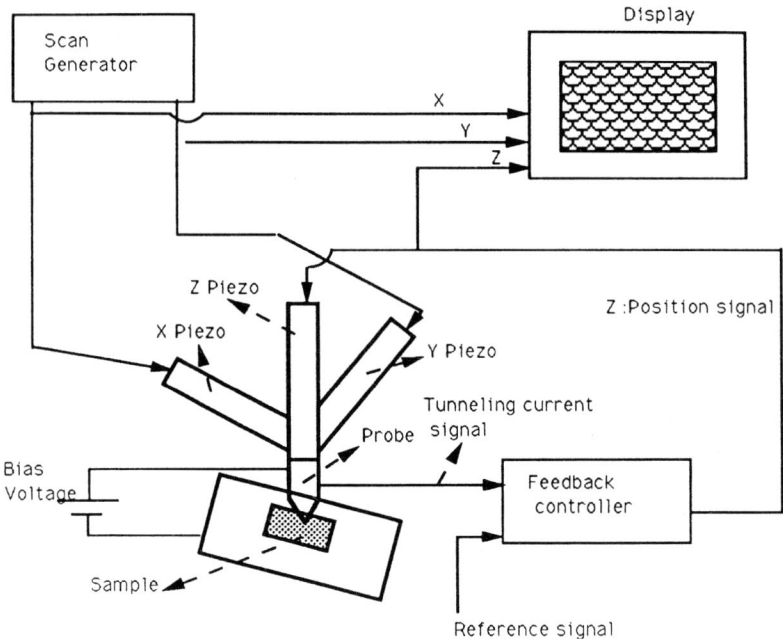

Fig. 1. Schematic diagram of a scanning tunneling microscope

obtain an image of the topography of the scanned surface. The ultrahigh resolution of the STM results from the use of a probe with an extremely fine (single-atom) tip, of piezo crystals that can move the probe by sub-nanometer distances, and of a sensing mechanism that is based on the tunneling current and is hence sensitive to movements of the order of the radius of an atom. A simplified expression for the tunneling current i_t is [177]:

$$i_t = \frac{e^2 \kappa_o V A_{eff} \exp(-2\kappa_o s)}{4\pi^2 hs} \quad (1)$$

where e is the electron charge, A_{eff} is the effective area through which the tunneling current flows, h is Planck's constant, V is the bias voltage (of the order of a few millivolts) between the probe and the sample, s is the distance between the probe and the sample, and κ_o is given by

$$\kappa_o = \sqrt{2m_e \phi / h^2} \quad (2)$$

where m_e is the electron mass and ø is the average "barrier height" above the Fermi level of the sample (i.e., the work function of the sample). κ_o is the decay constant of the electron cloud over the sample surface. The tunneling effect takes place when the probe and sample are at a distance within a few atomic diameters. Equation (1) shows the high sensitivity of the tunneling current to the distance s between the probe and the sample. The tunneling current changes by a factor of 2

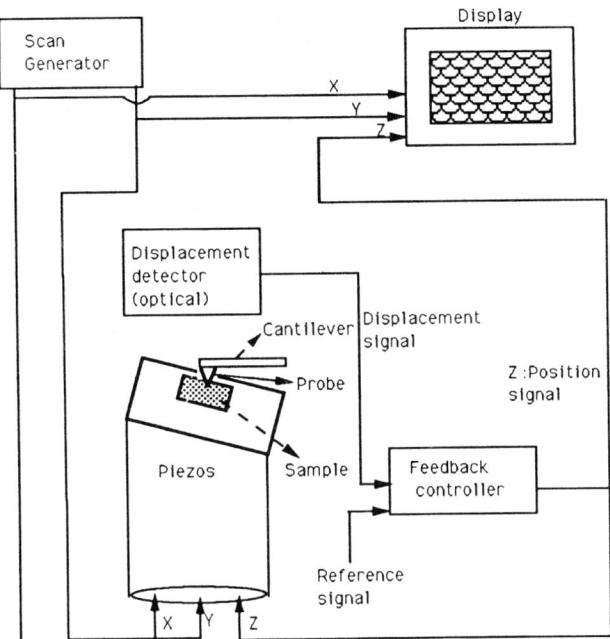

Fig. 2. Schematic diagram of an atomic force microscope

or more for a change of 0.1 nm in the distance between the tip and the surface. This expression assumes that both the probe and the sample can be represented as flat free-electron-like metals. However, the sensitivity of the tunneling current to distance remains valid even if this assumption does not hold.

One point to note here is that both the probe tip and the sampled material should conduct electricity if the tunneling effect has to take place. Hence, the STM can be used to image only conducting materials. This limitation is overcome by a variant of the STM, the atomic force microscope (AFM), that is discussed below.

2.2 The Atomic Force Microscope (AFM)

The principle of operation of the atomic force microscope (AFM) is very similar to that of the STM. However, rather than tunneling current, the physical effect that is monitored to keep the probe at a constant distance from the sample surface is the repulsive force between the probe tip and the sample surface due to the overlap of their electron clouds. The repulsive force is usually in the range of 10^{-6} to 10^{-9} N. For the operation of an AFM, it is not necessary that the surface should be conducting. The AFM can image both conducting and non-conducting specimens. Figure 2 shows a schematic of the atomic force microscope. The main components of the atomic force microscope are:

i) A probe attached to a cantilever
ii) A scanning system for rastering the sample relative to the probe tip.
iii) A sensing mechanism to measure the height of the probe over the sample surface.
iv) A feedback controller that maintains a constant distance between the probe and the scanned surface.
v) A display system for visualization of the measured topography of the surface.

The probe used in the AFM is attached to a cantilever, which acts as a spring and keeps the probe tip pressed against the surface being scanned. As the sample is scanned, the cantilever is deflected due to variations in the topography of the sample. A deflection sensing mechanism is used to measure these angstrom-level deflections of the cantilever. Different kinds of sensing mechanisms have been used to measure cantilever deflection. The original AFM developed by Binnig et al. [27] used an STM tip to measure the deflection of the cantilever. The most popular mechanisms today, however, are based on optical techniques. Optical detection schemes used are based on either interferometry or laser beam deflection and are capable of measuring cantilever deflections of the order of 0.1 angstrom. The scanning, feedback and display systems used in the AFM are very similar to those used in the STM.

2.3 Other Variants

Several variants of the STM have been developed which fall under the category of scanning probe microscopes. Some of these variants are simply the use of the STM or AFM in different modes to obtain other information besides topographic information. Table 1 summarizes the variants of the STM.

Laser Force Microscope. The laser force microscope (LFM) monitors the attractive force that develops between a surface and a probe that are 2 to 20 nanometers away [117]. The LFM detects the force by its effect on the dynamics of a vibrating probe. The probe is usually made of tungsten. Piezoelectric controls are used to vibrate the probe tip at just above its resonant frequency. When the tip is moved to within a few nanometers of the sample surface, the weak attractive force from the sample surface lowers the resonant frequency of the probe, thereby lessening the vibration amplitude. A laser sensor detects the changes in the amplitude of vibration of the probe by means of interferometry. The LFM is an example of a scanning probe microscope which scans in a "non-contact" mode keeping a constant non-negligible distance between the probe and the sample. The LFM can thus be used as a non-destructive surface profilometer.

Magnetic Force Microscope. The magnetic force microscope (MFM) is a variant of the laser force microscope that uses a magnetized iron or nickel probe [118]. In this case, the magnetic characteristics of the sample modulate the resonant frequency of the probe. The MFM can be used to image the strength and uniformity

Table 1. Scanning probe microscopes

Instrument	Physical effect	Probe material	Resolution	Applications
Scanning tunneling microscope (STM)	Tunneling current between charged tip and conducting sample	tungsten	0.2 nm (atomic)	Atomic to micron scale microscopy and spectroscopy of conducting surfaces
Atomic force microscope (AFM)	Repulsive force due to overlap of tip and sample atoms	silicon diamond silicon oxide silicon nitride	0.2 nm atomic	Atomic to micron scale contact mode imaging of non-conducting and conducting surfaces
Laser force microscope (LFM)	Attractive force between probe and sample when 2 to 20 nm away	silicon silicon nitride silicon oxide tungsten	5 nm	Non-contact surface profilometry, esp. for microelectronics
Magnetic force microscope (MFM)	Magnetic force between probe and magnetic sample	magnetized nickel or iron	20 nm	Imaging magnetic domain patterns of samples, eg., magnetic heads
Electrostatic force microscope (EFM)	Electrostatic force between charged probe and the sample	tungsten	5 nm	Measurement of electrical properties Dopant profiling in semiconductors
Scanning thermal microscope	Temperature change when probe approaches sample	tungstennickel junction (thermocouple)	30 nm	High resolution thermometry and profilometry of thermal insulators
Scanning ion conductance microscope (SICM)	Change in current between electrode (probe) and sample	glass micropipette containing an electrode	0.2 μm	Measurement of electrical activity in biosamples Imaging in electrolytes

of the magnetic fields produced by a sample. It is being used to image magnetic recording heads and magnetic media.

Electrostatic Force Microscope. The electrostatic force microscope (EFM) is another variation of the laser force microscope that uses an electrically charged probe (typically made of tungsten) [119]. The microscope measures electrical properties of the sample at very high resolution by means of changes in vibration amplitude of the probe due to electrostatic forces caused by charges in the specimen. The EFM is being used to measure electrical properties of microcircuits at a very fine scale.

Scanning Thermal Microscope. The scanning thermal microscope has a probe tip which is a tungsten-nickel junction that acts as a thermocouple. This microscope can measure surface temperature variations in thousandths of a degree at the nanometer level. By measuring the heat loss from the probe to the sample, which depends on the distance of the probe from the sample, the scanning thermal microscope can also be used to measure topography of the sample. The thermal microscope is being used for profiling insulating surfaces and for high resolution thermal microscopy, spectroscopy and thermometry.

Scanning Ion Conductance Microscope. The scanning ion conductance microscope (SICM) [189] scans a sample with a glass micropipette containing a tiny electrode. Using a feedback mechanism that maintains a constant ion current through the pipette opening, the SICM can profile a sample's topography. The SICM could also be used to measure electrical activity and one of its potential application areas is measurement of electrical activity in living cells.

Scanning Tunneling Spectroscope. The scanning tunneling microscope can also be applied as an analytical tool in a spectroscopic mode. In this mode, the tunneling voltage is varied in order to obtain current-voltage spectra from specific points on the surface. Peaks in the derivatives of these spectra are interpreted as corresponding to energies of high local density of electron states (LDOS). Images can also be taken at specific bias voltages to obtain spatial distribution of particular states [83, 190, 15]. In this mode the scanning tunneling microscope is often referred to as the Scanning Tunneling Spectroscope (STS).

Novel variants of these microscopes are being developed from time to time. Atomic force microscope and related force microscopies are collectively referred to as scanning force microscopy (SFM). The two most popular forms of scanning probe microscopy today are scanning tunneling microscopy (STM) and scanning force microscopy (SFM). This chapter focuses on these forms of scanning probe microscopy.

3 Attractive Features of SPMs

Scanning probe microscopes have several attractive features.

Resolution. Scanning probe microscopes represent a fundamental advance in microscopy as they achieve atomic resolution. SPM's overcome the "Abbe barrier" [30, 189, 190] that limits the resolution of any microscope that relies on lenses to focus light or other radiation. The Abbe limit on resolution is half the wavelength of the radiation used (wavelength of visible light is approximately in the range 400 to 700 nm). Scanning probe microscopes can analyze surface structures with a lateral resolution ranging from 5 micrometers down to 0.1 nanometer. The vertical resolution, measured perpendicular to the surface, can be better than 0.1 nm. Figures 3, 4 and 5 give an indication of the power of scanning probe microscopes. Figure 3 shows an AFM image of an image of an integrated circuit. The scan range here is 130 microns and the lateral resolution is about 0.5 microns. Figure 4 shows an image of a chemically textured hard disk. The scan range is 2.3 microns corresponding to a lateral resolution of about 0.02 microns. The scan range for Fig. 5 is 3.7 nanometers corresponding to a lateral resolution of about 0.15 nanometers.

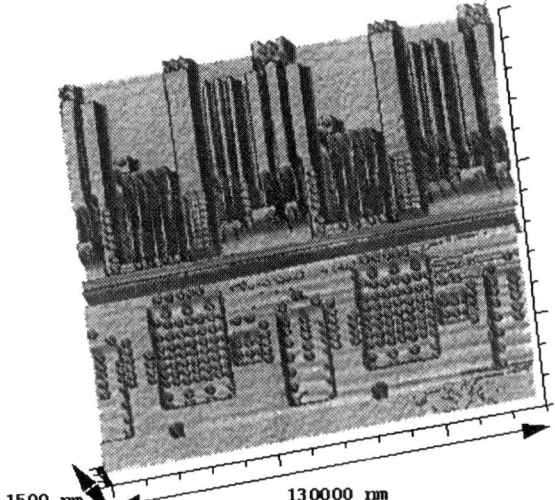

Fig. 3. AFM image of an integrated circuit

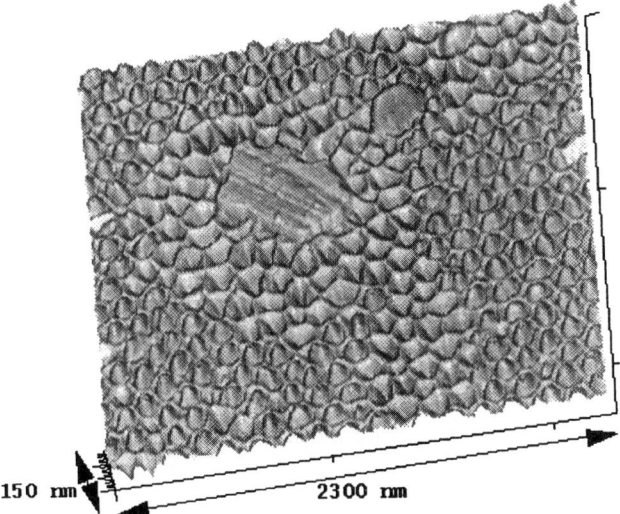

Fig. 4. AFM image of a chemically textured hard disk

This is an STM image of highly ordered pyrolitic graphite (HOPG). Individual carbon atoms can be seen in this figure.

Imaging Conditions. Another attractive feature of SPM's is that they can be designed to work under a variety of conditions – in ultrahigh vacuum (UHV), in moderate vaccum, in air (ambient conditions), and in liquids such as oil, water, liquid nitrogen, and in conductive solutions [83]. Although other techniques such as scanning electron microscopy (SEM) achieve atomic resolution in ultra high vacuum, only scanning probe microscopy achieves atomic resolution in ambient

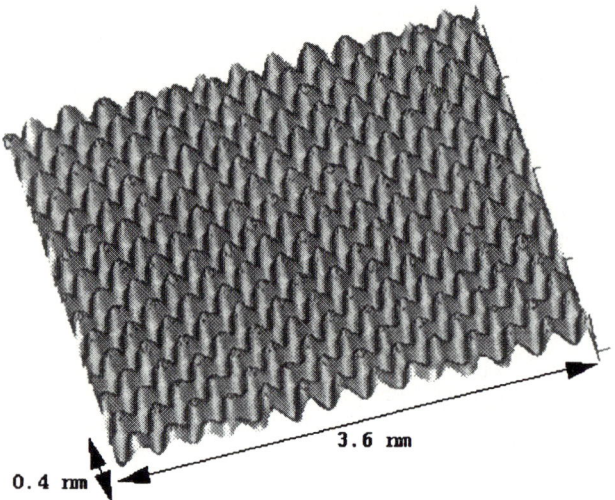

Fig. 5. STM image of graphite at atomic resolution

pressure and in water [83]. Besides, it is very difficult to achieve atomic resolution imaging of surface structure with methods such as SEM. The high energy electrons needed to achieve such high resolution tend to penetrate into the material making it hard to image the surface structure.

Compactness. Scanning probe micrscopes are very compact. The actual instrument is only about 30 cm tall and 15 cm wide. The whole set up including a PC for controlling the instrument, an optical microscope attached to the instrument and monitors for the optical microscope and SPM images can sit on a normal size table. Figure 6 shows an actual SPM. This is a commercially available Atomic Force Microscope. The compactness of the instrument is clearly seen in this figure. The compact design of the instrument also helps in vibration elimination.

Three Dimensional Digitized Data. Scanning probe microscopes give three dimensional digitized data of the topography of the surface scanned. The output can directly be processed by a digital computer. While methods such as SEM would match the resolution of some SPM images, SPM is attractive because of the ready availability of such digitally stored data which enables one to study any interesting cross section in profile with quantitative elevation data [43].

Imaging Modes. Scanning probe microscopes can function in different modes to yield different kinds of information. The imaged characteristics include surface topography of the sample, surface conductivity of the sample, magnetic domains on the surface of the sample, and the chemical structure of the sample.

Nanotechnological Instruments. Researchers have also started exploring the possibility of using such scanning probe instruments as tools to handle individual atoms and modify and manipulate single molecules. This promise of the blossom-

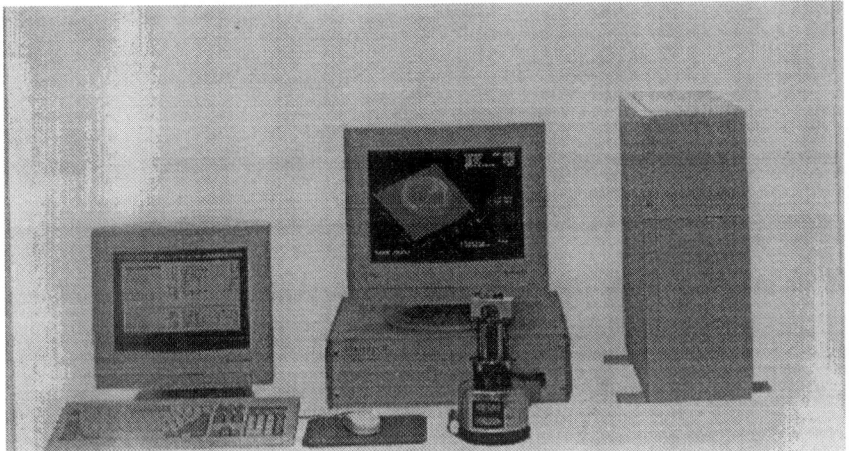

Fig. 6. Picture of an actual Scanning Probe Microscope (an Atomic Force Microscope)

ing of scanning probe microscopes into nanotechnological instruments continues to be a significant motivation for research in this area.

4 Sensor Technology Issues

A number of sensor technology issues arise in the development of ultra-high resolution instruments such as scanning probe microscopes. Some of the important issues are:

- Tip fabrication
- Tip shape characterization
- Positioning of the tip relative to the sample
- Isolation of the microscope from ambient vibrations
- Cantilever deflection detection systems for force microscopes
- Programmed scanning techniques: Programmed probe microscopy

4.1 Tip Fabrication

The most critical component of a scanning probe microscope is the probe that is used for scanning. The small portion at the end of the probe that is actually involved in imaging is referred to as the "tip" of the probe. The tip limits the lateral and vertical resolution of the scanning probe microscope. Two basic techniques are now being used for tip fabrication: erosion techniques, in which the probe of a

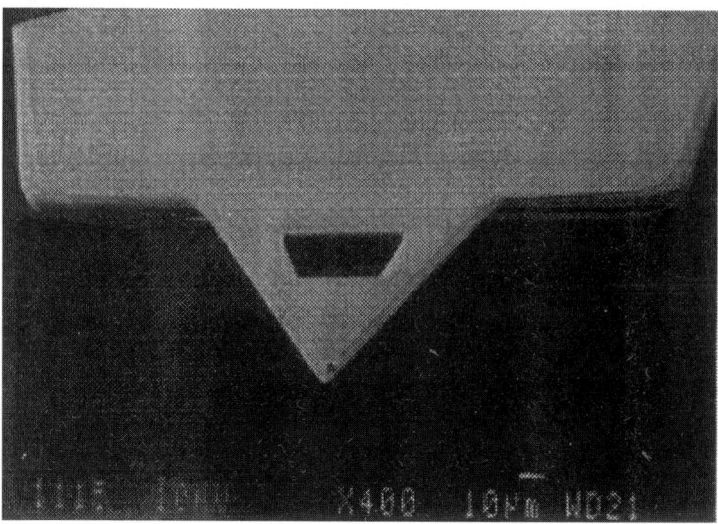

Fig. 7. Cantilever with probe tip

desired shape is obtained by eroding the surface of another shape; growth techniques in which a probe of desired geometry is grown. The commonly used materials for STM tips are tungsten, platinum and platinum-iridium. The tips are sharpened using cutting, grinding, and etching methods. Although several techniques have been successful in producing a tip that terminates in a single atom, precise control of the complete shape of the tip has been difficult. Electrochemical etching techniques are being used for microfabricating tips with desired geometries.

In atomic force microscopy, the probe tip is attached to a cantilever which acts as a spring and keeps the probe tip pressed against the surface being scanned. The most advanced cantilevers are microfabricated from silicon, silicon oxide or silicon nitride using photolithographic techniques. Typical lateral dimensions are of the order of 100 microns, with thicknesses of order 1 micron. This geometry gives spring constants in the range of 0.1 to 1 N/m and resonant frequencies of 10 to 100 kHz [158]. The cantilevers are often fabricated with integrated tips. In other cases, the tips are obtained separately by cutting, grinding or etching methods and then glued on to the cantilever. Figure 7 shows an image of a cantilever used in an atomic force microscope. The probe tip is attached to the cantilever as seen in the figure. Figures 8, 9 and 10 show scanning electron microscope (SEM) images of three different probe tip geometries. The most commonly used tip for AFMs is a pyramidal tip seen in Fig. 8. Much effort is being devoted to fabricating tips which have higher aspect ratios and which are mechanically stiff (so that they do not flex due to the probe-sample interaction forces).

Some of the best probe tips that act as force sensors for magnetic and electrostatic imaging are made by electrochemical etching techniques. The etched wires

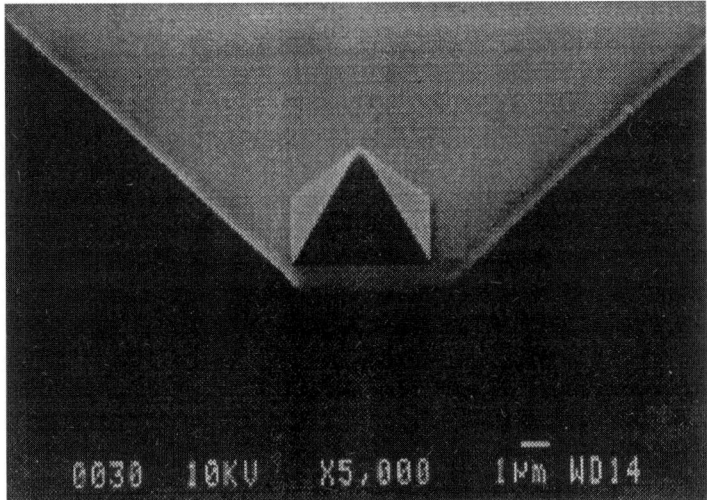

Fig. 8. SEM image of a pyramidal probe tip

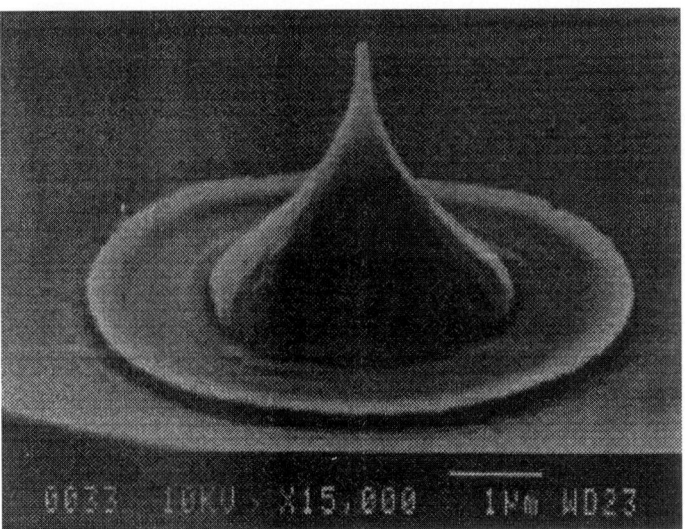

Fig. 9. SEM image of a hyperboloid probe tip

have a tapered geometry that varies from 10 microns in diameter at the point of attachment to less than 500 angstrom at the end. Novel techniques are being developed all the time for fabricating tips with higher aspect ratios. Keller et al. [96, 97] have developed an electron beam deposition process for growing "microtips" on top of the apex of a pyramidal probe. Microtips with a length of $2\,\mu m$ and end radius of $100\,\text{Å}$ have been produced. Kong et al. [103, 104] have developed a fine-

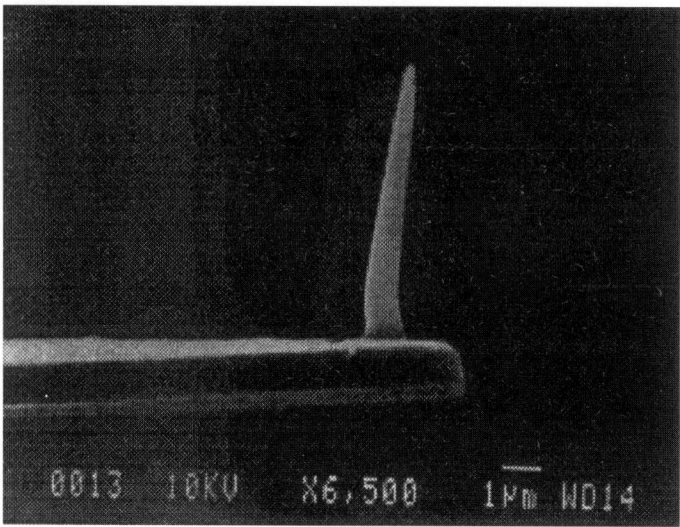

Fig. 10. SEM image of a electron beam deposited high-aspect ratio probe tip

grained polysilicon hyperbolic probe using reactive ion etching techniques (Fig. 9) as well as a high-aspect ratio tip grown using electron beam deposition (Fig. 10). Vasile et al. [183] have developed methods to controllably fabricate sharp tungsten and iridium tips using a focused ion beam (FIB) of Ga^+ ions. Some researchers [108, 130] are investigating the use of tips with flared ends for profiling undercut sidewalls.

Other researchers [102, 192] are developing integrated multi-channel scanning force microscopes. Figure 11 shows the schematic of such a device. As seen in the figure, multiple cantilever beams with attached styli, circuitry for driving the cantilever beams, optical fiber ports for optical readout of cantilever deflection, and electronic sensing circuitry are all integrated on a micromachined silicon substrate.

4.2 Tip Shape Characterization

The shape of the tip is the most important factor determining the quality of the image produced by a scanning probe microscope. However, the tip shape tends to be difficult to control during manufacture and may vary with usage. Several researchers are addressing the issue of *in situ* characterization of tips. Hashizume et al. [84] designed STMs operable in ultrahigh vacuum (UHV) and aqueous conditions. For UHV, they designed an STM combined with a field ion microscope (FI-STM). The FIM introduced inside the STM vacuum chamber is used for in situ characterization of the scanning tip. Though only a portion of the entire tip surface

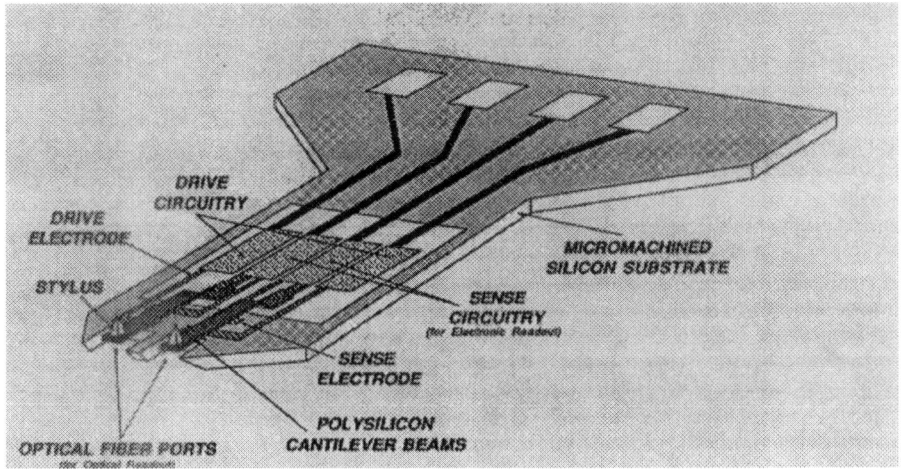

Fig. 11. Schematic diagram of a multi-channel scanning force microscope

is viewed by FIM, the details of the cap of the scanning tip can still be inspected on an atomic scale. The average radius and overall smoothness can be estimated. Several researchers have studied the in situ fabrication and regeneration of microtips for STM [24, 128]. Other researchers are exploring the possibility of recovering probe shape from scans of standard calibration surfaces using image processing techniques. [138, 146, 62, 65]. This is further discussed in Sect. 7.

4.3 Scanning and Positioning

One of the important issues in SPM imaging is positioning the probe tip relative to the sample. On a coarse scale, the tip needs to be moved in the millimeter range and positioned over the area of the sample that is of interest. On a fine scale, the tip needs to be moved over the sample in the lateral and vertical dimensions with nanometer or angstrom level accuracy. Piezoelectric ceramics are most popular for fine positioning. These materials expand and contract in a highly repeatable manner depending on the voltage applied. The commonly used configurations of piezoelectrics for fine positioning are the "tripod" configuration and the "tube" configuration [30, 31]. In the tripod configuration, separate piezoelectrics are used to control motion in each of the X, Y and Z directions. In the tube configuration a single type of piezoelectric material is expanded, contracted, or bent by applying a voltage to achieve the desired motion. The advantage of the tube configuration is that it is more rigid and hence less sensitive to vibration than typical tripod configurations. Tube nonlinearities such as hysteresis and creep are indeed a problem in SPMs. These nonlinearities can be reduced but cannot be eliminated. Hence, independent measures of the actual displacement of the tube are needed if the measurements from the instrument are to be reliable. Barrett and Quate [13] developed an optical system for independently monitoring the actuator position and correcting for nonlinearities. Grigg et al. [65] have developed a capacitor based system for independently monitoring the tube displacement.

Coarse positioning of the tip relative to the sample is a significant problem. The field of view in SPM is relatively small (typically $1\,\mu m^2$) due to the fine-positioning mechanisms used [66]. Hence, the chance of finding an object of interest within the range of the piezo scanner is very low. Coarse positioning mechanisms include piezoelectric walkers or "louses", screw-based micrometer type mechanical adjustments, lever mechanisms, and differential springs. Most of these are manually operated and cannot be controlled from data acquisition software. Laegsgaard et al. [106] developed an STM in which they use two piezoelectric ceramic tubes, one for the x-y-z motion of the tip and one for a linear motor ("nanoworm") used for the coarse positioning of the tip relative to the specimen. The nanoworm positioning implies that the STM is fully controlled by electronic means, and that no mechanical coupling is needed. Michel and Travaglini [122] presented an improved coarse positioning system with a large scan area. Commercial SPMs now provide coarse positioning systems that are mouse controlled and allow positioning anywhere on an 8 inch wafer with scan sizes up to 125 microns. The National Institute of Standards and Technology (NIST) is involved in the ambitious design of an instrument aimed at achieving 1 nm resolution over several centimeters [180].

4.4 Vibration Elimination

With imaging performed down to the scale of angstroms, vibration can severely affect the quality of the images produced in SPM. Hence, the design of a scanning probe microscope must compensate for various sources of vibration such as equipment vibration, building vibration, acoustic vibration and the vibrational response of the instrument. To isolate the scanning probe microscope head from vibrations, suspension systems based on springs, O-rings, eddy current damping mechanisms etc., are being used. Rigid components that have high resonant frequencies are used to minimize the effects of low frequency building and environment vibrations. Piezoelectric ceramics are particularly well-suited for positioning systems as they are inherently rigid.

4.5 Cantilever Deflection Detection Systems

In SFM, a critical component is the sensor that detects the cantilever's deflection. Early scanning force microscopes used a tunneling probe on top of the cantilever beam to detect the deflection of the cantilever beam. Although this method of detection has high sensitivity, the performance gets degraded when the tunneling surfaces become contaminated. Hence, most AFMs being designed now use some form of optical detection. Optical detection schemes are divided into two basic types: interferometry and beam deflection. Both of these methods are capable of measuring cantilever deflections of the order of 0.1 angstrom with a detection bandwidth of dc to 10 kHz [158]. Several cantilever driving systems and deflection detection systems used for scanning force microscopy are reviewed by Sarid and Elings [161].

4.6 Sample and Tip Orientation Mechanisms

In current SPM's, the sample is placed on a flat table and scanned. In an STM, the sample is kept stationary and the probe is moved during the scanning process. In an AFM, the probe is kept stationary and the sample is moved during scanning. In effect, in both the STM and the AFM, the sample is placed on an X-Y table and the probe scans the sample in a raster fashion. Currently, there is no provision for varying the *orientations* of the sample or the probe tip. Ability to control the sample and orientations provides additional degrees of freedom during scanning as shown in [142]. These issues are further discussed in Sect. 7.3.

4.7 Programmed Scanning Techniques: Programmed Probe Microscopy

Being a product of the 1980's, SPM's have been integrated with computer technology right from their inception. The scan range, speed of scanning, the resolution and other parameters are set in a computer which controls the scanning process. Over the years, an increasing amount of computer control has been incorporated into these instruments. Some instruments now provide a "step-and-scan" mode. In this mode, the instrument automatically scans adjacent areas in a sample and produces a series of images. The user can program in the size of each scan and the total width and length to be scanned. Instruments are also providing coarse positioning of the tip through mouse control. However, all SPM's scan the sample in a raster fashion. The scanning scheme itself is still not programmed. But researchers have begun to show that more accurate imaging is possible by appropriate variation of the scanning scheme. Nyysonen et al. [130] showed how a tip with a flared end could be used to profile sidewall information by moving the tip to the desired area and measuring the variation in its resonant frequency when it is vibrated in two orthogonal directions. A raster scan is not appropriate in this case. As discussed above, controlling the orientation of the probe and sample during scanning also provides additional degrees of freedom. The trend in SPM technology is towards having a suite of alternate scanning and positioning techniques pro-

Table 2. Comparison of commercial scanning proble microscopes

Instrument	Type	Medium of operation	Modes
Burleigh's Aris 2200	STM	Atmosphere	Topography, spectroscopy
Digital Instruments' Nanoscope	STM/AFM	Air, gases, liquids	Topography, spectroscopy
LK Tecnologies' STM 1000	STM	Atmosphere/liquid	Topography
LK Tecnologies' STM 5000	STM	UHV	Topography
McAllister's STM	STM	UHV	Topography, spectroscopy
Omicron's UHV STM	STM	UHV	Topography, spectroscopy
Park Scientific's STM-SU$_z$	STM	UHV	Topography, spectrosocpy
Park Scientific's Autoprobe	SFM/STM	Air	Topography, spectrosocpy
Perkin Elmer-Digital 301 STM	STM	UHV	Topography
RHK Technology UHV 635 STM	STM	UHV, atmosphere, liquid	Topography, spectroscopy
Topometrix' TMX 2000	AFM/STM	Atmosphere, liquid	Topography, spectroscopy, lateral force
Wyko's Microprobe	STM/AFM	Atmosphere	Topography

Table 3. Comparison of commercial scanning probe microscopes

Instrument	Vertical resolution	Lateral resolution	Scan range
Burleigh's Aris 2200	"Atomic"	–	–
Digital Instruments' Nanoscope	"Atomic"	–	$125\mu \times 125\mu$
LK Tecnologies' STM 1000	$0.1\,\text{Å}$	$2\,\text{Å}$	$10\mu \times 10\mu$
LK Tecnologies' STM 5000	$0.1\,\text{Å}$	$2\,\text{Å}$	$4\mu \times 4\mu$
McAllister's STM	$0.1\,\text{Å}$	$2\,\text{Å}$	–
Omicron's UHV STM	$<0.1\,\text{Å}$	$2\,\text{Å}$	$1.2\mu \times 1.2\mu$
Park Scientific's STM-SU2	$0.1\,\text{Å}$	$3\,\text{Å}$	$10\mu \times 10\mu$
Park Scientific's Autoprobe	"Atomic"	–	$100\mu \times 100\mu$
Perkin Elmer-Digital 301 STM	$0.5\,\text{Å}$	$1\,\text{Å}$	$12\mu \times 12\mu$
RHK Technology UHV 635 STM	$0.1\,\text{Å}$	$1\,\text{Å}$	$1\mu \times 1\mu$
Topometrix' TMX 2000	$0.1\,\text{Å}$	$2\,\text{Å}$	–
Wyko's Microprobe	$0.1\,\text{Å}$	$0.2\,\text{Å}$	$100\mu \times 100\mu$

grammed into the computer. The appropriate scanning and positioning strategy will be chosen based on the knowledge of the type of sample being imaged and the probe being used for imaging. Thus, the trend is towards programmed probe microscopy replacing the now prevalent scanning probe microscopy.

5 Commercial Scanning Probe Microscopes

There are several commercial manufacturers of scanning probe microscopes. Tables 2, 3, and 4 show the manufacturers of SPM's and summarize the features of the different microscopes.

Table 4. Comparison of commercial scanning probe microscopes

Instrument	Host computer	Image processing	Visualization
Burleigh's Aris 2200	IBM-AT compatible	Filtering, measurement of surface roughness, area and distance	2D, 3D plots
Digital Instruments' Nanoscope	IBM-AT compatible	Autocorrelation, FFT, various convolution filters, roughness measurements along a line or in an area	2D, 3D plots gray and color maps
LK Technologies' STM 1000, STM 5000	PC/AT 386 or Model 212 PC/AT	Histograms, line profiles, frequency analysis, distance, perimeter and area measurements, image rotation and scaling, low pass, horizontal, vertical edge filters	gray and color maps, perspective 3D
McAllister's STM	80386 CPU with 80387 coprocessor	Slope correction, FFT enchancement, 2D FFT, image editing, rotation, zoom cross-section, mean and median filters	False color top view, 3D solid modeling with movable light source, wire frame and filled
Omicron's UHV STM	HP 300 series workstation	drift correction, background subtraction, smoothing, image size	polygons, hidden line removal, line, contour plots grayscale, 3D plots
Park Scientific's STM-SU2	MC68040 CPU	Logarthmic scaling, rotation and zoom, background subtraction, FFT spectrumeditor, line, area analysis, notch and Wiener filters	gray, color plots, 3D rendering with height, curvature, shading user-defined viewing and light source angles
Park Scientific's Autoprobe	80486 CPU	Logarthmic scaling, rotation and zoom, background subtraction, FFT spectrum editor, line, area analysis, notch and Wiener filters	gray, color plots, 3D rendering with height, curvature, shading user-defined viewing and light source angles
Perkin Elmer-Digital 301 STM	–	–	–
RHK Technology UHV 635 STM	80486 CPU or Silicon Graphics IRIS workstation	FFT frequency analysis, image rotation, smoothing, median filtering, interpolation, Laplacian sharpening, interactive plane or paraboloid surbtraction, autocorrelation tilt and curvature removal	Gray scale, color maps, 3D surface and wire mesh plots, zooming, cross-sections, contrast manipulation
Topometrix' TMX 2000	IBM-AT compatible	Plane fit, FFT, line profile, fractal analysis, surface roughness	3D display, screen editing
Wyko's Microprobe	80486 CPU	Average, median, FFT filters, slope measurement, power spectrum, histograms, sub-area statistics (average, rms roughness, peak to valley difference,) least-squared tilt and curvature removal	Color maps, shaded 3D plots, zooming

Table 2 gives the instrument name, its type (STM, SFM etc.), the medium in which it operates, and its modes of operation (topography, spectroscopy etc.). Table 3 gives the maximum vertical resolution, which is the resolution measured perpendicular to the sample (i.e., in the z direction), and the lateral resolution, which is the resolution measured parallel to the sample (i.e., in the x and y directions). Table 3 also gives the maximum scan range of the instrument, which is the largest area that the instrument can image at a time. Several instruments come with alternate heads with different scan ranges. The table indicates the highest scan range available with a particular instrument. Table 4 indicates the host computer for each of the instruments and lists the image processing and visualization software available with each instrument. As seen in the table, most instruments now come with a library of image processing routines that include plane fitting and standard convolution filters. Some of them provide routines for computation of statistics along a line or in an area of the image. Blanks in these tables indicate that the corresponding information is not available.

Most commercial instruments come with a set of probes. The most commonly used probes are pyramidal in shape. Many of the instruments require manual operation for mounting the probe and for coarse positioning. The trend, however, is toward complete automated operation via software. Instruments are tending towards compact design and complete "mouse-driven" operation. Instruments are also incorporating increasingly sophisticated software for image manipulation, storage and analysis. Some instruments have a "step and scan" mode where a series of images of adjacent regions are automatically obtained in a sequential manner. Some vendors have started incorporating image databases for storage and retrieval of images and associated information such as values of various parameters (scan area, reference current etc.) corresponding to the image. Thus, scanning probe microscopes are incorporating sophisticated software both for instrument control and for acquisition, storage, and processing of images.

6 Application Areas

SPM is becoming increasingly popular in a number of application areas. The impact of SPM has been felt most in Materials Science where it has been used to obtain hitherto unseen images of the structure of surfaces of various materials. SPM has provided images of semiconductors, metals, superconductors and non-conducting materials. It has also been used to image cells and macromolecules in Biology but is still not a proven technique in this area. A few industrial applications that employ SPM have already been developed and it is being recognized as having immense potential in a number of industrial applications. Researchers are also working toward realizing the potential of scanning probe microscopes as nanotechnological instruments. Here we discuss some of the proven and potential application areas of SPM. Image processing and image understanding techniques can play an important role in many of these areas. Their use could range from enhancing the images using models of the physical processes involved, to making automatic measurements and detecting and classifying defects.

6.1 Semiconductors

SPM has been used to study semiconductor surfaces and surface reconstructions. The nature of the reconstructions have been studied on carefully prepared flat surfaces. The first STM images were of the 7 × 7 reconstruction of Si(111) [30]. Besides the topology of the Si(111) 7 × 7 surface, researchers have also succeeded in imaging the surface states [16] and electrical characteristics above individual atoms on the surface [70]. Besides giving such information on carefully prepared semiconductor surfaces, scanning probe microscopy can also be used to study and measure the microroughness of oxidized and ion-etched samples of semiconductors. SPM is also playing an important role in detecting sub-micron scale surface defects on semiconductors and semiconductor alloys [145]. Lipari [113] provides a good overview of the trends in the semiconductor industry and possible applications of SPM in the semiconductor industry. He points out that SPM can be used to advantage in both additive and subtractive processes in the manufacture of semiconductor devices. Some of the potential applications he identifies are surface preparation and characterization, thickness monitoring of thin films, surface device profiling, monitoring the dynamics of epitaxial growth, estimation of roughness of silicides, lithography mask characterization, and effects of reactive ion etching (RIE) on surface structure. Some of these predictions are already being realized. AFMs are being increasingly used for non-destructive metrology of sub-micron scale features on integrated circuits. Measurements made with SPMs include pitch, linewidth, microroughness and cirtical dimensions in the X, Y and Z directions [92, 133, 63].

6.2 Industrial Applications

Because of its great versatility as a metrology tool, SPM can be applied in product development and quality control in various industries such as the optical, semiconductor, and magnetic recording industries. One of the industrial applications of STM was in manufacture of a gold diffraction grating master. The SPM was used to measure the 120 nm high steps on the grating master and to guide the ruling machine to keep the blaze angle of the steps within a small range (about 3 degrees) [77]. STM has also been used in improving the manufacture of vertical recording thin film magnetic recording heads [77]. A potential application is quality control in the manufacture of compact-disk stampers. The raised bumps on such stampers can be imaged with SPM. SPM can also be used for defect detection at a micrometer scale on integrated circuit masks. The magnetic force microscope can be used to image magnetic fields above thin film magnetic recording heads. The most common application of SPMs today is the measurement of surface microroughness. SPM's are able to give direct measurements of roughness at high accuracy [133]. SFM can make atomic scale friction measurements or image the topography of surfaces such as photoresist on silicon. Another possible application is the measurement of lubricant thickness on surfaces. Other examples are imaging and analyzing fine grains on photographic film and various metals, and imaging localized charges on an insulated surface [61, 158, 43]. In the semiconductor industry, SPM's are being used for characterizing planarized structures and to optimize cleaning and etching processes. They are being used for critical dimension (CD) measurements and the detection of contaminants and defects on the nanometer or angstrom scales. With the ability to obtain three-dimensional profiles with a resolution ranging from the nanometer range to the micron range, scanning probe microscopy is bound to be widely employed in a variety of industrial applications. As discussed above, it is already being used, both in topographic and spectroscopic modes, for the surface characterization of various materials. Researchers are also trying to convert scanning probe microscopes into manipulation tools for manufacturing and repairing on a minute scale, as discussed below.

6.3 Polymers

With the advent of atomic force microscopes which are capable of imaging insulating surfaces, the study of polymers using SPMs is becoming increasingly common. SPMs are now part of the repertoire of Materials Scientists and Engineers along with instruments such as the SEM (scanning electron microscope), HREM (high resolution electron microscope) and TEM (transmission electron microscope). AFMs are being used in the study of microstructure of polymer surfaces. The great advantage with the AFM, compared to other techniques such as the HREM and TEM that are used for this purpose, is that sample preparation is relatively easy and imaging can be performed in vacuum, gaseous or liquid environments. AFMs are being used to characterize the microstructure of polymer thin films and interfaces [120]. The influence of various processing parameters on the local organization of polymer systems are being studied.

6.4 Metals

Several metals such as gold, platinum, iridium and silver have been studied using STM. Atomic resolution imaging has been performed. For example, images of single atom steps separating plateaus on a Au(100) surface have been obtained [26]. SPM is also useful in measuring the roughness of polished surfaces at a high resolution. The lateral resolution of SPM is much higher than conventional profiling instruments used for this purpose. SPM has a high potential for use in characterizing evaporated metal films. SPM may also be used in a spectroscopic mode to image the spatial variation in the electronic states of metal surfaces.

6.5 Biology

SPM has great potential for imaging biological samples. However, the success of SPM in this field has been limited due to the lack of appropriate specimen preparation methods. As most biological samples are non-conducting, the STM cannot be used to image them directly. Experiments with SFM are still being performed. While SFM has been used to image nonconductors such as boron nitride and nonconducting organic materials, smaller forces (10^{-10} N or less) may be required to image most biological specimens as they are fragile [77]. To image with the STM, the biological samples are coated with a conducting material or replicas of the sample are obtained. The STM has been used to image DNA in vacuum and in water, bacteriophage $\phi 29$, cell sheath, individual molecules of amino acids, macromolecules such as proteins, and porin vesicles [61, 158, 77, 43]. However, atomic resolution imaging has not been performed with biological samples. Specimen preparation techniques need to be developed further to obtain high resolution images. As SPM can perform imaging in water, it has the potential of imaging biomolecules in their active hydrated state. This potential is yet to be realized. Once SPM can image biomolecules in their active state, fast imaging techniques could be used to image biological processes in real time.

6.6 Superconductors

SPM is being used to study the spatial variations in superconducting properties on a microscopic scale. STM has been used in a spectroscopic mode to measure the superconducting energy gap of a thin film of Nb_3Sn [47]. STM can be used to measure the presence of superconductivity by measuring the ratio of the conductance of the sample at zero voltage to the conductance of the sample above the superconducting gap voltage [83]. This ratio is a sensitive indicator of superconductivity. As the STM can measure the conductance at high resolution, it can give a high resolution spatial map of the superconductivity of a sample. For such measurements, the STM is operated at low temperatures. At such low temperatures, the STM also has the potential of performing phonon spectroscopy and molecular vibration spectroscopy which might help in performing chemical analysis on a molecule by molecule basis [83].

6.7 Nanotechnology

It is being recognized that the STM can be employed as a nanoscale manipulation engineering tool to handle atoms and to modify individual molecules in a manner predicted by Feynman [165, 68, 15]. Becker et al. [16] placed a single atom onto a germanium surface. Foster et al [53] placed a single organic molecule at a particular location on a graphite surface. Some researchers are investigating the use of SPM for nanolithography. An STM tip has been used to draw lines 160 Å apart on glassy $Pd_{81}Si_{19}$ [152]. It is conceivable that SPM will evolve into a tool for manipulating atoms and molecules, and for removing and depositing material. An atomic processing microscope (AMP) which allows imaging selected atoms, stripping them off and replacing them with other atoms is already available [37]. It may also be possible to use the probe tip to test electronic circuits by using it as a local voltage probe and current source.

7 Image Processing and Visualization for SPM

Scanning probe microscopes yield digital images of the surfaces they scan. There is great scope for application of digital image processing techniques to the images produced by SPM. The development of new imaging devices (X ray imaging, MRI, electron microscopy ect.) in the past led to a tremendous amount of image processing activity – modeling the imaging process, enhancement and recovery of images, visualization techniques, and analysis of images to recover information relevant to different application domains. The techniques used for enhancement and restoration of SPM images differ considerably from those used for conventional images as the imaging process involved is very different. Image processing techniques can be very useful in the context of scanning probe microscopes. They can work hand in hand with sensor technology to develop SPM's that are more accurate and versatile.

7.1 Image Processing and Visualization in Current SPM's

7.1.1 Enhancement

Several researchers have worked on the computer automation of SPM [153, 17, 5, 19, 10]. Most of the systems developed provide image processing tools for image enhancement by means of various filters. These filtering techniques come from standard image processing theory. They are not based on models of the imaging process. They can be employed by the user to "improve" the quality of the image, often in a subjectively defined manner. All commercial scanning probe microscopes also come with image processing packages that provide such standard filters as discussed in Sect. 5. The enhancement techniques can be broadly divided into spatial domain and frequency domain techniques which are discussed below.

Spatial Domain

Spatial domain techniques directly operate on the pixels composing the image. Image processing functions in the spatial domain can be expressed as [59]

$$g(x, y) = T[f(x, y)] \tag{3}$$

where $f(x, y)$ is the input image, $g(x, y)$ is the processed image, and T is an operator on f defined over some neighborhood of (x, y). The most common approach is the use of "convolution masks". A convolution mask is a two-dimensional array whose coefficients are chosen to enhance or detect some property in an image. The size of the mask is usually small (eg., 3×3). To obtain the value of $g(x, y)$ for some (x, y), the mask is placed over the image $f(x, y)$ with the center of the mask over (x, y). Each pixel within the mask is multiplied by the corresponding coefficient and the results of the multiplications are summed. This weighted sum represents the value of $g(x, y)$. The coefficients of the mask and the size of the mask are chosen based on the type of processing that is desired. Most image processing packages allow the user to define convolution masks. The packages also provide some standard convolution masks. Examples of these are masks for image smoothing and masks for image sharpening and edge enhancement. A commonly used smoothing mask is one that obtains the average over a 3×3 neighborhood. This 3×3 mask has 1/9 as each of its coefficients. It is also referred to as the mean filter and is used to reduce the noise in the image. Masks used for sharpening the image typically approximate differentiation of the image by taking differences between pixels. Common masks include the Robert's cross operator and the Sobel operator. These and other edge detectors such as the Canny operator enhance the surface discontinuities in the image. Another commonly used spatial filter is the median filter which replaces each pixel by the median of the pixels over a certain neighborhood. This filter is particularly useful for eliminating salt and pepper noise.

Frequency Domain

In frequency domain techniques, the image is first transformed into the frequency domain by means of the two-dimensional discrete Fourier transform. The image is then processed in this domain and transformed back to the spatial domain. The fast Fourier transform. (FFT) is an efficient algorithm for obtaining the Fourier transform. Most image processing packages with SPMs provide the FFT and the inverse FFT. Most packages also provide an FFT spectrum editor which can be used to interactively modify the Fourier transformed image. Standard filters in the frequency domain are often provided. These include different kinds of low pass, high pass and band pass filters. The frequency domain techniques are used to enhance characteristics of the image that can easily be represented in the frequency domain. For example, noise that is associated with high frequency components can be eliminated by low pass filters.

The efficacy of enhancement using either spatial domain or frequency domain techniques is limited when it is not based on models of the imaging process. The filtering techniques could distort the actual topography in the image while producing aesthetically pleasing images. Filtering techniques that are based on models of the imaging process are being investigated by several researchers as discussed in Sect. 7.2.

7.1.2 Image Display and Visualization Techniques

An important feature of SPMs is that they are accompanied with graphics software that aids in the visualization of the data output by the microscopes [177, 174, 153, 19]. Although visualization does not fall under the category of image processing we include it here because of the similarity in the issues involved and because of the increasing interaction between image processing and visualization techniques. Besides two-dimensional gray scale maps, many microscopes provide increasingly sophisticated routines for three-dimensional visualization. The simplest case is a line plot where the scan lines output by the microscope are plotted in perspective. Hidden line removal is sometimes provided to enhance the three-dimensional appearance of the data. Contour plots are another technique for displaying the three-dimensional data. Here, contours join points at the same height. More sophisticated routines render the data as the surface of a 3D solid. Shading under simulated illumination is used to provide a "realistic" three-dimensional appearance. The user is allowed to position the light sources for the simulated illumination and also to define the viewing angle. In addition, the user may be allowed to define the color of the surface. In some cases, color information is superimposed to display other local physical quantities such as conductance that are obtained simultaneously from the microscope [177]. With the availability of more powerful graphics hardware and software, techniques such as Goraurd shading [52] are being used to render SPM data in a perceptually and aesthetically appealing manner. Most routines allow zooming to get a better view of an area of interest. Rotation is also provided to allow viewing the 3D surface from different angles.

7.2 Restoration of SPM Images

A very significant issue in Scanning Probe Microscopy is the appearance of artifacts in SPM images as a result of the imaging process. Correction of such artifacts requires a-priori models of the imaging process. Several researchers have addressed the problem of restoring images obtained from scanning tunneling microscopy and atomic force microscopy [177, 174, 175, 51, 49, 50, 40, 54, 150, 151, 99, 139]. Restoration techniques differ from the enhancement techniques discussed in Sect. 7.1.1 in requiring a model of the imaging process. The importance of restoration techniques cannot be overemphasized. When a naive user looks at an SPM image, he is inclined to believe that it represents true surface topography. Without restoration techniques imaging artifacts would be interpreted as features on the object being imaged. Hence, the research activity in image processing for SPM's has largely focused on the restoration problem.

Stoll et al. [177, 174, 175] developed a Wiener filter based approach for restoration that takes into account the significant noise sources in the imaging process and blurring due to the finite size of the probe tip. Feuchtwang et al. developed a linear response theory for the STM that takes into account the finite time constant of the instrument and the distortions due to the finite size of the tip. Other researchers [40, 150, 151, 54, 99, 139] have studied the effects of probe geometry on the image obtained in scanning probe microscopy and have addressed the issue of restoring an SPM image given the geometry of the probe used for scanning. Background plane subtraction techniques have also been developed which try to eliminate the tilt between the sample surface and the probe [19, 17, 153].

7.2.1 Restoration Using Linear Filters

Stoll et al. [177, 174, 175] use a Wiener filter based approach for image restoration. Their approach is developed chiefly for the STM operated in a topographic mode, although they claim that the approach can also be extended to atomic force microscopy and scanning tunneling spectroscopy. First, they identify the noise sources in the imaging process. The noise sources are [177]:

- the nonideal suspension system through which environmental vibrations could penetrate
- white shot noise accompanying the tunneling current (in STM)
- 1/f-like noise due to host or foreign atoms jumping on the tip or the sample
- 1/f-like noise due to the time-dependent aftereffects in the piezoceramic scanning actuators
- 1/f-like resistor and semiconductor noise in the operational amplifier and rectifier components of the feedback controller
- White Johnson noise in the operational amplifier component
- 1/f-like noise in the other electronic elements of the system.

They point out that the noise from the mechanical vibrations penetrating into the suspension system is usually negligible compared to other noise sources. Besides, the shot noise is negligible compared to the 1/f noise for tunneling currents in the nanoampere range. They argue that the low-frequency 1/f-like noise is the most significant component of noise in scanning probe microscopes and point out that the behavior of scanning probe microscopes is, hence, very different from scanning electron microscopes (SEMs) in which the high frequency shot noise due to high energy electrons is the main noise contribution. Thus, the noise elimination methods used for scanning probe microscopy need to be essentially different from those used in scanning electron microscopy.

They estimate the effects of noise by keeping the tip at a fixed position over a sample and recording the tip displacement signal as a function of time and displaying it as an image. They show that this noise image has stripes parallel to the "x" scan direction, caused by slow movements of the tip. They point out that such tip movements result in misleading artifacts in the background of STM images [175]. They account for such artifacts by fitting a $(1/f)^\beta$ law to the noise image. The value of β depends on the noise image and is obtained experimentally as outlined above. They report a value of 1.4 ± 0.2 for β in their experiments [175].

Stoll et al. obtain an expression for the point spread function (PSF) of the scanning process that takes into account the blurring due to the finite resolution of the probe. They derive the expression from the equation for the tunneling current (equation(1)). They consider the extent to which the profile produced by an STM reproduces the corrugation of the sample that is scanned. The ratio of the apparent corrugation amplitude imaged by the probe to the true corrugation amplitude of the surface is given by

$$\frac{\Delta s}{h_s} = exp\left(\frac{-\pi(r_t + s)}{\kappa_o a^2}\right) \qquad (4)$$

where r_t is the radius of the probe tip, s is the distance between the probe and the sample, a is the period of corrugation of the sample, and κ_o is a decay constant as in equation (1). Taking the Fourier transform of equation (4) they obtain the point spread function as

$$H(q) = exp\left(\frac{-q^2(r_t + s)}{4\kappa_o}\right) = exp\left(\frac{-q^2}{q_o^2}\right) \qquad (5)$$

where q_o is considered as an image processing parameter.

To restore an image produced by a scanning probe microscope, Stoll et al. employ a Wiener-filter based approach. Thus, if $G(q)$ represents the Fourier transform of the image produced by an SPM, the best least-squares estimate for the Fourier transform of the restored image is given by

$$F_e(q) = W(q)G(q) \qquad (6)$$

where the Wiener filter function is given by

$$W(q) = \frac{H^*(q)}{|H(q)|^2 + \phi(q)} \qquad (7)$$

where $\phi(q)$ is the noise to signal ratio.

Using the $1/f^\beta$ model for the noise, as discussed earlier in this section, they obtain the expression

$$\phi_\beta(q) = \frac{\alpha}{i_t^2 + (k/2L_y)^{2\beta/2}} \qquad (8)$$

for the noise to signal ratio [175]. For large tunneling currents, however, white noise dominates $1/f$ noise. Thus, to make the Wiener filter robust, they use

$\phi(q) = \phi_\beta(q)$ if $\phi_\beta(q) > \phi_o$
$\phi(q) = \phi_o$ otherwise.

where ϕ_o is the white noise estimate of the noise to signal ratio.

The important contributions of Stoll et al. are the careful consideration given to noise sources in the imaging process, and the development of an image restoration procedure. However, the approach of Stoll et al. works only with weakly corrugated samples. When the corrugation of the sample surface is large, and the sample has high steep features, the resolution function used by Stoll et al. is no longer valid. The nonlinear interaction of the probe and sample geometries becomes important in such cases.

Feuchtwang et al. [51, 49, 50] adapted and applied a linear response theory of measuring instruments to STM. Their basic assumption is that the instrumental artifacts in the imaging process are linear and translation invariant. They then try to model the effect of instrumental artifacts as a linear blurring operator. They chiefly consider artifacts due to the finite time constant of the instrument and the finite size of the tip. They describe both effects by partial instrument functions which can be combined into an overall instrument function. If the Fourier Transform of the measured output is given by $O_m(k_x, k_y; z)$ and the Fourier transform of the ideal output of the instrument is given by $O_i(k_x, k_y; z)$ and the instrument function (or the Fourier transform of the linear blurring operator) that accounts for instrumental artifacts is given by $L(k_x, k_y; z)$, then

$$O_m(k_x, k_y; z) = L(k_x, k_y; z) O_i(k_x, k_y; z) \tag{9}$$

Here, z is the tunneling gap between the tip and the surface and indicates that the outputs and the instrument function are dependent on the tunneling gap. When several independent mechanisms contribute to the blurring operator, the instrument function can be expressed as a product of several partial instrument functions. Hence,

$$L(k_x, k_y; z) = \prod_i L_i(k_x, k_y; z) \tag{10}$$

They model the partial instrument functions due to the finite time constant and finite tip size of the instrument. The partial instrument function accounting for the finite time constant τ is given by

$$L_\tau(k_x, 0; z) = \left[(\upsilon \tau i)\left(k_x - \frac{i}{\upsilon \tau} \right) \right]^{-1} \tag{11}$$

Here, υ is the speed of scanning, τ is the time constant of the instrument and i is the true input. To determine τ, they suggest scanning a sample along some crystallographic direction which has a lattice spacing R. Then, the Fourier transform of the ideal output has amplitudes which are integral multiples (space harmonics) of the fundamental wave number $G = 2\pi/R$. The relation between the measured corrugation amplitude z_m and true corrugation amplitude z_i is then given by

$$\left| \frac{z_m(n; \upsilon)}{z_i(n)} \right|^2 = [(nG\tau\upsilon)^2 + 1]^{-1}; \quad n = 1, 2, \ldots \tag{12}$$

To determine τ, they suggest scanning the sample at two different scanning speeds along the same crystallographic direction and use the ratio of the amplitudes for a given space harmonic. Thus,

$$\left|\frac{z_m(n;v_1)}{z_m(n;v_2)}\right|^2 = \frac{(nGv_2\tau)^2+1}{(nGv_1\tau)^2+1} = \left|\frac{L_\tau(n;v_1)}{L_\tau(n;v_2)}\right|^2 \tag{13}$$

from which τ and L_τ can be determined. Once L_τ is determined, the output can be corrected for the finite time constant.

To account for the finite size of the tip, the common approach is to have a model for the tip and to determine a blurring operator based on this model. This, for instance, is the approach taken by Stoll et al. Feuchtwang et al. recommend a different approach. They point out that it is very hard to model the tip accurately and that the tip may vary from run to run. Therefore, they suggest a semi-empirical calibration based approach. Their method involves (i) calculation of the Fourier expansion of the ideal output O_i of the STM for the particular STM being "calibrated"; (ii) Fourier expansion of the measured output O_m; (iii) evaluation of the Fourier expansion of the instrument function. If the Fourier expansion of the output is given by

$$O_i(x,0;z) = \sum_{G_x} A_{G_x}(z)e^{iG_x x} \tag{14}$$

and the partial instrument function corresponding to the tip size is given by $L_w(G_x; z)$, then the measured output is given by

$$O_m(x,0;z) = \sum_{G_x} A_{G_x}(z)L_w(G_x;z)e^{iG_x x} \tag{15}$$

If the Fourier coefficient $A_{G_x}(z)$ are known for the calibration surface, the coefficients $L_w(G_x; z)$ of the partial instrument function can be calculated from the measured coefficients $A_{G_x}(z)L_w(G_x; z)$. Once this is done, for any other (sample) surface, this instrument function permits the determination of the ideal corrugation from the measured, blurred one. They suggest that such calibration procedures should be performed before every run to account for variation between runs.

Feuchtwang et al. showed that similar linear models can be applied to the STM run in a spectroscopic mode. They also derive limits on the reolution of the instrument in terms of the linear response theory and random errors involved in imaging.

Feuchtwang et al. develop a good method for characterizing and calibrating an STM. However, the method requires standard surfaces for which a reliable calculation of local density of states (LDOS) is available. Besides, the model is chiefly for atomically flat samples and fails to account for geometric interactions of the probe and the sample in samples with steep and high structures. The linear response theory fails to account for nonlinear interactions of the probe and sample geometries.

7.2.2 Geometric Restoration

The linear filtering techniques discussed in Sect. 7.2.1 do not account for the interactions fo the probe and sample geometries. This interaction is nonlinear and becomes more and more significant as the sample feature sizes approach the size of the tip used for scanning. Artifacts due to geometric interactions can be very serious. Geometric restoration procedures are needed to correct for such artifacts.

Chicon et al. [40] developed a geometry based algorithm for surface reconstruction in STM. They point out that the data obtained by an STM represents some kind of convolution of the probe tip and the sample surface. They address the problem of reconstructing the actual sample surface given the apparent surface "seen" by the microscope. They make the following assumptions:

i) The probe tip can be assumed to be spherical.
ii) The probe scans the surface keeping a constant tunneling current.
iii) The tunneling current depends only on the minimum distance between the probe tip and the sample. Hence, tunneling is assumed to be a local rather than a non-local phenomenon.
iv) The probe tip maintains a constant distance "d" from the scanned surface.
v) The probe tip is at a distance "d" from only one point on the scanned surface.

They point out that different points on the probe tip may be at a distance d from the sample surface when the probe scans the surface. However, the center of the spherical probe tip is always at a distance $d_{eff} = d + R$ from the surface, where R is the radius of the spherical probe tip.

To reconstruct the original surface from the apparent surface, which is the surface traced by the center of the probe tip, each point on the apparent surface is moved a distance $d_{eff} = d + R$ in a direction normal to the apparent surface at that point. Thus, if $(x, y, f(x, y))$ is a point on the apparent surface, the corresponding point $(\tilde{x}, \tilde{y}, \tilde{z})$ on the real surface is given by:

$$\tilde{x} = x + \frac{\partial f/\partial x}{\sqrt{1 + \partial f/\partial x^2 + \partial f/\partial y^2}} * d_{eff} \qquad (16)$$

$$\tilde{y} = y + \frac{\partial f/\partial y}{\sqrt{1 + \partial f/\partial x^2 + \partial f/\partial y^2}} * d_{eff} \qquad (17)$$

$$\tilde{z} = f(x, y) - \frac{\partial f/\partial y}{\sqrt{1 + \partial f/\partial x^2 + \partial f/\partial y^2}} * d_{eff} \qquad (18)$$

They point out that the result they derive is an exact one when the assumptions they make are valid. They also note that the reconstruction procedure fails when there are discontinuities in the derivatives of the apparent surface. Such discontinuities could be due to the existence of deep cavities in the real surface.

The work of Chicon et al. is significant in that it was the first work to consider the effects of the probe tip geometry on the surface obtained by an STM. Their work is applicable to other scanning probe microscopes. However, the algorithm they develop is severely limited by the assumptions they make. The assumption of a spherical probe tip and the assumption that the tip is at a distance d from only one point on the surface, rarely hold in practice. Thus, they show results only with a simulated smooth surface for which the assumptions they make are valid. Besides, their algorithm does not take the effect of noise into account.

Reiss et al. [150] developed a geometric restoration procedure that is valid for a wider class of probe tips. If the image height function is given by $i(x, y)$, the true surface height function by $s(x, y)$ and the tip height function by $t(x, y)$, the restoration problem is to determine $s(x, y)$ given $i(x, y)$ and $t(x, y)$. They point out that if tunneling between the tip and the surface occurs at some point $S = (x', y', s(x', y'))$ on the surface, the corresponding image point $I = (x_o, y_o, i(x_o, y_o))$ is in general different from S. That is, $(x' \neq x_o, y' \neq y_o, s(x', y') \neq i(x_o, y_o))$. Thus, it is necessary to find the transformation

$$x_o \to x'$$
$$y_o \to y'$$
$$i(x_o, y_o) \to s(x', y')$$

in order to restore the image.

To do this, they use the fact that the local normals to the image at I are parallel to those of the tip and the surface at the contact point S. If the contact point on the tip is denoted $T = (\Delta x, \Delta y, t(\Delta x, \Delta y))$, then they point out that

$$n_i(x_o, y_o) = \begin{pmatrix} \frac{\partial i}{\partial x}\big|_{x=x_o} \\ \frac{\partial i}{\partial y}\big|_{y=y_o} \\ 1 \end{pmatrix} = \begin{pmatrix} \frac{\partial t}{\partial x}\big|_{x=\Delta x} \\ \frac{\partial t}{\partial y}\big|_{y=\Delta y} \\ 1 \end{pmatrix} = n_t(\Delta x, \Delta y) \quad (19)$$

where n_i and n_t denote the normals to the image and the tip surfaces respectively. S is then given by

$$S = (x_o + \Delta x, y_o + \Delta y, i(x_o, y_o) + t(\Delta x, \Delta y)) \quad (20)$$

Thus, their procedure is to (i) find the normal at each point on the image; (ii) determine the point on the tip that has the same normal direction; (iii) determine the corresponding surface point using equation (19). The shortcomings of this method are discussed below.

Keller [99] derived essentially the same method for restoration as Reiss et al. but expressed it in terms of a local nonlinear transform called the Legendre Transform. Keller derives conditions for surface recovery from the image of a surface that is scanned by a probe in a contact mode with a single point of contact. Figure 12 shows the model used by Keller.

The conditions derived by Keller are:

$$\frac{di(x')}{dx'} = \frac{dt(\Delta x)}{d\Delta x} \quad (21)$$

and

$$s(x) = i(x') + t(\Delta x(x')) \quad (22)$$

where $i(x')$ is the image height at x' (see Fig. 12), x represents the point of contact of the probe and the true surface, and is given by

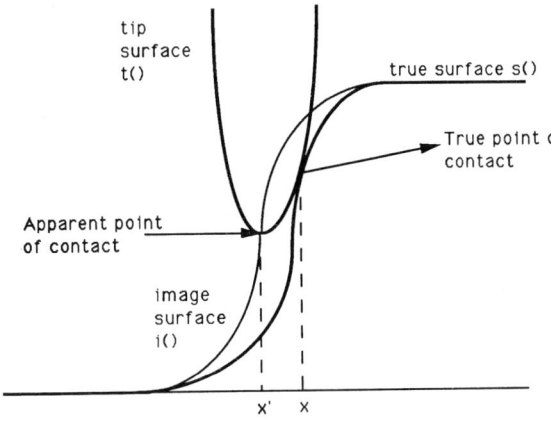

Fig. 12. Imaging model used by Keller (see text)

$$x = x' + \Delta x \tag{23}$$

$s(x)$ represents the true surface height at the point of contact and $t(\ )$ represents the probe shape function.

Keller then applies the Legendre transform $L[\ ]$ to equation (22) to obtain

$$L[s(x)] = L[i(x')] + L[t(\Delta x)] \tag{24}$$

where all Legendre transforms are evaluated at $m = \frac{di}{dx}$. The Legendre Transform of a function $f(x)$, $L[f(x)]$ is defined as the intercept with the y-axis of the line tangent to $f(x)$ at x. Thus,

$$L[f(x)] \equiv b(m) = f(x(m)) - mx(m) \tag{25}$$

where

$$m = \frac{df(x)}{dx} \tag{26}$$

The inverse Legendre Transform is given by

$$f(x) = m(x)x + b(m(x)) \tag{27}$$

Using these relations, Keller gives the following algorithm for true surface recovery:

For each image coordinate point x'

i) Obtain the slope m of the image surface at x'
ii) Determine the Δx for which the slope of the probe function $t(\Delta x)$ is equal to m.
iii) Use equation (24) to obtain the Legendre transform of the reconstructed surface corresponding to a coordinate x.

The reconstructed surface is then obtained by taking the inverse Legendre transform of the values obtained in step (iii) above.

Reiss et al. and Keller derived some useful theoretical conditions and gave an accurate algorithm for surface reconstruction in the case of imaging in a contact mode with a single point of contact. However, the class of probes for which these methods work is limited. These methods fail when the probe function $t(\ )$ has the same slope at more than one point. For example, the methods would fail with a commonly used probe shape such as a pyramidal probe with constant slope. Besides, these methods fail when there are discontinuities in the image surface, as they require computation of derivatives of the image surface at every point. These approaches do not handle cases involving multiple points of contact. As the reconstructions in these methods involve a many to one mapping, these methods often leave "holes" in the recovered surface.

Geometric restoration techniques can, in fact, be developed for tips represented by arbitrary height functions. The shortcomings of techniques that require the computation of partial derivatives can also be overcome. Gallarda and Jain [54] suggested that a model of the imaging process in SPM and geometric restoration techniques can be based on gray scale mathematical morphology. We formally developed such techniques [139]. We developed an imaging model for the interaction of probe and sample geometries in SPM imaging. Restoration techniques were then developed based on this model.

We make the following assumptions in modeling the imaging process for topographic imaging with an SPM.

- The surface that is being scanned, and the tip used for scanning, can be represented as finite single-valued function $S(x, y)$ and $P(x, y)$ with finite domains D_S and D_p respectively.

    The imaging model can, in fact, account for surfaces that do not satisfy this assumption of being single-valued. When the surface has multiple finite values corresponding to some point (x, y) in D_S, these surface values can be replaced by their supremum (i.e. maximum), as far as the imaging process is concerned. This is because only the highest value of the surface corresponding to a given point (x, y) affects the position of the tip during raster imaging. Thus, the surface can be converted into a single valued function. Similarly, the tip shape can be converted into a single valued function by replacing multiple values corresponding to some point (x, y) with their infimum.
- The tip used for scanning and the sample being scanned are perfectly rigid.
- Hysteresis effects during scanning can be ignored.
- During the scanning process, the tip is rastered across the surface of interest and the image output gives the height of a certain point on the tip.
- In contact mode imaging, each image point $I(x, y)$ corresponds to the height of the monitored point on the tip, when the tip is aligned to (x, y) and the tip just touches the surface S. A schematic of contact mode imaging is seen in Fig. 13a.
- In non-contact mode imaging, each image point $I(x, y)$ corresponds to the height of the monitored point on the tip when the tip is aligned to (x, y) and the tip is at a specified distance "d" above the actual surface. At present, the non-local interactions of the tip and the sample are not considered. A schematic of non-contact mode imaging is seen in Fig. 13a.

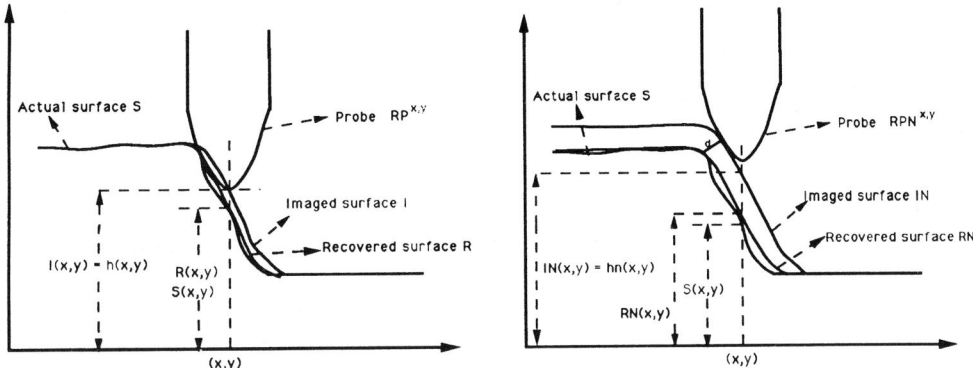

Fig. 13. a Schematic of contact mode imaging; **b** Schematic of non-contact mode imaging

The assumptions we make are quite general. Notice that we allow for arbitrary tip shapes and only assume that there is some point on the tip whose height is monitored during the scanning process. We make no assumptions regarding what the position of this point should be relative to the domain of the tip and can, therefore, allow for asymmetric tips.

Expressions for the image obtained in either contact or non-contact mode can be derived from the constraints imposed by the imaging process. These constraints follow from the assumptions stated above.

Constraint 1. In contact mode, corresponding to every image point, the probe touches the actual surface at least at one point. This constraint can be expressed as follows. $\forall (x, y) \varepsilon D_I, \exists (x_a, y_a) \varepsilon D_S$ such that

$$I(x, y) = S(x_a, y_a) - P_{x,y}(x_a, y_a) \tag{28}$$

where we use the notation

$$f_{a,b}(x, y) = f(x - a, y - b) \tag{29}$$

to denote the translation of function f by (a, b) and D_f to denote the domain of the function f.

The corresponding constraint in non-contact mode, where the probe maintains a constant distance "d" from the sample, is stated as follows. Corresponding to every image point, at least one point on the probe is exactly at a distance "d" from at least one point on the actual surface. This can be expressed as $\forall (x, y) \varepsilon D_{IN}, \exists (x_a, y_a), (x_b, y_b) \varepsilon D_S$ such that

$$IN(x,y) = S(x_b, y_b) + g^d_{x_b, y_b}(x_a, y_a) - P_{x,y}(x_a, y_a) \tag{30}$$

where the function g^d gives the height at coordinates (x, y) of a hemisphere of radius d centered at the origin and is defined as $\forall (x, y): x^2 + y^2 \leq d$

$$g^d(x,y) = \sqrt{d^2 - x^2 - y^2} \tag{31}$$

Constraint 2. Corresponding to every image point in a contact mode image, the raised probe height is always greater than or equal to the corresponding surface height. This can be expressed as $\forall (x,y), (x_1, y_1) \varepsilon D_S$

$$I(x,y) \geq S(x_1, y_1) - P_{x,y}(x_1, y_1) \tag{32}$$

In non-contact mode, the corresponding constraint is as follows. Corresponding to every point in a non-contact mode image, the raised probe height is always at a distance greater than or equal to d from actual surface. This can be expressed as $\forall (x,y), (x_1, y_1), (x_2, y_2) \varepsilon D_S$

$$IN(x,y) \geq S(x_2, y_2) + g^d(x_2 - x_1, y_2 - y_1) - P_{x,y}(x_1, y_1) \tag{33}$$

Using the two constraints, a model for the imaging process in contact mode is given in terms of gray scale morphological dilation as

$$I(x,y) = [S \oplus P^\wedge](x,y) \tag{34}$$

The morphological operation of gray scale Minkowski addition or gray scale dilation of two functions f and g is defined as [58]

$$f \oplus g = EXTSUP_{(x,y) \varepsilon D_f}(f(x,y) + g_{x,y}) \tag{35}$$

where the symbol EXTSUP is used to denote the *extended supremum* and is defined as [58]

$$[EXTSUP(f_k)](x,y) = \begin{cases} \sup[f_k(x,y)], & \text{if there exists at least one } k \text{ such that } f_k \\ & \text{is defined at } (x,y), \text{ and where the} \\ & \text{supremum is over all such } k \\ \text{undefined}, & \text{if } f_k(t) \text{ is undefined for all } k \end{cases}$$

The notation $f^\wedge$ is used to denote the reflection of function f about the origin. That is,

$$f^\wedge(x,y) = -f(-x,-y) \tag{36}$$

The imaging model for non-contact mode is given as

$$IN(x,y) = [S \oplus g \oplus P^\wedge](x,y) \tag{37}$$

Therefore, in non-contact mode, the imaging process can be modeled as a two step process. In the first step, the original surface is dilated with a positive hemisphere of radius d centered at the origin. In the second step, the result of the first step is dilated with the reflection of the tip shape about the origin. The result of the first step in this two-step process can be considered as the surface resulting from a non-contact mode scan at a distance "d" by an ideal (single-point) tip. This is indicated in Fig. 13b.

Numerous experiments were performed to test the efficacy of the model of the imaging process and the methods for surface and tip shape recovery. Here, we

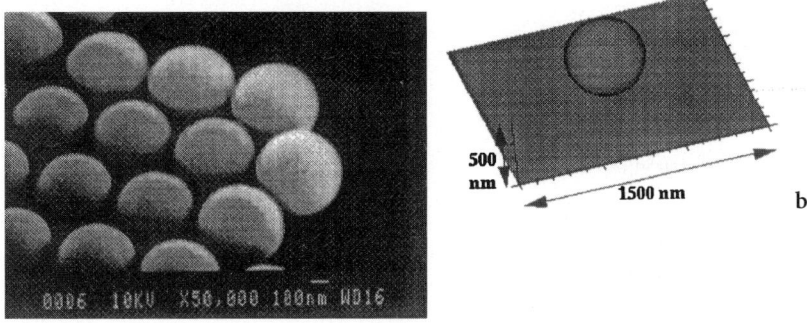

Fig. 14. a SEM image of polystyrene spheres; **b** Synthetic model of an individual sphere

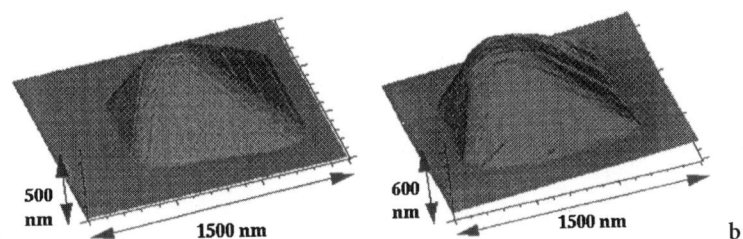

Fig.15. a Predicted SPM image of a sphere with a pyramidal tip; **b** True SPM image of a sphere with a pyramidal tip

present sample results with images obtained using a commercial pyramidal tip. The real scans were performed using a Digital Instruments' Nanoscope III Atomic Force Microscope.

Figure 14a shows a scanning electron microscope image of polystyrene spheres prepared by latex polymerization. These are commercially available spheres with a diameter of 482 nm. Figure 14b shows a synthetic model of an individual sphere. Figure 15a shows the SPM image that would result when the sphere is imaged by a commercial pyramidal tip. A SEM image of a commercial tip is seen in Fig. 19b. This is the image predicted using the model of the imaging process. Figure 15b shows an actual atomic force microscope (AFM) image of an individual polystyrene sphere using a pyramidal tip. Comparison of Fig. 15a,b indicates the efficacy of the imaging model. The figure also shows the considerable distortion that can occur in an SPM image due to the finite geometry of the scan tip.

We have developed image restoration techniques to correct SPM images for distortion due to tip geometry. Figure 15 shows the distortion that occurs in an SPM image due to the interaction of the geometries of the scan tip and the sample and summarizes our approach to restoration. We use the constraints imposed by the imaging process (discussed above) to derive a better estimate of the true surface. Given the function representing the image I of the sample being scanned and the shape P of the probe used for scanning, a better estimate R of the true surface of the sample that was scanned is given by

$$R(x, y) = [P \ominus I](x, y) \tag{38}$$

where the symbol $\ominus$ represents Minkowski subtraction [58] defined as [58]

$$g \ominus f = INF_{(x,y) \varepsilon D_f} (f(x,y) + g_{x,y}) \tag{39}$$

where the operation INF is an extension of the infimum operation (inf) and is defined as [58]

$$[INF(f_k)](x, y) = \begin{cases} inf[f_k(x,y)], & \text{if } f_k(t) \text{ is defined for all } k \\ undefined, & \text{otherwise} \end{cases}$$

In non-contact mode imaging, a better estimate RN to the true surface, given the image IN and the minimum distance d between the probe and sample, is

$$RN(x, y) = [q^d \ominus [P \ominus IN]](x, y) \tag{40}$$

The greatest problem in SPM imaging is that given an SPM image, the user does not know which parts of the image represent the true surface topography and which parts do not. We have derived a necessary condition [137] for determining where the recovered surface R in equation (38) represents the true surface topography S. The condition is:

$\forall (x, y) \, \varepsilon \, D_R$
$R(x, y) = S(x, y)$
if $\exists (x_1, y_1) \, \varepsilon \, D_I$ such that
$R(x, y) = I(x_1, y_1) + P_{x1,y1}(x, y)$
and $\forall (x_2, y_2) \, \varepsilon \, D_R$ and $\neq (x, y)$
$R(x_2, y_2) \neq I(x_1, y_1) + P_{x1,y1}(x_2, y_2)$

Here, the notation D_f is used to denote the domain of function f. Hence, D_I denotes the domain of the image while D_R denotes the domain of the recovered surface. However, this condition is not a sufficient condition. Hence, the points on the recovered surface that are marked as identical to the original surface are definitely so but some points on the recovered surface may not be marked even when they are identical to the original surface. A similar condition was derived for the non-contact mode. Based on this condition, we have developed software by which the SPM user can determine which parts of an SPM image represent reliable data. Figure 16 (above) shows the image of an integrated circuit scanned with a pyramidal probe and the lower part of Fig. 16 shows the regions of the image which do not represent the true surface topography.

7.3 Correction for Sample Tilt

SPM samples are rarely positioned exactly normal to the probe tip, even for atomically flat surfaces. This results in a background slope or tilt of the surface

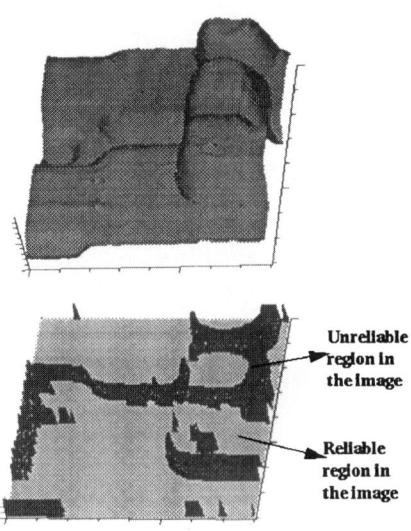

Fig. 16 SPM image of integrated circuit (*top*) and map indicating reliable regions in the image (*bottom*)

which must be measured and subtracted to maintain consistent contrast in the resulting image. One of the commonly used image processing operations for scanning probe microscopy is background plane subtraction. Bejar et al. [19] fit a plane to the entire image by least-square methods and subtract this plane from the image. Becker [17] developed a plane fit procedure to approximate the sample tilt. His algorithm works on one scan line at a time without requiring the complete image so that data can be displayed as it is acquired in gray scale. Robinson et al. [153] calculate a linear regression fit for each scan line in both the X and Y directions. The results for all lines along each axis are averaged, giving the average slope and dc offset of the surface along the X and Y axes. Linear ramps calculated from the X and Y average slopes and intercepts are subtracted from each axis of the data. Most commercial scanning probe microscopes now provide a plane subtraction routine.

Surprisingly, it has not been previously noted in the STM community that background plane subtraction is not a rigid body transformation. Background plane subtraction, in fact, distorts sample features. The correct method for correction for sample tilt is background plane rotation. This was pointed out in [142]. Besides, if care is not taken in the estimation of the background plane, the image after either background plane rotation or subtraction would be severely distorted. Hence, it is important to scan planar calibration areas on the sample to estimate the background plane orientation. In the background plane subtraction technique, a plane is fit to the SPM image using the least mean squares technique and this plane is subtracted from the image [17]. Thus, if (x, y, z) are the original image coordinates, the transformed coordinates (x', y', z') are given by

$$x' = x \tag{41}$$

$$y' = y \tag{42}$$

$$z' = z - ax - by - c \tag{43}$$

where the background plane is given by

$$z = ax + by + c \tag{44}$$

where x and y represent the coordinates of a pixel in the image and z represents the recorded height of the pixel in the SPM image. If the sample imaged is just a plane at a certain inclination, this background subtraction method would result in the plane being flat or parallel to the x-y plane in the image. However, problems arise when the sample is not just a single plane. First, the inclination of the sample has to be estimated from a portion of the image that is known to be flat. Second, and more serious, the correction by subtraction distorts features in the image. This is because background plane subtraction is not a rigid body transformation – it does not preserve the original sizes and angles between features. The distortions become negligible only when the background plane inclination is small. Hence, background plane subtraction is an inappropriate technique when the background plane inclination is large.

The correct method of compensating for sample inclination is background plane rotation. If the inclination of the sample is given by that of the plane in equation (44), the image has to be rotated so that the background plane of the sample is given by

$$z = k \tag{45}$$

where k is a constant. This is achieved by performing the following transformation:

$$\begin{bmatrix} x' \\ y' \\ z' \end{bmatrix} = \begin{bmatrix} R_{11} & R_{12} & R_{13} \\ R_{21} & R_{22} & R_{23} \\ R_{31} & R_{32} & R_{33} \end{bmatrix} \begin{bmatrix} x \\ y \\ z \end{bmatrix} \tag{46}$$

where

$$R_{11} = \frac{c}{\sqrt{a^2 + c^2}}$$

$$R_{12} = 0$$

$$R_{13} = \frac{-as_x}{s_z\sqrt{a^2 + c^2}}$$

$$R_{21} = \frac{-abs_y}{s_z\sqrt{a^2 + c^2}\sqrt{a^2 + b^2 + c^2}}$$

$$R_{22} = \frac{\sqrt{a^2 + c^2}}{\sqrt{a^2 + b^2 + c^2}}$$

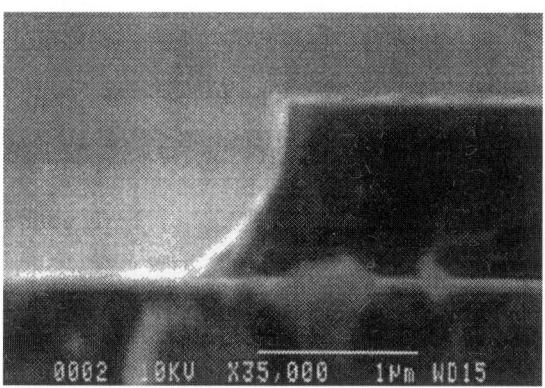

Fig. 17. SEM image of an RIE-etched polysilicon sample

$$R_{23} = \frac{-bcs_y}{s_z\sqrt{a^2+c^2}\sqrt{a^2+b^2+c^2}}$$

$$R_{31} = \frac{as_z}{s_x\sqrt{a^2+b^2+c^2}}$$

$$R_{32} = \frac{bs_z}{s_y\sqrt{a^2+b^2+c^2}}$$

$$R_{33} = \frac{c}{\sqrt{a^2+b^2+c^2}}$$

(x, y, z) represent the coordinates of a point in the original image and (x', y', z') represent the coordinates of the corresponding point in the rotated image. s_x, s_y and s_z represent the scaling factors along the x, y and z axes respectively. This method preserves the angles between sample features unlike the background plane subtraction method. However, the x-y spacings in the transformed image will not, in general, be the same as those in the original image. The spacings become irregular and the ranges of x, y and z in the two images will be different. Several z values may correspond to one (x, y) pair in the transformed image and the transformed image needs to be represented by (x, y, z) triplets unlike the original image which is usually represented as a raster depth map. The background plane subtraction technique preserves the depth map representation at the expense of distortion in image features. The background rotation technique loses the depth map representation but *preserves all the feature information that was present in the original image while correcting for sample inclination.* Hence, SPM images can be displayed and analyzed in the new representation although they are obtained from the microscope as raster depth maps.

Figure 17 shows the SEM image of the sidewall of an RIE-etched polysilicon sample. Figure 18 (above) shows the SPM image of the poly line obtained from a pyramidal scan tip. Comparison with the SEM image shows that the SPM image

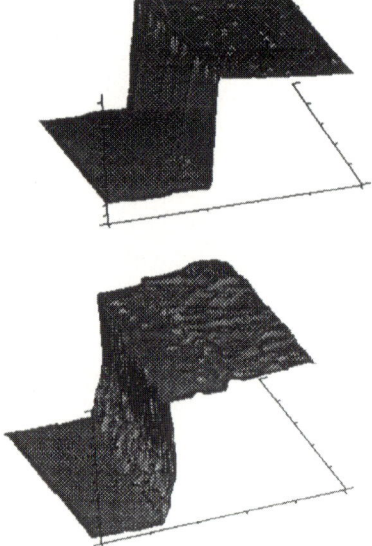

Fig. 18. SPM image of a polysilicon line edge using a pyramidal probe (*top*) and SPM image of the inclined sample after inclination compensation (*bottom*)

represents the shape of the pyramidal probe used for scanning rather than the concave sidewall. One way to improve the capture of the sidewall information is to appropriately tilt the sample. The lower part of Fig. 18 shows the SPM image obtained with a pyramidal tip when the sample is inclined at 24° to the horizontal. This image has been compensated for sample inclination by background plane rotation. The concave sidewall information is captured in this figure. As discussed above, we have established reliable procedures for estimating the inclination angle from the image of a calibration area. Once the angle is determined from such a calibration area, the SPM images can be corrected automatically for inclination. Thus, we have demonstrated that the SPM can profile sidewalls accurately. Even some undercut structures can be accurately imaged with low-aspect ratio tips using low-angle scans. The images shown here have a typical vertical resolution of 1 nm and a lateral resolution of 10 nm.

7.4 Probe Shape Recovery

All geometric restoration procedures discussed in Sect. 7.2.2 require knowledge of the shape of the probe used for scanning. As the shape of the probe plays a vital role in determining the quality of the output image and th probe shape could change over time, an important calibration step in SPM's is to determine the three-dimensional shape of the probe. Some researchers have addressed the issue of recovering the shape of the probe used in imaging from an image of a known surface. Since the image obtained from an SPM is distorted due to the probe shape, it should be possible to estimate the probe shape from the distortions of a known surface. Grigg et al. [64, 65, 62] suggested that images of known structures can be used for in-situ characterization of probe shape. They show results of probe shape recovery in STM [64]. They use the sidewall profiles of images of square pillars to estimate the shape of the probe. They give no computational algorithm. They manually segment out the sidewall profiles and manually combine them. A similar technique was used by Reiss et al. [151] to obtain a cross section of the tip from a single line scan of a cleavage step by an STM. They use this method to obtain a two-dimensional view of the probe. They show that the shape thus obtained is in qualitative agreement with the SEM image of the probe. They do not give a quantitative measure of the accuracy of recovery. We have developed an algorithm for recovering probe shape given the shape of the surface that is being imaged.

Probe shape recovery can be based on the constraints imposed by the imaging process which were discussed in Sect. 7.2.2. Given the image I obtained from an SPM and the true surface S that was scanned, an estimate of the probe shape is given by

$$EP(x, y) = [I^\wedge \oplus S](x, y) \tag{47}$$

where the symbol $\oplus$ is used to indicate gray scale morphological dilation. Equation (47) suggests that an estimate of the true probe shape can be obtained from an image obtained using the probe if the true surface is known. The probe shape estimate is given by the dilation of the reflection of the image function about the origin with the shape of the true surface. The equation states that the probe shape is recovered by scanning the true surface using the image as a probe. One great advantage of this equation is that it does not require that we explicitly identify the distorted regions in the image. The dilation based method automatically gets the estimate of the probe shape given the image and the model of the true surface. Clearly, the greatest demand made by this algorithm is that the true surface should be known. Besides, the true surface shape and the image should be aligned to each other for the method to work. Even if the true shape of a calibration pattern is known, alignment poses a difficulty. A solution would be to use a matching algorithm to match the model shape with the image in order to align them. Future research will have to address this issue.

Figure 19a shows the SEM image of a microfabricated silicon dioxide cylinder of 4 micron diameter and height 1.3 microns. Figure 19b shows the scanning electron microscope (SEM) image of a commercial pyramidal probe used in an AFM. The image was taken before the probe was mounted on an atomic force microscope. Figure 20a shows the real AFM image resulting from a scan of the cylinder in Fig. 19a with the probe in Fig. 19b. Figure 20b shows the probe shape recovered from the AFM image shown in Fig. 20a using a model of the cylinder shown in Fig. 19a. Comparison of the recovered probe shape with the actual shape in Fig. 19b shows the power of the probe shape recovery algorithm. The algorithm yields the three-dimensional shape of the probe from a single scan of the cylindrical surface. The orientation of the probe during the scan is also recovered. Thus, the algorithm can be used to image the shape and orientation of the probe *in situ* without having to dismount the probe from the microscope.

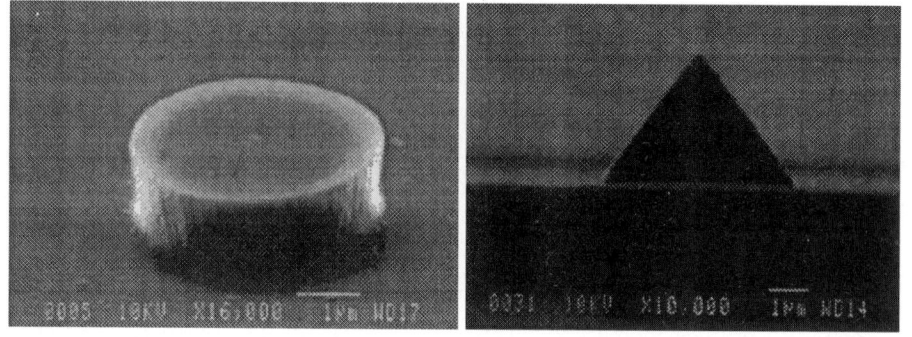

Fig. 19. a SEM image of microfabricated cylinder; **b** SEM image of commercial pyramidal probe

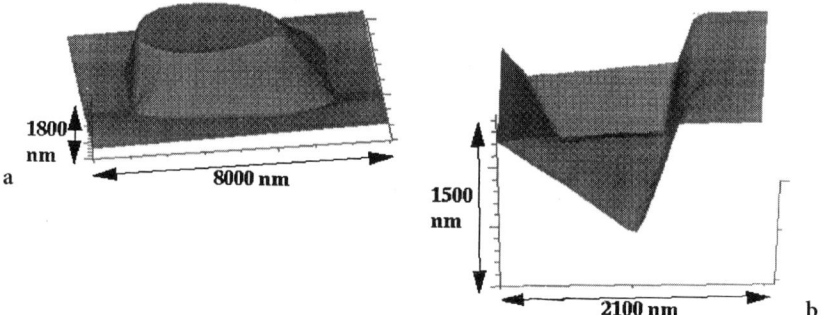

Fig. 20. a AFM image of microfabricated cylinder; **b** Probe shape recovered from the image of the cylinder

7.5 Image Processing Based Metrology

One of the greatest advantages of SPMs is that quantitative measurements can be made in any interesting area of the image. Image processing packages in SPMs are being designed for this purpose. Most packages allow the user to interactively define a line or area in the image and make some simple measurements from the image. The measurements that are commonly provided are:

- Three dimensional distance from one point in the image to another.
- Angle between any three points.
- Peak to valley difference along a line or in an area.
- Perimeter of a marked area
- Average and r.m.s. roughness along a line or in an area.

The roughness measurements are made in terms of the mean deviation in height (average roughness) or the root mean square variance in height (r.m.s. roughness) over the specified line or area. However, very little work has been done to obtain such measurements automatically. Domain specific automatic measurement techniques are a rich area for future research. Another important issue to consider is the variation in measurements with resolution. Measurements such as roughness can vary considerably with the scale of resolution.

7.6 Simulation and Animation of SPM Imaging

Computational models of the imaging process can significantly extend the design and use of scanning probe microscopes (SPMs). An imaging model allows the simulation of the imaging process given the imaging conditions. In the case of scanning probe microscopy, it would predict the image that would be produced given the appropriate imaging conditions i.e., sample shape, probe shape etc. Such a simulation tool would allow SPM users and designers to visualize the artifacts that would be produced in SPM images under certain imaging conditions. Simulation can play a crucial role in the design of SPMs. As we discussed in Sect. 7.2 several researchers have realized that tip-sample interactions can lead to serious artifacts in SPM imaging. Tip fabrication technology is also rapidly progressing toward the stage where a tip of desired geometry can be fabricated [62, 97, 103]. Simulation tools become important in this context. On the one hand, users can assess the utility of an SPM for a particular application by first studying the kind of images that would be produced when sample surfaces are imaged with commercially available scan tips. On the other hand, designers can study the effects of different tip shapes, possibly yet to be fabricated, on samples of interest. Designers can also vary other imaging parameters in the simulation environment and study their effects on SPM images. Some of these parameters may not even be controllable in existing instruments. For instance, we have developed a simulation environment that allows variation of sample and tip shapes as well as the sample and tip inclination angles. Sample and tip inclination angles cannot be controlled in currently available SPM's. The simulation environment allows the designer to study the significance of varying such parameters without having to modify the instrument to provide control over the parameters. Suitable modifications to the instrument design can be made on the basis of the results of simulation experiments. Thus, the simulation environment is a cost-effective means of experimenting with the features of an SPM and improving its design. Besides, users who do not own an SPM can experiment in such an environment to determine whether an SPM would meet the imaging needs of their applications.

Computationally efficient imaging models allow the animation of the SPM imaging process. In an animation environment, the user can actually see the tip scanning a surface and the image being produced. The user can see how and where distortions are occurring due to tip-sample interactions. The microscope designer can more easily identify which microscope scan parameters need to be adjusted to improve the imaging of a particular surface. Such animation environments could also provide for alternate scanning strategies besides the raster scan that is

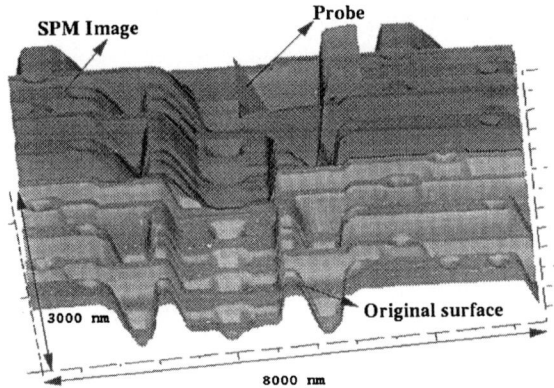

Fig. 21. Still from an animation showing an inclined pyramidal probe scanning an IC wafer

currently the only mode of scanning. They can pave the way to *programmed probe microscopy* where the user programs the appropriate scan mode based on his application needs and animation experiments. We have developed an animation environment based on our model of the imaging process. Figure 21 shows a still frame from the animation of a scan of an integrated circuit with a synthetic pyramidal probe. The probe is inclined at 12 degrees to the horizontal as in a real scan with an AFM. The true sample surface, the inclined pyramidal probe and the partially generated SPM image are seen in this figure.

8 Future Research

Image processing techniques can play a vital role in making scanning probe microscopes more powerful tools. Further work can be done in the area of enhancement and restoration of SPM images. Image processing techniques can be an important part of standard calibration procedures for vSPM. Surface characterization methods akin to those used with range imagery can be developed for SPM. Image analysis and understanding techniques could be developed for a wide variety of application domains. Image processing techniques can combine information from SPM images obtained in different modes such as topographic and spectroscopic modes. Auxiliary techniques that do not directly deal with SPM images could also be very important to SPM. Simulation and modeling techniques can play a significant role in the effective development and use of SPM. Scanning probe microscopes may soon evolve into programmed probe microscopes where they are not limited to just the raster mode of scanning.

Image Enhancement and Restoration. In this chapter, we have reviewed the work done to date in the area of enhancement and restoration of SPM images. Though some work has been done in this area, there is considerable scope for further research. Restoration methods are very important as they can be used as standard tools irrespective of the application for which the microscope is used. Some of the restoration methods, such as those that take into account purely geometric effects, can be applied to a wide class of scanning probe microscopes. Other restoration methods take into account the physical effects involved and the characteristics of a particular type of scanning probe microscope. Most of the restoration methods that account for distortion due to probe geometry do not take into account the noise sources involved in the imaging process. Besides, most models assume that non-local effects in the imaging process are negligible. Accurate models of the physical processes (such as tunneling, van der Waal interaction etc.) involved in imaging need to be developed. A more precise description of STM imaging in the so-called topographic mode is that the tip follows contours of constant electron density at a particular energy [83]. This energy depends on the bias voltage of the tip. Hence, detailed models have to be developed for the tip-sample interaction for different materials in order to accurately obtain information such as surface topography from an STM image. Such models need to be combined with those for geometric effects. Although some computational models have been developed for the physical processes involved in STM, none have been developed for SFM.

- **Calibration**

  A calibration procedure in which image processing techniques could play an important role is one that determines the distance between the probe tip and the surface in a non-contact mode of imaging. The SPM user varies a parameter such as the reference current or voltage value of the feedback controller in order to vary the constant distance between the probe tip and the sample. However, the actual distance between the probe tip and the surface is not known. Image processing techniques could be of help here. Imaging models have already been developed that predict the distortion in the geometry of a surface when imaged by a probe at a particular distance from the surface. By imaging a calibration surface with a known shape by means of a probe with known shape, and measuring the distortion in the resulting image, such models can be used to recover the distance between the probe tip and the surface. By carrying out this procedure with different reference current or voltage values and with calibration surfaces of different materials, look-up tables could be developed that give probe to sample distances corresponding to different reference signal values for diferent materials. Extensive experiments and accurate imaging models are needed to develop such calibration procedures. Once developed, such calibration procedures would be extremely useful in a wide variety of application domains involving SPM.

- **Surface Characterization Methods**

  SPM images are similar to range images in that they are dense depth maps. The wealth of surface characterization methods developed for range images [4, 22, 21, 20, 33, 48, 89, 93, 126, 167, 168, 184, 185] can, therefore, be extended to SPM images. However, the application of surface characterization methods to SPM images is a virtually unexplored area. Methods can be developed for surface

roughness measurements, fitting surface patches to image data, metrology of surface features, and detection of surface defects.
- **Image Analysis and Understanding Techniques**
  SPM has opened a whole new world in microscopy by providing depth maps at very high resolution. New applications are being identified in fields such as surface science, semiconductor manufacturing, biology and chemistry. Scanning probe microscopes are fast becoming industrial instruments. Automated analysis of SPM images in place of human analysis is, therefore, very important. As with any type of images, there is vast potential for development of a variety of image analysis and understanding techniques in SPM that are geared to different applications. Film thickness monitoring on semiconductor devices, identification of cracks, crevices and other surface defects, and identification and measurement of topographical structures are but a few examples.
- **Integration of Information from Different Modes**
  One of the powerful features of scanning probe microscopes is that they can operate in different modes. The scanning tunneling microscope, for instance, can be operated in both topographic and spectroscopic modes. It is possible to get closely registered scans of the same area in different modes. Most image processing work concentrates on SPM images of topography. But image processing techniques could also be applied to images obtained in other modes such as the spectroscopic mode. Processing images obtained in different modes and combining information obtained from such processing could lead to powerful techniques for characterization of materials and for defect identification. For instance, it is possible to obtain highly detailed, site-specific information on electronic states.
- **Study of Frequency Domain Artifacts**
  Most analysis of the geometric probe-sample interactions has been carried out in the spatial domain – the models, artifacts, restoration techniques and reliability indicators were developed in the spatial domain. An interesting research area is to perform the corresponding analysis in the frequency domain. This is particularly useful in Materials Science applications where the dominant frequencies are used to determine parameters such as crystal spacings, molecular spacings etc. Thus, models which predict how frequency information is distorted and techniques that can indicate which frequencies are reliable are invaluable in such applications.
- **Simulation Environments**
  With the development of good models of the imaging process, simulation environments could be developed, for instance to study the image that would be produced by a particular probe shape when used to image a particular surface. Such simulation environments would be useful both to the microscope and probe designers and to microscope users. Environments can be developed to maintain alternate physical models of surfaces of different materials and to allow the selection of the most likely model of an imaged surface from the candidate models. Simulation environments could also be developed with specific application areas in mind. For example, an environment for

nanolithography can allow simulation of different test patterns and display the results of imaging these test patterns. Such an environment can show images of test patterns or results of applying current pulses in different areas of these test patterns.
- **Image Databases**
  SPM's can produce hundreds of digital images per day. As in many other fields of imaging, SPM users are faced with the problem of storing and organizing thousands of images and queryign and retrieving images of interest. Image databases which help in these tasks and which allow querying based on the contents of the image will play a verry important role in SPM's.
- **Auxiliary Image Processing**
  Besides image processing techniques that directly deal with SPM images, auxiliary techniques that deal with other images such as optical or SEM images could be very useful in SPM. An example is *in situ* characterization of probe shape from images obtained by another microscope such as an optical microscope or field ion microscope. Image processing techniques that routinely process images from such microscopes and recover probe shape would be extremely useful.
- **Alternate Scanning Strategies**
  Currently, SPM's use only the raster mode of scanning. This type of scanning limits them to imaging only surfaces that can be expressed as single valued height functions in the scan coordinate system. Our work with orientations has shown that imaging can, in fact, be extended to more general surfaces by taking advantage of the probe and sample orientations. Thus, an interesting question that arises is how the scanning process can be varied to improve imaging. Scanning for instance, can be performed with the probe and sample at different orientations at different instances during scanning. Interesting questions arise regarding the optimal scan strategy for scanning a particular class of sample shapes. At this point, it almost seems certain that scanning probe microscopy will have to change to programmed probe microscopy where the appropriate scan strategy will be programmed based on the kind of sample being scanned.

9 Conclusion

In this chapter, we have reviewed the field of scanning probe microscopy with emphasis on issues related to image processing. Scanning probe microscopes are becoming increasingly popular in a number of application areas. They have caused a revolution in microscopy and promise to have an impact on a number of key areas in technology. The work done to date in image processing has shown that image processing techniques are an invaluable companion to scanning probe microscopy. Future work should see sensor technology and image processing working hand in hand to make scanning probe microscopes better metrological tools. Image analysis and understanding techniques will be used for automatic interpretation of SPM images in a number of application areas. Image databases that help in querying and retrieval of SPM images of interst will soon become coomonplace.

References

[1] Abraham, F.F., Batra, I.P., and Ciraci, S., "Effect of tip profile on atomic-force-microscope images: a model study," *Physical Review Letters*, Vol. 60, No. 13, March 1988, pp. 1314–1317.

[2] Abraham, F.F., and Batra, I.P., "Theoretical Interpretation of atomic-force-microscope images of graphite," *Surface Science*, 209 (1989) L125–L132.

[3] Abrahams, D.W., Williams, C.C., and Wickramasinghe, H.K., "Differential scanning tunnelling microscopy," *Journal of Microscopy*, Vol. 152, Pt 3, December 1988, pp. 599–603.

[4] Agin, G.J., and Binford, T.O., "Computer description of curved objects," *Proceedings of 3rd International Joint Conference on Artificial Intelligence*, Stanford, CA, pp. 629–640, August 1973.

[5] Aguilar, M., Garcia, A., Pascual, P.J., Presa, H., and Santisteban, A., "Computer system for scanning tunneling microscope automation," *Surface Science*, 181 (1987) 191–199.

[6] Akama, Y. and Murakami, H., "New scanning tunneling microscopy tip for measuring surface topography," *Journal of Vacuum Science and Technology*, A 8 (1), Jan/Feb 1990, pp. 429–433.

[7] Allison, D.P., et al. "Scanning tunneling microscopy and spectroscopy of plasmid DNA," *Scanning Microscopy*, Vol. 4, No. 3, 1990, pp. 517–522.

[8] Altschuler, T.L., "Atomic scale materials characterization," *Advanced Materials and Processes*, 9/92.

[9] Anders, M., Muck, M., and Heiden, C., "SEM/STM Combination for STM tip guidance," *Ultramicroscopy*, 25 (1988) 123–128.

[10] Bapst, U.H., "Automated scanning tunneling microscope," *Surface Science*, 181 (1987) 157–164.

[11] Bard, A.J. and Chang, H., "Formation of monolayer pits of controlled nanometer size on highly oriented pyrolytic graphite by gasification reactions as studied by scanning tunneling microscopy," *Journal of American Chemical Society*, Vol. 12, No. 11, 1990.

[12] Barrett, R.C. and Quate, C.F., "High-speed, large-scale imaging with atomic force microscope," *Journal of Vacuum Science and Technology*, B 1990.

[13] Barrett, R.C. and Quate, C.F., "Optical Scan-Correction System Applied to Atomic Force Microscopy," *Review of Scientific Instruments*, Vol. 62, 1991, pp. 1393–1399.

[14] Bauer, E., Mundschau, M., and Swiech, W., "Low energy electron microscopy of nanometer scale phenomena," *J. Vac. Sci. Technol.*, B 9 (2), Mar/Apr 1991.

[15] Baumeister, W., "Tip microscopy – top microscopy? An Introduction," *Ultramicroscopy*, 25 (1988) 103–106.

[16] Becker, R.S., Golovchenko, J.A., Hamann, D.S., and Swartzentruber, B.S., *Physical Review Letters*, Vol. 55, p. 2032, 1985.

[17] Becker, J., "Scanning tunneling microscope computer automation," *Surface Science*, 181 (1987), pp. 200–209.

[18] Behm, R.J., Garcia, N., and Rohrer, H., *Scanning tunneling microscopy and related methods*, Kluwer Academic Publishers, 1990.

[19] Bejar, M.A., Gomez-Rodriguez, J.M., Gomez-Herrero, J., Baro, A., and Entel, S.A., "New developments in fast image processing and data acquisition for STM," *Journal of Microscopy*, Vol. 152, Pt 3, December 1988, pp. 619–626.

[20] Besl, P.J., and Jain, R.C., "Three dimensional object recognition," *ACM Computing Surveys*, vol. 17, no. 1, pp. 75–145, March 1985.
[21] Besl, P.J. and Jain, R.C., "Invariant surface characteristics for three dimensional object recognition in range images" *Computer Vision, Graphics, Image Processing*, Vol. 33, no. 1, pp. 33–80, Jan. 1986.
[22] Besl, P.J. and Jain, R.C., "Segmentation through variable-order surface fitting," *IEEE Transactions on Pattern Analysis and Machine Intelligence*, Vol. 10, No. 2, March 1988.
[23] Betzig, E., Isaacson, M., Barshatzky, H., Lewis, A., and Lin, K., "Super-resolution imaging with near-field scanning optical microscopy (NSOM)," *Ultramicroscopy*, 25 (1988) 155–164.
[24] Binh, V.T., "In situ fabrication and regeneration of microtips for scanning tunneliing microscopy," *Journal of Mcroscopy*, Vol. 152, Pt 2, November 1988, pp. 335–361.
[25] Binnig, G., Rohrer, H., Gerber, Ch., and Weibel, E., *Physical Review Letters*, Vol 49, 57.
[26] Binnig, G., Rohrer, H., Gerber, Ch., and Stoll, E.P., *Surface Science*, Vol. 144, p. 321, 1984.
[27] Binnig, G., Quate, C.F., Gerber, C, *Physical Review Letters*, Vol. 56, 930 (1986).
[28] Binnig, G., Gerber, Ch., Stoll, E., Albrecht, T.R., Quate, C.F., "Atomic resolution with atomic force microscope," *Surface Science*, 189/190 (1987) pp. 1–6.
[29] Binnig, G., Rohrer, H., Scanning tunneling microscopy," *IBM Journal of Research and Development*, Vol. 30, No. 4, July 1986.
[30] Binnig, G. and Rohrer, H., "The scanning tunneling microscope," *Scientific American*, August 1985.
[31] Binnig, G. and Smith, D.P.E., "Single-tube three dimensional scanner for scanning tunneling microscopy," *Review of Scientific Instruments*, August 1986.
[32] Blaustein, P., "Full-field submicron visual wafer inspection," *Microelectronics Manufacturing Technology*, October 1991, pp. 41–45.
[33] Brady, M., Ponce, J., Yuille, A., and Asada, H., "Describing surfaces," *Computer Vision, Graphics and Image Processing*, Vol. 32, pp. 1–28, 1985.
[34] Bryant, P.J., Miller, R.G., Deeken, R., Yang, R., and Zheng, Y.C., "Scanning tunneling and atomic force microscopy performed with the same probe in one unit," *Journal of Microscopy*, Vol. 152, Pt 3, December 1988, pp. 871–875.
[35] Bustamante, C. and Dunlap, D., "Images of single stranded nucleic acids by scanning tunneling microscopy," *Nature*, Vol. 342, No. 6246, pp. 204–206, 9 Nov. 1989.
[36] Butt, H-J., et al. "Imaging cells with the atomic force microscope," *Journal of Structural Biology*, 105, 54–61, 1990.
[37] Cassidy R., "Ingenious STM puts atoms right where you want them," *R&D Magazine*, April 1993, pp. 71.
[38] Chesters, S., Wang, H-C., and Kasper, G., "Atomic force microscopy of gas-surface corrosion in stainless steel," *Solid State Technology*, June 1991, S9–S12.
[39] Chesters, S., Wang, H.C., and Kasper, G., "A fractal based method for describing surface texture," *Solid State Technology*, January 1991, pp. 73–77.
[40] Chicon, R., Ortuno, M., and Abellan, J., "An algorithm for surface reconstruction in scanning tunneling microscopy," *Surface Science*, 181 (1987) pp. 107–111.
[41] Demuth, J.E., Koehler, U., and Hamers, R.J., "The STM learning curve and where it may take us," *Journal of Microscopy*, Vol. 152, Pt 2, November 1988, pp. 299–316.
[42] Denley, D.R., "Scanning tunneling microscopy of rough surfaces," *Journal of Vacuum Science and Technology*, A 8 (1), Jan/Feb 1990, pp. 603–607.
[43] Denley, D.R., "Practical applications of scanning tunneling microscopy," *Ultramicroscopy*, 33 (1990) pp. 83–92.
[44] Dietzm P., and Herrmann, K.-H., "A scanning tunneling microscope," *Ultramicroscopy*, 25 (1988) 107–110.

[45] Ducker, W.A., Senden, T.J., and Pashley, R.M., "Direct measurement of colloidal forces using an atomic force microscope," *Nature*, Vol. 353, 19 Septembet 1991, pp. 239-240.
[46] Edstrom, R.D., Elings, V.B., "Direct Visualization of phosphorylase-phosphorylase kinase complexes by scanning tunneling and atomic force microscopy," *Biochemistry*, March 5, 1990.
[47] Elrod, S.A., de Lozanne, A.L., and Quate, C.F., *Applied Physics Letters*, Vol. 45, p. 1240, 1984.
[48] Fan T.G., Medioni, G., and Nevatia, R., "Description of surfaces from range data using curvature properties," *Proceedings of Computer Vision and Pattern Recognition Conference*, IEEE Computer Society, Miami, FL, pp. 86-91, June 1986.
[49] Feuchtwang, T.E., Notes, A., and Cutler, P.H., "The linear response theory of the scanning tunneling microscope II. Determination of the phenomenological and semiempirical instrument function," *Surface Science*, 207 (1989) pp. 558-572.
[50] Feuchtwang, T.E., Notes, A., and Cutler, P.H., "The linear response theory of the scanning tunneling microscope III. Analysis of resolution and its achievable bounds," *Surface Science*, 207 (1989) pp. 573-585.
[51] Feuchtwang, T.E., Notes, A., and Cutler, P.H., "The linear response theory of the scanning tunneling microscope I. General metrological considerations in the interpretation of experimental data," *Surface Science*, 207 (1989) pp. 547-557.
[52] Foley, J.D., vanDam, A., Feiner, S.K., and Hughes, J.F., *Computer Graphics: Principles and Practice*, Allison-Wesley Publishing Co., 1990.
[53] Foster, J., Frommer, J.E., and Arnett, P.C., *Nature*, Vol. 331, p. 324, 1988.
[54] Gallarda, H., and Jain, R., "A computational model of the imaging process in Scanning X Microscopy," Proceedings of Conference on Integrated Circuit Metrology, Inspection and Process Control V, *SPIE Symposium on Microlithography*, San Jose, March 1991.
[55] Garfunkel, E., et al. "Scanning tunneling microscopy and nanolithography on a conducting oxide $Rb_3M_oO_3$," *Science*, 6 Oct. 1989, v. 246, 99-100.
[56] Garnæs, J., Hansma, P., Gould, S., et al., "Ultrafine particles of North Sea illite/smectite clay minerals invistigated by STM and AFM," *American Mineralogist*, Vol. 76, pp. 1218-1222, 1991.
[57] Ghosh, A.P., Dove, D.B., Wickramasinghe, H.K., "Application of atomic force microscopy to phase shift masks," *Proceedings of the SPIE Conference on Integrated Circuit Metrology, Inspection, and Process Control VI*, Vol. 1673, 1992, pp. 255-265.
[58] Giardina, C. R. and Dougherty, E. R., *Morphological Methods in Image and Signal Processing*, Prentice Hall, 1988.
[59] Gonzalez, R.C. and Wintz, P., *Digital Image Processing*, Second Edition, Addison-Wesley Publishing Company, 1987.
[60] Gould, S.A.C., et al. "Simple theory for the atomic force microscope with a comparison of theoretical and experimental images of graphite," *Physical Review B*, Vol. 40, No. 8, 15 Sep. 1989, pp. 641-643.
[61] Gould, S.A.C., Drake, B., Prater, C.B., Wiesenhorn, A.L., Manne, S., Kelderman, G.L., Butt, H.-J., Hansma, H., Hansma, P.K., Magonov, S., and Cantow, H.J., "The atomic force microscope: a tool for science and industry," *Ultramicroscopy*, 33 (1990) pp. 93-98.
[62] Griffith, J.E., Grigg, D.A., Vasile, M.J., Russell, P.E., and Fitzgerald, E.A., "Characterization of scanning probe microscope tips for linewidth measurement," *Journal of Vacuum Science and Technology*, B 9 (6), November/December 1991, pp. 3586-3589.
[63] Griffith, J.E., Grigg, D.A., Kochanski, G.P., Vasile, M.J., and Russell, P.E., "Metrology with Scanning Probe Microscopes," *The Technology of Proximal Probe Lithography*, edited by C.K. Marrian, SPIE Institute for Advanced Technologies, 1993.

[64] Grigg, D.A., Russell, P.E., Griffith, J.E., Vasile, M.J., and Fitzgerald, E.A., "Probe characterization for scanning probe metrology," *Ultramicroscopy*, Vol. 42–44, Part B, September 1992, pp. 1616–1620.
[65] Grigg, D.A., Griffith, J.E., Kochanski, G.P., Vasile, M.J., and Russell, P.E., "Scanning probe metrology," *Proceedings of the SPIE Conference on Integrated Circuit Metrology, Inspection, and Process Control VI*, Vol. 1673, 1992, PP. 557–567.
[66] Guckenberger, R., Kosslinger, C., Gatz, R., Breu, H., Levai, N., and Baumeister, W., "A scanning tunneling microscope (STM) for biological applications: design and performance," *Ultramicroscopy*, 25 (1988) 111–122.
[67] Habib, K., Elings, V., and Wu, C., "Measuring surface roughness of an optical thin film with scanning tunneling microscopes," *Journal of Materials Science Letters*, 1990, 1194.
[68] Hameroff, S., Schneiker, C., Voelker, M., He, J., Dereniak, E., and McCuskey, R., "Scanning tunneling microscopy (STM) applications to molecular electronics," *IEEE Engineering in Medicine & Biology Society 10th International Conference*, pp. 1009–1011.
[69] Hamers, R.J., Tromp, R.M., and Demuth, J.E., *Physical Review Letters*, Vol. 56, p. 1972, 1986.
[70] Hamers, R.J., Tromp, R.M., and Welland, M.E., "A scanning tunneliing microscope for surface science studies," *IBM Journal of Research and Development*, Vol. 30, No. 4, July 1986.
[71] Hamers, R.J., "Atomic resolution surface spectroscopy with the scanning tunneling microscope," *Annual Reviews in Physical Chemistry*, 1989.
[72] Hansma, P.K., Elings, V.B., Marti, O., and Bracker, C.E., "Scanning tunneling microscopy and atomic force microscopy: application to biology and technology," *Science*, Vol. 242, 14 October 1988, pp. 209–216.
[73] Hansma, P.K., et al. "The Scanning Ion-Conductance Microscope," *Science*, Vol. 243, 3 Feb. 1989, pp. 641–643.
[74] Hansma, P.K., *Scanning probe microscopy of liquid-solid interfaces*, Kluwer Academic Publishers, 1990.
[75] Hansma, P.K., et al. "Imaging nanometer scale defects in Langmuir-Blodgett films with the atomic force microscope," *Langmuir*, Vol 7, No. 6, pp. 1051–1054, 1991.
[76] Hansma, P.K., Albrecht, T.R., and Quate, C.F., "Imaging crystals, polymers, and processes in water with the atomic force microscope," *Science*, Vol. 243, pp. 1586–1589, 24 March 1989.
[77] Hansma, P.K., Elings, V.B., Marti, O., and Bracker, C., "Scanning tunneling microscopy and atomic force microscopy: application to biology and technology", *Science*, Vol. 242, No. 4876, October 14 1988.
[78] Hansma, P.K., Elings, V.B., Massie, J., and Maivald, P., "Imaging and manipulating molecules on a zeolite surface with an atomic force microscope," *Science*, Vol. 247, 16 Mar. 1990, pp. 1330–1333.
[79] Hansma, P.K., Helen, G., et al. "Atomic Force Microscopy: Seeing molecules of lipid and Immunoglobin," *Clinical Chemistry*, VOl. 37, No. 9, 1991, pp. 1497–1501.
[80] Hansma, P.K., Massie, J., Longmire, M., Elings, V., Northern, B.D., Mukergee, B., and Peterson, C., "From atoms to integrated circuit chips, blood cells, and bacteria with the atomic force microscope," *Journal of Vacuum Science and Technology*, A8(1), pp. 369–373, Jan/Feb 1990.
[81] Hansma, P.K., Northern, B.D., and Peterson, C.M., "Imaging molecules and cells with the atomic force microscope," *XIIth International Congress for Electron Microscopy*, San Francisco Press, Inc., 1990.
[82] Hansma, P.K., Prater, C.B., Tortonese, M., and Quate, C.F., "Improved scanning ion conductance microscope using microfabriacated probes," *Review of Scientific Instruments*, 62 (11), November 1991, pp. 2634–2638.

[83] Hansma, P.K. and Tersoff, J., "Scanning tunneling microscopy," *Journal of Applied Physics*, January 15, 1987.

[84] Hashizume, T., Kamiya, I., Hasegawa, Y., Sano, N., Sakurai, T., and Pickering, H.W., "A role of a tip geometry on STM images," *Journal of Microscopy*, Vol. 152, Pt 2, November 1988, pp. 347–354.

[85] Henderson, E., "Imaging and nanodissection of individual supercoiled plasmids by atomic force microscopy," *Nucleic Acids Research*, Vol. 20, No. 3, 445–447.

[86] Hietschold, M., Hansma, P.K., and Wiesenhorn, A.L., "Scanning probe microscopy and spectroscopy in materials science," *Microscopy and Analysis*, Sept. 1991, pp. 25–27.

[87] Hochella, M.F., Elings, V.B., Wu, C.M., Kjoller, K., "Mineralogy in two dimensions: scanning tunneling microscopy of semiconducting minerals with implications for geochemical reactivity," *American Mineralogist*, Vol. 74, pp. 1233–1246, 1989.

[88] Hochella, M.F., Johnsson, P.A., and Eggleston, C.M., "Imaging molecular scale structure and microtopography of hematite with the atomic force microscope," *American Mineralogist*, Vol. 76, pp. 1442–1445, 1991.

[89] Hoffman, R. and Jain, A.K., "Segmentation and classification of range images," *IEEE Transactions on Pattern Analysis and Machine Intelligence*, vol. PAMI-9, no. 5, pp. 608–620, Sept. 1987.

[90] Horgan, J., "DNA unveiled; tunneling microscope offers a closer look at the stuff of life," *Scientific American*, November 1987.

[91] Howells, S., "Enhanced effects with scanning force microscopy," *Journal of Applied Physics*, 69 (10), 15 May 1991, pp. 7330–7332.

[92] Howland R., "Materials Characterization in Semiconductor Fabrication: Scanning Force Microscopes Extend Profilometry to the Angstrom Scale in Three Dimensions," *Microelectronics Manufacturing Technology*, January 1992, pp. 38–39.

[93] Jain, R.C., and Jain, A.K., *Analysis and Interpretation of Range Images*, Springer-Verlag 1988.

[94] Kaneko, R., et al. "Direct Observation of the configuration, adsorption, and mobility of lubricants by scanning tunneling microscopy," *Advanced Information Storage Systems*, Vol. 2, 1991, pp. 23–34.

[95] Kaneko, R., "A frictional force microscope controlled with an electromagnet," *Journal of Microscopy*, Vol. 152, Pt 2, Nov. 1988, pp. 363–369.

[96] Keller, D. and Jobe, R., "Enhanced imaging with sharp AFM tips," *Topometrix Applications Newsletter*, Volume 91-3, Fall 1991.

[97] Keller, D., Deputy, D., ALdvino, A., and Luo, K., "Sharp, vertical walled tips for SFM imaging of steep or soft samples," *Ultramicroscopy*, in press.

[98] Keller, D. and Chih-Chung, C., "Imaging Steep, High Structures by Scanning Force Microscopy with Electron Beam Deposited Tips," *Surface Science*, in press.

[99] Keller, D., "Reconstruction of STM and AFM images distorted by finite size tips," *Surface Science*, 253 (1991), pp. 353–364.

[100] Kino, G.S., Corle, T.R., "Scanning optical microscopes close in on submicron scale," *Circuits and Devices*, March 1990, pp. 28–36.

[101] Koch, R.H., and Hamers, R.J., "Characterization of electron trapping defects on silicon by scanning tunneling microscopy," *Surface Science*, 181 (1987) 333–339.

[102] Kong, L.C., Orr, B.G., and Wise, K.D, "A micromachined silicon scan tip for an atomic force microscope," *Technical digest of the IEEE Solid State Sensor and Actuator Workshop*, Hilton Head Island, South Carolina, p. 28, June 1990.

[103] Kong, L. C., Orr, B.G., and Wise, K.D., "An Integrated Electrostatically-Resonant Scan Tip for an Atomic Force Microscope," *Journal of Vacuum Science and Technology B*, May/June, 1993, p. 634.

[104] Kong, L. C., Pingali, G.S., Orr, B.G., Jain, R., and Wise, K.D., "Inspection of a Reactive-Ion Etched Sample by SFM," *Journal of Vacuum Science and Technology B*, May/June, 1993, p. 634.

[105] Kordic, S., van Loenen, E.J., Dijkkamp, D., Hoeven, A.J., and Moraal, H.K., "Scanning tunneling microscopy on cleaved silicon pn junctions," *IEEE International Electron Device Meeting IEDM 89*, PP. 277–280.
[106] Laegsgaard, E.L., Besenbacher, F., Mortensen, K., and Stensgaard, I., "A full automated, 'thimble-size' scanning tunnelling microscope," *Journal of Microscopy*, Vol. 152, Pt 3, December 1988, pp. 663–669.
[107] Laloyaux, Th., Lucas, A.A., Vigneron, J.-P., Lamban, Ph., and Morawitz, H., "Lateral resolution of the scanning tunneling microscope," *Journal of Microscopy*, Vol. 152, Pt 1, October 1988, pp. 53–63.
[108] Lee, K.L., Abraham, D.W., Secord, F., and Landstein, L., "Submicron Si Trench Profiling with an Electron-beam fabricated Atomic Force Microscope Tip," Journal of Vacuum Science and Technology, B 9, pp. 3562–3568, 1991.
[109] Lieber, C.M., Wu, X.L., and Zhou, P., "Surface electronic properties probed with tunneling microscopy and chemical doping," *Nature*, 335, 55 (1988).
[110] Lieber, C.M. and Kim, Y., "Chemically etched silicon surfaces viewed at the atomic level by force microscopy," *Journal of the American Chemical Society*, Vol. 113, No. 6, 1991.
[111] Lindsay, S.M., Thundat, T., Nagahara, L., Knipping, U., and Rill, R., "Images of the DNA Double Helix in Water," *Science*, Vol. 244, No. 1063, June 2, 1989.
[112] Lindsay, S.M., et al. "Sequence, Packing and nanometer scale structure in STM images of nucleic acids under water," *Journal of Biomolecular Structure and Dynamics*, Vol. 7 (2), 1989/1990.
[113] Lipari, N.O., "STM Applications for semiconductor materials and devices," *Surface Science*, 181 (1987) pp. 285–294.
[114] Maivald, P., Gurley, J.A., and Elings, V.B., "Using force modulation to image surface elasticities with the atomic force microscope," *Nanotechnology*, 1991.
[115] Manne, S., Hansma, P.K., Massie, J., and Elings, V., "Atomic resolution electrochemistry with the atomic force microscope: copper deposition on gold," *Science*, VOl. 251, 11 January 1991, pp. 183–186.
[116] Manne, S., Butt, H.J., Gould, S.A.C., and Hansma, P.K., "Imaging metal atoms in air and water using the atomic force microscope," *Allied Pyhsics Letters* 56 (18), 30 April 1990, pp. 1758–1759.
[117] Martin, Y., Williams, C.C., and Wickramasinghe, H.K., "Atomic force microscope-force mapping and profiling on a sub 100-Åscale." *Journal of Applied Physics*, Vol. 61, May 1987, pp. 4723–4729.
[118] Martin, Y. and Wickramasinghe, H.K., *Applied Physics Letters*, 50, 1455, 1987.
[119] Martin, Y., Abraham, D.W., and Wickramasinghe, H.K., *Applied Physics Letters* 52, 1103, 1988.
[120] Martin, D.C., Ojeda, J.R., Anderson, J.P., and Pingali, G.S., "Atomic Force Microscopy of Polymers Near Surfaces," *Atomic Force Microscopy/Scanning Tunneling Microscopy Symposium*, U.S. Army Natick Research, Development and Engineering Center, Natick, Massachusetts, June 8–10, 1993.
[121] Meepagala, S.C., Real, F., and Reyes, C.B., 'Tip-sample interaction forces in scanning tunneling microscopy: Effects of contaminants," *J. Vac. Sci. Technol.*, B 9 (2), Mar/Apr 1991, 1340–1342.
[122] Michel, B., and Travaglini, G., "An STM for biological applications: Bioscope," *Journal of Microscopy*, Vol. 152, Pt 3, December 1988, pp. 681–685.
[123] Mogren, S. and Steckl, A.J., "STM Characterization of focused ion beam profiles," *Materials Research Society Extended Abstracts*, (EA-26), 1990 MRS, pp. 103–106.
[124] Moreland, J. and Rice, P., "High-resolution tunneling-stabilized magnetic imaging and recording," *Applied Physics Letters*, 57 (3), 16 July 1990, pp. 310–312.
[125] Muralt, P., "Semiconductor interfaces studied by scanning tunneling microscopy and potentiometry," *Surface Science*, 181 (1987) pp. 324–332.

[126] Murray, D.W., "Model-based recognition using 3D shape alone," *Computer Vision, Graphics and Image Processing*, vol. 40, pp. 250–266, 1987.

[127] Nagai, K., Suzuki, M., Maruno, T., and Yamamoto, F., "Surface roughness of rubbed polyimide film for liquid crystals by scanning tunneling microscopy," *Journal of Vacuum Science and Technology*, A 8 (1), Jan/Feb 1990, pp. 631–634.

[128] Nishikawa, O., Masahiko, T., and Katsuki, F., "Arrangement and stability of atoms at the apex of a scanning tip," *Journal of Microscopy*, Vol. 152, Pt 3, December 1988, pp. 637–641.

[129] Nonnenmacher, M., Greschner, J., Wolter, O., and Kassing, R., "Scanning force microscopy with micromachined silicon sensors," *J. Vac. Sci Technol.*, B 9 (2), Mar/Apr 1991, pp. 1358–1362.

[130] Nyysonen, D., Landstein, L., and Coombs, E., "Two-dimensional atomic force microprobe trench metrology system," *Journal of Vacuum Science and Technology*, B 9 (6), November/December 1991, pp. 3612–3616.

[131] Parkinson, B.A., 'Discrimination of atoms on the surface of a two-dimensional solid solution with scanning tunneling microscopy," *Journal of the American Chemical Society*, Vol. 112, No. 3, 1990.

[132] Parkinson, J., "Layer-by-layer nanometer scale etching of two dimensional substrates using the scanning tunneling microscope," *Journal of the American Chemical Society*, Vol. 112, No. 21, 1990.

[133] Peters, L., "AFMs: What will their role be?," *Semiconductor International*, Aug. 1993, pp. 62–68.

[134] Peterson, C., Northern, B., Hansma, P.K., Gray, E.D., and Massie, J., "Direct observation of human blood cell surfaces using the atomic force microscope," *Proceedings of the STM/Spectroscopy Conference*, Japan, July 89.

[135] Pickering, H.W., Sakurai, T., "In situ scanning microscopy of inhibited Cu and Cu-Au electrodissolution in aqueous media," *Journal of Vacuum Science and Technology*, B9 (2), Mar/Apr 1991, pp. 976–983.

[136] Pickering, H.W. and Sakurai, T., "Scanning tunneling microscopy and its applications in corrosion science," *The NACE Annual Conference and Corrosion Show*, Cincinnati, March 1991.

[137] Pingali, G.S. and Jain, R., "Restoration of scanning probe microscope images" *Proceedings of IEEE Workshop on Applications of Computer Vision*, Palm Springs, CA, November 30-December 2, 1992, pp. 282–289.

[138] Pingali, G.S. and Jain, R., "Probe Shape Recovery in Scanning Probe Microscopy," *Proceedings of MVA '92 IAPR Conference on Machine Vision Applications*, Tokyo, Japan, December 7–9, 1992, pp. 639–642.

[139] Pingali, G.S. and Jain, R., "Imaging Models and Surface Recovery Methods for Scanning Probe Microscopy," *Computer Science and Engineering Technical Report CSE-TR-137-92*, Department of Electrical Engineering and Computer Science, The University of Michigan, Ann Arbor, 1992.

[140] Pingali, G.S. and Jain, R., "Surface Recovery in Scanning Probe Microscopy," *Proceedings of SPIE Conference on Machine Vision Applications, Architectures, and Systems Integration*, Boston, MA, November 17–18, 1992, pp. 151–162.

[141] Pingali, G.S. and Jain, R., "Image Processing Based Calibration of Scanning Probe Microscopes," *Proceedings of ISIR '93 International Symposium on Intelligent Robotics*, Bangalore, India, January 7–9, 1993, pp. 135–144.

[142] Pingali, G.S. and Jain, R., "Estimation of Sample and Probe Tilts in Scanning Probe Microscopy," *IMTC/93 IEEE Instrumentation/Measurement Technology Conference*, Irvine, CA, May 18–20, 1993.

[143] Pingali, G.S., Jain, R. and Kong, L.C., "Simulation and Animation of Scanning Probe Microscope Imaging," to appear in *Journal of Vacuum Science and Technology B*, March/April 1994.

[144] Pingali, G.S. and Jain, R., "Image Modeling and Restoration for Scanning Probe Microscope Imaging," submitted to *IEEE Transactions on Image Processing*.

[145] Pingali, G.S., Kong, L.C., Orr, B.G., Wise, K.D., and Jain, R., "Nondestructive Profiling of Submicron Surface Features Using Scanning Force Microscopy," submitted to *IEEE Transactions on Semiconductor Manufacturing*.
[146] Pingali, G.S., Kong, L.C., Jain, R., Orr, B.G., and Wise, K.D., "A technique for in-situ reconstruction of three-dimensional tip shape in scanning probe microscopes," submitted to *Nanotechnology*.
[147] Pohl, D.W., Fischer, U.Ch., and Durig, U.T., "Scanning near-field optical microscopy," *Journal of Microscopy*, Vol. 152, Pt 3, December 1988, pp. 853–861.
[148] Pohl, D.W., "Some design criteria in scanning tunneling microscopy," *IBM Journal of Research and Development*, Vol. 30, No. 4, July 1986.
[149] Quate, C.F., "Vacuum Tunneling: A new technique for microscopy," *Physics Today*, August 1986.
[150] Reiss, G., Schneider, F., Vancea, J., and Hoffmann, H., "Scanning tunneling microscopy on rough surfaces: Deconvolution of constant current images," *Applied Physics Letters*, 57 (9), 27 August 1990, pp. 867–869.
[151] Reiss, G., Vancea, J., Witmann, H., Zweck, J., and Hoffmann, H., "Scanning tunneling microscopy on rough surfaces: Tip-shape limited resolution," *Journal of Applied Physics*, 67 (3), February 1990, pp. 1156–1159.
[152] Ringger, M., Hidber, H.R., Schlogl, R., Oelhafen, P., and Guntherodt, H.J., *Applied Physics Letters*, Vol. 46, p. 832, 1985.
[153] Robinson, R.S., Kimsey, T.H., and Kimsey, R., "Desktop computer-based management of images and digital electronics for scanning tunneling microscopy," *J. Vac. Sci. Technol.*, B 9 (2), Mar/Apr 1991, pp. 631–635.
[154] Robinson, R.S., "Increasing the scanning speed of scanning tunneling microscopes," *Journal of Microscopy*, Vol. 152, Pt 2, November 1988, pp. 387–397.
[155] Robinson, R.S., "Real-time scanning tunneling microscopy of surfaces under active electrochemical control," *Journal of Microscopy*, Vol. 152, Pt 2, November 1988, pp. 541–546.
[156] Rodgers, M.R. and Yashar, F.D., "Recent developments in atomic force microscopy applicable to integrated circuit metrology," *Proceedings of the SPIE Conference on Integrated Circuit Metrology, Inspection, and Process Control VI*, Vol. 1673, 1992, pp. 544–551.
[157] Rudd, G., Saulys, D., and Garfunkel, E., "Scanning tunneling microscopy assisted oxide surface etching," *Apllied Physics Letters*, 1990.
[158] Rugar, D., and Hansma, P., "Atomic Force Microscopy," *Physics Today*, October 1990, pp. 23–30.
[159] Salmeron, M., Ogletree, D.F., Ocal, C., Wang, H.-C., Neubauer, G., Kolbe, W., and Meyers, G., "Tip-surface forces during imaging by scanning tunneling microscopy," *J. Vac. Sci. Technol.*, B 9(2), Mar/Apr 1991, pp. 1347–1352.
[160] Sarid, D., et al. "High resolution images of single C_{60} molecules on gold (111) using scanning tunneling microscopy," *Surface Science*, 1992.
[161] Sarids, D., Elings, V., "Review of scanning force microscopy," *J. Vac. Sci. Technol.*, B 9 (2), Mar/Apr 1991, pp. 431–437.
[162] Sarid, D., *Scanning force microscopy with applications to electric, magnetic, and atomic forces*, Oxford University Press, 1991.
[163] Sattler, K., "Scanning tunneling spectroscopy of graphite using an oxidized silicon tip," *Journal of Vacuum Science and Technology*, B9, No. 2, 1052, 1991.
[164] Sattler, K., "Scanning tunneling microscopy and spectroscopy for cluster and small particle research," *Journal of Physics D – Atoms, Molecules and Clusters*, 19, 287, 1991.
[165] Schneiker, C., Hameroff, S., Voelker, M., Jackson, H., Dereniak, E., and McCuskey, R., "Scanning tunneling engineering," *Journal of Microscopy*, Vol. 152, Pt 2, November 1988, pp. 585–596.
[166] Scott, E.R., White, H.S., and McClure, D.J., "Scanning tunneling microscopy of platinum films on mica: evolution of topography and crystallinity during film growth," *Journal of Physical Chemistry*, 93, 1989, pp. 5249–52.

[167] Smith, D.R. and Kanade, T., "Autonomous scene description with range imagery," *Computer Vision, Graphics, Image Processing*, vol. 31, pp. 322–334, 1985.

[168] Solina, F. and Bajcsy, R., "Recovery of parametric models from range images: The case for superquadrics with global deformations," *IEEE Transactions on Pattern Analysis and Machine Intelligence*, vol. 12, no. 2, pp. 131–147, Feb. 1990.

[169] Stedman, M. and Lindsey, K., "Limits of topographic measurement by the scanning tunneling and atomic force microscopes," *Journal of Microscopy*, Vol. 152, Pt 3, December 1988, pp. 611–618.

[170] Stedman, M., "Limits of Surface Measurements by Stylus Instruments," *Proc. SPIE*, Vol. 1009, 1988, PP. 56–61.

[171] Stedman, M., "Mapping the performance of Surface Measuring Instruments," *Proc. SPIE*, Vol. 83, 1988, pp. 138–142.

[172] Stedman, M., "Limits of topographic measurement by the scanning tunneling and atomic force microscopes," *Journal of Microscopy*, Vol. 152, Pt 3, December 1988, pp. 611–618.

[173] Stemmer, A., and Engel, E., "Imaging biological macromolecules by STM: quantitative interpretation of topographs," *Ultramicroscopy*, 34 (1990) 129–140.

[174] Stoll, E., and Baratoff, A., "Restoration and pictorial representation of scanning-tunneling-microscope data," *Ultramicroscopy*, 25 1988, pp. 149–154.

[175] Stoll, E., and Marti, O., "Restoration of scanning-tunneling-microscope data blurred by limited resolution, and hampered by 1/f-like noise," *Surface Science*, 181 (1987), pp. 222–229.

[176] Stoll, E.P., "Why do 'dirty' tips produce higher-resolution images when graphite is scanned in a scanning tunnelling microscope?" *J. Phys. C: Solid State Phys.*, 21 (1988) L921–L924.

[177] Stoll, E.P., "Picture processing and three-dimensional visualization of data from scanning tunneling and atomic force microscopy," *IBM J. Res. Develop.*, Vol. 35 No. 1/2 January/March 1991, pp. 67–77.

[178] Strecker, H. and Persch, G., "Application of STM in magnetic storage device manufacturing," *Journal of Vacuum Science and Technology*, 1991.

[179] Sullivan, T.E., Kuk, Y., and Cutler, P.H., "Proposed planar scanning tunneling microscope diode: application as an infrared and optical detector," *IEEE Transactions on Electron Devices*, Vol. 36, No. 11, November 1989, pp. 2659–2664.

[180] Teague, E.C., "The National Institute of Standards and Technology molecular measuring machine project: Metrology and precision engineering design," *Journal of Vacuum Science and Technology B*, Vol. 7, pp. 1898–1902, 1989.

[181] Thomson, D.J., "The STM as an information storage device," *Journal of Microscopy*, Vol. 152, Pt 3, December 1988, pp. 627–630.

[182] Uosaki, K., and Hideaki, K., "In situ, real-time monitoring of elecrde surfaces by scanning tunnelin microscopy, III. Surface structure of Pt and Pd electrodes," *Journal of Vacuum Science and Technology*, A 8 (1), Jan/Feb 1990, pp. 520–524.

[183] Vasile, M.J., Grigg, D., Griffith, J.E., Fitzgerald, E., and Russell, P.E., "Scanning probe tip geometry optimized for metrology by focused ion beam ion milling," *Journal of Vacuum Science and Technology*, B 9 (6), November/December 1991, pp. 3569–3572.

[184] Vemuri, B.C., Mitiche, A., and Aggarwal, J.K., "Curvature-based representation of objecs from range data," *Image and Vision Computing*, Vol. 4, no. 2, pp. 107–114, May 1986.

[185] Vemuri, B.C. and Aggarwal, J.K., "Representation and recognition of objects from dense range maps," *IEEE Transations on Circuits and Systems*, vol. CAS-34, no. 11, pp. 1351–1363, Nov. 1987.

[186] Wadas, A., and Grutter, P., "Theoretical approach to magnetic force microscopy," *Physical Review B*, Vol. 39, Number 16, June 1989, pp. 12013–12017.

[187] Wadas, A., "Description of magnetic imaging in atomic force microscopy," *J. of Magnetism and Magnetic Materials*, 78 (1989), pp. 263–268.

[188] Weihs, T.P., et al. "Limits of resolution for atomic force microscopy of molecules," *Applied Physics Letters*, 59 (27), 30 Dec. 1991, 3536–3538.
[189] Wickramasinghe, H.K., "Scanned-probe microscopes," *Scientific American*, October 1989, pp. 98–105.
[190] Wickramasinghe, H.K., "Scanning probe microscopy: Current status and future trends," *J. Vac. Sci. Technol.*, A 8 (1), Jan/Feb 1990.
[191] Williams, C.C. and Wickramasinghe, H.K., *Applied Physics Letters*, 49, 1587, 1986.
[192] Wise, K.D. and Najafi, K., "Microfabrication techniques for integrated sensors and microsystems," *Science*, Vol. 254, pp. 1335–1342, 29 November 1991.
[193] Wolter, O., Bayer, Th., and Greschner, J., "Micromachined silicon sensors for scanning force microscopy," *J. Vac. Sci. Technol.*, B 9 (2), Mar/Apr 1991, pp. 1353–1357.
[194] Wu, X. and Lieber, C.M., "Determination of the structural and the electronic properties of surfaces using scanning tunneling microscopy coupled with chemical modifications," *Journal of the American Chemical Society*, 110, 5200, 1988.
[195] Yi, L., Gallagher, M., Howells, S., Chen, T., and Sarid, D., "Combined STM/AFM and AFM for magnetic applications," *AIP Conference Proceedings*, Scanned Probe Microscopy, 241, 537, 1992.
[196] Yuan, J., and Shao, Z., "Simple model of image formation by scanning tunneling microscopy of non-conducting materials," *Ultramicroscopy*, 34 (1990), pp. 223–226.
[197] Zasadzinski, J.A.N., "Scanning tunneling microscopy with applications to biological surfaces," *Bio Techniques*, Vol. 7, No. 2 (1989).

Advances in Image Information Modeling

W.I. Grosky and R. Mehrotra

1 Introduction

With recent advances in computer technologies, numerous new application areas requiring management of non-alphanumeric data such as images, videos, graphs, and audios have evolved. Examples of such applications include weather information management, medical information management, environmental pollution information systems, space exploration, manufacturing information management, genome research, training and educational systems, entertainment applications, and defense applications.

Traditional alphanumeric data and information management techniques are not effective for these applications. This paper is concerned with the modeling and representation of images so that both image and alphanumeric information can be managed in an integrated information environment. Information modeling and representation is a key component of any information management system. Most of the new nontraditional applications mentioned above require representation, storage, and management of image data and associated information. In fact, stored images are the central source of information for many such applications. In many cases, the stored images are themselves the entities or objects to be represented and managed by the system. To effectively utilize the information present in an image, it must be processed (automatic or semiautomatic processing may be employed) in order to extract application or domain dependent useful information. The process of transforming image data to domain dependent information generally involves several stages where the form and information content of the data keeps changing from stage to stage. Furthermore, the processing required to transform an input image into desirable application dependent information varies from application to application.

Therefore, from an information modeling viewpoint, an image information management system must be able to efficiently represent image data, processed data, and extracted information at various stages of processing, as well as various application dependent views of an image, the domain specific information, and the data to domain information transformation procedures. Traditional alphanumeric information modeling and representation techniques are not designed to meet the complex requirements of image information management. This paper describes key issues involved in image information modeling and representation and the various types of image information which is generally required to be represented in image information management systems.

The remainder of this paper is organized as follows. In Sect. 2, we present key issues in image information modeling. Section 3 discusses generic types of image information which must be managed. In Sect. 4, a survey of existing approaches to image information modeling is presented. Finally, in Sect. 5, we present our ideas on future directions in image information modeling.

2 Key Issues in Image Information Modeling

An input image must be manually or automatically processed to obtain its meaningful components and the information they convey. Examples of such information are regions of uniform intensity, curve segments, and regions of uniform texture. To effectively manage these components, the extracted information is typically converted into a suitable representation which can be easily managed, queried, combined, processed further, or displayed. We refer to these extracted components of the image as *image objects*. Image objects contain no semantic information other than basic image feature identification; e.g., a boundary segment or a rectangular region.

However, given an application domain such as medical imaging, cartography, or meteorology, additional semantic information can be associated with an image object. That is, each of the image objects which comprise an image corresponds to some object or semantic category in that application domain. We call these domain-dependent categories *domain objects*. Each application domain typically has a reasonably well-defined set of domain objects which provide useful domain dependent information about the image. For example, in medical imaging a domain object might be a ventricle or a tumor. The image object to domain object correspondence is the most important type of information in the majority of image management applications.

Some of the key challenges posed by image data from a representation and management viewpoint are as follows:

1. In general, several different techniques exist for the same generic image processing or machine vision task. Usually, image objects and their associated descriptions, such as boundaries of detected regions, which are extracted from an image using different feature-based representations of an image and/or image object are possible, depending upon the techniques employed for their extraction. An image information management system should provide a way for the user to associate a group of operations for the same generic task with a data type. The desired image object can be extracted from an image, or an image object definition can be developed, by selecting the associated techniques from different generic task groups. In other words, the image processing component should be fully integrated into an image data management system. Also, with

each advance in the areas of image processing and machine vision, new techniques should be able to be added to a generic task group or an existing technique should be able to be modified or deleted. An image information management system should accommodate and manage such changes with ease.
2. As mentioned earlier, for each application domain, the correspondence between the image objects of each stored image and the set of domain objects must be correctly established. In a large image information management system, this correspondence needs to be established either automatically or semi-automatically, via interaction with the user through an interface, using image processing and machine vision techniques. The overall process of labeling an image and its components in terms of domain-based semantic categories (or domain objects) generally involves a sequence of processing tasks. These processing tasks change the data content. An image data management system should be able to represent and manage the entire transformation process as well as the data contents at each stage of this process.
3. The semantic information or interpretation associated with an image or its components generally varies considerably from domain to domain. In other words, the set of valid domain objects which can be used to label image components are domain dependent. Since, in a database environment, data can be shared among many applications, stored images should also be capable of being shared among many applications, which implies that multiple domains for an image are possible. Thus, any image information management system should be able to efficiently store and manage multiple image object to domain object correspondences and the associated data to information transformation processes.
4. In some application domains, the definition and representation of domain objects are not very precise, and as a result, the same image object can be assigned different domain objects by different users. For example, in radiology, the semantic category of *large ventricles* cannot be precisely defined due to imprecisions in the specifications of the prototypical member of the category as well as the fuzziness of the category boundaries. In other words, for a given domain object, the recognition methods or definitions used by different users may vary in some applications. Each such variation defines a new user of the image data within the same domain. Thus, even for an application domain specific image database system, one which has only one set of valid domain objects, multiple image object to domain object correspondences and transformation processes are possible.
5. In several application domains, the associated semantic categories (i.e., the set of valid domain objects) or the definitions of domain objects (i.e., image object to domain object correspondences or user views of an image) evolve or significantly change during the lifetime of the system. Such situations quite commonly occur in the areas of space exploration, genome research, and medical information management. In these cases, new image object to domain object correspondences and their associated transformations may have to be added or the existing ones may have to be modified or deleted. An image information

management system should be able to represent and handle such changes. Hence, an ideal image information management system should be flexible enough to effectively and efficiently manage differing semantic views of the same image and dynamic enough to handle advances in image processing techniques ad well as in the various managed application domain areas, along with the resulting view changes and schema evolutions.

3 Generic Types of Image Information

As mentioned in the previous section, a semiautomatic or fully automatic process which extracts desirable image objects from a stored image and associates the extracted image objects with the correct domain objects is necessary in a large image database management system. This process generally involves a sequence of processing steps. A typical image to application dependent semantic information transformation process involves enhancement/restoration, feature extraction, image object identification, and domain dependent image object labeling stages.

The enhancement/restoration stage is responsible for improving the overall quality of the input image for human or machine interpretation. Examples of the type of processing used at this stage include such tasks noise removal, contrast enhancement, and motion artifacts removal. A symbolic description of each of the detected features is then developed. Examples of such descriptions include line or curve equations for boundary components, area, perimeter, average intensity, or intensity variance of a region. Image objects formed by detected features are identified using feature descriptions and their relationships together with some a priori knowledge and described in the image object identification stage. Finally, each of the image objects is labeled with the corresponding domain object names. If needed, domain objects can be grouped to create higher level semantic categories or to assign a semantic label to the entire image.

In light of the above discussion on the different stages of processing involved in establishing the correspondence between image objects and domain objects, we can say that the following eight types of information are generated or available in the transformation process and are required to be modeled in an image information management system:

1. *Iconic.* This information consists of the images themselves, which are stored in a digitized format.
2. *Image registration data.* This is the information found in the header and trailer files of the images.
3. *Enhanced iconic.* These are enhanced or restored images obtained by applying some enhancement or restoration techniques to the input images.
4. *Feature (segmented) images.* These are feature maps (e.g., edge maps, uniform intensity regions, and histograms) corresponding to the input or processed images.

5. *Image object descriptions.* This is symbolic data representing properties of image objects, their components, and their interrelationships.
6. *Image object to domain object correspondences.* This information consists of the relationships between various image objects and their corresponding domain objects.
7. *Higher level domain objects.* These are semantic classes which are defined in terms of the domain objects and their relationships (over one or more images).
8. *Domain object information.* This is conventional alphanumeric data describing the domain objects.

The above information is an abstraction of the real-world. As such, it follows the standard database three-level architecture which consists of the external level, the conceptual level, and the physical level. See Fig. 1.

As mentioned earlier, in addition to facilitating the representation of all these types of information, an image information modeling system should be capable of modeling the image data to domain dependent semantic category transformation process. Associated with each of the aforementioned types of information and data is a valid set of operations. Some of these operations may use input information which belongs to one category and produce information belonging to some other category.

These operations can be grouped into generic classes such that operations in a given generic class perform the same function but employ different algorithms. For example, several different edge detection techniques can be grouped into a

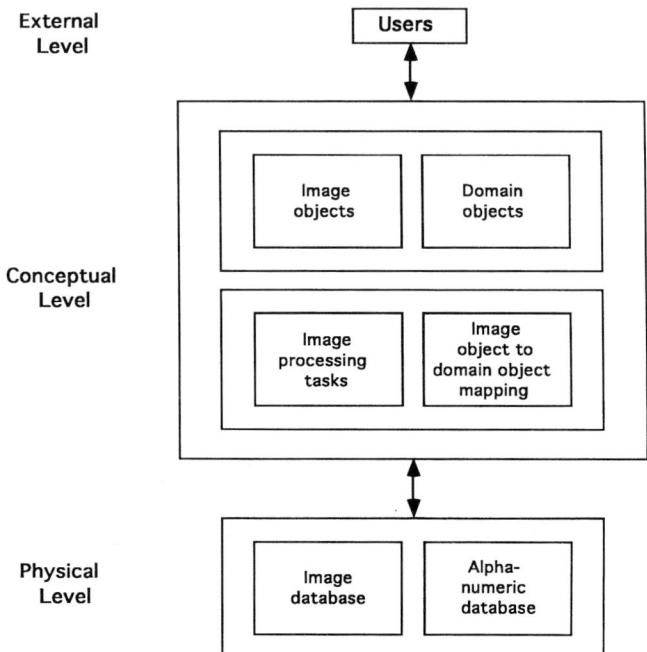

Fig. 1. Three-level database architecture for an image information management system

generic class called *edge detectors*. Thus, associated with each class of information is a set of valid operation groups. In general, each application determines the set of valid operation groups which need to be associated with a given information class. Also, the domain dependent interpretation of an image is implemented from these operations by selecting appropriate tasks from these operation groups associated with the information at different stages of the transformation process. Therefore, an image information management system should be capable of representing and managing both the operation groups themselves along with their interrelationships.

In general, image data is semi-structured. It is a hierarchically structured encoding of information, where the semantics of an image entity is a function of the semantics of its parts. This semantics can be inserted into a image information system manually, by having a human being doing the decoding process, or can be semi-automated through the mediation of various algorithmic decoding procedures, some of which are quite difficult to construct.

Each component of an image entity has attributes and can participate in relationships. These attributes and relationships are of two types: those which utilize the appropriate decoding procedures and those which do not. Those attributes and relationships which utilize any decoding procedures are *content-based*, while those which do not are *content independent*. Content-based attributes and relationships are further subdivided into *information-bearing* and *non-information-bearing* varieties. An attribute or relationship is information-bearing if the information it conveys is not explicitly encoded in the data. We note that, informally speaking, all content independent attributes and relationships are information-bearing.

For example, an image of a particular boat can participate in an information-bearing content-based many-to-many relationship from images to the building headquarters of the companies which manufacture these boats. A range image can participate in a non-information-bearing content-based one-to-many relationship from images to a set of edge maps using a particular edge operator at different resolutions. An image can participate in a content independent one-to-many relationship from photographers to the images which were shot by the given photographer. An example of a content independent attribute of an image could be the number of bits used to represent a pixel. An information-bearing content-based attribute of an image could be the bounding box coordinates of a particular scene of interest to a user. A non-information-bearing content-based attribute of an image could be the bounding box coordinates of a rectangular region which encompasses a particular person who appears in the image.

4 Existing Approaches

We propose to characterize image data models based on how content-based retrieval is supported. The initial impetus for image databases originated with the pattern recognition and image processing community. Most of the proposals from this community, however, were quite narrowly conceived and hence, after a brief flurry of activity in the late 1970's and early 1980's, interest dissipated due to its unsophisticated conception. This community conceived of an image database management system as just a way of managing images for image algorithm development test-beds and did not give serious thought to image data modeling. Images were retrieved based on information in header files, which contained exclusively alphanumeric information. Systems in this first image database generation were characterized by being implemented using the relational data model. As such, any image interpretation tasks associated with their use were either non-existent or hard-wired into the system and, if under user control, were extremely rudimentary. There was no notion of new image feature detectors being composed during run-time by the user nor of any support for intelligent browsing. At this time, the database community largely ignored such non-standard applications due, we believe, to the unsophisticated nature of the then current database management systems. It has only been since the development of the object-oriented data model that the database field has seriously considered these areas.

In the last half of the 1980's, however, the situation was reversed. The database community expressed much interest in the development of non-standard database management systems, including image and document databases, due, as just mentioned, to the development of the object-oriented data model as well as various data-driven approaches to iconic indexing, while the interest of the image interpretation community wavered. Systems developed during this second generation were characterized by being designed either in a more object-oriented fashion or utilizing an extension of the relational model having richer semantics. In this approach, image interpretation routines were, more or less, the methods and, as such, were packaged along with their respective objects. Still, there was no notion of the user composing new image feature detectors in a user-friendly and interactive fashion during run-time.

The decade of the 1990's has seen the two communities converge on a common conception of what an image database should be. This has been due to the belief that image and alphanumeric information should be treated equally. Images should be able to be retrieved by content and should also be integral components of the querying process. Thus, image interpretation should be an important component of any query processing strategy. We are now into the third generation of image databases. These systems will allow the user to manage image sequences [SSJ93], interact with the image interpretation module and compose new image feature detectors interactively and during run time [GWJ91a, GWJ91b], allow schema evolution and management of data and associated semantics at different stages of a data to domain-dependent semantics transformation process [GMY93a, GMY93b], as well as conduct knowledge-based browsing [WuS91]. The latter feature will be accomplished through the mediation of a tool-box of elementary features and their associated detectors (methods) as well as connectors of various sorts which will allow the user to build complex features and detectors from more elementary ones through an iconic user interface.

4.1 First Generation Systems and Their Data Models

These systems were specifically designed for pattern recognition and image processing applications [Cha81]. The image data modeling in these systems consisted mostly of encodings of the positional information exhibited in the images. These systems were not capable of handling the retrieval of image data by content. They could not be called integrated image database systems as they did not treat images equally with alphanumeric information. The only two attempts towards the design of integrated image database systems were described in [Gro84, Tan81].

The pioneering work in this generation was done by Kunii and his colleagues [KWT74]. In their system, a relational database schema was utilized to describe images as superimposed objects and objects as superimposed parts. Some additional relations were used to describe the color, texture, and regions of the objects. A weakness of this approach was that the image data modeling aspect did not address the issues concerning methods of extracting information from images and mapping them into the description schema.

The next system we discuss is the Graphics Oriented Relational Algebraic Interpreter (GRAIN), developed by Chang and his colleagues [CRM77, LiC80]. The main characteristic of the image data modeling in this system was the distinction of logical images from physical images. Logical images were a collection of image objects which could be considered as masks for extracting meaningful parts from an entire image. These were defined in three relational tables – the *picture object* table, the *picture contour* table, and the *picture page* table. Each physical image was stored as a number of picture pages which could be retrieved from image storage. In this approach, no methods were developed to transform an image into its corresponding tuples in the above relational tables; the image description was manually entered.

Another important first-generation system was the Relational Database System for Images (REDI) developed by Chang and Fu [ChF80, ChF81]. REDI was designed and implemented for managing LANDSAT images and digitized maps. In this approach, the database management system was interfaced with an image understanding system. The image features were extracted from images and image descriptions were obtained by using image processing operators supported by the system. Image descriptions and registrations of the original images were stored in a relational database. The original images were stored in a separate image store. This system made the first effort to manage the image processing routines as well as the image data through the use of *image processing sets*. Each image processing set was an ordered sequence of image processing operations which accomplished recognition tasks for various domains. There were processing sets for roads, rivers, cities, and meadows. All processing sets were packaged together into the LANDSAT Processing Package. This concept anticipated the emerging concepts of object-oriented design and is interesting for that reason.

Tang [Tan81] extended the relational data model to allow an attribute of a relation to have a data type of *picture* or *device*. The *picture* data type was characterized by three numbers: m, n and b, where the size of the image was $m \times n$ and the maximum allowed number of gray levels was b. The *device* data type could take as values only operating system recognizable I/O device names. The weakness of this approach was that an image could not stand by itself in the database and that an entity could not have more than a single associated image. Grosky [Gro84] proposed a logical data model for integrated image databases which overcame these weaknesses. He proposed three entity sets: one consisting of individual analog images, another consisting of individual digital images, and the last consisting of digital subimages. The relationships among various entities are represented by three tables: one connecting an analog image to its various digitized counterparts, another connecting digital subimages to the digital images in which they occur, and another connecting a digital subimage to the subject entities appearing in it.

The last first generation system we discuss is the PICture Database Management System (PICDMS) of Chock and her colleagues [CCK81, CCK84]. Its most interesting property is how image information is represented. At each point in an image, different attributes are generally recorded. In a generic image, these attributes comprise such data as region segmentation data, boundary data, or optic flow data. Rather than record this information for each point, however, the image is subdivided into a grid-like pattern, where each grid element is of some equal small area, and the above attributes are recorded for each entire grid element. Rather than store particular attribute values for the entire image in an individual record, however, a record consists of all the attribute values for the same grid element. Thus, if an image consists of g grid cells, each grid cell having a attributes, rather than having an image file consisting of a records, each record having g fields, this approach has an image file consisting of g records, each recording having a fields.

4.2 Second Generation Systems and Their Data Models

Systems in this generation are characterized by using more powerful data modeling techniques. Either various semantically rich extensions of the relational model or an object-oriented model is used.

The system REMINDS [MeG85] discussed a generic image data model which also included aspects related to image interpretation tasks. Although relational in implementation, it had many structural object-oriented aspects to it. The modelbase, which contained logical descriptions of image entities consisted of two parts: the *generic entity descriptions* and the *functional subschema*. The generic entity descriptions consisted of hierarchical descriptions of entities which the system is expected to manage. A model of an entity consisted of descriptions of its parts and their interrelationships. Methods are also objects. The functional subschema logically managed the descriptions of all the image interpretation procedures available in the system. For each image interpretation task, a control structure describing how a set of procedures combine to perform that task resided here. This feature of their system makes the image interpretation system highly modular, which, in turn, makes it easily modifiable: the procedures could be shared among various tasks, new procedures could easily be added, and old procedures could easily be replaced or removed. Thus, the duplication of efforts in the development of new image analysis techniques could be avoided.

Goodman, Haralick, and Shapiro [GHS89] indicated for a particular image interpretation task not only the image modeling which was necessary, but also the associated processing steps, what we previously called the functional subschema. The functional subschema was developed utilizing data structures called the *relational pyramid* and the *summary pyramid*. The former data structure defined level-k features in terms of features of level less than k, while the latter data structure captured various properties of the former. Their data model was described in the context of the *pose estimation* problem. This problem concerned determining the location and orientation of an object from its 2-D image.

In Jagadish and O'Gorman [JaO89], there was the notion of a physical hierarchy and a logical hierarchy as part of image data modeling. The physical hierarchy started at the pixel level, advanced to the chain level, the line level, the composite level, the structure level, and finally to the entire image level. Orthogonal to this, the logical level provided the semantics of the corresponding physical hierarchical structures. As an implementation of this general concept, the authors introduce the *Thin Line Code* image model. This model had a physical and logical hierarchy of 4 levels each, the primitive chain-code level, the line level, the composite level, and the structure level. The line level entities represented connected chains between various types of line junctions. The composite level entities represented one or more connected lines, such as loops. Finally, structure level entities corresponded to complete structures, such as object boundaries. Entities at each level have their own associated attributes and methods. Different concepts of inheritance were discussed depending on the application domain.

4.3 Third Generation Systems and Their Data Models

In all previous systems discussed, the user could formulate a standard database schema related to the aspect of the world to be modeled. This schema could, of course, include images. However, the user has no control over the module of the system which performs the actual image interpretation. Third generation systems allow the user some control over this module. There will be some sort of functional subschema which the user can formulate.

Initial work in this area has been done by Gupta, Weymouth, and Jain [GWJ91a, GWJ91b]. The discussion in these papers is extremely comprehensive with respect to data model design as part of the implementation of a very general image database management system called VIMSYS (Visual Information Management System). This is the only prototype system in which managing information from image sequences has also been addressed. VIMSYS has a layered data model which is divided into an image representation and relation layer, an image object and relation layer, a semantic object and relation layer, and a semantic event and relation layer, each layer being implemented via object-oriented techniques. In the image representation and relation layer, each image object has multiple representations which are mutually derivable from each other. The image object and relation layer concerns itself with image features and their organization. Examples of such features are those of texture, color, intensity, and geometry. New features can easily be formed from given features. Using supplied constructors, one can define such features as an *intensity histogram* by the expression *graph_of(intensity,integer)* as well as a *texture field* by the expression *matrix_of(append (orientedness,point))*. The latter definition illustrates the process of combining two existing features into a composite feature through the use of the operator *append*. The semantic object and relation layer is used to connect real-world entities with various objects in the preceding two layers. Finally, the semantic event and relation layer is used to construct so-called temporal features, a collection of features over an image sequence. An example of a temporal feature is that of a *rotation*.

The I-see knowledge-based software environment for image database research [FVS92] defines a *representation pyramid*, a series of progressively more abstract descriptions of an input image, where the input image itself is on the bottom of the pyramid and the domain objects and events are on the top of the pyramid. This system supports *precompilation*, the automated extraction of the representation pyramid from each input image. In conjunction with some clever means of interfacing with the user, this allows the user to issue queries pertaining to each level of the representation pyramid.

Recently, Griffioen, Mehrotra, and Yavatkar [GMY93a, GMY93b] proposed an object-oriented multimedia information modeling approach based on data semantics, called MOODS (Modeling Object-Oriented Data Semantics). In MOODS, an object consists of three components: a data structure, a set of methods (functions), and a data semantic specification. Methods associated with an object can change both the data and the semantics. Semantic changes affect the class to which an object belongs. Thus, a mapping from image data to domain dependent semantics can be specified in terms of a sequence of class transformations. MOODS supports immutable objects; i.e., methods which do not modify the current object but instead produce a new object. This feature permits storage and management of data obtained at different stages of a given data to domain dependent semantics transformation. In MOODS, operations on an object are defined in terms of generic functions, called *function groups*. These are defined globally. Each group consists of a set of methods which perform the same logical task. New objects can be dynamically created by combining two or more existing objects and new classes and methods can be added dynamically. Thus, MOODS supports schema evolution.

5 Future Directions

Each third generation system discussed above describes an environment more suited to a non-naive, knowledge intensive, application. More support needs to be designed for the naive user as well. Such a user should be able to seamlessly navigate between images and alphanumeric information. A hypermedia-based browsing environment and its associated data modeling should be supported [WuS91].

Consider the scenario of a student perusing a database concerned with the history of Rome which contains alphanumeric information, images, and videos of various buildings and people of historical interest. The student issues a filtering operation which states that he is interested in information pertaining to Julius Caesar. This filters out any entities from which a path of edges do not exist to the entity Julius Caesar. He then browses the resulting subweb. An example browsing path through which he navigates is from an image containing Julius Caesar in front of a particular building to an image showing the architectural details of that building to a video concerning the main architect of that building. After viewing various sorts of information in this browsing process, the student then has a better idea concerning the nature of the information he really wants. He then issues another filtering operation, resulting in a smaller subweb which is again explored via browsing.

The above scenario indicates the type of interactions with image information systems which should be possible in the not too distant future, if not at present. It is no coincidence that this scenario illustrates machine-guided exploratory behavior on the part of the user. Image output is so much richer than standard alphanumeric output that information systems which manage such data will have to support the filtering/browsing/composing paradigm illustrated above instead of the standard database paradigm which just consists of filtering operations.

In some future system, clicking a mouse on an image region of interest might indicate to the system that the user wants to know the attributes of the region in question or the nature of all relationships in which that region participates. However, the nature of these attributes and relationships are quite ambiguous. For example, clicking on the eye of a facial image of some person could mean many things. At a lower level of semantics, the region itself in which the user clicked could be of interest. That is, the user could be interested in queries concerning, say, the shape or texture of the region of interest; perhaps the user wants to find persons having eye regions of similar properties. Perhaps the entire eye is of interest. On the other hand, perhaps the person itself on whose eye region the user clicked is of interest. In this case, it was just happenstance that the user indicated this by clicking over the person's eye; the click might as well have occurred over the person's arm or leg. This motivates the problem of determining on what level of the representation pyramid [FVS92] the querying is to take place. Even after this level has been determined, there is still some ambiguity concerning at what level of the *part-of* hierarchy we are. For example, clicking on the window of a building in a city scene could mean that the user is interested in the given window, in the wall in which the window resides, in the building in which the aforementioned wall resides, or, perhaps, in the city block in which the previously mentioned building resides.

After determining the application domain object with which the user is concerned, a pop-up menu might appear which asks the user whether he is concerned with attributes of the object in question or with relationships in which that object participates. If the former is the case, the necessary attributes are displayed. If the latter is the case, the names of these relationships are displayed. After choosing the appropriate relationship, the user is then taken to a list of images, each containing the image of an entity which is related to the initial entity by the chosen relationship. For example, if after clicking on a particular building and choosing the relationship *rents*, the user might see all stored images of the tenants of that particular building. These images could, of course, be ordered through the mediation of particular filtering operations.

From the above discussion, it is clear that one of the important challenges for the future is how to seamlessly integrate hypermedia data models which support browsing for naive users [WuS91] with image data models which describe images at all levels of the representation pyramid [FVS92] along with the dynamics of moving from one level to another. Some other important topics for future research in the area of data model design are the following (see also [Cha92, GrM92, Jai93]):

1. Provide a rich set of simple features and a robust set of constructor operators for complex feature construction for images. Is there a minimal set of such entities which are domain independent? How can one design an appropriate set of simple features and constructors so they can be shared by as many domains as possible?
2. Can we support generic constructor operators, such as a generic edge map operator, without specifying a particular one, in a richer fashion that is capable in MOODS [GMY93a, GMY93b]? Which one is to be used in which context is left to the system to determine based on the context in which it is to be applied.
3. Develop a user-friendly approach to define the various mappings between the real-world application entity semantics and the feature semantics.
4. How does one support the insertion and deletion of features during run-time? Is this a wise thing to do?
5. Should the concept of views be supported which extend to the definition of features?
6. What are the real tradeoffs between user specified information-bearing content-based approaches and totally automated approaches which combine information-bearing with non-information-bearing content-based information? Is a semi-automated approach the way to go? If so, how can such an approach be supported?
7. How do we manage evolution [GMY93a, GMY93b] in our data model, especially with regard to complex feature definitions which serve to define infor-

mation-bearing content-based relationships between image objects and real-world application entities?
8. How does one efficiently manage histories of transformations of image objects such as MOODS [GMY93a, GMY93b] proposes? Should the user be allowed to backtrack to any previous state of a multimedia object? Are previous states saved in the system for future use? Can an active database environment be useful here?
9. How do integrity conditions carry over to a image environment? How can content-based integrity conditions be efficiently exploited?
10. Formalize the notion of content-based views which define virtual image objects.

Acknowledgements. We acknowledge the support of NASA Grant #NAG-1-1276.

References

[CCK81] M. Chock, A.F. Cardenas, and A. Klinger, "Manipulating Data Structures in Pictorial Information Systems," *IEEE Computer*, vol. 14, no. 11 (November 1981), pp. 43–50

[CCK84] M. Chock, A.F. Cardenas, and A. Klinger, "Database Structure and Manipulation Capabilities of a Picture Database Management System (PICDMS)," *IEEE Transactions on Pattern Analysis and Machine Intelligence*, vol. 6, no. 4 (July 1984), pp. 484–492

[Cha81] S.K. Chang (ed.), "Pictorial Information Systems," *IEEE Computer*, vol. 14, no. 11 (November 1981)

[Cha92] S.K. Chang, "Image Information Systems: Where Do We Go From Here?," *IEEE Transactions on Knowledge and Data Engineering*, vol. 4, no. 5 (October 1992), pp. 431–442

[ChF80] N.S. Chang and K.S. Fu, "Query-by-Pictorial-Example," *IEEE Transactions on Software Engineering*, vol. 6, no. 6 (November 1980), pp. 519–524

[ChF81] N.S. Chang and K.S. Fu, "Picture Query Languages for Pictorial Data-Base Systems," *IEEE Computer*, vol. 14, no. 11 (November 1981), pp. 23–33

[CRM77] S.K. Chang, J. Reuss, and B.H. McCormick, "An Integrated Relational Database System for Pictures," *Proceedings of the IEEE Workshop on Picture Data Description and Management*, Chicago, Illinois, April 1977, pp. 49–60

[FVS92] F. Fierens, J. Van Cleynenbreugel, P. Suetens, and A. Oosterlinck, "A Software Environment for Image Database Research," *Journal of Visual Languages and Computing*, vol. 3, no. 1 (March 1992), pp. 49–68

[GHS89] A.M. Goodman, R.M. Haralick, and L.G. Shapiro, "Knowledge-Based Computer Vision – Integrated Programming Language and Data Management System Design," *IEEE Computer*, vol. 22, no. 12 (December 1989), pp. 43–54

[GMY93a] J. Griffioen, R. Mehrotra, and R. Yavatkar, "An Object-Oriented Model for Image Information Representation," *Proceedings of the 2nd International Conference in Information and Knowledge Management*, Arlington Virginia, November 1993, pp. 393–402

[GMY93b] J. Griffioen, R. Mehrotra, and R. Yavatkar, *A Semantic Model for Embedded Image Information*, Technical Report, Computer Science Department, University of Kentucky, 1993

[GrM92]   W.I. Grosky and R. Mehrotra, "Image Database Management," In *Advances in Computers*, vol. 34, Marshall Yovits (ed.), Academic Press, New York, 1992, pp. 237–291

[Gro84]   W.I. Grosky, "Toward a Data Model for Integrated Pictorial Databases," *Computer Vision, Graphics, and Image Processing*, vol. 25, no. 3 (1984), pp. 371–382

[GWJ91a] A. Gupta, T. Weymouth, and R. Jain, "Semantic Queries in Image Databases," *Proceedings of the IFIP 2nd Working Conference of Visual Database Systems*, Budapest, Hungary, September 1991

[GWJ91b] A. Gupta, T. Weymouth, and R. Jain, "Semantic Queries with Pictures: The VIMSYS Model," *Proceedings of the 17th International Conference on Very Large Databases*, Barcelona, Spain, August 1991, pp. 69–79

[Jai93]   R. Jain (ed.), "NSF Workshop on Visual Information Management Systems," *SIGMOD Record*, vol. 22, no. 3 (September 1993), pp. 57–75

[JaO89]   H.V. Jagadish and L. O'Gorman, "An Object Model for Image Recognition," *IEEE Computer*, vol. 22, no. 12 (December 1989), pp. 33–41

[KWT74]   T. Kunii, S. Weyl, and J.M. Tenebaum, "A Relational Database Schema for Describing Complex Pictures with Color and Texture," *Proceedings of the Second International Joint Conference on Pattern Recognition*, Lyngby-Copenhagen, Denmark, August 1974, pp. 310–316

[LiC80]   B.S. Lin and S.K. Chang, "GRAIN – A Pictorial Database Interface," *Proceedings of the IEEE Workshop on Picture Data Description and Management*, Asilomar, California, August 1980, pp. 83–88

[MeG85]   R. Mehrotra and W.I. Grosky, "REMINDS: A Relational Model-Based Integrated Image and Text Database Management System," *Proceedings of the Workshop on Computer Architecture for Pattern Analysis and Image Database Management*, Miami Beach, Florida, November 1985, pp. 348–354

[SSJ93]   D. Swanberg, C.F. Shu, and R. Jain, "Knowledge Guided Parsing in Video Databases," *Proceedings of the SPIE IS & T Symposium on Storage and Retrieval for Image and Video Databases*, San Jose, California, January 1993

[Tan81]   G.Y. Tang, "A Management System for an Integrated Database of Pictures and Alphanumerical Data," *Computer Graphics and Image Processing*, vol. 16, no. 3 (July 1981), pp. 270–286

[WuS91]   V. Wuwongse and S. Singkorapoom, 'An Object-Oriented Data Model for Hypermedia Databases," In *Object Oriented Approach in Information Systems*, F. Van Assche, B. Moulin, and C. Rolland (eds.), North-Holland Publishers, Amsterdam, 1991, pp. 403–417

Lossless Compression of Medical Images by Content-Driven Laplacian Pyramid Splitting[1]

B. Aiazzi, L. Alparone, and S. Baronti

Abstract. An efficient scheme based on an enhanced Laplacian pyramid (LP) is proposed for *lossless/lossy* compression and *progressive* transmission of medical images. The entropy of the LP is reduced by adopting two filters different for reduction and expansion. Encoding priority is given to major details through a hierarchical *content-driven* decision rule defining a binary *quad-tree* of split nodes, which is *run-length* encoded. The root layer of the pyramid is optimally chosen for spatial DPCM encoding. *Error feedback* along the layers of the LP ensures *lossless* and *semi-lossy* reconstruction capability and improves the robustness of the overall scheme. Reversible compression of scanned RX images, achieved at ratios of about 6:1, establish improvements over both DPCM and pyramid schemes. High-quality lossy versions at 60:1 compression ratio outperform JPEG both visually and quantitatively. Also results of NMR images are presented and discussed.

1 Introduction

Lossless image compression is recently gaining attention over a wider audience in the field of Medical Imaging and particularly of *teleradiology*, where a huge amount of digital imagery or volumetric data (tomographic sections) must be stored, retrieved and transmitted (Kuduvalli 1992). However the *error-free* requirement severely reduces the compression performance attainable, due to the intrinsic noise level introduced by the imaging system, that must be coded as well (Roger 1994). Therefore, it is justified only if all the bits in the binary representation of the image samples are recognized to be significant, i.e., the quantization step is comparable to the *root mean square* (RMS) value of noise. This reason explains why a certain loss of information or *distortion* is usually tolerated whenever significant compression ratio is requested, provided that high reconstruction quality, as absence of visual, or better diagnostic, artifacts is fully guaranteed (Cosman 1993). Consequently, control of the maximum absolute error, or *Peak Error* (PE), instead of globally averaged measures like *Mean Square Error* (MSE) or *Peak Signal-to-Noise Ratio* (PSNR) is recommended.

Most of the classical image compression techniques based on control of MSE or PSNR, like *Vector Quantization* (VQ) (Nasrabadi 1988), *Transform Coding*

---
[1] Work partially supported by a grant of the National Research Council of Italy (CNR) within the framework of the Telecommunications Project.

(Netravali 1988) and *Sub-Band Coding* (SBC) (Woods 1986), even if effective for *lossy* coding, are not suitable by themselves for reversible compression and must be followed by an encoding process of the residual error, with performance penalty. Perhaps the only methods intrinsically capable of performing fully reversible image compression are 2-D *Differential Pulse Code Modulation* (DPCM) schemes, some of which extremely specialized to medical images (Das 1993), in which prediction errors are rounded and encoded.

Progressive image coding is growing in interest as well, as an alternative to *block* or *raster* image coding, for transmission over *low* and *medium bit-rate* channels. Applications range from image data retrieval and *telebrowsing* of *Picture Archival and Communication Systems* (PACS), to remote monitoring and low-rate video coding (Uz 1991). In the basic scheme (Sloan 1979) a coarse but compact and whole version of the image is transmitted first; refinements are attained by encoding gradually subtler details, up to the full reconstruction, if requested. In this framework, a compact representation of the 2-D information is a crucial point, since the performance of the entropic coder increases as the spatial decorrelation procedure is designed to reduce the *zero-order* entropy of the source.

In this paper, a complete adaptive system is proposed for both *lossless* and *semi-lossy* compression of medical images (RX, NMR) and monochrome still pictures in general, as well as for their progressive transmission on digital channels at any rate. The term *semi-lossy* denotes that a prefixed number of the MSBs of the samples are reconstructed without loss, and has been introduced when dealing with image data of variable word-length whose bits are not all meaningful. The outline is based on an enhanced *Laplacian pyramid* (LP) designed in order to possess lower correlation between adjacent layers, and consequently lower *zero-order* entropy, than the classical LP (Burt 1983), which is a representation of the (zero-mean) detail content of the original image, at increasing spatial resolution. The main innovations concern the adoption of two different filters for the two pyramid generating procedures: *reduction* (filtering, and decimation or *down-sampling*) and *expansion* (zero interleaving or *up-sampling*, and interpolation). A polynomial *half-band* kernel is used for 2-D interpolation, while the classical Burt's kernel (Burt 1981) is employed for reduction. Encoding priority is given to major details by a hierarchical *content-driven* decision rule (Dreizen 1987; Mongatti 1989, 1992) defining a binary *quad-tree* of split nodes (one for each quartet of nodes), which is *run-length* encoded. The split rule is based on a simple activity measure on *2 × 2* clusters of the LP. Feedback along the LP layers of the values of unsplit nodes, as well as of quantization errors (Wang 1991), ensures *lossless/semi-lossy* reconstruction capability and improves robustness of the scheme with respect to different image types and choices of pyramid-generating kernels. The *error-feedback* mechanism also reduces the overall *zero-order* entropy of the LP, by modifying the *data* distributions at each pyramid layer.

The complete outline is a hierarchical *non-causal* spatial DPCM, with the advantages of differential schemes in terms of error control and a source decorrelation more effective than that of a spatially predictive (i.e., *causal*) method, due to the intrinsic capability of coping with nonstationarity of the data field. Moreover, control of the maximum absolute reconstruction error prevents the introduction of visual artifacts, like tiling and ringing effects, in textures and homogeneous regions of *lossy* versions also for relatively high compression ratios, because the algorithm neither operates on blocks, like *JPEG* (Wallace 1987) and other *DCT-based* schemes, nor utilizes frequency selective filters, that may cause the onset of correlated artifacts in the neighboring of step edges, as in *SBC*.

Fully reversible compression of 8-bit RX image data, achieved at ratios of about 6:1, establishes improvement over 2-D DPCM, as well as over existing schemes based on *quad-trees* and on the classical LP; high-quality *lossy* versions are produced at less than 0.2 *bit/pel*. Lossy coding outperforms JPEG both visually, for the absence of tiling effects, and quantitatively, resulting in far lower global and local errors. Also versions of reduced sizes (*token* images) are made available at no additional cost, as an intermediate reconstruction step. Besides the efficiency and progressiveness features, a simple and fast algorithm recommends this method for *PACS* organization, and image browsing and retrieval from remote terminals connected by digital networks. As no *floating-point* computation is required, *on-line* compression and reconstruction are feasible on general-purpose computers.

2 Image Pyramids

2.1 Generalized Gaussian and Laplacian Pyramids

Let $\{G_0(i,j), i=0,\ldots M-1, j=0,\ldots,N-1\}$, with $M = p \times 2^T$ and $N = q \times 2^T$, be the input image, p, q and T being a triplet of nonzero integers. G_0 plus the set of recursively down-sampled images $\{G_k(i,j), K=1,\ldots T, i=0,\ldots M/2^k-1, j=0,\ldots, N/2^k-1\}$, where

$$G_k(i,j) = \sum_{m=-M_1}^{M_1} \sum_{n=-N_1}^{N_1} W_1(m,n) G_{k-1}(2i+m, 2j+n) \qquad (1)$$

constitute the *Generalized Gaussian Pyramid* (GGP); k identifies the current layer of the pyramid and $T > 0$ the top or *root*, of size $p \times q$.

From GGP a *Generalized Laplacian Pyramid* (GLP) is recursively defined as:

$$L_k(i,j) = G_k(i,j) - \sum_{m=-M_2}^{M_2} \sum_{n=-N_2}^{N_2} W_2(m,n) G_{k+1}\left(\frac{i+m}{2}, \frac{j+n}{2}\right) \qquad (2)$$

for $i=0,\ldots,M/2^k-1, j=0,\ldots,N/2^k-1$, and $k=0,\ldots,T-1$; G_{k+1} is taken to be null for noninteger values of $(i+m)/2$ and $(j+n)/2$, corresponding to zeroes samples are interleaved by. $L_T(i,j)$ is taken equal to $G_T(i,j)$, for $i=0,\ldots,p-1$ and $j=0,\ldots,q-1$; hence, the total number of nodes of both the pyramids is given by the sum of the truncated geometric series:

$$N_T = \sum_{k=0}^{T} \frac{M \times N}{4^k} = \frac{4}{3} M \times N \left(1 - \frac{1}{4^{T+1}}\right) \tag{3}$$

The terms *Gaussian* and *Laplacian* pyramids find their origin in Marr's vision theory (Marr 1982): the former represents the whole original image at different resolutions; the latter contains the contour sketch of the input image at the various resolutions. The attribute of *generalized* has been introduced because in the original definitions only *Gaussian-shaped* kernels were used for both reduction and expansion. A bank of linearly independent, yet non-orthogonal, band-pass filters may be defined from the basic Gaussian kernel (Ranganath 1991), in accordance with Marr's theory.

The purposes of the spatial filters $W_1(m,n)$ and $W_2(m,n)$ are the following: the former introduces a lowpass effect to prevent spatial frequency aliasing from being generated by decimation; the latter provides interpolation of the upper level of the GGP, whose difference from the current level recursively makes up the GLP. Both these functions are critical for the entropy and energy content of the resulting GLP, as it will be shown in Sect. 2.2.

$W_1(m,n)$ and $W_2(m,n)$, 2-D transformation kernels with support regions of sizes $(2M_1 + 1) \times (2N_1 + 1)$ and $(2M_2 + 1) \times (2N_2 + 1)$, respectively, are taken to be separable as product of two one-dimensional symmetric kernels:

$$W_1(m,n) = W_{1y}(m) W_{1x}(n) \text{ and } W_2(m,n) = W_{2y}(m) W_{2x}(n).$$

In the following it is assumed that

$$W_{1x}(n) = W_{1y}(m) = w_1(n) \text{ and } W_{2x}(n) = W_{2y}(m) = w_2(n).$$

Due to its extremely favorable properties, the parametric kernel of size 5, introduced by Burt (Burt 1981), stated as

$$w(0) = a, \ w(\pm 1) = 0.25, \ w(\pm 2) = 0.25 - a/2 \tag{4}$$

has been massively used for both reduction (1) and expansion (2) with equal values of parameter a (Burt 1983; Mongatti 1989,1992; Wang 1991); a gain factor 4 is added to $W_2(m,n)$ in (2), as samples to be interpolated are zero interleaved along each coordinate axis.

2.2 Enhanced Laplacian Pyramid

An improved pyramid scheme has been recently proposed (Unser 1992) by adding two filtering patches, specifically designed to optimize the reduction and expansion phases of Burt's pyramid. Such a pyramid results to be almost independent of the kernel parameter a, but the performance gain over the classical LP is poor, with increased computational cost.

Considerations on the frequency response properties of pyramid generating filters, as well as on computational complexity, suggest using *half-band* filters

(Meer 1987). However, from the analysis of the spectral distribution of up-sampled signals we recognized that the half-band requirement is tighter for expansion than for reduction (Crochiere 1983). In fact, the reduction filter must achieve a tradeoff between delivering the maximum amount of spectral energy to upper layers, simultaneously reducing the contribution of aliasing noise; for natural (correlated) images this implies that the filter passband may also exceed $f_S/4$, where f_S denotes the sampling frequency. Instead, the interpolation filter must cut at exactly $f_S/4$, and also exhibit vestigial symmetry of the response between *pass-band* and *stop-band*, for best removal of the spectral images centered at odd multiples of $f_S/2$.

Burt's kernel is not *half-band* except for $a = 0.5$, value which is not optimal for the coding scheme, when used for both reduction and expansion, as shown by the authors themselves (Burt 1983). Instead, in this work a *half-band* parametric kernel of size seven, with the same number of nonzero coefficients as for (4), has been applied for expansion (2):

$$w_2(0) = 1, \ w_2(\pm 1) = b, \ w_2(\pm 2) = 0, \ w_2(\pm 3) = 0.5 - b \tag{5}$$

whose DC gain equals 2, since samples to be interpolated are zero-interleaved. Suitable values of b range in $0.5 \div 0.625$, resulting in linear and cubic interpolation, respectively.

The parametric frequency responses of (4) and (5), shown in Fig. 1*a,b*, respectively, contribute to explain the reasons of the improvements. In fact, adopting different kernels makes reduction and expansion independent of one other, introducing a separate adjustment that significantly decreases the *zero-order* entropy, as well as the variance, of the resulting *enhanced* LP (ELP) (Baronti 1994) with respect to the classic LP. This is shown in Fig. 2*a*, reporting, for the test image *Lena*, the equivalent *zero-order* entropy (Wang 1991; Unser 1992), defined as

$$H_{eq}(L) \triangleq \sum_{k=0}^{T} \frac{H_0(L_k)}{4^k}$$

and in Fig. 2*b*, showing the equivalent amplitude, similarly defined as

$$\sigma_{eq}(L) \triangleq \sqrt{\sum_{k=0}^{T} \frac{\sigma^2(L_k)}{4^k}}$$

where $H_0(L_k)$ and $\sigma^2(L_k)$ respectively denote the *zero-order* entropy and the variance at the kth layer of the LP, measured with the same quantization as for the original (i.e., with *unitary* steps); $b = 0.578125$ has been chosen for the interpolation kernel, as the value (in *7-bit* arithmetics) that minimizes H_{eq} of the test image. When image changes, the lowest H_{eq} and σ_{eq} always exhibit a gain over Burt and Adelson's LP. The minimum H_{eq} and σ_{eq} of four images from our test set, *Lena*, *Harbor*, a chest RX and a head NMR, are reported in Table 1, both for LP, with the related value of a, and for ELP, with the values of a and b, in a 7-bit representation as well. From the plots of Fig. 2, it is evident that for the ELP, minimizing the

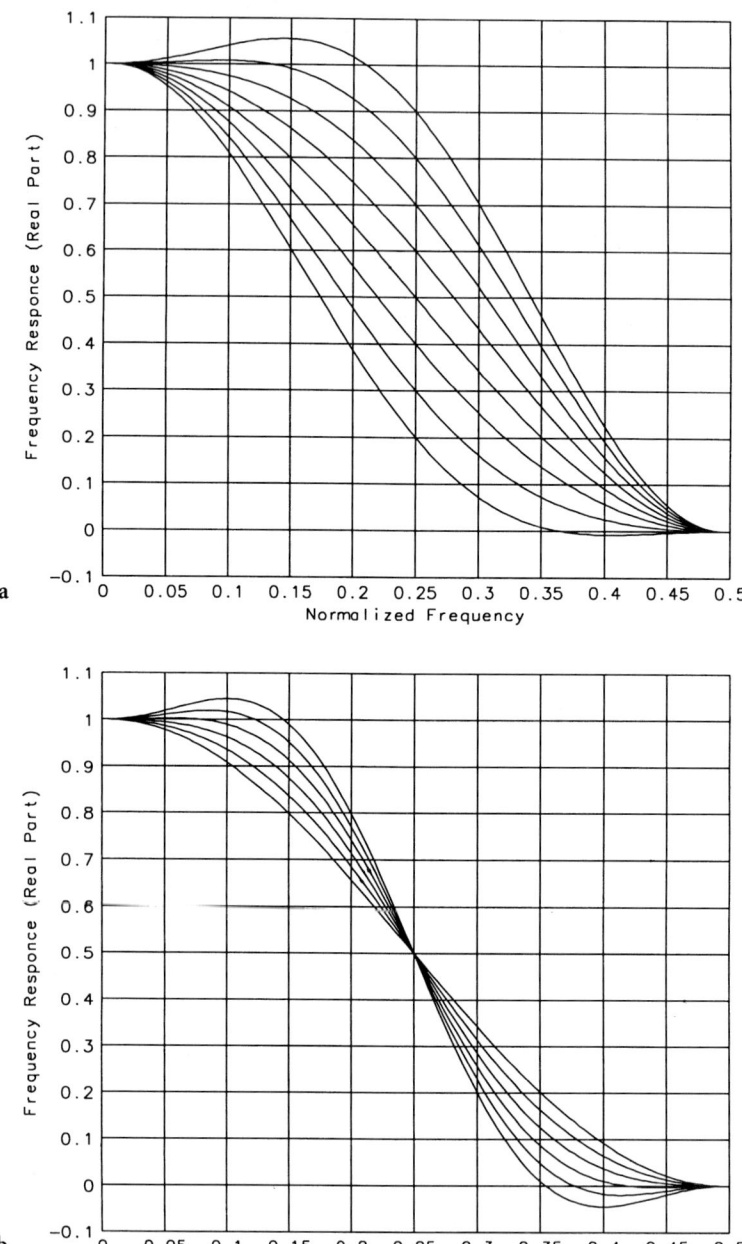

Fig. 1. Frequency responses of parametric filters for decimation **a** and interpolation **b**. Parameter ranges in 0.35 ÷ 0.7 left-to-right at steps of 0.05 **a**; in 0.5 ÷ 0.625 left-to-right in passband, step 0.025 **b**

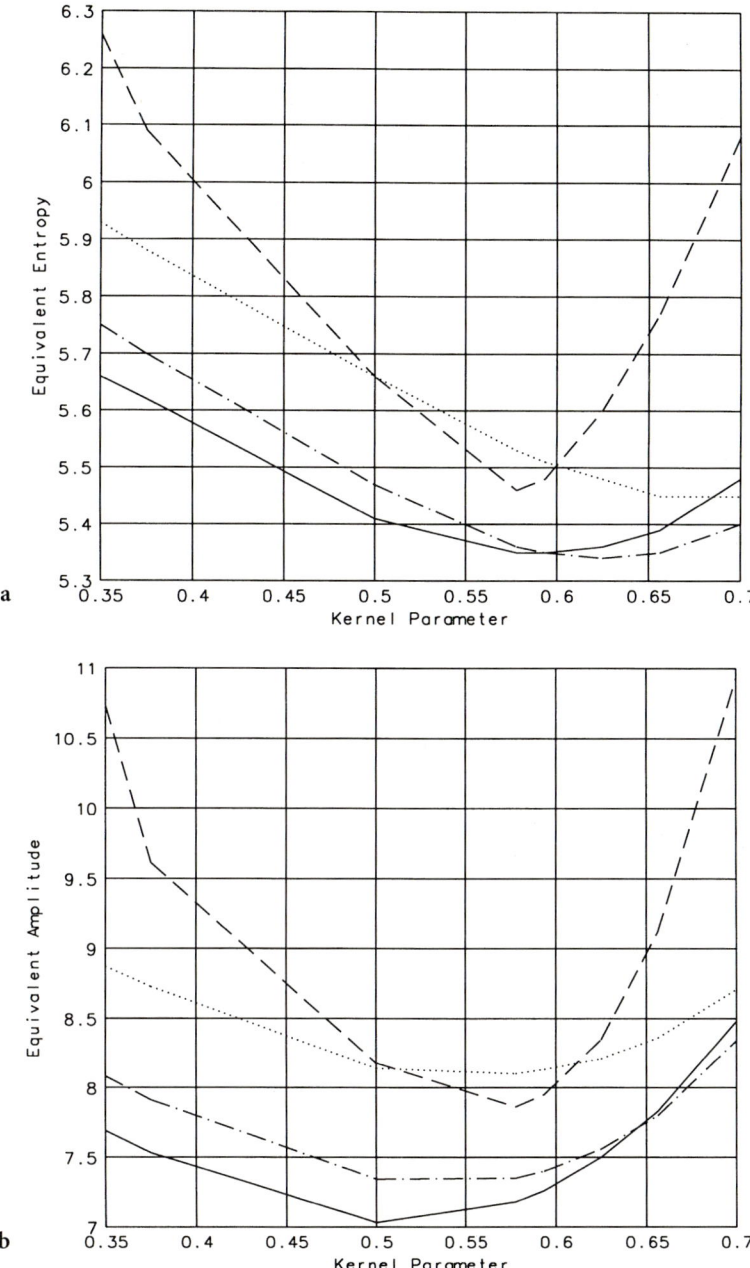

Fig. 2. Zero-order equivalent entropy **a** and equivalent amplitude **b** versus a, parameter of Burt's kernel used for reduction in all schemes (test image: *Lena*). Three curves correspond to different values of parameter b of the half-band kernel used for interpolation. Dotted line: $b = 0.5$; dashed-dotted: $b = 0.578125$; solid $b = 0.625$. The dashed line refers Burt & Adelson's LP: interpolation with same kernel and value of parameter a as for reduction

Table 1. Minimum equivalent entropy H_{eq} and amplitude σ_{eq} of Burt's LP and of enhanced pyramid (ELP), for several test images. H_0 stands for zero-order entropy of the original image

Image		Lena	Harbor	RX	NMR
H_0		7.45	6.76	6.71	6.49
H_{eq}	LP	5.45 a = 0.578125	6.70 a = 0.578125	2.03 a = 0.578125	6.06 a = 0.578125
	ELP	5.34 a = 0.625 b = 0.578125	6.67 a = 0.5 b = 0.625	1.81 a = 0.65625 b = 0.578125	5.98 a = 0.5625 b = 0.59375
σ_{eq}	LP	7.86 a = 0.578125	14.77 a = 0.578125	2.12 a = 0.578125	11.62 a = 0.578125
	ELP	7.02 a = 0.5 b = 0.625	14.58 a = 0.5 b = 0.625	1.99 a = 0.5 b = 0.625	10.32 a = 0.5 b = 0.625

energy does not correspond to optimum coding performance, as for LP; in fact, minimum energy is attained for $a = 0.5$, resulting in filters both *half-band* (see Fig. 1), while minimum entropy is for $a = 0.625$. Both H_{eq} and σ_{eq} are minimized by the same value $a = 0.578125$, when a single parameter may be tuned, as for LP (Burt 1983). Instead, for ELP, the minimum H_{eq} may occur for *a* ranging in $0.5 \div 0.65625$, and *b* in $0.578125 \div 0.625$: as a general rule, the frequency response of the two cascaded filters should be as flat as possible, as frequency approaches the DC; also the optimum value of *a* increases with the spatial correlation of the input image. A notable case is for *Harbor*, where the best reduction filter is *half-band* as well ($a = 0.5$); in this case, the reduction kernel has its minimum length (*3 nonzero* coefficients) to cope with the extreme nonstationarity of the image field. Minimum σ_{eq} of ELP is always attained with filters both *half-band*. Kernels designed for minimum energy (Chin 1992) or approaches based on interpolation error (Denatale 1991) may fail in minimizing the entropy, which is the main requirement of lossless compression.

3 Encoding Algorithm

3.1 Basic Definitions

The fundamental scheme consists of transmitting the *T*th layer of the GP (root image) followed by the quantized and coded LP at layers from $T - 1$ to 0 (Burt 1983). To introduce a selection criterion for information to be coded, each layer of the LP is divided into adjacent sub-images of 2×2 *nodes* (pixels if $k = 0$), that are information atoms to be considered. With reference to Fig. 3, a quartet of nodes at layer k is taken to have one father node at layer $k + 1$, and each node of a quartet at layer $k > 0$ is regarded to be the father node of a 2×2 cluster at layer $k - 1$. In this way a quad-tree *hierarchy* is introduced in the context of LP, that enables the use of a *content-driven* split decision rule.

3.2 Content-Driven Split Decision Rule

Content-driven transmission, introduced for *quad-tree* structured grey-level images (Dreizen 1987), and by two of the authors (Mongatti 1989) in the framework of Laplacian pyramids, consists of multiple *breadth-first* scanning steps driven by multiple sets of thresholds, one for each pyramid level. The thresholds identify those parts of the LP that are most meaningful. On each 2×2 block an *activity* function is computed. If this measure is lower than the current threshold, the subimage is skipped; otherwise, interpolation errors (LP quartet) are considered for transmission. The basic principle is the same as in Recursive Block Coding (Farelle 1990), where, however, a two-source decomposition is considered, and the stationary part of the image is reconstructed by means of a bilinear interpolator.

In the former works (Mongatti 1989,1992; Baronti 1994) the activity function was actually computed only for *expandable* quartets (i.e., quartets whose ancestors had been split as well), skipping all the others; therefore, the content-driven feature prevented the error-free reconstruction capability. In this work *all* the quartets at any layer of the LP are checked for splitting from their father node, regardless their ancestors have been split as well, or not. Moreover, the present work features a *single-step* pyramid scanning, aiming more at the efficiency of lossless compression than at the full progressiveness.

A crucial point of the above outline is the choice of an efficient *information* measure. Several functions have been reviewed by two of the authors (Mongatti 1992). In the present work $E_k(i,j)$, activity function of node (i,j) at layer k, is defined as the *maximum absolute value* of four adjacent interpolation errors on the next lower layer.

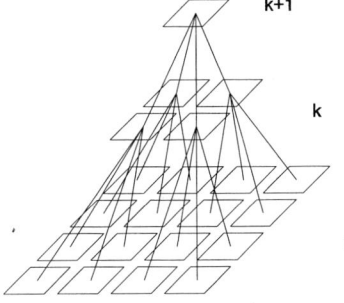

Fig. 3. Quad-tree hierarchy for content-driven pyramid split

$$E_k(i,j) \triangleq \max_{m,n=0,1} | L_{k-1}(2i+m, 2j+n) | \quad (6)$$

This choice represents a very simple yet efficient selection, both in terms of visual quality and objective errors (MSE). In fact, due to the inherent residual space correlation of the LP, four neighboring values are likely to be of similar magnitude; therefore, thresholding the maximum absolute value guarantees an efficient selection of the whole quartet.

3.3 Quantization and Error Feedback

Quantization is critical in pyramid schemes, because errors at higher layers can spread down over lower ones. Since differential schemes must ensure the predictor (or interpolator) to produce the same output both in compression and in reconstruction, quantization errors at upper layers must be *fed back* at lower ones. Hence, the actual LP to be encoded L_k^* is

$$L_k^*(i,j) = G_k(i,j) - \sum_{m=-M_2}^{M_2} \sum_{n=-N_2}^{N_2} W_2(m,n) G_{k+1}^* \left(\frac{i+m}{2}, \frac{j+n}{2} \right) \quad (7)$$

The term $G_{k+1}(.,.)$ in (2) has been replaced in (7) by $G_{k+1}^*(.,.)$, which recursively accounts for the quantization errors from the root down to layer $k + 1$. $G_k^*(.,.)$, reconstructed GP at layer $k < T$, is given by the sum of $L_k^*(.,.)$ rounded to an integer multiple of the quantization step Δ_k and the interpolated up-sampled G_{k+1}^*:

$$G_k^*(i,j) = \left\lfloor \frac{L_k^*(i,j) \pm \frac{\Delta_k}{2}}{\Delta_k} \right\rfloor \Delta_k + \sum_{m=-M_2}^{M_2} \sum_{n=-N_2}^{N_2} W_2(m,n) G_{k+1}^* \left(\frac{i+m}{2}, \frac{j+n}{2} \right) \quad (8)$$

This strategy has the effect of damping the propagation of errors due to quantization at upper layers and allows the control of the reconstruction error up to lossless performance by acting only on Δ_0. Moreover, the activity function (6) is computed on the actual LP (7), thus improving the efficiency of the *content-driven* decision rule.

In a practical implementation the values of G_k (1) and of the interpolated version of G^*_{k+1} (8) are rounded to integers and their differences L_k^* (7) are uniformly quantized with odd integer steps, roughly doubling for decreasing k to avoid accumulation of the reconstruction error in the lower spatial frequencies (Uz 1991). The uniform quantizer is known to minimize the entropy of the Laplacian source (Netravali 1988). The selection criterion based on thresholding the maximum absolute value of the LP (6) introduces a *dead-zone* in the quantizer, that decreases the entropy of the quantized source at the cost of a moderate additional distortion (Woods 1986). Quantization levels of split nodes are encoded through *Huffman* codes fitting the statistics of each pyramid layer.

The content-driven decision rule with fixed quantization of the retained quartets may be regarded as a *space-variant* quantization, in which the quartets to be skipped are quantized with so large steps that the quantized values are zero and the quantization errors are equal to the quartet itself. Therefore, also all the errors introduced by the *split/unsplit* decision rule can be recovered at lower pyramid layers, thus generalizing the mechanism of quantization error feedback also to content-driven schemes.

3.4 Coding of the Root Layer

As for the basic scheme, the $p \times q$ root level $\{G_T(i,j)\}$ is coded first. The optimal choice of T usually varies from an image to another. As a tendency, for a given image, increasing T decreases the mean correlation length of the root level image. However, due to *accumulation of aliasing* introduced by recursive low-pass filtering, the increase of T makes the LP to be extremely *energetic* at high layers; hence, it is suitable to keep T reasonably low and exploit the residual correlation of the root image by *spatial DPCM* encoding, also because progressiveness is of little use in the very early retrieval/transmission stages. Good results have been attained with a scheme using the values of four neighboring pixels for the causal prediction. $\hat{G}_T(i, j)$, predicted value at (i, j), is given by:

$$\hat{G}_T(i, j) = \alpha G_T(i-1, j-1) + \beta G_T(i-1, j) + \gamma G_T(i-1, j+1) + \delta G_T(i, j-1) \quad (9)$$

Optimal coefficients $\alpha, \beta, \gamma, \delta$ are found by minimizing the mean square prediction error:

$$E\{[G_T(i,j) - \hat{G}_T(i,j)]^2\} \simeq \frac{1}{p \times q} \sum_{i=0}^{p-1} \sum_{j=0}^{q-1} [G_T(i,j) - \hat{G}_T(i,j)]^2$$

where $E[.]$ is the expectation operator. The solution of this problem is well known in literature (Netravali 1988); for an *auto-regressive* (AR) model of the field it involves the inversion of a correlation matrix of size equal to the prediction length, 4×4 in this case. Nonzero prediction errors are Huffman coded as well, while the positions of their zero/nonzero values are *run-length* encoded in the same way described in Sect. 3.5.

The best choice of T for the above predictor, considering only 8-neighboring pixels, is the value for which the resulting root image exhibits a mean correlation length as close to unity as possible. Since the mean correlation length halves as k increases by one from 0 to T, T should be greater for more correlated (e.g., RX) and smaller for less correlated images (e.g., NMR), as experimentally verified. However, as T attains zero, the integrated scheme becomes a plain 2-D DPCM, thus losing its progressiveness feature.

3.5 Run-Length Encoding of the Split Quad-Tree

The introduction of a selective choice of the nodes to be split is effective in the coding scheme, but needs a synchronization overhead. Flag bits constitute a binary *quad-tree*, whose root corresponds to the *T*th layer, and whose bottom to the 1st layer of the LP. Each *one* marks the split of a pyramid node into the quartet of its sons, as outlined in Fig. 3.

However, a direct encoding of the *split-tree* is not efficient for the strong correlation existing within each of its layers, reflecting the features of the LP: contour positions and *active* regions are marked by clustered *ones*, homogeneous areas by gatherings of *zeroes*.

An easy way to exploit such correlation is to *run-length* encode the sequences of *zeroes* and *ones*. Each layer of the quad-tree is divided into square blocks; each block is *zig-zag* scanned to yield sequences of *zeroes* or *ones* (i.e., the *runs*), in case continuing inside the next block. This scan rule is more advantageous than the traditional *raster* scan, since it takes into account not only correlation along rows but also along columns: tests on RX images have shown that the average lengths of runs is optimal for *zig-zag* scan, with 8×8 block size.

Run lengths of *zeroes* and *ones* are separately coded with Laemmel (*A*) and Hasler (*B*) codes (Meyr 1974). These are more efficient than Huffman's for *run-lengths*, because for decoding they do not require the knowledge of the run length occurrences, whose number may be extremely large. A level by level check states which type of code is more suitable: while *the former* is efficient for short runs, *the latter* better fits longer ones. Also the optimal size of the code is chosen on a tree-level basis. With the integrated use of *A* and *B* codes the average coding length approaches the entropy of the run lengths (*first-order* Markov source), with a redundancy lower than 3% and very little additional information to be specified.

4 Coding Results

Results have been evaluated by considering the total bit-rate (BR) in bits per pixel, including side information like a header, occurrences of the quantized values at each LP layer for building Huffman codes, and sizes for *A* and *B* run-length codes. Distortion has been measured by means of the *Mean Square Error* (MSE), the *Peak Error* (PE), and the *Peak-to-Peak Signal-to-Noise Ratio* (PSNR). If $G_0(i,j)$ (zeroth layer of the GP) denotes the original image and $\hat{G}_0(i,j)$ its reconstructed version, then

$$MSE \triangleq \frac{1}{MN} \sum_{i=0}^{M-1} \sum_{j=0}^{N-1} [G_0(i,j) - \hat{G}_0(i,j)]^2$$

$$PE \triangleq \max_{i=0,M-1; j=0,N-1} |G_0(i,j) - \hat{G}_0(i,j)|$$

$$PSNR \triangleq 10\log_{10}\left(\frac{G_{fs}^2}{MSE}\right)$$

where G_{fs} denotes *full-scale*, namely 255 for *8-bit* images.

Figure 4a shows a 768 × 832 chest RX image, scanned at 60 *dpi* (dots-per-inch). Only the 8 *MSBs* have been selected for lossless compression as well as for display; the zero-order entropy of the image source is $H_0 = 6.71$ *bit/pel*. Figures 4b,c display reconstructions after applications of the proposed ELP scheme, ($a = 0.625$, $b = 0.578125$, $T = 4$, *content-driven* split and error feedback) at two different rates. Figure 4d portrays the result of *JPEG* scheme at the same rate as in Fig. 4b. Visual judgement confirms that significant features, like grey-level shades and textures, are preserved, while no appreciable artifacts are introduced in homogeneous regions. The compression performance of the tests of Fig. 4 (*lossless* case first) is quantitatively reported in Table 2.

Rate Distortion plots are drawn in Fig. 5 relatively to four different compression methods on the test RX image:

1) Burt's LP (with quantization error recovery);

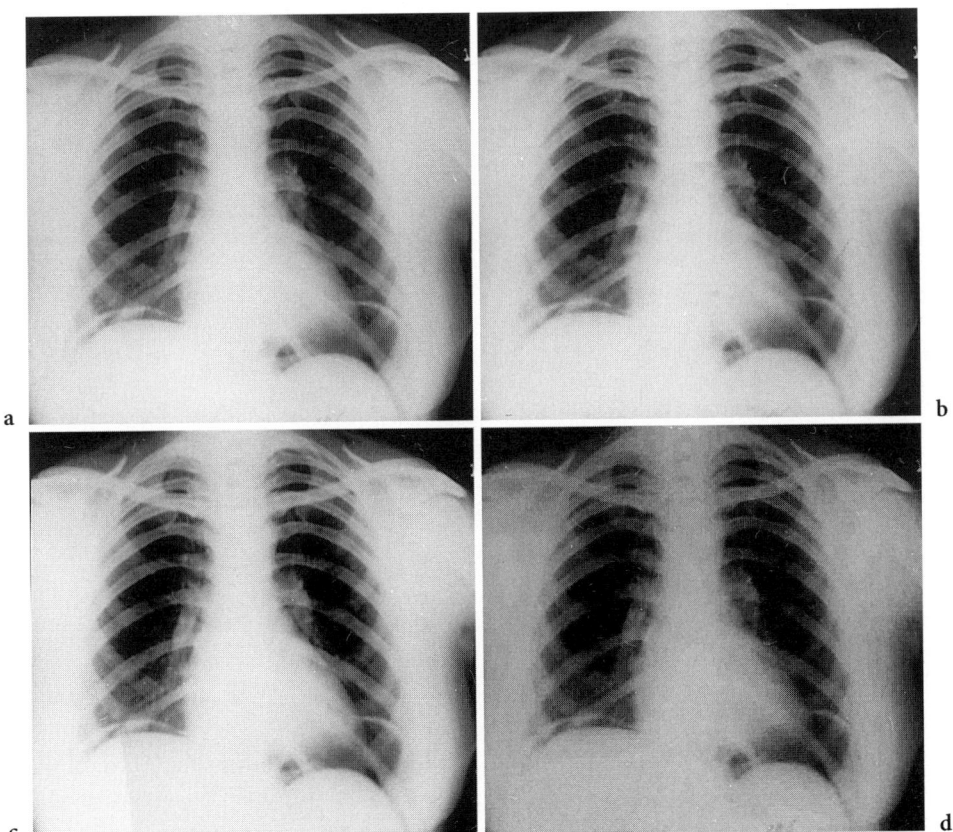

Fig. 4. Encoding results from original 8 bit/pel RX **a** of ELP scheme with Burt's kernel for reduction and half-band interpolator (a = 0.625, b = 0.578125), content-driven split and error feedback **b, c,** and JPEG **d**

Table 2. Bit-Rates and distoritons for the tests shown in Fig. 4

Fig. 4	BR(b/pel)	PE	MSE	PSNR(db)
a	1.65	0	0	∞
b	0.15	5	0.94	48.42
c	0.08	8	1.94	45.26
d	0.15	25	7.87	39.17

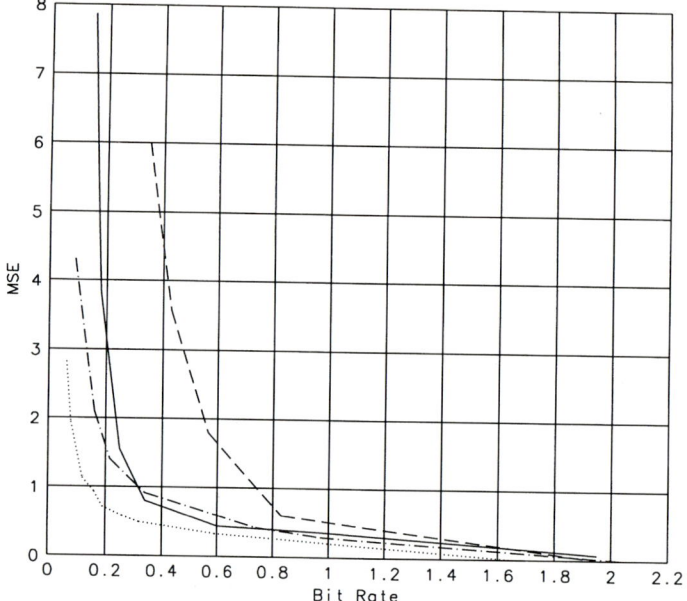

Fig. 5. Rate Distortion performance for test RX image: Burt's LP (*dashed-dotted line*); DPCM (*dashed line*); JPEG (*solid line*); ELP (*dotted line*)

2) DPCM with optimum AR predictor (9) and *run-length* coding of *zero/nonzero* errors;
3) JPEG;
4) Content-driven split of ELP (with feedback of both quantization and decision errors).

Due to the error feedback capability, lossless reconstruction is achieved by both the pyramidal schemes *1*) and *4*), by coarse quantization at upper layers and recovery of errors at the zeroth layer, by setting the quantization step Δ_0 to unity. Also DPCM is capable to attain reversible compression through a unitary step. On the contrary, JPEG cannot provide *error-free* results, as widely known. It appears that the pyramid scheme proposed in this paper (ELP) is more efficient than the classical LP with error feedback, as well as than DPCM and JPEG. Moreover, the MSE-BR performance of both the pyramid schemes is steady for low, medium and high rates, without critical points and cutoffs. The superiority of the novel pyramid scheme is stressed not only in terms of global (MSE, or equivalently PSNR) but also of local error (PE), which is kept reasonably low by the error feedback mechanism, also at extremely low BR. This trend is fully exposed in the plots of Fig. 6, in which PE of the reconstructed RX image is reported against BR.

The above improvements have been verified also for different test images, like the NMR mentioned in Table 1, a *256 × 256 8-bit/pel* T1 head section shown in Fig.

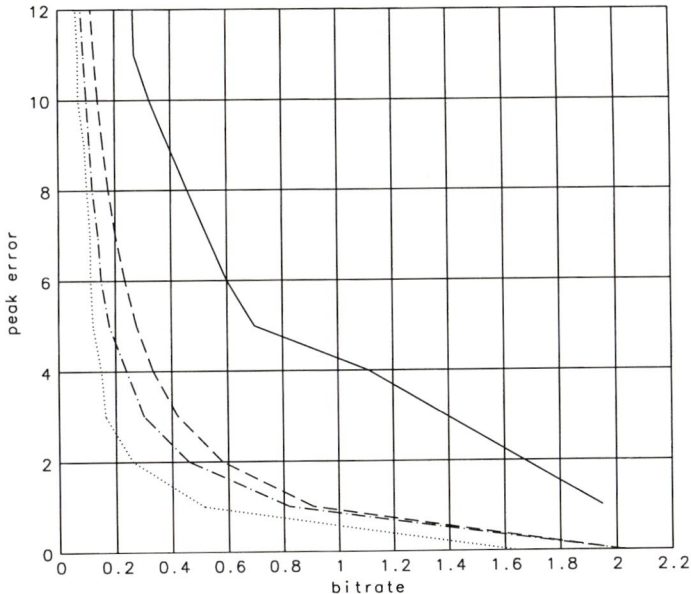

Fig. 6. Peak Error versus Bit Rate of compression schemes for test RX image; legends as for Fig. 5

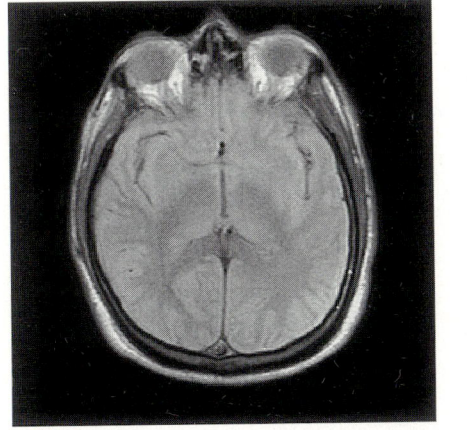
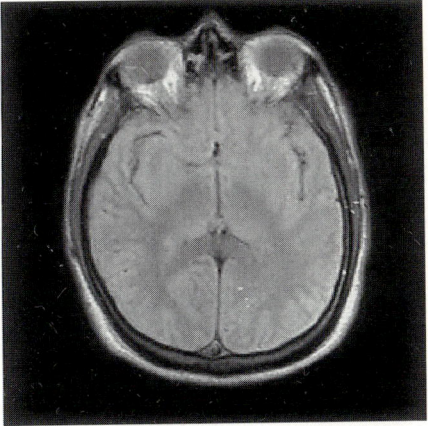

Fig. 7. Original 8 bit/pel NMR **a** reconstructed version after ELP compression (parameters for kernels a = 0.5625, b = 0.59375) at BR = 0.8 bit/pel, MSE = 20.22, PSNR = 35.07 dB, PE = 13

7a. A *semi-lossy* version is depicted in Fig. 7b at a compression ratio of about 10. Again, significant features, like contours and textures, are adequately preserved.

5 Conclusions

A novel encoding scheme has been proposed for reversible compression of medical images. It exploits an enhanced Laplacian pyramid (ELP) with entropy and energy lower than the classical LP, at comparable computational cost, by means of different *reduction* and *expansion* filters. The scheme features a *content-driven* decision rule based on a simple activity measure on 2×2 clusters of the ELP. Errors due both to quantization and to values skipped by the decision mechanism, are fed-back at lower pyramid levels. This strategy ensures the control of the maximum absolute reconstruction error up to full reversibility. Also robustness is improved to changes in numerical precision of kernel parameters and quantization steps. Synchronization of the quartet values is provided by a *quadtree* structure efficiently implemented on a layer basis through *run-length* encoding of *split/unsplit* nodes by means of *A* and *B* codes. Reversible results are superior to those of DPCM schemes, whereas lossy coding outperforms JPEG, as well as the classical pyramid scheme. Moreover, no *floating-point* computation is required and *real-time* compression/reconstruction is feasible on general-purpose computers.

Acknowledgements. The authors wish to gratefully acknowledge the valuable support of Dr. Franco Lotti and Dr. Andrea Casini of IROE – CNR in Florence, for careful revision of the manuscript and useful suggestions throughout the work.

References

Baronti S, Casini A, Lotti F, Alparone L (1994) Content-driven differential encoding of an enhanced image pyramid, Signal Processing: Image Communication, Vol. 6(5):463–469

Burt PJ (1981) Fast filter transforms for image processing, Computer Vision, Graphics, and Image Processing, Vol. 16:20–51

Burt PJ, Adelson EH (1983) The Laplacian Pyramid as a Compact Image Code, IEEE Communications, Vol. 31(4):532–540

Chen D, Bovik AC (1992) Hierarchical Visual Pattern Image Coding, IEEE Communications, Vol. 40(4):671–675

Chin F, Choi A, Luo Y (1992) Optimal Generating Kernels for Image Pyramids by Piecewise Fitting, IEEE Pattern Analysis Machine Intell., Vol. 14(12):1190–1198

Cosman PC, Tseng C, Gray RM, Olshen RA, Moses RE, Davidson HC, Bergin CJ, Riskin EA (1993) Tree Structured Vector Quantization of CT Chest Scans: Image Quality and Diagnostic Accuracy, IEEE Medical Imaging, Vol. 12(4):727–739

Crochiere RE, Rabiner LR (1983) Multirate Digital Signal Processing. Englewood Cliffs, NJ: Prentice-Hall

Denatale FGB, Desoli GS, Giusto DD (1991) Hierarchical Image Coding via MSE Minimizing Bilinear Approximation, Electronics Letters, Vol. 27(22): 2035–2037

Das M, Burgett, S (1993) Lossless Compression of Medical Images Using Two-Dimensional Multiplicative Autoregressive Models, IEEE Medical Images", Vol. 12(4):721–726

Dreizen HM (1987) Content-Driven Progressive Transmission of Grey-Scale Images, IEEE Communications, Vol. 35(3):289–296

Farelle PM (1990) Recursive Block Coding for Image Data Compression, Springer Verlag

Kuduvalli GR, Rangayyan RM (1992) Performance Analysis of Reversible Image Compression Techniques for High-Resolution Digital Teleradiology, IEEE Medical Imaging, Vol. 11(3):430–445

Marr D (1982) Vision, Freeman, New York

Meer P, Baugher ES, Rosenfeld A (1987) Frequency Domain Analysis and Synthesis of Image Pyramid Generating Kernels, IEEE Pattern Analysis Machine Intelligence, Vol. 9(4):512–522

Meyr H, Rosdolsky HG, Huang TS (1974) Optimum Run Length Codes, IEEE Communications, Vol. 22(6):826–835

Mongatti G, Alparone L, Baronti S (1989) Entropy Criterion for Progressive Laplacian Pyramid-Based Image Transmission, Electronics Letters, Vol. 25(7):450–451

Mongatti G, Alparone L, Benelli G, Baronti S, Lotti F, Casini A (1992) Progressive image transmission by content driven laplacian pyramid encoding, IEE Proceedings–I, Communications, Speech and Vision, Vol. 139(5):495–500

Nasrabadi NM, King RA (1988) Image Coding Using Vector Quantization: A Review, IEEE Communications, Vol. 36(8):957–971

Netravali AN, Haskell BG (1988) Digital Picture Representation and Compression, Plenum Press, New York

Ranganath S (1991) Image Filtering Using Multiresolution Representations, IEEE Pattern Analysis and Machine Intelligence, Vol. 13(5):426–440

Roger RE, Arnold JF (1994) Reversible Image Compression Bounded by Noise, IEEE Geoscience and Remote Sensing, Vol. 32(1):19–24

Sloan KR, Tanimoto SL (1979) Progressive Refinement of Raster Scan Images, IEEE Computers, Vol. 28(11):871–874

Unser M (1992) An improved least squares Laplacian pyramid for image compression, Signal Processing, Vol. 27(2):187–203

Uz KM, Vetterli M, LeGall DJ (1991) Interpolative Multiresolution Coding of Advanced Television with Compatible Subchannels. IEEE Trans. Circuits and Systems for Video Technology, Vol. 1(1):86–99

Wallace GK (1991) The JPEG still picture compression standard, Communications of ACM, Vol. 34(4):30–44

Wang L, Goldberg M (1991) Comparative Performance of Pyramid Data Structures for Progressive Image Transmission, IEEE Communications, Vol. 39(4):540–548

Woods JW, O'Neil SD (1986) Sub-band Coding of Images, IEEE Acoustic Speech and Signal Processing, Vol. 34(10):1278–1288

Video Compression for Multimedia Applications

A.A. Rodriguez, C.E. Fogg, and E.J. Delp

1 Introduction

Rapid continual advances in computer and network technologies coupled with the availability of high-volume data storage devices have effected the advent of multimedia applications in desktop computers, workstations, and consumer devices. Digital video data poses many challenges due to its inherent high bandwidth and storage requirements. For example, uncompressed 640 by 480 digital video (i.e., the screen size of typical desktop computers) at 30 frames-per-second (fps) in RGB24 color format requires a bandwidth approximately equal to 26.37 Megabytes/second (MB/sec), while HDTV requires a data rate larger than 1.5 Gigabits/second (uncompressed). These video data rates are prohibitive for transmission over networks like the Integrated Services Digital Network (ISDN) that will support bandwidths from approximately 64 Kilobits/sec (Kb/sec) to 1.920 Megabits/sec (Mb/sec) [1, 2]. They are also forbidden in desktop computers, some which have an *effective bandwidth* as low as 500 Kilobytes/second. Even high capacity storage devices, like CD-ROMs that can hold up to 650 MB of data, could only store a few seconds of uncompressed digital video. It is then apparent that in order to transmit, store, or display real-time digital video, some form of compression is necessary.

Although advances in video compression algorithm research have resulted in lower data rates with better preservation of image fidelity, as Rodriguez [3] pointed out, better video compression and better image fidelity are attained by performing more elaborate compression methods which typically result in higher computational complexity. As systems continue to attain increased performance levels, real-time digital video decompression and playback, and in some cases capture and encoding, have become feasible to reduce these gargantuan data rates and storage requirements.

The goal of video compression, or *video coding* as it is often referred, is to represent digital video data with as few bits as possible while simultaneously attempting to preserve the original video data fidelity. Consequently, most video compression schemes are typically *lossy* rather than *lossless*. Lossless data compression methods guarantee the exact numerical representation of the original data when the compressed data is reconstructed. On the other hand, the objective of lossy video compression schemes is to obtain higher compression by sacrificing the reproduction of the exact numerical representation without introducing noticeable degradation in the reconstructed, decoded video data. Lossless methods, such as variable-length coding methods like Huffman encoding [4], Lempel-Ziv Welch coding [5], and arithmetic coding [6, 7], are based on information theoretic approaches and tend to compress data to about half the original data rate. They are more appropriate for text compression and for compression of images (or video) in some biomedical applications, where the data must be kept intact. However, lossless compression methods often serve as one (or more) of the components of lossy video compression methods. In particular, variable-length coding is often used as the last step in hybrid video compression schemes.

At a high level, video coding can be categorized as a two-step process: *source coding and entropy coding*. Source coding is a lossy compression scheme that typically consists of two sequential steps:

1. a transformation that results in a reduction of information redundancy, or a data representation that can be compressed more efficiently, and
2. quantization.

Source coding maps digitized video frames (i.e., images) to a set of *codewords*, often referred to as *messages* or *tokens*. This mapping can be chosen in a wide variety of ways; however, it must be chosen so that the codewords form a reasonable approximation of the original video data to reduce visually apparent degradations.

The second step of the compression process, entropy coding, is a lossless process that exploits the statistical properties of the codewords to reduce redundancy and hence the data rate. This is typically a variable-length coding method such as Huffman coding [4], Lempel-Ziv Welch coding [5], or arithmetic coding [6, 7], that strives towards the information theoretic entropy of the quantized codewords.

Source coding can be further categorized as *intraframe* or *interframe* coding. *Intraframe* compression is the process of removing the spatial data redundancy of a frame independent of other frames. Typically, it is used to compress the first frame of a sequence of video frames and frames where a scene change occurs. *Interframe* compression is the process of removing data redundancy in the temporal domain – where possible, it exploits data redundancy in a frame relative to the data in one or more other frames in the sequence of video frames. Interframe compression methods typically employ an intraframe compression scheme in those areas of the frame where it is not feasible to use interframe compression.

A video compression method that analyzes and compresses data by considering how the human visual system perceives the video information, and not necessarily by the actual numerical representation of the data, is said to exploit *data irrelevancy* as well as data redundancy. Commonly, this is incorporated in the quantization process.

Any intraframe compression method can be broadly classified as being either statistically-based (algebraic) or symbolically-based (structural) [8, 9]. The statistical approach to intraframe compression is based on information theoretic principles and the methods used usually involve very localized, pixel-oriented features of video frames. Symbolically-based intraframe compression methods employ computer vision and image understanding techniques and human visual system properties to achieve very low data rates. Hence, they exploit data irrelevancy. The geometric structure of the image scene is emphasized in symbolically-based compression methods, as opposed to the algebraic structure of the pixels used by statistically-based compression methods. Due to their high computational complexity, symbolically-based video compression methods are impractical for multimedia applications and thus are not covered further in this chapter.

Digital video in desktop computers currently consists of two categories of video codecs (compressor/decompressors). The first category consists of video coding algorithms that exhibit low complexity for playback and therefore produce compressed video streams that can be decoded and displayed in desktop computers without special hardware assistance – the computer's CPU performs all of the decompression and display tasks. This set of video codec algorithms is typically referred to as *algorithms amenable for software-only video playback*, or *software-only video codecs*. The side effect of low playback complexity algorithms is that they tend to exhibit limited image quality. The second category of video codecs in desktop computers is typically referred to as *hardware-assisted video codecs*. As the video coding algorithm described by the Moving Pictures Expert Group (MPEG) [10, 11], hardware-assisted codecs are capable of providing a substantial increase in image quality, and in coding and playback performance, in comparison to software-only video codecs.

Figure 1 depicts the *image quality* versus *playback complexity* space spanned by the two sets of video codecs. Notice that software-only video codecs are within incremental quality of each other. An imaginary horizontal line above the domain spanned by the software-only video codecs reminisces the limited quality they provide. Likewise, an imaginary vertical line to the left of the domain of hardware-assisted codecs, indicates that these algorithms are too complex for software-only playback in today's desktop computers.

Software-only video codecs today are capable of decoding and displaying compressed video streams containing frames of size equal to 320 by 240 (or larger), at 15 (or greater) frames-per-second (fps), on desktop computers with a 486 or 68040 CPU running at 33 MHz. Video playback performance will improve in the

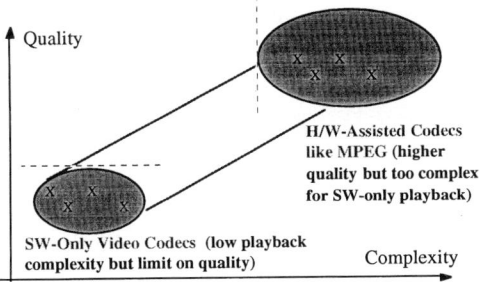

Fig. 1. The two categories of video codecs for desktop computers span different image quality and playback complexity domains

future with the introduction of more powerful CPUs, wider data buses (i.e., 64-bit data buses), 64-bit operating systems, local video buses, and additional cache memory. As computer technologies continue to advance, the general computational capabilities of desktop computers will project into the current playback complexity domain occupied by high-quality codecs, thereby rendering today's hardware-assisted codecs to become amenable for software-only playback in the future.

Hardware-assisted video codecs are desirable in multimedia applications that require higher quality video and better coding or playback performance (e.g., 30 fps). As VLSI chips reach one million transistors at speeds of up to 50 MHz in 0.5 micron technology, coding of digital video into narrow bandwidths have become economically viable and preferable to traditional analog means of video storage and delivery. In 1988, a group of international companies and academic institutions, under the auspices of the International Organization for Standardization (ISO), agreed to develop a digital video and associated audio standard to foster interoperability and avert a potentially disastrous format incompatibility war. This standard, which is known as MPEG (Moving Pictures Expert Group), addresses digital video compression [11], associated audio compression [12], and system-level functions like synchronization of audio and video, multiplexing, clock recovery, and guaranteed buffer behavior [13]. As a result of this effort, the MPEG syntax has become the de facto standard for consumer distribution of digital video over satellite, HDTV terrestrial broadcasts, cable TV, and compact discs intended for consumer devices.

MPEG has evolved over two phases: MPEG-1 which was officially released as a standard for video, audio, and systems in 1993 for an aggregate bit rate of about 1.5 Mbits/sec, and MPEG-2 for a broader scope of applications ranging from 1 Mbits/sec to 100 Mbits/sec. MPEG-2 [82] reached Committee Draft status in November 1993 and was projected to reach the International Standard status by the end of 1994. Work on a new MPEG initiative, MPEG-4, for very low bit rate coding of audiovisual programs to enable a new spectrum of applications, including interactive mobile multimedia communications, began in late 1993. MPEG-4 will require the development and validation of new algorithmic techniques and its draft specification is projected for 1997.

In this chapter, we describe algorithms and techniques commonly used in both video compression categories that are suitable for multimedia applications. For hardware-assisted video codecs we have opted to describe MPEG since it is destined to become the video codec of choice for years to come due to that it is a standard which is widely endorsed and to its significant momentum in the multimedia community. The focus of the chapter is on presenting how these methods work, referencing the theory when appropriate. We believe this complies with much of the attention that Multimedia Computing has received in every realm of computer engineering and science, where the emphasis is on making algorithms perform real-time. Hence, this chapter serves as a technology transfer conduit to computer engineering students and practitioners, whom with adequate programming skills should be able to implement the methods described herein.

In Sect. 2, we examine the general issues of assessing video codecs for multimedia applications, namely: image fidelity (i.e., quality), bandwidth (i.e., compression), ease-of-decoding (i.e., playback performance), memory consumption, compression to decompression asymmetry, scalability, and delay. We discuss the tradeoffs among these variables, quantitative distortion measures, and suggest rules for subjective quality evaluations. Section 3 covers software-only video codecs. We describe the significance of simplifying the complexity of color conversion operations, and present frame-differencing methods typically employed in software-only video codecs and intraframe compression techniques that exhibit low computational complexity for software-only video playback. In Sect. 3, we also discuss the bandwidth that Motion JPEG and MPEG would provide in a byte-oriented video stream. Section 4 presents video codec approaches for multimedia applications, including MPEG video, that are more likely to be implemented with hardware assistance due to their higher computational complexity. Finally, Sect. 5 contains a summary and conclusions.

2 Assessment of Video Codecs for Multimedia Applications

In this section we discuss the set of characteristics that must be considered in the selection of a video codec for a multimedia application and the tradeoffs among these characteristics. The issue of evaluating the image quality that video codecs produce is described by discussing quantitative image distortion measures and by suggesting rules for subjective image quality evaluations. Other video compression issues that are of importance but not addressed in this chapter, include coding algorithm complexity and susceptibility of coding techniques to transmission channel errors.

2.1 Video Codec Characteristics

All video codec algorithms exhibit a set of characteristics by which they can be assessed. Traditionally, video codec algorithms are judged by the image quality they produce when video content is compressed to a required bandwidth (i.e., data rate). Hence, two of the characteristics of video codecs are *image fidelity* (i.e., image quality) and *compressed bandwidth*. However, in multimedia applications a major part of the emphasis is on attaining real-time video performance. Thus, other characteristics of a video codec must be considered. For instance, software-only video codecs must have low decompression numerical complexity to provide good playback performance. Hence, the most crucial aspect of a software-only video codec is its *ease-of-decoding* characteristic (i.e., the ease of decompressing the compressed video stream). In practice, ease-of-decoding is typically measured by the frame rate and frame resolution that a software-only video codec can attain in a typical desktop computer.

An aspect of video codecs that contributes to ease-of-decoding is the average number of *color conversion* operations required. As discussed in Sect. 3, some video codecs inherently require less number of color conversion operations than others.

Memory consumption is another important characteristic of video codecs. Software-only video codecs are expected to execute in many existing desktop computers that have a limited amount of RAM. Hardware-assisted codecs often run on DSP's that have limited instruction RAM and data RAM. Whereas non-real-time capture and compression of digitized video could potentially rely on storage devices as a repository for interim computations and results, the real-time decompression and display process must execute within the bounds of the available RAM. Furthermore, video playback may be desirable for hand-held computer devices (e.g., personal digital assistants) and consumer devices (e.g., CD-ROM players) that have limited amount of memory. Memory consumption is measured by summing the number of bytes consumed by:

1. the *footprint* (i.e., the number of bytes consumed in the decompressor executable),
2. lookup tables (e.g., quantization tables or codebooks, or lookup tables used for color conversion and thus dependent on the native display format of the computer), and
3. working buffers (e.g., frame-differencing, described in Sect. 3, may require that one or more previous reconstructed frames be stored in memory).

A video codec is also characterized by its *compression to decompression asymmetry*. Formally, this means the amount of time it takes to compress an N number of frames rersus the time it takes to decompress them with the same computing resources. However, in practice the real measures are the time it takes to compress a single frame in software and whether real-time capture and compression can be performed with low-cost hardware.

A highly desirable feature for video codecs is *intrinsic algorithm scalability*. In the context of software-only video codec algorithms, scalability is often a misused term in the desktop computer industry. The misconception is that the capabilities provided by *scalable hardware* and the process of *frame dropping* are often associated with the video codec algorithm and consequently the video codec is deemed as a scalable one. However, special hardware that can scale a frame to any size (e.g., by using bilinear interpolation circuitry) or perform color conversions, can provide the same capabilities to all software-only video codec algorithms. Hence, it is the special hardware that provides the scalability aspect rather than the video codec algorithm. Likewise, any software-only video decoder can be implemented so that frames can be dropped when it cannot attain its target playback rate, and to provide playback of video at lower frame rates in desktop computers with lesser computational capabilities. Intrinsic scalability signifies that the video codec algorithm compresses the video in multiple frame resolutions, multiple sets of frequency bands, or multiple representations of pixel color depth, and that this information is organized in the compressed video stream in a hierarchical fashion. Ideally, the compressed video stream produced by an intrinsically scalable video codec can be decompressed and displayed in a range of different computers at different quality levels and/or frame rates. The more computational power the computer has, the more information that can be decompressed from the hierarchically organized video data, and consequently the more fine detail that can be added to obtain better image quality, and the more that the frame resolution of the original video can be approached.

Scalable video codecs are often based on subband coding methods [19, 20], wavelets [21–23, 67, 68], or pyramids [24, 66]. The video codec approach described by Taubman and Zakhor [20] could be considered as an coding method that uses multiple representations of pixel color depth. Specifically, they use a sequence of quantization layers, each representing progressively finer quantization step sizes.

Delay is another important characteristic to consider when evaluating video codecs. Multimedia applications such as video conferencing must exhibit minimal latency. It can also be very annoying to the user of a multimedia application if he or she has to experience considerable delay (e.g., more than half a second) when the video player is first launched. With software-only video codecs, such delay could be due to the computation of lookup tables that are used during playback to perform color conversion.

In summary, the characteristics of video codecs that must be considered for multimedia applications are:

1. image fidelity (or image quality),
2. bandwidth (or data rate),
3. ease-of-decoding,
4. memory consumption,
5. compression to decompression time asymmetry,
6. intrinsic scalability, and
7. delay.

2.2 Tradeoffs Between Characteristics

There are many tradeoffs among the characteristics of video codecs. As a rule, the *quality versus bandwidth* tradeoff dictates that the more compression that a video codec attains, the greater the likelihood of degrading the image quality. Better video compression and better image fidelity can always be attained by performing more elaborate compression methods (e.g., image analysis) which typically result in higher computational complexity. Except for vector quantization methods, increasing the compression complexity typically results in an increase of the decompression complexity. Consequently, *asymmetry* and/or *ease-of-decoding* are being compromised for *image fidelity* and/or *bandwidth*. Numerical computations can always be implemented with lookup tables thus *memory consumption* can be traded for *ease-of-decoding*. Further compression can be obtained by exploiting data redundancy in one or more frames. For instance, in MPEG [10, 11], the bi-directional frames (i.e., B frames) depend on a previous frame and a future frame that must be stored in RAM in order to decompress the B frame. Although this is not a complete list of all the potential tradeoffs that exist for characteristics of video codecs, it serves to exemplify the idea that when any video codec gains on any particular front, one or more of the other characteristics are being likely compromised.

2.3 Quantitative Video Distortion Measures

A common practice in development and assessment of video codec algorithms is to employ quantitative distortion measures. Ideally, a quantitative distortion measure should model human judgment of video distortion. The development of such a measure is not easy since it is usually very difficult to derive an analytical expression that quantifies degradation of important video characteristics, both in the spatial and temporal domain. This difficulty in quantifying the distortion of important video characteristics has led to the use of traditional mathematical measures of image distortion. The specific method used to measure the distortion in reconstructed video can vary greatly, depending on the application. However, this distortion measure is necessarily a function of the comparison of each original frame and its corresponding reconstructed, decompressed frame in the video sequence. For example, in some applications, such as *whiteboard videoconferencing* where the video consists of inscriptions on a white background, edges in the frames may be very important. In such cases it is vital that edges be unaffected by the coding and decoding process. Hence, the image distortion measure used to evaluate coding schemes for such applications should weigh heavily the accuracy of the edges in the decoded frames. The image features that are important for a given application should be reflected in the image distortion measure used to evaluate video coding schemes for that application. In other applications, such as *videophone*, where a talking head with a stationary background is typically transmitted, it is more significant to assess distortions according to their spatial location relative to the overall frame than by their local image features. In such cases, it is assumed that a talking head is centered on the video picture and that the most important information in the video, such as movements of lips and changes in facial expressions, will occur towards the center of the picture. Consequently, distortions should be penalized greater towards the center of the frame than towards its periphery.

One frequently used measure is the mean-square error (MSE) of the luminance between each original frame, I, and its corresponding reconstructed frame, D:

$$MSE = \frac{1}{N} \sum_{y=1}^{Y_s} \sum_{x=1}^{X_s} [D(x,y) - I(x,y)]^2 \qquad (1)$$

where the size of the frame is Y_s by X_s, and $N = Y_s X_s$. The MSE is often normalized by the variance of the original frame:

$$NMSE = \frac{MSE}{\sigma_I^2} \qquad (2)$$

or by the square of its dynamic range:

$$PMSE = \frac{MSE}{(I_{max} - I_{min})^2} \qquad (3)$$

In comparison and analysis of video codec algorithms, these measures are typically expressed as signal-to-noise ratios at different data rates. Signal-to-noise ratios can be computed in decibels (dB) by:

$$SNR = -10 \log_{10}(measure) \quad (dB) \qquad (4)$$

Although these methods do not typically correlate well with human judgment of picture fidelity, they serve a purpose in the fine tuning of video (or image) compression algorithms.

Luminance image data should be non-linearly transformed prior to computing the above measures to simulate the logarithmic sensitivity of the Human Visual System. Color image distortion can be quantified by measuring the mean Euclidean distance between each pixel in the original frame and its corresponding pixel in the reconstructed frame when expressed in their CIE L*u*v* color space representation [25].

Additional examples of mathematical image distortion measures can be found in [26]. As stated above, traditional distortion measures are often modified in simple ways that take into account the application or reflect an assumed Human Visual System model [27, 28]. However the Human Visual System is very complex, and the visibility of distortion in video is a function of many variables. For example, it is a function of the nature of the distortion itself, the image intensity in a space-time neighborhood of the distortion, the ambient illumination, and the *busyness* of the image in a space-time neighborhood of the distortion. If more than one distortion is introduced into the video, as is usually the case, the interplay of these multiple distortions can be very complicated. The complexity of the Human Visual System makes the incorporation of its characteristics into video compression algorithms difficult. A major shortcoming of traditional mathematical measures of image quality is that they are applied to the individual pixels of the image. Few pixel-wise mathematical image quality measures have consistently high correlation with human judgment of image quality. Measures that correlate well with human judgment of image quality need to be more globally-based [29]. Examples of image distortion measures tailored to the requirements of a human observer are found in [30] and [28]. Examples of various other image distortion measures are found in [31–33]. Measures that attempt to incorporate the Human Visual System's response to temporal frequencies (i.e., video) are discussed in [29] and [34].

2.4 General Rules for Subjective Evaluation of Video Quality

The lack of a widely accepted and reliable image fidelity metric that correlates well with subjective assessment of video quality often causes the method of choice to become a subjective evaluation of image fidelity. Obviously, a video codec can be fine-tuned by comparing the image fidelity of the produced decompressed video to the original video content. The image fidelity of multiple video codecs can be compared by compressing sample video clips that contain varied information to approximately the same bandwidth and comparing their produced results visually. Sample video clips for evaluation purposes should consist of *high-action* digitized movies that contain a significant number of scene changes, and scenes that exhibit camera panning and zoom. In addition, such video clips should exhibit variations in colors, multiple types of regions or objects (e.g., different textured and homogeneous regions), and varied illumination.

Since it is often desirable to compare the characteristics exhibited by the candidate video codecs for a multimedia application, exercising a fair comparison requires that video clips relegated for evaluation purposes be compressed to approximately the same bandwidth by the candidate video codecs, and then decompressed and displayed on the same computer under the same operating conditions, and assessed under the same viewing conditions. A common mistake is to assess the ease-of-decoding of different software-only video codecs based on the software-only playback performance attained in similar computers (e.g., same host CPU and CPU clock) and/or "same brand" desktop computers. However, playback performance is affected by many of the components and subsystems of a desktop computer, and the operating environment. In particular, playback performance is dependent on:

1. The *storage device* of the desktop computer. Different storage devices have:
   A. Different bandwidth and different cache and/or buffer architectures.
   B. Not all storage devices are DMA enabled.
   C. Different storage devices have different sustained read rates; even two storage devices that were manufactured to the same specifications may exhibit natural variabilities within the acceptable manufactured tolerance.
2. The *data bus* of the desktop computer – different desktop computers could have 16-, 32-, or 64-bit wide data buses.
3. Operating System – some operating systems perform 16-, 32-, or 64-bit data transfers, regardless of whether the internal data bus of the desktop computer is wider.

4. *Video hardware architecture* – some desktop computers have a local "video" bus that is physically dedicated to handle all of the data traffic from and to the video RAM. Consequently, a software-only video codec can write decompressed data to the video RAM without having to contend with other data traffic on the data bus (e.g., the transfer of compressed data from the storage device to system RAM). In addition, some video architectures have bus mastering capabilities and function support, like color conversion and frame scaling, which alleviate some of the tasks required for video playback.

Subjective evaluations and comparisons of image fidelity are often laborious but without a dependable metric, algorithm designers and product competitors resort to their visual sensation to form an independent, but perhaps biased, opinion. In addition to the factors discussed above, unbiased visual evaluations and comparisons require that a significant number of unbiased subjects rate the video at the same viewing distance under the same ambient illumination and display settings (i.e., contrast and brightness settings).

All conditions being equal, a subjective evaluation of video codecs should result in quantifying the *distortion threshold*, or equivalently, the *quality saturation*, of each candidate video codec. Video compression methods usually attain lower data rates at the risk of introducing perceptual artifacts or distortion. Many compression algorithms can be tweaked to the point where further compression results in noticeable distortions. Whereas the range of values of the parameters of a video codec prior to the *distortion threshold* does not tend to produce discernible visual distortions, the produced data rate is not optimal until immediately prior to this point. Hence, decompressed video can be considered to be perceptually lossless in that an observer will not notice appreciable distortion when the original data is compressed to a data rate higher than its *distortion threshold*. However, the *distortion threshold* is dependent on the video content and thus will vary for video clips that are representative of different applications.

Netravali and Limb [35] discussed formalization of subjective image evaluation by human viewers. There are two basic types of subjective evaluations: rating-scale methods and comparison methods. In the rating-scale method, the subject views a sequence of images and assigns each image a qualitative judgment such as *good*, *fair*, or *poor*. The rating scale may also take a form of an impairment scale such as *imperceptible*, *slightly annoying*, or *very annoying*. In the comparison method, the subject compares the distorted image to a reference image and judges the distorted image using a scale that ranges from *much better* to *same* to *worse*. The comparison method can also be implemented by allowing the subject to add impairment of a standard type to a reference image until the reference image is judged to be of the same quality as the distorted image. As mentioned above, there are various factors that affect the perceived image quality when performing subjective video evaluation, such as ambient illumination, viewing distance, and viewer fatigue. These factors have been investigated and some standardization has taken place for the subjective assessment of image quality [36]. An example of an experiment involving subjective evaluation of images distorted by the coding-decoding process is found in [27].

More recently, Apteker et al. [37] investigated subjective video quality in the context of a multimedia environment. Viewer acceptance of multimedia, such as clarity and interpretation of audio, continuity of visual messages, synchronization, and the general relationship between visual and auditory components were studied under classification of temporality, and visual and auditory message contents.

3 Algorithms Amenable for Software-Only Playback

Software-only video codecs were born from efforts to provide video playback in existing desktop computers. They have evolved by modifying and tailoring existing compression methodologies to suit video playback in desktop computers. The most crucial requirement that a software-only video codec must satisfy is high *ease-of-decoding* (i.e., low computational complexity of decompressing the compressed video stream and displaying the decompressed video data). To attain high ease-of-decoding, most software-only algorithms are designed to comply to a *byte-oriented* video stream syntax rather than the typical compressed bit stream definitions employed for compression and transmission of video over a channel. This simplifies the decompression task since CPU's are typically architected for manipulating data in a multiplicity of bytes (i.e., 2^n bytes, where n = 0, 1, 2, 3). A byte-oriented video stream definition thus typically prohibits the employment of a lossless variable-length coding method at the tail end of a software-only video compression method.

Generally, software-only video codecs sustain some degree of playback performance degradation when fully integrated to a desktop computer's multimedia software environment (e.g., Kaleida's ScriptX, Apple's Quicktime, or IBM's OS/2 Multimedia Presentation Manager). This however is valuable since the multimedia software environment in return provides various functionalities and services like: the user interface, the data streaming and parsing mechanism, the synchronization mechanism, color conversion and dithering, window scaling and clipping, and under certain conditions, it assumes responsibility for transferring the decoded video data from system RAM to the video RAM. Hence, the multimedia software environment provides the support that makes a usable product out of a video codec technology.

Typically, playback of compressed video can be categorized into three primary tasks:

1. The actual decoding of the compressed video stream,
2. Color conversion, and
3. The transfer of decoded and color converted video data from system RAM to video RAM. (This is usually referred to as *blitting data to the video display buffer*)

Digital video data is typically represented in a YUV color format for compression objectives. The YUV color format results in a more compact representation of color data as a result of the Human Visual System's lesser acuity for spatial variation of color than for luminance. Consequently, YUV data must be converted to the native display format of the desktop computer (e.g., RGB color space) before transferring decompressed frames to the video display buffer. Since YUV to RGB color conversion requires multiplies and adds, lookup tables are often employed to perform color conversion operations and therefore enhance playback performance. One such method for converting *YCrCb* to RGB is described in the U.S. Patent by Rodriguez et al. [38]. The *YCrCb* color format, used in MPEG video [10, 11] and often in JPEG [52, 71], can be converted to RGB format using the following equations:

$$R = MIN[255, MAX[0, Y + 1.402(C_r - 128)]] \tag{5}$$

$$G = MIN[255, MAX[0, (Y - 0.714(C_r - 128) - 0.344(C_b - 128))]] \tag{6}$$

$$B = MIN[255, MAX[0, Y + 1.772(C_b - 128)]] \tag{7}$$

where 8-bit values are assumed. Use of these equations requires six comparisons, four multiplies, and six adds per color conversion operation. However, we note that the *R* and *B* components depend on two of the *YCrCb* components and *G* depends on all three components. If each component of *YCrCb* is expressed as an 8-bit value, then two 16-bit addresses could be composed by concatenating *Y* with *Cr* and *Y* with *Cb* to obtain the *R* and *B* components, repectively, from two independent 64 KB lookup tables. The values stored in the lookup tables are computed a priori. The *G* component would require composition of a 24-bit address to obtain its value from a 16 MB lookup table. The total RAM consumption for obtaining the three RGB components would then be 16.25 MB which is excessive in most desktop computers where 4 MB of RAM is common. Rodriguez et al. [38] proposed that equation (6) be decomposed into two green components, one a function of *Y* and *Cr*, and the other a function of *Y* and *Cb*:

$$G = G_0(Y, C_r) + G_1(Y, C_b) \tag{8}$$

Each color conversion operation then only requires the composition of two addresses for retrieving information from two lookup tables. Each of the two lookup tables is loaded a priori with 16-bit wide information: the first table with the 8-bit *R* component next to the 8-bit value of G_0, and the second table with the 8-bit value of G_1 next to the 8-bit *B* component. However, composing 16-bit addresses would then require a total of 256 KB of storage for the two 16-bit wide lookup tables. This is still unacceptable in many multimedia applications. Moreover, the dynamic range of neither G_0 or G_1 is likely to fit in an 8-bit value. For instance, consider the following equations to compute G_0 and G_1:

$$G_0 = 0.5Y - 0.714(C_r - 128) \tag{9}$$

$$G_1 = 0.5Y - 0.344(C_b - 128) \tag{10}$$

The dynamic range of G_0 is approximately (–91, 219); for G_1 it is (–44, 172). Without appreciable color loss, the seven most significant bits of each *YCrCb* component can be used to reduce the amount of memory consumed for the lookup tables to 64 KB and to represent the dynamic range of G_0 and G_1 with two's complement 8-bit values. If the six most significant bits of each component are used, the size of the lookup tables becomes 16 KB.

The value of each component in the lookup tables are computed and stored within the available eight bits in a manner that facilitates the final color value composition required for the native display format of the desktop computer. For instance, if the display format is RGB16 (5:6:5) or RGB15, the *R* and *B* component values in the lookup tables are stored as 5-bit values; the *R* values left-shifted in the 16-bit entry of the first lookup table, and the *B* value right-shifted in the second lookup table. The *G* component is obtained from:

$$G = MIN[255, MAX[0, G_0 + G_1]] \tag{11}$$

The end result is one add and two compares per each color conversion operation.

Some software-only video codecs inherently require less number of color conversion operations than others. For instance, a video codec that generates a YUV color value for each pixel in the decompressed frame, will then require an RGB color conversion operation per pixel in the frame. For a 320 × 240 frame, such methods would require 76,800 color conversion operations. On the other hand, video codecs that are based on *binary pattern image coding* (e.g., based on methods described in [14–16]) or *vector quantization* (e.g., in [17, 18, 49]), require a much lower number of color conversion operations. If 4 × 4 blocks are used with a binary pattern image coding approach, the 320 × 240 frame will contain 4,800 non-overlapping blocks, each that can be represented with one or two colors, which results in at most 9,600 color conversion operations. If a vector quantization approach has a single codebook of 256 vectors representing 4 × 4 blocks, the number of color conversion operations required will be equal to 4,096. In the former case the saving in number of color conversion operations is 87.5 percent; in the latter case it is approximately 94.7 percent. Moreover, in vector quantization methods, the codebook does not necessarily change from frame to frame thus the average number of color conversions may be even less.

A problem often encountered in many existing desktop computers is limited bandwidth to the video display buffer. Such problems can often be attributed to computer display architectures that were not originally designed nor intended to handle the inherent high bandwidth of digital video. The norm for video playback performance by software-only video codecs in desktop computers is a video window of size equal to 320 by 240 at 15 frames-per-second. This requires that 1,152,000 pixels be displayed per second. For an RGB16 display mode (i.e., two bytes per pixel), the required bandwidth becomes approximately 2.2 Megabytes per second. The *effective bandwidth* of some existing desktop computers can be as low as 500 Kilobytes per second in IBM-compatible personal computers containing an Industry Standard Architecture (ISA) bus. Systems with higher bandwidth do not necessarily provide a solution to the bottleneck to the video display buffer since they could still be subject to latencies caused by memory setup time, wait states, lack of bus-mastering capabilities, and contention with the vertical blanking signal to avoid tearing artifacts.

All video codecs, hardware-assisted video codecs and software-only video codecs, attempt to exploit the temporal redundancy of the video with some form of interframe compression. A form of intraframe compression is typically employed in those areas of a frame where it is not feasible to use interframe compression.

In this section, we describe *frame-differencing*, a form of interframe compression that is typically employed by software-only video codecs to relieve the bottleneck to the video display buffer. A frame-differenced compressed frame is often referred to as a *delta frame*. Intraframe compression methods are used to compress those areas of a delta frame where it is not feasible to use interframe compression and to compress *keyframes*. A keyframe is compressed by exploiting its internal spatial redundancy independently of other frames. The first frame of a sequence of video frames is always a keyframe. After discussing frame-differencing methods, we proceed to describe intraframe compression techniques used in software-only video codecs, namely: spatial DPCM methods, vector quantization, interpolative coding, 1-D video compression methods, lossy Lempel-Ziv encoding, and binary pattern image coding. Finally, we discuss the bandwidth that Motion JPEG and MPEG would provide in a byte-oriented video stream.

3.1 Frame Differencing (Temporal DPCM)

Software-only video codecs rely on Temporal Differential Pulse Code Modulation (DPCM), or frame-differencing, as an instrument for interframe compression.

Frame-differencing methods for software-only video codecs exploit redundancy and irrelevancy between frames without searching for potential motion displacement. In order to keep the numerical complexity during video playback at a minimum, software-only video codecs are typically restricted to performing frame-differencing:

1. between consecutive frames, and
2. within corresponding spatial locations in the frames.

There are two general types of frame-differencing methods. One is obtained by *subtraction* and the other by *comparison*. Frame-differencing can be performed on a pixel by pixel basis or on a block to block basis. A block is typically a small rectangular image region. In the former case, pixels at every corresponding spatial location between consecutive frames are subtracted or compared by *predicting* the value of the information in the current frame from the values in the previous reconstructed frame. Frame-differencing on a block to block basis is performed by considering pixels at the corresponding spatial locations within the blocks or by considering the similarities between local image properties measured within the corresponding blocks. Alternatively, frames can be first compressed as keyframes. Frame-differencing is then performed by considering the similarities between the data representation produced by the intraframe compression method in each pair of spatially corresponding blocks in the two consecutive frames. A smaller block size tends to exhibit more temporal redundancy but larger blocks are simpler to "skip" during playback and produce better compression.

Frame-differencing by subtraction is performed on each of the three corresponding planes, Y, U, and V, between consecutive frames, whereas frame-differencing by comparison methods typically base decisions on whether information *changed* or *did not change* by only considering the luminance plane, Y. Although studies [39, 40] suggest that detection of large changes in luminance can generally serve to encapsulate detection of any possible large changes in chrominance (i.e., all large variations in chrominance exhibit corresponding large luminance variations, but not vice-versa), more elaborate frame-differencing methods also consider the chrominance planes, U and V, in their comparisons to reduce the introduction of artifacts.

3.1.1 Frame-Differencing by Subtraction

Figure 2 depicts a block diagram of a common algorithm used for frame-differencing by subtraction. In this approach, pixels in the current frame F_i are subtracted from the corresponding pixels in the previous reconstructed frame D_{i-1}. The residual difference, E_i, which is typically called the *error image plane*, or *differential image plane*, then undergoes further processing to obtain further compression. F_i and D_{i-1} represent corresponding planes (either Y, U, or V) which typically consist of 8-bit pixel values. In its simplest case, the quantization process, Q, truncates the 9-bit difference into an 8-bit value ranging from -128 to $+127$. Formally, the task of quantization is to represent a range of values by a single value in the range. For example, mapping a real number to the nearest integer is a form of quantization. More comprehensive quantization methods can be used to further reduce the number of bits. However, such quantization methods should be carefully designed to maintain a byte-oriented compressed video stream.

More generally, quantizer design involves in projecting coarse quantization in those parts of the video picture that are expected to be unimportant to the viewer, while projecting fine quantization in the parts that are important. For instance, in applications like *videophone*, where a talking head with a stationary background is typically transmitted, it is assumed that the talking head will be centered on the video picture and the viewer will focus his attention towards the center of the picture. Finer quantization should then be used towards the center of the video frame than towards its periphery. This results in fewer bits to encode the video information that is less important to the viewer.

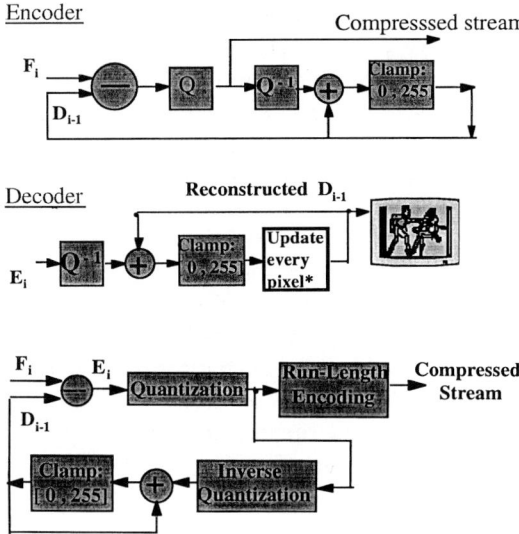

Fig. 2. Example of encoder and decoder for frame-differencing by subtraction

Fig. 3. Example of a frame-differencing by subtraction encoder followed by RLE

When there is little change from frame to frame, E_i will exhibit many values near zero. Hence, the next step in the encoder is to exploit this redundancy by employing run-length encoding (see Fig. 3). Since run-length encoding (RLE) is a lossless method, it does not need to be included in the simulation of the decoder process in the encoder. Such simulations are required to reconstruct the previous frame (D_{i-1}) in the encoder.

The output of the inverse quantization process reconstructs the error image plane that will be decompressed during video playback. Since quantization is an approximation step, large errors can potentially accumulate over a number of consecutive frames resulting in pixel values that are outside the dynamic range. Hence, clipping is performed after summing the previous reconstructed frame to the error image plane. Typically, keyframes are inserted at a specific periodicity in the compressed video stream so that the decompressor can replenish the complete video window periodically. Frames where a scene change occurs are also keyframes.

When high temporal redundancy is expected as in the case of *talking head video clips*, tokens can be used in the video stream to indicate conditions that relieve run-length encoding and result in greater compression. For instance, special tokens can be used to signify that the subsequent byte in the stream represents the consecutive number of rows to skip, the consecutive number of pixels to skip, the location of the first pixel to be displayed within a frame, or to skip the remainder of the frame.

The problem with frame-differencing by subtraction for software-only video is that its numerical complexity is not sufficiently small. During playback, the decoder has to perform inverse quantization, add the difference image to the previous reconstructed frame to recover the frame, and clamp to within the acceptable range of values. If the encoder does not employ run-length encoding or the special tokens described above, the decoder has to either write every pixel of the frame to video RAM or check for zero differences to avoid writing every pixel.

3.1.2 Frame-Differencing by Comparison

Frame differencing by comparison is better suited than frame-differencing by subtraction for software-only video playback because of its lower playback complexity. In reference to Fig. 4, the decoder determines the location of where it needs to update pixels in the current frame from information provided in the compressed video stream, and updates the corresponding non-zero pixels with data decoded from the compressed video stream. The *similarity test* performed at the encoder is typically the absolute value of the difference between the value of the two spatially corresponding pixels (or blocks) in F_i and D_{i-1}. If the absolute difference is less than a specified threshold, the pixel is then deemed to not have changed from the previous reconstructed frame. Local and global rules that allow a degree of lossiness are used when spatially corresponding blocks are compared. The local rules govern the maximum absolute difference between the values of pixels that can be tolerated as a function of the values of the two pixels. The global rules monitor the overall accumulated difference that can be tolerated in the set of pixels in the block. Alternatively, the global rule may simply state that if K or more percent of the pixels in the block satisfied the local rule (i.e., did not change), then the complete block is deemed to not have changed in relation to the spatially corresponding block in the previous reconstructed frame. This global rule can be enhanced to reduce visible *tiling* artifacts by enforcing that all pixels along the block boundary satisfy the local rule. Smaller blocks tend to exhibit more temporal redundancy but since one-bit token is required per block to specify whether information *changed* or *did not change*, the number of tokens increases.

If the pixel to pixel comparison (i.e., the local rule) is performed by only considering luminance information, the threshold value should vary as a function of the information being compared to simulate the logarithmic sensitivity of the Human Visual System. Alternatively, luminance image data can be non-linearly transformed prior to the comparison. Comparison of color information can be performed in their CIE L*u*v* color space representation [25].

A drawback of the frame-differencing by comparison method is that it tends to introduce speckle noise in the background as a result of accumulated changes over time that suddenly don't satisfy the similarity test. This could be partially attributed to consistent illumination variations over time. Frame differencing by comparison also yields less compression than frame differencing by subtraction. However, on the positive side, frame-differencing by comparison offers:

Video Compression for Multimedia Applications

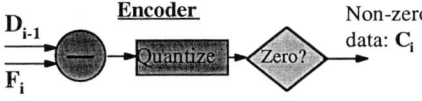

Fig. 4. Frame-differencing by comparison

1. better ease-of-decoding, and
2. lower bandwidth requirements to write pixels to the display buffer. This is significant for desktop computers with poor display architectures or low effective bandwidth.

In typical color video clips of 320 × 240 frames, the percentage of redundant pixels from frame to frame is:

15.3 % at high quality settings (i.e., low frame-differencing threshold value)
36.3 % at medium quality settings, and
58.4 % at low quality settings (i.e., high frame-differencing threshold value)

These percentages represent an average over many compressed video clips and are video content dependent.

3.1.3 Frame-Differencing with Exclusive-or Operator

Frame-differencing algorithms can be implemented at the bit-level with the exclusive-or operator rather than at the pixel level as described by the U.S. Patent by Pietras, Rodriguez, and Saenz [81]. This form of lossless compression uses the exclusive-or operator on spatially corresponding pixels of every pair of consecutive frames, F_i and F_{i-1}, to produce an exclusive-or plane, P_i. The exclusive-or operator exhibits the following properties:

If $F_i \veebar F_{i-1} = P_i$, then

$P_i \veebar F_{i-1} = F_i$ and

$P_i \veebar F_i = F_{i-1}$

By coding the video data with exclusive-or planes (P), the second equation can be used to play the video forward and the third equation to play the video in reverse. If a bit is *on* in the exclusive-or plane, P, it signifies that the bit of the other input must be inverted, else if a bit is *off*, it signifies no change. The location of the pixels that changed and their values are recoverable from the information in P. A pixel that does not need to be updated will exhibit a value equal to zero in P. Depending on the color format of the video data, the pixel value is either a byte (i.e., luminace or RGB8) or a 16-bit word (e.g., RGB16). Hence, a lossless coding scheme based on run-legth encoding can be used to encode P at the byte level.

This approach equips a video player with the capability to play the video in reverse as well as forward and thus provides good random access for interactive viewing and video editing.

Higher temporal redundancy can be obtained by spatially smoothing the frames with a low-pass or median filter prior to frame-differencing. However, this tends to compromise the image quality of the video.

3.2 Intraframe Compression Methods

Statistically-based image coding techniques address the intraframe compression problem from an information theoretic point of view, with the focus on eliminating the statistical redundancy among the pixels in the frame. These compression algorithms are characterized by an initial preprocessing step. The "ideal" preprocessor is one where the pixels are mapped into independent data. Typically, the best one can do is find a preprocessor that makes the data uncorrelated. For example, the mapping might be to take the Discrete Fourier Transform of the image pixels. The desire for the pixels to be independent is based on rate-distortion theory. *Rate distortion theory* defines the optimum coder to be the coder that attains the best possible data rate for a given image distortion [49]. Smaller data rates can be achieved by coding blocks of data, rather than individual pixels. In fact, the optimal coder is achieved as the size of the block approaches infinity. However, large blocks are impractical for multimedia applications.

Most intraframe compression methods used in software-only video codecs are block-based algorithms. In block coding methods, the video data is typically partitioned into non-overlapping spatial blocks with each of these blocks being coded separately. One reason why block coding methods are desirable is that decomposing the frame into blocks facilitates making the intraframe compression method adaptive to local image statistics. One disadvantage of block compression techniques is that the borders of the blocks are often visible in the decoded image. This type of artifact is often called *tiling* and results because the distortion introduced in adjacent blocks is discontinuous. Tiling is often resolved by maintaining the block size small, by pre- or post-processing the video data, by using overlapping blocks [45], or by sharing the block boundary between adjacent blocks [46].

3.2.1 Spatial DPCM

One category of intraframe compression techniques consists of spatial predictive methods, also known as spatial Differential Pulse Code Modulation (DPCM) [55]. The philosophy behind predictive image compression techniques is that if the

Video Compression for Multimedia Applications

pixels can be modeled as Markov sources [54], then the differences between consecutive pixels are statistically independent, and a simple quantizer will be nearly optimum. For predictive coding techniques, the value of a pixel is predicted based on the values of a neighboring group of pixels. The group of pixels on which the prediction is based can be spatially distributed or, for digital video, temporally distributed. Traditionally, the error in the prediction is then quantized and coded in the video stream.

Predictive coding results in data rates from one to two bits-per-pixel (bpp) for luminance images; for color images the data rate could be anywhere between 1.5 bpp to 6.0 bpp, depending on the statisitical complexity of the data. Predictive coding methods can be made adaptive by varying the prediction algorithm or the quantization of the difference [56]. Adaptive predictive coding achieves data rates ten to twenty percent lower than non-adaptive predictive coding.

Faced with the constraint of maintaining high ease-of-decode, predictive coding techniques used in software-only video codecs typically conform to simple implementations. For instance, some of the frame-differencing techniques described above can be implemented in the spatial domain. The simplest approach is to consider the similarities between pixels in consecutive rows, singly or as a set. Each pixel in the current row of the frame is predicted from the pixel directly above it in the previous row. Local and global rules that allow a degree of lossiness are used when pixels are compared rather than subtracted as a set of consecutive pixels. The local rules govern the maximum difference between pixel values that can be tolerated as a function of the values of the two pixels. The global rules monitor the overall accumulated difference that can be tolerated in the set of pixels.

In practice, row to row spatial DPCM is implemented by considering a set of a pre-specified number of pixels at a time. Smaller sets tend to exhibit more spatial redundancy. However, if the comparison approach is implemented so that higher ease-of-decoding can be attained, a one-bit token is required per set to specify whether information *changed* or *did not change*. Thus the number of tokens increases with smaller sets.

3.2.2 Block-Based Spatial DPCM

On a block basis, the simplest spatial DPCM approach is to consider the similarities between the properties of the current block and those of the previous block (directly to the left). This requires that a bit per block be allocated as a token to indicate if the block is coded relative to the previous block or independently with some other intraframe compression method. To exploit redundancy along the vertical, the block directly above the current block can be considered as well. This now requires that two bits be allocated to indicate the best matching block: the block directly above the current block, the block directly to the left, the block in the previous frame, or no match. In the latter case, the block must be compressed with some other intraframe compression method. The block directly to the northwest and northeast of the current block could also be used to predict the properties of the current block in conjunction with the left or top block. For instance, if image analysis is performed to determine that the entire area under consideration is homogeneous in some sense but changing slowly, the representative values of the block can be predicted by using bilinear interpolation. Yet another approach is to predict the values of the block by comparing it to the previous N blocks to find the best matching block. This last approach would then exhibit characteristice of a Lempel-Ziv encoding implementation (see below) except that the items are blocks rather than pixels.

3.2.3 Vector Quantization

As mentioned above, one of the advantages of vector quantization, or VQ, for software-only video playback is that it inherently requires few color conversion operations during video playback. Despite that it is a very numerical intensive video compression method, VQ decompression additionally offers very low computational complexity.

VQ coding is essentially N-dimensional statistical clustering. In software-only video codec implementations, the frame is typically decomposed into non-overlapping blocks. Each block is represented with an N-dimensional vector. The color format of pixels and the block size determine the dimension, N, of the vectors. Formally, N equals the total number of color components required to represent all the pixels in a block. For instance, if 4×4 blocks are used with RGB color data, N becomes equal to 48. In practice, the YUV 4:2:0 color format is used in association with every 2×2 non-overlapping image region. Each 2×2 image region is represented with four Y values, one for each pixel, a single U value and a single V value. Hence, if 2×2 blocks are used, the six values comprising the YUV information dictate 6-dimensional vectors. If 4×4 blocks are used, N becomes 24. Methods that find the color map, or palette, of a frame (or image) are categorically vector quantization methods where the block size is one pixel and $N = 3$ (i.e., the RGB triplet).

The objective in VQ coding is to find the best K blocks, or vectors, that represent the complete set of blocks in the frame in N-dimensional space. The K representative vectors could potentially be found by creating a histogram of all the N-dimensional vectors in the frame in N-dimensional space. The job is then to find the best set of K representative vectors, which may not necessarily be in the frame, that best minimize a distortion measure (see Sect. 2) over the complete frame. Typically, the distortion between two vectors is measured by the square of the N-dimensional Euclidean distance between them. The set of the K representative vectors, called the *codebook*, must be included in the compressed video stream. The representative vector of a block is specified by its codebook index in the video stream. Compression results when K is much less than the total number of blocks in the frame, B. However, better image fidelity is attained as the value of K increases. In software-only video codecs implementations, K is typically equal to 256 to obtain a byte-oriented video stream syntax. When 4×4 blocks are used (i.e., 24-dimensional vectors) for a 320×240 frame, the number of non-overlapping blocks is 4,800. The one byte index contributes an average of 0.5 bits-per-pixel (bpp). The codebook contributes 6144 (24×256) bytes per frame which results in a contribution of 0.64 bpp. The average compression is thus 1.14 bpp. If 2×2 blocks are used, the average compression becomes 2.16 bpp. Either way, the codebook does not necessarily change from frame to frame. Thus, it does not need to be specified completely in some frames. Frame differencing, which adds a one-bit token per block, reduces the average bandwidth further.

For a codebook of 256 vectors, a bit map of eight bytes is employed to indicate which vectors need to be updated for the frame. When a frame requires that the codebook be updated with a significant number of vectors, better ease-of-decoding may result by specifying the complete codebook and omitting the eight-byte bit map. A token at the beginning of a frame can specify whether its codebook needs to be partially or completely replenished, or not replenished at all.

Given that the best representative vector for any block depends on a global mapping (i.e., mapping the B blocks in the frame into the K representative blocks), VQ methods do not tend to preserve local image features as well as other compression methods that preserve local information statistics (e.g., binary pattern image coding). Consequently, VQ implementations of software-only video codecs tend to compute a codebook per frame, or per sections of a frame, to reduce the introduction of artifacts that arise as a result of minimizing the distortion measure in a global sense. A smaller block size also helps preserve local image features.

The major drawback of VQ coding is its asymmetry. Typically, the codebook is generated with the iterative algorithm described by Linde, Buzo, and Gray [47]:

1. A set of K initial codebook vectors, $T \in \{T_0, T_1, \ldots, T_{K-1}\}$ is chosen by sampling the frame at K different locations. The iteration index i is set to 1 and the average distortion measure, $D_{avg}(0)$, is initialized to a large value.
2. For each of the B vectors representing the blocks in the frame, $V \in \{V_0, V_1, \ldots, V_{B-1}\}$, perform the following steps:
   A. Compute the distortion measure between V and each of the K codebook vectors.
   B. Map V to the codebook vector exhibiting the minimum distortion. V becomes part of the cluster of that vector.
3. Compute the average distortion, $D_{avg}(i)$, of the B vectors for the ith iteration.
4. Terminate the algorithm if the fractional change in distortion is less than a prespecified threshold:

$$\frac{D_{avg}(i-1) - D_{avg}(i)}{D_{avg}(i-1)} < \text{threshold} \qquad (12)$$

If equation (12) is satisfied, the K vectors become the entries of the final codebook for the frame.
5. Find the centroid of the K clusters and use them as the new set of codebook vectors.
6. Increment the iteration index and go to step 2.

Obviously, steps 2 and 5 are very numerical intensive. To overcome this problem, codebooks can be generated using a *tree structure* [17, 18, 49] at the expense of more memory consumption and potentially worse distortion.

VQ coding is desirable for software-only video because it offers high ease-of-decode: low decompression complexity and few color conversion operations. Since the compressed data is represented with codebook indices, decompression is essentially looking up data in a table. If a vector quantization approach has a single codebook of 256 vectors representing 4×4 blocks, the number of color conversion operations required will be equal to 4096. With 2×2 blocks it is 1024. For a 320×240 frame, the saving in number of color conversion operations is approximately 94.7 percent for the 4×4 blocks and 98.6 percent with 2×2 blocks. Again, the codebook does not necessarily change from frame to frame thus the average number of color conversions may be even less.

There are many flavors of VQ coding. Some reduce the asymmetry (i.e., compression complexity) in exchange for higher decompression complexity. For instance, in *product-structure VQ coding* [17], independent image features of blocks, such as block gradient and magnitude, could be represented in different codebooks. Hence, the decoder has to perform numerical computations after retrieving the vectors from the independent codebooks to reconstruct the final block. In addition, color conversion operations may have to be performed for each pixel in every intraframe compressed block in the frame.

3.2.4 Differential Vector Quantization

The mean (or DC) value of each color component within a block can be subtracted from the respective color components contributing to the mean prior to performing VQ compression and encoded separately [48]. Any of the block-based spatial DPCM methods described above can be employed to encode the vector means of the color components. Although, this method results in better compression since the residual vectors can be represented better by the codebook, it adds complexity to software-only video playback. The decoder would have to add the quantized base value to each pixel in every intraframe compressed block of the frame to reconstruct the frame and perform color conversion on each of those pixels.

3.2.5 Interpolative and Extrapolative Coding

In interpolative and extrapolative methods [35], a subset of the pixels is obtained by subsampling the frame. This subset is then specified in the compressed video stream, and the decoder interpolates or extrapolates to fill-in the missing pixels. The subsampling of the frame can be done in either of the spatial dimensions, in the temporal dimension, or in any combination. The interpolation function can use straight lines or higher order polynomials. If higher order polynomials are used in the interpolation, it may be necessary to transmit polynomial coefficients in addition to the subset of sampled pixels. This class of compression techniques can be made adaptive by varying the degree to which the image is subsampled, the direction of the subsampling, or the function used to do the interpolation and extrapolation. For luminace images, interpolative compression techniques achieve bit rates in the neighborhood of two bits-per-pixel. Examples of interpolative image compression techniques can be found in [58–60].

3.2.6 1-D Video Intraframe Compression Approaches

Video codecs could be designed to only exploit data redundancy in one dimension (i.e., treating video as a 1-D raster signal). The original motivation behind these approaches was for video implementations in DSP-assisted hardware but as CPU's became more computationally efficient, these methods have been attempted as software-only video solutions on desktop computers. One dimensional video compression tends to yield poor reconstructed image quality – a common artifact is horizontal streaks. This however presents simplicity since each row of a video frame can be compressed independently.

Interpolative coding can be used in one dimension [58–60]. Here the signal is sampled at a pre-specified periodicity that satisfies the compression target. The samples can be quantized. The decoder reconstructs the intermediate values by interpolation. However, this results in blurred information since edge information is not necessarily preserved. A slightly different approach is to detect 1-D edge transitions and for each detected edge, specify in the compressed video stream:

1. two adjacent pixel values that represent the edge, and
2. the location of the left-most pixel value.

The pixel values can be quantized. Except for the first detected edge in the frame, the location of an edge is specified relative to the previous specified edge. Once again, the decoder reconstructs the missing intermediate values between different pairs of specified edge values by interpolation.

Piecewise approximation of the 1-D signal can be slightly more intricate. Line segment information, length and slope, could be stored in lookup tables. In particular, if a lookup table is used for the lengths and another for the slopes, this conforms to *product-structure VQ coding* [17].

Yet another approach is to find the average pixel value over a finite interval and encode the residual information. Storing both, the average value and the difference in two different (or concatenated) codebooks conforms to *differential VQ* [48].

In *1-D model coding*, every set of N samples is modelled with one of a set of pre-determined 1-D patterns (ramps, vertical edges, hats, U's, cones, etc.), where each pattern only requires one or two ordinate values associated with the points of inflection or end points in the pattern. The ordinate values and the patterns are stored in codebooks.

3.2.7 Lossy Lempel-Ziv Encoding

Lempel-Ziv encoding methods [5] are string matching techniques that can be employed as a form of spatial DPCM. For intraframe compression, a *string of pixels* is any set of consecutive pixel values in the raster representation of the frame. A sliding history buffer of reconstructed pixel values in the frame (i.e., compressed and decompressed data) is maintained in memory. In concert with frame-differencing, when the current data matches a string in the previous frame of significant length, a one-bit token representing that the data *did not change* is specified in the compressed video stream followed by the length of the matched string. Else, the method resorts to Lempel-Ziv encoding: if the current data matches a string in the sliding buffer, a *pointer* representing an offset to where the match occurred in the buffer is specified in the compressed video stream as well as the *length* of the string. The matching is employed by implementing a set of local and global rules to allow a degree of lossiness. A second bit is required as a token at the beginning of each intraframe encoded string to specify when a non-compressed pixel follows.

More recently Williams [44] described a Lempel-Ziv implementation that maintains a byte oriented data stream for high ease-of-decoding that can be extended to implement the method we have described. This method is protected with Patents issued to STAC Electronics. Tokens are grouped into 16-bit words and are followed by a sequence of 16-bit instances, each that is either a (length, pointer) pairs or non-compressed pixel information according to the value of their corresponding token. If the pixels are 8-bit color values, the string length is bound between three and 18 pixels, inclusive, so that they can be encoded with four bits. The four bits for the string length is concatenated with its corresponding 12-bit offset to form a 16-bit word. Hence, the maximum sliding buffer size equals 4 KB. Uncompressed 8-bit pixel values always appear in pairs to form a 16-bit word. Finally, if 16-bit color values are used, the length of a matched string is bound between two and 17 pixels and uncompressed pixel values appear singly.

3.2.8 Binary Pattern Image Coding

Block truncation coding (BTC) was first described by Delp and Mitchell [14] for monochrome images and instigated what we more generally refer to as binary pattern image coding (BPIC). Similar to halftoning and ordered dither displaying mechanisms, BPIC methods rely on the Human Visual System's capability to perform local spatial integration over the displayed image (or frame). When viewing the displayed area from a distance, our eyes average fine detail within the small area (i.e., block) and perceive the local statistics of the information.

In addition to offering low decompression complexity, one of the advantages of BPIC for software-only video playback is that it inherently requires few color conversion operations during video playback. BPIC methods also tend to have low compression complexity (e.g., see [15]).

Moment-Preserving BTC

The basis of the moment-preserving BTC algorithm [14] is the preservation of luminance or color moments of the pixel values in the decompressed image. BTC has been shown to preserve edge structure in the decompressed images and exploit aspects of the Human Visual System [69]. At moderate data rates, BTC performs favorably when compared to block-based transform coding [70]. BTC was a finalist for the ISO DIS 10918-1 standard that eventually chose discrete cosine transform coding for JPEG [71]. BTC offers low asymmetry and is unique in that the compression ratio (i.e., data rate), is independent of the image to be compressed.

The basic BTC algorithm requantizes each nxn non-overlapping block of pixels in an image into two luminance values. These values are chosen such that the sample mean and mean square value (or sample standard deviation) are identical with the original nxn block.

First, the original picture is decomposed into non-overlapping $n \times n$ blocks. A typical value of n is four. Blocks are then coded individually, each into a two level signal. The levels for each block are chosen such that the first two sample moments are preserved. Let $k = n^2$ and let $x_1, x_2, \ldots, xk$ be the values of the pixels in a block of the original picture. Let

$$\overline{m}_1 = \frac{1}{k} \sum_{i=1}^{k} x_i \qquad (13)$$

be the *first sample moment* (i.e., the *sample mean*). Let:

$$\overline{m}_2 = \frac{1}{k} \sum_{i=1}^{k} x_i^2 \qquad (14)$$

be the *second sample moment* and let

$$\overline{\sigma}^2 = \overline{m}_2 - \overline{m}_1^2 \qquad (15)$$

be the sample variance.

The sample mean is chosen as the threshold to obtain the two output levels for the quantizer. Other choices of thresholds are discussed in [14, 69]. Therefore, for $i = 1, \ldots k$, if

$$x_i \geq \overline{m}_1, \quad output = y_2 \tag{16}$$

else if

$$x_i < \overline{m}_1, \quad output = y_1 \tag{17}$$

where y_1 and y_2 are the desired "low" and "high" output levels, respectively. The output levels y_1 and y_2 for a two-level non-parametric moment preserving quantizer are found by solving the following equations. Let q = number of x_i's greater than or equal to $\overline{m}_1$. We then have:

$$k\overline{m}_1 = (k-q)y_1 + q y_2 \tag{18}$$
$$k\overline{m}_2 = (k-q)y_1^2 + q y_2^2 \tag{19}$$

Equations (18) and (19) are readily solved for y_1 and y_2:

$$y_1 = \overline{m}_1 - \overline{\sigma}\left[\frac{q}{k-q}\right]^{\frac{1}{2}} \tag{20}$$

$$y_2 = \overline{m}_1 + \overline{\sigma}\left[\frac{k-q}{q}\right]^{\frac{1}{2}} \tag{21}$$

Each block is then described by $\overline{m}_1$, $\overline{\sigma}$, and an $n \times n$ binary pattern consisting of 1's and 0's depending on whether a given pixel is above or below $\overline{m}_1$.

When $n = 4$, each block is coded with the quantized sample mean, the sample standard deviation, and a 16-bit binary pattern that contributes 1 bit-per-pixel (bpp). The sample mean and sample standard deviation could be jointly quantized to 10 bits using an empirically derived quantization scheme detailed in [69] but this would prevent a byte aligned video stream. The scheme in [69] is based on the fact that if $\overline{m}_1$ is very small or very large then $\overline{\sigma}$ will be small and hence fewer bits can be assigned to $\overline{\sigma}$. In such scheme, the original 16 pixels are represented by 26 bits or 1.625 bpp compared to the original 8 bpp in the luminance frame. A variable length coding extension of BTC yields further compression by representing those blocks where the sample standard deviation is zero (or very small) with the sample mean only. This variation on the BTC algorithm allows the average data rate to be reduced to a value between 0.5 bpp and 1.625 bpp for luminance images.

The BTC decoding algorithm consists of computing the luminance values y_1 and y_2, for each block from equations (20) and (21) and reconstructing the block in accordance with the bits in the binary pattern. The sample mean and sample standard deviation of the reconstructed luminance data are the same as those of the original block of pixels. For a suitable block size (see below), the reconstructed image appears slightly enhanced but not blocky, as would be expected, because the brightness has been preserved.

To illustrate coding a 4 × 4 block using moment-preserving BTC, let us quickly review the basic algorithm:

a) the luminance image is decomposed into small non-overlapping blocks such as 4 × 4.
b) The first and second sample moments are computed with equations (13) and (14).
c) A binary pattern is constructed such that each pixel location is coded as a "one" or a "zero" depending on whether that pixel is greater or less than $\bar{m}_1$.
d) The binary pattern, and values of $\bar{m}_1$ and $\bar{\sigma}$, potentially quantized, are specified in the compressed video stream.
e) The picture block is reconstructed such that $\bar{m}_1$ and $\bar{\sigma}$ (alternatively $\bar{m}_2$) are preserved. That is, pixels in the binary pattern that are 0's are set to y_1 and the 1's are set to y_2 according to equations (20) and (21).

For example, suppose a 4 × 4 picture block is given by the following:

$$X_{ij} = \begin{bmatrix} 121 & 114 & 56 & 47 \\ 37 & 200 & 247 & 255 \\ 16 & 0 & 12 & 169 \\ 43 & 5 & 7 & 251 \end{bmatrix} \qquad (22)$$

From equations (13), (14) and (15), we obtain:

$$\bar{m}_1 = 98.75 \qquad (23)$$
$$\bar{\sigma} = 92.95 \qquad (24)$$

and from equations (16), (17), (20) and (21), we obtain:

$$q = 7 \qquad (25)$$
$$y_1 = 16.7 \cong 17 \qquad (26)$$
$$y_2 = 204.2 \cong 204 \qquad (27)$$

the binary pattern is:

$$\begin{bmatrix} 1 & 1 & 0 & 0 \\ 0 & 1 & 1 & 1 \\ 0 & 0 & 0 & 1 \\ 0 & 0 & 0 & 1 \end{bmatrix}$$

the reconstructed block becomes:

$$\begin{bmatrix} 204 & 204 & 17 & 17 \\ 17 & 204 & 204 & 204 \\ 17 & 17 & 17 & 204 \\ 17 & 17 & 17 & 204 \end{bmatrix}$$

and the sample mean and variance are preserved.

BTC is obviously a form of block adaptive PCM, although it has been extended to use with DPCM [74]. BTC has also been used with multiresolution techniques [66]. BTC has been used successfully to code various types of pictures including aerial reconnaissance images, multilevel graphics, and video signals using a multitemporal extension of BTC [72, 73]. A variation of BTC has also been used in speech coding at low bit rates.

A drawback of moment-preserving BTC for software-only video playback is that it requires the square root operations and the determination of q from the binary pattern. This can be simply avoided by computing the two luminance levels during compression and specifying them in the stream. The need to code the mean of the block and its standard deviation is eliminated and a byte-oriented stream is obtained.

Absolute Moment BTC

It can be shown that absolute moment BTC [75], which preserves the mean and first absolute central moment of the block, has lower numerical complexity than moment-preserving BTC and provides the minimum MSE when the threshold is set at the sample mean. The compression algorithm is computed by the following steps:

1. For each block, the mean luminance value, Y_{avg}, is found.
2. For all pixels in a block whose luminance values are less than or equal to Y_{avg}, find the average luminance Y_{low}.
3. For all pixels in a block whose luminance values are greater than Y_{avg}, find the average luminance Y_{high}.
4. Construct a binary pattern for each block by representing pixels associated with Y_{low} as a "0" in the binary pattern, and pixels associated with Y_{high} as a 1.

Visual Pattern Image Coding

Chen and Bovik [15] introduced visual pattern image coding (VPIC) as a basis for preserving the local gradient and mean value. For each 4 × 4 block, the gradient direction of the block is found from the angle specified by the arc tangent of the vertical change in the information over the horizontal change. The vertical change is the sum of the pixels in the two top rows of the block minus the sum of the pixels in the two bottom rows of the block; the horizontal change is the sum of the two right columns minus the sum of two left columns in the block. The angle is quantized to the nearest 45 degree increment. For each possible quantized gradient direction there is a small set of binary patterns (a total of three or four), each which exhibits the same gradient direction. For instance, for the 90 degrees quantized gradient direction, the three possible binary patterns are:

$$\begin{bmatrix} 1 & 1 & 1 & 1 \\ 0 & 0 & 0 & 0 \\ 0 & 0 & 0 & 0 \\ 0 & 0 & 0 & 0 \end{bmatrix} \begin{bmatrix} 1 & 1 & 1 & 1 \\ 1 & 1 & 1 & 1 \\ 0 & 0 & 0 & 0 \\ 0 & 0 & 0 & 0 \end{bmatrix} \begin{bmatrix} 1 & 1 & 1 & 1 \\ 1 & 1 & 1 & 1 \\ 1 & 1 & 1 & 1 \\ 0 & 0 & 0 & 0 \end{bmatrix}$$

Likewise, the three possible binary patterns representing a quantized gradient direction of 270 degrees are:

$$\begin{bmatrix} 0 & 0 & 0 & 0 \\ 0 & 0 & 0 & 0 \\ 0 & 0 & 0 & 0 \\ 1 & 1 & 1 & 1 \end{bmatrix} \begin{bmatrix} 0 & 0 & 0 & 0 \\ 0 & 0 & 0 & 0 \\ 1 & 1 & 1 & 1 \\ 1 & 1 & 1 & 1 \end{bmatrix} \begin{bmatrix} 0 & 0 & 0 & 0 \\ 1 & 1 & 1 & 1 \\ 1 & 1 & 1 & 1 \\ 1 & 1 & 1 & 1 \end{bmatrix}$$

The eight quantized gradient directions are represented by a total of 28 different binary patterns that serve as a codebook in the decoder. However, note that the codebook does not have to be specified in the compressed video stream since it's known a priori.

The best binary pattern within the representative set of a quantized gradient direction is found by binary pattern matching. The binary pattern in the set that is selected is the one that best matches the binary pattern that would typically be computed for BTC by thresholding with Y_{avg}.

The two luminance levels associated with the binary pattern are computed by preserving the mean value of the original block and its gradient magnitude. These two luminance values are quantized and specified in the video stream along with an index for binary pattern in the codebook. For a codebook of 28 binary patterns five bits-per-block are required to specify the index. Blocks of low gradient magnitude are simply specified by a token that signifies that the block is represented by a single luminance value (i.e., the block is uniform). However, to keep decoding simplicity for software-only video playback, the two luminance levels should be computed during compression and each specified as 8-bit values in the video stream. The codebook can now be reduced to 14 binary patterns since for each binary pattern, there exists a dual corresponding binary pattern in its opposite direction that can be obtained by logical negation. For instance, each binary pattern in the set of 90 degree patterns above has a dual in the set of 270 degree patterns. Consequently, patterns can be specified with 4-bit indices which preserve byte alignment in the compressed video stream. The order of how the luminance levels are specified in the compressed video stream is simply swapped in order to benefit from the smaller codebook.

Color BPIC

The extension of BTC to color images can be described as follows [16]:
1. Decompose the image into non-overlapping n × m blocks.
2. For each block, find the mean luminance value, Y_{avg}.
3. For all pixels in a block whose luminance values are less than or equal to Y_{avg}, find the average color C_{low}.
4. For all pixels in a block whose luminance values are greater than Y_{avg}, find the average color C_{high}.
5. Construct a binary pattern for each block by representing pixels associated with C_{low} as a "0" in the binary pattern, and pixels associated with C_{high} as a 1.

For 4 × 4 blocks and RGB16 color values, color BTC yields a compression of 3.0 bits-per-pixels (bpp) since four bytes are required to store the two RGB16 color values and two bytes for the 4 × 4 binary pattern. If the color values in the block are represented with two luminance values, Y_1 and Y_2, and a single U and V pair, such that the quadruple $\{Y_1, Y_2, U, V\}$ is represented in three bytes (6 bits each), the attained compression becomes 2.5 bpp. Similarly, for 4 × 6 blocks, the compression with the RGB16 and Y_1Y_2UV color formats are 2.33 bpp and 2.0 bpp, respectively. And for 8 × 8 blocks, it respectively becomes 1.5 bpp and 1.375 bpp. However, recall that frame differencing reduces the bit rate further.

As pointed out by Chen and Bovik [15], for BPIC methods to work, the block size that can be employed depends on the viewing distance to the display monitor and the pixel resolution and physical dimensions of the display monitor.

Assuming typical viewing distances in desktop computers and typical dimensions of display monitors, these dependencies translate to limiting the block size used in BPIC according to the screen resolution (in pixels) of the display monitor. In practice, larger blocks (e.g., 8 × 8) can be used with larger screen resolutions (e.g., 1024 × 768, 800 × 600) and smaller blocks (e.g., 2 × 2) must be used with 320 × 200 screen resolutions.

Methods that suggest an alternative to adaptively select the BTC block size have been proposed in the literature. Roy and Nasrabadi [76] proposed a hierarchical BTC approach to code larger blocks that exhibited little variation with BTC. Blocks with large variations undergo quadtree decomposition and the same rule is recursively applied to the resulting quadrant blocks. Kamel et al. [77] proposed setting an interval, $[Y_{avg} - t, Y_{avg} + t]$, around the average luminance value of the block to find the best threshold value that minimizes the color mean-square-error. They proceeded to combine this approach with hierarchical BTC.

A variation of color BTC uses vector quantization to code each of the two color values with an 8-bit index [72]. Note that two codebooks, each of 256 vectors, can be used to preserve color fidelity and that the codebooks could change or be partially modified from frame to frame. Another BTC interframe approach codes three frames at a time using $4 \times 4 \times 3$ blocks [73] (i.e., instead of a 2-D binary pattern, a 3-D binary cube is produced analogous to the binary pattern above).

Pixel Distribution Image Coding

Rodriguez [3] introduced a novel approach to BPIC called pixel distribution image coding (PDIC). PDIC is based on testing blocks for homogeneity with a robust *homogeneity test*. If a large block is homogeneous (i.e., it has a unimodal distribution that exhibits low variance), it is coded with the mean color value of the block and a token that signifies that the block is represented by a single color value. Blocks that are not homogeneous are *split* into two pixel distributions: P_{low} and P_{high} by using the average luminance value of the block, Y_{avg}, as a threshold. Hence, rather than decomposing the block into quadrants, the block is decomposed into two separate pixel distributions. P_{low} and P_{high} are then respectively tested for homogeneity. The same rule is recursively applied until homogeneous pixel distributions are found. A *merging test* is applied to merge homogeneous distributions that were separated by the splitting process. For instance, if *Plow* or *Phigh* are further split into sets of two distributions: $\{P_{low,low}, P_{low,high}\}$, and $\{P_{high,low}, P_{high,high}\}$, respectively, because they did not satisfy the homogeneity test, $P_{low,high}$ and $P_{high,low}$ are merged and checked to determine if they comprise a single homogeneous pixel distribution. Likewise, if P_{low} is homogenous whereas P_{high} is not (i.e., *Phigh* is split), *Plow* and $P_{high,low}$ need to be checked to determine if they can be merged into a single homogeneous pixel distribution.

The overall block in PDIC is coded with tokens that signify the number of distributions in a block, and with the corresponding n-ary patterns to represent the associated color values, and the color values (one per distinct homogeneous pixel distribution in the block). In practice, the image could be initially decomposed into non-overlapping 16×16 or 32×32 blocks. With PDIC, objects and regions with arbitrary borders tend to retain their original borders within the blocks since the decomposition is performed on pixel distributions rather than on a superimposed structure (i.e., quadtree).

If a block exhibits a bimodal distribution, PDIC can be construed as essentially testing the appropriateness to code that block with color BTC. If a block has a trimodal distribution, PDIC will recursively split the pixel distributions and perform a merge operation if necessary.

BPIC methods are desirable for software-only video playback because they offer high ease-of-decode: low decompression complexity and few color conversion operations. The compressed data is amenable to a byte-oriented video stream syntax. The computational complexity of decompression is merely one comparison per pixel. In conjunction with frame differencing, which is simple to incorporate because of BPIC's block structure and byte-oriented stream, the average number of operations required per pixel is even less. If 4 × 4 blocks are used with a binary pattern image coding approach, a 320 × 240 frame will contain 4,800 non-overlapping blocks, each that can be represented with one or two colors, which results in at most 9,600 color conversion operations. The saving in number of color conversion operations is at least 87.5 percent. When frame differencing is considered, the average number of color conversions will be even less.

3.3 Bandwidth Comparison to Motion JPEG and MPEG

Low playback complexity algorithms tend to exhibit higher bandwidth and limited image quality in comparison to hardware-assisted video codecs. The higher data rates can be often attributed to the fact that variable-length coding (VLC) is not incorporated in software-only video codecs to preserve a byte-oriented compressed video stream. VLC methods [4–7] typically provide a *2X* compression improvement – they tend to compress data to about half the original data rate. In the case of JPEG and MPEG, the improvement tends to range between a factor of *1.3X* to *1.9X*.

Figures 5 and 6 depict high-level block diagrams of the baseline JPEG image encoder [52, 71] and the MPEG-1 video encoder [10, 11], respectively. A JPEG encoder for intraframe compression of digital video is described in [53]. The JPEG encoder consists of a forward Discrete Cosine Transformation (FDCT) step that is performed on each non-overlapping 8 × 8 block of information in the image.

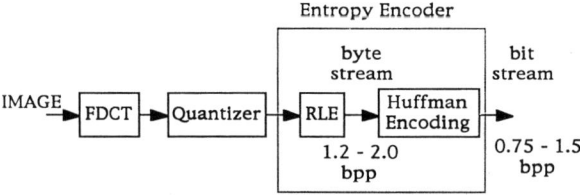

Fig. 5. High level diagram of JPEG image encoder for comparing bandwidth to software-only video codecs

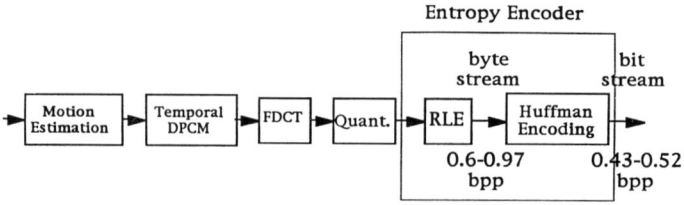

Fig. 6. High level diagram of MPEG-1 video encoder for comparing bandwidth to software-only video codecs

Except for the DC coefficient, which is coded using the difference between its quantized value and the quantized value of the DC coefficient in the previous 8 × 8 block (i.e., spatial DPCM), the DCT coefficients produced then undergo quantization and are ordered in a zig-zag sequence representative of non-decreasing spatial frequencies (see Sect. 4). The output of the quantization step is a byte stream that is input to the entropy coding block. The entropy coding step incorporates run-length and Huffman encoding. The bandwidth produced by software-only video codecs can be compared to the average compression that a motion JPEG encoder would provide if it had to adhere to a byte-oriented stream syntax. Empirical measurements of the average bandwidth of JPEG at acceptable quality, expressed in bits-per-pixel (bpp), immediately prior to converting the video stream to a *bit stream* – after simulating run-length encoding but before Huffman encoding – are shown in Fig. 5.

Likewise, the high-level block diagram of the MPEG-1 video encoder in Fig. 6 shows the compression that would be attained if it had to adhere to a byte stream syntax.

4 Hardware-Assisted Video Codecs

In this section we discuss video codec approaches for multimedia applications that are more likely to be implemented with hardware assistance due to their higher computational complexity. As mentioned in the previous section, according to rate-distortion theory, it is desirable for the pixels in the frame to be statistically independent. However, the best one can do in practice is to make the data uncorrelated. Smaller data rates can be achieved by decomposing the frame into large blocks and coding the blocks of data rather than individual pixels. However, video codecs for large blocks are impractical because they are difficult to design and implement. It can be shown that if the pixel values are statistically independent, a sequence of small blocks provides nearly as good compression (within about 0.25 bits-per-pixel) as a block that spans the same spatial domain when the MSE is used as a distortion measure [50]. Block-based intraframe compression methods are desirable because they are adaptive to local image statistics. Also, they are amenable to be implemented in parallel [41–43]. This is especially attractive when using a very computationally intensive block-based intraframe compression algorithm. These facts form the theoretic basis for all types of statistically-based intraframe compression.

For Gaussian distributed pixels, the Karhunen-Loeve transform (KLT) [51] can be employed to obtain independent data. These transformed pixels can be coded nearly optimally using a simple quantizer. Another example of this type of reasoning is with predictive coding (e.g., see spatial DPCM above), if the pixels can be modeled as a Markov random process, then the differences between consecutive pixels are independent [54]. These differences can be coded nearly optimally using a simple quantizer. Unfortunately, there are problems with the application of rate-distortion theory to video compression for multimedia applications. A major component of multimedia is on attaining real-time performance rather than merely finding an optimal coder based on minimizing a distortion measure for a particular data rate. Moreover, finding a valid random field model for digital video data (or images) of widely varying characteristics is difficult. Finally, as discussed in Sect. 2, there is no widely agreed quantitative distortion measure.

In this section, intraframe compression methods suitable for hardware-assisted multimedia applications are described. We begin by describing *transform-based* compression in preparation for a detailed account of the MPEG video compression algorithm. We then go on to discuss fractal image coding, and subband and wavelet coding prior to presenting the MPEG video coding algorithm.

4.1 Transform-Based Compression

Another category of compression techniques is transform coding methods [51, 57]. The motivation behind applying a transformation to a frame before coding is to take the statistically dependent image pixels and convert them into independent transform coefficients. Since with almost no exception it is impossible to obtain independent transform coefficients, one usually settles for a transform which results in nearly uncorrelated transform coefficients. The most popular form of transform coding in multimedia applications is the Discrete Cosine Transform (DCT). The objective of the Discrete Cosine Transform, and for that matter all orthonormal transforms, is to obtain a frequency representation of the data. Such transforms do not produce compression but merely decorrelate the data to achieve better compression. They reduce redundancy in the data in two ways. First, much of the information gets concentrated in a few of the transform coefficients. Second, transform coefficients that have small values typically get ignored as a result of quantization. The DCT is implemented by decomposing the frame into non-overlapping blocks and then performing the transform within each block. The block size is usually 8×8.

After performing the transformation on the frame's pixels, the next step in a transform coding algorithm is to quantize the transform coefficients. The quantized values of the coefficients and the coefficients' locations are then encoded in the video stream. Alternatively, vector quantization can be employed on the coefficients in the blocks or by computing four separate codebooks for the coefficients in the respective quadrants of the blocks. Except for the DC coefficient, methods like JPEG [52, 71] quantize the 8×8 DCT coefficients with an 8×8 quantization matrix and order the quantized coefficients in a zig-zag sequence representative of non-decreasing spatial frequencies (see Fig. 7). The DC coefficient is encoded using the difference between its quantized value and the quantized value of the DC coefficient in the previous 8×8 block.

The tail end of transform-based methods like JPEG [52, 71] and MPEG [10, 11] consists of an entropy encoding step that incorporates run-length and variable-

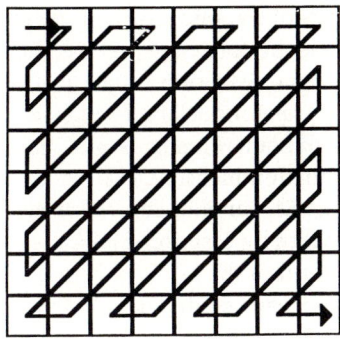

Fig. 7. Zig-zag ordering of 8 × 8 DCT coefficients

length coding after the quantization step (see Figs. 5 and 6). Data rates from 0.75 to 1.5 bpp can be achieved with DCT-based intraframe compression methods like JPEG [52] at very high image quality.

A disadvantage of transform coding is that the number of computations required to perform the block transformation can be quite large. For this reason, fast transform algorithms have been developed and are often used in transform-based compression. Transform coding algorithms are nearly always implemented on a block-wise basis [51].

The 8 × 8 DCT offers the right compromise for data redundancy. DCT transformation of larger blocks offer little improvements for the increased complexity. Fast DCT algorithms approximately double the number of arithmetic operations required per data sample when the block size is doubled. The best compaction efficiency results can be obtained by using locally adaptive block sizes (e.g., 16 × 16, 16 × 8, 8 × 8, 8 × 4, and 4 × 4). DCT transformation of larger blocks tends to absorb high frequency information (e.g., edge information) resulting in ringing artifacts (Gibbs phenomenom). Also, the DC coefficient is more sensitive to quantization noise with larger DCT transform sizes.

The DCT as it relates to MPEG is discussed in Sect. 4.4. Two software-only video codec approaches based on 4 × 4 DCT's are covered in [78] and [79].

4.2 Fractal Image Coding

The basis of fractal image coding [61–65] is on finding contractive affine transformations during intraframe compression and executing them iteratively during decompression to reconstruct the frame. A contractive transformation is one that reduces the distance between points. With a contractive affine transformation, a larger block in the frame, called a *domain* block, can be mapped into a spatially contracted *range* block. In practice, the frame is partitioned into 4 × 4 non-overlapping range blocks [61, 64]. Domain blocks can be obtained by decomposing the frame into overlapping 8 × 8 blocks that start at every 4 pixel increments. The number of available domain blocks can be increased by considering their reflection about the horizontal or vertical axes, and/or with rotations at pre-specified increments (e.g., 90 degrees). Every range block must be coded with a *fractal transform* – the coefficients of the contractive affine transform that maps the best matching domain block into the range block and the location of that domain block. This obviously would be very computational intensive since a least-squares method would need to be executed to find the best matching domain block for each range block in the frame. However, note that only a subset of all the domain blocks may end up being useful.

The computational complexity of the compression process can be significantly reduced by limiting the search for the best matching domain block and settling for a good matching domain block in the vicinity of the range block. Hence, for each range block, a subset of the available domain blocks may be considered to find a good match. Beaumont [64] used overlapping 12×12 domain blocks that started at every 4 pixel increments so that:

1. the center of every domain block would be coincident with the center of a range block, and
2. a domain block would perfectly tile nine range blocks.

The search for a good matching domain block starts at the domain block centered on the range block and extends out in a spiral fashion. Similar spiral searches have been employed in other pattern matching applications [80]. Although it is very likely that a good matching domain block will be found in the vicinity of the range block, the search is not necessarily constrained; it continues until a good matching block is found. Since the domain block tends to be found in the vicinity of the range block, its location relative to the range block can now be specified with fewer bits using variable-length coding. A distortion measure (e.g., MSE) could be used to signify a good match. However, to reduce the number of domain blocks that must be tested, it is preferable to measure and compare local image properties to determine a good match between a domain block and a range block [61]. Once a good matching domain block is found, the contractive affine transform is computed. Alternatively, matching can be performed by applying an orthonormal transform to the frame on a block basis and comparing the blocks in their frequency representation [64]. Range blocks that are uniform can be tagged with a token and their fractal transform do not need to be computed nor specified.

During decompression, the contractive affine transforms are executed iteratively to reconstruct the original frame. In theory, the starting domain blocks can have random pixel values during decompression because the transformations are contractive; the error is reduced at every iteration depending on the extent of the contractivity. Jacquin [61] started with blank domain blocks and required four to eight iterations to reconstruct each corresponding range block. Convergence can be achieved in one or two iterations if the process starts with the mean pixel value of the domain block [64]. For this purpose, the mean value of each range block can be computed and encoded using spatial DPCM methods (see Sect. 3). The decoder then reconstructs a low-pass filtered representation of the frame by decompressing the mean value of every range block and the mean value of each domain block is computed by averaging the mean values of the nine range blocks that it encloses. This does not necessarily result in extra bandwidth because the pixel intensity translation that would have been required in the contractive affine transformation is no longer required [64].

Beaumont [64] reported compression of 0.8 bits-per-pixel on color images with his fractal intraframe compression approach. In general, fractal image coding is very asymmetrical.

4.3 Subband and Wavelet Compression Techniques

Intrinsic video scalability signifies that the video codec algorithm compresses the video in multiple frame resolutions, multiple sets of frequency bands, or multiple representations of pixel color depth, and that this information is organized in the compressed video stream in a hierarchical fashion. Ideally, the compressed video stream produced by an intrinsically scalable video codec can be decompressed and displayed in a range of different computers at different quality levels and/or frame rates. The more computational power the computer has, the more information that can be decompressed from the hierarchically organized video data, and consequently the more fine detail that can be added to obtain better image quality, and the more that the frame resolution of the original video can be approached.

Intrinsic scalable video codecs are often based on subband coding methods [19, 20], wavelets [21–23, 67, 68], or pyramids [24, 66]. These video compression methods use multiresolution techniques whereby the frame is represented by a group of spatially (and possibly temporally) filtered versions of itself. The oldest version of this approach is pyramid image compression [24]. In this method the image is blurred by Laplacian spatial filters of larger and larger support. Each of these blurred images (low resolution images) are sub-sampled and compressed using DPCM, although other compression techniques such as Block Truncation Coding have been used [66].

Subband coding [19, 20] and wavelet coding [21–23, 67, 68] are newer approaches of scalable video coding and are very popular. Both methods have been used extensively in audio compression. Wavelet approaches have the promise of representing images very compactly. These compression approaches can be viewed as filtering the image through a bank of filters. That is, the frame is decomposed into different frequency bands by successive applications of low-and high-pass filters. Typically, at each stage the low-pass filtered representation of the previous stage (or initially, the original frame) is separated into four data representations:

1. high-pass filtered information in the vertical and horizontal directions,
2. high-pass filtered information in the vertical direction and low-pass filtered in the horizontal direction,

3. low-pass filtered information in the vertical direction and high-pass filtered in the horizontal direction, and
4. low-pass filtered information in the vertical and horizontal directions.

These subbands, which do not provide any inherent compression, are subsampled by 2 (demodulated) in each direction and then compressed. All subbands can be compressed with the same compression method or each can be potentially compressed with a different compression method. One common approach is to quantize the resulting subbands and subsequently employ variable-length coding. Spatial DPCM prior to quantization and vector quantization are other alternatives. The decompressed frames are upsampled and band-passed filtered to remove aliasing components and then the results are added together. Subband encoding is illustrated in Fig. 8. The reconstruction algorithm is simple up-sampling and addition. This is illustrated in Fig. 9.

The design of the filter structures for both the encoder and decoder is very important. The filters must not introduce distortion in the subimages such that perfect reconstruction is possible if the compression step is removed [55]. The most popular filters used in subband coding are the two-dimensional quadrature mirror filters (QMF) [19]. These filters reduce aliasing errors in the reconstructed images and can be designed to satisfy separability properties allowing for easy implementation [19].

Taubman and Zakhor [20] describe a subband video codec approach that uses multiple representations of pixel color depth. Specifically, they use a sequence of quantization layers, each representing progressively finer quantization step sizes.

Wavelets can be perceived as a form of subband coding that adds the concept of a multi-resolution pyramid. They can also be perceived as a form of transform coding. In the wavelet approach a filter bank structure is also used however the filters are replaced by wavelet transforms. The QMF structure used in [19] for

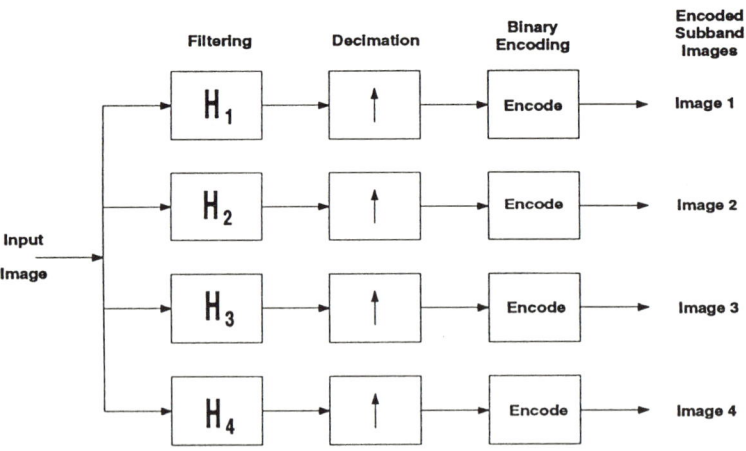

Fig. 8. Typical structure of a subband image encoder. (Similar structures are used in wavelet encoding techniques)

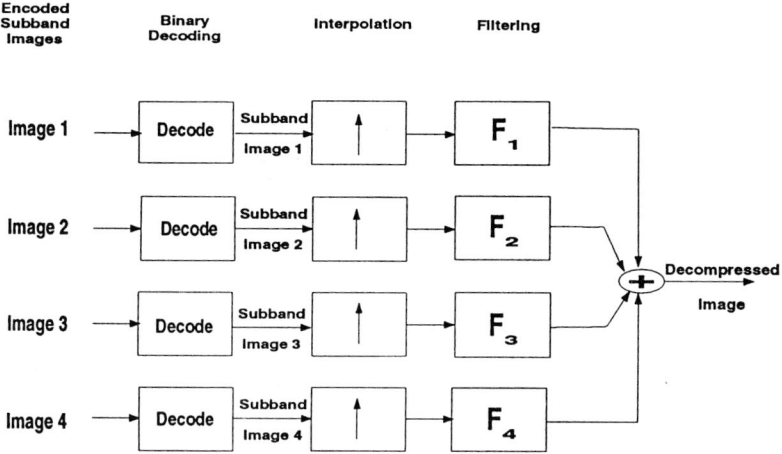

Fig. 9. Typical structure of a subband image decoder. (Similar structures are used in wavelet encoding techniques)

subband coding requires filters with 32 taps while in [67] only seven taps were necessary for the wavelet filters hence the compression and decompression algorithms are much faster. Lewis [21] only uses four taps. An approach based on wavelets that is suitable for software-only video playback is covered in [23]. The use of wavelets in image and video compression is still an open research problem, particularly relative to the design of the wavelet filters.

4.4 MPEG Video Compression

MPEG is destined to become the video codec of choice for multimedia applications for years to come due to that it is a widely endorsed standard with significant momentum in the multimedia community. This can be attributed to the fact that MPEG is a technically robust video solution contributed by prominent video engineering practitioners and researchers – it includes video, audio, and systems at high quality for a broad scope of applications ranging in data rates from 1.5 Mbits/sec (MPEG-1) to 4 to 100 Mbits/sec (MPEG-2). The MPEG video standard [11] specifies the syntax and the semantic rules by which bitstreams are generated in the encoder, and the arithmetic rules by which frames are reconstructed in the decoder. The MPEG syntax was designed to achieve high compression efficiency with as much simplicity as possible. An MPEG decoder implementation must be designed by choosing among a combination of algorithms that produce identical results to the normative MPEG specification [11]. Thus, it has limited flexibility. On the other hand, the encoder is widely open to the designer with the exception that the bitstreams it produces must conform to the syntactic rules. Hence, the designer of an MPEG encoder can choose among different cost and quality tradeoffs.

MPEG is designed to normalize computational complexity, buffer size, and memory bandwidth while still addressing the widest possible range of applications. MPEG-1 video, typically coded with 352×240 frames at 30 fps or 352×288 frames at 25 fps, was designed for compression of progressive (i.e., non-interlaced) video signals to approximately 1.5 Mbit/sec. MPEG-2 supports both interlaced and progressive video. An interlaced video signal has two fields per frame: the *odd field* contains the odd numbered rows of the frame; the *even field* contains the even numbered rows. We limit our discussion of MPEG-2 Video to Main Profile at Main Level. *Profiles* in MPEG-2 limit the syntax, whereas *Levels* limit parameters (e.g., sample rates, frame dimensions, compressed data rates). MPEG-2 Main Level consists of 720×480 (or lesser) interlaced frames at 30 fps.

MPEG video is a hybrid compression method designed with a suite of compression techniques to offer high image quality at low bandwidth (i.e., high compression) while simultaneously providing random access capability. Compression methods employed in MPEG video include: block-based motion compensated prediction for interframe compression (i.e., temporal DPCM), DCT transformations, quantization, spatial DPCM, run-length encoding, and variable-length coding (VLC).

This section serves as an informative tutorial of the algorithmic aspect of the MPEG video standard. The material presented herein should not serve as the source material for an MPEG design implementation; the reader must refer to the actual MPEG-1 video standard specification [11] to implement or design MPEG-1. Although MPEG-2 video [82] reached Committee Draft status in November 1993, it has not reached the International Standard status. The reader must refer to the MPEG-2 video standard specification to implement or design MPEG-2.

4.4.1 MPEG Color Format

MPEG-1 makes exclusive use of the *YCrCb* 4:2:0 color format. The *YCrCb* 4:2:0 color format is used in association with every 2×2 non-overlapping pixel region: each pixel in the 2×2 is represented with a *Y* value, whereas the entire 2×2 region is represented by a single *Cr* value and a single *Cb* value, both assigned to the center of the 2×2 region. MPEG-2 employs the *YCrCb* 4:2:0 color format in the Main Profile but it also supports *YCrCb* 4:2:2 and *YCrCb* 4:2:4. The *YCrCb* 4:2:2 color format is used in association with every 2×1 non-overlapping pixel region: each pixel is represented with a *Y* value; a single *Cr* value and a single *Cb* value are assigned to the left pixel of the 2×1 region. The *YCrCb* 4:2:4 color format consists of assigning the *YCrCb* triplet to each pixel. A minor difference between the *YCrCb* 4:2:0 color format in MPEG-1 and MPEG-2 is the location of the chrominance components as shown in Fig. 10.

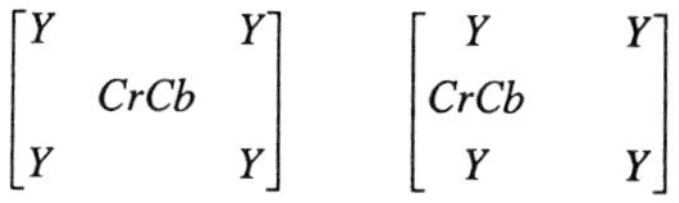

$$\begin{bmatrix} Y & & Y \\ & CrCb & \\ Y & & Y \end{bmatrix} \quad \begin{bmatrix} Y & & Y \\ CrCb & & \\ Y & & Y \end{bmatrix}$$

Fig. 10. Position of the chrominance components of *YCrCb* 4:2:0 within a 2 × 2 pixel region in MPEG-1 (left) and MPEG-2 (right)

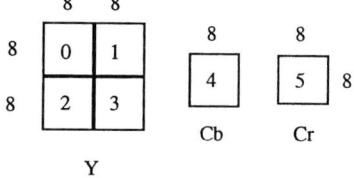

Fig. 11. Sequence of how the six 8 × 8 blocks of a macroblock are encoded in the video stream

The precision of each *YCrCb* component is strictly 8–bits. The *YCrCb* 4:2:0 color format is assumed for MPEG throughout the rest of this section.

4.4.2 The MPEG Macroblock

MPEG achieves compression through a number of tools and practices applied over various granularities or clusters of data samples. Every frame in MPEG is decomposed into non-overlapping 16 × 16 blocks that serve as the units to perform block-based temporal prediction for interframe compression. Each 16 × 16 block is referred to as a *macroblock* that consists of six 8 × 8 blocks – the four 8 × 8 blocks in the 16 × 16 luminance information of the block and the spatially corresponding 8 × 8 blocks of the *Cr* and *Cb* components. Figure 11 depicts the sequence of how the six 8 × 8 blocks are encoded in the video stream.

The size of the macroblock, 16 × 16, achieves good piecewise approximation for temporal prediction in frames of size equal to 352 × 240 or greater. Finer blocks for motion compensation typically yield small increases in compaction efficiency at the expense of increased compression and decompression complexities and syntax overhead (i.e., side information). Given the normative YCrCb 4:2:0 color format, the 16 × 16 pixel area also corresponds to the least common multiple of 8 × 8 blocks to perform 8 × 8 DCT transformations for decorrelation of the data.

The six 8 × 8 blocks within a macroblock share *side information* such as macroblock type, quantization scale factor, and motion vectors (see below). *Intra coded macroblocks* are compressed using the intraframe compression methods while *non-intra coded macroblocks* are interframe compressed macroblocks.

4.4.3 The Slice Layer

By following a raster-scan order, macroblocks are grouped into sets to form the *slice layer*. The objective of the slice layer is to serve as a re-synchronization unit [10] in the presence of errors in the compressed video stream (e.g., errors acquired in a noisy transmission channel). If an error causes the decompressor to become incapable of reading the compressed video stream, the decompressor merely jumps to the subsequent slice without having to discard the remainder of the frame. Slices do not necessarily have to begin and end on the same horizontal row of macroblocks in MPEG-1. As matter of fact, all of the macroblocks of a frame may be in a single slice (i.e., when not expecting errors) or each macroblock may constitute a slice. Slices can be of different sizes within a frame and the number and sizes of slices may change from frame to frame. However, in MPEG-2, a slice of macroblocks is only permitted within the same horizontal row of macroblocks.

4.4.4 Frame Types in MPEG

MPEG consists of three predominant frame types. *Intraframes*, or *I frames*, are compressed by exploiting their internal spatial redundancy independently of other frames and thus can serve as entry points in the compressed video stream for random access operations. The first frame of a sequence of video frames is always an *I* frame.

P frames are frames in which macroblocks can be interframe compressed by predicting their value from a *past reference frame*. A *past reference frame* is a frame, either an *I* or another *P* frame that is to be reconstructed and displayed prior to the current frame. Information in past reference frames is used to predict macroblocks in *P* or *B* frames. In a *P* frame, each 16 × 16 non-overlapping block in the frame (i.e., macroblock) is matched to a potentially displaced 16 × 16 pixel region in the past reconstructed reference frame. The resulting prediction error and *motion vector* specifying the relative displacement from the macroblock to the matched macroblock are then compressed and encoded, respectively. This operation is called *forward prediction* and is shown in Figs. 12 and 29.

Macroblocks in *B frames* are eligible for interframe compression in reference to both a *past* and a *future reference frame*. A *future reference frame* is a frame, either an *I* or *P* frame, that is to be displayed after the current frame. A future reference frame must be decompressed and reconstructed prior to its targeted

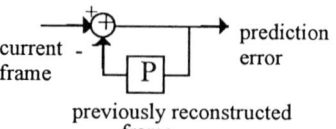

Fig. 12. Forward prediction from a past reconstructed reference frame in *P* and *B* frames

```
Frame     Type                         I  B  B  P  B  B  P
Display   order    (frame   no.)       0  1  2  3  4  5  6

Frame     Type                         I  P  B  B  P  B  B
bit  stream  order   (frame  no.)      0  3  1  2  6  4  5
```

Fig. 13. A video sequence example showing the order of how frames are displayed (top) and the order of how they are specified in the compressed video stream (bottom)

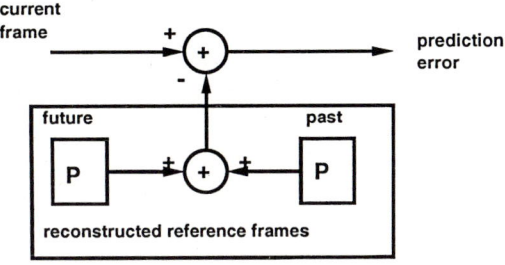

Fig. 14. Interpolative motion compensation in encodling B frames results from forward and backward prediction from a past reconstructed reference frame and a future reconstructed reference frame, respectively

display time so that its information is available to decode non-intra coded macroblocks in B frames. Consequently, frames in MPEG video are specified in the compressed video stream in the order that they are required to be decompressed and reconstructed rather than on the order that they are to be displayed. One of the functions of the decoder is to re-arrange frames to their proper display order. Figure 13 exemplifies the order of how frames are specified in the compressed stream for a given video frame sequence in display order.

I and P frames serve as reference frames for motion compensation in B frames. For B frames, the block matching is done relative to the past or future reference frames, or both. B frames provide the ability for *interpolative motion compensation* of macroblocks (see Figs. 14 and 27). Bi-directional macroblock prediction is the process of averaging the macroblock's prediction from a past reference frame (i.e., *forward prediction*) with its prediction from a future reference frame (i.e., *backward prediction*). The averaging helps reduce noise at low bit rates since it naturally acts as a low-pass filter.

B frames do not serve as reference frames so their information does not propagate into other frames.

B frames attain higher compression than I and P frames at the expense of higher computational complexity and delay for both compression and decompression. Obviously, computational complexity is increased in the encoder with dual block matching tasks. Computational complexity in the decoder is also increased since some macroblocks are coded with interpolative motion compensation which requires the averaging of two macroblocks. Extra delay is introduced in the compression process since the frame used for backward prediction (i.e., the future reference frame) needs to be transmitted to the decompressor before the intermediate B frames can be decompressed and displayed. Memory consumption is also increased since both, the past and future reference frames, must be retained during compression and decompression.

Without noticeable artifacts, I frames can be typically compressed to approximately 1.2 bpp whereas P and B frames can be compressed to 0.35 bpp combined. Generally, MPEG video can achieve very good video quality when compressed to an average of 0.3 to 0.6 bits-per-pixel.

4.4.5 Group of Pictures

A closed *Group of Pictures* (GOP) consists of an arbitrary number of compressed frames that depend only on reference frames within the group. Each closed GOP must commence with an I frame. A GOP may contain multiple I and P frames while multiple B frames may be interspersed between pairs of successive reference frames in display order. That is, B frames may exist between two I frames, two P frames, one I frame followed by a P frame, or by a P frame followed by an I frame. The presence of an I frame signifies:

1. the resetting of temporal predictions and dependencies between frames, and
2. a point in the video stream for random access.

Each frame type is typically allocated a target number of bits based on typical interframe redundancy in B and P frames and typical intraframe redundancy in I frames. Obviously, frame redundancy will vary with video content but this helps set the relative frequency of frame types in the video sequence for a target bit rate. In a typical scenario, I, P, and B frames will have a compressed size approximately 3, 1.5, and 0.5 times the average size of a compressed frame, respectively. The lower the target bit rate becomes, the higher the number of B frames and the lower the number of I frames that must be employed. Figure 15 exemplifies the relative frequency of the frame types based on their target compressed frame size. The period between I frames is called the N parameter and the period between P frames is called the M parameter.

In high action video clips that contain significant changes and scenes that exhibit camera panning and zoom, the P and B frames will consume more bits

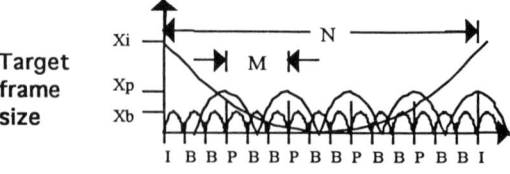

Fig. 15. Relative frequency of I, P and B frames is determined based on the desired bit rate and by projecting their respective compressed frame sizes

since many of the macroblocks may have to be intraframe compressed. They should get more than their usual share of allocated bits and the *I* frames should get less. Conversely, in video clips with little motion (i.e., talking heads), the *I* frames should get more than their usual portion of bits since the *P* and *B* frames will require fewer bits.

The number of consecutive *B* frames can vary if need be. Alternatively, a compressed video stream may not have any *B* or *P* frames between successive reference frames. This of course would not result in optimized compression.

4.4.6 The DCT in MPEG

MPEG employs 8 × 8 DCT transformations to decorrelate spatial data. As mentioned previously, the resulting frequency representation can be compressed better due to that much of the information gets concentrated in a few of the DCT coefficients and coefficients that have small values typically get ignored as a result of quantization. The DCT allows the subsequent quantization stage to spread quantization errors over an 8 × 8 spatial area.

MPEG employs the DCT for decorrelation of intraframe compression (i.e., intra coded macroblocks) and interframe compression (i.e., non-intra coded macroblocks). The precision of the input samples for *Intra* and *Non-intra* macroblocks is 8-bit and 9-bit, respectively. Output coefficients are 11-bit and 12-bit values. respectively, due to the expansion resulting from the DCT. In MPEG-1, the DCT coefficients of intra and non-intra coded macroblocks are clamped to 9-bit precision as part of the quantization process, whereas in MPEG-2, up to 12-bit precision can be retained. With the exception of differences in sample precision, the MPEG DCT is the same algorithm as found in H.261 [2] and JPEG [52, 71]. The 2-D 8 × 8 DCT is expressed by:

$$F[u][v] = \frac{1}{4} C_u C_v \sum_{x=0}^{7} \sum_{y=0}^{7} f(x,y) \cos\left[\frac{(2x+1)u\pi}{16}\right] \cos\left[\frac{(2y+1)v\pi}{16}\right] \quad (28)$$

where $C_u, C_v = 1/\sqrt{2}$ For u, v = 0,
      = 1   otherwise.

During compression, execution of equation (28) is typically referred to as the forward DCT (FDCT). During decompression, the inverse DCT (IDCT) is computed from the following Equation:

$$f[x][y] = \frac{1}{4} \sum_{u=0}^{7} \sum_{v=0}^{7} C_u C_v F(u,v) \cos\left[\frac{(2x+1)u\pi}{16}\right] \cos\left[\frac{(2y+1)v\pi}{16}\right] \quad (29)$$

Other than for errors produced due to finite precision, the DCT is a lossless transformation; the lossiness transpires in the quantization process (see below). Figure 16 shows the DCT coefficients that would result for a typical 8×8 block of information. Except for truncation effects when integer arithmetic is used, the IDCT reconstructs the exact 8×8 data block. The frequency representation has compacted the 64 data values into 14 transform coefficients. The DC coefficient, which is in the top-left, is proportional to the average value of 64 data samples (i.e., the DC value equals eight times the average of the 8×8 block). The other non-DC coefficients are called the AC coefficients.

The 2-D DCT requires 64 multiplies and 63 additions to compute each of the 64 transform coefficients. The orthogonal properties of the 2-D DCT can be exploited to separate the transformation into two 1-D transformations (a horizontal 1-D DCT followed by a vertical 1-D DCT, or vice-versa). The 1-D DCT for eight points is given by:

$$F[u] = \frac{1}{2} C_u \sum_{t=0}^{7} f(t) \cos\left[\frac{(2t+1)u\pi}{16}\right] \qquad (30)$$

where $C_u = 1/\sqrt{2}$ for $u = 0$,
$= 1$ otherwise.

Through this separation, the computational complexity is reduced to 16 multiplications and 14 additions to produce each of the 64 coefficients. The 8-point 1-D DCT above produces only seven unique constants that allow equation (30) to be described in matrix notation as:

$$\begin{bmatrix} F_0 \\ F_1 \\ F_2 \\ F_3 \\ F_4 \\ F_5 \\ F_6 \\ F_7 \end{bmatrix} = \begin{bmatrix} +d & +d & +d & +d & +d & +d & +d & +d \\ +a & +c & +e & +g & -g & -e & -c & -a \\ +b & +f & -f & -b & -b & -f & +f & +b \\ +c & -g & -a & -e & +e & +a & +g & -c \\ +d & -d & -d & +d & +d & -d & -d & +d \\ +e & -a & +g & +c & -c & -g & +a & -e \\ +f & -b & +b & -f & -f & +b & -b & +f \\ +g & -e & +c & -a & +a & -c & +e & -g \end{bmatrix} \cdot \begin{bmatrix} f_0 \\ f_1 \\ f_2 \\ f_3 \\ f_4 \\ f_5 \\ f_6 \\ f_7 \end{bmatrix} \qquad (31)$$

where a, b, c, d, e, f, g are scaled $\cos(i\pi/16)$ terms, $i = 1, 2, 3, 0, 5, 6, 7$, respectively. Each row of the 2-D matrix in equation (31) represents a basis vector.

As clearly visible from the 2-D matrix, some form of symmetry is evident for each of the basis vectors, F_0 through F_7. By exploiting this symmetry, equation (31) can be expressed as:

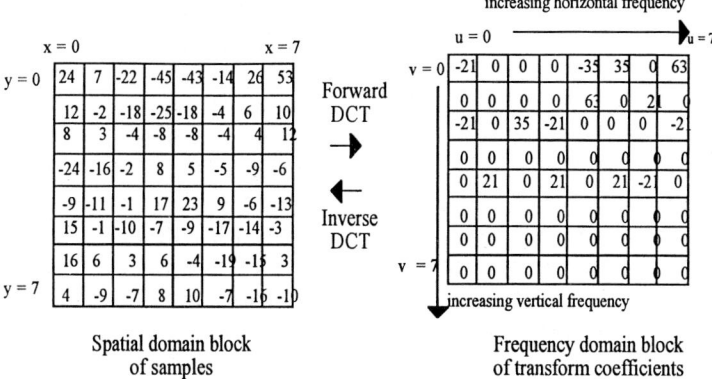

Fig. 16. Example of spatial to frequency 8 × 8 DCT transformation

$$\begin{bmatrix} F_0 \\ F_4 \\ F_2 \\ F_6 \\ F_1 \\ F_3 \\ F_5 \\ F_7 \end{bmatrix} = \begin{bmatrix} +d & +d & 0 & 0 & 0 & 0 & 0 & 0 \\ +d & -d & 0 & 0 & 0 & 0 & 0 & 0 \\ 0 & 0 & +b & +f & 0 & 0 & 0 & 0 \\ 0 & 0 & +f & -b & 0 & 0 & 0 & 0 \\ 0 & 0 & 0 & 0 & +a & +c & +e & +g \\ 0 & 0 & 0 & 0 & +c & -g & -a & -e \\ 0 & 0 & 0 & 0 & +e & -a & +g & +c \\ 0 & 0 & 0 & 0 & +g & -e & +c & -a \end{bmatrix} \cdot \begin{bmatrix} f_0 + f_7 + f_3 + f_4 \\ f_1 + f_6 + f_2 + f_5 \\ f_0 + f_7 - f_3 - f_4 \\ f_1 + f_6 - f_2 - f_5 \\ f_0 - f_7 \\ f_1 - f_6 \\ f_2 - f_5 \\ f_3 - f_4 \end{bmatrix} \quad (32)$$

Through this simple factorization, the complexity of each of the even numbered coefficients: $\{F_0, F_2, F_4, F_6\}$ is reduced to 2 multiplies. Likewise, 4 multiplies are required for the odd numbered coefficients. The DC coefficient (F_0) can be reduced to additions and a single shift. The overall result is an average of six multiplies per each of the 64 transform coefficients of the 2-D DCT.

Fast algorithms such as the one described by Loeffler et al. [83] can reduce the computational complexity by another factor of two, averaging three multiplies and eight additions per transform coefficient. In addition, fast DCT algorithms can improve signal accuracy since the number of multiplies present in the signal path is substantially reduced, thereby eliminating most points where quantization round-off error could be introduced. Such fast algorithms achieve further reduction over factorization through symmetric reduction between basis vectors. The partial product of one or more vectors can be substituted, for example, through rotation, for a partial product of another basis vector computation.

As the symmetry of the DCT is progressively decomposed, costly multiplication operations are exchanged for additions, negations, shifts, and data re-ordering (i.e., address mapping). Nonetheless, the total number of operations can be significantly reduced. Fast DCT algorithms rarely benefit from floating point arithmetic.

4.4.7 Quantization

Compression is facilitated by quantization of the DCT coefficients. An 8 × 8 *quantization matrix*, Q[u, v], is employed to exercise independent quantization of the transform coefficients and enable control over those coefficients that contribute the greatest subjective image quality. A *quantization stepsize* is associated with each coefficient of the 8 × 8 DCT. For intra coded blocks, each independent quantizer exhibits the characteristic of a *mid-step uniform* quantizer as shown in Fig. 17. That is, the coefficient dynamic range is partitioned into equal intervals and zero is one of the quantized coefficient levels.

The characteristic of the quantizer employed for each coefficient of non-intra compressed blocks in *P* and *B* frames is also of a mid-step uniform quantizer with the exception that it exhibits a larger interval to produce more zero coefficients (i.e., a *dead zone*). This is shown in Fig. 18.

The stepsize of each of the 64 entries in the quantization matrix ranges from 1 to 255. The stepsize represents the relative perceptual weight given to the corre-

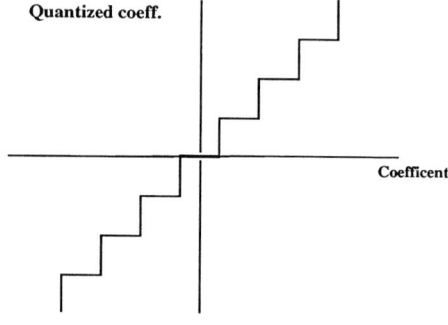

Fig. 17. Uniform quantization is performed in intra coded macroblocks

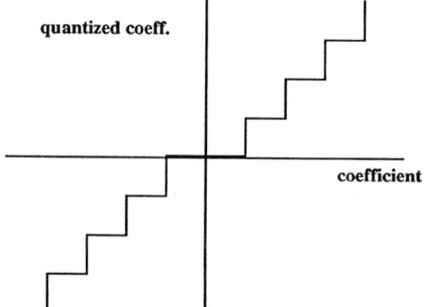

Fig. 18. Uniform dead zone quantization used in non-intra coded macroblocks of *P* and *B* frames

```
 8  16  19  22  26  27  29  34
16  16  22  24  27  29  34  37
19  22  26  27  29  34  34  38
22  22  26  27  29  34  37  40
22  26  27  29  32  35  40  48
26  27  29  32  35  40  48  58
26  27  29  34  38  46  56  69
27  29  35  38  46  56  69  83
```

Fig. 19. Default quantization matrix for intra compressed macroblocks

```
16  16  16  16  16  16  16  16
16  16  16  16  16  16  16  16
16  16  16  16  16  16  16  16
16  16  16  16  16  16  16  16
16  16  16  16  16  16  16  16
16  16  16  16  16  16  16  16
16  16  16  16  16  16  16  16
16  16  16  16  16  16  16  16
```

Fig. 20. Default quantization matrix for non-intra compressed macroblocks in P and B frames

sponding DCT coefficient. The smaller the weight the more accurately the coefficient is preserved. With the exception of the DC coefficient of intra coded blocks, which must be quantized with a weight equal to eight, in MPEG-1 and eight, nine, or ten in MPEG-2, the 64 weights of the quantization matrix can be modified by specifying them in the compressed video stream. However, it is atypical to use any table other than the *default quantization matrix*. The default quantization matrix for *intra* coded macroblocks is shown in Fig. 19. It was designed to resemble the response of the Human Visual System to spatial frequencies. The default quantization matrix for the prediction error of *non-intra* coded macroblocks (Fig. 20) can be perceived as a derivative of the default quantization matrix for *intra* coded macroblocks that statistically reduces the mean-square error.

The 64 stepsizes of the quantization matrix can be universally modified with the *quantizer scale factor (QSF)*. This allows values in the quantization matrix to be increased or decreased at the macroblock level and consequently the bit rate can be controlled within a frame by modifying the QSF. To increase the number of zero coefficients in non-intra coded macroblocks, the QSF expands the size of the deadzone. The overall coefficient quantization is performed by the following equation:

$$\text{quantized } F[u, v] = 8 * F[u, v]/(QSF * Q[u, v]) \tag{33}$$

This equation is not applicable to the DC coefficient since it is always quantized by by a fixed stepsize as described above.

The QSF is specified with five bits that relate to either uniform adjustments ranging from 1 to 31 (MPEG-1 and MPEG-2) or non-uniform adjustments ranging from 0.5 to 56 (MPEG-2 only). The wider range of the non-uniform partitioned scale permits finer rate control at low and high compression ratios. The desired QSF scale can be selected in MPEG-2 on a frame or field basis. An intra coded macroblock does not have to specify a QSF and thus can settle for the current QSF.

-1	0	0	0	-2	2	0	4
0	0	0	0	4	0	1	0
-1	0	2	-1	0	0	0	-1
0	0	0	0	0	0	0	0
0	1	0	1	0	1	-1	0
0	0	0	0	0	0	0	0
0	0	0	0	0	0	0	0
0	0	0	0	0	0	0	0

Fig. 21. Quantized DCT coefficients

The same quantization matrix and QSF are used to quantize the coefficients of the luminance (Y) and chrominance (Cb, Cr) information.

Assuming that the QSF = 1, Fig. 21 shows the quantized DCT coefficients obtained when the 8×8 block of DCT coefficients in the right half of Fig. 16 are quantized by the Q[u, v] in Fig. 20.

Performance in software MPEG implementations will benefit by storing 31 expanded quantization matrices in memory, rather than executing equation (33) per each DCT coefficient. Furthermore, the DCT transformation could be integrated with the quantization stage [84].

4.4.8 Compressing the DC Coefficient of Intra Coded Blocks

I Frames

Each quantized DC coefficient is compressed losslessly by using predictive coding (i.e., spatial DPCM). Within a macroblock there are six 8×8 blocks (see Fig. 11). In an I frame, the quantized DC coefficient of an 8×8 luminance block is predicted from the quantized DC coefficient of the previous luminance block in the macroblock. The value of the first luminance block in a macroblock is predicted from the value of the quantized DC coefficient in the last luminance block of the previous macroblock. The quantized DC coefficients of the Cr and Cb luminance blocks are respectively predicted from the corresponding values in the previous macroblock. Each resulting DC prediction error is coded using variable-length coding.

The quantized DC coefficients of the six 8×8 blocks of the macroblock at the beginning of a slice are predicted with a value of 128.

P and B Frames

The quantized DC coefficient of intra coded macroblocks in P and B frames are predicted with a value of 128, unless the previous macroblock was also intra coded, in which case the prediction approach becomes the one used for I frames.

There is no spatial prediction of the DC coefficients of non-intra coded blocks in P and B frames.

4.4.9 Zig-Zag Coefficient Ordering

To statistically increase the runs of zero DCT coefficients so that they can be more effectively compressed with run-length encoding, the quantized DCT transform coefficients are re-ordered into a sequence representative of non-decreasing spatial frequencies. The *Zig-Zag scanning order*, shown on the left of Fig. 22 is employed for progressive video in MPEG-1 and MPEG-2. The *alternate scan* on the right of Fig. 22 is suitable for interlaced video in MPEG-2. The Zig-Zag scan is identical to that used in H.261 [2] and JPEG [52, 71].

4.4.10 Run-Length Encoding

To reduce the number of symbols in the compressed video stream, the DCT coefficients of the scanned block are compactly translated into pairs of:

1. run-length of zero coefficients, and
2. the amplitude of the non-zero coefficient that immediately follows (i.e., terminates) the run-length of zero coefficients.

The run of zero DCT coefficients and the amplitude of the non-zero coefficient are concatenated into a composite token known as a *run-level event*. With the 9-bit truncated representation of quantized DCT coefficients in MPEG-1, 511 possible non-zero coefficients and 63 possible runs of zeros, there is a combination of 32,193 unique tokens. In MPEG-2, the maximum number of possible run-level events is 257,985. Slightly more than 100 of the most frequent events have corresponding variable-length codes (VLC). The remaining events are signaled to the decoder through an *escape code* followed by the 6-bit run and the coefficient amplitude (eight or nine bits in MPEG-1 and 12 bits in MPEG-2). Run-length

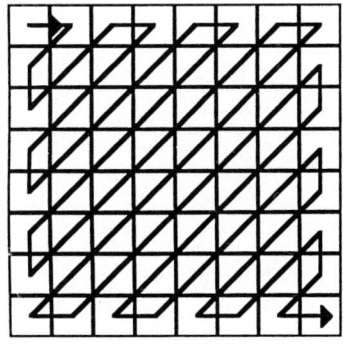 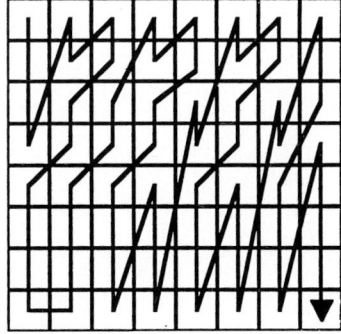

Fig. 22. Coefficient scans used for progressive video in MPEG-1 and MPEG-2 (left) and interlaced video in MPEG-2 (right)

encoding in MPEG is position-independent. An *End of Block* (*EOB*) code terminates all non-zero blocks regardless of the position of the last event. This semantic rule can also be employed as an inexpensive error checking mechanism.

4.4.11 Variable Length Coding

Unlike the JPEG standard, all variable-length coded side information in MPEG is assumed to have stationary probability and is therefore assigned stationary codes. This practice enables storage and implementation of VLC tables in Read Only Memory (ROM) which is significantly less expensive than Random Access Memory (RAM).

Intra and non-intra coded AC events share a single VLC table in MPEG-1. The MPEG-1 table that is optimized for collective intra and non-intra coded frame statistics can be selected in MPEG-2. The average length of the VLC of non-intra coded information is approximately 2.3 bits. The shortest variable-length codeword is 2 bits and the longest is 17 bits.

Due to the fact that the length of a VLC is not known until the boundary of the codeword has been detected, variable length decoding presents a significant bottleneck in both hardware and software implementations of MPEG. Fast decoders take advantage of the table entropy by attempting to "look-up" the 4 to 8-most significant bits in a table. If the codeword length is within the look-up size, it will be mapped immediately. If the codeword length is greater than the first look-up window, escape tables can be employed to map the remaining bits to the run-level event.

Figure 23 depicts the entropy coding process. After quantizing the DCT coefficients, the coefficients are scanned according to the scanning pattern table, then

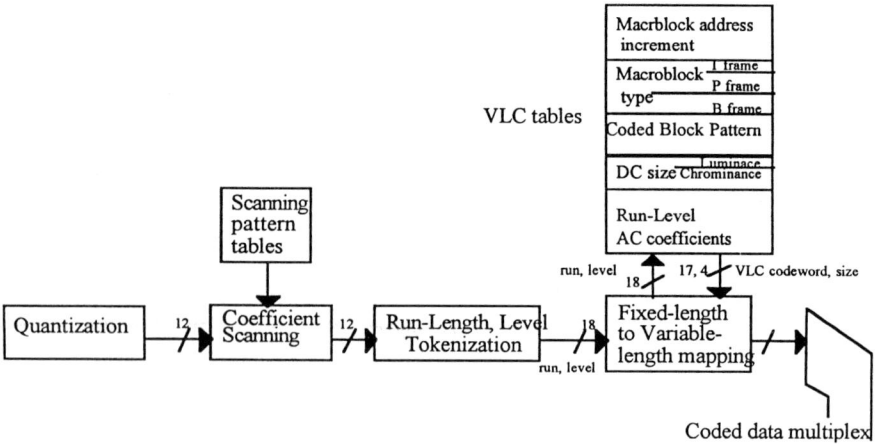

Fig. 23. Stages of Entropy encoding

they are concatenated into composite token events, and finally they are variable-length coded.

4.4.12 Macroblock Coding

A macroblock contains both side information and spatial energy. The encoder is given the freedom to select the macroblock coding method that yields the greatest contribution in image quality with respect to cost in bits. In a typical scenario, the encoder independently processes each macroblock in a series of fundamental stages. In the non-intra frame coding strategy presented in Fig. 24, the first stage, *Rate Control*, estimates the number of bits that should be expended for the current macroblock based on the fullness of the compressed video buffer. The second stage, *Decision*, determines the optimal prediction mode for the macroblock by performing block matching and delivers the motion vector to the *Motion Compensated Prediction* (MCP) unit. Finally, the *Coding* stage encodes the current macroblock into bitstream elements based on the modes selected in the Rate Control and Decision stages.

Adaptive Quantization and Rate Control

Rate control carries has two primary objectives in MPEG video coding:

1. To achieve the target bit rate with the highest possible video quality while preventing buffer overflow and underflow, and
2. To maintain uniform perceived image quality.

The target bit rate of the compressed video stream cannot be exceeded, otherwise frames would have to be dropped to prevent buffer overflow. This would result in some form of discontinuity in video playback. At the same time, the encoder should achieve the best possible image quality for the target bit rate using the set of syntax tools designed for MPEG. The macroblock quantization scale factor serves as an elegant control mechanism for achieving both goals.

Figure 25 depicts an example of an overall rate control strategy. The left part acts as the buffer rate control. The remainder of the diagram exemplifies the overall rate control mechanism. Local macroblock activity is measured to estimate

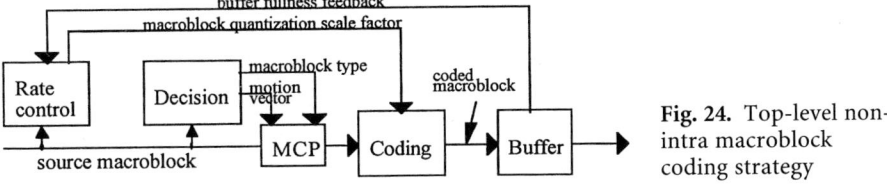

Fig. 24. Top-level non-intra macroblock coding strategy

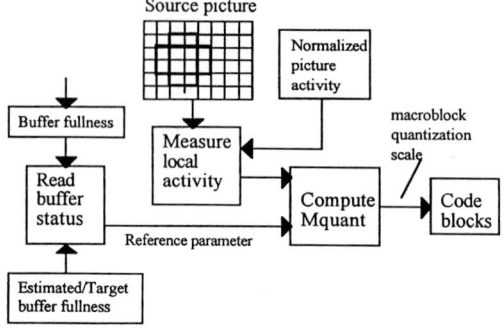

Fig. 25. Overall rate control strategy

the quantization scale factor (i.e., Mquant in Fig. 25). The rate control strategy must first start with a global estimate of bit distribution for the three frame types.

Global Rate Control

In most applications, a sequence of frames must be mapped into a constant rate bitstream. However, the coded size of each frame will vary depending on the degree of correlation with nearby frames (i.e., interframe redundancy) and the importance of the frame's information to human perception. The simplest strategy for encoding a sequence of frames is to establish a regular pattern of frame types (see section on GOP), and then to adjust the estimated target size for each frame based on a moving average of frame coding complexity (i.e., average frame size). In the most simple scenario, the target frame size, T_i, of the ith frame can be estimated as:

$$T_i = \frac{R_{GOP}}{N_{GOP}} \qquad (34)$$

Equation (34) would assign a constant number of bits to each frame based on the remaining number of frames in the group of pictures (GOP), N_{GOP}, and the remaining number of bits available, R_{GOP}. However, a periodically adjusted complexity measure that is frame type dependent would better adapt the allocation of bits to the statistics of the current sequence. This can be expressed by equation (35).

$$T_{I, P, \text{ or } B} = \frac{R_{GOP}}{W_I + W_P + W_B} \qquad (35)$$

where W_I, W_P, or W_B is a weight determined by:

1. The visual and statistical significance of the frame in relation to the other frame types, and
2. The number of respective frame types that remain to be compressed in the GOP.

For example, the weight for a P frame can be computed as:

$$W_P = N_P \qquad W_B = N_B \cdot \frac{K_P}{K_B} \cdot \frac{X_B}{X_P} \tag{36}$$

Where it is assumed that the only I frame in the GOP has already been coded and thus W_I is zero. K_P and K_B represent the relative visual importance of their respective frame type. X_P and X_B represent the coding complexity of the respective frame type. N_P and N_B are the number of respective frame types that remain to be coded in the GOP. The coding complexity can be updated as the product of the coded frame size and the average macroblock quantization stepsize. In the end, the target frame size becomes an important frame normalization parameter for the coding of individual macroblocks.

Local Rate Control

When the generated number of bits for a local window of contiguous macroblocks begins to significantly deviate from the estimated bit distribution model for the frame, the macroblock quantization stepsize can be increased or decreased to attain the target compressed frame size for the current frame. The number of bits generated by the current macroblock can be anticipated through pre-analysis of local regions in the current frame. For example, the local activity measure can be modeled by the spatial sample variance, or by performing a first-pass coding of the region to estimate how many bits are generated. The activity measurement should be normalized against the activity over the scope of the entire frame. If the global normalization factor is unavailable, as might be the case for encoders without a *priori* measurements, the average activity from the previous frame of the same type can be used as a reasonable estimate. To improve image quality, a smoothness constraint can be added to the activity measurement that reflects the surrounding areas of the current macroblock.

Macroblock Types and Decision Making

The encoder can select macroblock types using a number of different cost models. The simplest model is the *path of piecewise least distortion*. Prediction modes are tested against each other to find the mode that yields the least distortion or prediction error. The thresholds that determine whether the encoder takes one path or another should reflect the cost penalties of sending any side information associated with the respective prediction mode.

In MPEG-1, the number of possible macroblock modes for I, P and B frames are two, seven, and eleven, respectively. Since side information can comprise a significant portion of the compressed video stream, the *macroblock type*, which is highly statistically correlated, is variable-length coded.

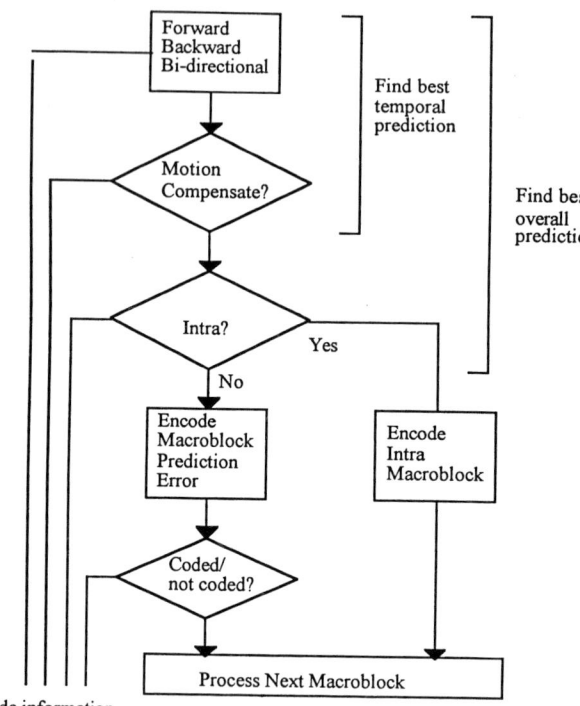

Fig. 26. Overall macroblock decision strategy for P and B frames

Figure 26 demonstrates a flow chart for the macroblock decision strategy for P and B frames. The *side information*, shown in the bottom-left, is generated at each stage of the decision tree and will eventually comprise a codeword that signifies the macroblock type and other side information. The following sections discuss the processes in Fig. 26.

Motion Estimation

The first stage of the macroblock coding decision in P and B frames, *Motion Estimation*, attempts to find the best matching motion compensated block between a reference frame and the current macroblock. The best matched block is specified by a *motion vector* that provides the relative displacement between the macroblocks. The motion vector *search range* has a great impact on image quality. Depending on motion activity, a search range between +/− 15 and +/− 32 samples has been empirically demonstrated to achieve very good results.

Exhaustive *search patterns* may be considered optimal, since they test all possible candidate displaced blocks in the reference frame, however in the context of MPEG video, hierarchical patterns have been shown to reduce motion vector entropy and to naturally limit sub-block motion divergence from the assumed uniform vector field within the block.

The *matching criterion* most often used in MPEG video is the minimum sum of the absolute value of the error between the matched blocks. Although the minimum mean square error is mathematically superior, it does not provide practical improvements in most situations. The luminance of the macroblock is the information commonly used to estimate the motion displacement of macroblocks between frames.

Once the best motion vector has been determined, half-pixel displacements of the motion vector (e.g., eight different half-pixel displacements in an 8-neighborhood sense) can be considered in the block matching process to increase the temporal prediction precision. Ideally, half pixel accuracy should be attained for the motion vector.

Once the best matching region is found in the reference frame, the prediction error is coded by performing 8×8 DCT transformations on each of the six 8×8 blocks of residual information. Most of the residual values will be small and become zero after quantization. In addition to coding the prediction error, the motion vector(s) representing the relative displacement of the best matching block(s) in the reference frame(s) must be specified with the non-intra coded macroblock.

A 2-D motion vector is used during decompression as an offset to retrieve the best matched information from the reference frame.

Forward, Backward, Bi-directional Temporal Prediction

P frame macroblocks employ only forward prediction. B frame macroblocks may be temporally predicted in the forward, backward, or bi-directional sense. If a macroblock of a B frame is predicted from both reference frames, the two predictions are averaged. This is referred to as *interpolative motion compensation.*

In the most simplified scheme, the encoder would choose the prediction mode that produces the least prediction error between the matched region in the reference frame and the current macroblock. The additional motion vector introduced by bi-directional prediction should be considered in the cost model. Bi-directional motion compensated prediction is exemplified in Fig. 27.

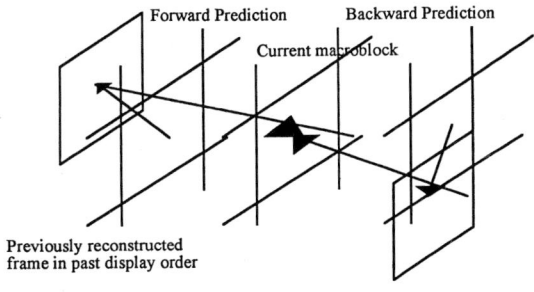

Fig. 27. Bi-directional prediction in B frames from two reference frames

Coding of Motion Vectors

Motion vectors are compressed losslessly using spatial DPCM. In P frames the motion vector is predicted from the value of the previous macroblock. In B frames, forward and backward motion vectors are respectively predicted from the values of the corresponding motion vectors in the previous macroblock. Predictions are reset at the beginning of each slice and in other situations.

Motion or No Motion Compensation

If a zero displacement prediction provides a close enough match to the desired fidelity of the current macroblock, then the coding of the motion vectors can be spared, saving a few bits. Further, a zero-motion compensation condition is a precursor to having *skipped macroblocks* in P frames. Figures 28 and 29 show forward prediction without and with motion compensation, respectively.

Intra/Non-Intra Coding Decision

The non-intra coding process of a macroblock is depicted in Fig. 30. Once the best temporal prediction of a macroblock is determined, the number of bits required to code the macroblock in non-intra mode is compared to its intra mode representation. The projected distortion of each mode should also be considered. If

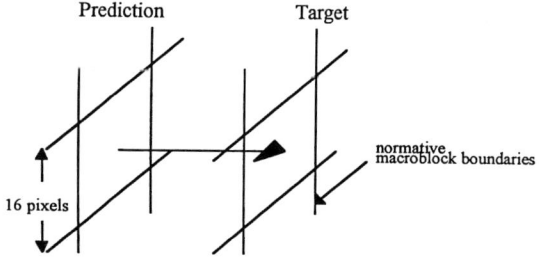

Fig. 28. Non-motion compensated forward temporal prediction

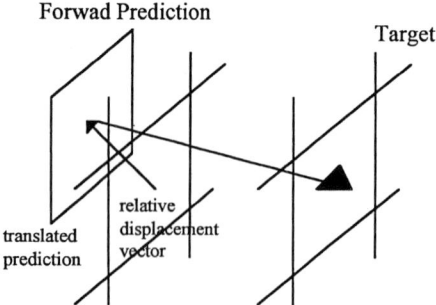

Fig. 29. Compensated temporal forward prediction

Video Compression for Multimedia Applications

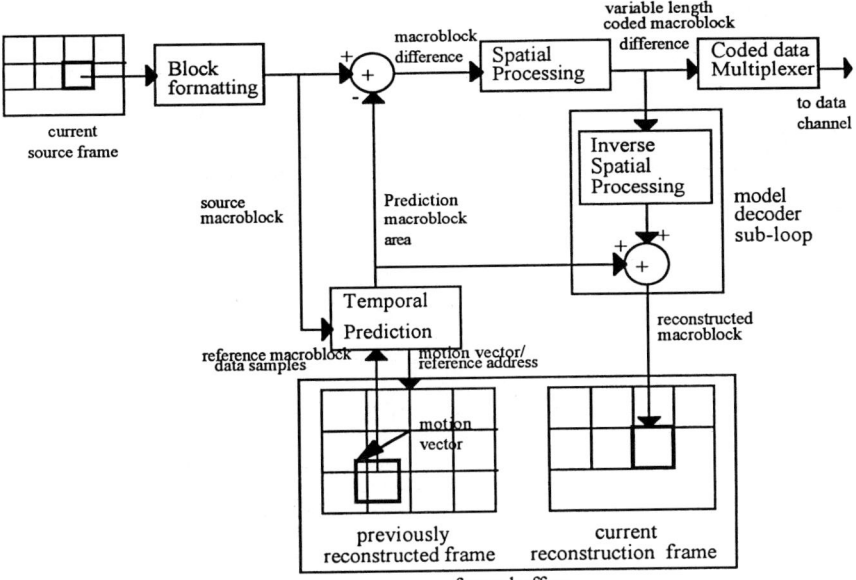

Fig. 30. Non-intra macroblock coding process

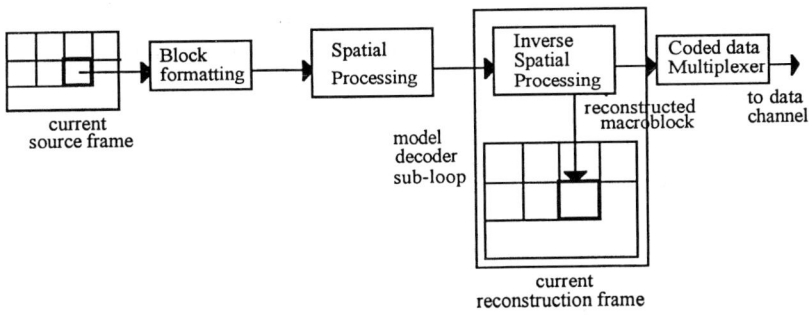

Fig. 31. Simplified diagram of intra coding of macroblocks

the compressor deems that a good temporal match does not exist, the macroblock is intraframe compressed. A simplified non-intra coding process of a macroblock is depicted in Fig. 31. The overall macroblock coding process is shown in Fig. 32.

The non-intra macroblock coding process of Fig. 30 is incorporated in Fig. 32 in the top-left box of the diagram. The intra macroblock coding process encompasses the remainder of the diagram. Both coding modes result in employment of the DCT to decorrelate the data. As mentioned previously, the DCT coefficients undergo quantization and are then re-ordered to implement entropy encoding (see Fig. 23).

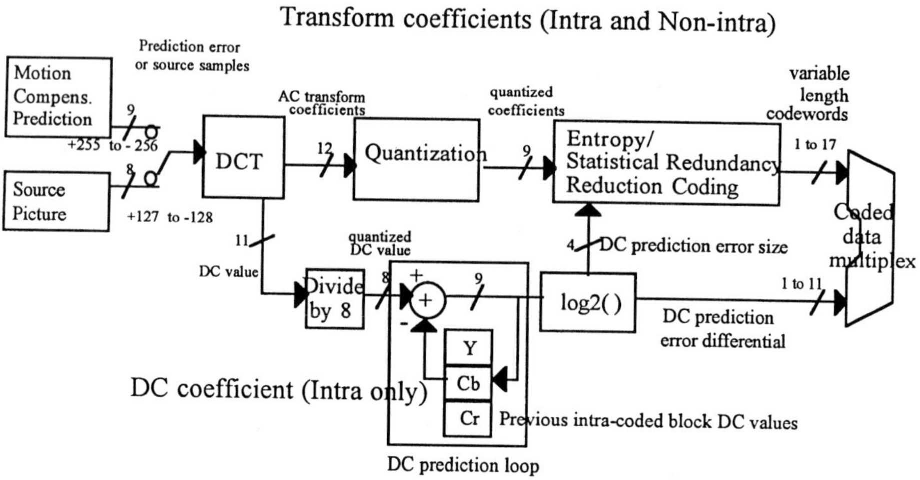

Fig. 32. Overall macroblock encoding process for MPEG-1

Skipped Macroblocks in P and B Frames

A skipped macroblock in a P frame is a macroblock with a zero motion vector that also has a zero prediction error. This is similar to the effects of the frame-differencing methods discussed in Sect. 3. During decompression, a skipped macroblock of a P frame is reconstructed by copying the information in the spatially corresponding macroblock in the previous reference frame.

A skipped macroblock in a B frame is a macroblock that has a zero prediction error and the same motion vector as the previous macroblock.

Hence, skipped macroblocks in P and B frames have different meanings but they both require the specification of very few bits in the compressed video stream.

Coded Block Patterns in P and B Frames

A *coded block pattern* (*CBP*) is used in P and B frames to specify which of the six blocks in the macroblock are coded versus which have zero prediction errors. In fixed length form, the CBP is a 6–bit token with each bit associated with corresponding 8 × 8 block in the macroblock (see Fig. 11). The 6-bit CBP is variable-length coded.

5 Conclusions

In this Chapter we have examined video compression algorithms for multimedia applications. We have given a detailed account of the general issues related to assessing video codecs for multimedia applications. The characteristics of video codecs that must be considered for multimedia applications were discussed. This discussion included references to image fidelity (i.e., quality), bandwidth (i.e., compression), ease-of-decoding (i.e., playback performance), memory consumption, compression to decompression asymmetry, scalability, and delay. We discussed the tradeoffs among these variables and suggested rules for subjective video quality evaluations. Quantitative distortion measures were also discussed but not emphasized since multimedia is a completely different problem than rate distortion theory.

The reality of digital video is that there are two camps: software-only video codecs and hardware-assisted video codecs that require hardware assistance for execution. Software-only video codecs have marked an era where a computer user does not have to purchase any special hardware to playback video on low-end personal computers. Hardware-assisted video codecs provide much higher image quality and better performance and will eventually be implementable in software as technological advances continue.

Ease-of-decoding is crucial for software-only video codecs. The significance of simplifying the complexity of color conversion operations for software-only video codecs and maintaining a byte aligned compressed video syntax was emphasized. We also examined the primary tasks required for software-only video playback. Frame-differencing approaches were described as they are an integral part of software-only video codecs. Intraframe compression techniques that exhibit low computational complexity for software-only video playback were presented. The bandwidth that Motion JPEG and MPEG would provide in a byte-oriented video stream was provided for comparison to software-only video codecs.

Video codec approaches for multimedia applications that are more likely to be implemented with hardware assistance were discussed in Sect. 4. A detailed account of the fundamentals of MPEG video compression was provided since MPEG is destined to become the video codec of choice for years to come due to that it is a standard that is widely endorsed and to its significant momentum in the multimedia community.

Acknowledgements. We wish to express our gratitude to many of our colleagues for many stimulating discussions. Kaleida Labs helped make this work possible. A.A. Rodriguez acknowledges his Lord and Savior, Jesus Christ, for making this work possible and for the light and strength needed in carrying out this endeavor. And to his wife, Judy, he expresses his deepest gratitude and love for her patience, understanding and strong support.

7 References

[1] W. Stallings, *Integrated Services Digital Network (ISDN)*. IEEE Computer Society Press, Washington, D. C., 1985.
[2] Video Codec for Audiovisual Services at p X 64 kbits/s. CCITT Recommendation H.261, International Telegraph and Telephone Consultative Committee (CCITT), 1990.

[3] A. A. Rodriguez and K. Morse, "Feasibility of video codec algorithms for software-only playback," in *Digital Video Compression on Personal Computers: Algorithms and Techniques*, A. A. Rodriguez, Editor, Proc. SPIE 2187, (1994).

[4] D. A. Huffman, "A Method for the Construction of Minimum Redundancy Codes," *Proc. IRE*, Vol. 40, No. 10, pp. 1098–1101, Sept. 1952.

[5] T. A. Welch, "A Technique for High-Performance Data Compression," *IEEE Computer*, Vol. 17, pp. 8–19, June 1984.

[6] G. G. Langdon, "An introduction to arithmetic coding," *IBM Journal of Research and Development*, Vol. 28, No. 2, pp. 135–149, 1984.

[7] W. B. Pennebaker, J. L. Mitchell, G. G. Langdon, and R. B. Arps, "An overview of the basic principles of the Q-coder adaptive binary arithmetic coder," *IBM Journal of Research and Development*, Vol. 32, No. 6, pp. 717–726, 1988.

[8] M. Kunt, A. Ikonomopolous, and M. Kocher, "Second generation image-coding techniques," *Proc. of the IEEE*, vol. 73, pp. 549–574, April 1985.

[9] H. A. Peterson and E. J. Delp, "An overview of digital image bandwidth compression," *Journal of Data and Computer Communications*, vol. 2, no. 3, pp. 39–49, Winter 1990.

[10] D. LeGall, "MPEG: A video compression standard for Multimedia Application," *Communications of the ACM*, Vol. 34, No. 4, pp. 46–58, April 1991.

[11] ISO/IEC International Standard IS 11172-2 "Information technology – Coding of moving pictures and associated audio for digital storage media at up to about 1.5 Mbits/s – Part 2: Video," 1993.

[12] ISO/IEC International Standard IS 11172-1 "Information technology – Coding of moving pictures and associated audio for digital storage media at up to about 1.5 Mbits/s – Part 3: Audio," 1993.

[13] ISO/IEC International Standard IS 11172-3 "Information technology – Coding of moving pictures and associated audio for digital storage media at up to about 1.5 Mbits/s – Part 1: Systems," 1993.

[14] E. J. Delp and O. R. Mitchell, "Image compression using block truncation coding," *IEEE Trans. on Communications*, vol. COM-27, No. 9, pp. 1335–1342, September 1979.

[15] D. Chen and A. C. Bovik, "Visual pattern image coding," *IEEE Trans. on Communications*, vol. COM-38, No. 12, pp. 2137–2146, Dec. 1990.

[16] G. Campbell, et al., "Two bit/pixel full color encoding," in *Proc. ACM Computer Graphics*, Vol. 20, No. 4, pp. 215–223, Dallas, Aug. 1986.

[17] R. M. Gray "Vector Quantization," *IEEE ASSP Mag.*, pp 4–29, April 1984.

[18] K. S. Wang, J. O. Normile, and H-J. Wu, "A high performance video codec for CD-ROM based video playback," in *Digital Video Compression on Personal Computers: Algorithms and Techniques*, A. A. Rodriguez, Editor, Proc. SPIE 2187, (1994).

[19] J. W. Woods and S. D. O'Neil, "Subband coding of images," *IEEE Trans. on Acoustics, Speech, and Signal Processing*, vol. ASSP-34, No. 10, pp. 1278–1288, October 1986.

[20] D. Taubman and A. Zakhor, "Rate and resolution scalable 3-D subband coding of video," in *Digital Video Compression on Personal Computers: Algorithms and Techniques*, A. A. Rodriguez, Editor, Proc. SPIE 2187, (1994).

[21] A. S. Lewis and G. Knowles, "Video Compression Using 3D Wavelet Transforms," *Electronic Letters*, Vol. 26, No. 6, pp 396–398, 15 March 1990.

[22] K. H. Goh, J. J. Soraghan, and T. S. Durrani, "New 3-D Wavelet Transform Coding Algorithm for Image Sequences," *Electronic Letters*, Vol. 29, No. 4, pp. 401–402, 18 Feb. 1993.

[23] A. Sengupta, M. Hilton, and B. Jawerth, "A computationally fast wavelet-based video coding scheme," in *Digital Video Compression on Personal Computers: Algorithms and Techniques*, A. A. Rodriguez, Editor, Proc. SPIE 2187, (1994).

[24] P. J. Burt and E. H. Adelson, "The Laplacian pyramid as a compact image code," *IEEE Trans. on Communications*, vol. COM-31, no. 4, pp. 532–540, April 1983.

[25] A. R. Robertson, "The CIE 1976 Color-Difference Formulae," *Color Research and Application*, vol. 2, No. 1, Spring 1977.

[26] Z. L. Budrikis, "Visual fidelity criterion and modeling," *Proc. of the IEEE*, vol. 60, pp. 771-779, July 1972.
[27] J. L. Mannos and D. J. Sakrison, "The effects of a visual fidelity criterion on the encoding of images," *IEEE Transactions on Information Theory*, vol. IT-20, pp. 525-536, July 1974.
[28] N. Jayant, J. Johnston, and R. Safranek, "Signal compression based on models of human perception," *Proceedings of the IEEE*, vol. 81, no. 10, pp. 1385-1422, Oct. 1993.
[29] D. J. Sakrison, "On the role of the observer and a distortion measure in image transmission," *IEEE Transactions on Communications*, vol. COM-25, pp. 1251-1267, Nov. 1977.
[30] D. J. Granrath, "The role of human visual models in image processing," *Proceedings of the IEEE*, vol. 69, pp. 552-561, May 1981.
[31] G. C. Higgins, "Image quality criteria," *Journal of Applied Photographic Engineers*, vol. 3, pp. 53-60, Spring 1977.
[32] J. O. Limb, "Distortion criteria of the human viewer," *IEEE Transactions on Systems, Man, and Cybernetics*, vol. SMC-9, pp. 778-793, December 1979.
[33] K. Hosaka, "A new picture quality evaluation method," *Proc. of Int'l Picture Coding Symposium*, Tokyo, Japan, April 1986.
[34] D. J. Sakrison, M. Halter and H. Mostafavi, "Properties of the Human Visual System as Related to Encoding of Images," in *New Directions in Signal Processing in Communication and Control*, J. K. Skwiyzyinski (Editor), Noordhoff and Leyden 1975.
[35] A. N. Netravali and J. O. Limb, "Picture coding: A review," *Proceedings of the IEEE*, vol. 68, pp. 366-406, March 1980.
[36] C. C. I. R, "Method for the subjective assessment of the quality of television pictures," 13th Plenary Assembly, Record 500, vol. 11, pp. 65-68, 1974.
[37] R. T. Apteker, J. A. Fisher, V. S. Kisimov, and H. Neishlos, "Distributed Multimedia: User Perception and Dynamic QoS," in *High-Speed Networking and Multimedia Computing*, A. A. Rodriguez, M-S. Chen, and J. Maitan, Editors, Proc. SPIE 2188, (1994).
[38] A. A. Rodriguez, et al., "Method of Converting Luminance-Color Difference Video Signal to a Three Color Component Video Signal," United States Patent No. 5,262,847, Nov. 16, 1993.
[39] J. O. Limb and C. B. Rubinstein, "Plateau Coding of the Chrominance Components of Color Picture Signals," *IEEE Trans. on Communications*, Vol. COM-22, pp. 812-820, July 1974.
[40] A. N. Netravali and C. B. Rubinstein, "Luminance Adaptive Coding of Chrominance Signals," *IEEE Trans. on Communications*, Vol. COM-27, pp. 703-710, April 1979.
[41] K. Shen, G. W. Cook, L. H. Jamieson, and E. J. Delp, "An overview of parallel processing approach to image compression," in *Image and Video Compression*, M. Rabbani and R. J. Safranek, Editors, Proc. SPIE 2186, (1994).
[42] G. W. Cook and E. J. Delp, "The use of high performance computing in JPEG image compression," *Proc. Twenty-Seventh Asilomar Conference on Signals, Systems, and Computers*, Pacific Grove, CA, Nov. 1993.
[43] G. W. Cook and E. J. Delp, "An investigation of JPEG image and video compression using parallel processing," *Proc. IEEE International Conference on Acoustics, Speech and Signal Processing*, Adelaide, South Australia, April 19-22 1994.
[44] R. N. Williams, "An Extremely Fast Ziv-Lempel Data Compression Algorithm", *IEEE Proc. of the Data Compression Conference*, Snowbird, Utah, pp. 362-371, April 8-11, 1991.
[45] H. C. Reeve and J. S. Lim, "Reduction of blocking effect in image coding," *Proc. IEEE International Conference on Acoustics, Speech and Signal Processing*, pp. 1212-1215, 1983.
[46] P. M. Farrelle, "Recursive Block Coding for Image Data Compression," Springer-Verlag, Heidelberg, Germany, 1990.

[47] Y. Linde, A. Buzo, and R. M. Gray, "An algorithm for vector quantizer design," *IEEE Trans. Commun.*, Vol. COM-28, No. 1, pp. 84–95, Jan. 1980.

[48] R. L. Baker and R. M. Gray, "Differential vector quantization of achromatic imagery," *Proc. Int. Picture Coding Symposium*, Davis, CA, pp 105–106, 1983.

[49] A. Gersho and R. M. Gray, *Vector Quantization and Signal Compression*, Dordecht: Kluwer, 1992.

[50] J. Y. Y. Huang and P. M. Schultheiss, "Block quantization of correlated gaussian random variables," *IEEE Transactions on Communication Systems*, vol. CS-11, pp. 289–296, September 1963.

[51] P. A. Wintz, "Transform picture coding," *Proceedings of the IEEE*, vol. 60, pp. 809–820, July 1972.

[52] G. K. Wallace, "The JPEG Still Picture Compression Standard," *Communications of the ACM*, Vol. 34, No. 4, pp. 30–44, April 1991.

[53] D. H. Lee and S. Sudharsanan, "Design of a Motion JPEG (MJPEG) adapter card," in *Digital Video Compression on Personal Computers: Algorithms and Techniques*, A. A. Rodriguez, Editor, Proc. SPIE 2187, (1994).

[54] E. J. Delp, R. L. Kashyap, and O. R. Mitchell, "Image data compression using autoregressive time series models," *Pattern Recognition*, vol. 11, no. 5/6, pp. 313–323, 1979.

[55] N. S. Jayant and P. Noll, *Digital Coding of Waveforms: Principles and Applications to Speech and Video*. Englewood Cliffs, New Jersey: Prentice-Hall, Inc., 1984.

[56] A. Habibi, "Survey of adaptive image coding techniques," *IEEE Transactions on Communications*, vol. COM-25, pp. 1275–1284, November 1977.

[57] W. H. Chen and C. H. Smith, "Adaptive coding of monochrome and color images," *IEEE Transactions on Communications*, vol. COM-25, pp. 1285–1292, Nov. 1977.

[58] L. Ehrman, "Analysis of some redundancy removal bandwidth compression techniques," *Proc. of the IEEE*, vol. 55, pp. 278–287, March 1967.

[59] L. D. Davisson, "Data compression using straight line interpolation," *IEEE Trans. on Information Theory*, vol. IT-14, pp. 390–394, May 1968.

[60] D. Gabor and P. C. J. Hill, "Television band compression by contour interpolation," *Proc. of the IEE*, vol. 108B, pp. 303–313, May 1961.

[61] A. E. Jacquin, "A novel fractal block coding technique for digital images," Proc. IEEE ICASSP, pp. 2225–2228, 1990.

[62] A.E. Jacquin, "Fractal image coding: A review," *Proc. of the IEEE*, vol. 81, no. 10, pp. 1451–1465, Oct. 1993.

[63] J. Waite, "A Review of Iterated Function System Theory for Image Compression," *Proc. IEE Colloquium on "The application of fractal techniques in image processing,"* London, 3 Dec. 1990.

[64] J. M. Beaumont, "Advances in Block Based Fractal Coding of Still Pictures," *Proc. IEE Colloquium on "The application of fractal techniques in image processing,"* London, 3 Dec. 1990.

[65] J. M. Beaumont, "Image data compression using fractal techniques," *British Telecomm Technology Journal*, Vol. 9, No. 4, pp. 93–109, Oct. 1991.

[66] L. A. Overturf, M. L. Comer, and E. J. Delp, "Color image coding using morphological pyramid decomposition," *To appear in IEEE Trans. on Image Processing*, 1995.

[67] M. Antonini, M. Barlaud, P. Mathieu, and I. Daubechies, "Image coding using wavelet transform," *IEEE Trans. on Image Processing*, vol. 1, no. 2, pp. 205–220, April 1992.

[68] R. A. Devore, B. Jaweth, and B. J. Lucier, "Image compression through wavelet transform coding," *IEEE Trans. on Information Theory*, vol. 38, no. 2, pp. 719–746, March 1992.

[69] O. R. Mitchell and E. J. Delp, "Multilevel graphics representation using block truncation coding," *Proc. of the IEEE*, vol. 68, no. 7, pp. 868–873, July 1980.

[70] O. R. Mitchell, S. C. Bass, E. J. Delp, T.W. Goeddel, and T. S. Huang, "Image coding for photo analysis," *Proceedings of the Society for Information Display*, vol. 21/3, pp. 279–292, 1980.

[71] W. B. Pennebaker and J. L. Mitchell, *JPEG Still Image Data Compression Standard*. Library of Congress Cataloging-in-Publication Data, New York: Van Nostrand Reinhold, 1993.

[72] Sun Microsystems, California, *Solaris XIL1.0 imaging library: Programmer's guide* February 1993.

[73] B. K. Neidecker-Lutz and R. Ulichney, "Software motion pictures," *Digital Technical Journal*, vol. 5, no. 2, pp. 19–27, 1993.

[74] E. J. Delp and O. R. Mitchell, "The use of block truncation coding in DPCM image coding," *IEEE Trans. on Signal Process.*, vol. 39, no. 4, pp. 967–971, April 1991.

[75] M. D. Lema and O. R. Mitchell, "Absolute moment block truncation coding and its application to color images," *IEEE Trans. Commun.*, Vol. COM-32, No. 10, pp. 1148–1157, 1984.

[76] J. U. Roy and N. M. Nasrabadi, "Hierarchical block truncation coding," *Optical Engineering*, Vol. 30, No. 5, pp. 551–556, May 1991.

[77] M. Kamel, C. T. Sun, and L. Guan, "Image compression by variable block truncation coding with optimal threshold," *IEEE Trans. on Signal Processing*, Vol. 39, No. 1, pp. 208–212, Jan. 1991.

[78] C. Pitts, J. M. Beaumont, S. Cozens, N. A. Emms, and D. J. Myers, "A software codec for personal computers based on the discrete cosine transform," in *Digital Video Compression on Personal Computers: Algorithms and Techniques*, A. A. Rodriguez, Editor, Proc. SPIE 2187, (1994).

[79] R. Wilson, "Using 4 × 4 DCTs and moving 4 × 4 blocks for software-only video decompression," in *Digital Video Compression on Personal Computers: Algorithms and Techniques*, A. A. Rodriguez, Editor, Proc. SPIE 2187, (1994).

[80] A. A. Rodriguez, J. R. Mandeville, and F. Y. Wu, "Calibration and Alignment Techniques for Automated Inspection of Printed Circuit Patterns," Industrial Metrology Journal, Vol. 1, No. 4, pp. 293–307, 1991.

[81] M. A. Pietras, A. A. Rodriguez, and A. J. Saenz, "System and Method for Frame-Differencing Based Video Compression/Decompression with Forward and Reverse Playback Capability," United States Patent No. 5,298,992, March, 1994.

[82] Committee Draft of ISO/IEC International Standard 13818-2 "Information technology – Generic coding of moving pictures and associated audio," ITU-T Draft Recommendation H.262, Nov. 25, 1993.

[83] C. Loeffler, A. Ligtenberg, G. S. Moschytz *Practical fast 1-D DCT algorithms with 11 multiplications Proceedings* IEEE ICASSP-89, Vol. 2, pp. 988–991, Feb. 1989.

[84] E. Feig and E. Linzer, "Scaled DCT Algorithms for JPEG and MPEG Implementations on fused multiply/add Architectures," Image Processing Algorithms and Techniques II, Proc. SPIE 1452, pp. 458–467, (1991).

Directionality and Scalability in Subband Image and Video Compression

D. Taubman, E. Chang, and A. Zakhor

1 Introduction

Broadly speaking, data compression strategies may be classified as either lossless or lossy. As its name suggests, the primary goal of lossless compression is to minimize the number of bits required to represent the source data without any loss of information. For image, and particularly video sources, however, some loss of information can usually be tolerated. There are three reasons for this. Firstly, significant loss of information can often be tolerated by the human visual system, without interfering with perception of the image or video sequence. Secondly, in many cases the digital input to the compression algorithm is, itself, an imperfect representation of a real-world scene. Thirdly, lossless image or video compression is usually incapable of satisfying the high compression requirements of most storage and distribution applications. In this chapter we are concerned only with lossy compression.

For any particular data source, the compression performance of a lossy compression scheme may be described in terms of its so-called rate-distortion curve, representing the potential trade-off between the bit rate and the distortion associated with the lossy representation. We must be careful, however, to identify what is meant by *rate* and *distortion*. In image compression applications, rate is usually taken to mean the average number of bits per image pixel. The exact rate of interest to video applications, where the number of pixels is effectively unbounded, is usually determined by distribution or storage issues such as buffer capacity. For example, the average number of bits per pixel over an entire video sequence is usually of much less interest than the maximum number of bits used to encode any frame or small collection of frames. For video applications, rate is usually expressed in terms of bits per second, rather than bits per pixel. Similarly, the average distortion over an entire video sequence is rarely of interest, whereas a local distortion average, taken over each frame or perhaps smaller regions of a frame or an image, is often much more relevant. Moreover various definitions of distortion may be taken, from the most simplistic Mean Squared Error (MSE), to a variety of measures which attempt to approximate the subjective nature of distortion.

Subject to these considerations, we may say that the primary goal of lossy compression is to optimize the rate-distortion curve over some range of rates and distortions of interest. In addition to good compression performance, however, many other properties may be important or even critical to the applicability of a given compression algorithm. Such properties include robustness to errors in the compressed bit stream, limited computational requirements for the compression and/or the decompression algorithms and, for interactive video applications, restrictions on the overall latency associated with compression, distribution and decompression of the source material.

One particular property which has attracted considerable attention in recent years is *scalability*. Generally speaking, scalability refers to the potential to effectively decompress subsets of the compressed bit stream in order to satisfy some practical constraint. Constraints may include display resolution – i.e., frame or image dimensions or frame rate –, decoder computational complexity, and bit rate limitations. More specifically, we refer to the ability to satisfy these various constraints, by extracting subsets from the compressed bit stream, as *resolution-scalability*, *complexity-scalability* and *rate-scalability*, respectively. The significance of scalability is that an image or video sequence need only be compressed, and possibly stored, once. Practical constraints may then be satisfied as they arise during distribution or decompression of the compressed data. Unfortunately, standard video compression algorithms currently provide only limited scalability, if at all.

In Sect. 2 we provide a brief overview of some of the conventional building blocks used in image and video compression algorithms. In Sect. 3 we then review the key compression standards, JPEG, MPEG and H.261. The objective in these first two sections is not just to provide an overview of compression techniques, but also to indicate the implications of particular techniques for the properties of the overall compression algorithm.

Most conventional image and video compression algorithms involve the quantization and coding of coefficients obtained from some separable image transformation – that is, a transformation obtained by separable application of a one dimensional operator in the horizontal and vertical image dimensions. As such, these algorithms fail to take full advantage of exclusively multi-dimensional features such as orientation and velocity. In Sect. 4 we present a novel approach to subband image compression, which specifically exploits local orientational features to reduce subjective distortion. Then, in Sect. 5, we present an approach to exploit velocity in a three dimensional subband setting.

As already mentioned, scalability is often an important goal for image and video compression. In Sect. 6 we present an algorithm for the progressive quantization and coding of subband coefficients, thus realizing the rate-scalable property. Finally, in Sect. 7, we present an efficient rate-, resolution- and complexity-scalable algorithm for compressing both video and still image material.

2 Conventional Building Blocks

The purpose of this section is to briefly present some of the conventional building blocks used in standard video compression algorithms and to stress their impact

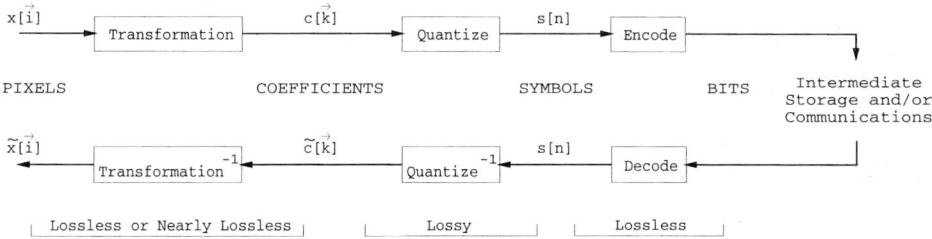

Fig. 1. General lossy compression model

upon the various compression goals outlined in Sect. 1. Ignoring, for the moment, the possibility of predictive feedback, Fig. 1 provides a useful framework for understanding lossy compression algorithms. A transformation is first applied to the source pixels, which are represented by the multi-dimensional source sequence, $x[\vec{i}]$. The output coefficients of this transformation, $c[\vec{k}]$, are scanned and quantized to yield a one-dimensional sequence of quantizer symbols, $s[n]$, which is encoded into a bit stream. The encoding block of Fig. 1 is assumed to be lossless, in that the symbol sequence, $s[n]$, can be exactly recovered by decoding the bit stream. The transformation block is usually also lossless, or at least approximately so. The information loss in a lossy compression algorithm is primarily attributable to quantization, so that the recovered coefficients, $\tilde{c}[\vec{k}]$, and pixel values, $\tilde{x}[\vec{i}]$, are only approximately equal to $c[\vec{k}]$ and $x[\vec{i}]$. Although this lossy quantization operation cannot be strictly invertible in the mathematical sense, the inverse notation of Fig. 1 is used for traditional reasons.

In Sect. 2.1 we review the two most commonly employed transformations, namely the Discrete Cosine Transform (DCT) and subband decomposition. In Sect. 2.2 we introduce a variety of conventional approaches to the quantization and coding of the transformation coefficients. Finally, in Sect. 2.3 we discuss predictive feedback for improving compression performance, with particular reference to its implications for scalability.

2. Transformations

As indicated by Fig. 1, most image and video compression schemes apply a transformation to the raw pixels before quantizing and coding the resulting coefficients. Although shape and texture modeling are sometimes used to obtain very low bit rates, the most common transformations are the Discrete Cosine Transform (DCT) and a variety of Subband Decomposition techniques. These are linear transformations which preserve the total number of samples, so that the multi-dimensional sequence of input pixel values, $x[\vec{i}]$, may be represented in terms of the transform's coefficients, $c[\vec{k}]$, via

$$x[\vec{i}] = \sum_{\vec{k}} c[\vec{k}] w_{\vec{k}}[\vec{i}] \tag{1}$$

for some $w_{\vec{k}}[\vec{i}]$ or, equivalently, regarding x and $w_{\vec{k}}$ as vectors in the linear space of multi-dimensional sequences,

$$x = \sum_{\vec{k}} c[\vec{k}] w_{\vec{k}}$$

The input image is thus represented as a linear combination of basis vectors, $w_{\vec{k}}$. The coefficients, $c[\vec{k}]$, are obtained as linear combinations of the source pixels, according to

$$c[\vec{k}] = \sum_{\vec{i}} \tilde{w}_{\vec{k}}[\vec{i}] x[\vec{i}] = \langle \tilde{w}_{\vec{k}}, x \rangle \tag{2}$$

for some sequences $\tilde{w}_{\vec{k}}$, where $\langle \cdot \rangle$ denotes inner product. In the case of the DCT and for some subband decompositions the $w_{\vec{k}}$ form an orthonormal set of basis vectors and so we have $\tilde{w}_{\vec{k}} = w_{\vec{k}}$.

The basis vectors, $w_{\vec{k}}$, are usually selected to have approximately bandpass frequency characteristics, so that the transformation may be viewed as a segmentation of the image or video sequence into a collection of bands, representing different spectral regions. The motivation for such transformations in compression applications is twofold. In the first place, the transform bands usually possess widely differing statistical properties, allowing the quantization and coding blocks, depicted in Fig. 1, to be appropriately tailored to the statistics of each band, in order to optimize compression performance. The second primary motivation for employing transformations, such as the DCT or subband decomposition, in compression algorithms is that they allow the distortion in individual bands to be independently adjusted according to the highly non-uniform frequency response of the human visual system. Transformations also have potential advantages for the robustness of the compression algorithm to errors in the bit stream, in that different emphases can be given to the protection of different bands of coefficients against communication errors, according to the visual significance of those coefficients.

The DCT

In our discussion of the DCT we begin by considering only a one dimensional source sequence, $x[i]$. The DCT is a block based transform in that the source sequence is first divided into segments of some fixed length N, which are then processed independently, The DCT coefficients, $c^{DCT}[k]$, are given by

$$c^{DCT}[Nb+k] = \frac{1}{\sqrt{N}} \begin{cases} \sum_{i=0}^{N-1} x[Nb+i], & k=0 \\ \sqrt{2} \sum_{i=0}^{N-1} x[Nb+i] \cos\frac{(2i+1)k\pi}{2N}, & 1 \leq k < N \end{cases} \forall b \tag{3}$$

where b denotes block number. Although equation (3) may seem somewhat complicated, the block terms, 'Nb', appear only for notational consistency. It is clear that each block of N DCT coefficients, $c^{DCT}[Nb+k]$, $0 \leq k < N$, depends only on a corresponding block of N sample values, $x[Nb + i]$, $0 \leq i < N$. In practice, then, we usually think of segmenting the input into blocks of N samples at a time, and applying the DCT transformation to each block, according to equation (3) with $b = 0$.

The orthonormal basis vectors associated with the one dimensional DCT transformation of equation (3) are

$$w_{Nb+k}^{DCT}[Nb' + i] = \frac{\delta(b' - b)}{\sqrt{N}} \begin{cases} 1, & k = 0,\ 0 \leq i < N \\ \sqrt{2} \cos \frac{(2i+1)k\pi}{2N}, & 1 \leq k < N,\ 0 \leq i < N \end{cases} \quad \forall b, b' \quad (4)$$

which are readily shown to satisfy equations (1) and (2) with $\tilde{w}_k^{DCT} = w_k^{DCT}$. Several of these basis vectors are illustrated in Fig. 2 for $N = 8$. The DCT is described as a block transform because the basis vectors occur in non-overlapping blocks of N vectors at a time. For obvious reasons, the coefficients, $c^{DCT}[Nb]$, are referred to as the DC coefficients, while the remaining coefficients are referred to as the AC coefficients.

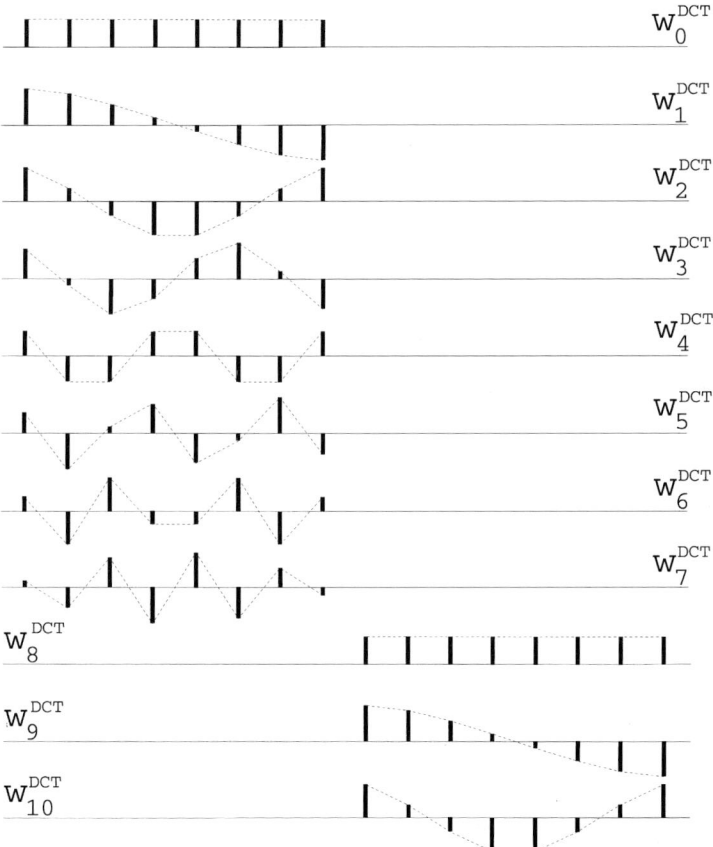

Fig. 2. DCT basis vectors with $N = 8$

The one dimensional DCT described above is usually separably extended to two dimensions for image compression applications. In this case, the two dimensional basis vectors are formed by the tensor product of one dimensional DCT basis vectors. This means that the basis vectors occur in non-overlapping $N \times N$ blocks, with the $N \times N$ basis vectors in each block given by

$$\omega_{\vec{k}}^{\text{DCT}}[\vec{i}] = \omega_{k_1,k_2}^{\text{DCT}}[i_1,i_2] \triangleq \omega_{k_1}^{\text{DCT}}[i_1] \cdot \omega_{k_2}^{\text{DCT}}[i_2]; \qquad 0 \leq k_1, k_2, i_1, i_2 < N$$

The separable, two dimensional DCT coefficients may be found by first applying the one dimensional DCT to each image row and then using corresponding coefficients from each row as input to a one dimensional DCT applied along the columns.

Fast DCT algorithms exist, analogous to the well-known Fast Fourier Transform (FFT) algorithms, when N is not prime and, in particular, when N is a power of 2. In the latter case, these algorithms require $O(N_p \log N)$ arithmetic operations to transform N_p image or video pixels, using a block size of N. For a thorough review of these algorithms, as well as variants on the most popular DCT transformation presented here, [31] is one of many useful references.

The major objection to the DCT in image or video compression applications is that the non-overlapping blocks of basis vectors, $w_{\vec{k}}^{\vec{i}}$, are responsible for distinctly "blocky" distortion characteristics in decompressed images or video when sufficiently low bit rates are demanded. Figure 13 in Sect. 3.1 provides a good illustration of these annoying artifacts.

Subband Decomposition

As for the DCT, we begin our discussion of subband decomposition by considering only a one dimensional source sequence, $x[i]$. Figure 3 provides a general illustration of an N-band one dimensional subband system. We refer to the subband decomposition itself as *analysis* and to the inverse transformation as *synthesis*. The transformation coefficients of bands $1, 2, \ldots, N$ are denoted by the sequences $u_1[k], u_2[k], \ldots, u_N[k]$, respectively. For notational convenience and consistency

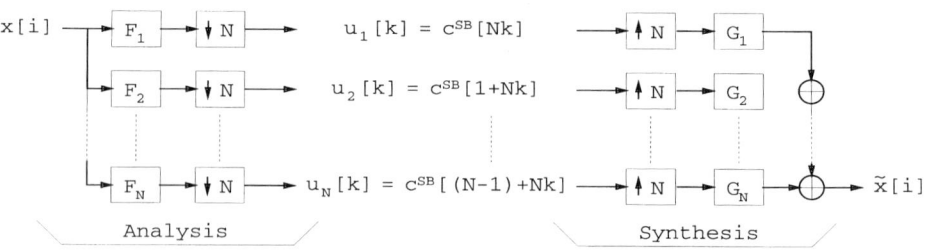

Fig. 3. 1D, N-band subband analysis and synthesis block diagrams

with the DCT formulation above, we write $c^{SB}[\cdot]$ for the sequence of all subband coefficients, arranged according to $c^{SB}[(\beta-1)+Nk] = u_\beta[k]$, where $1 \leq \beta \leq N$ is the subband number. These coefficients are generated by filtering the input sequence with filers $F_1, \ldots, F_N$ and downsampling the filtered sequences by a factor of N, as depicted in Fig. 3. The downsampling operator, $\boxed{\downarrow N}$, converts its input, $a[n]$, into a sequence, $b[n]$, with $\frac{1}{N}$ as many samples, according to $b[n] = a[Nn]$ – i.e., only every N'th sample is kept. In subband synthesis, the coefficients for each band are upsampled, interpolated with the synthesis filters, $G_1, \ldots, G_N$, and the results summed to form a reconstructed sequence, $\tilde{x}[i]$, as depicted in Fig. 3. The upsampling operator, $\boxed{\uparrow N}$, converts its input, $a[m]$, into a sequence $b[m]$ with N times as many samples, according to $b[mN] = a[m]$ and $b[mN+n] = 0$ for $1 \leq n < N$ – i.e., $N-1$ zeros are inserted after every sample of $a[m]$. If the reconstructed sequence, $\tilde{x}[i]$, and the source sequence $x[i]$ are identical then the subband system is referred to as Perfect Reconstruction (PR). Although Perfect Reconstruction is a desirable property, Near Perfect Reconstruction (NPR), for which subband synthesis is only approximately the inverse of subband analysis, is often sufficient in practice. This is because distortion introduced by quantization of the subband coefficients, $c^{SB}[k]$, as discussed in Sect. 2.2 usually dwarfs that introduced by an imperfect synthesis system.

The filters, $F_1, \ldots, F_N$ are usually designed to have band-pass frequency responses, as indicated in Fig. 4, so that the coefficients $u_\beta[k]$ for each subband, $1 \leq \beta \leq N$, represent different spectral components of the source sequence. The actual design of the analysis and synthesis filters is not discussed here, however [43] is a useful reference, among many others, for the design and application of subband filters, with image compression as a specific goal. The basis vectors for subband decomposition are the N-translates of the impulse responses, $g_1[i], \ldots, g_N[i]$, of synthesis filters $G_1, \ldots, G_N$. Specifically, denoting the k'th basis vector associated with subband β by $w^{SB}_{Nk+\beta-1}$, we have

$$w^{SB}_{Nk+\beta-1}[i] = g_\beta[i - Nk] \tag{5}$$

The corresponding "analysis" vector, $\tilde{w}_{Nk+\beta-1}$, of equation (2) is given by

$$\tilde{w}^{SB}_{Nk+\beta-1}[i] = f_\beta[Nk - i]$$

where $f_1[i], \ldots, f_N[i]$ are the impulse responses of the analysis filters, $F_1, \ldots, F_N$.

It is interesting to observe that the DCT may be viewed as a special case of subband decomposition. In particular, equating the basis vectors, w^{SB}_k and w^{DCT}_k of equations (5) and (4) for all k, and noting that $w^{DCT}_k = \tilde{w}^{DCT}_k$, reveals that the DCT

Fig. 4. Typical analysis filter magnitude responses

with block size N is nothing other than an N-band PR subband decomposition with the N-tap cosine filter impulse responses

$$g_\beta^{DCT}[i] = f_\beta^{DCT}[-i] = \frac{1}{\sqrt{N}} \begin{cases} 1 & \beta = 1,\ 0 \leq i < N \\ \sqrt{2}\cos\dfrac{(2i+1)(\beta-1)\pi}{2N}, & 2 \leq \beta \leq N,\ 0 \leq i < N \\ 0, & i < 0 \text{ or } i \geq N \end{cases}$$

Despite this connection, the term 'subband decomposition' is usually reserved to describe systems with a relatively small number of bands – e.g., $N = 2$, 3 or 4 – and whose filter impulse responses have more than N taps. Figure 5 illustrates five of the basis vectors for a particularly simple, yet useful two-band PR subband decomposition, with symmetric FIR analysis and synthesis impulse responses. Figure 5 is clearly distinguished from Fig. 2 on the basis of having overlapping rather than blocked basis vectors. N-band subband decompositions for which the analysis and synthesis filter impulse responses have support of more than N taps, necessarily have this property and are often referred to as *lapped transforms*.

For block transforms, such as the DCT, image boundaries require no special attention, provided the image dimensions are divisible by the block size, N. This is not the case with the lapped transforms, where some of the basis functions are guaranteed to overlap the boundaries. Three important approaches exist to preserving the PR or NPR properties of a lapped subband transformation in the vicinity of boundaries. The first approach is to retain all coefficients, $c^{SB}[k]$, whose corresponding basis vectors, w_k, intersect with the region of support of the source

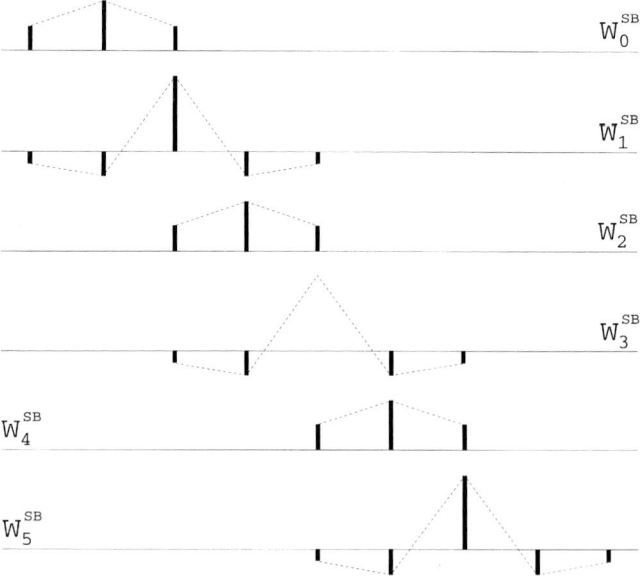

Fig. 5. Subband basis vectors with $N = 2$, $f_1[-2\ldots 2] = \sqrt{2} \cdot (-\frac{1}{8}, \frac{1}{4}, \frac{3}{4}, \frac{1}{4}, -\frac{1}{8})$, $f_2[-2\ldots 0] = \sqrt{2} \cdot (-\frac{1}{4}, \frac{1}{2}, -\frac{1}{4})$, $g_1[-1\ldots 1] = \sqrt{2} \cdot (\frac{1}{4}, \frac{1}{2}, \frac{1}{4})$ and $g_2[-1\ldots 3] = \sqrt{2} \cdot (-\frac{1}{8}, -\frac{1}{4}, \frac{3}{4}, -\frac{1}{4}, -\frac{1}{8})$

sequence, $x[i]$. In this case, the image can always be reconstructed correctly according to equation (1), however the number of transformation coefficients is larger than the number of support samples in $x[i]$. For the example of Fig. 5, supposing that $x[i]$ has support $0 \leq i \leq 4$, this approach would require coefficients $c^{SB}[k]$ to be retained for $-1 \leq k \leq 5$. This approach is often referred to as *expansive*. The sample rate expansion associated with the technique can prove very damaging to typical subband compression applications, in which the basis vectors can have quite large effective support – e.g., 100 taps. Such large effective basis vector supports arise from recursive subband decomposition in pyramid structures, to be discussed shortly.

The second approach to ensuring the PR or NPR property of a lapped subband transform near image boundaries is to periodically extend $x[i]$. In particular, if $x[i]$ has support $0 \leq i < P$, we apply the subband decomposition to the periodically extended sequence, $x^{PE}[nP+i] = x[i]$, $0 \leq i < P$, $\forall n$. When P is divisible by N, it may readily be shown that the sequence of all subband coefficients, $c^{SB}[k]$, is also periodic, with period P, and so only P coefficients need be retained in the representation of $x[i]$. This approach avoids sample rate expansion, however the periodic extension of $x[i]$ commonly has an adverse effect on compression performance due to the introduction of high frequency transients at the replication boundaries, $i = nP$. A third approach avoids this transient difficulty by symmetrically extending [38] the source sequence. Unfortunately, this method is only applicable when the subband analysis filters have symmetric impulse responses. By way of example, assume that the impulse response, $f_\beta[i]$, of each analysis filter, F_β, $\beta = 1, 2, \ldots, N$, is symmetric about $i = \beta - 1$. We may construct the symmetrically extended sequence, $x^{SE}[i]$, satisfying $x^{SE}[i] = x[i]$, $0 \leq i < P$, and

$$x^{SE}[-i] = x^{SE}[i] = x^{SE}[2P - 1 - i], \quad \forall i$$

It is readily shown that the sequence of all subband coefficients, $c^{SB}[k]$, obtained by subband decomposition of $x^{SE}[i]$, possesses the same symmetries, namely

$$c^{SB}[k] = c^{SB}[-k] = c^{SB}[2P - 1 - k], \quad \forall i,$$

and hence only P coefficients need be retained in the representation of $x[i]$. In addition to avoiding the boundary transient difficulties of periodic extension, this approach places no restriction on the relationship between P and N. In practice, therefore, symmetric extension with symmetric subband filtering is the preferred approach to handling image boundaries. When non-symmetric filters must be used, periodic extension is usually preferred over an expansive approach.

As for the DCT, one dimensional subband decompositions may be separably extended to higher dimensions. By this we mean that a one dimensional subband decomposition is first applied along one dimension of an image or video sequence. Any or all of the resulting subbands are then further decomposed into subbands along another dimension and so on. In addition to separable extension to multiple dimensions, it is common to recursively extend a subband decomposition in a so-called pyramid structure. By this we mean that the lowest frequency subband obtained from one "stage" of subband analysis is applied to a second subband

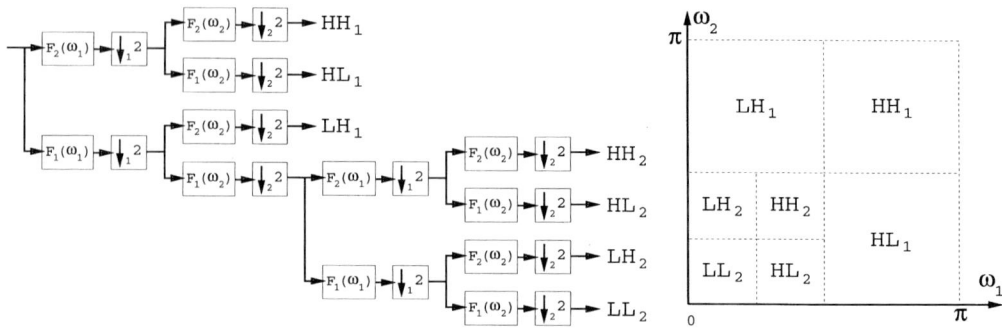

Fig. 6. Separable spatial subband pyramid. Two level analysis system configuration and subband passbands shown

analysis stage, whose lowest frequency subband may be applied to yet third stage of decomposition, and so on. Figure 6 illustrates the analysis system for a common, separable, spatial subband pyramid configuration, with two pyramid levels, built from two channel, one dimensional subband decompositions. In the figure, ω_1 and ω_2 denote horizontal and vertical frequency respectively, and $\boxed{\downarrow_1 2}$ and $\boxed{\downarrow_2 2}$ denote horizontal and vertical subsampling by 2, respectively. Figure 31 of Sect. 7 provides an example of a much more complex separable subband decomposition pyramid for video compression applications. In this figure HH_l denotes the horizontally and vertically high frequency subband at level l in the hierarchical decomposition; HL_l denotes the horizontally high frequency and vertically low frequency subband at level l; and so on.

Although we have discussed only one dimensional subband decomposition and its separable extension to multiple dimensions, it is possible to design non-separable multidimensional subband transformations. Such transformations are generally characterized by non-separable analysis and synthesis filters, $F_1, \ldots, F_N$, and $G_1, \ldots, G_N$, and generalized multi-dimensional downsampling and upsampling operators. D-dimensional downsampling and upsampling operators are described by a $D \times D$ matrix, S, with integer valued entries and a determinant of N. The downsampling operator converts a D-dimensional sequence, $a[\vec{n}]$, into a sequence, $b[\vec{n}]$, with $\frac{1}{N}$ as many samples, according to $b[\vec{n}] = a[S\vec{n}]$. Both the matrix, S, and the analysis and synthesis filter coefficients enter into the design problem for non-separable subband decompositions. Among other references, the interested reader is referred to [21] for more information. Non-separable subband transformations have the potential to exploit specifically multi-dimensional features in image and video signals, such as orientation and velocity, however the non-separable filtering operations involved usually render them considerably more computationally intensive than their separable counterparts. Moreover, the symmetric extension approach for handling image boundaries, discussed above, does not generalize to non-separable subband decompositions when image support is rectangular, as is almost always the case in practice.

Two dimensional, lapped subband decompositions have the advantage that they do not suffer from the disturbing blocking artifacts exhibited by the DCT at high compression ratios. Instead, the most noticeable quantization-induced distortion tends to be "ringing" or "rippling" artifacts, which become most bothersome in the vicinity of image edges. Figures 19, and 21 in Sect. 4 provide examples of such artifacts. Three dimensional subband transformations for video compression are of considerable interest, as discussed in Sect. 7, however they have the drawback that temporal filtering introduces significant overall latency, a critical parameter for interactive video compression applications.

2.2 Quantization and Coding

Quantization is the principle "lossy" element in lossy compression[1]. The objective of quantization is to generate a sequence of symbols, $s[n]$, which represents an approximation to the transformation coefficients, $c[\vec{k}]$, each symbol being selected from a finite *alphabet*. The objective of coding is to generate a sequence of binary digits to represent the symbols $s[n]$. We refer to this sequence of binary digits as the bit stream. Due to the intimate connection between quantization and coding, we discuss them together in this section. Although $c[\vec{k}]$ is a multi-dimensional sequence, the bit stream is a one dimensional pattern of 1's and 0's and so it is convenient, for our purposes, to think of the transformation coefficients as being scanned in some fashion so that the quantization symbol sequence, $s[n]$, is one dimensional. The nature of this scanning can be critical to the success of particular quantization and coding approaches.

Quantization

The simplest from of quantization independently assigns one symbol, $s[n]$, to each transformation coefficient, $c[\vec{k}]$. This is known as *scalar* quantization. For historical reasons, scalar quantization in the absence of predictive feedback, described in Sect. 2.3, is often referred to as Pulse Code Modulation (PCM). *Vector* quantization, on the other hand, collects the transformation coefficients into blocks and assigns one symbol to each block. The assumption of vector quantization is that the coefficients are not independent and that underlying redundancy can be exploited by carefully designing the quantizer alphabet and symbol definitions[2], often collectively referred to as the *codebook*. Vector

---

[1] Some distortion may be introduced by the non-ideal arithmetic used to compute transformation coefficients or by using a subband decomposition without the PR property, however these are usually negligible.
[2] Because vector quantization is capable of exploiting spatial redundancy, a function also served by the transformation block of Fig. 1, vector quantization is often applied directly to the image or video pixels, rather than to transformation coefficients.

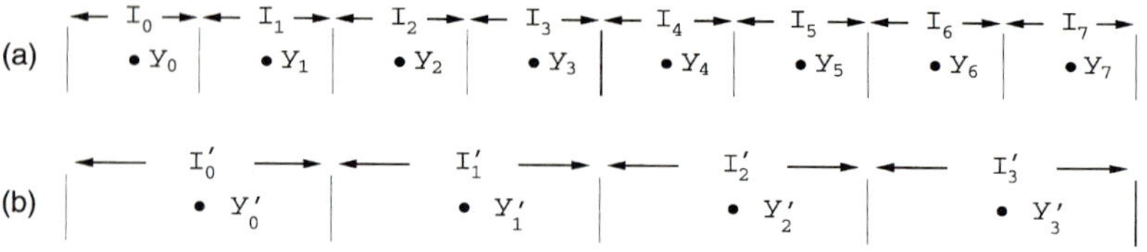

(a) | ←I_0→|←I_1→|←I_2→|←I_3→|←I_4→|←I_5→|←I_6→|←I_7→|
•y_0 •y_1 •y_2 •y_3 •y_4 •y_5 •y_6 •y_7

(b) | ←I'_0→ | ←I'_1→ | ←I'_2→ | ←I'_3→ |
•y'_0 •y'_1 •y'_2 •y'_3

Fig. 7. a 8 intervals of a uniform quantizer with quantization intervals, I_p, and representation levels, y_p; **b** 4 intervals of the coarser uniform quantizer obtained from **a** by bit planing, as described in text

quantization does have a number of drawbacks, however. A much larger alphabet is generally required than for scalar quantization and the selection of optimal symbols from amongst this alphabet is not trivial, imposing significant computational requirements for the compression algorithm – although not for the decompression algorithm. Among other references, the reader is referred to [12] for a comprehensive discussion of vector quantization.

Scalar quantization is characterized by a finite collection of intervals, I_p, forming a disjoint cover of the set of real numbers[3]. Each quantization interval, I_p, is associated with a particular symbol value, S_p. The quantizer may be regarded as a map, Q, from coefficient values, c, to symbol values, s, such that

$$Q(c) = S_p, \quad \text{for} \quad c \in I_p$$

Inverse quantization is characterized by a matching set of representation levels, $y_p \in I_p$ such that symbol, S_p, is mapped into y_p. Quantizer design involves the joint optimization of these quantization intervals and representation levels subject to the statistical distribution of the coefficients being quantized, the distortion measure of interest, and the coding method to be applied to the symbols. These issues are addressed in [18] among other references. The simplest scalar quantizer, illustrated in Fig. 7a, for which each interval, I_p, has the same length, and y_p is the midpoint of I_p, is optimal when the coefficients have a uniform distribution. For this reason it is referred to as a *uniform* quantizer.

Coding of Quantization Symbols

The simplest coding strategy is to assign a fixed number of bits to each symbol, $s[n]$. For an alphabet of L symbols, this approach requires $\lceil \log_2 L \rceil$ bits per symbol. As such, fixed length coding tends to be relatively inefficient from a compression point of view, however it has the advantage of simplicity. Moreover, fixed length coding offers maximum error resilience in that the code bits corresponding to each

---

[3] i.e., $I_p \cap I'_p = \emptyset$ for $p \neq p'$ and $\cup_p I_p = R$, the set of all real numbers.

symbol are independent. Fixed length coding can also provide a simple mechanism for rate-scalable compression. In particular, suppose that scalar quantization is employed and the quantization symbol indices are ordered so that the representation levels satisfy $y_{p+1} > y_p$, $\forall\ p$. Suppose also that the code word corresponding to S_p is simply the $\lceil \log_2 L \rceil$-bit, two's complement, binary representation of the symbol index, p. Then if l least significant bits are dropped from each code word, the remaining bits represent the symbols, S'_p, generated by a coarser quantizer with the quantization intervals, $I'_p = I_{2^l p} \cup I_{2^l p+1} \cup \ldots \cup I_{2^l p + 2^l - 1}$. In this way, up to $\lceil \log_2 L \rceil$ fixed bit rates can be made available by taking subsets of the bit stream corresponding to all but the l least significant bits of each code word, for $l = 0, 1, 2, \ldots$. This technique is often referred to as bit planing. It is illustrated in Fig. 7, where the coarse quantizer of Fig. 7b is obtained by dropping the least significant bit of the code words corresponding to the finer quantizer of Fig. 7a.

Significantly improved compression performance can often be obtained by assigning a variable number of bits to each symbol. In variable length coding, each symbol, S_p, is represented by a pattern consisting of b_p bits, where b_p is smaller for symbols with high probability of occurrence and larger for symbols with low probability of occurrence. Huffman [17] has described a simple algorithm for generating symbol bit patterns with optimal lengths, b_p. By optimal, we mean that there exist bit patterns of length b_p for each symbol, S_p, such that no bit pattern is a prefix of another and the average pattern length per symbol is minimum. Consider, for example, an alphabet of four symbols, occurring with probabilities $P(S_1) = 0.6$, $P(S_2) = 0.2$, $P(S_3) = 0.15$ and $P(S_4) = 0.05$. In this case the optimal pattern lengths are $b_1 = 1$, $b_2 = 2$, $b_3 = 3$ and $b_4 = 3$. Example bit patterns are (1), (01), (001) and (000) for S_1, S_2, S_3 and S_4, respectively. Observe that no bit pattern is a prefix of another and so the bit stream is guaranteed to be uniquely decodable. The average number of bits per symbol is $\Sigma_p b_p P(S_p) = 1.6$, which is lower than the 2 bits per symbol required for fixed length coding.

Unfortunately, variable length coding is highly susceptible to errors in the bit stream. A single bit error always results in at least one symbol being misinterpreted by the decoder, however if this erroneously decoded symbol has a different pattern length – number of bits – from the originally encoded symbol then the decoder will lose synchronization with the bit stream and every symbol decoded thereafter will be unreliable. Some degree of error robustness may be restored by frequently resynchronizing the decoder, however this also reduces the compression efficiency. Variable length coding also lacks the inherent rate-scalability of fixed rate coding. This is because there is, in general, no simple relationship between an optimal set of bit patterns for one quantizer and that for a coarser quantizer.

If we consider each symbol, $s[n]$, to be an independent outcome of a random variable, s, then it is known that the average number of bits required to code each symbol has a lower bound, given by the entropy [26],

$$\varepsilon(s) = -\sum_p P(s = S_p) \log_2 P(s = S_p)$$

While Huffman coding approaches this lower bound more closely than fixed length coding, a technique known as arithmetic coding [33] allows us to approach this lower bound arbitrarily closely. In fact for most practical applications, the bit rate associated with arithmetic coding deviates negligibly from the entropy bound. Ignoring this deviation, arithmetic coding requires $-\log_2 \mathbf{P}(s = S_p)$ bits to encode the event $s[n] = S_p$. Thus the minimum number of bits required to encode the sequence, $s[n]$, is effectively achieved by arithmetic coding and is given by

$$C(s[n]) = -\sum_n \log_2 \mathbf{P}(s = S_p) \qquad (6)$$

Arithmetic coding is particularly useful when one symbol has probability close to 1, permitting average rates of less than one bit per symbol, whereas Huffman coding requires at least one bit to encode each symbol. In arithmetic coding, symbols are not identified with particular bit patterns. Instead, the complete sequence of symbols is used to build a single arithmetic code word, whose value identifies each of the encoded symbols and whose binary digits are the bit stream. As such arithmetic coding is highly susceptible to errors in the bit stream – a single bit error invariably renders the remainder of the bit stream useless. To minimize this effect, it is important to break symbol sequences down into smaller segments, each of which is used to generate an independent arithmetic code word. Arithmetic coding is somewhat more computationally demanding than Huffman coding, and very much more so than fixed length coding. As for variable length Huffman coding, it lacks the inherent rate-scalability of fixed rate coding, in that subsets of an arithmetic code word cannot, in general, be used to decode more coarsely quantized versions of the transformation coefficients, $c[\vec{k}]$. In Sect. 6, however, we show how this rate-scalable property may be achieved while still requiring only the minimum number of bits, $C(s[n])$, to encode the symbol sequence $s[n]$.

Zero Coding

The coding techniques discussed above do not exploit any statistical dependence between the symbols. Moreover, if scalar rather than vector quantization is used to generate the symbol sequence, then no means is provided at all to exploit statistical dependence between the transformation coefficients, $c[\vec{k}]$. For this reason, zero coding techniques are commonly used to enhance compression performance when scalar quantization is employed. For convenience we identify I_0 as the quantization interval containing 0 and refer to the corresponding symbol, S_0, as the zero symbol. The AC coefficients of the DCT, as well as the high frequency subband coefficients of a subband decomposition typically have zero mean and small variance, leading to a high incidence of the zero symbol. In addition, incidences of the zero symbol are usually well correlated both in space and across frequency bands. The purpose of zero coding is to exploit this correlation in efficiently encoding which symbols

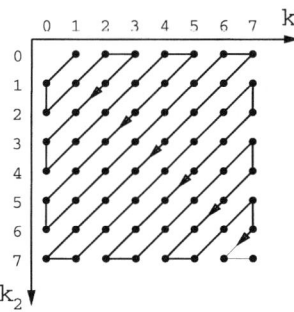

Fig. 8. Scanning of $c^{DCT}[Nb_1 + k_1, Nb_2 + k_2] - b_1, b_2$ denote the $N \times N$ block location, where $N = 8$ here

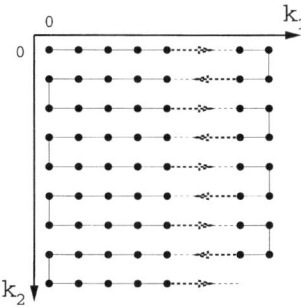

Fig. 9. Scanning of $c^{SB}[Nk_1 + \beta_1, Nk_2 + \beta_2] - \beta_1, \beta_2$ identify the subband channel in a separable $N \times N$-band subband decomposition

are zero and which are not. One or other of the techniques discussed above are then used to encode the actual value of any non-zero symbols.

Perhaps the most common zero coding technique is run-length coding. In run-length coding the locations of zero symbols are coded implicitly via so-called white and black runs, representing the lengths of contiguous non-zero symbols and contiguous zero symbols, respectively. The lengths themselves may be coded with any of the techniques discussed above. Run-length coding is inherently capable of exploiting correlation only in one dimension. As such, its success depends upon the scanning order associated with the symbol sequence $s[n]$. The AC coefficients of the DCT are usually quantized and coded using the zig-zag scanning order depicted in Fig. 8, the correlation being strongest between coefficients of adjacent frequency bands from the same DCT block. On the other hand the scanning order depicted in Fig. 9 is typically used for high frequency subband coefficients, the correlation being strongest between spatially adjacent coefficients of the same subband. Vertically and diagonally oriented variants of the horizontally oriented subband scanning order in Fig. 9 are also common [43, Sect. 6.4]. In Sect. 6 we present a zero coding approach that is capable of exploiting correlation in two dimensions. As such, it does not have the same dependence upon a one dimensional scanning of the transformation coefficients. Moreover, this approach turns out to be well suited to rate-scalable compression.

Optimal Quantizer Weightings for the Coefficients

The transformation coefficients, $c[\vec{k}]$, may be organized into collections of coefficients sharing common statistical properties and common significance to the human visual system. We shall refer to these collections of coefficients as bands. For the DCT each band is formed from coefficients corresponding to a particular frequency. In subband decomposition the bands are simply the subband channels. Since they share common statistical properties. it makes sense to apply the same quantizer to every coefficient in a given band, however different quantizers should be assigned to different bands. In this section we discuss, in very general terms, the relationships governing optimal quantization of these bands. For more comprehensive discussions of this topic the reader is referred to [18, Sect. 11.2] and the work of Pearlman [43, Sect. 1.3].

We consider that the coefficients are collected into N bands, $B_1, \ldots, B_N$, each consisting of $j_1, \ldots, j_N$ coefficients, respectively. To each band, B_b, we may assign a rate-distortion function, $D_b(r_b)$, where r_b is the average number of bits spent encoding each sample of B_b and D_b is the average distortion introduced into the reconstructed image or video sequence by quantizing each coefficient in B_b. This rate-distortion function is determined by the particular choice of quantization and coding strategies selected for the band of coefficients. We make the assumption that the distortion introduced by each band is additive, so that the overall distortion introduced into the reconstructed image or video sequence is given by

$$D = \sum_{b=1}^{N} j_b D_b(r_b) \tag{7}$$

and the total number of bits required to achieve this distortion is given by

$$R = \sum_{b=1}^{N} j_b r_b \tag{8}$$

In general, we wish to find the optimum operating point on each of the N rate-distortion curves, $D_b(r_b)$, so that the overall distortion, D, is minimized for a given bit budget, R, or, alternatively, so that the bit rate is minimized for a given allowable distortion. In either case, the method of Lagrange multipliers, applied to equations (7) and (8), establishes that the optimal operating point satisfies

$$\frac{dD_1}{dr_1} = \frac{dD_2}{dr_2} = \cdots = \frac{dD_N}{dr_N} \tag{9}$$

Equation (9) is of particular interest when the distortion measure of interest is MSE and the transformation basis vectors are orthogonal. In this case, our assumption of additive distortion is valid. For more psychovisually relevant distortion measures or for non-orthogonal transformation, equation (9) can at best be approximately valid.

The MSE based rate-distortion function associated with scalar quantization can be modeled by [43, Sect. 1.3]

$$D_b(r_b) = g_b(r_b)e^{-ar_b}$$

where $g_b(r_b)$ is usually a slowly varying function of bit rate, r_b, and a is a constant, usually close to 2. If we approximate $g_b(r_b)$ by a constant, equation (9) leads to the conclusion that

$$D_1(r_1) = D_2(r_2) = \ldots = D_N(r_N) \tag{10}$$

In other words, the average distortion introduced per coefficient should be identical for every band. If all the transformation basis vectors have identical 2-norms, $\|w_{\vec{k}}\|_2$, and quantization is sufficiently fine, we may assume that the distortion introduced by each coefficient depends only on the quantizer itself and is independent of the band. In this case, the implication of equation (10) is that exactly the same quantizer should be used in every band. It should be noted, however, that this conclusion is only valid for high average bit rates and when MSE is the distortion measure of interest.

2.3 Predictive Feedback

Predictive feedback techniques are commonly employed to improve upon the compression performance achievable using the straightforward compression model of Fig. 1. In Delta Pulse Code Modulation (DPCM) and more complex Linear Predictive Coding (LPC) strategies [15], the feedback loop is placed around the quantizer. Figure 10 illustrates the predictive feedback arrangement for the simplest case of DPCM. In the figure, Q and Q^{-1} indicate quantization and its inverse respectively and D indicates a delay of $\vec{d}$ in the multi-dimensional sequence of recovered coefficients, $\tilde{c}[\vec{k}]$. The scanning order associated with the one dimensional sequence of symbol values, $s[n]$, must be such that $c[\vec{k}]$ is always quantized and coded after $c[\vec{k} - \vec{d}]$. The idea behind DPCM, is that $c[\vec{k} - \vec{d}]$, and hence its approximation, $\tilde{c}[\vec{k} - \vec{d}]$, should be a reasonable predictor for the value of $c[\vec{k}]$, so that the *prediction error* values, which are quantized and coded, are relatively small. Typically $\vec{d}$ corresponds to a unit horizontal or vertical displacement. When $\vec{d}$ is a unit displacement in time, the predictive scheme is traditionally referred to as Conditional Replenishment (CR), rather than DPCM.

Motion Compensation (MC) is a predictive technique in which the feedback loop contains both the transformation and quantization blocks of Fig. 1, as shown

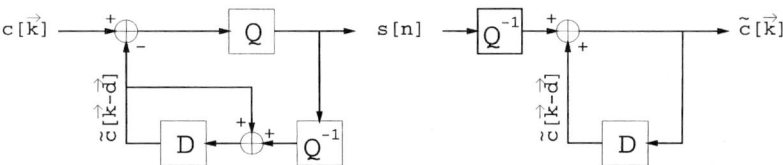

Fig. 10. DPCM feedback strategy. Q and Q^{-1} indicate the quantizer and inverse quantizer respectively. D indicates delay by $\vec{d}$

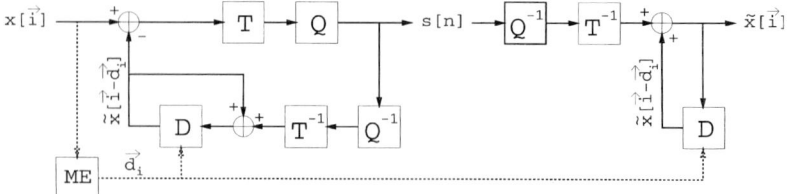

Fig. 11. MC feedback strategy. T, T^{-1}, Q and Q^{-1} indicate the transformation, the quantizer and their inverses. ME denotes motion estimation and D indicates delay by $\vec{d}_{\vec{i}}$ for pixel $x[\vec{i}]$

in Fig. 11. In this case the delay represented by the D block is not fixed and must be encoded as side information in the bit stream. The displacement vectors are given by $\vec{d}_{\vec{i}} = (h_{\vec{i}}, v_{\vec{i}}, 1)$ denoting a horizontal displacement of $h_{\vec{i}}$, a vertical displacement of $v_{\vec{i}}$, and a temporal displacement of one frame. Intuitively $x[\vec{i}]$ is to be predicted from some pixel, $\tilde{x}[\vec{i} - \vec{d}_{\vec{i}}] \approx x[\vec{i} - \vec{d}_{\vec{i}}]$, in the previous frame, where $(h_{\vec{i}}, v_{\vec{i}})$ represents the local motion field, at location $\vec{i}$. To minimize the amount of side information which must be included in the bit stream and to simplify the motion estimation task, represented by the ME block of Fig. 11, motion estimation is usually block based. That is to say that every pixel $\vec{i}$ in a given rectangular block, is assigned the same motion vector, $\vec{d}_{\vec{i}}$. [27] is one of many sources of information regarding block matching strategies.

DPCM and MC prediction techniques generally offer significant improvements in compression and are thus widely used. Predictive feedback has the serious drawback, however, of being inherently incompatible with scalable compression. To understand this, observe that the delay block, D, of Figs. 10 and 11 is essentially a memory element, storing values $\tilde{c}[\vec{k}]$ or $\tilde{x}[\vec{i}]$, recovered during decompression, until they are required for prediction. In scalable compression algorithms, the value of $\tilde{c}[\vec{k}]$ or $\tilde{x}[\vec{i}]$, obtained during decompression depends on constraints which may be imposed after the bit stream has been generated. For example, if the algorithm is to permit rate scalability then the value of $\tilde{c}[\vec{k}] \; \tilde{x} \; \tilde{x}[\vec{i}]$ obtained by decompression of a low rate subset of the bit stream can be expected to be a poorer approximation to $c[\vec{k}]$ or $x[\vec{i}]$, respectively, than the value obtained by decompressing from a higher rate subset of the bit stream. This ambiguity presents a difficulty for the compression algorithm, which must select a particular value for $\tilde{c}[\vec{k}]$ or $\tilde{x}[\vec{i}]$ to serve as a prediction reference. This inherent non-scalability of predictive feedback techniques is particularly problematic for video compression where scalability and motion compensation are both highly desirable features. Two approaches have been presented to resolve this difficulty, both of which permit only a small number of different "scales" and typically exhibit degradation in compression performance due to the introduction of scalability. Vandendorpe [42] advocates an approach in which multiple predictive feedback loops are used, one for each potential sequence of values that could be recovered during decompression. Unfortunately, the multiple symbol sequences produced by these predictive feedback loops tend not to be well correlated with one another, and hence are difficult to code efficiently. For high motion video sequences Vandendorpe reports an increase of as much as 60% in overall bit rate in a scalable system with three resolution scales, as compared with a conventional non-scalable motion compensated compression scheme.

An alternative approach proposed for scalable motion compensation has been suggested by Civanlar and Puri [8]. In this approach a single predictive feedback loop keeps track of the values recovered at the scale of highest resolution and quality, using these for the prediction of all scales. The symbol sequences corresponding to the various scales are now much more highly correlated and may be more efficiently coded than in the multiple feedback loop approach. This generally leads to only small loss of compression performance for the scale of highest resolution and quality, however the other scales suffer from *prediction drift*. The recovered values at these scales drift further and further away from the true values because the prediction values used during compression are only approximately available during decompression.

3 Compression Standards

In this section we review three major compression standards. Essentially, these schemes are based on the building blocks introduced in Sect. 2. Our objective is not only to impart a conceptual understanding of the various compression algorithms embodied in these standards, but also to reflect on their implications for the various compression goals introduced in Sect. 1. The Joint Photographics Experts Group (JPEG) still image compression standard is discussed in Sect. 3.1. In Sect. 3.2 we review the CCITT standard H. 261 for digital video communications and then, in Sect. 3.3 we outline the Motion Picture Experts Group (MPEG) standard for video compression.

3.1 JPEG

JPEG is commonly misunderstood to be a specific compression algorithm. Instead, perhaps the most flexible of the three compression standards discussed in this section, JPEG is better understood as a family of compression algorithms [30]. The standard defines a bit stream syntax which describes the configuration of a variety of different building blocks as well as the necessary code bits to represent the image. The JPEG syntax includes a lossless coding mode which we shall not discuss here, as we are only concerned with lossy coding. The lossy compression modes employ the 8×8 two-dimensional DCT discussed in Sect. 2.1, uniform scalar quantization of the DCT coefficients and either Huffman or adaptive arithmetic coding of the quantization symbols. The uniform quantization intervals for each of the DCT coefficients may be independently specified. Subjective assessment is often employed in selecting appropriate quantizer interval sizes to reflect the perceptual significance of the various DCT coefficients. The predictive feedback technique of DPCM is used to enhance compression of the DC coefficients, whereas a variant of run-length coding is employed together with the zig-zag scanning order of Fig. 8 to enhance compression of AC coefficients. The uniform quantization intervals and Huffman code tables may be specified by the application and, if desired, may be recorded in the bit stream.

Both the Huffman and arithmetic coding modes use conditional coding to improve compression efficiency. By conditional coding we mean that the Huffman code words, or arithmetic probability tables, depend upon a context, which is determined from coefficient values already coded and available at both the encoder and decoder. The conditioning employed in the arithmetic coding mode, however, is much more extensive than that in the Huffman coding mode. Partly because of its increased complexity, the majority of JPEG implementations do not support arithmetic coding. Improvements of approximately 10% to 15% in the bit rate have been observed at rates of about 0.8 bits per pixel, by using the arithmetic coding mode instead of Huffman coding [30, p. 255].

As well as describing either lossless or lossy transformation modes and either Huffman or arithmetic coding modes, the JPEG standard also describes three modes which govern the scalability of the compression algorithm. the most familiar of these is the *sequential* mode, in which each DCT block is completely coded one after the other to form a non-scalable bit stream. In the *progressive* mode, each DCT block is coded roughly in a first pass, with subsequent passes refining the DCT coefficient values. This mode introduces scalability in that not all the bit stream need be received and decoded in order to obtain a partial reconstruction of the image. The refinement may be based on successively quantizing the coefficient values to higher precision (successive approximation), or on successively increasing the number of AC DCT coefficients coded (spectral selection), or on a combination of both spectral selection and successive approximation. The primary emphasis of the progressive mode is rate-scalability, although some measure of resolution-scalability may be introduced in the case of spectral selection. The *hierarchical* mode provides for resolution-scalable compression. In this case a first pass compresses a spatially subsampled copy of the image. Subsequent passes compress the difference between higher resolution versions of the image and a prediction obtained by upsampling and interpolating the compressed image from the previous pass. For a thorough discussion of the JPEG compression family, [30] provides a useful reference.

Due to the diversity of compression algorithms in the JPEG family, the standard does not require implementations to support all the modes discussed above, but enforces the support of a minimal subset known as the *baseline system*. The baseline system supports the most well-known JPEG compression algorithm, which involves 8×8 DCT transformation blocks and Huffman coding according to the non-scalable, sequential mode. To demonstrate the performance of this baseline JPEG compression algorithm, we use the 512×512 pixel standard test image, "Lena", with 8 bit grey scale, as depicted in Fig. 12. Table 1 presents distortion

Fig. 12. Original 512 × 512, 8 bit grey scale "Lena"

Table 1. Rate-distortion performance of baseline JPEG compression, with 512 × 512, 8 bit grey scale "Lena"

Rate (bits per pixel)	0.127	0.249	0.508	1.000
PSNR(dB)	27.76	30.40	33.95	37.19

values, measured in PSNR[4], for the reconstructed images corresponding to compressed bit rates of $\frac{1}{8}$, $\frac{1}{4}$, $\frac{1}{2}$ and 1 bit per pixel. A set of quantization step sizes, optimized for natural image compression, is uniformly scaled in order to obtain a variety of compression rates, while the Huffman code words are separately optimized for each individual bit rate using training statistics from 28 natural images of similar dimensions to the "Lena" image itself. Figure 13 depicts the reconstructed image corresponding to $\frac{1}{4}$ bit per pixel, clearly revealing the blocking artifacts common to DCT based compression at low bit rates.

3.2 CCITT H.261

Recommendation H.261 of the CCITT Study Group XV, was adopted in December 1990 [4] as a video compression standard for use in the Integrated Services Digital

---

[4] Peak Signal to Noise Ratio (PSNR) is defined in terms of Mean Squared Error (MSE), according to $PSNR = 10\log_{10}\frac{255^2}{MSE}$.

Fig. 13. 512 × 512, 8 bit grey scale "Lena" compressed to $\frac{1}{4}$ bit per pixel using baseline JPEG algorithm

Network (ISDN). Two objectives are primarily responsible for shaping this compression standard. The first is that total latency associated with compression and decompression should not exceed 150 ms, so as to be useful for interactive applications such as videoconferencing. The second objective is that the compressed bit stream should have a rate of $p \times 64$ kbits/s, where the value of p is a parameter of the compression algorithm. Unlike the family of algorithms covered by the JPEG standard, H.261 defines a much less flexible compression scheme. The approach is most easily understood in terms of the Motion Compensation (MC) predictive feedback loop depicted in Fig. 11. The transformation block, in this case, consists of the same 8×8 DCT used in all JPEG lossy compression modes. The quantization and Huffman coding approaches are also essentially the same as those used in baseline JPEG, except that the step sizes associated with each of the uniform quantizers are uniformly scaled from one DCT block to another so as to avoid excessive fluctuations in the bit rate and hence limit the amount of bit stream buffering required to achieve a constant rate of $p \times 64$ kbits/s.

Chrominance components are required to be subsampled by two in both the vertical and horizontal directions so that there are four luminance (Y) DCT blocks for each pair of U and V chrominance DCT blocks. These six DCT blocks are collectively referred to as a *macro-block*. Each macro-block may individually be specified as intra-coded or inter-coded. Intra-coded blocks are coded independently of the previous frame and so do not conform to the model of Fig. 11. They are used when successive frames are not related, such as during scene changes, and to avoid excessive propagation of the effects of communication errors. Inter-coded blocks use the MC predictive feedback loop of Fig. 11 to improve compression performance. The Motion Estimation (ME) scheme is based on 16 × 16 pixel blocks so that each inter-coded macro-block is assigned exactly one motion vector. The reader is referred to [4] for further details of the H.261 video compression standard. It should be noted that H.261 defines an inherently non-scalable compression algorithm. All decisions regarding spatial resolution, frame rate and bit rate are fixed at the time of compression.

3.3 MPEG

The first MPEG video compression standard, now known as MPEG-1, is shaped by significantly different compression objectives to H.261. Specifically, MPEG-1 is intended primarily for non-interactive applications, for which the low latency constraint of H.261 is not so important. In addition, the bit rate target for MPEG-1 is in the range 1.0 to 1.5 Mbits/s. This target bit rate is partly motivated by existing laser recording technology used in the familiar audio compact disc. Despite these different objectives, MPEG-1 has much in common with its forerunner, H.261, as well as the baseline JPEG compression algorithm, so that decompression hardware supporting a subset of all three standards is not inconceivable. The algorithm is based on the 8 × 8 block DCT; 16 × 16 motion compensated macro-blocks; dynamically scaled quantization for bit rate control; zig-zag scanning of the AC coefficients, as in Fig. 8; DPCM prediction for the DC coefficients; and Huffman coding.

The most significant departure from H.261 in the MPEG standard is the introduction of the concept of bi-directional prediction, together with that of a Group of Pictures (GOP). These concepts may be understood with the aid of Fig. 14. Each GOP commences with an intra-coded picture (frame), denoted I in the figure. The motion compensated predictive feedback loop of Fig. 11 is used to compress the subsequent inter-coded frames, marked P. Finally, the bidirectionally predicted frames, marked B in Fig. 14, are coded using motion compensated prediction based on both previous and successive I or P frames. Bidirectional prediction conforms essentially to the model of Fig. 11, except that the prediction signal is given by

$$a\tilde{x}[\vec{i} - \vec{d}_{\vec{i}}^{\,f}] + b\tilde{x}[\vec{i} - \vec{d}_{\vec{i}}^{\,b}]$$

In this notation, $\vec{d}_{\vec{i}}^{\,f} = (h_{\vec{i}}^{f}, v_{\vec{i}}^{f}, n^{f})$, where $(h_{\vec{i}}^{f}, v_{\vec{i}}^{f})$ is a forward motion vector describing the motion from the previous I or P frame, and n^{f} is the frame distance to this previous I or P frame. Similarly, $\vec{d}_{\vec{i}}^{\,b} = (h_{\vec{i}}^{b}, v_{\vec{i}}^{b}, -n^{b})$, where $(h_{\vec{i}}^{b}, v_{\vec{i}}^{b})$ is a backward motion vector describing the motion to the next I or P frame, and n_b is the temporal distance to that frame. The weights a and b are given either by

$$\begin{array}{c} a = 1 \\ b = 0 \end{array}, \quad \begin{array}{c} a = 0 \\ b = 1 \end{array}, \quad \text{or} \quad \begin{array}{c} a = n_b/(n_f + n_b) \\ b = n_f/(n_f + n_b) \end{array}$$

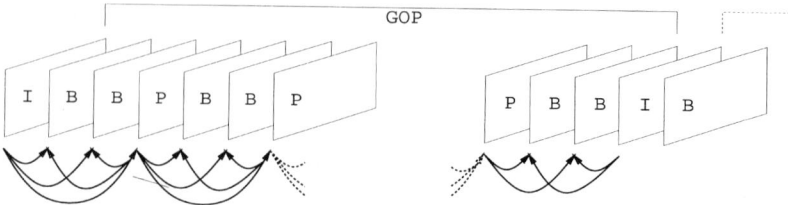

Fig. 14. MPEG's Group Of Pictures (GOP). Arrows represent direction of prediction

corresponding to forward, backward, and average prediction respectively. Each bidirectionally predicted macro-block is independently assigned one of these three prediction strategies. It is important to appreciate that compression performance can vary from one MPEG-1 implementation to another depending on such factors as the motion estimation approach and the bit rate control strategy.

The introduction of bidirectional prediction significantly increases the latency associated with MPEG video compression, however it can lead to improved compression efficiency while permitting a form of resolution-scalability, based on frame rate. In particular, it is possible to independently decompress only the I and P frames, or even just the I frames in order to obtain successively lower frame rates. The MPEG-1 standard supports scalability in this respect only. More recently, work is in progress to finalize the MPEG-2 standard for interlaced video compression, with target bit rates of approximately 4.0–10 Mbits/s. This standard may be regarded largely as an extension of MPEG-1 and makes some provision for spatial resolution-scalability. For further details of the MPEG-1 and MPEG-2 compression algorithms, we refer the interested reader to [9, 22] and [16], respectively. Some MPEG-1 compression results are provided in Sect. 7.

4 Orientation Adaptive Subband Transformation for Image Compression

In image and video compression applications, directionality arises as an important, yet specifically multi-dimensional attribute, that cannot adequately be exploited by the separable composition of one-dimensional transformation operators featured in Sects. 2 and 3. In this section, we propose an adaptive image transformation, based on subband decomposition, which exploits local directional image features in order to improve overall compression performance.

Adapting subband transformations according to the properties of the signal being compressed is not a new concept. Delsarte et al. [11] have developed a "ring algorithm" to optimize the basis vectors in one dimensional, two channel subband systems for which these basis vectors are orthogonal. Their algorithm finds a local minimum to the non-linear objective function expressing mean squared reconstruction error as a function of analysis filter tap values and signal statistics.

Taubman and Zakhor [32, 39] describe an algorithm for global minimization of the same objective function and also consider the adaptation of certain non-separable two dimensional subband systems. Gurski et al. [14] solve a related problem, again in the one dimensional case. Nayebi et al. [28], on the other hand, take a different approach in which they maintain a library of pre-optimized, compatible, one dimensional, FIR subband filters, from which an optimal selection is made. Their work tackles the issue of preserving perfect reconstruction when the filter impulse responses vary with location. Chung and Smith [7] have proposed a similar one dimensional adaptive subband transformation, in which the library consists of two or more pre-optimized IIR subband filters. They present a particularly attractive application of this concept to image compression by separably extending their one dimensional adaptive transformation to two dimensions. In particular, they propose a library consisting of two different analysis filters and corresponding synthesis filters. The first filter has good magnitude response – i.e., it is a good approximation to an ideal bandpass filter –, but exhibits significant "ringing" when presented with a step input. The second filter has a poorer magnitude response, but a better step response. Good magnitude and step response properties are generally mutually exclusive. By selecting the first filter for use in relatively smooth regions of the image and the second in the neighbourhood of image edges, perceptual quality at low bit rates can be significantly improved over the quality obtained with a non-adaptive subband transformation.

As mentioned, directionality is a purely multi-dimensional attribute. A number of non-separable two dimensional subband transformations have been proposed, whose subband channels have psychophysically meaningful orientation sensitivity. Mahesh and Pearlman [23] and Simoncelli and Adelson [37] propose non-separable subband transformations for hexagonally sampled images, leading to subbands whose orientational sensitivities, while fixed, are more closely related to the sensitivity of the human visual cortex than are the conventional separable subband passbands shown in Fig. 6. Bamberger and Smith [2, 3], on the other hand, demonstrate non-separable subband transformations, based on conventional rectangular image sampling, which are capable of resolving images into many different fixed directional components. Shapiro [35] has proposed a truly adaptive, non-separable subband transformation based on a McClellan Transform [25] approach to directional filter design, however this work has a number of unresolved practical difficulties.

The orientation adaptive approach proposed in this section is based on the observation that natural images commonly contain approximately linear edges, on a local level at least, and that conventional separable subband transformations perform best when such features are oriented either horizontally or vertically. There are two reasons for this favouring of horizontal and vertical features. The first reason is that edges with these orientations affect the least number of high frequency subbands in a separable decomposition. To understand this, consider the passbands depicted in Fig. 6. A horizontal edge segment will affect only the LL and LH subbands, whereas a vertical edge segment will affect only the LL and HL subbands. Edges with different orientations, however, contribute to all subbands to varying degrees. By concentrating their signal information into the fewest subbands, horizontally and vertically oriented features produce less non-zero quantization symbols, $s[n]$, than features with different orientations. In combination with any or all of the variable length coding, arithmetic coding and zero coding techniques introduced in Sect. 2.2, this translates into improved compression performance for vertically and horizontally oriented features.

The second reason for favouring horizontally and vertically oriented features when the transformation is separable is that these features produce the least disturbing "ringing" artifacts for low bit rate compression. The objectionable nature of subband ringing artifacts in the neighbourhood of image edges has already been mentioned in relation to the work of Chung and Smith [7]. Empirically, the ringing is found to be least noticeable in reconstructed images when edges are oriented along one of the horizontal and vertical principal axes of the separable subband basis vectors.

Unfortunately, natural images contain oriented features which do not have strictly horizontal or vertical alignment. For this reason, we propose pre-distorting the image itself so that the dominant features in any local region are reoriented to be either horizontal or vertical. Naturally the pre-distortion must be reversed during decompression.

In overview, our proposed compression algorithm consists of the following elements, schematized in Fig. 15. We first partition the image into smaller rectangular regions, which are to be considered independently. This is necessary so as to minimize the number of distinct orientations presented to the adaptive subband transformation. For each partition, we then determine the two dominant feature orientations using an algorithm outlined in Sect. 4.2. The partition is then reoriented, using the approach described in Sect. 4.1. A separable, pyramidal subband transformation, in the form of Fig. 6, is applied to the reoriented partition. Finally, conventional quantization and Huffman and run-length coding techniques are applied to the subband coefficients. The Huffman code bits are combined with the reorientation parameters to form the compressed bit stream. During decompression, each reoriented partition is reconstructed using conventional separable subband synthesis, after which the reorientation applied during compression is reversed. Finally, to remove artifacts resulting from independent processing of the image partitions, a local smoothing algorithm is applied at the partition boundaries, which also exploits directional attributes of the image. For a

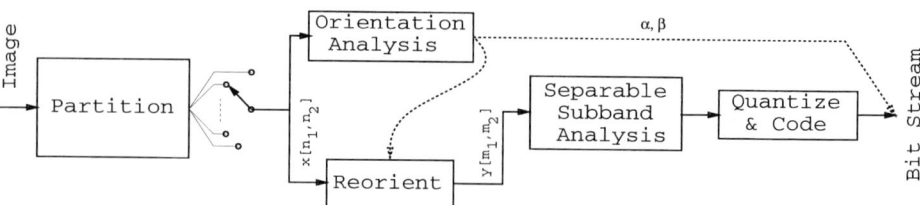

Fig. 15. Schematic of orientation adaptive compression algorithm

discussion of this partition boundary smoothing algorithm and a more detailed discussion of the other algorithmic features, the reader is referred to [40]. In Sect. 4.3 we present a comparison of reconstructed image qualities resulting from conventional and orientation adaptive subband compression.

4.1 Reorientation of Partitions

This section is devoted to a discussion of the reorientation block in Fig. 15, by which we achieve orientational tuning of our otherwise conventional subband transformation. We adopt the philosophy that the decompression algorithm should be able to perfectly reconstruct an image from its subbands if quantization is sufficiently fine, which imposes the constraint that the reorientation operator be invertible. Such an invertibility requirement immediately rules out image rotation, for example, as the aliasing distortion associated with discrete space rotation prohibits exact inversion.

In place of rotation, we implement an invertible reorientation by means of skewing operators. As indicated in Fig. 15, we denote the partition samples by the sequence $x[n_1, n_2]$, where n_1 and n_2 are column and row indices respectively. The reoriented partition is denoted by the sequence $y[m_1, m_2]$. The skewing operator, $\mathbf{R}_\alpha$, simply shifts every row of the partition to the left by αn_2 pixels. More precisely,

$$y[m_1, m_2] = x[n_1, n_2]\,|_{n_2=m_2, n_1=m_1+\alpha m_2} \tag{11}$$

This skewing operator may also be viewed as a resampling of the image partition. By this we mean that $x[n_1, n_2]$ corresponds to the rectangular sampling of an underlying spatially continuous image, which we assume to be ideally bandlimited to the frequency region $(-\pi, \pi)^2$, and that $y[m_1, m_2]$ is a non-rectangular sampling of the same underlying spatially continuous image, with sampling lattice vectors of $(1, 0)$ and $(\alpha, 1)$. This is still a Nyquist sampling of the underlying continuous image and so $\mathbf{R}_\alpha$ can be inverted, unlike rotation. The operation of $\mathbf{R}_\alpha$ is indicated in Fig. 16a. The figure shows how image features not aligned with the cardinal directions – i.e., horizontal and vertical – in the n_1, n_2 domain, become oriented vertically in the m_1, m_2 domain. The cardinal axes of the non-rectangular resampling lattice corresponding to this skewing operator are also depicted in the figure. We may similarly define a skewing operator, $\mathbf{R}_\gamma$, which shifts the columns of the image partition. The operation of $\mathbf{R}_\gamma$ is depicted in Fig. 16b, together with its interpretation in terms of non-rectangular resampling axes. Finally, these two skewing operators may be cascaded, as illustrated in Fig. 16c, so as to reorient two distinctly oriented features to the horizontal and vertical directions in the m_1, m_2 domain.

From the resampling interpretation of these skewing operators, we see that the cascade of any number of $\mathbf{R}_\alpha$ and $\mathbf{R}_\gamma$ stages possesses exactly two degrees of orientational freedom. These are the orientations of the two resampling axes. Our goal is to align these resampling axes with the two most significant linear features

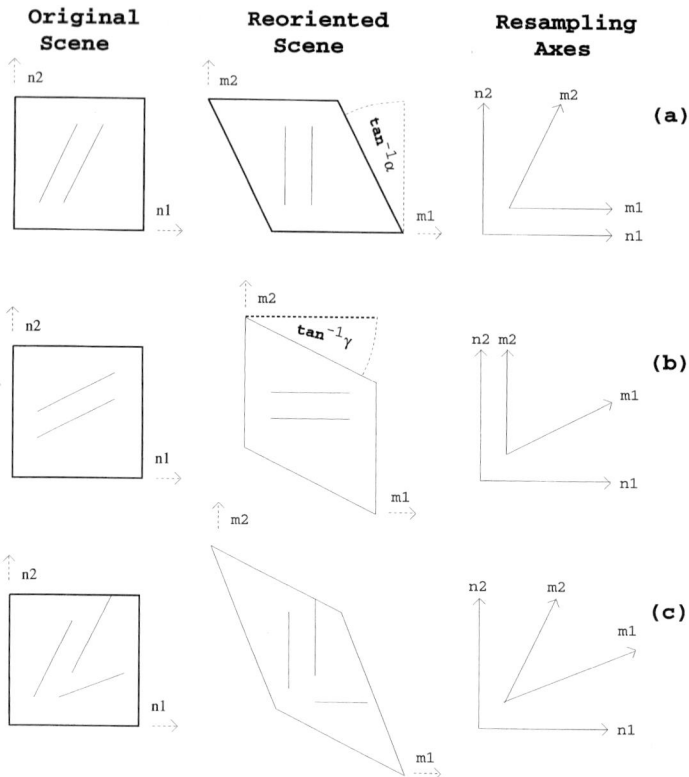

Fig. 16. Pictorial illustration of skewing operators, together with resampling interpretations for **a** R_α; **b** R_γ; and **c** R_α followed by R_γ

in the image partition. As we are only interested in orientation, we restrict ourselves to the consideration of cascades of the form shown in Fig. 17. The optional transposition of the image partition, indicated in Fig. 17, effectively allows us to consider column skewing followed by row skewing as well as row skewing followed by column skewing. We restrict the parameters α and γ to the range

$$-1 \leq \alpha, \gamma < 1$$

Together with the optional transposition, the range $-1 \leq \alpha < 1$ is sufficient to allow the m_2 resampling axis to be aligned with the most significant linear feature in the image partition, regardless of its orientation. On the other hand, the restriction, $-1 \leq \gamma < 1$, is included to prevent the m_1 and m_2 resampling axis orientations from approaching one another too closely, a condition which can severely degrade the compression performance of the orientation adaptive algorithm.

In defining the resampling operator, R_γ, according to equation (11), an important detail has been glossed over; namely $x[n_1, n_2]$ is a discrete space signal and so the right hand side of the equation is not defined for non-integral values of α. To address this problem, we modify equation (11) to

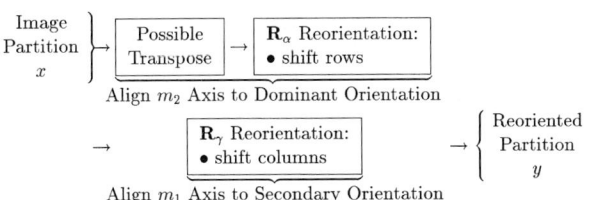

Fig. 17. Expanded schematic of reorientation block

$$y[m_1, m_2] = \hat{x}[n_1, n_2]\big|_{n_2=m_2, n_1=m_1+\langle\alpha m_2\rangle} \tag{12}$$

where $\langle \cdot \rangle$ represents rounding to the nearest integer, and $\hat{x}[n_1, n_2]$ is obtained by applying a one dimensional, linear interpolative filter, $F_{\sigma_{n_2}}$, to each row, n_2, of the image partition, $x[n_1, n_2]$. The purpose of $F_{\sigma_{n_2}}$ is to interpolatively shift its image row to the left by an amount, σ_{n_2}, where

$$\sigma_{n_2} = \alpha m_2 - \langle \alpha m_2 \rangle$$

is at most half a pixel spacing.

Noting that equation (12) represents no more than a relabeling of the indices, which is trivially reversible, the invertibility of our skewing operators and hence of the reorientation block in Fig. 15, depends entirely on the invertibility of the interpolative row shifting filters $F_{\sigma_{n_2}}$. As already mentioned, invertibility is an important property because the reorientation of each image partition must be reversed during decompression. Following our assumption that $x[n_1, n_2]$ represents Nyquist sampling of an underlying, ideally bandlimited, spatially continuous image, we conclude that $F_{\sigma_{n_2}}$ should ideally have the sinc impulse response, $f_{\sigma_{n_2}}[i] = \frac{\sin \pi(i+\sigma_{n_2})}{\pi(i+\sigma_{n_2})}$. Unfortunately, this infinite impulse response is not practically realizable. In its place we use an interpolative filter with the all-pass transfer function

$$F_{\sigma_{n_2}}(z) = \frac{S_{\frac{1}{2}\sigma_{n_2}}(z)}{S_{-\frac{1}{2}\sigma_{n_2}}(z)} \tag{13}$$

where $S_{\frac{1}{2}\sigma_{n_2}}(z)$ is an FIR filter obtained by applying a Hanning window, of width 2τ, to the ideal sinc interpolative filter corresponding to a shift by $\frac{1}{2}\sigma_{n_2}$. $S_{\frac{1}{2}\sigma_{n_2}}$ has impulse response

$$s_{\frac{1}{2}\sigma_{n_2}}[i] = \begin{cases} \frac{1}{2} \frac{\sin\pi(i+\frac{1}{2}\sigma_{n_2})}{\pi(i+\frac{1}{2}\sigma_{n_2})}\left[1+\cos\left(\pi\frac{i+\frac{1}{2}\sigma_{n_2}}{\tau}\right)\right] & , \left|i+\frac{1}{2}\sigma_{n_2}\right| < \tau \\ 0 & , \left|i+\frac{1}{2}\sigma_{n_2}\right| \geq \tau \end{cases}$$

The filter, $F_{\sigma_{n_2}}$, given by equation (13), may thus be implemented by means of recursive filtering. The handling of boundary effects is discussed in [40]. This interpolative filter has a simple inverse given by

$$F_{\sigma_{n_2}}^{-1}(z) = \frac{S_{-\frac{1}{2}\sigma_{n_2}}(z)}{S_{\frac{1}{2}\sigma_{n_2}}(z)} = F_{-\sigma_{n_2}}(z) \tag{14}$$

In this way the image transformation depicted in Fig. 15 is realized by the operations of one dimensional filtering and index relabeling only.

4.2 Finding Dominant Partition Orientations

An appropriate choice of reorientation parameters, α and γ, or equivalently, resampling axis orientations, is clearly essential to the success of our orientation adaptive compression algorithm. Our objective is to locate the dominant linear image features within each image partition and to select α and γ so that the two resampling axes lie parallel to one or another of these features. As it stands, however, this is too vague an objective. In particular, it is not clear at which resolution we should search a partition for its linear features. If we are interested in very low bit rate compression then the linear features of interest are those that appear at low spatial resolutions. This is because the necessarily large quantization step sizes, required to keep the bit rate down, suppress the high frequency subband coefficients – high frequency subband coefficients typically exhibit the lowest variances and are quantized most coarsely. At higher bit rates, however, we are more interested in the higher resolution linear features. To accommodate these considerations we approach the selection of reorientation parameters in two distinct stages. In the first stage we examine each image partition at several different resolutions, collecting feasible α and γ pairs. In the second stage we decide which of these to actually employ in reorienting the image partition.

In the first stage we adopt a resolution dependent feature extraction approach first introduced by Marr and Hildreth [24]. We apply Gaussian low pass filters to the original image partition prior to a simple edge detection scheme. This edge detection scheme sets all pixel values to zero except for those at which the spatial gradient is a local maximum, the latter pixels assuming a value equal to the square of the local gradient. In this way we generate a so-called edge gradient field corresponding to the resolution associated with each level in the spatial subband pyramid used in the subband analysis block of Fig. 15 – Fig. 6 is an example of such a spatial pyramid decomposition with two levels.

To each of these edge gradient fields we apply an orientation analysis strategy which bears a strong resemblance to the Hough Transform approach described by O'Gorman and Clowes [13] for linear edge enhancement. In our case we are interested only in orientation information and not edge location. Our approach relies upon index relabeling, as in equation (12), to skew the vertical axis of the gradient field by an angle $\theta \in [-45°, 45°]$, in a similar fashion to the skew operators described in Sect. 4.1 except that the linear interpolative filtering phase is omitted here for efficiency – i.e., we approximate $\hat{x}[n_1, n_2] = x[n_1, n_2]$ in equation (12). Orientations, θ, in the range [45°, 135°] relative to vertical are obtained by first transposing the edge gradient field and then making the substitution $\theta \leftarrow 90° - \theta$. An objective function described in [40] is selected to respond to the vertical alignment of any edge segments in the skewed – and possibly transposed – gradient field. Essentially, by summing the squared average gradient value in each column, weighted by the column's length, over each column of the skewed gradient field, our objective function gives its maximum response when skewed edges intersect with a minimal number of columns. The angles, θ, for which this objective function is locally maximum correspond to the orientations of linear edge segments. Similar to the Hough Transform approach [13], this strategy does not rely upon edge continuity and so is highly immune to image noise.

The first stage in the determination of dominant feature orientations concludes with the selection of one or more pairs of resampling parameters, α and γ, for each image partition and at each resolution. For a full discussion of the collection of candidate pairs of reorientation parameters, based on the local maxima of the orientation objective function described above, the reader is referred to [40]. In the second stage a single α-γ pair is selected from this collection of candidates. The selection is made by quantizing and coding the partition subband coefficients obtained when using each of the candidate pairs of reorientation parameters. The parameters selected are those which minimize the bit rate. An obvious justification for such a selection procedure is that it prevents the bit rate associated with the orientation adaptive subband transformation from exceeding that associated with a conventional separable subband transformation. This is guaranteed by always considering $\alpha = \gamma = 0$ as candidate resampling parameters. The fact that this option, corresponding to conventional subband coding, is rarely selected as optimal – see Fig. 23 – is one indication of the prevalence of useful directional information in natural images. A further justification for resampling parameter selection on the basis of bit rate is due to our observation that the resolution of interest in linear feature detection is dependent on quantization and coding parameters. For a more detailed discussion of these justifications the reader is referred to [40].

4.3 Compression Results

In order to demonstrate the efficacy of our orientation adaptive subband transformation, we adopt a conventional approach to quantization and coding of the subband coefficients. Quantization is scalar, with DPCM predictive feedback employed for the lowest frequency subband – i.e., the LL subband of Fig. 6 – and run-length coding used to efficiently code the locations of zero symbols in the other subbands. The performance of DPCM and run-length coding both depend on the scanning order used to convert the two dimensional subband coefficients into a one dimensional sequence. We identify four different scanning orders: the horizontal pattern of Fig. 9; a vertical pattern obtained by transposing axes in Fig. 9; a top left to bottom right diagonal pattern similar to that of Fig. 8; and a top right to bottom left diagonal pattern similar to flipping that of Fig. 8 about the vertical axis. The compression algorithm examines each of these four scanning orders for each subband of each image partition, selecting the one which minimizes the bit rate. All symbols are Huffman coded with Huffman codes optimized using training statistics from the same 28 natural images used to train the baseline JPEG compression algorithm in the example of Sect. 3.1.

The image partitions used are 64 × 64 pixel blocks and the separable spatial subband pyramid has three levels, but is otherwise identical to the two level pyramid illustrated in Fig. 6. We use the nine tap, linear phase, nearly orthogonal. NPR subband filters of Adelson et al. [1] and the symmetric extension approach, discussed in Sect. 2.1, for subband filtering in the neighbourhood of the partition boundaries. The α and γ reorientation parameters for each partition are uniformly quantized with 128 levels over the range $-1 \leq \alpha < 1$. These quantized values, together with an extra bit to signal the optional transposition of Fig. 17, are included in the bit stream. A further two bits are required for every subband of every partition to indicate the scanning order used for DPCM and run-length coding – i.e., horizontal, vertical, or one of the two diagonal approaches. The overhead associated with encoding α and γ parameters as well as scanning orders for each subband is thus 0.0085 bits per pixel.

The scalar quantizer associated with each subband, b, is uniform with step size, δ_b, everywhere except around zero, where a dead zone of width v_b is used. This means that the quantization intervals, I_p, associated with each quantizer are as shown in Fig. 18. Dead zone sizes, v_b, larger than the step size, δ_b, are commonly used to enhance the compression gains provided by run-length coding, or, more generally, any zero coding approach. As discussed in Sect. 2.2, the appropriate selection of quantization parameters for the different subbands is an important task, which should, in general, take into account the spectral sensitivity of the human visual system. In order to accommodate such considerations, we specify the complete set of quantizers by four parameters which are then tuned in subjective experiments to obtain approximately optimal reconstructed images at each of the bit rates considered. Specifically, we specify the step size and dead zone of each subband's quantizer according to

$$\delta_b = \Delta(\Gamma_\delta)^{L_b} \quad v_b = Y(\Gamma_v)^{L_b}$$

where L_b is the total number of one dimensionallow pass filtering stages used to generate the subband b, as in Fig. 6. The four subjectively tuned parameters are the base step size and dead zone parameters, Δ and Y, and the scaling parameters Γ_δ and Γ_v. The subband filter tap values are normalized so that the subband basis vectors form an approximately orthonormal set. The analysis of Sect. 2.2 then suggests that the MSE distortion measure should be approximately minimized, for a given bit rate, by setting $\Gamma_v = \Gamma_\delta = 1$. However we are interested in minimizing perceptual distortion for which we expect the scaling parameters to be less than 1

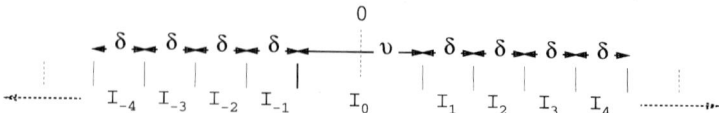

Fig. 18. Quantization intervals for uniform quantizer with dead zone

so that the lower frequency subbands, to which the human eye is generally more sensitive, are more finely quantized than the higher frequency subbands. This reasoning is born out in our subjective experiments, where values of $\Gamma_\delta = 0.8$ and $\Gamma_\upsilon = 0.8$ are found to be approximately optimal.

Numerical and visual experimental results are obtained both for the orientation adaptive subband algorithm and conventional separable subband compression. The conventional subband compression algorithm is identical to the orientation adaptive algorithm except that the image is considered as one big partition and its reorientation parameters are forced to $\alpha = \gamma = 0$. The three level spatial subband pyramid and all quantization and coding techniques are thus identical for the two systems. The source material for these results is the 512×512, 8 bit grey scale, standard test image "Lena", shown in Fig. 12. Figures 19 and 20 illustrate the reconstructed images obtained at $\frac{1}{4}$ bit per pixel using the conventional and orientation adaptive subband approaches respectively. The reduction in ringing artifacts around image edges due to orientation adaptation is marked. In particular, this effect is quite pronounced in the regions of the hat, the shoulder and the mirror edge. Interestingly, both subband algorithms provide significantly higher image quality than the baseline JPEG compression algorithm – cf. Fig. 13. The ringing artifacts common to conventional separable subband compression are more evident in Fig. 21, corresponding to a bit rate of $\frac{1}{8}$ bit per pixel. These ringing artifacts are, again, all but absent in Fig. 22, which is obtained at the same bit rate using orientation adaptive compression. Similar improvements are ob-

Fig. 19. Figure 12 compressed to $\frac{1}{4}$ bit per pixel using conventional subband scheme

Fig. 20. Figure 12 compressed to $\frac{1}{4}$ bit per pixel using orientation adaptive scheme

Fig. 21. Figure 12 compressed to $\frac{1}{8}$ bit per pixel using conventional subband scheme

Fig. 22. Figure 12 compressed to $\frac{1}{8}$ bit per pixel using orientation adaptive scheme

Table 2. Quantization parameters, bit rates and distortions for conventional and orientation adaptive subband compression

Algorithm	Figure	Bit rate	PSNR (dB)	Quantization parameters			
				Δ	Γ_δ	γ	Γ_v
Conventional	2.21	0.124	30.34	146	0.8	244	0.8
Adaptive	2.22	0.125	30.16	149	0.8	250	0.8
Conventional	2.19	0.249	33.24	67	0.8	98	0.8
Adaptive	2.20	0.251	32.82	69	0.8	100	0.8
Conventional	–	0.497	36.23	28	0.8	44	0.8
Adaptive	–	0.498	35.77	29	0.8	45	0.8

served at $\frac{1}{2}$ bit per pixel, although the overall distortion at this bit rate is much less apparent.

The quantization parameters and PSNR values corresponding to these reconstructed images are tabulated in Table 2. Interestingly, the subband compression algorithms also significantly outperform the baseline JPEG compression algorithm with respect to PSNR – cf. Table 1. The curious reader may wonder why conventional subband compression should achieve slightly higher PSNR values than orientation adaptive subband compression. The explanation for this lies principally in the fact that symmetric extension compromises the orthogonality of the subband basis vectors in the neighbourhood of partition boundaries. The conven-

Fig. 23. Dominant orientations in 512 × 512 Lena image with 64 × 64 partitions

tional subband algorithm, for which the entire image is considered as one partition, suffers much less from this effect than the orientation adaptive algorithm with its 64 image partitions.

Figure 23 reveals the dominant orientations determined by the orientation analysis algorithm described in Sect. 4.2, corresponding to the $\frac{1}{4}$ bit per pixel image shown in Fig. 20. The dominant and secondary orientations for each partition are identified by the white and black lines respectively. Note that the algorithm is highly successful in locating the dominant linear features in the image, often exploiting the availability of both axis orientations to capture as much directional information as possible.

4.4 Summary of Orientation Adaptive Algorithm

In this section, we have demonstrated the value in adapting an image compression algorithm to the local orientational features of the image. At low bit rates we are able to achieve considerably cleaner edges than conventional algorithms, in which orientation is not considered. For natural images, Table 2 reveals that this subjective improvement in edge quality is not associated with significant changes in quantization precision, but arises instead from directional attributes of the quantization noise. In the light of such results, we consider directional shaping of quantization noise to be the most compelling motivation for orientation adaptive subband image compression.

The particular orientation adaptive transformation outlined here is capable of exploiting up to two distinctly oriented features in each region of an image and may be implemented using only the operations of one dimensional filtering and index relabeling. The compression algorithm is necessarily much more complex than that for conventional separable subband compression, however the decompression algorithm need only be about twice as computationally intensive as a conventional subband decompression algorithm. For further discussion of these implementation issues, the reader is referred to [40].

5 Velocity-Based Subband Transformation for Video Compression

The concept of exploiting directionality, introduced in Sect. 4, can be extended into the temporal dimension for video compression. In this case, orientations in space and time correspond to velocities of moving objects. Many of the traditional techniques such as CCITT H.261 and MPEG, described in Sects. 3.2 and 3.3, take advantage of motion in an explicit but artificial manner. Even so, they achieve results that represent the current standard in video compression. This section introduces work in which non-separable subband decomposition is used to partition the source video sequence into subbands according to velocity. Our motivation for such a velocity-based subband transformation is twofold. In the first place, there is much evidence to suggest that the human visual system has pathways that respond specifically to motion [19]. A subband transformation with similar characteristics should be well-suited to perceptually relevant compression. Our second motivation arises from the observation that individual regions in video sequences are typically characterized by a limited number of distinct velocities, often only one. By concentrating signal information into subbands with specific velocity sensitivity, the number of non-zero quantization symbols, $s[n]$, can be minimized. In combination with any or all of the variable length coding, arithmetic coding and zero coding techniques discussed in Sect. 2.2, this velocity sensitivity translates into improved compression.

Traditional subband compression techniques use one dimensional filters to partition an image or video sequence into low and high frequency components along two spatial dimensions and time. As a result they divide up the 3-D spectrum into regions of high and low spatial and temporal frequency, without separating motion along opposite directions. Consider the separable subband transformation shown in Fig. 6. By adding a stage of temporal subband decomposition to each spatial subband, we obtain a 3-D separable subband transformation. Figure 24 shows the regions in the spatio-temporal frequency cube, which correspond to the HLH subband of such a transformation. In the figure, w_1, w_2 and w_3 denote horizontal, vertical and temporal frequency respectively. In the notation, HLH, the first

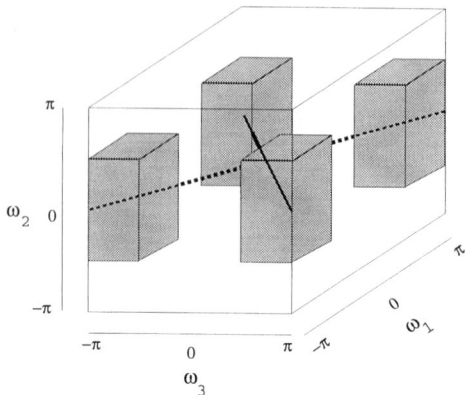

Fig. 24. HLH subband of traditional 3-D separable subband decomposition

H stands for high pass in the horizontal direction, the L stands for low pass in the vertical direction, and the final H stands for high pass in the temporal direction. A vertical line stimulus moving at +1 pixel per frame (p/f) in the horizontal direction will have a Fourier Transform given by the solid line in the figure. The same line stimulus moving at −1 p/f in the horizontal direction will have a Fourier Transform given by the dashed line. Because both stimuli activate regions in the HLH band, the subband transformation does not distinguish between the two signals. In a directional subband transformation, stimuli moving in opposite directions should excite different bands.

In Sect. 5.1, we show how a set of nonseparable 2-D checker filters may be used to further partition the bands of a separable subband transformation into subbands that respond to motion in only one direction. Then, in Sect. 5.2, we briefly review extensions of this concept, which lead to enhanced velocity discrimination. Finally, in Sect. 5.3, we propose a velocity adaptive subband transformation, in similar vein to the orientation adaptive transformation of Sect. 4, to enhance the compression efficiency associated with signal components of low spatial frequency.

5.1 The Checker Filter Approach

Observing that the velocity of a moving object specifies some region of support in the spatio-temporal frequency cube, our main goal is to use subband filters which are capable of separating this region from the rest of the cube. The approach proposed in this section is to use the two band, two dimensional checker filter described in [3], whose passbands are shown in Fig. 25c. When used in conjunction with a conventional separable subband decomposition, the checker filters are capable of further subdividing frequency bands into diametrically opposed pairs of cubes in the frequency space. The pairs correspond to opposite directions of motion over a small range of speeds. An analysis architecture which demonstrates

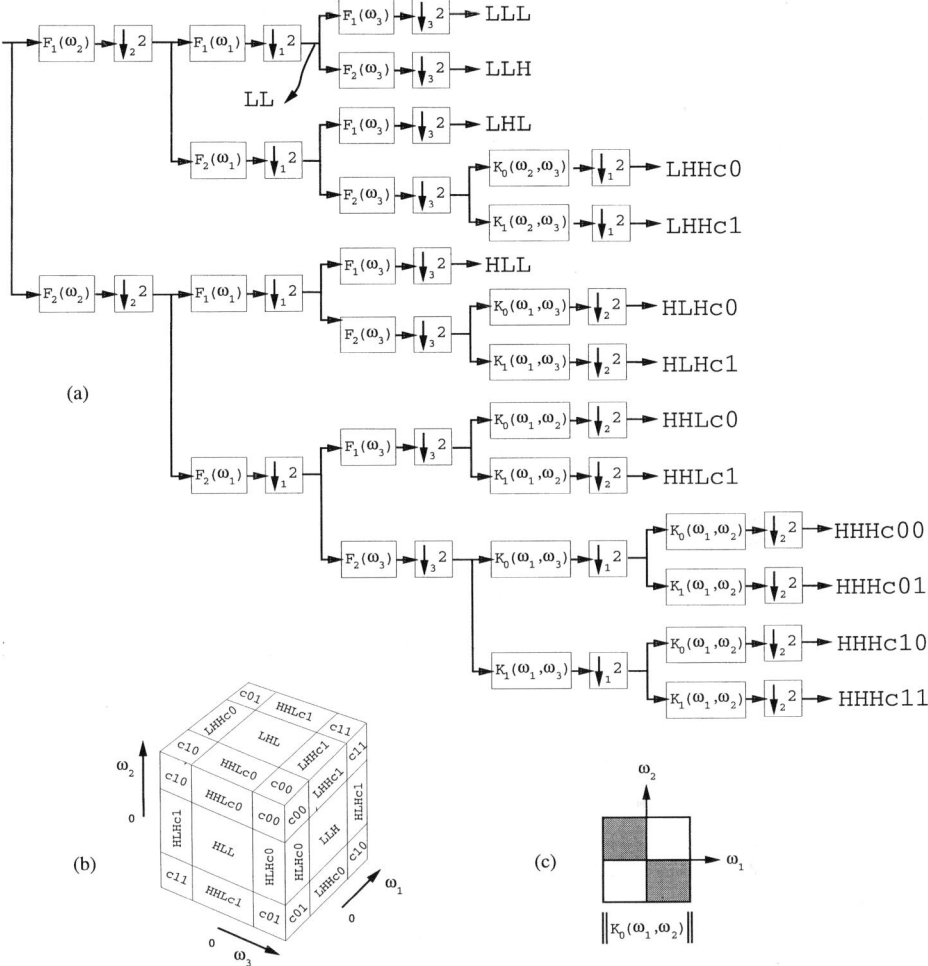

Fig. 25. a Directional subband analysis system architecture; b Subband partitioning of the frequency cube by the analysis system of a; c Passbands of the checker filter, K_0, used in a

this concept is shown in Fig. 25a. In this figure, the first three stages consist of one dimensional lowpass and highpass filters, F_1 and F_2 respectively, constituting a separable subband decomposition. The checker filters in the fourth and fifth stages are denoted by K_0 and K_1. K_0 denotes the filter which passes signal components in the second and fourth frequency quadrants, as shown in Fig. 25c, while K_1 denotes the filter which passes signal components in the first and third frequency quadrants.

The initial, separable subband decomposition partitions the input sequence into eight subbands, each representing a different region in the frequency cube. In this case, the LLL band is not subject to checker filtering. The LLH, LHL, and HLL bands are each already composed of two diametrically opposed regions in the

Table 3. Direction sensitivity associated with HHH_c** subband pairs

Active bands	Inactive bands	Sensitivity
c00 c11	c01 c10	vertical motion at -1 p/f
c01 c10	c00 c11	vertical motion at $+1$ p/f
c10 c11	c00 c01	horizontal motion at $-$p/f
c00 c01	c10 c11	horizontal motion at $+1$ p/f
c01 c11	c00 c10	stationary feature with $-45°$ orientation
c00 c10	c01 c11	stationary feature with $+45°$ orientation

frequency cube, as required for velocity discrimination. The LHH, HLH, and HHL bands are each composed of four regions in the frequency cube. In any one of these bands, the four regions do not correspond to any single specific direction. One-stage of checker filter decomposition is applied to each of these bands to create pairs of diametrically opposed regions, such that each pair is tuned to one direction. For example, the pair of regions comprising LHHc0 covers the second and fourth quadrants in the w_2-w_3 plane, as shown in Fig. 25b. Therefore, an object moving in the horizontal direction at $+1$ p/f will have a Fourier transform which lies on a plane that passes through LHHc0 but not LHHc1.

The final band, HHH, is composed of eight separate regions in the frequency cube. Two levels of checker filter decomposition are needed to separate these eight cubes into four pairs of diametrically opposed corner cubes. With this cube partitioning scheme, uniform motion activates only two of the four sets of cubes. For example, an object moving at -1 p/f in the vertical direction will have a spectrum constrained to the plane satisfying $w_2 = w_3$. This plane passes through bands HHHc00 and HHHc10, but not bands HHHc01 and HHHc11. Therefore the checker filtering makes the bands sensitive to changes in direction of motion. Each combination of two pairs of bands corresponds to a different motion or spatial orientation, as shown in Table 3.

In order to demonstrate the performance of this velocity sensitive subband decomposition, we use as source material a synthetic video sequence in which a 5 × 5 pixel white square moves across a 64 × 64 pixel dark frame at a variety of different velocities. Table 4 reveals the signal variance measured for coefficients in each of the subbands obtained by checker filtering. The variance figures in the table reveal that the velocity-based subband transformation is able to resolve velocities at speeds of approximately 1 p/f. At higher speeds such velocity discrimination does not exist. In the next section we present solutions to this problem.

5.2 Alternative Velocity-Based Subband Transformations

As demonstrated above, the problem with the approach outlined in Sect. 5.1 is that it only captures motion reliably in the neighborhood of 1 p/f. At faster or slower

Table 4. Subband variances for subband decomposition of Fig. 25a with synthetic video sequences

Subband	Horizontal		Vertical		Diagonal
	+1 p/f	−1 p/f	−1 p/f	−4 p/f	(−1, −1) p/f
LHHc0	283	85	1	78	92
LHHc1	85	283	1	78	237
HLHc0	1	1	85	34	92
HLHc1	1	1	283	41	237
HHLc0	1	1	1	22	12
HHLc1	1	1	1	3	8
HHHc00	21	6	26	5	6
HHHc01	21	6	1	1	10
HHHc10	6	21	1	3	1
HHHc11	6	21	26	3	4

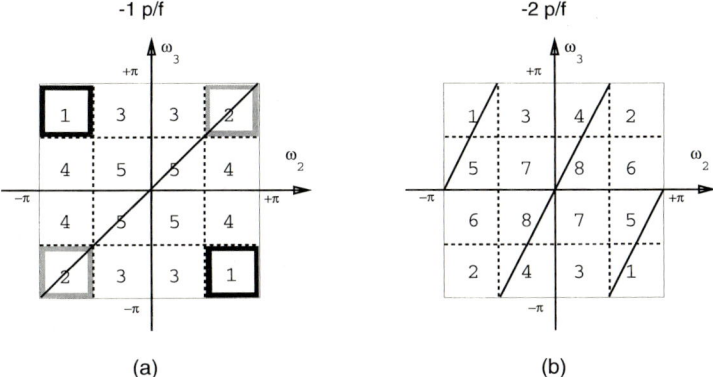

Fig. 26. Two dimensional slice of spatio-temporal frequency cube through $w_1 = 0$. Numbered regions represent subband passbands for **a** the transformation of Fig. 25a, and **b** a more complex transformation for discriminating higher velocities

speeds, the spectrum of a moving object has a steeper or shallower angle in the frequency cube. In addition, higher speeds cause aliasing [10], which results in duplicate copies of the spectrum appearing at different frequencies, as shown in Fig. 26b. Figure 26a,b corresponds to the $w_1 = 0$ plane in the spatio-temporal frequency cube. The Fourier Transform of a point source object moving in the vertical direction at −1 p/f and −2 p/f, are indicated by the diagonal lines in Figs. 26a and b, respectively. The numbered regions, 1, 2, ..., 5, in Fig. 26a correspond to the subbands HLHc0, HLHc1, LLH, HLL, and LLL, respectively, in the subband transformation discussed in Sect. 5.1. Ignoring the aliased spectral regions, this transformation is not capable of distinguishing between velocities of ±2 p/f. On the other hand, a transformation with the frequency partitions shown in Fig. 26b would be capable of distinguishing between velocities of ±1 and ±2 p/f. It is possible to construct such a subband transformation by appropriately combining checker filters with separable subband decompositions. A variety of subband transformations based on this approach are proposed in [5].

Jonsson and Mersereau [20] have proposed an alternative subband transformation to partition the spatio-temporal frequency cube in a similar manner to that depicted in Fig. 26b. Their approach is based on non-separable cosine modulated subband filtering. In this case, the subband analysis filters, $F_{\vec{b}}$, have impulse responses of the form

$$f_{\vec{b}}[\vec{i}] = f_1[i_1]f_2[i_2]f_3[i_3]\cos(2\pi\vec{b}^t\mathbf{M}^{-1}(\vec{i}+\vec{h})) \cdot \begin{cases} \frac{1}{2}, & \vec{b}=0 \\ 1, & \vec{b} \neq 0 \end{cases} \quad (15)$$

where f_1, f_2, f_3 are appropriate one dimensional low pass filter impulse responses, $\vec{h} = (\frac{1}{2},\frac{1}{2},\frac{1}{2})$, $M = \text{diag}(N_1, N_2, 2N_3)$ and the decimation matrix, $D = \text{diag}(N_1, N_2, N_3)$. The index, $\vec{b}$, identifying the subband channel takes on values in the range $0 \le b_1 < N_1$, $0 \le b_2 < N_2$ and $0 \le b_3 < N_3$. The analysis filters given by equation (15) have approximately cube shaped passbands centered at the frequencies $\pm 2\pi(\mathbf{M}^{-1})^t\vec{b}$ in the spatio-temporal frequency cube, exactly as do the HHHc00, HHHc01, HHHc10 and HHHc11 subbands of Fig. 25b, for example. By appropriate design of the baseband filter impulse responses, f_1, f_2 and f_3, Jonsson and Mersereau exhibit a perfect reconstruction subband transformation with $N_1N_2N_3$ subbands tesselating the spatio-temporal frequency cube, each of which consists of the diametrically opposed passband regions required for velocity discrimination. Moreover, FFT techniques may be used to significantly reduce the computational demands associated with this transformation.

At higher velocities, aliasing components, distributed throughout the spatio-temporal frequency cube, account for an increasing proportion of the total signal energy. As such, the signal information cannot be concentrated in a small number of subbands, and compression performance is correspondingly degraded. For this reason, the velocity-based transformation systems discussed in this section are particularly appropriate when scene velocities are not too high.

5.3 Velocity Adaptive Subband Transformation

The subband transformations discussed in Sects. 5.1 and 5.2 both suffer from an inability to resolve velocities at low spatial frequencies, where a significant proportion of the signal information is commonly to be found. As indicated by Fig. 26a, the transformation of Sect. 5.1 suffers from this difficulty because signal components of low spatial frequency are all captured by the subband marked "5" in the figure, regardless of the direction or speed of motion. In the more complex transformations discussed in Sect. 5.2 the same difficulty arises because the subband filters do not have ideal bandpass responses. In Fig. 26b, for example, the subbands labeled "7" and "8" would respond approximately equally to a vertically moving stimulus, regardless of its speed, provided the spatial spectrum of the stimulus is

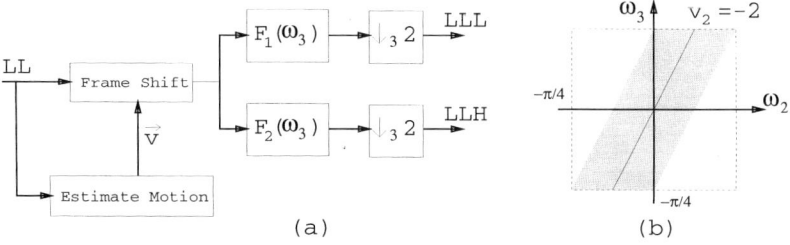

Fig. 27. Velocity adaptive subband transformation: **a** schematic; **b** passband of LLL subband, projected onto $w_1 = 0$.

sufficiently low pass. In this section we propose a simple velocity adaptive subband transformation to enhance compression performance associated with these components.

As for the orientation adaptive transformation of Sect. 4, the velocity adaptive approach is best understood as a pre-distortion, followed by conventional temporal subband decomposition. Whereas the pre-distortion of Sect. 4 is intended to align oriented features to one of the two cardinal spatial directions, the pre-distortion here is intended to align moving objects to the cardinal temporal direction, i.e. to remove the motion. For a scene velocity of $\vec{v}$ p/f, this is accomplished by shifting frame n by $\vec{v}$ pixels relative to frame $n-1$, prior to the application of a conventional temporal subband decomposition. Note that this scheme may also be thought of as a non-separable subband transformation of the undistorted video sequence with the non-zero filter tap values confined to a line in space-time whose orientation is adapted according to $\vec{v}$. Such a transformation is illustrated in Fig. 27a and is applied to the LL subband shown in Fig. 25a. The motion vector, $\vec{v}$, is adapted at each frame so as to capture a single, dominant component of velocity, e.g., camera pan, at any point in time. The passband associated with the LLL subband of this adaptive decomposition is indicated in Fig. 27b. Such a response is clearly able to offer superior velocity discrimination to the subbands "7" and "8" of Fig. 26b. When the transformation of Fig. 27a is applied to 40 frames of the standard ISO video test sequence, "football"[5], with the velocity parameter, $\vec{v}$, adapted to the single dominant component of scene motion, the variance of the LLL subband coefficients is found to exceed that of the LLH subband coefficients by a factor of 6.97:1. On the other hand, by fixing $\vec{v}$, corresponding to conventional temporal subband decomposition, the variance ratio between these two subbands is reduced to 4.52:1.

The simple velocity adaptive transformation shown in Fig. 27a may be extended in several ways by the addition of further levels of hierarchical temporal subband decomposition and by applying the scheme to smaller frame regions, as

---

[5] We use a monochrome version here with dimensions of 352 × 240 pixels at 30 frames per second.

in Sect. 4, so as to capture more local velocity components. For further details of such velocity adaptive transformations, the reader is referred to [6] and [29].

5.4 Summary of Velocity-Based Subband Transformation

In this section, we have introduced subband transformations which are capable of discriminating between different velocities. In relation to Fig. 1, the material in this section is concerned only with the transformation block itself. Although actual quantization and coding results are not provided here, the implications of velocity discrimination for efficient, psychovisually relevant video compression, as outlined at the beginning of the section, provide significant motivation for such transformation techniques.

6 Progressive Coding of Subband Coefficients

As mentioned in Sect. 1, scalability can be an important goal for image or video compression. This is particularly true for video compression where issues of resolution compatibility and real time distribution can render resolution- and rate-scalability indispensable features for certain applications. We recall that scalability essentially means that the bit stream can be manipulated in a simple way in order to satisfy some constraint on bit rate, display resolution or decompression hardware complexity. The power of scalable compression lies in the fact that this manipulation takes place at any point *after* the compression itself, thus satisfying constraints which may not be known during compression. In general this manipulation consists of the extraction of relevant subsets of the bit stream, which should each represent an efficient compression of the image or video sequence for some resolution or distortion. In rate-scalability, appropriate subsets are extracted in order to trade distortion for bit rate at a fixed display resolution. Resolution-scalability, on the other hand, means that subsets may be extracted which represent the image or video sequence at a variety of different resolutions. Rate- and resolution-scalability usually also provide a means of scaling the decompression algorithm's computational demands, as demonstrated in Sect. 7.3. In order for the complete bit stream to also represent an efficient compression of the source material at the maximum resolution and bit rate, these subsets must be embedded within one another, rather than independent as in a simulcast.

Resolution-scalability is best thought of as a property of the transformation block of Fig. 1. Both the DCT and subband transformations may be used to provide resolution-scalability. In Sect. 7 we present an image and video compression algorithm in which two and three dimensional subband decomposition is used to provide resolution scalability. Rate-scalability, however, is best thought of as a property of the quantization and coding blocks of Fig. 1. Of the techniques discussed in Sect. 2.2, only fixed length coding is inherently rate-scalable, however it also exhibits the worst compression performance. In this section we show how rate-scalability may be introduced without making such sacrifices in compression performance. Our approach is specifically directed towards rate-scalable quantization and coding of subband coefficients in that the rate-scalable zero coding algorithm described in Sect. 6.2 is not very suitable for use with DCT coefficients.

In our proposed approach the coefficients of each subband are progressively quantized and encoded in a sequence of N layers, representing successively finer quantization. In this regard, our approach bears a significant resemblance to the embedded image coder described by Shapiro [36][6]. We refer to a set of N scalar quantizers, $Q_1, \ldots, Q_N$ and N quantization layers $L_1, \ldots, L_N$. As described in Sect. 2.2, each quantizer operates on the subband coefficients to produce a sequence of symbols. The symbols for quantizer Q_1 are encoded into layer L_1, while the information necessary to recover the symbols for quantizer Q_n, given that the symbols for quantizers $Q_1, \ldots, Q_{n-1}$ are already known, is encoded into layer L_n. In this way the decoder is able to recover quantization symbols for any of the quantizers, Q_n, by decoding layers $L_1, \ldots, L_n$ only. A reasonable goal for such a layered coding scheme is that the total bit rate associated with layers $L_1, \ldots, L_n$ be approximately the same as that associated with coding the symbols produced by quantizer Q_n alone. This means that we do not sacrifice compression efficiency in obtaining rate-scalability. We refer to this compression efficiency goal repeatedly in the remainder of this section.

In order to achieve such a goal it is necessary to exploit statistical dependencies existing between the quantization layers. In Sect. 6.1 we discuss layered PCM coding, while in Sect. 6.2 we present an efficient zero coding strategy which is well suited to our layered quantization approach. The layered coding strategies developed in this section are employed in the fully scalable image and video compression algorithm presented in Sect. 7.

6.1 Layered PCM

Throughout this section $u[k]$ is used to denote an observed sequence of subband coefficients[7], each element of which is an outcome of a random variable, U. This sequence might, for example, be one of the sequences, $u_1[k], \ldots, u_N[k]$, in the subband system of Fig. 3. Each quantizer, Q_n, is characterized by its quantization intervals $I_{n,p_1}, I_{n,p_2}, \ldots$, emitting a symbol, p, whenever the subband coefficient, u, lies in $I_{n,p}$. In the functional notation developed in Sect. 2.2, we write $Q_n(u) = p | u \in I_{n,p}$.

---

[6] We note, however, that our layered coding techniques differ significantly from those in [36]. In particular, the approach described here permits both rate- and resolution-scalability, rather than just rate-scalability.

[7] $u[k]$ actually represents some scanning of the multi-dimensional subband coefficient sequences. The scanning order is not important for this discussion.

We begin our discussion by imposing the following important condition on the set of quantizers, $Q_1, \ldots, Q_N$.

$$P(U \in I_{n,Q_n(u[k])} \setminus I_{n-1,Q_{n-1}(u[k])}) = 0, \quad \forall u[k] \text{ and } \forall n \geq 2 \tag{16}$$

Where $P(\cdot)$ refers to the probability of an event and $\setminus$ is the set subtraction operation. Equation (16) states that every fine quantization interval, $I_{n,Q_n(u[k])}$ containing any coefficient $u[k]$, is almost entirely contained in the coarser quantization interval, $I_{n,Q_{n-1}(u[k])}$, containing $u[k]$. The probability that U lies in any part of $I_{n,Q_n(u[k])}$ not contained in $I_{n-1,Q_{n-1}(u[k])}$ is zero. For all practical purposes, it is sufficient to think of equation (16) as the requirement that every quantization interval of Q_n is contained in some quantization interval of Q_{n-1}.

In this section we first prove that our scalable compression efficiency goal can be achieved if and only if equation (16) is satisfied. We then show how this condition can be applied to the design of a useful set of quantizers.

Assuming that each subband coefficient, $u[k]$, is a statistically independent outcome of the random variable, U, the minimum number of bits required to encode the sequence of quantization symbols generated by Q_n is found, from equation (6), to be

$$C(Q_n(u[k])) = -\sum_k \log_2 P(U \in I_{n,Q_n(u[k])}) \tag{17}$$

Moreover, this minimum number of bits may effectively be achieved by using arithmetic coding. For $n \geq 2$, layer l_n must encode the symbols $Q_n(u[k])$, given that layers $l_1, \ldots, l_{n-1}$ and hence $Q_{n-1}(u[k])$ are known. The minimum number of bits required to encode layer l_n, then, is

$$C(L_n) = -\sum_k \log_2 P(U \in I_{n,Q_n(u[k])} | U \in I_{n-1,Q_{n-1}(u[k])}) \tag{18}$$

$$= -\sum_k \log_2 \frac{P(U \in I_{n,Q_n(u[k])} \cap I_{n-1,Q_{n-1}(u[k])})}{P(U \in I_{n-1,Q_{n-1}(u[k])})}$$

$$= -\sum_k \log_2 [P(U \in I_{n,Q_n(u[k])}) - P(U \in I_{n,Q_n(u[k])} \setminus I_{n-1,Q_{n-1}(u[k])})]$$

$$+ \sum_k \log_2 P(U \in I_{n-1,Q_{n-1}(u[k])}) \geq C(Q_n(u[k])) - C(Q_{n-1}(u[k])) \tag{19}$$

where equality holds if and only if $P(U \in I_{n,Q_n(u[k])} \setminus I_{n,Q_{n-1}(u[k])}) = 0$ – i.e., if and only if equation (16) is satisfied. Noting that layer L_1 simply encodes the sequence $Q_1(u[k])$, using $C(Q_1(u[k]))$ bits, equation (19) leads, by induction on n, to the result

$$\sum_{m=1}^{n} C(L_m) \geq C(Q_n(u[k])) \tag{20}$$

with equality if and only if equation (16) is satisfied. Equation (20) states that our compression efficiency goal is satisfied for layered PCM coding, provided arithmetic coding is employed so that the minimum number of bits, $C(L_n)$, is achieved in coding each quantization layer, L_n, and provided equation (16) is satisfied. In this case the number of bits required to encode the first n quantization layers, from which the symbols, $Q_n(u[k])$, may be recovered, is exactly the same as the number of bits required to encode the symbols $Q_n(u[k])$ directly. This means that we need not sacrifice compression efficiency to obtain rate-scalability.

We turn our attention now to design of the quantizers. From a mean squared error perspective, the minimum entropy is achieved for a given distortion by uniform quantization [18, p. 154][8]. As already noted in Sect. 4.3, however, the introduction of a larger dead zone, as in Fig. 18, commonly enhances the compression gains provided by zero coding. In Sect. 6.2 we present an appropriate layered zero coding technique. Using the notation of Fig. 18, we denote the step size for quantizer Q_n by δ_n, and the width of its deadzone by v_n. For a set of N such uniform quantizers with dead zones, it can be shown that equation (16) holds if and only if the following two conditions are satisfied:

$$\delta_{n-1} = K_n \delta_n \tag{21}$$

$$v_n = v_{n-1} - 2K'_n \delta_n \tag{22}$$

where $K_n > 0$ and $K'_n \geq 0$ are arbitrary integers. Equation (21) indicates that the quantization step size must be divided by an integral factor from layer to layer. In practice we choose the smallest useful factor, $K_n = 2$, in which case *each successive quantization layer doubles the precision to which subband coefficient values are quantized*. Equation (22) arises from the fact that the quantizer dead zone must be centred about 0. For consistency and ease of implementation, we would like to halve not only the quantization step size, δ_n, but also the dead zone threshold, v_n, in each successive quantization layer. One way to arrange this is to set $v_n = 2\delta_n$, in which case equation (22) is satisfied with $K'_n = 1$. This means that *each quantizer has a dead zone twice as large as the other quantization intervals*. From an implementation perspective, these quantizers may be realized simply by discarding least significant bits in an appropriately scaled, sign-magnitude representation of the subband coefficients, $u[k]$.

6.2 Layered Zero Coding

As mentioned in Sect. 2.2 high frequency subband coefficients typically exhibit zero mean and relatively low variance. These coefficients most frequently lie within the quantizer dead zone, $I_{n,0}$ – cf. Fig. 18 – leading to a high incidence of the zero symbol. Occurrences of the zero symbol generally correspond to smooth regions in the image or video source being compressed. In these smooth regions,

---

[8] This comment is only strictly correct at relatively high bit rates.

the assumption made in Sect. 6.1, that the subband coefficients are statistically independent, is unreasonable. For this reason, we separate the coding of the quantization symbols, $Q_n(u[k])$, into two phases. The first phase codes whether the symbol is zero or non-zero – i.e., whether $u[k]$ lies in $I_{n,0}$ or not. The second phase then codes the particular value of each non-zero symbol, using the layered approach developed in Sect. 6.1. The first phase, which we refer to as zero coding, attempts to exploit spatial or some other dependencies amongst the quantized coefficients. Its task is to encode the binary valued sequence, $\sigma_n[k]$, given by

$$\sigma_n[k] = \begin{cases} 0, & Q_n(u[k]) = 0 \\ 1, & Q_n(u[k]) \neq 0 \end{cases} \qquad (23)$$

Run-length coding, described in Sect. 2.2, is a simple zero coding approach, capable of exploiting statistical dependencies between quantized coefficients in one dimension only. In this section we propose a zero coding technique capable of exploiting statistical dependencies in two dimensions, which is also well suited to our layered quantization environment. The approach may readily be extended to incorporate dependencies between quantized coefficients in different subbands. The reader is referred to [41] for a discussion of this extension.

The idea behind our proposed zero coding algorithm is to use conditional arithmetic coding, to encode the sequence $\sigma_n[k]$, given a sequence of conditioning terms, $\kappa_n[k]$, which are functions of the quantized subband coefficients in the neighbourhood of $u[k]$. The value of $\kappa_n[k]$ forms the conditioning context for encoding the value of $\sigma_n[k]$, which then requires exactly $-\log_2 P(\sigma_n[k] | \kappa_n[k])$ bits. Naturally, this conditioning context, may be based only on symbols already encoded. Our proposed definition of $\kappa_n[k]$ is provided presently, however we first indicate how these conditioning terms are employed in a layered coding scheme.

Given the quantizer constraints represented by equations (21) and (22), zero sequences associated with successive quantization layers are strongly correlated according to the relationship

$$\sigma_n[k] \geq \sigma_{n-1}[k]$$

This means that there is no need to encode $\sigma_n[k]$ if $\sigma_{n-1}[k] = 1$ is already known from quantization layer L_{n-1}. Thus, when layered zero coding is combined with layered PCM coding of the non-zero symbols, the total number of bits required to encode layer L_n is

$$C(L_n) = -\sum_{k \ni \sigma_{n-1}[k]=0} \log_2 P(\sigma_n[k] | \sigma_{n-1}[k]=0 \ \& \ \kappa_n[k])$$
$$+ -\sum_{k \ni \sigma_n[k]=1} \log_2 P(Q_n(u[k]) | \sigma_n[k]=1 \ \& \ Q_{n-1}(u[k])) \qquad (24)$$

The first term in equation (24) represents the number of bits required to encode the zero sequence, $\sigma_n[k]$, given $\sigma_{n-1}[k]$ and $\kappa_n[k]$, whereas the second term represents the number of bits required to refine the values of the non-zero symbols to quantization precision, Q_n. In Sect. 6.1 we proved that no loss in compression efficiency is suffered by using layered PCM coding instead of conventional single quantizer PCM. It would be nice to be able to prove a similar result when PCM coding is combined with zero coding, as given by equation (24). In the degenerate case of $\kappa_n[k]$ a constant, the result may readily be obtained by combining equations (20), (23) and (24). In the more useful case, however, when $\kappa_n[k]$ is anything but constant, we are not able to prove anything conclusive about the compression performance of the overall layered system. In practice, though, we find that the layered system almost always exhibits superior compression performance to an equivalent single quantizer system. The reason for this is that the layered system is able to exploit spatial correlation at a variety of quantization precisions via layered zero coding, whereas a single layer system is able to exploit spatial correlation only in coding the zero sequence associated with a single quantizer. We find, therefore, that in practice we almost always exceed our scalable compression efficiency goal. Results presented in Sect. 7.3 demonstrate this remarkable fact.

We turn our attention now to the definition of the conditioning terms, $\kappa_n[k]$. Although numerous possibilities present themselves, the definition proposed here has been found to offer good compression performance with a relatively simple implementation. Largely for convenience, we adopt a fixed lexicographic scanning order for the sequence of subband coefficients, $u[k]$, and hence $\sigma_n[k]$. In our proposed definition for $\kappa_n[k]$, the basic idea is to first consider coefficients adjacent to $u[k]$. We refer to this as local scale conditioning. Only if all the quantization symbols available for these coefficients are zero do we resort to wider scale conditioning. Figures 28a and 28b provide frameworks for understanding the local and wide scale approaches, respectively. We first collect local conditioning information in $\kappa'_n[k]$, defined by

$$\kappa'_n[k] = 2^0 \cdot \sigma_n[k-1] + 2^1 \cdot \sigma_n[k_p] + 2^2 \cdot (\sigma_n[k_p-1] \; \wr \; \sigma_n[k_p+1])$$
$$+ 2^3 \cdot \sigma_{n-1}[k+1] + 2^4 \cdot \sigma_{n-1}[k_f] + 2^5 \cdot (\sigma_{n-1}[k_f-1] \; \wr \; \sigma_{n-1}[k_f+1]) \qquad (25)$$

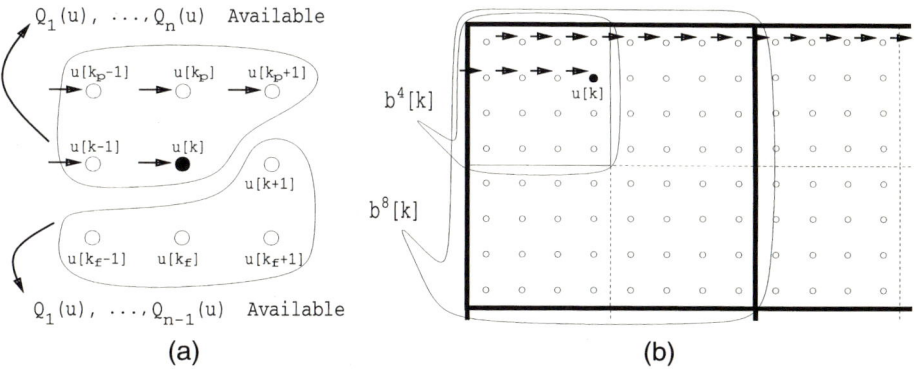

Fig. 28. Subband coefficients used to build the conditioning term, $\kappa_n[k]$, for coding whether $Q_n(u[k])$ is zero or not: **a** local scale; **b** wide scale. Arrows indicate lexicographic scanning order followed in coding the coefficients

where $\wr$ denotes logical "or", and k_p and k_f denote the indices of adjacent coefficients to $u[k]$ on the previous and future scan lines respectively, as depicted in Fig. 28a. The binary representation of $\kappa'_n[k]$, as defined in equation (25), consists of 6 binary digits. Each of $u[k]$'s most immediate neighbours, $u[k-1]$, $u[k+1]$, $u[k_p]$ and $u[k_f]$, corresponding to the first, fourth, second and fifth terms in the right hand side of equation (25), respectively, independently determines the value of a single digit in the binary representation of $\kappa'_n[k]$. The corner neighbours, $u[k_p-1]$, $u[k_p+1]$, $u[k_f-1]$ and $u[k_f+1]$, however, are grouped into pairs, corresponding to the third and sixth terms in equation (25), via the logical "or" operator. These pairs determine the remaining two binary digits of $\kappa'_n[k]$. This pairing limits the total amount of correlation information and hence the size of the conditional probability tables in a practical implementation.

When $\kappa'_n[k] = 0$, we resort to wider scale conditioning information, which is based on fixed blocks of 4×4 and 8×8 coefficients. In particular, let $b^4[k]$ be the collection of coefficient indices, j, belonging to the 4×4 block containing the coefficient $u[k]$, as depicted in Fig. 28b. Similarly, let $b^8[k]$ be the collection of coefficient indices, j, belonging to the 8×8 block containing the coefficient $u[k]$. We define wide scale conditioning terms, $B^4_n[k]$ and $B^8_n[k]$ by

$$B^4_n[k] = \max_{k>j\in b^4[k]} \sigma_n[j] \wr \max_{k<j\in b^4[k]} \sigma_{n-1}[j]$$

and

$$B^8_n[k] = \max_{k>j\in b^8[k]} \sigma_n[j] \wr \max_{k<j\in b^8[k]} \sigma_{n-1}[j]$$

The binary valued terms, $B^4_n[k]$ and $B^8_n[k]$, indicate whether any non-zero quantized coefficients have already been coded in the 4×4 and 8×8 blocks, respectively, containing $u[k]$. The local and wide scale terms are combined to form our ultimate sequence of conditioning terms, $\kappa_n[k]$, according to

$$\kappa_n[k] = \begin{cases} 2+\kappa'_n[k] & \text{if } \kappa'_n[k] \neq 0 \\ \max\{B^4_n[k], 2B^8_n[k]\} & \text{if } \kappa'_n[k] = 0 \end{cases} \quad (26)$$

In practice, we find that most of the compression gain is obtained from conditional coding of $\sigma_n[k]$ conditioned by the local scale term, $\kappa'_n[k]$. The incorporation of wide scale terms, $B^4_n[k]$ and $B^8_n[k]$, in equation (26) typically reduces the bit rate by only a few percent, however an efficient implementation of the wide scale conditioning has negligible impact on the computational demands of our algorithm, justifying its incorporation.

7 Fully Scalable Image and Video Compression

The concept and benefits of scalability have already been described in Sects. 1 and 6. In this section we describe a rate-, resolution- and complexity-scalable image and video compression algorithm based upon subband decomposition and progressive quantization and coding of the subband coefficients. Our approach involves two dimensional subband decomposition for still images and three dimensional subband decomposition for video, followed by progressive coding of each subband independently, using the algorithm described in Sect. 6. The fact that each subband is coded independently of higher frequency subbands introduces resolution-scalability. Resolution-scaled, embedded subsets of the bit stream are simply obtained by discarding the code bits corresponding to high spatial and/or temporal frequency subbands. On the other hand, the progressive coding of each subband, as discussed in Sect. 6, introduces rate-scalability. In general, the computational demands associated with decompression depend on both the number of subband coefficients from which the image or video is to be synthesized and the number of quantization layers which must be decoded for each coefficient. Thus complexity-scalability may be achieved by appropriate selection of resolution and rate limited subsets of the bit stream. In Sect. 7.1 we present our proposed subband transformation, which uses a pre-distortion approach similar to that of Sect. 4 to compensate for camera pan motion in video compression. In Sect. 7.2 we describe the composition of a realistic bit stream so as to support these modes of scalability. Finally, in Sect. 7.3 we present results to demonstrate the performance of the scalable algorithm, including a comparison with the inherently non-scalable MPEG-1 video compression algorithm. For further details regarding the work presented in this section, the reader is referred to [41].

7.1 Subband Transformation

In this section we discuss the subband transformation approach adopted for our fully scalable image and video compression algorithm. For still images, we simply use the spatial subband pyramid depicted in Fig. 6 except that five levels of pyramidal decomposition are employed rather than the two indicated in the figure. Although the orientation adaptive transformation discussed in Sect. 4 could also be used to improve compression performance, our aim here is to investigate scalability and we do not wish to over complicate the algorithm. As evidenced by Sects. 3.2 and 3.3, the most common means of exploiting temporal redundancy in video compression is to use motion compensation. In Sect. 2.3, however, we showed that motion compensation is an inherently non-scalable compression technique. For this reason we adopt a three dimensional separable subband decomposition approach to exploit spatial and temporal redundancy.

In Sect. 4 we demonstrated that a two dimensional separable subband transformation is best suited to image features that are oriented in the vertical or horizontal directions. With the addition of temporal subband decomposition this effect is even more pronounced so that the compression performance associated with three dimensional separable subband decomposition degrades significantly with scene and camera motion. Ohm [29] has proposed a temporal subband

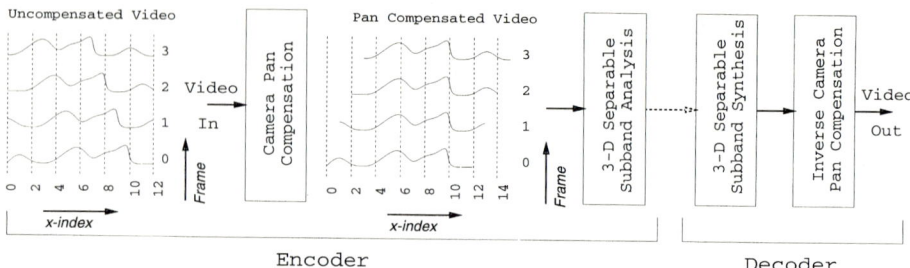

Fig. 29. Separable subband system with camera pan compensation. For clarity, only one spatial dimension is shown. Operation of camera pan compensation is demonstrated with four frames of a hypothetical sequence, in which the camera pans to the right at a rate of one pixel per frame

transformation incorporating motion vectors to alleviate this difficulty. Chang and Zakhor [6] have also proposed an approach in which low pass spatial subbands are shifted before the application of temporal subband analysis, in order to partially compensate for camera pan motion, as described in Sect. 5.3. On the other hand, the approach adopted here is to pre-distort the entire video sequence, in an analogous manner to that introduced in Sect. 4, so as to compensate for camera pan. Figure 29 is helpful in understanding this approach. The figure portrays four frames of a hypothetical video sequence, with no scene motion, in which the camera pans to the right at a constant rate of one pixel per frame. For clarity, only one spatial dimension is shown. Our pan compensation strategy consists of a skewing of the video sequence, analogous to that depicted in Fig. 16a, in which n_1 and m_1 may be associated with the spatial dimension and n_2 and m_2 with the temporal dimension. In this case, however, we allow the skew parameter, a camera pan vector, to change from frame to frame. In order for this pan compensation approach to be successful, all spatial and temporal filtering and subsampling operations must be performed in the coordinates of the skewed sequence.

Exactly as described in Sect. 4.1, the skewing operation may be implemented in two phases. In the first phase camera pan motion is approximately compensated merely by index relabeling, analogous to the relabeling described by equation (12). In a practical implementation what this means is that we record the spatial indices of, say the top left hand corner of each frame, in the skewed coordinate system and use these indices to align all filtering and subsampling operations. These indices are obtained directly from the camera pan vectors. In the example of Fig. 29, the relabeled pixel indices associated with frame 0 run from 0 to 12, those of frame 1 run from 1 to 13 and so on. In this example, in which the camera pans by an integral number of pixels per frame, relabeling is sufficient to completely compensate for camera pan. In general, for arbitrary camera pan, the frames must first be shifted by up to half a pixel in the vertical or horizontal direction. Shifting and relabeling together allow arbitrary skewing of the video sequence, so as to compensate for arbitrary camera pan. We use exactly the same linear interpolative all-pass filtering approach described in Sect. 4.1 to accomplish the fractional frame shifts.

Luminance (Y)

352x240, 30 fps

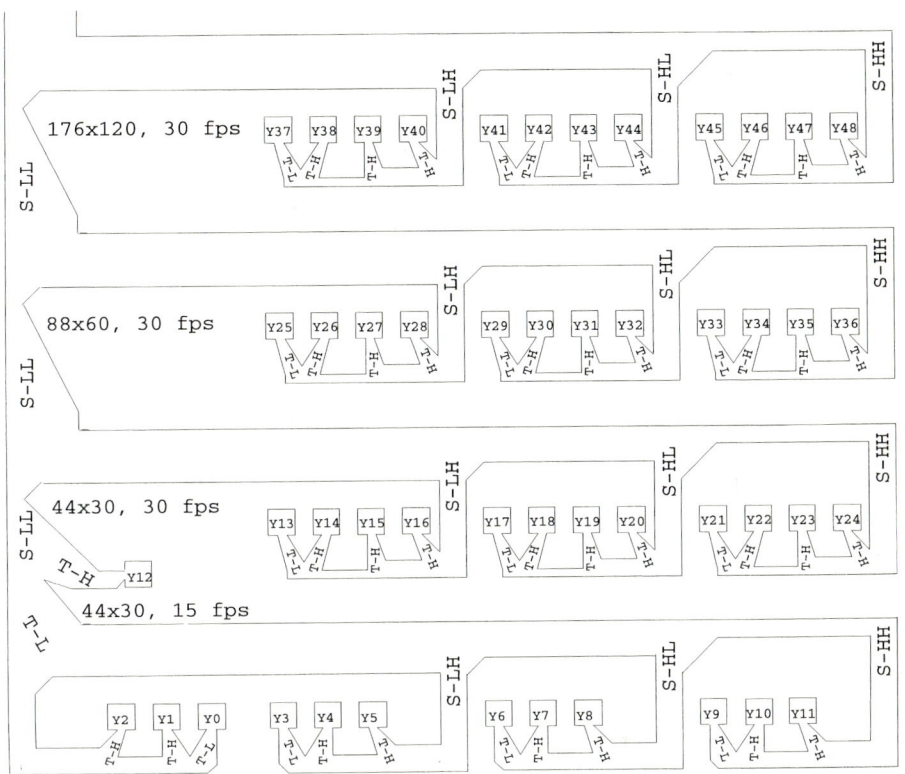

Fig. 30. Spatio-temporal subband structure. S-LL, S-LH, etc., denote spatial subbands. T-L and T-H denote temporal low and high pass subbands, respectively. Only luminance component is explicitly shown. U and V chrominance components are subsampled by two, horizontally and vertically, and so their subband structures are missing subbands 37 ... 48

For details of the approach used to determine camera pan vectors the reader is referred to [41].

For the subband decomposition of Fig. 29, we propose the structure depicted in Fig. 30. In this figure, S-LL denotes the horizontally and vertically low pass spatial subband, S-LH denotes horizontally low pass and vertically high pass spatial subbands, and so on. These are obtained by separable application of a one dimensional, two channel subband decomposition, exactly as in Fig. 6. Each of the spatial subbands may be applied to one or more temporal subband decomposition stages, organized in a temporal pyramid. In Fig. 30, T-L and T-H denote the low and high pass temporal subbands in such pyramids respectively. This subband decomposition is used in obtaining the scalable video compression results of Sect. 7.3, having been selected over about 30 other investigated configurations for its broadly optimal compression performance with the video sequences considered.

This subband structure provides a wide range of resolution-scalability including many different frame sizes and frames rates. By way of example, a monochrome display of frame size 176×120 at 15 frames per second only requires the decoding of code bits representing the subbands Y0-Y11, Y13-Y15, Y17-Y19, Y21-Y23, Y25-Y27, Y29-Y31 and Y33-Y35.

7.2 Bit Stream Composition

The combination of subband decomposition and progressive coding of the coefficients of each subband provides the framework for a fully scalable compression algorithm, however scalability ultimately requires a simple mechanism to extract appropriate subsets from the compressed bit stream. In this section we briefly describe a realistic organization for such a bit stream, together with a subset extraction approach. These are used to acquire the experimental results of Sect. 7.3. Our bit stream syntax may be described in terms of two basic constructs, which we refer to as the *code block* and the *transmission block*. Each code block contains a single, independent arithmetic code word, which encodes the N quantization layers, for a fixed number of coefficients of a particular subband. Code blocks are then collected into transmission blocks, each of which represent a fixed number of frames, F, of the video sequence. For video compression results presented in Sect. 7.3 we use $F = 32$, while for still image compression, $F = 1$.

Code blocks provide a very useful way to introduce parallel computation into the compression algorithm, in that the quantization layers associated with each code block may be independently encoded or decoded. In order to best accommodate such parallel implementations, each code block should ideally require approximately the same amount of work to encode or decode, implying approximately equal numbers of coefficients in each code block. For this reason, we allow our code blocks to represent either a fraction of a subband frame or many frames, not exceeding F, depending on the number of coefficients in each subband frame. The arithmetic code word contains an encoding of quantization layer L_1 for all coefficients represented by the code block, followed by L_2 for all coefficients and so on. Each code block also contains a header specifying the number of bytes of the arithmetic code word required to unambiguously decode the first n quantization layers, for $n = 1, 2, \ldots, N$. The number of coefficients in each code block should be large enough to prevent this header information from consuming too much of the overall bit rate. Apart from this consideration, however, smaller code blocks are to be preferred as they increase the potential for large scale parallelism as well as the opportunity for effective bit rate control, as discussed below. For the experimental results presented in Sect. 7.3, the code blocks represent 5280 coefficients, wherever this value size can be accommodated without exceeding the transmission block size, F.

The transmission block is the basic unit of synchronization and bit rate control for our bit stream. In addition to the code blocks themselves, each transmission block contains camera pan vectors and information identifying the subband structure used for encoding. Resolution scalability is readily accomplished by discarding code blocks whose subbands are not required for a particular display resolution. We implement a very simple algorithm for bit rate control. We first translate a limit, B_r, on bit rate into a limit, $T_B = (F \cdot B_r)/(8 \cdot \text{frame rate})$, on the number of bytes for each transmission block. We then examine the headers associated with every code block in the transmission block to determine the number n_l such that n_l quantization layers may be retained for each code block[9] without exceeding the limit, T_B. Finally, after n_l layers of all code blocks have been incorporated, code blocks are considered one at a time as candidates for an extra quantization layer, so as to use up as much as possible of the T_B available bytes. In this process, code blocks representing subbands of lower spatial and temporal frequency are considered first.

7.3 Experimental Results

In this section we present experimental results to indicate the performance of our scalable image and video compression algorithm. Some additional experimental results may be found in [41]. The spatial subband filters used for our experiments are the same nine tap, symmetric NPR filters used in Sect. 4.3. Temporal subband decomposition is accomplished with the simplest possible two channel subband filters, having tap values of $(\frac{1}{\sqrt{2}}, \frac{1}{\sqrt{2}})$ and $(\frac{1}{\sqrt{2}}, \frac{1}{\sqrt{2}})$. The current work does not include psychovisual optimization of the quantization coefficients. Instead, we select exactly the same set of $N = 9$ quantizers for every subband in both the still image and video compression experiments. As discussed in Sect. 2.2, this selection should be approximately optimal from the perspective of mean squared reconstruction error, or, equivalently, Peak Signal to Noise Ratio (PSNR).

Table 5 indicates the performance of our fully scalable image compression algorithm applied to the 512 × 512, 8 bit grey scale, standard test image "Lena" of Fig. 12.

The fixed probability tables required for the progressive arithmetic coding described in Sect. 6 are obtained using the same 28 natural images used to train the baseline JPEG and orientation adaptive image compression algorithms in Sects. 3.1 and 4.3. The different bit rates indicated in Table 5 are obtained by extracting appropriate subsets from a single compressed bit stream using the rate control algorithm described in Sect. 7.2. Our results are compared with those obtained by Shapiro [36] and Said and Pearlman [34], using a rate-, but not resolution-scalable compression strategy originally developed by Shapiro. Quite apart from the

---

[9] Concerns over the wisdom of allocating approximately the same number of quantization layers from each code block should be allayed by the observation that the relative significance of quantization layers in different subbands is determined by the quantization parameters selected for each subband.

Table 5. Still image compression performance with 512 × 512 grey scale "Lena" test image. Comparison with rate-scalable algorthms by Shapiro [36] and Said and Pearlman [34]. CPU decoding times reported for uni-processor Sparc 10/41

Bit per pixel	Shapiro PSNR	Said PSNR	Taubman CPU*	PSNR	CPU+
1.0	39.55 dB	40.04 dB	4.2 s	40.35 dB	3.0 s
0.5	36.28 dB	36.84 dB	2.0 s	37.25 dB	2.6 s
0.25	33.17 dB	33.67 dB	0.9 s	34.12 dB	2.2 s
0.125	30.23 dB	–	–	30.96 dB	1.7 s

* Does not include subband transform!
+ All-inclusive!

scalability features, the PSNR values quoted in Table 5 are some of the best image compression results mentioned in the literature.

The video compression results presented here use the 264 frame, standard colour test sequence, "pingpong", in SIF525 format[10], as source material. The probability tables for the arithmetic coder are trained using the "pingpong" sequence as well as two other standard SIF525 test sequences, "flower garden" and "football". Figure 31 illustrates the mean luminance and chrominance distortions, taken over the entire video sequence, as a function of bit rate limit. Also shown are three measured points on the rate-distortion curve obtained with an MPEG-1 implementation from Bellcore[11]. It is important to realize that a separate bit stream must be generated by the non-scalable MPEG-1 encoder for each of the three bit rates indicated, whereas the scalable algorithm generates just a single bit stream, from which subsets are extracted to satisfy the bit rate requirement. The rate limiting algorithm is so effective that for subsets corresponding to bit rates in excess of 30 kbps, the number of bytes, T_A, allocated to any transmission block always satisfies $T_B \geq T_A > 0.999 T_B$, with T_A often equaling the limit, T_B, defined in Sect. 7.2.

Figure 32 gives a clearer indication of the performance of the scalable video compression algorithm as compared with MPEG, by showing the frame-by-frame luminance distortion at a bit rate of 1.0 Mbits/s. Clearly the subband system significantly outperforms MPEG during regions when the camera is still or panning. During camera zoom, however, the motion compensation approach of MPEG definitely provides superior compression. It can be argued that panning is by far the most common form of camera motion experienced in entertainment video.

As a visual demonstration of the quality tradeoff inherent to rate-scalable

---

[10] 30 progressively scanned 352 × 240 frames per second with chrominance U and V components subsampled by two both horizontally and vertically.
[11] MPEG parameters: half pixel accuracy motion compensation with search window of ±7 pixels per frame; 15 frame GOP with 1 I-frame, 10 B-frames and 4 P-frames.

Directionality and Scalability in Subband Image and Video Compression

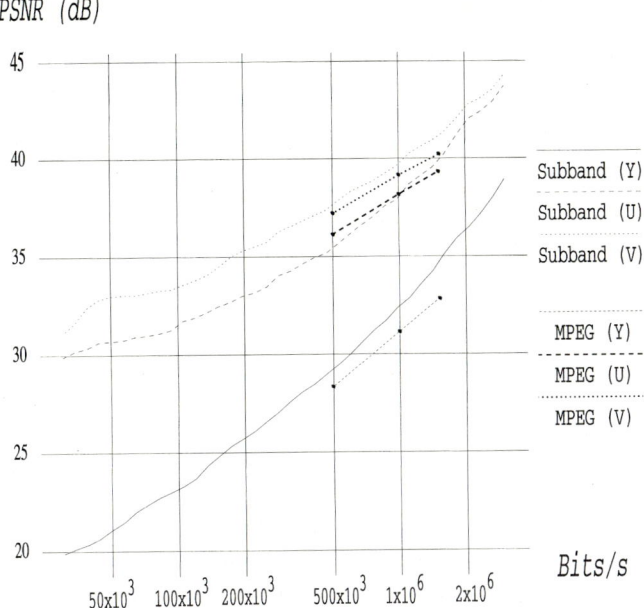

Fig. 31. Rate-distortion curves for "pingpong" sequence. Overall PSNR values for Y, U and V components are plotted against the bit rate limit imposed upon the rate-scalable bit stream prior to decompression. MPEG-1 distortion values are also plotted for reference

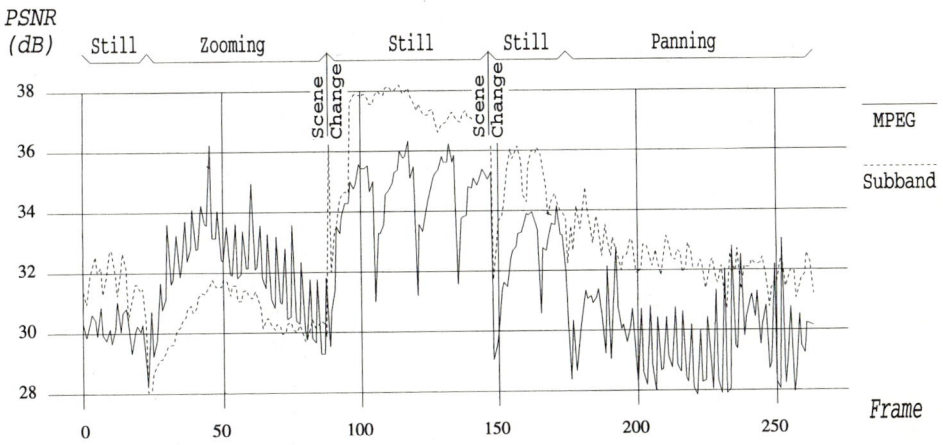

Fig. 32. Frame-by-frame distortion for luminance component of the "pingpong" sequence, reconstructed from 1.0 Mbps MPEG bit stream and from the subband bit stream, rate limited to 1.0 Mbps. Annotations indicate camera motion present during each segment of the sequence

Fig. 33. Frame 210 of "pingpong" sequence decoded from scalable bit stream at 1.5 Mbit/s

video compression, Figs. 33, 34, and 35 show frame 210 from the panning segment of the "pingpong" video sequence, decompressed at bit rates of 1.5 Mbits/s, 300 kbits/s and 60 kbits/s for monochrome display.

Figure 36 reveals the interesting property alluded to in Sect. 6.2, that it is possible to encode the first n quantization layers of a subband, from which quantization symbols, $Q_1(u[k]), \ldots, Q_n(u[k])$ may be recovered, with less bits than are required to encode the symbols, $Q_n(u[k])$, alone. The figure indicates the reduction in average bit rate obtained by the layered coding strategy of Sect. 6 versus the average bit rate obtained by using only a single quantizer for each subband, for fixed values of n from 1 to N, where $N = 9$ in our case. Improvements are indicated both for the "pingpong" sequence and for the still image, "Lena".

Finally, Fig. 37 demonstrates the complexity-scalability of our algorithm. The computational requirements of the decompression algorithm may clearly be traded for reconstruction quality by adjusting the bit rate, the resolution or both. The plotted decoding CPU times do not take into account the need to invert any fractional pixel interpolative frame shifts introduced during camera pan compensation, as discussed in Sect. 7.1. On the Sparc 10/41 CPU, this operation consumes an average of 2.2 seconds for each 352×240 colour frame during panning, regardless of bit rate. The inverse shift, however, may be completely omitted at the expense of a slight, apparent camera jitter (within ±0.5 pixels) during camera pan.

Fig. 34. Frame 210 of "pingpong" sequence decoded from scalable bit stream at 300 kbit/s

Fig. 35. Frame 210 of "pingpong" sequence decoded from scalable bit stream at 60 kbit/s

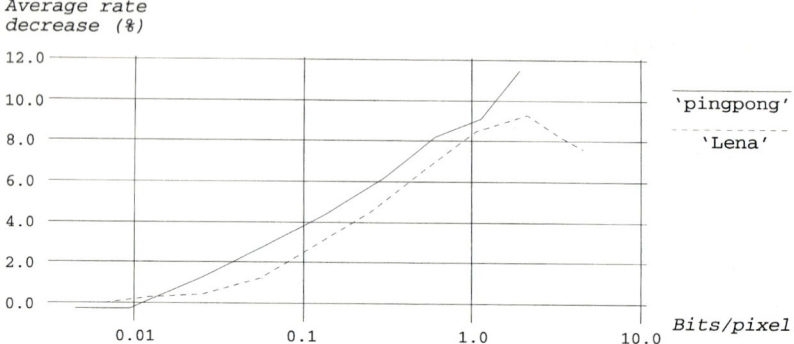

Fig. 36. Decrease in average bit rate achieved by progressive coding of subband coefficients rather than conventional single layer quantization

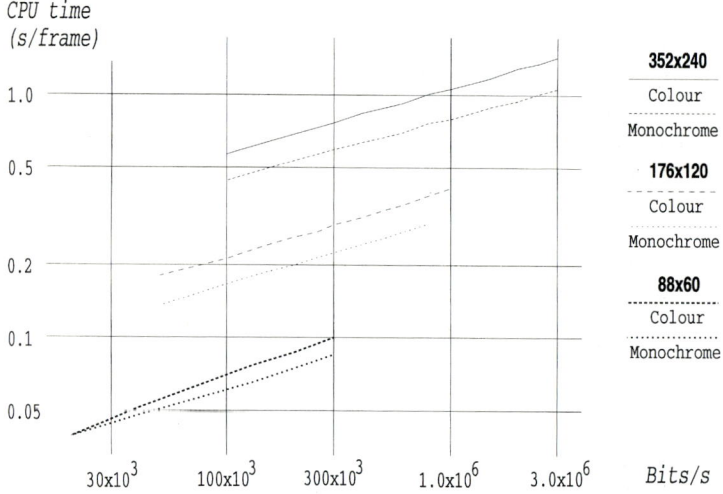

Fig. 37. CPU time per frame, measured on uni-processor Sparc 10/41 for decompression at various bit rates and display resolutions

7.4 Summary of Scalable Compression Algorithm

In this section, we have presented a rate-, resolution- and complexity-scalable compression algorithm for still images and video sequences. The still image compression performance ranks amongst the best results reported in the literature. When camera motion conforms to a pan model, as is common, the video compression performance has been shown to exceed that of the non-scalable MPEG-1 compression standard. We stress, however, that the primary value of this algorithm lies not so much in compression performance as it does in scalability. A useful attribute of the bit stream organization described in Sect. 7.2 is that it is well suited to a parallel implementation.

8 Conclusions

In this chapter we have presented a general model for lossy image and video compression algorithms, in which a transformation operator enables spatial and temporal redundancy in the source signal to be exploited by the ensuing quantization and coding stages. This model is depicted in Fig. 1. With the addition of predictive feedback this model is sufficient to describe the well known compression standards. Although the various compression standards discussed in Sect. 3 are the culmination of much high quality research, they do not by any means conclude research on compression algorithms. In the first place, there is still, and perhaps always will be, much room for the investigation of more effective transformation operators. The orientation adaptive subband transformation of Sect. 4, the velocity based subband transformation of Sect. 5 and the camera pan compensation strategy of Sect. 7.1 provide examples of transformation operators that are found to be particularly effective in exploiting directionality, a specifically multi-dimensional property, which cannot adequately be exploited by the separable transformations common to standard compression techniques. Moreover, the quantization and coding strategies associated with conventional compression algorithms are not necessarily able to satisfy important auxiliary compression goals such as acalability. The scalable quantization and coding algorithm presented in Sect. 6 is of particular interest in this regard. The standard H.261 and MPEG video compression algorithms are based upon motion compensation, a popular predictive feedback strategy which is inherently incapable of providing the scalability required by many emerging applications in video storage and communications. It is of considerable interest, then, that the fully scalable compression algorithm presented in Sect. 7 is able to compete with these non-scalable standards in compression performance.

References

[1] E. H. Adelson, E. Simoncelli, and R. Hingorani, "Orthogonal Pyramid Transforms for Image Coding," *Proc. SPIE*. Vol. 845, Cambridge, MA, pp. 50–58, Oct. 1987.
[2] R. Bamberger and M. Smith, "A Filter Bank for the Directional Decomposition of Images: Theory and Design," *IEEE Transactions on Signal Processing*. Vol. 40, No. 4, pp. 882–893, April 1992.
[3] R. Bamberger and M. Smith, "A Comparison of Directionally-Based and Non-Directionally-Based Subband Image Coders," *Proceedings of SPIE, VCIP Conference No. 1605 (Boston)*. Vol. 2, pp. 757–768, November 1991.

[4] *CCITT Recommendation H.261, Video codec for audio visual services at $p \times 64\,kbit/s$*, 1990.
[5] E. Chang and A. Zakhor, "Velocity-based Architectures for 3-D Subband Video Coding," *IEEE Visual Signal Processing Workshop (Raleigh)*. pp. 245–251, September 1992.
[6] E. Chang and A. Zakhor, "Scalable Video Coding using 3-D Subband Velocity Coding and Multirate Quantization," *Int. Conf. Acoustics, Speech and Signal Processing (Minneapolis)*. Vol. 5, pp. 574–577, April, 1993.
[7] W. Chung and M. Smith, "Spatially-Varying IIR Filter Banks for Image Coding," *Proc. Int. Conf. Acoustics, Speech and Signal Processing (Minneapolis)*. Vol. 5, pp. 570–573, April 1993.
[8] M. R. Civanlar and A. Puri, "Scalable Video Coding in Frequency Domain," *SPIE Symp. Visual Communications and Image Processing (Boston)*. Vol. 1818, pt. 3, pp. 1124–1134, November 1992.
[9] *Committee Draft of Standard ISO11172, Coding of Moving Pictures and Associated Audio*, ISO/MPEG 90/176, December 1990.
[10] G. Cortelazzo, R. Manduchi, and C. Monti, "On the Relationships between Motion and Aliasing in Typical Video Sequences," *IEEE Int. Conf. on Circuits and Systems (San Diego)*. pp. 1689–1692, May 1992.
[11] Philippe Delsarte, Benoit Macq, and Dirk T. M. Slock. "Efficient Multiresolution Signal Coding via a Signal-Adapted Perfect Reconstruction Filter Pyramid," *Proc. Int. Conf. Acoustics, Speech and Signal Processing (Toronto)*. pp. 2633–2636, 1991.
[12] A. Gersho and R. Gray, *Vector quantization and signal compression*, Kluwer Academic Publishers, 1992.
[13] F. O'Gorman and M. B. Clowes, "Finding Picture Edges Through Colinearity of Feature Points," *IEEE Trans. Computers*. Vol. C-25, 4, pp. 449–456, April 1976.
[14] G.C. Gurski, M. T. Orchard and A. W. Hull, "Optimal Linear Filters for Pyramidal Decomposition," *Proc. Int. Conf. Acoustics, Speech and Signal Processing (San Francisco)*. Vol. 4, pp. 633–636, 1992.
[15] S. Haykin, *Modern Filters*, Macmillan Publishing, 1989.
[16] T. Hidaka and K. Ozawa, "ISO/IEC JTC1 SC29/WG11; report on MPEG-2 subjective assessment at Kurihama," *Signal Processing: Image Communications*. Vol. 5, pp. 127–157, February 1993.
[17] D. Huffman, "A method for the construction of minimal redundancy codes," *Proc. IRE*. pp. 1098–1101, September 1952.
[18] N. Jayant and P. Noll, *Digital Coding of Waveforms*. Prentice-Hall, New Jersey (1984).
[19] E. Kandel, J. Schwartz and T. Jessell, *Principles of neural science*, Elsevier, 1991.
[20] R. H. Jonsson and R. M. Mersereau, "Efficient Motion-Oriented Filter Banks for Video Coding," em Int. Symp. on Circuits and Systems (Chicago). May 1993.
[21] J. Kovacevic and M. Vetterli, "Non-separable multidimensional perfect reconstruction filter banks and wavelet bases for R^n," *IEEE Trans. Inform. Th., special issue on Wavelet Transforms and Multiresolution Signal Analysis*. Vol. 38, pp. 533–555, March 1992.
[22] D. Le Gall, "The MPEG Video Compression Algorithm," *Image Communication*. Vol. 4, pp. 129–140, 1992.
[23] B. Mahesh and W. A. Pearlman, "Hexagonal sub-band coding for images," *Proc. Int. Conf. Acoustics, Speech and Signal Processing (Glasgow, U.K.)*. Vol. 3, pp. 1953–1956, May 1989.
[24] D. Marr and E. Hildreth, "Theory of Edge Detection," *Proc. Royal Society of London*. Vol. B 207, pp. 187–217, 1980.
[25] J. McClellan, "The Design of Two-Dimensional Digital Filters by Transformations," *Proc. 7'th Annual Princeton Conf. Information Sciences and Systems*. pp. 247–251, 1973.
[26] R. McEliece, *The Theory of Information and Coding: a mathematical framework for communication*, Cambridge University Press, 1984.

[27] H. Musmann, P. Pirsch and H. Grallert, "Advances in Picture Coding," *Proc. IEEE.* Vol. 73, pp. 523–548, April 1985.
[28] K. Nayebi, T. Barnwell and M. Smith, "Analysis-Synthesis Systems with Time-Varying Filter Bank Structures," *Proc. Int. Conf. Acoustics, Speech and Signal Processing (San Francisco).* Vol. 4, pp. 617–620, 1992.
[29] J. Ohm, "Temporal Domain Sub-band Video Coding with Motion Compensation," *Int. Conf. Acoustics, Speech and Signal Processing (San Francisco).* Vol. 3, pp. 229–232, March 1992.
[30] W. Pennebaker and J. Mitchell, *JPEG Still Image Data Compression Standard.* Van Nostrand Reinhold, 1993.
[31] K. Rao and P. Yip, *Discrete Cosine Transform – algorithms, advantages, applications*, Academic Press, 1990.
[32] R. Rinaldo, D. Taubman and A. Zakhor. "Applications of Multi-Resolution Analysis to Images," *Seventh Workshop on Multidimensional Signal Processing.* September 1991, Lake Placid, New York.
[33] J. Rissanen and G. Langdon, "Arithmetic Coding," *IBM Journal of Research and Development.* Vol. 23, No. 2, March 1979, pp. 149–162.
[34] A. Said and W. Pearlman, "Image Compression Using the Spatial-Orientation Tree," *Int. Symp. Circuits and Systems (Chicago).* Vol. 1, pp. 279–282, May 1993.
[35] J. M. Shapiro, "Adaptive Multidimensional Perfect Reconstruction Filter Banks using McClellan Transformations," *Proc. IEEE Int. Symp. Circuits and Systems (San Diego).* Vol. 2, pp. 939–942, 1992.
[36] J. M. Shapiro, "An Embedded Hierarchical Image Coder using Zerotrees of Wavelet Coefficients," *3'rd Data Compression Conference (Snowbird, Utah).* pp. 214–223, 1993.
[37] E. P. Simoncelli and E.H. Adelson, "Non-separable extensions of quadrature mirror filters to multiple dimensions," *Proceedings of the IEEE.* Vol. 78, no. 4, pp. 652–664, April 1990.
[38] M. J. T. Smith and S. L. Eddins, "Analysis-synthesis techniques for subband image coding," *IEEE Trans. Acoustics, Speech, and Signal Processing.* Vol. 38, pp. 1446–1456, August 1990.
[39] D. Taubman and A. Zakhor, "A Multi-Start Algorithm for Signal Adaptive Subband Systems," *Proc. Int. Conf. Acoustics, Speech and Signal Processing (San Francisco).* Vol. 3, pp. 213–216, 1992.
[40] D. Taubman and A. Zakhor, "Orientation Adaptive Subband Coding of Images," *IEEE Trans. Image Processing (to appear).* July 1994.
[41] D. Taubman and A. Zakhor, "Multi-Rate 3-D Subband Coding of Video," *IEEE Trans. Image Processing, special issue on image sequence compression (to appear).* 1994.
[42] L. Vandendorpe, "Hierarchical Transform and Subband Coding of Video Signals," *Signal Processing: Image Communication.* Vol. 4, pp. 245–262, 1992.
[43] John Woods (ed.), *Subband Image Coding*, Kluwer Academic Publishers, 1991.

Springer-Verlag and the Environment

We at Springer-Verlag firmly believe that an international science publisher has a special obligation to the environment, and our corporate policies consistently reflect this conviction.

We also expect our business partners – paper mills, printers, packaging manufacturers, etc. – to commit themselves to using environmentally friendly materials and production processes.

The paper in this book is made from low- or no-chlorine pulp and is acid free, in conformance with international standards for paper permanency.

Printing: Saladruck, Berlin
Binding: Buchbinderei Lüderitz & Bauer, Berlin